MEDIEVAL HAGIOGRAPHY
AN ANTHOLOGY

EDITED BY
THOMAS HEAD

ROUTLEDGE
NEW YORK & LONDON

Medieval Hagiography

Published in 2001 by
Routledge
29 West 35th Street
New York, NY 10001

Published in Great Britain by
Routledge
11 New Fetter Lane
London EC4P 4EE

Routledge is an imprint of the Taylor & Francis Group.

Copyright © 2000 by Thomas Head

Printed in the United States of America on acid-free paper.

All rights reserved. No part of this book may be reprinted or reproduced or utilized in any form or by any electronic, mechanical, or other means, now known or hereafter invented, including photocopying and recording, or in any information storage or retrieval system, without permission in writing from the publisher.

10 9 8 7 6 5 4 3 2 1

Library of Congress Cataloging-in-Publication Data

Medieval hagiography : an anthology / edited by Thomas Head
    p. cm.
    Includes bibliographical references.
    ISBN 0-8153-2123-6 (alk. paper) / ISBN 0-415-93753-1 (pb)
    1. Christian saints—Biography. 2. Christian saints—Cult—History of doctrines—Middle Ages, 600–1500. 3. Literature, Medieval—Translation into English. 4. Hagiography. I. Head, Thomas (Thomas F.) II. Series.

BR1710.M39 1999
270.3'092'2—dc21
[B]

99-045450

Dedication

He gained such praise for his skillful teaching of the arts and of scripture that at length he became recognized by many as almost a father, a guide to tradition, and a master among teachers. Yet he never disdained being one student among others. For it is a part of monastic tradition that a man who refuses to place himself under others should not presume to place himself over others.

WILLIBALD, *LIFE OF ST. BONIFACE*, CHAPTER 2

This collection is dedicated to my first guides to the monastic tradition, the monks of the Abbey of Saint Gregory, Portsmouth, Rhode Island, and, most especially, to Dom Ansgar Nelson, bishop of Stockholm (RIP).

Contents

Acknowledgments	xi
Introduction *Thomas Head*	xiii
Note on the Translations	xxxix
Contributors	xliii
Chapter 1: Athanasius of Alexandria, *Life of St. Antony of Egypt* Translated by David Brakke	1
Chapter 2: Victricius of Rouen, *In Praise of the Saints* Translated by Philippe Buc	31
Chapter 3: Mark the Deacon, *Life of St. Porphyry of Gaza* Translated by Claudia Rapp	53
Chapter 4: Constantine the Great, the Empress Helena, and the Relics of the Holy Cross Edited and translated by E. Gordon Whatley	77
Chapter 5: *Life of the Holy Virgin Samthann* Translated by Dorothy Africa	97
Chapter 6: Jonas of Bobbio, The Abbots of Bobbio from the *Life of St. Columbanus* Translated by Ian Wood	111
Chapter 7: Dado of Rouen, *Life of St. Eligius of Noyon* Translated by Jo Ann McNamara	137
Chapter 8: Bede, *Martyrology* Translated by Felice Lifshitz	169

CHAPTER 9: EINHARD, *TRANSLATION OF THE RELICS*   199
OF STS. MARCELLINUS AND PETER
Originally translated by Barrett Wendell
and edited by David Appleby

CHAPTER 10: RAGUEL, *MARTYRDOM OF ST. PELAGIUS*   227
Translated by Jeffrey A. Bowman

CHAPTER 11: HROTSVIT OF GANDERSHEIM,   237
The Establishment of the Monastery of Gandersheim
Originally translated by Mary Bernadine Bregman
and edited by Thomas Head

CHAPTER 12: ODILO OF CLUNY,   255
Epitaph of the August Lady, Adelheid
Translated by David A. Warner

CHAPTER 13: THE CULT OF RELICS IN THE ELEVENTH CENTURY   273
Edited and translated by Thomas Head

CHAPTER 14: PETER DAMIAN, *LIFE OF ST. ROMUALD OF RAVENNA*   295
Translated by Henrietta Leyser

CHAPTER 15: *LIFE OF ST. ALEXIS*   317
Translated by Nancy Vine Durling

CHAPTER 16: *The Miracles of St. Ursmer on His Journey*   341
through Flanders
Translated by Geoffrey Koziol

CHAPTER 17: DROGO OF SINT-WINOKSBERGEN,   359
Life of St. Godelieve
Translated by Bruce L. Venarde

CHAPTER 18: HARTVIC, *LIFE OF KING STEPHEN OF HUNGARY*   375
Translated by Nora Berend

CHAPTER 19: GUIBERT OF NOGENT, *ON SAINTS AND THEIR RELICS*   399
Translated by Thomas Head

CHAPTER 20: *A Tale of Doomsday Colum Cille*   429
Should Have Left Untold
Originally translated by Paul Grosjean
and edited by Dorothy Africa

Contents ix

CHAPTER 21: *Life of the Dear Friends Amicus and Amelius* — 441
Translated by Matthew Kuefler

CHAPTER 22: *The Book of Ely* — 459
Translated by Jennifer Paxton

CHAPTER 23: *The Tract on the Conversion of Pons of Léras and the True Account of the Beginning of the Monastery at Silvanès* — 495
Translated by Beverly Mayne Kienzle

CHAPTER 24: Thomas of Monmouth, *Life and Passion of St. William of Norwich* — 515
Originally tranlated by Augustus Jessopp and Montague Rhodes James, and edited by John M. McCulloh

CHAPTER 25: *The Jewish Martyrs of Blois* — 537
Edited and translated by Susan Einbinder

CHAPTER 26: *Liturgical Offices for the Cult of St. Thomas Becket* — 561
Edited and translated by Sherry Reames

CHAPTER 27: *Saga of Bishop Jón of Hólar* — 595
Translated by Margaret Cormack

CHAPTER 28: Gautier de Coincy, *Miracles of the Virgin Mary* — 627
Translated by Renate Blumenfeld-Kosinski

CHAPTER 29: *The Cult of Mary Magdalen in Late Medieval France* — 655
Edited and translated by Raymond Clemens

CHAPTER 30: *The Lives of St. Margaret of Antioch in Late Medieval England* — 675
Edited and translated by Wendy R. Larson

CHAPTER 31: *The Middle-English version of Jacques de Vitry's Life of St. Marie d'Oignies* — 709
Translated by Sarah McNamer

CHAPTER 32: Peter of the Morrone (Pope Celestine V), *Autobiography* — 729
Translated by George Ferzoco

CHAPTER 33: THE *LIFE OF ST. DAVID* SET DOWN BY AN ANCHORITE   745
AT LLANDDEWIBREFI
Translated by Elissa R. Henken

CHAPTER 34: THE OLD CZECH *LIFE OF ST. CATHERINE OF*   763
ALEXANDRIA
Translated by Alfred Thomas

CHAPTER 35: THE CANONIZATION PROCESS FOR ST. VINCENT FERRER   781
Translated by Laura A. Smoller

CHAPTER 36: THE MISSION OF JOAN OF ARC   805
Edited and translated by Nadia Margolis

Acknowledgments

The completion of a collaborative project involving years of work by dozens of scholars necessitates an expression of gratitude far beyond the scope permissible here. Let me first thank the thirty-two friends and colleagues who have contributed chapters to this volume. They have shared the fruits of their own research and devoted time painfully wrenched from their own teaching and administrative duties in a manner which has continuously amazed me. In addition to the contributors to the volume, I would particularly like to thank Peter Brown, Caroline Bynum, John Coakley, Sharon Farmer, Katherine Gill, Cynthia Hahn, Paul Halsall, Dorothy Head, Susan Hellauer (and the other members of Anonymous 4), Richard Kieckhefer, Richard Landes, Harry Liebersohn, Guy Lobrichon, Barbara Newman, Thomas Noble, Monika Otter, Frederick Paxton, Peter Potter, Virginia Reinburg, Dorothy Schneider, Nancy Sevcenko, Barbara Welter, and André Vauchez for their advice and encouragement in this endeavor. At various points in its inception and development, I have relied on the institutional support of the Institute for Advanced Study, Hunter College, Washington University, and Yale University. I have been allowed to focus the volume on the development of Western Christian hagiography not only because of the limitations of my own knowledge, but because of the extraordinary publication venture—in essence to produce a set of English translations of Byzantine hagiography—currently appearing under the direction of Alice-Mary Talbot and the aegis of Dumbarton Oaks. As the dedication to this volume I hope makes clear, I would never have envisioned this project—or, indeed, most of my academic ventures—had I not studied at a school, that is Portsmouth Abbey, sponsored by a monastery which consciously and conscientiously follows the *Rule of St. Benedict*. In addition to Bishop Ansgar Nelson, whom I singled out in the dedication, I also wish to thank all of the members of that community who have been my teachers, in particular Dom Caedom Holmes and Dom Damian Kearney. I would have been unable to compile this volume without the very existence of the Hagiography Society and the active cooperation of much of its membership, most particularly Sherry Reames—its president—and George Ferzoco—who was most responsible for organizing a wonderful conference of its members at Ammerdown. In New York the Friends of the Saints, organized by Jo Ann McNamara, have provided wonderful company. I would like to add a particular note of thanks to the Jewish contributors to this volume, whose interest in Christian hagiography—with its often virulently anti-Semitic overtones—has immeasurably added to its whole. Fittingly I have completed the edition of this volume while ensconced in living quarters enclosed within a former church, the Spencer Memorial, in Brooklyn Heights. I would like to end my acknowledgments with a nod to those Presbyterians who once sang hymns (certainly free of reference to the medieval saints described in this volume) in the space which now houses my computer, my books, and myself.

Thomas Head
December 15, the feast of St. Maximinus of Micy

Introduction
Thomas Head

When Eddius Stephanus, an Anglo-Saxon priest, sat down to write *The Life of Bishop Wilfrid* in the early decades of the eighth century, he mused, "This very task of preserving the blessed memory of Bishop Wilfrid is of great gain and value to myself. Indeed it is in itself a ready path to virtue to know what [Wilfrid] was."[1] And so he did not simply record the actions of Wilfrid, but did so both to advance the cause of his own salvation and to educate his audience in the proper practice of Christianity. Those spiritual and pedagogic concerns lie at the heart of the genre, or more properly genres, of hagiography. Works of hagiography can thus tell us at least as much about the author and about those who used the text—their ideals and practices, their concerns and aspirations—as it does about the saints who are their subjects. Hagiography provides some of the most valuable records for the reconstruction and study of the practice of premodern Christianity.[2]

This volume attempts to chart the development of hagiography though the Middle Ages by presenting a set of important exemplary texts in English translation. With the exception of a few of the earliest texts in the collection—works which were formative in laying the groundwork for later developments—they are works which either appear here for the first time in English or which are no longer readily available in translation. Thus many well-known hagiographic texts are absent from this collection, because they are available with reasonable ease to students and teachers. Some of those translations will be pointed out in the notes to this introduction or in the introductions to the individual chapters. I have deliberately adopted an expansive chronology of the Middle Ages: the texts range from the fourth through the fifteenth centuries. The medieval world represented, while broad in geographical and thus cultural scope, is nonetheless largely confined to Western or Latin-speaking Christendom. One of the chief reasons for omitting Byzantine Christendom and the Eastern worlds it influenced is a practical one: Dumbarton Oaks has recently begun a laudable and ambitious project to translate a large and representative group of Greek *Lives* of saints into English.[3] Although explicitly Christian in its origins, the term "hagiography" has also been adopted by scholars of other religions, most notably Judaism and Islam, to refer to analogous writings in those traditions. For a variety of practical reasons, examples of such non-Christian writings have also been omitted from this collection, with the notable exception of Jewish martyrological literature which memorialized Jews slaughtered at the hands of Christians.

Hagiography is quite simply "writings about the saints." It is a word of relatively modern vintage coined from Greek roots: *hagios*, that is, holy, or by extension, saint, and *graphē*, that is, writing. (Medieval writers, in contrast, tended to use similar words derived from the same roots to mean the books of the Bible, literally "holy writings.") The sorts of literature which fit under the rubric of hagiography are extremely varied, including *Lives* of saints, collections of miracle stories, accounts of the discovery or movement of relics, bulls of canonization, inquests held into the life of a candidate for canonization, liturgical books, sermons, and visions. Hence it is best to consider hagiography not so much as a single genre, but as a collection of genres, many of which are represented in the texts below. It is only possible to understand the term, and the works included in this collection, with reference to the Christian concept of sanctity. Saints were quite literally holy men and women (holy is the root meaning of *sanctus* and *sancta* in Latin, from which our English word "saint" is derived via medieval vernacular usages). But the word "saint" came to have the status of a title designating those who had lived a life of heroic virtue and then been posthumously judged by God to be worthy of entrance to the kingdom of heaven. In theory all who resided in the divine court were saints, but in practice Christian churches accorded a relatively small number of people the title of saint and, with it, public veneration. (In this collection, the translators have attempted to distinguish between these different meanings by use of the abbreviation "St." in reference to the title and of the simple word "holy" where they think no such official meaning is implied, thus glossing over an often deliberate ambiguity which exists in many medieval texts.)

The veneration of those people deemed to be saints lay at the core of the practice of medieval Christianity. For saints were, both during their lives and after their deaths, key members of the Christian community. Saints demonstrated their holiness through their actions, whether it be in the willingness to accept martyrdom, in the rigors of extreme asceticism, in the wise exercise of episcopal office, or in the heroic defense of their virginity. With God's assistance they could turn that holiness into miraculous actions, such as curing the sick, defeating their enemies without the use of force, and exorcising demons. Those miraculous powers were not extinguished by death, for posthumously the saint was a resident of God's court, whose intercessory powers could be invoked by living Christians through prayer and pilgrimage, donation and devotion. There could be no better advocate at the final judgment than someone who already belonged to the "fatherland" of heaven. It is no accident that in Latin the single word *virtus* (which can be translated variously as virtue or power) was used to denote both pious actions and miracles which transcended the rules of nature.

Only a limited number of holy people came to be recognized and honored with the title of saint. The means by which that recognition was officially granted developed significantly over the course of the Middle Ages, and even differed regionally. Central to any official recognition of sainthood, however, was the celebration of a feast which marked the day of the saint's death, that is, of his or her birth into the divine kingdom. In practical terms then, the living holy man or woman only gained sainthood when accepted by a community of believers and blessed by an ecclesiastical authority. In one important sense sanctity is thus a social construct, and it is texts such as those which follow that allow the student of Christian history to reconstruct the evolution of the ideals and practice of holiness.

One of the most important factors in the changing character of sanctity over the course of the Middle Ages was gender. The recognition of, or more importantly the failure to recognize, women as saints betrays many of the misogynist traits typical of medieval society and culture. While most medieval theologians conceded a theoretical equality between men and women in their ability to be saved, they almost uniformly saw men as more likely to practice the virtues necessary for salvation. Moreover women were excluded from the Christian clergy and thus from the callings which produced the majority of saints recognized during certain periods. Throughout the Middle Ages women were a distinct minority among those Christians whose reputation for holiness received public celebration and thus earned for them the title of saint.

The first Christians to be honored as saints were martyrs, who had died for giving witness to the faith during the periodic persecutions which oppressed the new religion throughout the Roman empire.[4] While many stories of martyrs and their relics are included within this collection, they all come from later periods. I have decided to omit the authentically early stories of martyrs—that is, the earliest form of Christian hagiography—and begin the "long" Middle Ages represented in this collection after the official acceptance of Christianity by the emperor Constantine through the Edict of Milan in 313. Over the course of the fourth and early fifth centuries, the development of new types of accepted sanctity, beyond the ideal of martyrdom, and the development of the public veneration of the relics of saints laid the foundations for the medieval traditions of hagiography and the cult of saints. The first four chapters in this collection illustrate these developments: they therefore deserve a more detailed introduction. Two of them are Greek texts from the eastern Mediterranean, for during this period—despite the many differences already developing between Latin and Greek speaking Christians—the world of Christianity was still largely integrated with that of the Roman Empire.

It was the burgeoning ascetic movement, in which lay the beginnings of Christian monasticism, in the Egyptian desert that provided the first new ideal of sanctity.[5] Rejecting the norms of society, monks (the word comes from a Greek term meaning "those who live alone") left the settled communities of the Nile valley for desolate places where they created an alternative society centered on prayer and rigorous ascetic practice (including fasting, chastity, and poverty). Around 360, Bishop Athanasius of Alexandria (d. 73) composed the *Life of St. Antony of Egypt* (Chapter 1), one of the first and most charismatic members of the nascent monastic movement. The *Life* was soon translated from Greek to other languages in order to communicate and disseminate the ideals of monasticism. Soon ascetic holy people began to set up hermitages and monasteries in the deserted outback of Palestine, Syria, and Anatolia. Many works were written concerning the practices of these monks, not only in Greek, the official bureaucratic and ecclesiastical language of the eastern Roman provinces, but in the vernacular languages of Coptic and Syriac.[6] The traditions of ascetic hagiography and with it the practice of monasticism penetrated into the western provinces of the Roman Empire through the translation of some of these works about Eastern monks into Latin, as well as through the writings of two westerners who sojourned for long periods in the East, Jerome (d. 419/20) and John Cassian (d. ca. 433).[7] The heart of the new hagiography was didactic; the new type of saints came to be known as confessors, those who confessed or taught the faith. Indeed Augustine of Hippo (d. 430) heard the *Life of St. Antony* during the winter of 386, quite possibly through the mediation of Jerome, and counted it as a crucial influence in his conversion to Christianity and celibacy.[8] Athanasius's *Life* was to remain a central reference points for all writers of hagiography, both Eastern and Western, throughout the Middle Ages.

It was in 386 that Bishop Ambrose of Milan (d. 397), Augustine's friend and mentor, discovered the relics of two martyrs named Gervasius and Protasius and enshrined them in a church within the center of that city.[9] While this was hardly the beginning of the public veneration of relics (Constantine himself had had several basilicas built over the tombs of martyrs in and around Rome), Ambrose's actions did much to excite widespread interest in the discovery and acquisition of the relics of martyrs. About a decade later, Bishop Victricius of Rouen wrote *In Praise of the Saints* (Chapter 2) to commemorate the arrival in his diocese, located far from Rome in the western reaches of the empire, of a group of martyrs' relics which were immediately enshrined in a central church in that city. It is one of the earliest pieces of hagiography to document the practice of the cult of relics. The decades around the year 400 witnessed many attempts to disinter or discover, distribute, and enshrine relics of the saints. Typical of these were the stories—told about this time first in Greek, but soon translated into Latin, Syriac, and virtually every language of the Christian world—which attributed the discovery (technically known as an *inventio*) of the relics of the most important of all martyrdoms, that is the True Cross of Christ, to the emperor Constantine and his mother, Helena. These traditions were told and retold many times over the course of the coming centuries. E. Gordon Whatley has collected several Latin versions of these traditions (Chapter 4), beginning with an account from the late fourth century and ending with one from the tenth century.

Sometime around 396, a learned Christian layman named Sulpicius Severus composed his *Life of St. Martin of Tours*. Although Sulpicius Severus acknowledged the importance of the *Life of St. Antony* as a model and while much of the work was centered upon Martin's vigorous asceticism, Martin (d. 397) was also bishop of Tours and Sulpicius's work inaugurated yet another type of hagiography celebrating yet a new type of saint. In time this work became for Western hagiographers perhaps an even more important model than the work of Athanasius. Over the course of the next few decades, four more *Lives* of bishops—Ambrose of Milan, Augustine of Hippo, Epiphanius of Salamis, and Porphyry of Gaza—were written.[10] It is the last of these, a Greek composition from Egypt, which is included in this collection (Chapter 3), but the genre was to have a long and important life in both Eastern and Western hagiography.

All these works were written by men who were members of the Christian elite of the Roman Empire. They reflect the extraordinary power and influence which Christianity had gained during the century following the edict of Milan, as well as the variety of practices and pieties in that world. It was, however, a world which was on the cusp of an enormous transformation. Already in the final decades of the fourth century, Germanic peoples such as the Goths had begun to migrate into the western regions of the empire. In 410 a Gothic army sacked Rome; in 456 Rome, now in theory protected in part by Goths, was sacked by Vandals. Even as the Germans slowly carved up the western empire into successor kingdoms each dominated by a different Germanic people, these peoples were undergoing conversion to Christianity and accepting the Latin language as the most important medium of writing. In the process, Christianity and its notions of sanctity were translated into new cultural idioms, eventually in areas well beyond the western and northern boundaries of the Roman Empire.[11] For the fifth and much of the sixth century, however, most of the Christians recognized as saints in the former western provinces of the empire continued to be Romans who followed traditional monastic and episcopal roles, albeit in a manner tailored to changing circumstances.[12] Traditionally recognized Roman saints also continued to be important through their relics, as well as through the liturgical commemoration of their feasts. One of the best cases in point is the cult of St. Martin of Tours, who came to be seen as a patron of Gaul by both Romans and Franks. As Martin's reputation grew over the course of the fifth century, pilgrims flocked in increasing numbers to his tomb outside of Tours, where an important new church was built over the shrine in the 460s. On the outside of that building an inscription read, "When you have bowed down to the earth, your face sunk in the dust, your wet eyes pressed to the beaten ground, raise your eyes, and, with a trembling glance, perceive wonders and commit your cause to the best of patrons . . . Ask for [Martin's] assistance: it is not in vain that you knock at this door."[13]

The hagiographers themselves also continued to be men of the Roman elite, most notably Gregory of Tours (d. 593/4) in Gaul and Gregory the Great (d. 604) in Italy.[14] They wrote not simply to record and preserve the past, but to influence the present, holding up their stories of holy men and women as examples of Christian conduct. Gregory of Tours introduced one of his works by saying, "I have recently discovered information about those who have been raised to heaven by the merit of their blessed conduct here below, and I thought that their way of life, which is known to us through reliable sources, could strengthen the Church . . . because the life of the saints . . . encourages the minds of listeners to follow their example."[15] In the later sixth and the seventh centuries, sanctity came to be accorded to men and women of the barbarian peoples, whose modes of holiness reflected much of the distinctive styles Christianity was developing in their kingdoms.[16] Not just the nature, but even the language of Western hagiography was slowly changing. In Ireland, a land never part of the Roman Empire, hagiography was appearing both in Latin and in Old Irish by the seventh century.[17] And in Anglo-Saxon England, works of hagiography, a staple of local Latin literature from the seventh century, were appearing in Old English by at least the ninth century.[18] As the notes to this paragraph indicate, much of the hagiography extant from the barbarian kingdoms has already been made available in English translation. But three important new translations are included here. The *Life of the Holy Virgin Samthann* (Chapter 5) provides a window into the novel forms of monasticism in Ireland, marked by a particularly rigorous asceticism and an acceptance of women such as Samthann. As is seen in sections of Jonas of Bobbio's *Life of St. Columbanus* (Chapter 6), the influence of that Irish monasticism spread in the seventh century to the European continent, particularly in the kingdoms of the Franks. Dado of Rouen's *Life of St. Eligius of Noyon* (Chapter 7) concerns a member of the Frankish nobility who chose an ecclesiastical rather than a military career, one which documents the ways in which the customs of the Roman episcopate had been altered to fit the realities of the Frankish kingdoms.

The public cult accorded to saints in the early medieval west took many forms. One pervasive mode was liturgical. During the Mass and the monastic office, a list of the martyrs and other saints whose feasts fell on that day was read. Lists covering the entire liturgical year were developed which included short biographical entries for some of the more important saints. These works, known as martyrologies, varied greatly according to the local needs of individual dioceses or monastic houses. One of the most influential, the so-called *Martyrologium Hieronymianum*, was incorrectly attributed to the fifth-century Christian scholar Jerome. Another particularly influential version was that compiled by the seventh-century Anglo-Saxon monk Bede (Chapter 8), a work which shows how hagiographic traditions from all over the ancient Roman Empire had traveled to England, whence they would be brought back to the continent via copies of Bede's work. Relics of the saints continued to be important foci for the devotions of Christians both Roman and barbarian. In many areas which had been part of the Roman empire, such relics were plentiful in the cemeteries and shrines which surrounded old Roman cities. In more newly converted areas, however, relics had to come either from saints of a more recent vintage or to be obtained elsewhere. Martyrs' relics from Rome itself acquired a particularly high status in the barbarian kingdoms. Einhard, a Frankish noble and member of the court of Charlemagne, told in the *Translation of the Relics of Sts. Marcellinus and*

Introduction   xix

Peter (Chapter 9) how his agents had gone to Rome and there acquired the relics of two martyrs through means perhaps best described as "holy theft." Einhard had the relics brought back to a chapel constructed on his own lands, located in what is now Germany. The expansion of Western Christendom into newly converted lands and its encounter with powerful non-Christian peoples resulted in a renewal of the oldest form of Christian sanctity, that is, martyrdom. It was still defined as a death incurred because of witness to the Christian faith. Many sorts of Christians could still encounter this violence: missionaries such as Boniface, killed during the eighth century by polytheists resisting conversion; kings such as Edmund of East Anglia, slain in the ninth century by marauding Vikings; common laypeople who lived under non-Christian rule such as Pelagius, executed in the tenth century by the Muslim caliph who ruled the Iberian peninsula.[19] It is this latter's story which was recorded by a Spanish priest named Raguel in the *Martyrdom of St. Pelagius* (Chapter 10) and which stands in this collection for an extremely varied phenomenon, as well as for western Christendom's often violent encounter with Islam.

During the late eighth and early ninth centuries, Charlemagne created an empire based on the old Frankish kingdoms and revived the use of the Roman imperial title in the West. It was this Carolingian Empire, named after and ruled over by Charles's family, that served to organize much of the basic political structures of continental western Europe for centuries to come. Even as it fractured into many constituent kingdoms, the most important (most accurately denoted during this period as the western and eastern Frankish kingdoms) became the seeds for the kingdoms of France and Germany (and through the latter for the so-called Holy Roman Empire). The powerful ecclesiastical hierarchy of the Carolingian empire and its successors did much to clarify the traditions around the recognition of saints and the practice of the cult of relics, as is reflected in Einhard's above-mentioned *Translation of the Relics of Sts. Marcellinus and Peter*.[20] From the ninth through the twelfth centuries, monasteries became the chief custodians of the cult of relics. Several chapters present texts which illustrate different aspects of this intimate relationship between monastic communities and the liturgies and relics of the saints. In Chapter 13, I have gathered together a group of short texts to illustrate the processes through which relics were enshrined and pilgrims came to visit them. In Hrotsvit of Gandersheim's *The Establishment of the Monastery of Gandersheim* (Chapter 11), the bones of deceased saints and the actions of living holy women are central to the foundation and development of a community of nuns. In *The Miracles of St. Ursmer on His Journey through Flanders* (Chapter 16), a group of monks take the relics of their patron saint on what amounts to a fund-raising tour. And in *The Book of Ely* (Chapter 22) the monks discuss how the miraculous powers of their long-dead patron help them in the acquisition and defense of property. These are but a few examples of what was an enormous monastic literature composed about the miraculous powers of saintly patrons over the course of these four centuries.[21] These traditions and practices were not, however, universally accepted. Abbot Guibert of Nogent—himself a monk and occasionally an ardent believer in the efficacy of certain saints' cults—produced one of the most sustained critiques in *On Saints and Their Relics* (Chapter 19). Clerics were also not above using hagiography as a vehicle for satire, as in *A Tale of Doomsday Colum Cille Should Have Left Untold* (Chapter 20), an entertaining and perplexing adaptation of the forms of Old Irish bardic poets to a Christian purpose.

The cults of long-dead saints enshrined in monastic churches provided a continuity with the past. And new saints continued to be recognized in accord with traditional paradigms of sanctity.[22] New forms of sanctity, however, were also emerging over the course of these same centuries. One important form was the association of sanctity with the royal dynasties of certain barbarian kingdoms.[23] During the late tenth century, Odilo of Cluny detailed in his *Epitaph of the August Lady, Adelheid* (Chapter 12) the importance of women as bearers of children and of memory to the Ottonian clan of the eastern Frankish or German kingdom. Over a century later, a priest named Hartvic celebrated the holiness of the first Christian king of the newly converted Hungarians in the *Life of King Stephen of Hungary* (Chapter 18). Opponents of royal power could also occasionally gain sainthood through martyrdom, as in the famed case of Archbishop Thomas Becket of Canterbury, murdered by barons in his church.[24] The liturgical offices for feasts of this saint presented below (Chapter 26) provide a sense of how that man was memorialized, as well as how hagiography was regularly incorporated into the liturgy. A second form of new saints were those associated with the many new forms of reform monasticism which began during these centuries. One important development within this movement was a revival of eremitic monasticism, whose practitioners intended to return to the ascetic practice of the earliest monks in the eastern deserts. Over the previous two centuries hagiography had come to focus ever more exclusively on the miraculous powers of the saint, but in the *Lives* of these men hagiographers returned to an interest in the spiritual life and ascetic exercises of saints, including frequent comparisons to such ancient hagiography as the *Lives of the Desert Fathers*. Peter Damian described one of the most influential of these hermits in the *Life of St. Romuald of Ravenna* (Chapter 14).[25] The most important by far of the new orders of the twelfth century was the Cistercians. Works in many genres, including hagiography, depicted the spiritual practice and thus the lives of such abbots as Bernard of Clairvaux (d. 1153) and Aelred of Rievaulx (d. 1167) as ascents to God in a manner characteristic of Cistercian psychology and spirituality.[26] The Cistercian monks and saints were thus portrayed as imitators of their ancient predecessors in works like *The Tract on the Conversion of Pons of Léras and the True Account of the Beginning of the Monastery at Silvanès* (Chapter 23). Latin had by this time become a learned language, used throughout western Christendom by priests and monks, scholars and bureaucrats, but spoken nowhere as a native tongue. A third innovation was that hagiography in the Romance vernacular languages began to appear in the eleventh century; as it did it took on many of the traits of the genres of vernacular literature.[27] The *Life of St. Alexis* (Chapter 15), one of the earliest surviving and most important pieces of vernacular hagiography, details the story of the conversion of a nobleman who gives up wealth and marriage for a life of voluntary poverty and severe asceticism. In an analogous manner, the thirteenth-century author of the *Saga of Bishop Jón of Hólar* (Chapter 27) used an Old Icelandic form usually employed to tell the stories of heroes and villains to narrate the career of a bishop creating ecclesiastical structures in a land which had been Christian for only a couple of centuries. Much vernacular hagiography was based on Latin originals. One such Latin source, later translated into several vernacular versions, was the *Life of the Dear Friends Amicus and Amelius* (Chapter 21), which portrays—using conventions shared with vernacular romances—the almost paradoxical problems which the practice of Christianity posed for members of a secular nobility based on military power and the making of war.

It should also be noted here that collections of miracles associated with that very special female saint, the Virgin Mary, became a staple of both Latin and vernacular literatures over the course of the twelfth and thirteenth centuries. The example which appears in this collection, some selections from Gautier de Coincy's *Miracles of the Virgin Mary* (Chapter 28), is one of the most important Old French texts concerning the cult of the Virgin, but similar examples could be found in virtually every language of Latin Christendom. The cult of the Virgin itself was one of the oldest in Christendom, her feasts were an important part of the calendar, and a prayer invoking her aid (the Ave Maria or "Hail Mary") was one of the best known Latin prayers among the laity. But literary expressions of the legends about the Virgin's life and her miraculous powers tended to be restricted, in the West at least, to the liturgy until the twelfth century. The flowering of a Marian devotional literature coincided with the rise of a number of important pilgrimages to shrines featuring relics of the Virgin, such as Rocamadour and Chartres in France, Walsingham in England, or Montserrat in Spain.

During the eleventh and twelfth centuries, members of the Christian clerical hierarchy worked at consolidating the power of the institutional Church in part by attacking vulnerable or outcast members of society. One major component of this process was the development of the clerical campaign against heresy, which included the prosecution and often execution of religious dissidents. The attempt to control, indeed eradicate, certain alternative forms of Christianity at times amounted to a campaign of persecution directed by the Church. The stories of heretics, preserved in trial transcripts as well as narrative works, were in an almost literal way the very anti-type of the stories of the saints.[28] Three very disturbing sets of stories translated below show how hagiography can also document aspects of these processes. In the *Life of St. Godelieve* (Chapter 17), the eleventh-century priest Drogo narrated the story of a noblewoman whose entanglement in a brutally abusive marriage led to her death.[29] While the male cleric's depiction of this violent death as a form of martyrdom is undoubtedly sympathetic to the female victim, it is just as surely steeped in the deep misogyny of his culture. Anti-semitism was also dramatically on the rise, linked at least in part to the development of the Crusades.[30] The twelfth-century cleric Thomas of Monmouth recorded the first known accusation against Jews with the so-called blood libel in the *Life and Passion of St. William of Norwich* (Chapter 24). The accusation of Jews with the murder of Christian infants or other trumped-up charges often led to the execution of numbers of Jews. A series of Hebrew works memorializing as martyrs the Jews murdered in the French town of Blois in 1171 (Chapter 25) provides a poignant and telling counterpoint to Thomas of Monmouth's blood libel. The saints who are the subject of these works, the only examples of non-Christian hagiography included in this collection, were the victims of Christian executioners.

New religious movements developed in the thirteenth century which transformed the practice of the religious life, and with it the face of sanctity. Indeed, in Western Christendom, the thirteenth century produced more Christians celebrated by their contemporaries as saints than any other period of the Middle Ages, one tally puts the number at over five hundred. A remarkably high percentage, over a quarter, of these "modern" saints were women. The most influential of the new movements were the mendicant orders, particularly the Franciscans and Dominicans. The primary ideal of these movements was voluntary poverty. The elevation of the ideal of poverty helped to break down some of the distinctions between the religious and the lay life. Christians of both sexes used the mendicant ideal—both formally, within the orders, and informally, in associated confraternities and other groups—to live a religious life in the ordinary world, outside the walls of the monastic cloister. One important lay leader, a merchant from Lyon named Peter Waldes, was moved in part by hearing a performance of the *Life of St. Alexis* (Chapter 15) to use his wealth for the alleviation of famine and poverty. Over the course of the later middle ages, informal groups of so-called tertiaries or third orders—such as the vowed virgins known as beguines in the cities of the Low Countries or those known as *beatae* in the cities of Italy—would become almost as influential in matters of religious practices as the formal orders of priests and nuns. Many of the leading figures of these movements came to be celebrated as saints. Few figures of the Middle Ages were to produce such a large and complex hagiographic tradition as Francis of Assisi (d. 1226), and many other members of the Franciscans and Dominicans had their chroniclers. A significant amount of this hagiographic literature from the mendicant orders already is available in English.[31] It was not only the men (and women) of the formal orders who were celebrated as saints. Clerics such as Jacques de Vitry and Thomas de Cantimpré were drawn to Flanders by stories of sanctity and there lovingly recorded the careers of a number of Beguines and nuns in the region of Liège, including Mary of Oignies, Christina of Saint–Trond, and Lutgard of Aywières. In championing this novel approach to the religious life, which combined traditional asceticism with charitable works and teaching, these hagiographers provided a model for late medieval female sanctity whose characteristics included strenuous fasting, ecstatic visions, devotion to the Eucharist, and service to the urban poor. Once again much of this remarkable literature has been made available in English translation.[32]

The tombs of some new saints, such as Bernard of Tiron (d. 1117) and Louis of Anjou (d. 1297), enjoyed brief vogues in attracting pilgrims, but more commonly the importance of these new saints was linked to their holy example—as transmitted in hagiography—and powers of intercession—as sought in private devotional prayer—rather than to pilgrimage to their shrines. This does not mean that the physical remains of these holy men and women were not prized. The Dominican confessor of Margaret of Ypres (d. 1237) asked the saint's mother to provide him with some of her possessions, such as headresses and shoelaces, after the young girl's death.

Because such good examples of the hagiography of the new religious orders from the thirteenth and even fourteenth centuries are available in English and because these *Lives* tended to be lengthy works, only two examples of these genres are included in this collection. The first (Chapter 31) is a translation into Middle English of Jacques de Vitry's *Life of St. Marie d'Oignies*, one of the most influential of the Flemish Beguines. As a translation of Latin hagiography into a vernacular language, this text provides an example not only of the ideals of voluntary poverty and feminine sanctity so important in the thirteenth century, but also of the efforts made to make these stories available to a wider audience. The second (Chapter 32) is the so-called *Autobiography* of Peter of the Morrone, a noted Franciscan ascetic who briefly became pope as Celestine V. This document reminds us that there is a rich tradition extant from the later Middle Ages of self-reflective spiritual and mystical texts written by men and women who came posthumously to be considered saints, a tradition of writing which some scholars have called "auto-hagiography."[33]

The proliferation of such contemporary saints caused clerics to become anxious about their control over the legends and the cults of the new saints. Beginning in the eleventh and twelfth centuries, but decisively in the thirteenth century, the papacy moved to take control of the legal means by which new saints were officially recognized. Such papal canonization involved legal inquiries into the lives of reputed saints: not all such inquiries, known technically as *processus canonizationis* or "processes of canonization," resulted in a positive verdict. The records of these inquiries, conducted by clerics who interviewed witnesses, represent a new form of hagiography and one of the most precious sources for information about religious practice in the later Middle Ages. Extracts from one such process, which resulted in the canonization of the French Dominican preacher Vincent Ferrer (d. 1419), is included in this collection (Chapter 35).[34] Relatively few individuals actually achieved such papal canonization (some seventy-two between 1198 and 1418) and so many of the "holy people" of the later Middle Ages, although celebrated like the saints in local liturgies, curing shrines, and hagiography, should technically be known under the title "blessed" according to the practices of the Roman Catholic Church. Such are the inherent ambiguities of the term "saint."

The cults of these new saints did not by any means supplant the cults of traditional saints. Indeed the cults of many martyrs and other saintly patrons drawn from the early centuries of Christianity became even more important and widespread through liturgical commemoration and iconographic representation over the course of the later Middle Ages. Relics came to be displayed more prominently in the churches of the later Middle Ages than they had been in earlier periods. New fragments of saintly bodies were eagerly sought and placed in ornate reliquaries. Many relics were brought to Western Christendom as spoils from the East during the course of the crusades. In 1248, for example, that vigorous crusader King Louis IX of France (who was later considered to be a saint) had the beautiful Sainte Chapelle in Paris built as a form of relic treasury: the building even imitated a reliquary in its very shape. Other forms of church ornamentation also celebrated the cult of saints, as hagiographic legends were prominently displayed in stained-glass windows and painted tryptychs. Pilgrimage to the shrines of certain saints of the traditional order also remained important. Raymond Clemens has gathered a group of documents (Chapter 29) illustrating how the Dominican order cultivated the cult of the biblical figure Mary Magdalen, particularly around the shrine of her relics which the Dominicans controlled in Provence. It is a useful reminder that pilgrimage to shrines of local significance remained important, although they were superseded by shrines of transregional meaning, such as those of the martyrs in Rome, the many Marian shrines, or the Holy Sepulchre of Jesus and other sites connected with His life around Jerusalem.[35]

Another means of inculcating the correct practice of Christianity, and one which particularly developed in association with the mendicant orders, was preaching. One of the reasons for the success of those orders was the vigorous attempts being made on the part of the ecclesiastical hierarchy to reach the urban laity. Preachers needed collections of exemplary stories of a sort different from that produced for monastic novices. Many such collections which made use of hagiographic traditions were gathered for preaching purposes. The most influential hagiographic compendium in Western Christendom during the later Middle Ages was the *Golden Legend*, completed by Jacapo da Voragine, an Italian Dominican, in 1258.[36]

The translation of legends concerning traditional saints into the vernacular languages served as an important part of this widespread clerical effort to disseminate and inculcate proper religious practice. Although written in Latin, for example, the *Golden Legend* became available in virtually every vernacular language of western Christendom by the fifteenth century. These and the translations of many other works into the varied vernaculars greatly dominated, in terms of the sheer number of texts, the hagiographic production of the later Middle Ages.[37] Hagiography thus became much more available to an audience of religious women and laypeople who were literate only in the vernacular. "Translation" is often not an accurate term for these works, which were often very free in their rendering of the Latin originals. Often the authors of these vernacular legends followed the style of contemporary epics and romances, although they also self-consciously attempted to produce a morally uplifting rival to such secular works. The author of a *Life of St. Barbara* in Old French claimed, contrasting the heroines of her tale to the heroes of the popular *Song of Roland*, "I want to tell a new kind of story, / Never heard before. / Know that it does not concern Ogier, / Nor Roland, nor Olivier, / But a most holy maiden / Who was very courteous and beautiful."[38] The moralist Thomas of Chobham specifically exempted those *jongleurs*, or minstrels, who performed works about the saints from his general condemnation of that profession. In the process of adaptation, the legends often changed, and it is often important to study what authors of vernacular hagiography omitted from or changed in their traditional sources. In a compelling illustration of this process, Wendy Larson has brought together several significantly differing versions of the legend of the martyr Margaret of Antioch (Chapter 30) which circulated in England, both in Middle English and in Latin (specifically the relevant section from the *Golden Legend*), during the latter part of the thirteenth century. The legends of the early Christian martyrs were also differentiated by the linguistic and national context within which they appeared in the vernacular. An excellent example is provided by the Old Czech version of the *Life of St. Catherine of Alexandria* (Chapter 34), who was, like Margaret, purported to be a martyr on slim historical evidence. One of the earliest pieces of hagiography extant in Czech, this work—composed by a cleric, quite possibly a Dominican preacher, in the entourage of Emperor Charles IV—gives evidence not only of a desire to make the teachings of the *Golden Legend* available to a wider public, but also distinctly nationalist concerns related to the status of the Slavic languages. Similarly, but on the other side of Western Christendom, the Old Welsh version of the *Life of St. David* (Chapter 33)—a sixth-century missionary bishop and the national patron of Wales—also betrays a complex combination of religious and political concerns as it provides access to ancient Latin traditions for a fourteenth-century audience literate in the vernacular. Through texts like these, saints from the ancient past continued to be present and active for pious Christians of the late medieval West.

The celebration of traditional saints certainly remained an important element in the culture of devotion practiced by pious laypeople not only in churches and other public religious spaces, but also in the home. Preachers used exemplary stories gleaned from the lives of the saints to spice up their sermons. Glass-fronted reliquaries made bits of holy bodies visible to the faithful. Confraternities adopted appropriate saints as their patrons and celebrated their feasts in elaborate fashion. Books of hours promoted the observance of many feasts, as well as the cult of the Virgin Mary, in the home. Individuals and communities sought the aid of "specialist" saints with particular problems, such as St. Roch for the plague and St. Margaret of Antioch for difficult childbirths.

Over the course of the fourteenth and fifteenth centuries, however, devotion to the passion of Christ and bodily mortification, accompanied by a heightened emotionalism often expressed in the so-called gift of tears, began to take a more central place in spiritual and penitential practices.[39] The varied reformations of the sixteenth century, both Protestant and Catholic, brought with them radical changes in the practice of the cult of saints. Protestant theologians and preachers rejected the idea of saintly intercession, which was thought in Lutheran terminology to constitute a reliance on works rather than on faith. Reformers of all stripes—Desiderius Erasmus and Thomas More, Martin Luther and John Calvin—composed, generally in the vernacular, critiques of the cult of relics.[40] Theological opposition often turned to violent iconoclasm during the Wars of Religion. Relic collections were destroyed and the statues of the saints in many churches still bear the scars of attack. In the mid-sixteenth century, the Council of Trent took many steps to reorganize the practice of the cult of saints and the means by which saints were canonized within early modern Catholicism.

In the midst of these conflicts and changes, a person's holiness was often examined by hostile secular courts or religious tribunals for conformity to a prevalent orthodoxy. Well before the Protestant Reformation, some who claimed visionary or miraculous powers—women more often than men—were burned for heresy or witchcraft, even when their claims and practices did not vary greatly from those of some saints canonized by the Church. The final texts in this collection come from just such a case in the fifteenth century. Joan of Arc was a visionary who used her prophetic powers as a means of brilliantly, if evanescently, rallying the military fortunes of the kingdom of France against the English forces which occupied much of its territory. Sentenced to death by a corrupt ecclesiastical tribunal dominated by English interests, she was burnt at the stake for heresy in 1431. Virtually from that moment she was treated by the French as a saint and national patron. Almost five hundred years later, her visions and actions served as the basis for an official inquiry which led to her canonization as a saint in 1920. Nadia Margolis has collected a dossier of texts (Chapter 36) to illustrate Joan's varied trials. It provides an appropriate, if ambiguous, note on which to conclude this collection.

Guide to Further Reading

In this guide, I seek to provide information about some important reference works and general studies in the field of hagiography. Much in the way of more specific references may be found in the guides which accompany each chapter. I will emphasize works available in English. (For translations of primary sources into English, one may consult the notes to this introduction.) Unfortunately no adequate general guide to the history, study, and use of hagiography exists in English. The best introduction to research in hagiographic sources currently available is Jacques Dubois and Jean-Loup Lemaitre, *Sources et méthodes de l'hagiographie médiévale* [Sources and methods of medieval hagiography] (Paris, 1993), which includes an extensive, but largely Francophone, bibliography. René Aigrain, *L'hagiographie: ses sources, ses méthodes, son histoire* [Hagiography: its sources, its methods, its history] (Paris, 1953) remains useful, particularly on the history of hagiographic scholarship. David Knowles, *Great Historical Enterprises* (London, 1962) and several of the chapters in *Medieval Scholarship: Biographical Studies on the Formation of a Discipline*, ed. Helen Damico and Joseph Zavadil (New York, 1995) provide much information on the early history of hagiographic scholarship.

A major scholarly enterprise under the direction of the Belgian scholar Guy Philippart is currently collecting a series of surveys of medieval hagiographic sources and the scholarly study of them; two of its volumes have already been published. When complete, it will be the most comprehensive guide to hagiographic scholarship: *Hagiographies. Histoire internationale de la littérature hagiographique latine et vernaculaire en Occident des origines à 1500* [Hagiographies: an international history of the Latin and vernacular literature of hagiography in the West from its origins to 1500], ed. Guy Philippart, 4 vols. (Turnhout, 1994-present). The individual articles are in English, French, German, and Italian. Philippart himself has written a thorough study of the etymology and development of the term "hagiography," see Guy Philippart, "Hagiographes et hagiographie, hagiologes et hagiologie; des mots et des concepts" [Hagiographers and hagiography, hagiologers and hagiology: concerning words and concepts], *Hagiographica* 1 (1994): 1–16.

For over three and one-half centuries, the Jesuit members of the *Société des Bollandistes* [Society of Bollandists], founded by Jean Bollandus (d. 1665), have been at the forefront of hagiographic scholarship. It is they who have edited the single most important collection of hagiographic sources, that is the *Acta Sanctorum* [Acts of the saints], the first of whose sixty-eight immense folio volumes appeared in 1643. They continue their efforts to this day through the edition of the journal *Analecta Bollandiana* [Bollandist gleanings], which contains regular bibliographies and summaries of hagiographic scholarship. Their work is well documented at the site which they maintain on the World Wide Web: http://www.kbr.be/~socboll. Members of this group have compiled and regularly updated the standard guides to the primary sources of hagiography written in the clerical languages of Latin and Greek, as well as those of the Christian East: *Bibliotheca hagiographica latina antiquae et mediae aetatis*, 3 vols., Subsidia Hagiographica 6 and 70 (Brussels, 1898 and 1986); *Bibliotheca hagiographica graeca*, third edition (with supplement) by François Halkin, Subsidia Hagiographica 8 and 65 (Brussels, 1957 and 1984); *Bibliotheca hagiographica orientalis*, ed. Paul Peeters, Subsidia Hagiographica 10 (Brussels, 1910). In these reference works, each hagiographic source is provided a distinct number, and all extant editions of it (as well as important manuscripts in some cases) are listed. In the chapters which follows, every Latin or Greek primary source is identified by its number in the *Bibliotheca hagiographica latina* or the *Bibliotheca hagiographica graeca*. Few equivalent standard references yet exist for hagiography written in the vernacular languages, although several important projects to catalog such vernacular literature are currently in process. An exception is Ole Widding, Hans Bekker-Nielsen, and Laurence Shook, "The Lives of the Saints in Old Norse Prose: A Handlist," *Mediaeval Studies* 25 (1963): 294–337. Documentation of other projects may be found in the articles of Philippart's *Hagiographies* and in recent numbers of the journal *Hagiographica*. The problems faced in one such project are well described by E. Gordon Whatley in "An Introduction to the Study of English Prose Hagiography: Sources and Resources," in *Holy Men and Holy Women: Old English Prose Saints' Lives and Their Contexts*, ed. Paul Szarmach (Albany, NY, 1996), pp. 3–32. On the same problem, also see Michael Lapidge, "The Saintly Life in Anglo-Saxon England," in *The Cambridge Companion to Old English Literature*, eds. Malcolm Godden and Michael Lapidge (Cambridge, 1991), pp. 243–63.

Two useful dictionaries providing information about specific saints are available in English: Donald Attwater, *The Penguin Dictionary of Saints* (Harmondsworth, 1965) and David Farmer, *The Oxford Dictionary of Saints*, revised edition (Oxford, 1992). Anglophone readers might also consult the volumes of the *New Catholic Encyclopedia*. Unfortunately the well-known work by Alban Butler entitled *The Lives of the Saints* (revised edition by Herbert Thurston and Donald Attwater [London, 1926–38; reprint, New York, 1956]) is largely based on secondary sources and is often unreliable. A new revision of Butler's work currently being undertaken by David Farmer promises more accurate information. For those beginning to undertake serious research into hagiographic sources, further references and bibliography may be found in: *Bibliotheca Sanctorum* [Library of the saints], eds. Iosepho Vizzini et al., 13 vols. (1961–69); *Vies des saints et des bienheureux par les reverends pères bénédictins de Paris* [Lives of the saints and of the blessed by the Reverend Benedictine priests of Paris], eds. Jules Baudot, Paul Antin, and Jacques Dubois, 13 vols. (1935–59); *Histoire des saints et de la sainteté chrétienne* [History of Christian saints and sanctity], eds. André Mandouze, André Vauchez, et al., 11 vols. (Paris, 1986–88). The best guide to the iconography of symbols associated with the saints available in English is *The Bible and the Saints*, ed. Gaston Duchet-Suchaux and Michel Pastoureau, trans. David Howell (Paris, 1994). Much more complete is Gertrud Schiller, *Ikonographie der christlichen Kunst* [Iconography of Christian art], 5 vols. (Gütersloh, 1966–91). For a useful bibliography of works on pilgrimage, consult Linda Kay Davidson and Maryjane Dunn-Wood, *Pilgrimage in the Middle Ages: A Research Guide* (New York, 1993).

In the decades around 1900, a Bollandist named Hippolyte Delehaye laid the foundations for modern hagiographic scholarship. Although Delehaye wrote in French, his seminal essay on hagiographic method has appeared in two separate English translations, see *Legends of the Saints*, trans. V.M. Crawford (from the first French edition; London, 1907; reprint, Notre Dame, IN, 1961) and trans. Donald Attwater (from the fourth French edition; New

York, 1962). Also available in English is Delehaye's history of the Bollandist enterprise, see *The Work of the Bollandists Through Three Centuries, 1615–1915* (Princeton, 1922). Approaches to the history of medieval Christianity have changed greatly since the time of Delehaye, who was concerned to provide a Catholic response to positivist historicism. One of the most influential works in the development of medieval religious history has recently been translated into English; see Herbert Grundmann, *Religious Movements in the Middle Ages*, trans. Steven Rowan (German original, 1935; Notre Dame, IN, 1995). For an interesting, but controversial, study of these historiographical developments, see John Van Engen, "The Christian Middle Ages as an Historiographical Problem," *American Historical Review* 91 (1986): 519–52.

The formative work in applying these new methodologies in religious history to the subject matter of medieval hagiography was written, ironically enough, by a Czech Marxist. František Graus, *Volk, Herrscher und Heiliger im Reich der Merowinger. Studeien zur Hagiographie der Merowingerzeit* [People, lords, and saints in the kingdom of the Franks: studies on the hagiography of the Merovingian period] (Prague, 1965) remains one of the most innovative and important studies of medieval history written in the second half of the twentieth century, although it has lamentably never been translated into English. In essence Graus challenged historians to use the then relatively neglected genres of hagiography to serve as sources for the social history of Western Christianity. That challenge has been taken up explicitly or implicitly by a wide variety of scholars of medieval religion, society, literature, and art over the course of the last three decades. The chapters of this collection bear eloquent witness to the fruits of that scholarship.

Recent studies of medieval hagiography, however, would be almost literally inconceivable were it not for the pioneering work of three magisterial scholars—Peter Brown, André Vauchez, and Caroline Bynum—published initially over the course of the 1970s and 1980s. Peter Brown investigated the function of sanctity as a form of social or political power in the later Roman Empire. He first explored the role of living ascetic saints in the villages of fifth- and sixth-century Syria in "The Rise and Function of the Holy Man in Late Antiquity," *Journal of Roman Studies* 61 (1971): 80–101, which is more easily available as reprinted in a collection of his articles entitled *Society and the Holy in Late Antiquity* (Chicago, 1982), pp. 103–52. He thus coined an important scholarly concept which has influenced virtually all later Anglophone scholarship on hagiography—that is "holy man"—through the brilliantly simple expedient of taking his sources literally. Since the original publication of that article, he has regularly reevaluated his findings in the light of newer scholarship: "The Saint as Exemplar in Late Antiquity," in *Saints and Virtues*, ed. John Hawley (Berkeley, 1987), pp. 3–14; "Arbiters of the Holy: The Christian Holy Man in Late Antiquity," in Peter Brown, *Authority and the Sacred* (Cambridge, 1995), pp. 55–78; "The Rise and Function of the Holy Man in Late Antiquity, 1971–1997," *Journal of Early Christian Studies*

6 (1998): 353–76. (The autumn number of the *Journal of Early Christian Studies* for 1998, in which the latter essay appeared, is a special issue, edited by Susanna Elm, devoted to analyses and reconsiderations of the scholarly heritage of Brown's original article.) Brown also analyzed the posthumous role of saints in *The Cult of the Saints: Its Rise and Function in Latin Christianity* (Chicago, 1981), a pathbreaking work on the beginnings of the cult of relics in Western Christendom. Secondly, André Vauchez interrogated the ways in which hagiographic sources themselves were produced and how this process in turn formed ideas of sanctity in *La sainteté en occident aux derniers siècles du moyen âge d'après les procès de canonisation et les documents hagiographiques*, Bibliothèque des Ecoles françaises d'Athènes et de Rome 241 (Rome, 1981; second edition, 1987), which has been translated as *Sainthood in the Later Middle Ages*, trans. Jean Birrell (Cambridge, 1997). In it Vauchez examined the records of the formal processes initiated for the canonization of saints between 1198 and 1431 in the hope of illuminating the practices of Western Christianity—and the attempted control of those practices by the papacy—during those centuries. Anglophone readers may garner a sense of his extensive work on related topics from the essays collected in *The Laity in the Middle Ages: Religious Beliefs and Devotional Practices* (Notre Dame, IN, 1993). Finally, Caroline Bynum highlighted gender as a crucial category in the analysis of hagiography and sanctity in *Holy Feast and Holy Fast: The Religious Significance of Food to Medieval Women* (Berkeley, 1987). She has further explored and deepened her analysis in the articles collected in *Fragmentation and Redemption: Essays on Gender and the Human Body in Medieval Religion* (Boston, 1991).

Much innovative scholarship has appeared on saints and their cults since the publication of Brown's article on the "holy man." The following short list includes some of the most significant, listed in chronological order, although it necessarily omits much by including only works in English and emphasizing books over articles: Patrick Geary, *Furta Sacra: Thefts of Relics in the Central Middle Ages* (Princeton, 1978; second edition 1990); Jean-Claude Schmitt, *The Holy Greyhound: Guinefort, Healer of Children Since the Thirteenth Century* (French original, Paris, 1979; Cambridge, 1983); Phyllis Johnson and Brigitte Cazelles, *Le vain siècle Guerpir: A Literary Approach to Sainthood Through Old French Hagiography of the Twelfth Century* (Chapel Hill, NC, 1979); Donald Weinstein and Rudolph Bell, *Saints and Society: The Two Worlds of Latin Christendom, 1000–1700* (Chicago, 1982); Clare Stancliffe, *Saint Martin and His Hagiographer: History and Miracle in Sulpicius Severus* (Oxford, 1983); Richard Kieckhefer, *Unquiet Lives: Fourteenth-Century Saints and Their Religious Milieu* (Chicago, 1984); Sherry Reames, *Legenda Aurea: A Reexamination of its Paradoxical History* (Madison, WI, 1985); Alison Elliott, *Roads to Paradise. Reading the Lives of the Early Saints* (Hanover, NH, 1987); Thomas Heffernan, *Sacred Biography. Saints and Their Biographers in the Middle Ages* (Oxford, 1988); Susan Ridyard, *The Royal Saints of Anglo-Saxon England* (Cambridge, 1988); David Rollason,

Saints and Relics in Anglo-Saxon England (Oxford, 1989); Katrien Heene, "Merovingian and Carolingian Hagiography. Continuity or Change in Public and Aims?" *Analecta Bollandiana* 107 (1989): 415–28; Jeffrey Hamburger, "The Use of Images in the Pastoral Care of Nuns: the Case of Heinrich Suso and the Dominicans," *Art Bulletin* 71 (1989): 20–46; Thomas Head, *Hagiography and the Cult of Saints: The Diocese of Orléans, 800–1200* (Cambridge, 1990); Gabor Klaniczay, *The Uses of Supernatural Power: The Transformation of Popular Religion in Medieval and Early-Modern Europe*, trans. Susan Singerman (Princeton, 1990); Paul Fouracre, "Merovingian History and Merovingian Historiography," *Past and Present* 127 (1990): 3–38; Sharon Farmer, *Communities of Saint Martin: Legend and Ritual in Medieval Tours* (Ithaca, NY, 1991); Cynthia Hahn, "Picturing the Text: Narrative in the *Life of the Saints*," *Art History* 13 (1990): 1–33; Julia Smith, "Oral and Written: Saints, Miracles, and Relics in Brittany, c. 850–1250," *Speculum* 65 (1990): 309–43; Lisa Bitel, *Isle of the Saints: Monastic Settlement and Christian Community in Early Ireland* (Ithaca, NY, 1991); John Coakley, "Gender and the Authority of Friars: the Significance of Holy Women for Thirteenth-Century Franciscans and Dominicans," *Church History* 60 (1991): 445–60; Aviad Kleinberg, *Prophets in Their Own Country: Living Saints and the Making of Sainthood in the Later Middle Ages* (Chicago, 1992), Dyan Elliott, *Spiritual Marriage: Sexual Abstinence in Medieval Wedlock* (Princeton, 1993); Pamela Gehrke, *Saint and Scribes: Medieval Hagiography in its Manuscript Context* (Berkeley, 1993); Susanna Elm, *"Virgins of God": The Making of Asceticism in Late Antiquity* (Oxford, 1994); Barbara Abou-el-Haj, *The Medieval Cult of Saints: Formations and Transformations* (Cambridge, 1994); Michael Goodich, *Violence and Miracle in the Fourteenth Century: Private Grief and Public Salvation* (Chicago, 1995); Yitzhak Hen, *Culture and Religion in Merovingian Gaul, A.D. 481–751* (Leiden, 1995); Julia Smith, "The Problem of Female Sanctity in Carolingian Europe c. 780–920," *Past and Present* 146 (1995): 3–37; Amy Hollywood, *The Soul as Virgin Wife: Mechtild of Magdeburg, Marguerite Porete, and Meister Eckhart* (Notre Dame, IN, 1995); Cynthia Hahn, "The Sight of the Saint in the Early Middle Ages: The Construction of Sanctity in Shrines East and West," *Speculum,* 72 (1997): 1079–1106; Jane Schulenburg, *"Forgetful of Their Sex": Female Sanctity and Society, ca. 500–1100* (Chicago, 1998).

Also see the articles collected in *The Church and Healing*, ed. W.J. Sheils, Studies in Church History 19 (Oxford, 1982); *Saints and Their Cults*, ed. Steven Wilson (Cambridge, 1983); *Images of Sainthood in Medieval Europe*, eds. Renate Blumenfeld-Kosinski and Timea Szell (Ithaca, NY, 1991); *Women and Religion in Medieval and Renaissance Italy*, eds. Daniel Bornstein and Roberto Rusconi (Italian original, 1992; Chicago, 1996); *Martyrs and Martyrologies*, ed. Diana Wood, Studies in Church History 30 (Oxford, 1993); *Creative Women in Medieval and Early Modern Italy: A Religious and Artistic Renaissance*, eds. E. Ann Matter and John Coakley (Philadelphia, 1994). Finally, two catalogs of art exhibits which have made particularly interesting use of objects connected to the cult of saints are: *The Art of Devotion in the Late Middle Ages in Europe, 1300–1500,* ed. Henk van Os (Princeton, 1994) and *Memory in the Middle Ages*, eds. Nancy Netzer and Virginia Reinburg (Chestnut Hill, MA, 1995).

NOTES

1. Eddius Stephanus, *The Life of Bishop Wilfrid by Eddius Stephanus*, ed. and trans. Bertram Colgrave (Cambridge, 1927; reprint 1985), preface, p. 3.

2. In this introduction, I have provided foonotes only to translations of primary sources, in order to cite the source of quoted passages and, more importantly, to provide the reader a number of works in English translation which can serve as useful comparisons and adjuncts to the present collection. I have adapted some of the essay which follows from articles on "Hagiography" which I have written for two reference works also published, like the present collection, by Garland Press: *Medieval France: An Encyclopedia*, eds. William Kibler and Grover Zinn (New York, 1995), pp. 433–37 and *Encyclopedia of Medieval Women*, eds. Katherina Wilson and Nadia Margolis (New York, in press). In addition to the printed works below, a large number of hagiographic works are available via the Internet; it should be noted that, due to copyright laws, many of the works thus available are somewhat dated. An extraordinarily useful catalog and guide to these works (including active links to them) is maintained by Paul Halsall on the World Wide Web as "The Internet Medieval Sourcebook: Saints' Lives" (http://www. fordham.edu/halsall/sbook3.html).

3. The first two volumes in the series Byzantine Saints' Lives in Translation have appeared: *Holy Women of Byzantium: Ten Saints' Lives in English Translation*, ed. Alice-Mary Talbot (Washington, D.C., 1996) and *Byzantine Defenders of Images: Eight Saints' Lives in English Translation*, ed. Alice-Mary Talbot (Washington, D.C., 1998). Some useful collections presenting translations of representative works of hagiography from various areas of the Eastern Christian world include: *The Life and Times of St. Gregory the Illuminator: The Founder and Patron Saint of the Armenian Church*, trans. S.C. Malan (London, 1868); *The Book of the Saints of the Ethiopian Church: A Translation of the Ethiopic Synaxarium*, ed. and trans. E A. Wallis Budge, 4 vols. (Cambridge, 1928); *Lives of the Serbian Saints*, ed. and trans. Voyeslav Yanich and C. Patrick Hankey (London, 1921); John of Ephesus, *Lives of the Eastern Saints*, ed. and trans. E.W. Brooks, 3 vols., Patrologia orientalis 17–19 (Paris, 1923–25); *Three Byzantine Saints: Contemporary Biographies*, ed. and trans. Elizabeth Dawes and Norman Baynes (Oxford, 1948; reprint, Crestwood, NY, 1977); *Lives and Legends of the Georgian Saints*, ed. and trans. David Lang, Ethical and Religious Classics of East and West 15 (London, 1956); *Holy Women of the Syrian Orient*, ed. and trans. Sebastian Brock and Susan Harvey (Berkeley, 1987); *The Hagiography of Kievan Rus*, ed. and trans. Paul Hollingsworth, Harvard Library of Early Ukranian Literature 2 (Cambridge, MA, 1992). Also, much of the hagiography concerning early asceticism and monasticism listed below in note 5 was written in the Christian East. For a complete listing of translations of Byzantine Greek hagiography into modern languages, see the extremely useful "Survey of Translations of Byzantine Saints' Lives" maintained online (and regularly updated) by Alice-Mary Talbot at the Dumbarton Oaks site on the World Wide Web (http://www.doaks.org/translives. html).

4. Translations of all "authentic" acts of martyrs (that is those by roughly contemporary authors), both Greek and Latin, may be found in *The Acts of the Christian Martyrs*, ed. Herbert Musurillo (Oxford, 1972). Many other translations exist of several of these texts, such as *The Martyrdom of St. Polycarp* and *The Passion of Sts. Perpetua and Felicity*. The development of traditions about the martyrs in the Christian West during the later fourth and early fifth century can be seen in *The Works of Prudentius*, ed. and trans. H.J. Thomson, 2 vols., Loeb Classical Library (Cambridge, MA, 1953). Traditions about Christian martyrs were also preserved outside the orthodox Church, see *Donatist Martyr Stories: The Church in Conflict in Roman North Africa*, ed. and trans. Maureen Tilley, Translated Texts for Historians (Liverpool, 1996).

Introduction

xxxiii

5. Asceticism itself, of course, predated monasticism and even Christianity. A number of important texts on asceticism in the late antique world (including some that are hagiographic) have been collected in *Ascetic Behavior in Greco-Roman Antiquity: A Sourcebook*, ed. Vincent Wimbush (Minneapolis, MN 1990).

6. Some fourth- and fifth-century works which record the development of monasticism in the Christian East and are available in translation include: Palladius, *The Dialogue Concerning the Life of Chrysostom*, trans. Herbert Moore (London, 1921) and *The Lausiac History*, trans. Robert Meyer (Washington, DC, 1964); Gregory of Nyssa, *Life of St. Macrina* in *Ascetical Works*, trans. V.W. Callahan (Washington, DC, 1967) or, alternatively, *The Life of Saint Macrina*, trans. Kevin Corrigan (Toronto, 1987; reprint, Toronto, 1997); *Pachomian Koinonia, vol. 1: The Life of Saint Pachomius and his Disciples*, trans. Armand Veilleux, Cistercian Studies 45 (Kalamazoo, MI, 1980); *The Sayings of the Desert Fathers: The Alphabetical Collection*, trans. Benedicta Ward (London, 1975; reprint, New York, 1980); *The Lives of the Desert Fathers*, trans. Norman Russell, Cistercian Studies 34 (Kalamazoo, MI, 1981); Theodoret of Cyrrhus, *A History of the Monks of Syria*, trans. R.M. Price, Cistercian Studies 88 (Kalamazoo, MI 1985); *The Lives of Simeon Stylites*, ed. and trans. Robert Doran, Cistercian Studies 112 (Kalamazoo, MI 1992); *Histories of the Monks of Upper Egypt and Life of Paphnutius*, trans. Tim Vivian, Cistercian Studies 140 (Kalamazoo, MI, 1993). A useful selection of works of early monastic hagiography from the Christian East is *Journeying into God: Seven Early Monastic Lives*, ed. and trans. Tim Vivian (Minneapolis, MN, 1996).

7. English translations of a Latin version of the *Sayings of the Desert Fathers* (see above note) and of John Cassian's *Conferences* (which, although not hagiography, did draw deeply on the eastern hagiographic traditions discussed in the above note) may be found in *Western Asceticism*, ed. and trans. Owen Chadwick, Library of Christian Classics (London and Philadelphia, 1958). Some of the hagiographic works of Jerome may be found in *Early Christian Biographies*, ed. Roy Deferrari, Fathers of the Church 15 (New York, 1952), pp. 217–97. A fuller selection of Jerome's hagiography, but in a dated translation, may be found in Jerome, *Letters and Select Works*, ed. and trans. W.H. Fremantle, et al., Library of Nicene and Post-Nicene Fathers, second series 6 (Edinburgh, 1893). Jerome described the lives of many ascetics in his *Letters*. Works specifically about early female ascetics, from both East and West, have been collected in *Handmaids of the Lord: The Lives of Holy Women in Late Antiquity and the Early Middle Ages*, ed. Joan Petersen, Cistercian Studies 143 (Kalamazoo, MI, 1996), which includes useful translations of Jerome's most important letters concerning female ascetics.

8. Augustine, *Confessions*, Book 8, Sections 15–17. There has been much speculation that Jerome was one of the three anonymous companions of Ponticianus mentioned by Augustine.

9. Ambrose described his discovery of the relics in a letter to his sister (*Letter 22*) which may be found in Ambrose, *Select Works and Letters*, ed. and trans. H. de Romestin, Library of Nicene and Post-Nicene Fathers, second series 10 (Edinburgh, 1896).

10. Translations of the *Lives* of Martin, Ambrose, and Augustine may be found in *Early Christian Biographies* (see note 7 above) and in *The Western Fathers*, ed. F.R. Hoare (New York, 1954); those of Martin and Augustine appear in updated versions with fuller notes in *Soldiers of Christ: Saints' Lives from Late Antiquity and the Early Middle Ages*, eds. Thomas Noble and Thomas Head (University Park, PA, 1995), pp. 1–74. In addition to her translation of the *Life of St. Porphyry* which appears here, Claudia Rapp is preparing a translation of the *Life of St. Epiphanius* to be published in the Translated Texts for Historians series published by the University of Liverpool Press.

11. A useful collection of translated texts concerning this process of Christianization is *Christianity and Paganism, 350–750: The Conversion of Western Europe*, ed. and trans. J.N. Hillgarth, revised ed. (Philadelphia, 1986).

12. An interesting comparison to the episcopal lives written ca. 400 (listed in note 9) might be made to the *Lives* of bishops in the western Roman provinces during the fifth and first half of the sixth century—such as Honoratus of Arles (d. ca. 430), Germanus of Auxerre (d. 446), Epiphanius of Pavia (d. 496), and Caesarius of Arles (d. 542)—who largely had to deal with barbarian rather than imperial civil authorities: Hilary of Arles, *Life of St.*

Honoratus in *The Western Fathers*, pp. 247–80; Constantius of Lyon, *Life of St. Germanus of Auxerre* in *Soldiers of Christ*, pp. 75–106 (see note 10 above); Ennodius, *Life of St. Epiphanius*, trans. Genevieve Cook (Washington, D.C., 1942.); *Life of St. Caesarius of Arles* in *Caesarius of Arles: Life, Testament, Letters*, ed. and trans. William Klingshirn, Translated Texts for Historians (Liverpool, 1994). Honoratus was abbot of Lérins before becoming bishop of Arles. And one might also examine the *Lives* of such ascetic saints as Severinus of Noricum (d. 482) and Genofeva (or Geneviève) of Paris (d. ca. 500): Eugippius, *Life of St. Severinus*, trans. George Robinson (Cambridge, MA, 1914) and *Life of St. Genofeva* in *Sainted Women of the Dark Ages*, eds. and trans. Jo Ann McNamara and John Halborg, with E. Gordon Whatley (Durham, NC, 1992), pp. 17–37.

13. As quoted in Raymond Van Dam, *Saints and Their Miracles in Late Antique Gaul* (Princeton, 1993), p. 314.

14. All the hagiographic works of Gregory of Tours have been translated: *Life of the Fathers*, trans. Edward James, Translated Texts for Historians (Liverpool, 1986); *Glory of the Martyrs*, trans. Raymond Van Dam, Translated Texts for Historians (Liverpool, 1988); *Glory of the Confessors*, trans. Raymond Van Dam, Translated Texts for Historians (Liverpool, 1988); *The Suffering and Miracles of the Martyr St. Julian* and *The Miracles of the Bishop St. Martin* in Van Dam, *Saints and Their Miracles* (see above note). There are numerous translations available of Gregory the Great's *Dialogues*, particularly of the second book which concerns the life of St. Benedict of Nursia; perhaps the best is that by Odo Zimmerman, The Fathers of the Church 39 (Washington, DC, 1959).

15. Gregory of Tours, *Life of the Fathers*, p. 27.

16. There are a number of good collections of hagiography in translation from the barbarian kingdoms. For the kingdoms of the Franks, see *Sainted Women of the Dark Ages* (see note 12 above) and *Late Merogingian France: History and Hagiography, 640–720*, eds. and trans. Paul Fouracre and Richard Gerberding (Manchester, 1996). For Visigothic Spain, see *Lives of the Visigothic Fathers*, ed. and trans. A.T. Fear, Translated Texts for Historians (Liverpool, 1997). For the Anglo-Saxon kingdoms, see *Two Lives of Saint Cuthbert*, trans. Bertram Colgrave (Cambridge, 1940; reprint 1985); *Anglo-Saxon Saints and Heroes*, ed. and trans. Clinton Albertson (New York, 1967); *The Age of Bede*, ed. and trans. David Farmer (Harmondsworth, 1983); as well as Eddius Stephanus, *The Life of Bishop Wilfrid* (see note 1 above). In Italy one of the most important hagiographic works of the early Middle Ages was the periodic compiling of the *Liber Pontificalis* or *Lives of the Popes*. The earlier sections of this work have appeared in two volumes of the Translated Texts for Historians series (see note 10 above), both translated by Raymond Davis: *The Book of Pontiffs (Liber Pontificalis)* (Liverpool, 1989) and *The Lives of the Eighth-Century Popes (Liber Pontificalis)* (Liverpool, 1992).

17. Much Irish hagiography (both Latin and Celtic) has been translated, but the originals are often difficult to date with precision and the translations from older scholarly works now often sound quite dated: *Lives of the Saints from the Book of Lismore*, ed. Whitley Stokes (Oxford, 1890); *Lives of Irish Saints*, ed. and trans. Charles Plummer, 2 vols. (Oxford, 1922); M. A. O'Brien, "The Old Irish Life of St. Brigit," *Irish Historical Studies*, 1 (1938–39): 121–34, 343–53; *St. Patrick: His Writings and Muirchu's Life*, ed. and trans. A.B.E. Hood (Totowa, NJ, 1978); Adomnan, *Life of Columba*, ed. and trans. Alan Anderson and Marjorie Anderson, second edition (Oxford, 1991); *Saint Patrick's World: The Christian Culture of Ireland's Apostolic Ages*, ed. and trans. Liam de Paor (Dublin, 1993), which includes Tírechán's *Account of St. Patrick's Journey*, Muirchú's *Life of St. Patrick*, and Cogitosus's *Life of St. Brigid the Virgin*, perhaps the three oldest pieces of hagiography from Ireland.

18. Old English hagiographic poetry, such as Cynewulf's *Juliana* and *Guthlac*, may be found in modern English in many anthologies, including *Anglo-Saxon Poetry*, ed. and trans. R.K. Gordon (London, 1926 and reprints).

19. Willibald's *Life of St. Boniface* in *Soldiers of Christ*, pp. 107–40 (see note 10 above) and Abbo of Fleury's *Passion of St. Edmund* in *Corolla Sancti Eadmundi. The Garland of St. Edmund, King and Martyr*, ed. and trans. Francis Hervey (London, 1907), pp. 8–59. Aelfric's rendering of Abbo's work into Old English may be read in modern English in *The Anglo-Saxon World: An Anthology*, ed. and trans. Kevin Crossley-Holland

(Oxford, 1984), pp. 228–34. For other ninth- and tenth-century accounts of martyrdom from the Scandinavian and Slavic lands, see *Anskar, the Apostle of the North (801–865): Translated from the Vita Anskarii by Bishop Rimbert*, ed. and trans. Charles Robinson (London, 1921) and *The Origins of Christianity in Bohemia: Sources and Commentary*, ed. and trans. Marvin Kantor (Evanston, IL, 1990). Also of interest is the *Life of Otto, Apostle of Pomerania*, ed. and trans. Charles Robinson (London, 1929), which traces the career of the German bishop Otto of Bamberg (d. 1139) who worked for decades developing the Christian church in Poland.

20. A direct comparison to Einhard's text may be found in the selections from Ermentarius's *Translation and Miracles of St. Philibert* found in *The History of Feudalism*, ed. David Herlihy (New York, 1970), pp. 1–7. Although no *Lives* from the Carolingian period are included in this collection, a number of them exist in English translation. Several, such as Alcuin's *Life of St. Willibrord* and Rudolf of Fulda's *Life of St. Leoba*, may be found in *Soldiers of Christ* (see note 10 above). Also see, *Charlemagne's Cousins. Contemporary Lives of Adalhard and Wala*, trans. Allen Cabaniss (Syracuse, 1967), for *Lives* of two noble courtiers who later became abbots of Corbie; Alcuin, *The Bishops, Kings, and Saints of York*, ed. and trans. Peter Godman (Oxford, 1982); Rabanus Maurus, *The Life of Saint Mary Magdalene and of Her Sister Saint Martha*, trans. David Mycoff, Cistercian Studies 108 (Kalamazoo, MI, 1989); *The Monks of Redon: The Gesta sanctorum Rotonensium and Vita Conuuoionis*, ed. and trans. Caroline Brett (Woodbridge, Suffolk, 1989). Although not all technically works of hagiography, the lives of Charlemagne and his family provide excellent comparisons to the works included in the present volume: *Two Lives of Charlemagne*, ed. Lewis Thorpe (Harmondsworth, 1969); *Son of Charlemagne. A Contemporary Life of Louis the Pious*, trans. Allen Cabaniss (Syracuse, 1961). A wealth of useful sources on the Carolingian period may be found in *Carolingian Civilization: A Reader*, ed. Paul Dutton (Peterborough, Ontario, 1993).

21. Three collections of miracle stories made at important shrines—those of St. Faith in Conques, St. James in Compostella, and St. Erkenwald in London—during the eleventh and twelfth centuries have recently appeared in excellent annotated translations: *The Book of Sainte Foy*, ed. and trans. Pamela Sheingorn (Philadelphia, 1995); *The Miracles of Saint James: Translations from the Liber sancti Jacobi*, ed. and trans. Thomas Coffey, Linda Kay Davidson, and Maryjane Dunn (New York, 1996); *The Miracles of St. Erkenwald* in *The Saint of London: The Life and Miracles of St. Erkenwald*, ed. and trans. E. Gordon Whatley (Binghamton, NY, 1989), pp. 100–165.

22. See, for example, the *Lives* of monastic leaders, such as Odo of Cluny (d. 942) and Hildegard of Bingen (d. 1179), or of bishops, such as Aethelwold of Winchester (d. 984), Anselm of Canterbury (d. 1109), Hugh of Lincoln (d. 1200), and Edmund of Abingdon (d. 1240): *St. Odo of Cluny*, ed. and trans. Gerard Sitwell (New York, 1958); Gottfried of Disibodenberg and Theodoric of Echternach, *The Life of the Saintly Hildegard*, trans. Hugh Feiss (Toronto, 1997); Wulfstan of Winchester, *The Life of St. Aethelwold*, ed. and trans. Michael Lapidge and Michael Winterbottom, Oxford Medieval Texts (Oxford, 1991); Eadmer of Canterbury, *The Life of Saint Anselm Archbishop of Canterbury*, ed. and trans. R.W. Southern (London, 1962); Adam of Eynsham, *The Life of St. Hugh of Lincoln*. ed. and trans. Decima Douie and Hugh Farmer, 2 vols. (London, 1961–62); Matthew Paris, *The Life of St. Edmund*, trans. C.H. Lawrence (Oxford, 1996).

23. Other examples available in translation include the *Lives* of King Edward the Confessor of England (d. 1066) and Queen Margaret of Scotland (d. 1093): *The Life of King Edward who rests at Westminster, attributed to a Monk of St. Bertin*, ed. and trans. Frank Barlow, second edition, Oxford Medieval Texts (Oxford, 1992) and Turgot, *The Life of St. Margaret* in *Ancient Lives of Scottish Saints*, ed. and trans. W.M. Metcalfe (Paisley, 1895), pp. 297–321. An interesting comparison can be made to *Lives* of contemporary kings and queens who were not considered to be saintly, such as that of Queen Emma of England (d. 1052) in *Encomium Emmae reginae*, ed. and trans. Alistair Campbell, Camden Society 3.72 (London, 1949) and those of King Conrad II (d. 1039) and Henry IV (d. 1106) of Germany, both of which are contained in *Imperial Lives and Letters of the Eleventh Century*, ed. and trans. Theodor Mommsen and Karl Morrison (New York, 1962).

24. Translations of various records of Thomas Becket's martyrdom and miracles may be found in Edwin Abbott, *St. Thomas of Canterbury: His Death and Miracles*, 2 vols. (London, 1898); *The Life and Death of Thomas Becket, Chancellor of England and Archbishop of Canterbury*, ed. and trans. George Greenaway (London, 1961). (Edwin Abbott is better known as the author of the novel *Flatland*.)

25. An excellent comparison can be found in the story of a female hermit (or anchoress) from twelfth-century England, *The Life of Christina of Markyate, a Twelfth-Century Recluse*, ed. and trans. C.H. Talbot, Oxford Medieval Texts (Oxford, 1959; reprint, Toronto, 1998). A new and slightly more readable translation is now available in the Visionary Women series by Monica Furlong (Berkhamsted, 1997). Also see the selections from Reginald of Durham's *Life of St. Godric of Finchale*, another English hermit of the twelfth century, which appear in *Social Life in Britain from the Conquest to the Reformation*, ed. and trans. G.G. Coulton (Cambridge, 1918), pp. 415–20.

26. *Bernard of Clairvaux: The Story of his Life as Recorded in the Vita prima Bernardi by Certain of his Contemporaries*, trans. Geoffrey Webb and Adrian Walker (London, 1960) and Walter Daniel, *The Life of Ailred of Rievaulx*, ed. and trans. F.M. Powicke (London, 1950). Bernard himself also wrote an important piece of hagiography which well illustrates his attitudes toward the monastic life: *The Life and Death of Saint Malachy, the Irishman*, trans. Robert Meyer, Cistercian Fathers Series 10 (Kalamazoo, MI, 1978).

27. The oldest known literary document in Old French is in fact a brief hagiographic poem, the *Séquence de Ste. Eulalie* which dates to about 880. Significant numbers of vernacular hagiographic works, however, were not produced until the late eleventh century. They concerned such diverse subjects as St. Leodegar, a seventh-century bishop of Autun; St. Brendan, an Irish missionary; and St. Mary the Egyptian, a prostitute turned hermit. Two collections which contain hagiography written in Romance languages during the twelfth and early thirteenth centuries are *The Lady as Saint: A Collection of French Hagiographic Romances of the Thirteenth Century*, ed. and trans. Brigitte Cazelles (Philadelphia, 1993) and *Virgin Lives and Holy Deaths: Two Exemplary Biographies for Anglo-Norman Women*, ed. and trans. Jocelyn Wogan-Browne and Glyn Burgess (London, 1996).

28. For translated sources on medieval heresy, see *Heresies of the High Middle Ages*, ed. and trans. Walter Wakefield and Arthur Evans (New York, 1969); *The Birth of Popular Heresy*, ed. and trans. R.I. Moore (London, 1976); *Heresy and Authority in Medieval Europe*, ed. and trans. Edward Peters (Philadelphia, 1980); *Other Middle Ages; Witnesses at the Margins of Medieval Society*, ed. and trans. Michael Goodich (Philadelphia, 1998).

29 The story of Christina of Markyate—a woman who successfully used a prior vow of virginity to annul her engagement to a man named Burthred which had been forcibly extracted by her parents and later went on to a successful monastic career, first as a hermit and then as prioress of a convent of nuns—provides a poignant comparison to the story of Godelieve. See *The Life of Christina of Markyate* (see note 23 above). Another interesting comparison to a woman of the contemporary nobility is that provided by the widowed mother of Abbot Guibert of Nogent. The first book of Guibert's *Monodiae* is available in several translations: *The Autobiography of Guibert, Abbot of Nogent-sous-Coucy*, trans. C.C. Swinton Bland (London, 1926); *Self and Society in Medieval France: The Memoirs of Abbot Guibert of Nogent*, ed. and trans. John Benton (New York, 1970; reprint, Toronto, 1984); *A Monk's Confession: The Memoirs of Guibert of Nogent*, trans. Paul Archambault (University Park, PA, 1996).

30. For an interesting collection of translated documents concerning the relations between Jews and Christians, see *Church, State, and Jew in the Middle Ages*, ed. and trans. Robert Chazan (New York, 1980).

31. The hagiographic traditions surrounding St. Francis of Assisi have appeared in numerous translations, but the most comprehensive collection remains *St. Francis of Assisi: Omnibus of Sources*, ed. Marion Habig (Chicago, 1973). A similar collection of contemporary documents both by and about Francis's disciple Clare is to be found in *Clare of Assisi: Early Documents*, ed. and trans. Regis Armstrong (New York, 1988). Other examples of mendicant hagiography include: *The Life of Saint Thomas Aquinas: Biographical Documents*, ed. and trans. Kenelm Foster (London, 1959); *Saint Dominic: Bio-

graphical Documents, ed. and trans. Francis Lehner (Washington, DC, 1964); *Consolation of the Blessed,* ed. Elizabeth Petroff (New York, 1979); Raymond of Capua, *The Life of Catherine of Siena,* trans. Conleth Kearns (Wilmington, DE, 1980); *Early Dominicans: Selected Writings,* ed. and trans. Simon Tugwell (New York, 1982).

32. A number of the *Lives* of thirteenth-century-Flemish holy women have appeared through the Peregrina Translation Series: Thomas of Cantimpré, *The Life of Christina Mirabilis,* trans. Margot King (Toronto, 1986); Thomas of Cantimpré, *The Life of Lutgard of Aywières,* trans. Margot King (Toronto, 1991); Thomas of Cantimpré, *The Life of Margaret of Ypres,* trans. Margot King, second edition (Toronto, 1996); Jacques de Vitry, *The Life of Marie d'Oignies,* trans. Margot King, fourth edition (Toronto, 1998); *The Life of Blessed Juliana of Mont-Cornillon,* trans. Barbara Newman (Toronto, no date). For more on the activities of this publishing house, which does much to promote scholarship about the female saints of the Middle Ages, see their World Wide Web site at http://www.peregrina.com/index.html.

33. Many of these works are available in English translation (particularly through the efforts of the Cistercian Studies Series of Cistercian Publications and the Classics of Western Spirituality Series of Paulist Press). Some good examples include: Gertrud of Helfta (d. 1302), *Spiritual Exercises,* trans. Gertrud Jaron Lewis and Jack Lewis (Kalamazoo, MI, 1989); Angela of Foligno (d. 1309), *The Complete Works,* ed. and trans. Paul Lachance (New York, 1993); Catherine of Siena (d. 1380), *The Dialogue of Divine Providence,* trans. and ed. Suzanne Noffke (New York, 1980). A particularly valuable collection of selections from sources concerning female sanctity may be found in *Medieval Women's Visionary Literature,* ed. Elizabeth Petroff (Oxford, 1986). It contains selections from contemporary works both about and by holy women, that is both hagiography and autohagiography. Although the collection begins in the early Christian period, it focuses on the later Middle Ages. Also see the earliest piece of English autobiography, the *Book of Margery Kempe* (ca. 1438), which records the process by which its author tried, and largely failed, to become accepted as a holy woman by her community. It is available in several modern English versions, the best being that by Barry Windeatt (Harmondsworth, 1986).

34. One of the formative cases of papal canonization concerned Gilbert of Sempringham (d. 1189). The documents concerning this case have been collected and translated in *The Book of St. Gilbert,* eds. and trans. Gillian Keir and Raymonde Foreville, Oxford Medieval Texts (Oxford, 1987). Other examples of canonization processes available in English translation include those held concerning St. Dominic in 1233 (in *Early Dominicans* [see note 31 above], pp. 66–85) and St. Clare in 1253 (in *Clare of Assisi* [see note 31 above], pp.125–75).

35. A fifteenth-century pilgrim to the Holy Land by the name of Felix Fabri, who was an Italian Dominican, left a detailed and delightful account of his voyages, which have been summarized with much commentary and direct translation in Hilda Prescott, *Friar Felix at Large: A Fifteenth-Century Pilgrimage to the Holy Land* (New Haven, CT, 1950) and *Once to Sinai: The Further Pilgrimage of Friar Felix Fabri* (New York, 1958). English translations of most extant medieval accounts of pilgrimage to the Holy Land, from the fourth through the fifteenth centuries, are available in the thirteen volumes of "The Library of the Palestine Pilgrims' Text Society." The translations, while useful, are somewhat ponderous and dated (notably that of Felix Fabri's account, for which Prescott is a more entertaining, and usually reliable, source).

36. An excellent English translation is available of this extremely important text: Jacobus de Voragine, *The Golden Legend: Readings on the Saints,* trans. William Granger Ryan, 2 vols. (Princeton, 1993). Two, slightly earlier, collections of exemplary stories have been translated into English: Jacques de Vitry, *The Exempla or Illustrative Stories from the Sermones vulgares of Jacques de Vitry,* ed. and trans. Thomas Crane (London, 1890) and Caesarius of Heisterbach, *The Dialogue on Miracles,* trans. H.V.E. Scott and C.C. Swinton Bland, 2 vols. (London, 1929). An imperfect sense of late medieval preaching may be obtained from the extracts translated in *Medieval Sermon-Stories,* ed. and trans. Dana Munro, Translations and Reprints from the Original Sources of European History 2.4 (Philadelphia, 1901) and Bernardino of Siena, *Sermons,* ed. Nazareno Orlandi, trans.

Helen Robins (Siena, 1920). For two excellent collections of translated documents which illustrate the practice of Christianity in late medieval England, both the efforts of the clergy at educating the laity and the response of those laypeople, see *Catholic England: Faith, Religion and Observance Before the Reformation*, ed. and trans. R.N. Swanson, Manchester Medieval Sources (Manchester, 1993) and *Pastors and the Care of Souls in Medieval England*, eds. John Shinners and William Dohar, Notre Dame Texts in Medieval Culture 4 (Notre Dame, IN, 1998).

37. Relatively little of this prodigious output has been translated into modern English, but examples do exist for several languages. For Old French, see the texts collected in *The Lady as Saint* (see note 27 above). For Italian, see *The Life of Saint Mary Magdalen*, trans. Valentina Hawtrey (London, 1904). For Middle English, see Birger Gregersson and Thomas Gascoigne, *The Life of Birgitta of Sweden*, trans. by Julia Bolton Holloway (Toronto, 1991); *A Legend of Holy Women. A Translation of Osbern Bokenham's Legends of Holy Women*, ed. and trans. Sheila Delany, Notre Dame Texts in Medieval Culture 1 (Notre Dame, IN, 1993); *Medieval English Prose for Women: Selections from the Katherine Group and Ancrene Wisse*, ed. and trans. Bella Millett and Jocelyn Wogan-Browne (Oxford, 1990).

38. As translated by Brigitte Cazelles in *The Lady as Saint*, p. 102 (see note 27 above).

39. Some sense of the literature intended to inform late medieval preachers about the traditions surrounding the Virgin Mary and Christ may be obtained from Evelyn Underhill, *The Miracles of Our Lady Saint Mary* (London, 1905); Johann Herolt, *Miracles of the Blessed Virgin Mary*, trans. C.C. Swinton Bland (London, 1928); Mary Bodenstedt, *The Vita Christi of Ludolphus the Carthusian* (Washington, DC, 1944); *Meditations on the Life of Christ: An Illustrated Manuscript of the Fourteenth Century*, ed. and trans. Ira Ragusa and Rosalie Green (Princeton, 1961); *Praying the Life of Christ: The Prayers Concluding the 181 Chapters of the Vita Christi of Ludolphus the Carthusian*, trans. Mary Bodenstedt, Analecta Cartusiana 15 (Salzburg, 1973).

40. Some sense of the critiques leveled against traditional religious practice may be gleaned from the texts collected in *Culture and Belief in Europe, 1450–1600: An Anthology of Sources*, ed. and trans. David Englander, Diana Norman, Rosemary O'Day, and W.R. Owens (Oxford, 1990), section 1.

Note on the Translations

It is important for the reader to remember that all the texts included in this collection are translations and that the process of translation inevitably involves interpretation. The translators and editors of the chapters which follow have provided many aids to understanding the context and meaning of the original texts through their introductions, their guides to the sources, and their notes. A few general conventions adopted by the scholars involved in this collaborative venture should be noted. Any problems created by these conventions should be ascribed to the editor of the volume and not to the scholars whose long and devoted labors produced the contents of its individual chapters. Those scholars have provided introductions and notes to explain the specific context and nuances of their texts. Such apparatus cannot, however, substitute for a reading of the text in the original language. One of the most important purposes that a collection such as this can serve is to interest students in the study of medieval European languages so that they can experience directly the enjoyment and inspiration of reading texts such as these in the original language.

The thirty-six chapters comprising this volume have been arranged in roughly chronological order, although the uncertainty surrounding the dates of many texts necessarily renders that order inexact. The majority of the chapters provide translations of complete texts. Eight chapters (1, 3, 6, 7, 22, 27, 28, and 35) have omitted certain parts of the texts due to the constraints of space. In all cases the translators have indicated and summarized the excised sections in notes contained within brackets. Six chapters (4, 13, 25, 26, 29, 30, and 36) present a collection of different texts—in whole and in part—on a coherent theme. The editors have explained the relationship of the various texts in detail in the introductory matter to the chapter.

The majority of the chapters also present works which have never appeared previously in English translation. There are a few exceptions. Five of the chapters (9, 11, 20, 23, and 24) provide newly revised and annotated versions of previous translations that are significantly out of date, or, in one case (23) difficult to obtain. The first three chapters (1, 2, and 3) provide original translations of texts that are available in alternate English translations. All three are foundational texts for medieval hagiography. In these cases the versions provided here add substantial new material based on recent textual and historical scholarship.

Each chapter consists of three parts: an introduction, a guide to sources and further reading, and the translated text or texts themselves. Endnotes have been allowed to accompany only the translations. The introductory matter to each chapter is the result of careful synthesis on the part of the scholar responsible. The sources for their research may be easily identified from the works cited in the section entitled Sources and Further Reading. Many of the texts included in this collection underwent significant evolution over the course of their use. Medieval texts also varied considerably over time through the vagaries introduced by scribal copying in a preprinting technology. Some of the texts which follow, such as Jonas's *Life of St. Columbanus*, were copied and used in significantly different versions. Others, such as Bede's *Martyrology*, were altered through use in differing circumstances. Still others, such as the anonymous Old Czech version of the *Life of St. Catherine of Alexandria* and the anonymous Middle English version of Jacques de Vitry's *Life of St. Marie d'Oignies*, were adapted from Latin originals into vernacular languages. The scholars responsible for each chapter have indicated the base texts from which they have made their translations, once again in the section entitled Sources and Further Reading. In the notes that accompany the translations, the suggestions of the editor of the primary source (or variances from that editor's work) are indicated simply with reference to the name of the editor. References to the work of other scholars are given in full according to the ordinary usage of scholarly notes. These conventions have been adopted to minimize clutter and repetition.

The reader must keep in mind that the originals of the texts included in this collection come from a number of extremely varied linguistic traditions. The process of translation into modern English necessarily flattens the inherent differences between, for example, Latin and Old Irish, Hebrew and Old French, or even Middle English and its modern successor. The translators have indicated, in the apparatus to the individual chapters, many matters of interest in the specific language of the original text. In certain specific cases they have provided, either in brackets within the translated text or in the notes to it, words or phrases from the original, usually to clarify particularly difficult translations or technical vocabulary. The words or phrases from the original language are always placed in italic type. In general, scholars who have translated from languages such as Greek and Hebrew which do not use the Latin alphabet have transliterated their citations of the original language. The conventions of languages which primarily employ the Latin alphabet, however, have been observed as carefully as possible, as in the case of the extra characters used to render Icelandic or the accent marks used in Romance and Slavic tongues.

The rendering of proper names into English poses special problems. The honorific title "Saint" has been abbreviated throughout as "St." when it refers to a person. Places—particularly churches and monastic communities—were often named after such persons. In those cases, the full "Saint" has been retained (an important exception is the episcopal see of St. David's in Wales). The names of places with a modern equivalent are given in accord with contemporary American usage as reflected in the *Hammond Ambassador World*

Note on the Translations

xli

Atlas (Maplewood, NJ, 1990). That usage sometimes prefers the native modern language over customary British translation (as in Reims, rather than Rheims) and sometimes accepts translations (as in Rome, rather than Roma). The names of places without modern equivalents are provided in the original language. The identification of many place names is further clarified in the notes accompanying the translation. Churches and monasteries known by their dedication to a certain saint are identified either in the vernacular language proper to the modern country in which they are to be found (as in Saint-Denis, the abbey located near Paris) or by a full English phrase (as in "the monastery of Saint Bavo," located in Ghent). In general, those personal names (such as Peter or Patrick, Agnes or Margaret) for which there exists a modern English equivalent have been so rendered, while those for which there is no such ready equivalent (such as Maximinus or Rhigyfarch) have been left in the original language. In cases of historical personages from the later Middle Ages who are known to have used a specific name in the vernacular, that original name is retained even when there is an acceptable English rendering (as for authors such as Gautier de Coincy or Jacopo da Voragine). Medieval writers and scribes usually did not follow set rules of capitalization. In the following translations, most nouns and third-person pronouns referring directly to God (as in "the Father"), to the Virgin Mary (as in "Our Lady"), and to the institution of the Christian Church (as in "the holy Church") have been capitalized. In an era of religious pluralism and multiculturalism, these uses of the upper case may seem redolent of the outdated Christian triumphalism of older translations. These usages has been retained for the sake of clarity, distinguishing these key figures and institutions from other fathers and spirits, ladies and virgins, and individual church buildings.

All writers work with reference to systems of chronology with which they are familiar. There were a bewildering number of such systems in use during the Middle Ages: the so-called Anno Domini (literally "Year of Our Lord" and abbreviated as A. D.) system which is so familiar to us (and now often referred to as the "Common Era" and abbreviated as C. E.) was only one among many competitors. All dates in the translations which follow have been rendered into contemporary American usage, either in the text itself or sometimes—when the original version of the date is particularly significant—in the accompanying notes. Unless specifically identified as B. C. E. ("Before the Common Era"), all dates are C.E./A. D. Medieval writers identified the hours of the day according to two systems, one natural, the other liturgical. According to the first, the periods of light and of darkness were each divided into twelve equal segments. Thus the "third hour of the day" is midmorning. Where our use of the hour is to an absolute period of time, medieval hours varied in length according to the season. The second type of hour (in part related to the first) was that of the monastic liturgy, also known as the Divine Office. These hours of the office were the times when the monastic community gathered together in prayer: Matins (or the "morning office," also called Vigils) and Lauds (or the "office of praise") usually celebrated together in the middle of the night; Prime (or the "first hour") at dawn; Terce (or the "third hour") at midmorning; Sext (or the "sixth hour") at mid-day; Nones (or the "ninth hour") at midafternoon; Vespers (or the "evening office") around sunset; Compline (of the "final office") said before sleep.

Finally, all of the authors translated in this collection made use of the Bible in their work. This is so common and so important in many of the texts which follow that all biblical citations are provided in brackets within the text rather than in notes. Where the author directly quotes from the Bible, the scriptural passage is put into italics. Where an allusion to a biblical passage is implicit in the text, the reference begins "see." When the author differs significantly from a biblical passage, the reference begins " cf." or "compare."

There were, however, many different versions and translations of the Bible in circulation during the Middle Ages and used by our various authors. These differed significantly in terms of the canon of the books included, the division of those books into subsections, and the text itself. Even the so-called Vulgate (that is the translation of the Christian Bible from Greek into Latin made by St. Jerome in the fifth century), which was accepted as the normative Latin text of the Bible in Western Christendom for much of the Middle Ages, could vary significantly from copy to copy due to the errors of scribes. The authors themselves were often working without reference to a written text of the Bible, but rather citing from memory, and hence fallibly. Despite the wide variance of the texts of the Bible thus used by our authors, each was seeking to refer to a text familiar to and held in common with the audience who was to read or hear that author's composition. Thus it seemed desirable to choose a base text of the Bible for reference in this volume. All biblical citations are therefore provided in reference to the English translation known as the Revised Standard Version (or RSV). The abbreviations of biblical books is that employed by the editors of the RSV (such as "Gen" for Genesis or "1 Cor" for the First Letter to the Corinthians). Where such citations differ significantly from the Bible used by the author (as in the slightly different numbering system used for the Psalms in the Vulgate of Jerome), a variant reference is specified after the reference from the RSV. The most important alternate versions of the Bible are the Vulgate, the Septuagint (the Greek version of the Hebrew Bible, or Old Testament, which circulated in both Jewish communities of the Diaspora and in Christian communities of the eastern Roman Empire), and the Hebrew Bible (abbreviated below as "Heb"). In a few cases, specified by the translators (in particular, David Warner's translation of Odilo of Cluny and Susan Einbinder's translation of Hebrew texts), the difference between the RSV text and that employed by the author is so great as to require a direct translation of the biblical quotation. Italics are still employed to distinguish the biblical material. The imposition of the RSV translation does slightly but artificially alter the texts, yet it is hoped that the introduction of a version familiar to many in a contemporary audience will make up for what is lost in the process.

Contributors

Dorothy Africa is an independent scholar residing in Bedford, MA. She received her Ph.D. from the Centre for Medieval Studies at the University of Toronto. Her publications include articles on the *Confessio* of St. Patrick and on St. Malachy of Armagh. Currently she is working on the *vitae* and communities of two Irish female saints, Samthann of Clonbroney and Moninne of Killevy.

David Appleby is Associate Professor of History at the United States Naval Academy. He received his Ph.D. from the University of Virginia. He has published many articles on spirituality and religious practice in the Carolingian Empire, including "Sight and Church Reform in the Thought of Jonas of Orléans," *Viator* 27 (1996): 11–33 and "Holy Relic and Holy Image: Saints' Relics in the Western Controversy over Images in the Eighth and Ninth Centuries," *Word and Image* 8 (1992): 333–43. He is currently preparing a study of the understanding of sensory and supersensory beauty in the Carolingian period.

Nora Berend is Lecturer in History at Goldsmith's College, University of London. She received her Ph.D. from Columbia University. Her publications include "Medieval Patterns of Social Exclusion and Integration: The Regulation of Non-Christian Clothing in Thirteenth-Century Hungary," *Revue Mabillon*, new series 8 (1997): 155–76 and "Hungary in the Eleventh and Twelfth Centuries," forthcoming in the *New Cambridge Medieval History* 4.2. She is currently completing a book entitled *Coexistence in a Frontier Society: Jews, Muslims and "Pagans" in Medieval Hungary*, to be published by Cambridge University Press.

Renate Blumenfeld-Kosinski is Associate Professor of French and Director of the Medieval/Renaissance Studies Program at the University of Pittsburgh. She previously taught at Columbia University from 1981–93. She received her Ph.D. from Princeton University. She is the author of *Not of Woman Born: Representations of Caesarean Birth in Medieval and Renaissance Culture* (Ithaca, NY, 1990) and *Reading Myth: Classical Mythology and its Interpretations in Medieval French Literature* (Stanford, CA, 1997), as well as numerous articles on medieval French literature. She is also the editor (with Timea Szell) of *Images of Sainthood in Medieval Europe* (Ithaca, NY, 1991), the translator of the works of Margaret of Oingt (1991), and the editor and translator (with Kevin Brownlee) of *The Selected Writings of Christine de Pizan: A Norton Critical Edition* (New York, 1997). Her current work focuses on Christine de Pizan's religious and political thought.

Jeffrey Bowman is Assistant Professor of History at Kenyon College. He received his Ph.D. from Yale University. His publications include "Do Neo-Romans Curse? Law, Land, and Ritual in the Midi (900–1100)," *Viator* 28 (1997): 1–32. He is currently writing a book on the transmission of law and the settlement of disputes in Languedoc and Catalonia during the tenth and eleventh centuries.

David Brakke is Associate Professor of Religious Studies at Indiana University. He received his Ph.D. from Yale University. He is the author of *Athanasius and the Politics of Asceticism* (Oxford, 1995)—which has been released in paperback as *Athanasius and Asceticism* (Baltimore, 1998)—and articles on early Christianity in Egypt and asceticism, such as "The Problematization of Nocturnal Emissions in Early Christian Syria, Egypt, and Gaul," *Journal of Early Christian Studies* 2 (1995): 419–60. He is currently completing a critical edition and translation of a Syriac treatise *On Virginity*, which has traditionally and falsely been attributed to Athanasius.

Philippe Buc is Associate Professor of History at Stanford University. He received his doctoral degree from the École des Hautes Études en Sciences Sociales. His publications include *L'Ambiguïté du Livre: Prince, pouvoir, et peuple dans les commentaires de la Bible au moyen âge* (Paris, 1994) and many articles on medieval political culture, such as "David's Adultery with Bathsheba and the Healing Power of the Capetian Kings," *Viator* 24 (1993): 101–20 and "Conversion of Objects: Suger of Saint-Denis and Meinwerk of Paderborn," *Viator* 28 (1997): 99–143. He is currently writing a book entitled *The Dangers of Ritual: The Politics of Medieval Anthropology*.

Raymond Clemens is Associate Professor of History at Illinois State University. He received his Ph.D. from Columbia University. Currently he is at work on a book examining the cult of Mary Magdalen in southern France and the history of relic authentication in the later Middle Ages.

Margaret Cormack is Assistant Professor in the Department of Philosophy and Religious Studies at the College of Charleston. She received her Ph.D. from Yale University. Her research centers on the cult of saints in Iceland. Her publications include *The Saints in Iceland: Their Veneration from the Conversion to 1400*, Subsidia Hagiographica 78 (Brussels, 1994). She is currently preparing a continuation of that work which will cover the period from 1400 to the Reformation, as well as translating the major narrative sources pertaining to the medieval Icelandic saints.

Nancy Vine Durling is an independent scholar residing in Berkeley, CA. She received her Ph.D. from Princeton University. She has taught French and Comparative Literature at the University of California, Santa Cruz and

Florida Atlantic University. Her articles include "Hagiography and Lineage: The Example of the Old French *Vie de saint Alexis*," *Romance Philology* 40 (1987): 451–69. She has also translated (with Patricia Terry) Jean Renart's *Romance of the Rose or Guillaume de Dole* (Philadelphia, 1993) and edited *Jean Renart and the Art of Romance: Essays on "Guillaume de Dole"* (Gainesville, 1997). She is currently collaborating with Patricia Terry on a composite English version of selected Old French Grail narratives.

Susan Einbinder is Associate Professor of Hebrew Literature at the Hebrew Union College—Jewish Institute of Religion in Cincinnati, OH. She received her Ph.D. from Columbia University. She is the author of many articles on Hebrew literature and Judaism, including "Pucellina of Blois: Romantic Myths and Narrative Conventions," *Jewish History* 12 (1998): 29–46 and "The Troyes Elegies: Jewish Martyrology in Hebrew and Old French," forthcoming in *Viator* 30 (1999). She has also translated Shimon Ballas's novella *Iya* in *New Writing from Israel*, ed. Ammiel Alcalay (San Francisco, 1996), pp. 69–99. She is currently working on a study of medieval Jewish martyrology.

George Ferzoco is Lecturer and Director of Italian Studies at the University of Leicester. Following a first degree at St. Michael's College, University of Toronto, and a Master of Arts from Trent University, he pursued graduate courses at the École des Hautes Études en Sciences Sociales, the Pontifical Institute of Mediaeval Studies, McGill University, and the Institut d'études médiévales, Université de Montréal. His recent publications include "Sermon Literatures concerning Late Medieval Saints," in *Models of Holiness in Medieval Sermons*, ed. Beverly Mayne Kienzle, Textes et études du moyen âge 5 (Louvain-la-Neuve, 1996), pp. 103–125 and "Preaching by Italian Hermits," in *Medieval Monastic Preaching*, ed. Carolyn Muessig, Brill's Studies in Intellectual History 90 (Leiden, 1998), pp. 145–159. He is currently working on an edition of a collection of articles on the construction of medieval sanctity, a study of the canonization of Peter of the Morrone, and an analysis of the preaching of James of Viterbo regarding saints and sanctity.

Thomas Head is Professor of History at Hunter College and the Graduate Center, the City University of New York. He has previously taught at Washington University, Yale University, and the Claremont Colleges. He received his Ph.D. from Harvard University. He is the author of *Hagiography and the Cult of Saints. The Diocese of Orléans, 800–1200*, Cambridge Studies in Medieval Life and Thought, fourth series 14 (Cambridge, 1990) and articles on the practice of medieval Christianity, such as "The Marriages of Christina of Markyate," *Viator* 21 (1990): 71–95. He has also edited (with Richard Landes) *The Peace of God: Social Violence and Religious Response in France Around the Year 1000* (Ithaca, NY, 1992) and (with Thomas Noble) *Soldiers of Christ: Saints' Lives from Late Antiquity and the Early Middle Ages* (University Park, PA, 1994). He is currently working on a history of the development of the cult of saints from late antiquity through the twelfth century.

Elissa R. Henken is an Associate Professor teaching Folklore and Celtic literature in the Department of English at the University of Georgia. She received her Ph.D. from the Folklore Institute at Indiana University. Her publications include *Traditions of the Welsh Saints* (Cambridge, 1987), *The Welsh Saints: A Study in Patterned Lives* (Cambridge, 1991) and *National Redeemer: Owain Glyndwr in Welsh Tradition* (Cardiff and Ithaca, NY, 1996). She is currently researching a book on folktales in medieval Wales.

Beverly Mayne Kienzle is Professor of the Practice in Latin and Romance Languages at Harvard Divinity School; she also currently serves as President of the International Medieval Sermon Studies Society. She received her Ph.D. from Boston College. She is the author of many articles on medieval Cistercian preaching, including "Hélinand de Froidmont et la prédication cistercienne dans le Midi, 1145–1229," in *La prédication en Pays d'Oc (xiie-début xve siècle)*, Cahiers de Fanjeaux 32 (Toulouse, 1997), pp. 37–67. She has also edited *Models of Holiness in Medieval Sermons*, Textes et études du moyen âge 5 (Louvain-la-Neuve, 1996) and (with Pamela Walker) *Women Preachers and Prophets through Two Millennia of Christianity* (Berkeley, 1997). She is currently working on a guide to *The Sermon* (for the series *Typologie des sources du moyen âge*), a bilingual edition/translation of the Gospel homilies of Hildegard of Bingen, and a history of twelfth-century Cistercian preaching against heresy.

Geoffrey Koziol is Associate Professor of History at the University of California, Berkeley. He received his Ph.D. from Stanford University. The author of *Begging Pardon and Favor: Ritual and Political Order in Early Medieval France* (Ithaca, NY, 1992), he is writing a new book on marriage and political order.

Mathew Kuefler is Assistant Professor of History at San Diego State University. He has previously taught at Yale University, Rice University, the University of British Columbia, and the University of Alberta. He received his Ph.D. from Yale University. He is the author of *The Manly Eunuch: Masculinity, Gender Ambiguity, and Christian Ideology in Late Antiquity*, forthcoming from the University of Chicago Press. His publications include "Castration and Eunuchism in the Middle Ages," in *Handbook of Medieval Sexuality*, eds. Vern Bullough and James Brundage (New York, 1996) and "Male Friendship, Sodomy, and Masculine Identity in Twelfth-Century France," in *Difference and Genders*, eds. Sharon Farmer and Carol Braun Pasternack (forthcoming). He is currently working on a critical edition with a translation and commentary of Odo of Cluny's *Life of Gerald of Aurillac*.

Wendy Larson is Assistant Professor of Humanities in the School of General Studies at Boston University. She received her Ph.D. in medieval English literature from the University of Wisconsin, Madison. Currently, she is working on the history and material culture of the cult of St. Margaret of Antioch.

Henrietta Leyser is a Fellow and Lecturer in Medieval History at St. Peter's College, Oxford. Her publications include *Hermits and the New Monasticism* (London, 1984) and *Medieval Women* (London, 1995), as well as articles on religious history such as "Hugh the Carthusian," in *Hugh of Lincoln*, ed. Henry Mayr-Harting (Oxford, 1986), pp. 1–18 and "Piety, Religion and the Church," in *The Oxford Illustrated History of Medieval England*, ed. Nigel Saul (Oxford, 1997), pp.174–206.

Felice Lifshitz is Associate Professor of History and Religious Studies at Florida International University. She received her Ph.D. from Columbia University. She is the author of *The Norman Conquest of Pious Neustria: Historiographic Discourse and Saintly Relics, 684–1090*, Studies and Texts 122 (Toronto, 1995) and articles on medieval religious and cultural history, such as "Is Mother Superior? Towards a History of Feminine *Amtscharisma*," in *Medieval Mothering*, eds. Bonnie Wheeler and John Carmi Parsons (New York, 1996), pp. 117–38 and "Beyond Positivism and Genre: 'Hagiographical' Texts as Historical Narrative," *Viator* 25 (1994): 95–113. She is currently working on a book entitled *Women, Men and the Figure of the Martyr. Essays on the Religious Culture of East Francia*.

Nadia Margolis is an independent scholar residing in Amherst, MA. She has studied various aspects of medieval history, literature, and philology at universities in both the United States and France and received her Ph.D. from Stanford University. Her publications include a sourcebook, *Joan of Arc in History, Literature, and Film* (New York, 1990), translations of works by Christine de Pizan, and articles on such topics as Joan of Arc's reception history and Christine de Pizan's humanism. She is currently co-editing the *Encyclopedia of Medieval Women* for Garland Press.

John McCulloh is Professor of History at Kansas State University. He received his Ph.D. from the University of California, Berkeley. He is the editor of *Rabani Mauri Maryrologium*, Corpus Christianorum, Continuatio Mediaevalis 44 (Turnhout, 1979), and the author of many articles on relics and martyrologies, such as "The Cult of Relics in the Letters and *Dialogues* of Pope Gregory the Great: A Lexicographical Study," *Traditio* 32 (1976): 145–84 and "Herman the Lame's Martyrology Through Four Centuries of Scholarship," *Analecta Bollandiana* 104 (1986): 349–70. He is currently working on a study of Thomas of Monmouth's *Life and Miracles of St. William of Norwich*.

Jo Ann McNamara is Professor Emerita of History from Hunter College and the Graduate Center, the City University of New York. Her many publications on the history of hagiography, monasticism, and spirituality include (with John E. Halborg and E. Gordon Whatley) *Sainted Women of the Dark Ages* (Durham, NC, 1991) and *Sisters in Arms: Catholic Nuns through Two Millennia* (Cambridge, MA, 1996).

Sarah McNamer is Assistant Professor of English at Georgetown University. She received her Ph.D. from the University of California, Los Angeles. Her publications include an edition of *The Two Middle English Translations of the Revelations of St. Elizabeth of Hungary*, Middle English Texts 28 (Heidelberg, 1996). She is currently writing a book on pathos and gender in late medieval literature of the Passion.

Jennifer Paxton is an adjunct lecturer in History at Georgetown University. She recently received her doctorate from the Department of History at Harvard University. Her dissertation was entitled "Charter and Chronicle in Twelfth-Century England: The House-Histories of the Fenland Abbeys" which analyzes the uses of historical and hagiographic sources in the history-writing of twelfth-century English monks.

Claudia Rapp is Assistant Professor of History at the University of California, Los Angeles. She has previously taught at Cornell University. She received her D.Phil. from Oxford University. Her publications include "Byzantine Hagiographers as Antiquarians, Seventh to Tenth Century," in *Bosporus*, eds. Stephanos Efthymiadis, Claudia Rapp, and Dimitri Tsougarakis, Byzantinische Forschungen 21 (Amsterdam, 1995), pp. 31–44, "Figures of Female Sanctity: Byzantine Edifying Manuscripts and Their Audience," *Dunbarton Oaks Papers* 50 (1996): 313–44, and "Storytelling as Spiritual Communication in Early Greek Hagiography: The Use of Diegesis," *Journal of Early Christian Studies* (forthcoming). She is currently working on a critical edition of the Greek *Life* of Epiphanius and a study on holy bishops in late antiquity.

Sherry Reames is Professor of English at the University of Wisconsin; she also currently serves as President of the Hagiography Society. She received her Ph.D. from Yale University. Her publications include *The Legenda Aurea: A Reexamination of Its Paradoxical History* (Madison, 1985) and numerous articles on such topics as liturgical offices of saints and the retelling of saints' legends in Latin and Middle English. She is currently working on a descriptive inventory of the hagiography texts in Sarum breviary manuscripts.

Laura Smoller is Assistant Professor of History at the University of Arkansas at Little Rock. She received her Ph.D. from Harvard University. She is the author of *History, Prophecy, and the Stars: The Christian Astrology of Pierre d'Ailly, 1350–1420* (Princeton, 1994) and a number of articles on topics related to science and religion in the later Middle Ages, such as "Miracle, Memory, and Meaning in the Canonization of Vincent Ferrer, 1453–54," *Speculum* 73 (1998): 429–54 and "Defining the Boundaries of the Natural in the Fifteenth Century: The Inquest into the Miracles of St. Vincent Ferrer (d. 1419)," *Viator* 28 (1997): 333–59. She is currently at work on a study of the meanings of sanctity and the miraculous in the later Middle Ages, focusing on the canonization of St. Vincent Ferrer.

Alfred Thomas is John L. Loeb Associate Professor of the Humanities at Harvard University. He received his Ph.D. in Slavic Languages and Literature from Trinity Hall, Cambridge University. The author of *The Czech Chivalric Verse Romances; Vévoda Arnošt and Lavyrn in Their Literary Context* (Göppingen, 1989), *The Labyrinth of the Word: Truth and Representation in Czech Literature* (Munich, 1995), and *Anne's Bohemia: Czech Literature and Society, 1310–1420* (Minneapolis, 1998), he is presently working on a book entitled *Our Bohemia: Modernity and Tradition in Czech Literature, 1774–1989*, the third volume in a projected trilogy of new readings of Czech literature from the late Middle Ages to the present.

Bruce L. Venarde is Associate Professor of History at the University of Pittsburgh. He received his Ph.D. from Harvard University. He is the author of *Women's Monasticism and Medieval Society: Nunneries in France and England, 890–1215* (Ithaca, NY, 1997). His sourcebook on Robert of Arbrissel is forthcoming from the Catholic University of America Press, and he is at work on a study of ecclesiastical culture in western France centered on the lives and writings of Robert of Arbrissel and Marbode of Rennes.

David Warner is Associate Professor of History at the Rhode Island School of Design. He received his Ph.D. from the University of California, Los Angeles. His publications include articles on Ottonian political and religious life, such as "Thietmar of Merseburg on Rituals of Kingship," *Viator* 26 (1995): 53–76 and "Henry II at Magdeburg: Kingship, Ritual and the Cult of Saints," *Early Medieval Europe* 3 (1994): 1–31. He is presently completing a translation of and commentary on another important Ottonian literary source, the *Chronicle* of Thietmar of Merseburg.

E. Gordon Whatley is Professor of English at Queens College and the Graduate Center, the City University of New York. He received his Ph.D. from Harvard University. His publications include *The Saint of London: The Life and Miracles of Saint Erkenwald* (Binghamton, NY, 1989) and articles on hagiography such as "The Figure of Constantine the Great in Cynewulf's 'Elene,'" *Traditio* 37 (1981): 161–202 and "Late Old English Hagiography, ca. 950–1150," in *Hagiographies. Histoire internationale de la littérature hagiographique, latine et vernaculaire, en Occident, des origines à 1550*, ed. Guy Philippart, vol. 1 (Turnhout, 1996), pp. 429–99.

Ian Wood is Professor of Early Medieval History at the University of Leeds. He received his D. Phil. from Oxford University. He is the author of numerous articles, as well as books such as *The Merovingian Kingdoms, 450–751* (London, 1994) and *Gregory of Tours* (Bangor, 1994). He has recently been a coordinator of a European Science Foundation program on the Transformation of the Roman World, and is writing a book on the hagiography of the Christian missions from 400 to 1100.

Chapter 1
Athanasius of Alexandria, *Life of St. Antony of Egypt*
Translated by David Brakke

Introduction

Athanasius was bishop of Alexandria, the leading city of late ancient Egypt, from 328 until his death in 373. His career coincided with one of the most significant and tumultuous periods in the history of Christianity. During Athanasius's youth Christianity went from being an illegal, persecuted sect to the favored religion of the Roman emperor Constantine. Although from their earliest days Christians had claimed to form one Church throughout the world, they actually had existed in multiple diverse groups. Now with the support of the emperor, Christian leaders could work to form one international Church that would truly be *catholic* or "universal." Athanasius was a vigorous participant in this effort, and his most famous work, the *Life of St. Antony*, was intended to define the rightful place of the superior monk in Christian thought and practice. The *Life* was translated from its original Greek into several other languages, including Latin. Countless later Christians used Antony's *Life* as a model for their own asceticism, and the biography became the primary model for later Christian hagiographers.

Antony was born around 250 to a prosperous family in one of the villages that lay along the Nile River south of Alexandria. Orphaned as a young man, Antony devoted his life to service and contemplation of God through a program of "discipline" (in Greek, *askesis*, and hence "asceticism"), consisting of celibacy, poverty, fasting, and the like. For years Antony was just one of several such "zealous ones" who lived in and around Egyptian towns; but eventually he entered a deserted military fort, and, supported with food from visitors, he seldom saw or was seen by anyone for nearly 20 years. This spectacular feat made Antony famous, and he soon inspired numerous imitators, who abandoned city life for devotion to God in the desert. Ordinary Christians greatly admired these "solitary ones" (in Greek, *monachoi*, and hence "monks"), sometimes to the annoyance of their local priests and bishops. As more and more people came to Antony for spiritual guidance or supernatural aid (such as healings), he retreated to a remote oasis deep in the desert ("the inner mountain"), where he remained (except for occasional trips to "the world") until his death around 356.

Also in 356 the imperial government for the third time forced Bishop Athanasius to relinquish control of the churches in Alexandria. Athanasius had troubled the emperors for decades due to his steadfast opposition to a form of theology called (somewhat misleadingly) "Arianism," which taught that the Son of God who became incarnate in Jesus Christ was divine, but less divine than God the Father. Athanasius insisted on a much stronger interpretation of a creed that had been adopted at the Council of Nicea in 325, which declared that the Son was "of one substance (*homoousios*) with the Father." To Athanasius's mind, the Son was fully God, just as divine and eternal as the Father, although together the Father, Son, and Holy Spirit formed one God. Only through the incarnation of the fully divine Son or Word (*Logos*) of God in a human body could humanity be saved from sin and death. The Roman emperors wanted Athanasius to compromise with his theological opponents, but he never would, so the government repeatedly sent Athanasius into exile away from Alexandria. In February of 356 soldiers tried to arrest Athanasius, but he escaped into the desert with the help of supportive monks. He spent the next six years hiding from the police and writing numerous works in defense of his views, including the *Life of St. Antony*.

Athanasius wrote the *Life*, then, at a time of personal crisis: he designed his picture of Antony so that the recently deceased famous monk would exemplify Athanasius's views on the ascetic life, the place of monks in the church, and salvation through the Son of God. How did Athanasius get his information about Antony? In the preface, Athanasius states that he saw Antony "often," but this is a lie, designed to lend his account great authority: he probably met Antony only once (see Chapters 69–71). (Athanasius was a brilliant polemicist who did not hesitate to bend the truth if he thought it would serve the cause of "orthodoxy.") Athanasius refers also to what he learned from another source, a person "who followed him (Antony) for no short period of time and who poured water on his hand," an allusion to 2 Kings 3:11 and the relationship between the Israelite prophet Elijah (Antony) and his disciple Elisha (the unnamed person). Some scholars have guessed that this anonymous follower of Antony may be Bishop Serapion of Thmuis, an ally of Athanasius and a former monastic leader in his own right: Serapion is later described as being present when Antony had a vision (Chapter 82), and he is named along with Athanasius as a recipient of a "sheepskin" from the dying Antony (Chapter 91), another allusion to Elijah and Elisha (see 2 Kings 2:12–14). It is likely, then, that Athanasius learned about the basic events of Antony's career and gathered most of the stories he tells from Serapion and other monks who had known Antony. But many episodes and probably all of Antony's speeches must have been invented by Athanasius in order to create his picture of the ideal monk.

The *Life of St. Antony* was something new for Christians: the first extended biography of a holy person or "saint." To be sure, earlier Christians had written books about important persons in the faith: these include the Gospels about Jesus, popular novels about the journeys of the apostles (the "apocryphal acts," such as the *Acts of Thomas*), accounts of the trials and execution of martyrs, and a short biography of the Christian scholar Origen that Bishop Eusebius of Caesarea included in his *Ecclesiastical History*. Athanasius borrowed from these works and from biographies of "pagan" holy men to do something innovative: tell the story of an ordinary Christian who, through the hard work of ascetic discipline, achieves such holiness that he can do miraculous deeds and provide spiritual guidance to others. The result was a new form of Christian literature that was imitated and revised for centuries.

The Antony that we find in Athanasius's *Life* is the model of what a bishop thought a Christian monk should be. Indeed, Athanasius presents his work as a response to a request from "foreign monks" for information about Antony so that they can imitate him. As Bishop Athanasius presents it, Antony's decision to become an ascetic is prompted not by a private call from God, but by the public reading of the Gospel in church. Antony creates his virtue by resisting temptations from the devil, but Athanasius attributes this success to the victory that Christ won over evil and the flesh in his incarnation, death, and resurrection. Antony achieves such a level of virtue and purity of soul that he is able to benefit others in miraculous ways, such as healings and exorcisms, and in less spectacular fashion, through spiritual advice and exhortation. Athanasius describes numerous miracles in great detail, but Antony never claims to perform such deeds himself: only Christ can heal the sick, and so they should give thanks to him, not to Antony. Despite his superior virtue, Antony remains obedient to the organized Church and submissive to priests and bishops. He refuses to have any dealings with "heretics" and "schismatics" and even appears briefly in Alexandria to show support for Athanasius's theology and to condemn that of the Arians. When he dies, Antony forbids the establishment of any cult devoted to his own corpse, which he commands to be buried in a secret location. In this way, Athanasius creates a significant, but carefully limited, role for the charismatic monk within the wider Christian community made up of bishops, priests, and ordinary lay people. Salvation depends not on contact with Antony, but on living a Christian life as Antony did.

Modern readers of the *Life* find most striking the prominent role of demons, who oppose Antony at every turn. Ancient people believed that there were numerous supernatural beings that were less divine than God, but more powerful than human beings. Demons (in Greek, *daemon*) could be good or bad; they were invisible and everywhere (like germs to us), responsible for everything from illnesses to good weather. Although ancient Christians believed in angels (which were good), they considered all demons to be evil allies of Satan, a fallen angel. The gospels in the New Testament present Jesus as coming to earth to defeat the devil and his demons by resisting their temptations and casting them out of people. Egyptians believed that demons populated the arid desert, and so the decision of monks like Antony to move into the desert represented an attempt to reclaim for God territory that had belonged to the devil.

In the life of the ascetic, demons form the resistance that he must overcome in order to shape himself into a virtuous person. If the goal of the Christian life is to ascend to God and to reach heaven, the demons try to prevent the monk from reaching this goal (Chapters 65–66). Demons represent the ambiguity of temptation: although it originates from external forces of evil, it nonetheless derives also from the monk's internal fears and insecurities. Demons not only tempt Antony, but they also try to frighten him and so to undermine his confidence in God; Antony, however, remains serene and untroubled, secure in his faith in Christ. As Athanasius presents it, the monk's discipline replaces the struggle of the martyrs in the post-Constantinian era (Chapter 47): just as the martyrs had to resist the power of the Roman state, so too the monks must resist the power of the demonic hosts.

The accuracy of Athanasius's presentation of Antony is open to question because little evidence remains with which we can compare Athanasius's version of events. Seven letters that Antony wrote to his followers do survive: although their teachings are similar to those in the *Life* in several respects, there are also striking differences. While Athanasius presents Antony as a simple, uneducated man whose ascetic life is a struggle against demons, the Antony of the letters is an educated, philosophically astute teacher who sees the ascetic life as a means of transforming the self into a higher spiritual state. Demons play a much more subtle role. These letters reveal that Athanasius did not hesitate to present Antony as he wanted him to be, not necessarily as he really was.

Still, the *Life of St. Antony* is a brilliant work whose influence in Christian history and thought cannot be overestimated. Its story of a simple Christian who achieved great holiness with God's help inspired numerous ancient and medieval men and women to serve God in monasticism. Great artists have attempted to capture the drama of Antony's struggles with demons. Most important for the theme of this collection, Athanasius's engaging narrative became one of the most influential examples of how to write the *Life* of a saint for all later hagiographers in Western as well as Eastern Christendom.

SOURCES AND FURTHER READING

The following translation of Athanasius's *Life of St. Antony* (*Bibliotheca hagiographica graeca*, no. 140) is based on the text provided in Athanase d'Alexandrie, *Vie d'Antoine*, ed. and trans. G.J.M. Bartelink, Sources chrétiennes 400 (Paris, 1994), which marks a significant improvement on all previous editions. For the sake of brevity, many passages are provided in summary form only, marked by square brackets. An excellent translation of the entire *Life* is provided by Robert C. Gregg in Athanasius, *The Life of Antony and the Letter to Marcellinus*, Classics of Western Spirituality (New York, 1980). Like all previous translations, however, Gregg's is based on an unsatisfactory edition of the Greek text.

An outstanding study of Antony's life and thought, complete with English translations of his letters, is Samuel Rubenson, *The Letters of St. Antony:*

Monasticism and the Making of a Saint, Studies in Antiquity and Christianity (Minneapolis, 1995). Athanasius's presentation of Antony in the *Life* and his wider ascetic teachings are studied in David Brakke, *Athanasius and the Politics of Asceticism*, Oxford Early Christian Studies (Oxford, 1995), which has been reprinted as *Athanasius and Asceticism* (Baltimore, 1998). On the spirituality of the Egyptian desert monks, see the relevant chapters in Peter Brown, *The Body and Society: Men, Women, and Sexual Renunciation in Early Christianity*, Lectures on the History of Religions, new series 13 (New York, 1988).

Athanasius of Alexandria, *Life of St. Antony of Egypt*

Letter of Athanasius, Archbishop of Alexandria, to the Monks in Foreign Places Concerning the Life of the Blessed Antony the Great

(Preface.) It is a good competition that you have begun with the monks in Egypt by seeking either to equal or surpass them in your discipline in virtue.[1] For at last there are monasteries among you as well, and the reputation of the [Egyptian] monks is the basis of their organization: therefore, this plan [of yours] deserves praise; may God bring it to completion through your prayers.

Inasmuch as you have asked me about the blessed Antony's way of life and want to learn about how he began the discipline, who he was before this, what the end of his life was like, and if the things that have been said about him are true, so that you might guide yourselves by imitation of him, I have received your charge with great enthusiasm. Indeed, for me as well it is of great profit just to remember Antony, and I know that once you have heard about him, in addition to admiring the man, you too will want to imitate his determination, since monks have in Antony's lifestyle a sufficient pattern for their discipline.

Therefore, do not disbelieve what you have heard from those who have brought reports of him; rather, think that you have heard only a little from them, for even they scarcely can have completely related such great matters. And since I too, urged by you, am telling you what I can by letter, I am sending only a few of the things that I have remembered about him. You for your part should not stop questioning those persons who sail from here, for it is likely that after each person tells what he knows, the account concerning him will still hardly do him justice. Therefore, when I received your letter, I decided to send for certain monks, particularly those who had spent the most time with him, in the hope that I could learn more and send you the fullest possible account. But since the sailing season was coming to an end and the letter carrier was ready to go, I hurried to write to your piety what I know—for I saw him often—and what I was able to learn from the man who followed Antony no short period of time and who poured water on his hand [see 2 Kings 3:11].[2] I have in every place kept my mind on the truth, so that no one, having heard too much, would disbelieve it, or, having learned less than necessary, would look down on the man.

(1.) Antony was an Egyptian by birth, and his parents were well-born and possessed considerable wealth. Since they were Christians, he was raised in a Christian manner. As a child, he lived with his parents and was familiar with nothing other than them and their house. When he grew to become a boy and became older, he did not put up with learning letters because he wanted to be removed even from the companionship of children. It was his complete desire, as it is written, to live in his house as an unformed person [see Gen 25:27]. He would go to church with his parents. As a boy, he was not lazy, nor did he become rude as he got older. Rather, he was obedient to his parents, and by paying attention to the readings [see 1 Tim 4:13], he preserved in himself what was beneficial in them. Although as a boy he lived in moderate wealth, he did not trouble his parents for diverse and expensive foods, nor did he seek such pleasures. He was happy merely with whatever he found and asked for nothing more.

(2.) After the death of his parents, he was left alone with one small sister; he was about eighteen or twenty, and it was his responsibility to care for the house and his sister. Not six months after his parents' death, he was going to church as usual, and he was thinking to himself and considering all this: how the apostles abandoned everything and followed the Savior [see Mt 4:20; 19:27]; how the people in Acts [of the Apostles] sold their possessions and brought the proceeds and laid them at the feet of the apostles for distribution to the needy [see Acts 4:35–37]; and how such a great hope was stored up for these people in heaven [see Col 1:5]. Considering these things, he entered the church, and it happened that just then the Gospel was being read, and he heard the Lord saying to the rich man, *If you wish to be perfect, go, sell all your possessions, and give the proceeds to the poor, and come, follow me, and you will have treasure in heaven* [Mt 19:21]. And Antony, as if the remembrance of the saints had been placed in him by God and as if the readings had been made on his account, left the church immediately and gave to the villagers the possessions he had received from his ancestors—three hunderd *arourae* of fertile and very beautiful land—so that they would no longer trouble him and his sister.[3] He sold all their other movable possessions, collecting a sizable sum of money, and gave it to the poor, although he kept a little for his sister's sake.

(3.) But when he again entered the church and heard in the Gospel the Lord saying, *Do not worry about tomorrow* [Mt 6:34], he could not stay: he went out and gave even that [little money remaining] to the common people. When he had delivered his sister to known and faithful virgins in order to be brought up for virginity, he at last devoted himself to the discipline outside the house, attending to himself and guiding himself with patience. For there were not yet so many monasteries in Egypt, and no monk knew the great desert; rather, each of those who wanted to attend to himself practiced the discipline alone, not far from his own village. Now, at this time there was an old man in the neighboring village who had practiced the solitary life from his youth: when Antony saw him, he imitated him in virtue [see Gal 4:18]. At first he too began by remaining in the places around the village; then if he heard of some zealous one somewhere, like the wise bee, he went and sought that person, and he did not return to his own place until he had seen the man and had received from him, so to speak, travel supplies for the road to virtue.

And so, spending time there at first, he strengthened his intention never to return to the things of his parents nor to remember his relatives, but he directed all his desire and all his zeal toward the effort required by the discipline. Therefore, he worked with his hands, since he had heard, "Let not the idle one eat" [see 2 Thess 3:10], and he spent some of the money on bread and some for the needy. He prayed continuously since he knew that it is necessary to pray in secret without ceasing [see Mt 6:6; 1 Thess 5:17]. For indeed he so devoted himself to the reading that nothing of what is written fell from him to the ground [see 1 Sam 3:19], but he retained everything, so that his memory replaced books for him.

(4.) Conducting himself in this way, then, Antony was loved by everyone. He sincerely submitted to the zealous ones whom he visited, and he learned thoroughly the advantage in zeal and discipline that each one possessed in comparison to himself. He contemplated the graciousness of one and the devotion to prayers of another; he observed one's lack of anger and another's love of people; he attended to the one who kept vigils and the other who loved to study; he admired one for his perseverance and another for his fasting and sleeping on the ground; he watched closely the gentle nature of one and the patience of another; but in all he noticed piety toward Christ and love for one another. And when he had been filled in this way, he returned to his own place of discipline, and then he gathered into himself the virtues of each and strove to display them all in himself. Indeed, he was not contentious with those of his own age, except only that he should not appear to be second to them in the better things. And he did this in such a way that he did not hurt anyone's feelings; rather, they rejoiced in him. And so when the people of the village and the lovers of virtue with whom he associated saw that he was this kind of person, they all called him "Beloved of God"; some welcomed him as a son, others as a brother.

(5.) But the devil, who hates and envies the good, could not bear to see such resolution in a young man, but set out to do against Antony the kinds of things he usually does. First he tried to dissuade him from the discipline by suggesting the memory of possessions, the care of his sister, the intimacy of family, love of money, love of glory, the varied pleasure of food, and the other indulgences of life—and finally the difficulty of virtue and the great effort that it requires. He introduced the weakness of the body and the long duration of time. In short, he raised up a dust cloud of thoughts in Antony's mind, desiring thereby to separate him from his upright intention.

But the enemy saw that he himself was weak in the face of Antony's resolve and saw instead that he was defeated by the other's stubbornness, overthrown by his faith, and falling due to Antony's constant prayers. Then he took confidence in the weapons of the belly's navel [see Job 40:16] and, boasting in these—for they are his primary means of trapping the young—he advanced against the youth, troubling him at night and harassing him by day so that those who watched could sense the struggle that was going on between the two. The one would suggest dirty thoughts, and the other would turn them back with prayers; the one would titillate, and the other, as if seeming to blush, would fortify his body with faith and fasts. And the miserable devil dared at night to dress up like a woman and imitate one in every way merely to deceive Antony. But Antony, by thinking about Christ and the excellence one ought to possess because of him, and by considering the soul's rational faculty, extinguished the ember of the other's deception.

Once again the enemy suggested the ease of pleasure. But Antony, like someone fittingly angry or grieved, thought about the threat of fire and the torment of the worm, and by setting these thoughts against [those of the enemy], he passed through these things unharmed. All this was a source of shame for the enemy, for he who had considered himself to be like God [see Is 14:14; Ezek 28:2] was now being mocked by a youth, and he who boasted over flesh and blood was being overthrown by a human being who wore flesh. For working with Antony was the Lord, the one who for our sake took flesh and gave to the body the victory over the devil, so that each of those who truly struggle says, *Not I, but the grace of God that is with me* [1 Cor 15:10].

(6.) At last, when the dragon could not defeat Antony in this way but instead saw himself thrust out of his heart, he gnashed his teeth, as it is written [see Ps 35:16; 37:12; 112:10]. As if he were beside himself, he finally appeared to Antony in his form just as he is in his mind, as a black boy. And as though he had fallen down, he no longer attacked Antony with thoughts—for the crafty one had been tossed down—but finally he used a human voice and said, "Many people I have deceived, and most I have defeated, but now coming against you and your efforts as I have against others, I have been weakened." Antony asked, "Who are you who say such things to me?" Immediately he answered with a pitiful voice, "It is I who am fornication's lover. It is I who have been entrusted with its ambushes and its titillations against the youth, and I am called the spirit of fornication. How many persons who desired to be prudent I have deceived! How many persons who professed to be so I have persuaded to change by titillating them! It is I on whose account even the prophet blames those who have fallen, saying, *You have been deceived by the spirit of fornication* [Hos 4:12]. For it was through me that they were tripped up. It is I who so often troubled you and who as often was overthrown by you." But Antony gave thanks to the Lord and took courage in him, and he said to him, "You are very despicable then, for you are black in your mind and as weak as a boy. From now on I will have no anxiety about you, *for the Lord is my helper, and I will look down on my enemies* [Ps 118:7]." When he heard this, the black one immediately fled, cowering before these words and afraid even to approach the man.[4]

(7.) This was Antony's first struggle against the devil, or rather this was the achievement in Antony of the Savior, *who condemned sin in the flesh so that the righteousness of the Law might be fulfilled in us, who walk not according to the flesh, but according to the spirit* [Rom 8:3–4]. But Antony did not, because the demon had fallen, now become negligent and take no thought of himself, nor did the enemy, because he had been defeated, stop lying in ambush. For the enemy went around again like a lion, looking for some opportunity against him [see 1 Pet 5:8]. But Antony, since he had learned from the Scriptures that the wiles of the enemy are numerous [see Eph 6:11], practiced the discipline intensely, figuring that, even if the enemy had been unable to deceive his heart through bodily pleasure, he would attempt to trap him by another method. For the demon is a lover of sin.

Therefore, Antony more and more punished his body and enslaved it [1 Cor 9:27], so that, even though he had triumphed in some ways, he would not be overcome in others; he resolved, then, to accustom himself to more severe training measures. Many people were amazed, but he himself endured the labor with ease, for his soul's intention, which had lasted for a long time, created in him a good habit so that, when he received even slight encouragement from others, he would show great enthusiasm for the task. He would keep vigil to such an extent that often he spent the entire night without sleep, and when he did this not once but many times, people were amazed. He ate once a day after sunset, but there were times when he went two days and often four days without eating. His food was bread and salt; his drink, only water. Indeed, it is superfluous even to speak about meat and wine, for nothing of the sort was ever found among the other zealous ones. For sleeping he was content with a rush mat, but mostly he lay upon the bare ground. He would not anoint himself with oil, saying that young men ought to pursue the discipline with zeal and should not seek what would pamper the body, rather that they should accustom the body to labors and consider the Apostle's statement, *Whenever I am weak, then I am strong* [2 Cor 12:10]. For at that time he used to say that the soul's intellect grows strong when the body's pleasures are made weak.

He had this truly wonderful thought: that one should not measure progress in virtue or withdrawal made for this purpose by the length of time, but by the desire and intention. Therefore, he himself did not keep track of the time that had gone by; rather, every day, as if he were just starting the discipline, he would make his effort toward advancement greater, constantly saying to himself Paul's statement, *forgetting what lies behind and straining forward to what lies ahead* [Phil 3:13], and remembering also the voice of the prophet Elijah, saying, "The Lord lives, before whom I stand today" [see 1 Kings 17:1; 18:15].[5] He observed that in saying "today" he was not measuring the time that had gone by, but, as if he were always making a new start, he was zealous every day to show himself to God to be such that one should appear to God: pure in heart and ready to obey his will and nothing else. He would say to himself, "The ascetic ought always to observe his own life in the conduct of the great Elijah as if in a mirror."

(8.) Having constrained himself in this way, Antony departed to the tombs, which happened to lie far outside the village. He commanded one of his acquaintances to bring him bread every several days, and he himself entered one of the tombs; when the other had shut the door, he remained inside by himself. Then, when the enemy could not bear this but was afraid that in a short time Antony would fill the desert with the discipline, he came one night with a crowd of demons and so cut Antony with wounds that he lay on the ground speechless from the tortures. For he used to maintain that the pains were so severe that he would say that blows inflicted by human beings could not have inflicted such torture. But by God's Providence—for the Lord does not neglect those who hope in him—his acquaintance came the next day to bring him the bread. When he opened the door and saw Antony lying on the ground as if dead, he lifted him up, carried him to the village church, and laid him on the ground. Many of his relatives and the villagers sat around Antony as if beside a corpse. But around midnight Antony came to himself and got up; when he saw everyone asleep and only his acquaintance keeping watch, he motioned with his head for him to approach and then asked him to pick him up again and carry him to the tombs without waking anybody.

(9.) And so he was carried back by the man, and as usual, the door was shut, and he was once again inside by himself. He was unable to stand because of the blows from the demons, and so he prayed lying down.[6] After the prayer, he said with a loud voice, "Here I am: Antony! I do not flee from your blows. For even if you do more, nothing shall separate me from the love of Christ" [see Rom 8:35–39]. Then he sang, "*Though an army encamp against me, my heart shall not fear*" [Ps 26:3]. This is what the ascetic thought and said.

But the enemy, who hates the good, was amazed that he dared to return after such blows. He called together his dogs and burst out, "See that we have not stopped this one with the spirit of fornication or with blows; rather, he bravely comes against us. Let us attack him in some other way." It is easy for the devil to change forms for his evil purposes, and so at night they raised such a tumult that it seemed as though that entire place was being shaken by an earthquake. The demons, as if they had shattered the four walls of the dwelling, seemed to enter through them, transformed into the appearance of beasts and serpents. And the place was immediately filled with the appearances of lions, bears, leopards, bulls, snakes, asps, scorpions, and wolves, and each of them was moving according to his own form. The lion was roaring, wishing to attack; the bull seemed to butt with his horns; the serpent writhed but did not approach; and the wolf rushed forward but was restrained. Altogether the ragings of their apparitions and the sounds of their voices were completely terrifying. Antony, whipped and tortured by them, felt even more severe bodily pain; but his soul was not trembling, and he remained vigilant. He groaned because of his body's pain, but he was sober in his thinking, and as if to mock them, he said, "If you had had the power, it would have been enough for one of you to come alone. But since the Lord has made you weak, you are trying to frighten me by your number. But it is a proof of your weakness that you imitate the shapes of irrational beings." And again he took courage and said, "If you are able and have received authority against me, don't delay, but attack! But if you cannot, why are you harassing me in vain? For faith in our Lord is our seal and wall for safety." And so after many attempts, they gnashed their teeth against him because they were making fools of themselves rather than of him.

(10.) Meanwhile the Lord had not forgotten Antony's struggle, but came to him in assistance. Thus, Antony looked up and saw the roof as if it were being opened [see Acts 7:55–56] and a certain ray of light coming down to him. The demons suddenly vanished; his body's pain immediately stopped;

and the building was once again intact. When Antony perceived the assistance, got his breath back, and was relieved of his pains, he asked the vision that appeared to him, "Where were you? Why didn't you appear at the beginning and make my pains stop?" And a voice came to him, "Antony, I was here, but I waited to see your struggle. Because you endured and were not beaten, I will always be your help, and I will make you famous everywhere." When he heard this, he got up and prayed, and he became so strong that he felt that he had more strength in his body than he had had before. At this time he was around thirty-five years old.

(11.) The next day Antony went out even more enthusiastic about the piety, and when he came to that old man [whom he had imitated earlier],[7] he asked him to live with him in the desert. But when this man declined due to his age and because there was not yet such a custom, immediately he himself set out for the mountain. Yet again the enemy, when he saw his zeal and wanted to impede it, cast in his way an apparition of a large silver disk. But Antony recognized the trick performed by the hater of good; he stood and said to the disk, because he saw the devil in it: "How did a disk end up in the desert? This path is not well-trod, nor is there any trace of people having traveled through here. If it had fallen, it would have been missed thanks to its size; rather, the one who lost it would have turned back, searched, and found it since the place is a desert. This is the devil's work. You will not impede my intention in this way, devil! Indeed, let this go with you into destruction" [see Acts 8:20]. When Antony had said this, it vanished like smoke from before a fire [see Ps 68:2].

(12.) Next, as he went along, he again saw this time not an apparition, but real gold scattered in the path. He himself has not said nor do we know whether it was the enemy who showed this to him or whether it was some better power who was training the athlete and showing the devil that he truly did not care about money at all, but what appeared really was gold. Antony marveled at the amount, but as if stepping over fire, he passed by it so as not to turn back; rather, he ran so fast that the place became hidden and forgotten.

Having intensified his resolve more and more, he hurried to the mountain. On the other side of the river he found a deserted fort, abandoned for so long that it was full of serpents; he situated himself there and lived in it. The reptiles, as if someone were chasing them, immediately withdrew, but he barricaded the door, and since he had stored up enough bread for six months—the people of the Thebaid do this, and their bread often stays fresh for a year—and since he had a water supply inside, he descended as if into a shrine, and he remained alone inside the monastic retreat, neither going out himself nor seeing anyone who came.[8] And so in this way he devoted himself to the discipline for a long time, receiving only bread let down from above the house twice each year.

(13.) Those of his acquaintances who came, since he would not allow them to enter, often used to spend days and nights outside, and they would hear what sounded like crowds making a commotion, clamoring, raising up pitiful voices and crying out, "Leave our places! What have you to do with the desert? You cannot endure our attack!" At first those outside thought that there were certain people fighting with him and that these people had gone in to him by ladders. But when they stooped and peeped through a hole and saw no one, then they reckoned that they were demons; they became frightened and called for Antony. He heard them, although he did not give a thought to the demons: coming near to the door, he exhorted the people to withdraw and not to be afraid, for he said, "In this way the demons create apparitions against the cowards. Therefore, seal yourselves [with the sign of the cross] and depart with courage, and let these [demons] make fools of themselves." And so they went away fortified with the sign of the cross, but he stayed behind and was in no way harmed by the demons, nor did he grow weary of fighting them. Indeed, the assistance of the visions that came to his intellect and the weakness of the enemies gave him much rest from his labors and made his intention even greater. For his acquaintances would always come, expecting to find him dead, but instead would hear him singing, "*Let God rise up, and let his enemies be scattered; and let those who hate him flee before him. As smoke disappears, let them disappear; as wax melts before fire, let the wicked perish before God*" [Ps 68:1–2]. And again: "*All nations surrounded me; in the name of the Lord I repelled them*" [Ps 118:10].

(14.) For nearly twenty years he continued to discipline himself in this way, not going out himself and being seen by others only rarely. After this, when many eagerly desired to imitate his discipline, and others of his acquaintances came and were pulling down and wrenching out the door by force, Antony emerged, as if from some shrine, initiated into the mysteries and filled with God. Now for the first time he appeared outside the fort to those who had come to him. And they, when they saw him, were amazed to see that his body had its same condition: it was neither fat as if from lack of exercise nor withered as if from fasting and fighting demons, but it was such as they had known it before his withdrawal. The disposition of his soul was pure again, for it was neither contracted from distress, nor dissipated from pleasure, nor constrained by levity or dejection. Indeed, when he saw the crowd, he was not disturbed, nor did he rejoice to be greeted by so many people. Rather, he was wholly balanced, as if he were being navigated by the Word and existing in his natural state.

Therefore, through Antony the Lord healed many of the suffering bodies of those present, and others he cleansed of demons. He gave Antony grace in speaking, and thus he comforted many who were grieved and reconciled into friendship others who were quarreling, exhorting everyone to prefer nothing in the world to the love for Christ. While he discussed and recalled the good things to come and the love for humanity that has come to us from God, *who did not withhold his own son, but gave him up for all of us* [Rom 8:32], he persuaded many to choose the solitary life. And so at last there came to be monasteries even in the mountains, and the desert was made a city of monks, who left their homes and enrolled in the heavenly commonwealth [see Phil 3:20; Heb 12:23].

(15.) When it was necessary for him to cross the canal of Arsinoë—he needed to visit the brothers—the canal was full of crocodiles. Simply by praying, he entered it, he and all those with him, and they crossed it safely. When he returned to his monastic retreat, he resumed the same holy and vigorous labors. By his constant discourses he increased the zeal of those who were already monks, and most of the rest he moved to a love for the discipline. Soon, thanks to the drawing power of his speech, there came to be many monasteries, and he directed them all like a father.

[**Translator's note**: In chapters 16–43 Antony delivers a long address on the monastic life concerned mostly with the monk's struggle with demons.]

(44.) While Antony was discussing these matters, everyone rejoiced. In some persons the desire for virtue increased; in others, negligence receded; and in still others, conceit came to an end. Everyone was persuaded to despise the demonic scheming, and they marveled at the grace that the Lord had given to Antony *for the discernment of spirits* [1 Cor 12:10]. In the mountains the monastic dwellings were like tents filled with divine choirs: they were singing Psalms, studying, fasting, praying, rejoicing in the hope of the things to come, working so as to be able to give alms, and maintaining love and harmony with one another. Truly it was like seeing a land all its own, a land of piety and justice. For there was no one there who was the victim of injustice, and there was no complaint about the collection of taxes; rather, there was a multitude of ascetics, all of whom shared a single purpose: virtue. Anyone who saw again the monasteries and the ranks of the monks would cry out and say, *How beautiful are your dwellings, Jacob, and your tents, Israel: like shady glens, like a riverside garden, and like tents that the Lord has pitched, like cedars beside waters* [Num 24:5–6, Septuagint].

(45.) Antony, as was his custom, withdrew by himself in his own monastic retreat, intensified his discipline, and sighed daily as he thought of the heavenly dwelling places [see Jn 14:2]: he desired them and kept in mind the brevity of human life. In fact, when he was about to eat, sleep, or go about the other bodily necessities, he would be ashamed as he considered the soul's rational faculty. Often, therefore, when he was about to eat with many other monks, he would recall the spiritual feast [see 1 Cor 10:3], ask to be excused, and go far away from them, since he thought it would be embarrassing if he were seen by others while eating. Therefore, he ate by himself for the sake of the body's need, and also with the brothers, out of respect for them, but freely offering words for their benefit. He used to say that one should give all one's attention to the soul rather than to the body, although on account of necessity it is permitted to give a little time to the body. But on the whole one should devote oneself to the soul and seek its benefit, so that it will not be dragged down by the body's pleasures, but rather so that the body will be enslaved to it. For this is what was said by the Savior: *Do not worry about your life, what you will eat, or about your body, what you will wear. And do not keep striving for what you are to eat and what you are to drink, and do not keep worrying. For it is the nations of the world that strive after all these things, and your*

*Father knows that you need them. Instead, strive for his kingdom, and these things will be given to you as we*ll [Lk 12:22, 29–31].

(46.) After this the persecution that took place during the time of Maximinus seized the church.[9] When the holy martyrs were being led to Alexandria, Antony himself left his monastic retreat and followed them, saying, "Let us go, so that we may contend if we are called or we may contemplate those who are contending." He desired to be martyred, but since he was not willing to turn himself in, he ministered to the confessors both in the mines and in the prisons.[10] He showed great zeal in the courtroom: he stirred up the enthusiasm of those who were called while they were contending, and he received those who were being martyred and accompanied them until they were perfected.[11] Therefore, when the judge saw the fearless zeal of Antony and those with him, he commanded that none of the monks should appear in the courtroom or remain in the city at all. All the others thought it wise to hide that day, but Antony gave such heed to this command that he washed his outer garment and the next day stood on an elevated place before them and appeared before the governor clearly visible. And as everyone marveled at this and the governor saw and passed by after his audience, Antony stood without trembling and so demonstrated the zeal of us Christians. For indeed he himself prayed that he would be a martyr, as I said, and he seemed to grieve that he had not been martyred. But the Lord was preserving him for our benefit and that of others, so that he might become a teacher to many in the discipline that he had learned from the Scriptures. For many people, just by seeing his conduct, became eager to imitate his way of life. And so again, as was his custom, he ministered to the confessors, and as if he were their fellow prisoner, he labored in their service.

(47.) When at last the persecution ceased and the blessed Bishop Peter had been martyred, Antony departed and withdrew again to his monastic retreat, and there he was daily a martyr to his conscience and a contender in the struggles of the faith [see 1 Tim 6:12].[12] For he practiced the discipline even more and treated himself even more severely. He was always fasting, and he wore a shirt that was hairy on the inside, but leather on the outside, which he kept until the end. He did not wash his body with water because of dirt, nor did he wash his feet or even put them in water unless it was necessary. No one saw him unclothed, nor did anyone ever see Antony's body naked except when he died and was being buried.

(48.) While he was withdrawn and determined to spend a certain length of time without going out himself or receiving anyone, a certain Martinianus, a military officer, came and bothered Antony, for he had a daughter who was harassed by a demon. For a long time he kept knocking on the door and asking for Antony to come out and pray to God for his child. Antony could not bear to open the door, but looked down from above and said, "Man, why are you crying to me? I too am a human being as you are. But if you have faith in Christ, whom I serve, go and as you believe, pray to God, and it will be so." Immediately Martinianus had faith, called upon Christ, went away, and found his daughter cleansed from the demon. Many other such things the Lord did through Antony, the Lord who says, *Ask, and it will be given you* [Mt 7:7; Lk 11:9]. Many of the sufferers, when he would not open his door, simply slept outside the monastic retreat, and because they had faith and prayed sincerely, they were cleansed.

(49.) Antony saw that he was troubled by many people and was not permitted to withdraw as he desired, and he became apprehensive about the things that the Lord was doing through him, worrying either that he would become conceited or that someone else would think he was greater than he was. He thought about it and decided to depart to the Upper Thebaid, where people did not know him.[13] And so when he had received bread from the brothers, he sat by the bank of the river, watching to see whether a boat might come by so that he might get in and go up with them. While he was thinking about this, a certain voice from above came to him: "Antony, where are you going, and why?" He was not disturbed; rather, since he was used to being called in this way often, he paid attention and answered, saying, "Because the crowds do not permit me to live quietly, I want to go up to the Upper Thebaid, because of the many troubles that happen to me here and especially because they ask me for things beyond my power." But the voice said to him, "Even if you were to go up into the Thebaid, or even if, as you are thinking, you were to go down to the Bucolia,[14] you will have to endure more, even double the toil. If you really wish to live quietly, depart now for the inner desert."[15] Antony said, "Who will show me the way? For I do not know it." Immediately the voice showed to him Saracens about to travel on that way.[16] Therefore, Antony approached, drew near to them, and asked to go with them into the desert. And they, as if commanded by Providence, welcomed him enthusiastically. After he had traveled with them three days and three nights, he came to a very high mountain. Below the mountain there was a very clear spring of water, sweet and very cold, and farther off there was a plain with a few neglected palm trees.

(50.) Then Antony, as if moved by God, loved the place, for this was what the one who had spoken to him by the banks of the river had meant. At first, since he had received bread from his fellow travelers, he remained on the mountain alone, with no one else there. Since he recognized it to be his own home, he at last kept to that place. But the Saracens themselves, when they saw Antony's zeal, would travel that route on purpose and would joyfully bring him bread. At that time he had also small and meager relief from the palm trees. But later, when the brothers learned of the place, like children remembering their father, they took care to send to him. When Antony saw that some of them were troubled and endured hardship on account of the bread, to spare the monks this, he resolved within himself and asked some of those who came to supply him with a hoe, an ax, and a little grain. And when these were supplied, he went about the land around the mountain; when he found a small piece of suitable land, he began to cultivate it, and since he had plenty of water for irrigation, he sowed. Doing this every year, he got his bread from there, rejoicing that no one would have any trouble because of this and that he kept himself from being burdensome. But later, when he saw that people were coming again, he cultivated a few vegetables as well, so that anyone who came might have a little relief from the toil of that difficult journey. At first the wild beasts of the desert would come because of the water and often damage his seed and cultivation. But he gently took hold of one of the beasts and said to them all, "Why are you hurting me when I have caused you no harm? Go away, and in the name of the Lord, do not come near here any more." And from then on, as if afraid of his command, they no longer approached the place.

(51.) Thus he was alone at the inner mountain, occupied with prayers and the discipline. The brothers who were coming asked him for permission, and they served him by supplying him monthly with olives, legumes, and oil, for by then he had become old. And so, living there, he endured very great struggles, as it is written, *not against flesh and blood*, but against the adversarial demons [Eph 6:12], as we have learned from those who went to him. For indeed they heard there tumults, many voices, and clashes of weapons, and at night they saw that the mountain was full of sparks, and they beheld him fighting as if against visible beings and praying against them. He encouraged those who came to him, and he himself contended by kneeling and praying to God. It was truly marvelous that, although he was alone in such a desert, he was not afraid of attacking demons, nor did he fear the ferocity of such wild beasts as were there, four-footed ones and reptiles. Rather, truly, as it is written, because he was confident in the Lord, he was *like Mount Zion* [Ps 125:1], with an immovable and undisturbed mind, so that the demons instead fled from him, and the wild beasts, as it is written, made peace with him [see Job 5:23].

(52.) Therefore, the devil, as David says in the Psalm, closely watched Antony and gnashed his teeth against him [see Ps 35:16]. But Antony was consoled by the Savior and remained unhurt by the devil's villainy and diverse forms of craftiness. So when he was keeping watch at night, the devil sent wild beasts against him, and nearly all the hyenas in that desert came out of their dens and surrounded him, and he was in their midst. When each of them was opening its mouth and threatening to bite him, he recognized the enemy's trick and said to them all, "If you have received power against me, I am ready to be eaten up by you, but if you were sent by demons, do not stay, but withdraw, for I am a slave of Christ" [see Rom 1:1]. When Antony said this, they fled, driven away by that utterance as if by a whip.

(53.) A few days later, as he was working—for he was careful to work hard—someone stood at the door and pulled the cord with which he was working, for he used to weave baskets, which he would give to those who came to him in exchange for the supplies they brought him. Getting up, he saw a beast that was like a human being down to his thighs but had legs and feet like those of an ass. Antony just signed himself and said, "I am a slave of Christ. If you have been sent against me, look, here I am!" But the beast ran away with his demons so fast that he fell down and died. The beast's death was the downfall of the demons, for they were zealous to do everything to make him leave the desert, but they were unable to do so.

(54.) Once when he was asked by the monks to come down and visit them in their places for a while, he traveled with the monks who had come to him. A camel carried the bread and water for them, for that entire desert is dry, and there was no drinkable water at all, except only in that mountain from which they had drawn their water, the one where his monastic retreat was. And so when the water ran out and the heat was very oppressive, everyone was in danger. When they had gone around the area and had not found any water, they at last could not even walk; rather, they threw themselves on the ground and in despair let the camel go off on its own. But when the old man saw that everyone was in danger, he became very distressed and groaned, and moving a brief distance away from them, he knelt, stretched out his hands, and prayed. And immediately the Lord created water right there where he stood praying, and so they all drank and were revived. When they had filled their water-bags, they sought and found the camel, for it happened that its rope had become caught on a stone and was held fast. Thus, when they had brought it back and had given it water, they put the water-bags on it, and they traveled unharmed.

When he came to the outer monasteries, they all greeted him, looking on him as a father. And he, as if he were bringing travel supplies from the mountain, gave them hospitality with words and shared what was beneficial. Once again there was joy in the mountains, along with zeal for progress and consolation through mutual faith. He too rejoiced when he saw the monks' enthusiasm and that his sister had grown old in virginity and was herself directing other virgins.

(55.) After some days, he returned to the mountain. From then on many people would come to him, and others who were suffering were brave enough to come. He always had this precept for the monks who came to him: to have faith in the Lord and to love him; to keep themselves from impure thoughts and fleshly desires and, as it is written in Proverbs, *not to be led astray by the belly's feasting* [Prov 24:15, Septuagint]; to flee vainglory and to pray continually [see Lk 18:1; 1 Thess 5:17]; to sing Psalms before and after sleeping; to repeat by heart the commandments in the Scriptures; and to remember the actions of the saints so that the soul, reminded by the commandments, might be brought into harmony with their zeal.

Especially he counseled them to meditate continually on the Apostle's saying, "*Do not let the sun go down on your anger*" [Eph 4:26], and to reckon that this was said likewise about every commandment, so that the sun should go down neither on anger nor on any other sin of ours. "For it is good and necessary that the sun should not condemn us concerning any daytime evil, nor the moon concerning any nocturnal sin or even thought. Therefore, so that this disposition might be preserved in us, it is good to listen to the Apostle and to keep his word, for he says, *Examine yourselves, and test yourselves* [2 Cor 13:5]. Therefore, every day let each person take an account of his daytime and nighttime activities. If he has sinned, let him cease; but if he has not sinned, let him not boast; rather, let him continue in the good without becoming negligent, condemning his neighbor, or justifying himself, as the blessed Apostle Paul says, until the Lord comes who searches out what is hidden [see 1 Cor 4:5; Rom 2:16]. For often we forget even what we ourselves do: we ourselves do not know, but the Lord comprehends everything. Therefore, giving the judgment to him, let us show sympathy to one another *and bear one another's burdens* [Gal 6:2], but let us examine ourselves and be zealous to fill up what we lack.

"May this form of surveillance serve as a safeguard against sin: let each of us mark and write down his actions and the motions of his soul, as if we were going to tell them to each other. Be assured that since we would be ashamed if such things were to become known, we will stop sinning and even conceiving of anything foul. For who wants to be seen while sinning? Who, when he has sinned, would not rather lie since he wants to go unnoticed? Therefore, just as we would not fornicate if we were watching one another, if we write down our thoughts as if we were going to tell them to one another, we will all the more keep ourselves from impure thoughts, since we would be ashamed for them to become known. Let the act of writing serve for us in place of the eyes of our fellow ascetics, so that, by being as embarrassed to write as to be seen, we will never think dirty thoughts. By forming ourselves in this way we will be able to enslave the body [see 1 Cor 9:27], *to please the Lord* [1 Cor 7:32], and to trample under feet the machinations of the enemy."

(56.) These are the things that Antony taught to the people who visited. He sympathized and prayed with those who were suffering; often and in many cases the Lord listened to his prayers. Antony did not boast when his prayers were answered, nor did he grumble when they were not. Rather, he always gave thanks to the Lord, and he exhorted those who were suffering to be patient and to know that healing did not come from him or from any human being, but only from God, who acts whenever he wishes and for whomever he chooses [see Rom 9:15–18]. Therefore, the sufferers received even the words of the old man as healing and learned not to be negligent, but to be patient. And those who were healed were taught to give thanks not to Antony, but to the Lord alone.

[**Translator's note**: Chapters 57–64 illustrate Antony's special connection with God with stories in which sick persons are healed, Antony miraculously knows future or geographically distant events, and demons are exorcised. Chapter 58 is representative.]

(58.) A certain young woman from Busiris in Tripoli suffered from a terrible and extremely pitiful condition: when her tears, mucus, and discharges from her ears fell to the ground, they immediately became worms. Even more, her body was paralyzed, and her eyes were abnormal. Her parents had faith in the Lord who healed the woman with the flow of blood [see Mt 9:20], and so when they learned about some monks who were going out to Antony, they asked that they might go with them and bring their daughter, and the monks consented. The parents and the child remained outside the mountain with Paphnutius, the confessor and monk, while the others went in. Just as the monks were about to tell Antony about the girl, he beat them to it and told them all about the girl's illness and how she had traveled with them. Still, when they asked that these people be allowed to come in, he would not permit it, but said, "Go, and you will discover that she has been healed, unless she is dead. For this achievement is not mine so that she should come to me, a pitiful human being. Rather, healing belongs to the Savior, who bestows his mercy everywhere on those who call upon him. Therefore, it is to that girl's prayer that the Lord has consented, and it is to me that his love for humanity has revealed that he has healed the girl's illness where she is." In this way the miracle happened, for when the monks went out, they found the parents rejoicing and the girl completely healthy.

[**Translator's note:** We now continue with the main line of the story.]

(65.) Numerous monks have harmoniously and consistently reported many similar such things that happened through Antony, but these accounts do not appear so amazing in comparison with other even more marvelous things.

Once when he was about to eat, as he got up around the ninth hour to pray, he sensed that he had been snatched away in thought. And what is amazing is that while he was standing he was looking at himself, as if he were outside of himself and being led up into the air by certain beings. Next certain harsh and fearful beings in the air wanted to prevent him from passing through. And when the ones that were guiding him fought back, the others demanded an explanation as to why Antony was not accountable to them. When these other beings wanted to take an account of Antony's life from his birth, the ones guiding Antony would not let them, saying to them, "The Lord has done away with the things that date from his birth, but you may take an account of things from the time when he became a monk and devoted himself to God." Then, when they made accusations but could not prove any of them, Antony's way became free and clear. And immediately he saw himself as if he were coming and standing with himself, and once again he was truly Antony.

Then he forgot to eat and spent the rest of the day and the entire night groaning and praying, for he was amazed to have seen with how many opponents we must wrestle and how many toils a person must face to pass through the air. He remembered that this is what the Apostle said: *following the prince of the power of the air* [Eph 2:2]. For the enemy's power consists in this: that he fights and tries to stop those who are passing through (the air). Therefore, Antony used to exhort particularly, "*Take up the armor of God so that you may be able to withstand on the evil day* [Eph 6:13], so that, *having nothing evil to say of us* [Tit 2:8], the enemy might be put to shame. And having learned this, let us remember what the Apostle said, *whether it was in the body, I do not know; whether it was outside the body, I do not know; God knows*" [2 Cor 12:2]. But while Paul was snatched up to the third heaven, heard ineffable words, and came down [see 2 Cor 12:2–4], Antony saw himself arrive as far as the air and struggle until he appeared to be free.

(66.) He also possessed this spiritual gift: when he was sitting alone on the mountain [see 2 Kings 1:9], if he was at a loss seeking the answer to something in himself, this would be revealed to him by Providence while he was praying. Indeed, the blessed one was, as it is written, *taught by God* [Jn 6:45; 1 Thess 4:9].

Later he had a discussion with some persons who had come to him about the passage of the soul and what sort of place it will have after this life. The following night someone called to him from above, "Antony, get up, come out, and look!" When he went out—for he knew whom he ought to obey—and looked up, he saw someone huge, ugly and terrifying, standing and reaching up to the clouds, and he saw certain other beings ascending as if they had wings. The giant was stretching out his hands: he prevented some, but others flew by, passed through, and ascended without anxiety. The giant gnashed his teeth over such as these, but he rejoiced over those who fell back. And immediately a voice came to Antony: "Understand what you are seeing!" And his mind was opened [see Lk 24:45], and he understood that this was the passage of the souls and that the giant who was standing there was the enemy who envies the faithful. Those persons accountable to him he seizes and prevents from passing through, but he cannot seize those who do not submit to him, and they ascend past him. Seeing this as a kind of reminder, Antony each day strove all the more to advance to *what lies ahead* [Phil 3:13].

Antony did not voluntarily speak about such things. He spent time praying and marveling about these things privately, but when those who were with him asked and pressed him, he felt compelled to speak, just as a father cannot hide anything from his children. On the contrary, he judged his conscience to be pure and the report of these things to be profitable to them since they would learn that the fruit of the discipline is good and that visions often are a relief from its labors.

(67.) How patient his character was, and how humble his soul! For even though he was so great, he scrupulously honored the rule of the Church, and he wanted every member of the clergy to be held in higher regard than himself. He was not ashamed to bow his head before bishops and priests. If a deacon came to Antony for some edification, he would discuss what was beneficial, but in matters of prayer he would defer to the deacon, since he was not ashamed to learn himself. For indeed he would often question and ask to hear from those who were present, and he acknowledged that he had benefited if someone said something useful.

Moreover, what remarkable grace Antony's face had! He had this wondrous spiritual gift from the Savior: if he was present among a great number of monks and someone who had not previously known him wished to see him, as soon as that person arrived he would pass by the other monks and run to Antony, as if drawn by his eyes. It was not in his height or his weight that Antony differed from the other monks [see 1 Sam 16:7], but in the stability of his character and the purity of his soul. For since his soul was undisturbed, he kept his external senses serene, so that because of his soul's joy he had a cheerful face, and from the movements of his body one could perceive and understand the stability of his soul: as it is written, *When the heart rejoices, the face blooms, but when it is grieved, the face is sad* [see Prov 15:13, Septuagint]. This is how Jacob recognized that Laban was devising a plot and said to his wives, *Your father's face is not as it was yesterday and the day before* [Gen 31:5, Septuagint]. This is how Samuel recognized David, for his eyes brought joy [see 1 Sam 16:12], and his teeth were as white as milk [see Gen 49:12]. And this is how Antony was recognized. For when was he troubled when his soul was so calm? Or when was he sad when his thinking was so joyful?

(68.) In matters of the faith, he was completely marvelous and pious. For he never communed with the Melitian schismatics since he saw their wickedness and apostasy from the beginning.[17] Nor did he have friendly conversation with Manichaeans or any other heretics, except only to admonish them to convert to piety, for he thought and affirmed that friendship and conversation with such persons was harmful and destructive to the soul.[18] Therefore, in the same way he abhorred the Arian heresy, and he commanded everyone neither to go near them nor to hold their evil faith.[19] So when some of the Ariomaniacs came out to him and he had questioned them and learned that they were impious, he chased them from the mountain, saying that their words were worse than serpents.

(69.) Once when the Arians were falsely claiming that Antony shared their views, he became vexed and astonished when he heard. Then, summoned by the bishops and all the brothers, he came down from the mountain. When he entered Alexandria, he publicly renounced the Arians and said that this was the last heresy and the forerunner of the Antichrist. He taught the people that the Son of God is not a creature and had not come into being from what was non-existent, rather that he is the eternal Word and Wisdom from the substance of the Father: "Therefore, it is impious to say, 'There was when he was not,' for the Word was always co-existent with the Father. Therefore, have no fellowship with the supremely impious Arians, for light has no fellowship with darkness [see 2 Cor 6:14]. Indeed, you are pious Christians, but as for them, when they say that the Son who comes from the Father, the Word of God, is a creature, they differ in no way from the pagans since they worship the creature rather than God the Creator [see Rom 1:25]. Believe that even the entire creation itself is vexed with them because they include among the things that came into being the Creator and Lord of all, in whom all things came into being" [see Jn 1:3].

(70.) And so all the people rejoiced to hear the Christ-fighting heresy anathematized by such a man, and all the residents of the city ran together to see Antony. The pagans and their so-called priests came into the church and said, "We ask to see the man of God," for they all called him this. In that place, the Lord cleansed many people of demons through him and healed those who were insane. Many pagans asked if they could just touch the old man, believing that they would be benefited. No doubt as many people became Christian in those few days as one sees do so in a year. Then, when some people thought that he was disturbed by the crowds and so were turning them all away from him, he himself, not disturbed, said, "These people are not as numerous as those demons with whom we do battle on the mountain."

(71.) When he was leaving and we were escorting him, as we approached the gate, from behind us a woman cried out, "Stay, man of God! My daughter is cruelly harassed by a demon! Stay, I beseech you, so that I will not endanger myself by running!" When the old man heard and was asked by us, he willingly stayed. As the woman approached, the child was cast to the ground. But when Antony had prayed and pronounced the name of Christ, the child got up healthy, for the unclean demon had departed. The mother blessed God, and everyone gave thanks. And he himself rejoiced, going off to the mountain as if to his own home.

[**Translator's note**: In chapters 72–80, Antony debates the truth of Christianity with pagan philosophers, who are impressed by the "unlearned" monk's philosophical sophistication and even more by his ability to cast out demons. Even the emperors write to Antony, who responds reluctantly with letters of spiritual exhortation (Chapter 81). Antony receives a vision that presages the destructive activities of the Arians, but also their eventual downfall (Chapter 82).]

(83.) Such was Antony's life. We should not doubt that such marvels happened through a human being. For it is the promise of the Savior, who said, *If you have faith the size of a mustard seed, you will say to this mountain, "Move from there," and it will move; and nothing will be impossible for you* [Mt 17:20]. And again: *Very truly, I tell you, if you ask anything of the Father in my name, it will be given to you. Ask and you will receive* [Jn 16:23–24]. And it is he who says to the disciples and to all who have faith in him: *Cure the sick; cast out demons. You received without payment; give without payment* [Mt 10:8].

(84.) It was not by giving commands that Antony healed, but by praying and saying the name of Christ, so that it was clear to everyone that it was not Antony who was doing this, but the Lord, who was, through Antony, expressing his love for humanity and healing those who suffered. Only this belonged to Antony: the prayer and the discipline, on account of which he sat on the mountain.

Antony rejoiced in the contemplation of divine matters, but he grieved that he was troubled by so many visitors and drawn to the outer mountain. For even all the judges demanded that he come down from the mountain because they could not come there on account of the accused persons who followed them around. Nevertheless, they would demand that he come so that they might at least see him. But when he turned aside and refused to make such journeys to them, they persisted and even sent to him accused persons in the custody of soldiers so that he might come down on account of them. When Antony saw these persons lamenting, he was affected by this pressure and came to the outer mountain. Once again his effort was not without profit, for his arrival resulted in benefit and advantage for many. He benefited the judges by advising them to put justice before everything else, to fear God, and to know that by the measure with which they judge they shall be judged [see Mt 7:2]. Still, he loved the time he spent on the mountain above everything else.

(85.) Once he was subjected to this kind of pressure by those who had need of him, and the military commander asked him through many messengers to come down. After Antony had come and had spoken briefly about what pertains to salvation and about those persons in need, he hastened to return. When the one who was called the duke asked him to stay, he said that he could not stay long with them and convinced him with this charming analogy: "Just as fish that stay too long on dry land die, so too monks who stay with you and spend time among you slack off. Therefore, we must hurry back to the mountain, just as a fish must to the sea, so that we do not, by lingering, forget the interior matters." When the commander heard this and many other things from him, he marveled and said, "Truly this man is a slave of God [see Mt 27:54; Mk 15:39]. For how could an uneducated man have an intellect of such quality and magnitude unless he is loved by God?"

(86.) A certain military commander named Balacius was brutally persecuting us Christians because of his zeal for the hateful Arians. Since he was so savage that he beat virgins and stripped and flogged monks, Antony sent to him and wrote a letter that said: "I see wrath coming upon you! Stop persecuting Christians or the wrath will seize you! Indeed, already it is about to come!" But Balacius laughed, threw the letter to the ground, and spat on it; then he insulted those who had brought it and commanded them to tell Antony this: "Since you are concerned about the monks, I am going to come after you too right away!" And five days had not gone by before the wrath seized him. For Balacius and Nestorius, the prefect of Egypt, went out to the first stopping-place beyond Alexandria, called Chaireu, and both were riding horses. The horses belonged to Balacius and were the gentlest of all those that he had trained. But before they got to the place, the horses began to play with each other, as they do, and suddenly the gentler one, which Nestorius was riding, seized Balacius by biting him and attacked him. And it mangled his thigh with its teeth so badly that he was immediately carried back into the city, and in three days he died. Everyone marveled that what Antony had predicted had come to pass so quickly.

(87.) In this way, then, he warned the cruel, and he so exhorted those who came to him that they immediately forgot their lawsuits and blessed those who withdrew from this life.[20] He so defended those who were being wronged that one would think it was he and not other people who was suffering. Moreover, he was of such benefit to everyone that many soldiers and persons who had lots of possessions renounced the burdens of life and at last became monks. Truly it was as if a physician had been given by God to Egypt. For who came to him grieving and did not return rejoicing? Who came to him mourning for their dead and did not immediately cast off grief? Who came angry and was not converted to friendship? What poor and weary person came and did not, after hearing and seeing him, despise wealth and become consoled in his poverty? What neglectful monk came to him and did not become even stronger? What young man who came to the mountain and saw Antony did not immediately find the pleasures to be dried up and begin to love self-control? Who came to him tempted by demons and did not find rest? Who came to him troubled by thoughts and did not become calm in his mind?

(88.) For this indeed was the great thing about Antony's discipline: that, as I said before, he had the gift of discerning spirits [see 1 Cor 12:10]; he recognized their movements and toward what end each of them focused its intention and zeal for attack. Not only was he himself not mocked by them, but he also taught those who were troubled by thoughts from them how they could turn back their attacks, explaining the tricks and weaknesses of the spirits that were working against them. Thus, each person, as if he had been oiled up for battle by Antony, departed ready to take on the plans of the devil and his demons. How many girls who had suitors ready to marry them, just by seeing Antony from afar, remained virgins for Christ! People would come to him even from foreign lands: they too, with all the others, received benefit and returned, as if sent off by a father. No doubt when he died, they all, like orphans deprived of a father [see Jn 14:18], consoled themselves only with his memory, preserving both his admonitions and his exhortations.

(89.) It is worthwhile for me to recall, and for you to hear as you would like, what the end of his life was like, for this too is worthy of emulation. As was his custom, he was visiting the monks of the outer mountain, and when he had learned in advance about his end from Providence, he said to his brothers, "This is the last visit to you that I shall make, and I shall be surprised if we see each other again in this life. At last it is time for me to depart, for I am nearly 105 years old." When they heard this, they wept and embraced and kissed the old man. But he, as if he were sailing from a foreign city to his own, discoursed joyfully and exhorted them not to be negligent in the labors nor to grow weary in the discipline, but to live as if they were dying daily [see 1 Cor 15:31]. And as he had said before, he told them to guard zealously their soul from impure thoughts and to have a rivalry with the saints, not to approach the Melitian schismatics—for you know their wicked and impure intention—nor to have any fellowship with the Arians, for their impiety is *plain to everyone* [2 Tim 3:9]. "Even if you should see the government officials acting as their patrons, do not be disturbed, for it shall cease, and their appearance is mortal and of short duration. Therefore, keep yourselves pure of these things, and preserve the tradition of the fathers and especially the pious faith in our Lord Jesus Christ, which you have learned from the Scriptures and of which I have often reminded you."

(90.) But when the brothers were pressing him to stay with them and to die there, he would not for many reasons, as he indicated by keeping silent, but especially for this reason. The Egyptians like to honor with funeral rites and to wrap in fine linens the bodies of the zealous ones who have died, and especially those of the holy martyrs, but they do not bury them under the ground; rather, they place them on stretchers and keep them inside among themselves, supposing that in this way they honor those who have departed.[21] But Antony often demanded that the bishops command the people concerning this, and he shamed the laity and chastised the women, saying that it was neither lawful nor pious to do this. For the tombs of the patriarchs and prophets are preserved until today, and the body of the Lord himself was placed in a tomb, and a stone was placed there and hid it until he arose on the third day. And by saying these things, he showed that that person transgresses who does not after death bury the bodies of the departed, even if they happen to be holy. For what is greater or holier than the Lord's body? And so many people, when they heard this, thereupon buried their dead under the ground and gave thanks to the Lord that they had been taught so well.

(91.) But since Antony knew this and was afraid that they would do the same thing to his body, he left quickly after he said farewell to the monks on the outer mountain. And after he had arrived at the inner mountain, where he was accustomed to remain, he became sick a few months later. When he had called those who were with him—there were two who stayed there, practicing the discipline for fifteen years and attending to him on account of his old age—he said to them, "As for me, as it is written, I am going the way of the fathers [see Josh 23:14; 1 Kings 2:2], for I see that I am called by the Lord. As for you, be watchful and do not ruin your discipline, which has lasted so long, but as if you were starting now, be zealous to preserve your intention. You know the scheming demons: you know how fierce they are, but how weak they are in power. Therefore, do not be afraid of them: rather, always breathe Christ and have faith in him. Live as if you were dying every day [see 1 Cor 15:31] by paying attention to yourselves and remembering the exhortations that you heard from me. Have no fellowship with the schismatics and not at all with the heretical Arians, for you know how I myself turned away from them because of their hostility to Christ and their heterodox policy. Rather, be zealous to attach yourselves chiefly to Christ and next to the saints, so that after death they may receive you as familiar friends into the eternal tents [see Lk 16:9]. You too: consider these things and reflect upon them.

"If you care about me and remember me like a father, do not permit anyone to take my body into Egypt lest they deposit it in houses, for this is why I entered the mountain and came here. You know also how I rebuked those who do this and commanded them to stop this custom. Therefore, bury my body yourselves, and hide it under the ground. Closely guard what I am saying, so that no one will know the place except you alone. For I myself at the resurrection of the dead will receive my body back from the Savior incorruptible. But divide my clothes, and to Athanasius the bishop give the first sheepskin and the garment on which I lay, which he himself gave to me new and which has grown old with me. And to Serapion the bishop give the other sheepskin, and you yourselves keep the hair garment. And finally, farewell, children! For Antony departs and is with you no more."

(92.) When he had said these things and they had kissed him, he lifted up his feet, and as if he saw friends coming to him and was glad because of them—for he appeared to lie there with a cheerful face—he expired and was himself gathered to his fathers [see Gen 49:33]. And then they, as he had commanded them, buried, wrapped, and hid his body under the ground, and no one knows, even until now, where he is hidden except these two alone.[22] But each of those who received the sheepskin of the blessed Antony and the garment he wore guards it as a great possession, for just seeing them is like gazing at Antony, and wearing them is like bearing his admonitions with joy.

(93.) This was the end of Antony's life in the body, and the preceding has described the beginning of the discipline. Even if this account has been brief in comparison to his virtue, nevertheless consider from it for yourselves how great was this man of God, Antony: from his youth to such a great age he kept the same enthusiasm for the discipline; he neither was lessened by extravagance in food on account of old age, nor did he, because of his body's weakness, change his way of dressing or wash even his feet in water. Yet he remained completely healthy in every way. For even his eyes were unharmed and healthy: he could see clearly [see Deut 34:7]. He had not lost even one of his teeth, but they had become worn down to the gums because of the old man's great age. He remained healthy in both his feet and hands, and while everyone else was making use of varied foods, baths, and different kinds of clothing, still it was he who appeared more cheerful and more ready for exertion.

It is proof of his virtue and of his soul's friendship with God that he is proclaimed everywhere, that he is the object of everyone's amazement, and that even those who have not seen him long for him. For Antony has become famous not through writings, nor through external wisdom, nor on account of any skill, but solely because of his piety. That this was a gift of God no one will deny. For how did news about a man who settled and was hidden in a mountain make it to Spain and Gaul, how to Rome and Africa, unless it was the God who makes his own people known everywhere who promised this also to Antony at the beginning?[23] For even if they work in secret, even if they want to be ignored, still the Lord reveals them like lamps to all people, so that in this way those who hear might know that the commandments can be performed successfully and so receive zeal for the path to virtue.

(94.) Therefore, read this to the remaining brothers, so that they might learn what sort of life the monks ought to lead and they might be persuaded that our Lord and Savior Jesus Christ glorifies those who glorify him [see 1 Sam 2:30]. He not only leads into the kingdom of heaven those who serve him to the end, but even in this place, those who hide themselves and are eager to withdraw he makes famous and proclaimed everywhere because of their virtue and for the benefit of others. And if there is need, read this even to the pagans, so that even in this way they might recognize not only that our Lord Jesus Christ is God and Son of God, but in addition that the Christians, those who serve him truly and believe in him piously, not only prove that the demons, whom the Greeks themselves consider gods, are not gods, but also tread on them and chase them away as deceivers and corrupters of humankind, in Christ Jesus our Lord, to whom be the glory for ever and ever. Amen.

Notes

1. Athanasius presents his biography in the form of a letter to monks in places outside Egypt, most likely in areas of the western Mediterranean, such as North Africa and southern Europe. Many of the sentences in this opening section appear complicated and obscure to us because we do not know the exact situation in which Athanasius writes and because such a style is typical of prefaces to ancient works, in which the writer hopes to impress his readers with his rhetorical skill.

2. See the introduction for an explanation of this obscure reference.

3. Three hundred *arourae* may have been around two hundred acres; thus, Antony is portrayed as very wealthy by the standards of third-century Egypt.

4. The symbolism of this scene is on two levels. First, the appearance of the devil as a boy reflects the homoerotic interest in male adolescents pervasive in the ancient world and condemned by Christian leaders like Athanasius. Second, the devil's black skin illustrates the prejudice based on skin color present in late antique Egypt, which was a multiethnic society. Most Alexandrians like Athanasius were descendants of the Greeks who founded the city in the fourth century B.C.E. and so were of lighter skin color than persons of more sub-Saharan African descent.

5. Athanasius has conflated and abridged the two passages. The word "today" appears in 1 Kings 18:15, which reads: *As the Lord of hosts lives, before whom I stand, I will surely show myself to him today.*

6. It was contemporary custom to pray standing with one's arms extended.

7. See Chapter 3.

8. Athanasius uses the Greek term *monasterion* ("monastery") to refer both to a building or set of buildings that housed several monks, as in the preface, and to a small dwelling that Antony lived in by himself, as here. In the latter case, I will use the English phrase "monastic retreat" so as not to imply the larger kind of structure.

9. Maximinus Daia became Caesar (junior emperor) in 305 and governed Syria, Palestine, and Egypt. After becoming Augustus (senior emperor) in 308, he renewed the persecution of Christians that had been initiated by the emperor Diocletian, but in 313 he was defeated and removed from office by the emperor Licinius.

10. Most Christian leaders taught that, although one should submit to martyrdom if it should come, a Christian should not actively seek arrest and martyrdom. "Confessors" were persons who were imprisoned for their Christian faith.

11. That is, until the time of their execution.

12. Here Athanasius marks the transition from the age of the martyrs, who died for the faith in persecution, to the age of the monks, who suffer for the faith in their ascetic labors. Bishop Peter of Alexandria was martyred in November 311; Athanasius was probably about fifteen years old at the time, and Antony about sixty years old.

13. The Upper Thebaid is the more southern region of Egypt; it is called "upper" since it is upstream on the Nile River, which flows north. Thus, to go south on the river is to "go up."

14. The Bucolia is a marshy region in the Nile Delta, in the north of Egypt.

15. The dialogue to this point may be compared to 1 Kings 19:13–15.

16. Although the Saracens were a specific Arab tribe, at this time Greek writers used the term for Arabs in general.

17. The "Melitians" formed a church organization in Egypt, complete with bishops and priests, separate from the one headed by Bishop Athanasius; they owed their allegiance to a Bishop Melitius, who broke with Bishop Peter of Alexandria around 305 over matters of church administration and discipline. Because they did not differ with Athanasian Christians over doctrine, they were considered "schismatics" rather than "heretics."

18. Manichaeism was a worldwide missionary religion, founded by Mani in the third century, which emphasized the salvation of the spiritual element within humanity. In Chris-

tian areas Manichaean missionaries presented their religion as the true "inner meaning" of Christianity and thus often appeared to be Christian heretics.

19. Arian Christians, Athanasius's primary enemies, followed the doctrines of Arius, a priest who taught that Christ, the Son or Word of God, is not as divine as God the Father is. In the Arian view, while the Father is eternal, without any beginning, the Son came into being by the father's will at some point in time: hence, the slogan, "There was [a time] when he [the Son or Word] was not," mentioned by Antony in the next chapter. In the Athanasian view, the Father and Son both have no beginning: they are "eternally co-existent." The Arians appeared to make the Son a being created by God, rather than "begotten" by the Father, so that when they worshiped Christ, they were not worshiping the Creator, but a creature. During Athanasius's lifetime it was not clear which view would prevail.

20. That is, who became monks. Evidently some who took up the monastic life left behind debts or other legal difficulties.

21. Christians extended the traditional Egyptian practice of keeping mummified bodies of dead family members in the home to the most valued members of the Christian "family": ascetics and martyrs. Athanasius vigorously opposed this practice not only here, but in other writings as well.

22. Despite this claim, Antony's body was "discovered" in 561 and moved to Alexandria. After the Arab conquest of Egypt in the seventh century, Antony's bones were taken to Constantinople, where they remained until 1070, at which time they were moved to southern France, where they were kept at a church and hospital devoted to the cure of ergotism or St. Antony's fire.

23. See Chapter 10.

Chapter 2

Victricius of Rouen, *In Praise of the Saints*

translated by Philippe Buc

Introduction

Bishop Victricius composed the so-called *De laude sanctorum* for the festive arrival of relics into the city of Rouen (in the Roman province of Gaul, modern France), ca. 396/7. The ceremony of "transfer" or "translation" was patterned after the *adventus*, the reception into a city of the emperor or his representative, in which groups of citizens, organized in agegroups and professional groups, greeted the incoming power. This latter procession was called the *occursus*. In 396/7, the relics advent probably culminated in the consecration of a church's inner hall (*aula*) where these objects were to be deposited and permanently venerated. These relics consisted of small fragments of the bodies of several saints, apostles as well as martyrs, who had died a violent death for the Christian faith. They seem to have been transported in containers or reliquaries, which Victricius calls *templa*, that is, temples. Victricius weaves his *De laude sanctorum* among three (to us) distinct levels of discourse: on the orders of society, on Christology (the theology bearing on the God-Man Christ's nature), and on Trinitarian thought (the Unity of the three divine persons, that is Father, Son, and Holy Spirit). A metaphor, that of Christ's body, connects together those (to us) different narratives. First articulated by the apostle Paul, it will become a root metaphor for the medieval notion of the Christian Church: the saints, united in the "communion of the saints," are par excellence the body of Christ, to which all good Christians also belong. To argue for this notion and to explain the presence of the saints' power everywhere that their relics happen to be, Victricius makes heavy use of Christian Neoplatonism: God as Unity which diffuses itself throughout the Whole, binding together apparently disparate parts; presence of the logical subset, the species, in the superordinate set, the genus; belief in the substantial reality of such categories as "human nature" or "animality." Given the technicality of these considerations, I have chosen to stick as closely as possible to the Latin text when translating them into English. For this reason I have chosen to capitalize God's attributes and the pronouns referring to Him (typographically unpleasant, but a help in following Victricius's syllogisms). Victricius uses as well the contemporary Roman language of law and power: the saints, whom he also calls "the just" or "powers" (*potestates*) are advocates and judges as well as patrons endowed with majesty. One owes them "military service" (*militia*) as well as a client's service (*obsequium*). As such, the text provides an extraordinary and unequalled point of entry into the theology of relics in its relation to the theology of power and of the social body.

We know very little about Bishop Victricius (or for that matter about fourth-century Rouen). Victricius's main claim to fame consists in this exceptional text, and in a handful of letters addressed to him (see note 15 to the text below). From these sparse documents historians have surmised that he may have been born ca. 330 and died between 404 and 409. We can, however, reconstruct something of Victricius's social position. He belonged to the generation of prelates which had seen, between 381 and 385, Emperor Theodosius I (who reigned 379–94) proclaim Christianity the exclusive religion of the Roman Empire. In this era bishops, showered with imperial privileges, could aspire to become the dominant figures in late Antique cities, mediators between the imperial administration and the citizenry, and prime patrons of urban life. Their office was increasingly integrated in the *cursus honorum* an aristocrat would try to climb—to the point that the late sixth-century *Histories* of Gregory of Tours portray numerous counts or governors intriguing to become bishops as the culmination of their careers. Sociologically seen, in the western half of the Roman Empire at least, the episcopate was claiming the place once held by the senatorial class in the social pyramid. As such, in the best tradition of Mediterranean urban elites, bishops continued to erect buildings for the community; now, however, the more conspicuous civic monuments were Christian churches (as Victricius's new *aula*), not temples, theaters, or amphitheaters. To pursue further the comparison with earlier elites, one might see in the *adventus* of 396 a spectacle of power—not unlike circus games—seeking to institutionalize these recent developments. Finally, like Roman magistrates before them, bishops sought to monopolize access to the holy, including the remains of martyred saints. The desire to stabilize this social and religious position explains the importance of relic translations—and of the desire of Bishop Victricius to provide an authoritative interpretation of this rite which might place him squarely in the center.

By the ninth century (the date of the two earliest preserved manuscripts now extant), Victricius's text was joined to two treatises penned by Ambrose of Milan. These codices opened with the *On the Holy Spirit*, continue with the *On the Lord's Incarnation*, and conclude with Victricius's work. In other words, for the people who put the manuscripts together, saints' relics constituted the lower rung of a continuum which comprised the Trinity and the Incarnation. And, like the Spirit and the Incarnate Christ, they mediated between Heaven and earth.

The two ninth-century manuscripts are quasi-twins, in the sense that they were copied in two monasteries, Saint-Germain in Auxerre (Auxerre, Bibliothèque Municipale MS 27) and Saint Gall (Sankt Gallen, Stiftbibliothek MS 98), associated with two rival half-brothers, King Charles the Bald of the western Frankish kingdom (d. 877) and King Louis the German of the eastern Frankish kingdom (d. 876). Both rulers are known to have participated actively in relic cults. The first Saint Gall manuscript was, in fact, dedicated to Louis the German. Interestingly, Ambrose had dedicated the two treatises found in these codices to another ruler, Emperor Gratian (d. 383). It is tempting to connect the ninth-century production of copies of Victricius's text with the general increase in relic translations and narratives recounting them under the Carolingian kings. The dynasty and the leading families of the empire (the so-called imperial aristocracy) collected relics with a passion, and found them mainly (as Victricius had) in Italy. Thus Victricius's text can serve historians as a double monument, to both the beginnings of the cult of relics in Latin Christendom during the late fourth-century and to the reworking of relic cults under the Carolingians during the ninth century.

SOURCES AND FURTHER READING

The following translation is based on the text provided in Victricius of Rouen, *De laude sanctorum*, eds. Jacques Mulders and Roland Demeulenaere, Corpus Christianorum Series Latina 64 (Turnhout, 1985). Their introduction provides a full bibliography of recent works. They indicate that the title *De laude sanctorum* may have been added to the text well after its composition. An earlier edition accompanied by a translation into French can be found in René Herval, *Origines Chrétiennes. De la IIe Lyonnaise gallo-romaine à la Normandie ducale (IVe-XIe siècles)* (Rouen and Paris, 1966), pp. 109–153. Herval's edition, based on Sankt Gallen, Stiftbibliothek MS 98 (ninth-century), while imperfect, superseded the text to be found in *Patrologia latina*, ed. Jean-Paul Migne, 221 vols. (Paris, 1844–64), 20: 443–58. The two other known manuscripts are Sankt Gallen, Stiftbibliothek MS 102 (a tenth-century copy of Sankt Gallen, Stiftbibliothek MS 98) and Auxerre, Bibliothèque Municipale MS 27 (a mid-ninth-century copy from the monastery of Saint-Germain which is incomplete at the end).

Peter Brown, *The Cult of the Saints: Its Rise and Function in Latin Christianity* (Chicago, 1981) provided a pioneering study on the cult of relics in late antiquity, especially good on the saint's fashioning as a Roman patron. On the modeling of relic advents after imperial entries into cities, see Nikolaus Gussone, "Adventus-Zeremoniell und Translation von Reliquien. Victricius von Rouen, *De laude sanctorum*," *Frühmittelalterliche Studien* 10 (1976): 125–33. A complete synthesis on relic translations is provided by Martin Heinzelmann, *Translationsberichte und andere Quellen des Reliquienkultes*, Typologie des sources du Moyen Age occidental 33 (Turnhout, 1979). And more generally on the Christianization of late Antique ceremonial forms, see Sabina McCormack, *Art and Ceremony in Late Antiquity* (Berkeley, 1981). Jacques Mulders, "Victricius van Rouaan. Leven en Leer," *Bijdragen. Tijdschrift voor filosofie en theologie* 18 (1957): 19–40 and 270–89 provides the best account of Victricius's Neoplatonic metaphysics. Claudia Santosa, in her Stanford University (Religious Studies) Ph.D. dissertation (currently in process), "The Reception of Victricius of Rouen in Carolingian Political Culture," will offer a study of the role of the *In Praise of the Saints* for the ninth-century political culture which produced the work's surviving copies.

Finally, the author wishes to express his gratitude to the Netherlands Institute for Advanced Studies for its support.

Victricius of Rouen, In Praise of the Saints

(1.) Most beloved brothers,[1] even the presence of abundant spiritual goods admonishes us that we depend on God's mercy and on the Savior's omnipotence.[2] We cannot see any executioner, we are not aware of any naked sword [drawn] out of its scabbard, and we are present before the altars of the divine powers. Today, there isn't any bloodstained enemy, and yet we are enriched by the passion of the saints. Today, there isn't any torturer who might throw himself on us, and yet we carry the martyrs' trophies. Presently, no blood is being shed, no persecutor persecutes, and yet we are filled with the joy of [martyrdom's] triumphs.[3] We should therefore immerse ourselves in weeping, and release our great joys in an abundance of tears. Behold, the greater part of the celestial army deigns to visit our city; and as a result we must now dwell among the throngs of the saints and the illustrious powers of Heaven. To have with us persons to whom we can reveal our faults and who can soften them is not a meager help for these faults. And indeed, the present joy allows me to fathom what I lacked up until now. Please, pardon my impatience: a happiness without measure cannot weigh its words. I grieve, and in some way, according to human reason, I am sad, that these [saints] came so late to inhabit our chests: had they come sooner, they would have found fewer faults.

Thus, most beloved, let this be our first petition to the saints: may you [the saints] excuse our sins in the fashion of a piously merciful advocate rather than lead an inquest into them in the spirit of a judge. As for myself, as far as I can tell, I have for my belatedness an excuse which is worthy of pardon. It was to execute your orders that I went to Britain and remained there for a while.[4] My episcopal colleagues, bringers of salvation, called me there for the sake of peacemaking. I could not refuse this, I who had served with you. To obey orders is not to abandon a client's service.[5] I knew that you are everywhere owing to your virtue's deserts [*merito virtutis*].[6] For no terrestrial distance can hurt celestial clarity. You must therefore forgive that I rushed to meet you so late, and only to the fortieth milestone.[7] I had been serving you as a client in Britain. I may have been separated [from you] by the ocean which surrounded me, but it was your service which detained me there. This delay hurt my desire; it did not set aside my service. Anyway, I attribute everything to your majesty given that you are Christ's body,[8] and that divine is the Spirit which inhabits you. It was owing to you that I went away, owing to you that I returned. An orderly reckoning, then, of this excuse remains to be given. You are the founders of God's peace, and you delegated me to be, as it were, the interpreter of its verdicts. I fulfilled this salvation-bringing order of God and yourself, if not as I should have, at least as I could. I infused the wise with the love of peace. I lectured on it to those who could be taught; inculcated it to those who did not know it; forced it upon those who refused it. Following the Apostle, I stood opportunely inopportunely, and reached in the soul of these people through teaching and touching. Yet whenever circumstances and human frailty led me into temptation, I implored your spirit's protection. I did what those who navigate in the strongest force of a tempest do: they do not rely on the helmsman's experience but implore the Supreme Majesty's mercy. Indeed, Jesus, Who is in you, knows how to appease the flow and moderate the winds; earthly skill does not. But what need do I have now to labor for those who fell completely from the bond of the faith? I have the presence of your majesties. Let the authority of your power make up for those things in which [I], the usher of your cult, fail.

(2.) With which veneration shall I now embrace you, blessed Ambrose? With which love shall I kiss you, Theodule? With which spiritual embrace shall I glue you to my senses, Eustachius? With which worshipfulness of a born-again mind and with which admiration shall I receive you, Catio? In truth, I do not know, I do not know how to pay back such deserts. The sole thing which can repay your benefactions is if you demand our debts from the holy apostles and martyrs so that you do not lack in those you wanted to be with us.[9] As for you, most beloved brother Aelianus, I render thanks for both your zeal and patience.[10] Yet the apostles and martyrs have already handed out [to you] the reward of your labor and service: they were with you for a long time. Give [them to us], therefore, give [them to us]. Why are you tarrying? Hand over the saints' temples. It behooves us to act, it does not behoove us to speak. For if the contact, even light, of the coatfringes of the Savior, cured, without doubt the embrace of the bodies which underwent martyrdom will cure. And it is for this reason that this labor does not make one feel any fatigue.

Before today, we carried our apostles and martyrs by faith. So the saints have come twice to Rouen. Then, they entered our chests; now they crowd the city's church. Behold, every age hurries to your [the saints'] service; each one strives to surpass the other in the zeal of religion. Priests, deacons, and every minister known to you through his daily service, rush from the town to meet you. The clientship of known people is all the more welcome, for they do not begin to be loved but acquire an increase in [an already existent] love.

(3.) This is why an army composed of known veterans fears more the Lord; an increase in the military stipend increases the veteran's fears, for he who has something to lose through a transgression fears more. Such is indeed he who is hurrying to meet you: a soldier tried by time at your service, tested by labor and vigils. Such a one, I say, hastens to minister, who transforms labor into desire, who ignores the name of Fortune, who measures this life not according to its present brevity but to eternal felicity. He who is in such a disposition of mind considers that he is enriched with an immense benefit as often as his hands are honorifically burdened with the saints' relics.[11]

From the city, there gathers the troop of monks emaciated by fasts. From there, resonates the loud joy of innocent children. From there, the choir of devoted and spotless virgins bears the sign of the cross.[12] From there, the multitude of the chaste and of the widows accompany them, worthy of such an office. These women's lives shines forth in proportion to the harshness of their condition over and above the common lot of humankind. Indeed, to resist a known pleasure is a burdensome combat: if you do not know it, the nature of this very ignorance protects you, but if you know it, the very knowledge of this desire fights against you. A dead husband's cold [body] extinguishes the fire of this one woman, and all her desire is enclosed in a mournful memorial.[13] The husband of another woman is still alive, but having been stroked by the hand of eternity's promise, holds back from lovemaking. Despite their unequal fates, they have an equal palm of virtue:[14] this one woman condemned with horror and modesty sexual intercourse while remaining in a marital union; that other woman entrusted [her chastity] to her dead [husband]. And it is not undeservedly that they show zeal only for religion. Where there is no thought of pleasures, there dwells chastity. Since a good conscience bears nothing that gossip could tear at, or that unspoken insulting thoughts might bother, it serves the saints freely. To demonstrate sexual modesty and abstinence is part of a client's assiduous service.[15]

For this reason, no one's dress exhales the intensity of Tyrian purple, nor does anyone, walking affectedly, make quiver waves of rustling silk. Pearls and circlets of gold are unknown. Indeed, in comparison to divine matters, human things are like filth, as the Apostle [Paul] teaches: "[I] *count them but as dung, that I may gain Christ*" [Phil 3:8, Vulgate]. These women proceed, resplendent and burning with the drunkenness of chastity; these women proceed, wreathed with God-given ornaments. Their chests are dense with the Psalms' riches. At every nocturnal vigil, such a gem shines; at every holy place of religion, such a brocade gleams. A crowd of chaste human beings makes the saints rejoice. The multitude of the widows and the continent invites the powers in. Owing to this, the old shed tears mixed with joy; owing to this, these joys draw out the vows of the mothers as well as the minds of the children. From this, finally, derives the whole people's unanimous affection for your majesty.

(4.) Have mercy, therefore, have mercy! You have what you can pardon. We confess God the Father; we confess God the Son; we confess God the Holy Spirit. We confess that these three are one. I said, one: indeed, they come from the One, just as the Son [comes] from the Father, thus the Father is in the Son; and just as the Holy Spirit [comes] from the Father and the Son, so the Father and the Son are in the Holy Spirit. They are one divinity and one substance, because there is one principle and one perpetuity, both existing before all things, and through whom all things were done. They are True God from True God because just as the one comes from the other so is the one in the other, Living One from the Living One, Perfect One from the Perfect One, Light from Light and Light in Light. Thus this Trinity's divinity comes from the One and resides in the One. The Father is the Father; the Son is the Son; the Spirit is the Spirit. Three names, three by one principle, three by one power, three by one action, three by one substance, three by one perpetuity. Indeed, just as they are three from one, so there is unity in these three. We confess the Trinity in this way because we believe it to be this way: undivided, to Whose level nothing can reach, and Whom the mind cannot conceive, through Whom *all things*, visible and invisible [were created] be they Thrones, be they Dominations, be they Principalities, be they Powers. *All things were made by Him, and without Him nothing was made* [Jn 1:3]. It is He who descended from on high for the salvation of the human race, received His flesh from Mary the Virgin to take on humanity, suffered His passion, was crucified and was buried, resurrected from the dead on the third day and rose up into heaven. He sits at the right hand of God the Father. He will come from there to judge the living and the dead. [We confess belief] in the Holy Spirit as well, because He Himself declared this mystery to the apostles when He said: When I rise up to my Father who is your Father *I will pray the Father that He will give you another counselor, to be with you forever, the Spirit of truth, whom the world cannot receive, because it neither sees Him nor knows Him; but you know Him, for He dwells with you, and will be in you* [Jn 14:16–17]. And elsewhere: *When they will make you stand before the powers of this world, do not worry about what you shall speak out. For on that hour what you are to speak out will be given to you; your Father's Spirit will speak out in you* [Mt 10.19].

In this unity, we confess the lights of your venerable passions. We read in the Gospel that *You are the lights of the world* [Mt 5:14]. We preach this in [time of] dangers and in [time of] happiness. This confession benefits sinners, because he who requests is heard, as the Lord says in the Gospel [see Mt 7:7–8]. For indeed when the robber, hanging on the cross, requested that the Savior would remember him, He answered: *Truly I say to you, today you will be with me in Paradise* [Lk 23:43]. Let no one investigate faults; let us implore pardon.

(5.) Most beloved brothers, let us now pour in libation to the sacrosanct relics the words of the Psalms, kneaded with milk and honey. Let a sobriety inebriated by vigils and psalms implore the washing of our sins. Let us make the saints' favor incline toward us while their advent is still fresh. Their dwellings may be celestial, but we pray them as their hosts. It is often advantageous to dissimulate what one knows; they know their own secret. Those who preserve mysteries and do not inquire into secret things request with more effect. And you as well, sacred and inviolate virgins, sing psalms, sing psalms, dance in choirs, and strike with your foot the paths through which one ascends to Heaven! I say, wear down with your soles and tire through your leaps those [paths] which in Paradise's perpetual spring enjoy a clear light and are troubled by no clouds. And should someone having erred seek [the way], the Savior's mercy has added on other guides for us.

(6.) For indeed, dearest ones, what else is a martyr if not an imitator of Christ, a tamer of frenetic sensuality, one who tramples ambition underfoot and seeks death, is contemptuous of riches, suppresses lasciviousness, and persecutes intemperance? Neither anger nor cupidity ever snatched away or won from him/her the scepter of prudence. S/he ascended through the stairs of the virtues to the place from which the Savior came down, as the Apostle teaches: *He who descended is this same one who ascended above all heavens*

[Eph 4:10]. And through those [stairs] He took up with Himself those he had predestined, saying: *Father, I want that those Whom You gave me be where I am and that they be with me* [Jn 17:24]. Prudence, justice, fortitude and temperance are the celestial road. The Savior opened it when He said, *I am the way and the truth* [Jn 14:6]. The merchant of celestial pearls and of eternity wore it out. The prophets show it to the Christian travelers. It is the one the Apostles followed. Cold never freezes it over and heat never makes it burning hot. The Psalms assure us that: *By day the sun will not burn [nor] the moon by night* [Ps 120:6]. For this reason, let us pray, dearest ones, let us pray that should the heap of our sins prevent us from ascending we may warm up with more pressing kisses the footsteps of those who ascended. These people are to be venerated; these are the saints who inflicted death upon Death, as we have read: *Whomsoever believes in Me, even though he may die, lives* [Jn 11:25].

O how *precious in the sight of the Lord is the death of His saints* [Ps 115:15], to whom the threatening persecutor gave more [rewards]! The torturer feels dread, [the martyr] laughs when submitted to judicial torture; the executioner trembles, and s/he who is about to die helps the right hand of this trembling man.[16] The ferocious beast refuses [the martyr]; thrown to it, s/he provoked it, not because his/her nature had lost corporeal pain but because the Savior, director of this all-important fight, brandished the palm and offered the victory of immortality.[17]

Although these things may be so, nevertheless, in this passion which limbs suffered, your bodies bore the fight with you. Therefore, prostrate on the earth and bathing the ground with tears we shout together one acclamation: May you, who will always occupy your sacred relics, cleanse our bodies. Nor shall our offering pollute you.[18] A dwelling which such victors inhabit has great dignity. Here you will find John the Baptist, that man, I say, who covered with blood made his stand in the public stadium, and ascended to Heaven with the crown [of victory], he whom the Lord Himself declares to be the best of all the children born of women. Here is Andrew, here is Thomas, here is Gervasius, here is Protasius, here is Agricola, here is Euphemia—the virgin who, her spirit having been made male [*masculato animo*], did not blanch under [the tortures of] the executioner. In other words, there is here so large a multitude of heavenly citizens that one would need to search for another place for your majesty's advent if your mystery and the unity of your power did not bind you together.

Such are your decrees: charity should engender neither jealousy nor swelling pride, nor the demand for those things which are one's own [see 1 Cor 13:4–5]. Hence I am certain that you do not feel it an insult that this place (according to human opinion) is humble. Humans consider that these spaces are too exiguous, [but] divinity is indifferent to scale, and is not limited by time or place. Unity is subjected to nothing. And one should not be amazed that there is no difference between you in terrestrial substance given that in the Spirit's light you hold everything in common. But nevertheless the glory of your powers will be greater if you defend those who labor and if you protect those who bar the road to the enemy. Let those who want shield themselves with a weapon; as for us, your battle line and your [military] insignia will protect us. If you give out your pardon for our sins, there is no enemy. Your hands hold the tethers of our life. Pardon our crimes and no wars will disturb us. But why should I, your devotee the powerless Victricius, have fears concerning the quality of this place? From yourself, you came to yourself.[19] Here you will find those who minister to the altars of the Lord Jesus Christ. Arms stretched out toward you, John the Baptist awaits you; Thomas awaits you; with an equal desire, Andrew, Luke, and the rest of the heavenly multitude call you into their bosom. No new host will receive you: these saints are those with whom you serve in Heaven. But it will be an especial grace if those persons whom a spiritual clarity joins together are joined in their relics.

(7.) And indeed we are one corporeal lump (as we gather from the Scripture's hints). For can one find anyone so brutish in nature or so devoid of reason to deny that woman took her origin from man's side [see Gen 2:21–23]? From this arises the following: we should understand that the flesh took its origin from the flesh and that the flesh was the flesh's own nature. Thus, should anyone energetically focus his/her mind and look carefully for some kind of genus to the [human] genus, he/she will find that Adam, who had been a species, was made a genus. Indeed, Adam cannot but be a genus, he from whose matter and image the human body was produced, diffused itself through all humans, and increased. Therefore, most holy brothers, the first thing we must know is that human beings do not differ [from one another as individuals] owing to nature, but owing to time, place, operation, and thought. Indeed, Unity does not allow diversity; Unity diffuses itself widely without losing anything of itself. And if the eyes of reason see clearly that all humans belong to a single body, by the same reasoning it follows that we believe that thanks to their adoption [by God] those who live in Christ and in the Church have a single substance of flesh, blood, and vital spirit. The starting point of the New Law is the washing away of past crimes. Furthermore, the Savior, although He belonged to the earlier [Law], guaranteed this better Testament. It is therefore necessary that there should be a single power in those in whom there is a single perfection of the mysteries. Indeed, the Apostle says, *You are Christ's body and His members, and God's Spirit dwells in you* [1 Cor 1:17, 3:16]. Now given that the Scripture's teaching assures us that we can be joined to the Divine Spirit through the mystery of baptism, let us learn, using the same reasoning, that even our bodies are tightly tied to the Son's members through the glue of our persevering profession [of the faith], and that, thanks to grace, nothing of this unity perishes. How could one then doubt that our apostles and martyrs deserved to be in a perfect and undivided concord? Indeed, God's Spirit is also God the Son, Christ, Whose equitable power shatters the idea of an injurious subordination,[20] Whose venerable triumph left his members no room for death, Who refuses the concept of singularity, nor feels in any of His parts an end or a beginning. Consequently, the apostles and saints, through the spiritual mystery's power, through the immolation of the body,[21] through a price in blood and the sacrifice of the passion,[22] ascended the Redeemer's throne, as He Himself says in the Gospel: *When the Son of Man sits on the throne of His glory, you as well shall sit, on twelve judge-seats, to judge the twelve tribes of the children of Israel* [Mt 19:28]. And again: *Sins will be remitted to whomsoever you remit them to, and whomsoever you shall bind shall be considered bound* [Jn 20:23]. We must therefore conclude that they are wholly with the Whole Savior, since those for whom nothing is dissimilar in their profession [of faith] hold everything wholly in common within the Deity's Truth. Furthermore, justice makes them the Savior's war companions;[23] prudence, His imitators; the usage of their limbs, one body with Him; blood [shed in martyrdom], His blood brothers; and the consumption of the Host, sharers of the Cross in eternity. Indeed, it is written: *I am ascending to My Father Who is your Father* [Jn 20:17]. Therefore, if they have in common a Father, they have "being sons" in common. If they commune in filiation, they have a common inheritance. But the saints' victory has devoted them to immortality. There follows that the authority of their will is not divided but one, as the Lord Himself pleads before His Father: *Father, sanctify them in Truth. Your Word is Truth. Just as You sent me into the world, I too have sent them into the world. And I sanctify myself for them so that they too may be sanctified in Truth. I beseech You not only for them but as well for those who will believe in me through their words so that they all may be one—just as You, Father, are in me and I in You, let them as well be in Us so that this world may believe that You sent me and that I am sending them. I gave them the light You gave me so that they may be one just as We are one: I in them and You in me that they may be made full into a unity and the world may know that you sent me and that You loved them as You loved me* [Jn 17:17–23]. Indeed, those who are worthy (that is, whomsoever wears the sacred confession's insignia) will take the salvation-bringing Empire by force.

(8.) Dearest ones, there are two different immortalities, one sempiternal and free of the weakness of conception,[24] the other granted by [God's] generosity. We cannot deny that immortality was granted to the apostles and martyrs, but we hold the following: that after they have earned divinity, there is nothing that separates the Trinity from the saints' offering, given that it is the very Trinity's Truth which has revealed them [as saints]. Indeed, it is necessary to proclaim that God's nature is full and perfect; otherwise, were we to deny it, it would be an insult. Yet the Lord says: *Whomsoever denies me and my teachings before human beings, I too shall deny him before My Father and His angels* [Mt 10:33]. On top of this, fullness cannot take in anything beyond itself. Yet after martyrdom blood enflames itself with the reward of divinity. Therefore, let the insult of a distinction disappear, given that the bond of light [which binds them] is the same. *I go*, He says, *to My Father Who is your Father*. Therefore, most beloved one, you see that what belongs to the saints owing to the unity of the reward they received belongs to the Father and to the Son as a property of Their nature.[25] God diffuses Himself far and wide and, without loss to Himself, lends out His light. In any part He is whole intellect, whole sight, whole mind, whole Himself. Therefore, He Who is perfect in the whole cannot fail to be perfect in the apostles.

But maybe someone at this point will clamor out and say, "Is a martyr therefore that: the Deity's first power and Its absolute and unaccountable substance?" I say that they are the same through a grant and not as a property, by adoption and not by nature, and that it is so in order that when the great day occurs he who received power shall not seem to have acquired it and He Who gives it shall not seem to have been diminished.[26]

It belongs to a clement and good legal arbitrator (*disceptator*) to warn [you] in advance of what you should fear. Behold, the just, sending ahead, as it were, their relics' light, show us the path of Truth. They teach reverence, faith, prudence, justice, fortitude, concord, continence, and chastity, while they punish in possessed bodies vices contrary to these virtues and remove their stains.[27] But even when the just begin to weigh our faults, they hold in themselves this mercy and this desire to teach as well as this abundance of relics and these burning rays of light. A good king judges without favor; one finds pure truth when the advocate (*cognitor*) does not lean toward any side. But those very [martyrs], whose gifts we now use, shall grant us a hearing. Therefore, all the saints' goodness, which is now spread out, shall be gathered into, as it were, one heap, so that they may hold the judge's scepter without favor or the insult of an appeal [to another court].[28] Sins belong to darkness; light is innocence. Therefore, the jail of darkness shall necessarily appear when what belongs to the sun's light begins to return from itself into itself. The gifts have been spread widely. The sun fills and illuminates all the earth's surface, all the dwellings, [all] eyes, yet it does not recede from itself through its [giving's] abundance. It pours out its presents and receives them back, possessing as much as it had previously lavished. It donates, and [yet] it is found to be the owner of the things it donated.[29]

(9.) It is hardly otherwise, dearest ones, that before judgment day the splendor of the just is poured out into all the basilicas, into all the churches, and into the chests of all the faithful, but it will return into itself when it takes on the person of the Judge. Should this comparison seem lowly to anyone, let this person understand that it is owing to majesty, and not to some mistake, that we make things of the corruptible sphere meet divine matters and small things great ones: primordial things, given that they do not belong to a genus, cannot be defined.[30] The Deity's substance, when it bends down [toward the created world] retains in itself the image of its dignity. We cannot find a quantity or quality to which the Trinity can be equaled. A concept of the celestial is not acquired by comparison; it is taught. It is a subject one suggests indirectly, not one which one adorns [with attributes]. Therefore, the sun served as an example to teach us about Divinity, but was not confused with this Unity.

It is now evident to all that God created out of nothing what had not been. This evacuates the dialecticians' poison. Indeed, if the Founder and Lord of all things shaped this spiritual vessel and its limbs out of emptiness, why could He not translate to His light's substance an animate body made one through, as it were, blood's ferment?[31]

In the midst of so much gratitude, we crammed a book with a jumble of questions –not groundlessly, for the hunt for Truth delights the questioner.[32] In this way, one acknowledges God; in this way, one acknowledges the Savior; in this way, one meets a triumph offered to salvation-giving arms; in this way, bodies acquire the Eternal Splendor. The celestial prayer [of the Psalms] makes us understand that angels contain the spirit of the Flamboyant Majesty. Indeed, we read: *He Who makes His angels into spirits and his ministers a burning fire* [Ps 103:4]. Therefore, if there is blood in a body, this very blood mixes with the supernal fire. The conclusion of our question, then, is that there is one and the same concord [joining] the saints to the Universal All. We must now, dearest ones, destroy and banish from our minds a doubt. No one (perhaps deceived by the error of the rabble) should fail to believe that the essence of the just ones' whole passion in the body is present in their minute relics and in this apostolic consecration.

As for us we proclaim with all our faith and authority the following: that in relics there is nothing if not fullness; indeed, where healing is full, the limbs are whole. We say that the flesh is contained in the glue of blood, and we affirm that the Word's flaming ardor directed a spirit soaked in the dew of blood.[33] And since it is so, it is beyond any doubt that our apostles and martyrs have come to us with their full powers. The gifts here present admonish us further that this is so.[34] Indeed, when we acknowledge that their "translation" occurred according to their will and according to the law,[35] we understand that they are not inflicting upon themselves any loss by being dispersed, but that, enriched by the [Supreme] Unity, they are spreading their gifts. A flame pours and gives out its brightness, yet this bestowing does not make it suffer any loss. Similarly, the saints are munificent without loss, full without having been added to. Similarly, they reached us without aversion at having traveled. Thus, in relics, there is an exhortation to perfection and not the harm of a division. Whatever is shaped out of, and conceived in dissimilitude, and is not irrigated with the First Fount's flow, is by necessity perishable. The sun and the stars, the earth and the other vain entities suffer corruptibility because they do not originate in the Spirit.[36]

(10.) Furthermore, the saints' passion is an imitation of Christ, and Christ is God. Therefore, one should not introduce division into fullness, but rather worship the essence of fullness in this very division which lies before our eyes.

Why then do we call relics "relics"? Because words are the images of things (*res*) and their designations.[37] Blood and dirt lie before our eyes; because we cannot do otherwise, we designate them, as through stamping them with a vivid language, by the name of "relics." But when we speak the whole through the part we open the eyes of the heart rather than that hindrance which physical eyes are. Indeed, things do not serve words, but words serve things. Hence, having removed the traps of language, let us compare thing with thing, concept with concept. Each part called a species necessarily receives in itself the meaning and definition of its genus. For when I state that an animal is an animate substance and a sensitive substance, I state simultaneously the definition of "human beings" (since the human being does not perceive what belongs to God)[38] and of "cattle" as well as of other animated beings.[39] If the variations within the species are included in the definition of the genus, how can it be that there is not a physical fullness in relics given that they have the same spiritual concept? We have thus shown that the whole can be in the part. Hence we cannot marvel now at the relics' smallness. Indeed, when we say that, as in the case of the genus, nothing perishes in sacrosanct bodies, we shall have expressed merely that what is divine cannot be diminished because it is whole in the whole, and because the whole is present wherever something is.[40] Furthermore, we gather from the holy scriptures that a body imbued with the Spirit is rendered eternal.[41] Therefore, one can conclude that wherever the Fullness makes itself felt nothing more can be wished for.

For the sake of instruction let us insist on the following example, an easy and most common one. We speak of the radiance of fire, we speak [as well] of its color, and yet fire and radiance are one and the same entity—this is what nature orders—and the one is separate from the other only through a nominal distinction. Light gives birth to brightness, nevertheless there is not any divide between light and brightness. The human being itself, in that it is a human being, belongs to a single community with all by sharing in the fact of being born.[42] Even though avarice's crooked talons tear apart copper, gold, and other kinds of metals into plurality, nevertheless [each part] has the qualities of the indivisible substance. It is therefore evident that a species is defined by its nature; it is therefore evident that in relics each part possesses perfection because their spiritual consecration entails a sharing (*consortium*) in possessions.[43] Indeed, the celestial ones are akin to the Celestial One. Were we to say that relics are separated from the Spirit, it would be right to seek every joint of their vitals and their bodily integrity. But, in fact, since we realize that a substance has unity, it is useless to seek the whole [body] to get the whole [power]. A search for greater power is an insult to unity. It is an optical illusion. The eyes of the concepts see more clearly. We behold small relics and a little blood. But Truth sees that these small fragments shine more than the sun, as the Lord says in the Gospel: *My saints shall blaze like the sun in My Father's Kingdom* [Mt 13:43]. And then the sun will shine more fully and more brightly than now.

(11.) For this reason, the parts cure no less than the integral body. Do they hand out remedies to the wretched differently in the East, in Constantinople, Antioch, Thessaloniki, Naissa, Rome, and Italy? Do they purify bodies in pain differently? John the Evangelist cures in Ephesus and in several other places as well (he whom we learned did not leave Christ's breast before his consecration and whose very remedies are among us). Proculus cures in Bologna, Agricola likewise, and we behold their majesty here as well. Antonius cures in Piacenza; Saturninus and Throianus cure in Macedonia;

Nazarius cures in Milan; Mucius, Alexander, Datisus and Chinedeus's generous power pour out the grace of salvation. Ragota, Leonida, Anastasia, and Anatoclia[44] cure, as the Apostle says, [made] *into the perfect man (vir), measured according to Christ's plenitude in age* [Eph 4:13], by the One and same Spirit *which operates everything in everything* [1 Cor 12:6].[45] I ask you whether the aforementioned saints' curative power is different among us than among others. If there is any part of the saints anywhere, they defend, purify, and protect their worshipers with an equal loyalty. This should augment their worship, not fragment their majesty. If relics did not contain the full weight of [the saints'] power, it still would not behoove a good mind to diminish in anything their great dignity. It does not benefit one to know, but rather to fear. Indeed, we are warned that *Fear of the Lord casts out sin. For one will never be able to render just he who is without fear* [Sir 1:27–28].

The matters which confront us are without number, but we only watch for the course and motions of a pure stream. The syllogistic knot of the categorical and hypothetical thinker does not entangle me; the empty sophisms of the philosophers do not deceive me. Truth Itself reveals Its face. Faith spurns arguments. Crime looks for hiding places, innocence, for publicity. Therefore, I show with my hand what we are investigating, I touch these fleshy sheddings, and I affirm that there is in these relics (*reduviae*) a perfect grace and a perfect power.[46] And were it necessary at this point to declare the truth through an assemblage of words, I would state that the relics are identical to one another in genus, species, and number. It is a person in doubt who will, in a faithless and malicious accusation, doubt this, nay perhaps, not a person in doubt but a person lacking in love. But since I believe by faith this whole matter, I consider that one should refrain for the moment from superfluous questions. For these are things to be seen and not questioned.

Behold, an executioner applies himself to an impure and polluted demon, yet this torturer does not appear to our eyes.[47] There are no chains, yet the victim is bound. Heavenly Anger uses a torture rack made of air. There are no iron talons, yet the crimes of those confessing are so many. No wound appears, yet one hears teeth grinding. No judge interrogates, yet [the interrogated] gives ground and surrenders unconditionally. No one, assuredly, no one will be so devoid of intelligence as to say that Fullness lacks in anything when s/he sees that everything is subject to its judicial examination. Indeed, without any doubt it is God, it is God who is the torturer and the judge of invisible beings. An imperfect nature cannot wound a spirit. Alone He Who cures interior matters can judge them. Alone He Who tramples the scepter underfoot commands to the elements. Alone He Who is entire in His parts and whole in the whole belongs to the Trinity. The First Intelligence needs no addition. But the apostles and the saints not only do not seek additions but also bestow the gifts of health and salvation. Therefore, they have one intelligence, one spirit, and one complete merging with the Truth. He Who cures is also the Living One. He Who lives is in the relics. But the apostles and the martyrs cure and purify; they are therefore bound in the relics by the bond of full eternity. Death's gloom darkens any partition; but we have sufficiently made clear that the saints do not suffer any loss in being partitioned. Therefore, it remains that we should understand that the just bestow themselves to all the faithful out of mercy and not to create a question.

Whomsoever loves believes. Whomsoever believes examines the faith, as opposed to the words, of the orator and bishop. Hence, should our discourse seem vile to someone, certainly our zeal shall displease this person in no way, when s/he sees that we composed this book out of a simple faith, not words, out of worshipfulness, not for argument, with veneration, not out of inquisitiveness. Whomsoever shows reverence is a lover of Truth; whomsoever raises questions hates It.

(12.) For this reason, most loving ones, since the troop of the saints has just arrived, let us bend low to it, and draw sighs from the depth of our veins. Advocates have arrived; let us reveal in our prayer the sins we have committed. These judges favor us; they can mitigate our sentence, they to whom it was said: *You shall sit on twelve judgment-seats, and you shall judge the twelve tribes of the sons of Israel* [Mt 19:28]. They are forever judges because they are forever apostles. But it is not so much the zeal to speak as duty toward faith which has taken me to these greater lengths.

A boundless gratitude does not know how to remain silent. It is detrimental to joy if an audience is lacking. If I could remain silent among such a multitude of rejoicers, I would be liable to be charged with sadness. The apostles and the martyrs are coming; it is not fitting for the bishop to be silent. Altars are erected; let the people's joy take its starting point in that of the bishop. I ask: who shall be so brutish, who shall be so profane, who shall be so ignorant about law and religion not to feel these joys?

Were any among the princes of the world to visit our city now, immediately all its spaces, crowned with wreaths, would smile.[48] Mothers would crowd up rooftops; gates would pour out a flow of people. Each age group divided according to its pursuits would sing his praises and his war deeds; one would marvel at the flames of the prince's war mantle and at his Tyrian purple. One would be astonished at the yield of the Red Sea and at the frozen tears of monsters.[49] And were you to see these objects, you might be struck with wonder; yet if you reflected upon them you should condemn them, for after all they are called stones. These things, I say, would captivate the people and make it gape. But in truth, most blessed ones, now that the triumph of the martyrs and the procession of the powers enters under our roofs, why don't we dissolve in rejoicing?

We are not seeking here eloquence, but the pure simplicity of joy. We are not lacking in things to marvel at: instead of a royal vestment we have at hand the garb of eternal light. The saints' togas have imbibed this purple. Here are diadems adorned with the various splendors of the gems of wisdom, intellect, science, truth, counsel, fortitude, endurance, temperance, justice, prudence, patience, and chastity. In each precious stone one of these virtues is inscribed and expressed. The Savior crafted and adorned the martyrs' crowns with these spiritual gems. Let us stretch the sails of our souls toward these gems. In them, nothing is frail, nothing diminishes a greater thing, nothing feels a loss. They flower ever increasingly in beauty. Even blood, which still stamps the Holy Spirit's fire onto these very bodies and the relics of their limbs, makes manifest that the battle standards of Eternity are being brought forth. Let us rejoice, dearest ones, whenever we see light scattering darkness. Why don't we rush with more effusion into rejoicing when we behold the radiance of salvation-bringing and eternal lights being brought forth? It seems to me that this day has taken on the joy of a brighter serenity, and not undeservedly, for (as I said) the martyrs are seven times brighter than the sun.

But now, most loving ones, it behooves us to pray, not to give the conclusion of a discourse. We must pray, I say, so that every attack of the devil may be repelled away from us, the devil who enters our chest by slipping in it clandestinely. Strengthen thus, o saints, strengthen your worshipers, and fit out our chest on [Christ] the Cornerstone. The enemy is dangerous and strong. He explores all the accesses and all the entryways, but we should not fear anything: great is the multitude of the saints who are marching out [against him]. Therefore, since such a great number of celestial soldiers and kings have come to us from the camps, let us seize the weapons of justice and prudence, protect ourselves as well with faith's shield, and fortify our chests not with the scales of a breastplate but with the armor plates of temperance and modesty. Let us always brandish in our right hands the javelins of faith and patience. Let us swiftly strike back if some enemy should strike us. Back in the past, the apostles bore such arms, yes, such arms. Thus fitted out, they broke the necks of intemperance, lasciviousness, greed, ambition, anger, and pride. Therefore the Savior's mercy did not deny us anything: neither weapons nor defenses. Hence, we should as well take care again and again lest the slumber of vices invade us as if we yawned, lest either incredulity, faith's enemy, snatch us secretly, or anger scatter us, or greed harass us, or ambition wrestle us to the ground. The martyrs will willingly side with us if we betake our pure conscience to their service. If by any chance this military service should seem harsh and impossible to anyone, let this person not throw away the lance before the signal of battle rumbles, let death's coldness not invade him/her before combat. Let no one desert the Savior's battle standards. He gave the example, sent reinforcements; victory is assured when one fights alongside such fellow soldiers and with Christ as military leader. Then, assuredly, a bishop's helmet shall glimmer on my head when your charity sees me in the battle line. To fight in your sight and with you as followers inflames me to glory.

An unshaken faith and spiritual constancy are a safe position and the best fortified harbor for salvation. A good life won't be of any advantage if you do not know for what you live. The winds' whirlwind ravishes to the heights a fickle and incredulous mind. Faith is what transported the saints to Heaven. Faith is what unlocked the tombs of the dead. Faith is what changed flames into dew and instilled a salvation-bringing coolness into balls of fire [see Dan

3]. Faith is what solidified the agitated waves' waters under the steps of those who walked them. Faith is what displays the martyrs consecrated to the model of the Lord's death. Faith is what fortified the confessors' souls in the struggle of passion. Faith is what nourishes itself in humility on fasts as well as on late and meager foods. Faith is what guards virginity, widowhood, and continence in chaste integrity. Faith is what takes away physical concupiscence and infuses one with love for the Celestial Empire. Faith is what conjoined us with the Lord onto immortality through His death on the cross. Through the world's hatred, it presents to the Lord those who are hated with Him. In prisons, it revives confessors locked together in the repulsive horror of darkness. While they are thrown in filth and garbage, and pierced by their own beds of earth, they cannot rest in carefree sleep for the smallest length of time. While every kind of torments thus shreds them daily, while all sorts of tortures pressure them, their virtue journeys toward the crown of martyrdom. Faith is what in such confrontations demonstrates a unity dear to God, and by dying for Him renders to Christ what one owed Him. Just as the Head of that body died for the members, so the members die for the Head, in order that just as the Head lives, so the members may be made alive with the Head. The most blessed Paul confirms this: *If we die together for Christ*, he says, *We live together. If we suffer, we shall reign together with Him* [2 Tim 2:11–12].

Most loving ones, there remains now to follow up with the confession of our sins. It is not that divine powers do not know the recesses and secrets of minds, but an unprovoked confession easily elicits the judge's mercy. Let there be no day, dearest brothers, on which we do not remind ourselves of these dramatic plays.[50] That martyr did not blanch under torture; that man anticipated with haste his murderer's tarrying; that man avidly drank the flames [of the pyre]; that man was mutilated yet stood up whole; that man stated that he was blessed in that he happened to be tortured;[51] that man, in the executioners' hands, ordered the rivers to return [to their bed] lest the journey be delayed.[52] That woman mourned her father's tears as a daughter, spurned them as a martyr; that woman, avid for death, excited the lion's anger against herself; that woman, while her infant fasted, presented her full breasts to the wild beasts;[53] that virgin, adorned with Eternity's neckpiece, submitted her neck to the assassin.[54] Dearest brothers, the sacred writ commemorates thousands of examples of virtues, but for the sake of exhortation more than for that of teaching we have selected a few among that multitude. Indeed, a few will suffice to the faithful, but more will not help the infidels.

We should not tarry in fulfilling the saints' wishes. Why do we delay? Let the inner hall be opened wide to the divine martyrs. Let the relics be gathered; let their graces be gathered as well. Let the starting points of the first resurrection come together and be one. Let our confession be made secretly in their midst; to pardon crimes gives joy to the powers. Dearest brothers, greedy for an edifice I snatched this space for the basilica, and fittingly. Let the saints' advent excuse my greed. They themselves ordered an inner hall to be prepared for them, through a secret order they gave to my desire. It is undeniably so; it is undeniably so. For we threw up the foundations; we lengthened the walls; and today we have learned for whom arose the intention for this work of ours. For this reason, all delays have been blamed and repelled. I do not delight in anything lazy or slow. It pleases me to roll huge stones by hand and carry them on my shoulders. The earth drinks my sweat, and if only it could drink my blood in the Savior's name! For the time being, the earth which shall receive the altars drinks sweat. If our apostles and martyrs see us faithful in this labor, they shall call in others.

NOTES

1. In the text, Victricius will move from exhorting his brethren to addressing directly the saints, and back.

2. This chiastic structure plays on the coinherence of the first and second person of the Trinity, for the Savior is traditionally merciful, and God (as Father), almighty.

3. Here Victricius develops the theme of the eternal "presence" of the saints' triumphal passion: their victories against pagan persecutors where theierelics are—especially on the day of their advent into Rouen.

4. Victricius probably visited Britain in order to fight against the Pelagian heresy, much like Germanus of Auxerre.

5. Victricius employs the term *obsequia* which literally means the service owed by a client to his patron.

6. This Latin phrase could also mean "owing to your miraculous power."

7. In the late Antique ritual of *adventus*, the distance traveled out in procession from a city to meet the incoming ruler (here the saints) served as a measuring rod for the respect shown by the greeting party (here Victricius).

8. Compare Augustine, *City of God*, trans. Henry Bettenson (Harmondsworth, 1972), bk. 22, chap.10, p. 1049.

9. Here Victricius thanks Ambrose of Milan and the other bishops who gave him the relics, and tells them that in giving these relics they have not lost the martyrs. Prayer to the martyrs makes them present in the place where they had once been and whence they were translated.

10. Aelianus was a member of the Milanese clergy, who seems to have taken a leading role in the transfer of relics.

11. I have rendered as "burdened" the variant Latin words *onustatas* (as found in the edition from the *Patrologia Latina*) or *onestatas* owing to the classic wordplay between *onus* (burden) and *honor*.

12. "Devoted" (*devotarum*) probably means "vowed to God," that is consecrated women.

13. That is, the tomb.

14. The palm is a symbol of victory, here over carnality.

15. Victricius' interests in chastity parallels those of Pope Innocent I, in a letter directed to this same bishop of Rouen (*Patrologia latina*, ed. Jean-Paul Migne, 221 vols. [Paris, 1844–1864], 20:468–481). If obeyed, the rules he transmits, Innocent asserts, will create order, unanimity, orthodoxy, concord, and peace. I translate here passages bearing on Victricius' speech: ". . . (2.) Furthermore, should anyone receive the belt of secular office (*cingulum militiae secularis*), he must in no way be admitted into the clergy . . . (4.) A cleric shall not take a woman as a wife, since it is written [see Lev 21:13–14 and Ez 44:22], Let the priest take a virgin for his wife, but not a widow nor a woman who was cast aside . . . (5.) He who takes a woman as a wife either before baptism or after baptism shall, even though he was a layman, not be admitted into the clergy, because he is excluded owing to the same vitiation. Indeed, baptism remits sins, but does not dissolve one's association with one's wife. (6.) He who takes a second wife shall not be made a cleric . . . (9.) Bishops and clerics shall not have intercourse with their wives, since they are daily busy with their office's needs . . . (13.) Women who married Christ spiritually and merited to be veiled by the bishop but later either married publicly or secretly corrupted [their chastity]

shall not be allowed to perform penance unless he to whom they joined themselves leaves the world. Indeed, if the rule applies to all that whomsoever marries another man while her husband lives is considered adulterous and is not allowed to perform penance unless one of them dies, it should apply all the more to her who had first joined herself to the immortal groom and then moved on to a human wedlock. (14.) Women who had not yet been covered with the sacred veil yet had sworn that they would remain in the calling of virgins shall do penance for some time. If they marry, because, even though they were not veiled, their promise was made to God . . ."

16. See the scene in *The Martyrdom of Sts. Perpetua and Felicity*, chapter 21 (*Acts of the Christian Martyrs*, ed. and trans. Herbert Musurillo [Oxford, 1972], pp. 128–31) where the martyr offers her neck to the trembling gladiator and guides his hand for the fatal blow.

17. Possibly as well a reference to *The Martyrdom of Sts. Perpetua and Felicity*, chapter 10.

18. The term "offering" (*oblatio*) could refer to the new church building or to the offerings laid on the altar during mass.

19. As the following sentence explains, the incoming saints are met by other saints to whom they are essentially associated in God, and who are therefore also "themselves."

20. That is, the subordination of one person of the Trinity to another, as the Arians taught.

21. It is unclear whether Victricius is speaking here of Christ's passion or about its imitation, the martyrdom of the saints and apostles.

22. Following a correction (*ac* instead of *ad*) made to the text in Sankt Gallen, Stiftbibliothek MS 102. The translation otherwise would be: "through a price in blood [paid to arrive] to (*ad*) the sacrifice of their passion."

23. The term "war companions" (*comites*) can suggest membership in the military bodyguard of an emperor, here the spiritual emperor, Christ.

24. This may be a reference to original sin or to the eternity of the Word (against the Arians, who believed that "there was when He was not").

25. That is, the saints receive unity as a reward, this unity that the Trinity has by nature.

26. The "great day" or last judgment is the time when the saints will sit, alongside Christ, in judgment with a power they seem to have had forever without diminishing that of the Supreme Judge.

27. I understand this to mean that the ability of saintly relics to torture the demons who control possessed human beings on account of the latter's vices serves a pedagogical function. Perhaps the saints force the demoniacs to confess the vices which allowed the demons to take hold of them.

28. That is, all the saints will judge as a collective in Christ, leaving no other power to which the damned or the condemned might appeal.

29. This is the original chapter division in the two ninth-century manuscripts.

30. That is, God being the greatest possible entity as the principle of all things is not encompassed by categories, and therefore cannot be grasped by apt comparisons, but only approached through necessarily clashing similes.

31. That is, an extreme wonder, human being's creation *ex nihilo*, explains that God has the power to spiritualize the saints' bodies and unite them to Himself, pure Spirit.

32. Here and elsewhere Victricius means a theological question.

33. For Neoplatonism, a guiding principle logically contains the entity it directs. Hence for Plotinus the soul contains the body, which it animates as the sea moves the net plunged in it. Here blood as an animating principle contains the body, and the Word this blood.

34. The "gifts" are the relics, both gifts of fellow bishops and God's gifts to Rouen.

35. I here follow René Herval's French translation (*Origines Chrétiennes. De la IIe Lyonnaise gallo-romaine à la Normandie ducale [IVe-XIe siècles]* [Rouen and Paris, 1966]) of the phrase: *cum ius translationis, ipsis volentibus, agnoscamus*.

36. This is the original chapter division in the two ninth-century manuscripts.

37. The term *res* can mean things, essences, or realities.

38. This is a confusing allusion to 1 Cor 2:14, *the animalistic human being does not perceive those things which pertain to God's Spirit*, to justify that the species "human" is included in the genus "animal."

39. Jacques Mulders, "Victricius van Rouaan. Leven en Leer," *Bijdragen. Tijdschrift voor filosofie en theologie*, 18 (1957): 29 and note 76, draws attention to Victricius' debt to Neoplatonism, specifically Porphyry's *Commentary on Aristotle's Categories*, possibly mediated by the lost Christian commentary owed to Victorinus (preserved fragmentarily in Boethius' own commentary on Porphyry): "'animal' which is a genus, is the predicate of both cattle and horse" (*animal vero, quod genus est et bovis et equi praedicatio est*). Just as the genus "animal" contains the species "humanity" and "cattle," the whole body of the saint contains the relics (that is parts, or members) of that saint.

40. That is, just as the genus animal, in being logically divided into the species it comprises (cattle, human, etc.) still remains whole animality in each of them, so a saint's body, when it is divided into relics, is fully in each relic.

41. Auxerre, Bibliothèque municipale, MS 27 provides "a Head" instead of "a body."

42. It is unclear whether by *communione nascendi* Victricius means the communion of human beings or the genus including all things that are born.

43. *Consortium* means community, literally a sharing (*sors* means "share") in common, and could be translated as well "joint ownership" or "living together."

44. Mulders, "Victricius van Rouaan," pp. 23–24, seeks to identify all the saints in the foregoing list.

45. Even female saints are made perfect by being the vessels of the Spirit, a perfection gendered masculine since it is Christ's perfection. Compare the discussion in Augustine, *City of God*, book 22, chapter 17 as to whether women will retain their sex in the resurrected body.

46. The rare Latin term *reduviae* means literally "flesh around the fingernails" or "a snake's shed skin." Victricius asserts here demonstratively that even in the smallest bodily remnants there is perfect (understand, full) power.

47. Here Victricius describes how the presence of the saints, through whom God works, tortures judicially the demons who possess with their vices human beings.

48. Here Victricius develops the analogy of the imperial *adventus*.

49. Some pearls and precious stones were thought to be produced by sea monsters, like whales' amber.

50. The metaphor of martyrdom as spectacle is an old one. See, for example, Werner Weismann, *Kirche und Schauspiele. Die Schauspiele im Urteil der lateinischen Kirchenväter* (Würzburg, 1972), pp. 108 ff., and more recently David Potter, "Martyrdom and Spectacle," in *Theater and Society in the Classical World*, ed. Ruth Scodel (Ann Arbor, 1993), pp. 53–88, as well as Philippe Buc, "Martyre et ritualité," *Annales* 52 (1997): 63–92 (English version forthcoming in his *The Dangers of Ritual*).

51. Victricius uses the verb *cruciari*, which can literally mean to be crucified.

52. The journey in question may be that of the martyr to his/her death.

53. See *The Passion of Sts. Perpetua and Felicity*, chapter 20 where Felicitas, having just given birth, is thrown into the arena her breasts still dripping with a young mother's milk.

54. Jacques Mulders and Roland Demeulenaere, in their edition of Victricius' text, suggest the following reading: "virgin, adorned with the neckpiece of Eternity."

CHAPTER 3

MARK THE DEACON, *LIFE OF ST. PORPHYRY OF GAZA*

Translated by Claudia Rapp

INTRODUCTION

When Porphyry died in 420, Christianity had been on the rise for over a century. Twenty-five years earlier, when Porphyry became bishop of Gaza, Theodosius I had just begun to pass legislation aimed at outlawing pagan observances and closing pagan temples. But paganism was not eradicated overnight, nor could it be obliterated simply by imperial decree. Throughout his episcopate, Porphyry's efforts to expand the Christian Church in Gaza met with the vehement opposition of the local pagans. If by the time of Porphyry's death the Christian community had registered exponential growth, this was not due entirely to the inner strength and external appeal of the new religion, nor was it alone attributable to the superior qualities of Porphyry as a saint and bishop, as his hagiographer would have us believe. In fact, it depended in large part on the tangible support for his cause which Porphyry skillfully wrested from Theodosius's son and successor Arcadius (383–408) and his wife Eudoxia in the form of legislation, finances, and military protection.

Gaza, a thriving city of about twenty thousand inhabitants, was located in the Roman province of First Palestine with its capital in Caesarea Maritima, which was also the seat of the metropolitan (archbishop) of the Christian Church. It commanded a large rural hinterland, dotted with pagan shrines and villages whose agricultural production contributed to the prosperity of the city. A further source of wealth was Gaza's location in the vicinity of the major overland trade routes to Arabia, as well as its easy access to the nearby harbor town of Maioumas, another stronghold of paganism. A few decades earlier, Maioumas had been the center of activity of the saintly monk Hilarion. His struggle on behalf of the nascent monastic movement in this region is described in a biography by Jerome. Gaza was thus an economic and cultural hub. It had a famous school which in the sixth century brought forth the rhetoricians Procopius and Choricius whose speeches paint a colorful picture of the city's monuments. Gaza also boasted a population of diverse backgrounds: Jews, Samaritans, Egyptians, Greeks, and Romans, in addition to many foreign traders. Two languages were spoken, Greek and Aramaic, a Semitic language closely related to Syriac. Counterbalancing this diversity and providing a sense of civic cohesion were the numerous pagan cults with the attendant opportunities for processions and festivals. The most prominent of the eight pagan temples in Gaza was that of Zeus Marnas, the so-called Marneion, where the god also gave oracles. Its enormous size and unusual circular shape, itself surmounted by a large dome, distinguished it as a local landmark.

By background and training, Porphyry was quite unsuited for managing a city of this stature. He was an outsider in every way: born in the imperial city of Thessaloniki, and hence without knowledge of the local Aramaic tongue in Gaza, he heeded a call for the desert in his youth. For a few years, he joined the monastic settlements in Egypt, then lived as a hermit in the Jordan valley, until finally settling in Jerusalem, where he frequented the holy places, at first depending on the charity of others and later earning his keep as a cobbler. In the meantime he had distributed his considerable inheritance to worthy Christian causes.

Uneducated and poor, as well as lacking any previous experience in ecclesiastical administration, Porphyry may have seemed an unlikely candidate for the episcopal see of Gaza when it fell vacant in 395. His episcopate would be marked by the continued confrontation with pagans which often erupted into violence affecting the whole community. But as an "athlete for Christ," Porphyry could count on powerful allies, divine and human, in his quest to foster the growth of Christianity. By 403, halfway through his episcopate, he had succeeded in increasing the Christian community more than threefold, from two hundred and eighty to eight hundred and forty-seven members, and it continued to attract new members thereafter. Even then, Christianity still represented a minority of little over 4 percent of the total population of Gaza.

A large part of the *Life of St. Porphyry* is taken up with the saint's greatest success, the destruction of the Marneion and the construction of an enormous church on its foundations. This feat could only be accomplished with imperial help. It took two embassies to Constantinople, and the prophecy of the birth of a son for the empress Eudoxia, followed by some clever manipulation of the emperor by his wife, to gain the support of Arcadius. He then not only issued an order for the closure and destruction of the temple, but also dispatched a military force to oversee these measures and to maintain calm in the city. Arcadius, and especially the grateful Eudoxia, also made available funds and privileges for the Church, thus laying the basis for its continued prosperity.

While the confrontation and eventual triumph over paganism makes for the most spectacular scenes in the *Life of St. Porphyry*, which are therefore selected for translation here, this was not the only issue with which Porphyry had to contend. Like many other bishops of the late fourth and early fifth centuries, he was concerned about defending the right faith against the Christian heresy of Arianism, and against the teachings of the Manichaeans.

As an administrator, Porphyry made every effort to give the Christian community the structure, organization, and economic foundation that it needed to ensure its continued growth. He had a numerous clergy, appointed deacons, and was in close contact with the monastic establishments in the area. He established a processional route in the city, devised his own system of liturgical chant and of the order of the liturgy, and laid the groundwork for the administration of Christian charity through the hospice for strangers attached to the new church and the regular donations to the poor that he instituted at the inauguration of his church. The greatest monument of Porphyry's episcopate was the construction of the new church. When it was built, its size appeared excessive for the congregation, but Porphyry felt justified in his hopes that it would soon be filled to capacity.

The *Life of St. Porphyry* can thus serve as a lively and vivid account of the unsteady progress of Christianity and the resistance with which it met in the eastern provinces of the Roman Empire. But a serious word of caution is in order. Like all hagiographic accounts, the *Life of St. Porphyry* contains the usual stereotypes of an exemplary lifestyle, miraculous powers, divine gifts of foreknowledge, exceptional piety and devotion. In contrast to many other saints who are independently attested as historical figures, there is no other evidence that Porphyry ever existed. No other author utters so much as a word about him, no inscription mentions his name, and nor have archaeologists found any trace of the large church which he is purported to have built. This total silence is even the more suspicious since it cannot be attributed to a general lack of evidence, literary or archaeological, for that period and region. The period of late Antiquity is unusually rich in documentation, thanks to the prolific output of Christian writers, and it is surprising to find that Porphyry's political connections in the capital of Constantinople and his enormous building project find no reflection in the sources.

Not only is the historicity of the story in question, the text of the narrative itself poses great problems. Its author purports to be a certain Mark. He introduces himself early on in the text as a younger contemporary of Porphyry who composed his account on the basis of his own personal recollections after the saint's death. A good estimate for the time of composition would thus be the two decades after Porphyry's death, that is, between 420 and 440. But for an eye-witness, Mark is remarkably inaccurate. The sequence of events is garbled, and he attributes the wrong names to well-known ecclesiastical figures. Moreover, the *Life of St. Porphyry* as it has come down to us begins with a prologue that is clearly plagiarized from Theodoret of Cyrrhus's *History of the Monks in Syria*, which wasn't composed until 440.

The textual problems can be resolved if we assume that the *Life of St. Porphyry* was composed in two successive stages: the original notes by a contemporary and eyewitness (whom we may chose to call "Mark") were later, perhaps in the 450s, given their final shape and put into circulation by another author who does not appear in the text. This later redactor would be responsible for the addition of the borrowed preface and for the systematic elimination of the names of all those people with whom Porphyry was in contact, but who had in the interim fallen under suspicion of harboring heretical beliefs. This would explain why the name of John, the bishop of Jerusalem who ordained Porphyry to the priesthood in 392 and who was known as a supporter of Origenist and Pelagian ideas, was replaced by that of Praylios. At the same time, this explanation allows us to recognize that the *Life* contains a historical core. Even though the absence of external attestations for Porphyry and his church somewhat mitigates this assertion, the text abounds with such convincing historical detail and shows such an intimate knowledge of the region of Gaza in late Antiquity, that at the very least the general storyline merits our confidence.

The *Life of St. Porphyry* also is significant for the development of hagiography in that it is one of only five *Lives* of holy bishops that survive from the late fourth and early fifth centuries. Like hermits and monks, bishops came to be regarded as potential saints in this period after the cessation of the persecutions had eliminated the possibility of martyrdom as a means to sainthood. Along with Augustine of Hippo, Ambrose of Milan, Martin of Tours, and Epiphanius of Salamis in Cyprus, Porphyry represents a new type of holiness that is acquired not by fleeing the world and its temptations, but by working within it for the progress and improvement of the Christian Church. The *Life of Porphyry* thus stands at the beginning of the development of episcopal hagiography which was to become immensely popular in the Latin West during the Middle Ages.

SOURCES AND FURTHER READING

The following translation of the *Life of St. Porphyry of Gaza* (*Bibliotheca hagiographica graeca*, no. 1570) is based on the text provided in Marc le Diacre, *Vie de Porphyre, évêque de Gaza*, eds. Henri Grégoire and Marc-Antoine Kugener (Paris, 1930) which makes use of four manuscripts dating from the eleventh to fourteenth centuries. A translation into rather antiquated English—Marcus Diaconus, *The Life of Porphyry, Bishop of Gaza*, trans. G.F. Hill (Oxford, 1913)—has also been consulted. For the sake of brevity, some passages have not been translated, but are given in summary form only, marked by square brackets. I have tried to remain faithful to the style, vocabulary and syntax of the Greek. For the sake of consistency, I have adopted the narrative past tense throughout, despite the frequent erratic changes of tense in the Greek. Although the written language of the eastern Roman Empire was Greek, the vocabulary for the imperial administration and bureaucracy was borrowed from Latin. Such official titles are indicated in square brackets, in their original Latin form.

The *Life of St. Porphyry* also survives in a translation into Georgian. In the Middle Ages, several monasteries in the Holy Land were populated with monks from the Caucasus region of Georgia. Hence, there was considerable interest among Georgians in the history of Christianity and the stories of saints, especially of Palestine. The Georgian version has been shown by its editor, Paul Peeters, "La vie géorgienne de saint Porphyre de Gaza," *Analecta Bollandiana* 59 (1941): 65–216, to be based on a Syriac original, which is now lost. Since the Georgian version differs considerably from the Greek, there has been a great deal of debate among scholars whether (1) the lost Syriac version is a translation from the extant Greek version; (2) the extant Greek is a translation from the lost Syriac version; or (3) an equally lost "Ur-version" in Greek was the common basis of the lost Syriac as well as the extant Greek. The tendency in recent years has been to postulate a straightforward progression: the extant Greek version was translated into Syriac, and that (lost) version was then translated into Georgian. Since each translator would have taken certain liberties in altering the text, this would account for the differences between the Greek and Georgian versions.

The historical context of Porphyry's struggle with paganism is discussed by Raymond Van Dam, "From Paganism to Christianity in Late Antique Gaza," *Viator* 16 (1985): 1–20, and by Frank Trombley, *Hellenic Religion and Christianization, c. 370–529*, 2 vols. (Leiden, 1993). A detailed history of the urban setting is given by C.A.M. Glucker, *The City of Gaza in the Roman and Byzantine Periods*, BAR International Series 325 (Oxford, 1987).

Mark the Deacon, Life of St. Porphyry of Gaza

(1.) It is a fine thing to contemplate with our own eyes the contests of the holy men, their divine zeal and yearning—for by being seen, they become worthy of love. However, accounts by accurate informants also bring not a little benefit, as they infiltrate the souls of the listeners. For sight is more reliable than hearing, and persuades the ear if the words are uttered by trustworthy men. And so if the narrative of beneficial things remained free from fraudulence and falsehood did not infiltrate truth, the written account of such matters would be superfluous, truth being sufficient for edification, constantly infiltrating the ears of succeeding generations in turn. But since time corrupts, either through oblivion or fraudulence, I have come to the present account from necessity, so that over the course of time oblivion should not come upon such a holy man—I mean St. Porphyry. For to recall his righteous deeds is a preventive medicine for those who hear about them.

(2.) It will not do that tragic poets and other such authors lavish their words on ridiculous topics and old wives' tales, while we disregard and condemn to oblivion men who are holy and worthy of commemoration. For what kind of punishment would I not justly suffer, if I failed to commit to writing the life of this god-pleasing man, the life of someone who had set his sights on the heavenly way of life—a lesson in philosophy. Let us recount in detail his campaigns and his resistance not only against the leaders and the vanguard of those who are mad about idols, but also against an entire populace filled with utter folly. For he was mindful of the words of the blessed apostle in which he says: *"Take up the whole armor of God, so that you may be able to withstand on that frightful day, and having done everything, to stand firm"* [Eph 6:13]. Clad in such armor, that apostle entered into the contests. But Porphyry, with adversaries of such character and number, having on his hands a fight similar to that of the apostle also carried off an equal victory. As a sign of victory he set up in the middle of Gaza the holy church of Christ recently built by him. However, it was not human nature that provided him with the victory, but his mental disposition which attracted the grace of God. Since he was a most ardent lover of Christ, he was able to suffer and manage everything. How many hostile attacks did this man undergo at the hands of his adversaries, how many plots and mockeries did he endure!

(3.) Since it is impossible to enumerate everything accomplished by this famous man—for his feats are numerous and will appear unbelievable to most—I will set out a few of those feats which I recall myself, having lived with him for a very long time and having enjoyed the presence of that blessed and awesome soul who is now a companion of the angels. Who would not justly sing the praises of this man who had achieved every form of virtue? Now, I know that no account can do justice to the virtue of such a man. Still, I must attempt it, emboldened by his holy prayers. I shall not write his praise in pompous language; for beautiful language does not normally adorn the life of such men, but the virtue of their deeds elevates the style itself. Hence I begin writing this account, putting my faith in the holy prayers of this courageous man, asking through them for the grace and the succor of the Lord Jesus Christ that I may be able, in whatever manner, to narrate the virtue of the holy man. I beg those who come across this piece of writing not to disbelieve my words. For I witnessed his virtue with my own eyes, having lived with him, joined him on his travels, and endured maltreatment with him until the last day of his life here on earth. So let me now begin my narrative.

(4.) Gaza is a city of Palestine, located on the border of Egypt, not without distinction, on the contrary densely populated and counting among the renowned cities. At that time, the madness of the people for idols was at its height there. Porphyry, the subject of our eulogy, became bishop of that city. His homeland was the heavenly Jerusalem (for there also he had enlisted himself as a citizen), but his city of origin on earth was Thessaloniki. He came from a distinguished family. A divine desire overcame him to leave his homeland, his illustrious family and its boundless wealth and to embrace the monastic life, so he sailed off from Thessaloniki and went to Egypt. Immediately upon his arrival, he made his way to Scetis,[1] and after a few days was deemed worthy of the venerable monastic habit. And having spent a period of five years there with the holy fathers, he was again seized by divine desire, this time to venerate the holy and revered places of God [in Jerusalem]; and after he had gone there and venerated them, he left for the regions of the river Jordan where he lived in a cave, similarly spending five years there, enduring much hardship. He fell gravely ill because of the excessive dryness and the climatic contrasts in those regions. When he saw that he was in mortal danger, in accordance with divine dispensation, he asked one of his acquaintances to take him to Jerusalem. The affliction was a tumor of the liver, accompanied by a very light continuous fever. Although this affliction grew stronger, piercing his intestines unremittingly, and his body was wasting, he did not desist from making his daily round of the holy places, bent and without the strength to keep his young body upright, but leaning on a staff.

[**Translator's note**: In Chapters. 5–16 Porphyry sent Mark to Thessaloniki to claim his considerable inheritance. The money was given to charitable causes, and Porphyry earned his keep as a cobbler, maintaining an ascetic lifestyle. During Mark's absence, he was miraculously cured from his liver tumor by a vision of the crucified Christ. He was appointed guardian of the wood of the Holy Cross by Praylius, bishop of Jerusalem. When the episcopal see in Gaza fell vacant, it was revealed to John, metropolitan of Caesarea, that Porphyry should be the appointed. At John's request, Porphyry, accompanied by Mark and the young servant Barochas, traveled to Caesarea. In the presence of a small delegation from Gaza, Porphyry is taken by surprise and forcibly ordained bishop.]

(17.) He [John, the metropolitan of Caesarea] enjoined us to leave as soon as possible, and after one further day, we departed. We took our rest in Diospolis and, having spent the night there, we arrived in Gaza late in the evening, extremely worn out and tormented. Now the reason for our torment was this: in the vicinity of Gaza, there were villages along the road which were given to idol-madness. By mutual agreement, the inhabitants of these villages had strewn the whole road with thorns and brambles, so that it was impossible for anyone to pass. They had also poured out mire and burned other foul-smelling substances so that the stench caused us to choke and put our eyesight at risk. Having barely escaped, we reached the city at around the third hour of the night. This obstacle was put in the way of the blessed man as a demonic assault. But he was not aggrieved. For he recognized the snare of the devil who wanted to avert the arrival of the just man.

[**Translator's note:** In Chapter 18 Porphyry established himself in the exceedingly small episcopal residence which had been founded by Bishop Irenios, adjacent to the church of Irene or "Peace."]

(19.) In that same year, there happened to be a drought, and everyone in the city ascribed this to the arrival of the blessed man, saying: "It was prophesied to us by Marnas that Porphyry would bring bad luck to the city." As God continued to stall the rainfall for the first month, which they call Dios,[2] and then also in the second month of Apellaios,[3] all were afflicted. So the idol-maniacs, having gathered at the Marneion, offered up many sacrifices and prayers because of this. For they said that Marnas is the lord of the rains; and Marnas, they say, is Zeus. Thus for seven days they were continually reciting hymns and going to what is called "the place of prayer" outside the city; discouraged, they then returned to their private affairs, having accomplished nothing. When these things had taken place in this way, the Christians, having gathered a total number of two hundred and eighty men, women, and children, entreated holy Porphyry to go out with them in procession and pray that the rains be sent down (for already there was a famine), the more so because they ascribed the drought to the arrival of the blessed man.

(20.) The holy man was persuaded, announced a fast, and then ordered all to gather in the evening at the holy church, so that we might hold a vigil there. In the course of the whole night, we performed thirty prayers, and an equal number of genuflections, not to mention choral chants and readings. When dawn broke, we took the sign of the precious cross, which was leading our way, and then went out, chanting hymns, to the old church in the west of the city which, they say, was founded by the most holy and blessed Bishop Asklepas, who had endured many persecutions on behalf of the orthodox faith, and whose life and deeds are recorded in the paradise of delights. Having thus reached this church, we performed there the same number of prayers; and departing from there, we went to the holy martyrion of the glorious martyr Timothy, in which repose also other precious relics of the martyr Maiouros and of the woman confessor Thee.[4] After we performed there also the same number of prayers and genuflections, we returned to the city, completing three prayers and three genuflections on the way. But when we arrived at the city gate, we found it closed (it was the ninth hour). The idol-maniacs had done this, wanting to disperse the congregation, to prevent us from concluding our procession. But after we remained for two hours outside the gate, and there was nobody to open it, God seeing the perseverance of the congregation and their groans and their untold tears, especially of the holy man, was moved to pity, and as he had done at the time of the great Elijah, the prophet, he raised a stormy wind from the south; and the sky was covered with clouds, and thunder and lightning began to strike while the sun was setting, and a great torrent was brought down [see 1 Kings 18:45] so that one would have thought that these were not raindrops, but hail falling from heaven. And we in our joy almost did not notice it, for we were holding each other embraced.

(21.) Now some of the pagans,[5] seeing what great miracles God did for us and becoming believers, opened the gate and mingled with us, shouting: "Christ alone is God; only He has conquered." They went with us to the holy church, and there the blessed man dismissed them in peace, sealing them with the sign of the cross. They were one hundred and twenty-seven in number, seventy-eight men, thirty-five women, fourteen children, of whom five were girls. And we, having completed the perfect Eucharist, departed with joy and peace each to his own place. In that night and on the following day, such a torrent came down that everybody feared that the houses would collapse; for most of them were built of unbaked bricks. Our Lord Jesus Christ made it rain unremittingly from the eighth to the tenth day of Audynaios. For them Audynaios is the month of January in Roman reckoning; their months anticipate those of the Romans by five days. On the eleventh day, we celebrated the day of the Epiphany of our Lord Jesus Christ, joyously singing hymns and giving thanks for all that His mercy had done for us. In that year, there were added to the flock of Christ, in addition to the two hundred and eighty, a further thirty-five.[6] But the idol-maniacs did not cease to harry the blessed man and the other Christians. When they got hold of a pagan magistrate, they secretly persuaded him, either with bribes or with the help of their godless cult, to oppress the Christians; and this resulted in considerable affliction for the most blessed man. Therefore, he incessantly, day and night, beseeched the merciful God to turn them from their error to His truth.

[**Translator's note**: The narrative for Chapters. 22–36 can be quickly summarized. Outside the city, Barochas was beaten senseless by the pagans. A tumult ensued when the pagans, anxious to avoid pollution of the city, vehemently protested that his (apparently) dead body was carried back into the city by fellow Christians.[7] He was restored to health by Porphyry's prayers. Mark and Barochas were ordained deacons. Mark was sent to Constantinople to petition the emperor Arcadius on behalf of the Christians in Gaza. He found supporters in John [Chrysostom], the bishop of Constantinople,[8] and the chamberlain Eutropius. An imperial decree ordered the closure of the temples and the silencing of the oracles in Gaza. Its implementation was enforced by the presence of imperial officers and armed guards, who exerted pressure also on members of the city council. Nonetheless, the largest temple, that of Zeus Marnas, and its oracle were allowed to remain unaffected, due to the corruption of the imperial officer in charge. The entire household of the noblewoman Aelias, numbering sixty-four people, were converted to Christianity after Porphyry's prayers safely delivered her of her child. In order to obtain imperial support in counteracting the continued oppression of Christians in Gaza, Porphyry, Mark and John, the metropolitan of Caesarea, departed for Constantinople. On the island of Rhodes, the hermit Procopius instructed them to gain the favor of the empress Eudoxia by predicting the birth of a son.]

(37.) ... in another ten days, we reached Byzantium [Constantinople]; after taking lodgings, on the next day we went to the most holy bishop John. Informed who we were, he received us with great honor and attention. He asked us why we had undergone this hardship, and we told him; and when he had found out, he remembered that we had made the same request by letter the previous year; and, recognizing me, he gave me a friendly embrace. He encouraged us not to lose heart, but to put our hopes in the mercy of God. He said to us: "I cannot speak to the emperor. For the empress has incited his anger against me, because I objected to her appropriateion of a property she had set her heart on.[9] Yet to me, it is of no concern that she is angry over this, and I am not worried; for they have brought harm to themselves, not to me. Even if they should inflict harm on my body, they are bringing much greater benefit to my soul. But let us leave this to God's compassion. And regarding your business, God willing, tomorrow I will send for the eunuch Amantius, who is the personal servant [*castrensius*] of the empress and has great influence with her. He is truly a servant of God and I will present this business to him, and he will greatly expedite it with the help of Christ." With such instructions and a blessing, we went to our lodgings.

(38.) The next day, we went to the holy man and found with him the chamberlain [*cubicularius*] Amantius. He had already attended to our business, having sent for Amantius and instructed him regarding us. When we entered and Amantius recognized that we were the ones about whom John had spoken to him, he rose and did obeisance to the most holy bishops, bowing to the ground; and they also, having recognized him, embraced and kissed him. The most holy Archbishop John then invited them, too, to inform the chamberlain [*cubicularius*] in their own words about their business. The most holy Porphyry told him everything regarding the idol worshipers, how they were perpetrating illicit deeds with impunity and how they were inflicting suffering on the Christians. And he, on hearing this, shed tears and was filled with divine zeal and said to them: "Do not lose heart, fathers. For the Lord Christ shall guard his religion as with a shield. Therefore, you must pray, and I will speak to the empress [*augusta*], and I place my hopes in the God of the universe that once again He will show His mercy. And tomorrow, I will bring you to her, and you instruct her in your own words about everything you wish; if fact, you will find her already instructed by me." After saying this and bidding us farewell, he departed, but we engaged in conversation about many spiritual things with the most holy Archbishop John, and then left with his blessing.

(39.) The next day, the chamberlain [*cubicularius*] Amantius sent two court ushers [*decani*] to summon us to the palace and, after getting ready, we went in haste. We found him waiting for us, and he took the two bishops and then led them inside to the *augusta* Eudoxia. When she saw them, she embraced them first, saying: "Say a blessing, Fathers." They in turn paid obeisance to her. She was sitting on a golden couch and said to them: "Forgive me, priests of Christ, because of the weighty burden of my belly. For I should have met your holiness at the outer doors. But pray to the Lord on my behalf, that I may deliver the fruit of my belly with his mercy." The most holy bishops marveled at her deference and then said: "He who blessed the womb of Sarah, and of Rebecca, and of Elizabeth, will also bless the fruit of your belly and give it life."

(40.) After they had uttered some more pious words, she addressed them: "I have learned why you have taken the trouble of the journey. For Amantius the *castrensis* has already instructed me. But if you yourselves want to give me a report, please do so, Fathers." With that invitation, they gave a complete report about the idol-maniacs, how they were fearlessly perpetrating unholy deeds, and how they were oppressing the Christians, by not allowing them to stand for public offices, and by preventing the cultivation of their estates, "from which they pay the taxes to your Majesty." Upon hearing this, the empress said: "Do not lose heart, Fathers. For I hope in the Lord Christ, the son of God, that I can persuade the emperor to do right by your holy faith, and to dismiss you from here with your affairs attended to. Now go and recover yourselves (for you are exhausted), and pray that God may help my plea." Having said this, she ordered that money be brought in; and, having taken three handfuls for each, she gave them to the most holy bishops, saying: "Take this for the moment for your expenses." The bishops, after receiving the money and saying many blessings over her, departed. On their way out, they distributed most of the money to the *decani* who were standing at the doors, so that little was left for them.

(41.) When the emperor came to her, the empress reported to him the business about the bishops, then she asked him to overturn the temples of the idols in Gaza. But the emperor was displeased upon hearing this, saying: "I know that that city is prone to idolatry, but it is willing to pay its dues in public taxes, bringing in substantial amounts. Therefore, if we suddenly instill fear in them, they will take to flight and we will lose this great amount of tax income. But if it pleases you, we will gradually wear them down, stripping the idol-maniacs of dignities and of other public offices, and we will order that their temples be closed and not give oracles any longer. For when they are suffering under pressure in every regard, they will recognize the truth. For an extreme measure which is also sudden is hard to bear for the subjects." Having heard this, the empress was greatly aggrieved (for she was ardent in the faith); but she did not say a word in response to the emperor except this: "The Lord will come to the help of his servants the Christians, whether we want it or not." The pious Amantius the *cubicularius* told us this.

(42.) The next day, the *augusta* sent for us, and after she had embraced the holy bishops first as was her custom, she invited them to sit down. After speaking many spiritual words, she said to them: "I have spoken to the emperor and he was a little displeased. But do not lose heart. For, God willing, I will not rest until you have fulfilled your mission and depart, having accomplished your goal in accordance with God." Having heard this, the bishops paid obeisance. And deeply moved, our holy Porphyry, mindful of the words of the thrice-blessed hermit Procopius, said to the empress: "Trouble yourself, your majesty, on behalf of Christ, and he will grant you for your troubles a son who will live and reign as emperor, while you see him and take pleasure in him for many years." When the empress heard this pronouncement, she was filled with joy, and her face became rosy and greater beauty was added to her already beautiful countenance.[10] For external appearance makes visible those things which are invisible.

(43.) Then she said to the most holy bishops: "Pray, Fathers, that, God willing, I will give birth to a son, according to your word. If that will come to pass, I promise that I will do everything you ask. Furthermore, with Christ's approval, I will do even other things which you did not ask. For I am going to build a holy church in Gaza, right in the middle of the city. Now go in peace and be at rest, praying fervently for me, that I may give birth with mercy. For this is the ninth month and [my pregnancy] is coming to its term." Having taken their leave then and commended her to God, the bishops left the palace. Their prayer was that she might give birth to a son. For we believed the word of the holy recluse Procopius. Every day we went to the most holy Archbishop John, and we enjoyed his holy words which were *sweeter also than honey and drippings of the honeycomb* [Ps 19:10; 18:11, Vulgate]. Amantius the chamberlain [*cubicularius*], of eternal memory, visited us constantly, sometimes to convey messages from the empress, at other times also to enjoy our company.

(44.) And after a few days, the empress gives birth to a son;[11] and they gave him the name Theodosius, after his grandfather Theodosius the Spaniard, who ruled jointly with Gratian.[12] The newborn, Theodosius the Second, was born in the purple,[13] for which reason he was proclaimed emperor from the moment of his birth. And there was much rejoicing in the city [of Constantinople], and messengers were sent to the cities to bring the good news, along with donations and favors. But as soon as her majesty had given birth and raised herself from the delivery stool, she dispatched Amantius to us, saying to us through him: "I give thanks to Christ that through your holy prayers God has granted me a son. Pray now, Fathers, for his life and also for my humble self, that I may fulfill what I have promised you—again, according to Christ's will—through your holy prayers.

(45.) After the completion of the seven days of childbed, she sent for us and then received us at the door of her chamber, holding the baby in the purple. She bowed her head, saying: "Say a blessing, Fathers, over me and the child which the Lord has granted me through your holy prayers." She also gave them the baby so that they could seal him. The holy bishops sealed both her and the child with the seal of Christ[14] and, after saying a prayer, sat down. after they had said many words that were filled with contrition, her majesty said to them: "Do you know, Fathers, what I have planned to do about your business?" My lord Porphyry answered and said: "All that you have planned, you have planned with God. For this last night my humble self had a revelation in a vision. For I thought we were in Gaza, standing in the place of idol worship there, the so-called Marneion. I saw your piety handing me the gospel, saying to me: 'Take and read.' And upon opening it, I found the passage in which the Lord Christ says to Peter: '*You are Peter, and on this rock I will build my church, and the gates of Hades will not prevail against it*' [Mt 16:18]. And you, your majesty, answered and said: '*Peace be to you* [Judg 6:23, etc.], *be strong and courageous*,' [Josh 1:6]. At that moment, I woke up; and now I am convinced that the Son of God will assist you in your desire. Now tell us, your majesty, what you have planned."

(46.) The empress answered and said: "In a few days—Christ willing—the child will be deemed worthy of holy baptism. Go now and prepare a petition, making in it a list of all your requests. And when, after the precious baptism, the baby comes out, give the petition to the one who carries him; I shall have instructed him beforehand what to do; and I put my hope in the Son of God that He will direct this whole business according to the disposition of His mercy." With such instructions, and after saying many blessings over her and the baby, we departed; we then went and prepared the petition, making a long list on the sheet, not only that the sanctuaries of the idols be destroyed, but also that the holy church and the Christians be granted privileges and sources of income. For the holy church was poor.

(47.) After several days had passed, the day arrived when the new emperor Theodosius was to be baptized.[15] The whole city was wreathed with garlands, and adorned with silks and gold plate and many other kinds of decorations, so that one could not describe the beautiful decoration of the city. Indeed, the crowds of inhabitants offered a sight like waves, as they were wearing many different kinds of garments. To describe the splendor of this beauty is not in my power, but rather of those who are trained in speechmaking; I, for my part, shall continue with the present truthful piece of writing. After the baptism of the young Theodosius, as he was leaving the church in the direction of the palace, one could observe again the splendor of the crowd that was leading the procession and the brilliance of their dress. For all were wearing white garments,[16] so that the crowd appeared to be covered with snow. Leading the procession were the *patricii*,[17] the *illustres*,[18] and all dignitaries along with the divisions of soldiers, all holding candles, so that it seemed as though stars were shining on earth. Near the baby that was being carried was the emperor Arcadius himself, with a cheerful face that was shining more brightly than the purple he was wearing; and one of the grandees was carrying the baby in a shimmering garment. We marveled at this glorious sight. And St. Porphyry said to us: "If there is such glory among things of this earth that are vanishing after a short time, how much more will there be among the things in heaven that have been prepared for those who are worthy, and that *no eye has seen, nor ear heard, nor the human heart conceived* ?" [see 1 Cor 2:9].

(48.) We were standing at the outer doors of the holy church, holding the sheet with the petition, and as he came out from the baptism, we exclaimed, saying: "We appeal to your piety," while also holding out the sheet. When the man who was carrying the baby saw this, and recognized our business (for he had been previously instructed by her majesty), he ordered that the sheet be received and given to him; and upon receiving it, he halted in his path. He ordered silence and, after opening it, read it out in part. He then rolled it up, placed his hand under the head of the baby, made it nod in front of all, and shouted: "The power of his highness has granted the petition." All who saw this were amazed and paid obeisance to the emperor, calling him blessed that he was worthy in his lifetime to see his son exercising imperial authority. Upon hearing this, the emperor was swollen with pride. It was announced immediately also to the empress Eudoxia what had happened thanks to her child;[19] and she rejoiced and fell on her knees to give thanks to God.

(49.) After the child had entered the palace, the empress met and received him and covered him with kisses and, holding him in her arms, she also embraced the emperor, saying: "You are blessed, your majesty, because of what your eyes have seen in your lifetime." Hearing this, the emperor rejoiced. And, seeing that he was cheerful, the empress said: "With your permission, let us find out what the petition contains, so that the requests in it may come to pass completely." The emperor ordered the sheet to be read out, and when it was read, he said: "Heavy is the demand, but heavier yet its refusal, because it is after all the first order of our son." Her majesty says to him: "Not only is the order his first, but he also issued it in this holy garment, and the petition was made for the sake of piety and by holy men." Reluctantly, the emperor agreed to it, her ladyship having put much pressure on him. All this the God-pleasing Amantius announced to us.

(50.) The next day, the empress sent for us; and after she had embraced the holy bishops first as was her custom, she invited them to sit down and said to them: "Through your prayers, God gave me the idea how to deal with your business; and with His help, it has been fulfilled. You saw what method I have used. But with your permission, tomorrow I will send for the state secretary for finance [*quaestor*] and before your eyes, I will charge him to compose a sacred rescript in the name of the two emperors,[20] according to the substance of your petition; and, simply put, he will do whatever you will say to him." Having heard these words also, the bishops called down many blessings upon her, her son, and the emperor; and after further edifying remarks, they took their leave and departed. The next day, she sent for the *quaestor* and for us, and said to him: "Take this sheet, and draw up a sacred rescript according to its substance." The *quaestor* received the sheet and with great expeditiousness dictated the sacred rescript in our presence. We suggested that he appoint for protection military commanders [*duces*] and governors [*consulares*] and their divisions.

[(51.-62.) Eudoxia put the imperial officer Cynegius in charge of destroying the pagan temples in Gaza. After final audiences with Eudoxia, who gave Porphyry two hundred pounds of gold for the new church, along with other gifts and privileges, and with Arcadius, they departed. In a tempest at sea, Porphyry converted the ship owner from the heresy of Arianism to Orthodoxy. While the welcoming procession was on its way from the seaport to Gaza, the marble statue of Aphrodite suddenly broke into pieces, killing one pagan and injuring another. Thirty-nine pagans converted to Christianity as a result.]

(63.) The admirable Cynegius arrived after ten days, along with the provincial governor [*hypatikos*], the military commander [*dux*] and a great military and civilian host. But many of the idol worshipers knew this in advance and left the city, some going to the villages, others to other cities; these were the majority of the wealthy in the city. And this Cynegius requisitioned the houses of those who had fled. On the following day, Cynegius, having called together the inhabitants, in the presence of the *dux* and the *hypatikos*, promulgated the imperial rescript which ordered that the places of idol worship be torn down and given over to the flames. As soon as the idol worshipers heard this, they raised a loud lament, so that the leaders became angry and, with threats, sent soldiers against them to beat them with clubs and cudgels.

[**Translator's note**: In Chapter 64 they set out to destroy the temples. There were eight public temples in Gaza, in addition to countless idols in private dwellings and in the villages.]

(65.) Therefore, after the soldiers had been given the order, in company with the Christians of the city and of the coastal region that belonged to it, they moved against the places of idol worship; and having decided first to tear down the so-called Marneion, they were repulsed. For the priests of that place of idol-worship, having heard in advance, blocked from within the doors to the inner temple with large stones; and, having assembled all the precious furnishings that belonged to the temple and also the statuettes of their gods themselves in the so-called inaccessible [space], they hid them there; and they fled, by way of the "inaccessible" itself, through other exits. For they said that this "inaccessible" has many exits in different places. Since, as I said before, they had been repulsed, they set upon the other places of idol worship, and some they tore down, others they gave over to the flames, plundering all the precious furnishings in them. But St. Porphyry had pronounced in church a condemnation on any Christian citizen who took anything at all from the places of idol worship for his own gain. Therefore none of the faithful citizens took anything, except the soldiers and the foreign residents who were present there. For pious men of the clergy and the holy bishop Porphyry himself were going around together with the lay people, preventing them from appropriating anything. They spent ten days tearing down the temples of the idols.

(66.) After this number of days, they took counsel also about the Marneion, how they should deal with it. Some suggested razing it to the ground, others suggested burning it down, yet others suggested purifying the place and consecrating it for a church of God; and there was much debate about this. Finally, the holy bishop ordered a fast and supplication for the congregation, so that the Lord might reveal to them how it should be dealt with; and having fasted on that day and supplicated God in this matter, in the evening they celebrated the holy liturgy. After the conclusion of the liturgy, a child of about seven years, standing next to his mother, suddenly lifted up his voice, saying: "Burn the inner temple to the ground. For many terrible things have been done in it, especially human sacrifices.[21] Burn it in this manner: bring raw pitch, sulfur, and pork fat, and mix the three, and apply this to the bronze doors, and set them on fire, and thus the whole temple is going to burn. For it cannot be done in any other way. But leave the outer [temple] with the precinct. And after it has burnt, purify the place and build a holy church there." And he also said this: "I testify to you before God, it will not happen in any other way. For it is not me who speaks, but *Christ who speaks in me*" [see 2 Cor 13:3]. This he said in the language of the Syrians. When they heard this, all marveled and gave praise to God.

(67.) This miracle also came to the ears of the holy bishop and, stretching his hands up to heaven, he gave praise to God and said: "Glory be to you, Holy Father, *because you have hidden* [these things] *from the wise and the intelligent and have revealed them to infants* [Mt 11:25]." He ordered that after the dismissal from the church, the child and his mother be present in the episcopal residence; and, having sent the child aside, he said to the woman: "I beseech you in the name of the Son of the Living God, to say if your child has uttered what he said about the Marncion due to a suggestion of yours or of someone else whom you know." And the woman, upon hearing this, said: "I surrender myself to the fearful and terrifying judgment seat of Christ, if I had any previous knowledge of what my son has uttered today. But if you wish, here is the child, take him and examine him under threat, and if he has said this as the result of someone else's suggestion, he will admit it out of fear; but if he will not say anything else, then it is clear that he was inspired by the Holy Spirit." Having heard and approved the speech of the woman, he ordered that she be sent outside for a time and the child be brought in; and, with the child standing before him, he said to him: "Who has suggested to you to utter in the church those things that you have said regarding the Marneion?" The child remained silent. So the most holy bishop ordered that a whip be brought in and the child be set up [for a beating] in order to frighten him. And the man who was holding the whip shouted with a [loud] voice, saying: "Who told you to speak? Say it, so that you will not be beaten by the whip." But the child stood speechless, without uttering a sound. Then we who stood around him told him the same, accompanied by threats. But he remained steadfast.

(68.) Finally, after all had fallen silent, the child opened his mouth and said in the Greek language: "Burn the inner temple to the ground. For many terrible things have been done in it, especially human sacrifices. Burn it in this manner: bring raw pitch, sulfur, and pork fat, and mix the three, and apply this to the bronze doors, and set them on fire, and thus the whole temple is going to burn. For it will not happen in any other way. But leave the outer [temple] with the precinct. And after it has burnt, purify the place and build a holy church there. I testify to you once more before God, it will not happen in any other way. For it is not me who speaks, but *Christ who speaks in me*" [see 2 Cor 13:3]. The most holy Porphyry and all those with him marveled when they heard the bold speech of the child and how articulately he had held forth. Having called his mother, he asked her if either she or her son understood the Greek language. But she affirmed with oaths that neither she nor her child knew Greek. When the most holy Porphyry heard this in turn, he gave praise to God; and he took three gold coins [*nomismata*] and gave them to the woman. But when the child saw the *nomismata* in his mother's hand, he cried out in the Syriac language, saying: "Do not take it, mother; do not you also *sell God's gift for gold*" [see Acts 8:21]. But we in turn, when we heard this, marveled exceedingly. And the woman returned the three *nomismata* to the bishop, saying: "Pray for me and my child and commend us to God." And the holy bishop dismissed them in peace.

(69.) Early in the morning, having gathered the pious clergy and the devout congregation and also the admirable Cynegius and the magistrates, he told them how the child had given voice regarding the Marneion. They marveled hearing this, and by unanimous consent said that it should be burned according to the pronouncement of the child. So having brought the raw pitch, and the sulfur, and the pork fat, and having mixed the three, they applied this to the inner doors, and, after a prayer, set fire to them. Immediately the whole temple caught fire and burned. All those among the soldiers and the strangers who were able, wrested from the flames what they could find, either gold, or silver, or iron, or lead.

[**Translator's note**: In Chapters. 70–74 an officer, who was only nominally a Christian, found his just death in the fire. Idols and sacred books of the pagans were sought out in private dwellings and committed to the flames. Porphyry welcomed even those who converted to Christianity out of fear.]

(75.) When finally the Marneion had been burned and the city had calmed down, the blessed bishop decided with the pious clergy and the devout congregation to build a holy church in the place that had been burned, just as had been revealed to him when he was in Constantinople, for which purpose he had also received the money from the most God-pleasing empress Eudoxia. Having dismissed the magistrates and the devout congregation then, he held back part of the auxiliaries to prevent any uprising after their departure; and not only because of that, but also so that they could assist in gathering materials for the construction of this holy church. Now, some advised to build the church according to the plan of the burnt place of idol worship. It was of a circular shape, surrounded by two concentric rows of columns. Its center was a raised dome that extended to a great height; it also had other features that were appropriate for idols, and suitable for the abominable and illicit deeds of the idol-mad. According to this plan, then, some said the holy church should be built; but others disagreed, saying that even the very memory of this plan ought to be erased. Those who said this persuaded all, as they were speaking well. But the holy bishop said: "We shall also leave this to the will of God." And while the place was being cleared, an official of the Master of Offices [*magistrianus*] arrived, carrying an imperial letter from Eudoxia of eternal memory; and the letter contained a greeting and the request for prayers for herself and the emperors, her husband and her child. But on another sheet, inside the letter, was the sketch of the holy church in the shape of a cross, just as it can now be seen, thanks to God, and the letter specified that the holy church should be built according to the sketch. The holy man rejoiced when he read and saw the sketch. For he realized that this, too, had occurred according to divine revelation, and he recalled the Scripture which says: "*The king's heart is in the hand of God*" [Prov 21:1]. Included in the letter was the promise that, in addition, very valuable columns and marbles were about to be sent.

(76.) Now after the debris had been removed and all the abominations had been taken away, the remaining rubbish of the marble paving of the Marneion, which was said to be holy and in a location where it could not be trodden, especially by women—these the holy bishop ordered to be laid down as pavement of the street outside, in front of the temple, so that they would be trampled upon not only by men, but also by women, dogs, pigs, and beasts. This caused greater grief to the idol worshipers than the burning of the temple. Hence, the majority of them, especially the women, do not step on these marbles to the present day. And after a short time he announced a fast for one day and after the dismissal of the morning prayers, the God-pleasing bishop ordered all devout men to bring hoes and shovels and other such implements. This he had already announced in advance, since the previous evening, so that in the morning everyone would be ready, which is indeed what happened.

(77.) When the congregation had gathered with these implements in the holy church named "Peace" [*Eirene*], he ordered that all, chanting psalms together, proceed to the former Marneion; he followed behind, carrying the holy Gospel, surrounded by the pious clergy, truly imitating Christ with his disciples. Leading the congregation was Barochas of eternal memory, holding the form of the sign of the cross, while on either side of the congregation were the soldiers who had been left behind for the sake of good order in the city. They chanted psalms while they were walking, and at a set break in the psalm they said the Alleluia. And the psalm which they chanted was: "*O come, let us sing to the Lord; let us make a joyful noise to the rock of our salvation! Let us come into his presence with thanksgiving; let us make a joyful noise to him with songs of praise! For the Lord is a great God and a great King of the whole earth.*[22] *In his hand are the depths of the earth; the heights of the mountains are his also. The sea is his, for he made it, and the dry land, which his hands have formed. O come, let us worship and bow down, let us kneel before the Lord our Maker! For he is our God, and we are the people of his pasture, and the sheep of his hand*" [Ps 95:1–7]. And they chanted also other psalms until they arrived at the Marneion.

(78.) Now the holy bishop had commissioned Rufinus the architect from Antioch, a faithful and skilled man, through whom the entire building project was completed. This man took chalk and marked out the plan of the holy church according to the shape of the sketch that had been sent by the God-pleasing Eudoxia. And after the most holy bishop had said a prayer and made a genuflection, he ordered the congregation to dig. And immediately, with one soul and with the same zeal, all began to dig, shouting: "Christ has conquered!" And one could not see a difference between men and women, or old person and child, but their eagerness gave all the same strength; and some were digging, others were clearing away, so that within a few days all places of the foundation were dug up and cleared out.

(79.) And since the building material had been readied in advance, very large stones from the hill called Aldioma to the east of the city as well as other material, the holy man, after once again gathering the devout congregation and saying many prayers and chanting many psalms on the location, girded himself and was the first to begin carrying stones and throwing them into the foundations; then also the God-pleasing clergy and all the lay people, rejoicing and singing psalms with a loud voice, so that they could be heard at a distance of three miles from the city.

[**Translator's note**: In Chapters 80–83, three children who had fallen into a well in the temple precinct were rescued unharmed through Porphyry's prayers.]

(84.) In the following year, the empress Eudoxia sent the columns which she had promised, marvelous and large, thirty-two in number, of the kind known as Carystian, which are in the holy church shining like emeralds. When they arrived by ship, the zeal and eagerness of the devout congregation was again made manifest: upon the word [of the ship's arrival], all immediately ran to the seashore, not only men, but also women and children and old people (for the love of the faith gave strength to them all); and having brought wagons, and having laid one column at a time on them, they dragged it up and set it down in the open space of the sanctuary, and again they went away and brought up another one, until they had brought them all. And this is enough on this topic.

[**Translator's note**: In Chapters 85–91, Porphyry confronted the Manichaean woman Julia in a public debate. His prayer rendered her dumb, and she died. Her followers converted.]

(92.) After five years, the building of the holy and great church was completed; and it was named Eudoxiane after the name of the most God-pleasing Empress Eudoxia. And the most holy Porphyry held a lavish celebration for the inauguration on the Day of the Resurrection of the holy Eastertide, not sparing any expense; but having assembled all the monks of the surrounding area, about one thousand men, along with other pious clergy and lay people and bishops, he held festivities all the days of the holy Eastertide. And they were a sight to behold like angelic choirs, not only during the liturgy of the church, but also in those hours when they had a meal. For the fare was not only physical, but spiritual as well. After the food a Psalm was said and after the drink a hymn. And when the idol-maniacs saw what was happening, they were eating their heart out. For even strangers came from everywhere to see the beauty and size of this holy church. For it was said that it was larger than all the churches at that time.

[**Translator's note**: In Chapters. 93–94, Porphyry justified the excessive size of the church with his faith in the future growth of the congregation. To celebrate the occasion, he distributed money to visitors and the poor. Later, he stipulated in his pious testament the continued distribution of charity during Lent.]

(95.) But the more the idol-maniacs saw the growth of Christianity, the more they raged and were eager to harm the Christians, and especially their holy shepherd Porphyry. On one occasion, when a dispute had arisen about landed properties between the *oikonomos* [financial administrator] of the holy church and Sampsychus the head of the city council, the God-pleasing Barochas, observing how the *oikonomos* was being insulted, took up his cause and began to insult this Sampsychus. When the other members of the city council heard this, they gathered and moved against the *oikonomos* and the God-pleasing Barochas. And many of the citizens also went along with the magistrates, having found a pretext to inflict harm on those of the faith, and, as one might say, from a small spark such a fire was kindled and ignited that all the Christians were in danger even of perishing. For the rage of the idol worshipers was so intense that they took up swords and cudgels and killed seven people and beat many others.

(96.) And then, not being content with this, they moved against the shepherd himself. But some well-intentioned men hurried ahead and warned the most holy bishop of the attack of the mob. And when the blessed man heard this, he called me and said: "Let us flee, brother, and go into hiding for a while until the wrath of God has passed." And, by climbing walls, we escaped over the roofs. The idol-maniacs broke down the doors of the episcopal residence and went inside, and when they did not find holy Porphyry, they ransacked everything that was found there.

[**Translator's note**: In Chapters 97–98, Salaphtha, a pagan girl, hid them in her grandmother's attic for two days.]

(99.) And when we found out that the commotion in the city had calmed down, we went at night to the holy church, and, having gone up to the episcopal residence, we found nothing in it except the God-pleasing Barochas, who was lying there in extremely poor condition because of the wounds that had been inflicted on him by the godless and impious idol worshipers. After a few days, when the provincial governor (he was called Clarus) had heard about what had happened in the city, he sent a record keeper [*commentarensius*] with many soldiers and he arrested those whom the public officials identified, and sent them to Caesarea for trial, and some he punished, others he dismissed after a whipping, and, having caused not little fear, he thus restored calm to the city.

[Translator's note: In Chapters 100–102, Salaphtha, her aunt, and her grandmother converted and received remuneration from Porphyry. After her grandmother's death, Salaphtha became a nun, renowned for her asceticism.]

(103.) The most blessed bishop Porphyry, after establishing the ecclesiastical standard and the whole order of the liturgy and having lived another few years after the consecration of the great church, was afflicted by an illness and set down a pious testament, naming many legatees. And, having entrusted all of the devout congregation to God, he fell asleep in peace with the saints, on the second day of the month Dystros,[23] in the year 420 according to Gazan reckoning. He had been a bishop for twenty-four years, eleven months, and eight days, and carried on the good fight against the idol-maniacs until the day of his eternal rest. And now he is in the paradise of delight, interceding with all the saints on our behalf. Through their prayers may God the Father, and the Son and the Holy Spirit have mercy on us, to whom be praise and power from eternity to eternity. Amen.

Notes

1. There were several monastic settlements in this region, west of the Nile Delta.

2. The first day of the Gazan month of Dios corresponded to October 28 of the Roman calendar.

3. The first day of the Gazan month of Apellaios corresponded to November 27 of the Roman calendar.

4. Both were executed during the persecution of Christians under Emperor Diocletian, Maiouros in Gaza and Thee in Diocaesarea.

5. Literally "Hellenes." Among Christian authors of this period, the word specifically refers to pagans.

6. According to a different branch of the manuscript tradition, that number was one hundred and five.

7. The ancient Roman prohibition against the presence of dead bodies inside cities was reaffirmed in a law of 381: "All bodies that are contained in urns or sarcophaguses and are kept above ground shall be carried and placed outside the City, that they may present an example of humanity and may leave to the homes of citizens their sanctity." *The Theodosian Code*, trans. Clyde Pharr (Princeton, 1952), bk. 9, chap. 17, sec. 6, p. 240.

8. John Chrysostom became patriarch of Constantinople in 398. He was deposed in 404 and died in exile three years later, the victim of an extensive intrigue among imperial and ecclesiastical circles.

9. John's relationship with Eudoxia is described by Kenneth Holum, *Theodosian Empresses. Women and Imperial Dominion in Late Antiquity* (Berkeley, 1982), pp. 54–56, 72–78.

10. Eudoxia had three daughters before, and another one after the birth of her son Theodosius II.

11. Theodosius II was born on April 10, 401, and was proclaimed co-emperor with his father, Arcadius, the following year. He ruled the eastern Roman Empire from 408 to 450.

12. Theodosius I was born in 347 at Cauca in modern Spain. From 379 until his death in 395, he ruled over the eastern Roman Empire. Gratian ruled over the western Empire from 375 to 383.

13. The use of the color purple was strictly reserved for the emperor and his family. Thus, to be "born in the purple" indicated a claim to future rulership.

14. That is, they made the sign of the cross over him.

15. The baptism took place on January 6, 402.

16. Brilliant white was the color of the dress of angels and of the robes worn at baptism.

17. This is an honorary rank, assigned at the discretion of the emperor.

18. This is the highest hereditary social rank.

19. Purity regulations surrounding birth required that Eudoxia could only receive Porphyry in the palace after seven days (see Chapter 45) and could not attend the baptism of her son.

20. The law must have been issued in the name of the two ruling emperors, Arcadius and Honorius, before the official proclamation of Theodosius II as emperor which occurred four days after his baptism, on January 10, 402.

21. This is more likely polemical commonplace than historical fact.

22. The Septuagint has: "a great King above all gods."

23. Porphyry died on February 26, 420. The first day of the Gazan month of Dystros corresponds to February 25 according to the Roman calendar.

Chapter 4
Constantine the Great, the Empress Helena, and the Relics of the Holy Cross
Edited and translated by E. Gordon Whatley

Introduction

The texts translated in this chapter belong to a hagiographic subgenre, *inventio* (literally "finding" or "discovery"), which deals with the discovery of the relics of Christian saints. Modern historians have come to recognize how important such relics could be to a particular community, not only because they were regarded as sacred vessels or channels of divine grace and healing power, but also because of their potential economic and political uses. Narratives of their discovery can thus be of great historical and cultural interest. Early examples of the *inventio* genre survive from shortly before and after the turn of the fifth century and provide vivid evidence of the increasing commitment of the Christian hierarchy to relic cults. The *inventio* texts, which appear both as separate compositions and also as episodes embedded in larger literary contexts such as histories, sermons and letters, exhibit an array of shared narrative motifs, including visions or other divine promptings initiating the search for long-buried relics; episodes of obstruction, delay, and resistance; inscriptions and documents; prayers and miracles (including expulsion of demons) that facilitate the discovery, or help authenticate the relics; and the enshrinement and/or distribution of the precious remains.

The relic of the "Holy Cross" at the center of the *inventio* narratives below is the wooden gibbet on which, according to the gospels, Jesus was crucified and which bore the inscription "Jesus of Nazareth, Kings of the Jews." None of the gospels mentions what happened to the Cross after Jesus' death and resurrection. We are told how the Roman soldiers who executed him divided up his clothes between them by casting lots, but nothing is said about how the Cross and nails, the inscription, or the crown of thorns and other objects mentioned in the story, were disposed of. The silence of the gospels seems to have stimulated rather than impeded interest in such things. In succeeding centuries all the material relics of the Crucifixion were to become objects of religious devotion and the subjects of legends and miracle tales witnessing to their physical survival in different parts of Christendom.

The most important of the relics, however, was the Cross. Not only was it seen as the original agent of Christian salvation, but, as Bishop Cyril of

Jerusalem told his catechumens assembled in 348–50 in the basilica dedicated to it, the Cross like the Holy Places themselves was visible proof that the Crucifixion had taken place: "The holy wood of the Cross bears witness, seen among us to this day, and from this place now fills the whole world by means of those who in faith take portions from it." This clear statement that the wood was physically present in Jerusalem, and that fragments of it were taken home by pilgrims, has usually been regarded as the earliest reference to the Cross as a Christian relic. While Cyril says nothing about how the precious timbers came to light, it has been suggested recently, by Stephan Borgehammar among others, that one cryptic and reticent passage in the writings of Eusebius, a decade earlier than Cyril, is evidence that the wooden beams believed to be those of the Holy Cross were unearthed when Bishop Macarius of Jerusalem was clearing the site of Golgotha and the Holy Sepulcher under orders from the emperor Constantine (ca. 326).

It was not until seventy years after the putative discovery, however, around the turn of the century, when stories of relic discoveries had become fashionable among the clerical elite in the Latin West, that a spate of accounts of the discovery of the Cross issued from important authors such as Bishop Ambrose of Milan, Rufinus of Aquilea, and Paulinus of Nola. All of them credit the dowager empress Helena (ca. 250–330), Constantine's aging mother, with conducting the excavations on Golgotha and with the actual discovery of the Cross, albeit with Bishop Macarius's help. Most modern historians are skeptical about these accounts, agreeing only that Helena, as Eusebius relates in his *Life of Constantine*, made an imposing pilgrimage or "progress" to the Holy Places some years before her death. While there, she supervised construction of churches on the Mount of Olives, where Jesus is believed to have ascended to heaven, and in Bethlehem where he was born.

The late-fourth/early-fifth-century narratives that initiated the legend of Helena and the True Cross in the Latin West are represented below by the account of Rufinus, which comprises two chapters from Books 9 and 10 of his *Church History* (written ca. 402) and deals first with the emperor Constantine's vision of the Cross and his ensuing victory over his rival Maxentius, followed by Helena's finding of the Cross in Jerusalem. Rufinus, longtime friend of St. Jerome (who later grew hostile to him), spent much of his life studying monastic life and theology in Egypt and Palestine and publishing Latin editions of important Greek writings, including portions of the so-called *Lives of the Fathers* (*Vitae patrum*) and the works of Origen. He died in Sicily in 410. His *Church History* is a translation and continuation of the earlier *Church History* of Eusebius of Caesarea (written ca. 316/17). Rufinus's account of Constantine's victory over Maxentius draws on Eusebius's *History* but incorporates additional material from the latter's *Life of Constantine* (ca. 340) and other sources; for his story of the *inventio* proper, Rufinus drew on traditions current in Palestine or Jerusalem itself in the late fourth century (for example, a now-lost *Church History* written in the last quarter of the fourth century by Bishop Gelasius of Caesarea, nephew of

Cyril of Jerusalem). The result is an artful amalgam of history and legend making.

The anonymous *Inventio sanctae Crucis* (henceforth simply *Inventio*), retells the Cross story known to Rufinus and his contemporaries, incorporating many of the details they provided but also expanding and changing the story considerably. For example, Constantine's vision is reworked so that the enemy is now a barbarian horde, not a fellow emperor, while Helena's adventures now involve her in a series of stylized confrontations with the Jews, culminating in the resistance and conversion of Judas Cyriacus. The resulting hybrid legend moves away from historical verisimilitude toward myth in order to dramatize the process by which Christianity ousted Roman paganism as the religion of the emperors and appropriated for the new Romans the status and power of God's chosen people. Helena's speeches to the assembly of Jewish elders echo early Christian polemic in asserting that the Jews had willfully misinterpreted scripture, resisted the Old Testament prophecies, and crucified Christ, thereby forfeiting to the Gentiles their status as God's chosen. To signal the emergence of Christianity as the dominant religion of the empire, Helena's encounter with the hapless Judas wryly mimics the typical clash of pagan persecutor and Christian martyr by reversing the traditional pattern and values of the Christian *passio* or martyrdom narrative: here in the *Inventio* the misguided "martyr" capitulates and converts to the righteous persecutor's faith. The triumph of the Cross is thus seen to sanctify imperial power, deheroicize resistance to the state, and validate forced conversions of Jews.

The oldest extant version of the *Inventio* legend, represented by two Syriac manuscripts of the fifth-sixth century, was long thought to represent the original, but recent textual study by Borgehammar concludes that the work was composed not in Syria but in Palestine, in Greek, in the first half of the fifth century, and translated into Latin (and from Latin into Syriac) shortly afterward. The Latin rendering became known in the West at least by the first half of the sixth century, when it appears to have given rise to the Roman church festival or feast of May 3. During subsequent centuries both legend and feast became widely known across Europe. With its simple, repetitive, but far from artless style, the *Inventio* narrative would have been quite comprehensible to most inhabitants of the Latin parts of the former Roman Empire during the early Middle Ages. In my translation I have not tried to smooth away the crudity and rough music of this "Low Latin." Further, since an important element of the style is its frequent use of scriptural quotations and echoes, I have tried to signal as many of the borrowings as possible, either with italics where the correspondence seems fairly exact, or simply with references following the relevant passages. All the references are keyed to the Latin Vulgate text, which frequently differs from the standard modern translations based on the Hebrew and Greek originals.

The best modern edition of the *Inventio sanctae Crucis* is Stephan Borgehammar's eclectic reconstruction based on several Latin and Greek manuscripts (*How the Holy Cross Was Found: From Event to Medieval Legend*,

Bibliotheca Theologicae Practicae, Kyrkovetenskapliga studier 47 [Stockholm, 1991], pp. 154–61), but I have preferred here to translate a specific Latin manuscript version, complete with its variations and corruptions, as more typical of the sort of text in actual use in early medieval Europe (in a few instances where this version makes no sense, I have silently adopted readings from Borgehammar's edition). The text was transcribed in a monastery in Castile in northern Spain during the tenth century, as part of a large manuscript "legendary" containing saints' *Lives* intended for reading during church services or during meals in the monastery's refectory or dining room. The textual tradition represented in this manuscript probably derives from much older Spanish copies, since the legend would have been used for liturgical readings during the church services held on the May 3 festival of the Invention of the Cross in the late seventh century, when the feast was already among the most important in the Visigothic church calendar. Along with Easter and Christmas, it was one of a small group of feasts that the Jews of Spain, under the aggressively anti-Judaic Visigothic kings, were required by law to "observe with solicitous devotion." Since they spoke the local Latin dialect the Spanish Jews could not have avoided understanding the *Inventio*'s forcefully anti-Judaic message.

Copies of the *Inventio* text were known in England at least by the ninth century, if not earlier, but there only the best educated clergy could read it in Latin, with the result that it soon became the basis of an elaborate Old English verse rendering, Cynewulf's *Elene*, and a century or more later was translated into Old English prose. The tenth-century English homilist Ælfric, who scrupulously avoided translating works that seemed to him to lack proper "authority," pointedly chose Rufinus's version, which he believed to be by Jerome, as the basis for his brief Old English prose homily on the feast of the Cross Invention.

SOURCES AND FURTHER READINGS

Rufinus of Aquileia's Latin account of Constantine's vision of the Cross and of Helena's discovery of the Cross (*Bibliotheca hagiographica latina*, no. 4164) are in his *Historia Ecclesiastica*, ed. Theodor Mommsen, Die griechischen christlichen Schriftsteller der ersten drei Jahrhunderte 9.2 (Berlin, 1909), bk. 9, chap. 9 and bk. 10, chaps. 7–8, pp. 827–33, 969–71. The text of the anonymous *Inventio sanctae Crucis* translated here (*Bibliotheca hagiographica latina*, no. 4169) is that of *Pasionario Hispánico*, ed. A. Fábrega Grau, Monumenta Hispaniae Sacra, Serie Liturgica 6.2 (Madrid and Barcelona, 1955), pp. 260–66. The *Inventio* was most recently translated, from his own new edition, by Stephan Borgehammar in *How the Holy Cross Was Found: From Event to Medieval Legend*, Bibliotheca Theologicae Practicae, Kyrkovetenskapliga studier 47 (Stockholm, 1991), pp. 154–61. Borgehammar also discusses the other Latin and Greek versions of the Cross Invention, providing information and bibliography on their historical background and sources; see also Jan Willem Drijvers, *Helena Augusta: the Mother of Con-*

stantine the Great and the Legend of Her Finding of the True Cross (Leiden and New York, 1992). On Helena's visit to the East and other royal pilgrimages, see E. D. Hunt, *Holy Land Pilgrimage in the Later Roman Empire AD 312–460* (Oxford, 1982). On Christian anti-Judaism in general, see James Parkes, *The Conflict of the Church and the Synagogue: A Study in the Origins of Anti-Semitism*, revised ed. (New York, 1979); on the position of the Jews in Medieval Spain, see Roger Collins, *Early Medieval Spain. Unity in Diversity, 400–1000*, second edition (Oxford, 1995) pp.128–43. For the Old English versions, see P.O.E. Gradon, *Cynewulf's Elene* (Exeter, 1977), which is translated by S.A.J. Bradley, *Anglo-Saxon Poetry* (London, 1982) pp. 164–97; Benjamin Thorpe, *The Homilies of the Anglo-Saxon Church*, 2 vols. (London 1844–46), 2:302–06; Mary-Catherine Bodden, *The Old English Finding of the True Cross* (Woodbridge, Suffolk, 1987).

Constantine the Great, the Empress Helena, and the Relics of the Holy Cross

Rufinus of Aquileia, Church History, *Book 9, Chapter 9, Sections 1–11*[1]

Constantine, the most devout emperor, son of the most virtuous and excellent ruler Constantius[2], was at the head of his army preparing to do battle against Maxentius, the tyrant of the city of Rome.[3] At this time Constantine was already a supporter of the Christian religion and a worshipper of the true God but had not yet received the sign of the Lord's passion, which is our custom in the rite of holy baptism. During the journey, anxiously going over the many things needed for the approaching battle, and often raising his eyes to heaven to pray for divine aid, he fell into a trance and saw in the east the sign of the cross shining in heaven with fiery radiance. Then, terrified as he was by such a vision and such a strange sight, he saw angels standing near him and saying, "Constantine, conquer with this."[4] When he came to himself, feeling happy and already confident of victory, he marked on his forehead the sign of the Cross that he had seen in the sky.[5] It seems to me indeed, since he was brought into the faith in this way, by heavenly means, that he was no whit inferior to the man to whom a voice from heaven said, "*Saul, Saul, why do you persecute me? I am Jesus of Nazareth,*" [Acts 4:5] except that Constantine was brought in not as a former persecutor but as a follower.[6]

As a result he transformed the sign revealed to him in heaven into military banners, adapting what they call the *labarum* in the shape of the Lord's Cross.[7] And thus equipped with the arms and banners of religion, he set out to oppose the arms of the wicked. But also in his right hand he is said to have held the sign of the Cross fashioned in gold (I certainly do not think it unreasonable to make known a little more than has already been published of that devout general's exploits in this war). But even now that he had been assured of victory with the help of divine power, the mind of this devout ruler surged nonetheless with another sorrow: namely, that although he had been elected Roman emperor and father of the fatherland, and desired, if he could, to surpass in religion and virtue all those who had undertaken the leadership before him, he was being compelled to make war not only on the fatherland but also on the city of Rome itself, the capital of the Roman empire; for he could not restore the fatherland's liberty without attacking the fatherland that the tyrant occupied.[8] Hence his spirit was tormented, and day and night he prayed to the god whom he sensed was his friend, to avoid staining with Roman blood that right hand which he had strengthened with the saving sign. Day and night he begged for this, and divine providence granted his prayer.

And when Constantine had pitched his camp not far from the Milvian Bridge,[9] behold Maxentius, as if suddenly gripped by a divine force, felt impelled to attack. Rushing outside the gates of the city of Rome he ordered the army behind him to follow, for he had armed himself earlier than the rest and was running on ahead. Moreover, he had previously ordered ships to be strung out in a line abreast of one another, with pontoon bridges laid across them, as a trap.[10] But now he forgot about this plan and when he himself, as both cavalry and vanguard, rode onto the bridge with a few followers, the ships gave way and he was drowned in the deep water. Thus the slaughter that would have occurred in the war was thwarted by the death of its evil instigator, and the immaculate right hand of the devout prince was kept clean of the citizens' blood.

Indeed, it is just as appropriate to say of this event, as was said of what befell Moses and the Hebrew people: "*Pharoah's chariots and his host he cast into the sea, and his picked riders and their teams of equerries he has drowned in the Red Sea; the deep has swallowed them up*" [Ex 15:4, Septuagint]. And so Maxentius and his armored retinue were drowned in the deep, he was overthrown by the very bridges that he had devised for the destruction of the devout prince. Of this it would be fitting to say, "*He made a pit and dug it out, and fell into the hole he had made. His mischief returns upon his own head and his violence descends upon his own pate*" [Ps 7:16–17]. These words fit the wicked ones perfectly, but to Constantine, as to God's servant, one might apply those words that Moses sang after the victory when his enemies were destroyed: "*Let us sing to the Lord, for gloriously has he been honored; horse and rider he has cast into the sea. Who is like thee, Lord, among the gods? Who is like thee, glorious among the saints, wondrous in splendor, doing marvelous things?*" [Ex 15.11, Septuagint]. Thus Constantine entered the city of Rome in triumph, singing songs like these (not with these words, but with similar contents) in honor of God on high from whom he had obtained the victory. And then the happy Senate and the Roman people, all with their wives and children, freed from the great plague, redeemed from the yoke of tyrannical savagery, welcomed Constantine as the author of their safety and restorer of their liberty. He did not, however, let himself wallow in the praises that the people were shouting or in the applause of such a great city, nor did he attribute what he had just done to his own efforts, but rather to divine support. As a result, wherever the Senate set up statues of him to honor him in his triumph, he immediately ordered the standard of the Cross of the Lord to be sculpted in his right hand and inscribed beneath with these words: "By means of this extraordinary sign, the symbol of true power, I have rescued the city of Rome, and the Senate and the Roman people, from the yoke of tyranny and oppression, and I have restored them to their former liberty and dignity."

Rufinus of Aquileia, Church History, *Book. 10. Chapters 7–8*

Helena, the mother of Constantine, was a woman of unparalleled faith and religion, and of extraordinary greatness of soul. Constantine not only was believed to be, but really was, her son. Around this time,[11] prompted by divine visions, she went to Jerusalem and there made inquiries among the local inhabitants about the place in which the sacred body of Christ had hung, nailed to the scaffold. It was not easy to find, because a statue of Venus had been mounted there by the persecutors of old[12] with the intention that if any of the Christians of that place wanted to adore Christ, they would appear to be adoring Venus. And for that reason the place had fallen into disuse and was virtually forgotten. But when, as we said earlier, the devout woman had hastened to the place pointed out to her by divine guidance, and when she pulled down from there all the profane and polluting objects, and excavated all the rubble, deep down she found three crosses jumbled together. But her happiness at this precious discovery was disturbed by the fact that the crosses were indistinguishable from one another. It is true that the inscription was there, which had been written by Pilate *in Greek and Latin and Hebrew characters* [Lk 23:26, Jn 19:18–19],[13] but it did not give a clear enough indication as to which was the Lord's scaffold. So now human doubt and uncertainty needed to be resolved by divine testimony. It happened that in that same city a high-ranking woman resident had been stricken with a serious illness and was lying close to death. Macarius was bishop of the church there at that time and when he saw that neither the queen nor all those present could decide, he said, "Bring with us all the crosses that were found and God will reveal to us now which one carried God." And he went in, with the queen and the people as well, to the woman who was lying sick, and he fell to his knees and poured out his prayer to God in this way: "O Lord, who by your only-begotten son deigned to bring salvation to the human race through his passion on the Cross and now most recently have inspired the heart of your handmaid to seek out the blessed wood on which our salvation hung, show us clearly which of these three crosses was for the glory of the Lord, and which were merely for the punishment of wretched men, by causing this woman who lies here half alive to be called back to life from the doors of death the moment the wood of salvation touches her." And when he had said this, he touched her first with one of the three crosses and it did no good; he touched her with a second and nothing happened; but when he moved the third toward her, the woman suddenly opened her eyes and raised herself and, filled with health and strength much more vigorous than when she had been well before, she began to run about all over the house magnifying the power of the Lord.

And so, after this unmistakable demonstration, the queen's desire had been fulfilled, and she built a wonderful temple, royally ambitious in scale, on the site where she had found the Cross,[14] and the nails also, with which the Lord's body had been fastened [to the Cross] she carried back to her son. From these she fashioned a bridle, which he used in battle, and it is said that he also armed his helmet with them, ready for use in battle. She took part of the wood of salvation to her son, but part she left there, enclosed in a silver casing, and it is still honored on the feast day, with passionate veneration.[15]

The venerable queen also left behind her the following demonstration of her devout spirit. They say that she would invite to dinner the virgins whom she found there consecrated to God[16] and that she cared for them with such devotion that she thought it unfitting to make use of servants, but rather, donning a serving-woman's garb, she would lay out their food with her own hands, proffer them the cup, and pour water on their hands: thus the queen of the world, the mother of the empire, would assume the role of handmaiden to Christ's handmaidens.

These events took place in Jerusalem. Meanwhile Constantine, trusting in piety, overcame the Sarmatians, Goths, and other barbarian nations in battle on their own soil, except for those who made peace with him in friendship or by capitulation. And the more devoutly and humbly he submitted himself to God, the more freely God brought everything under his control.

Inventio Sanctae Crucis, from a Tenth-Century Spanish Legendary

(1.) The reading from the Ecclesiastical History, on the finding of the Holy Cross, which Elene Augusta discovered on the third of May. Thanks be to God.

(2.) In the two hundred and thirty-third year after the passion of our Lord Jesus Christ, in the reign of the venerable Constantine, a worshipper of God, a great man, in the sixth year of his reign, a great nation of barbarians assembled above the river Danube, assembled for war against Romania.[17] But this was made known to King Constantine. And he himself *assembled a host of troops* [Judg 9:29], and set off to meet them, and found them, for they had already crossed over into the territories of Romania, and they were beside the Danube. When he saw that they were a countless multitude, Constantine was *very sorrowful* and fearful *even unto death* [Mt 26:38; see also 1 Mac 9:6; Ex 14:10].

That very same night a most radiant man came and roused him and said to him, "Constantine, do not be afraid, but look up to heaven and see." And turning toward heaven, he saw the sign of the Cross, gleaming, made of light, and written upon it with letters was an inscription: "With this sign, conquer."[18] Seeing this sign, King Constantine bestirred himself and made a likeness of the cross which he had seen in the sky, and he rose up and launched an attack against the barbarians, and he caused the sign of the Cross to go before him, and overtaking the barbarians with his army at dawn, he began to cut them to pieces, and the barbarians were afraid and fled away along the banks of the Danube, and on that day died a great multitude; and on that day God blessed the victory of King Constantine through the power of the Holy Cross.

(3.) Returning then to his own city, King Constantine summoned all the priests of all the gods or idols: and he asked of them whose sign this Cross was or what it might be, and they could not tell him. But then certain of them answered and said, "This is the sign of the God of heaven." A few Christians there at that time heard about this and came to the King and *preached to him* [Acts 8:35] the mystery of the Trinity and the coming of the son of God, how he was born and was crucified and on the third day rose again. King Constantine then sent to Eusebius, the bishop of the city of Rome,[19] and made him come to him, and he taught him all the faith of the Christians, all its mysteries, and baptized him in the name of the Lord Jesus Christ and he was confirmed in the faith of the Holy Spirit. Then he gave orders for churches of Christ to be built everywhere, but for the temples of the idols to be destroyed. Then the blessed Constantine was perfect in the faith, and dedicating himself to the Holy Spirit he studied the holy gospels of Christ [see Rom 7:6; Ps 118:15]. When he had learned from the holy gospels where the Lord was crucified, he sent his mother, Helena, to seek out the holy wood of the Lord's Cross and to build a church of the Lord in that very place. And the grace of the Holy Spirit rested in the blessed Helena, mother of the emperor Constantine.[20]

(4.) She studied all the holy writings and took boundless delight in our Lord Jesus Christ. And henceforth she sought after the healing wood of the Holy Cross. When she had read intently of the coming of the savior of humankind, our Lord Jesus Christ, and how he was taken up on the cross and raised again from the dead, she would not be satisfied until she found Christ's victorious wood, to which the divine and holy body was nailed. She found it in this way.

(5.) On the twenty-eighth day of the second month,[21] she entered the holy city of Jerusalem together with a very great army. She assembled there a great assembly of the Jews, that most wicked nation, but she ordered not only those who were in the city to assemble but also those Jews who were in the strongholds, estates, and cities roundabout. But Jerusalem was deserted at that time, so on that day only three thousand men of the Jews were to be found.[22] When she had called them together, the most blessed Helena said, "From the books of the holy prophets I learned you were beloved of God. But you all rejected wisdom [see Hos 4:6]; you cursed him who wished to redeem you from the accursed one;[23] and him who lightened your eyes with his spittle, you defiled with your loathsome spitting; and him who raised your dead to life, you delivered to death [Mk 8:23, 14:65; Jn 11:44, 11:50]. And thus, in a word, you thought light was darkness and truth falsehood [see Is 5:20; Rom 1:25], and there came upon you the curse that is written in your law.[24] Now choose from among yourselves men who know your law thoroughly, to give me answers to the questions I will ask them." They withdrew in great fear, and after holding a great consultation among themselves, they found those who said they knew the law—in number a thousand men—and bringing them to the blessed Helena, they stood and bore witness that these men had great knowledge of the law.

(6.) Blessed Helena said to these men, "*Hear* my words and *give ear to my sayings* [Is 1:2; 28:23]. For you did not understand in the sayings of the prophets [see Mt 13:14] how they prophesied concerning the coming of Christ. It is because of this that I am questioning you today. Moses was the first to prophesy, saying, 'For a boy *will be born* and his mother will *not know a man*' [Lk 1:34–35]. And again David, the writer of hymns, says, '*I foresaw the Lord in my sight always; for he is on my right hand lest I should be moved*' [Ps 15:8].[25] And Isaiah says concerning you, '*I have borne sons and exalted them, but they have rejected me. The ox knows his owner and the ass his lord's crib. But Israel has not known me and my people have not under-*

stood me' [Is 1:2–3]. And every portion of Scripture has spoken concerning him. Therefore you who were learned in the law have erred. So now choose men who have gotten knowledge of the law and who might answer my questioning." And she commanded the soldiers to guard them with the utmost diligence.

(7.) Taking counsel with one another, they chose five hundred men, the best teachers of the law, and they came and stood in her presence. And she said, "Who are these?" and they said "They are the men who know the law best." And again most blessed Helena began to teach them: "O truly stupid men, you sons of Israel, you who according to the Scriptures followed the blindness of your fathers, who say that Jesus is not the son of God, who read the law and the prophets, and do not understand."[26] Then they answered, "Indeed, we read and we do understand; for what reason, lady, do you say such things to us? Reveal [it] to us plainly. Once we know, we can answer the things you are saying." But she said to them again, "Nevertheless, go and choose better men." And as they left, they said among themselves, "For what reason do you think the queen imposes this burden on us?" One of them, named Judas, said to them: "I know that she wishes to inquire about the wood on which our fathers hung up Christ. See to it that no one confesses to her: for surely the traditions of our fathers shall be destroyed [see Acts 6:16] and the law reduced to nothing. Zacheus, my grandfather, proclaimed to my father, Simeon, and my father in turn, when he was dying, proclaimed to me, saying, "Beware, my son, of the day when inquiry is made concerning the wood to which our predecessors condemned the Messiah: reveal it before you are tortured. For from that time the race of the Hebrews shall reign [no] longer, but the kingdom will belong to them who worship him who was crucified.[27] He himself *will reign world without end* [Rev 11:15] amen; for he himself is *Christ, the son of the living God*" [Mt 16:16]. But I said to him, "Father, if your fathers knew he was Christ, why *did they lay hands on him?*" [Mk 14:46]. And he said to me, "*Hear, my son* [Prov 1:8] and learn his ways and his indescribable name. I was never of their counsel, nor did I agree with them,[28] but several times indeed I spoke against them. But because he reproved the elders and chief priests, for that reason they condemned him to be crucified, thinking to put to death the deathless one [see Acts 3:15]. And after taking him down from the Cross, they buried him. But on the third day after he was buried he rose again and revealed himself to his disciples. Because of this your brother Stephen[29] believed and began to teach in his name. And after taking counsel with one another, the Pharisees and Sadducees condemned him to be stoned. And a crowd of people took him off and stoned him. But that blessed man, as *he gave up the ghost* [Jn 19:30], stretching his hands toward heaven, prayed and *said, 'Lord, blame not this sin on them'* [Acts 7:59]. *Hear me*, therefore, *my son* [Prov 1:8], and I will teach you about Christ and his goodness. For Saul, who would sit before the Temple and practice *the craft of tent-maker* [Acts 18:3], was also persecuting those who believed in Christ, and he stirred up the people against [your] brother

Stephen; and the Lord was moved by pity for him and made him one of his holy disciples. On account of this I and my fathers believed in him, that *truly he is the son of God* [Mt 27:54; Mk 16:39]. And now, son, do not blaspheme him or those who believe in him, and you will have life eternal."

(8.) "My father Simeon bore witness of these things to me. Now you have heard everything. What do you think should be done if she questions us about the wood of the Cross?" The rest of them said, "We have never heard such things as these from you today. But if there is an investigation concerning this (cross), see that you do not reveal it: yet from all you have said, it is clear that you know the place." Just as they were saying this, the soldiers came to them saying, "Come, the queen calls you." When they came before her, they were formally questioned by her, but they would say nothing of the truth. Then blessed Helena ordered them to be cast into the fire, and in their fear they surrendered Judas to her, saying, "This is the son of an *upright man and a prophet* [Mt 13:17], and he knows the law best. He will correctly show you this, lady, and everything your heart desires." And while they were all at once supplying this testimony, she dismissed them and kept Judas alone. And summoning him before her she said, "*Life and death are offered to you; choose* [Deut 30:19] for yourself which one you want: life or death." Judas said, "And what man, left alone in the desert, has eaten *stones* when *loaves* were offered to him?" [see Mt 4:3, 7:9]. Blessed Helena said, "If you wish to live on earth and in heaven, tell me where the precious wood of the Cross has been hidden away."

(9.) Judas said, "According to what is said in the memorials, it was two hundred years ago, more or less: and since we are not that old, how can we know?" Blessed Helena said, "How then is it that, though the war was waged in Ilium and Troy so many generations ago, yet all who died there are still remembered, and a record of their tombs and places of burial is preserved in writing?" Judas said, "Doubtless, my lady, because those events were indeed written down. But we do not have these other things written down." Blessed Helena said, "Only a short while ago, you yourself revealed that there are memorials: why do you now say that we do not have these things in written form?" Judas said, "I spoke in doubt." The blessed Helena said, "I have the blessed voice of the Gospels to tell me in which place he was crucified. Only make known to me *the place that is called Calvary* [Lk 23:33] and I will have the place purified[30] and perhaps I may find the object of my desire." Judas said, "I do not know the place either, because I was not alive at that time." Blessed Helena said, "By him who was crucified, I will have you starved to death if you do not tell me the truth." And with that she commanded him to be put in a dry pit and to stay there without food for seven days. And when the seven days had passed, Judas shouted from the pit, saying, "I beseech you, bring me out of here [see Ps 29:3–4], and I will show you the Cross of Christ."

(10.) When he had ascended from the pit he went straight to the place, and not knowing the exact spot where the Cross of Christ lay, he raised his voice to the Lord in the Hebrew tongue: "Hiit sata brimilas filo annobonaht biroheboem lemedoc eliazel zathfahic kautiubruc kata Hodonahi Heloy eloconas. Abraxio attedau baruhc Srahel athamas Trambizona mahcata David dabia haruel beelbemon seyrgemat Iesu."[31] Which means: "God, my God, *who made heaven and earth* [Is 37.16], who measured heaven with the palm of your hand and spanned the earth with your fist [see Is 40:12], *who sit upon* the chariot of *the cherubim* [Is 37:16], you who alone have immortality and dwell in unapproachable light, whom no man sees or is able to see, and for whom is honor and empire everlasting. With you are *four living creatures covered in front and behind with eyes* [Rev 4:6] and *having each six wings* [Is 6:2, Rev 4:8] flying on the courses of the air into the light immense where humankind cannot go; for you are he who made them to serve you; and of the living creatures who have six wings each, four of them, serving you as they fly, are *saying, "Holy, holy, holy"* [Rev 4:8] and are called Cherubim; but two of them that *you have posted in paradise to guard the wood of life* [Gen 3:24] are called Seraphim. *You are lord over all things* [1 Chron 29:12], for *we are* your *handiwork* [Eph 2:10], you who put away the unbelieving *angels, dragged down with chains, in* the depths of *Tartarus* and in the bottom of the abyss it is their lot *to be tortured* [2 Pet 2:4] by the fury of serpents [see Ps 57:5], and they cannot resist your command. And now, lord, if it is your will for the *son of Mary* [Mk 6:3] to reign, who was sent by you—for if he had not been of you, he would not have done such great wonders, if he had not been your child, you would not *have awakened him from among the dead* [Acts 3:15]— *make* this *miracle* for us, *lord* [Acts 4:30], and just as you heard the prayer of your servant Moses and revealed to him the bones of our father Joseph, in the same way, Lord, if it is your will, show us the hidden treasure: cause to arise, from the place where it lies, a fire that smells of spices of sweetness,[32] that I might believe in Christ crucified, that he is king of Israel now, and world without end, Amen."

(11.) And when Judas *had finished praying,* at once *the place shook* [Acts 4:31] and a great cloud of smoke, fragrant with sweet spices, ascended to the heavens; so that Judas, marveling, clapped his hands together and said: "In truth, O Christ, you are the savior of the world [see Jn 4:42]: I give thanks to you, Lord Jesus Christ, because, although I am unworthy, you have not cheated me of a share in your grace. I beseech you, Lord Jesus Christ, that, although I am unworthy, you will not be mindful of my sins, but number me with my brother Stephen, whose story is written in the Acts of the Apostles."[33] When he had said this, he took a spade and girded himself in manly fashion, and began to dig.[34] And when he had dug down thirty feet, he found the three crosses that had been hidden away, and bringing them out, he took them into the city. Blessed Helena questioned him then as to which cross was Christ's, saying, "We know that there were two others, belonging to *the thieves crucified with him*" [Mt 27:37]. And they put them down in the center of the city and awaited the glory of Christ. And about the ninth hour a young man who had died was carried past on a bier: Judas, filled with joy, said, "Now, my lady, you will recognize the most beloved wood and its power."

And Judas made them stop the bier and put down the dead man, and he laid (two of) the crosses over him one by one, and he did not arise; then he laid the third cross, the Lord's, upon the dead man, and at once the young man who had been dead arose, and all who were there glorified the Lord.

(12.) But the enemy, ever envious of all good things, in a fury cried aloud in the air, saying, "Who is this once again who does not let me claim their souls?[35] O Jesus of Nazareth, you have drawn all to yourself; and behold, now you have displayed your wood against me. O Judas, what have you done? Was it not by means of a Judas a while ago that I committed treachery and incited the people to do evil [see Lk 22:3; Jn 13:2]. And now, behold, by a Judas I am cast out of here. But I will find a way to oppose you: I will raise up another [ruler], who will abandon the crucified one and follow my counsels, and subject you to wicked torments, and after being tortured you will deny the crucified."[36] But Judas, *burning in the* Holy *Spirit* [Acts 18:25], said to him, "Christ himself, who raised up the dead, will damn you to the abyss of eternal fire." And hearing this, blessed Helena marveled at the faith of Judas. Then with great care she adorned the precious Cross with gold and precious stones, and made a silver casket in which she placed the Cross of Christ; and constructed a church on the site of Calvary itself. Judas received the baptism of incorruption in Christ Jesus; he was shown to be a believer by the preceding miracles and she commended him to the current bishop, who baptized him in Christ Jesus. While blessed Helena was still residing in Jerusalem, it happened that the blessed bishop fell asleep in Christ Jesus. Blessed Helen summoned Eusebius, bishop of the city of Rome,[37] and he ordained Judas bishop of the Jerusalem church of Christ, and changed his name, and he was called Quiriacus.[38]

(13.) Then the blessed Helena, filled with faith in God and understanding the scriptures of the Old and New Testaments, instructed and filled with the Holy Spirit, began in turn to seek for the nails which had been fastened to the cross, and with which the wicked Jews [had] crucified the Savior. And summoning Judas, who was also called Quiriacus, she said to him: "With regard to the wood of the Cross, my desire is fulfilled; but about the fastenings, the nails which were fastened to it, I have enormous sadness. I will have no relief from this until the Lord *fulfills my desire* [Phil 4:19]; you must set to and deal with this also by praying to the Lord." And so the holy bishop Quiriacus came to the site of Calvary, together with many brethren who had believed in the Lord Jesus Christ because of the finding of the Holy Cross and the miracle worked on the dead man. And *raising his eyes to heaven and striking his breast* [Lk 18:14] with his hands at the same time, he cried out to the Lord with all his heart [see Ps 118:145], confessing his *former ignorance* [1 Pet 1:14], and blessing all who had believed in Christ and who were about to believe in his name. And when he had prayed for a long time for some sign to be shown to him, just as happened with the Cross, so with the nails, at the end of his prayer, when he was saying "Amen," there occurred such a miracle that all of us present saw it. A great radiant light, brighter than the light of the sun, broke from the place where the Holy Cross was found, and straightway those nails appeared, which had been fixed in the Lord's body, shining like gold in the earth, so that everyone, believing and free from doubt, said, "Now we know in whom we believe" [see Jn 6:70]. Plucking them out (of the ground) with great awe, he carried them to the venerable Helena, who knelt and bowed her head, and adored them.

(14.) Filled with wisdom and with much knowledge, she then pondered deeply as to what she should do with them. But since she had taken upon herself to seek out *the whole way* [Bar 3:37] of truth, the grace of the Holy Spirit gave her the idea of making something as a memorial for the generations to come, which the prophets had foretold many generations earlier. Summoning therefore a man faithful and well-taught, of whom many people gave a good report, she said, "Obey the king's command and fulfill the meaning of a kingly mystery. Take these nails and make them into a bit for the bridle of the king's horse. It will be an invincible weapon against all adversaries, (ensuring) victory for the kings and peace instead of war, that the prophet's words might be fulfilled: *And in that day, that which is on the horse's bridle will be called sacred to the Lord* [Zech 14:20]. Blessed Helena then, strengthening the faith in Jerusalem, and making all things perfect, visited persecution on the Jews who had remained unbelievers, and expelled them from Judea.[39] And such grace attended the holy Bishop Quiriacus that he drove out demons by prayer and healed all the infirmities of men. And blessed Helena, leaving many gifts for Quiriacus the bishop to minister to the poor, slept in peace,[40] requiring all who love Christ, men and women, to celebrate the commemoration of the day on which the Cross was found: the fifth before the Nones of May [May 3]. Whoever commemorates the Holy Cross receives everlasting reward through our Lord Jesus Christ crucified,

(15.) Who lives and reigns with the Father and the Holy Spirit, world without end. Amen.

Notes

1. Rufinus's account is adapted from Eusebius of Caesarea's *Church History*, Book 9, Chapter 9, and *Life of Constantine*, Book 1, Chapters 28–40.

2. Flavius Constantius, better known as Constantine, was a professional soldier who rose to become Caesar (junior emperor) of Gaul and Britain (from 303 to 305), and then Augustus (senior emperor) of the western Roman Empire (from 305 to his death in 306) after the joint abdication of Diocletian and Maximian. He was notably more tolerant of Christianity than his eastern counterparts, which may have influenced his son's conduct later. Constantine spent part of his youth at the court of Diocletian (essentially as a hostage), was elected to succeed his father by the Roman legions at York in 306, when not much older than twenty.

3. Maxentius, son of the former emperor Maximian, was emperor of Italy and Africa 306–12. Natural rivalries between himself and Constantine, aggravated by the complicated politics of the four-emperor system, resulted (in 312) in all-out war for supremacy in the western Roman Empire.

4. The famous command is first recorded by Eusebius of Caesarea (ca. 340), in his *Life of Constantine*, Book 1, Chapter 28, where it is said to be an inscription on the heavenly cross. Rufinus includes the command in both Greek and a Latin translation: only the Latin

translation is reflected here. The first account of the vision itself, but lacking the command, is that of Lactantius (writing ca. 315–20) in his *On the Deaths of the Persecutors* (*De mortibus persecutorum*), Book 1, Chapter 44.

5. Rufinus may be suggesting a quasi-baptismal gesture here.

6. According to Acts, Saul of Tarsus after participating in the stoning of the first Christian martyr, Stephen, was active on behalf of the Jewish authorities in persecuting and arresting the Christians of Jerusalem, until his own conversion (Acts 7:57; 7:59; 8:3; 9:1–19).

7. The *labarum* was an elaborate Roman military standard carried before an army and often bearing the commander's portrait. Constantine's *labarum* (pictured on numerous early Christian sarcophagi) apparently had the words "In this (sign) conquer" inscribed on the banner portion, while at the top of the ceremonial spear, on which the banner hung on a crosspiece, was the Chi-Rho symbol (also known as the Christogram).

8. Rufinus's tortured prose here, the account of the bloodless battle later, and the repeated characterization of Maxentius as "tyrant," are all designed to exonerate Constantine of the responsibility for waging what was in reality a typical Roman civil war between ambitious rival generals.

9. Now Ponte Molle, just over a mile north of the ancient city wall.

10. Rufinus presumably means, following Eusebius's *Life of Constantine*, Book 1, Chapter 38, that Maxentius's pontoon bridge was designed to give way when Constantine's army crossed it to lay siege to Rome. In fact Maxentius was accidentally pushed off the bridge in the panic retreat of his routed army.

11. Rufinus is referring to the famous Council of Nicea (325), the subject of his previous chapter.

12. Eusebius (*Life of Constantine*, bk. 3, chaps. 26–27) describes how on Constantine's orders a shrine of Venus had been removed from the site of the Holy Sepulcher. But other evidence indicates that a statue of Jupiter surmounted this site, while the statue of Venus was on the rock of Golgotha.

13. Rufinus implies that the inscription tablet is no longer attached to the Cross, contradicting a somewhat earlier account by St. Ambrose of Milan.

14. This is the so-called *martyrium* church. Rufinus, followed by the *Inventio s. Crucis* legend below, is probably correct in giving the impression that the main church built on the site commemorated the discovery of the Cross and the site of the Crucifixion, not the Holy Sepulcher where Jesus was buried, as has usually been assumed.

15. Rufinus here seems to refer to the well-known exhibiting of the Cross to the pilgrim crowds in Jerusalem on the second day of the annual feast of the dedication of the church of the Holy Sepulcher (September 13–20).

16. "Consecrated virgins" is a technical term from the late-Roman era for a distinct class of dedicated Christian women (usually either virgins or celibate widows) living a life of service and chastity that anticipated in many respects that of medieval nuns.

17. The date (233) seems original and may derive from Syrian rather than Western chronology (see Stephan Borgehammar, *How the Holy Cross Was Found: From Event to Medieval Legend*, Bibliotheca Theologicae Practicae, Kyrkovetenskapliga studier 47 [Stockholm, 1991], pp. 181–82), but the author of the *Inventio* is hardly scrupulous about historical consistency. Thus he has anachronistically conflated the vision and battle of 312 with certain later episodes of Constantine's reign. A great Roman victory was won against an army of Goths along the Danube in 332, but by Constantine's son, Constantine the Younger. Constantine the Great had himself routed the Goths ten years earlier, driving them back across the Danube. *Romania* was a common fifth-century term for the Roman Empire.

18. See Rufinus's account above and note 4 above.

19. The only historically attested pope named Eusebius held the office for a short time earlier in Constantine's reign, from April to September of 308. During most of the reign, the pope was Silvester (who reigned from 314 to 335), and in some Latin manuscripts his name is substituted here and later. Constantine's baptism was actually performed on his deathbed in 337, by another Eusebius, the Arian bishop of Nicomedia, later Patriarch of Constantinople.

20. It is likely that the earliest versions of the *Inventio* began with this sentence, that is with Helena's resolve to seek the cross, and that the vision of Constantine was subsequently added as a prologue. Some awkward narrative duplication results in Chapters 3 and 4, where first Constantine, and then Helena, is credited with initiating the search for the Cross.

21. That is, April 28, in the Latin church calendar, although this does not allow a full week before May 3, when the Cross is found by Judas after his seven days in the pit.

22. After Emperor Hadrian's suppression of the Jewish uprising under Bar Kosiba (also known as Bar Kokhba, who led a revolt from 132 to 335), Jerusalem was rebuilt as the Roman city of Aelia Capitolana, and the centers of Jewish life shifted both to other parts of Palestine and abroad, especially to Babylon.

23. That is, Satan, as in Gen 3:14.

24. See 2 Chron 34:24, the words of the prophetess, Huldah.

25. This verse is repeated by Peter in his first Pentecost sermon (Acts 2:25), which Borgehammar suggests as one possible model for Helena's harangue.

26. Helena's language here, including her allusions to the "blindness" of the Jews, partly echoes Jesus' attacks on the Pharisees and Scribes in Mt 23:16–32 (echoed by Paul in Acts 13:27; see also Jn 12:40, alluding to Is 6:9–10, and Rom 11:10, quoting Ps 68:24), but it is also squarely in the tradition of early Christian anti-Judaic apology and polemic.

27. Israel had ceased to be an independent kingdom centuries before Helena's time, but in the Roman province of Palestine there was still a Patriarch, titular ruler of the Jewish "nation," although his authority was minimal and Jewish life in Palestine under the newly Christianized empire was becoming more and more difficult. The last vestige of "nationhood" in the Jews's homeland ended ca. 425 when the patriarchate was abolished by Theodosius II and the academic Sanhedrin forced to close.

28. See Lk 23:50, concerning Joseph of Arimathea. Borgehammar, in his edition, suggests a reference to Gen 49:5.

29. According to Acts 6–7, St. Stephen, the first Christian martyr, was a Hellenized Jew and a deacon of the Christian community in Jerusalem in the years following Jesus' death (see also note 6 above). His cult began to flourish in earnest after the supposed discovery of his relics in the early fifth century. The chronology of the *Inventio* legend at this point is strained, since Judas would have had to outlive his "brother" Stephen by almost three centuries. In another redaction of the *Inventio* legend Stephen is (somewhat) more plausibly the cousin of Judas's father. This whole section of the legend typifies its mythic, figural character.

30. *Calvary* (literally "the skull") is the Latin name for *Golgotha*. The site had to be "purified" because it had been polluted by a shrine to Venus; see Mt 27:33 and Rufinus's account (above).

31. In this strange passage, of which there are numerous variant versions in the manuscripts, there are some phrases of recognizably Hebrew origin (for example, *kautiubruc kata Hodonahi*), but the whole does not seem to make any sense.

32. For the image of a sweetly smelling sacrificial victim see Gen 8:21; Ezek 20:41, reinterpreted as Christ himself and the faith of his followers in 2 Cor 2:15; Eph 5:2; Phil 4:18. On Joseph's bones in the Old Testament, see Gen 50:25; Ex 13:19. Judas is also invoking a Rabbinic legend, according to which Moses miraculously retrieved Joseph's sweetly smelling coffin from the Nile or from a mausoleum of the Pharoahs.

33. See note 29 above.

34. The wording echoes Jn 13:4–5 (Jesus washing the feet of his disciples).

35. That is, the souls of the dead, whom, according to early medieval belief, the devil was permitted to claim as his own after the fall of Adam and Eve and up to the coming of Christ.

36. This all refers to the emperor Julian (who reigned from 361 to 363), the so-called Apostate. In an account of Judas's later life, which occurs as a sequel to the *Inventio* in some medieval manuscripts, Julian is Judas's persecutor and orders his martyrdom.

37. On the problem of "Pope Eusebius," see note 19 above. In the fourth century a new bishop of Jerusalem would normally be consecrated not by the Roman Pope, as here, but rather by the Jerusalem bishop's metropolitan or immediate superior, the bishop of

Caesarea, or by the bishop of Antioch, head of Jerusalem's patriarchal see. But Bishop Juvenal of Jerusalem (422–58), at the Council of Chalcedon in 451, engineered the elevation of the see of Jerusalem itself to the status of an independent patriarchate. The consecration episode here, in which Jerusalem is seen to be ecclesiastically subordinate only to Rome, may thus reflect the church politics of the time in which the work was composed.

38. Also spelled *Cyriacus*. The Greek word *kyriakos* means "belonging to the Lord."

39. This brusque detail reflects the increasing harshness of official Christian attitudes and legislation regarding the Jews in the late fourth century and later.

40. The exact year of Helena's death, at the age of eighty, is uncertain, but was probably ca. 330. She apparently died with Constantine at her bedside.

Chapter 5

Life of the Holy Virgin Samthann

Translated by Dorothy Africa

Introduction

This work survives principally in an early-fourteenth-century manuscript, Oxford, Bodleian Library, MS Rawlinson B.485. There are two other manuscript versions of it, but they are dependent upon this one. In the study of the great medieval collections of Irish saints' *Lives* done by Richard Sharpe, this manuscript is a witness for a textual tradition he calls the Oxford group. While the history of Rawlinson B.485 is obscure, Sharpe has argued for an origin in the region of the counties of Longford or Westmeath. Such an origin would certainly account for the inclusion of St. Samthann in the manuscript, since she was abbess of the women's community of Clonbroney in Longford. Whether the *Life of Samthann* was already part of the collection used as the exemplar for Rawlinson B.485 or whether it was added by one of the scribes cannot be determined.

Unlike most monastic Irish saints, Samthann was not the foundress of her community. She also belongs to a much later period than most of the saints whose *Lives* were gathered into the great collections. Ireland's great age of saints and monastic foundations was the sixth century, while Samthann was an eighth-century figure. Very few women appear among the saints of the great collections, and the others—Brigit, Moninne, and Íta—belong to the ranks of the sixth-century founders of monastic communities. It is possible that the *Life of St. Samthann* was a relatively late addition to the collection of the saints *Lives*, put in because of regional pride in a prominent ecclesiastic of fairly recent memory. It should be pointed out, however, that even if this is true, it does not mean the *Life of St. Samthann* was itself composed later than most of the other *Lives* in the collection. Indeed, many of the *Lives* of sixth-century saints were composed long after their deaths, though some of these are demonstrably based on earlier written material no longer extant.

In *The Annals of Ulster* the death of Samthann of Clonbroney is noted in the entry for the year 739. This obituary begins a series of entries in the annals pertaining to Clonbroney and two other communities with which it was sometimes connected, Clonguffin and Cloonburren. These entries appear sporadically from the mid-eighth through the early ninth centuries, and very rarely thereafter. The last obit for an abbess of Clonbroney appears in 1163. Though it drops out of annalistic record, the community may have survived in

97

some form or another through the medieval period. An evaluation of 1595 lists a hospital, Termon-Irenagh, or Corbeship at Clonebrone, as endowed with eight *cartrons* of land.

While no mention of the community appears in the annals prior to the obituary for Samthann, the *Tripartite Life of St. Patrick* asserted that it was founded by Patrick for two sisters, both named Emer, whose brother Guasacht he had made bishop of Granard. All three were the children of Milchú, the man whom Patrick had served in Ulster as a slave in his youth. While this story in not literally credible, the *Life of St. Samthann* does refer to a trip made by Samthann to Granard, confirming an association between it and Clonbroney. Further, Samthann herself is of Ulster origin, and the genealogies show her family to be one closely connected to Patrick in the *Tripartite Life*. In addition to the problems of separating and dating the various layers of composition and redaction in the Irish *Lives*, are the complexities of the language question. By 600 C. E. the Irish learned class had developed a written vernacular which gradually displaced Latin. In his study of early Irish hagiography, Richard Sharpe (*Medieval Irish Saints' Lives* [Oxford, 1991]) has suggested that Latin fell into decline in Ireland in the ninth century, reviving again in the eleventh and twelfth centuries. A number of Irish *Lives* survive in both Irish and Latin versions, while others show signs of translation from one to the other in their surviving texts.

The *Life of St. Samthann* shows only a cursory interest in the origins of Samthann, but it is possible that such material has been dropped by subsequent redactors who found it irrelevant. The *Life* names quite a different founder for the community, the virgin Fuinech. There are several religious women named Fainche recorded, but little is known of any of them. Of particular interest among these obscure figures is one of the five daughters of Fergne, Fainner at Clonbroney, listed as one of the communities subject to St. Brigit of Kildare. If this is a hint at the earlier situation of Clonbroney, the surviving *Life* gives no sign that the community was still attached to Kildare when Samthann was its abbess. There is also the possibility that St. Cainnech of Aghaboe was the original founder since his *Life* claims he once lived there.

Typically Irish saints' *Lives* follow a pattern similar to those of secular epic and romance heroes. Often the conception as well as the birth of a saint is attended by strange events, miracles, and portents. As a child the saint demonstrates his or her vocation with miracles, shows great piety and sagacity, and enters into the religious life as soon as possible. The Irish Church was predominately monastic in its focus rather than episcopal, so the career trajectory for most Irish saints is one of founding communities and fostering them. Attendant on these activities is the performance of miracles in the form of cures, the procurement of provisions, and acts of prophecy, defense, and rescue. The death of the saint is also attended by marvels and portents, and many *Lives* of Irish saints conclude with the recital of posthumous miracles and local customs concerning sites or objects connected with the saint. There are exceptions to the pattern, of course, but in general Irish saints were expected to follow such a course, and to be vigorous and efficient miracle workers.

Except for the omission of an account of her early life, the *Life of St. Samthann* follows the general pattern of Irish saint's *Lives*. It has, however, several distinctive features worthy of comment. Few saints *Lives* display such an opening sequence as this one, with the protagonist entering her own life sound asleep and hurtling within a few sentences into full dramatic action. It is common, however, in the *Lives* of women saints for the saint to struggle heroically to avoid a marriage forced upon her by parents and kin. Fosterage was a common practice in Ireland for children of both sexes. Usually a woman's own family, not her foster father, would make arrangements for her marriage, but if they were distant, as appears to be the case here, responsibility might pass to a fosterer.

In addition to the dramatic first section, the *Life of St. Samthann* is distinctive for its emphasis on her activities as a builder, and the threefold repetition of the motif of the captive released from his chains. Most of the miracles associated with these two themes are not unique to this *Life,* but the emphasis on them is unusual, especially when the saint is female. The various episodes concerning the building projects at Clonbroney are valuable in pointing out the special difficulties women's houses faced in assembling adequate manpower and materials needed in an agricultural society of scattered, isolated farmsteads. Surviving remains of Irish monastic sites show them to have been collections of small buildings. Only the more populous, wealthier communities were likely to have large structures in them, so the construction of a large hall for the sisters to work in that appears in section sixteen was an ambitious project indeed.

The question of why the sisters might need a large hall may be partly explained by section twenty-three, in which a load of wool is brought to Clonbroney from Iona, an island just off the southwestern coast of Scotland. While it is entirely reasonable to suggest that Clonbroney had been involved in textile production, it still seems implausible that wool would have been brought from such a distance as a matter of routine. This illustrates the difficulties of using hagiographic material for sociological information. While such texts do allow glimpses at the ordinary, their explicit purpose is to exhibit the extraordinary. The line between the two is not always clear.

A similar blurring of the lines surrounds the use of the motif of the bound prisoner miraculously freed which is used in Sections seven, twelve, and twenty-two. The biblical model for this miracle comes from Acts 12:5–10. The version closest to the biblical parallel in the *Life of St. Samthann* is the first one in Section seven. This section is also one of those in which the keen perception of human psychology the author of this *Life* had is displayed in the exchange between the guards and the departing prisoner Follomain. A similar display of the author's insight is in section six where the author uses the befuddlement of a laborer to illustrate the power of faith to work miracles and shows Samthann's sanctity in her laughter.

In the second use of the motif of the miraculously freed prisoner in Section twelve a more distinctively Irish feature is introduced, the *simulacrum*. In Irish hagiography the *simulacrum* is usually that of a funeral hearse carrying the body of a saint. Two groups contending for the privilege of burying the body are prevented from engaging in battle by the appearance of two identical hearses, and each group departs convinced that it has possession of the saint's remains. Once the legitimate party has reached safety, the *simulacrum* escorted by the rival group disappears. Objects can also have a *simulacrum*, but it is rare for a living person to have such a double. The use of the *simulacrum* in Section twelve is more like what one would expect to find in a popular tale than in a hagiographic text, though such motif crossing is not uncommon in saints' *Lives*.

In the *Life of St. Samthann,* section four is a prime example of such a usage. The destruction of a spell or magic protection by a foolish question or remark is very common in popular tale and romance. This incident in the life forms a contrasting pair with section six. Both feature miraculous occurrences connected to the saint showing her interaction, or better reaction, to the faith of those around her. In one instance it is with one who lacks faith and in the other with one who has it. Sections four and six apparently are used to frame section five in which the saint leaves her former home at Urney for Clonbroney. This frame provides the spiritual explanation for this divinely mandated change of location for Samthann. The virgin Funecha invites Samthann to Clonbroney as a consequence of a vision, but the framing episodes of section four and six demonstrate that the saint must leave a place where her faith cannot thrive for one in which it can. The episodes also make it clear that this spiritual prosperity has solid material benefits.

The final instance of the motif of the miraculously freed prisoner shows the least embellishment of the theme, though this might be the consequence of later editing and revision in the transmission of the text. It is surprising that the episode is located in the Corcaguiny area of County Kerry. This is certainly a considerable distance from Clonbroney in County Longford, and there is no ostensible connection between the two. It is possible, however, that this reference to Kerry comes from the influence of a version of the *Life of St. Íta*. There are several parallel episodes in the surviving *Lives* of these two female saints, and Kileedy, the community where St. Íta was abbess, is very close to Corcaguiny.

The overall construction of the *Life of St. Samthann* is similar to most of the others in the collections of Irish saints' *Lives*. It is a series of miraculous episodes loosely following the career path of the saint as founder and/or leader of a monastic community. The episodes have only a general chronology within the stages of the saint's career. While the order of episodes can often seem arbitrary, one can sometimes note a thematic or stylistic order in them, within the loose chronology of the saint's career. The miracles and marvels in the *Life* of one particular saint tend to be similar to those in the *Lives* of other saints, both male and female. Some miracles, especially provisioning miracles, appear in greater proportion in the women's *Lives*, but they are frequently found in the men's *Lives*. Both male and female saints extend their protection to the lives, property, and well-being of others, act as teachers and spiritual guides, oppose secular authority upon occasion, and travel when necessary.

The difference in men's and women's experience in the medieval Irish Church is reflected in its hagiographic literature not so much in its quality as its quantity. In contrast to the many *Lives* of male saints are the very few women's *Lives*. This would appear to reflect the historical record of the size and number of powerful men's communities like Clonmacnois, Kells, Armagh, and Glendalough as opposed to the obscurity of the small women's communities. Kildare is a notable exception, but it was also a double house. This difference in prominence in record in turn reflects, in large part, the greater difficulty women had in maintaining control of property in Ireland where property traditionally was a family possession passing in a patrilineal lineage.

While it is difficult to use stylistic or literary evidence to date the *Life of St. Samthann*, Section thirteen offers an important clue. This episode relates the miraculous rescue by Samthann and her nuns of the soul of one Flann son of Conla. While most of the ordinary folk named in saints' *Lives* are stock figures, this one has at least a family of historic record. *The Annals of Ulster* record the obituaries of many members of a family that held the kingship of Tethba, the part of Cairpre Gabra in which Clonbroney was located, from the late seventh century into the early tenth. Among these obituary records is one for Conla of Tethba in the year 771. The likelihood that he is to be equated with the father of Flann son of Conla in this section is confirmed by two other obituaries, one for Béc son of Conla, king of Tethba in 741, and another for Forblaith daughter of Conla, abbess of Clonbroney in 780. It was common for royal patrons to commission the writing of the *Life* of a saint for religious communities they favored, especially when their own relatives were prominent members of them. It is quite likely then, that a *Life* of Clonbroney's most important abbess of recent memory should be commissioned when it was enjoying such a period of royal favor and intimacy. Nor did the hagiographer miss the chance to impress upon these royal patrons the advantages their family members might enjoy in return when crafting section thirteen.

If an original *Life* composed within a couple of generations of the saint's death is well preserved in the text that survives to us, the *Life of St. Samthann* provides us with a late-eighth-century *Life* of an Irish female saint. As such it can be compared to the Carolingian women's saints' *Lives* studied by Julia Smith. Her study indicates a shift in these texts from the earlier paradigm for women's *Lives* followed by such texts as the *Life of St. Geneviève*, composed in the early sixth century, which drew upon a more or less unisexual model of sanctity; to one which sharply distinguished female sanctity in the late-ninth-century *Lives* of saints such as Hathumoda and Liutberga. The *Life of the Holy Virgin Samthann* clearly shows a preference for the unisex model, though the dearth of material precludes generalizing on views of female sanctity in Ireland as a whole for this period.

SOURCES AND FURTHER READING

The *Life of the Holy Virgin Samthann* (Bibliotheca hagiographica latina, no. 7486d) was edited by Charles Plummer, *Vitae Sanctorum Hiberniae* (Oxford, 1910, reprint 1968), 2:253–61. This work is currently available in a new 1997 reprint from Four Courts Press, Dublin. For a general history of the history and culture of early Ireland, see Dáibhí O Cróinín, *Early Medieval Ireland, 400–1200* (London, 1995). Lisa Bitel's *Isle of the Saints, Monastic Settlement and Christian Community in Early Ireland* (Ithaca, NY, 1990) contains much information on the material culture of monastic Ireland as reflected in the Irish saints' *Lives*. A thorough study of the uses made of hagiographic and popular literary motifs in the *Life of the Holy Virgin Samthann* is provided by Dorothy Bray in "Motival Derivations in the Life of St. Samthann," *Studia Celtica* 20–21 (1985–86): 78–86. The study by Julia Smith of hagiographic models referred to above was published as "The Problem of Female Sanctity in Carolingian Europe c. 780–920," *Past and Present* 146 (1995): 3–37. Richard Sharpe provides a wealth of detail about the development of the hagiographic tradition in *Medieval Irish Saints' Lives* (Oxford, 1991).

Life of the Holy Virgin Samthann

(1.) The holy and venerable virgin Samthann came from an Ulster family; her father was named Dyamranus, her mother, Columba.[1] When she came of age, her fosterer, Cridan king of Cairpre Gabra, betrothed her to a noble man.[2] On the night before the wedding, this man awoke in the middle of the night and saw a shaft of light like a sunbeam descending through the roof down onto the bed where Samthann and two of the king's daughters were sleeping. Amazed at this strange ray at such an hour, he arose and approached the bed, and saw that it suffused the face of his betrothed. He rejoiced that he merited a spouse so imbued with heavenly light. On the following night after the wedding had taken place, as is customary the pair went to bed, and her husband said to her, "Get undressed so that we may join as one." But she answered, "Please wait until the others in the house have fallen asleep." He agreed, and soon fell asleep. Then she began to pray, beating at the gates of divine charity, that it might save her virginity. God heeded her plight and granted the prayer, for near midnight a prodigious flame seemed to soar from her mouth to the roof of the house. To those outside, the compound appeared to burst into flame, and they raised a great outcry that roused those within, all rushing at once to put out the fire.

(2.) Meanwhile, the holy virgin Samthann fled and hid herself in a fern thicket nearby. The fire died out at once, without harming the compound. At dawn, her fosterer the king of Cairpre set out to find her, and, when he did, she said, "Your stronghold wasn't destroyed by the fire last night was it?" "No," he replied, and she said, "Thank God it was not. Why did you desire to give this poor servant of almighty God to another spouse without consent?" Then the king said, "I will not take you from another man, but let the judgment be yours." She said, "Here is my decision—that you shall offer me henceforth to God in marriage, and not to a man." The king knelt and said, "We bestow you in marriage, and join you to God, the spouse of your choice." Then with the consent of her husband she entered the community of the virgin Cognate which is called Urney.[3] She lived there for some time, and devoutly and faithfully served as steward.

(3.) One morning when the holy virgin Samthann arose at dawn, she heard the loud cry of a leper from the far side of a stream asking to be brought across. Obedient to his wishes, she ferried him across, guiding her little boat with her staff. He was complaining of poverty and nakedness, so she gave him a cow with its calf, and the greater part of her cloak, just as another Martin. She asked him where he had come from, and he answered from the monastery of St. Ultán [Ardbreccan] and left.[4] Then a marvelous thing happened, for the cow and calf given to the leper were found in the byre, and not even the trace of a tear was visible in Samthann's garment.

(4.) While Samthann was the steward at Urney, it was the case that through the agency of her blessing one vat of butter was sufficient for the sisters and their guests for a whole year. A certain girl who had recently retired from the secular life came into the sisters' cellar without Samthann knowing of it. She saw the vat of butter was nearly full, and remarked "This butter never seems to run out" and left. The holy virgin came in and found the vat empty. Amazed and stunned by this, she wondered what had happened. In the grip of a prophetic spirit she declared, "This place shall never be wealthy," and what she said proved true.

(5.) At that time the foundress of Clonbroney, the blessed virgin Fuinech, dreamt that sparks of fire in the likeness of St. Samthann came and consumed the whole monastery, and then rose up in a great flame. She told her dream to the sisters and gave this interpretation: "Burning with the fire of the Holy Spirit, Samthann will make this place shimmer by virtue of her merits and in the splendor of miracles." For that reason, Fuinech sent for Samthann and gave her the community.

(6.) After she had taken charge, first she wanted to construct an oratory of trimmed timber, and so she sent out carpenters and other workmen to bring in timber from forests nearby. One of the carpenters, observing the paucity of the provisions and the number of workers, thought to himself, "Oh, if only we could have forty wheaten loaves with butter and cheese and milk; for such a quantity of bread would suffice us!" Man is not frustrated in his desire for something his soul has desired. For through the merits of holy Samthann, all he had thought he saw placed before him. The intimate of Christ, giggling, said, "The thought of your heart is fulfilled, is it not?" And he said to her, "Indeed so, mistress, there is neither something in addition, or anything missing." Then all gave thanks to God and his servant, and ate their fill.

(7.) At another time, Samthann sent messengers to a king named Cennétig, asking him, at her request, to release a man he had defeated and was holding captive. But the haughty king, disdaining her plea, accorded nothing to them. So she sent messengers again, saying: "If he shall not have released him from his bonds, say to the prisoner 'In the name of the holy Trinity you shall be released from your fetters and come unharmed to Samthann, the servant of that same Trinity.'"[5] When the king persisted still in his impiety, the messengers spoke to the captive as the servant of Christ had ordered. He said to them, "I believe that it shall happen just as she has said." When the king heard this, in contempt of the virgin he doubled the fetters on him, and on the following night he placed eight guards at the gate of the prison and as many at the gate of the stronghold. In the middle of the night, the aforesaid captive arose, freed by divine aid. When he passed by the first guards, they said, "Hey! you, going by there, who are you?" He answered, "I am Follomain, the one who was imprisoned," for so this vanquished man was called. The guards said to him, "If you were he, you would not saunter by like this." Then he, avoiding the second watch, scaled the wall at another side and thus escaping reached Samthann on the third day without peril.

(8.) Also this virgin through the power of her prayers restrained beasts in a local lake. Prior to this they were dangerous to men and livestock, but afterward they harmed none.

Life of the Holy Virgin Samthann

(9.) Nor should it be left untold that once this virgin fed fifty guests sufficiently with the milk of a single cow, to the admiration of many. For she had nothing else with which she could refresh them at the time. So after she had prayed, the holy virgin milked the cow herself, and it put forth as much milk as would sustain such a quantity of people.

(10.) At another time she fed the abbot of Devenish and one hundred and forty others with food and drink for a week with a single measure of flour divided into two parts.

(11.) Once a lustful cleric came into the sisters' community and took a fancy to a young girl who caught his eye there. She in turn paid out love to the lover. So, he undertook to go off to the woods nearby, and the girl was to follow him. He first addressed himself to Samthann, seeking her prayer that his journey be unobstructed. When she asked him where he was going, he replied, "I wish to go to Connacht." Then the holy virgin said to him, "Where ever you may go, do not trouble my sisters with sweet talk or misdeeds." "Far be that from me, mistress," he responded, and with this remark, he left. He reached the river and began to cross it. The water had risen as high as his belt when a huge eel encircled his loins and cinched tightly around him. After this happened, he was so deeply terrified that he returned to the virgin of God, fell to his knees, and sought her pardon. After she had given it, the eel immediately fell away from his limbs. He took heed of his fright, and swore that he would never come again to a women's community.

(12.) At one time, the peoples of Connacht and Tethba made a treaty after a long struggle. In accordance with it, the king of Tethba seized the son of a widow whom he was going to hand over to them as a hostage. At the request of this widow, the blessed Samthann sent the prioress of her community with five other virgins and two men to the aforesaid king to seek his release. But the king would not agree and denied what they asked, but he said, "Whatever else she will have asked of me, she will certainly get." Then Nathea the prioress said to the captive: "In the name of our Lord Jesus Christ and the holy Samthann his servant, you shall come with us released from your fetters." After hearing this, the guards surrounded him more closely, fearing that he might be able to escape their clutches through the power of this prayer. Then the king set out toward the Shannon river, so that he might confirm the peace with the Connachtmen by handing over the hostage, the widow's son, to them. Then a miraculous event takes place. For as the holy virgin's messengers are on their way back; poof!, they behold the widow's son with them on the way. They rejoice greatly at the sight; and give thanks to God and Samthann his servant. Even so the presence of the very man so miraculously freed was not lacking to either the aforesaid king or his guards, or so they thought. However, when they had reached the Shannon, and wished to take that captive across by raft, the restraints, which they were thinking held him captive among them, fell down empty. There was no trace of the man whom, as they thought, the fetters had secured. Then all extolled God, shown so marvelous in his handmaiden.

(13.) Flann son of Conla was a nobleman who relied on the blessed servant of Christ in the cultivation of his great piety. For whenever he was about to set off into battle or on a foray, he would come to her to receive her blessing or a prayer. But then the Connachtmen attacked Tethba, and he, without Samthann's blessing, went out against them and was killed. In the very hour in which he was killed, she herself told the sisters of his death; for she said to them, "Hasten at once to prayer; even now the soul of our friend Flann is being led by demons to the places of punishment." After she said this, she went into a trance. After a short time she roused and said to the sisters: "Give thanks to God, for the soul for whom you pray was conducted from torment to rest through our intercession and the great mercy of God."

(14.) There came a time when the buildings of the monastery had to be changed to increase its space; but the oratory could not be moved without the aid of a vast multitude. Word went out to the local populace, so that they would come for this task. On the following night, however, when those who had been summoned had not yet arrived, the blessed Samthann invoked divine assistance and busied herself in prayer, that she might have the customary aid of its grace in this task. The very next day she asked the men, only eight in number, to move the oratory. Obedient to her order, they readily moved that oratory to where it was supposed to go without any hindrance.

(15.) At another time when this same oratory had to be renovated, the craftsmen went to the woods with the prioress Nathea to bring in suitable timber. And when they came upon a tree fit for the job, the builder said: "If the tree were to fall this way, it will be useless, but if it falls that way, it will serve." But the tree began to tilt in the direction that the workers did not want it to fall. When Nathea saw what was happening, she ordered that the blessed Samthann's belt which she had with her be placed away from this area. As soon as the belt was in place, a sudden violent gust of wind came up, and fell that tree in the opposite direction.

(16.) Once the holy servant of Christ desired to build a large hall for the work of the sisters, and sent Nathea the prioress with the craftsmen into the forest of Connacht for pine timber. When they had searched for three whole days without finding the wood, the weary group decided on the fourth day to return home. While they slept that night, the blessed Samthann suddenly appeared in a dream to her disciple, Nathea, saying: "Tomorrow morning cut down bog willows at the root, and you will find enough pine lying there." At daybreak, they did just as she instructed; and found the pine they desired. But the owner of the woods, seeing such a heap of pine, said, "Unless you buy them, you will not get these trees." Nathea said to him, "We will buy them willingly." The following night Samthann appeared in a vision to that man. She spoke in a threatening voice, saying, "What tempts you, fellow, to withhold things offered to God?" Then she struck his side with a staff, saying, "Wretch, unless you do penance, know that you will die very soon." Next morning, that man, stung by penance, gave them the lumber outright. When word got out, the inhabitants of the region praised God as manifest in the holy Samthann. They provided sixty yokes of oxen and conveyed all that wood back to the monastery.

(17.) Niall son of Fergal, king of Ireland, asked for the staff of the holy virgin Samthann so that he could decorate it with gold and silver. However, that rod was crooked and ancient, so that it seemed to the craftsmen perverse to labor at its ornamentation. On the following night, the staff was placed on the wall above the king's bed. Due to the devotion of the pious king, and the merit of his handmaiden Samthann, Christ corrected that rod, before so twisted, so that no trace of crookedness was visible in it. Then the king was gladdened with a great joy, since holy piety had done what human cleverness could not accomplish. For that very reason, the king himself and his entire populace held that staff in the greatest esteem.[6]

(18.) There were two religious women living near the monastery of Abbot Cainnech.[7] One of them yielded to evil suggestion, and subsequently bore a son. Yet she wanted to maintain public decency and did not want him to be reared in the vicinity. Having heard good report of Samthann and after consulting with each other, this pair of religious went to her with the infant. She sympathized with them, and undertook the child's rearing. In order for the women to avoid scandal and suspicion, she told them to leave at night. When they had set out and were making their way through the forest, they caught sight of some thieves advancing toward them whom they could not elude. But then, the right hand of the Lord showed its power; for a huge tree close by opened itself, revealing to them its hollow interior, and then reknit itself on the outside, thus enclosing them miraculously. Then while the brigands hunted for them here and there, an extremely dense fog enveloped them so they could see nothing at all until the women had left the woods and traveled a good part of the way. The blessed Samthann raised the baby, and saw to his instruction in letters. In the course of time, he became a famous abbot in the monastery of Saint Cainnech.

(19.) At one time Samthann was returning to her own community from the monastery at Grenard, and came upon a certain lofty oak which thrust out its branches across the path so as to make it impassable for those seated in the cart. But the blessed virgin, placing her staff against the obstacle, pressed on with the order that it give way to them. There was no delay. The branch, pliantly wrapping around its own trunk while lifting itself up, gave them an easy passage.

(20.) Once a monk consulted Samthann as to the proper manner in which to pray, whether one should be prone, seated, or standing. She replied to him that one ought to pray in every stance.

(21.) A petty king named Rectabra had a wife who was sterile, so she came to Samthann, hoping to bear a child when the shame of sterility had been expunged through her prayer. Samthann blessed the woman's womb, and said prophetically, "You will give birth to a son, and name him Inrechtach. He will be a wise man and the lord of his people," which all came to pass.[8]

(22.) There was a petty king of Corcaguiny who held a widow's son in fetters. At the request of this widow, the devout virgin was moved in sympathy to send messengers to this king so that in consequence of her intervention that captive would return to his mother after the king had freed him. When the cruel king would not comply with her prayers, his wife spoke as follows, "If you do not free this fellow at the behest of holy Samthann, God will free him at her prayer." Then the messengers said to the captive, "The virgin Samthann has ordered you to come to her tonight when you are freed." And behold, not long after this a cry resounded through the region that an enemy had arrived to ravage the territory. When he has heard that, the king has hastily rushed out with his men to confront the enemy. Meanwhile, the captive, quit of the restraint which held him, skedaddles. On the following night he reached the virgin without any difficulty.

(23.) Once the community of brothers on the isle of Iona sent some of their members to the holy Samthann with a boatload of wool. While they were cleaving the level surface (of the sea), the calm of the air changed suddenly. The waves, raised by the heightening of the winds, menaced them angrily with death. A lad among them spoke up foolishly, saying, "Let's throw the granny's wool overboard, lest we sink." The navigator of the ship refused to allow this, and said, "Certainly not. With the old lady's wool we shall either live or die." With this remark, such serenity of the sea ensued that the wind disappeared altogether and they resorted to rowing. Then the same boy piped up again, "Why can't the granny provide us any wind now?" The navigator responded, "We believe that God will assist us for the sake of her merits." At once the wind filled their sails and they capitalized on this gift for three whole days and nights until they reached the harbor at Colptha.[9] When they had arrived at the monastery of the blessed virgin, they saluted her as they entered and kissed her hand. When the aforesaid lad approached her, the virgin said "Now what was that you were saying about me at sea when the storm threatened you with death?" The boy was confounded into silence with shame. She said to him, "Never doubt this, if ever dangers corner you, call upon me boldly."

(24.) At one point Daircellach the teacher came to the virgin, and told her, "I propose to defer study, and leave off prayer." She said to him "What, then, can steady your mind lest it stray, if you shall have neglected spiritual cultivation?" The sage responded, "I wish to go abroad on pilgrimage." She retorted "If God is not to be found on this side of the sea, certainly we may go abroad. For since God is near all who summon him, no need of voyaging besets us. One can reach heaven from any place on earth."[10]

(25.) These few incidents, selected from many, have been related here. Who, indeed, could recite all the things with which God enriched her? She was full of the grace of good works, decked with the display of all virtues, and in her life fully endowed with good examples, a pious teacher of the lowly, but a most humble servant in the maintenance of the body. She was poor in spirit and in material things. She refused to hold fields; nor did she ever have more

Life of the Holy Virgin Samthann

than six cows at a time. Thus all goods, and especially her own household items, were solicited through charity. For, as this one instance from among the many illustrates, when alms offered to her were shared among the sisters, hers was reckoned among the individual huts.[11] For however many sisters lived together at one time, her share was added on to theirs. She was merry in adversity, modest in receiving, devout in empathizing, efficient in assisting. Why belabor the point by the recital of details? No labor of devotion passed her by. Thus she spent the course of this present life in holiness and justice in the sight of her spouse, Christ. On the eighteenth of December she received from him the crown which he has eternally ready for those who worship him.

(26.) On the very night in which (her) spirit returned to heaven, the holy abbot Lasran,[12] of whom we spoke earlier, awoke and saw two moons, one of which dipped toward him. He was mindful of his own request, for he had asked her that when she passed to the celestial realm she would bend toward him. Recognizing her in the guise of a star, he said, "Well done, Samthann, faithful servant of God, for now you are ushered into the rejoicing of the Lord your spouse." In this fashion she faded away, climbing into the sky, where eternal life is enjoyed forever and ever, Amen.

Notes

1. Her pedigree is given in the saints' genealogies as Samthann of Clonbroney the daughter of Díarán son of Ferdoman son of Dichu son of Trichem. In the *Tripartite Life* St. Patrick is befriended by two sons of Trichem, Dichu who gives him the site of Saul in County Down, and Ross who lives at Bright, also in County Down.

2. There is no record of a king of Cairpre Gabra of this name in the annals or genealogies, but they are by no means complete. Cairpre Gabra was the region around Granard. Tethba was the region next to it on the west.

3. The community was located in what is now County Tyrone. There are only a few references to it in the annals, but it appears to have become a male monastic community after Samthann's time.

4. The leper's reference to the monastery of Ultán could simply mean Ardbreccan in County Meath, but Dorothy Bray ("Motival Derivations in the Life of St. Samthann," *Studia Celtica* 20–21 [1985–86]: 78–86) points out that it could also mean Péronne in France. The reference to St. Martin of Tours was probably added by a later redactor in the opinion of Richard Sharpe (*Medieval Irish Saints' Lives* [Oxford, 1991]) who has studied the manuscript tradition of the large collections of saints' *lives* very carefully.

5. I have chosen to translate *catenae* and *vinculae* as bonds or fetters instead of the more customary "chains" because I am inclined to think that ropes or leather thongs may have been the more customary sort of restraint. Smithing was common enough in Ireland for chains to have been available, but they are likely to have been used for grander purposes. I have also elected to retain the use of the present tense in the sections of these escape miracles where it appears to have been used to provide emphasis and dramatic effect. Something more than classical tense sequence seems to stand behind it. Plummer suggests that the King Cennetig (Kennedy) in this episode is Cináed son of Irgalach, who died in 728.

6. Niall son of Fergal (718–78). In his edition of the text, Plummer offered the observation that this was probably intended as a posthumous miracle performed by the saint. Bray (see note 4 above) concurred with this opinion in her study of the motifs used in the *Life*. This episode may have come at the end of the *Life* originally.

7. This is probably a reference to Aghaboe in County Laois. The episcopal seat for the bishopric of Ossary was moved to Kilkenny, also founded by Cainnech, by the Council of Rath Breasail in 1111, but at the time the original *Life* of St. Samthann was composed Aghaboe was the more prominent community.

8. Plummer listed two possible identifications for Rectabra in his edition of the text. One was a king of Uí Tuirtri who died in 734, the other a chief of Cremorne who died in 759. The first is, in fact, the more likely since Rectabra of Uí Tuirtri appears in the genealogies as the father of a son named Inrechtach.

9. I have kept the spelling as Colptha to distinguish between the harbor and the religious foundation of Colp which was an Anglo-Norman foundation. It may have been a refounding of an earlier Celtic community at the same site, but there is no record of an earlier community there.

10. Daircellach or Tairchellach *sapiens* (the wise) died in 760 according to the *Annals of Ulster*. Plummer notes this obituary in his notes to his edition of the present text, while Bray (see note 4 above) points to the similar incident in the *Life of St. Íta*.

11. It is very difficult to tell what this sentence intends to say. Plummer offers the guess "that Samthann's share which she gave up to the other sisters was multiplied so as to give an extra portion to each," an interpretation that implies that there was something miraculous in the whole business. From other sources we know that the head of a religious community often has a separate dwelling, while the rest of the community shared living space. If alms were divided equally among the dwellings, as abbess Samthann may have been given a larger share than the others to begin with. Perhaps the sentence means that she kept only a portion equal to what the other sisters would receive as individuals, and gave the excess back to be distributed to the rest of the community.

12. Plummer points out that this identification of the abbot of Devenish is probably an error introduced into the *Life* by a later scribe because he was the only abbot of Devenish whom the scribe knew by name. Lasrán, or Molaisse, of Devenish died in 564 or 571. There is no surviving list of abbots for Devenish, and only a few references to members of the community there appear in the annals prior to the tenth century.

CHAPTER 6

JONAS OF BOBBIO, THE ABBOTS OF BOBBIO FROM *THE LIFE OF ST. COLUMBANUS*

Translated by Ian Wood

INTRODUCTION

The *Life of St. Columbanus and His Disciples* was written by Jonas of Bobbio around the year 640. From the point of view of the modern historian it is perhaps the most important hagiographic text to have been written in Western Europe during the seventh century. It was already a work of some significance in its own time, being used by the chronicler known as Fredegar within a quarter of a century of its composition. It also came to be cited frequently by other hagiographers, although this is more apparent in the eighth century than in the second half of the seventh.

For the modern historian the importance of the *Vita s. Columbani* rests on four principle factors. First, it is an account of the life of the Irish saint, Columbanus, who was one of the earliest insular holy men to work on the Continent, and who had a major impact on the spirituality of the Frankish and Lombard kingdoms. Second, it is unusual among hagiographical works in dealing not just with a single saint, but in adding the lives of the two generations of disciples who followed their founding father. Third, although it is a hagiographical text, and therefore, like all hagiographical texts concerned first and foremost with spiritual matters, it provides crucial information on the period between 590 and 615, and indeed on the following two decades. Finally the work is important because of Jonas and the time in which he was writing, for he himself was caught up in a movement for monastic reform, which in certain respects stemmed from Columbanus's monastic foundations, and he also provides us with valuable information on that movement. It is useful to take each of these points in turn, before concluding with a comment on the text of the *Vita s. Columbani* and the selection included in this translation.

Columbanus was born in southwestern Ireland, in the kingdom of Leinster. The date of his birth is unknown, and Jonas's information on his early career in Ireland is sketchy. We are told that he moved north, first to a community near Downpatrick and then to the great monastery of Bangor. In 590/1 he crossed to Francia (or Frankland), where he founded, a little while after, in the region of the Vosges, monasteries first at Annegray and then, more importantly at Luxeuil, with a further house at Fontaine-les-Luxeuil. These foundations seem to have had some royal backing, and this despite the fact that Columbanus followed a tradition of dating Easter which differed from that accepted in Francia, and which prompted some confrontation with the local bishops. Nevertheless Columbanus seems to have been well regarded in Francia. His monasteries were sought out for their high ascetic standards, which involved an unusual degree of separation from the world, while he himself seems also to have played a role in the promotion of the practice of private penance. Theoretically the standard form of penance in the Western Church was public and could only be performed once in a lifetime (though it is fairly clear that this system was already being undermined by the end of the sixth century). In the British Isles, by contrast, the notion of a tariff of penances, to be performed as and when necessary, had come into being. Lists of penances known as *Penitentials* started to be compiled, and that drawn up by Columbanus is the first that is known to have been used on the Continent.

Columbanus's position in Francia, however, depended upon royal support, and this came to an end at some point in the first decade of the seventh century, when the saint refused to bless the bastard children of King Theuderic II. By the end of 610 he had been forced out of Theuderic's kingdom by the king and his grandmother, the dowager queen, Brunhild. He passed through the courts of Theuderic's rivals, Chlothar II and Theudebert II, and paused briefly at Bregenz, where he decided not to carry out a mission to the pagans – a point of some interest in that Columbanus is often thought of as a missionary figure. Certainly he played a role in the evangelization of the countryside, but essentially he was what the Irish termed a pilgrim for Christ (that is a *peregrinus pro Christo*) rather than a missionary to the heathen. His stay in Bregenz was short-lived, because a civil war blew up between Theuderic II and Theudebert II; Columbanus found it expedient to move to Italy. This proved a wise decision, since Theuderic killed Theudebert in 612. Theuderic, however, died of dysentery in 613, and Chlothar II was able to destroy Theuderic's immediate family, including Brunhild, and to reunite the whole Frankish kingdom. He then turned to Columbanus, inviting him back to Francia. In 613, however, King Agilulf of the Lombards had given Columbanus the site for a monastery at Bobbio in the mountains southwest of Pavia, and Columbanus resolved to stay there. He did, however, ask Chlothar's support for his Frankish foundations. He died in 615.

Book 1 of the *Vita s. Columbani* ends with the saint's death. Book 2 takes up the story of his followers at Bobbio and Luxeuil, and also relates the history of a nunnery founded for Abbess Burgundofara, by followers of Columbanus himself, at Faremoutiers. In the text as it is now edited, Jonas begins by relating the history of Columbanus's successor as abbot of Bobbio, Athala (615–26). (This section, *Vita s. Columbani*, Book 2 Chapters 1–6, is translated below.) From Bobbio Jonas turns to Luxeuil, and the career of Eustasius (*Vita s. Columbani*, Book 2, Chapters 7–10, not included in the transatlions below), who became abbot there, after Columbanus's departure. The abbacy of Eustasius (ca. 610–629) saw a crisis within the Columbanian movement when a monk, Agrestius, began to challenge the traditions and the theology of Luxeuil and Bobbio. Unfortunately Jonas is our sole source for this challenge, and he is obviously a biased observer. It is possible that in some respects the views of Agrestius were closer to those of Columbanus than were those of Eustasius and Athala under whom Columbanian monasticism had certainly developed in terms both of monastic lifestyle and theology. Eustasius's abbacy seems to have had one other aspect of particular significance. It saw the organization of missions to the heathen *Baioarii*, inhabitants of modern-day Bavaria. Indeed it is Eustasius rather than Columbanus who seems to have placed Columbanian monasticism in the forefront of missionary activity.

Clearly Jonas is a mine of information on the nature of Columbanian monasticism as it was perceived in the mid-seventh century, indeed his work was almost certainly intended to be a work of spiritual edification, aimed primarily at the communities of Bobbio and Luxeuil. Nevertheless certain passages of the *Vita s. Columbani* are also important for historians in providing major sections of narrative relating to ecclesiastical and secular history. The most obvious section of importance in this respect is the account of the confrontation between Columbanus and Theuderic II, which was indeed taken over wholesale by Fredegar, the chronicler who provides us with the most extensive narrative of this period. Jonas, however, also provides important information on the growing conflict between Theuderic II, Theudebert II, and Chlothar II in 612–13. In Italy his account of the conflict between Abbot Bertulf and Bishop Probus of Tortona, culminating in the acquisition of a papal privilege from Pope Honorius, is of immense value for our understanding of the development of papal involvement in monastic immunities, and his information on Milan and Pavia provides useful details on those two royal cities.

Jonas himself makes a number of appearances in his narrative. We learn that he was born in Susa, a town in the Alps which was disputed among the Franks, the Lombards and—at one stage—the Byzantines. He joined the community of Bobbio under abbot Athala in ca. 618, as can be deduced from the anecdote relating to Jonas's visit to his mother just before the abbot's death in 626 (*Vita s. Columbani*, Book 2, Chapter 5). He seems to have been regarded with some favor in the monastery, even as a young man, for he accompanied Bertulf on his journey to Rome in 628, when Honorius granted his papal privilege (*Vita s. Columbani*, Book 2, Chapter 23, translated below). Thereafter he made a number of journeys, notably to Luxeuil, but finally left the community to work with the missionary bishop Amandus of Maastricht in what is now the northern parts of Belgium, a point that he records in the preface to the *Vita s. Columbani* (translated below). Jonas was, therefore, himself involved in missionary work. As a Columbanian monk—and perhaps also as a monk who was known to have been present at the securing of a papal privilege—Jonas also became involved in the monastic reform movement which developed around King Clovis II (639–57), and more importantly around Queen Balthild. This movement seems to have been concerned primarily with the legal status of monasteries and their relationship with, or (in the case of the most important monasteries) independence from, bishops. Here association with the acquisition of Honorius's privilege would have been of great importance. Jonas's association with Balthild is clearest in the preface to another work, the *Life of St. John of Réomé*, where he refers to a journey undertaken on the orders of the queen and her son, King Chlothar III (657–73). His involvement in the monastic reform movement may also be reflected in the third work attributed to him, the *Life of St. Vedast*, which is likely to have been commissioned by the reforming bishop Autbert of Cambrai, who had himself been a monk of Luxeuil. What happened ultimately to Jonas is unclear, but he has been identified with Jonatus, abbot of Marchiennes, a community associated with Amandus.

Jonas's oeuvre is important. It also poses difficulties. The *Life of St. Vedast* is not provably his, although the attribution is likely. More important, the manuscript tradition of the *Vita s. Columbani* raises considerable questions about Book 2. No early manuscript of the *Vita* includes the text as reconstructed by Bruno Krusch in his edition. Instead, manuscripts pick and choose between the sections relating to Luxeuil, Bobbio, and Faremoutiers. Krusch very reasonably took Jonas's comments in his introductory letter to Waldebert and Bobolenus to argue that Jonas intended Book 2 to cover all the surviving material relating to those three monasteries. At the same time the manuscript tradition may suggest that Jonas himself added to the *Vita* over a number of years, and, equally importantly, that the early readers of the *Vita* wanted an abridged text, which covered those of Columbanus's disciples who were of most immediate interest to them.

In choosing to translate the sections of the *Vita s. Columbani* which are concerned with Bobbio, I have, therefore, returned to a time-honored tradition. By choosing the Bobbio chapters, moreover, I have been able to set out a discrete block of evidence, and one which, in its emphasis on abbots of the second and third generation of a community, presents a slightly unusual picture of early medieval monasticism, whose hagiography is usually concerned with founding fathers.

SOURCES AND FURTHER READING

The best edition of the *Vita s. Columbani* (*Bibliotheca hagiographica latina*, no. 1898) remains Iona, *Vitae sanctorum Columbani, Vedastis, Iohannis*, ed. Bruno Krusch, Monumenta Germaniae Historica, Scriptores Rerum Germanicarum in usum scholasticum 37 (Hannover, 1905). (Note that this edition significantly surpasses that provided by Krusch in *Monumenta Germaniae Historica, Scriptores Rerum Merovingicarum*, vol. 4 [Hannover, 1902], pp. 61–108.) Recent studies of its language and structure have been largely in German: Christian Rohr, "Hagiographie als historische Quelle: Ereignisgeschichte und Wunderberichte in der Vita Columbani des Ionas von Bobbio," *Mitteilungen des Instituts für Österreichische Geschichtsforschung* 103 (1995): 229–64, and Walter Berschin, *Biographie und Epochenstil im lateinischen Mittelalter, II: Merowingische Biographie, Italien, Spanien und die Inseln im frühen Mittelalter*, Quellen und Untersuchungen zur lateinischen Philologie des Mittelalters 9 (Stuttgart, 1988). These authors discuss the manuscript tradition of Jonas's work, as well as Krusch's edition.

For more detailed historical commentary on Jonas's work, see Ian Wood, "The *Vita Columbani* and Merovingian Hagiography," *Peritia* 1 (1982): 63–80, and "Jonas, the Merovingians and Pope Honorius," in *After Rome's Fall: Narrators and Sources of Early Medieval History*, ed. A.C. Murray (forthcoming). More specifically on the influence of Jonas's work on later hagiography, see Wood, "The *Vita Columbani*," p. 69, and Berschin, *Biographie und Epochenstil*, pp. 25, 74, 98.

For Columbanus himself there is the useful edition of his writings (with English translation): *Sancti Columbani Opera*, ed. G.S.M. Walker (Dublin, 1970). These works have recently been the subject of an important volume of essays: *Columbanus: Studies on the Latin Writings*, ed. Michael Lapidge (Woodbridge, Suffolk,1997). Of particular interest in that volume for the issues raised above in the introduction are the articles by Donald Bullough on "The Career of Columbanus" and by T.M. Charles-Edwards on "The Penitential of Columbanus." More generally on Columbanian monasticism and its impact there is *Columbanus and Merovingian Monasticism*, ed. H.B. Clarke and Mary Brennan, British Archaeological Reports, International Series 113 (Oxford, 1981). Naturally general surveys of the Merovingian Church also comment on Columbanus and his disciples, see notably J.M. Wallace-Hadrill, *The Frankish Church* (Oxford, 1983). For the Merovingian kingdoms at the time of Columbanus the chief source is *The Fourth Book of the Chronicle of Fredegar*, ed. J.M. Wallace-Hadrill (London, 1960). Fredegar draws on the work of Jonas of Bobbio at Book 4, Chapter 36. Useful recent histories of the Merovingians can be found in Edward James, *The Origins of France: From Clovis to the Capetians, 500–1000* (London, 1982); Patrick Geary, *Before France and Germany: The Creation and Transformation of the Merovingian World* (Oxford, 1988); and, with more detail on the period in question, Ian Wood, *The Merovingian Kingdoms, 450–751* (London, 1994). On Merovingian hagiography in general, see Paul Fouracre, "Merovingian History and Merovingian Hagiography," *Past and Present* 127 (1990): 3–38, and Paul Fouracre and Richard Gerberding, *Late Merovingian France: History and Hagiography, 640–720* (Manchester, 1996).

For the Lombard kingdom the chief narrative source is Paul the Deacon's *Historia Langobardorum*, which was edited by Ludwig Bethmann and Georg Waitz in *Monumenta Germaniae Historica, Scriptores Rerum Langobardicarum et Italicarum, saec. VI-IX* (Hannover, 1878). There is a useful but rather old translation by F. W. Foulke: *Paul the Deacon, History of the Langobards* (Philadephia, 1907; reprint 1974). For a recent treatment of the Lombards themselves, see Neil Christie, *The Lombards* (Oxford, 1995).

Jonas of Bobbio, The Abbots of Bobbio from the Life of Columbanus

(Preface.) Jonas the sinner to the fathers Waldebert and Bobolenus, distinguished lords adorned with authority of sacred distinction and sustained by the force of religion.[1]

I remember that about three years ago, at the entreaty of the monastic community and the command of the blessed abbot Bertulf, while I was spending time with them in the countryside of the Apennines, staying in the monastery of Bobbio, I promised to attempt to compose an account of the deeds of the bountiful father Columbanus, especially since those who were with him during his lifetime and were present to see what he did, many of whom have survived among you, have described to me things that they did not merely hear about, but actually saw, while I have also learned things from the venerable men, Athala and Eustasius, the first of whom succeeded him at Bobbio, the second at Luxeuil, monasteries now ruled by you, and they passed on to his followers those institutes of the master which ought to be preserved.[2] And their lives as well as those of the many whom excellence has made memorable I have set down afterward, insofar as I am able. But while the love of the aforesaid brothers, and the compelling order of the previously mentioned abbot was thought to flow over like a stream, I find myself most unequal to the work. However, if I had not regarded myself as unworthy of this work I would have embarked on the account at once, albeit rashly. But for three years I was borne over the estuaries of the Ocean and the Scarpe, heavy with its boats, and the Scheldt wet me as I sailed along [literally, with the boat cutting] its gentle waterways, while the sticky marsh of the Elno wet my feet as I assisted the venerable bishop Amandus who had been placed over these regions to combat the old errors of the Sicambri with the sword of the Gospel.[3] And appreciation of the work that has been commissioned, of the properly venerated abbot and of your judgment will be such that if anything lacks elegance of speech, having been set out with inadequate ceremony, it will be clothed in your virtues, so that it seems fitting to the readers, and since the deeds are not equaled by the account of them,[4] and the virtues of holy men are not imitated by bearing oneself proudly, they should not be appalled by my lack of skill in composing and having been appreciative in their applause at the first appearance of the work, soon strive to withdraw their hands, stained with blood by the hardship of the path. It is right to say to them that swimmers thrown back onto the bank, exhausted by the waves of the sea, when all other help is lacking, are accustomed to seize thorn bushes with a sudden effort and that the stomachs of the rich, when there is an excess of other banquets, often long for country cooking, and many, when their ears have been satiated with the instruments of every musician, with the honey of the lute and the cithara, adapt their hearing frequently to the modulation of the soft pipe.

And if I am found to have praised someone who is still living let me not be thought a flatterer, but one who describes things well done, nor do I favor anyone with a panegyrical song, but commend things worthy of memory, and if such a man is living, let him not be proud in any way, if he sees the gifts given to him by the Creator described by me, lest he corrupt the upright firmness of the mind at the prompting of arrogance.[5] For there is no doubt at all that the approval of flatterers pollutes minds full of the grace of virtues, as the Lord said to Israel through Isaiah, "*O My people, they that call you blessed, the same deceive you and destroy the way of your steps*" [Is 3:12, Vulgate]. Truly, false praise is a reproof to the wise man, as the saying goes, but true praise leads him to strive after better things. A praiseworthy reputation therefore adorns men in what they have done well, and it reproves less blameworthy languor stains by the loss of fervor. Let them be esteemed by others if what they do is worthy of imitation and not draw to themselves the evils of pride perniciously afterward as a result of praise for the virtue shown.

Therefore I have included those things which I have found to have taken place according to reliable authority and which I have considered are being forgotten out of negligence, and I have passed over many things, which I have not been able to remember completely and I have decided to write down nothing where I have an incomplete record. I have divided the material into two volumes to remove the excess of putting all in one volume for the readers: the first sets out the deeds of the blessed Columba,[6] and the second has recorded the life of his disciples Athala, Eustasius, and others whom I have remembered.[7] I think that these things should be weighed in your scales so that, approved by you with wise examination, they may drive uncertainty from others, for if anyone at all has discovered points improperly set out and not zealously corrected, he will think that it should be rejected, especially if he is fortunate in being trained with the eloquence of the learned and abundantly equipped with knowledge. For he will have learned that we do not turn our steps to this in order to equal the steps of the learned. They have painted the damp green fields in flower with the dew of eloquence; the arid earth has scarcely learned to produce bushes as a result of our skill. They with their riches have portrayed the unguent of balsam from Engaddi and the flowers of spice trees from Arabia; butter from Ireland scarcely grows fat at our touch. They lay hold of pepper and aromatics [literally: nard, that is balsam] from India; the unconstrained summits of the Pennine Alps, home of the birds, where the cold grows rigid from the Zephyr winds, scarcely bring forth wild flowers [literally: the Celtic nard] for us. They boast of the variety of precious stones; it seems rash for us to delight in the amber of Gaul. They set out the exotic fruits of the palm tree zealously, the ripe fruits of the gentle chestnut are ripe for us as in the poet of Ausonia.[8] Farewell kindly fathers, vigorous men and strong, devoted to eternal God. Amen . . .

Here begins the second book.

(1.) Concerning the manner of life and election of abbot Athala and the punishment meted out on the wicked.

And therefore, after the venerable Columba had passed from this world,[9] Athala was elected in his place, a man praiseworthy for his absolute piety, whose notable virtues shone out in imitation of his master; he was a Burgundian by race,[10] and thus noble by his nationality but nobler in holiness, following in the footsteps of his master. But it is not right to pass over the ways in which his early interests from the very beginning led to mature success. And so, while he had been provided with a liberal and literary education by his noble father he was recommended to a certain Bishop Arigius by his parent.[11] But when he saw that no profit was coming of this, his uncultivated yearnings began to long for greater things and he made up his mind to attach himself to a group of monks, having set aside the pleasures of lay society. Therefore he secretly left his companions and content with only two servants (*pueri*) came to the monastery of Lérins.[12] Having lived there for some while and seen the others submit their necks in no way to the reins of the discipline of a monastic rule, he began to consider anxiously what additional and stronger council might provide him with access to the true way. And so he left there and came as far as Luxeuil to the blessed Columbanus. The holy man saw that he was shrewd and naturally intelligent, he included him in his ministry and tried to educate him in every divine command.

Therefore, when he was ruling the aforesaid monastery with distinction in succession to the blessed Columbanus and was guiding it in every discipline consonant with the tenor of a monastic rule, the subtlety of the old serpent[13] began to spread the fatal virus of discord with injurious blows, exciting the hearts of some of his subordinates against him so that they claimed that they could not bear the precepts of excessive ardor and that they were unable to sustain the weight of harsh discipline.[14] But he, being of a wise mind, was anxious to provide holy poultices and to give a health-giving antidote, by which the putrefied scab might be removed, and he strove to soften the hearts of the arrogant. For a long time while he was not strong enough to keep control of those he castigated, disturbed by the sorrow of his mind, he followed them with many prayers and with the indulgence of piety, so that they would not leave him, nor deviate from the route of the arduous path and that they should remember that the fathers came into possession of the kingdom of heaven through mortification and contempt for the present life. When he saw it was of no use and realized that those souls who were turning elsewhere could not be held back by the reins of his community, he allowed the pertinacious ones to leave and, of those who departed from him, some afterward were received by marine hiding places and others sought the region of the desert in order to gain liberty. Having reached these destinations they soon felt punishment for their arrogant temerity through an extension of justice, for while they resided in these places and were slandering the man of God, one who was with them, called Roccolenus and who had stoked up the quarrel, as it is believed, was burned up with a sudden blazing attack of fever and began to cry out from the fires of his punishment that he wished to go to the blessed Athala and assuage the evils of the crime which had been committed with the medicine of penitence. Without delay he fell silent, he scarcely had time to say what he did, and breathed out his final breath. But of those who were present to see the divine vengeance taken for the injuries to the man of God, many returned and confessed their faults and promised to be reformed in all things if he would receive them back. The holy man accepted them back with wonderful joy, like sheep retrieved from the mouths of wolves and restored them to their places as they acknowledged their faults. But truly, those who were stained with the vice of arrogance, being hindered by shame and by temerity, not wishing to return and despising the object lesson in penitence which they had been given, were destroyed in a variety of ways, so that it became apparent that they were companions in the increasing reservoir of contumacy of him whom divine vengeance had struck, since they did not merit pardon with the rest. For one of them, called Theudemund, was killed by the blow of an ax; another, while crossing the bed of a small stream, got his legs entangled in a net and was killed by the little waves of the river; a third, who was called Theutharius, was drowned when he believed that his boat would carry him. Seeing these things, the others who remained, their shame overcome, followed their companions back to the blessed Athala and were received and saved by him as the others had been before.

(2.) Concerning the recession of the river by divine power.

Another miracle performed by him is attested to by all the brothers in the aforesaid monastery, including myself, who had been allocated to the service of the holy man. When at a certain time a stream which we have already mentioned, known as Bobius,[15] flowing violently and in rapacious course with the pressure of swollen water, as happens with torrents falling from the summits of the Alps when filled by the rains, so this one collected piles of stones and bundles of wood as it swelled with excessive strength and it strove to undermine the mill of the monastery with its fast current and to submerge the workshop, beating against it. Having heard this battering noise, the guardian of the mill who was called Agibodus made his way to the mill to see whether so much pressure might lead to any destruction.[16] When he arrived there he saw that unless help came quickly all would be destroyed and he believed that the father should be told with all speed, so that he might bring relief and save the mill from the force of the waters with necessary aid. The man of God addressed him, "Go," he said, "and call to me the deacon Sinoald. As for yourself, go to your bed and get some sleep and do not give your heart over to sorrow, overcome as you are by fear." For it was morning and the dawn was pouring out the first pleasant light on the earth. Therefore Sinoald came to the man of God and blessed Athala said to him, "Take the staff with which I prop myself up, go to the Bobius and speak with commanding voice, making the sign of the lordly cross before, so that it ceases to break through the banks and flood them with presumptuous audacity, but removes to other slopes of the hill, leaving this unharmed and let it know that it will recede by the commands of God." Following this command of the man of God the aforesaid man set off with faith to support him and having planted the rod in the bank he ordered the stream to remove itself from that place following the orders of the man of God and with divine power agreeing, and to transfer itself with violent effort to other slopes of the hill. And soon, having abandoned its course with the waters leaving these slopes of the hill, the obedient river kept in check the torrent, as if constrained by wings, and flowed down the hard slopes of the hill to wherever channels, containing the water, provided a bed along which it might flow. And now with the dawn bursting forth to extend light to the world,[17] Sinoald arose and, thinking, began to say to himself, "I shall go and see if the flood is obedient to the wish of the man of God." And he came to the bank of the channel and, seeing it empty, he wondered how it had moved to the slopes of another hill, leaving the channel where it had flowed for him to see. He came quickly to the man of God and announced the triumph of the victory that had been obtained. The man of God said to him, "Never tell this to anyone during my lifetime," doubtless lest the approbation of sycophants might stain a heart full of virtues. This vice, although a man be endowed with all sorts of virtues, is to be avoided zealously by all holy men, for the cunning enemy strives maliciously so that while he cannot stain a holy man with great and obvious sins, he may pollute him at least in obscure matters which seem to be of no importance.

(3) Concerning the thumb that was cut off and cured by the man of God.

It then happened, when, at a certain time, one of the monks, called Fraimer was plowing the land in preparation for sowing, the roughness of the hard earth suddenly checked and broke the firmness of the stock, which, when the aforesaid brother tried to mend it, suddenly cut the thumb off his left hand with an unexpected blow of iron. He buried his thumb in the ground, and placed turf over it, as if giving it over to burial. Then having left the plow, he made his way to the monastery and prostrate on the ground told the father in confession. On seeing this, the man of God said, "Where is the part of the thumb which was cut off?" And he said that he had buried it in the ground, in a furrow. "You have acted wrongly," he said, "why did you not bring it to me? Therefore hurry, telling no one the reason, and having retrieved it, bring it here." He therefore went out to the place, and brought back the piece of his thumb, as commanded. The distance was about a mile with the path weaving its way over the hard shoulder of the mountain and across the course of the Trivea.[18] Then the man of God, taking the bit of the thumb joined it to the hand, sticking it with his saliva, and the thumb, joined to the flesh with this glue, stuck as it had before, and he ordered that he go away discreetly keeping silence. Oh wonderful virtue of the Almighty, that he glorifies his followers thus on earth, that cold and severed limbs return to previous beauty by their intervention.

(4.) Concerning the sick cured at Milan.

On one occasion when this same man had traveled to Milan, there was a small boy suffering from the last stages of fever, waiting for death. His parents, on hearing of the arrival of the blessed Athala, came to him quickly and begged him to go with them. When the man of God attempted to disguise himself, they compelled him with tears and terrible oaths, to go before the evil noxious fire deprived the boy of his final breath. Therefore, anxious to flee popular acclamations and rumors he said, "Go, I will follow you, as I am able." Coming therefore, he traveled round the basilicas and holy places, praying for the sick child, so that he might be restored to health immediately. Then to fulfill his promise he hurried to the invalid, entered the house secretly, lest any herald of the dispenser of the gift appear, and he touched the sick child and directly divine virtue showing favor to holy prayers returned the invalid to pristine health. At the same time the parents gave thanks to the creator, who had turned the ears of his piety to the petitions of his servants.

For this man was kindly to all, of singular fervor, quickness and love towards foreigners and the poor; he knew to resist the proud and to subordinate himself to the humble, to requite the wise with learning and open mysteries to the simple; sagacious in solving and asking questions, vigorous and reliable against the snares of the heretics,[19] strong in adversity, sober in prosperity, temperate in all, discreet in everything. Love and fear flowed over in those subject to him, doctrine was diffused in his disciples; no one before him was either worn down with sorrow or elevated with excessive joy.

(5.) Concerning the prophecy of his death.

When the inventor of things wanted to liberate him from the hardship of this life, he wished matters to be revealed in a vision, so that he might have a way prepared in all things, once he had left the world and that a space of fifty days might be created in which he might prepare the way. But the soul of the man of God did not know clearly whether this way was the end of life or that he would set out for another place, and the man of God prepared for both. He thickened the enclosure of the monastery, renewed roofs, strengthened all, so that if he were absent, none might depart foolishly; he surreptitiously attended to vehicles, he rebound books and ordered coverings to be washed, tears to be sown up, rotten things to be made good, shoes to be prepared so that all should be ready. He himself prepared his body with fasting, vigils, and prayers, so that he had never before been seen to perspire so much while praying.

And lest it seem ridiculous to anyone let me relate what this man did with regard to me. Since nine years had passed since I had entered the monastic life, during which time my parents had often asked that he might give me permission to see them, but without success, he then said, making no reference to these requests, "Go hurriedly, my son, and visit your mother and brother, admonish them and return without delay." And when I made excuses and said that an opportune time would arise in the near future—for it was a period of excessive cold, being February—he said, "Hurry; set out on the journey of which I have told you; you do not know whether it will be possible to undertake in future." Therefore, having been given as companions the priest Blidulf and the deacon Hermenoald, about whose devoutness there was no doubt, we came to our destination. The place, Susa, a noble city, once a colony of Turin was one hundred an forty miles from the monastery.[20] There, when we arrived, we were graciously received by my mother after an interval of so many years, but she did not benefit from the hoped for gift for long. For that same night I was overcome with fever and began to shout out in my feverish-ness that I was tortured by the prayers of the man of God and might not stay there at all against his command; if they did not move me quickly and if I could not retreat to the monastery by whatever effort, I would soon be taken by death. To this my mother said, "It is better to me, 0 son, to know you are there healthy, than to weep for you dead, here." I say that it was a long wait until the coming of day. Scarcely had dawn broken than we were at pains to return, nor did we take any food for three days, until we had more or less reached the midpoint of the journey. Hurrying and pushing on the journey I regained my health and coming to the monastery found the father already overtaken by fever and near to death; when he saw us he was glad. And thus we openly knew that the prayers of the man of God had prevailed in this, so that the strength of fever had forced me to return quickly to the monastery before his death.

(6) Concerning the opening of the sky, divine consolation, and death.

When he came to the last hours of this present life, while he still had strength and breath he ordered that he be carried out of his cell, and rising from his couch with what strength he could muster, with the brothers helping on all sides, he left the cell. Seeing the cross which he had ordered to be set up there, so that leaving and entering the cell he might protect his forehead by touching it,[21] he became sad and began to cry and remember the trophy of the cross. "Hail sweet cross," he said, "you who have carried the ransom of the world, and who bears the eternal standard; you bore the salve of our wounds, you were anointed with his blood, who came from heaven to this vale of tears to save the human race, who spread out in you the stain of the first Adam a while ago and now a second Adam washes away the blot." While he did this he begged all to leave him and return to their cells and to let him alone in the place for a while. Therefore, with all going, one, however, Blidemundus by name, stood without breathing behind the man of God, thinking that as the knees of the man of God were tired by his broken labors, they might give way and that he would be ready to sustain him. When therefore [Athala] thought that no one was present, he began to beseech the clemency of the Creator with a multitude of tears that he might grant him gifts even though he was unworthy of his bounty, and that wiping out old stains might restore him to full salvation, and showing his old mercy, might not cast him aside from celestial gifts. Among sad sighs and flowing tears, looking up he saw the heavens open to him; this he saw for a space of many hours and he let out a great roaring from his heart. Then he gave thanks to the Almighty, because he had showed the gates of heaven opened to him, which after a little while the soul, having left the limbs of the body, would enter, and then he gave a sign that the brothers might come to take him back to his cell. These things the aforesaid brother told us on the same day. He showed this consolation to his servant that with the final secure nourishment of future pardon or rather glory, he might depart rejoicing. This the man of God had wished to keep hidden, had the aforesaid Blidemundus not remained secretly behind his back. On the next day,[22] saying farewell to all the brothers and exhorting them so that they might not leave the journey they had started, but might confirm their undertaking, strengthened by better acts with daily perseverance, and having thus consoled all, he broke the bonds of the present life and returned his soul to heaven. Justly the Maker of all things adorns his saints with a host of virtues, as it is written, "*His spirit has embellished the heavens,*" [Job 26:3] for those thirsting after celestial life are zealous to obey his commands so that they might receive the fruit of eternal life from the labor of obedience . . .[23]

[**Translator's note**: In Chapters 7–22 Jonas treats a number of other monastic communities founded by Columbanus, before returning to Bobbio in Chapter 23.]

(23.) Concerning the life of Abbot Bertulf.

The community of the learned strives to make known to posterity how notable are the monuments of the just during the hardships of this life. Therefore what is now known to have happened in our times, we ought in no way to pass over because we are overcome by the silent sleep of negligence, so that just as the examples of our predecessors generate a richer zeal for religion among us, so afterward the profitable deeds of our times may be fruitful for posterity, and while we set out things worthy of imitation for others, we may more often set out things worthy of commemoration for ourselves.[24]

For who and how great was the venerable Bertulf, head of the monastery of Bobbio, of whom we have made mention before, should not be left out by us in what we pass on to memory. But first the quality of his conversion [*conversatio*][25] from the world and his religious life should be remembered. For he was noble by birth albeit a barbarian [*gentilis*][26] and was related to the blessed Arnulf, bishop of the city of Metz.[27] When the aforesaid Bishop Arnulf turned to inhale the cult of religion after honors at court and to be active in piety after the decorations and pomp of the world, he also strove to desire heavenly things, treading earthly things under foot.[28] He set behind himself father, place of birth, and the pomp of the world, following the command of the Gospel, and after losing his possessions, naked he followed Christ, by taking up the Cross and denying himself for his sake.[29] Having joined the aforesaid Bishop Arnulf, he stayed with him for a short time. Then he set out for Luxeuil and the venerable man Eustasius, and there he remained for a long time, subject to the holy rule [*sanctae regulae*] and religion and pleasing to all.[30] Next, when the blessed Athala came from the regions to the south, he joined his community with the agreement and bond of love of the holy man Eustasius, because they were of one heart and one soul, nor did any discord remain between them, since they exchanged those subject to them according to mutual agreement. Therefore, he followed after in the footsteps of the venerable Athala and was received into the folds of the South and remained in the monastery of Bobbio in obedience to the blessed Athala. And when the creator of all things drew the aforesaid father Athala to the heavenly kingdom after the hardships of this world, the whole assembly of the monks cried out, united in voice and mind, "We elect Bertulf to the paternal office." For thirteen years he did not cease from teaching his flock with all diligence and zeal and from imbuing them with lifegiving advice. But what he did during this period ought to be handed down to memory.

When he already governed the community with noble traditions, goodness and discipline with knowledge as a moderating force, the old serpent began to vex the quiet mind with the blows of adversity. He stirred up a certain bishop, Probus by name, bishop of the city of Tortona, who strove with all his power to make the aforesaid abbot, and the monastery in addition, subject to him.[31] First he approached the courtiers and neighboring bishops, tempting them with bribes, and when he was delighted that they had joined him, he went on to use them to persuade the king. At that time Arioald ruled over the Lombards.[32] But when they received nothing from the king by way of reply, except that they should prove by ecclesiastical law whether a monastery situated far from cities ought to be subordinated to episcopal jurisdiction, [Probus] associated all whom he could with his cause. And when these things were being declared one of the courtiers secretly told the aforesaid Bertulf what plots they were devising in the matter. He sent messengers to the king to test out the situation, to whom Arioald replied, "It is not for me to adjudicate in ecclesiastical cases, which a conciliar examination ought to pursue to the point of truth." Therefore, they wondered whether [Arioald] might be a supporter of their arguments. He said he was in no way favorable to those who wished to stir up troubles against the servant of God. And when they saw that he spoke such things, although [he was] a credulous follower of the Arians among the barbarians, they asked that they might be supported at public expense, so that they would be able to go to the apostolic seat in Rome.[33] Therefore, with aid granted, the aforesaid abbot [Bertulf] in whose company I traveled set out for Rome in royal style, to Pope Honorius.[34] When [Bertulf] had explained the case in hand to him, [the pope] inquired zealously what the custom of regular discipline might be. And when [Bertulf] had set out everything perspicaciously to the ears of his superior, the blessed Honorius was pleased by the signs of humility in [the monks'] regular pattern and reverence for religion. Therefore, [Honorius] kept Bertulf for a little while and strove to encourage him with daily suggestions, so that he might not forsake the hardship of the way he had set out on and might not cease from striking the perfidy of the Arian disease with the sword of the Gospel,[35] for Honorius was a venerable pontiff of wise mind, strong council, illuminating doctrine, and striking sweetness and humility. He was delighted to have found an ally for those in need, from whom he acquired sweet council, but he was not further pleased that he had quickly to leave his company. But since the considerable commotion prevented a long period of rest, he offered the hoped-for gift and granted a papal privilege so that no bishop might try to claim authority over the aforesaid community [Bobbio] by whatever right.[36]

Therefore, having obtained the gift we had hoped for, we attempted to return home. And when, having covered part of the journey and having set behind us the fields of Tuscany, we reached the countryside of the Appenines and had come close to the fortress known as Bismantova,[37] a fever of such great force afflicted Bertulf that it was thought that he had been altogether forestalled by death. For when he had left Rome he was already a sick man. Both the sorrows of the long journey and the hardships of the ailing abbot oppressed all, nor did anyone have any more hope for his recovery. When the tent had been pitched in a harsh location, hemmed in on all sides with sorrow, and not at all confident in the abbot's recovery, we were fearful. It was then the vigil of the [feast of the] passion of the blessed apostles, Peter and Paul.[38] And when black night had already fallen he summoned me, tormented by the blazing fever as he was, and his mind given over to cares enquired about the nocturnal vigil. And when I said that it was already arranged, he said, "Lie before my bed for the whole measure of the night, until the dawn of day breaks through." And when I had lain down, as the dead of night fell, so great sleep overcame me that I was not able to lift up my head, and all who lay in the tents, by the baggage or horses, were similarly overcome by sleep. And therefore when complete silence fell, the blessed prince of the apostles Peter came and stood over the bed of the sick abbot, "Rise," he said, "and give your help to your companions." And when [Bertulf] asked who he was, he said, "Peter. My glorious festivities are celebrated throughout the world today." And when he had said these things, he departed. The other, struck by fear, took care to question me with anxious and fearful heart, about the reason behind the event. For he thought I had heard the voice and seen the figure. And when I said that I had heard and seen nothing, he said, "Did you not see the yellow light in which the apostle Peter departed." And when I said that I had seen nothing at all, he began to be silent. And when I realized what lay behind the event, I was scarcely able to induce him by my prayers to expound the truth of the matter to me. He would have kept completely silent, if he had not thought that I heard and saw.

On a certain occasion, he together with the brothers went out of the church of the blessed Peter after the office of Psalms on the second hour of the day,[39] and on the way they encountered a man called Viaturinus, who was filled with demonic madness. Seeing him, he looked at the heavens and asked the Creator that He might be present and favorable to his request and might cure the man ailing from the demonic plague in response to his prayers. Then [Bertulf] ordered that the rabid power of the demon should leave the man and never again presume to soil the image of God.[40] The wicked disease, miserably flailing around, fled from the man, immediately a cure followed, and the fit man left the church with the brothers and continuing in health, gave thanks to the Creator, who had thus relieved his torment, thus quickly showing favor to his servant and responding to his prayers.

Then after a period of time, a child called Domnicus, the son of a certain Urbanus, oppressed with a savage demonic affliction, rushed to him for the favor of a cure. After reproaching him for a long time, [Bertulf] cured him and forced the savage plague to depart from the boy.

Another miracle followed. A certain leper, deeply afflicted by leprosy and not being given any assurance from the doctors that he would regain his health, came to the venerable man, Bertulf, and asked him if he might merit the riches of mercy through his prayers. When the man full of faith looked at him and saw that the man was subject to most painful torment, he sighed and ordered that he remain with him until health returned. He took pains so that the mind conscious of virtues, penetrating the heavens, might rouse the Creator of things to respond to his prayers. Having spent a two-day fast, he poured oil over [those] limbs covered in ulcers and soon the limbs learned to receive health, after the putrefaction of the intestines, and to return once again to pristine beauty, and thus the sick man was cured so that no trace of leprosy was visible on his body.[41] And thus the Creator of all brought relief, showing favor to his servants, so that strengthened more fully with the power of virtue trampling on slovenliness, they might always strive to fulfill the commands of heaven.[42]

(24.) Concerning the vengeance of the monk on the Arians.

And we know from experience that the virtues of numerous monks shine out and therefore we think it right to set down certain of the tales relating to them. When, on a particular occasion, the priest Blidulf, whom we have already mentioned above,[43] had been sent by the blessed Athala to the city of Pavia,[44] and had arrived there, while walking along a street in the center of the city, he met Arioald, duke of the Lombards, a most noble man by birth, son-in-law of Agilulf and a relative of Adalwald, a follower of the Arian sect, who, after the death of Adalwald, undertook the government of the kingdom of the Lombards.[45] Therefore, when he saw Blidulf, he said, "He is one of the monks of Columbanus and refuses to make appropriate responses to our greetings." And when he was already quite close, he greeted him derisively. To this Blidulf said, "I would look forward to your greeting if you did not support your heretics and doctrine alien from the truth. Those whom you have hitherto called bishops have deceitfully secured the title for themselves; further it is better to confess the Trinity which is beyond comprehension as one God; and not three powers, but three persons, nor one person with three names, but three persons in the truth of the Father, Son, and Holy Spirit, one in power, wish and essence." Listening to this for a little while he moved forward, then asked why he did not have servants of such cruelty, that they might attack the monk as he returned when the darkness of night had fallen and might deliver this monk to death, beaten with cudgels and staves. Then one, more depraved than the others, said he was prepared to do this deed if it was commanded. [Arioald] said truly, "If you do this, I will endow you with gifts on the following day." Therefore he set out having associated a likeminded companion in crime with himself, and kept watch over the route as night fell. The monk and priest, therefore, traveling along the same road, returning from a dinner to which he had been invited by a certain Christian,[46] suddenly fell unexpectedly among the ruffians and having been frequently hit and struck on every joint of his body, he died horribly beaten by the blows of cudgels and by staves, with none of the people knowing, it being an out-of-the-way place, but he did not stop from shouting out, fearing the lethal blows. Therefore, they then went away for a while, leaving the corpse lifeless, as they thought, and announced to its author that the crime had been committed. And when the man at whose house he was staying saw that the priest and monk was delayed, not knowing the outcome of things he was fearful—for he himself was a priest, called Iustus—that he might have fallen among the Arians, and, taking up his staff, Iustus followed the route for a while and found the man lying there, as if overcome by sleep and he tried to raise him. [Blidulf] truly rose from the road as if unharmed, with the traces of the blows scarcely visible. And together they went to their lodging. On being asked why this was, he said that "nothing more gentle had ever happened to me" and swore that he had never had a sweeter sleep. The other asked if any pain in the limbs afflicted him, he replied that he had never been healthier and did not know that anything adverse had happened to him. Having done his necessary business he returned to the monastery [of Bobbio]. He, however, who had shown himself ready to perform the deed, soon after the departure of the monk from Pavia, was seized by a demon and tormented by the flames of various punishments, confessed that he had performed the fatal crime. He shouted out to all the people that whoever perpetrated such deeds as he had against the monks of Bobbio was subject to similar vengeance and who fell in with the persuasions of the Arians, felt such anger of the just judge. Seeing this crime revealed by the divinity, the wretched Arioald, confused and fearful lest anything similar might happen to him sent the man tormented by this horrid force, together with his companions, to Athala and asked for himself that [the abbot] might overlook the evil committed, and that if they were willing to receive his gifts, [Arioald] was ready to provide them with great servitude. The blessed Athala, seeing the injuries of the man's body avenged by the divinity, asked that all pray for the afflicted so that the force of the adverse power might be driven from the wretched man. The gifts of the impious and heretical man, he replied, he would never receive in all eternity. Therefore, the Lord heard the prayers of all in the present time: having been restored to health, the fortunate man returned home immediately, but he did not long possess the riches of life. When he had returned to his lodging and was reproached by others about why he had done this, he said insolently that he had done it of his own accord. What then did they want? Suddenly seized by the fires of fever, shouting out among the punishments of the flames, he was deprived of life. They did not dare at all to bury him near the tombs of others, but far from all in a conspicuous place where those going by say, "Here lies buried that wretched man, who acted cruelly against a monk of Bobbio following his own lascivious nature."

(25.) Concerning the monk Meroveus and his vengeance and the death of the monk, Agibodus, and Theudoald, Baudacharius and Leubardus.

At that time then another monk, Meroveus by name, was sent by the blessed Athala to the city of Tortona and arrived there, but because of the business for which he had come he went on some way from the city, and came to a certain villa on the river Staffora, in which, as he was approaching, he saw a temple situated among the trees, and bringing fire, he set light to it and gathered together a pile of wood like a pyre.[47] The temple's disciples seeing this, seized Meroveus and having beaten him for a long while with cudgels and struck him with blows they tried to drown him in the river Staffora.[48] But the waves did not dare to receive the monk although he was utterly prepared to die for such a cause. And when they saw that they could not drown him whom the mercy of God protected, mad counsel took place among them. They threw Meroveus onto the waves and then heaped up stuff on top of him so that the great weight might force him below the waves. And when they thought the crime concluded, they left the corpse, as they thought and returned to their dwellings. When they had gone, Meroveus feeling no pain, rose unharmed from the river and having broken his bonds safely entered Tortona and afterward made the return journey to the monastery. But soon divine vengeance struck the ruffians after Meroveus had moved on. For all those who were in the gang which attempted this deed were afflicted with various plagues. Some went blind, some were burned by fire, the knees of some contracted, some were struck by debility in all their limbs, different men were tormented in diverse ways. But after they had discovered that Meroveus had returned safely to Bobbio, some of the sick among them were brought there. But a few of them were saved through the medicine of penitence; all the rest were destroyed in the same vengeance. The Creator of things pours out wonderful gifts to His servants, since after the torments of the flesh and injuries sustained by the body He provides strength through aid in the present life and he glorifies with future coronation after the strife and He notices those especially who receive injury on their own accord for His name.

We see a good life and an even better death achieved by other monks of the aforesaid monastery of Bobbio, who going from this life have left examples in diverse exhortation for those still alive. From among those some should be set forth so that the exhortation might grow among those still living who imitate their lives. For at a certain time a certain monk called Agibodus, whom we have already mentioned, who was in charge of the mill of the monastery at the time of the blessed Athala,[49] was placed in extreme anxiety and awaited the hour of his death. And when the crowd of brothers stood around to pay final honors to the soul leaving the world and were preparing themselves for the office of psalms as is the custom, the soul left the body and saw eternal light prepared for itself and the sun shining with a sparkling gleam. And when he saw and said that he had never seen such a sun or brightness that could equal it, one of the angels came to him and asked why he looked astonished. He said that he wondered at the radiance of the sun and that he had never seen anything comparable. The other said, "Know that today you come to us and will be an inhabitant of this golden light and, placed among the chorus of the just, will shine seven times more than this sun. Go back, say farewell to the company of your brothers and then return thus to us." The soul returned to the body; he said his last farewell to all. And when one of the bystanders asked why he had remained so long between life and death, he explained the matter of the event, related what he had seen and how much radiance had been promised to him, and announced that he would die that hour, having returned to take the great viaticum and to say farewell to the brothers. And when he had consumed the holy body of the Lord, he gave a kiss to all and asked that they might perform the duty of love to his body. The end soon followed the promise and having a happy death he left only longing to the living. The giver of rewards to the saints wished to leave this for posterity as an example, so that those who knew that his crown had been promised before his death might imitate his purity and religion in all things. For he had been brought up from boyhood under the maxims of regular discipline, having been converted from the world under the blessed Columbanus; he was held to be simple in all goodness among his brothers, shining in obedience and religion, and a child standing completely above malice in accordance with the New Testament. [see 1 Cor 14:20] For why was it that the most clement Creator of things wished to show him the quality of his future life, while he was dying, except that those, who live in similar simplicity and are voluntarily subject to obedience and mortification, might look forward to a similar reward and might obtain the brightness of eternal light?

We see another man, Theudoald by name, alike in obedience, piety, and gentleness, happily separated from the present life and hastening to eternal joys with all gladness and exultation. For as he lay happily on his bed he asked that all come and said a final farewell to each; that same hour he would leave his body. But how he foreknew his death he was completely unwilling to tell us. And when he had already said farewell to all, he asked for the viaticum and having received it, he himself began the antiphon, saying "The holy will go from virtue to virtue; the God of gods will be seen in Sion." [Ps 83: 8] When the tune of the antiphon was finished, joyfully and filled with all pleasantness, he returned his soul to its donor, so that we who were present were given to understand clearly that he was filled with joy by the sight of glory and the promise of a reward.

Under Abbot Bertulf, another monk called Baudacharius, was ordered to protect the vines at the time of harvest, lest damage might be caused by the arrival of birds or beasts, and it happened that thirty brothers came to protect the same vineyard. He, full of love, asked that there they might refresh their tired limbs after work having nothing other than a little bread which he had brought for his own use. When the overseer[50] reproached him not to continue with this plan because he could not provide bread, [Baudacharius] said, "I have plenty of food with me from which as many and more can be satiated." And when the overseer asked what they were, he said, nourishment given to him by God, which the common people call ducks because they swim.[51] He said, "As you have requested, set out food for the brothers." He exerted himself and divided between thirty and thus all were so satisfied that they said they had been filled with food at scarcely any other time. Faith increased what they did not have by supplementing the food.

Again, another monk called Leubardus, when on a different occasion he had been deputed to look after the vines found a little fox devouring the grapes. He castigated it with threats not to touch the grapes ever again and prohibited this by command. And when he went away the wild animal accustomed to live by theft, came to the food and when it had tasted, taking the prohibited food in its mouth it expired. Soon Leubardus, patrolling the vineyard according to his duty, discovered the fox dead, holding the prohibited food in its mouth.

On another occasion, the same Leubardus, together with Meroveus, whom we have already mentioned, were strengthening the enclosure of the vineyard and building it up on the abbot's orders. It happened that they cut a tree down with an ax and strengthened the fence by adding branches. And when they had denuded the trunk of branches they decided to prostrate themselves on the ground to ask God to increase their strength so that they could transport the complete tree trunk to the fence. And when they rose from prayer, they picked up the tree on invoking the sacred name of almighty God and tried to carry it to the agreed spot. And what many could scarcely have dragged to the place, two men, armed with faith, carried with light movement. Afterward, many brothers gathered and tried to move it all together and when they could not raise it, then finally they acknowledged the strength of the Almighty. And this virtue, when they returned, they each made known secretly to the others at the same time, not each ascribing it to himself, but the one to the other.

But perhaps someone will judge and condemn us, reprehending us and disparaging us for including such things. We, however, do not know how to hide those things which belong to divine glory. Let each judge for himself whether these gifts of the Creator are either meet to be received by him who denies them, or rejected by him who does not believe in the miracles of faith which have been performed.

Notes

1. Waldebert sreved as the second abbot of Luxeuil, from 629 until 670. He succeeded Eustasius, who had led the monastery after Columbanus's departure (ca. 610). Bobolenus became abbot of Bobbio on the death of Bertulf in ca. 639. Bertulf, the second abbot, followed Columbanus's successor, Athala, who served as abbot from 615 until 626.

2. "The institutes of the master (*magistri instituta*) which ought to be preserved" are clearly those aspects of Columbanus's own rulings on monasticism which were still acceptable a generation after his death. Two rules associated with Columbanus still survive, see *Sancti Columbani Opera*, ed. G.S.M. Walker (Dublin, 1970), pp. 122–69. It is clear, however, that these were rapidly adapted, just possibly while he was still alive, and that Luxeuil and Bobbio both used elements of the *Rule of St. Benedict* alongside the *Rule of Columbanus*. See Ian Wood, "The *Vita Columbani* and Merovingian Hagiography," *Peritia* 1 (1982): 74. On the *Rules of Columbanus*, see J.B. Stevenson, "The Monastic Rules of Columbanus," in *Columbanus: Studies on the Latin Writings*, ed. Michael Lapidge (Woodbridge, Suffolk,1997), pp. 203–16.

3. The Scarpe, the Scheldt, and the Elno are all waterways in present-day Belgium. Amandus, bishop of Maastricht, was one of the leading missionary figures in early seventh-century Francia. He has been seen as playing a major role in the development of the ideology of mission: see W.H. Fritze, "*Universalis Gentium Confessio*. Formeln, Träger und Wege universalmissionarischen Denkens im 7. Jahrhundert," *Frühmittelalterliche Studien* 3 (1969): 78–130. He was also associated with Columbanian monasticism, founding an

important monastery at Elno (also known as Saint-Amand-aux-Eaux). *Sicambri* is an archaic name for the Franks.

4. Jonas here echoes the words of both *The Conspiracy of Cataline* by the Roman historian Sallust (86–34 BCE) and the *Life of St. Hilarion* by the Christian scholar Jerome (ca. 341–420).

5. The question of pride was one that much concerned Jonas. It features strongly in the section of the *Vita s. Columbani* concerned with Burgundofara and Faremoutiers (bk. 2, chaps. 11–22), and may explain why Jonas says so little about Burgundofara herself.

6. Columba and Columbanus are one and the same person, Columbanus merely being the diminutive form of the name Columba. This diminutive form is used consistently by historians to distinguish Columbanus, the founder of Luxeuil and Bobbio, from his older contemporary Columba, the founder of the Scottish monastery of Iona who died there in 597. This second Columba was also known as Colum Cille, the name under which he appears in a work translated later in this collection: *A Tale of Doomsday Colum Cille Should Have Left Untold*.

7. Jonas's description of his work is an important clue to its original shape. No early manuscript includes the whole of Book 2, but each one concentrates on material relating to only one or two of the three communities of Luxeuil, Bobbio or Faremoutiers. The comment here provides some justification for Bruno Krusch's reconstruction of the text, but it should still be noted that from very early on the second book of the *Vita s. Columbani* seems to have circulated in a deliberately truncated form: see Christian Rohr, "Hagiographie als historische Quelle: Ereignisgeschichte und Wunderberichte in der Vita Columbani des Ionas von Bobbio," *Mitteilungen des Instituts für Österreichische Geschichtsforschung* 103 (1995): 229–64. Only the selection of chapters relating to Bobbio are included in the present translation.

8. That is, Vergil. *Ausonia* is a poetic word for Italy, Vergil's home. The citation in question is Vergil, *Eclogues*, book 1, line 80. The whole passage, with its self-deprecating set of comparisons between what a classical rhetorician could achieve (defined by exotic descriptions of the East) and the best that Jonas could do (defined by the more humble descriptions of the West), shows precisely how skillful Jonas was, despite his own rather idiosyncratic Latin, and the point is rubbed in with the final reference to Vergil. Unlike other authors Jonas makes no attempt to say that rhetorical language is inappropriate for Christian writing; instead he sets out to equal the classics.

9. Columba(nus) died on November 23, 615.

10. Burgundy was the Frankish kingdom whose center was Chalon-sur-Saône. On the changing meaning of Burgundian in this period, see Ian Wood, "Ethnicity and the Ethnogenesis of the Burgundians," in *Typen der Ethnogenese unter besonderer Berücksichtigung der Bayern*, eds. Herwig Wolfram and Walter Pohl (Vienna, 1990), pp. 53–69.

11. Arigius (sometimes spelled Aridius) was bishop of Lyon from 603.

12. The monastery of Lérins was founded in the early fifth century by the Gallo-Roman aristocrat Honoratus. For the first century of its existence it was one of the leading centers of monasticism in Gaul, and indeed of Western Europe, providing a model for abbots and monks elsewhere, while many of its own inmates also went on to become bishops in sees throughout southern Gaul: Ralph Mathisen, *Ecclesiastical Controversy and Factionalism in Fifth-Century Gaul* (Washington, DC, 1989), pp. 69–140. Although it continued to be cited as having a model monastic constitution in the seventh century, its standards declined dramatically: see Ian Wood, "A Prelude to Columbanus: The Monastic Achievement in the Burgundian Territories," in *Columbanus and Merovingian Monasticism*, ed. H.B. Clarke and Mary Brennan, British Archaeological Reports, International Series 113 (Oxford, 1981), p. 19.

13. The "old serpent" is, of course, the devil.

14. Although there are indications that Columbanian monasticism changed in the generation after Columbanus's death, it is far from clear whether the complaints against Athala's abbacy really were directed against a harshening of standards. What follows suggests that the rebels wanted to become hermits, and that the conflict was one between an abbot who insisted on the cenobitic life and monks who wished to live outside the community.

15. The stream known as the Bobius gave its name to Columbanus's monastery. Jonas describes it in *Vita s. Columbani*, Book 1, Chapter 30. For a translation of the passage in question, and commentary on it, see Ian Wood, "Jonas, the Merovingians and Pope Honorius: Diplomata and the *Vita Columbani*," in *After Rome's Fall: Narrators and Sources of Early Medieval History*, ed. A.C. Murray (forthcoming). Although Jonas talks of the Alps, Bobbio lies to the southwest of Milan, in what would now be regarded as part of the Appenines, and it must be to these mountains that he refers.

16. The death of Agibodus is related subsequently by Jonas, in *Vita s. Columbani*, Book 2, Chapter 25.

17. Jonas here recalls a phrase of Vergil, *Aeneid*, trans. Robert Fitzgerald (New York, 1981), bk. 4, line 585, p. 117: "Soon early dawn ... cast new light on earth."

18. The Trivea is also described in *Vita s. Columbani*, Book 1, Chapter 30. See Ian Wood, "Jonas, the Merovingians and Pope Honorius."

19. The heretics whom Jonas has in mind are almost certainly the Arian Lombards, although other heretical groups were present in northern Italy, among them the Tricapitoline schismatics. For Columbanus's own theological position with regard to these heretics, see Clare Stancliffe, "The Thirteen Sermons Attributed to Columbanus," in *Columbanus: Studies on the Latin Writings*, ed. Michael Lapidge (Woodbridge, Suffolk, 1997), pp. 187–8. On conflicts between the monks of Bobbio and heretics, see *Vita s. Columbani*, Book 2, Chapters. 24–5, which are translated below.

20. Susa is in the Alps, on the route from Italy to France. In the late sixth century it was disputed between the Byzantines, the Lombards, and the Franks: see Ian Wood, *The Merovingian Kingdoms 450–751* (London, 1994), p. 168. It is possible that it was Frankish when Jonas was born.

21 For this tradition see also Columbanus, *Regula Coenobialis*, chap, 3, ed. Walker, pp. 146–149 (see note 2 above).

22. March 10, 626 (?).

23. In Bruno Krusch's reconstruction of the text there follows a series of chapters, first on Luxeuil during the abbacy of Eustasius and then on the nunnery of Faremoutiers under Abbess Burgundofara. Although Athala appears again briefly in Chapter 9, the history of the abbey of Bobbio is not taken up again until Chapter 23, with the *Life of Abbot Bertulf*.

24. This reads like the opening of a new work, and indeed the title of the chapter, *De vita Bertulfi abbatis*, indicates that the chapter could have been read independently from the rest of Book 2 of the *Vita s. Columbani*. As mentioned above, the manuscript evidence suggests that the second book of the *Vita* was treated as a collection of detachable accounts of Bobbio, Luxeuil, and Faremoutiers: the *Life of Abbot Bertulf* could, therefore, have easily been treated as an independent portion of the text.

25. The word used by Jonas is *conversatio*, which really means religious or monastic lifestyle rather than conversion.

26. This must indicate that Bertulf was a Frank, but the description is rather surprising for a number of the saints, previously described by Jonas, including Burgundofara, were of Germanic extraction.

27. Bishop Arnulf of Metz (who served from 614 to 629 and died ca. 640) is given a high profile by many early medieval historians, as being an ancestor of the Carolingian family. Whether he was or was not is by no means certain, since the direct evidence for a family connection (that is, the marriage of Arnulf's son Ansegisel to Begga, daughter of Pippin I) comes only from the late eighth century. The fact that nothing is made of any relationship in seventh-century sources suggests that, if there was a family connection between Arnulf and Pippin I, it was not regarded as being of great significance before the reign of Charlemagne. Nevertheless Arnulf, who had been *domesticus* under King Theudebert II, who ruled Austrasia from 596 until 612, certainly played an important political role alongside Pippin I in the takeover of the kingdoms of Austrasia and Burgundy by Chlothar II in 613. Arnulf remained influential under Chlothar, until the king's death in 629, and under Chlothar's son, Dagobert I, who was raised by his father to be co-king in 623 and reigned until 639, as can be seen in the *The Fourth Book of the Chronicle of Fredegar*, ed. and trans. J.M. Wallace-Hadrill (London, 1960), Chapters 40, 52, 53, and 58. Arnulf was also closely associated with monasticism in northeastern Francia, having notable connections

with the monastery of Remiremont under Abbots Amatus and Romaricus, and he retired from his diocese to become a hermit in ca. 629. The *Life of St. Arnulf* has been seen as a key to the mid-seventh century (see Lellia Cracco Ruggini, "The Crisis of the Noble Saint: The Vita Arnulfi," in *The Seventh Century: Change and Continuity*, eds. Jacques Fontaine and Jocelyn Hillgarth [London, 1992], pp. 116–49), but its date of composition is uncertain and arguments about the text's value for interpreting the period should therefore be treated with caution. The *Life of St. Arnulf* has much in common with the *Lives* of Abbots Amatus and Romaricus, but these are sometimes seen as being eighth-century compositions, see Ian Wood, "Forgery in Merovingian Hagiography," in *Fälschungen im Mittelalter*, 5 vols., Monumenta Germaniae Historica, Schriften 33 (Hannover, 1988), 5:370–71. All three *Lives* are, nevertheless, earlier than the sources which emphasize Arnulf's Carolingian connections, and more certainly reflect a Merovingian assessment of his importance than do the later accounts of the marriage of Ansegisel and Begga.

28. Jonas's chronology appears to be faulty here: Arnulf seems to have set aside his episcopal office to enter the religious life in 629 (see the edition by Bruno Krusch of the *Vita s. Arnulfi*, chap. 7 in *Monumenta Germaniae Historica, Scriptores Rerum Merovingicarum*, vol. 2 [Hannover, 1888], pp. 434–35), whereas Bertulf had already become abbot of Bobbio in ca. 626.

29. This is, of course, a topos, derived largely from Mt 10:37–40.

30. The words *sanctae regulae* ("to the holy rule") should probably not be taken as a precise reference to a particular monastic rule, but rather as a more general reference to the lifestyle at Luxeuil.

31. Tortona lies between Genoa and Placentia. It was the center of the diocese in which Bobbio lay. The conflict between Bertulf and Probus which follows marks a crucial stage in the development of monastic immunity: see Ian Wood, "Jonas, the Merovingians and Pope Honorius" (see note 15 above).

32. Arioald was king of the Lombards from 626–36. Like most of his immediate predecessors he was an Arian, and indeed Jonas returns to his Arianism in Chapter 24. Here, however, Arioald acts with remarkable moderation.

33. This might suggest the functioning of some state transport system (a *cursus publicus*) not unlike that which had operated in the Roman world.

34. Pope Honorius I, who served from 625 until 638.

35. The papacy was clearly keen to exploit any connections it could, both to attack Lombard Arianism and also to counter Lombard military threats against Rome.

36. This is a reference to the granting of a papal privilege on June 11, 628. The grant to Bobbio became a model for subsequent papal privileges, and it is preserved as such in the papal formulary, the *Liber Diurnus*, where it is number 77: see *Codice diplomatico del monastero di S Columbani di Bobbio*, ed. Carlo Cipolla, 3 vols., Fonti per la storia d'Italia 52–54 (Rome, 1918), 1: 100–103.

37. Bismantova was a fortress in the region of Modena.

38. That is, June 28, 628.

39. The story of the papal privilege is now over, and Jonas is relating a miracle back at Bobbio. In the Columbanian Rule there were eight daily services, which were mainly concerned with singing of Psalms. The office at the second hour, that is 6 AM, was Prime: see, in particular, Stevenson, "The Monastic Rules of Columbanus," pp. 209–10 (see note 2 above).

40. The reference is to the notion that man is made in God's image.

41. Leprosy is mentioned in the Bible, but there it is unlikely to be the same as Hansen's disease, which is what we now term leprosy. This disease appears to have been extremely rare in the early Middle Ages. References to leprosy, therefore, may be references to one of a number of conditions which could be called "unclean," and because they were unclean they were often thought to have been caused by sin, hence, possibly, the strong element of spiritual instruction in this cure. For leprosy in the early Middle Ages, see R.I. Moore, *The Formation of a Persecuting Society* (Oxford, 1987), pp. 47–50.

42. This appears to be the end of the *Life of Abbot Bertulf*. One manuscript actually adds the statement, "Afterward the holy father Bertulf, having completed the thirteenth

year of his leadership, distinguished by his virtues and celebrated for his miracles, migrated to Christ."

43. Blidulf was one of Jonas's two companions, when he went to visit his mother, in *Vita s. Columbani*, Book 2, Chapter 5.

44. Pavia, like Milan, was one of the seats of the Lombard kings: see Neil Christie, *The Lombards* (Oxford, 1995), pp. 146–47.

45. Jonas seems here to assume that his readers are not aware of the involvement of Arioald in Chapter 23. Before becoming king he had been duke (*Dux*) of Turin (see Paul the Deacon, *Historia Langobardorum*, bk 4, chap. 41 in *Monumenta Germaniae Historica, Scriptores Rerum Langobardicum et Italicarum, saec. 1-IX*, eds. Ludwig Bethmann and Georg Waitz [Hannover, 1878]). As son-in-law of Agilulf, who reigned over the Lombards from 590 until 616, he was actually brother-in-law to Agilulf's son, Adalwald (also spelled Adaloald). The latter, who was brought up as a Catholic by his mother, Theudelinda, had reigned over the Lombards from 616 until 626 (see Christie, *The Lombards*, pp. 185–86, note 44 above).

46. Christian in this case meaning one of Catholic, not Arian, leanings.

47. For Tortona, see note 31 above.

48. This rather surprising account of pagans in Italy might be compared with the account in the *Vita s. Barbati* of pagans in the region of Benevento: see Christie, *The Lombards*, pp. 186–87 (note 44 above). Snake worship in Latium was not, however, a Lombard tradition, at least in origin, for it is well known in the classical period: see the entry under *Marsi* in Charlton Lewis and Charles Short, *A Latin Dictionary* (Oxford, 1879).

49. See above Book 2, Chapter 2.

50. Or "prior."

51. The point is clearer in Latin: *a nando anatem vulgo vocant*. This etymology for *anas*, the Latin for duck, was commonplace: see Isidore of Seville, *Etymologiae*, ed. W.M. Lindsay (Oxford, 1911), bk. 12, chap. 7, sec. 51.

Chapter 7

Dado of Rouen,
Life of St. Eligius of Noyon
Translated by Jo Ann McNamara

Introduction

Bishops bulked large among the individuals singled out as saints by early Christian communities. During the persecution period, they were the natural targets for Roman officials who understood that a flock without a shepherd is soon scattered. After Constantine, they were endowed with imperial dignities and privileges to enhance their spiritual leadership. Civic-minded congregations competed to elect the most eminent men they could find to their primacies. The most learned scholars, the most effective administrators, and the most morally rigorous men were promoted from the laity or wrested from monastic communities to take on the responsibilities of episcopal leadership.

As the effective power of the emperors and their secular representatives declined in the West, the prestige of bishops grew. During the fifth and sixth centuries, they experienced new avenues to sanctity as defenders and representatives of the Catholic Roman population in the face of Germanic invaders who were either pagan or adherents of Arian Christianity. In many cases they fell heir to the government of Roman cities and very frequently the new kings ratified that responsibility. Nevertheless, it was typical for bishops of that period to be subjected to heavy trials and even execution when they were suspected of treason. Thus the opportunity for martyrdom remained the basis for episcopal sanctity until the new principalities had stabilized and their rulers embraced Catholicism.

By the seventh century, at least in Merovingian Gaul, this had largely been effected. The kings were proud of their Catholicism and the fraternal wars that had persistently drawn bishops into deadly political strife were ended. The internal power struggles of the mid-seventh century lacked the religious components of the earlier period. Though a number of bishops died in the rivalries that forced Queen Balthild out of power in the years following the death of the hero of our story, they were not cast as martyrs. Nor were they representative of a "Roman" population as opposed to the conquering "barbarians." Dado, the author of the *Life of St. Eligius* was the scion of one of the leading families of the new nobility and he makes no distinction between Romans and the various Germanic peoples who appear in his narrative.

The canonical requirements that bishops be elected by the clergy and people of their communities had fallen into disuse and, probably as a result, the episcopacy was no longer monopolized by a Gallo-Roman clerical caste as it had been in the age of Gregory of Tours. Dado and Eligius (like most of their contemporary prelates) were appointed by the Frankish king from among his chief secular councilors. Unlike most of the saints and leading men of the day, Eligius apparently did not originate among the military, landed aristocracy but started life as an artisan. He came to prominence in the court of Chlothar II, whose own mother was a slave, flourished under Dagobert, and completed his bishopric during the regency of another former slave, Balthild, widow of Clovis II.

Chlothar II and his son Dagobert worked to centralize their government by creating a court nobility bringing men from the landed aristocracy together with talented newcomers like Eligius. Their career paths often ended with ecclesiastical office. As bishops, Eligius and other elder statesmen performed the dual function of representing royal interests in the outlying provinces and patronizing the Christianizing mission of the rural monasteries founded under the inspiration of the Irish missionary Columbanus and his successors. These functions are not particularly clerical in nature. The spread of rural monasticism is as strongly identified with noble lay patrons as with bishops. His liturgical and sacramental role is all but absent from his biography, though Dado does emphasize that, as a sign of his devoutness, Eligius delayed his installation until he could pass through the traditional *cursus honorum* of clerical ranking, following a hagiographic topos established in the *Life of St. Ambrose of Milan* in the fourth century.

Thus there is little in the career of Eligius that seems to qualify him for sanctity except his personal character as delineated by his friend Dado. The episcopal role, so strongly administrative in character, does not readily lend itself to the lineaments of sanctity. Where the possibility of martyrdom is not present, the hagiographer has to draw on two rather ill-fitting models: the monastic and the queenly. As the great monk-bishop Martin of Tours maintained, the prelacy weakened the single-minded devotion that had formerly made him so ready a conduit for divine power. The same anxiety appears in the letters of the first monastic bishop of Rome, Gregory I. Nevertheless, Dado freely endowed Eligius with some of the qualities of a monk: self-mortification and chaste celibacy. To balance the authority and wealth that went with his exalted position, he displays the characteristics of sainted queens: sobriety in the midst of worldly pomp, extravagant charity, patronage of relic cults, monasteries, and the subversion of royal justice through freeing prisoners. Aside from political differences that time has buried, this may account for the sense of rivalry that Dado conveys between Eligius and Queen Balthild (and her ally Erchenwald). She too capped a brilliant secular career with a somewhat formulaic sanctity and a comparison of the two lives reveals a startling similarity of activity between the two. (An English translation of the *Life* of St. Balthild is included in Jo Ann McNamara and John Halborg, with E. Gordon Whatley, *Sainted Women of the Dark Ages* [Durham, NC, 1992].)

This *Life of St. Eligius* was originally written by his close friend and partner Dado (Audoen or Ouen) who became bishop of Rouen after retiring from court. Dado was born at Soissons of Audechar and Aiga and his brothers were Ado and Rado. The whole family is mentioned in the *Life of St. Columbanus* (Book 1, Chapter 26). An epistle of Desiderius, bishop of Cahors, mentions him and his brothers in the "college of palatine friends." The friendship of these groups is mentioned in other letters of Desiderius and a Charter of Eligius. Rado became a treasurer under Chlothar II and *referendarius* under Dagobert. Dado was also a *referendarius* who, like Eligius, followed the monastic life. He founded Iotrum, a monastery of virgins, and founded Rebais. Not long after the death of Dagobert, Dado resigned his offices. When Romanus, bishop of Rouen died, the king ordered his election at about the same time that Eligius went to Noyon.

A "lord Audoenus" is noted along with Ebroin and Bishop Chrodobert of Paris as advisors to Queen Balthild during the regency of Chlothar III. His biographer says he made peace among warring factions in the palace. Indeed the last journey of his life, to Clichy in 684, was made for the purpose of peacemaking. In addition to the *Life of St. Eligius*, Dado wrote letters to Constantius of Albi and Desiderius. The monk of Saint-Denis who wrote the *Gesta Dagoberti I* in the ninth century, mentioned a charter at the monastery which he wrote. He was himself considered a saint and in 688, his successor, Ansbert translated his body. In the eighth century, Bishop Herlemund of Le Mans built an oratory in his memory and a church at the monastery of Rebais was dedicated to him. Alcuin established an altar to Remi and Ouen in the church of Saint-Vaast. The details of his life were firmly fixed in a biography composed at Rouen not long after his death which has been characterized by Ian Wood (*The Merovingian Kingdoms, 450–751* [London, 1994], p. 151) as "among the few hagiographic works that can be assigned with almost total certainty to the Merovingian period."

The same exacting author has faith in the historical value of Dado's *Life of St. Eligius*, though it has come down to us only in a Carolingian copy somewhat edited and probably embellished to make it more liturgically elegant.

SOURCES AND FURTHER READING

This translation of Dado's *Life of St. Eligius of Noyon* (*Bibliotheca hagiographica latina*, nos. 274–76) has been made from the edition by Bruno Krusch in *Monumenta Germaniae Historica, Scriptores rerum Merovingicarum*, vol. 4 (Hannover, 1902), pp. 669–742. That edition has numerous lacunae which we have indicated by notes within brackets in the translation below. Further omissions of extraneous material are also noted in brackets. A complete translation of the extant text by Professor McNamara may be found on the *Internet Medieval Sourcebook*, edited by Paul Halsall (http://www.fordham.edu/halsall/sbook.html). For a complete study of the other sources pertaining to the life and career of Eligius, see Elphege Vacandard, *Vie de Saint Ouen* (Paris, 1902), which collects a series of articles published by Vacandard in the *Revue des questions historiques*, vols. 63, 69, and 71 (1898, 1901, and 1902). The letter of Desiderius of Cahors mentioning Eligius may be found in an edition by Wilhelm Arndt in *Monumenta Germaniae Historica, Epistolae*, vol. 3 [*Epistolae Merowingici et Karolini Aevi*, vol. 1] (Berlin, 1892), p. 199, while the Charter of Eligius may be found in an edition by Bruno Krusch in *Monumenta Germaniae Historica, Scriptores rerum Merovingicarum*, vol. 4 (Hannover, 1902), pp. 749–61.

The essential foundation of all recent studies of Merovingian hagiography and its use to study social history is the remarkable work of Frantisek Graus, *Volk, Herrscher und Heiliger im Reich der Merowinger. Studeien zur Hagiographie der Merowingerzeit* (Prague, 1965). Good introductions to the subject in English are to be found in the introductions to two collections of translated sources: Jo Ann McNamara and John Halborg, with E. Gordon Whatley, *Sainted Women of the Dark Ages* (Durham, NC, 1992) and Paul Fouracre and Richard Gerberding, *Late Merovingian France: History and Hagiography, 640–720*, Manchester Medieval Sources Series (Manchester, 1996). Both of these collections contain a number of saints' *Lives* in translation which provide excellent comparative material to the *Life of St. Eligius*.

More specifically on Eligius and on Dado's *Life,* see Paul Fouracre, "The Work of Audoenus of Rouen and Eligius of Noyon in Extending Episcopal Influence from the Town to the Country in Seventh-Century Neustria," *Studies in Church History* 16 (1979): 77–91 and "Merovingian History and Merovingian Historiography," *Past and Present* 127 (1990): 3–38. More generally on the religious world of the Merovingian kingdoms see J.M. Wallace-Hadrill, *The Frankish Church* (Oxford, 1983). Friedrich Prinz has provided a good English summary of his ideas on the relationship of nobility to sanctity in "Aristocracy and Christianity in Merovingian Gaul: An Essay," in *Gesellschaft, Kulture Literatur. Beiträge L. Wallach gewidmet*, ed. Karl Bosl (Stuttgart, 1975), pp. 153–165.

Dado of Rouen, The Life of St. Eligius of Noyon

BOOK 1

(1.) Eligius sprang from the villa of Chaptelat about six miles toward the western shore from the town of Limoges in Gaul, which joins the Britannic ocean in the space of about two hundred miles. Thus the city sits in Armorican parts, in ulterior Gaul and prima Aquitaine which looks to the western shore. On the east, it is bordered by the province of Lyon and Gallia Belgica and to the west and south it has the province of Narbonne which also borders Ocean. In fact, Spain may be reached from the west.[1] So Eligius was born and raised in that region from free parents of an ancient Christian line. His father was called Eucherius and his mother Terrigia. By grace of divine prescience, he received the name Eligius, a fitting mirror of his mind.[2] And as a foretaste of what he would do, or indeed what God would do through him, it is fitting to tell what happened before he was born. For I should not omit the sign of his sanctity that was shown or the testimony of great men that I have heard.

(2.) For when the blessed man was still in his mother's womb, his mother (*genetrix*) had a vision ordained in this manner. She saw a splendid eagle wheeling above her bed crying out to her three times promising I don't know what. And when she awoke, terrified by the reverberating voice, she began to wonder much what the vision might mean. Meanwhile the hour of the birth approached and the mother was beginning to be endangered in the greatest pain. So they called a certain religious priest, a man of good repute, that he might pray for her. When he came to her, prophetic words soon seized him and he assured her: "Do not be afraid, mother, for the Lord has deigned to bestow a blessed birth upon you. He will be a holy man and chosen from all his people he will be called a great priest in the Church of Christ."

(3.) So Eligius was born and nurtured in the true faith and imbued by his parents with the Catholic Christian religion. When he had passed the years of boyhood, he entered adolescence with industry and took up whatever work suitable to his age came to his hand and completed it with wonderful aptitude. When his father saw that his son was so skillful, he apprenticed him to an honorable man, Abbo, a proven goldsmith who at that time performed the public office of fiscal moneyer (*fiscalis monetae*) in the city of Limoges.[3] Soon he was fully trained in the uses of this office and began to be honored with praises among the dwellers and neighbors in the lord. For he acted with dove-like simplicity, lest he bring pain to anyone and he had the wisdom of the serpent lest he fall into traps set by others.[4] He was worthy both in having his skills and in his easy and pure speech. Often he entered into the meetings of the Church giving gold to whomever was there reciting the sacred Scripture which he longed eagerly to bury within the memory of his heart so that even when he was absent he might ruminate with intense meditations on what he had heard.

(4.) Afterward some years went by until for some reason which I believe was guided by divine providence, he left his native land and his parents and went to the soil of the Franks. Only a few days passed before he came to the notice of a certain royal treasurer named Bobo, an honest and mild man, who committed him to his patronage and put him to work under his tuition. He strenuously employed himself at all work and won the love of everyone to whom he could speak.

(5.) After a while, a certain cause brought him to the notice of King Chlothar of the Franks.[5] For that king wanted a chair urbanely made with gold and gems but no one could be found in his palace who could do the work as he conceived it. But when the aforesaid royal treasurer [Bobo] had satisfied himself of Eligius's skill, he began to investigate whether he might complete the work as it was planned. When he was sure that [Eligius] could easily undertake it, [Bobo] went to the prince and indicated to him that he had found an industrious artisan who was at his disposal for the work without delay. Then the king most readily gave him a great weight of gold which he in turn gave to Eligius. Having taken it, he began the work immediately and with diligence speedily completed it. And from that which he had taken for a single piece of work, he was able to make two. Incredibly, he could do it all from the same weight for he had accomplished the work commissioned from him without any fraud or mixture of *siliquae*, or any other fraudulence. Not claiming fragments bitten off by the file or using the devouring flame of the furnace for an excuse, but filling all faithfully with gems, he happily earned his happy reward. For having brought the completed piece to the palace he gave one seat to the king and kept the other back. The king began to marvel and praise such elegant work and ordered that the craftsman be paid in a manner worthy of his labor. Then Eligius produced the other in their midst: "I have made this piece," he said, "from the gold which I might have lost through negligence." The king was thunderstruck with even greater admiration and questioned the other workmen whether any of them could do the same from the original weight and accepted the answer he got from them acknowledging the sublime favor of his skill: "From this, you will believe in the utmost." And indeed this was the origin in the royal palace of honoring and believing the testimony of Eligius. From this of course, the goldsmith rose and his work was always most wonderfully done with the most learned skill, and he began to find increased favor in the king's eyes and the presence of his *optimates*. By the Lord's will, his faith was strengthened and, stimulated by the king, he grew better every day.

(6.) For some reason unknown to me, unless it were to obtain greater proof of his fidelity, one day at Rueil in the fields, in my presence, while I was living among the king's boys, the king ordered some relics of saints brought to Eligius and ordered that he place his hands upon the sacred tokens and take an oath. But, moved by divine intuition, he humbly refused all attempted inducements. And when he was more urgently pressed, he soon burst into anxious tears fearing to offend the king but trembling sevenfold to impose his hands on the sacred tokens. Then the king, feeling his fear, and simultaneously marveling at the man's great devotion, desisted from forcing him but sent him away with a kinder and gentler manner. His face beaming, he declared him more worthy to be believed than if he had given his oath many times over.

(7.) When he reached the age of virility, desiring to show himself a vessel sanctified to God and fearing that some sin might stain his breast, he confessed his adolescent deeds to the priest. Imposing severe penances with mortifications on himself, he began to resist the flesh with the fires of the spirit in labors following the apostle, vigils, fasts, chastity, in much patience and unfeigned love. For he protected himself against the present ardors of the flesh with fires of future suffering and the memory of the ardors of Gehenna shut out lust . . .

(8.) Then calling on the Lord with a breast full of faith he asked that if his penitence were acceptable to God he might deign to give him a sign. Now, in the cubicle where he was accustomed to rest regularly he had tokens of many saints hanging from above and beneath that sacred covering he rested his head on a haircloth and spent the night in prayer. When as usual he lay prostrate in that place one night, praying on his haircloth, he was weighed down by descending sleep and dropped off for a moment and suddenly he saw someone standing before him who said: "Behold Eligius! Your prayers have been heard and the sign you asked for in the past will now be given to you." As soon as he heard this, he sensed a sweet odor, and the softest drops from the chrism of the reliquaries flowed smoothly upon his head. Exceedingly astonished by this he swiftly arose and careful investigation disclosed chrism like balsam distilled on the blanket that covered him. And such a sweet fragrance spread from there that it filled the room so that he could scarcely remain there. And then, mindful of his petition, and exceedingly amazed by the generosity of God's bounty, loudly weeping, he blessed Christ the faithful rewarder, who never fails those who hope in him, from the bottom of his heart. For indeed his power began with almighty God to whom all things are possible. The holy man secretly confided in his comrade named Ouen, cognomen Dado, whom he loved as his own soul, exacting a promise that as long as he remained in this body he would tell no one.[6] Hearing this, [Dado] immediately felt compunction in his heart and with the secret of these arcane [things] began to burn inside with love. Because of this he spurned secular blandishments and desired to emulate Eligius studiously to the good. And then they took Dado's brother Ado into their common counsel. These were men high among the *optimates* at court, the sons of Audechar.[7] With common counsel they both began to imitate what they had learned from Eligius and he was their familiar consort and they had *one heart and one soul* [Acts 4:32] in the Lord.

(9.) Therefore Eligius found grace in the presence of the Lord and in the presence of the king of the Franks. And he was held in such good repute by all that the king turned over to him a huge heap of gold and silver and gems without even weighing them. Day by day, he grew in honor with great favor and wholly tested in every respect he flourished, devout in the court. Meanwhile, Chlothar [II] died and Dagobert his son succeeded alone to the monarchy of the kingdom by whom Eligius was granted such familiarity that his happiness earned the hatred of many.[8] [**Tranlator's note:** There is a gap in the text.]

(10.) He grew more in vigils, in fasts, and in charity. For the king's use, he made many utensils from gold and gems. He sat fabricating in a mine opposite Thille, his apprentice [*vernaculus*] from the Saxon tribe who followed in his master's footsteps and led a venerable life.[9] Sitting at the work, he propped open a book before his eyes so that even while laboring he might receive divine mandates. Thus he performed double offices, his hands to the uses of man and his mind bound to divine use. His fame spread abroad so that Roman, Italian, or Gothic legates or those sent from any other province to make an alliance or on another mission to the palace of the king of the Franks, would not go first to the king but would repair first to Eligius asking him either for food or seeking healthful counsel. Religious men and monks also flocked to him and whatever he could collect, he gave to them in alms or gave for the ransom of captives, for he had this work much at heart. Wherever he understood that slaves were to be sold he hastened with mercy and soon ransomed the captive. The sum of his captives redeemed rose from twenty and thirty to fifty and finally a hundred souls in one flock when they were brought in a ship, of both sexes and from different nations. He freed all alike, Romans, Gauls, Britons, and Moors [*Mauri*], but particularly Saxons who were as numerous as sheep at that time, expelled from their own land and scattered everywhere.[10] If it should happen that the number of people for sale outweighed his means, he gave more by stripping what he had on his own body from his belt and cloak to the food he needed and even his shoes so long as he could help the captives. And often it was pilgrims of Christ that he rescued. Oh, daily did he not wish to be a debtor that his own debts might be forgiven? Daily did he not rip golden bracelets, jeweled purses, and other gold and gems from himself so that he might succor the miserable? Let me briefly comprehend how many multitudes of captives over successive periods of time he freed from the harsh yoke of dominion and how much alms he distributed to people of both sexes, diverse churches and monasteries, though no orator, however studious or eloquent, could tell the tale. Standing directly in the presence of the king, redeemed captives threw the deaneries before him and he gave them charters of liberty.[11] To all of them he gave three choices: since they were now free, they could return to their own country and he would offer them what subsidy they required; if they wished to remain he would accommodate them willingly and include them not among his servants but as his brothers; and if he could persuade them to embrace the venerable life of monks and take the cloister of a community, honoring those marked for the Lord, he would supply clothing and whatever else was needed for their care. He had several apprentices [*vernaculos*] in his workshop [*contubernio*] helping him with these needs. One was Bauderic, his countryman, who took care of his things with all honesty. Tituin of the Suevi tribe was a faithful lay attendant [*cubicularius*] who achieved the highest reward when he was later killed.[12] Buchin, converted from the gentiles, later lived at the community of Ferrières.[13] Andreas and Martin and John at his procurance deserved to come to the clergy. These and more others than I can count were in his chamber day and night striving to complete the solemn canonical course with all effort . . .

[**Translator's notes:** All but a few phrases have been lost from Chapter 11.]

(12.) He [Eligius] was tall with a rosy face. He had a pretty head of hair with curly locks. His hands were honest and his fingers long. He had the face of an angel and a prudent look. At first, he was used to wear gold and gems on his clothes having belts composed of gold and gems and elegantly jeweled purses, linens covered with red metal and golden sacs hemmed with gold and all of the most precious fabrics including all of silk. But all of this was but fleeting ostentation from the beginning and beneath he wore a hairshirt next to his flesh and, as he proceeded to perfection, he gave the ornaments for the needs of the poor. Then you would see him, whom you had once seen gleaming with the weight of the gold and gems that covered him, go covered in the vilest clothing, with a rope for a belt. Sometimes the king himself would see him despoiled for love and devotion to Christ, tearing from himself what he had given him even to his clothing and his belt. For he said that the ornaments that served his appearance to the world were worthless and all that which was inglorious he gave up for the sake of Christ.

While he was with the king he had a mansion carefully joined with Dado whom he loved as his own soul. From this, we could take many examples if we had enough time to repeat them. He had many tokens of saints hanging there in his cubicle and several holy books turning on an axis. Thus after exchanging Psalmody and prayers, like a careful bee, he secreted the choicest from a variety of flowers from different readings in the beehive of his breast. At night, it was his custom to stretch out before his bed on a haircloth and either from the first twilight or after a little rest rising from bed to pray prostrate with his head bowed and passing many nights in tears keeping watch. For he had the great grace of tears. In various ways, he determined as far as human nature could permit, that every night would be consumed in the service of God. So he would pray at length interrupting the prayers for some relief, reciting the Psalms in order and then turning to chanting or reading. And when he was struck by some sacred words, you would see him suddenly raise his eyes to the sky, joining sigh to sigh, mixing tears with the reading, striking his breast and pouring out an ocean of weeping. And when during this reading he was weighed down by invading sleep, he would meditate on the words in a sort of dream. Then starting awake he would finish the reading and according to custom turn to prayer in which work he strove with so much silence never moving his head or any other part that you could barely hear the fleeting breath. Often, for various reasons, he was called to the king's chamber at night but even when one messenger followed another, he would not go until he had completed his service to Christ. Then leaving the house, he was armed with the sign of prayer and the cross. Returning home he prayed first thing. And thus he did every day of his life longing for his eternal homeland. For he was affable in every way and subtle, with pious heart and a spirit strong for battle.

(13.) When the king asked him to lead a legation to Breton lands, he hastened there without delay, secure in the love of Christ. And when he met the prince of the Bretons, he indicated reasons for making a pact and received pledges of peace. And when some might have intended a quarrel or to declare mutual war on them, his gentleness attracted the aforesaid prince with so much benignity and mildness that he was easily persuaded to go with him. For after he had remained there for some time he returned home taking with him the king and many soldiers of his tribe. Presenting them in the villa of Creil to the king of the Franks, he negotiated peacefully. He who brought many gifts returned home even more heavily rewarded. [**Translator's note**: The remainder of Chapter 13 is missing.]

(14.) Indeed King Dagobert—swift handsome, and famous, with no rival among any of the earlier kings of the Franks—loved [Eligius] so much that he would often take himself out of the crowds of princes, *optimates*, dukes, or bishops around him and seek private counsel from Eligius.[14] And whatever Eligius requested, he would give without delay. Whatever he could gain, he expended in alms for the needy, ransom of captives and remedies for the weak, whence the prince rewarded him ever more freely because he knew that not one but many would profit by it.

(15.) Among other things, he acquired a villa in the neighborhood of Limoges called Solignac, saying: "May your serenity concede this place to me, lord king, so that here I may raise a ladder by which you and I may both succeed in climbing into heaven." [see Gen 28:12] As usual, the king freely granted his petition, agreed, and gave the order without delay that what he asked might be conceded. That was a time when a public census from the same region was exacted to be paid to the royal treasury. But when all the revenue collected together was ready to be brought to the king, the *domesticus* and *monetarius* wished to refine the gold by cooking in the furnace so that according to ritual only the reddest and purest metal would be brought into the king's presence. They did not know that it had been conceded as a reward to Eligius. Despite every strain and effort for three or four days, God hindered them so that they could not complete the work. At last, the arrival of a messenger from Eligius interrupted the work being done and asserted his ownership. As soon as the announcement was made, with the inhabitants rejoicing, the work was completed and his wealth committed. There in that place, first the most powerful man of God built a monastery.[15] Then having constituted an abbot, he freed many of his apprentices [*vernaculis*] to the number of a hundred from different provinces and added fifty monks with enough land to support them abundantly. He lavished so much love and devotion on the place that whatever he had, whatever the king gave him, whatever he could buy, whatever he was paid in gratuities by the powerful, he sent to that place. There you would see loaded carts, vessels for every use of both copper and wood, vestments and lectuaries and linens and volumes of sacred Scripture and all things needful for the use of a monastery in such profusion that it kindled the envy of many depraved great folk. He even thought that he would bind himself to that same monastery except that the dispensation of God obligated him to something else.

(16.) I saw, when I visited the place, such observance of the holy rule there that could hardly be matched in any other monastery in Gaul. For that large congregation is adorned with many different flowers of grace. And they had artifices by many skilled in different arts which were completed in fear of Christ and always prepared in obedience. For no one there claimed anything as their own but as we read in the Acts of the Apostles all things were all in common among them all. Such joy reigned in that fertile place that when anyone strolled among the orchards and the gardens flourishing with beauty, he knew the words to be completely fulfilled: "*How fair are your tents, O Jacob, your encampments, O Israel! Like valleys that stretch afar, like gardens beside a river, like aloes that the Lord has planted, like cedar trees beside the waters.*" [Num 24:5–6] Surely, of such was it said through Solomon: "the habitations of the just are blessed." [see Prov 3:33] That same community is undoubtedly about six miles from Limoges toward the southern shore. It is surrounded by a wall not just of stone but with a well-fortified ditch having the circumference of ten *stadia*. On one side it is strengthened by a river [the Briance], guarded by a high mountain covered with trees and sheer cliffs. And they filled the whole area of the monastery with orchards of diverse fruit trees. And so the sluggish soul is refreshed and rejoiced to occupy itself with the amenities of paradise.

(17.) When he had completed that monastery (*cenobium*) with all its works, and stabilized it with care, he thought to build a hospice for pilgrims (*xenodochium*) in the city of Paris. But God inspired him to conceive a more excellent plan. He began to raise in his own house which he had received as a gift from the king in that same city, a domicile of virgins of Christ. After long and sweaty labor, he constructed a monastery worthy of holy virgins.[16] There, constituting the strict discipline of the rule, he gathered thirty girls from diverse tribes, some from among his own *ancillae* and other more noble matrons of the Franks. He appointed an abbess fitting to God, a girl named Aurea, daughter of Maurinus and Quiria.[17] He assigned land with high revenue and turned it over from all his property. From hither and thither you could see deliveries of everything necessary or useful for a monastery, vessels and vestments, sacred books and other ornaments. The most pious father provided whatever things appropriate to the sex were needed, with the most solicitous and diligent care. And when all the house was complete and furnished with everything necessary to it and made perfect, one vile but necessary thing still remained for the building of the domicile. He had not enough land, for it was all filled by the house, but there was a small piece from the fisc lying adjacent for the necessary work. Therefore, he ordered the land cleared, so he might learn its dimensions and hurried off to the prince, suggested the area and without delay obtained what he asked. And when he returned home, the lines drawn, and the size of the habitation considered, he found that it was a foot greater in size than he had told the king. He was sad, for he who never wished to lie to anyone had lied to the king. Leaving the work completely, he went back to court and sought out the prince, threw himself on the ground and accused himself of lying asking for pardon or for death. But when the king learned the insignificance of the cause he condoled with his injury more in amazement and soon turning to the multitude of bystanders and said: "behold how bright and venerable is the faith of Christ! My dukes and domestics rob me of spacious villas and the servant of Christ because of the faith that he has in the Lord will not bear to hide a palm's breadth of land from us." And he consoled Eligius so kindly that he doubled the gift he had given him. This story makes clear how the holy man feared to be guilty of a lie and soil his conscience with the meanest fib kept from the king. So his faith raised him to heaven and that fidelity made him dear to God and famous among men.

(18.) When the monastery was done and the edifice for handmaids of God complete, for which the profit of the labor is its own reward, then he built a basilica for the interment of the bodies of God's handmaids. It was dedicated to the holy apostle Paul. The roof covered with lead in sublime elegance and Abbot Quintilianus lay buried there. Then he built and restored the basilica in honor of St. Martial, bishop and confessor, at Limoges. He also covered that roof with lead in urbane stability. When he bore the saint's relics there, fully devout with great triumph and a great company of both sexes, a chorus chanting melodies of psalms and sweet modulations of antiphons, the Lord declared a miracle worthy of memory. Eligius was inspired to direct that the relics be taken a certain way when he could have gone more directly by another. But on that path there were four enclosed dungeons where three guards held seven men, either innocent or guilty. When Eligius passed, exulting and dancing before the ark with the relics like David of yore accompanied by the exultant voices of his flock [see 2 Kings 6:14], they came to the dungeon. Suddenly depressed by a heavy weight, the bearer of the relics was fixed to the ground. However much they pushed and pulled, he could not move a step which he confessed in a stentorian voice. And while the witnesses were marveling at this, there came a sound like a thunderbolt from within the prison and the walls were burst with a great explosion from the ground. And immediately the prisoners appeared at the broken gate with all their bonds broken. Then the feet of the relic bearer lightened and they went on to the church with the former prisoners. And all who were there began in amazement to praise the new miracle and the joined merits of two saints, praise of Martial to declare the favor of Eligius. And all, seeing the fruits, praised Christ the Lord who does his work in his servants and raised their voices continually . . .

[**Translator's note:** At this point, Krusch's text begins to be punctuated by significant gaps. Of Chapters 19 though 29, there are only a few lines of

Chapter 21, praising Eligius's leadership of the monastery of Solignac, and a few lines of Chapter 27, describing Eligius's cure of a cripple.]

(30.) One day while [Eligius] was living in Paris, the custodian of the basilica dedicated to St. Columba the virgin sped to him at dawn trembling and falling all over his feet. He announced that, in the silence of the night, the basilica had been robbed of all its ornaments. The news deeply depressed Eligius but he swiftly reverted to his usual source of hope. He kindly comforted the custodian and then hurried to that same oratory where he prayed with these words: "Listen, St. Columba, to what I say. My Redeemer knows that unless you restore those stolen ornaments speedily to the tabernacle, I will have the entrance sown over with thorny plants so that veneration will never be offered to you again in this place."[18] He said that and left. And behold! the following day, when the custodian rose in the morning, he found all restored as before, down to the tiniest curtain. And his joy matched his former distress as he sped again to Eligius and announced that everything had been returned. Seeing everything in its place, he praised the martyr and as always magnified the name of Christ the Lord with growing hilarity.

(31.) Among the infinity of his other good works, he obtained license from the king that wherever he might find any human bodies executed by royal severity or judicial censure or from cases following any diverse arguments, whether in cities or villas, he might take them down from the gallows or the wheel or the noose and bury them. From among his companions, he appointed *respelliones* named Gallebodo and Vincent to whom he entrusted this care with their colleagues. Thus wherever they went whether in nearby towns or far away, they carried hoes with them so that they could immediately cover any corpse they found with earth. One day in the royal county of Austrasia, they came to a certain town called Stratoburg and outside the town on a height they saw a hanging man. The noose had taken his life on that very day. Going straight to the place, they removed the noose so that they might start the burial rites. But the venerable man felt power working. While the burial was being prepared, he approached the body and began to massage it gently from head to toe. When he felt the spirit to be present, denying the power that came from him, he said without delay: "Oh what a terrible crime, we have nearly perpetrated without the Lord's order! We nearly buried this body in the ground when the spirit is still within!" Saying this, he ordered the man covered with clothing and they waited. Refreshed in spirit, he arose from the ground having suffered no injury. When news of what had happened circulated in the town, hostile pursuers planned to seize him on the road and put him to death. But Eligius swiftly tore him from their hands and supplied royal letters of safe conduct for him and defended him. Not long after, he removed himself from his company, perhaps with Eligius's connivance. Lest the things he had done should spread among the people, he never appeared again among his servants. But enough about that. It is enough that what he did about this is known to God alone and not hidden whether he was in secular habit or under the venerable apostolic tonsure.[19] Meanwhile, I will try to be brief in telling what he achieved with his handiwork.

(32) Among other good works this same blessed man fabricated tombs for the relics of Sts. Germanus, Severin, Piaton, Quentin, Lucian, Genovefa, Columba, Maximian and Lolian, Julian and many more, with gold and silver and gems.[20] But above all, by order of King Dagobert, he covered blessed Martin of Tours' sepulchre with wonderful work of gold and jewels and he urbanely composed the tomb of St. Brice and another where the body of St. Martin had formerly lain.[21] And he obtained great benefices from the king for that same church. At Eligius's request, and for reverence to the holy confessor Martin, King Dagobert forgave the whole census that was released to the royal tax gatherer from that church and confirmed it by a charter. Thus the church claimed the whole use of the fiscal cents from him so that in that town even today it is decreed through obliging episcopal letters. Above all, Eligius fabricated a mausoleum for the holy martyr Denis in the city of Paris with a wonderful marble ciborium over it marvelously decorated with gold and gems.[22] He composed a crest [at the top of a tomb] and a magnificent frontal and surrounded the throne of the altar with golden axes in a circle. He placed golden apples there, round and jeweled. He made a pulpit and a gate of silver and a roof for the throne of the altar on silver axes. He made a covering in the place before the tomb and fabricated an outside altar at the feet of the holy martyr. So much industry did he lavish there, at the king's request, and poured out so much that scarcely a single ornament was left in Gaul and it is the greatest wonder of all to this very day.

(33.) At last, all these wonderful works were done and all the people about quieted, even the ferocious Gascons broken on their own hostile swords. Then the great and famous King Dagobert died and was buried in that same basilica of Saint-Denis under the arch in the right side. His son Clovis [II][23] still juvenile in age, succeeded him to the kingdom . . . [**Translator's note**: The remainder of Chapter 33 and all of Chapter 34 contain a digression on the heresy of Monolethitism, which has been omitted.]

(35.) While these things were happening in the city of Rome, a heretic from overseas struck a blow at the province of Gaul. He came to that city once called Aedua, now Auxerre, and began most fraudulently to preach nefarious dogma. And when this came to the ears of Eligius in the palace, vigilant as always, with Ouen [Dado] and other Catholic men, he began to seek out every manifestation of this plague. He did not stop reminding the bishop and the *optimates*, and by his order the sacerdotal princes were gathered in a council at Orléans.[24] The aforesaid heretic was led before them and they questioned him about different things, knowing him to be learned, but could reach no conclusion. He answered their questions so craftily that just where he seemed to be absolutely straight, he opened up holes, slithering like an oily snake. And when no one could stop him or overcome him in any way, a most learned bishop named Falvius emerged among us by God's Providence who was his match in everything and we rejoiced in his skill. Now all his previously hidden cunning and arts were revealed as dissimulation and his arguments were uncovered. Thus all the bishops imposed a sentence against him and sent a decree above his name to all the cities to eliminate the error to the ends of Gaul.

(36.) But when Eligius discovered another apostate disturbing the people of Paris, he energetically extirpated him from the city. Similarly, after long imprisonment, he ejected another man who circulated through villas and squares deceiving the populace by pretending to be a bishop from the boundaries of the kingdom of the Franks. And with great authority he pursued everyone else who attempted to subvert the people. For he hated all heretics, schismatics, and every figment beyond the Catholic doctrine and followed every trace of them with outrage. His eloquence flowed out and he was most subtle in the study of Scripture, and when he had been sufficiently instructed, he went everywhere preaching with the evangelical cohorts to the people to hold unshakably to their faith in Christ and take care to protect themselves from every contagion of heresy . . .

[**Translator's note**: Chapters 37 through 39 are missing.]

(40.) But it would take far too long to recount every sign of his virtue and it is time to put an end to this part of the book. Words fail and words attenuate our aridity and we will succumb long before we have exhausted all there is to tell of Eligius. Indeed, I will never tell even a hundredth part of all the ornaments of good which are so precious that he earned as his heavenly reward. And we have only covered part of his life. For now the time came when he put off the dress of a layman and so we can impose an end on this part of the book before our audience sinks into boredom. The things which he accomplished in his episcopacy and the way in which he migrated from this world and the virtues he performed after his death, if the lord grants me life and power, I will explicate in another book. For we do not confide in ourselves but his merits, to take the work happily begun faithfully even to the end. If Christ deigns, he will intercede for us in heaven who earned his reward to work such miracles on earth through the same our lord Jesus Christ, who with God the Father and the Holy Spirit reigns and lives through the cycle of the ages. Amen.
Here ends the first book of the Life of St. Eligius Bishop and Confessor.

BOOK 2.
(Preface.) Propitiating the Lord, I left the work I began on the life of the blessed confessor Eligius imperfect, lifting my weary and exhausted pen in the middle of the path. Now somewhat refreshed in strength, with desiring vow, joyful heart, and charming pen, I will attempt to go on with the work I began. The road may be hard and deep but I will walk willingly and where my feet cannot take me, love will guide me and so I will go with devotion where words cannot enter. I accuse myself of being unworthy to pass the life of such a man on to posterity's memory with the skill due to his literary monument which should draw from the narrative of deeds the maximum edification for those who read. But he did so much that I simply cannot surpass the magni-

tude of good. The multitude of deeds forces me to omit so much that my soul thirsts in doubt while I try to decide what to keep and what to leave out. For if I tell all I wish to add, the days will run out while I am still telling and I will far exceed the limit. But on the other side if I include less, I fear the laughter of *hypochritarum*,[25] who will say: "This man began a building and now he cannot finish it." I fear even more that I will offend the prelate, lest in struggling to expound his accomplishments within the limits set by the aridity of my eloquence, I will seem more to do him an injury than to reveal his life. So discreet on both sides, I concentrated the article to the membrane and what I rejected from the first book follows in this. So it was sufficient in the first book to reveal the things he did while in lay dress and now we will take up what he did as a bishop.

(1.) Eligius once served the eternal king of all princes, Christ, in the palace under secular habit. He remained in this way from the middle of Chlothar [II]'s time as king of the Franks, through the whole time of the famous prince Dagobert and his son Clovis [II] and even to the beginning of the reign of the junior Chlothar [III].[26] But in those days the simoniac heresy cruelly pullulated in the cities and even to the borders of the Frankish kingdom and most of the time the unhappy Queen Brunhild violated the Catholic faith with this contagion even to the time of King Dagobert.[27] The holy men Eligius and Ouen in common council with certain other Catholic men, warned the prince and his *optimates* that this death dealing virus must swiftly be eliminated from the body of Christ which is the universal Church.[28] Their pious petition had its effect and they freely obtained what they had requested devoutly. Thus a single counsel was pleasing to all, accepted in the Holy Spirit and by royal order, that no one who had paid a price should be admitted to sacerdotal offices, nor those who, like rapacious wolves, profited by putting the gifts of the Holy Spirit up for sale. But only men of good reputation and irreproachable life should be chosen for the pontifical offices.

(2.) And in that spirit they chose Eligius for the merits of his sanctity and good works, now radiating light, for the holy sacerdotal office. He was to preside over the church of Noyon after Acharius, the bishop [*antistes*] of that town, had died in the turning of his years.[29] And at the same time, they chose his comrade Ouen who is called Dado to preside over the church of Rouen. So the unwilling goldsmith was tonsured and constituted guardian of the towns or municipalities of Vermandois which include the metropolis, Tournai, which was once a royal city, and Noyon and Ghent and Courtrai of Flanders. They made him pastor in these places because the inhabitants were still caught in the errors of the Gentiles. Given over to vain superstition, they were wild peasants who could in no way comprehend the word of salvation. But when the blessed man recognized that he could in no way escape the imposition of the office, he would not permit himself to be consecrated priest until he had run the normal course and time of the clericature. And so there was some delay before he and Ouen were ordained by Deodatus of Matiscon from the lands across the Loire. But by his counsel, in the same day, they earned equally the grace of articulated apostolic benediction. For it was the time when all the people of Gaul celebrate the rogations. Therefore gathering together in Rouen on the fourteenth day of the third month, in the third year of the reign of the younger Clovis, the Sunday before the litanies, among crowds of people and flocks of priests and psalm-singing choirs of the consecrated, we had the grace to be made bishops by that bishop, I to Rouen and he to Noyon.[30] And being thus made bishop he removed to his see where he presided with more dignity than I can narrate.

[**Translator's note:** The remainder of Chapter 2, as well as Chapter 3, 4, and 5 are marred by significant gaps.]

(6.) Among other miracles of his virtue it was conceded to that most holy man from the Lord that the bodies of holy martyrs, which had until then been hidden from the people through many ages, were brought to light when he investigated and searched with the great ardor of his faith. Some had formerly been venerated by people in places where they were not while being completely ignored in the places where they were certainly buried. But from the time that Eligius, consecrated bishop, was given as pastor to the churches, not a few were declared found by the people. Among them first and foremost the holy martyr Quentin was sought with great urgency in the beginning of his episcopate. He who had been hidden in the past advanced openly in public. When Eligius was first given to that place as bishop, a certain unprincipled man called Maurinus, who wore a religious habit in public, was cantor in the royal palace. Having won praise for telling the king's fortune, he became swell-headed. His heart shameless and his actions dissipated, deceived with the audacity of his presumption, he began to clamor that he would seek and find the body of the martyr Quentin for himself.[31] But the Lord revealed his shamelessness and the merits of Eligius. As soon as he broke the earth with a hoe, the handle stuck to the digger's hands until the miserable man abandoned his presumptuous work. On the following day, he died miserably, his hands seething with worms. And after that, all the people were afraid and even men of respectable lives did not dare approach Eligius about this business. But as soon as he was ordained, Eligius began to search the place energetically. The saint had undoubtedly come from the town of Vermandois and had been buried on the mountain where the martyr was once raised from the flood by Eusebia.[32] But Eligius, instigated by God's nod, considered this in his mind and openly proclaimed to the people that his body was not where they had been venerating him but rather in another place altogether. And when his mind had thus been stimulated for some time, he began to launch a probing investigation through the pavements of basilicas here and there trying to sense some sacred tomb. But when no sign of a tomb appeared, the brothers began to abandon him, fearing among themselves that such an investigation betokened a proud mind which would end in a sorry death. Moreover, they tried to turn his mind from the idea because the antiquity of the body and the length of time assured that it must be consumed and reduced to dust. But when he realized this opposition by his brothers, he cried to them loudly: "Oh brothers, don't, I beg you, don't impede my devotion. For I believe my Creator will not deign to defraud me of such a treasure when I long for it so much." And persisting he went on a three-day fast praying loudly to Christ the Lord with tears and vowed that he would not take any food until he knew that he would deserve what he wanted. His faith and his constancy were so great that he might overcome in this way just as he believed it had been done [before], that sometimes he could speak with God as to his earthly lord and that he would decree what he proposed and indubitably he believed that God would complete it. Whence when he was drained by so much, he said: "You lord Jesus, Who know all things before they happen, You know that, unless You show me a sign of this witness's body who suffered for Your name's sake, unworthy as I am, I will never act as bishop to these people but rather I will be an exile from this province and take myself away somewhere to die among the beasts." What more? Persisting in the work begun, he went with his helpers to diverse churches where they hoped to find something. In one such place, which no one had suspected, he ordered digging in the back of the church. But when they had opened a trench nearly ten feet deep, their hopes vanished. But as the middle of the third night flowed by, Eligius grabbed the hoe and, throwing off his cloak, began with all his strength to dig at the holy ground with his hands by the light of candles and lamps. And soon at the bottom of the ditch, to the side, he began to scratch at the earth and uncovered the wrapping of the holy body. Then filled with great joy, he opened the tomb with the hoe he held in his hand and a fragrant odor with a great light spread from it so that Eligius could barely sustain his strength in the power of that odor and that light. A globe of splendor proceeded from the tomb at the striking blow. It shed the strength of its brightness so much that it blinded the eyes of those who were standing around and changed night to day in the greater part of the region. Whence all who had kept watch in that hour gathered. Though ignorant of the cause, they knew they had been given a great sign from Heaven. For this happened in the middle of night and the night was dark and stormy but the spreading radiance was like the light of day and it shone for some time before it grew dim. Having found the holy body, Eligius kissed it with tears of joy and raising it from the depths of the ground he divided the desired relics into eleven parts. As he extracted the teeth from the jaws, a drop of blood flowed out from the root of each tooth. He abstracted nails of wondrous magnitude which the persecutors had fixed into the body at the time of his passion from the head and other limbs and sequestrated them with the relics. He divided the hair and chose the most beautiful reliquaries to hold each one. And then he brought the body to the altar wrapped in the most precious silk and decently laid out. And he built a tomb wonderfully decorated with gold and gems. He widened the church to hold greater gatherings of people and decorated it. And then he distributed the relics which he had taken from the saint's body to many places where they healed many invalids praying for help.

[**Translator's note:** Chapters 7–14 contain a number of gaps. They narrate Eligius's discovery of the relics of other martyrs, his attempts to evangelize the Suevi around Flanders, and his ability to drive out demons.]

(15.) At that time, with the affection of piety and the solicitous care of a pastor, he came to visit his own paternal possessions in the city of Limoges. Hearing the holy fame of the monasteries constituted after his example in that same town, he greatly desired to cast his gaze on his own and particularly on all the institutions which imitated his own venerable monastery. When his company neared the city of Bourges, having directed each of his comrades on their way, he himself with a few others headed for the memorial of Sulpicius to adore the confessor. When he arrived there and had made his prayer, he heard that recently several persons condemned to death had been bound in the fiscal prison. They had killed a fiscal judge and therefore were held in chains. Eligius, mindful of the Lord's word, "I was in prison and you visited me," and "Whatever you do for one of the least of mine, you do for me," asked to be taken to them. But when he approached the prison guard, the soldiers rising soon obstructed him violently and would not permit him to come nearer. Sorrowful and indignant in spirit, he left and returned to the original road.

When he came to his destination, he remained there for some time near the city of Limoges, and made the circuit of all the monasteries in the city and its suburbs, listening devoutly to all their benedictions. He visited his own monastery of brothers and placed a second abbot over them—for the first had been captured to the episcopate—showing paternal solicitude for each of them, exhorting all to serve God in truth and simplicity of heart and daily come together in the better, to follow the accepted plan with all zeal even to the end. Then he went to the estate of his parents where his brother Alicius had built a monastery in his father's dwelling. There too he comforted the convent of brothers and then prepared to return to his own city.

And when the road passed Bourges, he wished again to turn off at that city. His spirit moved since he had not been of any help before to those who were held there in prison and could not free them. Acting on this, therefore, he prayed on the road that the Lord would not suffer his labor on behalf of the prisoners to be consumed in vain. Therefore on the day he entered the city, at dawn, he raised his eyes to the heavens which were exceedingly darkened with storm and clouds so that the city dwellers could barely see beyond a stone's throw. No sooner had Eligius entered the city than he approached the prison gates and, by God's nod, immediately with a great bang they were broken open, the hinges torn off, the gates yawned, and all the chains were loosened from the men's feet. Then Eligius pretending that the power conceded to him had nothing to do with himself, went swiftly away to the prison; he gave the prisoners advice that as soon as they left the prison they should seek refuge in the church. And coming out they hurried straight to the church of Saint-Sulpice and when they were all there they found the gates of the church barred. Though they searched high and low, they could find no way in until suddenly one of the largest windows in the front of the church burst and one of the side gates opened. They got into the basilica and hurried to the throne of the altar. So when Eligius came there in his circuit of all the places where he prayed, he found them all around the altar and before the sepulchre of the aforesaid primate. And when the soldiers found the prison emptied, they followed them to that place and entered the basilica, and attempted to lay hands on them and drag them into iron chains. Blessed Eligius spoke mildly to them saying: "Don't, I beg you, men of God, don't behave this way in a holy place. Why do you strain to slay those whom the pious Lord has freed? Wherefore do you act so impiously in the house of God? Why do you not fear the guilt of such wickedness? For this house is the house of life, not death. It is a refuge for the delinquent, not damnation for the refugee. This is the place of prayer, not a den of thieves." But when none of his words would move them, then he said, "The Lord God sees what you are doing. You, if you refuse to listen to me, must, I believe, hear him who never deserts those who trust him." So turning to his accustomed guide, he prostrated himself on the earth between the altar and the memorial of the confessor and prayed urgently to the Lord. And when he raised his head from prayer, immediately, the chains fell to the ground and all on whom they had been placed were instantly freed with a mighty blow. Seeing this, the soldiers were struck with fear and trembling threw themselves at the feet of Eligius praying for his pardon, saying: "We have sinned, lord father, we have done evil, we were stupid to try and contend with you. We admit that we have done wrong and pray you to overlook our impiety." And then he said to them: "and I realize that you have acted in ignorance. For the Lord works as he will. I pray that he who freed them give pardon to you and, propitiated, absolve you from all sin. For not I, as you suppose, but the holy Sulpicius defends those who flee to him." And in this way Eligius, or the Lord through Eligius, absolved criminals twice from dire danger of death. The pious one, the merciful one, who ripped Peter from raging Herod, putting his guards to sleep, now worked in Bourges with his servant Eligius. He who freed His vessel of election, Paul, from the chains of prison now emptied the prison to humble the arrogance of the proud. Therefore praise to him, glory to him through whom his servant can do such wonders in the world. So therefore, Eligius gave the freed criminals, who were practically naked, clothes and alms and ordered that in future they amend their lives as should many others as well, and that same day he distributed money to various paupers and monasteries.

Then he resumed his original path and at last came to his own. Every day attending to people entrusted to him, he tirelessly worked for their salvation. Evidently burning with zeal for the truth, he wished to show the people that they should maintain fearless faith, ordering all to serve God in truth and do justice at all times and that they should be mindful of the benefices of Christ and bless his name every day of their lives. Collecting crowds from all around into the church, he offered them many great admonitions encompassed in sermons that were brief but rich in spiritual edification, exalting his voice with prophetic assurance.

(16.) I ask you dearest brothers and admonish you with great humility to command your intent spirit to listen to what I wish to suggest to you for your salvation.[33] [**Translator's note**: There is a gap here in the text.] Before all else, I denounce and contest, that you shall observe no sacrilegious pagan customs. For no cause or infirmity should you consult magicians, diviners, sorcerers, or incantators, or presume to question them because any man who commits such evil will immediately lose the sacrament of baptism. Do not observe auguries or violent sneezing or pay attention to any little birds singing along the road. If you are distracted on the road or at any other work, make the sign of the cross and say your Sunday prayers with faith and devotion and nothing inimical can hurt you. No Christian should be concerned about which day he leaves home or which day he returns because God has made all days. No influence attaches to the first work of the day or the [phase of the] moon; nothing is ominous or ridiculous about the Calends of January. [Do not] make [figures of?] *vetulas*, little deer or *iotticos*, nor set tables at night, nor exchange New Years' gifts or supply superfluous drinks. No Christian believes impurity or sits in incantation, because the work is diabolic. No Christian on the feast of St. John [the Baptist] or the solemnity of any other saint performs *solestitia* [solstice rites?] or dancing or leaping or diabolical chants. No Christian should presume to invoke the name of a demon, not Neptune or Orcus or Diana or Minerva or Geniscus or believe in these inept beings in any way.[34] No one should observe Jove's day in idleness without holy festivities not in May or any other time, not days of larvae or mice or any day but Sunday. No Christian should make or render any devotion to the gods of the tritium, where three roads meet [*trivia luminaria*], to the fanes or the rocks, or springs or groves or corners. None should presume to hang any phylacteries from the neck of man nor beast, even if they are made by priests and it is said that they contain holy things and divine Scripture because there is no remedy of Christ in these things but only the devil's poison. None should presume to make lustrations or incantations with herbs, nor to pass cattle through a hollow tree or ditch [*terram foratam*] because this is to consecrate them to the devil. No woman should presume to hang amber from her neck nor call upon Minerva or other ill-starred beings in their weaving or dyeing but in all works give thanks only to Christ and confide in the power of his name with all your hearts. None should presume to shout when the moon is obscured, for by God's order eclipses happen at certain times. Nor should they fear the new moon nor abandon work because of it. For God made the moon for this, to mark time and temper the darkness of night, not impede work nor make men mad as the foolish imagine, who believe lunatics are invaded by demons from the moon. None should call the sun or moon lord nor swear by them because they are God's creatures and they serve the needs of men by God's order. No one should tell fate or fortune or horoscopes by them as those do who believe that a person must be what he was born to be. For God *desires all men to be saved and to come to the knowledge of truth* [1 Tim 2:4] and dispenses wisdom to all as he disposed it before the constitution of the world. Above all, should any infirmity occur, do not seek incantators, or diviners, or sorcerers, or magicians, do not use diabolic phylacteries through springs and groves or crossroads. But let the invalid confide solely in the mercy of God and take the body and blood of Christ with faith and devotion and ask the Church faithfully for blessing and oil, with which he might anoint his body in the name of Christ and, according to the apostle, "*the prayer of faith will save the sick man and the Lord will raise him up.*" [Jas 5:15] And he will not only receive health for the body but for the soul and what the Lord promised in the Gospel will be fulfilled saying: "*And whatever you ask in prayer, you will receive, if you have faith.*" [Mt 21:22]

Before everything, wherever you are, at home or on the road or at table, let no foul and lustful language drop from your mouth because the Lord announced in the Gospel: "*On the day of judgment men will render account for every careless word they utter.*" [Mt 12:36] Diabolical games and dancing or chants of the gentiles will be forbidden. No Christian will do them because he thus makes himself pagan. Nor is it right that diabolical canticles should proceed from a Christian mouth where the sacrament of Christ is placed, which it becomes always to praise God. Therefore, brothers, spurn all inventions of the enemy with all your heart and flee these sacrileges with all horror. Venerate no creature beyond God and his saints. Shun springs and arbors which they call sacred. You are forbidden to make the crook which they place on the crossroads and wherever you find one you should burn it with fire. For you must believe that you can be saved by no other art than the invocation and cross of Christ. For how will it be if groves where these miserable men make their devotions, are felled and the wood from them given to the furnace? See how foolish man is, to offer honor to insensible, dead trees and despise the precepts of God almighty. Do not believe that the sky or the stars or the earth or any creature should be adored beyond God for he created and disposes of them all. Heaven is high indeed, and the earth vast, and the sea immense and the stars beautiful but more immense and more beautiful by necessity is he who created them. For if the things seen are so incomprehensible, that is none of the variety of fruits of the earth, the beauty of flowers, the diversity of fruits, the types of animals, some on earth, some in water, some in the air, the prudence of bees, the breath of the wind, the dewy clouds and clashing thunder, the turning of the seasons, the alternation of days and nights, can be comprehended by the human mind. If all this is so, as we see, and we cannot comprehend them at any point, what should we think of those heavenly things which we cannot see? What of that artisan at whose nod all this was created and at whose will all is governed? Therefore, fear Him, brothers, above all; adore Him among all; love Him over all; hold to His mercy and never despair of His clemency.

[**Translator's note:** The end of the Chapter 16 is missing and there are only fragments of Chapter 17. Chapter 18 recounts of miracle involving wine. Chapter 19 provides another story of Eligius's powers of exorcism.]

(20.) Once when the diocese was celebrating the natal day of the most blessed Peter the Apostle in the town of Noyon, Eligius went to the *vicus* and preached as was his constant custom, the word of God with skillful constancy, denouncing all demonic games and wicked leapings and all remnants of inane superstitions as things to be thoroughly abominated. Some of the leading people in that place bore his preaching most grudgingly, resenting that he would upset their feasts and weaken their customs, which they deemed legitimate. Chief among these depraved ones were the servants of Erchenwald who, as *praepositus* of the palace at the time, emulated Eligius but not to the good.[35] They decreed together that, if Eligius should again attack their frivolities, they would kill him boldly. When Eligius learned of this, stimulated by the desire for martyrdom, he swiftly rose and ordered all his people that none should follow him but two priests and a deacon. So he went into the middle of a crowd of people and stood on a high place before the basilica where he began to preach urgently. Heatedly, he abjured the people that by turning their backs on his admonitions to salvation, they would be extremely threatened by diabolical phylacteries. Violently moved by this exhortation, the crowd answered him with shameful and impudent words, threatening him: "Never, Roman, however hard you try, shall you uproot our customs but we will attend our solemnities always and forever as we have done till now nor can any man forbid us our ancient and gratifying games." When he saw that he was getting nowhere and further games were being organized, he was moved with indignation and called forth to the Lord Jesus from his heart, saying: "Lord, I seek your divine clemency. May you permit these, who dare to contradict your holy admonitions with such pride and audacity and prefer the seductions of demons to your precepts, be given an example of such ferocity and terror that they shall know whose work they are and your Holy Name shall be glorified by men who believe in you." As soon as he spoke these words, many people were suddenly possessed by unclean spirits, particularly Erchenwald's partisans who, despising divine mandates, had been prepared to raise their hands against him and they began to rave. The whole crowd except those who were with [Eligius] were filled with terror and began to lick his footsteps showing reverence lest they suffer the same fate, each one begging to be enrolled among his sincere followers. To them, the blessed man said: "Don't be afraid, but rather glorify the just judgment of God, seeing that it is worthy of respect that he draws those who seem to run against his will to face what they love that their preceptors may feel whose cult they serve. You too, if you obey the precepts of Christ willingly, should fear nothing because you will always be safe from these robbers." Many then prayed for those who were being harassed but he did not wish to pray for them immediately. Rather, he said: "Let it be, let it be, they must bear it; they must bear it; they must know whom they have despised and whose orders they have obeyed until now." So when a year had passed and the anniversary of that festivity arrived, he ordered all the harassed to come to him. And when they were present, he prayed, exorcised some water, and gave it to them for a cure, freeing them immediately from the devil's traps. For there were more than fifty of them. Healing them in this way he corrected them and sent them home healed and punished.

(21.) Another time, when he was visiting his diocese following episcopal custom, he interdicted the course of the oblation being celebrated in a basilica for a particular reason.[36] For there was a priest there suffering in bad conscience whom he excommunicated because of his guilt. He took the bishop's words lightly, not thinking that he had to obey the order. When he thought [Eligius] had gone far enough away from the place, he began to ring the bell at the usual hour as was his custom. Then confuting the human presumption, the creature more insensible than rational heeded the bishop's words imposing silence on it and not a sound emerged from his strenuous ringing of the bell. For a long time the priest pulled at the rope, until he realized that the bells would remain mute. Then he went out of the basilica, the cause being made clear at the same time. Then mindful of Eligius's excommunication, he hurried after him praying that he would reconcile the basilica. But, although he was kind, he did not want to act hastily but first to have satisfaction that his sentence reflected. Thus a day and a night passed while the priest vainly tried to ring the bells and no sound attended his ringing. Then another night and day and still no ringing. A third day and night went by, still with no sound. But then nuncios came with letters from the *optimates* and seniors and at last their prayers overcame and the prelate was satisfied with the penitence and the place was reconciled with a single word from Eligius and soon, when the signal was touched, the bells were restored to their tintinnabulation.

[**Translator's note**: Chapters 22–26, which apparently narrate a set of miracle stories, are greatly marred by gaps in the text.]

(27.) Once a certain *praepositus* from Erckenwald's palace for some reason asked to travel to a town in his company. But considering the size of his group, he refused to accompany him. But the elders and abbots of his city pressed him to agree lest the man should use the excuse of the trip to take offense or become an enemy. At last, forced to answer them straightforwardly, he said: "What is the need, brothers, for us to get all upset about this? For unquestionably I know what none of you know, that if we hurry off there, we will suffer great injury. This man will get there in a hurry but he will not return alive but will die there." Indeed after several days his words were fulfilled for when they came in their own time to the said estate they learned that it had happened as he predicted. Then one night when everyone else was deep in sleep, Eligius happened to leave his tent and as he walked about before the vestibule, revolving I don't know what psalm internally, he suddenly saw a column of fire descend from heaven and violently penetrate Erckenwald's chamber. And silently considering the event within himself, he indicated the death of that beast to his deacon who was always with him at that time. Immediately struck with divine punishment, Erckenwald was afire with a sudden conflagration in his inmost bowels and straight off ordered that Eligius be called to him. When called, he came. Seeing him violently choking, he began to persuade him as he was about to die to do what he had not done willingly when he was alive, because faith had not been alive in him. Without delay, he must give the great sacks bursting with unrefined golden metal which traveled with him on horses to the poor for the refreshment of his soul. He added that nothing could be beneficial to him except to relinquish that treasure that had undoubtedly damaged his soul. But greedy as always, tenacious and avaricious, he kept dithering and in his long delay exhaled his spirit. Taking his corpse with him for mercy, Eligius brought him to burial and so the fulfillment of his prophecy was complete.

(28.) Similarly he foretold the death of a certain most cruel man, Flavadus, to his brothers.[37] For that tyrant most wickedly killed a Christian man, Willibad, a patrician of Burgundy and his death was announced to Eligius. He responded in opposition to that narrative, saying: "You tell me that Willibad is dead and Flavadus is alive. But I tell you that I know that he whom you have killed now lives more happily in heaven for his great merits; and he whom you applaud as still living will soon be dead in all his evil ways." And he remained unmoved, openly predicting: "I tell you this, because that dead man was a worshiper of the true God during his life, now he lives happily without end. But Flavadus who seems to be living for a longer time, will pursue evil for but ten more days and then, as is fitting, he will die." And it happened just as he said it would. For in seven days Flavadus was struck down and soon was miserably dead following the sentence of the man of God.

[**Translator's note**: Chapters. 29 and 31 tell other stories of Eligius's prophetic gifts. Chapter 30 is missing from Krusch's text.]

(32.) He predicted many other things in the course of familiar speech such as when he foretold the death of the former king Charibert [II] and it happened a little later and the death of the famous King Dagobert and the birth of Chlothar junior [III].[38] For when he was still in the womb and the queen was greatly afraid that she might have a daughter and the realm succumb because of it, Eligius came to her and reassured her. In the presence of the pregnant woman, he predicted a male birth to all and foretold her son from the mystery of regeneration. He then named the child in the womb and promised certain pieces of work that a child could use and had them made and ordered them to be kept against the birth. And all happened as he predicted which at last was attested by the king. For the queen brought forth a son and he was like a little son to Eligius. And the king called him by the name Chlothar which Eligius had bestowed upon him. After this, God multiplied his progeny and he sired two more sons. But in those days when the three procreated were still young and the king and queen remained peaceful and happy, Eligius predicted: "In a nocturnal vision, I saw the sun hurrying and shining brightly about the third hour of the day. Suddenly it disappeared into nowhere. And while I was still skillfully straining this formless prodigy, I looked there and behold, the moon sprang in the midst with three stars circling around, seemingly bound to that path where the returning sun turned daily. So I waited, astounded by this portent and soon before my wondering gaze, the moon was fortuitously removed leaving the stars remaining. After that, I earnestly watched the three stars until the noon hour came and their rays reflected one another in turn and one which seemed brighter than the others was unexpectedly withdrawn and the two openly poured out as much [light]. And then the same thing happened with the two: one of them was obscured or subtracted and only one remained in view which alone followed the path imitating the sun and shone with great brilliance and when it set in the west, great brightness was propagated on that side. And when at last it came to the final setting, so much brightness from its lamp was shed that it seemed to outshine the brightness of the sun. And this was therefore the order of the vision. After the death of King Clovis—for he soon will come to an end—this kingdom of the Franks will be left for some time to the queen and the three little boys. And after she will be removed from ruling, one of the three sons remaining will fall at last. And after no great time, one of the two will be deprived of the kingdom and the third will have the monarchy alone and will be magnified above all his affines and obtain the three kingdoms for his own. And so this vision will be consummated."[39] Thus spoke Eligius. It remains for us to see whether these words will come true for they are now only partially completed. But we do not doubt that consideration of the preceding which has been fulfilled, points to fulfillment of the rest. For following his sentence, King Clovis died at peace within thirty days. Then his widowed queen with her boys obtained the reign for a few years. She was afterward removed by law and left the principate to her sons, and, after a few years, the eldest born among them, who was seen to hold the most power, died one day after reigning peacefully and quietly and left his two surviving brothers. Now what will happen to them will only be decided by the judgment of God. Therefore this and similar other things which it would take too long to tell, were prophesied by Eligius.

[**Translator's note**: Chapter 33 is a fragmentary conclusion to Book 2. Chapter 36, which is also "The Death of the Holy and Blessed Eligius, bishop and confessor," opens with a summary of his merits and his prediction of his own death. A gap in the text ends with the death of Eligius. We will pick up the story there.]

(36.) . . . and this said, among these words he emitted his spirit.[40] And suddenly at the first hour of the night a blinding brightness was seen, shining like a great beacon from that house and among the wondering watchers a fiery orb taking on the shape of the cross scattered the density of the clouds with its swift course to penetrate the heavens on high. So in this manner his holy soul was liberated from the pressure of the abject flesh which encased it and flew joyfully to its author. After long wandering here, to the rejoicing of heaven, the weeping of earth, and the applause of the angels, it arose at last rejoicing to [its] ancient estate. So all the love that the blessed man had among the people was clearly demonstrated in his death. Hardly had he exhaled his spirit and rendered the soul he owed to Christ than, as the messengers ran, weeping resounded through the whole town to heaven and all the streets were suddenly filled with noise and in the city everyone mourned this death as a common disaster. What more? When the composed body was carried to the church on its bier, as is customary, the people came for vigil, keeping watch in turns, the clergy with hymns and the people lamenting through the night.

(37.) So by dawn a multitude of both sexes had gathered in the town. Queen Balthild was there with her sons and a multitude of nobles who speedily entered the town and went to the funeral course, and broke into tears weeping and wailing that she had known him so little in life. And when she had wept for a long time lying with laments on his bier, she asked that preparations be made for her to carry the body of the blessed man to her monastery of Chelles. But when she tried to raise him nothing could prevail to move him from the spot and with sorrow she ordered that the *triduum* of the Church be celebrated with fasts and psalm-singing. While that was done, she celebrated that *triduum* in continuous vigil with her *optimates* and clerks persisting in their longing. When this was over, the venerable queen weeping uncontrollably, could in no way keep back her tears. And since she could in no way bear the absence of the holy man because of her excessive sorrow, at last, to satisfy her desire, she revealed his face kissing it sorrowfully and began to wet his hands and breast and drown his cheeks with a sea of tears. And behold! suddenly as she was stroking the holy body with kisses, a miracle occurred. For it was winter time and the corpse lay frozen until fortuitously a flood of blood flowed from this nose and began to moisten the holy one's cheeks. Seeing this, the bishops and the most Christian queen quickly placed a linen napkin there. Diligently, they collected the blood wherever it ran and the better to conserve the gift separated it into three pieces. Meanwhile, with the fast finished, the queen was determined, as we said, to move the body of the holy man to her monastery at Chelles. But others wanted to bring him to Paris and yet more insisted that the city of Noyon most justly deserved the legacy of her *antistes'* limbs. Thus altercation arose among them all with pious devotion alternating with holy rapine, about who most justly deserved the relics and the sepulchre. When the bishops and forestanders (*praestantiores*) who were of the queen's party prepared to bear him to her monastery a great roar and tumult rose among the whole people of Noyon. Then the queen, taking more prudent counsel and committing the cause to God said: "Now let these tortuous debates be discarded and we will test whether it is the Lord's will that this holy man be there where I desire. In that case, [the bier] may be raised without difficulty, or otherwise." And when she had spoken they went to the bier and attempted to raise it but felt so much weight depressing it that they could not move it from that spot. Then in turn others tried but none could prevail. Finally the queen, wishing to prove it for herself, stretched out and turned up her forearm and began to push, trying to move a single corner of the bier. And when she had struck with all her strength radiating courteous-ness, [it was] like a giant mountain and she could accomplish nothing. Then turning to the *optimates* she said: "Behold! we must acknowledge that it is not his will that we take him away. Let us concede to this people what we still would not wish to accept." The counsel was acceptable and they all decreed with one voice that he should be buried in that city. And after that decision, when again they tried to lift the bier, they found it very light, carried easily by two people which before no number could move. What a miracle for the citizens! With the queen watching, they magnified the glory of the Lord saying: "Great and wonderful are your works, Lord" and "You are wonderful, God, in your saints."

(38.) So the corpse was brought to burial with all the city doing homage in tears. And the devout queen, though it was winter and very swampy, could in no way be persuaded that a vehicle and horses should be used but followed the bier on foot. With great labor, she went through the flood with continual lament with all his household. Oh how many tears of all, of monks and poor people, flowed together on that day echoing through all the streets. The chorus rendered psalms with sobbing voices, chants and weeping flocks resounded with sorrow through the air; all the people of the town quaked with tears and the highest peak of Olympus was filled with plangency. The rhythms of the antiphons rang in the choir and the sorrow of Noyon sounded in heaven. Every path gave forth the funeral chants, dire ululations filling every abode and the wailing of the people poured out over the entire globe: "and they filled waves of tears with golden voices."[41] What pomp the extinct pastor emanated all around! What crowds brought the body to the tomb, here preceded by the chanting choir, there with the flocks of the people in continued wailing! They complained that they had lost their father and nurse and quaking with sobbing, they could barely get out the words: "To whom, good pastor, will you commit the service of your people, or to whom will you entrust the pastoral care of your flock? Oh Eligius, you sweetener of the poor, strength of the weak, protector, comforter without peer! Who after you will give such great alms, who will be our protector, as you were, good pastor? Would it not be sweeter to die with you today than to live on without your presence?" In this way they proceeded to the grave, giving cries with all their voices mixed to the heavens so that it was not easy among so many tearful voices to separate the accents of the chant, the psalm-singing of the clergy, or the ululations of the people. For on that day who could be so heartless that, hearing the laments of the poor, he would not burst into tears himself? Or who could discern the vociferations of all the people and remain so merciless as not to begin roaring himself? Who had so iron and stolid a stomach that when he saw the weeping queen with the princes, he would not immediately break down into lamenting? Who now could record with dry eyes how he was brought to the sepulchre with such ardor of desire, such movement of love, such impulse of sorrow? The bier was held back, drawn away by the people to the rear so that for a moment the corpse might remain in the open and they might satisfy their desire. For they kept causing all these delays to keep the body from being enclosed in the sepulchre because no one could bear his absence. But finally the strength of the people ebbed and as I have said, rapt from strong to stronger, it was released to the bishops who had advanced to the sepulchre. And so the stone opened and it was kept with great honor, and with all surrounding the tomb he lay in glory. Thus while the venerable queen with the people buried him the prelates adoring his limbs, she returned to her own fasting, her tears preventing her from taking food until she had fulfilled the three days of mourning. [**Translator's note**: There is a gap here in the text.] This is enough for us to say about the death of the holy man. Otherwise we shall bore our readers. I had judged that, with the end of his life, our words should also end but the unwearying Lord did so many miracles through the holy body that I am impelled to go on talking. Therefore I shall take the opportunity to extend the reading and show some in this present book.

NOTES

1. Dado has adapted his geographic information from a number of Roman sources, including Pliny (d. 79) and Orosius (d. post 417).

2. Dado implies that Eligius's name was derived from *eligo* meaning chosen.

3. Abbo's name appears on many coins from this mint.

4. Dado adopts this common saying from the letters of the Christian scholar Jerome.

5. Chlothar II was king of Neustria from 584 to 629. He also exercised control over Austrasia and Burgundy for periods of time. He was one of the youngest sons of King Chilperic I (by Chilperic's second wife, Fredegund), but he was the only one to ascend to a royal title.

6. The author is describing himself in the third person.

7. The family of Audechar (or Autharius) was an important one in court circles which apparently gave its allegiance to King Chlothar II only after earlier supporting Chlothar's rival in Austrasia, Theudebert II. See Ian Wood, *The Merovingian Kingdoms, 450–751* (London, 1994), p. 151. The members of this family also appear in the *Vita s. Audoini*, Chapters 1, 4, and 7 and Jonas of Bobbio, *Vita s. Columbani*, Book1, Chapter 26.

8. Dagobert was the oldest surviving son of Chlothar II. Chlothar had made Dagobert his co-king in Austrasia in 623. On Chlothar's death in 629, Dagobert received the kingdoms of Burgundy and Neustria, while that of Aquitaine went to his younger brother (possibly a half-brother) Charibert II.

9. Like that of Abbo (see note 3 above), Thille's name has been found on coins of the period.

10. The Moors in question were refugees from Mauretania, a Roman province of North Africa. The same term *Mauri* was later applied by Western Christians to the Muslim conquerors of North Africa. The death of the prophet Muhammad, however, occurred in 632 and the expansion of Muslim military and political power had not yet taken place.

11. Bruno Krusch cites, in the notes to his edition, several such extant charters signed by Eligius.

12. That is, as a martyr.

13. The monastery of Ferrières was located in the Gatinais, near the Loire river.

14. Krusch points out that much of the physical description of the king is borrowed from the prologue of the *Salic Law*.

15. According to tradition, the monastery of Solignac was founded on November 22, 632.

16. Dado uses an arcane word, *archeterium*, to describe this convent.

17. The monastery founded by Eligius and its abbess Aurea are both also mentioned by Jonas of Bobbio, *Vita s. Columbani*, Book 2, Chapter 10. The community contained women of varied social rank. *Ancillae* are, strictly speaking, female slaves. In the seventh century slavery was still a living social reality in Gaul and much on the minds of St. Eligius and his contemporaries, as his energetic efforts to free captives illustrates. He may well

have intended his monasteries to shelter women whom he had freed. The same word, however, was commonly used in hagiography for holy women who had given themselves into God's service, often in commanding positions as abbesses of great monasteries. Gregory I used the term *ancillae Dei* for consecrated women who lived in their own homes serving urban churches in various capacities. Eligius's plan of grouping *ancillae* into monastic communities may afford an early glimpse of the women who emerge in eighth-century sources as canonesses. Such women were systematically monasticized under the Rule of Aachen in 816,

18. In this action, Eligius anticipated the later ritual of the humiliation of saints.

19. Krusch explains that Eligius bore an Irish, rather than a Roman or "apostolic," style of tonsure.

20. This list provides a litany of some of the most important saints' shrines in the region of Paris at this time. Germanus (d. 576) had been a bishop of Paris, who was buried in the monastery of Saint-Germain-des-Prés, which he had founded. There were a number of saints known by the name Severin, but Dado probably alludes to a sixth-century hermit whose relics were enshrined in a church in Paris. Quentin and his disciple Piaton were remembered as martyrs executed during their attempt to evangelize the region of Vermandois. Lucian was a third-century martyr venerated at Beauvais. Genovefa, or Geneviève, (d. ca. 500) was a virgin who was credited with saving the city of Paris at the time of the Hunnish attacks. She was enshrined on the top of the hill which bore her name in Paris. Columba was a third-century virgin and martyr from Sens who was also venerated in a basilica in Paris, mentioned above in Chapter 30. Julian was a fourth-century bishop of Le Mans whose relics were enshrined in that city.

21. All these tombs were located in or near the city of Tours. Martin (d. 397) had originally been buried in the monastery of Marmoutiers which he had founded to the east of the city. His relics were later moved to a new shrine located within the city walls. This quickly became one of the most important shrines in the Frankish kingdoms and continued to be an important center of pilgrimage throughout the Middle Ages. Martin's disciple Brice (d. ca. 444) succeeded him as bishop of Tours. Later he built a small basilica in honor of Martin which served as his own burial chapel.

22. The basilica of Saint-Denis, where the tomb of an early bishop of Paris was located, lay to the north of the city. It was greatly enriched during the reign of Dagobert.

23. Dagobert died and was succeeded by Clovis II in 639.

24. This passage provides the main evidence for the Council of Orléans, apparently convoked in either 639 or 640 to condemn a man who preached some version of Monolethism. See Odette Pontal, *Histoire des conciles mérovingiens* (Paris, 1989), p. 216.

25. Krusch suggests that this word has more the meaning of "hypercrites" than "hypocrites."

26. Chlothar III became king of Neustria and Burgundy in 657 on the death of his father, Clovis II.

27. Brunhild was the wife of King Sigibert I (d. 575), whose capital was at Reims. She continued to exert powerful influence over her sons and grandsons during her long widowhood. Sigibert was the brother of Chilperic I, and thus the uncle of Chlothar II. Bruno Krusch in his edition (p. 694, note 3) points out that there is no reason to classify Brunhild's appointments as simoniac in contrast to the similarly political appointments of her successors. In any case, Dado (or the ninth-century editor) makes an error here: Brunhild was executed by Chlothar II and therefore did not live into the reign of Dagobert.

28. This is apparently a reference to the Council of Chalons, which was held in 644.

29. Acharius is called Aigahard in the acts of the Council of Clippiac (626) and Aigatarius in the privileges of the monastery of Burgundofaro at Rebais (637).

30. The consecration occurred on May 13, 641.

31. On St. Quentin, see note 20 above.

32. See Gregory of Tours, *Glory of the Martyrs*, trans. Raymond Van Dam (Liverpool, 1988), Chapter 72.

33. It has been suggested that this chapter constitutes an actual sermon by Eligius which has been inserted into the text. On this problem, see the discussion by Joseph-Claude Poulin, "Eligius," *Lexikon des Mittelalters*, vol. 3 (Munich, 1986), columns 1829–30. It

Dado of Rouen, *Life of St. Eligius of Noyon*

provides important evidence for the attempts by the Christian ecclesiastical hierarchy to root out pagan and magical practices. A good overview of the efforts to convert the rural population of the Frankish kingdoms to Christianity, including several references to the present text, is provided by J.M. Wallace-Hadrill, *The Frankish Church* (Oxford, 1983), pp. 17–36.

34. Krusch suggests that Geniscus is a local genius or minor deity.

35. Erchenwald had been the original owner of Balthild when she was a slave. After she had married Clovis II, she and Erchenwald continued to cooperate.

36. This sentence echoes a phrase used by Sulpicius Severus to describe Martin of Tours.

37. That is, the monks at Noyon.

38. Charibert II died in 631/2; Dagobert died in 639; the exact date of the birth of Chlothar III is unknown.

39. This prophecy apparently refers to the consolidation of the Frankish kingdoms by Chilperic III from 687 until 690 (following the death of his brothers Chlothar III in 673 and of Childeric II in 675). These events most probably postdate Dado's composition of the original version of this text. See the fuller discussion by Krusch in his edition.

40. The most probable date for Eligius's death is 640.

41. This is quoted from Sedulius Scotus, *Paschale carmen*, book 4, line 34. See Sedulius Scotus, *Carmina*, ed. Jean Meyers, Corpus Christianorum Continuatio Mediaevalis 117 (Turnhout, 1991).

CHAPTER 8
BEDE, *MARTYROLOGY*
Translated by Felice Lifshitz

INTRODUCTION

Although Christianity was illegal in the Roman Empire before the year 313, persecutions of Christians occurred only sporadically and Christian groups were able to grow for much of the time. Still, anti-Christian legislation was sometimes enforced, for instance in the years 249—251 under the emperor Decius. England formed part of the Roman Empire from approximately 43 until 410. In Roman Britain, "pagan" religions were practiced by the majority of natives and immigrants, but there is also evidence of Christian missionary activity by Mediterranean churches. It appears that some Romano-British Christians (such as Albanus) may have fallen victim to the Decian persecution. Despite persecutions, when the emperor Constantine embraced Christianity early in the fourth century, churches in Britain, as elsewhere, were sufficiently organized to send delegates to conciliar gatherings. It would have been possible then to forget the sporadic persecutions of previous centuries, but some Christians preferred to commemorate those who had stood firm in their religious loyalties despite secular law. Christians executed by the Roman Empire were not remembered as criminals, which they technically were at the time of their legal punishments, but rather as "martyrs:" literally "witnesses" who had publicly testified, or borne witness, to their faith.

In the course of the fourth and early fifth centuries, remembrance of the martyrs became an integral part of developing Christian practice. The veneration of Roman-era martyrs was primarily organized around the tombs of those special dead, as "ordinary" Christians tried to arrange their own burials (or those of their loved ones) near the holy martyr tombs. However, the remembrance of the Roman-era martyrs did not remain confined to the burial locales of the individuals in question, or even to the territories which witnessed their persecution. Relics and written texts, both imminently portable, functioned as vehicles for the dissemination of martyr cults beyond their places of origin. The cults developed in the fourth and fifth centuries primarily in the Mediterranean, where the numbers of "actual" martyrs were much more elevated than, for instance, in Roman Britain. It was on the Italian peninsula, perhaps in Rome or in Aquileia, that an unknown fifth-century author compiled a massive list of martyrs, arranged in calendrical order with multiple entries for each day, and attributed this martyrological calendar, or martyrology, to the scholar St. Jerome (Hieronymus in Latin). Subsequent additions to the pseudo-Hieronymian martyrology were made primarily outside of the Italian peninsula, particularly in Gaul; those entries largely remained confined to the simple naming and localizing of each saint.

After 476, there ceased to be an effective imperial political center in the Latin West, as all the former Roman provinces joined Britain in falling to the control of regional elites, both Roman and barbarian. Despite the loss of political unity, the cultures of the sub-Roman successor realms on the Continent were marked by a consciously preserved *Romanitas*, one which included the Christian cult of saints. However, the persons commemorated as the Christian "special dead" included an increasingly smaller percentage of Roman-era martyrs, as communities throughout the Latin world focused remembrance on individuals more closely connected with local interests and present circumstances, such as missionaries and monastic founders, or martyrs to later, non-Roman political units. Such individuals were incorporated into the ever-evolving pseudo-Hieronymian martyrology, although martyrs still vastly predominated numerically in all the extant manuscripts of that enumerative martyrology. Unfortunately, the details of this double evolution (political and cultic) are much less understood for Britain than for the Continent. Indeed, the discontinuity between Roman and post-Roman forms seems to have been much more dramatic in Britain than on the Continent. For instance, only scattered clues, both archeological and literary, indicate the existence of memorial martyr shrines or other cultic installations in Britain during the fifth and sixth centuries.

As for the Continent, it is clear that by the end of the sixth century, the remembrance of martyrs was a standard feature of the liturgy, that is the formal celebration of the Christian cult, at least in the church of Rome. Pope Gregory I noted that the daily masses in his church were sung in veneration of the martyrs of each particular day, according to the entries in a codex which seems to have been a version of pseudo-Jerome. By the eighth century, at least in Gaul, the saints to be commemorated during the upcoming week would be announced from such a list as part of each Sunday's mass. Martyrologies were thus used in connection with the divine office from an early date, and in fact on a daily basis, but were not technically liturgical books; they had no official approval or status, but were composed by private initiative to serve local needs. Thus, each and every currently extant manuscript version diverges considerably from all the rest as a result of adaptation to local interests. Despite the lack of centralizing control, all the martyrologies used by Latin churches during Bede's lifetime descended from the pseudo-Hieronymian martyrology. The recitation of martyrs' names on and around their festival dates was probably introduced to the Anglo-Saxon churches by continental missionaries.

Despite geographical eccentricity and despite being relatively cut off from the Christian-Roman practices of the Mediterranean during the fifth century, when martyr veneration first truly flourished, it was Anglo-Saxon England that contributed the most lasting newer feature of the cult of the martyrs:

Bede's martyrology has been the basis for the most commonly used martyrologies since the ninth century and, as the foundation for the *Roman Martyrology*, continues to be so today. Bede (672/3–735) was an innovator who moved the Latin churches away from simple lists of saints and martyrs to the use of historical martyrologies. In 731 Bede described his project in the following terms: "A martyrology concerning the commemorative festival days of the holy martyrs, in which I have diligently striven to note down all those whom I was able to find, not only on what day but also through what kind of struggle and under which judge they vanquished the world" (*Ecclesiastical History of the English Nation*, bk. 5, chap. 24). In effect, Bede conveniently historicized the regular commemorative process; he injected specific substance into the daily remembrance of martyrs (and of the other nonmartyred individuals who were featured in the company of saints). That Bede should have made such a contribution is not surprising.

Günter Kotzor has suggested that the key to the switch from enumerative to historical (or narrative, or anecdotal) martyrologies is to be found in the monastic lifestyle, the one to which Bede adhered throughout his lifetime. Monastic communities had a tradition of communal daily readings, and such traditions would certainly have facilitated the incorporation of narrative into the martyr-remembrance portion of the daily liturgy. By the early eighth century, there were numerous male, female and mixed monastic communities in Latin Europe, but only one particular monk, Bede, took the step to incorporate historical information into the martyrologies that must have already been widespread. Bede may have been a monk, but he was also a historian, and a particularly creative one at that. Just as Bede alone took the step to develop the fifth-century Italian pseudo-Hieronymian martyrology along new lines, launching the genre to great heights of popularity, it was also Bede alone who saw the value in another late Antique Italian invention, the dominical or *Anno Domini* (Year of the Lord) chronology of the early-sixth-century Roman monk Denis the Short. Bede adopted *Anno Domini* (or A. D.) dating for his *Ecclesiastical History of the English Nation*, for it enabled him to orient all phenomena in relation to salvation history. The dating method spread along with copies of his masterpiece, after having been ignored for centuries by people who failed to see the utility in the innovation. Bede was, therefore, not just any monk. No evidence has ever been found for any pre-Bedan historical martyrologies, although Henri Quentin (who tended to see Bede as a copyist, not a creative thinker) suspected that Bede had followed some earlier model; in the absence of evidence, the innovation must be credited to Bede, and explained by reference to Bede.

In the initial conversion of the Anglo-Saxon ruling elite to Christianity, both *Romanitas* and continental culture (so wrapped up with Christianity by the seventh century) themselves formed part of the appeal of the new religion. To join "Christendom" in the seventh century meant, for Anglo-Saxons, to join a world of high culture and written history. Bede's activity belongs in this context. He was, more than most Angles and Saxons, attracted by *Romanitas*.

For instance, Bede's own *Ecclesiastical History of the English Nation* is a work with a distinctly pro-Roman (and anti-British) bias, ignoring any continuities from or contributions of the Romano-British churches to the ecclesiastical world of his lifetime, and instead highlighting the Romanization of the insular churches after the arrival of continental missionaries sent by pope Gregory I in 597. Bede spent his entire life at the monastic complex of Wearmouth-Jarrow, a community whose buildings were deliberately constructed to look like a Roman villa, whose own saintly patrons were the ultimate Roman saints, that is Peter and Paul, whose library was stocked with books brought from Rome by the founder, Benedict Biscop, and whose scriptorium imitated a Roman hand (Roman uncial) for its own book production. Although other libraries also benefited from the massive influx of Mediterranean books, Bede's was particularly richly endowed; the major literary resources available to him are evident from his many writings, including the martyrology, whose compilation required at least fifty *passiones* (accounts of a martyr's suffering or "passion") and the writings of twelve different ecclesiastical historians and chroniclers.

In the course of the seventh century, the connections between England and Italy (especially the Roman papacy, in some sense the heir of the Roman Empire) both multiplied and intensified. Numerous relics of Roman-era martyrs such as St. Lawrence were sent to the Anglo-Saxon kingdoms by Roman bishops, or brought there by Anglo-Saxon pilgrims and collectors such as Acca of Hexham and Benedict Biscop. Through the importation of these relics, the veneration of Roman martyrs flourished in Anglo-Saxon England; eastern Mediterranean relics, traditions, and practices also penetrated the British Isles from the latter part of the seventh century, particularly through the influence of Theodore of Tarsus, an Oriental refugee and Roman monk appointed archbishop of Canterbury by Pope Vitalian in 669. As Anglo-Saxons commemorated and remembered Roman-era martyrs, the Anglo-Saxon churches came to adopt Roman-Mediterranean history as part of their own genealogy. Bede's martyrology, written between 725 and 731, was both a product and a stimulator of the process whereby the Anglo-Saxon realms moved from a position of eccentricity and separation from Mediterranean-Roman culture to one of conceptual and actual integration into the Roman world.

The martyrology is a universal Church calendar which marks the commemorative festivals of individuals and groups drawn geographically from all over the known world, from Persia through Bede's own Northumbria, and chronologically from apostolic times through Bede's own contemporaries. Bede included martyrs from the British Isles, but not in any unusually high proportion; rather, just enough to give his homeland a presence. Bede exercised extraordinary selectivity in compiling his martyrology, leaving most days blank; those days would soon be filled in (from the pseudo-Hieronymian martyrology) by the authors of later martyrologies and indeed even by scribes whose task was supposedly only to copy Bede's text! Bede could have filled all the days; instead, from each source (all of which have been precisely identified) he only harvested a few entries. He exercised extraordinary restraint in limiting his entries, for he omitted from the martyrology many individuals whom he himself had celebrated elsewhere in his own writings; he was aiming for a particularly finely calibrated balance of contents, and was not merely adhering to strict scruples about potentially erroneous dates (as Quentin has argued). The pseudo-Hieronymian martyrology (like the lists of saints and their burial places common in Anglo-Saxon England) had conveyed no information about the past, or indeed about the present; in contrast, the narrative entries in Bede's martyrology added up to a story of the universal Church, the story of its progressive geographic spread up to the author's own lifetime against enemies who sought to stem the Christian tide through violence.

The key to Bede's martyrology is the universal Rome-centered story into which England, like other Christian nations, had finally been incorporated. Conspicuous by their absence, in what is usually regarded as a great "age of saints" in the Celtic world, are Irish and British saints; Bede omitted them from his martyrology, just as he had ignored or downplayed their contributions in his *Ecclesiastical History of the English Nation*, to emphasize their status as outsiders to the universal Roman Church, whose teachings they rejected. The martyrology is the liturgical pendant to the *Ecclesiastical History*; in fact, Bede located the martyrology immediately after the *Ecclesiastical History* on the list of his writings which he appended to the *Ecclesiastical History*. Both combine to tell the story of Britain from the perspective of, and as part of, the Roman Empire and Church, for it was only insofar as Britain participated in Roman history that it acquired historical, universal significance. Bede's position on such matters, his passion for the universal Church and for the fact of its diffusion across all parts of the globe, is easily grasped due to the numerous volumes of biblical commentary which he composed. The incorporation of England into the universal Church was but a stage in the unitary movement of the inexorable divine plan, which triumphed even over persecutions, and a particularly exciting stage at that, precisely because of the geographical remoteness and cultural distance of the British Isles from the Mediterranean center. The Church was approaching the periphery of the world, and the martyrology was a liturgical monument to the final stage of history. However, as a liturgical pendant the martyrology represented time differently from the linear chronology of the *Ecclesiastical History*. Unlike the *Anno Domini* dating system (used in the *Ecclesiastical History* but eschewed in the martyrology), a system which constructs time as linear and progressive, a calendar such as the martyrology emphasizes the circularity of the annual liturgical cycle.

All of Bede's works were "best-sellers" within decades of his death. In fact, demand for copies of his works was so high, particularly on the Continent, that it put a strain on the scriptorium at Wearmouth-Jarrow, so much so that a specially efficient hand was developed to speed the production process (a hand which, ironically, required abandoning the Romanist traditions of

Bede's lifetime). None of the extant manuscripts of Bede's martyrology (of which there are twenty-one) represents the text precisely as he composed it. Every manuscript contains at least one interpolation, a festival for the Anglo-Saxon missionary Boniface, who died in 755, twenty years after Bede. Every extant manuscript descends from a single archetype, one copied evidently after 755. There may have been an orchestrated campaign to reproduce and disseminate copies of the martyrology, since by the second decade of the ninth century at the latest the daily reading of the stories of the martyrs (and not just their names) was required by canon law. From this point onward, martyrologies technically became classifiable as liturgical books, and the standard martyrological form would ever after adhere to the template created by Bede. Terminologically speaking, however, ninth-century and later Christians did not always adopt Bede's designation of *martyrologium* or martyrology for such liturgical books; they were called by a variety of names, and most frequently simply "calendars."

One way Bede's reputation and martyrology were spread on the Continent during the eighth century was surely by the steady stream of Anglo-Saxon pilgrims and missionaries who journeyed through Gaul and Germany to Italy and above all to Rome. Bede's martyrology found its most welcoming home of all in Lyon, a major staging point on more than one of the standard routes between the British Isles and Italy. From the early ninth century, several clerics of the church of Lyon updated and expanded Bede's martyrology. It was, however, Usuard, a monk of the Parisian abbey of Saint-Germain-des-Prés, who around 875 produced (and dedicated to the emperor of the revived western Roman Empire, Charles the Bald) the updated version of Bede's martyrology that would be used by most Latin churches, in the British Isles and on the Continent, for centuries to come.

SOURCES AND FURTHER READING

Despite its importance in the liturgical history of the Latin churches, Bede's martyrology has been the object of virtually no scholarly attention, with the exception of some stylistic analysis by Günter Kotzor, "Anglo-Saxon Martyrologists at Work: Narrative Pattern and Prose Style in Bede and the Old English Martyrology," in *Sources and Relations: Studies in Honour of J.E. Cross*, eds. Marie Collins, Jocelyn Price, and Andrew Hamer, Leeds Studies in English, new series 16 (Leeds, 1985), pp. 152–73. Therefore, readers who wish to know more about the man and the environment which produced this first historical martyrology should begin with a survey such as David Rollason, *Saints and Relics in Anglo-Saxon England* (Oxford, 1989). There is no critical edition, indeed no real edition at all, of this martyrology; in what follows I have translated the entries as they were printed from what were believed to be the best available manuscripts—namely a ninth- or tenth-century partial copy from either Fulda or Mainz (now in the library of Saint Gallen, Stiftbibliothek MS 452), supplemented by a ninth-century copy from Salzburg (now in the Bavarian National Library in Munich, MS 15.818)—by

Henri Quentin in his meticulous study of Bede's sources which forms Chapter 2 of *Les martyrologes historiques du moyen âge. Etude sur la formation du martyrologe romain* (Paris, 1908). Also available is *Edition pratique des martyrologes de Bède, de l'Anonyme Lyonnais et de Florus*, eds. Jacques Dubois and Geneviève Renaud, IRHT Bibliographies, Colloques, Travaux Préparatoires (Paris, 1976); this is not a critical edition and contains a number of errors, however it is laid out in a much more convenient, reader-friendly format than is Quentin's work, for Dubois and Renaud organized calendrically (from Quentin's study) the entries which Quentin had printed alphabetically according to Bede's sources. Since making this translation, I have compared the entries from Quentin's work with all the oldest available manuscripts of the text, and have concluded that the versions which he used (that is, the manuscripts now preserved in Saint Gallen and Munich) are reasonably representative of the martyrology which circulated under Bede's name throughout western Europe during the ninth and tenth centuries.

Jacques Dubois, *Les martyrologes du moyen âge latin*, Typologie des sources du moyen âge occidental 26 (Turnhout, 1978) and Günter Kotzor, *Das altenglische Martyrologium*, Bayerische Akademie der Wissenschaften, Philosophisch-Historische Klasse, Abhandlungen neue folge 88.1-2 (Munich, 1981) contain the only major studies of early medieval martyrologies since Quentin's groundbreaking work of 1908. The only general study available in English is John M. McCulloh, "Historical Martyrologies in the Benedictine Tradition," in *Benedictine Culture, 750 – 1050*, eds. W. Lourdaux and D. Verhelst, Mediaevalia Lovaniensia 1.9 (Leuven, 1983), pp. 114–131. None of these authors pays particular attention to Bede.

Because of the complicated transmission history of the text, and particularly due to all the scribal interventions to update and expand the entries, the precise state of Bede's martyrology as it left his hands cannot be determined. All of the manuscripts contain large numbers of short notices, that is, mere indications of place and name such as had characterized the pseudo-Hieronymian enumerative martyrology; it is not clear which, if any, of those entries were the responsibility of Bede himself. The variety can be extreme from one manuscript to another, depending upon the local traditions of the churches where the manuscripts were originally produced and then used over succeeding centuries. Scholars do, however, agree that a core group of one hundred and fifteen developed historical entries (one hundred and four concerning martyrs) were penned by Bede; it is those that are translated here.

A few points are in order concerning the translation itself. Every entry begins with the phrase "the commemorative festival of" which corresponds to the Latin word *natale*. The word *natale* is sometimes expressed, but is just as frequently left unexpressed yet implicit in the fact that the name (or names) of the saint(s) in question is (are) always given in the possessive form, indicating that the day in question is the *natale* of that saint or those saints. *Natale* literally means "birthday," for the martyrs were believed to have been born into eternal life when they triumphed over bodily death. However, the actual dates on which martyrs died were rarely known, and the natal days tended realistically to correspond rather to the saints' memorial days, the days on which they were remembered in one place or another; those festival (or feast) dates could vary from church to church. The dates themselves have been translated to accord with modern convention and placed in parentheses at the beginning of the entry. The Roman dating system used by Bede reckoned days of the month by counting backward from set signposts, such as the "Kalends" or first day of each month; thus, March 27 was "VI Kalends of April" (or "sixth day before the Kalends of April"). The numbers preceding the entries in the following translation are the days of the month (according to modern usage) of the feast days. Latin personal names have been Anglicized when their English versions are so common that leaving them in Latin would only cause confusion; thus, Petrus is translated to Peter. Less well known Latin names are left in Latin; most have no English equivalent in any case. Finally, Bede's prose style is extraordinarily concise and compressed; most entries comprise a single syntactical unit filled with relative clauses and embedded subordinate constructions, yet effectively devoid of qualifying adjectives. Bede's hypotactic summary technique is most striking in connection with the asydetic string of nouns he consistently utilizes to summarize the torments faced by the martyrs. The Latin syntax used by Bede is linguistically impossible to reproduce in English, a language which requires a more unraveled style; nevertheless, I have tried to come as close to Bede's concision as possible.

There has been significant scholarly interest of late in somatic history, namely, the history of the body. This interest has included attention to themes such as torture. Also, as this anthology itself perhaps makes clear, there has also been a flourishing scholarly interest in the Christian cult of saints. Finally, the last few decades have also been characterized by a keen scholarly interest in the study of gender. The intersection of these trends has resulted in a number of studies concerning gender and physical violence in the cults of martyred saints. Some scholars, such as Caroline Walker Bynum, have emphasized the spiritual message of the martyrs' miraculous abilities to survive, often without pain, excruciating and repeated torments; see her collection of essays *Fragmentation and Redemption: Essays on Gender and the Human Body in Medieval Religion* (New York, 1992), particularly the essay "Material Continuity, Personal Survival and the Resurrection of the Body." Most authors, however, have found profoundly disturbing misogynistic traits in the Christian cult of martyrs, and have argued that female martyr bodies were regularly and disproportionally imagined—and imagined with pleasure!—as the victims of violence, particularly sexual violence. Such arguments are generally based upon twelfth- or thirteenth-century and later evidence, such as vernacular literature in the case of Brigitte Cazelles's *The Lady as Saint. A Collection of French Hagiographic Romances of the Thirteenth Century* (Philadelphia, 1991) or the Golden Legend in the case of Margaret R. Miles's *Carnal Knowing: Female Nakedness and Religious Meaning in the Christian West* (Boston,

1989). However, the evidence of Bede's martyrology has never been brought into the discussion.

Bede's compilation is eminently suited for the study of gender, torture, and martyrdom since Bede, much more than any other early martyrologist, focuses on the torments sustained by his holy hero(ine)s. It is hoped that readers will draw their own conclusions about how the evidence of Bede can contribute to the discussion. I would like, in closing, to offer some statistics in support of the argument that there is no such lurid or sensationalist association between female martyrs and (sexual) violence to be found in Bede's martyrology. Fifty-six male martyrs and twenty-four female martyrs have their tortures described, mostly in a dry, matter-of-fact manner amounting to little more than a string of nouns. Some entries, however, do aim to arouse emotional affect, and linger in more picturesque detail on the torture process. The proportions of those entries are nineteen out of fifty-six for the male martyrs and eight out of twenty-four for the female martyrs, approximately one-third for both groups. Only five of Bede's martyrs are said to have been naked during their public tortures: three male and two female saints. This issue is one theme to consider while reading the martyrology; I hope readers will find many others as well.

Bede, Martyrology

January

/1 The commemorative festival of Alamachius who, at the command of Alypius, prefect of the city [that is, Rome], since he had said: "Today is the octave of the lordly day:[1] do not engage in the superstitions of idols and polluted sacrifices!" was, for this reason, killed by gladiators.

/3 At Rome, the commemorative festival of Antheros, pope and martyr: who ruled the church for twelve years, and was buried in the cemetery of Callistus, on the Appian Way.

/10 The commemorative festival of Paul the first hermit: who remained alone in the wilderness from his sixteenth year until his one hundred and thirteenth: Anthony saw his soul carried by angels to heaven among a chorus of apostles and prophets.

/11 In Africa, [the commemorative festival] of St. Salvius. On his commemorative festival, St. Augustine gave a sermon to the people of Carthage.

/13 In Poitiers, the deposition of Hilary, bishop and confessor of Poitiers, about whom, among other virtues, it is said that he revived a dead man by praying.

/14 In Campania, the commemorative festival of St. Felix, priest and confessor: about whom Bishop Paulinus wrote, among other things, that when he was placed in prison by persecutors and was lying, chained up, upon snail shells and small potsherds, he was released and let out at night by an angel.

/16 The commemorative festival of St. Marcellus, pope, who was first beaten with clubs on the command of Emperor Maximianus, and then expelled from the sight of him whom he [Marcellus] had reproached. Then [Maximianus], hearing that [Marcellus] had made a church, and was celebrating masses in it in the middle of the city, in the house of the holy Lucina, whom [Maximianus] himself had condemned with confiscation of property because she kept giving donations to Christians from her own resources: commanded boards to be arranged in that same church for the draught animals of the public stable and condemned the bishop himself to servicing the animals, along with the regular public sentinels. Indeed after serving there for many years, clad in a mantle made of hair-cloth, he died and, having been preserved with spices by the priest John and blessed Lucina, was buried in the cemetery of Priscilla.

/17 And at Langres, the commemorative festival of the triplets Speusippus, Elasippus and Melasippus: who when they were twenty-five years old, with their grandmother Leonilla and Ionilla and Neon, were crowned by martyrdom, in the time of the emperor Aurelian. Indeed the triplets, hung in a single tree with their hands tied upward but their feet tied downward, were so stretched out that they were nearly reckoned to have been severed from the very joining of their limbs; and having been cast down headlong into the fire after these things, yet not harmed by the flames, between words of prayer they migrated together to the Lord. Ionilla, seeing these things, acknowledged that she was also a Christian and, having soon been apprehended by the crowd, hung from her hair and weakened by many torments, was slain by the sword together with Leonilla since she was unwilling to deny Christ. Neon, the scribe of their deeds, having himself also acknowledged Christ, was crowned with martyrdom. Moreover Benignus, a priest whom blessed Polycarp (disciple of the apostle John) sent from the East to Gaul with Andochius, a fellow priest, and Thyrsus, a deacon, instructed and baptized these triplets. Moreover those very same triplets were buried at the second milestone from the town of Langres.

/19 The commemorative festival of the holy martyrs Marius and Martha with their sons Audifax and Abbacuc, nobles of Persia, who came to Rome to pray in the time of Prince Claudius: after having endured clubs, the rack, fires, nails, the cutting off of their hands, Martha was drowned in a fountain, the rest beheaded, and their remains were all burned.

/20 At Rome, [the commemorative festival] of Fabian, bishop: who, when he had presided over the church for twenty-five years, suffered martyrdom in the time of Decius, and was buried in the cemetery of Callistus.

The commemorative festival of St. Sebastian of Milan, who was so dear to the emperors Diocletian and Maximianus that they gave over to him the post of commander-in-chief of the first division of the army. Diocletian, when he learned that [Sebastian] was a Christian, and could not be called away from the faith, ordered him to be tied up in the middle of a field as if he were the target for an arrow and to be shot with arrows by the soldiers. Reckoning [Sebastian] to be dead, since he was standing there filled with arrows as if he were a hedgehog, they went away. A certain woman, however, named Irene, coming at night to take away the body, found him alive, and led him to her own house, and worked to cure him. When he regained his health, he strengthened many in their faith; without delay, appearing before the very emperors themselves, he reproached them just as they deserved. Then Diocletian ordered him to be led into the hippodrome of the palace and to be tormented until he failed. They placed him, dead, in the largest possible sewer: but he appeared in a dream to the holy matron Lucina, saying: "Next to the circus you will find my body hanging on a hook: the filth has not touched it: and when you have raised it up, you will proceed to the catacombs, and you will bury me in a crypt next to the remains of the Apostles." She, coming that very night with her servants, completed everything precisely in that way.

/21 At Rome, [the commemorative festival] of St. Agnes who, under the prefect of the city, Symphronius, having been tossed into the fires, but those fires having been extinguished through her prayers, was pierced through with a sword.

/22 At *Aquas Salvias*,[2] [the commemorative festival] of St. Anastasius, monk and martyr of Persia: who, after the very many torments of imprisonments, lashings and chains which he had endured from the Persians in Caesarea of Palestine, afterward had many punishments inflicted upon him in Persia, and at last was beheaded by their king, Chosroes.

/23 At Rome, the commemorative festival of St. Emerentiana, virgin of Christ and martyr, who was the foster sister of St. Agnes and, while she was praying at the latter's sepulchre, defended others likewise praying there from injury by the Gentiles, and was herself stoned by them.

/26 The commemorative festival of St. Polycarp, bishop of Smyrna: who, as the incumbent proconsul together with the entire population of Smyrna scolded him, was surrendered to the fire under Marcus Antoninus and Lucius Aurelius Commodus.

/29 At Rome, in the time of Diocletian, the commemorative festival of Sts. Papias and Maurus, soldiers, who, seeing the constancy of the martyrs Saturninus and Sisinnius, converted to the faith, and immediately it was ordered by Laodicius, prefect of the city, that the holy men's mouths, by which they were confessing Christ, should be pounded with rocks, and that they should be thrust into prison: there they were baptized by Pope Marcellus. Led back out again after twelve days, [Laodicius] ordered them to be thrown to the ground and beaten with clubs, then lifted up from the ground and beaten with scourges with leaden balls attached until they breathed their last. John, a priest, collecting their bodies at night, buried them on the Nomentan Way at the fountain of blessed Peter, where he would perform baptisms. It is written in the deeds of the blessed Pope Marcellus.

FEBRUARY

/5 In Sicily, under the consul Quintianus, in the time of Diocletian [the commemorative festival] of St. Agatha: who after blows to the face and imprisonment, after the rack and tortures, after the cutting off of her breasts and being healed by the Lord, after rolling in burning coals and small potsherds, finally was made perfect in prison.

/14 At Rome, the commemorative festival of St. Valentine, priest: who after many public signs of healings and erudition, having been beaten with clubs, was also in this way beheaded, under Claudius Caesar.

The commemorative festival of St. Valentine bishop of Terni [in Italy]: who, detained by the pagans and beaten with rods and, after having been subjected to the long, slow slaughter of imprisonment, when he could not be vanquished, having been tossed out of the prison in the silence of the middle of the night, was beheaded at the command of Furiosus Placidus, prefect of the city. Then Proculus, Efybus, and Apollonius, his disciples, transferring his body by night to their church in the city of Terni, buried him: when they were abiding there with daily vigils, having been detained by the Gentiles, they were given over for guarding to the emperor's governing legate, Leontius: he ordered them to be presented before his tribunal in the middle of the night: and when they could not be called away from the faith either by allurements or by threats, he ordered them to have their heads cut off: they were buried not far from the body of St. Valentine.

/16 And in Cumae,[3] the commemorative festival of St. Juliana, virgin: who, in the time of emperor Maximianus, having first been beaten and seriously afflicted by her father Africanus, and having been beaten, naked, with rods and hung up by her hair, and drenched from her head down with molten lead by the prefect Eolesius, whom she had taken as her husband, and having been taken back again into prison where she openly contested with the devil; and having been called back out again, she vanquished the torments of torture wheels, the flames of fires, a boiling-hot pot and accomplished martyrdom by the cutting off of her head. Indeed, she suffered in Nicomedia; but after a short time, through God's disposition, she was transferred into Campania.

/17 In Babylon, the commemorative festival of Polychronius, bishop of that same city: who, in the presence of the persecutor Decius, his face having been crushed with stones, with his hands outstretched, lifting his eyes to heaven, sent forth his spirit. It is written in the passion of St. Lawrence.

MARCH
/7 At Carthage, [the commemorative festival] of Perpetua and Felicitas, who were condemned to the beasts, under Prince Severus: and since Felicitas was pregnant in prison, it was procured by the prayers of all the soldiers [of Christ] who were likewise suffering that she would give birth in the eighth month. Truly, among other things it was granted to Perpetua that her mind would somehow be turned away from her body, in which she endured the attack of a cow: in this way, in order that she might look forward to what was to come, she did not know what was then happening while she was still in herself.

/9 In Sebaste, in Lesser Armenia, in the time of King Licinius, under chief Agricolaos, [the commemorative festival] of the forty soldiers, who after chains and repeated imprisonments, after having their faces beaten with stones, were placed in a pond: where their bodies, contracted by the cold, were bursting asunder during the night, and in the morning they accomplished martyrdom by the breaking of their shins. Then their bodies were burned and tossed into the river; but due to divine direction their relics were found unmutilated and were buried with worthy honor. Moreover the more noble among them were Quirion and Candidus.

/16 At Rome, the commemorative festival of St. Cyriacus who, after wasting away under long imprisonment, which he endured under Maximianus, with Sisinnius his fellow deacon and Smaragdus and Largus, after many miracles had been done, among which he cured of a demon and baptized Artemia, the daughter of Diocletian, at that very man's request, also liberated from a demon and baptized Iobe, the daughter of Sapor king of the Persians, along with the king himself and another four hundred and thirty people, having been sent there precisely for that purpose by Diocletian. Returning to Rome after the death of Diocletian, he was detained along with other Christians by [Diocletian's] son Maximianus, and taken into custody, because he had made his sister a Christian. Then [Maximianus] commanded that he be dragged before his carriage on the day of his procession, naked and loaded with chains, and after these things, having been led out from the prison along with his companions Largus and Smaragdus and Crescentianus by the deputy Carpasius, his head was also drenched with melted pitch. And then again after four days, having been led out once more from prison, stretched out on a scaffold, drawn tight with fetters and beaten with clubs; after this his head was lopped off, along with Largus and Smaragdus and twenty others, on the command of Maximianus. It is written in the deeds of Pope Marcellus. At that same time Maximianus killed his sister Artemia.

/25 The commemorative festival of Dula, maidservant of a soldier, who was killed for the sake of chastity.

At Rome, [the commemorative festival] of Cyrinus, who was slain by Claudius and thrown into the Tiber, discovered on an island of the Lycaonians, and buried in the cemetery of Pontianus. It is written in the passion of St. Valentinus.

APRIL

/1 In Thessalonica, the commemorative festival of Agape and Chionia who, under Diocletian, first wasted away in prison, then were sent into the fire but, untouched by the flames, rendered up their souls after having poured forth a prayer to the Lord.

/5 In Thessalonica, the commemorative festival of Irene who, after supporting imprisonment, amidst prayers was pierced through by an arrow by Count Sisinnius, under whom her sisters Agape and Chionia also achieved martyrdom.

/9 In Sirmium,[4] the commemorative festival of the seven virgins, who deserved to be crowned as one group.

/12 At Rome, the deposition of Julius, bishop and confessor: who, under the Arian Constantine, son of Constantine, having endured ten months of tribulations and exiles, was returned to his see with great glory after [Constantine's] death.

/14 At Rome, the commemorative festival of Tiburtius, Valerian, and Maximus, under Almachius, prefect of the city, of whom the first two were beaten with clubs and pierced through with the sword, the last was lashed with scourges to which leaden balls were attached for as long as it took until he rendered up his spirit.

/15 In the city of Corduena [in Persia], the commemorative festival of Olympiades and Maximus, nobles: who, at the command of Decius, having been beaten with clubs and then with scourges with leaden balls attached, at last had their heads pounded with axes, until they sent forth their spirits.

/22 At Rome, the deposition of St. Gaius, pope: who, when he has ruled the church for eleven years, four months and twelve days, is crowned by martyrdom, under Prince Diocletian, along with his brother Gabinius.

In the city of Corduena, the commemorative festival of Parmenius, Helymas and Chrysothelus, priests, and of Lucus and Mucus, deacons, from Babylon, of whom the first kept speaking even though his tongue had been cut out. All were hung up on the rack and drawn close together by means of restraints, then scorched by red-hot plates applied to their sides, and mutilated with claws: at last butchered with the sword, in the presence of the persecutor Decius. It is written in the passion of St. Lawrence.

/25 In Alexandria, the commemorative festival of St. Mark the Evangelist: who, having established and strengthened churches throughout all Libya, Marmarica, Ammon, the Pentapolis, Alexandria, and Egypt, at the last was detained by the pagans who remained in Alexandria. They, seeing him performing masses on the holy day of Easter, April 24, threw a rope around his neck and dragged him to Boukolia, the pasturage which is near the sea, under the cliffs, where a church had been constructed; and his very flesh was pouring off onto the ground, and the stones were being discolored with blood. Moreover once evening had come, they placed him in prison, where around the middle of the night, having first been strengthened by an angelic visitation, then by the Lord himself appearing to him, he was called to the heavenly realm. And in the morning, while he was being dragged to Boukolia, giving thanks and saying: "Into your hands I commend my spirit," he died and was buried with glory by God-fearing men, in a place cut out from the rock. Moreover he had ordained Annianus in his place as bishop of Alexandria: he had also given bishops, priests, and deacons to other churches, far and wide.

/26 The deposition of St. Marcellinus, pope: who, when he had ruled the church for nine years and four months, in the time of Diocletian and Maximianus, had his head chopped off, for the faith of Christ, along with Claudius and Cyrinus and Antoninus, by that same Diocletian, and after thirty-five days he was buried in a small chamber on the Salarian Way by the priest Marcellus and by deacons, with hymns, on April 26.

May

/3 At Rome, [the commemorative festival] of Sts. Alexander, pope, and Eventius and Theodulus, priests: the first of whom was slain, after chains and prisons, the rack, claws and fires, by means of punctures repeated throughout all his limbs: and the following ones, themselves after the long endurance of prison, were tested by fires and at last beheaded under the judge Aurelianus, in the time of Prince Trajan.

/10 At Rome, the commemorative festival of the old man Calepodius, priest, under Emperor Alexander, who had him killed by Laodicius, and had his body dragged through the city and thrown in the Tiber, on May 1. Fishermen raised up the discovered body and reported to Bishop Callistus. And the latter preserved the body, which he had received, with spices and linen cloths, and buried it in his own cemetery, on the Aurelian Way, at the third milestone from the city, in a crypt, on May 10. Then the consul Palmatius was beheaded by Alexander, along with his wife and children and forty-two others of mixed sex, and with them the senator Simplicius, who had just recently been baptized through the teaching of Pope Callistus and the priest Calepodius. It is written in the passion of St. Callistus, pope.

/12 At Rome, [the commemorative festival] of St. Pancratius who, when he was fourteen years old, under Diocletian, completed his martyrdom by the cutting off of his head.

/14 [The commemorative festival] of our father, St. Pachomius, who, when he was distinguished by deeds of apostolic grace, and was the founder of the monastic communities of Egypt, wrote for those monasteries rules which he had learned from a dictating angel: and at the same time, he wrote about the Easter season.

In Syria, the commemorative festival of Victor and Corona, under Emperor Antoninus, when Sebastian was commander at Alexandria. Moreover Victor was a soldier from Cilicia, whom Sebastian had ordered, as a result of his confession of faith, to have his fingers broken off and pulled out by the skin. Then he ordered him to be put in a furnace of fire where, remaining for three days, he was not harmed. Next, having been ordered to drink poison, he did not die, but converted the poisoner to the faith. Then he was ordered to have the sinews of his very body removed, then to have boiling oil placed in his private parts. After these things, [Sebastian] ordered him to be hung up and have burning torches applied to his sides. After this, for vinegar and lime to be mixed together and given to him in his mouth; for his eyes to be plucked out; for him to be hung with his head downward for three days; and when he was still breathing, [Sebastian] ordered him to be skinned. Then Corona, although she was the wife of a certain soldier, began to bless St. Victor for the glory of his martyrdom. While she was doing that, she saw two crowns, which had fallen down from heaven, one sent for Victor and the other for her. And since she was declaring this in public to all who were listening, she was detained by the judge, and it was ordered for two palm trees to be bent toward each other, and for Corona to be tied with hemp ropes by her hands and feet to both of them, and thus for the trees to be released. When this was done, Corona was divided into two parts: moreover she was sixteen years old. Then Victor was also beheaded and himself earned the triumph of everlasting victory.

/19 At Rome, the commemorative festival of St. Urban, pope and confessor, through whose teaching many were crowned with martyrdom.

/22 In Africa, [the commemorative festival] of Castus and Aemilius, who accomplished the passion of martyrdom through fire. Cyprian wrote about them in the book *On the Lapsed*.[5]

/28 The deposition of St. John, pope: since he was orthodox and, when visiting Constantinople, had been gloriously received by the orthodox emperor Justin, having been taken into custody when returning through Ravenna, the Arian king Theoderic put him to death along with other, equally catholic men. St. Gregory mentions him in his book of *Dialogues*:[6] his body, having been transferred from Ravenna, was buried in the basilica of St. Peter the apostle, on May 28 when Olybrius was consul.

JUNE

/2 At Rome, [the commemorative festival] of Marcellinus, priest, and Peter, exorcist: who, educating many in prison to the faith, after abominable chains and very many torments were beheaded under the judge Serenus: and the one who beheaded them, Dorotheus by name, saw their magnificently adorned souls being carried to heaven by angels: and, doing penance under Pope Julius, was baptized in his old age.

In Lyon, [the commemorative festival] of St. Blandina with forty-seven martyrs: always renewing their torments from first light to evening, at last the torturers acknowledge that they themselves have been conquered: she is not vanquished, having been beaten with instruments of torture again for a second day. And also on the third day, having been bound to a stake and stretched out in the manner of a cross, she is set out as food for the beasts. Since none of the beasts would dare to touch her, she is called back again to prison; indeed on the fourth day, having gone through lashings, having been set on fire with small griddle-irons, and having steadfastly endured many other things, at last she is slaughtered by the sword. Then Ponticus, too, a boy of fifteen years, having gone through all types of torments with her throughout the circus, and having been strengthened by her maternal encouragement, accomplished martyrdom before her, under Antoninus Verus. It is written in the *Ecclesiastical History* [of Eusebius], Book five.[7]

/16 In the city of Besançon, [the commemorative festival] of Ferreolus, priest, and Ferrutio, deacon, who, under the judge Claudius, having been stretched out on hoisting pulleys and whipped, then shut up in prison and, in the morning, having had their tongues cut off, were preaching the word of God. After these things, once thirty awls had been driven into each of their hands and feet and breast, at last they were slain by the sword.

/19 In Milan, [the commemorative festival] of Sts. Gervasius and Protasius, whose sepulchres Ambrose discovered by the Lord's revelation, and their bodies were uncorrupted and just as they were on the very day they were killed: when they were brought into the town, a certain man who had long been blind recovered the light of his eyes at a touch of the bier.

/22 In Britain, [the commemorative festival] of St. Alban, martyr: who, in the time of Diocletian, in the city of *Verulamium*,[8] after lashings and bitter torments, suffered capital punishment: but as he was falling on the ground, the eyes of the one who killed him likewise fell to the ground. One of the soldiers also suffered with him, because he was unwilling to strike him when ordered to do so: for he was completely terrified by a divine miracle, since he had seen the blessed martyr, as he was hastening to the crown of martyrdom, render the bed of an interposed river passable for himself through prayer.

/23 In Britain, [the commemorative festival] of St. Aethelthryth, virgin and queen: whose body, buried when she was sixteen years old, was found uncorrupted.

/26 At Rome, [the commemorative festival] of John and Paul, of whom the first was the chamberlain, the second the chancellor of Constance, daughter of Constantine; they afterward, under Julian, deserved martyrdom through the cutting off of their heads by Terentianus, a battlefield instructor, who later became a Christian.

JULY
/8 In Palestine, the commemorative festival of Procopius who, having been led from Scythopolis to Caesaria, had his head lopped off when the judge Flavianus became angry at the confidence of his responses.

/9 In the city of Tora [on Lake Velino, Italy], under Emperor Decius, the commemorative festival of Sts. Anatholia and Audax: of whom Anatholia, when she had cured many sick, lunatics, and possessed in the region of Ancona, was led, on the command of Festinianus, to the city of Tora, and abused with various types of injuries. Then when, having been shut up all night with a serpent, she was unharmed: indeed, in the morning she even snatched the Marsian himself, named Audax, who had sent the serpent, away from being devoured by his own serpent, and converted him to the martyrdom of Christ. For he himself, after this, having been taken into custody because of his confession of truth, without delay, was crowned by a capital sentence. Also the virgin of Christ herself was transfixed with a sword as she stood with her hands stretched out in prayer, so that the sword, which had been placed through her right side, was coming out from her left. She suffered on July 9: moreover she was buried in the morning by the citizens of Tora. But Audax, since he was from the East, was transferred there by his wife and children.

/10 At Rome, [the commemorative festival] of the seven brothers, the sons of St. Felicitas, that is Felix, Phillip, Vitalis, Martial, Alexander, Silanus and Januarius, under the prefect of the city, Publius, in the time of Prince Antoninus. Of them, Januarius was killed after the lashings of rods and imprisonment and scourges with leaden balls attached. Felix and Phillip were offered up in sacrifice by cudgeling: Silanus was killed by being thrown off a precipice: Alexander, Vitalis and Martial were punished with a capital sentence.

/14 [The commemorative festival] of St. Phocas, bishop of Sinope [on the Black Sea], who under Emperor Trajan, when Africanus was prefect, vanquished prison, chains, the sword and even fire for Christ. His relics are held in the basilica of the Apostles, in Gaul, in the city of Vienne.

/16 In Ostia, [the seaport of Rome,] the commemorative festival of St. Hilarinus: who, under the persecution of Julian, when he was unwilling to sacrifice, having been beaten with clubs, chose martyrdom.

/17 In Carthage, under the prefect Saturninus, [the commemorative festival] of the Scillitans, that is Speratus, Martial, Cithius, Vesturius, Felix, Aquilinus, Lactantius, Januarius, Generosa, Vesta, Donata and Secunda who, after their first confession of Christ, having been placed in prison and fastened to a tree, in the morning were also beheaded by the sword.

/19 [The commemorative festival] of our father, St. Arsenius, about whom it is said in the *Lives of the Fathers*[9] that, because of the overflowing of tears needing to be wiped away, he always had a handkerchief in the bosom of his garment or in his hand.

/21 And at Tibur, a town in Italy, the commemorative festival of St. Symphorosa with her seven sons, Crescens, Julianus, Nemesius, Primitivus, Justin, Stacteus, Eugenius, together with whom she suffered by the doing of Prince Hadrian: he ordered Symphorosa herself to be beaten with palm branches, then to be hung up by her hair: but when she could in no way be vanquished, he ordered her, tied to a rock, to be thrown into the river: her brother Eugenius, the chief magistrate of the municipal council of Tibur, collecting her body, buried her. And in the morning the emperor ordered seven stakes to be driven into the ground and her sons to be stretched out there on pulleys: and for Crescens to be pierced through in the throat, Lucianus in the breast, Nemesius in the heart, Primitivus through the navel, for Justin—stretched out through all his limbs—to be cut through each of the joints and junctures of his body, for Stacteus to be transfixed in the ground with countless lances until he died, for Eugenius to be split open from his breast all the way to his nether regions. On another day, Hadrian commanded the bodies. . . .[10]

/23 The death day of St. Apollinaris, bishop, in Ravenna, who was ordained at Rome by the apostle Peter and sent to that place: who even preached in Aemilia and in the area of the Corinthians and in Mysia [in Asia Minor] and along the banks of the Danube and in areas of Thrace, into which places he was banished in exile. And wherever he came to, he worked countless miracles and withstood sufferings: for he was offered up in sacrifice with great carnage, both beaten repeatedly for a long time with clubs and placed upon burning coals with bare feet, beaten anew and hung up on the rack, he was twisted and his face was crushed with a rock, and with the heaviest possible weight of iron he was shut up in a horrific prison and stretched out on a wooden plank; there he was indeed disregarded by men, but publicly nourished by an angel. Next, chained and sent into exile, in which he was once more beaten for a long time with clubs and, back again in Ravenna, bound fast, beaten by pagans and wounded and once more sent into prison and beaten, in this way he accomplished martyrdom, under Vespasian Caesar, when Demosthenes was patrician. He ruled the church for twenty-eight years and four days.

/29 The deposition of St. Lupus, bishop of Troyes: who came to Britain with Germanus, and died after fifty-two years in the priesthood: who, just as is sung in his hymn, "Fortified Troyes by praying, While wars were ruining everything," in the time when Attila was ravaging Gaul.

/30 At Rome, [the commemorative festival] of Abdo and Sennes, petty princes whom, when they had already been afflicted with chains by the emperor Decius in Corduena, a city of the Persians, [Decius] at last led, bound in chains and having been wasted away through various punishments, to Rome where, having first been beaten with scourges with leaden balls attached, they were finally put to death by the sword.

August

/1 In Auxerre, [the commemorative festival] of bishop Germanus who, bright with many virtues, erudition, and continence, even defended the faith of the Britons on two occasions from the Pelagian heresy.

In Vercelli, [the commemorative festival] of Bishop Eusebius who, with the Arians stimulating a persecution, suffered martyrdom under Prince Constantius.

/2 At Rome, [the commemorative festival] of St. Stephen, pope: who was crowned with martyrdom in the persecution of Prince Valerian.

The commemorative festival of St. Theodota with her three sons, in the province of Bithynia, in the town of Nicaea, during the time of Diocletian, under Count Leocadius, who sent this woman, bound in iron, with her sons, to Nicetius, the emperor's governing legate of the province of Bithynia. And at first he had her firstborn son, Evodius, confidently acknowledging Christ, beaten with clubs, then finally had her consumed by fire with all her sons. It is written in the passion of St. Anastasia.

/6 At Rome, [the commemorative festival] of St. Sixtus, bishop, Felicissimus and Agapitus, deacons, who were beheaded, under Decius. Four other subdeacons,[11] Januarius, Magnus, Vincent and Stephen, were also beheaded with him, as is read in the *Pontifical Book*.[12]

/7 In Arezzo, [the commemorative festival] of Donatus, bishop and martyr, who, as Gregory mentioned in his books of *Dialogues*, restored the holy chalice, which had been broken by pagans, by praying at mass.

/9 At Rome, [the commemorative festival] of St. Romanus, a soldier who, goaded by the stings of conscience in the midst of St. Lawrence's acknowledgment of Christ, sought to be baptized by him, and soon, on the command of Decius, was displayed on clubs and beheaded.

/10 Under Decius, the commemorative festival of St. Lawrence: who, after the very many torments of prison, of various lashings, of red-hot plates, at last completed his martyrdom by being roasted on an iron griddle.

/12 In Sicily, in the city of Catania, the commemorative festival of Euplus, deacon: who, when he had been tortured for a long time, was beheaded by Calvisianus, the emperor's governing legate, in the time of Diocletian and Maximianus.

/13 At Rome, [the commemorative festival] of St. Hippolytus who, in the time of Decius, tied by his feet to the necks of unbroken horses, in this way having been dragged through wild thistles and thorns, sent forth his spirit. Also [the commemorative festival] of his nurse Concordia who, having been beaten by scourges with leaden balls attached, achieved martyrdom before him: Also [the commemorative festival] of nineteen others from his household, who were beheaded all together.

At Rome, the commemorative festival of St. Cassian who, when he was unwilling to adore idols, interrogated by a persecutor concerning what skill he possessed, replied that he taught letters to boys. And soon stripped of his clothes, and with his hands bound behind his head, he was set up in the middle, and the ability to slay him was given to boys who were called in, boys to whom he had made himself exceedingly hated by teaching them. And they, just as much as they had grieved when learning, that much were they rejoicing to be taking revenge; some would strike him with writing tablets and writing tablets made of boxwood, others would wound him with pens: however much weaker the hand of each boy was, that much more burdensome did it make the pain of martyrdom, as death was delayed. So wrote the poet Prudentius.[13]

/22 The commemorative festival of St. Timothy who, coming to Rome from Antioch under Pope Melciades, was received as the guest of St. Silvester, who was afterward made bishop: preaching there for an entire year and several months, when he had converted many people to Christ, he was detained by Tarquinius, prefect of the city, and, having wasted away in the long-standing confinement of prison, since he was unwilling to sacrifice to idols, having been beaten for the third time and handled with the most burdensome tortures, at last he was beheaded, and buried next to blessed Paul the apostle. It is written in the history of St. Silvester.

/26 At Rome, the commemorative festival of Sts. Irenaeus and Abundius: whom, in the Decian persecution, Valerian commanded to be drowned in a sewer, because they had raised up the body of blessed Concordia which had been thrown into the sewer. And Justinus the priest raised up their bodies as well, and buried them in a crypt near blessed Lawrence.

/28 In Africa, [the commemorative festival] of St. Augustine, bishop: who, having first been transferred from his own city to Sardinia because of the barbarians, was recently moved and honorably buried at Pavia by Liutprand, king of the Lombards.

/29 The beheading of St. John the Baptist: who was first preserved in Samaria, and now is in Alexandria; furthermore, his head was brought from Jerusalem to Emesa, a city in Phoenicia.

/30 In Venosa, a city of Apulia, [the commemorative festival] of Sts. Felix, bishop of the city of Thibiuca [in Africa], and Januarius, priest, and Fortunatianus and Septimus, lectors: who, in the time of Diocletian, having been detained in his city by the superintendent Magnellianus on June 14, then having wasted away under many chains and long imprisonments, both in Africa and in Sicily, finally were made perfect through slaughter by the sword. Felix died, a virgin, at fifty years of age. Moreover, there are thirty-five miles between Carthage and Thibiuca.

SEPTEMBER

/11 At Rome, [the commemorative festival] of Sts. Protus and Hyacinth, who were eunuchs of St. Eugenia.

/14 At Rome, the commemorative festival of St. Cornelius, pope: whose face was beaten with scourges with leaden balls attached, and in this way he was decapitated, along with twenty-one others of mixed sex, and a soldier Cerealis, and his wife, Salustia, whom Cornelius had healed of infirmity; they suffered under Decius.

The commemorative festival of St. Cyprian, bishop, who, under Prince Valerian, after a long exile, accomplished martyrdom through the lopping off of his head, at the sixth milestone from Carthage, next to the sea.

/16 The commemorative festival of St. Euphemia, virgin, who achieved martyrdom under Emperor Diocletian, moreover under Priscus the proconsul, in the city of Chalcedon: she, for Christ, vanquished torments and imprisonments, lashings and the arguments of wheels of torture, fires and the weights of square stones, beasts and the blows of rods, sharp saws and red-hot frying pans, and once again the biting of a beast, and was buried by her father Philosophron, a senator, one mile from the city of Chalcedon.

/19 In Naples, in Campania, the commemorative festival of Sts. Januarius, bishop of the city of Benevento, with Sosius deacon of the city of Misenum, and Festus [Januarius's] deacon, and Desiderius his lector: who after chains and imprisonments, had their heads lopped off in the city of Pozzuoli, under Prince Diocletian, with Dracontius as judge. When they were being led to death, Proculus, deacon of the city of Pozzuoli and two laymen, Eutyches, and Acutius, among others, saw and inquired why righteous men were commanded to be killed: the judge, as he saw the Christians, commanded them to be decapitated along with the others. In this way all seven were decapitated together. And Christians took up their bodies at night; and the Neapolitans placed Januarius in a basilica near the city, the Misenans likewise placed Sosius in a basilica, the Pozzuolans placed Proculus, Eutyches and Acutius near the basilica of St. Stephen: the Beneventans collected Festus and Desiderius.

/20 In Chizico [in Asia Minor], the commemorative festival of Sts. Fausta, virgin, and Evilasius, under Emperor Maximianus; Evilasius himself, when he was chief of the palace, commanded her to be shorn of hair and shaved to her dishonor: then to be hung up and tortured: at which time, a flash from the heavens smote many of his servants. Then he commanded caskets to be brought there and commanded her to be placed and fastened inside, and to be cut down the middle like a piece of wood; but the executioners did not have the power to harm her with their saws. In the middle of all this, Evilasius, astounded, began to believe in Christ: and when this was announced to the emperor, he sent a prefect who tortured [Evilasius], bravely hung up. [The emperor] also commanded Fausta, naked and without a struggle, to be led out from prison and her head to be bored through and nails driven into it. Afterward not only her head and face, but also her breast and her entire body up to her shins were filled with nails. After these things, he commanded a frying pan to be made red hot: but as she psalmodized, it became cold again. In the middle of all this, a voice coming from heaven called for them, and so they surrendered their spirits. Fausta, moreover, was thirteen years old, and Evilasius eighty.

/23 The commemorative festival of St. Sossius, deacon of the city of Misenum in Campania, who when he was thirty years old, chose martyrdom along with blessed Januarius bishop of Benevento, in the time of Emperor Diocletian. At a certain time, when he was reading the Gospel in the church of the city of Misenum, in the presence of Bishop Januarius (for he was accustomed to visiting him frequently because of [the deacon's] holiness and judiciousness), that same bishop suddenly saw a flame rise out from his head, which no one else saw, and he announced that [Sossius] would be a martyr. And after not many days, that same deacon was detained and placed in prison. When the bishop came to visit him, along with his own deacon Festus and his lector Desiderius, he himself was also detained along with them, and all were killed along with three others.

In the East, the commemorative festival of St. Thecla, virgin from the city of Iconium,[14] who, instructed in the confession of Christ by the apostle Paul, defeated fires and beasts: and coming, after many struggles and after having taught many people, to Seleucia [in Cilicia, Asia Minor], she rested in peace.

/24 In Autun, the commemorative festival of St. Andochius, priest, Thyrsus, deacon, and Felix: who, directed from the East by St. Polycarp for the purpose of instructing Gaul, were most gloriously crowned under Prince Aurelian. Indeed, beaten with whips, at last hung up for an entire day with their hands turned upside down, sent into the fire but not burned, in the end their necks are struck by strong poles. There Symphorianus, at the time twenty years old, who suffered later on, was performing prayers and vigils.

/26 [The commemorative festival] of the holy martyrs Cyprian, bishop, and Justina: Justina, having endured many things for Christ under Diocletian, also converted to Christ Cyprian himself, although he was a magician and was trying to bewitch her with his magic: under Prince Claudius she later achieved martyrdom along with [Cyprian], by then a bishop and a noble teacher.

/27 In the city of Aegea [a seaport in Cilicia, Asia Minor], when Lysias was its guardian, under the persecution of Diocletian and Maximianus, the commemorative festival of Sts. Cosmas and Damian: who, after having endured many torments, chains and imprisonments, after having by divine influence vanquished the sea and the fire, the cross, a shower of stones and arrows, were beheaded.

/30 At Bethlehem in Judaea, the deposition of St. Jerome, priest, who died in his ninety-first year.

OCTOBER

/3 Among the Old Saxons, the commemorative festival of the two Ewalds, priests: who, coming with bishop Willibrord into Germany, crossed over to the Saxons: and when they began there to preach Christ, they were apprehended by the pagans and thus were killed: a great amount of light, appearing frequently at night at their bodies, demonstrated both where they were and of what great merit they were.

/14 The commemorative festival of St. Callistus, pope: who, in the persecution of Emperor Alexander, long racked by hunger in prison and beaten daily with clubs, was strengthened and consoled in a vision by his priest Calepodius, who earlier had accomplished martyrdom: who, placed in that prison, cured a certain soldier, Privatus by name, both of the pain and filthiness of sores and likewise of unbelief. Hearing this, Alexander had that very soldier worn out with scourges with leaden balls attached: but he had blessed Callistus cast headlong through the window of a house and plunged into a well with a rock tied to his neck, and then he filled up the well with old rubbish. But after seventeen days, [Callistus's] priest Asterius, coming at night with clerics, raised up the body and buried it in the cemetery of Calepodius, on October 14.

/18 The commemorative festival of St. Luke the Evangelist. A Syrian from Antioch, a physician by profession, a disciple of the apostles, afterward having followed Paul until his confession, serving the Lord without fault. For, never having either a wife or children, he died in Bithynia at seventy-four years of age, filled with the Holy Spirit.

At Rome, [the commemorative festival] of St. Tryphonia, wife of the caesar Decius, who, once her husband had been punished by divine will after the murder of the blessed ones Sixtus and Lawrence, sought to be baptized, along with Cyrilla the daughter of Decius, by the priest Justinus, and she died on another day and was buried in the crypt next to St. Hippolytus.

/21 [The commemorative festival] of our father, St. Hilarion, whose *Life*, filled with virtues, Jerome wrote.

The commemorative festival of St. Asterius, priest of Callistus: whom Emperor Alexander, hearing about it after six days, instructed to be cast down headlong through a bridge, since he had buried Callistus's body which he had raised up from a well: his body was discovered in Ostia and buried in that same city by certain Christians. It is written in the passion of St. Callistus, pope.

/25 At Rome, on the Salarian Way, the commemorative festival of forty-six soldiers, who were baptized together by Pope Dionysius, and soon beheaded on the command of Emperor Claudius. Another one hundred and twenty-one martyrs were also placed there: among whom were the four soldiers of Christ Theodotius, Lucius, Marcus and Peter. It is written in the passion of St. Sixtus.

/28 At Rome, [the commemorative festival] of St. Cyrilla, daughter of the caesar Decius, who, under Prince Claudius, had her throat cut and was slain by the sword: and she was buried by the priest Justinus, with her mother, next to St. Hippolytus.

/31 In the Gauls, [the commemorative festival] of St. Quintinus, who suffered martyrdom under Emperor Maximianus: and after fifty-five years, through the revelation of an angel, his body was discovered and buried on June 24.

NOVEMBER

/1 In the stronghold of Dijon, the commemorative festival of St. Benignus, priest, who was sent from the East to Gaul by St. Polycarp, bishop, along with Andochius, a fellow priest, and Thyrsus, deacon, in the time of Aurelian who, once [Benignus's] preaching had been found out, instructed that he be brought to him, bound and beaten: and, once the constancy of his speeches was heard, had him beaten again with the roughest force possible, and gave him over to Count Terentius to be vanquished. By [Terentius], [Benignus] was stretched out on hoisting pulleys and beaten and again transferred to prison, in the morning destroyed idols by praying, and was brought back to prison. They drove ten glowing-hot awls into his hands, and drove his feet into a stone perforated by means of a slack scourge with a leaden ball at the end of it, and shut him in for six days with twelve savage dogs. And an angel took heavenly bread to him, took out the awls, and snatched him from the lead and iron. After this his neck is ordered to be buffeted with an iron pole and his body bored with a lance. When that was done, as the Christians were looking on, a snow-white dove ascended to heaven from out of the prison, and the most delightful fragrance possible, as if of paradise, followed. As Aurelian was going away from that place, blessed Leonilla arrived, and buried the body, preserved with spices, not far from the prison itself.

The commemorative festival of Sts. Caesarius, deacon, and Julian, priest: who, that is to say, Caesarius, coming from Africa to Tarracina, a city in Campania, in the time of Claudius, when he was crying out in public against idolaters, was detained by the Roman high priest Firminus, and shut up in confinement: having wasted away there for many days, he was then given over to Leontius, the emperor's governing legate of the province of Campania. When the latter was unable to vanquish him with words, he ordered him to be led, bound in front of a cart, his hands tied, naked, all the way to the temple of Apollo. When they came to that place, the temple tumbled down as a result of his prayer, and killed the Roman high priest Firminus. Shut up in prison after this, by Luxurius the chief of the city, he was there for one year and one month. Finally, led forth into the market place, he was surrounded by God with a heavenly light when he prayed, so that Leontius himself believed, then enveloped Caesarius (who was naked) with his own cloak, was baptized, received the body and blood of the Lord from the hands of the priest Julianus: with no delay, once a prayer had been said over him, he surrendered his spirit on October 30. Then Luxurius bade Julianus and Caesarius to be placed in a sack and cast down headlong into the sea. They, on that same day, were thrown back onto the shore, and were buried by Eusebius, a servant of God, near the town of Tarracina. And that same Eusebius afterward suffered martyrdom, with the priest Felix.

/5 In Tarracina, a city in Campania, the commemorative festival of Sts. Felix, priest, and Eusebius, monk, in the time of Emperor Claudius: who, that is to say, Eusebius, when he had buried the holy martyrs Julianus and Caesarius and, praying and fasting at their sepulchres, had converted to the faith many people, whom Felix the priest would baptize, were both detained by Leontius, the son of the emperor's governing legate Leontius, most of all for this reason, that Caesarius had made his father a Christian: and they were led to his marketplace, not vanquished, from that place shut up in prison and, that same night, when they would not sacrifice, beheaded and thrown into the river. Their bodies came all the way to the sea, and were thrown back onto the shore, and found by a certain priest from Capua, named Quartus: who soon led them, placed upon a wagon, into his own cottage and, searching inquisitively, also found their heads and, having joined them to the bodies, buried them near St. Caesarius.

/22 The commemorative festival of St. Cecilia, who thoroughly instructed her spouse Valerian and his brother Tiburtius both for belief in Christ and for martyrdom: and she herself finally achieved martyrdom, indeed vanquishing the fire, but killed by the sword, under Almachius, prefect of the city.

/23 At Rome, the commemorative festival of St. Clement, bishop, who on the orders of Trajan was sent into exile across the deep of the sea. There, having called many to the faith through his miracles and erudition, he was cast headlong into the sea, with an anchor tied to his neck. But the sea withdrew, at the prayers of his disciples, by three miles: and they discovered his body in a rocky coffin, in a marble temple, and next to the anchor.

[The commemorative festival] of St. Felicitas, mother of seven martyr sons, who was beheaded for Christ at the command of Antoninus.

/24 At Rome, the commemorative festival of St. Chrysogonus who, beheaded, completed his martyrdom under Diocletian. It is written in the passion of St. Anastasia.

On that same day, the commemorative festival of St. Crescentianus, who was with deacon Caesarius and Largus and Smaragdus in prison, under the persecution of Maximinus son of Maximianus, and, having been led out from prison on the command of the deputy Carpasius, was hung up on the rack and beaten with clubs and scraped with nails and then, once flames had been for a long time applied around his sides, having been scorched for a long time, sent forth his spirit, and was buried by the priest John in the cemetery of Priscilla. At that same time Maximinus killed his sister Artemia. It is written in the deeds of Pope Marcellus.

/25 The commemorative festival of St. Peter, bishop of Alexandria: who, when he was adorned with all the virtues, and inferior to none of the ancients in divine Scripture, a true priest and consecrated host of God, is suddenly seized and his head is lopped off at the command of Maximinus: and with him, very many other bishops from Egypt are likewise butchered. It is written in the *Ecclesiastical History* [of Eusebius], book nine.

/29 At Rome, [the commemorative festival] of St. Saturninus, martyr, and Sennes, and Sisinnius, deacon, under Maximianus, by whom they, among others, were first condemned to digging up the sandy wastes in order to build the Baths of Diocletian, then having wasted away for a long time in prison where, teaching, they kept baptizing many Gentiles: and having been led back out again, bound with chains and barefooted, before Laodicius the prefect of the city, they were ordered to be lifted up onto the rack and drawn tight with fetters, and beaten with clubs and scorpions:[15] after this he also ordered flames to be applied to their sides and for their heads to be lopped off once they had been removed from the rack. A most Christian man, Thraso, who had been ministering much to the martyrs out of his own resources, collecting the bodies along with John, a priest, buried them in his own estate on the Salarian Way. While [the martyrs] were still in the midst of their struggle, two soldiers, Papias and Maurus, believed; they were soon apprehended by Laodicius, and not long afterward were crowned with martyrdom. It is written in the deeds of Pope Marcellus.

DECEMBER

/10 In Barcelona, a city in Spain, under the ruler Dacian, the commemorative festival of St. Eulalia, virgin: who, when she was thirteen years old, after many torments, was beheaded; and as her head was springing away from her, a dove was seen to go out from her body.

/13 Under Paschasius, the emperor's governing legate, the commemorative festival of St. Lucy, virgin, from Syracuse: when the pimps wanted to ruin her, at the command of Paschasius, in no way were they able to move her, not by added ropes or by various teams of oxen; she endured pitch, resin, boiling oil without being harmed. Even when pierced through by a sword which had been plunged into her internal organs, she still did not die until, once priests had arrived, she had received the communion of the lord's body and blood. She suffered in the time of Diocletian and Maximianus.

/17 The commemorative festival of St. Ignatius, bishop and martyr: who, as the third bishop of Antioch after the apostle Peter, in the twelfth year of Trajan, was sent, chained, to the beasts at Rome. The relics of his body, having been brought back, lie at Antioch, in the cemetery of the church outside the Daphne gate.

/23 At Rome, under Decius, the deposition of St. Victoria: who, since she was betrothed to a pagan man, Eugenius, and was willing neither to marry nor to sacrifice, after having worked many miracles, including having attached many virgins to the Lord, was pierced through the heart with a sword, with Taliarchus overseer of the sanctuaries acting as executioner, at the request of her own fiancé: moreover, she was laid to rest on December 23.

/25 The commemorative festival of St. Anastasia who, in the time of Diocletian, first patiently suffered terrible and harsh confinement by her husband Publius, during which she was nevertheless much consoled and strengthened by Chrysogonus, a confessor of Christ. Next she wasted away in likewise extremely oppressive and lasting confinement by the prefect of Illyria: during which she was refreshed for two months with heavenly foods through St. Theodota who had already suffered martyrdom. Next, placed on a ship with twenty men and seventy women, so that they would be submerged in the sea, she was brought to the Isle of Palms where, stretched out and tied by her hands and feet to immovable stays, there was also kindled around her midsections a fire, in which she accomplished martyrdom; and all who had come with her engaged in martyrdom together through various forms of killing.

/31 At Sens, under Emperor Aurelian, the passion of St. Columba, virgin, who, having vanquished the fire, was slaughtered.

Notes

1. An octave is a secondary festival held one week after a major festival such as, in this case, Christmas.
2. A monastery in Rome dedicated to St. Anastasius.
3. Now Pozzuoli, in Italy. Juliana of Cumae is here confused with a different Juliana, of Nicomedia in Bithynia (Asia Minor).
4. Now Srijemska Mistrovica in modern Serbia.
5. Cyprian was bishop of Carthage from ca. 248 until 258. He survived one persecution and died in another. He composed *On the Lapsed* during the earlier persecution of 251; it is a treatise concerning the issues raised by those Christians who capitulated to imperial demands to sacrifice to traditional Roman deities.
6. Gregory I, also known as "the Great," was bishop of Rome or pope from 590 until 604. His *Dialogues* are four books describing the lives and miracles of holy men and women in Italy, especially those of Benedict of Nursia, founder of Monte Cassino and author of the *Rule of Benedict* for communitarian monastic observance.
7. Eusebius wrote the *Ecclesiastical History*, usually considered the first Christian history, in a number of drafts over a period of many decades, completing the final draft around 326, when he was bishop of Caesaria.
8. Now Saint Albans in Hertfordshire, England.
9. The *Lives of the Fathers* were a series of different collections of Latin translations from eastern monastic writings which were called the *Vitae Patrum* or *Lives of the Fathers* following the usage of St. Benedict of Nursia. It is possible that Bede is actually referring to the *Apophthegmata Patrum or Sayings of the Fathers*, a similar series of collections of proverbs from and anecdotes about the monks of the Egyptian, Syrian and Palestinian deserts.
10. All the manuscripts break off suddenly at this point.
11. This is an error in the manuscripts of Bede; there were no subdeacons in Rome at the time.
12. The *Pontifical Book* (*Liber Pontificalis*) was a collection of the lives of the bishops of Rome, or popes, arranged in chronological order from Peter to Pius II (d. 1464). The first stage of the original compilation was made in the sixth or seventh century, probably by a member of the Roman clergy; it was then continued by a variety of different authors.
13. Prudentius, who was born ca. 348 and died sometime after 405, was a Christian Latin poet from Spain. He wrote (between ca. 401 and 403), among other things, the *Liber Peristephanon* (*The Martyrs' Crowns*), a collection of fourteen hymns concerning principally Spanish and Italian martyrs.
14. In Galatia (Asia Minor), now Koniyeh in modern Turkey.
15. A Roman torture implement, not the animal.

Chapter 9

EINHARD, *TRANSLATION OF THE RELICS OF STS. MARCELLINUS AND PETER*

Originally translated by Barrett Wendell and edited by David Appleby

INTRODUCTION

Einhard, the author of the *Translation of the Relics of Sts. Marcellinus and Peter*, is best known as the friend and biographer of Charlemagne. He was born in about 770 to a noble family of the east Frankish region called the Maingau. His parents entrusted him to the monks of Fulda, who educated the young man in the liberal arts and put him to work in the monastery's chancellery. Einhard's aptitude for learning induced Abbot Baugulf to send him to the royal palace at Aachen in about 794 to continue his studies at the feet of the learned men who gravitated toward Charlemagne. There Einhard became a familiar member of the court and demonstrated such skill in craftsmanship and architecture that he was given oversight of the buildings of the palace complex and became known as "Beseleel," a reference to the builder and craftsman mentioned in Exodus. Charlemagne had enough confidence in Einhard to send him on at least one diplomatic embassy, namely in 806 to Rome to gain the assent of Pope Leo III to the *Divisio regnorum* [Division of the Kingdoms]. His service to the emperor continued under Charlemagne's son and successor, Louis the Pious (814–42). While the quality of Einhard's personal affection for the father may have found no counterpart in his relationship with the son, Einhard and his wife, Emma, were willing to accept the rewards proffered by an emperor who in the event needed all the friends he could get. Over the years Einhard accumulated a group of monastic houses which he held as lay abbot, the most important of these being in Ghent, Maastricht, Paris, Fontenelle, Fritzlar, and Pavia. But if Louis the Pious hoped that gifts would induce Einhard to take an active part on his behalf in the struggle between the emperor, his sons, and the Frankish magnates which unfolded in the later 830s, he must have been disappointed. Troubled by advancing age and physical illness, and deeply saddened by the death of Emma, Einhard spent the few years before his own death in 840 in prayer and the service of his saints.

Einhard acquired saints' relics for the dedication of churches he built on lands granted to him and Emma in 815 by Louis the Pious. The first of these was a modest chapel finished by about 827 at Michelstadt-Steinbach in the Odenwald of Hesse. The second was a more substantial structure located in the Maingau at a place called Ober-Mühlheim, where construction began around 830 and the dedication took place around 836. The historical irony of early medieval architecture is that while the most important sites were apt to be damaged by heavy use or later razed and reconstructed, churches that were less important and less frequented had a better chance of surviving in something approaching their original form. This is certainly the case at Einhard's churches. The small church at Michelstadt housed the miracle-working relics of Sts. Marcellinus and Peter only briefly and so stands today with much of its ninth-century structure intact. The basilica at Mühlheim, which became the permanent resting place of the saints and enjoyed so much success as a destination for pilgrims that its name was changed to Seligenstadt or "City of the Blessed," is an architectural conglomerate of various periods with few traces of the original Carolingian church. This is a pity because excavation has shown that the basilica at Mühlheim was among the first churches with a continuous transept built in Frankland since the late eighth century, and one of the earliest northern European churches to have a large crypt to house of the relics of its patron saints.

The four books of the *Translation of the Relics of Sts. Marcellinus and Peter* fill twenty-five pages in the folio edition. Einhard probably began the first book in the summer of 828 and finished it along with the second by the end of that year. Book 1 recounts Einhard's efforts to obtain the physical remains of a saintly patron for the church at Michelstadt by commissioning a shady Roman deacon named Deusdona to acquire relics in Rome and send them to Frankland. The relics he finally obtained were those of Marcellinus and Peter, a priest and an exorcist who had been martyred in the late-third- and early-fourth-century persecution of the emperor Diocletian and buried in the cemetery of the Via Labicanna in Rome. The story covers the journey to and from Italy, the difficulties Einhard's agents encountered and the miracles of the saints along the way. The first book ends with a description of the movement of the relics from Michelstadt to Mühlheim and their installation in the new church there. In a very interesting retrospective narrative passage, Book 2 reveals how some of the relics of St. Marcellinus had been stolen on the way from Rome by a priest whom Abbot Hilduin of the monastery of Saint-Médard in Soissons had sent along with Deusdona's party. Only after vigorous protest was Einhard able to recover the relics, which Hilduin finally transferred from Saint-Médard to the palace church at Aachen. Einhard then removed them to his private chapel at Aachen and from there to his estates in the eastern Frankish domains, where they were reunited with the other relics. This episode is prominent enough to suggest that the desire to crush the rumor that Saint-Médard held relics of St. Marcellinus was one of the main considerations that prompted the author to record the translation and miracles of the saints. Books 3 and 4, which Einhard probably wrote in 830 or 831, record the miracles performed at Mühlheim, Aachen, and other churches on Einhard's estates to which he loaned part of the relics. Sometime after August 834, he attached two final chapters to Book 4 describing miracles of Sts. Protus, Hyacinth, and Hermes performed after Deusdona brought their relics to Mühlheim.

The *Translation of the Relics of Sts. Marcellinus and Peter* must be understood in the context of the religious and literary culture of its time. Einhard received his education during the reign of Charlemagne, a period notable for the prevailing sense of optimism about the possibility of combining Christian wisdom and secular knowledge in the service of the church. No figure more clearly attests this wave of Christian humanism than Alcuin, the Anglo-Saxon scholar who served in the palace school and advised Charlemagne after 781. Einhard knew him and may have studied under his direction at Aachen. Echoing an idea expressed in the sixth century by Boethius, Alcuin identified the desire to know the truth as a characteristic feature of human nature. This conviction led Alcuin beyond Augustine of Hippo's cautious affirmation of the instrumental value of the liberal arts in the process of individual conversion to say that grammar, rhetoric, and the others arts possess an intrinsic value that corresponds to an innate human attraction to truth; like the seven columns of the porch of the temple of wisdom, the arts afford access to the sacred precinct. Another source that sheds light on Einhard's cultural horizon are the letters of his friend and younger contemporary Lupus, later the abbot of Ferrières. His view of the matter ranged from a youthful assertion that "knowledge should be sought for its own sake," to a more circumspect mature reflection on the difference between learning and moral goodness: "he who gives first place to erudition and not to saintliness shall be excluded by a deadly hunger from the banquet table of wisdom." In either case, however, the arts were considered indispensable in the pursuit of Christian wisdom.

The positive approach taken to the Christianized liberal arts left its imprint on every phase of Einhard's work. On one side, in the *Life of Charlemagne*, which appeared sometime between 817 and 825/6, the emperor's provision for the arts education of his children, and indeed his own efforts in that field seem to have an intrinsic value. On the other, his letter to a young protégé who had gone elsewhere to continue his studies resembles the remarks of the mature Lupus in its tendency to subordinate the liberal arts to an upright way of life; while both are important, in the absence of love that builds up, grammar, rhetoric, and the rest become nothing more than the knowledge that puffs up. It seems likely that Einhard's reading in *De architectura*, the handbook "On Architecture" dedicated to the emperor Augustus by the architect and engineer Vitruvius, influenced the work he did at the palace complex at Aachen and at his churches at Michelstadt and Mühlheim. A sketch of the silver base for a large altar cross attributed to Einhard that has survived from the seventeenth century offers another indication of the conscious synthesis of Christian and classical elements that characterized Einhard's milieu. Although designed in the form of an ancient Roman triumphal arch, it is decorated with three tiers of images, with military saints on the bottom, the evangelists and scenes from the life of Christ in the middle, and the enthroned Christ flanked by apostles on top.

The clearest sign of Einhard's formation in the tradition that placed the art of rhetoric in service of Christian wisdom is the contrast in style that distinguishes the *Translation of the Relics of Sts. Marcellinus and Peter* from the biography of Charlemagne. In the classical model of Cicero and Quintilian, the orator selects from a hierarchical register of styles the level of discourse that best corresponds to the gravity of the theme he means to address. Lupus echoed this underlying principle when he praised the pairing of style and subject in the *Life of Charlemagne* in which Einhard "gloriously set forth the glorious deeds of the emperor." Although often mentioned as an indication of early medieval enthusiasm for ancient literature, Einhard's use of the Roman imperial biographies of Suetonius in his portrait of Charlemagne also reflects his intentions regarding style and tone. The Roman principate's language of civic virtue and self-sacrifice, and the Stoic resonance of qualities such as "magnanimity" and "steadfastness" offered Einhard a fitting means of paying tribute to his friend and lord, a man who was neither a saint nor an ecclesiastic and so could not be described in terms borrowed from hagiography or episcopal biography.

But the lives and miracles of the saints were something else again. Efforts to represent in words the manifestation of divine power in the acts of God's chosen human agents seemed to dissolve the traditional register of styles in paradox and oxymoron. The theme was at once too lofty and too humble to fit any grade of the register: too lofty because of the radical transcendence and dazzling glory of the author of saintly goodness; too humble because the deeds of holy men and women showed that divine grace illuminates even the darkest recesses of fallen man's world. Reflection on the simple and direct expression of profound truth in the Gospels had led late Antique Christian authors to develop a mode of discourse known as *sermo humilis*, low or humble speech, which allowed them to address mixed audiences in terms that most people could understand. But *sermo humilis* was not only a means of accommodating the limited capacity of the uneducated; its very form conveyed a sense of the transformation and renewal made possible by the presence of absolute reality in an utterly contingent world. The power and love of God reach from alpha to omega, drawing goodness and order from history's chaos of sin and despair. No longer signs of a middling or low style, oxymoron and paradox here attest the miracle of the redemption achieved in Christ and reiterated though the saints. In effect the new rhetoric of hagiography showed that words and rhetoric themselves were parts of the created continuum and thus were encompassed by divine will.

Einhard mastered the *sermo humilis* of hagiography as well as the antique register of styles. Although the Germanic tongue was his own native language, he knew the difference between the colloquial Latin suited to the lives and miracles of saints and the more reserved and stately style appropriate to imperial biography. The syntax and vocabulary of the *Translation of the*

Relics of Sts. Marcellinus and Peter are more simple and direct than those of the *Life of Charlemagne*. Furthermore in the former Einhard discussed a number of "low" themes that had no place in the latter, such as the decomposed bodies of the saints, the illnesses and afflictions of those who visited Mühlheim, and the pious or impious deceit of those who pilfered holy objects. But the realism of the *Translation of the Relics of Sts. Marcellinus and Peter* should not be confused with naive simplicity of composition. The work is written in the first person, and this subjective perspective gives it an immediacy and experiential quality absent in most ninth-century hagiography. Even more than usual this text reveals its author's mind at work, exemplifying not only his stylistic range but his ability to deploy narrative, vivid description and an appeal to secondary causation in service of his saints and in defense of his claim to possess their relics.

SOURCES AND FURTHER READING

The standard edition of Einhard's work (*Bibliotheca hagiographica latina*, no. 5233) remains that by Georg Waitz in *Monumenta Germaniae Historica, Scriptores in folio*, vol. 15 (Hannover, 1887–88), pp. 238–64. Although he did not work from the best Latin edition, Barrett Wendell made a fine English language version, titled *The History of the Translation of the Blessed Martyrs of Christ Marcellinus and Peter* (Cambridge, MA, 1926), and the present translation of Books 1 and 2, and parts of Book 3, is simply a revision of his work against the edition of Waitz. The document's full text in English is available in Paul Edward Dutton, *Carolingian Civilization. A Reader* (Ontario, 1993), which is also a revision of Wendell's version. For the little we know about the martyrs Marcellinus and Peter, see *Bibliotheca hagiographica latina*, nos. 5230–33. As an introduction to Einhard's life and works, see Josef Fleckenstein, "Einhard," *Lexikon des Mittelalters*, vol. 3 (Munich, 1986), pp. 1737–39, and the chapter devoted to him by Eleanor Shipley Duckett in *Carolingian Portraits. A Study in the Ninth Century* (Ann Arbor, MI, 1969) is still useful. The most important sustained discussion of Einhard as hagiographer is Marguerite Bondois, *La translation des saints Marcellin et Pierre. Étude sur Einhard et sa vie politique de 827 à 834* (Paris, 1907). For an excellent study of the *Translation of the Relics of Marcellinus and Peter* in the context of pious thefts of relics, see Patrick Geary, *"Furta sacra": Thefts of Relics in the Central Middle Ages*, rev. ed. (Princeton, NJ, 1990). Sigmund Hellmann, "Einhards literarische Stellung," *Historische Vierteljahrschrift* 27 (1932): 40–110, examines Einhard's stylistic range, and Hans Liebeschütz, "Wesen und Grenzen des karolingischen Rationalismus," *Archiv für Kulturgeschichte* 33 (1971): 17–44, considers what the work reveals about the character and extent of what he calls the "rationalism" of the Carolingian era.

Einhard, Translation of the Relics of Sts. Marcellinus and Peter

(Preface.) To true worshipers of the true God, and to sincere lovers of our Lord Jesus Christ and his saints, Einhard a sinner.

Those who for posterity recorded in writing the lives and deeds of people who lived righteously in accordance with divine precept, seem to me to have wished to emend people's wicked lives and by the use of examples of this sort to encourage them to join in the praise of almighty God. They did this not only because they lacked spite but because they possessed abundant charity, which caused them to desire the good of all. Because their praiseworthy undertaking was openly inspired by this and no other desire, I see no reason why they should not be emulated by many people. And therefore, because I feel that these books, written as well as I could do it, on the translation of the bodies of the blessed martyrs of Christ, Marcellinus and Peter, and the signs and miracles that God desired to perform through them for the benefit of the faithful, were written with the same desire and intention, I have decided to release them and offer them for reading to those who love God. I think, moreover, that this work should not only not seem useless and empty to anyone of the faithful, but indeed fruitful and useful if it lifts up the reader's soul in praise of its Creator.

(Book 1, # 1) When, still at the palace and occupied with secular affairs, I often dreamed of the rest and withdrawal that I desired to enjoy, I came across an unknown place, removed from the beaten track; and thanks to the munificence of Prince Louis, whom I served at the time, received it as my own.[1] This place is in the German forest that lies between the rivers Neckar and the Main and in modern times is known as the Odenwald by those who live in and around it. When according to my skill and resources I constructed there not only domestic buildings and living quarters but also a reasonably nice basilica suitable for celebrating the Divine Office, I began to wonder in the name and honor of which saint or martyr I should best dedicate it. After a good deal of time had passed in this condition of indecision, it happened that a certain deacon of the church of Rome, named Deusdona, came to the palace to petition the king's support of his own needs.[2] When, having stayed there for a time and having finished the business for which he came, he was preparing to return to Rome, as a gesture of kindness to a traveler I invited him to share my humble dinner. During dinner we spoke of many things until at last we came to the subject of the transferal of the body of blessed Sebastian.[3] It emerged that in Rome there was a huge number of neglected burial places of the martyrs. I turned the discussion to the dedication of my new basilica and began to inquire how I might be able to bring it about that I should obtain some small portion of the true relics of the saints who are buried at Rome. At first Deusdona hesitated and responded that he didn't know how this could happen. Then when he became aware that I was eagerly interested in the matter, he promised to answer my question another day. Later, when again I had invited him to dine, he removed a booklet from the folds of his robe and gave it to me saying that I should read it when I was alone, and that I should tell him whether I was pleased with what I found in it. I took the booklet and as he had urged read it in private. It said that at home he had access to the relics of many saints and that he wished to give them to me, if he could return to Rome with my support. He understood that I had two mules, and if I gave him one and sent along a trustworthy man of my own who could bring relics received from him back to me, he would immediately send them to me. This offer pleased me, and I resolved to test his promise straight away; so, having given him the aid he sought, and adding money for the expenses of the trip, I ordered my notary Ratleic, who wished to go to Rome to pray, to travel with him. So having set out from the palace at Aachen—for at that time the emperor and his entourage were there—they came to Soissons. There they spoke with Abbot Hilduin of the monastery of Saint-Médard, because the deacon had promised him that he would try to send the body of blessed Tiburtius to him.[4] Enticed by these assurances Hilduin sent with him a priest, a shrewd man by the name of Hunus, ordering him to bring to him the body of that martyr once he had received it. From there they set out and reached Rome as quickly as they could.

(2.) After they entered Italy it happened, however, that Reginbald, the servant of my notary, was taken with a tertian fever and significantly impeded the progress of their journey, for they could not travel during the hours when the fever's grip on him was strongest. Since the party was small they preferred not to be separated from one another. While their journey was slowed not a little bit by this problem, they made such progress as they could. Three days before they came to the city, a certain man dressed as a deacon appeared to the feverish servant in a vision, questioning him as to why his master hastened to Rome. When he explained as much as he knew about the promise of the deacon and the relics of the saints that were to be sent to me, and about those that had been promised to Abbot Hilduin, "The outcome of the venture that brings you," he said, "will be quite different from what you anticipate. For the deacon who urged you to come to Rome will do little or nothing of what he promised; and therefore I want you to follow me and carefully consider what I shall show and say to you." Then having taken his hand, as it seemed, he led him to the top of the mountains where the two stopped and he said: "Turn to the east and look at the country before your eyes!" When he turned and directed his gaze at those lands he saw huge constructed, citylike shapes, and when questioned whether or not he knew what this was he responded that he did not. Then his companion said, "It is Rome that you see." And he immediately added, "Look at the farther part of the city and see if you can make out any church there." When he said that he could see a church, his companion said: "Go and tell Ratleic that in the church you now saw that thing lies that he should convey to his master. He should strive to obtain it as soon as possible and return to his master." And when he said that none of those he was traveling with would believe what he said about such things, his companion responded saying: "You know that those who travel with you are troubled because for many days you have struggled with a severe fever, and that you have had no remission." And he said, "It is as you say." "For that reason," said his companion, "I wish it to be a sign to you and to those to whom you will relate what I have said, that from this hour through the mercy of God you will be so relieved of the fever that until now has burdened you, that it will not bother you again on this journey." With that the boy awoke and hastened to relate to Ratleic all that he seemed to have heard or seen. When Ratleic told these things to the priest traveling with him, it seemed to both that the experience of the dream was proven by the realization of the promised cure. For on that same day according to the nature of the disease from which he had been suffering, a fever should have attacked him who had seen the vision. And that it was not a vain illusion by rather a true revelation was clear, for neither on that day nor on those that followed was there any sign of the fever in his body. Thus it happened that they believed his vision and put no more faith in the promises of Deusdona, the deacon.

(3.) So coming to Rome, they lodged near the basilica of the blessed apostle Peter, which is called In Chains, in the home of the deacon with whom they had come.[5] They stayed with him for some days, urging him to make good his promises. But he, who was unable to do what he had promised, excused himself for not doing so by various pretexts of delay. At last they spoke with him and asked why he wished to mislead them in this way, at the same time warning him against detaining them any longer with deception and impeding their return with false hopes. When he had heard them, and perceived that this sort of deception would no longer work, the deacon first informed my notary concerning the relics promised to me that he could not have them, because his brother, to whom upon leaving Rome he had entrusted the house and its contents, had gone to Beneventum on business, and that he had almost no idea when he would return. Because he had given him those relics and other household items for safekeeping, he didn't know what had become of them, since they were no longer in the house. And so my notary should fend for himself because there was nothing more to hope from him. After he said all this to my notary, who complained at being deceived and tricked by him, he talked in I know not what vain and frivolous terms with the priest of Hilduin, and deprived him of any similar hope. But the next day, when he saw them quite despondent, he urged them to accompany him to the cemetery of the saints; for it seemed to him that there they might find something that would satisfy their desires, and thus prevent them from returning home empty-handed. But when this suggestion pleased them, and they wanted as quickly as possible to do what he had suggested, in his usual way he delayed the business, and by this delay cast down their spirits, which had briefly risen, into such disappointment, that in Deusdona's absence, they resolved to return home with their mission incomplete.

(4.) But my notary, remembering the dream of his servant, urged his companion that they should go to the cemetery without their host and see what he had promised to take them there to see. So having found a guide to show them the place, they came first to the basilica of the blessed martyr Tiburtius on the Via Labicana, about three miles from the city, and examined the tomb of the martyr as carefully as they could; and discussed with the greatest privacy whether it might be opened in such a way that nobody else would notice the fact. Then they went down into a crypt next to the basilica, in which the blessed martyrs of Christ Marcellinus and Peter were buried; and having examined the security of this monument too they withdrew, reckoning that what they had done could be kept secret from their host. But it turned out otherwise than they wished. For, although they knew not by what means, knowledge of their movements soon reached him; and fearing that they might accomplish their desires without him, he decided to hasten to anticipate their purpose. And since he had a thorough familiarity with those holy places, he spoke to them gently and urged that they all go there together; and, if God desired to favor their wishes, together they should decide what to do. They agreed to his plan, and by common consent fixed on a time for beginning it. Then, after fasting for three days, they went by night, unnoticed by any of the inhabitants of Rome, to the place I have mentioned. Having entered the basilica of St. Tiburtius, they first tried to open the altar below which his body was believed to lie. But they made very little progress in this attempt, for the monument was built of hardest marble and easily repelled the inexperienced hands of its assailants. Therefore, leaving the burial place, they went down to the tomb of the blessed Marcellinus and Peter; and there, having invoked our Lord Jesus Christ and having prayed to the holy martyrs for help, they tried to lift the stone that sat on top of the tomb. When they had raised it, they saw the most holy body of St. Marcellinus placed in the upper part and close to his head a marble tablet which attested in writing the name of the occupant whose body lay in this grave. So, they raised the martyr's body with the greatest reverence, as was fitting, wrapped it in a pure muslin cloth, and gave it to the deacon to carry and hold. And replacing the stone so as to leave no sign that the body had been removed, they returned to their quarters in the city. The deacon, affirming that he would and could keep the body of the blessed martyr that had been given him in his house near the basilica of the blessed apostle Peter, called In Chains, entrusted it for safekeeping to his brother, named Luniso; and thinking that this would satisfy my notary, he began to urge him to take the body of blessed Marcellinus and return to his own country.

(5.) But he had an altogether different plan in mind. For, as he later told me, it seemed to him not right to return home only with the body of blessed Marcellinus, and positively unacceptable that the body of blessed Peter the martyr, who was his companion in martyrdom and for more than five hundred years had shared the same burial place with him, should stay behind with Marcellinus gone. Once having conceived this idea, he was so vexed by its growth and restlessness within him, that neither taking food nor relaxing in sleep seemed attractive and easy to him, unless the bodies of the martyrs, as they had been joined in their passion and place of burial, so too could be joined in the journey he was about to undertake. But how he might achieve this he was totally uncertain. For he was aware that no one could be found in Rome who might help him in this undertaking, nor even anyone to whom he might reveal his secret plan. Burdened by this anxiety, he found a certain foreign monk, by the name of Basil, who had come to Rome from Constantinople two years before and along with four disciples was staying on the Palatine Hill with other Greeks of the same persuasion as he.[6] He went to him and disclosed his burdensome trouble. Then, encouraged by his advice and trusting in his prayers, his heart was so strengthened that he decided to attempt the thing as soon as possible, even though the effort put him at grave risk. Having summoned his companion, the priest of Hilduin, he proposed that once again they go to the basilica of blessed Tiburtius, in secret go to the tomb in which the body of the martyr was believed to rest, and once again try to open it. The plan seemed good; and taking along the servants, they set out secretly at night, their host having no idea where they were going. And when they had come to the church, having made prayers for the success of the operation outside the doors of it, they entered. Then, dividing the company, the priest remained with some in the basilica of blessed Tiburtius to seek that saint's body; Ratleic with others went down to the body of the blessed Peter, in the crypt that adjoined the church; and easily having opened the sepulchre, he took out the holy remains of the blessed martyr, with no problem, and put them into a silken bag, which he had prepared for this purpose. Meanwhile the priest who was searching for the body of blessed Tiburtius, having gone to great trouble for nothing, saw that the effort was pointless and, giving up on the job, came down into the crypt to Ratleic and began to ask what he should do. When he answered that he thought that the relics of St. Tiburtius were found, and explained what he meant, for a little before the priest had come to him in the crypt, he had found, in the same tomb in which the bodies of Sts. Marcellinus and Peter lay, a certain hole, round in form dug to the depth of three full feet, and a foot wide, and placed in it was quite a bit of very fine dust. It seemed to them both that this dust could have been left from the body of the blessed Tiburtius if his bones had been taken from there. And, to make it harder to find, it might have been placed just between the blessed Marcellinus and Peter, in the same tomb. They agreed that the priest should take it and carry it away with him as the relics of the blessed Tiburtius. With these things carried out and arranged, they returned to their lodgings with what they had found.

(6.) After that Ratleic spoke with his host, asking that he return the holy ashes of the blessed Marcellinus which he had given to him for safekeeping, and saying that he wished to be held up by no unnecessary delay. The deacon not only restored to him at once what he sought, but gave him a substantial number of the relics of saints gathered in a bundle to be brought to me. When asked to provide their names he answered that he would tell me himself, when he came to see me. He recommended, however, that these relics should receive the same veneration that was shown to the other holy martyrs, because their merit was not less in the eyes of God than blessed Marcellinus and Peter; and that I would believe this as soon as knowledge of their names came to me. Ratleic took the offered gift, and, as he was advised, put it with the bodies of the blessed martyrs. On the advice of his host, the holy and much-desired treasure was placed and labeled in bags and sent ahead to Pavia with Luniso, the deacon's brother whom I have already mentioned, and the priest of Hilduin, who came with him. Ratleic stayed with the host in Rome, looking and listening for seven days, to discover if the citizens learned anything of the stolen bodies of the saints. And when he had seen that there was no mention anywhere of this deed, and deeming it safe, he set out after those who had gone ahead, taking his host with him. When they found them awaiting their arrival at Pavia in the basilica of blessed John the Baptist, which is commonly called Dominarum [of the ladies], and at that time by a royal grant which was in my power, they decided to wait there a few days both to refresh their horses and to prepare themselves for the long journey ahead.[7]

(7.) At the time of their delay, a rumor spread that legates of the holy Roman Church, sent by the Pope to the emperor, were coming there soon. Thus fearing that their arrival could bring some inconvenience or obstacle to themselves if they should be found there, they decided that some of them should leave quickly to avoid the embassy's arrival; the rest should stay there, and having diligently looked into the matter about which they were concerned, after the departure of the legates they would follow their companions, whom they had sent on ahead. When this was settled among them, Deusdona with the priest of Hilduin went ahead of the legates coming from Rome, and as quickly as possible made for Soissons, where Hilduin was thought to be. Ratleic stayed at Pavia with the treasure he had with him, waiting, until the legates of the Apostolic See should pass by, so that, when they had crossed the Alps, he might make his own journey more safely. But fearing that the priest of Hilduin, who with Deusdona had gone ahead, and who had full knowledge of all that had happened and been discussed between them, because he seemed crafty and slick, might have contrived to place some obstacle for him in the road by which he planned to travel, he decided it would be best to go another way. So, after sending on to me the servant of our procurator, Ascolf, with a letter in which he informed me both of his own return and that he was bringing the treasure which divine assistance had discovered, he himself, once the Romans had left their lodgings and he thought they had crossed the Alps, left Pavia and in six days came to Saint-Maurice [d'Agaune]. And there, having gathered the things that seemed necessary for it, he enclosed the holy bodies in a little casket and placed it on a bier; and from that point onward he began to carry them publicly and openly with the help of the people who flocked to meet them.

(8.) When however he had passed the place that is called the Head of the Lake, he came to the crossroad where the roads leading into Frankland divide.[8] Taking the path on the right, through the territory of the Alemanni, he came to Soleure, a town of the Burgundians. There he met a greeting party which I had sent from Maastricht after news of his arrival reached me. For when the letter of my notary was brought to me by the servant of my procurator, whom I mentioned above, I was in the monastery dedicated to St. Bavo, on the river Scheldt.[9] Informed by the letter of the arrival of the saints, right away I ordered one of my household to go to Maastricht, and there to gather priests and other clerics as well as laymen, and to hurry out to greet the saints. And he, making no delay, together with those he brought, in a few days met, in the place which I have named, those who were bringing the saints. Together with the throngs of hymn-singing people who accompanied, with everyone rejoicing they swiftly came to the city of Argentoratum, which is nowadays called Strasbourg. From there sailing down the Rhine, when they came to the place called Portus, they disembarked on the east bank, and after five days journey, with a great multitude of people singing the praises of God, they came to the place called Michelstadt. This is the place in the German forest which in modern times is called Odenwald and is about six leagues distant from the Main River. When they found there the church newly built by me, but not yet dedicated, they carried the holy ashes into it and placed them there as if they would remain there forever.

(9.) When word of this was brought to me, without delay I hastened to come as quickly as I could. There, three days after our arrival, when at the end of the office of vespers a certain servant of Ratleic, under his instructions, when everyone else had left, remained alone in the church and with the doors closed was sitting down in the chancel next to those holy bodies, to keep watch over them, he was weighed down by a sudden drowsiness, and sleeping he saw two doves fly in through the right-hand window of the apse and land on top of the platform above the same bodies of the saints: one of them looked all white, the other a combination of gray and white. When they had walked around on top of the platform for some time and called back and forth as if speaking to one another in the way that doves do, they left through the same window and were no longer visible. Above the head of the servant a voice spoke as follows: "Go," it said, "and tell Ratleic, that he should inform his master that those holy martyrs do not want their bodies to rest in this place; for they have chosen another to which they desire to be taken." He could not see whose voice this was, but when the speaking ceased, he awoke and told Ratleic, when he came back to the church, what he had seen. The next day at his earliest opportunity Ratleic carefully informed me of what his servant had related. But I, though not daring to spurn the mystery of this vision, nevertheless determined that it must be confirmed in some more definite manner; and meanwhile I had the holy ashes removed from the linen wrappers in which they had traveled and placed in new silk containers. And when, upon examining them, I saw that the remains of the blessed Marcellinus were less in quantity than those of St. Peter, I reckoned that he had simply been a smaller man than St. Peter. But that this was not the case, the theft that was later exposed made plain: where, and when, and by whom, and how this was accomplished and was discovered, I shall relate in due course. For now, the proper order of the story I have begun should be maintained and continued.

(10.) Now after I had carefully looked at that great and admirable treasure, more precious than any gold, the casket in which it was contained began to displease me greatly because of the cheap material from which it was made. Desiring to put this right, on a certain day after the completion of the office of vespers I instructed one of the sacristans to take the dimensions of the casket by measuring rod and bring them to me. When he was about to do this he lit a candle and lifted up the enveloping drapery that covered the casket, he saw that the casket was everywhere exuding moisture the color of blood in a miraculous way; and deeply alarmed by the shock of such a sight, he quickly told me what he had seen. Then I, along with the priests who were on hand approached and looked at this stupendous and admirable miracle. For, just as water often condenses on and runs down columns and the square slab that sits on top of them or marble images, so the casket that contained the most holy bodies in truth was found to be wet with blood over all its surface. The appearance of this unusual and unheard of miracle frightened us. For this reason, after consultation, we decided to pass three days in fasting and prayer, so that we might be worthy to know through divine revelation what this great and unspeakable sign meant, and what we were intended to do. And having passed the three days fasting, when evening was approaching, that horrible bloody moisture suddenly began to dry and, in a wonderful way, that which had for seven straight days dripped like a permanent spring of water, within a few hours was so dry that in that hour of the night—for it was Sunday—when the bell summoned us for the celebration of the predawn office and we entered the church, no trace of it was to be found on the casket. But the linen cloth which was draped around the casket and had been sprinkled with the same moisture such that it was stained with bloody marks, I ordered to be saved. To this day in those stains there is impressive evidence of that unheard-of sign. For it established that the moisture tasted rather salty, in the way that tears do, and had the consistency of water but the color of real blood.

(11.) In the quiet of that same night two youths were seen standing beside him by one of our servants, named Roland, and, as he himself affirmed, they ordered him to say many things to me about the transferal of the bodies of the saints; and they revealed the place where they should be moved and how it should be done; and they warned him with frightening threats that this should be reported to me without delay. As soon as he could go to me he carefully recounted all he had been told. When I heard these things, I became very worried, and began to wonder what I should do: whether again fasting and prayer should again be observed, and God once more appealed to for the settlement of my questions; or whether some devout and faultless servant of God should be sought, to whom I might reveal the anxiety of my heart and the complaints of my cares, and whom I might ask, that through his prayers he should obtain from God a clarification of the matter for me. But where or when I might find such a servant of Christ the Lord, above all in that region? For although there were some monasteries located not far from where we were, nevertheless because of the rude way of life in these places, there were few men or none of whom anything of the kind or even the slightest rumor of it was reported. In the meantime, while thus troubled, I was praying for the assistance of the holy martyrs, and was repeatedly urging everyone who was with me to do the same, it happened that for several days running no night passed in which there was not revealed in dreams either to one or two or even three of my companions that those bodies of the saints must be transferred from that place to another. And at last, as he himself confirms, there appeared in a vision to a certain priest among those who were with us there, by name Hiltfrid, a certain man in priestly dress, remarkable for his venerable whitish-gray hair, dressed in white clothing, who rebuked him in these words: "Why," he said, "is Einhard so hard-hearted and stubborn, that he will not believe so many revelations, and despises so many divine admonitions sent to him? Go and tell him that what the blessed martyrs desire to be done with their bodies cannot remain undone. And although he has so far postponed carrying out their will in this matter, now, if he does not want the credit for this deed to go to someone else, let him hasten to obey their command, and not fail to remove their bodies to the place that they selected."

(12.) After these and other sorts of warnings had been sent to me, it seemed to me that the transferal of the holy ashes should be delayed no longer; and so, in consultation with others, we decided that we should hasten the process as much as possible. Therefore, having made ready everything that seemed necessary for this removal quickly and with careful attention, at first light after the morning office, with great lamentation and sadness of those who were to stay in this place, we lifted that holy and most precious treasure and began to carry it along the road, accompanied by a throng of the poor, who in those days had come there from everywhere to receive alms; for the people of the neighborhood knew nothing about our intention. The sky was heavy with dark clouds which might quickly have turned into a heavy rain, had divine power not prevented it. For all night long it had rained so much that it seemed we would hardly be able to begin to travel that day. But our doubt, which came from weakness of faith, supernal grace resolved through the merits of the saints far otherwise than we expected; for we found little mud and discovered that the streams, which are apt to rise in such a heavy and continuous rain as there had been the night before, were hardly swollen at all. And when we left the forest and approached settlements, we were received by great crowds of greeting people singing praise to God. They accompanied us for a distance of about eight leagues, devoutly helping us carry the holy burden and diligently joining us in singing God's praise.

(13.) But when we saw that we could not reach our destination on that day, we turned aside at the village called Ostheim which was within sight of our route. With evening settling in we carried those holy bodies into the church of Saint Martin which is in the village; and leaving most of our company there to keep watch, I and a few others hastened on to the journey's end;

and throughout the night we worked to prepare the customary reception of the bodies of saints. But in the church in which we left the sacred treasure, a certain crippled nun by the name of Ruodlang, of the convent Machesbach [Mosbach], which is located a distance of one league from that church, who had been brought in a cart by her friends and relatives, and who had spent the night among the other people keeping watch and praying beside the bier of the saints, recovered the health of all her limbs; and the next day with no one's help and no assistance of any kind, on her own feet she returned to the place she had come from.

(14.) Rising before dawn, we went out to greet our companions coming this way, and accompanied by a very large group of people from the neighborhood who, excited by word of the arrival of the saints, had assembled outside our doors at dawn so that together with us they might go out to greet the saints. And we hastened out to them in the place where the brook Gernsprinz flows into the Main. From there marching together and in unison singing the praise of the mercy of our Lord Jesus Christ, we carried those holy remains of the most blessed martyrs, amid the great delight and exultation of everyone who was there, to Upper Mühlheim, for thus in modern times the place is called. But, because of the vast multitude of people who going ahead filled the entire area, we could neither go to the church nor take the bier into it; so we set up an altar under the open sky on a rise in the field adjacent and, resting the bier behind the altar, we celebrated mass. After that, and when the crowd had gone about their business, we carried the most holy bodies of the saints into the church that they had chosen, and with the bier near the altar again we celebrated mass. Present during the rite was a certain boy about fifteen years old named Daniel, from the Portian country, who came there begging among the other poor people, and was so hunched over that unless he was leaning backward and lying down he could not see the sky. He approached the bier and was suddenly knocked down as if pushed by someone, and when for a long time he had lay like one sleeping, before our very eyes he rose up unharmed and with all his members healed and the vigor of his sinews restored. These things happened on the sixteenth day before the Kalends of February [January 17], a day so fair and clear that it matched the radiance of the summer sun, and whose calm air was so gentle and pleasant that in alluring warmth it surpassed the mildness of spring.

(15.) The next day we placed the sacred bodies of the blessed martyrs, enclosed in a new shrine, in the apse of the basilica; and as is the custom in Frankland, we put over it a wooden frame and for decoration covered it with fine linen and silk. And placing on either side of the altar two standards of the Lord's passion which on the road had gone before the bier, we took care, as much as our means would allow, to make a suitable and fitting place for the celebration of the Divine Office. Having appointed clerics who would keep watch there and whose responsibility it was to sing divine praises, with great joy and with God speeding our journey, we returned to the palace, not because we wished to, but having been summoned by an imperial letter which had reached us on the road.

(Book 2, 1) A few days after my arrival, I rose early, as is usual for courtiers, and at dawn went to the palace. There having entered I met Hilduin, whom I have already mentioned, sitting outside the doors of the royal chamber and awaiting the emergence of the prince. Having greeted him politely I asked him to rise and come with me to a certain window which looks onto the lower part of the palace. Leaning against it side by side, we spoke a good deal about the transferal of Sts. Marcellinus and Peter, and of the miracle of the flow of blood that their casket exuded for seven days. And when we came in our conversation to the place where I mentioned the clothing in which their bodies was found, and I said that the clothing of blessed Marcellinus was of wonderful delicacy, Hilduin, responding as though he knew this as well as I, affirmed what I said about the clothing. Stunned and perplexed by this, I began to inquire from what source this knowledge of the clothing which he had never seen might have reached him. But he, looking at me, kept silent for a little and then said: "I suppose it is better that you should learn from me what you will soon learn from others if I do not speak, and that I should exactly inform you of a matter which any other informer will not tell you with exactness, nor indeed can, because nature arranged it that no one can speak the whole truth whose knowledge of a thing depends on the account of others rather than his own experience. I have enough confidence in you that I believe you will deal justly with me when by my story you know the whole truth about what has been done." And when I had responded briefly that I would not do otherwise than we agreed between ourselves, "That priest," he said, "who went to Rome under orders from me to remove the relics of blessed Tiburtius, was unable to accomplish that which he had come to do. After your notary had received the relics of the holy martyrs about which we have been talking and had decided to go home, he decided to stay in Rome a little longer, while the priest himself, with Luniso the brother of Deusdona, and his men would carry those holy ashes ahead to Pavia and there await the arrival of the notary and Deusdona. This suggestion suited both of them, and leaving the two in Rome, the priest, with Luniso and his servants who carried the relics, set out for Pavia. Once they arrived there, the caskets containing the holy ashes were placed next to the altar in your church and diligently guarded by clerics and laymen standing watch. But one night, when among others the priest was keeping watch over the relics in the church, it happened in the middle of the night that he observed that, with sleep gradually stealing upon them, everyone other than himself who had gathered in the church for the vigil was asleep. Then the idea occurred to him that it had not happened without some great cause that such a sudden sleep had taken by surprise so many people; and deciding to take advantage of the opportunity, he got up and with a lighted taper silently went to the caskets. Then, burning the cords of the seals by putting the flame of the taper close to them, he

quickly opened the caskets without a key; and taking a share from each body, he restored the seals as they were on top of the burned cords; and, with no one aware of the deed, he sat down again in his place. Later, when he had returned to me, he brought the relics of the saints stolen in this fashion, and at first he declared that they were not those of St. Marcellinus or Peter, but of St. Tiburtius. Then, apprehensive of something, when he spoke with me in private, he openly explained which saints these relics belonged to and how he had obtained them. I have them in a suitably honorable place at Saint-Médard where they are worshiped by the entire populace with great veneration. But whether I may keep them is up to you." When I heard all this, I remembered what I had heard from a certain man I had stayed with on my way to the palace. Among other things he said to me: "Have you heard," he said, "the rumors about the holy martyrs Marcellinus and Peter spreading through this region?" When I said that I did not know, he said: "Those who come from Saint Sebastian say that a certain priest of Abbot Hilduin went to Rome with your notary.[10] When they were on their way back, and had lodgings together, and all your men were drunk or asleep and completely oblivious to what he was doing, he opened the caskets that held the bodies of the saints, removed parts, and leaving carried them to Hilduin, and that they are now at Saint-Médard. By contrast in your caskets little of the holy ash remains, which was brought you by your notary." Remembering these things and comparing them with what Hilduin had said, I was more than a little disturbed, especially because it had not yet occurred to me how I might combat this execrable and infernally widespread rumor, and drive it from the minds of gullible people. Nevertheless I judged it best that I should ask Hilduin to return to me that which, after his willing confession he could not deny to have been taken from my caskets, and carried to him, and received by him. I did this with as much forcefulness as I could. Though for a short time he was harder and slower to comply than I would have liked, he was overcome by the determination of my requests, and yielded to my disapproval, though a short time before he had declared that especially in this case he would yield to the demands of no one.
(2) Meanwhile, letters having been sent to Ratleic and Luniso—for they were in that place where I had situated the bodies of the martyrs [that is, at Mühlheim]—I informed them of the rumor about those same holy martyrs that was spread through most of Gaul, urging them to consider whether they could think of any such incident on their journey, or recall anything like what Hilduin claimed his priest had done. Coming immediately to me at the palace, they recounted a story that was quite different from what Hilduin said. For to begin with they attested that everything that the priest had said to Hilduin was false; and that after they had left Rome, there had been no occasion for that priest or anyone else to gain access and accomplish such a deed. Yet at the same time it was clear that this very thing had happened to the holy ashes of the martyrs, but at Rome, in the house of Deusdona, through the avarice of Luniso and the cunning of the priest who has been mentioned, at the time when the body of the blessed Marcellinus, removed from its tomb, was hid-

den in the house of Deusdona. They said that the manner of the deed was as follows. Frustrated in his hope of acquiring the body of St. Tiburtius, and to avoid returning to his master emptyhanded, that priest of Hilduin contrived to obtain by fraud what he had failed to obtain honestly. So, approaching Luniso, for he knew him to be poor and consequently eager for gain, with the offer of four gold coins and five of silver he entangled him in the betrayal. Taking the proffered money, he opened the ark in which the body of blessed Marcellinus was placed and shut up by Deusdona, and gave the power of stealing whatever he fancied whenever he wished to that worst of scoundrels. Nor was he sparing in this wholesale theft: for he took enough of the holy ashes of the blessed martyr to fill a vessel that could hold a pint and a half. That it was done in this manner, the same Luniso who had conspired with the priest attested through tears as he lay at my feet. With the truth of the matter revealed, I then instructed Ratleic and Luniso to return whence they came.

(3) Thereafter, when I had talked with Hilduin, and an agreement had been made between us as to when the holy relics were to be returned to me, I ordered two clerics from our household, namely Hiltfrid and Filimar, the former a priest and the latter a subdeacon, to go to Soissons to receive them, sending with them to the place from which the relics were to be removed a goodwill offering of one hundred golden coins. They came to the monastery of Saint-Médard on Palm Sunday and stayed there for three days; and having received the incomparable treasure that they had been sent for, with two of the brothers of the same monastery accompanying them, they returned to the palace as quickly as they were able. Nevertheless they brought the relics not to me but to Hilduin. And he, receiving them, put them under guard in his private chapel until, after celebration of the feast of Easter was done, he should have free time in which he could show me what was to be returned before actually returning it. About eight days after holy Easter, when the king had left the palace to go hunting, Hilduin, according to an agreement between us, having taken the same relics from his oratory where they were being held and carried them into the basilica of the Holy Mother of God and there placed them upon the altar, had me summoned to accept them. Then opening the coffer in which the relics were contained, he showed me so that I might see what it was he was returning and I was receiving. Then, lifting the same coffer from the altar he placed it in my hands, and having made a suitable prayer, he acted as choirmaster, assigning a fitting antiphon in praise of the martyrs to the clerics who were skilled in song; and so singing he followed us with the priceless treasure as far as the doors of the basilica. We processed from there little by little with crosses and candles, praising the mercy of God, to the simply constructed chapel in our residence, and because there was no other place for them, we brought the holy relics into it.

(4) I think the miracle that happened in this procession of ours which I said we made from the basilica to our chapel should not be passed over in silence. For when we had left the church and were loudly singing in praise of the Lord our God, a smell so pleasantly sweet filled the whole part of the town

of Aachen that looks westward from the church, that the fragrance attracted nearly all the inhabitants of the neighborhood and everyone who happened to be there for whatever reason and business. So powerful was the divine force impelling them that dropping the work that was in their hands, everyone ran swiftly first to the church, then as if following the scent to our chapel, into which they heard the relics had been taken. The concourse of exulting and admiring people became too large for our enclosure. Although the greater part of those who gathered did not know what it was that had taken place, nevertheless filled with joy and exultation, they were joining in the praise of the mercy of Almighty God.

(5) But, after the spreading rumor made it widely known that the relics of St. Marcellinus the martyr had been carried to that place, such a numerous and vast multitude gathered not only from the town of Aachen and its immediate neighborhood and nearby hamlets, but from far-off places and villages, that there was scarcely room to enter the chapel to say the office except in the evening and at night. From everywhere the weak and those suffering from various illnesses were gathered there by their families and friends around the walls of the oratory. You could see there nearly every type of infirmity in people of both sexes and all ages cured by the power of Christ the Lord and through the merit of the most blessed martyr. Sight was restored to the blind, walking to the lame, hearing to the deaf, speech to the mute; even paralytics and those deprived of all strength of the body were carried by the hands of others and, with health restored, returned home on their own feet.

(6) When these things were related by Hilduin to the king, he first decided that on returning to the palace he would hasten to our chapel, where these things had happened, and there venerate the martyr. But advised by Hilduin not to do so, he ordered that the relics be carried to the larger basilica, and once they were brought there he venerated them with humble supplication, and after mass had been said, he offered to the blessed martyrs Marcellinus and Peter a certain small estate, located by the River Aar, by the name of Ludolvesdorf, comprising fifteen farms and nine acres of vineyards. And the queen offered her belt made of gold and jewels, weighing three pounds.[11] When these things were accomplished, the relics were carried back again to their proper place, that is to our chapel, and were there for forty days or more, until the emperor left the palace and entered the forest in the beginning of the customary hunt. When this was done, we too, after preparing the things necessary for our own departure, set out with those same relics from the town of Aachen.

(7) At the very moment of our departure, during the celebration of mass, a certain old woman well known in the palace, about eighty years old, who was suffering with paralysis, was cured before our eyes. As we learned from her own lips, she had been in the grip of this illness for fifty years, moving around by creeping like an animal on hands and knees.

(8) Taking to the road from there, with the help of God and by the merits of the saints on the sixth day we reached the village of Mühlheim, in which when

we had set out for court we had left the holy ashes of the blessed martyrs. And in that journey how much joy and delight the arrival of those relics occasioned among the people along the route, I should neither hush up, nor can it be reported and described as it really was. Yet I must try to tell it, so that something pertaining directly to the praise of God not appear to be passed over in neglectful silence. And first indeed my mind stirs me to tell of what, when we left the palace, I remember that I myself saw in the presence of many people. Reaching the bridge on the stream called Worm that lies about two thousand paces from the palace of Aachen, we stopped for a short while because the crowd that had followed us that far from the palace now wished to return. And there one of the people offering prayers approached the relics with another and addressing his companion said: "For the love and honor of this saint I forgive you the debt of money you owe me." As the man himself attested, he owed him a half pound of silver. And again, another man drew his associate by the hand to the relics: "You murdered my father," he said, "and so we have been enemies; now, however, for the love and honor of God and this saint, putting aside the feud, I wish to enter into and join with you in a truce, so that from now on there may be a lasting friendship between us: and may this saint be the witness of our mutual love, and take vengeance on him who first breaks this peace."

(9) And from this point, the crowd that had set out from the palace with us, after worshiping and kissing the holy relics, returned home so filled with joy that its tears could not be kept back. Another throng rushed out to greet us there, and continually singing the *Kyrie Eleison* accompanied us until we were received by others hurrying toward us; and then as before, with its supplication made the throng returned home. In this way each day from sunrise to evening with crowds of people accompanying and singing praise to Christ the Lord, we traveled from the palace of Aachen to the village of Mühlheim, with the Lord hastening our journey. And there we placed the relics in a jeweled box on the altar, behind which was placed the casket holding the holy ashes of the martyrs.

(10) They stayed there until, in November, when we were preparing to go to the palace, we were warned in a vision not to leave that place before uniting the relics with the body from which they had come. But how it was revealed that I should do this should not be passed over in silence, because not only in a dream, as is usual, but in certain signs and threats it was made clear to those on watch that the blessed martyrs were determined that their commands should be obeyed to the letter.

(11) There was one of the clerics who were assigned to keep watch in the basilica, by name Landolph, whose task was to sound the bell and whose bed was near the eastern door. When he had risen in solemn fashion for Vigil and Matins and had sounded the bell as usual, and the office being finished before dawn, he wished to return to bed, and with the doors of the church closed, he prostrated himself for the purpose of supplication before the holy ashes of the martyrs. There, as he himself affirms, when he began to recite the fiftieth

Psalm, he heard what sounded like the footsteps of a person walking here and there next to him on the floor. Alarmed with not a little fear, he raised himself onto his knees and began to look all around, supposing that one of the poor had been shut in and had gone to a corner. When he saw that no one else but he alone was inside the basilica, again he bowed in prayer and again said the Psalm he had begun. But before he could finish a single verse of it, the jeweled box on the altar containing the holy relics of blessed Marcellinus sounded so sharply with repeated rattling that you would have thought it was being broken apart by hammer blows. Also the two doors of the basilica, the west and east, which were then closed, emitted a similar noise as if someone were knocking and beating. Frightened and confused by these things, when he found that he didn't know what else to do, Landolph got up from the altar and shaking with fear threw himself onto his bed; and overcome by a deep sleep, he saw next to him the face of someone he did not know, who addressed him in these words: "Is it true," he said, "that Einhard is in such a hurry to go to the palace that he will not first restore the relics of St. Marcellinus, which he brought here, to the place whence they were taken?" When Landolph responded that he didn't know about this: "Get up," he said, "at first light and tell him by order of the martyrs not to dare leave here or go anywhere before he has restored those relics to their place." He sat up wide awake, and when he could first see me he related what he had been told. Nor did I think that slow action was called for in this matter, and deciding to obey the order without delay, on that very day I commanded that the necessary arrangements be made; and next day, with due care, I restored those holy relics to the body from which they had been taken. How pleasing this was to the most blessed martyrs is clearly shown by the plain witness of the miracle that ensued. For that night, when we were sitting in the basilica at the solemn office of Matins, a certain old man, deprived of the use of his legs, entered the oratory crawling on hands and knees. Through the power of God and the merits of the most blessed martyrs, in the presence of everyone and within an hour of his arrival, he was so fully cured that for walking he did not need so much as a crutch. He had also been deaf for five straight years, and he affirmed that his hearing was restored at the same time as was the use of his feet. With these things done, I set out, as I said above that I wished to do, for court, there to pass the winter, pondering many things in my mind.

(Book 3, Preface.) I am about to record the cures and miracles worked in various placed by the most blessed martyrs of Christ Marcellinus and Peter after their most holy bodies were brought from Rome to Frankland; or, as I should say, which, through their blessed merits and devout prayers, God the king of martyrs himself and our Lord Jesus Christ desired to work in various places for the salvation of human beings. Before doing so, I have decided to note in a short preface that most of those things which I have made ready to write about were brought to my attention by the reports of others. That I might have confidence in them, however, I was so firmly persuaded by the things which I myself saw and knew to have occurred in my presence that without the slightest scruple of doubt I could believe to be true what was said by those who bore witness that they had seen these things, even though of the persons from whom I heard it I might have either little or no knowledge up to that time. But of all these things it seems to me that those should first be written down which occurred and were seen by myself in that place [that is, Mühlheim] to which those same most blessed martyrs directed that their most holy ashes should be translated. Then those things which were done in the palace at Aachen, under the very eyes of the court, are to be recorded. Then, I thought, should be put down the things done in various places to which, at the request of religious men and by my assistance, the holy relics of those saints were carried; so that, following this order of narration, nothing should be omitted of all the signs and miracles which could possibly have come to my attention, unworthy though I am. And so, now that the preface is finished, let us set forth the miracles that should be related . . .

[**Translator's note**: In the first twelve chapters, Einhard relates a set of miracles performed through the relics and the patronage of Sts. Marcellinus and Peter.]

(13.) Not long afterward Ratleic, who, as has been mentioned before, brought the holy ashes of the martyrs from Rome, arrived, having been ordered, as he said, to bring me a little book containing many chapters; and the account he gave for this was as follows: that blind man whom we have just mentioned had advised on the authority of the martyrs that those chapters should be written down and brought me, and he said that I should take them and offer them to the emperor to read.[12] I took the little book from him and read it, and when it was corrected and a fresh copy made, I offered it, as he had instructed, to the emperor. And he also took it and read it, but of the things which in this little book he was ordered or advised to do he took the trouble to accomplish very few. Now what those chapters contained, or what they recommended to be done or what left undone by him, may better be discussed in some other place. Nevertheless I think that the way in which it was revealed and ordered that the little book ought to be made and to be given the king not only should not be passed over but should be written down as openly and as clearly as it can be. Ratleic said that these things came about in this way: "A few days ago," he said, "when we met to celebrate the night office, that blind man whom you know came to me, begging that I step aside with him into a more secret place. I did as he wished, and with him entered the cell where I sleep. He spoke first, saying 'Tonight, a little before we were awakened by the sounding of the bells, there appeared to me in a vision a certain man, with venerable white hair who was clothed in a white garment, and held in his hand a golden wand. He spoke to me in these words: "Be sure, Aubrey," he said, "that you fully understand all that I shall say to you, and hold it so fast in memory that you can also make it clear to others, who are to write it down. For it is my will that these things be written down and shown by your master to Louis, the emperor, that he may read them. For truly it is very necessary that this should be not only known but also done by the prince to whose realm those same martyrs have come by the order of God." Then he dictated one after another a dozen or more chapters; and he ordered that I should tell and explain them one by one to you and to four others whom I will name to you; and that after this you should make a little book of them and carry it to your master, who is now staying at the palace; and that you should tell him, on the authority of the martyrs, to present it as soon as he possibly can to the emperor. Thereafter he added, "Do you know who I am, who command you to do these things?" Then without hesitation I answered that he was St. Marcellinus. And he said to me: "It is not as you suppose, but I am Gabriel, the archangel; and I have taken on the shape and form of Marcellinus because the Lord God has committed to me the charge of all things and matters concerning these same martyrs; and I have come now to tell you what I have instructed you to write down, because it is the will of God that those things shall be brought on their authority, without delay, to the knowledge of the king. And go, as I have told you, at dawn after Matins is over and tell what you have heard to those to whom I have ordered you tell it." Then I said, "There is no one who will believe that an angel has spoken to me, or has ordered me to relate such things." And he answered and said: "It will not be so, for I will give you a power which you shall exercise in their presence, and when they have seen this they will have no more doubt about the things you relate to them on my command. So therefore I want you to ask Ratleic to put before you two new candles which have not yet been lit; and taking one in the right hand and the other in the left go stand before the altar; and when you have finished telling everything I have ordered you to say, tell those who heard them that by this sign they may believe these things which you have spoken to be true and ordered by the angel of God, that is, if the candles in your hands shall be lighted while they are watching, without the use of visible fire.'" When all this had happened, the little book was written and brought to me, and by me offered to the king, and also by him received and read through. So it has appeared right to me to mention this little book among the other miracles; for on the occasion when it was ordered to be written that marvelous and unprecedented lighting of candles occurred which the angel who lighted them declared should be accomplished through the merits of the blessed martyrs.

(14.) At about the same time, when Ratleic left us and returned to the basilica of the martyrs, another little book was brought to us from there containing the words and discourse of a certain demon who called himself Wiggo. He spoke in the presence of many witnesses before the altar next to which the holy ashes of the martyrs were placed, under the interrogation of the priest who read the words of exorcism over the one who was possessed. It recounts the story as follows. There is a manor in the country of Niedgau called Höchst, belonging to the monastery of Saint-Nazaire, from which a certain girl, of about sixteen years, possessed by that wandering spirit, was brought by her parents to the basilica of the martyrs. And when she came before the tomb containing the holy bodies, and the priest had read above her head the words of exorcism, in the proper manner, and thereafter began to question the demon as to how and when he had entered into her, he answered the priest not in the barbarous tongue which was all the girl knew but in Latin. And when the priest was struck with wonder and asked after the source of this knowledge of Latin, when the girl's parents, who were present there, were completely ignorant of that language, the demon answered and said: "You have never seen any of my kin." Then the priest said: "Who then are you, and where do you come from, if these are not your family?" And, speaking with the lips of the girl, the demon said, "I am an officer and disciple of Satan, and for a long time was a doorkeeper in the underworld, but for the last years, along with eleven friends, I have laid waste the kingdom of the Franks. Following our instructions, we destroyed the grain, grapes, and all the earth's produce that is useful to mankind. We slaughtered the stock with disease and even directed plague and pestilence against human beings. All the adversities and every evil that mankind has rightfully suffered lately, we have executed and accomplished." And when the priest asked him why a power of this kind had been granted him, "By reason of the perverseness," he said, "of this people, and of the manifold sins of those who are set up to rule over them. For they love profits and not justice, and they fear man more than God, and they oppress the poor; they will not listen to widows and orphans crying out to them for aid, and they do justice to none except for pay. Besides these there are many and almost innumerable other sins which are daily committed both by the people themselves and by their rulers: no one forbids perjury, drunkenness, adultery, murder, theft, or rape, and no one punishes those who commit them. Those in power serve like slaves for base profits; and they abuse the higher place, which they received that they might justly rule their subjects, giving themselves up to pride and vainglory; hatred and malice they direct not only against those who are far off but against their neighbors and those with whom they are allied; friend mistrusts friend, brother hates brother, and father has no love for son. There are few who faithfully and devoutly pay tithes, fewer still who give alms; and this because they view as a loss to themselves whatever they are told to give to God or to the poor. They do not fear to have short measures and false weights, against the command of God; they are not ashamed to bear false witness; they do not keep Sundays and feast days, but then, just as on other days, they work as much as they are inclined. For these reasons and many more, which God has either commanded men to do or not to do, and because this people by disobeying His commands is guilty of contumacy, we have been allowed and even ordered to do those things among men which I have named above, one by one, so that they may suffer the deserts of their faithlessness. For those are faithless and lying who take no pains to keep the promises they have made in baptism." All this the demon said in Latin through the lips of the girl who knew none. And when the priest began to command that he come forth from her, "I will leave her," he said, "not because of your command, but because of the power of the saints, who will not allow me to stay in her any longer." With these words he cast the girl down on the pavement, and made her lie there for a little while, face down, as if asleep. But a little while after, when he had left, the girl, as if waking from sleep, by the power of Christ and the merit of the blessed martyrs, rose up sound, and all who were there saw her and marveled, and after the demon was cast out of her she could not speak Latin; so that it is plainly evident that not she but the demon through her lips had spoken it. Ah for pity! Into what great miseries our times have sunk, when evil demons rather than good men are teachers, and the proponents of vice and inciters of crime admonish us for our own correction.

NOTES

1. Throughout the text, Einhard refers to the royal palace at Aachen where he spent at least a part of each year down until soon after 830. Although Einhard refers to him variously as prince (as here), king, and emperor, Louis the Pious reigned as emperor from the death of Charlemagne in 814 until his own death in 840

2. Patrick Geary, *"Furta sacra": Thefts of Relics in the Central Middle Ages*, revised edition (Princeton, NJ, 1990), pp. 45–49, discusses what we know about Deusdona.

3. In 826 Abbot Hilduin had acquired the relics of St. Sebastian (*Bibliotheca hagiographica latina*, nos. 7543–49), who was martyred in Diocletian's persecution, and installed them in the church of the monastery of Saint-Médard in Soissons.

4. Hilduin, the imperial archchaplain under Louis the Pious, had been a student of Alcuin and became abbot of the monasteries of Saint-Denis near Paris and Saint-Médard in Soissons. He died in ca. 840. Tiburtius was another martyr from the reign of Diocletian whose remains were buried near those of Sts. Marcellinus and Peter in the cemetery next to the church of Santa Helena—that is St. Helen, mother of the Emperor Constantine—on the Via Labicana in an eastern suburb of Rome. On the topography of Rome in late antiquity and the Middle Ages, see Richard Krautheimer, *Rome, Profile of a City, 312–1308* (Princeton, NJ, 1980).

5. The church of San Pietro in Vinculo (or "Saint Peter in Chains") was built around 400 on the western spur of the Esquiline Hill that reaches toward the valley of the imperial forum. Dedicated to the apostles Peter and Paul during the pontificate of Pope Sixtus III (432–40), it was known for the greatest of its relics, the chains of St. Peter. Judging by the list of restorations and gifts made by eighth- and ninth-century popes, it must have been an impressive church at the time of Einhard's visit.

6. Although the presence of Greek monks in ninth-century Rome is well known, this particular monk named Basil is otherwise unattested.

7. Pavia was the seat of the Lombard kings until Charlemagne toppled the monarchy and turned the city into a Frankish administrative center and way station for travelers moving between Frankland and Rome. There seem to have been at least two churches dedicated to John the Baptist in ninth-century Pavia. It may be that Einhard held the one built in the mid-seventh century by Queen Gundiperga, the daughter of Queen Theudelinda, both of whom the late-eighth-century Lombard historian Paul the Deacon mentioned in his *History of the Lombards*, Book 4, Chapter 47 as endowers of churches. (The best edition of the *Historia Langobardorum* is by Ludwig Bethmann and Georg Waitz in *Monumenta Germaniae Historica, Scriptores Rerum Langobardicarum et Italicarum, saec. VI-IX* [Hannover, 1878]).

8. The "Head of the Lake" is modern Villeneuve in Switzerland.

9. The cloister that came to be dedicated to St. Bavo in Ghent was founded in the period between 630 and 639 at the confluence of the Lys and Scheldt Riversby the missionary Amandus. Although originally dedicated to the apostle Peter, in the early ninth century it received the relics of St. Bavo (or Adlovinus), a student and disciple of Amandus, and thereafter was associated with his name. On St. Bavo, see *Bibliotheca hagiographica latina*, nos. 1049–60. During his tenure as lay abbot, a period of some twenty years before his death in 840, Einhard instituted important administrative and fiscal changes in the monastery, and it may be that he was responsible for the translation of St. Bavo's relics from the saint's burial church where they had originally been interred.

10. The reference is actually to the monastery of Saint-Médard in Soissons, which possessed relics of St. Sebastian.

11. The queen in question is Judith, the second wife of Louis the Pious and mother of Charles the Bald. She is first mentioned in 819, and her death is recorded in 843.

12. At this point in the narrative, Einhard was at the palace at Aachen.

CHAPTER 10
RAGUEL,
THE MARTRYDOM OF ST. PELAGIUS
Translated by Jeffrey A. Bowman

INTRODUCTION

Raguel is an obscure figure. The only surviving reference to him identifies him as a priest in Córdoba who wrote *The Martyrdom of St. Pelagius*. Raguel composed this work not long after Pelagius was tortured and executed in July 925. Raguel's narrative begins by stressing the importance of writing with appropriate models, and the work as a whole certainly relies on a long tradition of Christian martyrdom narratives. But the events Raguel relates are also grounded in the complexities of Iberian history.

The Córdoba in which Pelagius died and Raguel wrote had been under Islamic rule for more than two hundred years. Within a few years of invading in 711, armies from northern Africa had toppled the disorganized Visigothic kingdom and occupied most of the peninsula. Only a narrow shelf of beleaguered kingdoms in the north remained under Christian rule. The greater part of the peninsula, under Muslim rule, was known to its inhabitants as al-Andalus.

During the ninth and tenth centuries, armies from al-Andalus regularly raided the Christian kingdoms, destroying fortresses, seizing booty, and taking prisoners. The fragmented kingdoms in the north undertook similar raids into Muslim territory, but the Christian armies usually lacked the resources and organization needed to make these raids anything more than an occasional annoyance to the rulers of al-Andalus. The tenth century was, in the words of Joseph O'Callaghan, "a bleak period in the history of Christian Spain." (*A History of Medieval Spain*, [Ithaca, NY, and London, 1975], p. 120). In 920, during one particularly crushing defeat, Bishop Ermogius of Tuy, Pelagius's uncle, was captured and taken to Córdoba as a prisoner. The bishop's health deteriorated in prison and Pelagius was offered as a substitute for him.

The interaction of Christians and Muslims on the frontier centered on military alliances and antagonisms, but in Córdoba and the other cities of al-Andalus, Muslim-Christian interaction was considerably more complicated and, in general, more peaceful. During the tenth century, there were significant Jewish and Christian communities in most major cities. Islamic law granted Jews and Christians the right to observe their religions and to govern themselves. Some of these religious minorities even rose to prominent positions in government.

The Islamic policy toward Christians and Jews was one of toleration, not equality. Minority communities were subject to special taxes and were at times obligated to wear distinctive clothing. While allowed to observe their own religions, they were required to do so discreetly, without drawing attention to themselves or challenging Islam. Negotiating this policy of toleration was a delicate business for both the dominant Muslim population and for tolerated religious minorities. Relations between Muslims and Christians were often respectful, but they were not without tensions. Pelagius was, in fact, far from being Córdoba's first Christian martyr. During the 850s, several waves of Christians openly criticized Islam and defamed Muhammad. When these Christians persisted in their public attacks on Islam and its Prophet, the rulers of Córdoba had them executed for blasphemy or apostasy. Christians in Córdoba and elsewhere did not universally endorse the martyrs' actions. Some accused the martyrs of needlessly inviting trouble by provoking a relatively benign government.

At the time of Pelagius's imprisonment and martyrdom roughly seventy-five years later, the ruler of al-Andalus was the caliph Abd al-Rahmann III. His reign lasted nearly fifty years, during which time he earned an enduring reputation as one of the greatest rulers of medieval Spain. He brought unprecedented political unity to al-Andalus, linking together fragmented city-states and restraining the different ethnic and tribal rivalries which divided the Muslim population. Having consolidated his control over al-Andalus, he assumed a more aggressive attitude toward the neighboring Christian kingdoms, increasing both the frequency and the intensity of the raids into the north. The caliph's achievements were not, however, exclusively political and military. In Córdoba he undertook vast building projects, adorning the city with new palaces, mosques, fountains, and baths. His court attracted the greatest scientific and artistic talents of the Islamic world. During the caliph's reign, Córdoba was the most sophisticated and vibrant city in Europe. In general the caliph's treatment of Christians and Jews seems to have been particularly open-minded. Pelagius's bloody execution certainly reveals the dangers of scorning the caliph's attentions, but it does not reflect any programmatic oppression of Christians during Abd al-Rahmann III's reign.

When Raguel wrote *The Martrydom of St. Pelagius*, he had little interest in cataloging the caliph's many accomplishments, but his text can be seen as the product of a Córdoba shaped by Abd al-Rahmann III and his immediate predecessors. Raguel's concerns about Christian-Muslim interaction must have been widely shared by other Christians living in al-Andalus. Raguel displays a sensitivity to the precarious situation of the Christian kingdoms in the north. He deplores the cramped and unhealthy conditions in Córdoba's prisons. The splendor of the caliph's court offers a vivid contrast to the squalor of the prison in which Pelagius languished for three and a half years. The delicacies, the luxurious clothing, and the throngs of young attendants which

Raguel describes all reflect a new opulence at the caliphal court. Raguel's attitude toward this sumptuous display and ceremony is unremittingly hostile, but he does offer some idea of how innovations in court protocol under Abd al-Rahmann III appeared to disapproving Christian clerics.

Raguel's anxieties about caliphal conduct extend well beyond the court's opulence and formality. The caliph promises to shower Pelagius with honors, gifts, and attendants if he will renounce Christ. Pelagius patiently refuses to do so. When the caliph tries to touch Pelagius, Pelagius lashes out. He calls the caliph a "dog," and suggests that he (Pelagius) is not "effeminate," like the caliph. Raguel wants the reader to see the caliph's thwarted groping as an index of the boundless depravity of the court. Raguel's insinuations about the intense physical interest that the caliph takes in Pelagius's beauty are, in part, conventional. Accusations of lasciviousness and aberrant sexual practices featured prominently in the rhetorical arsenal of Christian polemicists during the Middle Ages, and such accusations were hurled with special frequency at Muslims. But while his description of the caliph's touch is, in part, a time-tested slander with little historical specificity, it is also true that the sexual mores of the caliphal court varied considerably from those of priests like Raguel.

Raguel doubtless expects the reader to find the caliph's caress shocking, but it would be a mistake to understand the attempted seduction of the beautiful Pelagius only in sexual terms. In addition to being a paean to Pelagius's strength and beauty, Raguel's narrative is also testament to the anxieties of a minority religious community living under the rule of a dominant religion that was economically, politically, and culturally superior. As Raguel wrote, Christians in al-Andalus were converting to Islam in increasing numbers. Christian leaders complained that young Christians were more interested in learning Arabic than Latin. Embattled communities of religious minorities struggled to maintain traditions and coherent identities. *The Martyrdom of St. Pelagius* is not only the story of heroic resistance to the fleshy enticements of this world; it is also, more generally, a story of the refusal to assimilate. For Raguel, the caliph's court was the center of a complex web of interrelated seductions—economic, cultural, religious, and sexual—which drew Christians away from their faith. When Pelagius strips himself of the fine gown in which he had been dressed, his nakedness in the midst of the court's garish luxury marks his refusal to participate in the pleasures of the caliph's court and, more generally, the dominant Islamic culture of al-Andalus.

After Pelagius's death, his cult spread from Córdoba to his native Galicia and beyond. A liturgical office for St. Pelagius appeared in León before 970. At around the same time, his remains were moved from Córdoba to León. Pelagius became a popular patron for religious communities in the Christian kingdoms. His fame even reached as far as Saxony, where the Hrosvit of Gandersheim wrote a metrical *Life of St. Pelagius*. Raguel's narrative ends with the request that Pelagius become the patron and advocate of religious communities. While Raguel remains an obscure figure, his work seems to have served the purpose he intended. His account of Pelagius's martyrdom fueled enthusiasm for the saint's cult and inspired religious communities to adopt Pelagius as their advocate.

Sources and Further Reading

The text of *The Martyrdom of St. Pelagius* (*Bibliotheca hagiographica latina*, no. 6617) has been most recently edited and translated into Spanish by Celso Rogríguez Fernández: *La Pasión de S. Pelayo: Edición crítica, con traducción y comentarios*, Monografías da Universidade de Santiago de Compostela 160 (Santiago de Compostela, 1991). The following translation is based on that edition. A thorough discussion of the texts can be found in Manuel C. Díaz y Díaz, "La Pasión de S. Pelayo y su difusión," *Anuario de estudios medievales* 6 (1969): 97–116. For overviews of the history of the Iberian peninsula in the early Middle Ages, see Joseph O'Callaghan, *A History of Medieval Spain* (Ithaca, NY, and London, 1975); Roger Collins, *Early Medieval Spain: Unity in Diversity, 400–1000* (New York, 1983); and Thomas Glick, *Islamic and Christian Spain in the Early Middle Ages* (Princeton, 1979). Older, though still valuable for an understanding of Córdoba in the tenth century, is Evariste Lévi-Provençal, *L'Espagne musulmane aux X siècle* (Paris, 1932). Mark Jordan devotes the first chapter of *The Invention of Sodomy in Christian Theology* (Chicago, 1997) to an examination of the permutations in Pelagius's story during the tenth century. He discusses Raguel's narrative, Hrosvit's poem, and liturgical references, focusing on how these sources portray same-sex desire. John Boswell discusses the accusations of sexual misconduct which were often aimed at Muslims in *Christianity, Social Tolerance, and Homosexuality* (Chicago, 1981). The ninth-century Cordoban martyrs have attracted a great deal of scholarly attention, see Kenneth Baxter Wolf, *Christian Martyrs in Muslim Spain* (Cambridge, 1988) and Jessica Coope, *The Martyrs of Córdoba: Community and Family Conflict in an Age of Mass Conversion* (Lincoln, NE, 1995).

Raguel, The Martyrdom of St. Pelagius

The Life and Passion of St. Pelagius, Martyr, who suffered in the city of Córdoba under Abd al-Rahmann on the 26th of June.

Every written work corresponds to some clear model. A written narrative should have a carefully chosen beginning, since it is especially from such a beginning that a favorable attitude develops toward whatever follows. In this way, endings will not be out of tune with beginnings. Whatever is chosen as the motive at the beginning of the work should be the same at the end. Although our text hopes to present the martyrdom of its most faithful witness, it is nevertheless not disconnected from beginnings, since Christians were threatened with torture. Therefore, we should pray to the Lord that, in speaking to us, he grant us a beginning to the story such that when the work is completed there should be absolutely no discrepancy. In this way, he who remains inwardly the mover of our conscience should sound outwardly in our tongue.

In those times when the most savage trials affected the Christians, their enemies from Hispania moved against Galicia.[1] If Galicia were entirely overthrown, these outsiders would have wielded power over all the faithful. But divine help, restraining the unwarranted boldness of those coming against the Christians, did not abandon them completely. When these enemies arrived, the army of Christians charged against them and both parties came together in battle.

It is customary for the king of the faithful to bring his bishops with him on campaign. Because of this, after the battle had begun and the people of God turned in flight, even these bishops were taken as prisoners along with other faithful. Among these, one named Ermogius, who was bound in irons with the others, remained locked up in a prison in Córdoba.[2] Later, because divine influence gives different signs to each of those whom the Almighty God calls to the celestial kingdom, Bishop Ermogius, exhausted by the cramped prison and the weighty chains, offered his nephew Pelagius as a hostage for himself, hoping that he would later be able to send prisoners to redeem his nephew.

The customary gifts of God truly made themselves known. They inspired Pelagius so much that he accepted prison as a test or file for those daily sins without which human weakness cannot live. In this way prison would lead him to the absolution of those sins committed earlier, when he was unable to lead his life in the world without giving in to temptations. Indeed, one is in a poor position to please God when one wants to claim for oneself all that is God's. For this reason the Lord said that the path to life is narrow, while the path which leads to perdition is wide and ample [see Mt 7:13–14]. Truly, the more it is pleasant to fall into hell through prosperity, the more it is fitting that one should reach sublime heights through trials and tribulations. In death one resembles the Lord, and from this one reaps the great benefit of joining the host of angels.

The most holy Pelagius, divinely inspired by these lessons, as his actions show, lived prudently in prison, where he was firmly shut away at the age of ten. Neither his friends nor fame remain silent about how he conducted himself there. He was chaste, sober, gentle, and meek. He was vigilant in prayers, constant in reading, not unmindful of the Lord's commands, taking part in good conversations, free from sins, and slow to smile, for he had read Paul as his constant master of doctrine. He was quick to prayer. He shared in the sufferings of others and did not fail in difficulties. Because of this, he was skillful in reading and expert in doctrine. This same teaching stood out clearly in his normal conversation no less so than in the responses he strove to make when some chattering person outside the faith by chance accosted him.

Enriched both by his virginity and by the crown of his suffering, he bore a double victory against the enemy. Scorning riches and not giving way to vices, he would be crowned by the Lord because of his contempt for those things in which the devil rejoices greatly. A double reward went to him who vanquished the loathsome enemy and his servants. Truly, holy Pelagius steadily kept his promises and remained worthy of praise by not giving in to vices. To whatever extent this old foe tried to snare Pelagius—sometimes secretly, sometimes openly—with wicked schemes, he became wretched through his own evil. That is, through God's will he was tossed to his feet, *for he is a liar and the father of it* [Jn 8:44].

One day, after Pelagius had been accomplishing such feats for three and a half years, some enterprising henchmen of a young recruit of the king's were in the prison. They described the beauty and charm of the blessed Pelagius's features to their master. It was not without reason that he appeared outwardly beautiful, since he had been made still more beautiful within by Lord Jesus Christ. These foolish and ignorant men thought they would conceal his true form with their torrents of raging vices, even though our Lord had promised Pelagius that he would stand at His right among the choirs of holy virgins. These wretches did not understand that they could not oppose the mercy of the Lord, for they *can not ever make even a single hair either light or dark* [Mt 5:36].

When this report reached the king's ears, it pleased him greatly (although not rightly) that Pelagius, the servant of God, appeared beautiful even amid the rigors of prison. In the middle of a banquet, he sent some of his servants to make him who would be a victim for Christ appear in his presence so that he might gaze at him. Since all things remain possible to the almighty God, these men, making orders deeds, quickly seized the servant of God Pelagius in chains, so that they might stride into the king's palace, cut off the rattling pile of chains and, in spiritual blindness, joyfully offer to a mortal king one whose soul Christ Himself had already betrothed to His own in inseparable faith. They presented him before the king's gaze in a royal robe, murmuring in the ears of the most holy boy that his beauty had raised him to this great position.

The king spoke to him immediately: "Boy, I will raise you up to the honors of a high office, if you are willing to deny Christ and to say that our

Prophet is true. Don't you see how great and how many are my realms? Moreover, I shall give you a great deal of gold and silver, fine clothing, and costly baubles. You will also take whichever of these young knights you should choose to serve you according to your tastes. I will give you companions to live with, horses to ride, and luxuries to savor. Then, I will release from prison whomever you choose. If you wish, I will bring members of your family here and confer great honors upon them."

Holy Pelagius, seeing all of this and knowing it to be ridiculous, said: "The things that you show me, king, are nothing. I will not deny Christ. I am a Christian. I have been a Christian and will always be a Christian. All things have an end and pass in their own time [see Eccles 3:1]. But Christ, whom I cherish, can have no end because he has no beginning. For he is, along with the Father and the Holy Spirit, the one true God, who made us from nothing and who holds everything in his power."

Then, when the king tried to caress him playfully,[4] holy Pelagius said, "Get back, you dog! Do you think that I am effeminate like yourselves?" Pelagius ripped off the robes in which he had been dressed and made himself like a bold athlete in the arena, choosing to die honorably for Christ rather than to live shamefully with the devil and to be defiled by his vices. The king, still thinking that he could persuade him, instructed his attendants to seduce him with pandering speeches, so that he might apostatize and submit to his royal vanities. But Pelagius, with the help of God, stood strong and remained undaunted, professing only Christ and saying that he would always obey his commands alone.

The king, seeing this passionate spirit resisting him and recognizing that he was thwarted in his desires, was moved to rage. "Hang him up high with iron tongs," he said, "and then drop him down again and again until he gives up the ghost or denies that Christ is God." Unafraid, the blessed Pelagius, who had never refused to suffer for Christ, endured the test with an unshakable spirit. When the king saw his constant perseverance, he ordered him to be cut into pieces with a sword and thrown into the river. Having received this order, the torturers raged like the Bacchae. They embarked on such savage derisions of Pelagius that it was as if they were unknowingly offering the sacrifice that was necessary in the presence of Our Lord Jesus Christ.

He was chosen in heaven, and for this he suffered intensely on earth. One of the torturers chopped off his arm at its base, another cut off his legs, and a third struck his neck. Meanwhile the intrepid martyr remained standing, blood, rather than sweat, flowing drop by drop from his body [see Lk 22:44], calling only on his Lord Jesus Christ, for whom he did not refuse to suffer, saying: *Lord, deliver me from the hand of my enemies* [Ps 30/31:15]. Truly divine power did not forsake him, making him a confessor in his trials and, under the point of the sword, a glorious martyr in heaven. The hands which he had raised to God, they wickedly cut off with a sword. Then the most blessed Pelagius gasped, exhausted. Because not a single person there took pity on him, he called on the Lord alone. The strong athlete cried out, but the

Lord was already present as a principal in this struggle, saying: "Come. Take the crown which I promised you from the beginning." [see 1 Cor 9: 25] Then his spirit departed to God, while his body was tossed into the river.

Even so, there were still some faithful who sought his body and bore it solemnly to a sepulcher. The cemetery of Saint Cyprian now holds his head, while the field of Saint Genesius has his body. What a martyr truly worthy of God, who began his suffering at the seventh hour and fulfilled it the late afternoon of the same day! Who will ever be able to do justice to this gift in speech? From the squalor of prison, he was restored to the glory of heaven. Because of his worldly sufferings, he deserved heavenly rewards. For the nation which he left, he possessed the paradise that he desired. Truly, he abandoned his relatives and brothers, but now he has angels as companions. The divine word says, *everyone who leaves father, mother, etcetera, in my name, shall receive a hundredfold and will possess eternal life* [Mt 19:29]. He who endured the sword in his limbs now has the kingdom of heaven.

Most holy witness Pelagius, in the midst of threats and temptations you confessed Christ. You did not give in to flatteries, choosing to die for truth rather than to live in this world and lack justice. He whom Christ had already among his chosen did not submit to the promises of the condemned. Therefore, holy martyr, we ask that you defend and cherish without rest the Church which you see honors you with prayers and offerings, so that it will have you, raised in Galicia but glorified through martyr's blood in Córdoba, as an advocate before God. The most holy Pelagius, at roughly the age of thirteen and a half years, suffered martyrdom in the city of Córdoba, as it is said, during the reign of Abd al-Rahmann, certainly on a Sunday, at the tenth hour, the twenty-sixth of June, in the era 964 of our Lord Jesus Christ,[5] who lives and reigns with God the Father in unity with the Holy Spirit, one God in the Trinity for ever and ever. Amen.

Notes

1. The inhabitants of the northern Christian kingdoms, and of Latin Europe more generally, referred to the southern, Muslim-ruled, part of the Iberian peninsula as "Hispania." The modern English word "Spain," is an obvious cognate. It would, however, be inaccurate to translate "Hispania" as "Spain," since the former refers only to that part of the peninsula under Muslim rule. Galicia, Pelagius's native province in the northwestern corner of the peninsula, is part of modern Spain, but would not have been considered part of Hispania.

2. Ermogius was the bishop of Tuy in Galicia. In addition to being mentioned here by Raguel, his name appears in a number of contemporary documents. After Pelagius's death, his cult enjoyed great popularity around Tuy.

3. This is a complicated sentence. Raguel understands Pelagius's bodily perfection as an apt reflection of having been chosen as Christ's spouse. Pelagius's beauty shows that he is betrothed to Christ, and that Pelagius and Christ would celebrate their union in Pelagius's martyrdom. The obvious contrast with Pelagius's beautiful "habit" or "vessel" is the splendid robe which Pelagius wears before the caliph and which he eventually rips off as he rejects the caliph's offers. Raguel wants the reader to find the caliph's advances particularly repugnant since Pelagius is betrothed to Christ. The embraces of Christ, for which Pelagius is predestined, stand in contrast to the embraces of the caliph, which he rejects.

4. This passage in difficult to translate. In Latin the caliph's action is described as *tangere ioculariter*. A literal translation of this might be something like, "to touch playfully." Pelagius's response, however, suggests that he understood the caliph's touch as not "playful," but, as quite serious and, most likely, sexual. *Ioculariter* could have figurative meanings related to sexual intercourse. See Mark Jordan, *The Invention of Sodomy in Christian Theology* (Chicago, 1997), pp. 12–13.

5. Dating systems varied considerably in medieval Europe. Christians in Spain often used a dating system which identified years according to an "era." Designations of year by era varied by thirty-eight years from those calculated *Anno Domini* (or "in the year of the Lord"), the system more widely used in Latin Christendom. The "era 964" thus corresponds to the year 925 or, possibly, 926 according to modern usage.

Chapter 11
Hrotsvit of Gandersheim, *The Establishment of the Monastery of Gandersheim*

Originally translated by Mary Bernadine Bregman and edited by Thomas Head

INTRODUCTION

Hrotsvit of Gandersheim (ca. 935-ca. 1001/1003) is the only female author included in this collection and one of only a handful of women who are known certainly to have composed hagiographic works in the Middle Ages. (A large amount of medieval hagiography, including a number of works included in this collection, remain anonymous, and some of those unknown authors were surely women.) Hrotsvit was a very accomplished poet who composed works of hagiography, drama, and history during the 960s and 970s. Her monastery of Gandersheim was located in the duchy of Saxony and she wrote in the very decades during which the members of the Ottonian dynasty—themselves Saxon in origin—were creating an empire (later known as the Holy Roman Empire) from what had been the eastern Frankish kingdom of the Carolingian Empire. The foundation and construction of Gandersheim was the work of the direct ancestors of Emperors Otto I and Otto II, during whose reigns Hrotsvit composed her poems. It was Otto I's great-grandparents—a Saxon nobleman named Liudolf and, even more importantly, his wife, Oda—who first undertook the establishment of a convent at Gandersheim in the 840s. The community, however, did not fully come into being until 856 and its church was not consecrated until 881. The founders' eldest daughter, Hathumoda, became the first abbess at Gandersheim (856–74), followed by her sisters Gerberga (874–96) and Christina (896–919). It was around 959 that Gerberga II became abbess of Gandersheim. This Gerberga was a niece of Emperor Otto I (936–73), and thus related by marriage to Otto's second wife, Adelheid (whose *Life* by Odilo of Cluny is translated by David Warner in the following chapter), and thus also a great-great-grand-niece of Liudolf and Oda. Hrostvit, who herself came from a noble family, was probably already a member of the community, but it was under the rule of Gerberga II that she received most of her education and composed her extant poetry, including her story of the foundation of Gandersheim. As the presence of Gerberga II as abbess suggests, the imperial family still retained

237

strong ties to Gandershein in the time of Hrotsvit and long thereafter. Hrotsvit compressed some eighty years of complicated history—from the very inception of the desire to create a community of nuns at Gandersheim to the death of Abbess Christina—into the relatively brief narrative translated below.

Hrotsvit's name was indicative of her character. She proudly referred to herself in the preface of one of her works as *clamor validus Gandeshemensis*, that is, "the strong voice of Gandersheim." That phrase is simply a rendering into Latin of her name, which is a combination of the Old Saxon (the vernacular language spoken in that region) words *hruot* (*clamor* in Latin) and *sui*[n]*d* (*validus* in Latin). (That name has in turn been rendered into modern languages in a confusing number of variants including Hrosvita, Hrotswitha, Roswitha, and Rotsuith). The learning which Hrotsvit imbibed through her schooling at Gandersheim was rich and diversified. In addition to a thorough grounding in the liberal arts, she appears to have been familiar with much classical poetry, including Vergil's *Aeneid* and *Eclogues*, Ovid's *Metamorphoses*, and Terence's comedies. She also had read widely among Christian writers such as Prudentius (along with Terence her most important model), Sedulius Scottus, Venantius Fortunatus, and Boethius. Her works (all of them in poetry, despite the prose of the translation provided here) are usually grouped into three books: the first consisting of eight legends about saints; the second including six dramas followed by a poem of thirty-five lines on a "Vision of St. John"; and finally a pair of historical works, the *Gesta Ottonis*, (or *Deeds of the Emperor Otto I*) and the *Primordia coenobii Gandeshemensis* (or *Establishment of the Monastery of Gandersheim*). On the basis of these works, Hrotsvit has generally been deemed the most learned woman of the tenth century. One must remember, however, that her works survive largely because of a single manuscript. Her level of literary attainment coupled with the scanty dissemination of her works in the Middle Ages might argue that there were other equally learned female writers of this period, whose works have been lost or, consigned to anonymity, have been assigned to male authors.

Hrotsvit is best known as a hagiographer for the works about saints included among her legends and plays. According to certain strict definitions of genre, *The Establishment of the Monastery of Gandersheim* is more properly a work of history than of hagiography. It is, however, a work which well illustrates many of the connections between monasticism and the cult of saints. In it, Hrotsvit told the story of a group of three holy women who had ruled her community as abbesses. From a separate *Life* written by Agius of Corvey in the ninth century, it is known that at least one of them, Hathumoda, was posthumously celebrated as a saint. It would also be possible to read this entire work as a kind of argument for the sanctity of Oda, the remarkable wife of Liudolf of Saxony who according to Hrotsvit lived to the age of one hundred and seven and carefully oversaw the administration of Gandersheim for over six decades. Under her close care and supervision, the nuns of Gandersheim served as the spiritual guardians of the memory of Liudolf and Oda's clan, mourning the dead (as spectacularly happens in the case of Duke Otto) and praying for their memory.

The community of Gandersheim and the Liudolfing clan were thus in an important sense inseparable. While Hrotsvit explicitly told the story of the development of her own convent, she also implicitly told the story of the rise of the Liudolfings first to the position of dukes in Saxony and then to the rank of king and emperor over Germany. In order for the reader to understand the explicit level of Hrotsvit's story, it is important to review the history of the eastern Frankish realm which provides its implicit context. That context is further specified in the notes to the translated text.

The earliest member of the clan who founded Gandersheim known—either to Hrotsvit herself or to later historians—was a Saxon nobleman named Liudolf. The Saxons were themselves a German tribe who remained polytheists and unassimilated into Christian Europe until well into the eighth century. They regularly raided the neighboring kingdoms of the Franks, a Germanic tribe who had converted to Christianity in the early sixth century. Charles I, "the Great" (better known by the French equivalent of his name, that is Charlemagne), king of the Franks conquered the Saxons during several bitter campaigns in the 780s and forced them to convert to Christianity. Charles (a member of a royal dynasty called the "Carolingians," from "Carolus" the Latin word for "Charles") expanded the rule of the Franks over many other neighboring kingdoms. In 800, based largely on these military exploits, he claimed the title of western Roman emperor, a title which had not been in use for several centuries. His descendants ruled the empire created by Charles quite effectively for two generations. The empire remained unified under the rule of Charles's sole surviving son, Louis I, "the Pious" (d. 840). Louis divided his inheritance among his three surviving sons: Lothar (given the middle kingdom), Louis the German (given the eastern, or German kingdom), and Charles the Bald (given the western, or French kingdom). It is under the kingship of Louis the German—who is the Louis described by Hrotsvit below—that Liudolf came to have control over the Saxons and their lands (known simply as Saxony). Liudolf himself probably never used the official title *dux*, that is duke or literally the "leading man," of this people, but his sons certainly did and Hrotsvit, from over a century's distance, implicitly and explicitly applied this title to him. Liudolf died in 866 and was succeeded in turn by his sons Bruno (d. 880) and Otto (d. 912). When Duke Otto of Saxony died in 912, he was succeeded by his son Henry (d. 936). By this time, the last Carolingian claimant to the east Frankish, or German, throne had died and been replaced through election by one of the dukes of the kingdom, Conrad of Franconia. When King Conrad died in 919, Henry of Saxony (grandson of Liudolf and Oda) was elected in his place. At this time, the family held the duchy of Saxony, but not the royal title, by hereditary right. The family came to control the kingdom so thoroughly that Henry's son, Otto, was elected as his successor. Through the long and strong reign of Otto I—also known as "the Great"—this family came to be seen as the hereditary kings of Germany. They also laid claim to the title of emperor. This Otto is referred to as "the first" because he was the first member of the family to reign as king, rather than duke. Thus within a century this clan had increased their status from merely being one noble family among the Saxons, to being the leading family among the Saxons by hereditary right, to being the royal family of Germany, to replacing the Carolingians as the western imperial dynasty.

Under the Ottonians, certain female monastic communities, including Gandersheim, played an important role in the religious and cultural life of the kingdom. The importance of women within Ottonian politics and religion can also be glimpsed in the following chapter, Odilo of Cluny's *Epitaph* for the Ottonian empress Adelheid. Hrotsvit's literary creations carefully combine classical models with Christian content. They were made possible by the political culture of Ottonian Germany, where a conscious rebirth of Roman imperial power occurred in a society within which women participated in the responsibility of keeping alive the memory of the past.

SOURCES AND FURTHER READING

The basis for the following translation of the *Primordia coenobii Gandeshemensis* —which for the sake of simplicity renders Hrotsvit's technically fine poetry into what necessarily becomes rather flat and repetitive prose—is that of Sr. Mary Bernadine Bregman from her *Hrosvitae Liber tertius: A Text, with Translation and Commentary* (St. Louis, 1942). The volume is the published version of her Saint Louis University doctoral dissertation and is somewhat difficult to obtain. I have modernized, corrected, and annotated Bregman's translation with reference to the now standard edition of Hrotsvit's works: *Hrotsvithae Opera, mit Einleitungen und Kommentar*, ed. Helena Homeyer (Munich, 1970). Among other changes, I have specifically altered the paragraphs of the following translation to fit the divisions of the Homeyer edition. The corpus of her works is primarily known from a manuscript known as the Emmeran-Munich Codex (now Munich, Bayerische Staatsbibliothek, MS Clm 14485) which was copied ca. 1000. The *Primordia* is the only work not included in the present state of the codex, although Hans Götting (see below) has persuasively suggested that a copy of the *Primordia* was removed from that codex to serve as evidence in a legal dispute during the eleventh or twelfth century. Thus all editions of the *Primordia* are in essence reconstructions, based on early modern manuscript and printed copies.

While there is as yet no single scholarly monograph that provides a comprehensive analysis of Hrotsvit's writings, the essays collected in *Hrotsvit of Gandersheim: Rara avis in Saxonia?* ed. Katherina Wilson, Medieval and Renaissance Monograph Series 7 (Ann Arbor, MI, 1987), treat many aspects of her works and their reception. Peter Dronke offers a brilliant introduction in *Women Writers of the Middle Ages: A Critical Study of Texts from Perpetua (d. 203) to Marguerite Porete (d. 1310)* (Cambridge, 1984), pp. 55–83.

See also Katharina Wilson, *Hrotsvit of Gandersheim: the Ethics of Authorial Stance* (Leiden, 1987). The fullest treatment of the complex textual history of the *Primordia* and of the controversy which probably provided Hrotsvit's motivation for composing it, remains Hans Götting, "Das Überlieferungsschicksalvon Hrotsvits *Primordia*," in *Festschrift für Hermann Heimpel zum 70. Geburtsag am 19. September 1971*, 3 vols. (Göttingen, 1972), 3:60–108. For a comparison of this work to other accounts of the foundations of monastic communities, see Thomas Head, "Hrotsvit's *Primordia* and the Historical Traditions of Monastic Communities," in *Hrotsvit of Gandersheim: Rara avis in Saxonia?* pp. 143–55.

All of Hrotsvit's works are available in English translation. Bregman's work remains the only complete translation of Hrotsvit's historical works. The only complete translation of Hrotsvit's hagiographic legends similarly remains a published doctoral dissertation from Saint Louis University: *The Non-Dramatic Works of Hrosvitha: Text, Translation, and Commentary*, ed. and trans. Sister M. Gonsalva Wiegand (St. Louis, 1936). The dramas of Hrotsvit, on the other hand, have appeared in several English translations, the best and most recent being *The Plays of Hrotsvit of Gandersheim*, trans. Katharina Wilson (New York, 1989). Selections from all three groups of works may be found in *Medieval Women Writers*, ed. Katharina Wilson (Athens, GA, 1984), pp. 30–63 and *Hrotsvit of Gandersheim: A Florilegium of Her Works*, ed. and trans. Katharina Wilson (Woodbridge, Suffolk, 1998). For comparative purposes, in addition to Hrotsvit's other works, one might consult hagiographic works known to have been written by female authors during the earlier periods: Baudinovia's *Life of St. Radegund* in *Sainted Women of the Dark Ages*, ed. and trans. Jo Ann McNamara and John Halborg, with E. Gordon Whatley, (Durham, NC, 1992), pp. 86–105, and Hugeburc of Heidenheim's *Hodoeporicon of St. Willibald* in *Soldiers of Christ: Saints' Lives from Late Antiquity and the Early Middle Ages*, ed. Thomas Noble and Thomas Head (University Park, PA, 1994), pp. 141–64. Unfortunately Agius of Corvey's *Life of St. Hathumoda* (*Bibliotheca hagiographica latina*, no. 3763) has never been translated into English.

On the politics of this period, one can consult in English: Karl Leyser, *Rule and Conflict in an Early Medieval Society: Ottonian Saxony* (Oxford, 1979); Rosamond McKitterick, *The Frankish Kingdoms Under the Carolingians, 751–987* (London, 1983); Timothy Reuter, *Germany in the Early Middle Ages 800–1056* (London, 1991). Julia Smith has studied hagiography written about and by women in the period immediately before that of Hrotsvit (including Agius of Corvey's *Life of St. Hathumoda*) in "The Problem of Female Sanctity in Carolingian Europe c.780–920," *Past and Present* 146 (1995): 3–37. The most important study of hagiography written about women in the Ottonian Empire, however, remains Patrick Corbet, *Les saints Ottoniens. Sainteté dynastique, sainteté royale et sainteté féminine autour de l'an mil*, Beihefte der Francia 15 (Sigmaringen, 1986). Using in part Corbet's study, Patrick Geary has presented a compelling picture of the ways in which the female monastic communities of the Ottonian Empire, such as Gandersheim, mourned and memorialized the dead through their prayers in *Phantoms of Remembrance: Memory and Oblivion at the End of the First Millennium* (Princeton, 1994), pp. 48–80, although he does not explicitly discuss Hrotsvit's *Primordia*.

Hrotsvit of Gandersheim, The Establishment of the Monastery of Gandersheim

>Behold, the suppliant devotion of my humble mind ardently longs to recount the establishment of the blessed monastery of Gandersheim, which was erected with unstinting care by the leading men [*duces*] and lawful potentates [*iure potentes*] of the Saxons, that is the great and illustrious Liudolf as well as his son, Otto, who brought to completion the commemorative work which had already been begun.[1]
>
>Due order in this account now demands that the earlier erection of our renowned monastery of Gandersheim be recounted in a fitting poem.[2] For it is agreed that this Liudolf, leader [*dux*] of the Saxons, whom I previously mentioned, reverently built it. Born of very noble lineage and equaling his birth in the exemplary ways of his own virtue, he grew in distinction among all the Saxons. For he was of splendid physique and exceedingly handsome in appearance, skilled in speech, and careful in all his actions: the sole hope and the whole splendor of his race. From almost his earliest years, he was enlisted in the military service of the great Louis, king of the Franks,[3] and was elevated by him to distinguished honors. Soon he received the leadership over the march (*comitatus*) of the Saxon people; steadily he was granted the profits of greater jurisdiction, becoming equal to the men of first rank (*principes*) and not inferior to dukes (*duces*).[4] And as he surpassed all his ancestors in holiness, no less did he outshine them in magnificence of his honored rank.
>
>His wife, the distinguished Oda, was descended from a famous line of the mighty Franks, the daughter of Billung, a kindly ruler, and of Aeda, a lady reputed to be good and generous.[5] Now this Aeda was frequently accustomed to resign herself and her whole life to the Lord in prayer. Through the frequent and painstaking care of her pious actions, she merited—being well-versed in heavenly promises—to learn through the revelation of [John] the Holy Baptist of Christ, the fact that her progeny would at some time in future ages achieve the luster of imperial authority.
>
>Once, when dawn was piercing the nocturnal darkness with the brilliancy of its ruddy shafts, she lay prostrate in her accustomed fashion before the holy altar dedicated to the honor of St. John the Baptist, assailing with prayer the deep recesses of heaven. And when she had poured out her soul in these fervent devotions, she saw, as she lay prone there, the feet of a man standing close beside her. Greatly perturbed, she pondered deeply in her heart as to who this man could be who had presumed to disturb her seclusion in this hour so well suited for prayer. And raising her face from the ground and turning it a little, she saw a youth resplendent with wondrous beauty, robed in a mantle [the color] of yellow hair, as if clothed with the hair of a camel.[6] On his wondrously bright and beautiful face, a small beard harmonized in color with his black hair which afforded a crown of resplendent radiance. The matron, seeing him and not believing that he could be mortal, was dumbfounded and following the way of women fainted away under the sudden compulsion of

great terror. But he allayed her fear with kindly address and said, "Do not be afraid, nor be distressed and terrified; but put aside the weight of your fears and learn who I am. I come to you bringing great consolation. For I am John, who was deemed worthy to baptize Christ with the flowing waters. Since you have frequently venerated me, I announce that your famous descendent will establish a cloister for holy virgins and a triumphant peace for his realm, provided his piety remains duly steadfast. Hence, your posterity at some time in future ages will come to such a pinnacle of fame that no sovereign among earthly rulers will try to rival them in lawful power." And when he had said this he immediately withdrew into heaven, leaving tender solace in the heart of the benevolent lady. The grand promise of this magnificent honor singled out the famed offspring of Lady Oda: for it was her son, the illustrious Duke Otto, who begot King Henry, a monarch so well suited to rule. [Henry] was the father of the revered and august Otto, who, supported by the strength of the Eternal King, after assuming the rule of the Saxons in his father's place, had—under the benign blessing of the will of God—worthily succeeded to the same throne of the Roman Empire and the administration of imperial power, [and later] caused his son (who bore the same name and was his equal), under the disposing goodness of the Eternal King, to mount the same throne of empire and to enjoy a like splendor of dominion.[7] The pages of a modest book which we have written regarding these matters describes them more fully.[8]

Now our zealous pen must be turned to the accomplishment of the task dutifully begun. When the venerable Oda had been united in lawful wedlock to Liudolf, her lord, she tread the path of holiness and exceeded all the people of our country in reputation for both her bearing and her actions. And living in accordance with the example of her venerable mother, she commended herself entirely to the Lord in fervent prayer, retaining in her heart the admonition of her mother to build a convent. For she frequently in loving and persuasive speech urged her lawful lord to erect a monastery suitable for divine praises of God, using the wealth of their own treasures, so that in it chaste girls consecrated to the Lord by the holy veil could dwell and be free for the service of their divine Spouse. Her faithful husband, then, yielding to these counsels, duly complied with the petitions of his chosen spouse. Thus by the joint endeavor of like purpose, they both began to serve God.

[Liudolf and Oda] held possession of a small church situated across the banks of the Ganda River on a mountain; hence they named the renowned place Gandersheim. There worthily paying homage to the Lord until a place better suited could be found, they united many girls in community life, and they decreed that their own daughter, Hathumoda, would be like them in habit and their lifelong companion. And in order that she could be the first superior of the convent of young maidens, they first reverently handed her over for instruction to a certain holy abbess, who, succeeding in turn to prior prelates, had been elected abbess of Herford.[9] With such effort, Liudolf and his eminent wife planned their service to God.

After this, upon receiving the written approvals their superior—namely, the kind and pious King Louis [the German]—with his permission and a considerable retinue they proceeded to Rome and approached the throne of the Holy Father.[10] With worthy offerings and kindly entreaties they urged that with his support they would be able fulfill their vows in accordance with the will of God. Now at this time the blessed Pope Sergius held the primacy of the Church.[11] When he had perused the letter the king had sent to him, he realized that a leader (*dux*) worthy of the highest honors was coming to his abode. And after inquiring the reason for [Liudolf's] coming, [Sergius] presented himself with kindly address to his visitor. Showing the reverence worthy to the supreme pontiff, Duke Liudolf, prostrate with his wife, directed words of supplication mingling them with all tenderness: "Esteemed father, do not be austere to us, your guests from afar, who have come from the remote corners of the earth to pay homage to you with the gifts of our fealty. With all the energy of zealous hearts, we are striving to found a monastery devoted to the service of God. Therefore, indeed, it seemed especially fitting to seek your advice and by due entreaty to profess our zeal to you, who, as the head of the Church, has dominion throughout the whole world. Thus, if our devotion should happen to please you, we shall, with whatever help your paternal piety provides, quickly bring to completion in deed that which we are urging in our prayers. May you, whose counsel we rightly seek, receiving with compassionate heart our offerings and responding to the love of the eternal King, grant us sacred relics of saints, to whose honor the whole monastery may be fittingly dedicated and by whose blessed merits [it may be] protected. And that it may be free from the yoke of mighty rulers of this world and may not suffer from the power of earthly lords, we grant it to the authority of the apostolic ruler alone for protection and likewise for government." Thus the duke spoke. Sergius, the supreme bishop, replied as follows: "Son, I embrace you with a kindly heart, and I embrace as well your spouse, who is equally worthy of affection, and in happiness I rejoice at your holy zeal, and I believe it wrong to refuse your petitions. Here at one time there were two mighty shepherds, Anastasius, the most holy bishop of this throne, and his fellow apostle, the sacred Innocent.[12] They were conspicuous for their preeminent services to the Church, second only to the shepherd Peter and the teacher Paul. Their bodies until now have been safeguarded with such zealous care by all the rulers of this city so that no one has taken the tiniest particle from them, and they remain completely intact. But in as much as I ought rightly to comply with your pious prayers, I shall freely give you relics of both of them, removed in your presence from their own bodies, if upon solemn oath, you assure me that these relics will be perpetually venerated in a chapel of the aforesaid monastery built through your munificence, with the chanting of sacred hymns there night and day and with the constant illumination of a bright lighted taper. This monastery we consign, as you have requested, to the control of our apostolic authority, that it may be secure from the domination of earthly sovereigns." The duke, joyous in heart at these venerable promises, affirmed that he would soon comply with zealous acts, that he might be worthy of soon completing the holy structure.[13]

As the many who know would tell you, there was at that time a small forest near the monastery surrounded by shady hills, the very ones by which we are ourselves now surrounded. In the forest, moreover, there was small farm (*villa*) in which the swineherds of Liudolf were accustomed to finding shelter and in the enclosure of which the men rested their wearied limbs for the hours of night during their duty of caring for the pigs entrusted to them. Here, on one occasion when the holy feast of All Saints was to be celebrated two days later, these very swineherds saw in the forest many lights gleaming brightly in the darkness of the night. All were astounded by what they saw and wondered what was signified by this strange spectacle of the resplendent light, piercing the darkness of night with amazing brilliance. Alarmed they related to the father of the house what had occurred, pointing out the very place that the brightness had illuminated.[14] As he wished to verify what he had heard with his own eyes, he joined them out of doors and began to keep vigil upon the following night. He did not close his eyes, even though they were heavy with sleep, until [the swineherds] again saw the glowing lights—which even surpassed in number the earlier ones—in the very same place, although at an earlier hour than previously. As Phoebus [the sun] diffused his first rays from heaven's ether, it became known, as the happy rumor spread to everyone. It could not remain concealed from the worthy Liudolf, but came to his ears more quickly than one could say. [Liudolf] himself, on the holy vigil of the feast,[15] noting carefully whether the vision would thereafter reveal any manifest sign from heaven, watched with many companions the very same forest during the whole night. Nor did he have long to wait, for when night had shrouded the earth with dark shadows, everywhere within the circuit of the forested valley in which the renowned church was to be established, numerous lights were seen in orderly array. They sliced through the leafy shades and nocturnal darkness with the dazzling radiance of their gleaming splendor. Thereupon at once, all those who were present gave thanks to the Lord and asserted that the place must be dedicated to the service of Him who had filled it with light. Accordingly the duke, grateful for the kindness of heaven, and with the approval of his beloved wife, Oda, gave orders that the valley should be entirely cleared, and that its trees should be cut down and its underbrush removed. He cleansed the wooded spot, filled with Faunus and monsters, so that it was appropriate for the divine praises.[16] Then, using the funds which he had already set aside for the work, he straightway built the walls of the beautiful church [on the spot?] which the radiance of the glowing lights had indicated.[17] For this reason, therefore, the construction of our monastery was begun under God's patronage. Meanwhile, stones suitable for building were not able to be obtained in this region; a delay therefore ensued in the completion of the church. But the Abbess Hathumoda, hoping that those who believe can obtain through faith all things from the Lord, wearied herself with continuous and unstinting labor, serving God night and day with holy ardor. Many of her community joined her, while she begged that the solace of heavenly assistance would be granted in order that the work so well begun might not remain unfinished. Nor was it long before she perceived that the heavenly support that she was seeking was at hand, quick to take pity on her requests. She gave herself over to fasting and holy prayers when, one day as she lay prostrate before the altar, a pleasing voice ordered her to rise and follow a bird which, at some length, she again saw perched on the pinnacle of a large rock. She, embracing [the omen] with an already eager spirit, set forth, trusting in her heart what the voice had commanded. Taking skilled stone cutters with her, she proceeded rapidly where the Holy Spirit had led, until she arrived at the site of the notable temple now begun. There she saw the white dove which had previously nestled on the lofty apex of the stone. Presently it spread its wings and led the way, slowing its flight in unaccustomed fashion, in order that the spouse of Christ, walking with her companions, might be able to follow, its aerial course in a direct path. And when the dove in its flight had come to that place which we now know is not barren of large stones, it descended and struck with it beak an elevated spot under which many stones lay concealed. After this sure indication the worthy virgin of Christ ordered her companions to clear the place and by digging to cut through the mass of earth. When this had been accomplished, through the kindness of divine generosity, a great abundance of large rocks was uncovered. From this source the walls of the monastery and church could derive their full supply of stone. From that time the builders of the church that was to be dedicated to the glory of the Lord applied themselves more and more wholeheartedly, night and day to the new work.

But Duke Liudolf—who was its founder and under whose care the commencement of the whole structure had progressed, in accord with the entreating prayers of Oda—was not able (for shame!) to bring the zealous work to completion, but, stricken by the harsh doom of our common mortality, he was compelled to render up his soul to his Maker, before the honored house of the Lord could be completed. At death he entrusted the whole weight and responsibility of the momentous undertaking to his dear surviving wife and to his sons, the leaders [*duces*] mentioned above, beseeching them with zealous prayers to complete the whole construction of the monastery which remained to be built. His revered remains were then duly entrusted to the bosom of earth in an ancient church; but after the passing of several years his bones were removed from there to be placed in the new church.[18] Perhaps God took [Liudolf] from this world when he had scarcely attained the warmth of middle age, in order that thereafter the heart of the eminent lady Oda would be intent upon God and, with no further thought of earthly love whatsoever, might be able to devote itself more fully to the things of God. Yet [God] did not refuse her consolation, but with accustomed divine kindness provided her fresh riches, so that with such support she might be able to enrich her nuns with all that our needs required.

Her daughter, named Liutgard, through the kindly will of the Eternal King, was chosen to be the queen and wife of the famed Louis, king of the Franks.[19] He was the son of that ruler by whose gift Liudolf had first established dominion over his own people. After [Liutgard] had became queen, much to our advantage, she granted great benefits to our monastery as a worthy service to her holy mother and with the consent of the king, her proper lord. Meanwhile, Hathumoda, the happy spouse of Christ after bearing the responsibilities of her flock for two times eleven years, died in Christ and immediately passed to heaven.[20] She entrusted to Gerberga the governance of the tender flock. Now Gerberga was betrothed to a distinguished and exceedingly influential man named Bernard, but she had secretly consecrated herself by means of the sacred veil to Christ, with an ardent love for her heavenly Spouse and a complete disdain of heart for any mortal lover.[21] Yet, because of her desire to avoid charges of disobedience, she was not at once able to lay aside the garments resplendent with gold, and she continued to attire herself in costly raiment. Meanwhile, Bernard, whom this bride of Christ had rejected, came, seeking to consummate the union, but he heard that she herself had made a vow expressing her intention to preserve untainted her maidenly chastity. Now when Gerberga delayed and was not willing immediately to join him, he began to be very much afraid that the story he had heard might prove to be true. And brooking no delay, he won over the lady Oda with entreaties, until she herself bade her daughter to go forth beautifully clad in costly apparel and with jeweled adornments such as brides are accustomed to wear. When Bernard saw the dear object of his ardent love, he is said to have chided her in these words: "Often have I heard, the product of sinister rumors, that you are striving to disrupt our agreement and to dissolve the oath that should be faithfully preserved. Now, by order of the king, our lord, I am compelled to hasten speedily to an impending war, thus there is now no time to undo your vow. If I return uninjured and in full health, rest assuredly that I will join myself to you and utterly put to naught your vain vow [of chastity]." These were his words and in heartfelt fury he raised his right hand and swore by his sword and by her white throat that, so far as in him lay, the words he had spoken would be fulfilled in deeds. Responding, Gerberga spoke in a modest voice, "I entrust myself and my whole life to Christ, and pray that it be done unto me according to the will of the Lord." When they had finished their conversation, Bernard immediately departed and quickly realized by his own fate that no man of pride can prevail against the Lord. Since he had stupidly exceeded what may be lawfully spoken, he fell in battle, the heavenly power prevailing over him. The virgin soon united herself to the love of Christ, her heavenly Spouse, whom she had always cherished with chaste affection.

In the sixth year of his reign, if I am not mistaken, Duke Bruno, quick to defend the holy Church from the inroads of the savage Hungarians, was, alas, along with two esteemed rulers and likewise with all the men of his forces, slain by these same vicious enemies of the Lord.[22] Shortly after his death, his younger brother Otto was made leader of the people by the gift of King Louis. By his deeds [Otto] responded to the prayers of his holy mother, and with zeal like hers he strove to beautify the new church with becoming elegance and it was consecrated two years later. [Otto], moreover, completed the wall of our monastery, suitable for the girls who would live there over the centuries.

When these matters had been satisfactorily completed according to the wishes of his mother, [Otto] chose, at the request of the lady Oda, the very same day for the dedication of the church, in the midst of whose night lights had in an earlier year gleamed brightly to be beheld by many for the third time and on which the feast of All Saints was also duly celebrated the length and breadth of the spacious earth, [that is] first day of the month of November. As the fame of the dedication of the church echoed far and wide, very large crowds, wishing to be at hand for that eventful day, soon flocked together from all directions. In thanksgiving for having received the blessed remains of our holy patrons, the whole community of our sisters, at the first bright streak of dawn, collectively went forth amid the chanting of hymns to the location of the monastery which had been erected with such extreme solicitude. Then at length, when all preparations for the celebration of the festival had been duly made, Wicbert, blessed bishop of the Lord, dedicated this magnificent church to the glory of God for endless praise through the ages of all the saints whose feast was that day worthily commemorated.[23] The consecration of the famous church occurred on this feast in the eight hundred and eightieth yearly cycle, plus one, since a Virgin, without loss of her maidenly chastity, brought forth the one who was King of the ages and her own Lord.[24] Then for the first time in these wooded regions did hymns of divine praise begin to sound forth clearly. Thereafter the congregation of our community lived there in unceasing service to the Lord. Abbess Gerberga carefully safeguarded the young flock and instructed it by frequent exhortations to observe those things that were in harmony with its life and to avoid every profane deed. At the same time, the esteemed lady Oda, dwelling within the enclosure of the monastery, scrutinized with watchful solicitude the actions and zeal, the customs, and the mode of life of the community of sisters, lest any one of them should disdain the rule of her predecessors and presume to live wickedly by following a law of her own, and that there might be no occasion for the doing of any lawless deed, she by her own example led the way in what was to be done.[25] Just as the fond love of a wise mother sometimes restrains her daughter by fear from wrongdoing and sometimes draws them by kindly exhortations to the desire of virtue, so this holy woman instructed her dear foster children, sometimes by the impelling law of an authoritative mistress and sometimes in the soothing manner of an affectionate mother. She acted thus that they in community of life might serve the one King to whom the stars of heaven sing praise. Those, moreover, whom she reared with a love of maternal kindness, she truly reverenced with great regard, very frequently calling them her superiors. As often as her granddaughters and her noble grandsons, whom the dignity of great office exalted, came to do her a service and vied with one another in showering resplendent gifts upon her, in deference to her place as mother-in-law of the king and their own parent, she is said to have addressed them forthwith with these words: "I exhort and counsel you, my dear children, to hasten first of all to enrich abundantly with your gifts our mistresses, who must zealously serve our holy patrons in this place and by whose merits and holy prayers the success of our own aspirations to prosperity, as well as the dignity of the royal glory, have been increased." In this fashion she persuaded her whole family to provide dutifully for the upkeep of the monastery. The lands which she received by gift from her son-in-law, King Louis [the Younger] to possess for her own use, she caused with his permission to be handed over to the church of Gandersheim. And the king himself in reply to the kindly prayers of Queen Liutgard did not fail to enrich the estate [of that church], but he donated as gifts to it many farms, handing them over to the jurisdiction of our beloved Abbess Gerberga, the sister of the illustrious queen. And his successor, King Arnulf, confirmed these donations in law through royal statute, adding some vineyards as a gift on his own behalf.[26] The monastery continued to prosper in many ways by reason of the kindly intercessions of the popes, under whose authority the monastery had been founded.[27] Lest the fruits of such prosperity should bring about an undue insolence in weak minds, it was necessary that our blessed superior be tested, and the saving judgment of the heavenly judge took from this world many of those same people who had once been the main support of the monastery.

In this manner, pious King Louis died, who was first of the kings to hand over to us for our use many lands which had previously been under royal financial control and to establish with documents written under his name all the rights of our monastery.[28] A few years after his demise, Queen Liutgard, the worthy consort of his throne, who had been the cause of countless grants to us, departed (for shame!) from this world to our great fiscal detriment.[29] To this bereavement a similar cause for grief soon followed. Abbess Gerberga had dedicated her life to goodly concerns and had often –through the aid of the aforesaid kings and the ties of kinship with the queen, her sister—embellished the community with splendid gifts and had added ample substance for our use. After she had been for twice ten and two years in office, performing the duties of prioress as head of her community, she laid aside the mortal weight of the frail human body and returned to her Maker the spirit she had received from heaven. She entrusted the bereaved flock devotedly to be cared for and safeguarded by her sister, Christina.[30]

Christina followed the customs of her aforementioned sisters and carefully planned the conduct of her life. She, who was their equal in degree of nobility, also became like them by reason of her great virtue. No change of circumstance could affect the steadfast mind of her mother [Oda], who continued to be diligent in her service of the Lord. She encouraged her daughter by frequent word and example that, always wisely considering what she did, she should prudently safeguard the flock entrusted to her and, according to the merits of their various deeds, sometimes piously soothe those subordinate to her with loving counsels and sometimes justly to terrify them with reproachful words, lest the affection of her heart should grow lukewarm and allow any rite of divine worship to be disregarded. The lady Oda herself was preeminent in her zeal and resplendent in the bright radiance of wondrous integrity, beloved by God and of fair fame in the world. With her usual maternal piety and love, she was ever solicitous to obtain for her adopted daughters whatever she knew the needs of nuns required. And the great devotion of the illustrious Duke Otto, in accord with the wishes of his dear mother, mercifully cherished and lovingly advanced the cause of the virginal band of Christ's handmaids through aid of the kings to whom he tendered service. Nor could he be driven, even through love for his own life, either to harm them by causing any injurious loss or to withhold any gift that his worthy mother ordered him to give. Thus during the span of life allotted to him, he strove with all the effort of his zealous heart ever to provide for the monastery of his patrons with the constant protection of his unfailing aid. He sought not to be feared as a dread lord, but to be well loved after the fashion of a kindly father. Therefore, even to this day, the praise of his remarkable kindliness deservedly endures in this spot. We, too, influenced by the sweetness of his reputation, although not yet born in his day, but coming to the light of day long afterward, are warmed with a love of him no less enduring than that which was felt by those who beheld his presence and were enriched by the gifts of his benevolence.

This man of such distinguished piety [Duke Otto], who in his fervor had bestowed upon those dwelling with us gifts of high value, died before his mother, our powerful lady.[31] Because of the ancient crime of the fruit which our first parents tasted, he was loosed from his limbs fashioned from texture of clay and (for shame!) closed his eyes in the hour of death. With intense weeping, the community of our sisters surrounded the couch of their dying lord. From all directions our grief-stricken countrymen flocked together to attend his funeral which was to be celebrated with all due rites, and all in like degree mourned with unrestrained weeping the lamentable death of their beloved lord. But the plaintive wailing of his nuns surpassed the laments and grief of both the nobles (*proceres*) and the common people (*vulgus*) alike. In accordance with the accustomed weakness of their female hearts, they disdained to live, and longed speedily to die, not willing to place any bounds on their weeping. Hence, for three days they kept the corpse of their dear father and benevolent lord unburied, as if they hoped that by their flowing tears they could speedily recall the departed spirit of the deceased. At length, the wise counsel of those who had gathered persuaded them that they ought to relinquish vain hope; soon the body of the great leader (*dux*) was laid to rest in the center of the church that he himself had built, in a tomb made ready not without grief, but moistened with the lamentation of the bystanders. There, with our sisters zealously vying with one another in constant prayers, his beloved soul was commended to the mercy of [God] eternally enthroned on high, that He in His mercy might grant [Otto] eternal rest without end.

Eight days and as many nights before the unfortunate death of this leader (*dux*) occurred, a son was born to Henry—[Otto's] son and the future king—that is the famed Otto, who by the piety of the eternal King was chosen, like his father, first to be king (*rex*) of the vigorous Saxons and later emperor (*augustus*) of the mighty Romans.[32]

When six months had flown by in their course, after this renowned ornament of a great race had been born, in whom the happy promises of the Baptist of Christ were without doubt thought first to have been fulfilled—promises which I related at the beginning of my slight poem had been spoken to his ancestress, Aeda—the blessed Oda, our hope and protectress, after living ten decades and seven years, terminated her life with a happy close and passed to heaven, looking forward with hope to the time of returning breath, the rising of a glorified body from the dust, the body that now rests in a tomb under the hard earth near the graves of her daughters.[33]

Christina, who alone [of Oda's daughters] survived for her foster children and who was then a great consolation in the sorrow overwhelming them, lived not more than twice three years after her mother.[34] But she returned her blessed soul at the beckoning of her Maker and in the homeland of light and everlasting peace was united to her sisters, of whose nobility she was the heiress while she followed a holy path in life. Now that they are all united with their mother in heaven, do you kindly Father, grant that they may with you rejoice throughout eternity and forever enjoy the reward of that kingdom that you have safeguarded before all ages for those whom you love, in order that, in sweet utterance of blessed joy, they may praise you with the Son and with the Holy Spirit as the sole sovereign ruling in heaven.[35]

Notes

1. Hrotsvit begins by singling out the earliest known male of the Liudolfing (later known as the Ottonian) family, that is Liudolf (d. 866), and his second son, Otto (d. 912). Although she here implicitly and later explicitly assigns the title of duke (*dux*) to both men, it is doubtful that Liudolf himself was ever known by that title. Most contemporary sources refer to him as count (*comes*). It was probably his eldest son, Bruno (d. 880), who was the first of the family to hold the title *dux*.

2. Hrotsvit here plays with a phrase from Vergil's *Aeneid*, book 3, line 179.

3. Louis the German (806–76), king of the eastern Frankish kingdom.

4. Here I follow Homeyer's suggestion in her edition that *comitatus* refers to leadership over a march, that is a border region of the kingdom. This sentence implies the marginal relationship of Saxony to the eastern Frankish kingdom in the late ninth century and that Hrotsvit was aware that there was a time when Saxony was not a duchy.

5. Billung was the semimythical ancestor of a family who were of great importance among the Saxons during the late ninth, tenth, and eleventh centuries.

6. Hrotsvit here borrows an unusual word (*flavicomans* meaning "yellow haired") from the Christian poet Prudentius (d. post 405).

7. Hrotsvit here compresses the complicated lineage of the Liudolfing clan into a couple of sentences. Duke Otto (d. 912) is the same Otto to whom she referred at the beginning of the poem (see note 1 above). His son, Duke Henry (d. 936), succeeded him and was later elected king of the eastern Frankish kingdom in 919. As king, he is known as Henry I. Henry was succeeded in turn, both as duke of the Saxons and as king of the eastern Frankish kingdom, by his son Otto I, also known as "the Great" (d. 973). The numeral attached to his

name refers to his status as the first Otto to rule as king. Hrotsvit once again confuses the use of titles in hindsight. Otto I was crowned king of the eastern Frankish kingdom at Aachen following Henry's death in 936. He was only consecrated emperor at Rome in 962. Henry had certainly not claimed the imperial title before him. Otto was succeeded in turn by his son, Otto II (955–83), who was crowned co-king with his father in 961 and co-emperor in 967.

8. Hrotsvit here refers to one of her earlier poems, the *Gesta Ottonis* or *Deeds of Otto*. Hrotsvit composed that work around 968 at the request of Abbess Gerberga II and Archbishop William of Mainz.

9. The convent of Herford was located in Westphalia and had been founded by Emperor Louis the Pious ca. 800. The title "prelate" here is used as a synonym for "abbess," not "bishop." The same usage occurs as such in contemporary ecclesiastical legislation. Hathumoda, who was born in 840, was probably a very young girl when she was sent to Herford.

10. Their pilgrimage occurred in 845/6.

11. Pope Sergius II (844–47).

12. Pope Anastasius I (399–401) and Pope Innocent I (401–17).

13. Through the speeches contained in this paragraph Hrotsvit suggested that Pope Sergius had agreed to provide Liudolf not only with relics for his new monastic foundation, but also with a grant of immunity. It was the claim that Gandersheim had been placed under direct papal authority and thus removed from control of the local bishop—which Hrotsvit reiterates both explicitly and implicitly several times below—that had become in her time, and was to remain for decades, a bone of contention between the nuns of Gandersheim and the bishops of Hildesheim. Homeyer suggests that there is likely a single line missing from the final sentence of this paragraph. The foundation was by no means immediate. The community of nuns was first housed in the church of Brunshausen, to which Hrotsvit alluded earlier. Hathumoda was a mere twelve years of age when she assumed control of this community in 852. Construction of the buildings of Gandersheim itself did not commence for another four years.

14. The "father of the house" (*domus pater*) probably refers to a minor royal official who served as the manager of the farm.

15. The vigil is the night before a feast, in this case that of All Saints. Thus this is the second night following the original sighting.

16. Through her classical reference to Faunus—a rural deity of the Romans—and monsters, Hrotsvit implies that Liudolf has purified an ancient place of pagan ritual. It was common for Christian churches and monastic communities to be built on the sites of pre-Christian worship. The slender evidence which exists on the religious practices of the Saxons before their conversion in the late eighth century suggests that they often used wooded groves as ritual sites; see Ruth Karras, "Pagan Survivals and Syncretism in the Conversion of Saxony," *The Catholic Historical Review* 72 (1986): 553–72.

17. Homeyer follows most previous editors in suggesting that there are two lines missing from this sentence, thus rendering its precise grammatical structure, although not its meaning, obscure. The construction of the buildings of Gandersheim began in 856.

18. Liudolf died on November 2, 866. According to another source, Liudolf and Hathumoda (see note 20 below) were originally buried in the church of Brunshausen, only to have their remains later transferred to the completed church of Gandersheim.

19. Louis the Younger (d. 882) was the second son of Louis the German. On the death of his father in 876, Louis the Younger shared rulership over the eastern Frankish kingdom with his brothers, Carloman (d. 880) and Charles (d. 888). Louis's portion of the kingdom included the duchies of Saxony and Franconia; he inherited rule over Bavaria from Carloman on that brother's death in 880. Louis married Liutgard in 869.

20. Hathumoda died November 29, 874 at age thirty-four. She was buried, like her father, at the church of Brunshausen.

21. Gerberga was a third daughter of Liudolf and Oda. Her parents had apparently trusted that Hathumoda would live a longer life and so had made a marriage match for her with a nobleman similar to that arranged for Liutgard.

22. Bruno was the eldest son of Liudolf and Oda; he died in 880. Hrotsvit is mistaken about the opponent, for the raids of the Magyars, or Hungarians, did not begin until a

decade later. According to the *Annals of Fulda* for 880, Bruno died along with two bishops (Markward of Hildesheim and Theoderic of Minden) and twelve counts in a battle against raiding Northmen, or Vikings. See *The Annals of Fulda*, trans. Timothy Reuter (Manchester, 1992), p. 88.

23. Wicbert was bishop of Hildesheim.

24. That is, the dedication occurred on November 1, 881. Hrotsvit's remark above that the dedication occurred two years after the death of Bruno is explained by the fact that Bruno died in February, 880.

25. It was not unusual for noble widows to live in convents that they had founded.

26. Louis the Younger and Liutgard were apparently childless. After Louis's death in 882, his brother Charles III (also known as "the Fat") inherited his lands and served as sole ruler of the eastern Frankish kingdom. In 884, Charles also succeeded to the western Frankish throne and was the last member of the Carolingian family to hold the imperial title. He was a hopeless incompetent and was deposed by the nobles of both Frankish kingdoms in 887. Arnulf—the illegitmate son of Louis's and Charles's third brother, Carloman—succeeded to the throne of the eastern Frankish kingdom. Charles the Fat does not appear in Hrotsvit's narrative, but it is the chaos of his reign that probably necessitated the confirmation of royal grants to Gandesheim provided by Arnulf.

27. This is a none too subtle reference by Hrotsvit to Gandersheim's claim to possession of a papal immunity (see note 13 above).

28. King Louis the Younger died in 882.

29. Queen Liutgard died in 885.

30. Abbess Gerberga died on September 5, 896. Christina was the fourth daughter of Liudolf and Oda.

31. Duke Otto died on December 30, 912.

32. Hrotsvit compresses an extraordinary amount of information about the Liudolfing family and the politics of the eastern Frankish kingdom into this passage, while echoing Vergil (*Aeneid*, book 3, line 204) in its first line. Duke Otto's eldest son, Henry, succeeded him as duke. Eight days before Otto's death, Henry's wife Hatheburg had given birth to a son, whom they had named Otto after his (soon to be deceased) grandfather. Henry and his son would slowly advance the fortunes and position of their family, as Hrotsvit knew from her perspective writing in the 970s. In November of 911 the last Carolingian claimant to the eastern Frankish throne—Louis the Child, grandson of King Arnulf (see note 26 above)—died without issue. Duke Conrad of Franconia had been elected king in Louis's stead by his fellow dukes, including Otto of Saxony. Conrad died on Deceember 23, 918. Early the following year the dukes of the eastern Frankish kingdom chose Henry of Saxony to be king. His eldest son Otto—whose birth is signaled here—succeeded Henry both as duke and king. Otto, however, would go on—unlike his father, despite the retrospective claims of Hrotsvit—to gain the imperial title. For more detail, see note 7 above.

33. Oda died in 913 and was buried in the church of Gandersheim. Hrotsvit may exaggerate in giving her age as one hundred and seven, but she was certainly a woman of extremely advanced age.

34. Abbess Christina died in 919 and was also buried at Gandersheim. It was in this same year that her nephew, Duke Henry, was elected king.

35. The surviving text breaks off at this point, awkwardly in terms of the Latin grammar of the sentence. It is probable that some final lines, perhaps no more than one, are missing.

CHAPTER 12

ODILO OF CLUNY, *EPITAPH OF THE AUGUST LADY, ADELHEID*

Translated by David A. Warner

INTRODUCTION

In terms of its political geography, the world of Empress Adelheid (ca. 931–99) was defined by the breakup of the Carolingian Empire, a process which saw substantial pieces of the European landscape devolve into the hands of local dynasts. Among these pieces, the areas of modern day Switzerland and (somewhat later) the Rhone district of modern France were incorporated by King Rudolf I (888–912) and his descendants into a realm generally known as the kingdom of Burgundy. The first king of the Rudolfing line was succeeded by others of the same lineage: Rudolf II (912–37), Conrad (937–93), and Rudolf III (993–1032). It was to this lineage that Adelheid belonged, being the product of Rudolf II's marriage with Bertha, daughter of Duke Burchard II of Swabia. Through her first marriage, in 947, to King Lothar of Italy (947–50), Adelheid was allied with yet another parvenu dynasty. In contrast to Burgundy, the situation in northern Italy—that is, the former kingdom of the Lombards—was so fluid that no one family had succeeded (or ever would succeed) in establishing a claim to the throne for any length of time. King Hugh (926–47), Lothar's father, was a powerful nobleman in the Rhone district (so that he is sometimes referred to as Hugh "of Arles") who had taken up the office of king at the invitation of a faction within the Italian aristocracy. Lothar's inopportune death insured that both the marriage and the dynasty were rather short-lived.

The Ottonian dynasty, to which Adelheid was joined through her second marriage to Otto I (936–73), ruled over an expansive realm which extended more or less between the rivers Rhine and Elbe (that is, in contemporary terms, the eastern Frankish kingdom and its marches) and included parts of northern Italy. Its influence extended still farther, however, to encompass modern France (or, in contemporary terms, the western Frankish kingdom), the kingdom of Burgundy, and the emerging realms of central Europe. Though the effectiveness of their government would scarcely be comparable with that of any modern state or even a monarchy of the twelfth century, the Ottonians provided most of what their contemporaries expected from their kings. That success achieved one of its most obvious highpoints when Pope John XII bestowed the imperial crown upon Otto I in 962. Though possessors of this crown might be referred to as Emperors of the Romans, it was not the empire of Augustus to which they were heirs, but rather the renovated empire of Charlemagne. Though it did not increase their power in any substantial way, the title of emperor could be called upon to justify the Ottonians' intervention in Italy and Rome, and certainly increased their prestige. That Otto I would obtain a Byzantine princess as a bride for his son, Otto II, would seem almost in the nature of things though he was not the only western ruler to whom such a plan occurred. Theophanu (d. 997), Otto II's bride, would come to exercise a powerful influence at court and, as such, was Adelheid's most obvious rival.

Empress Adelheid was a woman of power and influence who had the good fortune to live at a time, and in a place, in which women had exceptional opportunities to exercise such qualities. In the Ottonian realm, customs of inheritance permitted highborn women to accumulate and dispose of substantial amounts of landed wealth. Wealthy heiresses figure prominently as benefactors of religious establishments and patrons of artists and writers. Women were equally prominent in the political life of the realm, and in ways that exceeded the traditional roles assigned them; cementing alliances, conveying property, and producing heirs. In the court of the Ottonians, imperial princesses and abbesses of the more important religious communities (the two conditions tended to overlap) played key roles as advisors, and occasionally as regents. Ottonian empresses were recognized as participants in the government of their husbands, a role embodied in their designation as *consors regni*. It is against this background that we must place both Adelheid's own accomplishments and the Epitaph composed ca. 1000 in her honor by Abbot Odilo of Cluny (993–1048). Indeed, for Odilo, the political aspects of the empress' career were no less noteworthy than her outstanding piety and miracles.

Through her two marriages Adelheid enhanced the territorial claims of her husbands, respectively, Lothar of Italy and Otto I. In the case of the former, these claims had been associated with the plans of King Hugh (who was Lothar's father) to seize the kingdom of Burgundy, then ruled by Adelheid's younger brother, Conrad. Hugh went so far as to marry Rudolf II's widow, Queen Bertha (who was Adelheid's mother). His plans were defeated when Otto I took Conrad under his protection, an act which also signaled a more intense involvement by the Ottonian dynasty in the domestic politics of the Burgundian kingdom. Following Lothar's death Adelheid found herself in a rather precarious position. Lacking a male heir and incapable of ruling in her own right, she became the focus of opposition to Berengar of Ivrea (also known as King Berengar II), an Italian magnate who had assumed a dominant position in the realm during her husband's brief reign. Odilo paints a lurid and undoubtedly much exaggerated portrait of her imprisonment and torture at the hands of Berengar and his wife, Willa (see Chapter 2 below). Somewhat later, Otto I's marriage with Adelheid enhanced his own claims to northern

Italy, the latter having been confirmed by his coronation in 951, at Pavia, the royal city of the Lombards. One should add, however, that Berengar was not completely excluded from power until 961, on the occasion of Otto's second Italian campaign.

For Otto, Adelheid produced the requisite male heir, Otto II (961–83) as well as a rather formidable daughter, Abbess Mathilda of Quedlinburg (d. 999). Her grandson ascended the throne as Otto III (980–1002). Hence, as Odilo observed, she could truly see the sons of daughters up to the third generation (see Chapter 4 below). Aside from these relatively traditional contributions, Adelheid was actively involved in the politics of the Ottonian court and served as the monarchy's representative in Italy and Burgundy. In particular, her influence in her Burgundian homeland appears to have been substantial. She was able to find refuge there after a falling out with Otto II (see Chapter 5 below). During this period of exile, she apparently visited Lyon and Vienne, major episcopal cities located in an area on the river Rhone which had only recently been incorporated into her brother's kingdom. Given the highly personal and proprietary character of medieval rulership, one might assume that her visits represented an assertion of Rudolfing authority. During her final visit to Burgundy, in 999, her stature was such that she could mediate a dispute between her nephew, King Rudolf III, and his unruly magnates (see Chapter12 below). She also engaged in high-level discussions regarding "matters of peace and honor" (see Chapter16 below). Odilo portrays the trip as a kind of pilgrimage to important churches and cult centers. Finally, along with Abbess Mathilda of Quedlinburg and Empress Theophanu, her daughter-in-law, she would later made up one-third of the regency that successfully governed the realm during the minority of Otto III. She endured setbacks and periods of exile, most notably at the hands of Theophanu, but ultimately, her greatest asset was her longevity which allowed her to survive every setback and outlive her most serious enemies.

Odilo, Adelheid's biographer, was an influential figure in his own right. Born into a noble family of Auvergne, he was a canon at Brioude prior to his entry into the monastery of Cluny. His elevation to the office of abbot was aided by his close relationship with his predecessor in that position, Abbot Mayeul. Odilo repaid his benefactor by compiling his *Life*. Befitting his status as head of the ever expanding monastic family of Cluny, Odilo was both well traveled and well connected. Cluniac daughter houses, such as Payerne, benefited from his ability to petition popes, kings, and emperors for privileges and gifts. Indeed, Odilo's observations regarding Adelheid's trials and tribulations are all the more valuable because of his connections with the Ottonian court and because he occasionally resided within the empress's inner circle. For Odilo Adelheid was the most "august of all empresses," and it is noteworthy that he essentially portrays her as the embodiment of the Ottonian claim to the imperial throne (see Chapters 3 and 7 and below). He was no less determined to make a case for her sanctity, in the customary fashion, by emphasizing her extraordinary devotions and generosity to monks and the poor.

Adelheid's posthumous miracles, the usual gauge of a saint's potential, were merely summarized by Odilo. They were given a more detailed treatment in a book of miracles compiled between ca. 1050 and 1057 at Selz which, as the repository of the empress's body, had a particularly compelling interest in keeping track of them.

Adelheid has been characterized by Patrick Corbet as the only unqualified success among the saints promoted within Ottonian circles, the others having failed to achieve any degree of popular veneration or, like St. (and King) Henry II, owing their promotion to a later period and different sponsors. That success, one might argue, achieved its highpoint during the reign of Pope Urban II (1088–99), when Adelheid was canonized at Rome. Odilo had every reason to contribute to Adelheid's fame. After all, she had displayed exceptional generosity to Cluny and to Odilo himself. It has been argued that he also had an ulterior motive, that being to enhance claims that Selz, the monastery founded by the empress in Alsace, was actually a daughter house of Cluny. Odilo does seem to dwell on that community's foundation in somewhat greater detail though, in contrast to the other foundations mentioned in the text, he does not expressly say that responsibility for implementing the rule was assigned to the Abbot of Cluny (see Chapter 10 below). At present, there seems to be general agreement that Selz was not a Cluniac house, at least not in any legal sense, but the evidence is far from clear and the fact that the community's status was always somewhat cloudy has insured that the issue continues to be debated.

The *Epitaph* itself displays the abundant biblical allusions that one would tend to expect from a literate cleric of the latter half of the tenth century. These have been noted, in great detail, in the standard edition by Herbert Paulhart. Insofar as these allusions are relatively straightforward and extend beyond two or three words, they have also been noted in the following translation. Odilo's allusions to classical literature tend to be rather less direct and have been excluded from the present text although they are noted in Paulhart. Among patristic authors, Odilo seems to have been particularly influenced by St. Jerome (ca. 342–420), of whom he speaks rather admiringly in his introduction. It has been argued, moreover, that Odilo found a model for the *Epitaph* in Jerome's letter to Eustochium, a text which focuses on the life of Paula. Paula was Eustochium's mother and, along with other aristocratic Roman women, a regular recipient of Jerome's spiritual guidance. Like Adelheid, Paula is characterized as a woman of high birth, a concerned if not devoted wife and mother, and a devout Christian with strong ascetic tendencies. These obvious similarities must be balanced by equally obvious differences in detail and, above all, by the absence of any political side to Paula's life.

SOURCES AND FURTHER READINGS

I have prepared this translation of Odilo's work (*Bibliotheca hagiographica latina*, nos. 63–66) from the now standard edition by Herbert Paulhart, *Die Lebensbeschreibung der Kaiserin Adelheid von Abt Odilo von Cluny*, Mitteilungen des Instituts für Östereichische Geschichtsforschung, Ergänzungsband 20.2 (Graz and Cologne, 1962). As far as further reading is concerned, as of this date, readers unfamiliar with French or German will find that the pickings are quite slim indeed. General information regarding Adelheid and events mentioned in Odilo's text can be gleaned from Timothy Reuter, *Germany in the Early Middle Ages 800–1056* (London, 1991) and Karl Leyser, *Rule and Conflict in an Early Medieval Society: Ottonian Saxony* (Oxford, 1979). An extended discussion of the *Epitaphium* and of Adelheid's place among the royal saints of the Ottonians, is included in Patrick Corbet, *Les saints Ottoniens. Sainteté dynastique, sainteté royale et sainteté féminine autour de l'an mil,* Beihefte der Francia 15 (Sigmaringen, 1986). On all questions relating to Adelheid's foundation at Selz, one should consult, Joachim Wollasch, "Das Grabkloster der Kaiserin Adelheid in Selz am Rhein," *Frühmittelalterliche Studien* 2 (1968): 135–43. The issue of Cluniac influence at Selz, one of Wollasch's main concerns, is also discussed by Karl-Joseph Benz, "À propos du dernier voyage de l'impèratrice Adelhaïde en 999," *Revue d'histoire ecclésiastique* 47 (1972): 81–91. Odilo is the subject of a monograph: Jacques Hourlier, *Saint Odilon, Abbè de Cluny*, Bibliothèque de la Revue d'histoire ecclésiastique 40 (Louvain, 1964). One final note on the translation itself. Although all translations of Scripture are mine, I have tried to stay as close as possible to the RSV.

Odilo of Cluny, Epitaph of the August Lady, Adelheid

(**Dedicatory Letter.**) To Lord Andrew, venerable Abbot, and to all the brothers commended to him, devoutly serving God and our Savior in the suburb of the city of Pavia, Brother Odilo of Cluny, the refuse of all paupers, sends prosperity in this life and joy in eternity.[1]

My brethren, we have sent this Epitaph of our lady, the august Empress Adelheid, written in a simple style, because we thought it appropriate that you constantly recall the memory of one whose zeal and prudence allowed the buildings of your monastery to rise from their foundations, and whose abundant generosity still assures your sustenance. We have treated such a serious matter, in a common and brief style, not because we believe that our speech suffices for the praise of such great virtue and nobility, but rather so that some other, more learned man might thereby find opportunity for writing. Insofar as this lofty material, freed from even more lofty words, may resound in the ears of empresses and queens, so too, by hearing great things of the great, and sincerely following the one of whom we have spoken, they may at least bring prosperity to domestic concerns, just as she spread prosperity throughout the realm.

(**Introduction.**) In our own lifetime, at the disposition of the Lord who bestows every honor and virtue, and with Otto I happily wielding the scepter, the august glory of the Roman Empire shone forth in the feminine sex. Adelheid, of divine and celebrated memory, was both empress and, on God's behalf, the author of many good deeds and miracles. Although we have eagerly committed all of this to writing, thereby commending it to the memory of future generations, I fear that we may rightly be criticized for having dared to discuss such a noble and virtuous subject in an inappropriately humble style. Although it is not unmerited, whoever offers such criticism, whether it be due to our uncultivated style, the newness of the material, or the simple and uncontrived character of our speech, should know and be absolutely certain that we were not motivated by any desire for mortal praise, but rather by the impulse of true and sincere love. Oh reader, you may disdain the crudeness of our all too limited talent, as indeed you should, but heed the nobility of mind and body possessed by the one whose life we have undertaken to relate. To find a man endowed with enough eloquence and wisdom to properly describe the life of this woman, you would either have to recall Cicero, the Rhetor, from hell, or have the priest, Jerome, sent down from heaven. Had Jerome been alive in Adelheid's day, moreover, this holy and sacred man, incomparable in divine and human wisdom, would certainly have devoted more that a few volumes to that august woman, since he devoted both books and letters to Paula and Eustochium, Marcella and Melania, Fabiola and Blesilla, Leta and Demetriade, and the woman who was struck seven-times.[2] In the absence of a Jerome or someone else, equally learned in the liberal arts, who might more worthily describe the customs and life of such a great woman, let us now proceed with this task, despite our lack of erudition, but to the best of our ability and with God's help.

(1.) Offspring of a lineage both royal and pious, she was still a young girl of sixteen years when, upon the bestowal of God, she was joined in a royal marriage with King Lothar, son of Hugh, the exceedingly wealthy king of Italy.[3] This union produced a daughter by whom King Lothar of the Franks had King Louis.[4] The latter died without issue and is known to have been buried at Compiègne, according to royal custom.[5] Less than three years after his marriage to Adelheid, the first Lothar also died, leaving his wife bereft of a husband, deprived of a kingdom, and altogether lacking in the good counsel of marriage. She endured that harsh persecution by which the souls of the elect are accustomed to be purified, even as a furnace refines gold [see Wis 3:6]. I do not believe that such treatment was demanded by her own sins, but rather that it was bestowed upon her as a gift by Divine Providence. I would truly affirm that God permitted the outward body to be afflicted, so that the urgent desires of the flesh might not burn this young girl within. The Lord wished her to be brought down by these many lashes so that, as the apostle Paul states, she might not die through self-indulgence while living as a widow [see 1 Tim 5:6]. With paternal love, he wished her to experience so many dangers that she might not be unworthy of that divine filiation of which the scriptures speak: "*The Lord chastises every son whom he receives.* [Heb 12:6]" She frequently gave thanks to God for this. With her closest companions, moreover, she used to discuss the duration and character of what she had suffered at that time, but also how mercifully the Lord had freed her from the hands of her enemies [see 1 Sam 10:1]. She judged that it was much better for her, at that time, to have been preoccupied with temporal anxieties than subjected to the laws of perpetual death by living in pleasure [see 1 Tim 5:6].

(2.) Following the death of Lothar, her husband, rulership over the kingdom of Italy passed to a certain man named Berengar who had a wife named Willa.[6] Though blameless, Adelheid was captured by those two and subjected to a variety of tortures. Her flowing hair was pulled out and she suffered frequent blows from the hands and feet of her tormentors. Finally, she was enclosed in a foul prison with only one serving woman for company. Following her miraculous liberation, with God ordaining, she was elevated to the throne of the empire. During the same night in which she was led forth from her place of imprisonment, she wandered into a swamp composed of reeds. She remained there, persevering for days and nights without food or drink, all the while beseeching God to send help. While she was detained in this perilous state, a fisherman suddenly appeared in a small boat into which, with the aid of a net, he was trying to pull a fish known as a sturgeon. As soon as he had seen her, he asked who she might be and what she might be doing there. The response she gave him was quite appropriate to her desperate situation: "Is it not obvious that we have wandered into this place quite unintentionally, and even worse, that we are suffering from loneliness and hunger. If you would, give us something to eat, but also grant us solace." The fisherman felt for

Adelheid that same compassion with which Christ himself, who sent him, had regarded certain hungry paupers in the desert. He responded: "Other than fish and water, we have none of the requisites for a meal [see Mt 14:15–17]." He had fire with him, as those who engage in the business of fishing are accustomed to do.

The fire was lit.
The fish was cooked.
The Queen got her supper.
The fisherman and serving woman waited table.

(3.) While they were eating, a cleric who had shared Adelheid's captivity and flight came to them and announced the arrival of a band of armed men. The latter happily accepted the young woman and took her with them, to a certain impregnable castle.[7] Afterward, by the grace of God and on the advice of the leading men among the Italians, she proceeded from the throne of the kingdom to the throne of empire.[8] She was worthy to be named and venerated as the most august of all empresses.

No one before her so increased the realm.
Stubborn Germany and fertile Italy,
She subjected to the Roman throne,
Along with their princes.
Otto, that noble king,
She installed as emperor of Rome,
And bore him a son worthy of the throne.[9]

(4.) Concerning the nobility of her lineage, enough has already been said. To describe how she exercised the nobility of her spirit, however, would exceed the capacity of any mortal. But if I may summarize as best I can: she was confident both in hope and faith, filled twofold with Christian love, very righteous, strong, prudent and extremely modest. Her life was blessed while she governed the world, with the aid of the Lord who rules the universe. Wise Solomon's words regarding neediness would be appropriate to this most holy woman: "*She opened her hands to the destitute and extended her palms to the pauper. She will not fear for her household in the frigid snow because all of her servants are clothed in doublets. She has made a covering for herself of blankets, her clothing is linen and purple. Her husband is noble in the gates when he sits with the elders of the land. Strength and beauty are her garments and she will laugh on the day to come. She has opened her mouth with wisdom and the law of clemency is on her tongue. She has considered the ways of her household and does not eat the bread of leisure. Her sons rise up and call her blessed and her husband praises her. Many daughters have gathered riches, but you surpass all of them* [Prov 31:20–29]." These things which we have said of her, we know not only from hearsay, but also by sight and experience. We have heard many salutary words from her, and received many gifts. She frequently made paupers wealthy with gifts of money and, on any given day, elevated those who were lacking in gold by granting them benefices. To the glory of all, this one, wife of the most famous emperor in the world, the first and greatest Otto, and mother of many future emperors, was found worthy to obtain the blessing enjoyed by Tobias, as we read in that same father's book, namely, that she might see the *sons of daughters up to the third generation* [Tob 9:11].

(5.) After the most august Otto went the way of all flesh, the empress and her son governed the Roman Empire in peace, for a long time.[10] But now that the supremacy of the Roman Empire had been consolidated, by the will of God and through the virtues and zeal of the empress, there was no lack of wicked men who aimed at nothing less than the planting of discord among them [viz. between the empress and her son; see Prov 6:19]. The mperor was deceived by their flattery and his affection for his mother waned. If we were to put down in writing the number and character of the events that then occurred, it would appear that we intended to diminish the reputation of this great family. We ought not to cause injury with the pen, however, since the situation was quickly resolved with a humble act of restitution. Loving her son and unable to bear the authors of discord, and also following the apostle's command to leave little room for anger [Rom 12:19], she resolved to return to her father's realm where she was accorded a kind and honorable reception by her brother, King Conrad, and his wife, the most noble Mathilda.[11] Germany mourned her absence, but all Burgundy rejoiced at her advent. Lyon was exultant, that illustrious city, once the mother and nurse of philosophy; likewise Vienne, that noble city of kings.

(6.) Later, moved by deep regret, Emperor Otto ordered messengers to make haste to his royal uncle and to Father Mayeul of holy memory; and to urgently request their intercession, to the end that he might regain his mother's favor, lost through his own misdeeds.[12] He also beseeched and begged that, in the company of his august mother, they might hasten to meet with him in Pavia. With the help of such great men, the meeting between mother and son took place, in Pavia, and at the time appointed.[13] Seeing one another, they fell prostrate upon the ground, crying and lamenting, and humbly offered their mutual salutations. The son expressed his humble regret, the mother, gracious forgiveness. For each of them, the bond of peace remained unbroken forever.

(7.) Somewhat later, she was deprived of her only son, who was then succeeded by a third Otto, born of a Greek woman.[14] Adelheid had long suffered under the recurring lashes of misfortune, but we cannot begin to describe, at least individually, the number and type of misfortunes that befell her now, following the death of her son. Although that Greek empress had been very helpful and most virtuous, both to herself and others, she was quite the contrary in regard to her imperial mother-in-law. At last, following the advice of a certain Greek, as well as that of other flatterers, she actually threatened her.[15]

Indeed, she might as well have pointed at her, as she announced: "If I survive the entire year, Adelheid will reign nowhere in the entire world, her dominion will not even fill the palm of one's hand." Through the judgment of God, that ill-considered statement came true. In less than four weeks, the Greek empress departed from this world, leaving august Adelheid alive and well.[16] Adelheid continued, nonetheless, to lament and weep for the pain of the world and, when necessary, saw to the welfare of the Roman Empire. The offspring of her only son, Otto III, studied the ways of nobility and virtue with the leading men of the realm. He ventured nothing in her regard, except that which did honor to both of them. Thus, through his grandmother's merits and the diligence of the leading men, he attained the throne of the Roman Empire.[17]

(8.) From her earliest years, the woman now called Empress endured the attacks of both foreign and domestic enemies, so that she could echo the words of the Prophet: *"They assaulted me from my youth"* and so on [Ps 129:1]. She also used to say, following the Apostle: *"I consider that the suffering of this present time is not worthy of the future glory which will be revealed in us"* [Rom 8:18]. As he says in another passage, moreover, If we suffer with him, *"we will also reign with him"* [2 Tim 2:12]. And elsewhere, *"as you share in our sufferings, you will also share in our comfort"* [2 Cor 1:7]. She frequently returned good for evil [see Prov 31:12] and, in accordance with the Lord's commandment, did not *let the sun set* without forgiving any who had sinned against her [Eph 4:26]. Regarding the injuries inflicted upon her, she reserved no right of accusation, but rather committed all to the Lord, knowing that he had declared, in the words of the prophet: *"Vengence is mine, I will repay"* [Rom 12:19]. I entreat you, spare those whom she has spared! Moreover, we should note that, as much as possible, she tended both to those who were in adversity and to those who were enjoying prosperity. With God willing, as long as she occupied the realm; first with the emperor, then with his son, then with the son's son—clearly, the imperial and august Ottos—for so long did she also exploit her own property to establish monasteries in honor of the King of Kings.

(9.) In the kingdom of her father, King Rudolf, and of her brother, Lord Conrad, there was a place called Payerne where her mother, Bertha, a woman devoted to God in all goodness, had been laid to rest. In this place, Adelheid founded a monastery in honor of the mother of God.[18] Through her generosity and at her brother's order, the community was then given to Father Mayeul, in perpetuity, that it might be organized according to the rule. Later, she took upon herself the task of establishing another monastery, dedicated to the Savior of the World, near the city of Pavia, in Italy.[19] By the authority of the emperor, and through her most generous donations, the foundation was brought to completion. Indeed, she endowed it amply with property and liturgical objects, and conveyed it to the same Father Mayeul who was to implement the rule. In Saxony, following the death of that ruler whom we have already mentioned, she cooperated with her wise and prudent daughter in bestowing gifts upon communities of nuns.[20]

(10.) Approximately twelve years before her death, in a place called Selz, Adelheid decreed that she would establish a monastery under the protection of the pope and, after that was done, brought it to completion.[21] In the same location, she also founded a new church, of marvelous design, and ordered Widerald, the august and devout bishop of Strasbourg, to dedicate it in honor of God and the Prince of the Apostles.[22] Adelheid's grandson, Otto III, joined her on this occasion. That, in days to come, the defense of this consecrated place might be supported by greater authority, Adelheid, the emperor's august grandmother whom we have often mentioned and often shall mention, convened a council of bishops in the emperor's presence. In the church itself, Adelheid prepared a cloister most suitable for monks and stipulated that it should be organized according to the rule of St. Benedict. She installed Ecceman as abbot, a man of good reputation, learned in both human and divine knowledge, to whom she had constantly turned for instruction in Holy Scripture. She endowed and increased the glory of this monastery with gifts of land, buildings, gold, gems, precious vestments, and a variety of other decorative objects. All of this was done, so that those who served God in that place would lack for nothing. During those four years, she had survived by dedicating both her property and herself to her Creator. She also acquired friends among Christ's paupers and servants, that they might welcome her at the eternal tabernacle when she departed from this world [see Lk 16:9].

(11.) Although involved in the highest matters of government, she did not think it unworthy to give support to the wretched and poor in their various misfortunes. If she could adorn her body with marvelous clothing and encircle her brow with precious gems, as was appropriate to her imperial dignity, she did not choose to weigh herself down with such bonds, but rather, living as a sincere imitator of her Redemptor who, though the highest of all, did not think it unworthy to experience the misery of humankind, she subsequently elected to use such things either to support paupers or to adorn the crosses of the Lord and the Gospel of Christ. She also bestowed benefits upon innumerable convents of canons, monks, and nuns, scattered here and there throughout the world, in the hope that this army of God's familiars, after being restored through her generosity, would more vigorously implore the divine favor for her and the realm. Moreover, in all that she did, she followed the model of righteousness and common generosity, trusting resolutely in that future judge who would not be deceived by things held in secret, and would find shameful things offensive, but delight in honorable ones. For this reason, she was viewed as exceedingly righteous and most gracious in her generosity, performing works of beneficence toward Christ whom the blessed apostle establishes as the foundation [see 1 Cor 3:11], wisely understanding that faith is the foundation of all virtue. She acted with perfect generosity in that, as much as possible, she concealed her good works with silence and ministered to the needs of individuals. Because of this, it was not by her own lips that she was praised [see Prov 27:2], but rather by the mouths of the paupers of Christ. And so, the saying proffered by the mouth of Job was fulfilled in her:

"the blessing of one about to perish came upon me" [Job 29:13]. With diligent consideration, she zealously considered that saying, along with the assertion of the prophet that a pauper should never leave her home with an empty bosom [Ecc 29:9], and similarly, that through such deeds, she might acquire the inheritance of heaven while residing in the land of the living [see Ps 27:13].

(12.) In the last year of her life, at a time when she must have been aware of her imminent departure from this world, as I believe, this constant friend of peace went to the land of her birth for the sake of peace and love. There, the vassals of her nephew, King Rudolf, were fighting among themselves. Among those who were agreeable, she established a sworn peace. Those who were not agreeable, she committed entirely to God, in her customary manner. For the rest, it would exceed our capabilities to relate how zealously, how devoutly she concerned herself to visit the places of the saints. For at that time she went to Payerne, a monastery which she herself had founded out of her own and her mother's property and had dedicated to the honor of the mother of God and the salvation of her mother who rested there.

(13.) At this point, there occurred something unusual which, in our judgment, ought to be inserted here. Fatigued from her journey, she could not give alms to the poor with her own hands, as she was accustomed to do. Thus, she summoned one of the brothers who was to distribute them in her place. As she had ordered, he approached the paupers, but found that their number exceeded the number of denarii allotted for them. He feared that there would not be enough. But, behold! The power of that one who satisfied a thousand people with five loaves of bread was with the august woman [see Mt 14:13]. The denarii multiplied, and the paupers went away happy with their gift.

(14.) After leaving Payerne, she sought out the church of *Agaunum* where the cliffs hold the thousand blessed bodies of the martyrs.[23] With how much devotion, with how much reverence she invoked the aid of that great martyr, Maurice, and his companions! How many sighs? How many lamentations? How many rivers of tears? At that time, so I believe, all of her sins were found worthy of eternal forgiveness. Indeed, if you were to gaze upon her face, you would say that it surpassed any human visage, and believe that if anything were to come forth from her lips, it would be nothing other than that prophetic dictum: *"I poured out my prayer in his sight, I declared my tribulation before him"* [Ps 142: 2]. Her greatest tribulation was her loving compassion on behalf of those who fell away from the law of God, so that she was able to say, with the Old Testament: *"I am seized by despair for the sake of sinners"* [Ps 119: 53], and with Paul, *"who is weak and I am not weak"* [2 Cor 11:29], and so on. She deplored the sins of others, in particular, because so many were incapable of deploring them on their own behalf. She rejoiced in the seriousness and accomplishments of the past, and was saddened daily by the faults of the present day, and especially of the future. In referring to the future, moreover, I declare that she undoubtedly possessed the spirit of prophecy. I might have neglected to mention it in this work, had I not seen it openly demonstrated.

(15.) When she was about to exit from that sacred place and, standing by herself, was praying in a corner of the church, a messenger came to her from Italy and announced that Bishop Franco of Worms had died at Rome.[24] Because Franco was a man of good reputation [see Acts 6:3], the august lady esteemed him highly, just as she was accustomed to esteem all good men. As soon as she heard of Franco's death, she summoned one of the retainers who had accompanied her and humbly requested that he offer prayers to God on the bishop's behalf. Then, she began to speak as if in trance, saying: "What shall I do, Lord, and what shall I say regarding that one who is both our lord and my grandson? I believe that many of those who are with him in Italy will die. And, so I fear, the august Emperor Otto will perish after them, alas for me, a wretch who shall remain bereft of all human consolation.[25] Oh Lord and eternal King, would that I did not have to be witness to so sad a loss." Then you would have seen that august woman with her whole body prostrate on the floor, and you would believe no less that her mind was completely fixed on heaven, and that she spoke with an anguished voice as if she had just discovered the path of the martyr Maurice. A little while later, after arising from her prayers, she gave gifts to the martyrs and alms to the poor.

(16.) From there, she went to the city of Geneva, desiring to see the hall of the victorious martyr, Victor.[26] From thence, she came to Lausanne where she devoutly observed the remembrance of the mother of God. In those places, she was received with honor by the king and the bishops, namely his nephews. Thereafter, she proceeded to a village called Orbe. She was delayed there for some time and, being descended upon by the needy and wretched, gave alms to as many of them as possible. Moreover, while she discussed matters of peace and honor with the king and the leading men of the realm, she also sent off diverse and various gifts to places of holiness. What churches were there, and what communities of monks that did not merit to receive her gifts and presents, regardless of whether they were joined to her by some affinity or merely by their physical proximity? Allow me to mention one example out of many: at the time in which her last day was fast approaching, she bestowed small but suitable gifts upon the blessed Father Benedict and also upon Father Mayeul, of blessed memory, who is presently crowned with the glory of heaven. While Mayeul dwelt within this mortal flesh, she loved him above all mortals of that order. Nor did she neglect the larger family of those dependent upon Cluny.

(17.) She set aside a substantial amount of silver for the restoration of the church of the blessed confessor of Christ, Martin.[27] It had recently caught fire and burned. And, for the ministry of its altar, she sent a piece of the cloak of her only son, Emperor Otto. Let us recall to memory her exceedingly sweet words to him, for whose service those gifts had been sent. Among other things, she said: I beseech you, dearest one, I beseech you to speak to that most holy priest. Along with this prayer, oh priest of God, may you receive the small gifts sent to you by Adelheid, empress by the gift of God, servant of the servants of God, and sinner. Receive also a piece of the cloak of Emperor

Otto, my only son, and pray for him to that Christ whom you yourself clothed, after dividing your own cloak, when he appeared to you in the form of a pauper.

(18.) On the very day and at the same hour in which she was supposed to leave the place mentioned above, as we sinners were standing by, she provided an example of perfect humility and also showed that she possessed the spirit of prophecy, and this without arrogance but rather in all meekness. There was a certain monk in her presence who, though unworthy to be called abbot, was thought by her to be of some importance. When she gazed at him, and he himself looked at her, each began to shed copious tears. I would say that she then accomplished more than if she had cured many people of their illnesses. She humbly grasped the rather simple garment in which he was clothed and, in exchanging kisses, marked those most holy eyes and most serene face. In a familiar fashion, and quietly, she said to him: remember me in your contemplations, my son, and know that I will no longer see you through my physical eyes. Moreover, at such time as I abandon this mortal world, I commit my soul to the prayers of the brothers. From there, following the same route by which she had come, she went to the place where, with God ordaining, she had ordered that a tomb be prepared for her.[28]

(19.) During this final journey of her temporal existence, she tried, as much as possible, to rise above her normal environment, scorning the rush of worldly matters, so that she might freely proceed to the contemplation of God. She viewed the business of the household as an inconvenience. Now, she worked strenuously to carry out the admirable task of Leah and Martha, and she wished to achieve the desirable leisure of Rachel and Mary. Therefore, intent on her readings and constant in her prayers, she rejected earthly things and focused her thoughts completely on heaven. If anyone interrupted her with some secular matter, she gave no response to this, but rather, mournfully repeated in her heart the complaint of the apostle: "*I am a wretched person; who will free me from the body of this death?*" [Rom 7: 24]. And, secure regarding the hope of divine recompense, she replied, "*the Grace of God through Jesus Christ*" [Rom 7: 25].

(20.) After being instructed by a message from Heaven, she went to the place where she was to return her last breath to God. The day was approaching, moreover, upon which the yearly devotions were offered up in memory of her son, the august Otto. Poor people rushed to her from nearby locations, as they always did. Such was her custom, that on the anniversaries of the deaths of her friends and familiars, she would disburse a donation to her spiritual warriors, as I would say, alms to the paupers of Christ. Indeed, a crowd of indigent folk had been gathered there in an orderly fashion. She came herself and humbly greeted them, following the example of Abraham the Patriarch by not doubting that God was among them [see Gen. 18:2]. Unmindful of her infirmity, she tried to approach these people, giving to each with her own hand, and when she saw some who were particularly wretched, adding clothing and other gifts. When these spiritual matters were finished, she had masses celebrated for her son by a certain venerable archbishop. That night, she was seized by a fever and, over a period of days, her illness worsened until she was almost at the end. Up to that point, as much as possible, she had been intent on prayer and, with her eyes desiring Christ, had refused to gaze at anything else. When the strength of her body had returned somewhat, she earnestly requested that she be protected by the mysteries of the Church. Thereafter, she was anointed with holy oil and humbly, with pious adoration, received the sacrament of the body of Christ in whom she always had hoped and believed. Fortified with such defenses and fed with such food, she said to her monks, who were standing by, and to the clergy, that they should sing the penitential Psalms and recite the names of the saints according to the custom of the Church. When they did so, she sang the Psalms along with those singing the Psalms, and prayed with those praying, until they reached the passage in which she asked God to be merciful to her. Aware that she was to hold the drum and choir with the sister of Moses [see Ex 15:20], with David the strings and the organum, and also take up the bright-sounding cymbals along with those who followed the lamb [see Ps 150:4], she was completely overcome with joy.

(21.) In the year 1000 of the Incarnation, desiring to see that one day in the court of the Lord which would be longer than a thousand [see Ps 84: 10], she often said, along with the apostle: "*I wish to depart and be with Christ*" (Phil 1: 23). This blessed woman died on the sixteenth day of December, as her joyful spirit anticipated the arrival of the feast of birth of the same Jesus Christ, our Lord. With the burden of her mortal flesh laid aside, she ascended to the pure radiance of that most pure ether. To her household she was pleasant though serious, to outsiders both serious and extremely forthright. Her concern for the poor was inexhaustible, and she displayed an abundant generosity in honoring the churches of God. Though unwavering in her kindness toward good people, she revealed her full severity to the wicked. Though timid in her own desires, she was nonetheless strong in desirable qualities. She greeted prosperity with true humility and endured adversity with abiding patience. Her daily repasts were marked by sobriety and her dress was modest. Zealous in reading, at prayer, and in observing vigils and fasts, she was of one and the same will in distributing alms. She was in no way bound by the glory of her earthly nobility, nor could any desire for human praise distract her from the goodness conceded to her by God. She displayed no arrogance regarding the virtues that God had granted her, and no despair regarding misdeeds that she herself had committed as the result of wicked counsel. The desire for honors, riches, or the luxuries of the world had no power over her, and discretion, the mother of all virtues, accompanied her every endeavor. She was securely resolute in her faith, resolutely secure in her hope, and generous in her love of God and those close to her, that being the foundation of all human goodness and principal cause of virtue.

(22.) Indeed, so I would truly declare, the worth and character of her life were revealed by the power of heaven through clearly miraculous events that occurred at her tomb. If they were to be described, they would require a volume in their own right. Moreover, human speech would scarcely have the capacity to explain them. That they might not remain entirely absent from the text, however, but also to avoid unduly lengthening it, I have summarized them briefly. At her tomb, through the grace and mercy of our Lord Jesus Christ, the blind received their sight, cripples had their bodily vigor restored, fevers were healed, and many sick persons were cured of different infirmities. The End.

Notes

1. Andrew was abbot of the monastery of San Salvatore in Pavia.
2. Here, referring to that circle of women for whom Jerome served as spiritual advisor.
3. King Lothar (947–50) and King Hugh (926–47) of Italy.
4. King Lothar (954–86) and King Louis (986–87) of the western Frankish kingdom.
5. At the abbey of Saint-Corneille in Compiègne.
6. That is, King Berengar II (950–64) of Italy.
7. The castle of Canossa in the Appenine Mountains of northern Italy.
8. Her husband, Otto I, was crowned emperor by Pope John XII in 962.
9. That is, Otto II.
10. Otto I died on May 7, 973.
11. King Conrad (937–93) of Burgundy.
12. Abbot Mayeul of Cluny was Odilo's predecessor.
13. That is, in December 980.
14. That is, Theophanu.
15. This "certain Greek" is usually identified with John Philagathos, who came from Calabria and held a number of important positions within the court and ecclesiastical hierarchies. He seems to have benefited to an extraordinary degree from Theophanu's patronage. His career came to an ignominious end after a brief term as pope. (Reigning as John XVI from 997 until 998, he died in 1001).
16. Theophanu died on June 15, 991.
17. Otto III was crowned emperor on May 21, 996, in Rome.
18. Bertha had died ca. 957. Payerne is in the canton of Vaud in modern Switzerland and in the diocese of Lausanne. The community was founded (ca. 962) by Adelheid, with some degree of cooperation from her mother.
19. San Salvatore was founded in 972.
20. That is, Abbess Mathilda of Quedlinburg (d. 999).
21. By placing the foundation under papal protection (i.e. *sub libertate Romana*), Adelheid attempted to free it from subjection to any other ecclesiastical authority. It remained subject to the emperor, however. Papal protection was, in a sense, a logical adjunct to royal protection.
22. Bishop Widerald of Strasbourg (992–99).
23. That is, the famous monastery of Saint-Maurice-en-Valais (d'Agaune), which rests on the purported site of the martyrdom of St. Maurice and his companions (that is, the Theban Legion), a group of late-Roman military saints. The Ottonian family seems to have had a more than passing interest in the saint who, for example, was chosen as patron of Otto I's foundation at Magdeburg.
24. Bishop Franco of Worms (999). Though his reign as bishop was relatively short, Franco seems to have enjoyed a long and rather close relationship with Otto III. He is reported to have joined the monarch in late night penitential exercises, in a cave near the church of San Clemente in Rome. Bishop Burchard of Worms (1000–1025), noted for his collection of canon law, was Franco's brother.
25. Here, Odilo presumably refers to the uprising which preceded the death of Otto III in 1002.
26. Here referring to a series of locations on the shores of Lake Geneva: the church and monastery of Saint-Victor at Geneva, the cathedral at Lausanne (dedicated to the Virgin Mary), and the then royal estate at Orbe, in the modern Swiss canton of Vaude.
27. This is the basilica of Saint-Martin in Tours.
28. Adelheid was buried at the monastery of Selz.

Chapter 13

The Cult of Relics in the Eleventh Century

Edited and translated by Thomas Head

Introduction

Writing in the 1030s, the French monk Ralph Glaber described the ecclesiastical landscape of Western Christendom at the turn of the first millennium:

> Just as the third year after the aforementioned millennium was at hand [that is, 1003], it transpired throughout the whole world—but particularly in Italy and Gaul—that ecclesiastical buildings were renovated, although most of the existing ones were in beautiful condition and not lacking the least thing. Nonetheless each tribe of Christians strove against the other to have the use of a more beautiful church. It was as if the whole world were shaking itself, shrugging off the past, and swathing itself all over in a shining mantle of churches. The faithful at that time remade almost all episcopal basilicas, as well as monastic churches dedicated to various saints . . . [*The Five Books of Histories*, 3.4.13].

The vivid terms of Glaber's description have become virtually canonical in textbook accounts of Europe in the decades around the year 1000. The rebuilding of churches which was correctly noted by Glaber—and which lies at the core of the development of what art historians know as the Romanesque style—also involved the cult of saints' relics and pilgrimage. Indeed, when Glaber himself returned to his image, he made the link explicit:

> When, as we have said, the whole world was clothed in a shining mantle of renovated churches, a little later, in the eighth year after the aforementioned millennium of the incarnation of the Savior, the relics of many saints were revealed by various indications where they had long lain hidden. It was as though they had been awaiting the honor of a resurrection and were now by God's permission revealed to the gaze of the faithful, to many of whose minds they brought solace . . . News of this attracted the faithful, not just from the provinces of Gaul, but from almost all of Italy and the lands beyond the sea. No small number of them were sick with fever, but they returned home cured by the intervention of the saints. [*The Five Books of Histories*, 3.6.19.]

The veneration of the relics of ancient saints had been part of the practice of Christianity in the West since the fourth century. But Glaber was correct in noting that in his lifetime there was a definite revival of interest in the cult of saints, which involved the alleged discovery of many new relics and an increase in the amount of pilgrimage to relic shrines.

The reasons for this revival are many and complex: the growth of a reform movement among the monks who largely controlled the cults of the saints; the desire of some monks to increase the prestige and revenues of their communities; a stabilization and rebuilding of shrines as the destructive raids of the Vikings came to an end; the interest of members of the secular nobility in securing the patronage of the saints through the foundation of new monasteries and the construction of new churches; the rise of certain millenarian expectations in conjunction with the anniversaries of Christ's birth and death in 1000 and 1032. What is indisputable is that clerics in these decades composed an unprecedented number of works concerning the relics of saints and the miracles associated with their shrines. (It has indeed been argued by some historians that the intensity of this revival of the cult of saints is more of a gauge of clerical literary production than actual increase in popular interest.) The texts collected in this chapter are a few very brief examples from this enormous literary output. They will serve, however, to illustrate some of the key aspects of the practice of the cult of saints in this period. All of them come from what Ralph Glaber would have recognized as Gaul, an area focused on, but larger than, the contemporary kingdom of France. This was a region of the old Roman empire and Christians had been burying their holy dead in special shrines outside the cities of Gaul since at least the fourth century. It was, simply put, a region which was richer than most in the legacy of the relics of ancient saints.

The first text comes from Trier, a city which had served as a regional capitol for the Roman emperors in late antiquity. Monumental buildings undertaken by the Emperor Constantine (d. 337)—a cathedral church and an imperial audience hall—still stand in the center of that city. There were major Christian cemeteries located on both the western and eastern edges of the city. Tombs of bishops and others celebrated as saints were located in both. During the early middle ages, churches and later monasteries were erected in the midst of these cemeteries which were dedicated to two early bishops of Trier, respectively St. Maximinus and St. Eucharius. In 979 a man named Egbert—the son of an important noble family with close ties to the Ottonian royal dynasty—was consecrated as archbishop of Trier. The monastery of Saint Maximinus had already undergone significant reform and was a thriving center both for the religious life and for pilgrimage to the shrine of its patron saint. Egbert undertook the reform and rebuilding of the monastery of Saint Eucharius. In the midst of the reconstruction of its church, a sarcophagus was found which was thought to contain the relics of another, previously unknown, saint named Celsus. (The discovery should not surprise us, as the workmen were digging trenches through an ancient cemetery which has since been excavated by modern archeologists.) The text included here—*The Discovery of St. Celsus*—was written (several decades after the event) by a monk of Saint Eucharius who detailed how Archbishop Egbert inaugurated the cult of this newly discovered saint.

Relics were ordinarily kept secure in their resting places. Monks and clerics did on occasion, however, bring relics of the saints outside of their shrines so that their power might be invoked for special circumstances, such as the cure of an epidemic, the solving of a blood feud, or the raising of revenues for a new ecclesiastical building. One text included elsewhere in this collection—*The Miracles of St. Ursmer on his Journey through Flanders* (Chapter 16)—details a particularly long journey undertaken by one group of monks with the relics of their patron saint. In the second text included in this chapter—*Journey of the Body of St. Junianus to the Council of Charroux*—Letaldus of Micy tells of how the monks of the abbey of Nouaillé brought the relics of their patron saint to a gathering of bishops and abbots in synodal council at the monastery of Charroux in June of 989. That council was one of the first and most influential gatherings in a movement which has become known as the Peace of God. That movement was an attempt by members of the ecclesiastical hierarchy to mobilize the sentiment of laypeople of both the noble and ordinary classes against the acts of violence being committed by members of the military elite. What is remarkable about this text, however, is that it provides details of how ordinary Christians reacted to the passage of the relics of saints through their home villages.

All of this attention, discovery, and movement doubtless provided the possibility of conscious deceit. The third text in this chapter is an excerpt from Ralph Glaber's *Five Books of Histories*, in which the same monk who often celebrated the discovery of relics condemns a specific instance of fraud. He gives a very different perspective than his contemporary Letaldus on the relations between clergy and laity around the relics of the saints. It was just such instances as these that gave rise to the critique voiced almost a century later by Guibert of Nogent in his *On Saints and Their Relics* (translated in Chapter 19 of this collection).

Our fourth and final text highlights pilgrimage, the process by which pious Christians came to the shrines of the saints in search of their intervention. Many collections of miracle stories were compiled in particular at monastic shrines in the eleventh and early twelfth centuries. The single story presented here, however, seems to have been placed in an archive for later inclusion in such a collection and is much more detailed about the processes of pilgrimage and cure than most of the stories in those collections in their final, edited form. It provides a particularly good look at the practice of pilgrimage and the ideology of saintly patronage.

This anonymous *Miracle of St. Maximinus* tells the story of a man named Henry who undertook a pilgrimage to the shrine of St. Maximinus at the abbey of Micy, which is situated on the southern bank of the Loire River near the city of Orléans (and home to Letaldus, author of our second selection).

According to tradition, Micy had been founded by Clovis (d. 511), the first Christian king of the Franks, as a gift to two holy men from Verdun, Euspicius and his nephew Maximinus. It was Maximinus who became the community's first abbot and was later celebrated as its chief patron saint. (Note, and this distinction is important to the story included here, that this St. Maximinus was a different individual from the bishop of Trier mentioned above.) During the wars of the eighth century, Micy was sacked and abandoned, only to be refounded around the year 800. It is clear that the sarcophagi containing the presumed relics of Maximinus and several disciples were enshrined in the monastic church by this time. The shrine was commonly visited by laypeople from the immediate region, most particularly (as in this text) on the feast days of the saint or in times of social crisis. During an outbreak of ergotism in the 990s, for example, numerous peasants from the surrounding countryside came to the abbey in search both of miraculous cures and handouts of food. The fortunes of the abbey of Micy improved considerably under the leadership of Abbot Albert, who rebuilt its church in the 1020s. A contemporary description indicates that the monks had forgotten the exact location of their patron's tomb. During the construction, however, Maximinus's sarcophagus was rediscovered and enshrined under the main altar.

It was to that shrine which Henry—the central figure of the text translated here—was to come, most probably (given internal evidence in the text) sometime during the 1060s. He did so in order to make reparation for his sins and thus to be cured of his lameness, an infirmity which he believed to have been inflicted on him by God in punishment for those sins. The text itself was composed by a monk of Micy who had heard it either from Henry himself or from other monks who were familiar with him. The pilgrim, after all, had resided in the abbey for a number of years. It was composed after Henry's departure from Micy in 1072/3. The sole extant manuscript of the text is apparently the author's original, for it is copied in an exceedingly rough hand on parchment which had previously been used for a charter or legal document pertaining to the abbey. In other words, the author raided the monastery's archives and scraped down some parchments which were no longer of use in order to provide himself with a kind of scrap paper for recording this story.

SOURCES AND FURTHER READING

The best edition of Theodoric of Saint Eucharius, *Inventio s. Celsi* (*Bibliotheca hagiographica latina*, nos. 1720–21) is to be found in *Acta Sanctorum quotquot toto orbe coluntur*, eds. Jean Bolland, et al., first edition (Antwerp and Brussels, 1643–1971), February III, pp. 402–6. I have analyzed the context for the discovery of the relics of St. Celsus, and other uses made of the relics of Trier by Archbishop Egbert in "Art and Artifice in Ottonian Trier," *Gesta* 36 (1997): 65–82. The most easily accessible edition of Letaldus of Micy, *Delatio corporis s. Juniani ad synodem Karoffensem* (*Bibliotheca hagiographica latina*, nos. 4562) is in *Patrologia latina*, ed. Jean-Paul Migne, 221 vols. (Paris, 1844–1864), 137:823–26 (which reprints the edition of Jean

Mabillon). I have analyzed the date at and circumstances under which the text was composed in "Letaldus of Micy and the Hagiographic Traditions of the Abbey of Nouaillé: The Context of the *Delatio corporis s. Juniani*," *Analecta Bollandiana* 115 (1997): 253–67. For more on the Peace of God movement, see the essays collected in *The Peace of God: Social Violence and Religious Response in France Around the Year 1000*, eds. Thomas Head and Richard Landes (Ithaca, NY, 1992). The best edition of Ralph Glaber's work is Rodulfus Glaber, *Historiarum libri quinque: The Five Books of Histories*, ed. John France (Oxford, 1989). France's edition provides a fine English translation, but the translations offered throughout this chapter are my own. For the context of Glaber's work, see John France, "Rodulphus Glaber and the Cluniacs," *Journal of Ecclesiastical History* 39 (1988): 497–507. The only edition of the *Miraculum s. Maximini* (*Bibliotheca hagiographica latina*, no. 5821b) is that which I have published from the only known manuscript (Vatican City, Biblioteca Apostolica Vaticana, MS Regenensis latinus, 621, fols. 29–33v) in Thomas Head, "'I Vow Myself To Be Your Servant': An Eleventh-Century Pilgrim, His Chronicler, and His Saint," *Historical Reflections/Réflexions Historiques* 11 (1984): 215–51 (the edition and an earlier English translation, here corrected and improved, are to be found on pp. 235–51). A full discussion of the text is to be found in that article. I have also discussed the development of the cult of St. Maximinus at the abbey of Micy in *Hagiography and the Cult of Saints. The Diocese of Orléans, 800–1200*, Cambridge Studies in Medieval Life and Thought, fourth series 14 (Cambridge, 1990), pp. 202–34. More generally on collections of miracle stories written in the eleventh and twelfth centuries, see Ronald Finucane, *Miracles and Pilgrims. Popular Beliefs in Medieval England* (Totowa, NJ, 1977); Benedicta Ward, *Miracles and the Medieval Mind* (Philadelphia, 1982); Pierre-André Sigal, *L'homme et le miracle dans la France médiévale (XIe-XIIe siècle)* (Paris, 1985); Head, *Hagiography and the Cult of Saints*, pp. 135–201. One complete collection of miracle stories, compiled in the early eleventh century at the southern French monastery of Conques, has appeared in an excellent English translation: *The Book of Sainte Foy*, trans. Pamela Sheingorn (Philadelphia, 1995).

The Cult of Relics in the Eleventh Century

1. FROM THEODORIC OF SAINT EUCHARIUS, *THE DISCOVERY OF THE RELICS OF ST. CELSUS*, CHAPTERS 1, 5, AND 12–24 [*BIBLIOTHECA HAGIOGRAPHICA LATINA*, NOS. 1720–21].

(1.) To the most excellent and magnificent builder and father Richard,[1] Theodoric—the least of his servants, than whom no one among the monks is held more contemptible—not unmindful of the monastic goal and hardly making any sort of roundabout apology, [presents this treatise] in compliance with the rule of obedience. Your paternal piety has asked—and inevitably it has been taken as a command—that I trace the origins of the discovery of the most sacred remains of the blessed confessor of Christ [named] Celsus and of his famed miracles. At the same time—mindful of the passage of heavenly time and how our days fritter away—[you have asked] that I add something about the pious memory of Egbert, archbishop of the city of Trier, because of the great service he performed for this church in fully discovering those blessed relics for the living. His actions in bringing to light the once-hidden treasure are known and their publication has been entrusted to relation by my own insignificant pen, for the purposes of the memory of posterity. No less, you [Richard] point out that the fame of the miracles performed by this great man [Celsus] will not allow us to remain idly silent. [**Translator's note**: In Chapters 2–4, Theodoric continues to introduce his work with similar protestations of his own insignificance and of the excellence of both Celsus and Egbert. The use of such a humility topos is common among medieval writers, but Theodoric extends it to an almost astonishing degree.]

(5.) In the year of the Lord's incarnation 978 when Prince Otto II—father of the Otto, emperor and monarch of Rome, who now actively holds the crown—held the scepter, Archbishop Egbert ruled over the holy church of Trier, which is preserved by God.[2] He was a man of blessed memory and a lamp of virtue, of high standing due to the generous bequest of his deceased parents, but of even higher standing due to the priceless dowry of complete uprightness. His reverence surpassed that of all the bishops and magnates of the kingdom [and] . . . he was the principle teacher and sustainer of monks, a special lover of the discipline of the *Rule* [of St. Benedict]. The humble heart of a devoted monk hid under the costume of a bishop, as if he frequently paraded with Martha in public in order to carry out the ministry of God, but nevertheless turned himself with Mary completely over to the study of the divine word. He made of himself a free sacrifice to the Godhead, in practical matters like a small bird, but in contemplative matters like a turtle-dove . . . [**Translator's note**: In Chapters 6–11, Theodoric describes how Archbishop Egbert undertook the reform of several monasteries in his diocese. In time he turned to the abbey of Saint Eucharius, located on the eastern side of Trier. The patron of this monastery was a saint celebrated as an early archbishop of the city. He installed a man named Gotherius, who had previously the monastery of Saint Bavo in Ghent, as the new abbot. With the permission and support of Emperor Otto II, they undertook to rebuild the monastic church.]

(12.) The glorious bishop was inspired by imperial support and accompanied by divine assistance. When he sought to implement the plan he had in mind for the church, however, his work met with a snare, for the place was strewn with many hard and sharp stones which hindered the digging of trenches. For many days the workmen labored at digging. Suddenly, on the third or forth day, a lucky blow in the trenches unearthed the grave of blessed Celsus, as was pleasing to God. As is read in the book of Job, nothing is in the ground without cause.[3] For it must be believed that it was not according to fate (which is abhorrent to Catholic ears), but according to divine providence that this discovery occurred, despite what was intended. For if blessed Celsus had not been buried in that very place, he would not have been found by any manner of excavation; also, if the workmen had not torn up the ground, the treasure would never have been found. For almighty God had allowed it to lie there for centuries, and to become known to the living at this time in accordance with His will. Behold how lifeless rocks cry out in praise of the Lord, and the rocks are found to be living [see Lk 19:40]. And so we see that the Divine does not live in temples built of stone, but rather we ought to make ourselves into living temples to God, because *the Word became flesh and dwelt amongst us* [Jn 1:14].

(13.) The sarcophagus, in which the naked seed lay awaiting for all time its flowering the grace of the resurrection, was stone of dazzling whiteness, which is called in the vulgar tongue *creta*.[4] On it lay a marble tablet on which an inscription concerning his sanctity was engraved. The funerary inscription ran thus: "To whomever anxiously wishes to learn about this tomb. Here lies the man Celsus [that is, noble one], who lived up to his name not only in word, but in his deeds. God has certainly inscribed this man in the roll of honor [in heaven], a man who was not lazy, but ever vigorous in his quest for his true fatherland. He drew his family and his birth from a distinguished lineage; he has been buried in this tomb with pious affection." . . . [**Translator's note:** In the remainder of Chapter 13 and in Chapter 14, Theodoric undertakes a lengthy exegetical digression in which he discusses the ways in which the verse from Job might be applied to the situation of Celsus.]

(15.) When the happy rumor of this discovery came quickly to the attention of the pious archbishop, [Egbert] blessed God by rendering much praise for the graces which had been granted by the giver of all good things. Giving no heed to appearances, he excitedly rushed off to the divine spectacle, where members of the clergy were standing around. Although he had been most eager to get on with the construction, he was nonetheless most happy to accept this interruption, which certified with good faith through the inscription that, in days gone by, the city of Trier had been held in the most dignified respect by God. [Egbert] diligently, but carefully rummaged around in the area where [the discovery] had taken place. He did not presume to move the coffin holding the sacred relics from the spot of its burial, but sought to place some sign of his authority on the watch kept over them. He brought together some monks who would unceasingly chant praises to God in thanks for the merits of such a just man. He also very much wished to learn the advice of his fellow bishops as to what ought to be done concerning the discovery; he had the matter written down in a book and sent his treasurer as a delegate.

(16.) Following the inviolable command of the bishop, the brothers [of the abbey of Saint Eucharius] chanted the office day and night without pause, sometimes in the open air, other times in the church. They sent their importunate prayers to God and hoped that He would hear them. Not much later, a synod of many bishops and abbots, including all the fathers of Belgium and Germany, was convoked by imperial edict at the royal palace, which is called in the vulgar tongue *Engilenheim*.[5] At that meeting, many pressing matters of concern to the Church [were addressed] and promulgations made according to the authority of holy canons which were to be inviolably observed by all posterity. Egbert—whose memory is always blessed when he is spoken of these days—was already scheduled, as metropolitan of the church of Trier, to take part in these proceedings. After the many matters had been discussed on which the synod promulgated edicts, when time had been set aside for him, Archbishop [Egbert], who held a high place among all those men, sought to speak, having brought forth a piece of parchment on which was written the inscription from the sarcophagus of blessed Celsus, as well as the story of how the relics had been found. Speaking before all with Ciceronian eloquence, he told what things divine grace had brought to light through the work of human hands in his city. When the emperor heard this, he was filled with a great joy and he spoke to the holy conclave dedicated to God.[6]

(17.) [**Translator's note:** Theodoric at this point places a long and wholly spurious speech into the mouth of Emperor Otto II, which was intended to bolster claims by the archbishop of Trier for authority over fellow archbishops.] After this the emperor promulgated a decree, accompanied by the bishops who provided their unanimous consent, that it was pleasing to the holy council that the archbishop of Trier ought to return to his see. There, along with his gathered clergy, he was to raise up the remains of blessed Celsus from their tomb; then he was to enclose them in a shrine, as if in a treasure chest of divine works; and finally he was to place the reliquary on the altar to receive the cult of full sanctity, as if it contained nothing less than the limbs of the highest king.

(18.) When the mandate [of the synod] and the order [of the emperor] had been received, Archbishop Egbert, like a prudent animal, had obtained for himself the blessings and prayers of his fellow bishops, and steadfastly joined to them a sign of imperial favor. Thus he prepared the way for favorable success, with divine patronage over his head and a crowd of important people at his side. After an interval of a few days, he called to his see all the leading abbots and monks, priests and clerics of his diocese. When he found that they all consented to the decree of the synod, he immediately arranged a festive procession with crosses, candles, censers, gem-encrusted Gospel books, and all ecclesiastical pomp, along with monks singing a sweet hymn to the Lord. The procession made its way step by step to the monastery of Saint Eucharius, filled with happy tears. After the bishop had simply commended himself and his vow to the holy confessors of Christ, he went trembling to the tomb, while the voices of all assembled gave praise which reached up to heaven. At the tomb, the bishop solemnly made supplication to God, that he be allowed to carry out his vow, inasmuch as it was not at odds with God's holy desires.

(19.) Since *in everything God works for good with those who love him* [Rom 8:28] after the bishop had brought this prayer to an end, this important task was undertaken in faith as a token to God. Having removed the seal, the bishop drew back the bolts from the sacred mausoleum. When it was opened, such a marvelously sweet odor escaped and such a fragrance of heavenly nectar came forth that all those who were present thought that they had come into the presence of God and entered into the delights of paradise. Thus struck with both fear and joy, they burst forth in praise of God as follows: "Blessed is the Lord of Israel, who never fails those who place their hopes in Him. God has decreed that His servant, who is Celsus [that is, noble one] in both name and deed, should be revealed in our days through the blessed efforts of our bishop. Blessed also, oh Lord, is he whom you have chosen and taken to yourself. You have appointed him to be a faithful guardian over all your goods and provided his most pious patronage to us in our poverty."

(20.) In the midst of these chants of sacred melody, Egbert reverently emptied the tomb, taking the dry, pale bones forth and placing them in shining white, clean linen. He sang out, accompanied by all the clergy, a verse most apt and fitting for this occasion: *Let the faithful exult in glory; let them sing for joy on their couches* [Ps 149:5].[7] Who is able to say how many tears, not of sadness, but of spiritual happiness then flowed? The archbishop was unable to restrain himself in the midst of the chanting voices and he devoutly watered his face with floods of tears in praise of the Redeemer. Among the joyful songs of the monks and the glad responses of the clerics, the voice of the crowd was everywhere mixed in, making a great and noisy song. Nothing was able to be heard in that large assembly of the faithful, other than the Kyrie Eleison and the Gloria. After having lain humbly hidden for so long, the bones of blessed Celsus were now gloriously revealed by the Lord. The eager servants of the bishops were employed to carry the coffin; so it was born in honor from its place of burial by God-fearing men and placed with the greatest reverence in the church of Saint Eucharius. When the archbishop, adorned with this dowry from heaven and surrounded by a great throng of believers, entered the monastery, he began to chant the first verse of the paschal hymn of joy, *Te Deum Laudamus*, and all those gathered there completed it in a glorious din. There were candles burning, church bells ringing, thuribles giving forth the fragrant scent of incense; all were agreed that in this procession of great joy the singing of angels as well as of humans was to be detected in the midst of that sweet odor of divinity.

(21.) After the most seemly procession of the blessed relics had been completed, they were reverently placed on the altar of Saint Eucharius by the blessed archbishop, accompanied by grateful applause and gushes of sweet tears on the part of all who were gathered giving thanks in common. Great and ineffable indeed was the cause of this joy, for the people of Trier had through divine grace acquired for their patron a citizen in the heavenly city. When the archbishop, surrounded by a crowd of priests, proceeded to the solemnities of the Mass, the devout congregation began to cry out sweetly to the Lord. Fear and reverence toward blessed Celsus swelled in the hearts of all those present. Earnestly entreating divine grace, they hoped that they might acquire some sign of his sanctity on that day. And their prayers were answered. After the passage from the holy Gospel had been read out, the bishop of the church spoke to the people in an admonitory manner. Just as nard gives off its odor, he told to all the story of the discovery of the holy relics. He exhorted the people that they not refrain from visiting blessed Celsus frequently and that in each future year they should celebrate the day of his birth, which happened to be January 4, with the greatest honor, as was ordered by apostolic authority.

(22.) When this sermon of doctrine was finished, Egbert returned from the pulpit to the altar in order to offer the host of our redemption up to Almighty God both for the honor of blessed Celsus and for the salvation of all Christian people. When the Offertory chant was finished with great jubilation, he began the Preface. At that point the priest of the Lord presumed to undertake an examination as to whether one could say that these relics seemed to be from blessed Celsus, lest the matter by chance seem to take place, or to have taken place, in a vacuum. In the eyes of all the clergy, he took a small piece of very thin cloth and he wrapped a piece of a joint from the saint's finger in it. He placed it in the live coals of the thurible, in which incense was burned, for the space of an hour, during which time he recited the mystical canon in its entirety. The relic remained intact in the fire. Since *the fire will test what sort of work each one has done* [1 Cor. 3:13], the degree to which there was apostolic character in blessed Celsus became most evidently clear through the material fire, which is generally predicted for all in the time of purgatory.[8]

(23.) Behold! the One who provided solace to the three boys in the fiery furnace [see Dan 3], that same One, in order to declare the merits of Celsus, has now removed from the coals the power to burn, lest the wrapping of the relic be consumed by fire. It is He who always was, always will be, and never will change, from Whom nothing is hidden, in Whose simple substance and nature nothing may suffer outrage, or is composite, or is created, or is there any particle of an earthly kingdom. He has not committed any fault, nor ever contemplated it. Nor has any sin impaired Him or altered His commands, from the beginning of time, forever. If the violence of material and extinguishable fire did not have the power to harm the wrapping, due to the magnitude of such merits, is it possible that on the day of the passion of the Lord, when the elements are aflame, the purgatorial fire will receive the power of doing any harm to blessed Celsus? For Celsus is the son of the Resurrection, who did not fail to build on that *foundation* over which the architect Paul placed *gold, silver*, [and] *precious stones*" [1 Cor. 3:12] and who, as long as he was in the flesh, lived contrary to the flesh.

(24.) After this miracle had been witnessed and the chanting of the Mass completed, the archbishop placed that relic, [now shown to be] acceptable to God on the altar along with the remaining bones in a seemly fashion. Having made a benediction, he dismissed the congregation in peace, giving praise to God, and saying, "Now we know what we have [in these relics]! How good is God! How great is His mercy for us in this world!"

2. LETALDUS OF MICY, *THE JOURNEY OF THE BODY OF ST. JUNIANUS TO THE COUNCIL OF CHARROUX* [*BIBLIOTHECA HAGIOGRAPHICA LATINA*, NO. 4565]. Brother Letaldus gives salutations to lord father Constantine and to the other brothers of the monastery of Nouaillé.[9] The angel Gabriel was once sent by the Lord to alleviate the labors of Tobias. The angel not only delivered him from toil, but also gave him the support of the kindness of divine piety. Then he returned to Him by whom he had been sent, going forth from Whom does not make one absent. Gabriel first taught those who had benefited from heavenly kindness and addressed them, saying, "*It is good to hide the secret of a king, but gloriously to reveal the works of God* [Tob 12:7]." Therefore it is fitting that we reveal and confess the works of Christ which are allowed to happen in our times through His most glorious confessor Junianus, both for the praise and glory of the saint's name and for the edification of those who will hear the story.[10] All people should learn these things, for such works as were done in the days of our fathers and are still done for us now do not happen on account of our own merits, but through the kindness of piety and the intervention of those fathers who are provided as intercessors for us. They provide something for us to copy in the important correction of our own lives.

We therefore approach the task of writing this work which we have promised, not trusting in the help of men, but supported by the aid of divine largesse, which comes from him who said, "*Open your mouth wide and I will fill it*" [Ps 81:10, 80:11 in the Vulgate]. Reverend fathers and brothers, you have begged us with your prayers and you have enjoined me by your charitable command. Do not allow our rustic speech to be displeasing to you, if only so that truth alone may bring forth the whole narrative, as it was told by you. At that time sinners were rising up like stalks of wheat. Evil people wasted the vineyard of the Lord just as briers and thorns choke the harvest of the land. Therefore it pleased bishops, abbots, and other religious men that a council be held at which the taking of booty would be prohibited and the property of the saints, which had been unjustly stolen, would be restored. Other evils which fouled the fair countenance of the holy church of God were also struck down by the sharp points of anathemas. I think that this council was held at the monastery of Charroux and that a great crowd of many people [*populus*] gathered there from the Poitou, the Limousin, and neighboring regions. Many bodies of saints were also brought there.[11] The cause of religion was strengthened by their presence, and the impudence of evil people was beaten back. That council—convoked, as it was thought, by divine will—was adorned through the presence of these saints by frequent miracles. Along with these various relics of the saints honored by God, the remains of the glorious father Junianus were brought with proper honor.

Several things occurred when the relics of the holy father Junianus were brought forth from their monastic enclosure. Not far from the monastery [of Nouaillé] those who carried the bundle containing the saint stopped and put down their holy burden. After the most holy relics departed, the faithful in their devotion erected a cross in order to memorialize and record the fact that the relics of the holy father had rested there. From that time to this, whosoever suffers from a fever and goes there is returned to their former health through the invocation of the name of Christ and the intercession of this same father Junianus. When the party came to the little village called Ruffiacus, they sought out the mansion house and passed the night there in a vigil singing hymns and praise to God. The next day they resumed their journey.[12] At the place where the relics had rested, faithful Christians erected a sort of fence from twigs, so that the place where the holy body had lain might remain safe from the approach of men and animals. Many days later a wild bull came by and wantonly struck that same fence with his horns and flanks. When suddenly he retreated from the fence, he fell down, and died. In that same place, a little pool was created by placing a gutter tile to allow runoff water to be stored up. Because of the reverence for the holy relics, this pool served as an invitation for many people to wash. Among these there was a woman who suffered from elephantiasis. When she washed herself with that water, she was returned to her former health.

3. From Ralph Glaber, *The Five Books of Histories*, Book 4, Part 3, Sections 6–8

(6.) Divine authority gave the Jews this warning through Moses: "If there is a prophet among you who speaks in the name of one of the gods of the foreign peoples and claims to know the future, do not believe him, even if by some fortune the event takes place, for the Lord your God is tempting you in order to know if you love Him or not" [see Deut 13:1–3].[13] In present times, there was a lowborn man who was the most skillful sort of swindler. He was of unknown name and origin, although in the many places where he sought refuge, he fraudulently gave himself names and invented the province from which he came, lest he be discovered. He used to rummage around in secret among tombs and take from them the ashes of men not long dead. Then he placed these in various urns and sold them to many people as if they were the relics of holy martyrs and confessors. After having pulled off innumerable such frauds in Gaul, he came for shelter to the Alps, which are mostly inhabited by primitive people who make their homes on the rugged slopes. There, giving up his former aliases of Peter and John, he called himself Stephen. According to his habit, in the dead of night he collected the bones of some anonymous man from the lowest of places, placed them in a casket, and then said that an angelic vision had revealed to him that they were the relics of a holy martyr named Just.[14] Soon all the common people flocked to this marvel, as usually happens in such matters as the people of rural areas are uneducated. They only regretted that they were not sick and so could not be cured. They brought the sick, offered small gifts, and held watch through the night, waiting for some miracle perchance to happen. As we have said, evil spirits are sometimes allowed to perform such miracles in order to tempt men to sin. These then seem to offer proof beyond a doubt. The mending of many limbs seemed to happen there and the people hung up many symbols of these cures. The bishops of Maurienne, of Uzès, and of Grenoble—whose dioceses were profaned by these events—did not show diligence in inquiring into the matter, the more so because they were convinced that their courts were nothing other than a means of seeking empty lucre from the people and so they at that time showed favor to the falsehood.

(7.) Meanwhile Manfred, the richest among local marquesses, hearing the reports of this matter sent some of his followers to take by force and bring back to him this simulacrum which they thought a martyr worthy of veneration. Now this marquess had begun to construct a monastery in the city of Susa, which is the oldest in the Alps, in honor of almighty God and His mother, the ever-virgin Mary. After the simulacrum had been seized, he sought to place it there along with many other relics of saints.[15] A little later, when work on the church had been completed and it came time for the day of dedication, the bishops of the region arrived and with them not a few abbots including the famed William of Saint-Bénigne.[16] The aforementioned swindler had meanwhile insinuated himself into the good graces of the marquess. To be sure he had then promised to reveal to him in the future relics of saints which were much more precious, but he had fallaciously confected the acts, names, and the facts of the passions of those saints, like that of St. Just. When the swindler was questioned by the learned men present as to how he was acquainted with such things, he prated on and spoke without any truth. I was there myself, for I had come with the aforementioned abbot. He said, "At night an angel appears to me, stays with me until I force him to depart, and tells me everything which he knows I wish to learn." When we replied to these claims, we asked him whether he saw this while in a vigil or during his sleep. He replied, "Most nights the angel takes me from my bed. Even my wife doesn't know. After saying many things, he gives me his salutations and a kiss, and departs." Recognizing that this lie had been polished with much cunning, we knew that this man was no angel, but rather a minister of lies and evil.

(8.) Meanwhile the bishops continued with the rite of the consecration of the church for which they had come, and they introduced the bones fabricated by the craft of this profane man among the other relics. This came to pass on the seventeenth of October. The perpetrators of this error asserted that they were the bones of the martyr Just, who had died that day in the city of Beauvais in Gaul and whose head was now held to be in Auxerre, where he had been born and raised. I, who knew the novelty of the matter, asserted the frivolity of what was said. Although men of higher rank also recognized the pretensions of this lying person, they gave credence to the story which I have related. The following night monstrous phantasms were seen in the church by some monks and other religious. The forms of black Ethiopians issued from the place in which the bones were buried and left the church. While some people of sound mind claimed that the bones were a detestable figment which should be abominated, the common lot of country folk accepted the corrupt swindler and continued in their error of honoring the name of an unjust man with the name of Just.

4. THE MIRACLE OF ST. MAXIMINUS [BIBLIOTHECA HAGIOGRAPHICA LATINA, NO. 5821B]

Since [Henry] had come to penance more through necessity than through desire and also, perhaps, in consideration of those who considered him unsuitable, whose sense of propriety was upset by his restless agitation, he undertook to help the unfortunate through the aid and merits of our most faithful father Maximinus and to preach with glorious song the sublime power of that faithful patron to people far removed from our home.[17]

One night while Henry was groggy in the midst of severe pain, a divine vision had appeared to him and spoken to him thus, "Search for the tomb of Maximinus, the beloved of God, wherever you meet people. You will return to health there through God's mercy." The vision both stirred him awake and made him happy. Henry gave thanks to the author of the vision and roused his men with news of the mercy which had been promised him. His men quickly collected horses and other things necessary for a journey and they took to the road. When they were under way, they asked Henry about the name and the location of the holy relics. While Henry remembered the name of St. Maximinus, he knew nothing about [his tomb's] location. Some were for pressing on, while others hesitated. The former said, "We have heard that there is in Trier a friend of God by the name of Maximinus, who is accustomed to providing protection and is held in great veneration by the faithful.[18] Surely he is the one about whom your vision spoke. He is the one to be approached in the manner in which you were directed, master, in order that he may help you." Accompanied by a party of servants and horses, Henry took the recommended route.

After he had at length arrived in Trier, he slept many nights at the tomb of the saint. The same divine vision appeared to him once more and spoke thus, "You are mistaken, brother. You were not told to come here. [It is God's will] that you regain your health in another place and through the merits of another person. In the inns of Gaul seek for a place where the body of the blessed man, whose name was revealed to you, rests. Make your petition [to

God] through his merits. You will receive help." Disturbed by this news, Henry awoke his companions and said, "My dear friends, trust me, our efforts here are worthless. Unless you now come to my assistance with full solicitude and forethought, this oracle of God's mercy will have aided us in vain. The most faithful Jesus has benevolently resolved to advise me through an angelic patron because he wishes to alleviate me of the burden of my unhappiness and he has again made clear to us the depth of our ignorance. For he speaks and we do not understand. We labor, but it does us no good. For it has not been ordained that we be helped through the holiness of this particular father [Maximinus of Trier]. Rather, our cause has been commended to another Maximinus. Get up, then, for the sake of God, and see if you might perchance hear of the shrine of another Maximinus on the western side of Gaul. For we hear nothing about him among our own people, but public recognition has recorded his name elsewhere."

After all this had occurred, the group departed early in the morning. When some of his companions inquired into the matter, both in their own country and abroad, they at length heard, "Not far from the city of Tours, where St. Martin is sought for his protection, there is another town on the Loire, called by the name of Chinon. One of the disciples of St. Martin is buried there and revered, so we believe, under this name. We have heard that this famous man is faithfully praised and visited by many people, since those who visit and pray [at his tomb] are accustomed to being aided miraculously. We do not, however, know for certain whether he is called Maximinus or Maximus, that is, properly called by the former or the latter name."[19] After the servants heard this, they returned to their master and made known to him the ambiguity both about the name and about the tomb of the holy man. After they had discussed the matter and pondered the closeness of these names for a long time, they exhorted him to seek out the truth hidden beneath the ambiguity of the pronunciation of the names. Then he bid a rather disagreeable good-bye to those who had told him [about the saint]. After he had chosen one of their number to accompany him on the long journey, he sent the others home and prepared himself to go on pilgrimage.

After Henry had covered the long distance and arrived in the region of Tours, he heard about the miraculous deeds of the saint. When he made sure about the [saint's] name, however, [he learned that] the saint was called Maximus, so that, as Henry approached the shrine, he was seized by doubt. After he had made his prayers at length and frequently visited the tomb as a suppliant, the above-mentioned divine vision once again spoke to him, "You are a man of little wisdom and one who in no way seeks after his health. Why do you force God to be angry with you? Why do you look upon that which God offers to you in kindness as if it were offered in jest? God directed you toward salvation, but you work against Him through your errant wandering. God advised you to halt earlier, but you, like one who is unwise and hollow, still continue your foolish wandering. You seek out Maximus, when God advised you to seek out Maximinus. Believe me when I say that if the Lord had not wished to reveal the glory of His faithful [saint], you would not have been able through your wandering to arrive at the cure promised to you. Nonetheless, lest you fail in this matter, I tell you to remain confident, for you will soon find comfort. Remember this, then, and exactly this: when you return to the city of Orléans, through which you have passed, you will find not far from that city the home, and there the aid, of this holy father.[20] Get up, therefore, and make haste, since you will attain rich rewards when you come to that holy tomb." After this speech and this threat, Henry awoke and roused up his traveling companion. He hastened to return in the opposite direction.

When Henry approached the vicinity of the city [Orléans], he heard for certain about the tomb of the saint [Maximinus] and came to the monastery [of Micy]. When he explained the reason for his coming to the brothers, he was received with charitable hospitality. Many fires were lit and Henry's strength—which the cold of winter had depleted, for it was in the month of December, namely the feast of St. Nicholas on the fifth day of the month—was renewed by their heat.[21] On the next day, when he was taken to be introduced to the chapter of the brothers, he told them the place of his birth, the cause of his fall, and the errors he had made concerning the faithful advice [of the divinely inspired visions]. When, at tearful length, he had spun out his story, the brothers, being delighted at such a report, first gave thanks to God and then said to him, "If the goodness of the Savior wishes to reveal this [plan] to you, brother, and our faithful God desires to glorify our holy father by [granting you a cure], then from now on it behooves you, who were led to this place by a gift of God, not to waste time in laziness and indolence, but to strike the heart of divine mercy with the most persisted prayer and to take part with us both day and night in the praise of God and hymns [which we sing] in the church. The kingdom of God does not come to the lazy and slothful." After they had instructed him in this manner, the monks sent him back to the guesthouse.

Henry—concerned about his redemption, overcome by the great stress of his recent labor, and terrified by the portentousness of the aforesaid visions—began, as he had been instructed, to enter eagerly into the service of God and to take part assiduously in the vigils and nightly labor of the brothers. Once, when he was weighed down with sleep, he was caught up in ecstasy beyond measure and heard, "Take heart, brother, take heart and persevere. Your redemption will occur with the coming of the saints." After he had heard these words, Henry faithfully awaited the feast day of the saint, which was only a few days off.[22] With almost incessant prayers he commended himself again and again to the holy patron, in the manner of the prophet, *here a little, there a little* [Is 28:10]. And so he persevered until the feast day of the holy father, which was awaited by all people, and most particularly by the brothers [of Micy] and by the whole people of the region surrounding Orléans.

Henry prepared himself for the coming vigils, at the same time anticipating the hoped-for restoration of his health. He subjected his body to a fast for the entire day, so that, thoroughly subdued by bodily torment, he would be prepared with a ready mind for the nightly prayers. When the psalmody and prayer began with the first coming of night, he placed himself as a supplicant between the two altars, calling out incessantly and imploring his sought-after patron.[23] He cried out himself, and if any one of the brothers looked at him, he beseeched [that monk] to cry out [as well]. Henry also lay prostrate—a fact which we have neglected to mention—in the sanctuary through the entire night as devoutly as possible. The monks out of habit chanted the [liturgical] responses without delay. Henry repeated without ceasing, "Have mercy on me father Maximinus," with a cry from his lips and from his heart. To be sure, he called out the name which he had long held fast, but, as he had many times been in error, perhaps he still had doubts concerning this place. Addressing [the monks] in tears, he told how he had erred grievously, and how he had deserved to suffer his fall, and how he had labored in vain, although through the goodness of God he had been called back and been told of the name of our holy father [Maximinus]. Having come at length to the opportune time, that is the feast day of the saint, he would now be able to rejoice in the benefit promised him through the prayers of the saint and the promise of God.

At length, however, Henry became wearied by the prolonged chanting of the hymns of Matins.[24] He began to fault himself for his lack of fervor, both in his present prayers and his past labors, with the result that he almost admitted, [giving in to] the increasing power of his rage, that the divine oracles had misled him. [He acted thus] because he perceived, at the moment when the holy *Te Deum Laudamus* was coming to an end—with the uneven harmony of laypeople singing psalms along with the monastic chant, their common rejoicing fittingly alternating with that of the churchbells being rung—that the completion of the vigil approached with the rising dawn and that still he was unable to bring his limb forth from its wrapping.[25] At that moment, he began to feel weakened, as if by some great terror, and to lose his senses. Seized by a debilitating power, he considered, as he trembled there, that he might flee in fear [to someplace] where no one could threaten him and make him fearful. He was afraid, yet he did not know why. He trembled, yet he did not know the cause. He was full of doubt, not knowing what would happen during the coming moments and dreading lest Matins would be completed. At that moment, as he later told us, he thought to himself, that, if it were possible, he would leave hidden in the departing crowd, and that, having left, he would not appear again in our region. After he had hesitated for a while thinking such absurd thoughts, he began to leave in stealth.

Coming at length to the exit doors of the sanctuary, he came upon a person of great reverence, with a bent and white-haired head, an old and smiling face, and a modest and hesitant gait. This man, who supported himself on a staff, came to meet him and, upbraiding him for his foolishness, said to him, "Where are you going, fool? Where are you going? Hang on a bit longer. Hang on, I tell you. I am here. Resist foolishness. The time has come. You will soon be cured." The [old man] spoke and struck the flat of his palm against

Henry's face. Marvelous to say, it was clear that only a light blow had been struck, but such power followed the lightness of that blow, that Henry fell over, as if dead, on the pavement and—oh new thing—his feeble, paralyzed feet were stripped of all covering. We must believe that in this event the story of Moses was, as it were, repeated. For, when Moses wished to approach the [burning] bush, it was said, *Put off the shoes from your feet, for the place on which you are standing is holy ground* [Ex 3:5]. In the same way, Henry was standing in the sanctuary when he came to be cured, as if coming to the bush, and his feet were forcibly unshod, although as the result of actions, rather than words. These things happened about the end of the morning office, as the precentor beautifully and melodiously intoned the beginning of the antiphon for the Gospel.[26]

At just that moment the lord abbot and some of the brothers proceeded according to custom to the altar with thuribles.[27] They saw that Henry lay immobile on the pavement and they learned from the tumultuous murmur of the people how his feet had been bared of their coverings. For Henry himself said nothing at all. Meanwhile the monks remained still until the solemnities of the vigils were completed. At the end of the Psalm singing, when the people made a great racket over the whole affair, the brothers came with the abbot, intending to investigate what had happened. After silence had been broken with [the abbot's] permission, the monks strove with one another to repeat Henry's name in a loud voice. When the remains of his shoes and bandages, scattered about by the miracle, had been collected, they tried to revive him with blessed water.

When the clamor continued to increase over the course of a long time to an almost infinite pitch, Henry—sighing greatly, his face wet from much exertion, and on bent knees—spoke, "Hasten with me brothers and fathers, hasten, I implore you, to give thanks to God and to this father [Maximinus] who has intervened on his feast in such a festive way and cured my infirmity. For the holy father has rebuked me like a son with a slap, and through the power of God has restored to me, his servant, my long sought-after health. Be assured that, in whatever land I will live, I vow myself to be [Maximinus's] servant. I will be so now and forever." When Henry had explained everything, both what he had heard from and what he had seen of Maximinus, he added, "But, fathers, what are you doing? Why do you not honor the patron who is present? Behold he is here. Look, he is admonishing you. Praise the Lord." Thus Henry spoke and, as if he had Maximinus before his eyes, he quickly prostrated himself in order to hold the saint's feet. The brothers quickly collected themselves in the choir and loudly sang the *Te Deum Laudamus* from the beginning, weeping as they sang. The bells were pealed and rang out. The voices of the elder [monks] and the younger [monks] without distinction tearfully praised God and their holy patron. Those who were outside [the church] were drawn in by the loud alternation of the bells with the glad cries of the laypeople and of the monks. They hastened with great tumult to the church, joined their voices to praise, and their tears flowed giving thanks.

Later the brothers, with the abbot, detained Henry in the monastery for a long time, until the aforesaid council of Paris held by Bishop Gerald of Ostia at the end of Septuagesima; he traveled there with the abbot of the monastery healthy and happy in all ways.[28]

NOTES

1. Richard was abbot of the monastery of Saint Eucharius in Trier from ca. 1006 until 1023.

2. Egbert served as archbishop of Trier from 978 until 993. Otto II (955–83) of Germany was crowned co-king with his father (Otto I) in 961 and co-emperor in 967, serving in both capacities until his death in 983. His young son, Otto III, succeeded him on the throne, despite some immediate opposition, but did not claim the imperial title until 996. He died in 1002.

3. I have provided a literal translation of the Vulgate, which differs significantly from the RSV in this passage [Job 5:6].

4. "Cretan earth" is chalk.

5. Otto II spent Easter of 980 at the imperial court in Ingelheim. After the feast, he summoned the ecclesiastical hierarchy of the east Frankish realm to a synod. The decisions of that episcopal synod concerning a dipute between the monks of Stavelot and Malmedy are described in a royal act dated 4 June 980.

6. It would seem that Egbert was following the guidelines concerning the cult of saints laid down a century and a half earlier by the Carolingian reformers in canon 51 of the Council of Mainz: "Henceforth let no one presume to move the bodies of saints from one place to another without the council of the prince or license from a holy synod of bishops." Prince (*princeps*) in this context meant a secular ruler, such as Otto II.

7. The word translated as "faithful" in the RSV is *sancti*, which can also mean "saints." Theodoric is clearly playing on that meaning of the term here.

8. Egbert was in essence applying the judicial ordeal by fire to the relics. This is the earliest surely recorded instance of the use of the ordeal to authenticate the relics of saints, but this ritual came to be employed for that purpose with some frequency in the following decades. On the development and spread of this ritual, see Thomas Head, "The Genesis of the Ordeal of Relics by Fire (c. 980-c. 1020)," in *Constructing Sanctity in Medieval Europe*, ed. George Ferzoco (in press). It should be noted that this is a very early mention of the concept of purgatory. On the development of the idea of the place of purgatory in the Christian afterlife, see Jacques LeGoff, *The Birth of Purgatory*, trans. Arthur Goldhammer (French original, Paris, 1981; Chicago, 1984).

9. The abbey of Nouaillé was located in a wooded area about ten kilometers from the city of Poitiers in central France. It was founded sometime before the last quarter of the seventh century.

10. St. Junianus was known as the monk who had founded the monastery of Mairé, which was located like Nouaillé in the Poitou, sometime in the seventh or eighth century. Nouaillé came to possess his relics in the ninth century.

11. The council in question was held at the abbey of Charroux on June 1, 989. It is the earliest council associated with the movement known as the Peace of God from which the synodal decrees survive. Letaldus here refers to those decrees, with which he was probably familiar. The decrees read: "Supported by the authority of the councils of our predecessors and in the name of God and of our saviour Jesus Christ, I Gunbaldus . . . along with my fellow bishops have gathered together in this court which is called Charroux on this first day of June. These bishops, as well as clerics and monks, not to mention laypeople of both sexes, have beseeched the aid of divine justice. Our purpose is that the criminal activity, which we know has for some time been sprouting up through evil habit in our districts because of our long delay in calling a council, will be rooted out and more proper activity implanted. Therefore we who are specially gathered together in the name of God decree, as will be made manifestly clear in the following canons, that: (1) If anyone attacks the holy church, or takes anything from it by force, and compensation is not provided, let him be

anathema. (2) If anyone takes as booty sheep, oxen, asses, cows, female goats, male goats, or pigs from peasants or from other poor people—unless it is due to the fault of the victim—and if that person neglects to make reparation for everything, let him be anathema. (3) If anyone robs, or seizes, or strikes a priest, or a deacon, or any man of the clergy who is not bearing arms (that is, a shield, a sword, a breastplate, or a helmet), but who is simply going about his business or remaining at home, and if, after examination by his own bishop, that person is thus found to be guilty of any crime, then he is guilty of sacrilege, and if he furthermore does not come forward to make satisfaction, let him then be held to be excluded from the holy church of God."

12. Data suggests that the monks of Nouaillé would have taken either two or three days to complete the approximately thirty-five-kilometer trip to Charroux. It is known from other documents that the monks possessed property in the village known as Ruffiacus, which is most probably to be identified with the modern of La-Roche-Gençay. It seems that the monks were choosing places where they possessed properties to serve as resting stops along their route.

13. Glaber, possibly quoting from memory, gives only a very free approximation of the biblical verses.

14. St. Just of Beauvais was allegedly a child martyred ca. 200. His cult was strong in the northern and eastern areas of France, including the foothills of the Alps where this story occurred.

15. Glaber is apparently referring to the church of the abbey of San Giusto di Susa, founded by Ulric-Manfred, marquess of Turin, in 1029. Located in the Val di Susa, it was on one of the chief routes through the southwestern Alps. *Marchio* or marquess was the title given to lords of borderland regions.

16. Abbot William (d. 1031) of Saint-Bénigne in Dijon was Ralph Glaber's own abbot. The monk wrote a work celebrating the reformer William as a saint: an edition and translation of it are included in John France's edition of Glaber's *The Five Books of Histories*.

17. Despite its rich detail, however, the sole manuscript lacks the beginning of the text and so our story begins *in medias res*. Some of the circumstances of Henry's pilgrimage have thus been lost. The rest of the story makes it clear, however, that Henry was a man of substantial wealth and social standing who attributed his apparently recent lameness to sins which he had committed. The geographic references in the story and the fact that Henry's servants have trouble understanding the accent of the inhabitants of Tours, suggest that Henry came from a distant region, most probably some western part of the kingdom of Germany not too far from the city of Trier. Thus he came as a foreigner to the shrines of St. Maximus at Chinon and St. Maximinus at Micy, both located in the kingdom of France.

18. St. Maximinus of Trier (d. 346/7) was an early bishop of that city, which had served as one of the Roman imperial capitals during the fourth century. His relics were enshrined in the church of an abbey dedicated to his memory in the western suburbs of the city.

19. St. Martin of Tours (d. 397) was famed as an ascetic monk and miracle-working bishop. His shrine, located in the outskirts of Tours, was one of the most important in the French kingdom. According to tradition, Maximus of Chinon was a disciple of Martin who left the Touraine for the monastery of Ile-Barbe, located in Lyon. Some years later, returning to the region, Maximus was miraculously detained on the banks of the Vienne at Chinon, where he then founded the abbey which was to hold his tomb.

20. Orléans is located on the Loire upriver (that is, northeast) of Tours. A medieval traveler from the direction of Trier would necessarily have passed through it on the way to Tours and Chinon.

21. The feast of St. Nicholas of Myra is December 6 and was celebrated on that date at Micy, according to several surviving eleventh- and twelfth-century-liturgical calendars from the abbey. Henry thus, in fact, arrived on the vigil, or day prior, to the feast. But, as we shall see below in conjunction with the feast of St. Maximinus of Micy, the celebration of the vigils was an integral part of the feast day.

22. The main feast of Maximinus of Micy is on December 15.

23. Although the church of Micy has not survived, several descriptions of it have. Henry was positioned between the main altar (under which Maximinus's relics were buried) and one in the apse, that is within the precincts of the monastic choir itself.

24. Matins, or the "morning" office, began about midnight. Henry had apparently begun his stay in the sanctuary during Vespers, which occurred at nightfall, that is around five o'clock in December.

25. In other words, that the liturgy of the feast was coming to an end and that he still had not been cured.

26. The precentor or *paraphonista* was the monk charged with leading the liturgical chant. The antiphon for the Gospel marked the beginning of the Mass for the feast day of the saint, and thus the end of the office of Matins, which preceded it.

27. The monks were blessing the main altar of the church with incense in order to prepare it for the sacrifice of the Mass.

28. The text refers to the ecclesiastical council in Paris as *dictum*, although it does not occur in the extant text. Presumably some mention of it had been made in the now-lost introduction to the text. Septuagesima is the period between Septuagesima Sunday and the beginning of Lent. Gerald of Ostia held a council in Paris during his mission to France as a legate of Pope Alexander II in the years 1072 and 1073, most probably the former. Alexander died in April 1073 and was succeeded by Gregory VII.

CHAPTER 14
PETER DAMIAN,
LIFE OF ST. ROMUALD OF RAVENNA
Translated by Henrietta Leyser

INTRODUCTION

Romuald, Italian hermit and monk of the late tenth and early eleventh centuries is most intimately known to us not through his own writings—none survive except possibly a commentary on the Psalms—but through his *Life* written by Peter Damian, presented here in abbreviated form. Damian was to become a prolific writer and major figure in the papal reform movement of the eleventh century, but the *Life of St. Romuald* belongs to an earlier period of his life. It is generally thought to be his first work and to have been written in 1042, the year before his election as prior of the North Italian house of Fonte Avellane, a house founded by a disciple of Romuald's where Damian had become a monk in 1035, putting behind him the potential for a successful career at the cathedral school of Parma where he had studied the liberal arts. Paradoxically, however, Romuald's reputation through the centuries rests on a tradition that Damian never mentions: that Romuald was the founder of the monastery of Camaldoli near Arezzo, a foundation comprising both hermitage and monastery which subsequently, in 1113, became the head a new monastic order. While this does not necessarily disprove Romuald's connections with Camaldoli—to this day his cell, bed, and vegetable mouli may be seen there and it is perhaps one of the "many other places" where Damian claims Romuald lived—it does compel us to ask: what, if it was not explicitly as the founder of Camaldoli, was Romuald's claim to fame in Damian's eyes?

For answer, we must return to Damian himself. In 1049, only six years after his election as prior of Fonte Avellane, the Council of Reims was held, an occasion conveniently and not unreasonably taken as marking the first signs of the papal reform movement that was subsequently to convulse Europe. At this council both clerical sodomy and simony were on the agenda; both were matters of close concern to Damian as his writings of the time show and as already adumbrated in his *Life of St. Romuald*. Damian's commitment to such causes led to his becoming cardinal bishop of Ostia in 1057; what is important here is to stress the ways in which the *Life of St. Romuald* was thus already programmatic. In Romuald, Peter Damian could see and doubtless to some extent create a figure of great charismatic force fearlessly and restlessly contesting conventional standards of morality while at the same time demanding that the greatest respect be paid to ordered lives. No one in Damian's *Life* is disobedient and gets away with it. There is no room for the self-styled hermit who all too easily might turn heretic. At the same time, there is no place for the sinner to hide however grand his worldly status. Rulers are expected to do what holy men tell them. This is not a world that in any way exalts the lay power. There is no attempt here to create a new secular ethic. On the contrary, the plan is to monasticize the world—to turn it all, indeed—and they are Damian's words as he describes the activities of Romuald "into a hermitage." Like his subject, Peter Damian came to be posthumously celebrated as a saint, both for his ascetic lifestyle as a hermit and for his efforts on behalf of ecclesiastical reform.

SOURCES AND FURTHER READING

The present translation of Peter Damian's *Life of St. Romuald* (*Bibliotheca hagiographica latina*, no. 7324) has been made from *Petri Damiani Vita beati Romualdi*, ed. Giovanni Tabacco, Fonti per la storia d'Italia 94 (Rome, 1957). Considerations of space have required numerous omissions in the text; they are indicated by ellipses. Occasionally summaries of the omitted material are included within brackets. An earlier translation into French may be found in *Saints Pierre Damien et Bruno de Querfurt*, ed. and trans. Louis Albert Lassus (Paris, 1962). Colin Phipps has translated the work into English as part of his unpublished doctoral dissertation, *St. Peter Damian's Life of Romuald* (University of London, 1988). A translation of the complete works of Damian by Owen Blum is in progress but does not yet include the *Life of St. Romuald*.

Comparatively little has been written in English about either Romuald or Damian. For an eremitic context for Romuald, see Henrietta Leyser, *Hermits and the New Monasticism* (London, 1984). For Damian and the reform movement, John Ryan, *Saint Peter Damiani and His Canonical Sources: A Preliminary Study in the Antecedents of the Gregorian Reform* (Toronto, 1956) is fundamental, but see now Conrad Leyser, "Cities of the Plain: The Rhetoric of Sodomy in Peter Damian's 'Book of Gomorrah,'" *Romanic Review* 86 (1995): 191–211. For a brief, but helpful study of the *Life of St. Romuald*, see Colin Phipps, "Romuald—Model Hermit: Eremitical Theory in Peter Damian's *Vita Beati Romualdi*, chapters 16–27," *Studies in Church History* 22 (1985): 65–77.

Peter Damian, Life of St. Romuald of Ravenna

(**Prologue.**) Foul world, our complaint against you is the company you keep . . . consorting as you do with types who know how to make long, fancy speeches in law-courts about sordid business quarrels while not one of them could give an account in church of the moral perfection and noble deeds of a single saint . . . Just think, it is already nearly fifteen years ago since blessed Romuald laid down the burden of this flesh to pass to the kingdom of heaven and yet up to now not a single wiseacre has penned a history, or even a brief notice, in celebration of such an amazing life.[1] To have had such a thing readily available for recitation in church would have helped to satisfy the devout piety of the faithful and been of general benefit . . . All year round, and especially on his feast day, a great crowd of the faithful come from far and wide to Romuald's tomb; they bear witness to the miracles God works through him, they earnestly seek and desire to hear the story of his life—but to no avail, for there is no script. We have good reason, then, to be sorely afraid lest his widespread fame, at present on the lips of everyone, be erased with the passage of time from the memory of man.

Nagged then by this anxiety and besieged by the prayers of many brethren . . . I undertake the task of writing about Romuald . . . My source for the life of this remarkable man is what I have learned from his distinguished disciples. Given my inexperience I intend to write not so much a history of his life, but something more like a short memoir . . . I would, however, like my reader to know one thing from the start. It is this: in this little work I am not attempting to make a collection of miracle stories but rather to tell of Romuald's way of life for the edification of us all. For the blessed man shielded himself from the winds of vainglory with such a thick cloak of modesty that whenever there was the slightest risk that he might look like a miracle worker he did his utmost to suppress any such report. And yet even if he had performed only a few miracles he would be no less worthy of veneration on that account; his life itself was miraculous. We do not read of John the Baptist performing miracles and yet truth itself bore witness that there was no one greater than he among the sons of men [see Mt 21:11].[2] There are those who think that they are honoring God when they make up lies about the saints whose virtues they are extolling. Unaware that God does not need their falsehoods such men abandon truth (in other words God Himself) on the mistaken grounds that they will please Him by their bogus fabrications . . . But we must move on to our narrative: may God and the prayers of him of whom we are about to speak grant us aid.

(1.) Romuald, a native of Ravenna, was born into an illustrious ducal family.[3] As an adolescent, he showed inclinations toward sins of the flesh, a common enough failing among men of his age—especially if they are rich. Yet because of his profound devotion to God, Romuald forever strove to correct himself and to harbor noble ambitions . . .

By contrast his father, Sergius, was a man completely caught up in worldly affairs. When a feud broke out between him and his brother over a piece of property he fomented the discord; on noticing that Romuald, terrified of the possibility of fratricide, was all for peace he threatened to disinherit him unless he changed his tune. And what happened? Both warring parties rushed out of town to the disputed site, seized arms and engaged in fraternal combat; in the midst of the fray Sergius killed his enemy by a sudden blow. Romuald had himself inflicted no wounds on the dead man, but because he had been present, he undertook the appropriate penance, hastening to the monastery of San Apollinare in Classe to spend a period of forty days in mourning as is customary in cases of homicide.[3]

(2.) Exhausted by the severity of his penance, Romuald began to have daily conversations with a certain monk ... Time and again, though to no avail, this monk advised Romuald to leave the world and to become a monk. At one point, as if in jest ... the monk said to him: "If I could show you a bodily apparition of St. Apollinare so that you could see him clearly, what would be my reward?" And Romuald replied, "I solemnly swear to you that if once I saw the blessed martyr I wouldn't stay in the world a moment longer." Encouraged by this conversation the monk persuaded Romuald to keep vigil with him that night in the church ... Both spent long hours in prayer; then at about cockcrow the blessed Apollinare appeared, as plain as day ... seemingly he had come from the east, without doubt from the place where his tomb of porphyry lies. Instantly the whole church was filled with such brilliance that it was as if the sun was concentrating all its rays within those walls. The blessed martyr, splendidly clad in his priestly vestments and holding in his hand a golden thurible, censed all the altars of the church; as soon as he had done this he returned from whence he had come; very soon all the splendor that had attended him faded away.[5]

The monk ... now demanded that Romuald keep his promise. But Romuald procrastinated, insisting that he see the same vision once more. So the two of them spent another similar night in prayer and they beheld the blessed martyr in exactly the same fashion as before. Thereafter if any question arose as to where the body of the blessed martyr lay, Romuald always affirmed that it was buried within the church itself and indeed as long as he lived he never held back from offering his story as proof ...

One day, after this vision ... when Romuald ... was at prayer, the Holy Spirit inflamed him with so powerful a spark of divine love that he instantly burst into tears. Quite unable to restrain his weeping he threw himself before the monks and ardently begged that they clothe him in the monastic habit. The monks, however, afraid they might incur the wrath of his father did not dare to clear the way for him. So Romuald hastened to the Archbishop of Ravenna and opened his heart to him; the archbishop at the time was Honestus, formerly abbot of the monastery at Classe.[6] Captivated by the sincerity of Romuald's wishes Honestus gave him every encouragement and ordered the monks to accept Romuald into their congregation forthwith . . . and that was where he spent the next three years.

(3.) It was not long before Romuald noticed that some of the monks were living rather slackly and that he was not going to be able to keep to the strict path of perfection that he had mapped out for himself. So he began to wonder what he should do and to torment himself with questions and anxieties. From time to time he would take it upon himself to sternly rebuke the way of life of his associates; often to support his case, and to their embarrassment, he would invoke the precepts of their rule. It got to the point where since he persisted in showing up their vices, they began to think of murdering him, considering him a prig, for they had no respect for the words of their junior—and a novice at that—and they were not prepared to put up with his criticisms since they had no intention of changing their way of life.

(4.) [A murder plot having failed] Romuald's desire for perfection grew stronger day by day and he could find no peace. At this point he heard about a certain holy man, by the name of Marin, who was living near Venice as a hermit. The permission of his abbot and brethren being readily granted he set off by ship to visit this holy man and he decided to put himself under his direction. Now Marin, among his other virtues, was a man of great simplicity and integrity. No one had taught him how to be a hermit, he had been driven to the way of life under the impulse of his own worthy desires . . . Every single day he sang the whole Psalter. But given his ignorance and complete lack of education in the ordering of the solitary life—as Romuald afterward related with some mirth—he would often leave his cell with his disciple and wander up and down the hermitage singing psalms everywhere, twenty under that tree, now thirty or forty under another . . .

(5.) At about this time, Peter—Orseolo by surname—was governor of the Duchy of Dalmatia.[7] He had come to attain this high office [of doge] chiefly because he had given protection to the assassins of his predecessor, Vitalis Candiano[8] . . . These assassins had hatched various plots against Vitalis but all had been abortive until finally they decided to set fire to Peter's house, it being right next to the doge's palace. In this way they reckoned they would be able to capture the doge and to reduce to ashes all his household. Peter, who shared the conspirators' confidences, gave his consent to this plan but at a price: it was agreed that in exchange for the burning down of his house the conspirators would entrust Venice to his governance . . . This is how Peter became ruler of Dalmatia but it must be said that once his ambition had been gratified then by the grace of God he suffered pangs of remorse.

Now it so happened there was certain venerable abbot, Guarin by name, who came from the furthest parts of Gaul, whose pious custom it was to make pilgrimages to various places.[9] He chanced to visit the doge who asked him what he ought to do to avoid the danger attendant upon the great crime he had committed. Guarin in turn sent for Marin and Romuald; all three agreed that Peter should give up both the world and the office of doge which he had unlawfully assumed and that since he had unjustly acquired for himself the lofty role of a despot he ought now to submit to the authority of another. Peter felt that someone in his position could not risk publicly undertaking a conversion of this kind but that the following plan was feasible: it was about to be the feast day of a certain holy martyr whose church was in his possession; on the day before the feast he would send his wife ahead of him, giving the impression that he would shortly follow . . . In fact once his wife had left he and a great friend, John Granedigo by name, an accomplice of the original plot, together with the three holy men already mentioned, would board ship, and set sail for Guarin's monastery in Gaul. This is how it came about that Peter and John became monks in the monastery of Saint-Michel-de-Cuxa while Romuald and Marin went on to a place not far from the monastery to resume the solitary life to which they were accustomed. A year had barely passed when Peter and John joined them in order to undergo with them the rigors of solitude.

(10.) [While at Cuxa] Romuald had working for him a certain peasant. This man made utensils for Romuald's cell and when need arose would cheerfully minister to him from the scant supply of his own meager resources, he being a fellow richer in charity than in possessions. On one occasion a proud and haughty count sent his minions to ruthlessly seize this man's cow and just to satisfy his great greed ordered that the carcass be prepared for a banquet. The peasant rushed to Romuald's cell, threw himself at his door . . . lamenting that now he and his family were ruined. Straightaway blessed Romuald sent a message to the count and asked him in the mildest manner possible to return the animal to the poor man. The count, a man who easily succumbed to violent moods rejected Romuald's request outright, saying how tasty the rich joints of meat which he was going to taste that very day would be. The time to eat duly came; the table was laid; the beef brought in—but divine retribution was at hand. As the meal began the count carved himself a piece of meat, and put it to his mouth. All at once it stuck in his throat so that he could neither swallow it nor try as he might spit it out. And so in the arms of his household he choked and met a horrible death; thus by the just judgment of God ended the life in this flesh of a man who despite Romuald's advice had been determined to glut himself on flesh—and he died without having tasted a single bite.

(11.) There was another count, by the name of Oliba, who lived in the same part of Gaul and who had jurisdiction over the land on which Abbot Guarin's monastery was built.[10] He had reached the highest rank of earthly dignity but nonetheless was weighed down by the gravity of his sins. One day he went to visit Romuald and leaving everyone else outside he entered his cell alone and as if at confession began to give him a full account of his past deeds. When Romuald had heard all he had to say he told the count that the only way he could hope to save his soul was by renouncing the world and hastening to a monastery. The count was greatly perturbed by this especially since, or so he said, his spiritual advisors who knew what he had been up to did not seem to be of this opinion and had never tried to persuade him to adopt so radical a course. Calling together all those bishops and abbots who had come with him he asked them whether they all agreed with what the holy man had said. With one voice they confirmed Romuald's opinion, excusing themselves for not having spoken up beforehand out of fear of the count. Dismissing them the count then made a secret pact with Romuald that he would set off for Monte Cassino on the excuse that he was going there to pray and that there in the monastery of Saint Benedict he would bind himself irrevocably to divine servitude.[11]

(12.) Romuald's father Sergius who meanwhile had become a monk... now began to regret his conversion. The monks of his monastery—it was the monastery of Saint Severinus which is not far from Ravenna—informed Romuald of what was afoot. Shaken by this bad news Romuald decided that Abbot Guarin and John Granedigo should accompany Count Olibano on his journey of conversion while he himself would go with all speed to help avert his father's destruction. As for Peter the doge, he had already happily concluded his days on earth...[12]

(13.) The natives of the region got to hear Romuald was about to leave and greatly perturbed, talked among themselves about how to frustrate his intentions. They finally made up their minds to send assassins to slay him... their reasoning being that if they could not have him alive they could at least keep his dead body to protect their lands. On discovering their plans, Romuald shaved all his hair off; when dawn broke and the assassins approached his cell he began to eat with frenzied greed. When the assassins saw this they concluded that Romuald had gone mad and decided that since his mind was unbalanced they would leave his body unscathed...

[**Translator's note:** In Chapters 14—17, Romuald successfully reconverts his father who dies soon afterwards. Romuald is himself assailed by demons whom he overcomes as indeed he does earthly foes.]

(18.) On one occasion Romuald crossed over to a place called Bagno... where he stayed for some time to build a monastery in honor of the archangel Michael.[13] He himself chose to live in a cell nearby. Hugh, Marquess [of Tuscany] sent him seven pounds to cover his needs, a gift he accepted so that with generous prodigality he could dispense alms. For example, when he heard that the monastery of Palazzolo had burned down he ordered sixty shillings of the aforesaid money to be sent to help the brethren, keeping the rest for similar causes. When they got to hear of this the monks of Saint Michael were furious with him, both because he had already on several occasions taken a stand against their evil customs and also because out of the money that had been sent to him he had not given them the lot but had spent some of it on others. They therefore plotted together, broke into his cell with sticks and staves, beat him many times and having stolen everything chased him ignominiously out of the region... Romuald went on his way plunged in deep depression, thinking to himself that never again would he worry about the salvation of anyone else but himself. But as soon as he decided this he was overcome with fear that if this was really how he chose to act in future then undoubtedly he would perish, damned by divine judgment. The monks on the other hand ... now behaved as if they had been liberated from a great burden and congratulated each other most heartily on their behavior. With joy and mirth they abandoned themselves to wild games and noisy laughter and then to crown their celebrations prepared for a lavish feast. Now it was winter at the time, an appropriate season indeed for men of such hard and callous hearts. One of the monks—one who had been particularly cruel to the most blessed soldier of Christ—wanted to get some honey so he could make mead for the feast. While on this errand he crossed the River Savio, stumbled on the bridge and was suddenly thrown from it; he died, helplessly swept along by the raging river ... Moreover, that night ... there was a huge snowfall, so heavy that the roof of the monks' dormitory came crashing down over them, breaking skulls, arms, legs and all manner of limbs. One man had an eye torn out and lost part of his vision—deservedly so, for divided from his neighbor he had already lost one of the lights of twofold charity, even if he kept the other [see Mt 22:37–40] ...

(22.) [Some while later] the emperor Otto the younger, wanting to reform the abbey of Classe, gave the monks the choice of electing as abbot whomsoever they pleased. Unanimously they voted for Romuald.[14] The emperor rightly doubting whether he would be able to summon Romuald to the palace simply by message decided to go and call on him himself. He arrived at his cell in the evening; Romuald thought so important a visitor to his little home should have his bed to rest on; but the king refused the coverlet because it was too scratchy. In the morning the king took Romuald with him to the palace and beseeched him to accept the abbacy. Romuald refused it outright; the king retaliated by threatening him with sentences of excommunication and anathema from all the archbishops, bishops, and the whole synod. At last Romuald had to consent and against his will took up this pastoral role. He did admit, however, that this was not a bolt from the blue, for five years earlier God had revealed to him in a vision that this would happen. He ruled the monks with strict discipline, allowing no one, however wellborn, however learned to stray from the path of righteousness ... When the brethren realized, rather late in the day, the character of the man they had chosen they blamed each other for having encouraged his election and thereafter began to wound him by whispering malicious calumnies ...

(23.) On realizing that his standard of perfection was slipping even by a little and that the morals of his monks were going from worse to worse Romuald resolutely set off to find the king. Despite the king's reluctance—echoed by the archbishop of Ravenna—Romuald laid his staff down before them both and left the monastery. Now the king at the time was laying siege to the city of Tivoli.[15] Its citizens had killed their duke, the renowned Mazzolino, and having taken up arms were driving back the king himself from their city walls. It is quite clear that it was by divine providence that Romuald arrived on the scene at this point for with the restoration of peace he was able to rescue many souls from imminent danger. The agreement reached was this:

the Tivolese would honor the king by destroying a part of their walls, and would hand over hostages. They would deliver up in chains Mazzolino's assassin to his mother; through Romuald's prayers she was persuaded to be merciful, to pardon the crime, and to allow the assassin a safe conduct home.

(24.) While the venerable man was at Tivoli he performed another good deed which I do not think should be passed over in silence. There was a certain holy man by the name of Venerius who had from the start lived in a monastery with such humility and simplicity that all the brethren despised him and made fun of him claiming that he was quite crazy. Some used to box his ears, others to tip over him the dirty water in which they had washed their hands and feet, others to injure him by hurling insults. It seemed to him that with so many terrible things going on he could find no peace, so leaving this company behind him he hurried off to live in solitude. For six years he followed a very strict ascetic regime drinking no wine and eating no cooked food. On being asked what rule he was following and to whom he owed obedience he replied that he was his own master and that he followed his own judgment as to what was profitable. To this Romuald replied: "If you carry the Cross of Christ it is essential that you do not forsake Christ's obedience. Go therefore and once you have obtained the permission of your abbot you may return and live here under his jurisdiction in a spirit of humility. And so the edifice of good works your noble intentions is building will become taller through humility and be beautified by the virtue of obedience. " By offering this advice and much more besides Romuald taught Venerius how to contend against mental temptations and how to repel the threats of evil spirits. He then cheerfully took his leave of a man now strengthened and enlightened in many ways.

(25.) When he was still at Tivoli the most blessed Romuald converted Tammus, of German origin, a man very close to the king . . . [The story is] that Crescentius, a Roman senator who had incurred the wrath of the king, had taken refuge on the Monte San Angelo, an impregnable fortress where he would be able to hold out against the king should he besiege him.[16] On the king's orders Tammus vouched on oath for his safety; in this way Crescentius was trapped and with the approval of the pope, who was his enemy, was sentenced to death for treason; meanwhile the emperor took [Crescentius's] wife to be his concubine. Since Tammus was both an accomplice to this crime and guilty of perjury, Romuald ordered him to leave the world. Tammus went to seek permission to do so from the king, a permission the king granted not just readily but even with enthusiasm.

The aforesaid emperor was indeed a great patron of the monastic order and showed much devotion to the servants of God. Himself shriven by the holy man for the crime concerning Crescentius he made a barefooted pilgrimage as penance setting out from the city of Rome and going as far as the church of San Michele on Monte Gargano.[17] For the whole of Lent he stayed with a few companions at San Apollinare in Classe. There he dedicated himself so far as his strength allowed to fasting and psalmody; next to his skin he wore a hair shirt over which was a covering of gold and purple. His bed was made with shimmering coverlets but in fact he lay on a mat made of reeds that rubbed and bruised his delicate limbs. He even promised Romuald that he would abdicate and become a monk and that he, to whom so many men were subject, would make himself answerable to Christ the poor man and begin life anew as a debtor in the service of Christ.

(26.) On leaving Tivoli Romuald was accompanied by Tammus and by a very famous man called Boniface—whom the Russian Church is now proud to claim as a most glorious martyr—and by a number of other German converts.[18] All made their way to St. Benedict's monastery at Monte Cassino. There Romuald fell gravely ill but by God's mercy he was soon cured . . . he then returned to Pereum, where he had already lived some time before, taking with him the above mentioned companions.[19] To each and to the many other brethren gathered there Romuald assigned a cell; together all observed the rigors of the eremitic way of life in such a way that everyone who came to hear of their manner of living was filled with admiration. Who indeed would not be awestruck, who would not proclaim the power of God's right hand to effect change at the sight of men who previously had been clad in silk, even in gold, surrounded by crowds of courtiers, accustomed to every luxury, at the sight of such men, I say, now content with one garment, living as recluses, barefooted, unadorned, worn out by severe abstinence? And all did their share of manual work, some making baskets, others nets.

(27.) Of this company the one who outstripped all the others in his manner of living was the blessed Boniface. Boniface was related to the king and particularly dear to him . . . While at the king's chapel he saw the church of the ancient and blessed martyr Boniface and inspired by the example of his namesake he was filled with a desire for martyrdom, saying to himself, "I too am called Boniface. Surely I too should become a martyr for Christ."[20] Thereafter he became a monk . . . Having finally decided that the time had come to preach he went first to Rome where he received consecration as archbishop from the pope[21] . . . On arriving in pagan territory he began to preach with such heartfelt fervor and dedication that no one could doubt that here was a man seeking martyrdom. But the pagans remembering how many people had been converted after the martyrdom of St. Adalbert as a result of the dramatic miracles that had occurred were afraid that the same thing might happen again, so for a long time they kept their hands off Boniface . . . most cruelly given that he desired death above all else.[22] When the blessed man reached the king of the Russians he demanded the right to preach. The king looking at this man, barefooted and dressed in rags, came to the conclusion that he really was a beggar . . . and he promised him that if he would give up this charade he himself would alleviate his poverty. Boniface's response was to go back in all haste to where he was staying, to dress himself in all his pontifical finery and so to present himself a second time at the king's palace. This time . . . the king said to him "Now we can see that it is not poverty which compels you to teach your nonsense but ignorance . . . but if you really want us to believe the truth of your words then let two big piles of wood be set up with just a narrow path between them, let them be set alight, and when the fire is going so well that it looks as if there is only one fire between them then you are to walk through the middle. And if you are at all harmed we will abandon you to the flames and you will be burnt to ashes; on the other hand, should it so happen—though I do not believe for a moment that it will—you emerge unscathed then with no difficulty at all will we all believe in your god." This pact was considered satisfactory not only by Boniface but also by all the pagans present so Boniface, dressed as if ready to celebrate Mass, started off by sprinkling the fire with holy water and censing it. He then strode quite unharmed through the crackling mass of flames—not a single hair of his head was burned. Then the king and all who had witnessed this sight, threw themselves in a body at the feet of the holy man, in tears begged his forgiveness and insistently beseeched him to baptize them.

So great a crowd rushed forward for baptism that the holy man set off in the direction of a large lake and there baptized the people in the abundance of its waters. The king decreed that he would abdicate in favor of his son; he himself as long as he lived was never going to leave Boniface's side. But the king had a brother who was living with him and since he was not willing to believe the new faith the king killed him while Boniface's back was turned. Another brother, who was already living apart from the king, was also not willing to listen to the words of the venerable man when he came to see him, but on the contrary was very angry with him on account of his brother's conversion and straightaway arrested him, but then, fearing that if he kept him alive the king would come to seize him back he ordered him to be beheaded in his presence and before quite a large assembly of people. Immediately the king was blinded and such astonishment struck him and all who were there that they were quite unable to speak, or feel anything or respond in any human fashion. All stood still as stone, frozen to the spot. When news of this reached the king he was stricken with much grief and resolved not only to kill his brother but also to put to the sword everyone who had been party to so terrible an event. Forthwith he reached the place of the crime; there he found his brother and everyone else still standing in a state of shock, the body of the martyr in their midst. As he took in the scene it occurred to him and his followers that a prayer should first be said for them on the chance that divine mercy might bring them out of their stupor. Thereafter if they chose to believe they could live and their crime would be forgiven; if not they would all be put to death by the avenging sword. Prayers were accordingly said by the king and by the rest of the Christians; after a little while not only did the men recover consciousness but besides they urgently sought the way of true salvation. They straightaway and in tears begged penance for their crime, with the greatest eagerness received the sacrament of baptism and built a church above the body of the most blessed martyr. If I tried to tell you all the manifestations of excellence that abound about this amazing man—and the stories can be verified—I would run out of words rather than material.[23] Now although the virtues of Boniface require special mention we must commemorate him along with Romuald's other disciples so that by praising them too we can show what a great man their magnificent master was; in this way when the achievements of his pupils resound in the ears of the faithful it will be noted how illustrious was the school's teacher.

(28.) It was while Romuald was at Pereum that King Boleslav beseeched the emperor to send him spiritual men who would call the people of his kingdom to the faith. So the emperor approached Romuald and begged him to supply him with monks who could usefully be entrusted with this mission . . . Romuald did not feel he knew the will of God in what was a perilous undertaking so he chose not to make the decision himself but to leave it entirely to his brethren; despite the king's entreaties in the end only two of the whole group were prepared to volunteer. One of these was called John, the other Benedict.[24] On reaching Boleslav and with his support the first thing they did was to set themselves up in a hermitage and so that they would be able to preach they began the laborious task of learning the Slav language. When six years had passed—by which time they could speak the native tongue fluently—they sent a monk to Rome and through him asked for a papal license to preach. They also asked this messenger to bring along some of Romuald's flock, well trained in the ways of the eremitic life, who could live with them in the Slavonic lands.

Now it was Boleslav's ambition to receive a royal crown from Rome and he put considerable pressure on these brethren to send gifts to the pope and to ask that a crown be brought back for him from the apostolic see. The brethren, however, absolutely refused to do this telling the king: "We belong to holy orders and it is not lawful for us to discuss secular affairs." And leaving the king they went back to their cells. Now certain men knowing what the king wanted but not knowing the response of the holy men imagined that a huge amount of gold, destined for Rome, had been taken back by the holy men to their cells so they plotted among themselves to secretly enter the hermitage at night, kill the monks, and carry off the treasure. When the holy men realized they were trying to break in and what was afoot they began to confess their sins to each other and to fortify themselves with the sign of the cross. Now there were two boys present, servants sent from the king's palace who with all their might tried to fend off the robbers and to protect the holy men but the robbers finally found an entrance and with drawn swords rushed in and killed everybody indiscriminately. They then began to look around anxiously for the treasure and turned everything upside down but found nothing. At this point they decided that as a way of covering up for so horrible a crime they would make it look as if what had happened had been caused not by arms but by fire so they set the cell alight and tried to burn the very bodies of the martyrs. But the flames had no strength, and however hard they tried, the men could get nothing to ignite . . . [**Translator's note:** At day-break the malefactors are caught; a wonder-working shrine is built above the martyrs' bodies.]

(30.) Romuald meanwhile was still in Pereum. At his suggestion the Emperor Otto endowed and built there a monastery in honor of St. Adalbert . . . [25] The abbot who was elected was a disciple of Romuald's and once a community had been assembled Romuald took them under his protection and began to teach them how to follow a life of regular discipline. He ordered the abbot to spend the whole week apart from the community in his cell and to come to the monastery only on Sundays to visit the monks. The abbot, however, took no notice of Romuald's commands and neglected his office . . . Romuald realizing that he could not work there on his own terms went to the king to remind him of his promise that he become a monk . . . The king replied that he would indeed do what was demanded but first he had to go to Rome since it was in a state of rebellion; thereafter . . . he would return to Ravenna. But Romuald told him "If you go to Rome you will never again see Ravenna." He made it absolutely plain that the king's death was fast approaching and I have no doubt that even though Romuald could not make him change his mind that the king hurried off to Rome in the knowledge that he was soon to perish. Romuald meanwhile took a ship and crossed over to Parenzo. The king fulfilled the prophecy of the holy man for he had barely started his return journey from Rome when he fell ill and died at Paterno.[26]

(31.) Romuald spent three years near Parenzo. During the first year he built a monastery; for the next two he lived as a recluse. It was there that his God-given piety brought him to the summit of perfection so that under the inspiration of the Holy Spirit he was able to see into the future and to penetrate with the rays of his intelligence many of the hidden mysteries of the Old and New Testament. For some time he had wanted the gift of tears but however hard he tried he could not experience the compunction of a contrite heart. One day, when he was singing the Psalter in his cell he fell upon the following verse: *I will instruct you and teach you the way you should go; I will counsel you with my eye upon you* [Ps 32:8]. Immediately an abundance of tears welled up in his eyes and he received such illumination in the understanding of divine Scripture that on that very day, and thereafter for the rest of his life and whenever he wanted, he could easily burst into tears and many mysteries of Scripture were no longer hidden to him . . .[27]

(35.) [After frustrating experiences in the Tuscan Apennines at the monastery of Biforco] Romuald . . . began an eager search for some place where his work would be more fruitful. He sent messengers to the counts of the province of Camerino. At the very mention of his name they were filled with joy and showered him with offers, not only of woods and mountains but also, should he want them, of fields. At last a site just right for the eremitic life was found surrounded on all sides by mountains and woods. In the middle was a large clearing suitable for cultivation and irrigated by an abundant supply of water. This place was formerly known by the name of Val di Castro and had already a small church where a community of holy women were living. These women relinquished the place, new cells were built, and Romuald settled down to live there with his disciples. Who has either the ink or the words to describe how great was the harvest of souls the Lord acquired there through his work? Men flocked to him to seek penance, to give alms to the poor, others left the world altogether and fervently hastened to adopt the monastic life. The most blessed Romuald was like a seraphim afire in the most remarkable way with divine love and wherever he went he set others alight with the fire of his preaching ... Among others whom he reprimanded he took to task especially those secular clerks who had gained ordination by paying money and unless they chose to resign he held them to be heretics and utterly damned. Because this was a revolutionary notion the clerks who got to hear of it endeavored to kill him. For throughout the whole region up to Romuald's time the custom of simony was so widespread that hardly anyone knew this heresy to be a sin. To those who argued with him Romuald said, "Bring me your books of canon law and from your own texts you can confirm whether the things I say are true or not." When they had carefully perused these they acknowledged the accusation and lamented the error of their ways. The holy man accordingly established certain rules and taught the clerks who had been living in a secular fashion to obey their superiors and to live together in communities. A number of bishops who had entered into their holy offices through the heresy of simony came flocking to him to do penance. They placed themselves in his hands, promising to relinquish their sees at a fixed date and claiming that they would not delay in taking up the monastic life. And yet out of all these I do not know whether the holy man, as long as he lived, was able to convert a single one. The poison of this heresy was so deep-rooted and so entrenched especially in the episcopal order that such heretics were always full of promises but always put off their execution from day to day, endlessly deferring any decision to the future; indeed it would have been easier to convert a Jew to the faith than to bring one of these heretical scoundrels to true repentance ...

(37.) ... Romuald went now to Orvieto where he built another monastery ... so heartfelt was his longing to do good that he was never satisfied with what he achieved; as soon as he had one project in hand, he would rush off to start another. Anyone might have thought that his plan was to turn the whole world into a hermitage and for everyone to become monks. As it was, he snatched away many from the world, settling them in a great variety of holy places ...

(39.) On learning how the most blessed Boniface had been martyred Romuald, inspired by his example, decided that he too would shed his blood for Christ and that he would go to Hungary[28] ... having got permission from Rome, he set off accompanied by two disciples consecrated as archbishops and by twenty-four monks but on reaching the borders of Pannonia he was suddenly taken ill, stricken with a long-lasting disease ... At last he called his brethren together and said to them, "I have to conclude that it is not God's wish that I go any further. Since I know, of course, how committed you are to this journey I will not insist on any of you returning. Many before us have assuredly done all they could to reach the heights of martyrdom, but since

God willed otherwise have been forced to stay in their own station. Now I do not think that any of you are destined to be martyrs but nonetheless everyone is free to make up his own mind, whether to go on, or whether to return with me." Fifteen accordingly went on to Hungary, two monks had already left to go elsewhere so barely seven disciples remained with their master. Of those who went on some were beaten, some sold, many were enslaved; however, as the holy man had foretold none of them achieved martyrdom . . .

[Romuald returned to Orvieto] In this monastery Romuald suffered much persecution. For he wanted the abbot, as befits a true monk, to love asceticism and to minister to the needs of the brethren and not to enjoy worldly business, nor to squander the monastery's resources on unnecessary expenditure. Since the abbot turned a deaf ear to all this Romuald and his disciples left the place and went to live not far from Preggio under the protection of Rainier who later became marquess of Tuscany . . .

(40.) This Rainier had repudiated his wife on the grounds of consanguinity and then had married his brother's wife—his brother he had accidentally killed . . . Not wanting to be a party to this crime, Romuald was anxious not to stay any longer on Rainier's property without making payment, so he weighed out for him a piece of gold for his water and another for his wood. Rainier absolutely refused to accept this gold explaining that he wanted to give to the holy man not take from him; but at last he capitulated rather than face the possibility of Romuald leaving. Rainier used to say, "There is no mortal being, not even the emperor who can instill in me such fear as does the mere sight of Romuald. When I look at his face I neither know what to say nor can I find any excuses with which to defend myself." The holy man did indeed have from God this particular gift that whenever sinners came into his presence—especially if they were important figures in the world—they would be struck with fear to the core of their being as if they were already facing the majesty of God. Assuredly it was the Holy Spirit, lodged within his heart, who by God's grace struck the unrighteous with these shafts of terror . . .

(49.) [After many travels, preaching and performing miracles] Romuald went to live on the mountain of Sitria.[29] A note of caution must be sounded here: no one who hears that the holy man changed places so often should conclude that his holy work can be tainted by the charge of levity. For I have no doubt that the explanation behind all these moves was simply that a crowd of men, far too big to count, was always running after the holy man wherever he went. Reason demanded therefore that whenever he saw that any one place had become full to the brim with inhabitants he would appoint a prior and hurry off to find somewhere else to colonize.

It is quite beyond my powers to tell you how much distress, how many problems and how much suffering his disciples at Sitria caused him. For the sake of brevity let me give you just one example. Romuald had a certain disciple by the name of Romanus, a man of noble birth but utterly ignoble in his way of life. The holy man used not only to chide him for his filthy habits, but would often discipline him by giving him a severe beating. This wicked man dared to bring a trumped-up charge against Romuald for a like offence claiming that he had shamelessly blasphemed against the temple of the Holy Spirit and that the holy man had sinned with him in the same kind of vicious companionship. At this all his disciples were enraged, all of them deeply distressed. Some cried out that the wicked old man should be hung, others thought it would be fitting to set fire to him and his cell. All of which was pretty remarkable when you consider that spiritual men were able to believe such a wicked crime of a decrepit old man who had passed a hundred and who, even had he had the desire, would have been denied its implementation by nature—for by now his blood was cold and his body shriveled and worn out. But there can be no doubt that the scourge of so great an ordeal was sent from heaven in order to increase the merits of the holy man. For he himself used to say that he knew that this kind of thing went on in the hermitage he had just left and that it was for this reason that he had had to readily suffer such shameful reproaches. As for the false sarabite who had leveled the charge against the holy man he soon got, through simony, the episcopal see of Nucero. He occupied it for two years; in the first year as he richly deserved everything got burned—books, bells, and other sacred trappings. The next year he lost both position and life, struck down by the judgment of God.

(50.) Romuald's disciples imposed a penance on the holy man, as if he had indeed committed the crime and took away his right to say Mass. He willingly accepted this decision and fulfilled the penance just as if he were truly guilty; for the better part of six months he did not presume to approach the holy altar. But at last, as he later told his disciples, he received a warning from God that unless he wanted to lose his favor he must give up meekly accepting this sentence and should confidently celebrate the sacred rites of the Mass. On the very next day therefore he began to celebrate. When he had reached the second secret of the Mass he was caught up in ecstasy and was silent for so long that all who were present were amazed. When he was later asked why he had taken so much longer than was usual in offering the sacrifice he replied, "In ecstasy I was carried up to heaven and placed before God; and straightaway a divine voice told me that with the understanding God had given me I was to expound the Psalms and I was to set down in writing my interpretations one by one. I was paralyzed with fear and quite unable to say anything except, "So be it. So be it."[30]

(51.) His disciples asked him once, "Master, at the day of judgment how will the age of a soul be determined and what will a soul look like?" Romuald replied, "I know a man dedicated to Christ whose soul was brought before God; the soul shone like snow but had a human form and the height of an adult." On another occasion his disciples asked him whose soul this was but the question made him angry and he perplexed them by saying he did not want to tell them. His disciples talking among themselves soon came to the conclusion, correctly as it happened, that the man was none other than Romuald himself; that this was so was proved to them by very convincing evidence.

(52.) In Sitria the venerable man spent nearly seven years as a recluse and for all that time observed a vow of silence. And yet even though his tongue was silent his life spoke, so tellingly indeed that scarcely ever before had he worked so hard at converting and bringing to repentance those who flocked to him. Although he was now advanced in years he lived with great asceticism despite the fact that holy men are known to have lived more comfortably in their old age and to have eased the former rigor of their way of life . . .

(57.) Another brother, by the name of Gaudentius, the father to wit of the abbot of the monastery of San Vincenzo[31] had taken up the monastic life with considerable enthusiasm and thereafter lived in the service of God with ever growing dedication. In time he asked Romuald for permission to give up all cooked meals and to live simply on bread and water together with fruit or raw vegetables. Leave was given and Gaudentius kept to his resolve with great determination. But there was another brother called Tedald who with lack of judgment took pity on Gaudentius's failing strength and went to Romuald to tell him that he did not think Gaudentius could cope with such a strict diet and that the obstinacy with which he was following it should in no way be tolerated. Romuald, being in certain ways rather naive, gave ear to Tedald and withdrew from Gaudentius the permission he had previously granted. Gaudentius took this badly; no longer able to bear living with Tebald in the hermitage in which Romuald had placed them both he went off to live with Engelbert [a rebel hermit] who had dissociated himself from Romuald. He put himself under Engelbert's authority and was allowed by him to resume his chosen way of life. A little while later Gaudentius died and was buried in the cemetery of San Vincenzo next to the body of venerable Berard who, too, had been a disciple of Romuald's. Since Gaudentius had died in a state of disobedience Romuald refused point blank to allow prayers to be said for him. A little while later a monk from San Vincenzo suddenly got toothache while celebrating Lauds with the rest of the community; it was so severe that he was quite unable to stand in choir for the psalmody. He went out and threw himself down in lamentation on the tombs of Berard and Gaudentius. He lay there, praying for some time and before long fell asleep. And there he saw clearly Berard in the splendid vestments of a priest, holding in his hand a book written in gold. He was standing before the altar, celebrating Mass. He spotted the worthy Gaudentius, looking sad, standing far off behind Berard, not daring to approach the holy mysteries as if he were an excommunicate. By and by Gaudentius began to speak and this is what he said: "Brother, do you see the book Berard has that is so beautifully illuminated? I could have had a book just like it but, alas! alas! the monk Tebald took it away from me." At this moment the brother awoke and jumped up to find himself in good shape and all his pain gone. In joyful mood he told his vision to his brethren point by point. When Romuald got to hear of this he instantly ordered the brethren now to extend their fraternal charity to Gaudentius and to pray zealously for him. It is thus not unreasonable to conclude that by being deprived of Romuald's fellowship he had lost the book he deserved but that now that he was restored to his favor and was supported by his prayers he was considered worthy to obtain it again. Just as Tebald would not have been able to take it away without Romuald's consent so now Romuald was able to return it by praying for him in the company of all his brethren.

(58.) Another time the venerable man had of necessity to go on a journey. He left his cell in the care of one of his disciples, with orders to stay there until his return. Now this was a reckless fellow who showed none of the respect due to his master, even presuming to take the liberty of stretching himself out on his bed. That same night evil spirits rushed upon him in the most barbaric fashion and pretty well beat him to death. They then threw him out of the bed and left him, semiconscious. Well did he deserve to suffer such insolent acts of vengeance for the offence he had committed, failing as he did to show due humility to a man of Romuald's stature. For it was as he was behaving disrespectfully toward his master that he was disciplined by cruel and impious hands. On a similar occasion when the venerable man had to go off on a journey he left another disciple in the same cell. When he said to Romuald, "Master I will not lie in your bed for I fear that what happened to your other disciple might happen to me too." Romuald replied: "My son, lie there and sleep in peace; the one who lay there and fell into the hands of enemies did so because he had not received my permission, insignificant though I am, whereas to you I give my consent; trust in God and you may rest without fear." And indeed he lay there just as he had been told to, and met with no ill fortune whatsoever.

(59.) A certain layman by the name of Arduin took himself off to Romuald to be clothed in the monastic habit. He then returned home in order to sort out his possessions. His wife saw him coming and in a great state of womanly fury she shouted out at him, "So, my good man, here you are, come from that heretic and old seducer and I suppose you are all set to leave me in misery and deprived of all human consolation." Having spoken thus she flew into a fit of madness and began to rage and shake as if truly possessed by a devil. Now the holy man made it his custom that whenever his brethren went on a journey he would give them by way of a blessing either a piece of bread or a fruit or something of that kind; on several occasions his disciples had discovered that they could be sure that if they proffered to a sick person anything that had been blessed in this way by their master that person would be restored to health. Even the water in which he had washed his hands had made very many sick people well again; but these occurrences could only happen stealthily because if the holy man noticed what was going on he would fall into a deep depression. Now when the aforesaid women had been horribly tormented for quite some time, certain brethren who had some of the bread which the master had blessed gave her a morsel. As soon as she had eaten it she became calm and completely free from any sign of madness. Forthwith she gave thanks to Almighty God and to his servant Romuald for restoring her sanity and thereafter she no longer tried to deny her husband permission to become a monk . . .

(64.) It was not just the likeness of name that made Sitria seem like Nitria; it was also the life there.[32] Everyone went about barefooted, neglecting their bodily needs, everyone was pale and lived with the utmost austerity. Some indeed behind the closed doors of their cells seemed so dead to the world that they might have been already lying in their graves. No one drank any wine not even if he was suffering from a severe illness. But why speak of the monks when even their servants, those who guarded their sheep observed rules of silence and disciplined each other and underwent penance for idle chatter? O golden age of Romuald, an age which even though it did not know the torments of persecution yet did not lack the spirit of voluntary martyrdom! A golden age, I say, nourishing among the wild beasts of the mountains and woods so many citizens of the heavenly Jerusalem!

(65.) Meanwhile the emperor Henry [II] came to Italy from Germany and sent the holy man a most humble message asking to be considered worthy to come to see him and promising that in return for an audience he would do whatever Romuald ordered.[33] Romuald resolutely refused to break his vow of silence; this provoked all his disciples who said: "Master, you can see that there are so many of us who follow you that there is hardly room for us to live here in a suitable fashion; please therefore go and see the emperor and ask him for some large monastery where you can settle your crowd of followers." ... [Romuald reluctantly agrees].

The next day as he was arriving at the palace, lo and behold, a great crowd of Germans came rushing out from every direction to meet him; they greeted him with humility, bowing their heads; they then frantically began to pluck hairs off the skin clothing he was wearing and to hide them to take them back home as holy relics. This occurrence threw the holy man into such a fit of depression that but for his disciples he would have gone straight back to his cell. As it was he went on to see the king and spoke to him at length about the restoration of Church rights, about the violence perpetrated by the powerful, and about the oppression of the poor and after much else he asked for a monastery for himself and his disciples. The king accordingly gave him the monastery at Mount Amiata, dispossessing the abbot, a man guilty of many crimes. How much the holy man had to suffer not only from this abbot but also from the man whom he himself chose from among his disciples to be abbot we could not begin to relate even if we had the eloquence; yet he himself bore all with the utmost patience ...

(69.) The holy man lived in many other places, he suffered much, especially at the hands of his own disciples. Many miracles were worked through him which nonetheless we are going to omit since we wish to avoid being long-winded. After having lived in so many places and seeing that his end was near he returned to the monastery which he had built in Val di Castro and there he waited for his approaching death. He asked for a cell to be built for him with an oratory in which he could be enclosed so that he could observe his vow of silence until his death. Twenty years before he died he had clearly foretold his disciples that it was to this monastery that he would retire and would there breathe his last; no one was to be present at his death or make anything of his burial. Now it was his intention to be enclosed as soon as his reclusory was made; already by then his body was becoming more and more debilitated by various troubles ... For about six months he expectorated heavily from a damaged lung and a severe cough caused problems for his breathing. Despite this the holy man neither took to his bed nor, as far as was possible, did he accept any relaxation of his fast. The day came when his strength was utterly sapped and he was overcome by the assaults of his illness. The sun was already setting when he gave orders to the two brethren with him to leave and to close the door of the cell behind them. They were to return after dawn when they had sung lauds. Unwillingly the two left but they were anxious lest Romuald was about to die and instead of going straight off to rest they hid near his cell so they could keep watch over this cache of precious treasure. After some time they began to strain their ears to catch any noise. They could hear neither bodily movement nor the sound of any voice. Rightly guessing what had happened they rushed forward, pushed open the door, lit the lamp and found him lying on his back, a holy corpse, his blessed soul transported already into heaven. The holy pearl lay there, as if of no importance, but destined thereafter to be placed in the most honored position in the king's treasury. Assuredly he died as he had foretold and had gone to where he wanted to be. This most blessed man had lived for one hundred twenty years; twenty of these he had spent in the world, three in a monastery, and ninety-seven living as a hermit. Now he glows wondrously among the living stones of the heavenly Jerusalem, he rejoices with the fervent throng of blessed spirits, he is clad with the whitest garment of immortality, and he is crowned by the king of kings with a diadem that will shine forever ...

(72.) Five years after the death of the holy man the apostolic see gave permission to the monks to build an altar above the body of the holy man. It was the task of one Azo to go to the wood to make a modest box just big enough to hold the bones and disintegrated remains of the holy confessor. During the following night a venerable old man appeared to one of the brethren and asked him, "Where is the prior of this monastery?" When the brother replied that he did not know the old man interjected "He wanted to go to the woods to make a box but the body of the holy man is not going to fit in such a little container." The next day the prior, with the box now completed, returned to the monastery. The brother who had had the vision saw him and asked him why he had gone to the woods. The prior, exhausted by his labors, was in no mood to answer him; whereupon the brother regaled him with the reason for his journey ... concealing nothing of his vision from him. The grave was then dug up and the body of the holy man found to be whole and unblemished just as on the day on which he had first been buried except that it looked as if a fine down had grown on some of his limbs. The little box that had been built was set aside and then and there they got ready a reliquary big enough for the size of the holy body. In this they placed the holy relics of their patron saint and in a solemn service of consecration placed them above the altar. The most blessed man died on June 19 in the reign of Our Lord Jesus Christ who lives with the Father and the Holy Spirit and is glorified forever. Amen.

Notes

1. Romuald died sometime between 1023 and 1027.
2. Damian does nonetheless includes a number of miracles believed to have been performed by Romuald both in his lifetime and posthumously. Most of these have been omitted from this translation for reasons of space, but it does also seem from his narrative as if the miraculous powers attributed to Romuald were not of primary interest to Damian.
3. In tenth-century Ravenna this is likely to mean that his father held some high administrative post.
4. San Apollinare is a sixth-century foundation about four kilometers southeast of Ravenna.
5. St. Apollinare was allegedly a disciple of St. Peter and the first bishop of Ravenna. He was believed to have been stoned to death.
6. Honestus was archbishop of Ravenna from 971until 982/3.
7. Peter Orseolo was doge of Venice from 976 to 978. The title "duke of Dalmatia" is an anachronism since it was only assumed by the doge of Venice in the time of Peter Orseolo II.
8. There is some confusion here: Vitalis Candiano was in fact Peter Orseolo's successor. His predecessor was Peter Candiano IV.
9. Guarin was abbot of Saint-Michel-de-Cuxa in the Pyrenees, near Perpignan in modern France, an area celebrated for its links with the learning of Arabic Spain.
10. Count Oliba held extensive lands in the Pyrenees. He was the second son of the count of Barcelona.
11. Monte Cassino, founded by St. Benedict of Nursia in ca. 529, is situated halfway between Rome and Naples.
12. Orseolo died on January 10, 997/8 (probably the former).
13. To be identified with the modern town of Bagno di Romagna in the region of Forlì in northern Italy.
14. Emperor Otto III beseiged Crescentius within a fortress built on the remains of the tomb of Hadrian, an ancient Roman emperor, in 996.
15. The dating here is confused. Romuald resigned as abbot in 998; the siege of Tivoli took place several years later in 1001. The archbishop in question is very possibly Gerbert of Aurillac, later Pope Sylvester II and former associate of Guarin of Cuxa (see note 9 above).
16. Crescentius had expelled Pope Gregory V, Otto III's nominee, from Rome. In 998 Otto restored Gregory whereupon Crescentius fled.
17. Monte Gargano forms a large peninsula on the Adriatic coast of the region of Apulia, in southern Italy. A shrine dedicated to Michael the archangel flourished there from at least the seventh century.
18. St. Boniface of Querfurt was martyred at Braunsberg in Prussia (modern Germany) in 1009. He is perhaps better known to modern audiences by his baptismal name, that is Bruno, than by the name of Boniface which he chose as a monk.
19. Pereum is 15 miles northwest of Ravenna in northern Italy.
20. The more ancient Boniface, to whom the royal chapel was dedicated and whom the present Boniface adopted as a model, was St. Boniface of Crediton, an Anglo-Saxon monk and missionary who was martyred in Frisia (modern Netherlands) in 755.
21. Boniface/Bruno of Querfurt was consecrated an archbishop in 1002.
22. St. Adalbert of Prague was martyred in Prussia, probably near the modern town of Königsberg, in 997. Boniface/Bruno of Querfurt wrote a *Life of St. Adalbert* (*Bibliotheca hagiographica latina*, no. 38).
23. The above account does not tally with details provided by Boniface/Bruno himself and with other known facts. Damian has confused the already Christianized Russians of Kiev with the still polytheist Prussian tribes of the Baltic. Boniface/Bruno was in fact martyred (like Adalbert before him) among the Prussians: see note 18 above.

24. The martyrdom of John, Benedict, and their three companions in Poland in the time of Duke Boleslav Chrobry (to whom Damian incorrectly attributes a royal title) was commemorated by Boniface/Bruno of Querfurt in a work entitled *Life of the Five Brethren*.

25. It was consecrated in 1001.

26. Otto died on January 23 or 24, 1002.

27. To possess the "gift of tears" was commonly recognized as a mark of sanctity.

28. Since Hungary was already a Christian country it is likely that it was neighboring pagans who were to be the object of Romuald's mission.

29. Sitria is in Umbria near Nocera in modern Italy.

30. The commentary on the Psalms subsequently attributed to Romuald relies heavily on the sixth-century commentary by the monk Cassiodorus.

31. The monastery of San Vincenzo is located on the Candigliano River.

32. Nitria was the Egyptian desert celebrated as the home of fourth-century ascetics. The description Damian gives (below) of the "servants" has been seen (controversially) by some historians as providing a model for the order of lay brethren so successfully developed in the twelfth century by the Cistercians.

33. This meeting would seem to have taken place on the occasion of the emperor Henry II's third visit to Italy in 1021–22. The identification of the monastery in question is disputed.

Chapter 15

LIFE OF ST. ALEXIS

Translated by Nancy Vine Durling

Introduction

The anonymous *Life of St. Alexis* is one of the earliest extant poems in Old French. The oldest surviving version (ca. 1120) is composed of one hundred and twenty-five five-line *laisses* (stanzas) consisting of ten-syllable assonanced lines; a retelling of the saint's legend, it is generally thought to be based on one or more Latin "originals," or perhaps vernacular translations of them, probably made in the mid-eleventh century. There has been considerable controversy concerning the provenance and the dissemination of the legend itself. Extant Greek and Syriac accounts, dating from the late fifth or early sixth century, show that the life of Alexis was widely known and admired in the East long before it made its way to Europe.

There exist two early tenth-century *Lives* of the saint in Latin, but it is believed that the first important cult devoted to Alexis was established in Western Christendom when Pope Benedict XII appointed Archbishop Sergius, who had been exiled from Damascus in Syria, to head the church of San Bonifacio in Rome in 974. Within a few years, the cult of Alexis became closely associated with this church; by 987, he was officially referred to as a titulary (along with its original patron, St. Boniface). Canonization procedures for Alexis were underway by 993, and it seems likely that a Latin version of the saint's life, now lost, was written in Rome at this time and circulated widely. The many surviving references and allusions to the saint, as well as sermons and hymns, reflect the popularity that led to his feast day (July 17) becoming a fixed part of the liturgical calendar in France and other countries in the eleventh century.

In all European versions of the legend, the city of Rome figures prominently as the home of Alexis's family and as the symbol of the worldly concerns that the saint is compelled to flee. The poem begins with a description of the social standing of Alexis's father, Euphemian, a wealthy and highly regarded Roman count. It is imperative that Euphemian and his wife produce children to inherit his extensive properties, but they remain childless for many years. At last, by dint of constant prayer, they are granted a son. The longed-for child is exemplary: intelligent and dutiful, he promises to enhance the reputation of an already prestigious lineage. It is only when Alexis has duly married the young noblewoman selected for him by his father that we hear his voice—raised in protest—for the first time. Confronted with the reality of the marital bed, Alexis experiences a profound spiritual crisis: to carry out his duties as a husband and Roman citizen will separate him irrevocably from God. He exhorts his bride to follow his example of chastity, urging her to take as husband "the one who redeemed us with his precious blood." Alexis flees and for seventeen years leads a life of utter self-abnegation. Divine providence at last brings him back to Rome to reside—unrecognized and uncomplaining—for another seventeen years under the stairs in his own family's house. During his final illness, the saint writes a letter which after his death reveals his true identity to both his family and the citizens of Rome, who have been ordered by a divine voice to seek out a "holy man." The revelation provides the occasion for all three members of the family to express, in deeply affecting language, their thoughts and feelings about the saint's life. For the father, Euphemian, the loss of his son represents the end of his line and the futility of all he has worked for; for the mother, her son's rejection shows the uselessness of maternity; for the abandoned wife, the saint's wasted body illustrates the fleeting nature of youth and physical beauty. The three end their days together piously; thanks to the intercession of the saint, the family is saved and experiences a joyful reunion in heaven.

Alexis's *Life* follows closely the fixed biographical framework of the "hagiographic paradigm": birth, youth, moment of saintly self-awareness, renunciation of the world, life of saintly self-denial, death, and "rebirth" (posthumous miracles). Part of the value of this paradigm is its flexibility; individual characteristics of different saints become more meaningful, and in a sense more truthful, when the general outline of the saint's *Life* adheres to a recognized pattern of saintliness. Adherence to the framework, however, does not explain the remarkable power of the poem, which has been called by one critic, Patrick Vincent, "an embryonic drama." Contemporary audiences would have been deeply moved by the elegant austerity of the narrative, and by the subtlety with which the vernacular poet weaves scriptural allusions into the narrative. Extant Latin versions show that the vernacular poet emphasized the theme of family conflict and, therewith, the dramatic impact of the saint's renunciation. The poet also knew and admired the epic poetry of the time (the *chansons de geste*), and made effective use of various oral epic formulae (notably the lyric *planctus* or lamentation). An extreme example of the impact of the vernacular *Life* on an early audience is attested in a late-twelfth-century chronicle that relates the conversion of the wealthy merchant Waldes in 1178. Waldes, who stopped to listen to a public recitation of Alexis's *Life*, was inspired to renounce his worldly possessions, leave his wife, and, ultimately, found a mendicant sect (later known as the Waldensians).

The theme of family renunciation also played a role in the transmission of the Old French poem. The earliest version (translated here) is contained in a Psalter composed for the personal use of the early-twelfth-century anchoress Christina of Markyate. Christina's own story has been viewed as a female version of the *Life* of Alexis: the child of wealthy parents who forced her to marry against her will, she sought refuge in the Benedictine monastery of Saint Albans in 1118 and remained there until her death in 1155. The Saint Albans Psalter (known as MS L, for Lamspringe, where it was later housed) is one of the most remarkable manuscripts of the twelfth century, containing some forty unrubricated full-page illuminations of scenes taken from the Gospel accounts of Christ's life, the *Life of St. Alexis,* excerpts from the writings of Pope Gregory the Great defending the use of images, three additional full-page drawings, and an elaborately illustrated Psalter. Scholars have become increasingly aware that the manuscript context in which the story of Alexis is recorded may yield important clues about the meaning of the work for contemporary audiences; in particular, the story and the images are now thought to interact in unexpected, meaningful ways.

Sources and Further Readings

In addition to the copy contained in Saint Albans Psalter (MS L), three other twelfth-century manuscript versions of the Old French *Life of St. Alexis* are extant, although they vary considerably in both quality and completeness: A (Paris, Bibliothèque nationale, MS français 4503), V (Vatican City, Bibliotheca Apostolica Vaticana, MS Vaticanus latinus 5334), and S (Paris, Bibliothèque nationale, MS français 12471). There are three additional manuscripts dating to the thirteenth century: P (Paris, Bibliothèque nationale, MS français 19525), Mb (Carlisle), and (thirteenth- or fourteenth-century) Ma (Paris, Bibliothèque nationale, MS français 1553). A later, dramatized version of the story in Old French is found in the fourteenth-century *Miracles de Nostre Dame par Personnages.* Although the vernacular tradition was most elaborately developed in French, there exist also versions in Italian, Spanish, German, and Middle English.

The present translation is based on Christopher Storey's edition of MS L: *La Vie de Saint Alexis: Texte du Manuscrit de Hildesheim (L)* (Geneva, 1968). Inverted lines and lines supplied by Storey from other manuscripts are identified; alternative readings from other manuscripts are also indicated. Translations and texts of some of the oldest versions of the poem (in Syriac, Greek, and Latin, as well as the Old French) are included in Carl Odenkirchen's *The Life of St. Alexius in the Old French Version of the Hildesheim Manuscript,* Medieval Classics: Texts and Studies 9 (Brookline, MA, and Leiden, 1978). The poem has been translated into modern French by Jean-Marie Meunier in *La Vie de St. Alexis* (Paris, 1933) and Guy René Mermier and Sarah Melhado White in *La Vie de saint Alexis: Poème du XIe siècle* (Paris, 1983). Karl Uitti gives a useful overview of the poem and its importance in the French Middle Ages in *Story, Myth, and Celebration in Old French Narrative Poetry, 1050–1200* (Princeton, 1973), pp. 3–64; for detailed discussion of the development of the legend in France, see Ulrich Mölk, "La *Chanson de saint Alexis* et le culte du saint en France aux XIe et XIIe siècles," *Cahiers de civilisation médiévale* 21 (1978): 339–55. Brigitte Cazelles situates the *Life of St. Alexis* within the broader context of medieval French versified *Lives* in her article,

"1050? An Unidentified Copyist from Normandy, Probably from Rouen, Writes the Hagiographic *Vie de saint Alexis*," in *A New History of French Literature*, ed. Denis Hollier (Cambridge, MA, 1989), pp. 13–18. On the relation of the French poem to the *chansons de geste*, see Jean Rychner, "La *Vie de Saint Alexis* et les origines de l'art épique," in *Du Saint-Alexis à François Villon: Etudes de littérature médiévale* (Geneva, 1985), pp. 47–63 and J.W.B. Zaal, *"A lei francesca" (Sainte Foy, v. 20): Etude sur les chansons de saints gallo-romanes du XIe siècle* (Leiden, 1962). Zaal also discusses the social context in which French vernacular saints' *Lives* were written and performed and the "hagiographic paradigm" referred to in the introduction. On the dramatic qualities of the poem, see Patrick Vincent, "The Dramatic Aspect of the Old-French *Vie de saint Alexis*," *Studies in Philology* 6 (1963): 525–41. On the role of the family in the poem, see Nancy Vine Durling, "Hagiography and Lineage: The Example of the Old French *Vie de saint Alexis*," *Romance Philology* 40 (1987): 451–69.

In *The Alexis in the Saint Albans Psalter: A Look into the Heart of the Matter* (New York, 1991), Rachel Bullington discusses the role of Psalters in the Middle Ages and provides an overview of earlier studies of the images in the L version of the *Life of Saint Alexis*. A strong case for the inseparability of text and image is made by both Laura Kendrick ("1123? A Richly Illustrated Latin Psalter Prefaced by a Vernacular *Chanson de saint Alexis* Is Produced at the English Monastery of St. Albans for Christina of Markyate," in *A New History of French Literature*, pp. 23–30), and Michael Camille ("Philological Iconoclasm: Edition and Image in the *Vie de Saint Alexis*," in *Medievalism and the Modernist Temper*, eds. R. Howard Bloch and Stephen G. Nichols [Baltimore, 1996], pp. 371–401).

For additional bibliography, consult Christopher Storey's *An Annotated Bibliography and Guide to Alexis Studies* (Geneva, 1987), along with Karl Uitti's review of Storey in *Romance Philology* 46 (1992): 188–97. On the vernacular Italian tradition, see *Bonvesin da la Riva: Volgari Scelti*, translated by Patrick Diehl and Ruggero Stefanini (New York, 1987), pp. 67, 73–89, 252–58, 336–57.

Life of St. Alexis

Life of St. Alexis [1]

(**Prologue**.)[2] Here begins the lovely and pious account of that noble lord, Euphemian by name, and his blessed son about whom we have heard the story read and sung. Through divine will, he engendered this much-desired son. After his birth, he was a child beloved by God himself and nourished by his father and mother with great affection. His youth was virtuous and pious. Through love of sovereign piety, he commended his young bride to the living Bridegroom of Truth, who is the one Creator and who reigns in the Trinity. This story is a lovely source of grace and a sovereign consolation to all pious minds that live purely, according to chastity, and worthily take delight in heavenly joys and the virginal wedding feast.[3]

(1.) The world was good in bygone days
for there was faith and justice and love;
there was also belief, of which there is now no great abundance.[4]
Everything has changed, has lost its brilliance;
never will it be as it was for our ancestors.[5]   5

(2.) In Noah's time, and in the time of Abraham
and of David whom God loved so much,
the world was good; never again will it be so worthy.
It is old and frail; everything is in decline
and so it has worsened, all good things coming to an end.   10

(3.) After the time when God came to save us,
and our ancestors had the Christian faith,
there lived a lord in the city of Rome,
a rich man, of great nobility;
I tell you this because I wish to speak of his son.   15

(4.) Euphemian (such was the father's name)
was a Roman count,[6] and one of the best of his time;
the emperor loved him more than all his peers.
He married a worthy and honored woman,
one of the noblest in all the land.   20

(5.) They lived together for a long time;
they had no child—this weighs heavily on them.[7]
Both of them call on God as they should:
"Ah, heavenly king! By your command
give us a child who will please you!"[8]   25

(6.) So often did they pray to Him, in great humility,
that He gave the wife fertility.

He gives them a son, and for this they were most grateful.
They had him reborn through holy baptism,
and give him a good Christian name. 30

(7.) He was baptized, and had the name Alexis.
The one who bore him had him gently brought up;
later, his good father put him to school;
he learned so much that soon he was filled with knowledge.
Then the boy goes to serve the emperor. 35

(8.) When the father sees he will never have another child
apart from the one whom he loved so much,
he thinks of future days,
and wants his son to take a wife during his own lifetime;
thus he selects[9] for him the daughter of a valiant nobleman. 40

(9.) The young girl was of distinguished family,
the daughter of a Roman count.
He has no other child; he wants her to have every honor.[10]
The two fathers come together to talk about it;
they wish to have their two children unite. 45

(10.) They name the day for their union;
when the time came to carry it out, they do it nobly.
Lord Alexis formally weds her,[11]
but this was the kind of contract from which he would not wish anything.
His desire is directed entirely to God. 50

(11.) When the day is over and it was night,
the father said this: "You must go to bed
with your wife, as God in heaven commands."
The youth does not wish to anger his father:
he came into the chamber where his noble wife was waiting. 55

(12.) When he sees the bed and looked at the maiden,
he remembers his heavenly lord,
more precious to him than all earthly wealth.[12]
"Ah God," he says, "how great a sin besets me!
If I do not flee from it now, I greatly fear that I may lose you." 60

(13.) When the two were left all alone in the chamber,
Lord Alexis began to appeal to her.[13]
He began most severely to criticize mortal life to her;
he shows her the truth about the heavenly one,
but all the while he is longing to get away. 65

Life of St. Alexis

(14.) "Hear me, maiden![14] Claim as your husband the one
who redeemed us with his precious blood.
In this world there is no perfect love;
life is fragile, there is no lasting honor in it.
This happiness turns into great sorrow." 70

(15.) When he has shown her all his reasoning,
he then gives her the straps of his sword
and a ring;[15] he has commended her to God's care.
Then he went out from his father's dwelling;
in the middle of the night he flees the land. 75

(16.) Then he traveled rapidly, straight to the sea.
The ship he was to take is ready;
he pays his passage and has gone on board.
They raise their sails, let the ship rush through the sea;
they landed where it was God's will to lead them. 80

(17.) Straight to Laodicea,[16] a most beautiful city,
the little ship goes; it arrives there safe and sound.
Then Lord Alexis surely disembarked.
I do not know how long he dwells there;
wherever he may be, he does not cease to serve God. 85

(18.) From there he went to the city of Edessa[17]
because of an image[18] there he had heard talk of,
made by angels at God's command
on behalf of the Virgin who brought salvation:
Holy Mary, who bore the Lord God. 90

(19.) All his wealth that he has brought with him,
he distributes throughout the city of Edessa;
generous alms, so that nothing remained to him,
he gives to the poor, wherever he was able to find them.
He does not want to be burdened by any possessions [see Mt 19:23–30;
Mk 10:25–31]. 95

(20.) When he has distributed all his wealth to them,
Lord Alexis sat down among the poor;
he received alms, whenever God sent them to him.
He kept just enough to sustain his body;
if anything is left over, he gives it to the poor. 100

(21.) Now I shall return to the father and mother
and to the wife he had wed.

When they learned that he had fled in this way,
it was great grief that they showed,
and great lamentation throughout the city. 105

(22.) The father said this: "Dear son, how I have lost you!"
The mother replies: "Unhappy me! What has become of him?"
The wife said this: "Sin has taken him from me.
Ah, beloved, how little I have had you!
Now I am as wretched as anyone can be."[19] 110

(23.) Then the father chooses among his best servants;
through many lands he has his child sought.
All the way to Edessa two of them quickly came;
there they found lord Alexis sitting among the poor,
but they did not recognize his face or his appearance. 115

(24.) So much has the youth changed his tender flesh,
his father's two servants did not recognize him.
They gave alms to him—the very one they were seeking;
he took them as the other brothers did.
The men did not recognize him; soon they returned home. 120

(25.) They did not recognize him nor did they question him.
Lord Alexis praises God in heaven for this—
for his own servants on whom he is now dependent.
He was their lord, now he is their almsman.
I can't tell you how happy this made him! 125

(26.) These men go back to the city of Rome
and announce to the father that they were unable to find him.
If he was wretched, there is no need to ask.
The good mother began to wail,
ceaselessly lamenting the loss of her dear son. 130

(27.) "Alexis! Son! Why did your mother carry you?
You have fled from me, and I am brokenhearted.
I do not know in what place or country
I should go to look for you; I am completely lost!
Never again will I be happy, dear son, nor will your father." 135

(28.) Filled with sadness, she came into the nuptial chamber
and strips it so that nothing remained:
no silk cloth, nor any ornament.
Her mind was consumed with such sadness,
from that day forth she was never joyful. 140

Life of St. Alexis 325

(29.) "Chamber," she said, "you will never be adorned!
There will never be joy in you."
She has torn it to pieces as though an army had pillaged it.
She has sackcloth hung, and torn curtains.
Her great honor has turned to great mourning. 145

(30.) In her grief the mother sat down on the ground,
and the wife of lord Alexis did just the same.
"Lady," she said, "how great is my loss!
Henceforth I will live like a turtledove.[20]
Since I do not have your son, I wish to be with you. [see Ruth 1:16–18]" 150

(31.) The mother says this: "If you wish to stay with me,
then I will keep you, for love of Alexis.
You will never know any suffering that I can heal.
Let us mourn together for our beloved—
you for your lord, I for my son." 155

(32.) It cannot be otherwise; they resign themselves to it,
but they cannot forget their sadness.
Lord Alexis, in the city of Edessa,
serves his Master with ready will;
his enemy[21] cannot deceive him. 160

(33.) For seventeen years there was nothing more to say;
he punished his body in the service of the Lord God.
Neither for love of man or woman,
nor for honors that might have been conferred on him,
does he wish to turn aside from it, for as long as he has to live. 165

(34.) When he has strengthened his heart so thoroughly
that never of his own volition will he leave the city,
God, out of love for him, made the image speak
to the servant who served at the altar.
He gives him this command: "Call the man of God." 170

(35.) The image said this: "Make the man of God come,
for he has served God well and willingly,
and he is worthy to enter paradise."
The man goes, and he looks for him, but does not know how to identify
this holy man of whom the image spoke. 175

(36.) The sacristan went back to the image in the church.
"Truly," he said, "I don't know whom to ask."
The image replies: "He is the one sitting near the door.

He is close to God and the kingdom of heaven;
in no way does he wish to distance himself from it." 180

(37.) The man goes; he looks for him, and has him come into the church.
Word soon spread throughout the land
that the image spoke for Alexis.
All honor him, great and small,
and all beg him to have mercy on them. 185

(38.) When he sees that they wish to honor him,
"Surely," he said, "I must stay here no longer;
I don't wish to be burdened again by this honor."
In the middle of the night he flees from the city.
His path led straight back to Laodicea. 190

(39.) Lord Alexis boarded a ship;
they had the wind and let the ship rush across the sea.[22]
Straight to Tarsus[23] he hopes to go,
but it cannot be; he must go elsewhere.
Straight to Rome the strong wind takes them. 195

(40.) At one of the ports closest to Rome,
the holy man's ship arrives.
When he saw his own country, he is very much afraid
of his parents, that they might recognize him
and with worldly honors burden him. 200

(41.) "Ah, God," he said, "gracious king who governs all things,
if it were pleasing to you, I would not wish to be here.
If my parents recognize me now, in this land,
they will take me, by pleas or by force.
If I'm right about this, they'll drag me to ruin.[24] 205

(42.) But, nevertheless, my father longs for me,
and my mother too, more than any woman alive,
along with my wife whom I have left with them.
Therefore I will put myself in their power;
they will not recognize me; they have not seen me for so long. 210

(43.) He leaves the ship and came straight to Rome.
He goes through the streets with which he was already so well acquainted,
one after another; but there he encounters his father,
along with a great crowd of his men.
He recognized him, calls out to him by name: 215

Life of St. Alexis

(44.) "Euphemian, gracious lord, rich man,
give me shelter in your house; do this for God.
Under your stairs make a pallet for me
for love of your son, because of whom you have such pain.
I am very ill; let me be fed, for love of him." 220

(45.) When the father hears his son's appeal,
his eyes stream tears; he cannot prevent it.
"For the love of God and for my dear son,
I will give you, good man, all you have asked of me:
bed and lodging and bread and meat and wine." 225

(46.) "Ah! God," he said, "if only I had a servant[25]
to watch over him for me! I would make him a free man for it."
One of his men immediately stepped forward.
"Take me," he said. "I'll watch over him at your command;
for love of you I will suffer the hardship." 230

(47.) Then this man led him straight to the place under the stairs,
makes for him a bed where he can rest;
he prepares everything he will need.
He does not wish to oppose his master;
in no way can any one reproach him in this. 235

(48.) Often they saw him, the mother and father,
and the maiden whom he had wed;
not once did they recognize him in any way.
He did not tell them, nor did they ask him
what man he was, or from what country he came. 240

(49.) Many times he sees them mourning,
tears of tenderness flowing from their eyes—
always for him, never for any other.
Lord Alexis considers this;
it is nothing to him, for he has turned toward God. 245

(50.) Under the stairs where he lies on his straw mat,
they feed him with leftovers from the table [see Lk 16:19–31].
In great poverty he lives his noble life.
He doesn't want his mother to know it;
he loves God more than all his lineage [see Mt 10:34–37]. 250

(51.) Of the food that came to him from the house,
he kept just enough to sustain his body.

If any is left, he gives it to the poor.
He doesn't hold any back to fatten his flesh,
but gives it to the poorest to eat.[26] 255

(52.) He willingly dwells in holy Church,
and on every feast day takes communion;
Holy Scripture was his counselor.
He wants to work hard in God's service;
in no way does he want to be distanced from it. 260

(53.) Under the stairs where he lies and dwells,
there he delights in his poverty.
His father's servants, who serve the household,
throw their slops on his head;
it does not anger him, nor does he report them. 265

(54.) Everyone makes fun of him, considering him a fool.
They throw water on him, soaking his little bed.
This most holy man does not become angry at all,
instead he prays God, in His mercy
to *forgive them, for they know not what they do* [Lk 34:26]. 270

(55.) He dwells there in this way for seventeen years.
No one among his relatives recognized him
nor did anyone know his sufferings,
except the bed where he has lain so long:
he cannot prevent it from knowing.[27] 275

(56.) For thirty-four years he has punished his body thus;
for his service God wishes to reward him.
His illness becomes much more serious;
now he knows he must depart.
He has called his servant to him.[28] 280

(57.) "Find for me, dear brother, ink and parchment
and a pen. I beg this of you, in your kindness."
The man brings them, and Alexis receives them.
He writes the whole letter about himself,
how he left and how he came back. 285

(58.) He kept it close to him; he does not wish to show it,
so that they may not recognize him until he has departed.
Wholly to God he has commended himself.
His end approaches, his body grew heavy;
he completely ceases all speech. 290

Life of St. Alexis

(59.) During the week when he was to depart,
three times there came a voice in the city,
outside the sanctuary—by God's command—
that has called all His faithful to Him.
The glory He wishes to give him approaches. 295

(60.) The second time the voice gives another summons:
that they seek the man of God who is in Rome,
and pray to him that the city may not fall
and that the people living there may not perish.
Those who have heard it are very much afraid. 300

(61.) St. Innocent was at that time pope;[29]
to him go the rich and the poor;
they ask his counsel about this thing
they have heard, that greatly distresses them.
They expect the earth at any moment to swallow them up. 305

(62.) The pope and the emperors
(the one was named Arcadius, the other Honorius)[30]
and all the people, in a common prayer,
beg God to counsel them
about this holy man through whom they will be healed. 310

(63.) They beseech Him, in His mercy,
that He teach them where they may find him.
A voice came that proclaimed to them:
"Look in the house of Euphemian,
for he is there; there you will find him." 315

(64.) All turn to lord Euphemian;
some begin to reproach him harshly:
"You should have told this to us—
to all the people who were perplexed.
In hiding him so long, you have greatly sinned." 320

(65.) He defends himself, as one who knows nothing about it,
but they do not believe him; they have gone to the house.
He goes ahead of them to make the house ready,
loudly inquires of all his servants;
they reply that none of them knows about it. 325

(66.) The pope and the emperors
sit down on the benches, disconsolate and weeping.
All the other lords are watching them there.

They pray God to counsel them
about this holy man through whom they will be healed. 330

(67.) While they were sitting there like this,
the soul separates itself from the body of St. Alexis.
From there it goes straight to paradise,
to his Lord whom he had served so long.
Ah! heavenly king, cause us to come there! 335

(68.) The good servant, who served him willingly,
announced it to his father Euphemian.
He calls him quietly, and has secretly advised him of it:
"Lord," he said, "the man you were feeding is dead,
and I can say this: he was a good Christian. 340

(69.) I have lived with him for a very long time,
and I can reproach him with nothing at all.
I believe he is the man of God."
All alone, Euphemian returned
and went to his son, where he lies under the stairs. 345

(70.) He lifts the cloths with which he was covered,
saw the radiant[31] and beautiful face of the holy man;
in his fist the servant of God held his letter
where he has written all about his life.[32]
Euphemian wants to know what it says. 350

(71.) He wants to take it, but the body doesn't want to let him have it.
In great distress he returned to the pope:
"I have just found the one we have sought for so long.
Under my stairs lies a dead stranger;
he is holding a letter, but I cannot take it away from him." 355

(72.) The pope and the emperors
come forward, and fervently begin to pray;
they make their bodies suffer great afflictions.
"Mercy, mercy, mercy, most holy man!
We did not know you, nor do we know you yet. 360

(73.) Here before you are two sinners
called emperors by the grace of God.
It is through His mercy that he grants us the honor.
Of all this world we are the judges;
we are in great need of your counsel. 365

Life of St. Alexis

(74.) This pope must govern souls;
this is his duty that he must carry out.
Give him the letter, in your mercy;
he will tell us what he finds written in it
and may God grant that we now be healed by it!" 370

(75.) The pope stretches out his hand to the letter;
St. Alexis allows his own to reach toward him,
he gives it to him who is pope in Rome.
The pope did not read it, nor does he look inside it;
he holds it out to a good and learned clerk. 375

(76.) The chancellor,[33] whose duty this was,
read the letter; the others listened to it.
Of this jewel that they have found there,
it told them the name of the father and the mother,
and it told them who his relatives were.[34] 380

(77.) And it told them how he fled by sea,
and how he was in the city of Edessa,
and that for his sake God made the image speak,
and to avoid being burdened with the honor
he fled again, to the city of Rome. 385

(78.) When the father hears what the letter has said,
with both hands he tears his white beard.
"Ah, son!" he said, "what a grievous message![35]
I waited for you to come back to me,
so that, by God's mercy, you might comfort me." 390

(79.) In a loud voice, the father began to cry out:
"Alexis, my son, what grief is given to me!
I gave you poor comfort under my stairs.
Ah! Wretched, sinful me; how very blinded I was!
I saw him so often, yet never recognized him! 395

(80.) Alexis, my son; how sad your mother is!
What great pains she has endured for you,
how much hunger and how many cares,
and how many tears she has shed for your body!
This grief will pierce her again,[36] right through the heart [see Lk 2:35]. 400

(81.) Oh my son! Who now will inherit my great wealth,[37]
my vast lands, of which I had so many,

my great palaces in Rome?
For your sake I bore the burden of them,
so that after my death you would be honored. 405

(82.) My head is white and my beard is silver:
I had reserved for you my high position
for your sake, but you cared nothing for it.
What great sorrow has come to me now!
Son, may your soul be absolved in heaven! 410

(83.) You should have worn a helmet and a coat of mail,
girded on a sword like all your peers,
and you should have governed a great household,
carried the banner of the emperor,
as your father did and your forebears. 415

(84.) In what grief and in what great poverty,
son, you have lived in foreign lands!
And that wealth that should have been yours—
why did you not partake of it in your poor dwelling?
Had it pleased God, you should have been lord of it all." 420

(85.) The father's raging grief
was so loud that the mother heard it;
she came running, like a madwoman,
beating her palms together, crying out, disheveled.
She saw her son, dead; she falls to the ground in a faint. 425

(86.) Whoever saw her then, giving way to her great grief—
beating her breast and throwing her body down,
tearing her hair and scratching her face,
seizing and embracing her dead son—
they would be hard indeed if they did not weep. 430

(87.) She tears her hair and beats her breast;
she subjects her own flesh to great pain.
"Ah, son!" she said, "how you must have hated me!
And—unhappy me—how very blind I was!
I knew you no more than if I had never seen you." 435

(88.) Her eyes stream tears and she hurls great cries;
ceaselessly she laments: "Alas that I bore you, handsome son!
Why did you not have mercy on your mother?
Since you saw me wish for death
it is a great wonder you were not overwhelmed by pity at the sight. 440

Life of St. Alexis

(89.) Alas, unhappy me! How horrible is my fate!
Here before me I see my only child, dead.
My long wait has ended in great affliction.
Why did I—grieving, miserable woman—bear you?
It is a great wonder that my heart endures so long! 445

(90.) Alexis, son, how hardhearted you were
when you brought low all your noble lineage!
If you had once spoken to me alone, just once,
you would have comforted your weary mother,
who is so unhappy! Dear son, you would have been so welcome! 450

(91.) Alexis, son, how tender was your flesh!
In what suffering you have spent your youth!
Why did you flee from me? I bore you in my womb
and God knows how full of grief I am;
I'll never again be happy because of any man or woman. 455

(92.) Before I saw you, I wanted you so much;
before you were born, I was so very anxious;
when I saw you born, I was happy and joyful!
Now I see you dead; I am overwhelmed with grief.
It is a burden to me that my death delays so long. 460

(93.) Lords of Rome, for the love of God, have mercy!
Help me to bewail my grief for my son.
Great is the grief that has fallen upon me;
I cannot do enough to sate my heart;[38]
and it is no wonder; no longer have I son or daughter." 465

(94.) Into the scene of parental mourning
came the maiden whom he had wed:
"My lord," she said, "how long a time
have I waited in your father's house,
where you left me, sad and bewildered. 470

(95.) Lord Alexis, for so many days have I longed for you
and wept so many tears for your body,[39]
and looked for you so many times in the distance
to see if you would come back to comfort your wife,
not out of wickedness, nor from weakness![40] 475

(96.) O beloved, how beautiful was your youth!
It weighs on me that it will rot in the earth.
Ah, noble man, how unhappy I am!

I was expecting good news of you,
but now I find it so harsh and cruel. 480

(97.) O, beautiful mouth, face, shape—
how changed is your beautiful appearance!
I loved you more than any other.
Such great grief has come to me today—
it would be better for me, my love, if I were dead. 485

(98.) If I had recognized you down there under the stairs,
where you were lying in long sickness,
no one could have prevented me
from dwelling there with you.
If it had been permitted, I would have watched over you. 490

(99.) Now I am a widow, my lord," said the maiden.
"Never will I have joy, for it cannot be,
nor will I ever have a husband on earth.
I will serve God, the king who governs all;
He will not fail me, if He sees that I serve Him." 495

(100.) So much did the father and mother weep,
and the maiden, that everyone grew weary from it.
Meanwhile all the lords prepared the holy body
and clothed it in fine garments.
How happy those who believed and honored him! 500

(101.) "My lords, what are you doing?" said the pope.
"What good is this cry, this mourning, and this noise?
Some of you are grieving, but this is for us a source of joy,
for through this man we shall have good help.
So let us pray to him to deliver us from all evil." 505

(102.) All who could get close, take hold of him;
singing, they carry off the body of St. Alexis,
and all beg him to have mercy on them.
No need to summon those who have heard of it;
all run there, the great and the small. 510

(103.) Thus were all the people of Rome moved by this news;
those who could run quickly got there first.
Through the streets such great crowds are coming
that neither king nor count is able to get through,
nor could they proceed further with the holy body. 515

Life of St. Alexis

(104.) Among themselves these great lords begin to talk:
"The crowd is so great; we cannot get through it.
For this holy body that God has given us,
the people, who have so desired it, are joyful.
They are all running to it, no one wants to turn aside." 520

(105.) The two men who govern the empire reply:
"Mercy, my lords! We will seek a remedy for it.
We will make a great distribution of our wealth
to the poor folk who desire alms.
Though they are crowding around us now, then we will be free
    of them." 525

(106.) From their treasures they take gold and silver
and have it thrown before the poor people;
in that way they believe they can get through.
But it cannot be; the people ask for nothing.
All their desire is on this holy man. 530

(107.) With one voice the poor people cry out:
"For this money, truly, we care nothing.
Such great joy has come to us
from this holy body, we care for no other gift;[41]
through him, if it pleases God, we shall have good help." 535

(108.) Never in Rome was there such great rejoicing
as there was on that day among poor and rich alike,
for this holy body they have in their care.
It seems to them that they hold God himself;
all the people praise God and thank Him. 540

(109.) St. Alexis had goodwill;
for this reason he is honored today, this very day.[42]
His body is in the city of Rome,
and his soul is in God's paradise;
one who is so placed can well be happy. 545

(110.) One who has sinned can well remember this;
through repentance a person can still be saved.
In this world, life is brief; expect a more lasting one.
Let us pray for this to God, the Holy Trinity,
that together with God we may reign in heaven. 550

(111.) Deaf, nor blind, nor withered, nor leprous,
nor mute, nor one-eyed, nor any paralytic,

nor especially any who are ailing—
there is no one who goes there suffering
who does not cast off his pain. 555

(112.) No one with any infirmity came who,
when he appeals to him, does not have health immediately;
some walk there, some have themselves carried.
God has shown them such true miracles,
that the one who came weeping, he causes to depart singing. 560

(113.) Those two lords who rule the empire,
when they see his power so openly,
receive him, beseech[43] him and thus honor him.
In part by pleas, but mainly by force
they push ahead, thus breaking through the crowd. 565

(114.) St. Boniface, on whom we call as martyr,
had a very beautiful church in Rome.[44]
It is there, truly, that they take lord Alexis
and gently place him on the ground.
Happy the place where his holy body dwells! 570

(115.) The people of Rome, who have so wished for him,
for seven days, by force, keep him above ground.
Great is the crowd—no need to ask;
they have surrounded him on all sides in such a way
that it seems one can hardly get near him. 575

(116.) On the seventh day, the resting place had been made
for this holy body, for this heavenly jewel.
The people pull back, and the crowd gives way.
Whether they wish it or not, they allow him to be put into the ground;
this grieves them, but it cannot be otherwise. 580

(117.) With censers, with golden candelabras,
the priests, dressed in albs and copes,
place the body in a marble sarcophagus.
Some there sing, most shed tears.
Never, if they had their wish, would they be parted from him. 585

(118.) With gold and jewels the sarcophagus was adorned
because of the holy body they are to place there;
into the ground they lower it with great effort.
The people of Rome weep;
there is not a man under heaven who can delay it.[45] 590

Life of St. Alexis

(119.) Now there is no need to speak of the father and of the mother
and of the wife, how they lamented him;
for they have merged their voices in such a way
that they all grieved for him and mourned for him together.
That day a hundred thousand tears were shed.   595

(120.) They were unable to keep him any longer above ground;
whether they wish it or not, they allow him to be buried;
they take their leave of the body of St. Alexis,
and beg him to have mercy on them,
to be a good advocate for them before his Lord.   600

(121.) The people depart. The father and mother
and the maiden never left one another.
They remained together until they returned to God.
Their companionship was good and honorable;
through this holy body their souls are saved.   605

(122.) St. Alexis is in heaven without doubt,
together with God, in the company of angels,
with the maiden from whom he estranged himself.
Now he has her with him; their souls are together.
I cannot tell you how great their happiness is!   610

(123.) What good effort, God, and what good service
this holy man gave in this mortal life!
For now his soul is filled with glory;
he has what he wants—there is nothing more to say.
Above all, and in this way, he sees God Himself [see Mt 5:8].   615

(124.) Alas! how unhappy, how blinded we are![46]
For we see that we have all gone astray;
we are so burdened by our sins
that they make us quite forget the straight path;
by this holy man we ought to be rekindled.   620

(125.) My lords, let us keep this holy man in memory!
And let us pray to him that he deliver us from all evil;
that in this world he obtain peace and joy for us,
and in that other one the most lasting glory.
On that word, let us say *Our Father, Amen.*[47]   625

NOTES

1. The translator thanks Robert M. Durling and Ruggero Stefanini for their very helpful, detailed comments on earlier versions of the translation.

2. The prose prologue is unique to MS L, and is generally thought to be an addition by the copyist. It is accompanied by a three-part line drawing illustrating the saint's farewell to his bride, his departure, and embarkation.

3. The prologue here anticipates the conditions of Alexis's marriage. It has been noted that the poem reflects the intensifying contemporary interest in spiritual or encratic marriage (marriage in which the spouses lived without sexual intercourse) as an expression of sanctity; notable examples include the eleventh-century canonizations of Emperor Henry II of Germany (d. 1024) and King Edward the Confessor of England (d. 1066), both of whom were said to have abstained from carnal relations with their wives. For a discussion of these and other cases and their relation to the Alexis legend, see Duncan Robertson, *The Medieval Saints' Lives: Spiritual Renewal and Old French Literature* (Lexington, KY, 1995), pp. 219–29; for in-depth discussion of encratic marriage in the Middle Ages, see Dyan Elliott, *Spiritual Marriage: Sexual Abstinence in Medieval Wedlock* (Princeton, 1993).

4. The precise meaning here of Old French *prut* ("abundance") has been the subject of considerable debate; see, for example, Jessie Crosland, "Prou, Preux, Preux hom, Preud'ome," *French Studies* 1 (1947): 149–56.

5. Regret for a lost golden age was a popular topos in medieval literature. For discussion, see Ernst Robert Curtius, *European Literature and the Latin Middle Ages* (Princeton, 1973) and "Zur Interpretation des Alexiusliedes," *Zeitschrift für romanische Philologie* 56 (1936): 113–37.

6. As Thomas Noble and Thomas Head have noted, exalted lineage was a typical feature of early hagiographic texts (*Soldiers of Christ: Saints' Lives from Late Antiquity to the Early Middle Ages* [University Park, PA, 1995], p. xxxiv). The emphasis on noble birth reflects, in part, the biblical genealogy of Christ within a line of kings; the saints' renunciation of privileged birth recalls the words of Paul in 1 Cor 1:26–29, reminding the faithful that *God chose what is weak in the world to shame the strong*.

7. The frequent switching between past and present tenses is a standard feature of Old French narrative and has been retained in the present translation.

8. The couple's desperate desire for a child recalls the biblical stories of Abraham and Sarah (Gen 15–22) and Hannah and Elkanah (1 Sam), as well as the legend of Joachim and Anna (who were the parents of the Virgin Mary). For discussion of the motif in the *Life of St. Alexis*, see Karl Uitti, *Story, Myth, and Celebration in Old French Narrative Poetry, 1050–1200* (Princeton, 1973), pp. 21–22. For a comparison of the Latin and French versions, see Nancy Vine Durling, "Hagiography and Lineage: The Example of the Old French *Vie de saint Alexis*," *Romance Philology* 40 (1987): 451–52. Anna Granville Hatcher discusses the irony of the parents' request; the "pious phrase," "Amfant nus done ki seit a tun talent," is "addressed to God by a wordly-minded father, who, no doubt, identified God's pleasure with his own" ("The Old-French Poem *St. Alexis*: A Mathematical Demonstration," *Traditio* 8 [1952]: 111–58, here pp. 118–19).

9. The verb *acater* literally means "to buy." As Storey observes in his edition, the use of this word reminds us of "the old Merovingian custom of paying a sum of money to the father of the fiancée prior to the marriage" (p. 94).

10. The line is ambiguous and may refer to Euphemian and his aspirations for Alexis.

11. The Old French term *belament* can mean "elegantly" or "obediently." It seems to carry a legal connotation here, thus the translation, "formally."

12. The abandonment of the virginal spouse was a frequent theme in medieval hagiographic texts, see Baudouin de Gaiffier, "Intactam sponsam relinquens: à propos de la *Vie de S. Alexis*," *Analecta Bollandiana* 65 (1947): 157–95.

13. A difficult line to translate. *La prist ad apeler* ("began to call [or speak, or appeal] to her") here suggests Alexis's forthcoming "sermon."

14. The line is perhaps an allusion to the *Rule* of St. Benedict of Nursia, which begins *Obsculta, o fili, praecepta magistri, et inclina aurem cordis tui*. (The monastery of Saint Albans followed the *Rule* of Benedict.) Note that Alexis's rejection of marriage (and future

progeny) contrasts dramatically with his father's preoccupation with lineage and wordly honors; Euphemian is styled "a lord of Rome" (*sire de Rome*), while Alexis is "the man of God" (*l'ome Deu*).

15. The straps of the sword and the ring are symbols of Alexis's worldly life as a citizen of Rome.

16. Laodicea is an ancient city in Asia Minor. The early Christian community there is criticized in Rev 3:14–16 as "lukewarm."

17. Edessa, an ancient city (and early capital) of Mesopotamia, is the town of Urfa in modern Turkey.

18. The Old French term *imagine* can refer to a variety of images (for example, statues, paintings, tapestries, etc.). In the present (Eastern) context it clearly refers to a painted icon of the Virgin Mary.

19. *Or sui si graime que ne puis estra plus* literally means "Now I am so sad I cannot be more so." Compare *La Chanson de Roland*, line 2929: *Si grant doel ai que jo ne vuldreie estre* ("My grief is so great that I would not wish to exist").

20. The composite Latin version of the *Life of St. Alexis* (*Bibliotheca hagiographica latina*, no. 286) makes the bride's comment clearer: *sed similabo me turturi, quae omnino alteri non copulatur, dum ejus socius captus fuerit* ("... but I will be like the turtledove that will not mate with another when its partner has been captured" [*Acta Sanctorum quotquot toto orbe coluntur*, eds. Jean Bolland, et al., first edition (Antwerp and Brussels, 1643–1971), July IV, pp. 251–53]).

21. That is, the devil.

22. As Storey has observed (p. 14), this second voyage is depicted in terms that closely resemble those used to describe the earlier one in Stanza 16.

23. Tarsus was the birthplace of St. Paul; it is located in modern Turkey.

24. Storey notes that the use here of the infinitive *a perdra* is rare. He suggests a clearer reading from MS P, *a perte* ("to ruin"), which I follow here.

25. The Old French term *sergant*, may also be translated as "serf." The *Life of St. Alexis* contains many words derived from social practices associated with lordship and the manor. For further discussion, see J.W.B. Zaal, "*A lei francesca*" (*Sainte Foy, v. 20*): *Etude sur les chansons de saints gallo-romanes du XIe siècle* (Leiden, 1962), pp. 62–72.

26. Storey notes that this line is missing in MS L and has been supplied from MS P.

27. Lines 274–75 are missing in MS L; Storey has restored them according to MSS A and S. The meaning of line 275 is somewhat obscure; the narrator seems to be saying that only the pallet witnesses Alexis's suffering.

28. The line presents an interesting ambiguity: as God calls his servant Alexis to Him, Alexis calls his own servant to bring writing materials to him so that he may write an account of his own life. His autobiography will furnish subsequent biographers with an "authorized" version of the saint's life.

29. Innocent I served as pope from 401 until 417.

30. Arcadius (eastern Roman emperor, ca. 377–408) and Honorius (western Roman emperor, ca. 395–423) were the sons of Emperor Theodosius I (the Great).

31. The Old French term *cler* (conventionally used to describe a beautiful woman's face) means "bright" or "shining." See Alice Colby, *The Portrait in Twelfth-Century French Literature: An Example of the Stylistic Originality of Chrétien de Troyes* (Geneva, 1965), pp. 47–48.

32. This line is missing in MS L and has been supplied from MS P.

33. The Old French word *cancelers*, derived from the late Latin *cancellarius*, probably refers here to a cleric in charge of official documents.

34. Storey rearranges the order of these lines following MSS P and A.

35. This stanza begins the most deeply moving portion of the poem, as the parents and spouse give way to their grief. It expands on the compact description of the family's lamentations after Alexis first disappears (Stanzas 22, 26–30). The father's extended *planctus* is reminiscent of Charlemagne's lament for Roland in the *Chanson de Roland* (Stanzas 206–10).

36. I have followed Meunier's reading of *en quor* as *encor* ("again"), noted by Storey, p. 113.

37. Euphemian's great wealth is discussed in some detail in a thirteenth-century Latin version of the *Life of St. Alexis* included in Jacapo da Voragine's *Golden Legend*; in that account Euphemian owns three thousand slaves who wear clothes of silk and gold.

38. Lines 463 and 464 are reversed in MS L; Storey follows the order of MSS P and V.

39. Line 472 is missing in MS L and supplied by Storey from MS A.

40. A difficult line that has been the subject of considerable discussion. Storey adopts an interpretation proposed by the French scholar Maurice Wilmotte: had Alexis returned to console his wife, it would not have been a dishonorable act. I understand the line to be the wife's assertion of the nobility of her love.

41. I follow the readings of MSS A and V.

42. The poem is being sung as part of the celebration of the saint's feast day, that is July 17.

43. I follow here the suggestion of Professor Stefanini that *plorent* should be read *implorent* (beseech).

44. On the role of the church of San Bonifacio in the dissemination of the legend, see the discussion above in the introduction.

45. I follow Storey's suggestion that the verb *atarger* (MS L) is here a scribal error for *atarder*.

46. Note the similarity to the descriptions of the parents in lines 394 and 434. The audience, like the worldly family of Alexis, is blinded by mortal sin. The blindness metaphor here is effectively echoed in the final line of the stanza, where the faithful are assured that they may be "rekindled," or "relit" (*ralumer*) by the example of the holy man.

47. The line is a strange mixture of Old French and incorrect Latin. The meaning is uncertain.

Chapter 16

THE MIRACLES OF ST. URSMER ON HIS JOURNEY THROUGH FLANDERS

Translated by Geoffrey Koziol

INTRODUCTION

It was one thing for western European kingdoms to adopt Christianity as a sort of totemic religion. That they had done, for the most part, during the sixth and seventh centuries. It was something entirely different for western Europeans to become deeply and profoundly Christian. Even Charlemagne understood this, calling on his bishops in 811 to ask themselves, "Are we really Christians?" and fully expecting the answer to be no. Recognizing this difference between *conversio* and *conversatio* (adherence to articles of the faith as opposed to living a moral life), Carolingian councils devoted a great deal of attention to the interface between the Church and the people, demanding repeatedly that bishops tour their dioceses, examine parish priests on their knowledge of the faith, devote funds to building and maintaining local churches, require parents to know the Creed and essential prayers and to teach their children what they knew. But one hundred, even one hundred and fifty, years later, there is no evidence that much had been achieved. Confronted with recurring invasions from Vikings, Moslems, and Magyars and constant civil war, Church leaders had enough trouble simply maintaining the status quo. Beginning in the second half of the tenth century, however, and especially in France after the 990s, things began to change. For the first time, society seemed to be becoming deeply and profoundly Christian, or at least concerned that it wasn't. And this time the concern was not limited to bishops and emperors. Now the concern came from ordinary men and women in small towns and villages. And the interface between Church and local lay society was no longer the parish priest. It was the monastery. For if the tenth and early eleventh centuries had done nothing else, they had created or reformed hundreds of new monasteries, each monastery in turn creating or taking over local churches, sometimes staffing them with monks, more often staffing them with priests whose appointment and training the monastery itself guaranteed. When, therefore, one sees signs of new or renewed Christian fervor among the laity in the eleventh century, it is almost always channeled through monasteries.

One of the most visible signs of this alliance between monks and Christian laity is the sudden popularity of monasteries as pilgrimage sites. It took a lot to get to Jerusalem or Rome (and even so, surprising numbers did). But anyone could travel the twenty or forty kilometers to the little Jerusalems in their midst. People therefore flocked to monasteries to pay tribute to the local saints whose relics the monks tended—so many that in 1018, some fifty persons were trampled to death in the crush around the tomb of St. Martial at Limoges. So many pilgrims came bringing so many offerings that the monasteries had to enlarge their churches to accommodate them, and could afford to do so. So great was the demand to come close to the saints' bodies that the crypts holding them were redesigned to allow visitors actually to see the tomb as they passed in front of the choir. Often the tomb itself seems to have been made directly accessible to the public, given the numerous stories of laymen and laywomen throwing themselves onto saints' tombs, pounding on them in grief over some lord's injustice or sleeping on them through the night in hope of awaking cured from some illness in the morning.

The faithful didn't just come to the saints. The saints started coming to them, as monasteries began to build portable reliquaries that could house their patrons' relics. Some were small gilt statues made in the image of the saint, complete with glass paste eyes and a hand raised in a gesture of blessing. The most common were no more than simple wooden caskets, enameled or gilded with gold or silver foil. In the twelfth century, such reliquaries were often taken about on summer tours to raise money to rebuild churches (sometimes just to rebuild the reliquaries). But when the custom began, the motives had been less mercenary. The relics were handed over to local lords to aid them in battle. They were paraded across lands that local knights had stolen from the monastery. They were placed in fields and at crossroads under open-air tents when disease and famine raged through the countryside. And they were brought en masse to the great regional councils that, beginning in the 990s, proclaimed the Peace of God, which required castellans and knights to swear on the relics that if they absolutely had to fight wars and feuds, they would restrict their attacks to other warriors and refrain entirely from attacking churchmen and church lands, pilgrims, merchants—the unarmed of any sort.

The Miracles of St. Ursmer on His Journey through Flanders intersects all these concerns. The devotion of ordinary men and women to the saints, their commitment to relics, the importance of monks, who seem to work with relics and processions the way shamans work with fire and drums—all this is here, along with wicked stepmothers, demonic black dogs, and faked miracles (but who is doing the faking?). The background was a war fought from 1046 to 1056 between Count Baldwin V of Flanders (1035–67) and Emperor Henry III (1024–56) over control of Lotharingia. Much of the fighting occurred in Hainaut, which as the western part of Lotharingia was subject to invasion from both Flanders and the empire. Within Hainaut, the monastery of Saint Peter at Lobbes had been particularly hard hit. As stated in Chapter 1, the war not only devastated the monastery itself, it also disrupted its control over its distant Flemish estates. In 1060, therefore, the abbot of Lobbes determined to send some monks through Flanders on a tour (formally known as a *delatio*) with the relics of their patron St. Ursmer (d. 713), who had played an important role in originally converting the Flemish to Christianity. The journey required just over two months for a complete circuit around Flanders of over three hundred miles. The monks' goal was to meet with the count of Flanders personally and get him to confirm their possessions. They also wanted to raise funds from the churches and people of Flanders to help in rebuilding their church. Along the way, the monks also tried to settle an epidemic of feuds that seems to have erupted in the aftermath of the war. Often they were successful; at least once they were not. But they always tried; and always the author lets us see with an unusual degree of sympathy and insight why these people fought, and how relics and monks might help them stop.

SOURCES AND FURTHER READING

The sole manuscript containing the *Historia miraculorum in circumlatione per Flandriam* (*Bibliotheca hagiographica latina*, no. 8425) no longer exists. Before being lost, it was edited completely by Godefroid Henschen (*Acta Sanctorum quotquot toto orbe coluntur*, eds. Jean Bolland, et al., first edition [Antwerp and Brussels, 1643–1971], April 2, pp. 573–78, [third edition, pp. 570–75]) and by Jean François Thys (*Acta Sanctorum Belgii selecta*, eds. Joseph Hippolyte Ghesquière, Corneille Smet, and Jean François [Isfridus] Thys, 6 vols. [Brussels, 1783–49], 6:256–308), a fuller edition but difficult to find. Otto Holder-Egger (*Monumenta Germaniae Historica, Scriptores in folio*, vol.15 (Hannover, 1887–88), pp. 831–42) excerpted much of the text from the latter, but in favoring stories of feuds and lords left out some of the most interesting miracles. The following translation has been made from the edition of Holder-Egger, supplemented by that of Henschen.

The most complete study of the text is Geoffrey Koziol, "Monks, Feuds, and the Making of Peace in Eleventh-Century Flanders," in *The Peace of God: Social Violence and Religious Response in France around the Year 1000*, eds. Thomas Head and Richard Landes (Ithaca, 1992), pp. 239–58. *Delationes* in general, with passing reference to Ursmer's, are discussed in two articles: Pierre Héliot and Marie-Laure Chastang, "Quêtes et voyages de reliques au profit des églises françaises du moyen âge," *Revue d'histoire ecclésiastique* 59 (1964): 789-822 and 60 (1965): 5-32 and Pierre-André Sigal, "Les voyages de reliques aux XIe et XIIe siècles," in *Voyage, quête, pèlerinage dans la littérature et la civilisation médiévale* (Paris, 1976), pp. 75-104. A superb recent history of Lobbes to the time of the *delatio* is given by Alain Dierkens, *Abbayes et chapitres entre Sambre et Meuse (VIIe-XIe siècles): Contribution à l'histoire religieuse des campagnes du Haut Moyen Age*, Beihefte der Francia 14 (Sigmaringen, 1985), chap. 3 (with a brief mention of this *delatio* on p. 134).

As to the translation itself, while trying to make it enjoyable to read, I have also tried to stay close to the rhythms and word choice of the Latin. The word choice is especially important. Early medieval clerical Latin was extremely formulaic. Hagiography, liturgy, and history shared a limited treasury of words, ultimately derived from the Old Testament and therefore sacred. But within this repertoire, words were chosen to be relevant to concrete aspects of contemporary experience and thereby validate contemporary social and political institutions. In this account of Ursmer's journey, for example, people did not simply die in a plague. Death "ruled" them (*regnabat*), as a king ruled his people (Chapter 2). The black dog through which the devil led some feuders astray (Chapter 5) is referred to as a *dux*, his power a *ducatus*—in other words, a "duke" and a "duchy." Devotion and anger "fought with each other in our hearts," until one "conquered" the other (*pugnabant . . . vicit*) (Chapter 6). A boy loved by a girl has "conquered her with love" (*amore devinxerat*) (Chapter 4). A church is not simply a church (*ecclesia*); it is an Old Testament temple (*templum*). Finally, the word the author uses for "feud" is usually some variation on *inimicitia*, a word most easily defined in terms of its opposite, *amicitia*, meaning not only "friendship," but more narrowly that peculiarly medieval kind of friendship established by public rites and relationships such as marriage.

The Miracles of St. Ursmer on His Journey through Flanders

(1.) Although praise from the mouth of a sinner may be worth little, praising God in the saints allows us to obtain some measure of merit. For if it is good to preach the works of God, it is surely bad to pass over the acts of the saints (*virtutes sanctorum*),[1] since they are the works of Christ, and in them we can only wonder in amazement at his good will. For these reasons, and also because we should disparage injustice and counsel obedience, we are eager to pass on to posterity how, with God's aid, St. Ursmer journeyed among the Flemish.

During the war between the emperor Henry and Count Baldwin, when justice had been besieged and vanquished and could not rule over the land, the monastery of Lobbes was so reduced from its noble status as to be little better off than a serf. Its peasants had died, its inhabitants had fled, and nothing remained to recall its former glory but the stones of the site itself. But after the emperor Henry died, a semblance of justice returned to the land, and peace reigned even over men of evil will, whether they wanted it or not. Pillaging ceased. The reign of Saturn seemed to return. And everyone regained their liberty, though in being freed they were also now impoverished. Having lived to see this so-called peace, Abbot Adelard, rector of Lobbes,[2] fretted over how to raise the church from its great decline, since it had been oppressed and devastated more than other places. Taking counsel with his men, he could think of nothing that could be done unless divine aid came to their rescue through the merits of the saints; for needs were great but means nonexistent. The temple of Saint Peter, which had been dismantled and rebuilt in more peaceful times, now seemed more like a decrepit ruin than any foundation for renewal; and partly because of the wars and partly because of the negligence of its custodians, the possessions of the church had been much diminished, especially in Flanders, whose inhabitants (that is, the Flemish themselves, as well as the *Menapes* and *Wasiani*) St. Ursmer had originally converted to the Lord from pagan error and where, thanks to his preaching, he had gained much land for [the monastery of] Saint Peter.[3] But all this the church had now almost entirely lost on account of its elders' lack of oversight and the great distance of these lands from Lobbes.[4] All this making it necessary, nothing else being possible, both the older and the younger count were consulted.[5] And so, with their urging and entreaty, and also with the permission and blessing of the bishops, St. Ursmer was brought forth, not just to redeem what was his but to raise it from decline. Raised up with honor, receiving the worthy veneration of his people, he allowed scarcely a day to pass without some sign of miracles.[6] No contagion of demons could rule before him, no feud command enemies, no physical suffering could prevail. But so as not to speak of everything at once, let us try to recount each in turn.

(2.) At that time the wrath of God came upon the sons of unbelief, as a dreadful plague oppressed humanity and killed many. It left several regions desolate, especially parts of Brabant, where sisters [*sorores*] had so little strength that they had to use both hands to break thread.[7] Death ruled over every age and both sexes. Even if it passed over some without harm, it still left them desperate with fear. But they did not fall apart, as the dying usually do. Instead, while still healthy, they received Communion, disposed of their property, and even feasted with their friends; then, free to die, they burdened the living in droves with the duty of burying them. But at last God's providence brought help through St. Ursmer: wherever the holy confessor's procession passed, he left some trace [*vestigia*] of his healing, because afterward no one incurred any danger of dying from the infection.

(3.) Moving on from there, we arrived one day at the castle called Lille, attended by a great concourse of people. How much love they bore the holy confessor, and how great his feeling was for them, he afterward showed clearly enough by piously interceding before God on their behalf: for before he left, every one of those suffering from some infirmity had been visited by the hand of God. When we departed the next day, all the townspeople, men and women, youth and elders, went with us. At their entreaty, we set down the body of the saint at a crossroads outside the town. Carefully noting the spot, they decided to set up a cross in that location. As they afterward related to us, once they had done this, whatever infirm persons slept on that spot received healing by the merits in the sight of God of him who had lain there.

(4.) On that same day a girl left with the others. Because she was pretty, one of the nobler of the young men was vanquished by love for her. The girl had a stepmother—usually the worst kind of woman—who also wanted to follow the saint. But seeing her stepdaughter go out first and not daring to leave the house alone, she remained home against her will. When the girl returned, the stepmother beat her so severely that for eight days she did not have the strength to rise from bed. The stepmother also abused her on account of the young man's love for her, over and over calling her a whore. "It wasn't any devotion that made you leave the other day, except for that boy who makes you burn with lust like a simple harlot." "O most wicked woman," the girl replied, "let St. Ursmer judge between us. If I did not follow him for the reason you say, may he strike the hand you raised against me with horrible paralysis." The girl prayed and beseeched: and at once such weakness came over her stepmother's entire arm that for forty days she couldn't raise it to her head. All the townspeople heard of this and later recounted the miracle to one of our monks who was passing through.

(5.) Resuming our journey, we came to a town called Strazeele, where some knights had entered into such hostile feuds against one another that no mortal was able to bring them to peace. For several years such discord had arisen among them that fathers lost sons, sons their fathers, and brothers lost each other, all through the instigation of the devil. So when people from everywhere flocked to the saint, it happened that these knights all came accompanied by their factions. Others, who were not part of the feud, informed us about matters. We began to gather the different groups together, but separately, pleading that they give over this dispute to God and the saint, so that the number of dead might increase no further. A few assented, though reluctantly, out of fear of God and love for the saint; but a minority utterly refused. "Eia!" said Baldwin, our dean. "Let us carry the saint around in a circle, so that they shall either consent and obey our counsel or, in dissenting, follow the devil who leads them, and be separated from our company."[8] And raising the saint from the ground, we processed carefully and sang psalms so that all might be included within the perimeter of the circuit. Only those enemies of peace stood aside, not knowing what to make of our people's actions; but this was our intent, so great was our trust in the saint whom we followed: if we could ever completely surround them in the procession, the enemy's power would no longer be able to prevail over them. But behold the devil's tricks! Crossing between us and them came the blackest of dogs to act as their leader and lead them away from us. Nor did he release them from his power, because almost three months later all were drawn into a battle, from which not one of those enemies of peace came out alive.

(6.) Since they would not be persuaded, we left off preaching peace; yet by the intervention of the saint we did instill peace in the hearts of many during the course of our journey. After a few days we decided to lodge at the castle called Blaringhem. Whether this was by chance or by God's providence we would not know until morning's light. A youth[9] named Hugh was the leader there, on account of his noble bearing no less than by reason of his birth. That very day he would be vexed with a judgment, and he would not be able to establish concord without the shedding of much blood, unless St. Ursmer were to succeed by the mercy of God. This Hugh had two knights in his household who often argued among themselves with acid words, as youths will do. Learning of the dispute, the lord summoned his knights and demanded a judgment concerning those two; and he succeeded in making peace between them, even getting them to kiss. But one of them, the one who had been more wounded by the words, harbored evil in his heart, only feigning the peace of that kiss until the right time and place. It was not long in coming, for though of lesser birth, his reputation as a knight was greater. Besides, few lack guile and strength when it comes to an enemy, and an opportunity was soon provided for the praiseless deed. So waiting two days after his lord Hugh had departed, he approached his enemy, unsuspecting because of the peace that had been made. He found him sitting in a cellar, and there treacherously struck him through the chest with a lance—killing him just for a single word.

Clamor and riot ensued. The killer immediately entered the church, not wishing to resist everyone all by himself. Some of the knights wanted to kill him in the church; but the knight who held lordship in Hugh's absence drew him out in exchange for hostages, on the condition that he would return him to the church with his weapons in a fortnight, when Hugh was supposed to return. As it happened, the holy Confessor made his entry [*adventus*] into the church on that night, the night, that is, of the Lord's Ascension.[10] In the morning, a great crowd of knights from both sides gathered in arms: here, those who were ready to seize the killer by force if they could not get him handed over by persuasion [*ratio*]; there, Hugh and his men, wanting to prevent inferiors from seizing the guilty party. The shields glinted red as the rays of the morning sun struck the courtyard of the church [*atrium*],[11] the steel of the weapons glistened, horses were snorting and whinnying, adding to the confusion. Hugh's men surrounded the church, swords drawn, all aching to shed the blood of one sinner. But then we moved right through their midst and entered the church. There we found the wretch prostrate before the altar as if already dead. We began by celebrating a Mass for all the faithful, chanting litanies to implore divine mercy in a time of such great danger.[12] After this, dressed in albs with hoods [pulled over our heads] as if for a solemn Mass, we made our procession outside. First we humbly admonished Hugh that he not allow the blood of knights to flow for just one sinner. But our prayers availed nothing, though in a voice breaking with sobs and tears he apologized both to the saint and to us. We then entered the church, and without their knowledge brought out the holy body and placed it in their midst. Astonished, all humbly lowered their eyes, showing by their restraint that they knew clearly enough who lay on the ground among them, even if they did not know him.[13] Tears flowed from the eyes of all; piety and wrath vied in their hearts. At last, piety won out in Hugh, who let that poor man depart with life, limbs, and even his grace.

Almost one hundred feuds were pacified on this occasion among knights gathered there that day. One was a famous knight, Boniface in both deed and name.[14] Two brothers had seized his castle and killed the wife whom he had only recently married and also his son, not yet a year old. One of these two Boniface had killed; the other had fled from his sight. But now, having heard of the saint's reputation, without intercession from any mortal, the mercy [the surviving brother] had not dared seek himself or through others he now presumed to beg through St. Ursmer.[15] And he found what he sought. Indeed, no one went away from the saint unpacified that day: once he was placed on the ground in their midst, such piety seized the hearts of everyone that no one could doubt that the grace of the Holy Spirit was present.

(7.) Leaving Blaringhem, we started the climb up to Cassel. After preparing a place for the saint inside his tent, we ourselves took lodging with an innkeeper. A girl living there had been bled from a vein in the middle of her forehead in order to escape an illness. Even though she appeared to have warded off the sickness, it still seemed she was going to die, because for a full forty days she bled continuously through the compress on her head. She was almost dead (and no wonder: for someone of the manly sex [*virilis*] could scarcely have borne this for so long, let alone someone of the weak [*fragilis sexus*]). But then she began to ask if any of us knew how to staunch the bleeding, insisting that for the love of God we tell her if we did. We replied that we knew nothing and no one—except St. Ursmer, he being our doctor. Make your demand of him, we advised, since he had brought merciful remedy in similar cases. At this she got up and, supported by four women, put her demand to the saint. Immediately so much blood gushed from her wound that she was brought outside the tent as if she were dead. But after a little bit she began to breathe. Then she asked for a candle to be brought to her. With her own hand she placed it before the saint, and the bleeding stopped, so that not a single drop of blood came out afterward. She returned to us right away, took some nourishment with us as a blessing, and joined us in praising her healer. What a wondrous doctor, who had no greed for money—who would deign to confer such healing [*salutem*] for a candle worth scarcely an obol, but really only for devout faith.[16]

(8.) Next we joined the count and countess at Bergues, presenting our complaint to them about the injustice committed against the lands of the saint. After being received by them with reverence befitting the saint, we departed for our lodging, the saint in the temple, we in the cloister.[17] A monk there had suffered from a toothache for nearly three years. And since the sick always hope for a remedy, he asked if we knew of any medicine that might help it. We knew nothing at all, but we gave him the life of the saint to read, where he could learn that Ursmer had suffered the same thing for nine years and seven weeks. That very night was the feast of the coming of the Holy Spirit, that is, the fiftieth day after the Lord's Resurrection.[18] Since the monk could scarcely sleep because of the pain, he kept vigil that night, standing with his candle before the saint. He had kept his vigil with prayers and tears for a long time, until he was finally overcome with sleep. And when he awoke, he arose cured completely by the grace of God, and he accompanied the other brothers to Matins in complete health.

(9.) We celebrated the feast day there. The next day we went outside the town followed by the count and countess, the bishops of London and Thérouanne, and all the Flemish nobility. A little outside the town, religion established her altar,[19] since God wanted to exalt his saint in the sight of the princes. Setting down our load of treasure, we spoke of concord and peace in everyone's hearing, recounting how divine grace had been present in the different stages of our journey. Then we invited them to peace; and since many among them were each other's enemies, we called out each one singly by name; and as much as each showed the desire and spirit to make a pact of peace, so much did St. Ursmer intercede before God on his behalf. Not a single one out of all the nobles [*optimates*] dared hold himself back from these exhortations of peace.[20] Indeed, so many pacts were made among them that day that no mortal could have arranged them, not for all the gold in the world, as Count Baldwin himself admitted publicly before them all. No one remained outside a pact, no one went away unkissed. Thus having made peace, we left with our great patron.

(10.) The following night we received lodging in a village from the castellan of Veurne, who was acting on the countess's orders. The castellan had a small son, scarcely five years old and blind since he was two. Hearing of the miracles being worked through St. Ursmer, the castellan sent to us, asking that we might intercede with our patron on his behalf. The tumor over the child's eyes had grown so large that you could not even see his eyes, only swollen flesh. He spent that night before the saint, returning the next night also. Before the third day his eyes had been restored to their full beauty and light.

(11.) Departing that place we went to Bruges, where we were received with due devotion. After setting up our site and placing the saint in his tent with honor, we were received as guests by the governors established in the area.[21] After we had all sat down to eat, the wind blew out the lamps in front of the saint. After the meal the guardian to whom we had entrusted the saint's care returned to the tent. When he saw the lamp out, he got angry at the cleric whom he had left in his place for letting the light in front of the saint go out. The cleric replied that he had often tried to relight it, but he could not carry a flame into the tent because of the force of the wind. "Go get a torch," said the guardian, "and make sure I don't find the tent without light again." The cleric obeyed and started to go outside. But the saint didn't even allow him to get all the way out. In fact, he had not yet left the tent when he saw the candle in his hands burning. He cried out in amazement, his shout scaring everyone there, because they did not know why he had called out. "I'm holding a light sent by God," he explained. "Glorify God with me." Everyone present inside the tent at that moment gave witness to this. And this very light sent by divine power was used for divine services until we arrived at Ghent a month later.

(12.) As we continued on our way, St. Ursmer never ceased to heal those who suffered from fevers, toothaches, and illnesses of many kinds. As a result, by the time we entered Oostburg a huge crowd of people preceded and followed us, all of them singing praises. Since they had sent messengers on ahead of them, the people of Oostburg came out to meet us.[22] We went first to the temple, and from there to the place of our lodging. For three straight days a continuous line of people came and went. God is witness to just how necessary the saint's arrival was, since we gathered there by His providence and care. There were almost forty knights in that stronghold, and such a storm of feuds among them that none of them dared leave or return to their homes without an armed escort. To slay kinsmen required slaying still more kinsmen. Vengeance only increased the weight of vengeance, because although everyone had the urge to fight, no one had the means to win. Since none of them could triumph, they finally gave hostages to ensure a period of truce until a set day when they all might meet to adjudicate matters. But when that day came, they gathered as one in body only, not in spirit, not loving peace but only wanting to impress others with a show of strength. Because they had not come in peace, they all went the way of evil. Their greed was the worst thing of all. Some were willing to sell the death of a brother; others defended themselves on oath, preferring to perjure themselves completely rather than part with any of their hoard. So some received oaths, while others pledged ten pounds, or twenty, or thirty, even one hundred pounds and more. At this point they separated for the day, planning to return the next. And if peace were not made then, the demand for vengeance would grow even fiercer.[23]

They gathered, therefore, the next day; but things worked out better because now St. Ursmer was present to act as mediator. They had parted from each other the night before on bad terms. They returned the next morning all armed. But when Ursmer was placed in their midst, he immediately recalled them to peace and harmony, so that everyone gave pledges and oaths, swore peace on the body of the saint, and casting aside their weapons embraced and kissed. Then they joyously entered the church along with the saint, so that we might beseech God to grant absolution and mercy to the souls of those who had died in the feuds; and they themselves began to sing the hymn, *Te Deum Laudamus*. We all sang together to the sound of the pealing bells, as people of both sexes praised God in the manner of the region.

(13.) In that town lived a woman, rich and noble but deprived of her sight for five years. Depressed in both mind and body, she always sat in the shadows. Hearing of the saint's arrival, she rose quickly and had herself led to the church. There she sat, night and day, with a candle before the saint, as with Mary at the feet of Jesus.[24] As others laughed, she wept; as others sang, she moaned; and a river of tears flowed from eyes that could not see. She moved everyone to devotion, and especially us who were doubtful about her chances for recovery.[25] When others left to eat, she stayed next to the altar, fasting. While others slept, she kept vigil and prayed. That very night, which was to be our last in the town, right about cockcrow, she cried out to her serving women like the Canaanite, "Lift me up and set me before the saint! I am sure I feel the aid of the Most Pious." More than fifty people of both sexes were in the church at that time, all holding lights in their hands and singing hymns to God (not hymns like women sing but lauds like those of canons).[26] All of them immediately came running, gathering around the woman who was lying prostrate in the form of a cross. They reached out to her, sighing along with her, hopeful for her tearful prayer and praying for her as well. After she had prayed a long time, she stood up. A substance like an egg's albumen ran from her eyes, and she exclaimed that she could see, though not completely. The next day she followed the saint without any attendants—a testimony to her cure.

(14.) After this news of our doings preceded us, and our entries were announced before us everywhere. People spoke of what the saint had done, and invented things he had not done,[27] so that from villages everywhere they came out to greet us eagerly. In one village whose name escapes us but where we were to be lodged for one night, a woman had a son, scarcely five years old, who had suffered from a debilitating fever for three years. At the very hour when we were about to arrive he threw himself on the ground, deaf and mute, thrashing about in agony. When we entered the village, the poor mother took her son in her arms and carried him around the saint's reliquary three times. Returning home, she laid him on the spot where he had lain before, and then ran to us in the church to beg us for some holy water, into which she dipped the saint's pastoral staff.[28] This she offered as a drink to her little one. Tasting it, he began to breathe more easily after a little; and when he was able to speak he called to his mother and told her with absolute certainty that the drink had filled him with great sweetness. Later he asked for some food. He ate what was brought for him, and then, comforted by the food, got up straightaway. When a little later we came to the house to buy some staples (for they had things to sell in the house) we found the boy playing with other boys—and the mother praising the Lord.

(15.) On the third day a knight named Baldrad gave us lodging. He had one club foot, but no one was more upright in mind and deeds. He was a noble youth, one of the wealthier of the rich, one of the wiser of the wise, of knights one of the best. He was also one of the foremost among the count's counselors. How much love he felt for the saint showed clearly enough in the way he received us and in the honor he paid to the saint by his gifts. Nor did he lose anything from this, although St. Ursmer played a pleasant enough game with him. For when we came there everyone was healthy—that is, he and his wife and their two sons. Two days later all of them had taken sick. On the third day he hastened to us and with tears and contrition of heart began to make a claim against the saint for his wife and sons,[29] beseeching us that we might kindly pray for them. Having received our agreement, he returned home, finding them fully restored to health by the work of St. Ursmer.

(16.) One morning while staying at the village of Lissewege, we began to invite enemies to make peace for love of the saint. More than fifty knights followed us then, some disputing but wishing to reconcile, still others asking their enemies for peace through the saint.[30] When we thought we had reconciled everyone by the grace of God, behold a man stole through the crowd and threw himself naked and barefoot before the feet of another man in the form of a cross, holding scissors and rods.[31] Crying out for mercy, he begged him a hundred times for forgiveness, because one day he had killed two knights who were his brothers. The man he was begging was named Robert, and he was a powerful youth, leader of a force of almost two hundred knights. Taken completely unawares by this act, Robert fell back supine, partly in shock, and partly in grief for the two knights. Everyone wept quietly. You would have to have been a stone not to have wept. At last some people helped the knight up; but at our entreaty he prostrated himself again. The impasse seemed serious to us, difficult to the point of despair, yet we had faith in our patron. We gathered around the youth, kneeling in prayer before his sublimity.[32] He countered us with the excuse of his grief. He resisted. We persisted in entreaty. And in the middle lay the guilty party, beseeching Robert for mercy for the sake of God and the saint. At this the youth fell silent and began to weep, his face changing color, now wan, now flushed, trying to resist, madly gnashing his teeth as if mad. What more can one say? He would have fled if he'd had the chance. Meanwhile, we left off our entreaties and, without letting them see, took up St. Ursmer and laid him on a *pallium* at his feet.[33] The youth was dumbfounded, and with great sobs cast his face to the ground, eating dirt in his grief and crying out that he was a pitiable wretch. So now three lay there, all prostrate alike and yet not at all alike: St. Ursmer, as if begging pardon for the guilty man; the guilty man begging pardon for himself; and the youth prostrate before the saint, who had been placed before him so he might beg pardon too. Although you could see devotion there, you could hear nothing, for there were no sounds but sobs, no voices only tears. The cheeks and beards of the knights ran with tears, tears that flowed for three hours while the silence lasted among us, for none of us could produce a single word, only cries and moans. But at last, St. Ursmer won, and by a marvelous sign seized the minds and attention of everyone: from the ground on which he had lain unwillingly,[34] he made himself levitate quickly! Wonder of wonders, smoke rose from the reliquary! Everyone stepped back and looked on in terror, then immediately fell with their faces to the ground, striking their breasts with pounding blows. We quickly lifted up the saint (not without great fear) and put him back on the altar. Led before him, the youth tearfully begged pardon; and so as to merit it himself, he gave his own pardon to the guilty man, confirming the peace with an oath and a kiss.

(17.) When we left the town everyone came out with us. We then received lodging at a village called Leffinghe. There nature itself was afflicted, as for three months earth and sky had waited for St. Ursmer. The sterile land was bone-dry. The heavens refused to release their waters—save by the intercession of the saint. For when the inhabitants processed out to meet us, they came with their litanies and songs begging for rain through the saint. Then behold, a flood of rain followed without any delay at all, so that there could be no doubt that it had come by the intervention and merits of the Confessor. First, however, he allowed us to enter the church, not wanting it to rain on his people, or the water to fall on us instead of on the land. All night it rained. In the morning it dawned clear. We rose, celebrated Mass, and composed pacts in our accustomed manner wherever God wanted. Then we departed, although the peasants [*rusticis*] wanted us to stay.

(18.) Daily our saint performed these works and others like them, rewarding his hosts with beautiful gifts. On a Sunday we came to Ghent, where townspeople of both sexes ran out to meet us like a swarm of bees. Having entered the castle we first went to pray at the church of Saint Pharahilde; then, after resolving more than twenty conflicts, we went to the monastery of Saint John the Baptist.[35] Lodged there that night, we sent word to the monastery of Saint Peter, asking if they would receive us the next day so that we might rest, because we were tired from our journey. They received the saint with due veneration, us with due charity.[36] We gave ourselves up to leisure; but St. Ursmer continued to work for us and for himself. Inspired by God, a girl entered the temple, and coming before the altar where the saint had been placed she began to pray. Her left side had begun to decay so much that its blackness made it seem more like coal than flesh. Her arm had grown into her side and her hand into her breast, and the arm and the muscle had all joined together, so that the shape of the entire bone looked like a sort of spigot. She arose after praying, and standing half-naked (for she was poor and a beggar) she crossed herself in a girlish manner [*puellariter*]. And behold, the arm separated from the ribs and the hand from the breast; the bone that had joined muscle and arm popped out and landed at the foot of the altar, and blood flowed freely from the wound. At once wonderful and wretched to see, the girl collapsed as if dead. And immediately, her healing being given in one instant, her blackness receded by the intervention of the saint. The bells rang for vespers. Several monks and lay people were about. We sang vespers, and afterward, as the people gathered, we sang the hymn *Te Deum Laudamus*. As for the girl, she followed us to Lobbes, providing holy testimony of her being saved,[37] not by telling her story but simply by showing herself.

(19.) It would have been wrong to omit prayers to St. Bavo,[38] and we decided to go there in a monastic procession. We again first celebrated Mass at the church of Saint John the Baptist. Along with many others who were present, there was a very old woman, blind in one eye for several years. She begged us to place the saint's pastoral staff over her. We began to laugh, since she had not lost her vision because of any disease but some twenty years earlier from old age. Still, St. Ursmer had pity on her; for when we placed the staff over her, she pointed to her eye and gave thanks, exclaiming that she had never seen so clearly. Some cried out of devotion. Others laughed that she pointed to her eye thus; in any case, all the townspeople confirmed that they did not know her.[39] After celebrating Mass we processed to the monastery of Saint Bavo accompanied by a crowd of people, where we were received with such veneration that it was as if we had all been saints.

(20.) Having received permission to leave Ghent, we came after a journey of eight days to a village called *Finia*.[40] People were suffering from the great heat of that summer. We sent word to the priest so that he might open the church and give us lodging. Although the priest's name was Paul, he did not at all conform to Paul [the Apostle], unless it was when Paul had been Saul [see Acts 8:1–3, 9:1–19]. For he locked all the doors to the church and fled at once, taking the keys with him. Only when we arrived and stood before the doors asking for the keys did we learn that the priest had fled. But as we were setting up our tents in the atrium, we heard a thunderous clap and saw the bolt fly off in the middle of the church, and the doors opened before the saint. We all entered with great joy, praising God and our doorkeeper, Ursmer. When the priest returned he was not a little confused, and begged pardon from the saint and from us, pouring out tears in satisfaction.[41] In the morning, he again prostrated himself before the saint and begged pardon in the sight of all the people. Absolved by us, he told the people what had happened to him in German [*Theutonice*].

(21.) Hastening our journey, we returned to Brussels. On the eighth day, in the midst of a thronging crowd, there was a lame woman who walked on crutches dragging one foot. Since she could not keep up with the others, she quickly fell behind. But she kept at it, while calling on the saint to let her walk by devotion alone. Soon feeling the help of God and the saint within her, she threw away one crutch, while still holding on to the other; and supporting herself on the ground with her knuckles she arrived at the church after us, praising God and speaking of the cure to everyone. She was known to everyone, since although a mime, she lived a chaste and upright life. Peace was established in the hearts of many that day; for no one could resist after kissing the staff of the saint, whether they had done so willingly or not. Departing from there, and passing through other places with great glory, we arrived at Lobbes after ten days, on the vigil of the apostles. And since it was a feast day we brought our patron to the chief temple, where he remained with us for several days.[42]

(22.) On the night before the dawn of the day when the saint was to be returned to his monastery, a man of Thuin came to the church with his young son, who had lost his eyesight a year before, I know not how. Setting him before the saint, he kept vigil and prayed until dawn. But the night brought nothing. When we returned the saint to the monastery that morning, he came with us, again bringing his son. And when we set the saint in his place, the man tossed down the staff that he held in his hand, invoked the saint, and said to his son, "Run and fetch me what I threw down over there [*illuc*] right away." Immediately the boy recovered his sight, and as we watched he brought back the staff that his father had thrown aside. This man is our neighbor. The boy still lives at Thuin. He does not have much, not being one of the richer people. But though he might live in need, yet he was enriched with the sight of his eyes, thanks be to God and St. Ursmer.

Notes

1. There is no exact English equivalent. *Virtutes sanctorum* are the virtues of the saints, also their beneficent acts, also the acts that reveal their power (*virtus*). They are, in other words, the saints' miracles.

2. Adelard served as abbot of Lobbes from 1053 until 1077/78.

3. The *Menapes* and *Wasiani* were tribes in the vicinity of Ghent and Tournai converted by Ursmer.

4. Twice in his opening paragraph the author singles out negligence as a reason for Lobbes's sorry state: the *negligentia majorum* and the *incuria priorum*. This language is highly ambiguous. *Priores* could refer to abbots, or to those specific monastic officials called "priors" who were responsible for most administrative matters, or to the elders of a monastery as a whole, or simply to those who had "gone before." Likewise, *majores* could refer to the leaders of the monastery (abbots, priors, cellarers, or simply elders generally) or to the officials (whether monks or laymen) who supervised its rural estates. Part of the unwritten code of tenth- and eleventh-century monasticism was that monks never openly criticized their living superiors. Another part of the code was that the memory of past superiors (as that of patrons and rulers generally) was perpetuated according to their merits. In other words, bad monastic officials were criticized after their deaths, not during their lifetimes. So the author may have been criticizing past leadership (and his audience would have known exactly whom he meant). He may only have been criticizing local estate agents. The vagueness of his criticism might also indicate the need to believe that someone had been responsible for the monastery's troubles, even when no one was.

5. The older count was Baldwin V, the younger his eldest son Baldwin VI. Baldwin VI had ruled the county of Hainaut since 1051, when his father married him to the widow of Count Herman of Hainaut and had the rightful heirs consigned to the church. He briefly ruled Flanders as well as Hainaut from his father's death in 1067 until 1071, when he was overthrown by his younger brother Robert. One of the Baldwin's is mentioned (although it is not certain which) in Drogo of Sint-Winoksbergen's *Life of St. Godelieve* translated by Bruce Venarde in the following chapter.

6. "Sign of miracles" (*signis miraculorum*) not in the sense of a "trace" of miracles but rather in the sense of a "proof" or "validation" of St. Ursmer's power.

7. "Sisters" are probably nuns. Brabant was the territory northwest of Hainaut, mostly east of the Escaut river (also known as the Scheldt) from Oudenarde.

8. *Divisi a nostro consortio*: contemporaries spoke of the saved as being "in the consort of God and the saints." Conversely, those excommunicated by bishops or cursed by monks were spoken of as being "cut off from the consort of God and the saints." The phrasing here therefore suggests a curse actually damning the recalcitrant.

9. Here and in most other passages, the Latin word translated as "youth" is *juvenis*. The word does not always refer to those simply young in age. Particularly when applied to nobles, it usually refers to those who have no land, no wife, and no position of authority—in other words, those who are under the control of those called *domini* ("lords") or *seniores* ("lords" or "elders"). A forty-year old man may therefore have been regarded as a "youth." Yet our author describes as *juvenes* men who are clearly in positions of command, and Hugh himself is called *dominus*. I suspect that these men really were relatively young and that their power was recent and still unstable. My assumption is that the combination of war, drought, famine, and disease (all of course interrelated) that lies constantly in the background of the narrative had carried off a number of established lords, sparking a succession struggle accompanied by an unusually large number of feuds.

10. An *adventus* was a formal processional entry made with incense, candles, and hymns.

11. The church and its courtyard (*atrium*) were a protected space within which all bloodshed was prohibited. Criminals trying to escape immediate vengeance (like our killer here) could therefore flee to it as a refuge; for that very reason, it was also a place where bloodshed was sometimes unavoidable.

12. A litany was a concentrated sequence of chanted petitions keyed to particular circumstances and asking for benefaction from God and those angels and saints associated with such circumstances. In this case, the litany would probably have included petitions for peace from saints who had missionized in Flanders and those who had ended wars or died as a result of wars.

13. Presumably this means that although the people had not "known" Ursmer because his was not a local cult, they still recognized his power.

14. The name *Bonifacius* literally means "good deed" or "doer of good deeds."

15. When seeking favors from a lord, forgiveness for a misdeed, or even when merely offering to negotiate an issue, those in inferior or weaker positions always made their approach through intercessors. In trying to understand the cult of saints, it is worth pointing out that, technically, saints were the intercessors between God and humanity, begging God for acts of mercy and forgiveness on behalf of humanity (see Chapter 3 above). Similarly, monks were the intercessors between saints and the faithful.

16. The word used here, *salutem*, can mean "salvation" as well as "health." The dual meaning allowed writers to play off all sorts of parallels between the health of the soul and the health of the body, with Christ and the saints being doctors of both.

17. The "cloister" was the monastery founded at Bergues-Saint-Winnoc by Baldwin V's father.

18. The fiftieth day after Easter is the feast of Pentecost.

19. *Fixit pietas gradum* literally means "devotion established her step," the step referring to the steps in front of the altar where most acts of special devotion to God and saints were performed.

20. *Optimates* is a word that usually refers to those nobles who frequently attend a ruler's court. The significance of the word choice here is that although these nobles may have been troublesome, they were not fully independent warlords. They had close ties to the count, which they needed to maintain.

21. *Statutis custodibus e regione*. The phrase probably refers to officials the count had established in the town and surrounding territory. It might conceivably refer to local religious leaders (the cleric in charge of the lamp is also called a *custos*), though for this meaning the phrasing would be odd.

22. The *adventus* of a lord (see note 10 above) entailed a reciprocating *occursus*, in which clergy and townspeople processed outside the walls to greet the lord and escort him

into the town. This is what is being described here. The "praises" (*laudibus*) were formal chants. To greet in an *occursus* was itself a "constitutive" act, in the sense that by granting such an honor, a city or church was publicly declaring that it was willing to recognize a lord's authority—or, as here, a saint's.

23. When a person had been killed, injured, or merely insulted, he, his kinsmen, or his lords or vassals could initiate a feud in revenge; but that only led to the revenge needing to be avenged in turn. There were several ways out of the vicious circle. The most common was for the two sides to agree on an offer of some sort of compensation (property, luxury items, or money). Although this had been going on for centuries, in the eleventh century people were beginning to look at the customs of feuding differently, this writer, for example, portraying the desire for compensation as simple greed (rather than as a desire for some sort of equalizing justice). Without minimizing the importance of Ursmer's presence, one should note that even before the monks' arrival, the enemies themselves had realized that their feuds had reached a point of stalemate and had begun negotiating, however mistrustfully.

24. *Quasi ad pedes Jesu cum Maria.*

25. One suspects that the monks were trying to downplay expectations of a miracle. In fact, cures worked at pilgrimage sites often involved what we would call traumatic injuries, brought about by a moment of severe physical or psychological stress. There may be a suggestion here that this woman's loss of sight was simply the result of old age, making a cure unlikely. The author admits as much when writing of another old woman's blindness (see Chapter 19 below).

26. The phrase in parentheses reads: *hymnizabant Deo, non quasi femineis, se quasi canonicis laudibus.* Because the miracle occurs in the very early morning, and because the author describes these *laudes* as *canonicae*, he is apparently referring not to generic vernacular songs of praise but to the morning office of Lauds, specifically the shorter, simplified office sung by such secular clerics as canons (and therefore more familiar to the laity) rather than the longer office chanted by cloistered monks. If so, it is interesting evidence for the laity's knowledge of a Latin office.

27. This phrase, *sicut facta ita et infecta de actibus sancti comminiscens*, is a rather surprising admission for a monastic writer of the period who wanted to spread the fame of his saint. Monks were pretty good inventors of fictions themselves.

28. The sentence reads: *Petiit a nobis benedictam aquam, cui intingens sancti confessoris pastoralem baculum, parvulo citissime detulit potum.* Another surprising statement, but this reading is what the grammar demands: the woman, not the monks, dipped the saint's pastoral staff in the holy water.

29. Although striking, the formulation (*uxorem et filios . . . a sancto coepit exigere*) is not unusual in hagiography of the period. Sources often speak of a saint's devotees making formal demands upon him as if in a court of law. Sometimes they even threaten to take their service to another cult if the saint does not fulfill his obligation to protect his clients.

30. The model is again intercessory (see note 15 above): enemies do not approach enemies directly. They go through an intercessor.

31. The translation of the final phrase (*cum forcipe et scopis*) is conjectural, the description uncommon. I assume that the man was offering himself up for punishment: being beaten and having his hair cut by the man whose brothers he had killed.

32. The epithet of *sublimitas* given to Robert and the prostration before him were part of the protocol monks adopted when making requests before kings and counts for benefactions. They were the same protocol adopted for praying to God and saints. Necessary when addressing kings and counts, they were quite rare when addressing castellans like Robert. The point was to flatter Robert, but also to hold him to account: if Robert wanted to rule like a lord and be honored like one, he would have to be beneficent like one, too.

33. Here *pallium* probably refers to a special embroidered rug used to keep the reliquary from coming in direct contact with the ground. The single word translated as "without letting them see" is *dissimulando*.

34. To place a saint on the ground is demeaning to the saint, hence Ursmer's unwillingness to lie there, and his anger at being forced to by Robert's stubbornness.

35. A small church dedicated to St. Pharahilde was attached to the count's castle in Ghent staffed with secular canons. The monastery of Saint John the Baptist is, to my knowledge, unidentified.

36. The charity was owed (*debita caritate*), because the religious of the monastery of Saint Peter at Ghent and the monastery of Saint Peter at Lobbes shared a common vocation as monks (also common patrons in Peter, and probably a formal prayer confraternity requiring each to pray for the other's dead). This made them spiritual brothers, and love (*caritas*) was the virtue that governed ideal relations between brothers. This confraternal love would have shown itself quite concretely by the monks of Lobbes being allowed to participate in the liturgical offices at Ghent on an equal footing.

37. In this phrase (*suae salutis testimonium*), the word *salus* again refers to both health and salvation (see note 16 above).

38. The two most important monasteries in Ghent were those dedicated respectively to St. Peter and to St. Bavo, each of them endlessly embroiled with the other over precedence. In order to avoid giving offense, the monks of Lobbes had to visit both. The fact that they visited the monastery of Saint Peter first probably reflects a special confraternal tie with that monastery. That the brothers of the monastery of Saint Bavo received the monks of Lobbes with extravagant honor (see the last sentence of this chapter) suggests their desire to one-up their rivals.

39. In other words, the reputation of the woman could not be validated, the state of her prior blindness could not be validated, and therefore the miracle could not be validated. See also note 25 above.

40. *Finia* is modern Finis, in the parish of Saint-Maurice in Lille.

41. "Satisfaction" is a technical term for the act that atones for a wrong, whether a criminal wrong (in which case satisfaction is owed to the victim, his agents, or a lord) or a religious wrong, that is, a sin (in which case satisfaction is owed to God and the saint offended).

42. St. Ursmer's relics were ordinarily housed not at the main church of Lobbes but in the church dedicated to St. Ursmer on the hill above. Founded as a parish church by Ursmer himself, at the time of the *delatio* it was run by a community of secular canons who performed parochial duties for the local laity under the direct supervision of the monks of Lobbes, who in fact held the offices of provost, *custos*, and treasurer. The church was rebuilt after the 1070s, probably in order to accommodate pilgrims and devotees of Ursmer (as well as to increase pilgrimages and devotions to Ursmer).

CHAPTER 17

DROGO OF SINT-WINOKSBERGEN, *LIFE OF ST. GODELIEVE*

Translated by Bruce L. Venarde

INTRODUCTION

Drogo's *Life of St. Godelieve* is a precious record of one woman's tragic and triumphant fate. Godelieve is a unique figure: the only married female martyr recognized as a saint by a medieval pope. She is also, in Drogo's account, a vivid character whose biography illuminates tensions and conflicts in her world. In particular, the *Life of St. Godelieve* provides a candid account of a disastrous marriage at a time when the joining of individuals and families was central to social, economic, and political organization. Godelieve's story tells something about the psychological implications of the arranged marriages that were the rule among the propertied classes of premodern Europe. Godelieve emerges as a victim of medieval marriage and an example of medieval religious devotion as practiced by a laywoman.

Much of the interest of Godelieve's story derives from the extraordinary sympathy of her biographer. Drogo of Sint-Winoksbergen is the only named Flemish hagiographer of the eleventh century. His origins are uncertain, but it appears that he was of relatively humble birth. Drogo probably entered the monastery of Sint-Winoksbergen, in present-day Belgium, as a child oblate around the time of the abbey's foundation ca. 1022. Drogo's education, perhaps continued at the renowned abbey of Saint-Bertin, gave him familiarity with the writings of the Church fathers as well as classical Latin orators, poets, historians, and playwrights. Sometime after 1058 Drogo journeyed to Denmark and possibly spent time in England as well. He died sometime between writing the *Life of St. Godelieve*, in about 1084, and 1098, when his name appeared on a list of the remembered dead of his monastery.

The *Life of St. Godelieve*, then, is the work of an old man. Drogo had already written other biographies of male and female saints and a book about the miracles of the patron saint of his monastery. Because he was writing less than twenty years after the death of his subject, and not far from the site of her martyrdom and center of her cult, Drogo was able to get much of his information directly from eyewitnesses. There are no dates in Drogo's account, but it seems likely that Godelieve was born in the late 1040s or early 1050s and died in or around 1070. Since Drogo wrote before her canonization in the summer of 1084, fresh memories of Godelieve lend to the *vita* a frankness and specificity rare in hagiography. Closeness of time and place could account for the admiration and empathy of the author for his subject. However, Drogo was also singularly free of the misogyny and fear of the human (especially female) body common among his monastic contemporaries. The only evil woman in his writings is Godelieve's mother-in-law; he does not shy away from intimate details and is sensitive to the beauty of female youth and the dignity of matronly age. Finally, Drogo was a born storyteller whose rather awkward Latin style did not prevent him from composing a fascinating and horrible tale of faith, abuse, murder, and miracles.

Perhaps partly because it is such a compelling story, scholars do not agree on its meaning. Godelieve's unwavering faith was an example for other Christians. She also exercised selfless charity, sharing even her meager portion of food with the poor and miraculously providing abundant bread for her own funeral feast. But other implications of her story are subject to debate. Why, for instance, did Godelieve's marriage go sour so quickly? Drogo wrote that her husband was possessed by the devil; modern observers have suggested that sexual dysfunction may have been at the heart of the initial alienation of the couple. Drogo's straightforward account does not claim virginity for his subject, and he does not take the opportunity to condemn sexual pleasure or praise chastity. Was the author trying to explain what a good Christian marriage should be by enumerating the failings of a bad one? Or was he moralizing about the final rewards of obedience, to God and his earthly representatives? Godelieve flees her abusive husband once but is returned to him at the instigation of her father and by the authority of a count and a bishop. In a sense, then, she is a martyr to arranged marriage and the failures of secular and ecclesiastical authorities to solve the problems it posed. Two of the four miracle stories have Godelieve healing peasants who are acting contrary to priestly direction. Was Godelieve's cult at first a focus of anticlerical, antimale, antinoble, or even quasi-pagan devotion on the part of peasants, appropriated by the Church for its own purposes when it proved unsuppressible? The ultimate question of Godelieve's character arouses conflicting interpretations—was she a courageous martyr or a too-submissive wife? Whatever the conclusions drawn from it, Drogo's *Life of St. Godelieve* provides a glimpse of a turbulent life in a dynamic society. Godelieve's cult remains lively in Flanders. A nunnery was founded in her honor near the site of her martyrdom, and her story has been the subject of numerous writings, artistic productions, and even an opera by Edgar Tinel.

SOURCES AND FURTHER READING

The best edition of Drogo of Sint-Winoksbergen's *Life of St. Godelieve* (*Bibliotheca hagiographica latina*, no. 3591t) is Drogo van Sint-Winoksbergen, *Vita Godeliph*, ed. Nikolaas-Norbert Huyghebaert and trans. Stefaan Gyselen (Tielt, 1982), which is accompanied by helpful introduction, notes, and a translation in Dutch. The text differs little from the more readily available version edited by Maurice Coens in *Analecta Bollandiana* 44 (1926): 103–37, with introductory material in French. On Drogo, see Nicolas Huyghebaert, "Un moine hagiographe: Drogon de Bergues," *Sacris Erudiri* 20 (1971): 191–256. Two different perspectives on Godelieve and her biography are offered by Georges Duby, "The Matron and the Mismarried Woman," in *Love and Marriage in the Middle Ages*, trans. Jane Dunnett (Chicago, 1994), pp. 36–55 and Renée Nip, "Godelieve of Gistel and Ida of Boulogne," in *Sanctity and Motherhood: Essays on Holy Mothers in the Middle Ages*, ed. Anneke Mulder-Bakker (New York, 1995), pp. 191–223.

Drogo of Sint-Winoksbergen, *Life of St. Godelieve*

Here begins Drogo's prologue to the *Life of St. Godelieve*.

To Lord Radbod, by the grace of God bishop of Noyon, Drogo the monk and unworthy priest, the good which surpasses all good.

The fame of your name and your nobility, most blessed father, is deemed great and worthy to be mentioned far and wide. You flourish in the knowledge of literature; you devote yourself to the needs and concerns of those around you, like Martha, and in equal measure you receive the words of God, remaining at his feet, like Mary [see Lk 10:38–42]. When these qualities are happily present together in one person, they are cherished by students of wisdom who rejoice because that which appears according to the distributions of God's grace has been granted by the good Creator to a fellow man. And not at all unworthily—an extraordinary seed of love grows in those who without hesitation wish for their neighbors what they want for themselves. Truly, best of prelates, I understand from often hearing the spoken praise of many that your reputation is outstanding. Thus I earnestly feel in my heart that you who are elevated by the gift of all virtues would have a care for me in my efforts and support my tottering footsteps with your sweet aid.[1]

For I am forced by a great exhortation of many faithful people to do something beyond my strength, to begin an account of the passion of St. Godelieve: first to tell about the parents to whom she was born, then the man to whom she as a young woman was betrothed, then by whose trickery and by whom and how she was martyred. I have transcribed these things as they really were, worthy to relate and fitting to remember, all together on parchment. I send this record to you, kindest father, so that by your authority, if in fact you deem it worthy, it might remain valid and true and have the force of pontifical decree for all to whom it comes. Nevertheless, venerable father, before these things are read by many people, first you yourself read over our writings, of whatever quality they are. Trim what is superfluous, add eloquence to what is less clear, so that by your agency the enlightenment that readers seek might shine forth more brightly.

These things which we have written we have heard and learned from people still living who were eyewitnesses. Therefore let no one take it amiss, because Holy Scripture cries out that many others would have done it had I remained silent.[2] By your judgment, then, and that of wise people—even if I am rebuked for taking up the task by some—I will leave off and begin my account as best I can. Farewell.

Here ends the prologue.

Here begins her life and passion, which is the 30th of July.

(1.) The benevolence of the Almighty calls each sex to His mercy. Sometimes He makes this one come to His kingdom through many difficult tribulations, then He crowns that one with victorious patience, then He repays another one, mighty in the peace of the Church by the increase of virtues and love of God and neighbor, with a worthy reward of goods. When all are crowned, these with roses, those with white lilies, the eternal and highest good awaits them all equally—although it is well known that the reward varies by the quality of merits, according to divine goodness: martyrdom for some, the pinnacle of peace for others.[3]

For the palm awaits martyrs and eternal glory in heaven awaits the confessors of the faith; how much and how great a glory it is hardly possible to say, nor is the human heart, soul, or mind able to contemplate. A faithful soul, undefeated and perseverant amidst many tricks of the crafty enemy, grows stronger; the more constant it remains among insults and disgrace, the greater the glory of its coronation. For as long as the soul puts on the shield of humility, it protects itself with the impenetrable breastplate of patient endurance. For surely when other virtues join together with these, they elevate the humble mind by their might and make it dwell in heaven. While that soul enjoys eternal glory, ashes and bones are venerated by signs on earth everywhere.[4]

Enough of this. From here on, let the succession of the account proceed to show the course of life and the time and place of the passion of St. Godelieve.

(2.) She was born in the territory of Boulogne, in the city itself, the scion of well-born parents.[5] Her father was Heinfrid, her mother Odgiva. Already in the tender years of girlhood she began to be devoted to God, obeying her parents' instructions to have pity on the oppressed and do her best to keep her childhood pure and righteous. Thus occupied she slipped into youth and then, made marriageable by the passing years, she was sought by many men, mighty as she was in honorable morals, so gentle and humble, sweet in her actions, and affable in prudent conversation. Among others who sought the hand of so outstanding a young woman was one called Bertolf. He was a powerful man, exalted in birth and wealth.[6] The dowry he offered made him much more pleasing to Godelieve's parents than the other noble suitors, and the girl was promised in legal marriage to him.[7]

But on the very day he took his fiancée home, Bertolf's mind was assaulted by the devil. He began to hate Godelieve, occasionally regretting his hatred, sometimes blaming himself for what had happened. Not only does "evil communication corrupt good morals," as the apostle says [see 1 Cor 15:33], but in fact wicked habits make the spirit of evil worse when it is provoked by curses and taunting. For Bertolf was also driven to hatred by the words of his mother, who should have rejoiced in the success of her son's suit, after the fashion of good mothers.

(3.) There is a popular saying in that part of the world, that all mothers-in-law hate their daughters-in-law.[8] They waste away in vice thus: they want their sons to wed, yet when it happens, they are jealous of them and the women they marry. Bertolf's mother said, speaking metaphorically, "Were you entirely unable, dear son, to find any crows in your homeland, and thus wanted to bring home a foreign crow? Why did you do it? Why did you want to do such a thing? Shouldn't you have instead sought the counsel of your mother and others who would have advised you, consulted with your father, before doing as whimsy took you? Mark my words: you'll figure out what you've done, and you won't be able to correct the blunder when you realize you've made it." Driven by these and other maternal words, Bertolf was burdened with sorrow, and sickness of soul grew greater in him each day. He complained, sometimes to himself, sometimes to friends who had been told of his plans. "I have provoked my mother by my engagement, and unless I take some kind of action for the better, I have destroyed myself, too."

His betrothed had dark eyebrows and hair but very fair skin, which is agreeable and pleasing in women, often highly prized. Indeed her looks were perfect for anyone who caught sight of her, and anyone who smiled at her: for you perceived that she rejoiced with you when you were happy, and she seemed truly sympathetic when you were sad.

(4.) Now Bertolf did not want to attend his own wedding, and behaved as if intent on other, preferable activities on his own behalf, now doing business, now meeting far-flung allies. All this he did in order to be absent, lest he see the woman he despised. His mother, although unwilling, celebrated the union in the husband's—her son's—place; she calmed her stormy brow, hiding the poison she bore in her soul. For three whole days the son was absent while the marriage was fêted by his mother and his enemies. He came back after the third day; forsaking his own home, wife, and household, he went to live at his father's house. The newly married wife, unworthy of this treatment and certainly worthy of a better husband, remained at home, managed the household, and consoled the grief in her soul with distaff, spindle and loom. She spent her nights alone, and poured forth prayers as well as tears, asking that God grant her husband a change of heart. When Bertolf saw this, he began to discuss with both parents how he might corrupt her way of living, since it was a disgrace and harmful to him. His father sympathized with Bertolf—if such can be called "sympathy"—and joined in his son's hatred of Godelieve. A servant was prevailed upon to maltreat her, offering her a loaf of bread once a day at an appointed hour and nothing else. Still the woman of God gave thanks to God for the bread bestowed on her. She gave half of it to the poor, keeping the other half for the nourishment of her own body. The crowning blow was to see her servants' abundant pleasures, since they got meat and plenty else to eat. She had only salted bread and water once a day. Her husband told the servant that if he did anything other than what had been ordered, he would be punished.

(5.) Still the enemy did not rest. He plotted worse dangers and prepared more atrocities with which to torment the servant of God and make her more distinguished in the eyes of almighty God and men. "This is too much, too much I've allowed my wife. Anything further will harm me. Now let half the loaf of bread reserved for the needy be taken away, and only the other part be given to her. I'll take away her healthy color and destroy her mind so that she cannot even think about God or herself." Bertolf turned these things over in his mind; then he spoke and in his speech told what was to be done. Half a loaf was given to Godelieve. She took it, gave thanks to God for such a quantity, and prayed this prayer: "I beseech you, God, Creator of all things, help me in my frailty. Consider the many miseries with which I am afflicted. Although, my holy Lord, my portion of rations is diminished by my husband, in no way is my good will diminished. So let a poor person take this half, or rather let it be given to you through the needy." So she spoke, and gave a scrap of the half-loaf to a pauper.

Oh pious will, oh patience enduring together in the same woman! You persist always in adversities. Your spouse curses you; you bless him. He grows envious of you; you reconcile him to God with prayers and determination—if the good can be reconciled with the wicked. He even hopes for your death and threatens it; you, as long as you live, always pray to God.

So the woman devoted to God complied with the pledge she had made, giving over half the bread allowed her to the needy. It was very difficult for her to subsist on so tiny a portion, but she did not want to break the promise she had made to God. Women of the neighborhood and in-laws took pity on her, and brought bread, meat, fish, and other things given by God for human consumption. She lived on these while her personal bodily needs were attended by the washing of rags.[9] Nor should it be kept silent that all people present and absent loved and pitied her—even those who knew her only by name. For God grants to each of the faithful that the better part of humanity loves and reveres him, just as light combines with light and is joined to it. For it would be monstrous if two opposites were in harmony.

(6.) But Bertolf, too, had his supporters, who stuck by him and plotted evil. They goaded a man violent enough on his own, inclined and prepared to perpetrate any sort of crime, against an innocent. Amid such wrongs done by her husband, Godelieve, along with most of her household, was forced to flee from him. Barefoot and hungry, she left the country altogether and went back to her homeland and her father, accompanied only by a servant.[10] There she complained about her husband's injustice and the harm done to the household, and that for her love of God Bertolf had conspired against her and cursed her piety. Heinfrid pitied his daughter's misfortune and gave Godelieve a place to live while he took wise counsel about what would be most fruitful with respect to his own honor and her needs. When at last he had decided on what seemed to him the best course of action, he went to Count Baldwin and told him in detail the story of the harm done him and his daughter. He explained how at last the husband had forced her to flee. The count, however, sent Godelieve's father to the bishop of the diocese in which Bertolf lived, since that prelate was mighty in wisdom and ready to advise any person in matters of all sorts. "It is the office of a bishop," said the count, "to rule Christendom as well as correct anything deviating from holy practice, and mine to help him in any difficulties which he is unable to overcome by himself. Episcopal authority should first compel this man to take back what is his. If he refuses, and considers the bishop's order of little significance, then I will address the matter and demand satisfaction for your cause with every resource available to me."[11] Why wait to get on with the story? The husband was forced by both parties to take back his wife. He swore that he would not treat her badly, received her lawfully, and took her back home. Still she lived alone in the house and prayed to the Almighty that she be deemed worthy of comfort, as He comforts His servants.

(7.) Some people, including certain of Bertolf's friends, censured undying anger and perpetual hatred of such a woman, and criticized him because neither the teachings of God, nor the authority of the bishop, nor the command of the prince made him gentler toward her—his ferocity was not softened by the marriage contract or his own reputation. When people hurled curses at her, the one dear to God opposed them with pious words. God's servant even forbade others to damn her husband. "To speak ill of someone," she said, "is not much of a crime or sin, but to curse is a very great sin. As I have heard, this is what the apostle taught: 'Bless those who persecute you, bless and curse not' [Rom 12:14]. By this means everyone can keep his mouth entirely clean of curses and his tongue free from slander. He is known to have sinned against me; so much less should I heap up curses. So that God may pour forth the grace and goodness of his heart, let such hatred of me cease, and let my husband cherish me accordingly." While some bewailed her harsh misfortune and ached for her miseries, Godelieve, filled with divine grace, consoled herself. She showed a smiling, happy face, because the spirit informing her heart made her ever cheerful. She clung to the Lord in adversity and loved his teachings with the fullest embrace of devotion. She served Him and was deservedly loved by Him. In fact this is what her name shows: it means "dear to God" in German.[12]

(8.) This, too, is wonderful to say and worthy to be committed to writing. Some people bewailed the causes of her misfortunes and said that she was all alone, not knowing and not to know pleasures of the body or the delights of the world.[13] Godelieve saw that those lovers of the world measured out pleasures in their minds as earthly people in pursuit of things of the earth. Smiling at the empty folly of such words, yet with modest visage and invincible in her faith and hope she refuted the lamenters with a brief speech and responded from a ready heart. "I don't care at all about the lures of the body and I value little the riches of the transient world. Whatever we see, whatever we have, whatever we desire that we don't have yet—all this is changeable. Not even man himself lasts. A swift hour will destroy him and, according to the perfect Truth, all flesh is as the flower of grass, which now blooms but soon after, mown down, withers away" [see Is 40:6–7]. Then, fired with prophetic spirit, she added the following. "Nobody should say I am unlucky, nor think it, although I am tempest-tossed on this sea of life and afflicted with what you call misfortune. For I am exalted over every woman who draws breath in all Flanders and I will appear richer to all than I can imagine. Let Him who is most powerful do what He will with me, He who endows whom He wishes with His virtues and who raises the poor man from the dirt of his misfortune" [see Lk 1:46–49]. Saying such things makes it evident that she was comforted by the Holy Spirit and her mind put at ease and strengthened by heavenly consolation. She had foreknowledge that she would inhabit heaven by means of the things she patiently endured if in fact, persevering to the end, she were distinguished by virtue and good works.

I call to witness for the universal belief of mortals—I, who compose this report, of whatever sort it may be—that I knew and saw monks, practiced in the height of modesty and endowed in all virtues, zealous in good will and resistant to everything contrary to good, who were edified by Godelieve's sweet exhortation and left her better equipped to withstand all vice. There was grace of such a sort in her, the gift of divine clemency, that whoever spoke with her took pity and rejoiced: pitied her for the unworthy things she had endured and was still enduring, but rejoiced upon seeing that she rose above, triumphing over adversity.

(9.) Concerning her life that much suffices. Henceforth the pen turns to how she crossed over from this life to God. Since every one of Bertolf's deceits and contrivances was foiled with God's help, such that he was unable to make the holy woman perish from hunger or any other trick his cunning could devise, he began to plot. He soon became distracted by the darting about of his thoughts. He burned inside, the goads of rage unbridled. Moving his lips, he pondered the following in his disturbed mind. "Is there any kind of human skill to be found that could bring my will to bear? I live, and live badly, as long as I see my every plan overcome. In her life my own rots away, and while she lives there is no vigor in my body. Hunger does not overwhelm her nor long fasting exhaust her body. Rather she thrives, unharmed, and the more she is crushed and worn down by trouble, the more powerful her youthfulness obviously is. So if my ability to impose my will does not proceed by this path, another way must be found, tried, undertaken. Either she can die by sword or flame or water or by some other torture our need invents." Bertolf was agitated by rage and moved first to wound, to tear her mind apart without a sword, before torturing her body. He called two servants, Lambert and Hacca, to ask their advice about what he could try doing to Godelieve, by what kind of torture he could kill her. They replied as they saw fit and offered useful counsel and encouragement. They set a day and contrived a kind of torture by which she would easily perish and the deed be hidden. They even considered what time of day or night would be most expedient and secretive for doing what they planned.

(10.) Now the day had come, and the time was at hand when it would be made clear what sort of woman she was and how filled with God. The glory of heaven would reward her whose heart shone with divine grace from heaven and who was equally remarkable for virtue and humble patience. On the very night when she was to be killed by the trickery of criminal sinners, before sunset her husband came home to Godelieve. First Bertolf kissed her with a lying mouth and embraced her, putting a smile on his face while he bore poison in his heart. When he did this unaccustomed thing, he sat down next to her with pretended cheerful face and happy heart. Both were sitting on a bench. Since she feared to approach her husband, and to show reverence to him (as some think it proper to do), he drew her toward him by the hand, and soothed her fears with soft words. Then he spoke to the handmaid of God. "It is no small grief to me that I am of such cruel spirit toward you and seem to be so unyielding that you are not accustomed to my presence and kind address and do not delight in mutual fleshly pleasure. I don't know what sort of misfortune has come between us, what discord has separated our minds, so that I have become alienated from you and not in control of my heart. It seems to me that the trouble has been fostered by the enemy. He destroys the hearts of mortals, now inciting this one to envy, now that one to hatred. But I want to put an end to this spiritual separation, to cherish you as a dear wife and thus, putting hatred behind us little by little, our minds and bodies will come together as one."[14] Oh heart infected with every wicked art, oh foul tongue of man! You imitate Judas, the betrayer of the Lord, in your crime. He kissed a gentle lamb in planned trickery; you offer kisses to your wife and talk to an innocent with treacherous heart. For a price, he handed over the King and Lord of all to the hateful crowds; you hand over your wife to serfs, who are to be rewarded with some prize. So if we are permitted to compare great things to small ones, the depths to the heights, there will be like punishment, equal burden for you for your own crime. "I have found a woman," Bertolf continued, "who considers that she will be able to join us together in steadfast devotion and have us unite in love constantly, cherishing each other like no couple anywhere in the world. This business I have committed to the servants Lambert and Hacca. They will bring the woman to you. I believe strongly in all this. Therefore I am telling you all about it in advance, so it is not unknown to you or cause for anxiety."

When the crafty man had finished, Godelieve replied, "I am a handmaid of the Lord, and commend everything to him. Therefore if this can be done without any crime, I accept." Oh fortunate woman, and devoted to God! You unite yourself to God before all, and He takes care of you. You fear lest you are separated from your true self by magic. For that reason you choose to honor your marriage, lest you lose the Lord, joiner of marriage.[15] When she had finished the words above, she was silent. Bertolf, hopping up from the bench on which he sat, mounted his horse and went off for the night to Bruges, where he would await word of his wife's death. Thus, he thought, he would be free from criminal suspicion.

(11.) Now darkness fell quickly after sunset. The bodies of all humans slept their cares away and lay quiet. Behold Lambert and Hacca, rousing their mistress from sleep. "Arise, my lady," they said. "We come solicitously, to take you to the woman of whom our master spoke. There she is, standing by the gates, already waiting for you. Come on, get up, hurry, lest you harm your own cause by delay." First Godelieve protected herself with the sign of the cross—thereafter she committed herself wholly to God. When it became clear that she wanted to dress, the servants forbade it. "Come with bare feet, loose hair, dressed only in a shift," they say. "It's quite certain that everything will work to your benefit. But it must be done now, in the dark of night, before first light." She subjected herself to their demands, saying, "I entrust myself to the Almighty. I am his creature, so let whatever becomes of me seem most merciful. Now I surrender myself to faith in you." Rising up, she went with the two men. What they said and did for the next little while was empty of meaning, more tricks and scheming which do not even seem worthy of recording.[16] But when they deceived her one last time, they put a noose around her neck and hands around her throat, so nobody could hear her scream. They squeezed with all their might. When they figured she was dead, they submerged her in water, so in case any breath of life was left, the water would smother it. By the miraculous power of God, it was brought about that if anything of our earthly form was blackened, it could be made clean and white with that water.[17]

(12.) Afterward the pair did their duty. They took Godelieve back to her bed, lay her in it, and drew up the covers. When the sun had climbed high in the sky, the household murmured about what might possibly be keeping their mistress from getting up. She had been in the habit of hastening to arise, either before dawn or at first light, alerting others, and going to church. So the servants wondered, but did not want to wake up their mistress, thinking her either sick or sleepy. As more time passed, someone went into her bedroom and tried to rouse her, but a dead woman cannot be roused. Word spread quickly and neighbors arrived. The body was examined but no wound or sign of a sword's work was found anywhere. There was only a red ring around her neck where the wicked men had put the noose. Some asserted that she had died from natural causes while others muttered otherwise. True understanding was granted according to the measure of love people had for Godelieve. Burial was accomplished hastily the same day. Because the bread to be doled out for her salvation ran short, somebody went to correct matters by buying grain. The grain was a gain for its purchaser, for it multiplied such that when ground into flour it exceeded its measure and the buyer marveled at this miracle. God be praised! In your honor she gave as much to the poor as she could, while alive, and you reminded everyone of the fact with this heavenly miracle.[18]

(13.) The spot of ground where she was killed was turned to white stone, in order that the Lord might show her merit and make known to all the faithful the place of her death. Some people took away souvenirs out of devotion to Godelieve, brought them home, and afterward marveled that the stone turned to gems. I who am writing this account went as a witness and saw the gems and blessed the name of the Lord. Almighty God converted another earthly element for Godelieve's glory, to show her great merit. All comers weighed down with fevers or suffering from other infirmities who drank the water in which she drowned rejoiced at once that they had received, through her merits, the cure they had hoped for. Likewise the Lord showed her standing in heaven at her tomb, when he singled out her grave and even her body with heavenly signs. But I will tell only a few of the things that happened, and bring proofs of these signs to the fore, so that in them anyone can easily believe how highly this daughter of God is regarded in heaven's glory.

(14.) A father brought to her tomb his son, crippled from childhood, and prayed for a cure through her merits. After a short time the cripple rose up, and the father took him home healthy. The boy was called Algotus. He began his education as a child, and when he had attained manhood, he ascended little by little to the rank of deacon.

(15.) A certain crippled woman lay before the gate of the monastery of Saint-Trond for nine years, staying closed up there in the hope of being cured as others had been.[19] Many had been cured and raised up there so only this one woman remained in order to fulfill God's plan of making known far and wide the power of one grave. In the end, having heard of Godelieve's reputation, the woman had herself moved to the tomb, and prayed there for the Lord's mercy. After remaining only a short time, she arose, healed, and happily returned to her birthplace, safe and sound and on her own two feet. So this miracle took place. Godelieve shows the same merciful piety toward the poor as she did while alive and still in her human body.

(16.) One sabbath, at a time when it is forbidden, a certain man was harvesting in the field when his hand became stuck to an ear of grain. He tried to pull it off with the other hand, but he could not. You would have seen that he wanted to shake it off, but could not; in fact the more he tried, the more firmly it stayed in place. Soon recognizing his guilt in the matter, he went to the tomb of the oft-mentioned woman and got down on the ground to pray. The prayer not yet finished, his fingers stretched out, the grain fell away from his hand leaving his palm again visible.

(17.) This occurred on a solemn holiday which the faithful celebrated.[20] After mass, the priest stood and warned that the day should be observed by all and nobody should do any work whatsoever. A woman of the village heard the priest's warning, but thinking it of little account, she prepared some dye in a kettle and picked up a stick for stirring. At once it stuck to both hands. She struggled, swinging her arms about this way and that, but in vain. Word of the event got out, her household gathered, and neighbors came running. Some of the onlookers tried to wrench off the stick with their hands; others feared to touch it. Finally, urged on by her punishment, the woman went to the grave of her helper, to pray at the site and seek the merits of God's holy woman. Amidst tears and words of prayer first her fingers, then her whole hand suddenly were freed. The stick fell to the ground and the woman went home healed.

NOTES

1. What appears to be simply a stereotyped paean to a patron is more appropriate than usual in this case. Radbod, bishop of the large diocese of Tournai-Noyon from 1068 to 1098 and member of the powerful Avesnes clan, was indeed a celebrated preacher, sponsor of literary studies, and ecclesiastical patron. For a less flattering portrait by a member of the clan that was the chief rival of the Avesnes in Tournai, see Herman of Tournai, *The Restoration of the Monastery of Saint Martin of Tournai*, trans. Lynn H. Nelson (Washington, DC, 1996), especially pp. 105–6.

2. In this difficult passage Drogo appears to suggest that like the authors of the Gospels, he is producing an account based on eyewitness testimony; since Godelieve's story needs to be told by someone, Drogo has reluctantly done what many people have urged.

3. Drogo distinguishes between two kinds of faith: martyrdom, the shedding of blood symbolized by the rose, and unquestioning faith in surrender to God's will, symbolized by lilies, to whose happy fate Jesus referred in the Sermon on the Mount [Mt 6:28]. Then by verbal sleight-of-hand, Drogo claims that the reward for the merit either kind of faith demonstrates is the faith itself. Godelieve's life embraces both kinds of faith.

4. That is, through the cult of the saints and their relics.

5. Drogo gives no dates anywhere in the *vita*. Women married young in this society, so Godelieve might still have been in her teens when she died about 1070. Boulogne is in the northern reaches of present-day France.

6. Bertolf was a member of a family of petty lords in coastal Flanders. This class of people, often called castellans because a fortified place or castle was the symbol of their domination of the surrounding countryside, were at the peak of their power in western Europe in the eleventh century. Godelieve's parents were of similar social standing. Bertolf took his fiancée about one hundred kilometers northeast to his family's territory around Gistel, in modern Belgium.

7. In the early Middle Ages, and in some regions up until the thirteenth century, the groom's family provided a marriage gift. By the later Middle Ages, the financial burden, sometimes very heavy, rested with the bride's family. Drogo calls Bertolf's offering a "dowry," and finds nothing unusual in it: the early medieval practice was still at work.

8. Popular wisdom this may have been, but Drogo is also quoting a line from the Roman comic playwright Terence. This is but one instance of the author's mingling of popular tradition with sophisticated Latin learning.

9. Although Drogo's language is somewhat vague, he exhibits characteristic frankness in explaining how Godelieve could survive with any measure of personal dignity in virtual imprisonment.

10. Godelieve has been reduced to near-beggardom as she trudges half-starved back to her father's house. For a woman of her station, this was a very humiliating situation; Bertolf has treated her wretchedly.

11. Drogo refers to one of two Flemish counts: Baldwin V (1035–67) or his son Baldwin VI (1067–70). The two are both mentioned in *The Miracles of St. Ursmer on his Journey through Flanders*, translated by Geoffrey Koziol in the preceding chapter. If the latter, the bishop might well have been the Radbod to whom Drogo dedicated his account (see the prologue). According to Georges Duby (see Sources and Further Readings, above), Drogo's is the first statement from this part of Europe that the Church rather than secular authorities had jurisdiction over marriage.

12. That is "Gode lief," which might also be translated as "God's favorite" or "friend of God." Drogo wrote in Latin, but the spoken language of his native Flanders was Germanic. Godelieve was likely bilingual, since names in her family were Germanic but she grew up in Romance-speaking Boulogne. Perhaps that is also why her mother-in-law called her, a dark-haired speaker of a different language, a "foreign crow."

13. However, Drogo never refers to Godelieve as a virgin, or notes chastity among her virtues. It seems most likely that Godelieve and Bertolf did have sex at least once, perhaps on the journey from her home to his. Interestingly, the speech which follows does not condemn sexual or other bodily pleasures as evil, only noting that they are fleeting distractions from more important eternal matters.

14. The account of Bertolf's speech, with its heavy emphasis on sexual pleasure in marriage, has led some modern scholars to speculate that sexual dysfunction, vaginism or impotence, incited Bertolf's rage in the first place.

15. Drogo justifies his heroine's willingness to submit to the ministrations of a female magic healer, what we might call a good witch or a sorceress. Godelieve hesitates at such a course, but chooses to trust that her God stands guard as she obeys her husband.

16. Does this labored preterition suggest that the two servants raped Godelieve, perhaps at Bertolf's orders, before proceeding with their ultimate commission?

17. The tradition quickly grew up that Godelieve was dumped in a well. Her murder is represented this way in later writings and in art, for instance a Flemish polyptych of the late fifteenth century now in the Metropolitan Museum of Art in New York.

18. That is, instead of being reduced in volume by milling, the grain produced a quantity of flour greater than its original measure. The funeral feast is another instance of concern for the poor evident throughout the *Life*.

19. It was a common practice in this era for lay men and women to live right outside monastic compounds, some praying for specific favors, others simply leading a hermit-like existence in what they regarded as a holy place. Some of these seekers built primitive shelters, which is probably what Drogo means when he refers to the woman outside Saint-Trond "covering" or "closing" herself up (*operiens*).

20. Was this perhaps an early manifestation of Godelieve's cult? The vague language here may suggest that the canonization of the abused wife was a calculated official appropriation of a cult with non-Christian and even pagan overtones.

Chapter 18

HARTVIC,
LIFE OF KING STEPHEN OF HUNGARY

Translated by Nora Berend

INTRODUCTION

Bishop Hartvic undertook to write this *Life* of St. Stephen of Hungary at the command of King Coloman (1095–1116), either around the year 1100 or between the years 1112 and 1116. He drew heavily on two previous *Lives*, the *Vita Maior* (composed between 1077 and 1083), and the *Vita Minor* (written during the reign of Coloman, but before the work of Hartvic). The *Life* written by Hartvic became the official text; it was used as the basis of liturgical readings, or *lectiones*. Innocent III approved it in 1201, except the use of the words *utroque iure* describing Stephen's power; this part was subsequently omitted from manuscripts.

Stephen I (997–1038) was the first Christian king of Hungary, and it was mainly during his reign that both the secular and ecclesiastical structure of the kingdom was established. A conglomeration of tribes, led by and adopting the name of the Magyar (Hungarian) tribe, migrated from the east and invaded the Carpathian Basin in the late ninth century. Eventually they settled, and during the rule of their chieftain Géza (c. 970–97), and especially under his son Stephen I (crowned king in 1000/1001), converted to Christianity.

Stephen encountered both internal and external resistance in his efforts to establish a unified and independent Christian kingdom. He incorporated the territories of his defeated relatives into the realm, and eliminated those who aspired to his power: one, Koppány, was quartered, while another, Vazul, was blinded. Stephen and his successors repeatedly confronted the German emperors to secure Hungary's position as a separate kingdom. Ottonian and Salian emperors attempted to enlarge their empire by incorporating the emerging political units (Poland, Bohemia, and Hungary) on their eastern borders. Stephen's—successful—countermeasures had two aspects, military and ecclesiastical. On the one hand, Stephen and his successors defended the kingdom against several German attacks. The first, during Stephen's lifetime, was in 1030; after Stephen's death, Henry III tried to incorporate the kingdom into the German Empire by backing one of the contenders to the throne in exchange for submission. On the other hand, Stephen successfully avoided the incorporation of Hungary as an ecclesiastical province of the German Empire. The missionary bishops sent to Hungary in the late tenth century were consecrated by the archbishop of Mainz, and during this period the bishopric of Prague in Bohemia was created as a dependent of Mainz, while that of Poznań in Poland had a similar relationship to Magdeburg. Stephen, however, established an independent Hungarian ecclesiastical hierarchy of ten dioceses, including the archbishopric of Esztergom. In the *Life*, there is no mention of the German missionaries who converted Géza and his family and continued their work in Hungary; instead, Adalbert's role is much exaggerated, in order to emphasize Hungary's ecclesiastical independence since the beginnings. Stephen also established the territorial base of royal administration, the counties, and a military organization based on the counties.

The authors of the successive *Lives* of Stephen put hagiography in the service of politics and formulated refutations of both German imperial and papal claims. Gregory VII asserted papal rights over Hungary, maintaining that the kingdom had been offered to St. Peter. Stephen was portrayed in his first *Life* as offering himself and the kingdom to the Virgin Mary, who successfully protected her patrimony against a German attack. Thus the author claimed that it was God's will that the Hungarian kingdom did not become part of the German Empire; he also put forward an argument against the pope by declaring that Stephen offered Hungary to the Blessed Virgin Mary, not to St. Peter. Hartvic, not content to repeat this story alone, added another about the crown sent to Stephen by the pope. That is, Hartvic maintained that the first Hungarian king received royal insignia from the pope just as German emperors did, elevating the kingdom to a position analogous to that of the empire, thus independent from it. At the same time Hartvic stated that a vision instructed the pope to send a crown to Stephen, and, more importantly, portrayed a pope who conceded that Stephen had both temporal and spiritual jurisdiction (including the right to appoint bishops and clerics) in his realm. This way, drawing on anti-Gregorian material, Hartvic used up-to-date arguments against papal claims. Hartvic's work set out to prove that the Hungarian kingdom was not a dependent of the empire by divine decision, nor was it a papal fief.

Stephen died in 1038, by which time he had no surviving sons. He appointed one of his nephews, Peter Orseolo, as his heir. Civil wars, fights for the throne, and pagan revolts (1046, 1060–61) ensued, but finally Ladislas I (1077–95) reestablished a strong monarchy. It was Ladislas who, in 1083, organized the canonization of Stephen by a local Hungarian synod, together with Stephen's son Emeric (Henry), the martyred bishop Gerard (Gellért), and two hermits, Zoerard-Andrew and Benedict. He may have been inspired by the Bohemian (St. Wenceslas) or Kievan (Sts. Boris and Gleb) example to seek sacral legitimization through elevating the founder of the kingdom.

The alleged relic of Stephen's right hand and arm (later the arm was detached and taken to Poland) became important not only in the cult of the saint, but also, in modern times, as a symbol of the kingdom. It is on view in the basilica of Saint Stephen in Budapest.

Besides the *Lives*, important primary sources survive from the earliest period of Hungarian history, notably the laws of Stephen regulating lay and clerical behavior; the *Admonitions*, advice to Prince Emeric on how to rule, attributed to Stephen but written by a Bavarian or Venetian cleric; and the *Deliberatio* by Gerard (Gellért), missionary and bishop in Hungary under Stephen's reign, martyred in 1046.

SOURCES AND FURTHER READING

I have relied on the edition of Hartvic's work (*Bibliotheca hagiographica latina*, no. 7921) by Emma Bartoniek, found in *Scriptores rerum Hungaricarum*, ed. Imre Szentpétery, 2 vols. (Budapest, 1937–38), 2:401–40. The most important work on Stephen, on Hartvic, and on eleventh-century Hungarian history remains in Hungarian. I primarily drew from *Doctor et apostol: Szent István tanulmányok* [Essays concerning St. Stephen], ed. Péter Erdf (Budapest, 1994); József Gerics, "A Hartvic-legenda mintáiról és forrásairól," [The models and sources of the *Life* of St. Stephen by Hartvic] *Magyar Könyvszemle*, 97 (1981): 175–188 [with French summary]; and *Egyház, állam és gondolkodás Magyarországon a középkorban* [Church, state, and political thought in medieval Hungary] (Budapest, 1995); György Györffy, *István király és müve* [King Stephen and his achievement] (Budapest, 1983); Gábor Klaniczay, "Az 1083. évi magyarországi szentté avatások," [The canonizations of 1083 in Hungary] in *Müvelfdéstörténeti tanulmányok a magyar középkorból*, ed. Erik Függedi (Budapest, 1986), pp. 15–32; Zoltán Magyar, *Szent István a magyar kultúrtörténetben* [St. Stephen in Hungarian cultural history] (Budapest, 1996); Zoltán Tóth, *A Hartvic-legenda kritikájához* [Critical analysis of the *Life* of St. Stephen by Hartvic] (Budapest, 1942). A brief summary of the significance of—and unresolved questions about—the *Life* can be found in Gábor Klaniczay and Edit Madas, "La Hongrie," in *Hagiographies. Histoire internationale de la littérature hagiographique, latine et vernaculaire, en Occident, des origines à 1550*, ed. Guy Philippart, 4 vols. (Turnhout, 1994-present), 2:109–12. In English, one may consult György Györffy, *King Saint Stephen of Hungary*, Atlantic Studies on Society in Change 71; East European Monographs 403 (Highland Lakes, NJ, 1994). For an overview of medieval Hungarian history, see *A History of Hungary*, ed. Peter F. Sugar (London and New York, 1990).

Bishop Hartvic, Life of King St. Stephen [1]

Here begins the *Life of St. Stephen*, king of the Hungarians and their apostle.

(1.) For his lord, the most excellent King Coloman, Bishop Hartvic, who attained spiritual office by the grace of God, [wishes] a happy everlasting life after the end of this one. As I was about to begin this work about the life of the blessed King Stephen—which you, my lord, famous king, forcefully enjoined me [to do] by your royal command—I steadfastly bore for a long time the rebellious ignorance of my meager wits, especially because Priscian,[2] the master of grammatical art, whom once I knew in my very bones, fled long ago and now makes his face very obscure to me in my old age, as if engulfed by clouds. On the other hand, vexed though I was, considering through uncertain meditations the reverence due to your dignity, obedience, the light and gem of all virtue, finally defeated the doubt of an anxious mind. Under its strong protection, self-confidence, wanting to forsake me, regained strength to begin the work. But because something accomplished with confidence often generates tinder for envy, I beg the sublimity of your triumphal magnificence on bended knees, that you take this little work under the protection of your royal hands, lest the use of ill-sounding sentences or the irregularities of the confused arrangement offend your eyes when you read it. Because, if perchance any unworthy blunder occurred [in it], I would rather have the flame of fire destroy the codex, than that it should come before the envious eyes of a third person. Therefore, because all good that exists originates from the mercy of the creator, the discourse taken up here resounds from His gift.

Every good endowment and every perfect gift is from above, coming down from the Father of lights [Jas 1:17]. The good endowment and perfect gift of that Father flows abundantly to all, because it does not scorn anyone, but *desires all men to be saved and to come to the knowledge of the truth* [1 Tim 2:4]; it also poured forth to the Hungarians, who, it is well known, had once been the scourge of Christians. We thought it fitting that the office of this pen entrust to memory how and when this was done.

(2.) That is to say, at the time when the said people were destroying the Church of God, they had a certain ruler, fourth from the one who had been the first chief at the entry of the Hungarians to Pannonia,[3] by the name of Geysa,[4] who was strict and cruel, acting in a domineering way, as it were, with his own people, but compassionate and generous with strangers, especially with Christians, although [he was] still entangled in the rite of paganism. At the approach of the light of spiritual grace, he began to discuss peace attentively with all the neighboring provinces, so that it could already be seen from this whose son he wished to become, according to the word of our Savior speaking in the Gospel: *Blessed are the peacemakers, for they shall be called sons of God* [Mt 5:9]. Moreover, he laid down a rule that the favor of hospitality and security be shown to all Christians wishing to enter his domain. He gave clerics and monks leave to enter his presence; he offered them a willing hearing, and delighted in the germination of the seed of true faith sown in the garden of his heart.

What more is there to say? The divinely appointed time arrived, Geysa along with his household believed, and he was baptized, promising that he would deliver all those subject to his rule into the service of the Christian name. And, since he was greatly concerned about the subjugation of rebels and destruction of sacrilegious rites and the establishment of bishoprics, according to his judgment, for the success of the holy Church, the Lord consoled him through a miraculous vision at night. He made a youth of delightful appearance stand before Geysa, who told him: "Peace to you, chosen by Christ. I order you to be free from your cares. What you have in mind has not been granted to you, because your hands are polluted by human blood. A son will be born of you who will go forth, to whom the Lord will entrust all these things to settle, according to the purpose of divine providence. He will be one of the kings chosen by the Lord to exchange the *crown of* secular *life* [James 1:12] for an everlasting one. So, you should receive the man sent to you on special legation with respect, and once having received him, keep him with reverence, listen to his exhortations with a faithful heart, and not with feigned assent."

(3.) On waking, the dazed ruler contemplating the vision, first by himself, then with those faithful to Christ and his family, humbly gave thanks to God, prostrating himself on the pavement, stretching out his hands, and shedding tears. He commended himself, his domain, and his son who was to be born to the protection of Him who neither sleeps nor slumbers. While he thus wondered about the man divinely prophesied, it was announced to him that the blessed Adalbert, prelate of the Bohemian Church,[5] was coming to him for his conversion, and for his profession of an *unfeigned faith* [2 Tim 1:5, Vulgate], in order to *offer up a sacrifice of praise* [Heb 13:15] to the Lord God. Unspeakable joy arose in Christ's new soldiers; the leader, with all the faithful, went to meet the champion of Christ, received him honorably, and, as he was bidden by the vision, demonstrated in every way that he would be an obedient son to him. Therefore, at the order of the ruler, the unruly people came together everywhere, the holy bishop and his companions made exhortations continuously, the people of the land were converted and baptized, churches were established in many places. For the *light that enlightens every man* [Jn 1:9], chasing away darkness, began to shine in Hungary, and in this the words of the prophecy were fulfilled, which say *the people who walked in darkness have seen a great light* [Is 9:2]. The light of the invisible light is Christ, whom the pagans deserved to see when, recalled from darkness, they truly and wholly believed him to be true God and man.

Nor should it be passed over in silence that, to dispel all doubt, lest perchance the above-mentioned vision, having appeared only to the husband, should seem to lack credibility, divine grace wished also to console his wife, who was near giving birth, by a similar vision. For there appeared to her the blessed Stephen, Levite and protomartyr,[6] adorned in the distinctive Levitical habit, who began to talk to her thus: "Woman, trust in the Lord, and be assured, for you will give birth to a son, to whom first from this people a crown and kingdom is due; and give him my name." To whom the astonished woman responded: "Who are you, my lord, and furthermore by what name are you called?" "I am," he said, "Stephen protomartyr, who was the first to suffer martyrdom for the name of Christ." And, having said that, he disappeared.

(4.) In the meantime, as foretold by the Lord, the son of the ruler was born, whom, according to the prophet, the Lord had known before he was conceived in the womb, and to whom, before he was born, He had given the name of His protomartyr. Bishop Adalbert, beloved by God, anointed him with the baptismal chrism according to the truth of his belief. The name Stephen was given him, which we do not believe to have been contrary to the purpose of God. Indeed "Stephanus" in Greek means "crown" in Latin.[7] For God wanted to crown him in this world to royal power, and determined to redeem him in the future one by the crown of everlasting beatitude, that he might receive unfailing glory after the yoke of this life.

He was born in the city of Esztergom, and, still a boy, he was fully instructed in knowledge of the grammatical art. The child grew, nourished by diligent education, and with the passage of childhood, as he ascended to the first stage of adolescence, his father convoked the chief lords of Hungary, together with the next order,[8] and through the counsel of common deliberation, placed his son Stephen at the head of the people to rule after him; and to confirm this, he exacted an oath from everyone. And reaching the end of his days after this, in the year 997 of the Incarnation of the Lord, he exchanged the worthless afflictions of the world for heavenly joy. In the same year the blessed bishop Adalbert entered Prussia in order to preach the word of God, and there he was crowned with the martyr's palm.

(5.) After the death of his father, Stephen, still an adolescent, by the favor of the princes and common people was laudably raised to the seat of his father and began with an ardent spirit to be the defender of truth, because, although he was in the bloom of his adolescence, he did not *have his* heart *in his mouth, but his mouth in his* heart [Sir 21:26]. Not forgetting the Holy Scriptures, for which he was zealous above all, he kept judgment and justice before his eyes, according to the words of Solomon: *The wise man also may hear* discipline *and increase in learning, and the man of understanding acquire government* [Prov 1:5]. Thus showing himself to be God's *faithful steward* [Lk 12:42] in all his mandates, he began to consider in his own mind how he could deliver the people subject to him to the worship of the one God. But because he considered that without the alliance of neighboring peoples he could not do this, he faithfully strengthened the peace established with the people of surrounding provinces, so that whatever he pondered in his mind, he would be able to complete more securely in the young implantation of Christianity.

(6.) But the enemy of all good things, the devil, full of envy and malice, stirred up an internal war against him, in order to disturb the holy plan of Christ's champion, for at his instigation the pagan commoners, refusing to submit their necks to the yoke of the Christian faith, tried with their leaders to withdraw themselves from his rule.[9] They began to destroy his cities, lay waste his estates, plunder his lands, chase away the servants of the Church, and taunt—I should be silent about the rest—even [the king] himself. And when they did not want to shun their perverse way, and their fury was not satiated, the leader[10] himself, trusting in eternal virtue, advanced with a multitude of his army under the banner of the prelate Martin,[11] beloved by God, and of the holy martyr George,[12] in order to overcome the madness of the enemy. By chance in those days they besieged the city called Veszprém in the vernacular, turning this into his shame, that is, they established themselves in the place where there used to be access to communication with the leader's court, so that entering the other fortifications they were to occupy would be found easier. But he rose up against them, led by divine mercy, and they fought, he trusting in faith, they only in arms. Finally, defeating the enemy, some of them having been killed and others captured, the victorious leader took home the gifts of victory with his troops. And so he disposed wisely of their possessions, both the fields and the villages, not as Saul had done when, having defeated Amalech, he chose the best of the spoils despite the Lord's prohibition [see 1 Sam 15:1–9].

But because Pannonia gloried in the birth of the blessed prelate Martin, and it was under the protection of his merits that the man faithful to Christ, as I already said, wrought a victory over the enemy, reserving nothing of their things for his own needs, and keeping counsel with those beloved by God, he began to build a monastery dedicated to him [Martin], next to the patrimony of the holy prelate, in the place called the Holy Mountain,[13] which St. Martin, when he still lived in Pannonia, assigned to himself as a place of prayer; he enriched it by lands and revenues and all the necessary things, and made it similar to bishoprics by his own judgment with a tithe from the victors, ordering that tithes be given from all their means in such a strict way that if someone should have happened to have ten children, he was to give the tenth offspring to the monastery of Saint Martin.

(7.) Thus the soldier of Christ, having defeated the enemy, filled with spiritual joy, decided by the counsel of his inmost being to be the receptacle of the evangelical seed; occupying himself by almsgiving and prayers, frequently prostrating himself on the pavement of the holy house, shedding tears, he entrusted the completion of his plan to the will of God, so that, unable to do anything without Him, with the help of His dispensation he could with satisfaction bring to its end with virtuous undertakings the good that he had planned. But it was necessary to consult the faithful of Christ in order to begin and consummate this, so he made known his wish by letters and messengers in all parts. Thereupon many priests and clerics, urged by the visitation of the Holy Spirit, the Comforter, leaving their own sees, chose to become pilgrims for the Lord's sake. Abbots and monks, not desiring to have anything of their own, decided to live according to their rules under the government of such a religious ruler.

Among them came Father Asericus, who was a monk,[14] with his disciples, one of whom, by the name of Boniface, was afterward made abbot in the place of the father; when he was sent to lower Hungary by the blessed king to preach, he was struck by a sword on the top of his head, and although he survived, he was not deprived of martyrdom.

Two others came as well, from the land of Poland, choosing the eremitical life for the sake of contemplation, one of whom, by the name of Andrew, was taken up into the choir of angels because of the merit of his confession, which is attested by the signs of miracles made by the Lord through him. The other, Benedict, having shed his blood for Christ, was mercifully crowned [as a martyr].

Abbot Asericus, having been respectfully received with his [people], built a monastery dedicated to the holy father Benedict at the bottom of the Iron Mountain,[15] where to this day a community blooms under monastic discipline, abounding in temporal riches [necessary] for its sustenance from the donations of the holy leader, not needing anything, except daily to wash the feet of their [people] and of others, amidst prayers and tears according to the Gospel.

(8.) The servant of God, the most Christian ruler, taking counsel with them, sometimes together with all, sometimes alone with one of them, made himself so praiseworthy in the eyes of God that he could convert all the leaders of his army to the worship of the true God. Those whom he noticed to be following another path, he subjugated by threats and terror. Teaching them according to ecclesiastical doctrine, he put the yoke and law of discipline onto their bent necks, and he utterly destroyed all the impurity of evil.

After this, having divided his territories into ten bishoprics, he made the church of Esztergom the metropolitan and master of the others. The prudent leader, recognizing the piety of the said Asericus, elevated him, decorated by the miter of pontifical dignity through canonical election, and bestowed on him the dignity of the bishop of Kalocsa.

(9.) In the fourth year after his father's death, prompted by divine mercy, he sent the same prelate Asericus who by another name is also called Anastasius, to the threshold of the holy apostles,[16] in order to ask from the successor of St. Peter, the prince of the apostles,[17] that he extend his abundant blessing to the young Christianity, rising in the parts of Pannonia, that he confirm the church of Esztergom as head by the authority of his signature, and that he fortify the rest of the bishoprics by his blessing. Also that he would deign to strengthen him [Stephen] by a royal diadem, so that, supported by that office, what he had begun by the grace of God he could stabilize more solidly.

As it happened, at this time, Mischa, leader of the Poles,[18] having embraced the Christian faith with his [people], sent envoys to the pontiff of the Roman See, and asked to be strengthened by apostolic benediction and to be crowned with a royal diadem. The pope, assenting to his petition, already had had a crown made, decorated with extraordinary craftsmanship, which he decided to send to him with a blessing and the glory of sovereignty. But because the Lord knows those who are His, who preferred Matthew out of the two chosen by the apostles to share the apostolic order and complete the apostolic number [see Acts 1:23–26], determined instead to distinguish favorably his chosen, Stephen, by this temporal crown, who afterward was also to be adorned more favorably by the eternal one. Thus during the night preceding the appointed day on which the completed crown would be sent to the above-mentioned leader of the Poles, the emissary of the Lord approached the pope through a vision and said to him: "You should know that tomorrow, in the first hour of the day the envoys of an unknown people will come to you, who will urge you to bestow on their leader a royal crown together with apostolic benediction. Therefore make sure to give the crown that you have had prepared to their leader without hesitation just as they ask. For know that this is due to him together with the glory of sovereignty for the merits of his life."

And in accordance with that vision, at the prescribed hour of the following day, the prelate Asericus reached the pope, prudently executing the office enjoined on him, and expounding the deeds of the holy leader in order, he requested the token that we mentioned from the apostolic see, showing him [Stephen] to be worthy of such honor and dignity, he who had subjugated several peoples with the help of God and by His power had converted many infidels to the Lord. Upon hearing this, the Roman pontiff, rejoicing, kindly granted all, just as they had been requested. Moreover, he sent the king a cross to be worn as a sign of apostleship, saying "I am apostolic, but he is truly by his own merit Christ's apostle, through whom Christ converted so many people. Therefore we relinquish to his disposition as the divine grace instructs him the churches together with the people, to be governed according to both laws [*utroque iure*]."[19] Having obtained everything just as he had requested, the happy prelate Asericus returned to his people, taking with him that for which he had completed the journey he had undertaken.

(10.) Thus having acquired the letters of apostolic benediction together with the crown and the cross, the beloved of God, King Stephen, anointed by unction with chrism, was propitiously crowned with the diadem of royal dignity while the prelates and the clergy, the counts and the commoners acclaimed unanimous praise.[19]

After the symbol of royal excellence had been accepted, it was made manifest what manner of man he was in conduct of life and judgment in the statutes which he decreed with the bishops and chief lords of Hungary; in which, namely, he formulated the antidote of each sin. And so that he would show himself to be the son of peace by which Christ bound the world together, he left an edict to his successors, by approving an enduring pact, that no one should invade another in a hostile way, nobody should harm a neighbor without the benefit of a trial, no one should oppress widows and orphans.

He joined himself in matrimony to the sister of Henry of Roman imperial dignity—who was called Pious because of the gentleness of his character—named Gisela, to be his consort in the kingdom, but above all to bear his offspring.[21] He made her, anointed by unction with chrism, his companion in wearing the crown of the kingdom. How she stood out in adorning the worship of God, and how fervent and beneficent she showed herself [to be] to the congregations serving God is proved to this day by many churches' crosses, vessels, and ornaments made or woven by marvelous work. And above all the building of the bishopric of Veszprém [proves this] which she adorned nobly, beginning from the foundations, with every necessary thing for the service of God in gold and silver, and a multiplicity of vestments.

And the king himself, having assigned ample dioceses to each of the recently founded bishoprics, that is, as much to the archiepiscopal as all the episcopal churches, and always appointing as head a suitable prelate for each one, royally endowed them, as well as the abbeys, with estates and manor houses, households and revenues. He sufficiently provided them with crosses and vessels and other furnishings pertaining to the service of God, according to their needs. And every year, while he was alive, he added gifts and offerings, so that those filling the office of sacristan would not ask for anything from outside. Investigating, he diligently examined, sometimes through others, sometimes by himself, the life and conduct of monks, rebuking the lazy ones and taking the vigilant ones into his love. He commended the service of canons to the care of bishops, because of the testimony of Christ and the Church, according to the apostle: *I have become all things to all men, that I might save* [1 Cor 9:22] all.

(11.) There was a certain monk, by the name of Sebastian, whose life was held to be commendable, and whose piety [was held to be] devoted to the service of God. The venerable king began to esteem him wonderfully with love, because the more pious someone was, the more welcome that person was to him. Judging him to be worthy of episcopal office because of his meritorious life, he appointed him to govern the archbishopric of Esztergom. But, because God *scourges every son whom he receives* [Heb 12:6, Vulgate], He deprived the said Sebastian of the light of his corporal eyes for a while to test his patience. But, so that the flock, new in the faith, would not deviate from the intended right path without the guidance of the shepherd, through the consent of the Roman pontiff he substituted in his place the above-mentioned Asericus, bishop of Kalocsa. After the passing of three years, Sebastian recovered his sight through the mercy of God, and through apostolic counsel his see was restored to him, and Asericus returned with the pallium to his own church, namely that of Kalocsa.[22]

(12.) In the meantime the king was faithful and completely devoted to God in all his acts. He transferred himself together with his kingdom by an oath and offering, with assiduous prayers, to the guardianship of the Mother of God, the ever Virgin Mary. Her glory and honor are so famous among Hungarians, that even the feast of the Assumption of this Virgin is called the Day of the Lady in their language, without the addition of her proper name.

And, in order to be able to win the greater mercy of her protection, he began to build a famous and large basilica by wonderful craftsmanship, dedicated to and in praise of that perpetual Virgin, in the city of the royal see itself, which is called Alba,[23] with carvings adorning the walls of the choir, and the floor paved with marble tiles. Whoever saw this can offer a testimony to the truth of our words, that there are innumerable types of palls and vestments and other ornaments; several panels made of the purest gold around the altars, containing rows of the most precious stones, and above Christ's table a canopy of marvelous craftsmanship was erected, and the treasury was crammed full with all sorts of vessels made of crystal, onyx, gold, and silver.

Keeping the above-mentioned church of such beauty as his own chapel, the king endowed it with such independence that none of the bishops could have any rights whatever over it. Nonetheless, so that the brothers of that place be no strangers to monastic discipline, they had to gather at the communal synod of the archbishop, in order to be trained by the education of ecclesiastical teachings. And, on the day of absolution and the consecration of chrism, the king, if present, would enjoin any bishop, or, if absent, would send him, and he would absolve the penitents there and consecrate the chrism. And that bishop would celebrate the divine solemn Mass if the king happened to be present there, whom the king—with the consent of the brothers and provost—would order to celebrate it. And in the absence of the king no bishop would usurp the license to celebrate Mass or exercise any episcopal office without the consent of the provost and the brothers. Moreover he ordered the people of that church to be so free that they would not have to give any tithe to any bishop, but only to serve the provost and the brothers in the way he had ordered.

Afterward the servant of God strove to confer all that he already had and what he could acquire to Christ, from whose gift those things had flowed, so that He who made him worthy of the glory and honor of this world, would mercifully consider him deserving of association among the inhabitants of the celestial city.

(13.) We read in the prophecy, written about the apostles that *their voice has gone out to all the earth and their words to the ends of the world* [Rom 10:5]. This was proved to be said not only about the twelve, but also about all those sent by God to evangelize, by whose faith, words, and conduct the Church grows. Among those, that most Christian king [Stephen] is acknowledged as not the most insignificant, he who spread the fame of his good will and works—that he exercised in building churches to the extent of his own authority—to far distant lands and very famous cities.

For he constructed a monastery of monks in that city of Jerusalem where Christ lived according to His humanity, and he enriched it with estates and vineyards, to provide abundant daily food. And he founded a congregation of twelve canons in Rome, the head of the world, dedicated in honor of the protomartyr Stephen, abounding in all belongings, and he erected a wall all around it, made of stone, with houses and hospices for the Hungarians seeking the threshold of the blessed Peter, prince of the apostles, in order to pray. He did not deprive even the royal city, Constantinople, of endowing it with benefactions; he donated a church of wonderful craftsmanship with everything that was necessary.

Therefore he deservedly gained the name of apostle within the boundaries of his dominion, because although he himself did not assume the office of evangelization, nonetheless, leader and master of preachers, he established the comfort of protection and support for them.

(14.) Among all the favors of heavenly compassion divinely granted to the blessed king, those that obtain the first place in earning the joy of eternal life, that is, mercy and truth are above all to be listed and committed to writing. For in all his auspicious deeds he strove particularly to be what was understood by the true insight of his heart in the Gospel, through the testimony of Truth [Christ] Himself, saying: *blessed are the merciful, for they shall obtain mercy* [Mt 5:7], and in another place *give and it will be given to you* [Lk 6:38]. Therefore he embraced the poor of Christ, or rather Christ in them [the poor], with such merciful and pious arms, that no guest or pilgrim left him sadly without some kindness or solace. He arranged for daily payments to be made without fail for the refreshment of the needy; he used to spend the nocturnal Vigils busily and joyously washing the feet of Christ's faithful and in concealing alms in the bosom of the poor, deciding to console the needy Christ through his members in the world, so that he would deserve to rejoice eternally, finding the treasury of celestial life filled with all delights.

And indeed one night, touched by spiritual admonition, he proceeded to visit Christ's little flock alone, without anyone's knowledge, as was his habit, carrying a purse filled with the gift of God; and immediately the poor disrupting the distribution of the money of the celestial storehouse, offered testimony to the merits of the man of God by pulling out his beard. Upon which, the soldier of Christ, infused with great joy, turned to the most blessed Mother of everyone's Creator, and prostrate on the ground, giving thanks, exclaimed: "Celestial queen, my queen, your soldiers thus honor him whom you made king. If this had been done by an enemy of mine, I would avenge the wrong [done to me] through your support. But knowing, my Lady, that I am repaid by eternal joy for this, I rejoice exceedingly, giving thanks for the consoling words of our Savior, by which he consoled his disciples, saying: *not a hair of your head will perish*" [Lk 21:18]. Having said these things, the man of God, understanding that he was visited by celestial grace and imbued with spiritual chrism, decided never to close the doors of his heart to those seeking help. Instead, in turn by himself and others, but especially by the servants and serving-people of Christ (that is, clerics and monks), he had the resources given to him by heaven laid into the eternal treasury through the hands of the poor.

Many offer testimony to this, but one of these, participating with him eternally in celestial life, [is] a monk and hermit, converted from the secular nobility, the blessed Gunter, who, drawn by the generosity of the charitable prince, used to visit him often from the land of the Czechs. For whenever he illuminated Stephen's court by the brightness of his arrival, the treasury of the king, placed at his disposal, was emptied in a short time of the things that it contained through their distribution to pilgrims, the poor, the needy, widows and orphans, monasteries and churches.

And at the command of the same servant of God, the king, devoted to God, founded a monastery that is called Bel, endowed it with all goods, where the monk Gerard, coming from Venice, began to lead a contemplative life. Elected as bishop by celestial order, he was stoned in the turmoil threatening Christianity after the death of the holy king. He was made worthy of the community of martyrs through the gift of spiritual grace.

(15.) Nor do I intend to omit that divine power wished to show in his life how many merits the man of God would have after death; indeed whenever the infirmity of some man was made known to his ears, he sent him as medicine that which he had at hand then, a piece of bread or fruit, or fragrant herbs, and sent over his command that he rise healthy. The reconciliation of God having accompanied his words [the sick] immediately recovered. Our Savior, after gloriously ascending to Heaven and sitting marvelously with the Father is held to have appeared to few people physically, but many were consoled by a vision, and he taught them to have foreknowledge of the future, as it also happened to this blessed king.

For one night suddenly awakened by some revelation, he ordered a courier to hasten in one day and night to Alba in Transylvania,[24] and gather all those living in the country within the fortifications of the city as fast as he could. For he foretold that the enemies of Christians would come upon them, that is, the Pechenegs, who then threatened the Hungarians, in order to plunder their estate.[25] Scarcely had the messenger completed the orders of the king, when behold the unexpected onslaught of the Pechenegs devastated everything by burning and plundering. Through the revelation of God, which was granted because of the merits of the blessed man, the souls of everyone were saved by the shelter of the fortifications.

(16.) After this, it happened that the pious Henry, of Roman imperial dignity, friend of the blessed king, died, and Conrad assumed the crown of imperial power through the election of the Germans. After he destroyed the tranquillity of peace, Conrad joined hands with all Teutonia,[26] and tried to invade the borders of Pannonia like an enemy.[27] Against him Stephen consulted bishops and chief lords, and drew together the armed men of the whole of Hungary for the protection of the country. First, however, recalling that he could do nothing without Christ's assent, lifting his hand and heart to heaven and commending his wrongs to his Lady, Mary the ever Virgin Mother of God, he burst out in such a cry: "If it pleases you, Lady of the world, to have a part of your inheritance devastated by enemies, and to have the young implantation of Christianity destroyed, I beseech you, let it not be ascribed to my idleness, but rather to the purpose of your will. If the sin of the shepherd would merit anything, let him atone for it. I beg you, spare the innocent sheep" [see 2 Sam 24:17]. Having said these things, as if consoled by her, he set out trustingly on the road against the enemy. Immediately the next day, a messenger came to each one of the German leaders in the camp, as if sent by the emperor, who gave them the order to go back. With the withdrawal of the enemy, the holy man, knowing himself to be visited by God's mercy, [lay] prostrate on the ground and gave thanks to Christ and His mother, to whose protection he entrusted himself and the rule of the kingdom through persistent prayers. Indeed, terrified by the sudden desertion of his soldiers, and inquiring how this had happened, the emperor, when he understood that the messenger of their return was indeed not his [follower], did not doubt that it was done through divine mandate, in order to strengthen the hope of the most faithful king; and from then on, Conrad abstained from attacking the kingdom [of Hungary], kept back by his fear of the eternal judge.

(17.) And that blessed king occupied by the cares of royal administration, passing the time by day with discussions and counsels, exerted himself in the silence of the night to be zealous in vigils and prayers, to have time for contemplation, to pour out tears, to address God by supplications, asking that the restraint of the just judge mercifully descend upon the daily scrutiny of his judgments. He frequently did this duty with diligent spiritual longing; a certain night, being very far away from a church of God, he in fact stayed with his great and noble retinue, setting up tents in large fields. The others having been weighed down by deep sleep, Stephen, getting up from his bed and entering the bedchamber of his heart, genuflecting, battered the door of eternal mercy amidst sighs and tears, with only the movement of his lips. And after his long persisting in supplications, when the servants of his Lord, the eternal king, had assembled to take up his prayers, the tent spread out over him was lifted up from the earth and was suspended in the air until the man of God, coming back to himself from contemplation, released his soul from prayer. This, although invisibly, was known only to those who know about things before they occur, and to the angels privy to His secrets. It was, however, visibly manifested to a certain man of great simplicity and innocence, who was perhaps zealous in similar duty at the same time. The holy king, informed by the Holy Spirit that he was privy to his secret, called the man to himself and first inquired by coaxing speech about what he had seen, then enriching him by royal gifts, forbade him to disclose it to anyone while he was alive.

(18.) The fame of his name reached the ears of many secular people, and the judgments from his mouth having become known everywhere by famous praise, sixty men from the Pechenegs, whom I mentioned above, with all their pomp, that is with chariots loaded with an abundance of silver and gold, and many types of ornaments, went out from the territories of the Bulgars, wanting to come to the king, and approached the boundaries of the Pannons.[28] But many of the servants whose mind is wax, bending to sin, kindled by the torch of malice, went out to meet them, killed some of them by sword, carried off everything they had, and left them half-dead and possessionless. They, keeping back for the judgment of the king what happened and what they endured, completed the journey they had started, and hastening to him, threw themselves at his feet. Upon seeing them, he said: "what is the cause of your adversity?" They replied: "My lord, we, your servants, with no evil intent, came to hear the teaching of your judgments, and by the hands of certain people the property that we brought with us was carried off, without any offense on our part. Moreover, they killed those they took hold of, and scarcely alive we come to report this to you." The king, because he was of a very prudent spirit, threatened them neither by expression, nor by words, but holding back—as it is written, *a wise man holds it back* [Prov 29:11]—very swiftly sent to that commander under whom they served as soldiers, and establishing the day, he ordered all the men [responsible for] their ruin to be brought before him. It was done as he had commanded, and they were brought into his presence, in order to be examined. Addressing them, he said: "Why, transgressing the law of the precepts of God, did you not choose mercy, and condemn innocent men? Just as you had done, let the lord so do to you today in front of me. For the transgressors of the law must be killed." Having received their sentence, they were led away, and throughout every region, at the beginning of roads, hanged two by two, they perished. It is to be believed that Stephen did this from the zeal of justice to inspire fear in the others, because he wanted his kingdom to be a refuge open to all foreigners, entry unrestricted for all, so that no one would dare harm or trouble in anything anyone who entered. And this was done. For as long as he lived, nobody dared cause any foreigner any harm.

(19.) And that apostolic prediction befitted the blessed king, that is *through many tribulations we must enter the kingdom of God* [Acts 14:22], and in the book of Wisdom: God chastises whom he loves [see Prov 3:12], and the father *scourges every son whom he receives* [Heb 12:6, Vulgate]. For he fell under many kinds of divine correction, being afflicted by continuous infirmity for three years. After he had recovered from that by the medicine of God's grace, again he felt the scourge to be near him through some test of the eternal judge's secret deliberation, in the death of his sons, whom He who gave them, took away innocent in their infancy. The father restrained the grief arising over their death by the solace on account of the love of his surviving son, the child Henry of good natural disposition. As already the only one, loving him dearly, he commended him daily in his prayers to Christ and his ever Virgin Mother. He desired with all his wishes that the child outlive him and be the heir to the kingdom. And, so that he would be more capable of holding the helm of such government, he made him listen with both [corporal and spiritual] ears to the daily exercise of reading about the examples of faithful men. And Stephen himself, prompted by the flame of paternal love, composed for him a little book on the principles of conduct, in which he faithfully and conscientiously addressed him in words of spiritual admonition. He instructed [him] how above all he should observe the Catholic faith, strengthen the condition of the Church, show honor to the dignity of bishops, love the chief lords and soldiers, respect judgment, have patience in all his acts, receive guests liberally, and nourish them even more liberally, do nothing without counsel, always keep his ancestors before his eyes as an example, resort to the office of prayer often, possess piety and mercy together with the other virtues. The noble young man, instructed with this and similar learning, obeying the command of eternal providence, to whom all are subordinate, exchanged this mortal life for an everlasting one, in the year 1031 of the

Incarnation of the Lord, and joined the communion of heavenly citizens. His soul was shown being carried by angels to the palace of heaven in the very hour of his passing to a certain bishop of the Greeks, a man of holy conduct. And truly, because he was loved with the greatest feeling by everyone for the merits of his holiness, all began to mourn greatly, but especially the chief lords, among whom the desolate father heaved deep sighs. For seeing himself alone, left without hope of offspring, he grieved with pious feeling, indeed knowing the Scripture, *There is no wisdom, there is no understanding, there is no counsel against the Lord* [Prov 21:30, Vulgate], and that in the canons: nobody should be exceedingly saddened by the death of their loved ones;[29] casting off his grief, he gave himself wholly to seeking the abundance of divine mercy. Consoling the servants of monasteries and churches, that is, monks and clerics, by various gifts of alms, he distributed all the already collected revenues which he had at hand at the moment to pilgrims, widows and orphans. And through his messengers he often visited the monasteries of foreign provinces with innumerable gifts of royal generosity.

(20.) He retained to the end of his life the gravity of manner that he adopted in his youth. His lips hardly ever moved to laughter, recalling Scripture: *laughter shall be mingled with sorrow, and mourning takes hold of the end of joy* [Prov 14:13, Vulgate]; always appearing thus as if he stood before the tribunal of Christ, in his mind's eye keeping His visage before him, he showed that he carried Christ in his mouth, Christ in his heart, Christ in all of his acts. Always keeping the last day before the eyes of his heart, with all the desire of his mind he wished to live among the inhabitants of the celestial city, as if in the garb of angelic conversation. Adorned with every type of virtue pleasing to God, he decided to live *in holiness and justice before him in all the days* [Lk 1:75] of his life, so that the splendor—as though of some future glory—would already appear to shine in him.

(21.) Not long afterward a disease set in, which later consumed his body, and growing worse by the long affliction of weakness, he was unable to stand on his feet. Four of the very noble palace officials, seeing him suffering severely for a long time, held iniquitous council, and tried to plot his downfall and his death, for they still strayed in the faithlessness of their heart. When the day was already fading, before the lamp would be lit in the house, one of them entered audaciously under cover of darkness, hiding a naked sword under his cloak in order to cut the king's throat. When he set foot where the king was resting, the sword fell, undoubtedly on an impulse from heaven, and made a clattering sound as it hit the ground. The king, hearing it at once, asked about its cause, although he already knew what had happened. That troubled man fell down, reconsidered the decision of his madness, was sorry, approached, lay down, embraced the feet of the king, confessed that he had committed a sin, and begged to be forgiven. The king did not spurn the requested pardon, and readily dismissed the villainy; at the same time by the order of the king those murderers were found and brought forth, and he pronounced judgment on them and punished them by a worthy sentence.

(22.) Finally by the mercy of God, the one worthy of the prize of a hundredfold reward, struck by fever, not doubting that the day of his death was approaching, summoned the bishops and the chief lords of his palace who gloried in the name of Christ, and discussed first with them who was to succeed him as king. Afterward in a fatherly way he admonished them to keep the orthodox faith which they had accepted, to love justice, to cherish the chains of heavenly affection and render what was done for that affection, to be vigilant and zealous in humility, and indeed above all to guard the young implantation of Christianity. After having said this, lifting his hands and eyes to the stars, he exclaimed thus: "Queen of heaven, renowned restorer of the world, I commit the holy Church with its bishops and clergy, the kingdom with its chief lords and people to your protection in my last prayers, and saying my final farewell to them, into your hands I commend my spirit."[30]

(23.) The solemn feast was then approaching, famous to angels and men, the day of the Assumption of the same perpetually Virgin Mary, and, hoping to have a hope of greater mercy were the dissolution of his body to take place during that rejoicing, he asked this by special prayers and by sighs and tears obtained it. Thus that auspicious day arrived, very soon made more auspicious through his death, and the congregation of bishops and clergy, the foremost troop of stewards and important attendants stood encircling the place where the king, beloved by God, lying in their midst, having accepted the sacrament of spiritual unction, restored his holy soul by the viaticum of the body and blood of our Lord Jesus Christ, in the year 1033 of the Incarnation of the Lord, and gave it into the hand of the perpetual Virgin and holy angels, to be brought to the peace of eternal celestial beatitude. There was great lamentation among his people, and joy among the angels, but this lamentation later turned into everlasting gladness both for those to be born, and those already alive. People assembled for his funeral procession from every region of Pannonia, the body was taken to the royal seat, that is Alba,[31] and because the church, built by him to the honor of the blessed Virgin was not yet consecrated, the prelates, having deliberated, decided first to consecrate the basilica, and then to commit the body [of Stephen] to the earth. Having accomplished the ceremony of consecration, the holy body was placed in a sarcophagus of white marble in the middle of the building, where for several years the Lord exhibited countless favors for his merits to many who suffered troubles, had fever, proclaimed their affliction and misery, and endured judgment. Often at night the melody of the song of angels was heard by many, and even more often the sweetness of the most pleasant scent spread to all corners of the church.

(24.) And thus the blessed body rested in the same place for forty-five years, by the wondrous secret of His will, who is praised in *His saints* and is *wonderful* [Ps 67:36, Vulgate], so that, pressed by the weight of the ground and reduced to dust, he would both be more worthy to be revealed here in the preordained time, and would merit to be recalled more gloriously on the day of resurrection. It is pleasing to spiritual eyes to seek out what the purpose of this might be, and what it might mean, since we do not think that it could have happened without the workings of divine preordination. Perhaps a sprinkling of earthly dust had remained in him, without which rulers, as if by some powerful law, are hardly or not at all able to lead this present life, [that had] to be purified by the fire of divine testing. And thus forty-five years having passed, when God already wished to reveal the merits of his saint in order to show the mortals the favors of his mercy through him, it was decreed by apostolic letter, by order of the Roman see, that they should have elevated the bodies of those who sowed the seeds of the Christian faith in Pannonia and had been converting to God by preaching or education. When the time came for his revelation and for the spreading of the praiseworthy grace, which the Hungarian people had earned in the world through Stephen, King Ladislas, who then governed the realm—[a man] whose character was distinguished by the complete respectability of morals and remarkable for the splendor of his virtues, and who was completely dedicated to the praise and service of God—was imbued with the Holy Spirit, the Comforter, and, after having consulted with the bishops, chief lords and wise men of all Pannonia, declared for all a fast of three days, for the benefit of the community of Catholics through the gifts of the Holy Spirit working for the salvation of souls and bodies; for it seemed to be beneficial that [Stephen's revelation as a saint] be sought from Christ through a manifestation of signs by common prayer, secured by the alms and fasting of all. But the Lord, in order to show how merciful the holy king had been while living in a mortal body, demonstrated his approval of it before all other works when [the king] was already reigning with Christ to the point that though for three days they struggled with all their might to raise his holy body, it was not by any means to be moved from its place. For in that time, because of the sins, a grave discord arose between the said king Ladislas and his cousin[32] Solomon, because of which Solomon, captured, was held in prison.[33] Therefore when they tried in vain to raise the body, a certain recluse at the church of the Holy Savior in Bökénysomlyó, by the name of Karitas, whose famous life at the time was held in esteem, confided to the king by a revelation made to her from heaven that they exerted themselves in vain; it would be impossible to transfer the relics of the holy king until unconditional pardon was offered to Solomon, setting him free from the confinement of prison. And thus, bringing him forth from the prison, and repeating the three-day fast, when the third day arrived for the transferal of the holy remains, the stone lying over the grave was lifted up with such ease as if it had been of no weight before. Thus having completed the office of Vespers the third day, everyone expected the favors of divine mercy through the merit of the blessed man; suddenly with Christ visiting his masses, the signs of miracles poured forth from heaven throughout the whole of the holy house. Their multitude, which that night were too many to count, brings to mind the answer from the Gospel which the Savior of the world confided to John, who asked through messengers whether he was the one who was to come: *the blind see, the lame walk, the deaf hear, the lepers are cleansed* [Mt 11:5, Vulgate], the crippled are set straight, the paralyzed are cured; of which however we endeavor to make known some, because we cannot [make] all [known].

(25.) A certain youth, all his limbs weakened, suffering paralysis for twelve years who was without the use of his hands and feet, who was carried there with the aid of his parents, having received the cure of all his body, was the first of the signs.[34] Running to the altar far from sluggishly, he increased the joy of all those shouting praises to Christ. And another seven-year-old boy, who had crawled on his hands and knees from birth, because of contracted sinews, was brought by his parents, full of faith, to be helped by the blessed man; they prostrated themselves next to the tomb and laid him down with them, to ask for grace. They immediately obtained it; they marveled that the contraction of the sinews stretched in their son, and everyone seeing him walking with his knees and soles having become firm, glorified the name of Christ in the merits of the blessed man by praiseworthy acclamation. The king, devoted to God, crying in his great joy, lifted him with his [own] hands from the ground and carried him to the altar, where, uttering hymns of praise, he gave thanks with applause, together with everyone present for the favors shown in the curing of the boy. Thus God wondrously illuminated the whole night through the veneration of his servant by the splendor of many signs, and indeed the people, earnest in vigils and prayers, did not cease to make each miracle clear by shouts of praise. It should be added that not only those present, but even those situated far away were affected by the well-known consequences of a cure through the intercession of his merits. For when the report of his elevation began to spread everywhere, those afflicted by various illnesses immediately began to hasten to his holy tomb from the very borders of Hungary, each as best he could. But while some preceded and others, handicapped by more serious disease were unable to arrive at the same time, through the same mercy many were nevertheless cured on the way. Hence, in order to preserve the memory of the favors given by the holy king, very many whose health was restored by him gathered large mounds of stones in the same place on the road where they were cured, which were there for a long time afterward. And even a certain woman at this time, when her son, her only one, gave up the ghost, placed the lifeless body of her offspring on the holy king's tomb, in order to implore the solace of God and His saint for him. A wonderful and in our times astounding thing occurred, the woman had not even stopped praying when she received back alive her son whom she had laid out dead.

(26.) The morning of the fifth day after the Assumption of the most holy Mother of God, Mary, having come, when the chief lords, with the clergy and prelates, gathered in the church with the king, first the Mass for the dead was celebrated, then the marble slab that projected above the pavement was lifted, and they came to the sepulcher; and at its opening such a powerful, sweet-smelling fragrance enveloped everyone who was there, that they imagined themselves to be carried away into the midst of the delights of the Lord's paradise. And the sepulchre itself was full of water, a little crimson as if mixed with oil, in which rested, as in liquefied balm, the precious bones; having collected them in the finest linen cloth, they searched for a long time in that liquid for the ring that had been put on the right hand of the blessed man. Not having found it, some people began to pour the water into silver cauldrons and large jars at the order of the king, so that having emptied the sarcophagus, the discovery of the ring would be made more certain. But, miraculously, the greater the quantity of liquid that was poured out, that much more of it welling up filled up the sepulcher again. Seeing this miracle they restored the water they had drawn off to its place, but by pouring it back the grave did not overflow. Then covering the sepulcher, proclaiming praises and thanks to the divine kindness, they returned to the altar of the most blessed Mother of God Mary with the treasure they had found.

In the meantime God, who is *wonderful in his saints* [Ps 67:36, Vulgate] pouring forth the favors of his bounty, made his presence known to those asking for health both outside and inside the basilica by the signs of his miracles to such an extent that the time of the Lord's presence among men seemed to have returned, of which we read that: *all those who had any that were sick with various diseases brought them* [Lk 4:40] to Jesus and were cured. The divine power graciously worked all this not only that day, but for a long time afterward because of the merits of his servant. So hearing the fame of God's favors, those suffering from the affliction of various infirmities flocked with great longing from other regions for the intercession of the blessed man in order to regain their health. Indeed, the wife of a certain steward, a matron of exceptional renown, by the name of Mathilda, burdened for three continuous years by a pain of the intestines was already close to death. Carried by her own people on a bier, immediately that same day when she touched the tomb of the blessed man, she gradually felt herself to be better, and shortly having regained the health of her previous life revealed the *majestic power of God* [2 Mac 3:34] that recompensed her for the merits of his servant. Now I do not leave in writing the other wonderful signs of God's miracles that were revealed by heaven for the sake of his servant, not because I scorn them, but because the Lord rains not only on me, He who makes his sun shine over the good and the bad, [see Mt 5:45] the multiplicity of his kindness working for the benefit of all; I have entrusted to the innumerable wise men whom Hungary fosters and embraces to declare [the other miracles] by [their] pen. I have decided only to add at the end of the codex how, by a wonderful gift of the kindness of God, the ring they searched for so long, but did not find, was revealed together with the right hand of the blessed man, three years after his translation.

(27.) A certain monk, by the name of Mercurius, who, in the clerical order was the guardian of the treasury of the perpetual Virgin, and for the love of the heavenly home renounced the world, was sent away far from there by royal rebuke in that hour when the tomb was opened, lest he carry off something from the holy relics. As he was sitting in the choir with a sad face, a certain young man dressed in white clothes gave him a rolled up piece of cloth, saying: "I entrust this to you to preserve, and when the time comes to reveal." After the completion of the sacred office, the monk unfolded the cloth in the corner of the building, and seeing the intact hand of the man of God with the ring of marvelous craftsmanship, he got frightened; and without anyone's knowledge, he brought it with him to the monastery which had been commended to his governing, awaiting the time foretold to him from Christ by the youth. Here for a long time he alone undertook the guarding and watching of the treasure buried in the field, afterward he made the founders of that monastery aware of it, finally at the approach of the time when it had to be declared, he brought it to the notice of the king. The king immediately, joined by bishops and the chief lords of Hungary, obtaining there many favors of miracles from Christ, appointed the day of celebration for elevating the right hand of God's man.

Why is it, brothers, that his other limbs having become disjointed and, his flesh having been reduced to dust, wholly separated, only the right hand, its skin and sinews adhering to the bones, preserved the beauty of wholeness? I surmise that the inscrutability of divine judgment sought to proclaim by the extraordinary nature of this fact nothing less than that the work of love and alms surpasses the measure of all other virtues. Whence the Truth [Christ] says in the Gospel: *blessed are the merciful, for they shall obtain mercy* [Mt 5:7]. And also *give and it will be given to you* [Lk 6:38]. Also in another place: as the water extinguishes fire, so alms extinguish sin [see Sir 3:33, Vulgate]. The right hand of the blessed man was deservedly exempt from putrefaction, because always reflourishing from the flower of kindness it was never empty from giving gifts to nourish the poor. Because he helped those who found themselves in need, freed those burdened by the yoke of captivity, offered clothes and hospitality to pilgrims, reckoned the misery and need of widows and orphans to be his own, daily repeated the Lord's supper and order in washing the feet of the poor, made the alms flow not from plunder or the damage of others, but at the cost of his own purses; renounced, in order to make the houses of God rich, the will to possess, and thus advancing in everything the will of the divinity, he crucified his flesh together with his vices and desires. Hence the delightful and wonderful reverence to his body and right hand, hence the sweet and happy reward of eternal life, hence the desirable cohabitation with the citizens on high, where the shining and unfailing splendor of the one and most high deity, Father and Son and the Holy Spirit, always shines on him forever and ever. Amen. It ends. Here ends the *Life of St. Stephen the king*.

NOTES

1. I thank Robert E. Bjork and Marjorie Chibnall for their help and kindness.
2. Priscian was a Latin grammarian of the late fifth century, his *Institutiones grammaticae* was widely used during the Middle Ages.
3. Pannonia was a Roman province, covering the territory that later became western Hungary (up to the Danube). After the establishment of the kingdom of Hungary, the name Pannonia was applied to the whole of the kingdom.

4. That is, Géza who was chieftain of the Hungarians from ca. 970 until 997.

5. Adalbert (Vojtěch) was a member of the Slavník family of Bohemia. Bishop of Prague, he spent time as a missionary in Poland. Although he visited the Hungarian court, his missionary activities there were not at all on the scale depicted in the *Life*. Many of his disciples, however, eventually moved to Hungary and filled important positions during Stephen's reign. Adalbert was killed in 997 when he was trying to convert the pagan Prussians. His body was buried in Gniezno. Quickly regarded as a saint, his cult flourished in Bohemia, Poland, and Hungary.

6. Levites (from Levi, son of Jacob) were members of the tribe of priests in ancient Israel. In the New Testament, the word acquired the meaning of deacon. Information concerning St. Stephen survived in the *Acts of the Apostles* (Chapters 6–7); he was a deacon and the first martyr of the Christian Church. His cult was widespread all over Christendom.

7. Greek στε′φανος (*stephanos*) and Latin *corona* both mean crown.

8. The "next order" would mean those of lesser social rank.

9. The pagan revolt led by Koppány in 997. Koppány, the eldest male of the Árpád line at the time of Géza's death, did not acknowledge Stephen, but wanted to rule in his stead, according to the traditional inheritance pattern.

10. Hartvic used a terminology to separate rulers who received unction and those who did not. He reserved *rex* only for the former, while using *princeps* or *dux* for the latter. Hartvic referred to Géza first as *princeps* then as *dux*, while to Stephen as *dux* prior to his receiving unction, and *rex* afterward. The Polish ruler also appeared as *dux* in the text. *Dux* was used in the sense of war leader prior to the development of its meaning as "duke."

11. St. Martin of Tours (ca. 316–397). Born in Pannonia (which became part of medieval Hungary), he was a soldier prior to his conversion. He became bishop of Tours (later part of medieval France) in 372.

12. St. George of Lydda, a martyr of the third or fourth century, was often represented in the mythical story of St. George and the dragon. He was patron saint of soldiers both in the Byzantine Empire and in medieval Europe.

13. That is, the monastery of Pannonhalma.

14. He was a member of St. Adalbert's circle and moved to Hungary after Adalbert's death. The correct form of his name is not known, Asric or Aseric (due to an erroneous reading often referred to as Astric).

15. That is, the Benedictine abbey of Pécsvárad.

16. That is, to the papal court in Rome.

17. That is, from the pope.

18. Mieszko I ruled from before 963 until 992; at this time the Polish ruler was Boleslaw I Chrobry, who ruled from 992 until 1025.

19. The phrase *utroque iure* implies both temporal and spiritual (or ecclesiastical) law. The idea of two types of power became important during the late eleventh-century ecclesiastical reform ("Gregorian reform") and Investiture Contest. Pope Gelasius I (492–96) stated that the sacred authority of popes and secular imperial power, dependent on each other, governed Christians. From the 1070s, contrary views developed concerning papal and imperial rights and power and their relationship to each other. Hartvic affirmed Stephen's sovereignty in the context of this debate, attributing to him the legitimate use of both powers. This assertion reflected the controversies at the time Hartvic was writing, and not those of the epoch of King Stephen. Pope Innocent III, while approving the *Life*, objected to the use of this phrase, which was omitted from subsequent manuscripts: Augustinus Theiner, *Vetera Monumenta Slavorum Meridionalium Historiam Illustrantia*, 2 vols. (Rome, 1863–75), 1:57, no. 77; *Scriptores Rerum Hungaricarum*, ed. Imre Szentpétery, 2 vols. (Budapest, 1937–38), 2:369.

20. Hartvic described here the ecclesiastical rite of anointing kings at the time of their coronation. The model for this unction was provided by the Hebrew Bible (Samuel anointed Saul and David) and represented a consecration to God and an endowment with God's gifts. From this point in the text Hartvic starts to call Stephen king (*rex*).

21. Gisela was the sister of Emperor Henry II, who ruled from 1002 until 1024.

22. Physical disabilities such as blindness disqualified a man from the priesthood. The story is an attempt to explain the creation of a second archbishopric, that of Kalocsa, in Hungary.

23. This medieval town named Alba in the region of Pannonia is Fehérvár in modern Hungary.

24. This medieval town named Alba in the region of Transylvania is Alba Iulia in modern Romania.

25. The Pechenegs were a Turkic nomad tribal confederation, migrating in the steppe area across the Volga River. In the late ninth century a Pecheneg attack forced the Hungarian tribes into the Carpathian Basin. After the formation of the Hungarian kingdom Pecheneg raids recurred, while some of the Pechenegs settled in Hungary. From the mid-eleventh century large groups also settled in the Byzantine Empire. In the late eleventh and early twelfth centuries the Pechenegs were decisively defeated by a Byzantine-Cuman alliance.

26. That is, the German Empire.

27. Emperor Conrad II attacked Hungary in 1030.

28. That is, the inhabitants of Pannonia, used here as a synonym for Hungary.

29. This is a reference to canon law, probably to an alleged letter of Pope Anastasius I included among the Pseudo-Isidorian Decretals. A similar scriptural passage (Thess 4:13) was also incorporated into canon law. Eventually both texts were included in the *Decretum* of Gratian (C. 13, q. 2. c. 27 and c. 28).

30. This phrase recalls the last words of Jesus; see Lk 23:46.

31. This Alba is the one located in Pannonia, that is Fehérvár in modern Hungary. See notes 23 and 24 above.

32. The text has *frater* which could be brother or cousin; in fact, Solomon was Ladislas's cousin.

33. Solomon, son of King Andrew I (who reigned from 1046 until 1060), attacked King Béla I (who reigned from 1060 until 1063) with the help of Emperor Henry IV. Béla died before the battle and Solomon became king in 1063. In 1074 war broke out between Solomon and Béla I's two sons. Solomon was defeated and King Géza I ruled from 1074 until 1077. After his death his younger brother Ladislas (László) I became king and reigned until 1095. Solomon, who had fled after his defeat, tried to regain the throne. Ladislas recalled him to Hungary, and then imprisoned him. After being released, Solomon left the kingdom and joined the Pechenegs; after an unsuccessful attempt to regain his crown, he died in a war against Byzantium.

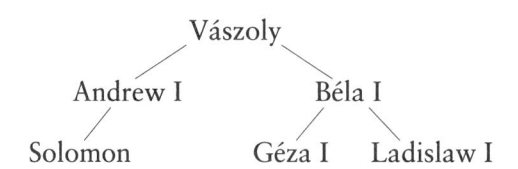

```
                    Vászoly
                   /       \
            Andrew I         Béla I
               |            /      \
            Solomon     Géza I    Ladislaw I
```

34. That is, miracles. Hartvic uses both *signa* and *miracula* to describe the miracles.

CHAPTER 19
Guibert of Nogent, *On Saints and Their Relics*
Translated by Thomas Head

INTRODUCTION

As works of hagiography, the works presented in this collection all naturally give praise, often extravagantly, to the virtues and miraculous powers of their saintly heroes. It is possible to forget that among medieval Christians themselves there was occasional criticism of—even opposition to or skepticism about—the cult of saints. Abbot Guibert of Nogent's *De pignoribus sanctorum* [*On Saints and Their Relics*] has become one of the most celebrated such critiques among modern scholars, although it apparently received only limited circulation at the time of its composition. It provides an important and interesting counterpoint to the stories told in other works contained in this volume. To appreciate Guibert's critique, however, it is important to know something of the circumstances of his life and of the composition of this work.

Guibert was born at Clermont, in northern France, most probably in 1055 to a family of the minor nobility. His father and brothers were knightly warriors, but his parents vowed Guibert to a religious vocation, mostly to save the life of a child weakened in the course of a difficult birth. His father died in captivity, likely from wounds received in battle, less than eight months later. His mother vowed, against the explicit desires of her in-laws, never to marry again. Persecuted by this family, she seems to have almost sequestered Guibert from his military relatives. As a child intended for the religious life he received an adequate, if harshly delivered, education from a private tutor at the family castle. In 1067 his mother finally fled the family to live as a virginal widow in association with the monastic community of Saint-Germer. A few months later, her young boy followed. He was to spend thirty-eight years in that monastery, first as a guest student, later as a monk. Over the course of that time he became a solid scholar, studying with no less a figure than Anselm of Canterbury, and attained some minor acclaim for his biblical exegesis and philosophical teaching. These decades, spent by Guibert in the relative seclusion of his monastery, were politically significant ones for the development of ecclesiastical power in Western Christendom, witnessing among other momentous events the launching of the First Crusade. During these years, such intellectual and religious luminaries as Peter Abelard, Suger of Saint-

Denis, and Bernard of Clairvaux were all born in what is roughly the northern half of modern France.

In 1104 Guibert finally achieved some measure of his long-held aspirations to a position of prominence, being elected abbot of Nogent, a monastery located about thirty kilometers west of Laon. At almost fifty years of age, Guibert began a two-decade career of real, if limited, public influence, both as a monastic leader and as a scholar. He wrote much over the course of those years, including a history of the First Crusade. All of his works are composed in an extraordinarily complex Latin filled with allusions (accurate and inaccurate) to works of the classical and Christian past, traits which indicate both the extent and the limitations of his schooling. In point of fact, Guibert was erudite, but pompous, and not very skilled stylistically.

Around 1115, a few years after a bloody revolt had shaken the secular and ecclesiastical politics of the nearby town of Laon, Guibert wrote a set of memoirs which he called his *Monodiae* and modeled on the *Confessions* of Augustine of Hippo (d. 430). This curious and deeply revealing work is one of the few autobiographical documents (another being the so-called *Story of My Misfortunes* of Peter Abelard) to survive from this period. It is because of these memoirs that we know so much about Guibert's career. The abbot of Nogent emerges from those as an ambitious and somewhat talented, but ultimately frustrated, man. Now an aging man, he realized that he would never go beyond the abbacy of Nogent, an institution of only middling consequence, and would never attain the prominence of a Suger in the political arena, of an Abelard in the scholarly academy, or a Bernard in reform monasticism, all of whom would begin to emerge in the public life of northern France in the next few years. He was judgmental in the extreme and often harshly critical of those he deemed his intellectual and spiritual inferiors. But he was also a man of strong and complex piety. He had been offended by the presumption of laymen in subverting the Church during the disastrous revolt in Laon and was now more than ever devoted to the idea of clerical authority. He was also deeply attached to the cult of many local saints, and believed in many miracles which had happened through their power.

His *On the Saints and Their Relics* was probably the last book he ever wrote, in ca. 1125 near the end of his life. He says in the introductory letter that he had in fact begun parts of it years earlier, but realized that his original argument was based in part on a faulty exegesis of Scripture. He had then returned to the abandoned project when the monks of a nearby monastery began to make much of their possession of a relic of Christ, to be specific a milk tooth shed by the boy Jesus. As he said in his introductory letter,

> Since many questions have been posed to me concerning a tooth of the Savior, which our neighbors the monks of Saint-Médard assert to have in their possession, and since they have expressed their opinions to many in the vulgar tongue [that is, French], I once decided to put a few thoughts into writing under this heading and so make known what is in my mind to

those who have kept silent on the matter. When I began to marshal my arguments at the very beginning of this small volume and had begun to dictate the first page, such a rich flood of thoughts on similar matters overcame me that the subject matter which I had undertaken was soon indefinitely postponed. At that time I followed these other matters, which were not alien from those of the original work, and hammered out a small volume, leaving unfinished the work on which I had embarked. In the course of things, my discussion touched on the body of the Lord and the work which I had begun on the tooth [of the Lord]—a matter on which I had vowed to have my say—came back to me. . . .

What resulted was an odd hodgepodge of a work, containing four books on different, although related, themes. It is the title of the first which came to stand for the work as a whole, but it is only that first book which he primarily devoted to the cult of saints and that is the only part of the work translated here. In the following books, he went on to consider the problem of alleged relics of Christ, in whose authenticity he did not believe, and even more importantly the nature of bodily resurrection. The preoccupation with death and resurrection is clearly that of an elderly theologian facing his own mortality.

The first book *On Saints and Their Relics* contains some harsh criticism of certain practices associated with the cult of saints and of the cults of specific relics. But it must be remembered that this was the work of a man who himself believed in the authenticity and miraculous power of many relics. It is also important to remember that this was a work which received only limited circulation in the Middle Ages. Although, as the introductory letter makes clear, Guibert distributed it among fellow clerics, only a single manuscript of it, that written by Guibert's own scribes, survives. The opinions of the abbot of Nogent expressed here were not commonly echoed until possibly the Protestant Reformation.

What Guibert is concerned to relay in this work is the importance of the clergy's authority in matters of religious practice and to urge the assertion of clerical control over the cults of relics. Guibert developed an explicit theory of the relationship of saints' relics to the saints themselves and the role played by written texts in that relationship. In Guibert's eyes, error, both stylistic and factual, was rampant in the traditions supporting the cult of certain saints. He went on to say that not only the falsification of evidence, but even the veneration of dubiously authenticated relics was sinful. Almost grudgingly he admitted that the pious veneration of inauthentic relics, when done in good faith, was meritorious. Guibert cannot simply be understood as a medieval skeptic, critical of the veneration of relics. For him, the combination of antique texts and contemporary miracles were the only trustworthy guarantee for the *auctoritas* of a saint. And in the end he grudgingly accepted the spiritual efficacy of many of the practices whose wisdom he questioned. The abbot of Nogent concluded this work on an uncharacteristically uncertain and almost self-questioning note, with a statement whose simple Latin may be understood even by those who are not familiar with that language: *Non est deus grammaticae curiosus.* God is not overly concerned about grammar.

SOURCES AND FURTHER READING

What follows is a translation of most of the first book of Guibert of Nogent, *De sanctis et eorum pigneribus* from the critical edition of the text found in Guibert of Nogent, *Opera varia*, ed. R.B.C. Huygens, Corpus Christianorum, Continuatio Mediaeualis 127 (Turnholt, 1993), pp. 79–175 (pages 85–109 for the portions translated here). (I have omitted a few anecdotes, summarized in brackets, for the sake of brevity.) Huygens's introduction to this work provides complete references to previous scholarship on the works of Guibert (most of which is not in English), a discussion of the sole surviving medieval manuscript of the work (pages 13–31), and an analysis of the date and process of Guibert's composition of the work (pages 32–36). Huygens argues very contentiously with previous scholars, in particular with Monique-Cecile Garand. As reflected in my remarks above, I accept the bulk of Huygens's conclusions.

Guibert wrote in an extremely convoluted style marked by sentences greatly lengthened through periodic construction, which are further complicated by dependent clauses—and who would not also mention his regular use of rhetorical questions?—as well as by subtle (not to mention parenthetical) allusions. In attempting to render the abbot of Nogent's words into comprehensible English, I have often had to expand upon their literal meaning. I have placed the most obvious expansions within brackets. In the course of this endeavor, I have made reference to Louise Catherine Nash, "Translation of *De pignoribus sanctorum* of Guibert of Nogent with Notes and Comments," Master's Thesis, University of Washington (1941), which is to my knowledge the only previous English translation of Guibert's work and which was necessarily dependent on the often defective text of Guibert's work found in Jean-Paul Migne's *Patrologia latina*, 221 vols. (Paris, 1844–64), 156:607–80 (pages 611–30 for the portions translated here). Nash's translation, while much more literal than that offered here, was often useful in providing ideas about the rendering of Guibert's complex Latin into comprehensible English. I wish to express my gratitude for the scholarly work of this nun, whose apparently considerable talents never to my knowledge found published expression. I am also extremely grateful to Robert Lamberton of Washington University for his help in tracking down information about, as well as acceptable translations of, those passages from works of classical antiquity to which Guibert alludes.

Guibert's *On the Saints and Their Relics* has yet to find an interpretation both compelling and comprehensive in modern scholarship. Huygens's edition is an important step toward such an interpretation. The fullest extant examination of Guibert's treatise is to be found in Klaus Guth, *Guibert von Nogent und die hochmittelalterliche Kritik an der Reliquienverehrung*, Studien und Mitteilungen zur Geschichte des Benediktiner-Ordens und seiner Zweige, Supplement 21 (Ottobeuren, 1970). The shortcomings of this work, however, have been noted in numerous reviews (see, for example, *Deutsches Archiv*, 26 [1970]: 649–50). For an Anglophone expression of the commonplace scholarly attitude toward Guibert's critique of the cult of the saints, see Colin Morris, "A Critique of Popular Religion: Guibert of Nogent on *The Relics of the Saints*," in *Popular Belief and Practice*, ed. Derek Baker, Studies in Church History 8 (Oxford, 1972), pp. 95–111. Similar sentiments are to be found in many other places, see for example Marie-Danielle Mireux, "Guibert de Nogent et la critique du culte des reliques," in *La piété populaire au Moyen Age Actes du 99e Congrès national des sociétés savantes, Besançon, 1974. Section de philologie et d'histoire jusqu'à 1610*, 2 vols. (Paris, 1977), 1:193–202. It should be noted that none of these three scholars enjoyed the benefit of the considerable fruits of Huygens's textual scholarship. My own interpretation of the text is at odds with their views. For a trenchant comparison of Guibert's opinions to others current in different regions of Western Christendom, see Julia Smith, "Oral and Written: Saints, Miracles, and Relics in Brittany, c. 850–1250," *Speculum* 65 (1990): 309–43. Smith suggests— correctly in my view—that Guibert is representative of an attitude toward the cult of saints developed in the Carolingian realm during the ninth century and perpetuated among members of the clerical elite for several centuries thereafter. For persuasive comments on Guibert's Eucharistic theory, which is dependent on his ideas concerning the relics of the saints, see Caroline Bynum, "Bodily Miracles and the Resurrection of the Body in the High Middle Ages," in *Belief in History: Innovative Approaches to European and American Religion*, ed. Thomas Kselman (Notre Dame, IN, 1991), pp. 68–106. Bynum, however, focuses on the latter three books of the treatise, which are not translated here. She greatly expanded the ideas which she introduced in this article in *The Resurrection of the Body in Western Christianity, 200–1336* (New York, 1995). While that book is essential to an understanding of the importance of the belief in physical resurrection to the material importance of saints' relics, it does not provide much in the way of new analysis of this specific work of Guibert of Nogent.

As suggested above, the reader should compare the attitudes on the relics of saints developed here to those which Guibert expressed in his so-called *Memoirs*, a work which he called the *Monodiae* and modeled on the *Confessions* of Augustine of Hippo. That work is currently available in two English translations: *Self and Society in Medieval France: The Memoirs of Abbot Guibert of Nogent (1064-c1125)*, ed. and trans. John Benton (New York, 1970; reprint, Toronto, 1984) and *A Monk's Confession: The Memoirs of Guibert of Nogent*, ed. and trans. Paul Archambault (State College, PA, 1996). The latter is significantly more readable and accurate, in part because based on a better edition, although Benton's psychohistorical critique of Guibert in his introduction remains of interest. The best edition of that work is accompanied by a French translation: Guibert de Nogent, *Autobiographie*, ed. and trans. Edmond-René Labande, Les classiques de l'histoire de France au Moyen Age 34 (Paris, 1981).

Guibert of Nogent, On Saints and Their Relics

Guibert—would that he were a true priest in the service of the Mother of God—[has written this treatise] for Odo, the lord abbot of Saint-Symphorien, [wishing that he might] gain progress and happiness in the service of God. . . .[1]

If it is regrettable to err concerning the status of the general resurrection of all people, then it is downright perverse to detract in any way from the resurrection of Him who is their Head. Since the efficacy of all hopes [of resurrection] hinge upon [Christ's] example, doubtless the entire meaning of His promise would be called into question if the possibility of doing [as He did] faded or if His own promise were in any way broken. For when people make promises and those promises do not come to pass, then those people are either accused of falsehood or it is said about them that they are unable to do that which they said they would do for others. Let no one, under the cloak of piety, impute to God any diminished power or any infidelity in carrying through on promises. One would shudder even to have such a thought, for it would most probably be considered impious in the minds of everyone and would seem an insult to universal belief. When people claim for themselves the excellence of their churches, then the laws of our faith lose their power. Any honor which they thus claim must be thought detestable, for it causes a decline or a failure in the hopes of all people. Surely if you so burden your right hand with gold that you weaken the power of your whole body through such ornament, then such a form of beauty, which harms the whole through the decoration of the part, is extremely impractical. In a similar fashion, an overabundance of twigs emerging from a branch causes it to wither, and with it the whole body of the tree. As regards those matters which are practiced and taught by the Church, such temperance has hitherto existed that no one would dare to promulgate [any teaching] except that which careful examination confirms as being [consistent] with the manner and example of Catholic authority. There are in addition certain other matters which are practiced, but not taught, such as the customs of fasting or the singing of psalms. Even though diversity [is allowed] in such practices, they may never disagree with the rule of faith. Those who diverge [from the norm] in fasting or the singing of psalms may not be condemned for acting differently in such matters. Otherwise those who, in a common faith, defended difference [in the practice] of asceticism or the liturgical office might be called, with some merit, a schismatic simply for such irregular practices. If you sing psalms or fast in some manner different [from the norm], however, it is not correct or suitable that you impose your way on others or that you say that they are doing some lesser good in their practice. For hear the [words of the] apostle: *He also who eats, eats in honor of the Lord . . . and he who abstains, abstains in honor of the Lord* [Rom 14:6]. Concerning analogous subjects, a similar judgment is readily made. On the other hand, there are those matters which are both practiced and taught, such as baptism and the sacrament of the Lord's host, which are so much the commonplaces of

Christianity that our faith would be unable to survive without them. These are by authority always practiced without difference and everywhere without change, so that they are the same in all times and all places, the doctrine which informs them and which is learned from them being identical. Identical, I say, so that what is pronounced publicly may be directly informed by the prayers of those who teach. There is, however, a difference between the two. Without [baptism through] water or blood a Christian cannot exist.[2] Without the Eucharist, however, a Christian is truly able to exist, if that Christian lives in constancy with the faith. This can be proven by the example of many martyrs and hermits, some of whom never received [the Eucharist], others only once or twice. Rather they incorporated this holy work into themselves through their long solitude and were thus sanctified.[3] There is a similar maxim which teaches that holding to the faith is sufficient for salvation even when other practices are lacking. Thus the Apostle [Paul] says: *And to one who does not work [. . .] his faith is reckoned as righteousness* [Rom 4:5]. An even greater standing is attributed to charity: since it is placed before faith and hope, it is valued above all other things. It is said of this *work* of charity: *establish thou the work of your hands upon us* [Ps 90:17], these being the actions common to any good profession [of the faith]. [The passage continues]: *yea, the work of our hands establish thou it* [Ps 90:17], that is, teach us the better gifts or, so to speak, the more noble path. These truths are taught because we believe them, and they [continue to be] believed by means of being taught.

Unlike the matters of which we have been speaking—things [that is, like baptism and the Eucharist] which are practiced and preached in church and without which it would not be possible to live an upright life—there are other matters which are not counted among the very highest necessities for our salvation, without the use and presence of which many people have led, and continue to lead, good lives. In this second category are numbered the bodies of the saint, as well as lesser relics taken from [those bodies] which are put to similar use. [The saints] are people who are worthy of our reverence and honor in exchange for their example and protection. As regards such people, the only method for considering a person to be a saint which should be considered authoritative is one that relies not on opinion, but on timeworn tradition or on the evidence of trustworthy writers. For why would you consider someone whom I sanctioned to be a saint,[4] if nothing was remembered of that person's dignity, still more if there were no texts or reliable reports of miracles to support [the claim of sanctity]? By texts, I mean those which are suitable for strengthening the faith! For there are many stories about the saints which would be more likely to cause their reputation to suffer an impious fate among unbelievers than to be at all illustrious. And even when stories about the saints are true, they can be expressed in such a ragged, pedestrian, or—if I might use a poetic expression—serpentine style and delivered with so much confusion that they are believed to be false, even though they are quite true.[5] And why should the tales of such authors, who put the very truth in doubt by means of their unbecoming crudeness, not be assigned [a place among those works] which ring falsely? Should we not regard it a slight upon the apostles when we read in the place of their true *Lives* some inanities about them that extinguishes the light [offered by their example]? What should we deem the *Acts of Thomas*—a work to which Augustine objects not just once, but in many places—except as a ringing in our ears?[6] Perhaps either God or the saints had need of a lie so that, in the words of Job [13:7], *they might speak deceitfully for him*! The holy apostles themselves, who were as close to Christ as a beard or hair are to the head, would not have need of such falsehoods. Such figments of the imagination would not disturb the spirits of some people, were our traditions [about the apostles] taken from the very Gospels and the *Acts of the Apostles*.[7] What should I say about [those saints whose lives] are not illuminated by any testimony or, even more, about one [whose life] is actually shadowed over by the very writings which are thought to celebrate it? What should I say about those saints whose births and mature lives are not known to anyone, and [the manner of] whose deaths, in which all praise is to be sung, are also completely unknown? And who would ask people, about whose merit in the eyes of God is uncertain, to intercede on their behalf? Would not the conscience of a man offer grave offense if he obtained as an intercessor with God someone who was not to be particularly trusted? Would not the sharpness of his prayer be blunted in its intention if he did not know whether the person whom he asked for help had anything in common with God? I knew some people who a long time ago brought the body of a man whom they took to be a confessor down from Brittany; then they suddenly underwent a change of heart and celebrated him as a martyr. When I demanded their reasons, they had nothing more dignified to say about this man's martyrdom than that which they had previously to say concerning his status as a confessor.[8] I swear to God that in the life of St. Samson, who is most famous among the Franks and the Bretons, I have read—and even had to reread with utter loathing to those who happened to be with me—a story about a certain abbot who was called St. Piro. When I inquired into the death of this man, whom I thought to be a saint on the basis of what I had read, I discovered the heights [to which] his sanctity [had risen], namely that he had drunk past the point of being sober, fallen down a well, and thus died.[9] Nor has the question escaped my memory which Lanfranc, archbishop of Canterbury in England, posed to his successor Anselm, then abbot of Bec, concerning one of his own predecessors who had been cast into prison and, since he was unable to pay money to ransom himself, died there.[10] What am I to say about those saints who are discovered to have died in sin, or about whom it is uncertain whether they died a good or evil death, or about whom there is some other doubt? Sweet Jesus! Is a person [to be considered] a saint, the manner of whose death remains ambiguous? Therefore, before one asks for the intercession of such a person, it is necessary that one ask about the truth of that person's sanctity. I dare say that it is a profanity to persist in placing among the highest thrones of heaven those people of whom no memory remains among the living as to their era, their birth, their life, the day of their death, or the manner in which they died. If the faithful honor such people with the name of sanctity, then priests—I say this for their own good—fail to act in an upright manner when they hear such vulgar opinion wafting on the breezes and fail to correct it. For when people are lawfully raised to the highest ranks [of sanctity] without written testimony and they are thus accidentally granted false, even sacrilegious, titles, then [it may be the case that] people are lifted up to a place of eminence among mortals who have, in fact, been relegated to a place of punishment or even been led to oblivion in Tartarus [that is, hell], people who would—like that rich man [see Lk 16:19–25]—beg help from ordinary mortals, if they knew their fate and were given a chance. The bishops, as the guardians of the people of God, ought to oversee [such matters]. They ought to care for their people so that, if [the people] have a "zeal for God," then [their zeal] is an enlightened one [see Rom 10:2], and so that they not err in offering righteous praise [to the saints] by failing to separate [the unrighteous] from the righteous. For, according to the prophet, *Woe to those who call evil good and good evil* [Is 5:20]. What greater perversity is there, than to place on the sacred altars those very things which ought to be kept outside the very church itself? Those who work miracles posthumously through their bodies were not free from punishment during their lifetimes; for we learn from our readings that the just are only saved with difficulty when they are put to trial. Ought we then to believe [in the sanctity] of someone for whom there is no evidence of holiness: neither what we see nor what we hear, neither written evidence nor miracles? And surely it would be difficult to believe in miracles [performed by] someone who has not lived a good life from birth to death. There are, I will admit, some ambiguous events, in which the [unrighteous] on God's left hand seem to be given as much glory as the [righteous] on God's right hand. For the same God who divided the Red Sea for the children of Israel, also held back the [sea at] Pamphylia for Alexander the Great.[11] You may read in Suetonius how Vespasian cured a lame man by touching him with the toe of his foot.[12] Miraculous signs have also surrounded the births of princes, such as the above mentioned Alexander, Julius Caesar, Octavian, and others.[13] Portents accompanied the deaths of Charles and his son Louis.[14] In our own times, we have often seen comets marking the deaths and even births of the kings of our own land, as well as of Lotharingia and England. And what are we to make of the fact that we regularly witness our lord King Louis [VI] working wonders? With my own eyes, I have seen people suffering from scrofula about the throat or elsewhere on their bodies crowd around him, seeking his touch, [to which] he added sign of the cross. I was near the king and shrank back, but he, with an inborn and elevated liberality, signaled them with his hand to come forward. His father Philip at one time frequently worked the glory of this same miracle, but he lost the power through some sins.[15] I omit what some other kings do in a like manner, but I do know that the English king never dares to try such things.[16]

It must be understood that the gift of miracles is distributed in many ways. There are certain persons through whom portents are delivered as if through canals and, while they thus serve a useful purpose in providing things for the sake of others, it is others who are held to be the true source of the things which happen through them.[17] This is the case when an ass speaks and when an angel is seen, [cases] to which the prophecies of Balaam [see Num 22:22–25] and of Caiaphas [see Jn 11:49–52] might be joined, [that is, cases in which] what sounds on the exterior is alien to what lies within.[18] Thus we see many things predicted about the future or announced about the state of the life to come by dying people who themselves are of indifferent merit. In the same way we are accustomed to placing value on the words of almost blameless infants, because words weighty with providence, both about their own lives and events which will befall others, are often thrust through them despite their dullness of mind. The following story will offer an example. Quite recently, that is to say last Easter, on the very day on which the feast was celebrated, in the nearby town of Soissons, a certain woman brought her own child to church for the purpose of receiving Communion.[19] When the moment for the consecration of the Eucharist had arrived, the small boy—who to this point had been unaware of anything—was standing in the presence of his mother, who had her back to the priest, and he saw in the middle of the altar, while the divine service was continuing, a young child more beautiful than any other being held aloft in the hands of the priest. While he gazed attentively, he could not remain silent in his childlike curiosity about what he saw, and, within the hearing of those gathered in the church, he said to his mother, "Lady, lady, don't you see what a beautiful boy the priest is holding above the altar?" When she turned around, the vision did not appear to her. A little while later, when the priest, following the elevation, put down the host and covered it with a cloth, the boy again cried out, "Look, [the priest] is wrapping [the baby] in a white tunic." Since he repeated these things in the hearing of those gathered around, some people of greater intelligence understood that the innocent boy had been gazing upon the beautiful baby with other eyes, and with those other eyes he had seen the material of the tunic in which the vision was wrapped. But consider that he who saw these things is now growing up in the world and is not considered to have a better hope of the life to come. Thus it is demonstrated beyond doubt that the vision did not add to the merit or increase the glory of the boy who saw it, but it did add distinction to the faith of those who heard him. How could it be said that the boy saw [the vision] for his own edification or glory, when he is barely—and in no reasoned fashion—able to remember that which he once saw? There are to be found yet other persons to whom merits come, not because of what they have done before, nor due to any exercise of reason on their part, in such a way that, without any learning or effort, a glory almost equal to that of the final judgment falls upon them. This happened most notably in the case of the Holy Innocents.[20] For they suffered without any thought of either God or of salvation, yet they obtained as a reward everything that God can give. For it is the right of the potter to make a vessel either for beauty or for menial use [see Rom 9:21]. For indeed it is He who objects: *Am I not allowed to do what I choose with what belongs to Me* [Mt 20:14]? For, *He has mercy upon whomever He wills, and He hardens the heart of whomever He wills* [Rom 9:18]. No different lesson is learned from a story from modern times. In the town of Saint-Quentin, there was once a certain young boy who was, in the judgment of his parents, called to the clerical life.[21] If I am not mistaken, he had already risen to the rank of acolyte. One feast day at the moment of consecration he stood in front of the choir, that is between the altar and the apse, poised to perform his office, holding the paten on which the Host was about to be raised. Nearby at the front of the sanctuary, not far from the tomb of the martyr St. Quintinus, a plaster image stood, presenting the likeness of the crucified Lord. As he stood next to the image carrying the offerings, he spoke to the image in a way which was boyish more in sound than in meaning: "Lord, do you want some of my bread?" The Lord was very clearly heard to reply to the boy, "Very soon I Myself will give you some of My bread." When the boy heard these words, he was seized by a sickness, and within a very few days the young man relinquished his hold on his short life and, having exchanged it for a heavenly garment, was buried in front of the statue which had promised it to him. I learned these things from the priest of that very church and I have seen the very grave from the story. Indeed, I believe that I first heard the story from Raoul, the archbishop of Reims; it is also told in Soissons, as well as by the clergy and people of Laon.[22] As Seneca said in his books *Concerning Reward*, a person who returns the largesse of another is to be considered like a merchant, but he who bestows freely imitates God.[23] I may safely and surely say that it is much more natural for God to bestow grace than for any human to use it worthily.

There is, on the other hand, another sort of person, whose faith merits so much from divine mercy that He, whose *food is to do the will* [Jn 4:34] of His Father, provides a most powerful ability in the working out of salvation to those very people whom He has found to be most full of courage in bringing to a conclusion what they had begun in faith.[24] Thus to many His words are familiar: *Your faith has made you well* [Mk 10:52]. Which is to say, "The assertion of your faith has been so pleasing to Me that your health now depends on Me rather than on yourself." And this can be illustrated by a novel story which has occurred in our own times. Around the neighborhood, unless I am mistaken, of Cambrai in the province of Artois, a young man and a young girl, very closely related by blood, lived together under the same roof in the country.[25] The very closeness of the living quarters led to familiarity, and the familiarity held forth the possibility of unseemly conduct, so that shortly a shameless incest spoiled the badly guarded relationship. Soon, when the young girl perceived the result of their lustful couplings, they began to complain loudly to one another, with not a few tears and shouts, fearing that infamy to be seen by their own people. So they decided to depart from their native soil, but the girl, full of fear because she realized her culpability in the matter, went to the priest and confessed her sin with deep sorrow. The night after this had been done, they departed their country, as if seeking sanctuary in another region. When they had not gone very far from their own fields, their way led them past the edge of a long-abandoned well. And the boy said, "Let us sit, so that you may lighten the heaviness of your uterus by pausing at the mouth of the well."[26] She believed his lie and when she sat down with the angry youth, he struck her on the chest and thrust her into the well. After a little time had passed, the girl returned to her senses and groaned from the pain [caused by] her long fall, then the boy began to call to her pretending to care whether she still lived. Learning that she was alive from the ragged murmuring of her plaintive voice, he began to gather stones [to throw] at her. Then the young woman, falling silent, withdrew into a projecting corner of the well, not seeking peace so much as to avoid the rocks raining down on her. When neither breath nor sob made by her reached his foul ears, the boy thought that she was dead, if not from the fall, then from being struck by the rocks. He then left and made his way to their home, more happy because of the crime. There was little talk about the girl, except to note that she had gone away unaccompanied. Meanwhile she was left in the curve of the cave in most desperate straights, not even expecting to receive help from God Himself. She then noticed that a drop of liquid frequently fell from the turf which hung over her head, and putting her lips to what little was there, she was refreshed by it, as if it were all of riches of Sardanapallus.[27] What more can I say? She lay there for almost forty days, with no other nourishment than the drops which I mentioned above.[28] At one point during those forty days, some swineherds and shepherds pasturing their flocks in the fields around there, happened by the well. While walking around the place, they heard a voice coming up from its depths. When they put their heads over the top of the well, they learned from the voice that some human being had fallen in there, whom they determined, after great shouting, to be a woman. They asked who she was, and with great cries she told them who she was and where she came from. When the shepherds heard this, they set off for the nearest village with the speed of Pegasus and said that they had found the girl who had been thought to have utterly perished or to have left the country in exile.[29] Without delay a crowd of peasants rushed off: a group of women gathered, small boys were not kept away by their age, and old women were not prevented by the sluggishness of their years from running there, one more quickly than the next. One man was let down by ropes to bring out the trapped woman and show her to the waiting crowd. When she came out and told the story of her rescue, the fame [*fama*] of the miracle [*miraculum*] was not confined within that area, but as a story of virtue [*virtus*] most unusual for that time, it circulated to regions far away.[30]

Behold how much value lies in faith in doing penance, as well as in persevering in the desire to correct oneself. A person who places faith in doing penance, having accepted the grace of confession and with it a trustworthy forgiveness, will never have to despair concerning indulgence. This is that very same faith which the apostle [Paul] commended in a long list of the patriarchs [Heb 11:32–34], among whom Rahab and Jepthah should be numbered, although the latter had more obscure reasons than the others for the aforementioned faith.[31] The faith of this young women seems to me to be particularly important, in that she faithfully and unswervingly turned to God in the moment of her need. Faith has such standing before God that He is not able to deny recourse to His infinite piety even to those whose repentance is by no means assured. For whom, I think, it was often said by the prophets: *delay not for Thy own sake* [Dan 9:19] and *help us . . . for the glory of Thy name* [Ps 79:9; 78:9 in the Vulgate]. Accordingly I will with utter certitude say that God, who is piety itself, is unable to deny even those who are likely to be banished from Him in the future, although He even more quickly assists the just. He tempts the just for reasons of health, as He movingly demands of them exactly what is required for their salvation.

Finally there are other people who in modern times merit heavenly rewards, not for some single instance of faith, but for a long lifetime of holy work.[32] In the church of Cambrai about two years ago, there was a dean, who was also the chief custodian of the church, by the name of Erlebald.[33] He used to preach through many sermons delivered to the populace throughout the region the results of true confession. In order to illustrate that point, we will now relate an exemplary story about Erlebald. He overcame his own body through the harsh burdens of abstinence and by always wearing a squalid hairshirt, in which he hardly ever washed and in which such an infestation of vermin swarmed that it burst forth like a bubbling stream, so that it was considered a marvel that human flesh was in any way able to endure it. He never took it off, not even when sleeping, and he never used a mattress, but for his bed used a bench without any support or covering, on which he always lay clothed. When he was reaching the end of his life, he began to be gravely tempted in his soul by demons, drawn by them, as it were, into the pigsty. When those who witnessed him inquired as to the cause of his suffering, he replied that it was inflicted on him by demons because he had not in the least corrected the clergy who had been given to his care. When death finally came to him, he then appeared to many people in a pleasing form. The first to whom he appeared in this manner was a bishop, who asked him how things were going for him. Erlebald replied, "For the past thirty days I have been flogged daily with whips." "Even you, my lord?" the bishop answered him, "For what reason?" Erlebald answered, "What you say surprises me, for you know that a man, however holy he may wish to be, is still subject to the lapses of fragility whether he wills it or not. You yourself ought to consider those things which you have confessed to me and to God, and you should correct them, just as you promised me. Do not delay in correcting them, for it is in your best interests to do so." Then on Christmas Day, [the bishop] met his end. In time this vision and those of other people were made public. The series of these stories and the piety of Erlebald's life seemed to give credibility to the fact that all things were favorable for him. Then the feast of Easter came to pass. In the monastery of Bourbourg, which is the home for many holy religious virgins, there were two young women of the finest character, one of whom died on the day before Easter.[34] She had been enjoined through many promises by her companion to return to her as soon as her body had been laid to rest, if her ghost was so permitted by God, and to tell her whether things went well or badly for her [in the afterlife]. They had so bound themselves together through love that they were unwilling to remain ignorant in death of those things which they always knew about one another in life. Therefore several days after the death of the girl and the feast of Easter, when the surviving girl had gone to the dormitory for I don't know what purpose, her most beloved companion unexpectedly stood before her, displaying nothing morbid or mournful, but appearing pleasing to the senses. [The living girl] was struck with amazement, and hesitatingly asked how things went with her. "I am happy," the dead girl replied. "For on this past Easter day, Lord Erlebald, the dean of Cambrai, and I along with him, were received into the great joy of the celestial throng in the presence of Almighty God." She spoke and disappeared, but not before embracing with some sadness the companion she had left behind. Erlebald was therefore truly a man of the clergy who served as a shining beacon, very learned in the study of Scripture and quite attached to me in friendship. I give thanks, as I ought, for the supreme honor which is his, would that I might become as pleasing [to God]. His faith equaled his works, and together they made God his debtor for his pious labors. I heard these things first from my lord bishop of Laon, Barthélemy.[35] In short order, so many good men came from the provinces as witnesses, all saying similar things about this matter, that I am unable now to keep them all in my memory.

We have spoken of these miracles not because of their novelty, but in order to give a sense of the diversity of such cases. It ought to be added that, just as that which is evident and undoubted must be accepted wholeheartedly, so too that which is not factual but fraudulent must be severely punished as being lies. For when a person ascribes to God that which God has not even thought, that person, inasmuch as it is possible, makes God out to be a liar. If anyone should accuse me, an insignificant man, of some falsehood or suggest that I had done what I had not, that person would be despicable and odious to me. And who can be more destructive, more hopeless, or more damnable than one who of his own accord dishonors God, the fountainhead of all that is pure. One time I saw—and it pains me to retell it—how a boy of the vulgar class, who was said to be the armor bearer of some knight, fell into a well on Good Friday, [that is] two days before Easter, near the city of Beauvais. This event happened to occur in the jurisdiction of a very well known abbot.[36] Sanctity began to be imputed to the dead [boy] just because of the holiness of the day on which he died. Since peasants are anxious to celebrate novelties, they came from all the neighboring districts to his tomb bearing offerings and candles. What more can I say? His tomb was covered [by their offerings]; a structure was built to surround the place. Whole battalions of peasants, but without anyone from the better classes, came there on pilgrimage, even from the furthest reaches of Brittany. The [above-mentioned] learned abbot, along with his religious monks, saw these things and, seduced by the gifts that the pilgrims frequently brought with them, allowed miracles to be faked. Vulgar common people are able to be duped in their greedy hearts by feigned deafness, affected madness, fingers pushed back into the palm on purpose, and feet twisted up under thighs. What should a modest and wise man do when a proposal of sanctity comes to his attention, before he allows himself to become the promoter of such a cult? We repeatedly see [the cult of saints] trivialized through gossip and made an object of ridicule through the dragging around of reliquaries. Daily we see someone's pockets completely emptied by the lies of those whom Jerome called "rabble rousers" from their rabid style of speech. We are bothered by their worthlessness but are also carried away by their praise of divine matters because they—according to that same learned man [Jerome]—excel gluttons and jesters in their appetite, and surpass ravens and magpies with their troublesome chatter.[37] But what should we number as a crime if not the erroneous [transformation] of something rather improbable into something special? A certain very famous church became involved in this sort of circumlocution, when it sought to raise funds for the repair of some damages by hiring a public relations specialist.[38] And when on one occasion he had gone on at length about the church's relics, he produced a box and said—for I was among those present—"You know that inside this little box is a piece of the very bread which our Lord chewed with his own teeth. If you do not believe me, behold this distinguished man (he referred to me) whom you know to be very learned. On my word, he will provide a witness for my claim." I confess that I blushed when I heard this. If it were not for the presence of those who seemed to be his employers, and for the fact that I would have seemed to have been attacking them rather than the man who spoke, I would have exposed the falsehood. What can I say? Neither monks nor clerics restrain themselves from [taking] such shameful profits, [with the result that] in my hearing they proclaim heretical things about our faith. As Boethius said, "I should be rightly set down as insane if I held out for being sane among those madmen."[39]

In order that the matter at hand may be seen more clearly, it is necessary to consider first those people who are called "saints." We number as saints first the apostles, and then those whom the whole church recognizes as martyrs. Surely the judgment can be extended to confessors as well.[40] The mark of blood is enough to distinguish martyrs, even if later writings are silent about them. Nor is it asked in the case of martyrdom what sort of life preceded it, since blood is sufficient to cleanse away the worst crimes. Sweet Jesus, why should it not? For is not such suffering capable of wiping away all sin and bringing the fullness of glory? Just as baptism is the agent for the complete cleansing of all prior faults, so, after baptism, martyrdom negates sins and washes away vices [and thus leads to] salvation. I should add that only a righteous cause removes all penalty. For in the canons it says that, should someone be apprehended while destroying idols and then be slain because of that action, that person should not be accounted a martyr for such a death.[41] Surely the result of such an action seems a worthy one, but cannot a bad intention pervert a good cause? Donatists suffered in the same manner as the martyrs, but, since they were excommunicated, they died in vain.[42] The Manichaeans [burned at] Soissons shone with the zeal of the people of God, but, as they had likewise been excommunicated with just cause, they were damned and their relics placed with the bodies of criminals. I have spoken about these things at greater length in my *Monodiae*.[43] If such ambiguities may be encountered in the sanctioning of martyrs, then what amount of care must be used in an investigation made into confessors, [the manner of] whose death provides less of a guarantee? Even if the common wisdom of the Church agrees on the cases of Martin [of Tours], Remigius [of Reims], and similar people, what will I say about those whom the common people daily make into saints in villages and small towns, cases similar to those I have already discussed?[44] When some people see that others have important patrons, they first wish that they could have similar patrons, and then they simply make them up. In the same way poets first produce noble works, and later others are led into unskilled work through imitation. As Horace said, "We all write poems, whether we know how to do it or not."[45] In ancient times artistic creators, who thought that they lived in the golden age, raised up human beings as gods and goddesses. Over time so many deities accumulated that eventually some were deprived of honor, while others were set aside and called select. When the Jews were exiled in Babylonia, the Samaritans made gods for themselves: "Every nation still made gods of its own . . . The men of Babylon made Succoth-benoth, the men of Cuth made Nergal" [2 Kings 17:29] and others made other gods. According to Gregory the Great it is evident that "when a person is out of favor and is sent to intercede, the mind of the incensed person is moved to greater anger."[46] But everyone denies that they have chosen patrons who are in disfavor [with God]. Let them tell me, then, how they can take as their patron someone about whom they don't even know the first thing, because they can find nothing written about their patron except a name. While the clergy keeps silence, old hags and crowds of vile little women chant fabricated stories about such patrons while working at their treadles and looms. If someone disputes their words, they will stand in defense of their patron saints not only with cries, but even brandishing their shuttlecocks. Who, other than someone completely demented, would call upon such patron saints—about whom there remains not the slightest trace concerning their identity—as intercessors? What good is a prayer in which uncertainty vexes the soul of the person praying, uncertainty concerning the very person held up as an intercessor with God? What profit is there, I say, in that which is never without sin? For, when you pray to someone whom you know not to be a saint, you sin in the very action through which you sought pardon, by failing to distinguish the righteous from the unrighteous, even though you are offering sacrifice in a righteous way. When you pray to a patron [whose sanctity] you doubt, you fail to please God. When you are distrustful of your petition, you irritate God, for God takes offense when you send as your spokesperson someone whom God does not know. Why should someone speak for you, about whom you harbor suspicions? If you do not hold a good opinion of your patron, why do you think you will gain merit through that patron? Somewhere Ambrose says, "He ought to be superior to me, if I am ready to trust myself to him."[47] In short, is it not the mark of a foolish mind to send a petition through someone of uncertain status? Why do you ask that someone should stand before God for you, when you are not even sure that that person is your better? See how the Lord has commended the power of faith to move mountains [see 1 Cor 13:2] and has clearly opposed any uncertainty of spirit. And so it is said: if you place before yourself some [target], however large, and if you hesitate, even if only a little, then you will miss [the mark]. It is much more tolerable for you to lose trust in your own merits, than to despair of the patron through whom you have placed your hopes before God. Since you trust yourself less, you call upon the patron, but surely you know that if your advocate is convicted of falsehood, then you stand to lose all that you have gained.

Why should I speak at such length on these matters when there is such modesty in the mouth of the whole holy Church that it does not dare to say that the body of the Mother of the Lord has been glorified by resurrection, on account of the fact that this cannot be proven by compelling arguments?[48] It would be wicked to believe that [the body of Mary]—that vessel, more fair than any creature other than her son, who bore the universal Lord of majesty, a privilege which has never been granted to anyone else, not even one of angelic nature—was put aside without reward or honor in order to undergo corruption. Christ would be obliged to renew the body of His Mother, the source of His own being to which He owed the glorification of His own body. Do we refrain from declaring that it was restored to life, as would be sensible, for any reason except that we are not able to offer convincing proofs of it? In commenting on biblical texts the exercise of reason alone is sometimes sufficient, indeed examples cited from Scripture often depend upon such a reasoned exegesis. Yet in this case, where the most exacting application of reason suggests that Mary was graced through the renewal of her body to wholeness, yet where the right sort of visible proof is lacking, we lack the authority to prove [the assertion], and so keep silent, even if we privately believe that she was so glorified. Reason, however, makes the truth of the matter evident. It is believed that the bodies of varied saints were resurrected along with her son. Yet Mary's flesh does not differ from that of her Son, for we know that nothing extra was provided by a father in the conception of Christ, except for the Holy Spirit. How could she reside in the dust of the earth according to the ancient law of malediction [see Dan 12:2], she who was personally selected to bear the Author of benediction? She could not have [experienced corruption] without injury [to Christ's flesh], if I might dare to say so! He [could not have] abandoned the flesh of His mother to the common fate, and granted to the flesh of strangers a privilege which He denied to His own mother, the very source of His own flesh! Yet we are prohibited from asserting this [teaching] publicly, since eyewitness testimony is lacking, although we are in no way forbidden from accepting it privately. Yet if we are not able to teach these assertions concerning a woman whose glory creatures are unable to value fully, are we able to enjoin anything except eternal silence concerning those people whose salvation or damnation is uncertain? There are some things written about saints which are worse than folk songs and which should not even enter the ears of swineherds. Since many people attribute the greatest antiquity to their patron saints, they urgently demand that modern versions of the lives of those saints be written down. I have often been asked to do such a thing. I, however, can make mistakes even about those things which have happened before my very eyes. How can I claim to be truthful about those things which no one ever saw? If I were to relate things which I have only heard said—and I have been asked to speak the praises of ignoble saints, even to preach their acts to the people—then both I myself, were I to do as asked, and those who suggested that I say such things would be equally worthy of public censure.

But let us be finished with those [saints] whose very obscurity deprives them of authority, and turn instead to those [saints] whom the certitude of faith upholds. Surely the errors [told about] them are also endless! For some say that they have the relics of a certain saint, while others claim to have the same relics. Let us take the example of the head of John the Baptist: the people of Constantinople say that they possess it, but the monks of Angély claim to have the very same head.[49] What greater absurdity can be preached about this man than that he be said by two groups to have two heads? But let us be done with absurdities and attend to the matter at hand. Since it is certain that a head is not able to be duplicated, and thus that the two groups are unable to have [what they claim], it is obvious that one group or the other has resorted to lies. When two sides contend with each other arrogantly and falsely about a pious matter, they substitute a devilish behavior for a godly one. Thus both the deceivers and the deceived vainly venerate the very relic about which they boast. Behold how, when some unworthy object is venerated, the whole crowd of supporters is subjected to a long chain of false reasoning. And even if one head is not that of John the Baptist, but in fact that of some other saint, still the claims made about it are no less sinful lies.

Why am I going on about the head of John the Baptist, when each day I hear the same thing said about innumerable bodies of other saints? When my predecessor, the bishop of Amiens, transferred what he thought to be the body of St. Firminus the martyr from one casket to another, he failed to discover any document inside, not even a single letter of testimony as to who lay there.[50] I have heard this with my own ears from the bishop of Arras, and even from [his successor as] bishop of Amiens. For which reason the bishop forthwith had an inscription made on a leaden plate, which would lie in the reliquary: "This is Firminus the martyr, bishop of Amiens." Not long afterward, the incident was repeated in a similar manner at the monastery of Saint-Denis.[51] Relics were taken forth from their resting place in order to be placed in a more ornate shrine, which had been prepared by the abbot. When the skull was unwrapped along with the bones, a slip of parchment was found in the martyr's nostrils, on which it was written that *this* body was Firminus, the martyr of Amiens. Things are not as those from Amiens claimed them to be in this matter, for written testimonies give voice to a contrary claim and reason, if you please, takes the seat of judgment. Will not the inscription placed on that metal plate by the bishop be judged legally null and void? Does his claim become valid merely by being written down? Surely those from Saint-Denis would object, and they at least have [older] writings on their side. So we see that those people who venerate a patron saint about whom they are unsure are always in great danger, even if that patron turns out to be ancient. For if that patron is not a saint, they have committed an enormous sacrilege. What is a greater sacrilege than to venerate as holy something that is not? For only those things which pertain to God are divine. And what pertains to God more than those who are united in one body with God? I have heard [a story] which will throw light on our concerns and help us to make judgments about those matters we are discussing. A certain Odo—bishop of Bayeux, bastard son of Robert, count of the Normans, and thus the natural brother of William, the senior king of the English—ardently wished to possess [the relics] of his holy predecessor Exuperius, which were enshrined with great honor in the city of Corbeil.[52] He paid a hundred pounds to the guardian of the church in which the saint was enshrined in order that he might receive [relics of the] saint from him. The custodian, cunningly asking the bishop to wait for him, dug up the tomb of a certain peasant who was also named Exuperius. The bishop asked him whether what had been brought [to him] were [the relics of] St. Exuperius and even demanded an oath from the guardian. The guardian said, "I swear under oath to you that this is the body of Exuperius, but I can say nothing about his being a saint, since that title has been given to many people whose reputation is far from being saintly." Thus the bishop, deceived by the thief, did nothing. When the townspeople learned how he had turned their patron into merchandise, the guardian became the object of scorn. When pressed by them, he responded, "Go back and check the seals of the saint's tomb, and if you do not find them unbroken, I will pay recompense." Behold how this acquisition of false [relics] by the bishop brought dishonor on all religion, by profanely promoting this peasant Exuperius to sainthood and placing his bones on the sacred altar of God, which may never be rid of this blasphemy. My memory is full of many similar events done in every quarter, but I lack both the time and the strength to recount them. Fraudulent deals are frequently struck—not so much in the case of whole bodies, as in the case of limbs and parts of bodies—and common bones are thus distributed to be venerated as the relics of the saints. These things are clearly done by those who, according to the Apostle [1 Tim 6:5], *suppose gain to be godliness* and turn those very things which should serve for the salvation of their souls into the excrement of bags of money.

But all such practices stem from a perverse root, which is nothing other than that [the bodies of the saints] are deprived of that which all [who share in] human nature ought to accorded as a common lot. For if it is more certain than certainty itself that the origin of humanity comes from the earth and, because of original sin, [humanity] will according to the law return to that same earth when the penalty of death is paid, it is most certainly said to human beings: "You are dust, and to dust you shall return."[53] As far as I know, God has not said to anyone yet living or to come: "You are gold or silver, and to gold or silver you shall return." So why, I ask, should a human being be removed from the natural elements (still less by the order of God) and be enclosed in gold or silver cases, which are not required for purposes of preservation. If the wise man knew of receptacles other than the earth for human bodies, he would not say: [A] *heavy yoke is upon the sons of Adam, from the day they come forth from their mother's womb till the day they return to the mother of all* [Sir 40:1]. Note how elegantly it is said: "*their mother*" and "*the mother of all.*" If [the word] "mother" is said to me, it means she who has given a place in her womb and that is an immutable fact which cannot be changed. Consequently she is even more a mother who has given to mortals the very material of their existence, and she is clearly more than a mother, because she receives us again, a thing which is not permitted to [mortal] mothers for a second time. No matter what type of coffin you use to seek to ward off the touch of the earth, you will become earth, whether you wish it or not. And why should anyone be granted the dignity of being enclosed in gold or silver, when the Son of God is buried in the lowliest rock? From the earliest centuries not even the proudest of kings has attempted such a thing; not a single example comes to my mind. Even when they invested infinite amounts of treasure in their tombs, I do not remember having read that they exchanged pure marble for coffins of gold or silver. What sort of an attempt is it to emulate God—certainly not one according to reason!—when faith, bearing no true fruit but bringing forth much that is unseemly, produces in our age [a practice] which we are unable to find in any other religion, indeed in any display of wealth, in this world? Surely if the bodies of the saints remained in the places assigned them by nature—that is, in their graves—then errors of the sort I have encountered would not exist. But, as it is, these bodies are removed from their tombs, their limbs carried in every direction, and, under the pretext of piety, opportunities arise to display them. Such a degree of wickedness has entered this practice and the uprightness of its original intention has been so distorted, that a general avarice has corrupted [a practice] which had been begun in good faith. Such merit was ascribed to Tobias for his burial of the dead, that, among his many humanitarian undertakings, [this burial] was particularly praised by the testimony of [the archangel] Raphael and was said to be entirely pleasing in the sight of God [see Tob 12:12–13]. What impiety and guilt, then, must we think obtains to those who deprive bodies of their natural right and disturb them on some slight pretext?

And what reason, I would say, is not only more trivial, but more unbecoming, than that a disciple may be placed above his Master? Why should He be thrust into stone, when [His disciples] are encased in gold? Why should He be skimpily covered in a simple shroud, while they are wrapped all around in robes woven with silk and gold? According to the most illustrious Pope Gregory, those persons who unintentionally looked upon the bodies of the apostle Paul and the martyr Lawrence were very severely punished.[54] What judgment will be imposed on those whose only reason is avarice, [those] who cause the bodies of the saints to have no rest and to be scattered about, even, as I have said, having them displayed on a daily basis for the sole reason of obtaining offerings? For they are accustomed to cover the bare bones of the saints in boxes made of ivory and silver, and then, when requests flow in on them, they uncover [those bones] at certain times and places. Did not the ghost of Samuel—which as a ghost was animated with a natural ability to move—complain, when he was called forth, that he had been disturbed through necromancy [see 1 Sam 28: 3–19]?[55] Would not lifeless bones, if they were able, most justly complain when they suffer dispersion in every direction? Jacob and Joseph made arrangements for their burial [see Gen 50]: many saints prepared their own tombs and thus assumed the task of turning their bones back into the fruitful soil, not being buried in their own home, that is among the bones of their ancestors or among those with whom they had lived, as if they feared being damned. What else is taught by this, but that they considered it very important that their bodies should be in all ways unchanged for the glory of the resurrection? People—at least those acting in accordance with reason—do not hate their own flesh, but rather provide portions of food and drink according to their daily requirements. Even more so, in a matter in which luxury cannot outstrip necessity, as so often happens in the consumption of food, did not [the saints] strive in a most heartfelt manner to build up—insofar as is possible within the circuit of what the poet [Vergil] calls this "sad duty"—hope of a better life in a place where, free from the storms of this world and protected from the hurly-burly of the present life, they might await the voice of the archangel bidding them to rise?[56] As the apostle [Paul] calls people of this sort "sleepers" [see 1 Thes 4:13–15], I consider it wrong to disturb them, since in their rest, they expect no one to force them to wake except God, who makes the dead alive [see Rom 6:13]. Say what you might, I feel sure in stating clearly that it has never been pleasing, either to God or to the saints, that the tomb of any one of them should be unsealed or their bodies wantonly divided. Among the pagans, whose hope [of salvation] is surely buried along with the body, it is the custom to provide bearers and a pauper's grave even for those who entirely lack the resources to pay for undertakers and a funeral. Why should we then excavate the tombs and dismember the bodies of those who, according to many documents, have clearly shown their anger with such actions. When Augusta—whom, unless I am mistaken, was born to Tiberius—asked Gregory for the head of the apostle Paul, he replied that he would in no way dare to do such a thing, once the reports which I mentioned above had been brought to his attention.[57] Edmund was a king and martyr of no small renown among the English, whose zeal in the care of his body I wish other saints would imitate.[58] To this very day he remains in a sleeplike state and will not allow anyone to see or touch him. Although I will not mention those things which may be read in his *Passion*, [I will tell how] in our own time an abbot of [Bury Saint-Edmunds], being more than a little curious, wondered whether the saint's head, which had once been cut off, was now reunited to the body, as popular opinion held. After having undertaken a fast with one of his monks, he tried, with that monk's help, to separate the neck [of the saint] from the shoulders. But he was instantly punished for his attempt with so great an infirmity that no movement remained in either of his hands. If [the saints] were allowed to rest in their graves, without any exchanges or transactions over their bodies and relics, then all dispute would cease. If the tombs of all the saints remained untouched, as is just, then one group of people would not be able to say that they had a certain relic which another group also claimed to possess. If all the saints were to rest unmoving in the earth to which they had been consigned, then frauds such as we have reported above concerning the distribution of their broken parts could not take place and unworthy people would not be held in high regard [as saints].

A question might also be posed by some people concerning relics: when they are honored as belonging to one saint but are those of another, and are not what they are thought to be, will something disastrous happen to the people who venerate [those relics], as is often thought. I do not agree. For our Lord says of the saints, *That they may be one, even as we are one* [Jn 17:22]. Their union under Christ as Head provides them, as it were, an identity of body and they join together to be one in spirit with God. Among the bones of those who truly are saints, there is no error if the bones of some saints are honored as being the bones of others who are recognized as their fellow members in the body of their Creator. According to this opinion, it does not seem to be problematic that the festival of the Four Crowned Martyrs is observed through the authority of Rome under the names of five other martyrs.[59]

But, given this, someone will doubtless ask whether God hears those simple folk when He is invoked by them through [the intercession of] those who do not number among the saints. One would answer that, although a person might annoy God when praying to Him through [a saint] of uncertain status, nevertheless when a person prays faithfully believing someone who is not [a saint] to be [a saint], then that person still pleases God. For the sake of argument, let us suppose that there is a person who thinks that giving alms is a sin. If that person were knowingly to give alms, and that person were to have done this deed with full attention to conscience, then that person would sin, even though for anyone else to act in this manner would be a good deed. Let us then take the case of people who value as a saint someone whom they have heard called a saint, but who is not truly numbered among the saints. If such people were to ask the aid of the [false] saint wholeheartedly and in accord with the faith, and if the entire intention of their prayer were to be fixed upon God, who is both the seed and the fruit of prayer, then—no matter the manner in which the soul may seem to have erred through simplicity concerning the choice of intercessor—their prayer would be honored [by God], for what is done with good intentions is never denied a good reward. If you receive a prophet in the name of a prophet, that is one who has only the name of a just man and prophet with none of the reality, then you share in the full merit of the prophet and just man, although the person who only has the name of just man and prophet, and who merely pretends [to possess] their habits, is himself left bereft [of any merit]. Surely many barely literate persons are frequently mistaken in their prayers, but the divine ear judges intentions rather than words. For if when you pray "Lord may the power of the Holy Spirit be with us," you were to say *absit* [be away from us] rather than *assit* [be with us], yet do so earnestly, it would not harm you.[60] God is not overly attentive to grammar. No voice comes to Him, that His heart does not embrace.

NOTES

1. This phrase is the opening invocation of the prefatory epistle, which was likely added to the treatise following the composition of all four books. Guibert was abbot of the monastery of Sainte-Marie in Nogent, that is, of a community dedicated to the Blessed Virgin. He here dedicated his treatise to Abbot Odo (d. post 1125) of the monastery of Saint-Symphorien in Beauvais, a town located about eighty-five kilometers west of Nogent.

2. Martyrdom was considered to be a form of baptism by blood.

3. Guibert momentarily loses the thread of his argument, referring here specifically to hermits, not martyrs.

4. This sentence employs a play on words: the similarity in meaning (not sound, as is moderately the case in my rendering of the phrase as a pun in English) of "sanctioning" (*ut ita dicam*) and "being considered a saint" (*sancitur*).

5. Guibert is here paraphrasing the Roman poet Horace (65–8 B. C. E.), *Ars Poetica* [The Poetic Art], 28: "We poets are too often tricked into trying to achieve / A particular kind of perfection: I studiously try / To be brief, and become obscure; I try to be smooth, / And my vigor and force disappear; another assures us / Of something big which turns out to be merely pompous. Another one crawls on the ground because he's too safe, / Too much afraid of the storm" (*Satires and Epistles of Horace*, trans. Smith Bovie [Chicago, 1959], p. 272.).

6. For a complete list of the places in which Augustine of Hippo (354–430), one of the most influential Christian theologians of the late Roman empire, criticized the *Acts of Thomas*, consult the notes in Huygens's edition (*De pigneribus*, p. 87).

7. Guibert here repeats a metaphor he had used earlier in this work, a metaphor which I have had to expand greatly in translation. He is comparing the canonical *Acts of the Apostles* (that is a work which orthodox Christians had traditionally accepted as part of the divinely inspired New Testament) to the apocryphal *Acts of Thomas* (that is a work which had been long rejected from the canon of the New Testament as not being of divine inspiration).

8. Guibert here refers to two separate categories of sanctity. A martyr was considered to be a saint for having died as a witness to the Christian faith, while a confessor was considered to be a saint for having taught the faith while living.

9. Piro was an abbot of a Welsh monastery whose death in a drunken stupor was recorded in the life of St. Samson (d. 565), bishop of Dol in Brittany. For the specifics of the hagiographic traditions surrounding Piro and Samson, see Julia Smith, "Oral and Written: Saints, Miracles, and Relics in Brittany, c. 850–1250," *Speculum* 65 (1990): 309.

10. Guibert here refers to a conversation between Lanfranc and Anselm (each of whom served first as abbot of the monastery of Bec in Normandy and then as archbishop of Canterbury in England) which was recorded by Eadmer, the latter's biographer. Lanfranc happened to question whether an Anglo-Saxon archbishop of Canterbury named Ælfheah was actually a martyr, as the man had died, not for confessing the name of Christ, but for refusing to pay ransom. Anselm defended Ælfheah's sanctity. For a full record of the conversation, see Eadmer of Canterbury, *Vita s. Anselmi*, ed. R.W. Southern (London, 1962), bk. 1, chap. 30, pp. 50–54. Guibert had himself been a student of Anselm of Canterbury, and thus probably knew of the conversation through the same oral tradition on which Eadmer relied, rather than through the writings of Eadmer.

11 Pamphylia was located on the coast of Asia Minor, in modern Turkey. A story of miraculous assistance granted to the army of Alexander the Great (356–323 B. C. E.) in the passing of a bay was included in medieval versions of the Alexander legend. See for example, *Leben und Taten Alexanders von Makedonien. Der griechische Alexanderroman nach der Handschrift L*, ed. Helmut van Thiel (Darmstadt, 1983), p. 40.

12. Emperor Vespasian ruled the Roman Empire for a decade, from 69 until 79. According to the Roman historian Suetonius (d. post 122), "[T]he god Serapis had promised them in a dream that if Vespasian would consent to spit in the blind man's eyes, and touch the lame man's leg with his heel, both would be made well." Suetonius, *The Twelve Caesars*, trans. Robert Graves (Harmondsworth, 1958), bk. 10, chap. 7, p. 279

13. Julius Caesar (100–44 B. C. E) and Octavian (63 B. C. E – 14 C. E.), better known as Augustus, were both rulers of the city of Rome and the empire which it had created.

14 Emperors Charles the Great (better known as Charlemagne) and Louis the Pious were both members of the Carolingian royal dynasty, who ruled the kingdoms of the Franks (and their subsequent empire), respectively from 768 until 814 and from 814 until 840. According to Einhard, *Life of Charlemagne*, Chapter 32 in *Two Lives of Charlemagne*, ed. and trans. Lewis Thorpe (Harmondsworth, 1969), p. 84, "Many portents marked the approach of Charlemagne's death, so that not only other people but he himself could know that it was near. In all three of the last years of his life there occurred repeatedly eclipses of both the sun and moon; and a black-coloured spot was to be seen on the sun for seven days . . ." Just before the death of Louis the Pious in 840, according to the *Annals of Saint-Berlin*, trans. Janet Nelson (Manchester, 1991), ". . . an eclipse of the sun was seen by a lot of people in many different places. The emperor, on his way back from pursuing his son, was stricken by illness."

15. Scrofula is a condition caused by a swelling of the lymph nodes due to chronic tuberculosis. This passage is the earliest certain attestation to a belief, later common, that a person suffering from scrofula could be cured by the touch of a monarch. Guibert is discussing Kings Philip I and Louis VI (also known as "the Fat") of France, a father and son who reigned respectively from 1060 until 1108 and from 1108 until 1137. On this passage, and more generally on the royal cure of scrofula, see Marc Bloch, *The Royal Touch: Monarchy and Miracles in France and England*, trans. J.E. Anderson (French original, Strasbourg, 1924; New York, 1961), pp. 12–14.

16. The "royal touch" was at a later time attributed to English kings as well, see Bloch, *The Royal Touch*, pp. 51–56.

17. This is the first of three different groups of people through whom "the gift of miracles is distributed," each of which will be discussed in turn by Guibert and illustrated by exemplary stories.

18. Guibert's point is that the voices heard by onlookers through Balaam's ass, through Caiaphas the high priest, or through any angel (whose very title means messenger), have a divine origin which lies outside the apparent mouthpiece.

19. The town of Soissons is located about twenty kilometers south of Nogent.

20. The Holy Innocents were the infants slaughtered by Herod in his attempt to kill the infant Jesus, see Mt 2:16.

21. The town of Saint-Quentin is located about forty kilometers north of Nogent. It was named after St. Quintinus, a martyr of the third century, whose relics were enshrined in its main church.

22. Raoul le Verd served as archbishop from 1108 until 1124. The archdiocese of Reims (located about sixty-five kilometers southeast of Nogent) encompassed the towns of Saint-Quentin, Soissons, and Laon (located about twenty kilometers northeast of Nogent), as well as the abbey of Nogent.

23. Guibert here freely paraphrases the Roman philosopher Seneca ("the Younger," ca. 4 B. C. E. – 65 C. E.), *De beneficiis*, bk. 3, chap. 15, sec. 4. Seneca, himself a polytheist, referred to "the gods" in the original text.

24. This is the second group through whom "the gift of miracles is distributed."

25. The town of Cambrai is located about seventy-five kilometers north of Nogent.

26. The explicit implication of the words placed here in the mouth of the boy (*uteris gravitudinis*), as well as the implicit implication of the phrase used above by Guibert to describe their fears (*infamiam suorum oculosque vereri*), is that the girl has become pregnant.

27. According to Greek legend, Sardanapallus was the last king of Assyria, who burned himself and his wives alive in their palace in order to prevent invading troops from capturing his wealth.

28. Guibert plays on the symbolism of Christ's stay in the desert (or the liturgical season of Lent which commemorated that exile), a period of forty days.

29. Pegasus was the winged horse which, according to Greek legend, sprang from the blood of Medusa.

30. Guibert here provides eloquent testimony to the power of gossip or rumor (that is, *fama*) in medieval society. There is also a rich ambiguity to his words, for *virtus* was often used to mean "miracle" as well as "virtue." There is no mention at the conclusion of the story of the girl's pregnancy, which had presumably terminated as a result of the physical deprivation she had suffered.

31. Rahab, although mentioned by Paul in this passage, was not a patriarch at all, but a prostitute of Jericho who hid the spies of Joshua in her house and was thus spared when the Israelites captured the city [see Josh 2:1–11, 6:17–25]. Jephthah was the leader of Gilead who was forced to fulfill an ambiguous vow made in war by executing his only child [see Judg 11:32–40]. Guibert's implication by coupling these two would seem to be that faith in God must transcend human bonds to city, tribe, and family; thus the reference he makes to the *obscuriores causae* which moved Rahab and Jepthah.

32. This is the third group of those through whom "the gift of miracles is distributed."

33. The dean of a cathedral was the chief assistant to the bishop. The custodian, or sexton, of the cathedral's building was another important office.

34. Bourbourg was a female monastic community in the diocese of Saint-Omer, located near the coast, almost one hundred kilometers northwest of Cambrai and over one hundred and fifty kilometers from Nogent.

35. Barthélemy de Joux (or de Jur) was elected bishop in 1112, following the disasterous events of the revolt of the Laon commune. A relative of St. Bernard of Clairvaux, he died well after Guibert in 1158.

36. Presumably Abbot Odo, to whom this treatise was addressed, would have understood Guibert's elliptical reference, for Odo's community of Saint-Symphorien was located in Beauvais.

37. Guibert is here referring to two passages from the *Letters* of the renowned Christian theologian Jerome (ca. 347–419). Huygens provides full details of the sources in the notes to his edition (*De pigneribus*, pp. 97–98). Even more importantly, Huygens notes how this passage betrays the pretension and fallibility of Guibert's classical learning. The phrase I have rendered as "gluttons and jesters" has, in fact, three elements in the original: *scurras, elluones et catellanos*. The third word in the phrase was a corruption of a personal name (*Attelanus*) introduced into the text of Jerome through scribal error and was essentially a nonsense word. Guibert included it, apparently thinking it a word known to Jerome whose meaning had been lost. I have simply omitted it from the translation.

38. The cathedral of Laon had suffered a disastrous fire in April of 1112 during the revolt of the Laon Commune, which was described in detail by Guibert in his *Monodiae* or *Memoirs*.

39. Boethius, *Contra Eutychen*, preface, lines 30–31 in *Tractates*, ed. and trans. H.F. Stewart, E.K. Rand, and S.J. Tester (Cambridge, MA, 1918), p. 75.

40. On the definition of martyrs and confessors, see note 8 above.

41. Guibert refers to a canon promulgated by the Council of Elvira (ca. 300).

42. Donatists were members of a separatist group among North African Christians during the later third and fourth centuries. Although they were considered heretics by contemporary members of the orthodox or Catholic Church, many were executed for their Christian beliefs by Roman imperial authorities. The Catholic Church did not accept these Donatists as true martyrs.

43. Guibert also discussed the heretics of Soissons in his *Monodiae* or *Memoirs*, Book 3, Chapter 17. For an English translation, see *A Monk's Confession: The Memoirs of Guibert of Nogent*, ed. and trans. Paul Archambault (State College, PA, 1996), pp. 195–98.

44. Martin of Tours (d. 397) and Remigius of Reims (d. 533) were the objects of two of the most traditionally important saints' cults in the French kingdom, both closely associated with royal patronage. Guibert is consciously choosing examples which no cleric would contest.

45. A quotation from Horace, *Epistola*, 2.1, line 117 (translation as in *Satires and Epistles of Horace*, p. 253 [see note 5 above]).

46. Pope Gregory I, the Great (ca. 540–604) was an important Christian theologian. The translation is from Gregory the Great, *Pastoral Care*, trans. Henry Davis, Ancient Christian Writers 11 (New York, 1950), bk. 1, chap. 10, p. 39.

47. Ambrose of Milan (ca. 339–97) was an important Christian theologian who also served as bishop of Milan. The quotation citation is of his *De officiis clericorum* [On the Duties of the Clergy], 2. 12. 62 as translated in Ambrose, *Selected Works and Letters*, trans. H. de Romestin, et al., A Select Library of Nicene and Post-Nicene Fathers of the Christian Church, second series 10 (New York, 1896), p. 53.

48. In this paragraph, Guibert discusses the doctrine of the Assumption of the Virgin Mary, which was being vigorously debated by theologians of the twelfth century. Guibert was clearly a partisan of the doctrine, which claimed that the body of the Virgin Mary had been physically taken whole into Heaven following her death. It was not accepted as dogma, that is as certain teaching, within the Catholic Church until the twentieth century.

49. Guibert made a similar criticism of the varied cults of the head of John the Baptist in his history of the First Crusade, see *The Deeds of God through the Franks: A Translation of Guibert de Nogent's Gesta Dei per Francos*, trans. Robert Levine (Woodbridge, Suffolk, 1997), pp. 37–38.

50. Bishop Godfrey of Amiens (d. 1115) had formerly been Guibert's predecessor as abbot of Nogent. According to tradition, St. Firminus was a bishop of Amiens who died during a Roman persecution in the early fourth century.

51. Saint-Denis was an important monastery located near Paris and closely associated with the royal family.

52. Guibert here refers in very unflattering terms to some of the most important members of the ducal house of Normandy, who successfully led the conquest of England: Bishop Odo of Bayeux (d. 1097); Robert I, who served as duke of Normandy from 1027 until his death in 1035; William I, better known as "the Bastard" or "the Conqueror," who served as duke of Normandy from 1035 until his death in 1087, and as king of England from the time of his victory at Hastings in 1066. Robert fathered William by his concubine Herleva, who was then married, after William's birth, to Herluin de Conteville, by whom she had two sons, Bishop Odo and Count Robert of Mortain. Thus while Odo was William's natural brother, the relationship was through their mother, not (as suggested by Guibert) their father. According to tradition, St. Exuperius had been bishop of Rouen in the fourth century.

53. This was a liturgical formula commonly used in burial rituals, which was derived from Gen 3:19.

54. Guibert refers, both here and below, to a letter written by Pope Gregory the Great (see note 46 above) answering a request by the Empress Constantina to send her the relic of the head of the apostle Paul for a new chapel being built in her palace in Constantinople. Constantina was the daughter of Emperor Tiberius II (d. 582) and the wife of Emperor Maurice (582–602), both rulers of the eastern Roman, or Byzantine, empire. Gregory

denied the empress's request, sending instead a relic of the chains of St. Peter. Throughout the letter, Gregory expressed his respect for the innate power of relics. He wrote in part, "[W]hen my predecessor, of blessed memory, was desirous of changing the silver which was over the most sacred body of the blessed apostle Peter, though at a distance of almost fifteen feet from the same body, a sign of no small dreadfulness appeared to him. Nay, I too wished in like manner to amend something not far from the most sacred body of St. Paul the apostle; and, it being necessary to dig to some depth near his sepulchre, the superintendent of that place found some bones, which were not indeed connected with the same sepulchre; but, inasmuch as he presumed to lift them and transfer them to another place, certain awful signs appeared, and he died suddenly. Besides all this, when my predecessor, of holy memory was desiring in like manner to make some improvements not far from the body of St. Lawrence the martyr, it not being known where the venerable body was laid, diggings were made in the course of search, and suddenly his sepulchre was unawares disclosed; and those who were present and . . . who saw the body of the same martyr, which they did not indeed presume to touch, all died within ten days." Gregory the Great, *Registrum epistolarum* [The register of letters], bk. 4, no. 30 as translated in *The Book of Pastoral Rule and Selected Epistles of Gregory the Great, Bishop of Rome*, trans. James Barmby, A Select Library of Nicene and Post-Nicene Fathers of the Christian Church, second series 12 (New York, 1895), pp. 154–6.

55. According to a well-known story from the Hebrew Scriptures, King Saul of Israel (ca. 1000 B. C. E. used the help of a necromancer (famously remembered as the "Witch of Endor") to summon the ghost of his predecessor, King Samuel, to provide him counsel during a war between the Israelites and the Philistines.

56. The allusion is to the description of the burial of Misenus, a companion of Aeneas, in Vergil, *Aeneid*, trans. Robert Fitzgerald (New York, 1981), bk. 6, 223, p. 167: "Bearers then took up / As their sad duty the great bier."

57. The woman whom Guibert refers to as Augusta was Empress Constantina. Guibert confuses her title with her proper name. On the letter of Gregory the Great to Constantina, see above note 54.

58 Guibert tells this same story about the relics of Edmund in almost identical terms in his *Monodiae* or *Memoirs*, Book 3, Chapter 20. For an English translation, see *A Monk's Confession* (see note 43 above), p. 209. King Edmund, who ruled the Anglo-Saxon kingdom of East Anglia, had been murdered by Danish raiders who attacked his realm in 869. Because Edmund died defending his Christian kingdom against pagan conquerors, he was regarded as a saintly martyr. The *Passion* to which Guibert refers is probably that by Abbot Abbo of Fleury (d. 1004), *The Passion of St. Edmund* (*Bibliotheca hagiographica latina*, no. 2392), which the French monk composed while visiting England in the 980s allegedly on the basis of the transmitted oral tradition of eyewitnesses. For an English translation of this work, see *Corolla Sancti Eadmundi. The Garland of St. Edmund, King and Martyr*, ed. and trans. Francis Hervey (London, 1907), pp. 8–59. According to a tradition attested by Abbo, Edmund's head had been severed from his body during the course of his execution, but the two parts of the corpse had been later miraculously reunited. The intact body was then buried at the church known as *Beadericesworth* in East Anglia, which later became the monastery of Bury Saint Edmund's. The examination of the relics by the abbot of that monastery, to which Guibert refers here, apparently occurred in the eleventh century. On the development of the cult of Edmund, see Antonia Grandsen, "The Legends and Traditions Concerning the Origins of the Abbey of Bury St. Edmund's," *English Historical Review* 100 (1985): 1–24.

59. A church dedicated to the Quattro Coronati, or "Four Crowned Martyrs," had existed on the Caelian Hill in Rome from at least the fifth century. Pope Paschal II (d. 1118), with whom Guibert had an audience in 1107, rebuilt that church into one of the most impressive in Rome. The four martyrs in question were Roman soldiers who had suffered execution (probably in 306) in the Roman province of Pannonia (modern Hungary) for refusing to worship a statue of a pagan deity. Their legend and their feast day had become confused with the group of five sculptors who had been executed for earlier refusing to make the statue in question, which had been finished by other hands. Unfortunately no concise discussion of this enormously complex tradition exists in English, but see the

excellent summary by Jacques Dubois in *Vies des saints et des bienheureux par les reverends pères bénédictins de Paris*, 13 vols. (Paris, 1935–59), 11:249–68.

60. Guibert here cites a section of the preparatory prayers from the Mass of the Roman rite current in his time. The prayer would have been recognizable to Guibert's literate clerical audience as one recited (and often incorrectly recited) on a widespread daily basis by illiterate laypeople throughout Western Christendom. In emphasizing that prayers are efficacious because of good intention and not betrayed by bad grammar, Guibert is following a long tradition which dates back to at least Augustine of Hippo. Pope Zacharias (d. 752), for example, had written to St. Boniface that a baptism was valid even if a priest incorrectly recited—in the place of the liturgical formula *in nomine patris et filii et spiritus sancti* ["in the name of the Father, and of the Son, and of the Holy Spirit"]—*in nomine patria et filia et spiritus sancti* ["in the name of the fatherland, and of the daughter, and of the Holy Spirit"].

CHAPTER 20
A Tale of Doomsday Colum Cille Should Have Left Untold

Translated by Paul Grosjean and edited by Dorothy Africa

INTRODUCTION

When the Bollandist Paul Grosjean, S J. published his edition and translation of this Old Irish text in 1929, he intimated his own unease about the tale when he characterized it in his introduction as "scurrilous and profane" to the contemporary mind. The brevity of his introduction provides a further indication of his reserve. In it he gave only the relevant particulars of his manuscript source, the mid-fifteenth century manuscript in the collection of the Royal Irish Academy known as the *Liber Flavus Fergusiorum;* a tentative dating to the eleventh or twelfth century of its base text (which is no longer extant); and the customary acknowledgment of the assistance of others. Father Grosjean was certainly accustomed to the heroic style of medieval vernacular Irish literature, and the degree to which it marked Irish hagiography in both Latin and Irish. One might hazard the guess, therefore, that it was not the heroic narrative style of the piece that disconcerted this learned Bollandist, or even the pride evinced in its portrayal of St. Patrick, but rather its presentation of saints and godhead as collegial adversaries.

Since Grosjean's time, much work in many areas of Celtic studies has been done, and readers of this text can draw upon assistance not available to the scholars of his day. In particular, recent work in the areas of early Irish law and ecclesiastical history can provide plausible contexts for some of the features which so affronted Grosjean. From this new perspective it would appear that the defining structures of this story are not theological, but legal. Using traditions about divine promises made to St. Patrick in exchange for undertaking the conversion of the Irish, the story appears to model this confrontation between Patrick and God along the lines of a contract dispute in Irish law. Its author, or redactor, dramatizes the positions of the opposing sides, but ends the tale abruptly with no hint of its outcome. As such, the story is loosely comparable to the *quod libets* ("what you please") of the medieval university, academic exercises which posed questions on legal, theological, or philosophical issues for debate in similar sorts of fanciful, and often impudent, terms. Whether the author of this Irish tale deliberately framed it to set up a debate or intended it more simply to be provocative, cannot be ascertained. The *Liber Flavus Fergusiorum* is a miscellany of tales sacred and profane, apparently drawn from a variety of sources. The manuscript contains scant information on these sources or the original contexts of its stories.

Since Grosjean's original publication of this story, scholars have also become more appreciative of the sophistication of Irish texts. The archconservativism of Irish literary culture in its forms and conventions is easily mistaken, on the literal level, as a naive primitivism. A deeper understanding of the culture evinced in more recent scholarship has moved the focus of research away from questions of survivals of archaic Indo-European features and toward the analysis of texts for more contemporary motivations. Irish learned culture was extremely conservative in its models, and commonly used revered figures and events from the past, both historical and mythical, to comment upon persons and events of the present. This veneer of antiquity often led scholars of the nineteenth century to assign to Irish texts dates of composition a century or so earlier than a modern scholar might date the same pieces. Modern scholars also allow for considerable alteration to such texts during the course of transmission, whether in copying from manuscript to manuscript, of transcription of an oral text into writing, or of translation from Old Irish into Latin.

Although the Irish learned class was accustomed to thinking of literature as multiform and often mutable, it sought for an ultimate unity. Throughout the medieval period, the learned Irish labored to produce a Christian culture that was yet consonant with their own learned traditions and social requirements. This story of Doomsday (that is, the day of judgment) is a good illustration of how difficult it can be to identify and date the various elements of a medieval Irish text. It is a prime example of the use of figures from Ireland's early Christian past to vivify questions of its creator's present. That "present" may well have been the first half of the twelfth century, and its anonymous author may have been speaking to the issues raised by the administrative reform movement of the Irish Church in that period. In all likelihood he was himself a churchman, and was therefore keenly aware of the political ramifications of the changes the reform movement both reflected and initiated.

The progress of this reform movement was the subject of intense study by the late Aubrey Gwynn, S.J., who analyzed and documented the earlier contacts between prominent Irish notables, lay and ecclesiastic, and churchmen in England and on the continent. By the end of the eleventh century, the Norse towns along the southeastern Irish coast—Dublin, Waterbury, and Wexford—had formed close ties to the Church in England. To the north, Armagh, the prestigious seat of the cult of St. Patrick, had formed an alliance with the Cistercian order through the personal friendship of its abbot, St. Malachy, with St. Bernard of Clairvaux during the early years of the twelfth century. (It was Bernard himself who would record Malachy's *Life* in a moving piece of hagiography.) At the same time, Ireland had renewed its ties with Rome through the visits of papal legates and the appointment of Irish ecclesiastics to serve as papal representatives in Ireland.

Leading Irish reformers, as Gwynn argued, were determined to bring the Irish Church into conformity with the governing structures of the Continental and English Church, but equally intent on preserving their own authority in Ireland. This story of Doomsday, with its careful assembly of the Irish under the leadership of their saints, certainly conforms to such a view of the ecclesiastic unity of the Irish. The union of culture and religion contrasts strongly with the political divisions that characterized Ireland throughout the medieval period. In trying to create a single ecclesiastical hierarchy for Ireland, the Irish reformers had to deal with the warring secular rulers around them and the inevitable disputes within their own ranks regional conflicts engendered.

The author of the tale had a rich store of material about Patrick and the early Irish saints more generally upon which to draw. The notion that Patrick had made a pact with for favorable treatment of the Irish in exchange for his services as a missionary is present in the earliest surviving Patrician hagiography, but most powerfully presented in the *Vita Tripartita* [known in English as the *Tripartite Life*]. Indeed, this text provides two stages to this pact. The first stage enumerates Patrick's three requests of God when the deity appears to him on Mount Hermon and asks him to undertake the conversion of the Irish: to sit at God's right hand in heaven, to judge the Irish on Doomsday, and to receive as much gold and silver as his nine companions could carry to give to the Irish for their faith. Later in the same text Patrick fasts on Croagh Patrick, apparently to win confirmation of these same conditions. In this second stage an angel acts as an intermediary between Patrick and God during protracted negotiations back and forth. At last the angel reports that the denizens of heaven, visible and invisible, have taken Patrick's side and prevailed upon God to give Patrick what he asks. The angel assures him that when Patrick strikes his bell (presumably on judgment day) heaven will accord him the means to consecrate all the Irish, both living and dead (*cosecrad* [*dferaib*] *dolucht inna hÉirend huli iter biú ocus marbu*). While the Doomsday story draws upon both these passages, the second provides the strongest support for its portrayal of the confrontation between the two contractual parties in the moment of truth.

The creator of the story also drew upon Christian tradition and some specific biblical passages. The closest biblical parallel to the negotiations between Patrick and Jesus can be found in Gen 18: 23–32, in which Abraham argues with God over the destruction of Sodom and Gomorrah. However, the cautious and deferential manner adopted by Abraham is in marked contrast to the stance of Patrick in the Irish story. The reference to twelve camels loaded with gold and silver may be also a biblical allusion, most probably to the arrival of the Queen of Sheba in the court of King Solomon with camels loaded with spices, gold, and precious stones (1 Kings 10:2; 2 Chron 9:1). Its more immediate antecedents, though, are the *Vita Tripartita,* and perhaps some references made by the historical St. Patrick in his surviving writings to the heavy expenditures required of him by his mission.

Two mountains of biblical significance are named in the Irish story, Mount Zion and the Mount of Olives just east of Jerusalem. The latter was associated with the ascension of Jesus (Lk 24:50) and is therefore an obvious place for our author to select for the departure point of St. Patrick and his Irish entourage. This is especially necessary in this tale which deliberately and carefully cultivates the notion, taken from the *Vita Tripartita,* that Patrick as redeemer of the Irish is a doppelgänger, of sorts, to Jesus as the redeemer of humankind. This parity has to be established for two reasons, to underscore Patrick's stature as an apostle, and to give him legal credibility in his dispute with God and Jesus about the contract between them.

In Irish law contractual obligations had a wide scope, extending even to some kinds of gifts and agreements. Irish law required some sort of public pledge between contracting parties of the terms of the agreement, and the naming of sureties, persons of good repute and property, who formally undertook varying degrees of responsibility to see that the terms agreed upon were honored. Generally speaking, the greater the disparity in rank between the two contracting parties, the greater the need for sureties to enforce compliance. Between two persons of suitably high rank, sureties were less important, and might not be needed at all. It is difficult to tell how literally this Irish tale parallels an actual legal procedure, for we have no record of how medieval Irish contract disputes were arbitrated.

There is, however, a surviving treatise (*Di Astud Chor*) on the principles of contract law, several of which could be relevant to the situation outlined in the tale. Of particular interest is the role of the *déorad Dé*, the hermit of God, when a contract has been made in the name of the men of heaven and the Gospel. In such a contract, the *déorad Dé* acts as an enforcing surety. The term *déorad* is itself a legal term for a person outside society, such as a stranger, foreigner, mercenary, or exile. Since persons entering the Church left secular society, the legal status of the *déorad* was easily applied to them. Prominent Irish ecclesiastics, however, such as the founders of the great monasteries, or the later twelfth-century reformers, could not hope to escape constant secular involvement in the course of their administrative duties. The marginal status of the *déorad* was an ideal, not a daily reality. The Irish annals contain numerous obituaries for ecclesiastics renowned for both religious learning and their proficiency in the secular fields of law, poetry, and history: skills necessary for maintaining their status and their communities within medieval Irish culture.

Another principle key to the Doomsday story is the Irish legal concept of *saíthiud*. There is no equivalent legal term in English; but it makes the crucial distinction, in Irish law, between a contract that is fraudulent and one that is unfair. A fraudulent contract can be repudiated by the injured party because crucial information was withheld or deliberately misrepresented to him when the contract was agreed upon. Irish law, however, held every competent adult responsible for his (or her) own *saíthiud*: disadvantageous commitments made in full possession of the facts. In Irish law, then, contractual obligations cannot be set aside purely on the grounds that they are injurious, disproportionate, or unfair if the aggrieved party was fully aware of the terms when the agreement was made.

In the present instance, the legal notion of *saíthiud* could be used to argue that God should have foreseen a possible disagreement over how Patrick exercised the power granted to him, and could not, therefore, repudiate his contractual agreement when Patrick rendered his judgement. This is especially so since Patrick, in successfully undertaking his part of the bargain to go to Ireland and convert the Irish, has satisfied his contractual obligations. Against this argument from Irish law can be posited Christian theological arguments that as a Christian Patrick was bound in his judgment to honor Christian principles, and that not to do so was fraudulent. In the tale Patrick counters the challenge that he has brought the wicked with him by asserting that they have done penance. The statement introduces yet another contentious topic, the efficacy of acts of penance and the expiation of sin.

The legal dimension gives the Doomsday story the twist that makes it so distinctively an Irish Christian puzzle. It pits the theological requirements of salvation for the good against the Irish legal conception of *saíthiud*, the validity of the injurious contractual promise. Indeed, one can imagine a discussion among Irish clerics well versed in Christian theology and Irish law on the precise definition of the *saíthiud* of an omniscient God lasting quite some time. It is particularly characteristic of medieval Irish Christian culture that, while it acknowledged a cosmic hierarchy, it envisioned a whole system, not one in which divine law simply overrode the human one.

Aside from the philosophical and legal debates offered by the story, the depiction it gives of the negotiations of the saints seems to reflect some of the political contemporary developments associated with the twelfth-century reform movement within the Irish Church. The tale gives an impression of "national" peace, uniting all the Irish under their saints. In fact there was no politically unified Irish nation in the twelfth century, and the saints named in the text are primarily connected with the region of Leinster. Those named as leading the Irish of Connacht and Munster are all saints associated with foundations on the western and southern border areas of Leinster.

Standing alongside this provincial preference in the text is the administrative structure of the Irish Church as organized by the twelfth-century reform movement in the councils of Cashel (1101) and Rath Breasail (1111). This scheme used the classic model of ancient Ireland which divided the island into northern and southern regions. The northern area of Ulster, Connacht, and Meath was headed by Armagh, which claimed primacy over all Ireland as the principal foundation of St. Patrick. The southern region of Munster and Leinster was under the aegis of Cashel, but the patron of Munster and of the southern region as a whole, remained St. Ailbe of Emly in order to give the southern region a patron of equal antiquity. This scheme was replaced with a more politically realistic division of Ireland into four provinces by the Council of Kells in 1152. It is likely, therefore, that this Doomsday tale dates to the interim period between 1111 and 1152.

As noted before, the saints prominent in the rally of the Irish in the Doomsday tale are the famous sixth-century founding saints of Leinster, but the hierarchy in the tale reflects early twelfth-century administrative divisions. Patrick leads, accompanied by Sts. Peter and Paul, whose relics were in the possession of Armagh cathedral. He is also accompanied by St. Martin of Tours who was greatly revered in the early medieval Church generally. In Ireland Martin was believed to be St. Patrick's maternal uncle. Aside from the Christian significance of the relationship, the maternal uncle was also of considerable importance in Irish society, especially in legal affairs. The southern contingent is lead by Ailbe of Emly, Ruadhán of Lorrha, and Brénainn of Birr, these last two being founders of communities on the northern edge of Munster bordering west Leinster. When the formal embassy goes from the Irish to greet Christ on Mount Zion, however, it is Ailbe who leads it "with seven bishops about him," an apparent reference to the division of Munster into seven dioceses devised at the Council of Rath Bresail.

The series of delegations Patrick sends out in this tale can be variously interpreted. Though each of the saints in the story has a personal significance in Irish hagiography, the tale itself gives no explication of the successive delegations sent by Patrick. It would appear, however, that each delegation represents a higher level of expertise and therefore importance. In that case, the author's or redactor's selection of the saints in these delegations becomes politically significant. After the first delegation led by St. Ailbe, Patrick sends a second composed of Ciarán of Clonmacnois, Cainnech of Kilkenny, and Colum Cille of Iona and Kells.

While Colum Cille and Ciáran are saints of considerable stature in Irish hagiography, it is clearly Cainnech who is the prominent member of the trio here. Cainnech, however, is not especially prominent in Irish hagiography, and the particular favor he is shown by Christ in this story may be due to the status given to his community at Kilkenny by the Council of Rath Breasail as one of the five bishoprics of Leinster. Some of the more prestigious communities may have regarded Kilkenny as somewhat undeserving of such an honor. If this tale intended to support the elevation of Kilkenny, that would explain the remarks made by Christ to the other saints concerning his welcome to Cainnech and his "little patch of desert ground."

A similar influence of twelfth-century ecclesiastical politics may also account for the decisive role St. Munnu mac Tulchain has in this tale as a member of the third delegation from Patrick to Christ. In Irish hagiography Munnu was famous for his school and his quick temper, but the significance of the saint in this tale may be the location of his community in what is now southern County Waterford. The port of Waterford was an Hiberno-Norse community, and as such its church was largely in the shadow of Lismore, a far more ancient native Irish foundation. The omission of Lismore's founder, St.

Mochuda, from the roster of saints in this tale may be a deliberate attempt to avoid exacerbating mistrust between Waterford and Lismore. At the Council of Rath Breasail the two were combined into the diocese of Lismore or Port Láirge (Waterford), an uneasy union which seems to have been successful only during the tenure of Bishop Maél Isu Ua h-Ainmire (1096–1135). The prominent role given Munnu in this tale, and the absence of Mochuda, therefore, may be an attempt to encourage the fragile unity of the region.

Without other manuscript witnesses of this tale, and contemporary comment upon it, we are left to guess about the date of its original composition, subsequent redactions, and what significance it might have had to its medieval audience. Though direct textual references to twelfth-century ecclesiastical politics are lacking in the story, some of its more cryptic dialogue and characterizations become more intelligible in that context. It may be that the story was intended for a restricted circle of churchmen, but whether for their amusement or something more deeply engaging remains mysterious.

In its narrative structure the story seems to deliberately evoke some native Irish genre types, but follows none. There are several Irish stories that use the frame of the *agallamh*, which is a colloquy or learned disputation. However, such meetings are direct discussions without delegations or mediation between the principals. In its opening section the Colum Cille story suggests the native Irish literary form of the *aisling*, a prophetic vision. Colum Cille was himself reputed to have knowledge of future events, but in this story Baíthíne also sees the apparition of the newly arisen dead. This event is found in lists of the signs and portents of Doomsday, and several such texts circulated in Ireland. Whether Baíthíne realizes the import of the sight, or its metatemporal status, is not clear from the text, but it is his dismay that prompts him to question Colum Cille.

Contrary to the purpose of such a vision, to provide knowledge of a future event, the story reveals nothing definitive. Indeed, as an *aisling* the tale seems a failure, ending in an abrupt loss of nerve, the more startling for its initial audacity. However, if the tale was deliberately crafted to frame a debate or raise some questions, it does so admirably. The literal panache that is so immediately obvious and amusing to a modern reader may not have been so to a medieval Irish one. The defensiveness of Christ and the anxiety of Patrick might have had greater significance for him, as indicative of the importance of their contract and its resolution. If Patrick could not hold heaven to its promise in his contract, what could any other individual believer hope for in his? In the end, the tale appears to offer the reader two options, to wait outside for the resolution, or to take up Christ's offer to debate the question with the nine hierarchies of heaven. The sound of a bell may end the vision, but it seems unlikely that the author of this tale intended it to end the debate as well.

Sources and Further Reading

The edition and translation of this tale was first published by Fr. Paul Grosjean in *Scottish Gaelic Studies* 3 (1929): 73–85. He published some corrections and notes in a subsequent number of the same volume (issued in 1931) on pages 188–199. Grosjean's translation has been slightly emended to fit the demands of modern usage and the present volume. The passages in parentheses come from the original text; the passages in brackets are interpolations by the translator and the editor. Uncertainties in the text or its translation are indicated by question marks in brackets. The names of all the saints are given in Irish, with the exception of Patrick himself (who is more properly Pátraic in Irish).

There has been no critical commentary on this tale since it was published by Grosjean. The *Vita Tripartita* of St. Patrick, which appears to have been the basis for this tale, was translated by Whitley Stokes for the Rolls Series with the title *The Tripartite Life of Patrick* (London, 1887; reprint, New York, 1965). This is a text with a complex manuscript tradition, which is discussed by Kenneth Jackson, "The Date of the Tripartite Life of St. Patrick," *Zeitschrift für Celtische Philologie* 41 (1986): 5–45. The articles written about the twelfth-century reform movement and its milieu by Aubrey Gwynn have been collected and edited by Gerard O'Brien under the title *The Irish Church in the Eleventh and Twelfth Centuries* (Dublin, 1992). A great deal of work has been done in recent years to examine early Irish legal texts and their social setting. For the social context of Celtic legal procedure and its evolution, see Robin Chapman Stacey, *The Road to Judgment: From Custom to Court in Medieval Ireland and Wales* (Philadelphia, 1994). A critical edition and translation of an Irish treatise on contracts, *Di Astud Chor,* has been published by Neil McLeod, *Early Irish Contract Law*, Centre for Celtic Studies (Sydney, no date).

A Tale of Doomsday Colum Cille Should Have Left Untold

(1.) On one occasion, Colum Cille and Baíthíne went to Armagh, and slept there. They arose on the following day and went to bless themselves [?] at the [sepulchral] stones and the cemeteries and crosses of Patrick. Thus then Baíthíne saw all at once men stark naked and what remained about them of their winding sheets after their awakening. Baíthíne expressed disapproval of that, for he did not like it. "What is it we see?" said Baíthíne to Colum Cille. "If you had any thing of Patrick's feelings for the clerics and Psalm-singing hermits, in regard to their assistance," said Colum Cille, "you would not behave thus; and I shall serve the winding sheets which you see, so that a reliquary shall be filled with them by me; it will cure the men of Ireland and of Scotland from every sickness and labor." Baíthíne asks Colum Cille how the patronage of Patrick should affect the men of Ireland. [And Colum Cille said:]

(2.) "Well, O Baíthíne, great will be the reverence and honor [bestowed] on Ciarán above all the other saints of Ireland, since it will be about him that shall be the muster of the men of Ireland in the day of judgment, O Baíthíne.[1] The muster of the men of Ireland will assemble to meet Patrick at Clonmacnois, and the end of them at Dun Coilli [Dunkeld] in Scotland.[2] Then shall the bell be struck in Croagh Patrick, and the men of Ireland, both quick and dead, will awake at the voice of the bell, namely [the bell known as] the Bernan of Patrick,[3] which was broken on [the heads of] the demons at Croagh Patrick. Then messengers will go from Patrick to the Patrick of Munster—that is to Ailbe of Emly of the Yew Tree—and to Ruadán of Lorrha, and to Brénainn of Birr, and they will come to Clonmacnois with the men of Munster around them. Other messengers will be sent then to the saints of Leinster and Connacht, [that is to] Ciarán [of Saighir] and Brénainn of Clonfert; and to the saints of Ulster, that is to Comgall [of Bangor] and to Finnian of Moville; and to the saints of Leinster, [that is to] Brigit and Colum mac Crimthainn, and Cóemgen [or Kevin] of Glendaloch, and Máedóc of Ferns; and to the saints of the North of Ireland, [that is to] Cainnech moccu Dalann, and Molaisse of Devenish [and Nainnid Faeburderg]; and that number shall go from him all over Ireland.[4]

(3.) After all the men of Ireland will have gone to Clonmacnois, happy the men of Ireland on that day, O Baíthíne [said Colum Cille], for good are the relics that I have. Happy the men of Ireland on that day, if only they satisfy Patrick. But woe on the men of Ireland who do not keep the feast of Patrick, and who do not give anything in his name, because it is he that shall be judge and that shall be debtor for the men of Ireland on the day of judgment. Then we men of Ireland shall go together with Ciarán [of Clonmacnois] to Patrick at Crossakeel to the east of Ross. It is then the sun shall go in front of Ciarán, son of the Wright.[5] Then Martin and Patrick will go together to meet Peter and Paul. Peter and Paul and Martin and Patrick with all their hosts will proceed to Mount Zion, and Patrick and the men of Ireland will hold a consultation by themselves. Then Patrick will tell Peter and Paul and Martin, after that consultation, to go and treat with the Lord on Mount Zion.

(4.) Patrick will proceed with the men of Ireland to the Mount of Olives. Ailbe, with seven bishops about him, will go from Patrick to negotiate with Christ on Mount Zion. The Lord will give him welcome, and Christ will ask: "Where is the lightning of the western world today? He is long in coming to this assembly." "He will come," Ailbe will say. Christ will say, "He brought many sinners with him and many bad men." "That is not as *he* thinks," Ailbe will say, "[according to him] they are penitents, who have been under the waves of the sea for the space of seven years."[6] "Tell him," Christ will say, "to leave behind the third part of the host, whoever is worst, and let the other two-thirds come with him." "That is not a command I can take [?]," Ailbe will say, "because the fellow [Patrick] is wrathful and choleric, and no one of the men of Ireland who are with him will dare bring him such a message. However, it is not for negotiating that I am come," Ailbe will say, "but to greet thee and to find out for [Patrick] how matters stand. Other messengers will come from him, and it is full of reproaches that he has them [?]."

(5.) Ailbe went to Patrick. "Have you had a talk with the Lord?" Patrick will say. "I have," Ailbe will say. "Is He friendly to me?" Patrick will say. "He is," Ailbe will say; "He sent a message for you that two thirds of your host should come, with you, and that you should leave one third of them." "That is not the beginning of a welcome, O Ailbe," Patrick will say. Then Ciarán son of the Wright will go (says Colum Cille), and Cainnech moccu Dalann and I will go to the Lord. Then the host asks: "Who are you?" "'We are of Patrick's people," Colum Cille will say. "Make way for them," the host will say, "for the book-singers [?] of Patrick, the lightning of the western world." We shall go to Christ (says Colum Cille), and He will welcome me, and Ciaran, and Cainnech. "I shall reply," Cainnech will say, "as soon as there will be welcome; until there shall be welcome I shall not."

(6.) It is then the Lord will say three times: "Welcome [to you], Cainnech!" The [rest of the] saints of Ireland are annoyed that this should be said to Cainnech. "Be not annoyed," Christ will say, "Cainnech is my beloved companion. He was not annoyed with me for the little patch of desert ground I gave him. But as for you, it is a great deal of the land of Ireland and Scotland you have received." "Ask Patrick," Christ will say, "if he will leave behind one-fourth of yonder host?" "He won't," Colum Cille will say. "Will he leave one-fifth?" Christ will say. "He won't," Colum Cille will say. "Will he leave one-sixth?" Christ will say. "He won't," Colum Cille will say. "Will he leave one-seventh?" Christ will say. "He won't," Colum Cille will say. "Will he leave one-eighth?" Christ will say. "He won't," Colum Cille will say. "Will he leave one-ninth?" Christ will say. "He won't," Colum Cille will say. "Will he leave one-tenth?" Christ will say. "He won't," Colum Cille will say. "Tell him then," Christ will say, "To abandon one-hundredth of the host, all the worst of them; and let him bring the rest with him." "He won't," Colum Cille will say. "Let him then leave behind his druids, and his satirists, and his female satirists, and his adulterers,[7] and his lampooners, and all those who went under the heels [?] of the Church and forsook the hierarchies of heaven."

(7.) "Then we shall go," Colum Cille will say, "to Patrick with that message, and we shall report to him the whole affair." (And they told the whole tale to Patrick.) "Arise again [and go] to Him," Patrick will say, "and tell Him: 'My druids and my satirists, and all that have come with me will follow me, so that the men of the [whole] world may know today my household.'" "He shall not have the power," Christ will say, "though My love for him is great, to let come his druids and his satirists to penance without contrition." News of that is brought to Patrick. "Arise again [and go] to Him," Patrick will say. "I shall go with them this fourth time," Munnu mac Tulchain will say. "There will be a bargain about the matter," Patrick will say. "You shall bring a token to Him," Patrick will say. "The day I came from the east to the [meaning of text uncertain] and quiet [?] country, to Ireland, and when I received from him the twelve camels with all they could carry of gold and silver,[8] [and] He told me on that day that I should make the awards of doom to the men of Ireland on this present day."

(8.) Then they will come to Christ. "Well then?" Christ will say. "Well," Ciarán will say. "Patrick said," Ciarán will say, "You promised him on the day he left You to go to Ireland, with the load of twelve camels of gold and silver, [and] that he should be judge today. And when he was on the great fast on Croagh Patrick, it was said to him on Your behalf that he should be judge today over the men of Ireland. And it was said to him that he would bring to Heaven today seven sinners for each small hair of his chasuble, and seven every Thursday, and twelve every Saturday, together with every man who should keep his feast, and who should give something in [Patrick's] honor and in his name, and every man who should recite the last three stanzas of his hymn on getting up and on lying down." "You found the recital an easy task," Christ will say. "Let every one tell his own tale," Ciarán will say. "I ask then," Munnu will say, "is it meet that You should feel grief in respect of Patrick?" "Who has said that?" Christ will say. "Munnu mac Tulchain here," Munnu will say. (He was a druid even when he was young.) "By my druidhood," Munnu will say, "the men of Ireland will not leave the hill on which they are, until [Patrick] has secured their safety [?]." "This consultation here is no fit subject of decision for one man," Christ will say. "Let Patrick come here with all his hosts. Where are the nine hierarchies of Heaven that we may admit him into the assembly there?"[9] It is then the [sound of the] bell for midday was rung.[10] "This is to make me hurry up,"[11] Colum Cille will say, "because it is from Heaven [that] the tale I tell you has been revealed [and it should be left untold on earth]."[12]

NOTES

1. That is, the muster will take place around Ciarán's abbey of Clonmacnois.
2. The "end of them" means the end of the line. Dun Coilli is most probably to be identified as Dunkeld on the river Tay in central Scotland.
3. The reference is to the well-known story of St. Patrick's fast on Croagh Patrick, as told, for example, in the *Vita Tripartita* (translated by Whitley Stokes as *The Tripartite Life*

of Patrick [London, 1887; reprint, New York, 1965]), where, however, the bell in question is called the Bernan of St. Brigit.

4. This last phrase is probably a reference to the messengers of the saints.

5. That is, Ciarán of Clonmacnois.

6. This is an allusion to the belief that St. Patrick had obtained as a boon from the Lord that Ireland should be submerged by the sea seven years before Doomsday, lest the Irish people should have to suffer persecution from the Antichrist and become involved in the curse which is to fall on the last generations of humanity.

7. That is those, probably both men and women, who still practiced polygamy, a pre-Christian custom in Ireland.

8. This an allusion to the vision, recorded for example in the *Vita Tripartita*, St. Patrick had of the Lord on Mount Herman. For further details, see the introduction above.

9. The translation of this last phrase is problematic. It could mean, "admit them to the dwellings there."

10. The reading of this sentence is a mere conjecture.

11. It would seem that the bell had been made to ring earlier than it should, precisely in order to interrupt the story of Colum Cille.

12. Perhaps we should translate: "because the tale I tell you is meet for Heaven." Such an unhappy ending with a reticence seems to be a feature of visions ascribed to Colum Cille. See, for example, the *Colloquy of Colum Cille with the Young Warrior* which has been printed in *Analecta Bollandiana* 45 (1927): 74–83.

CHAPTER 21

LIFE OF THE DEAR FRIENDS AMICUS AND AMELIUS

Translated by Mathew Kuefler

INTRODUCTION

The title of this anonymous work itself indicates what it is about: friendship. Indeed, it is probably no more than a legend about friendship which, because it was set within a context of miracles and faith in God, was reworked as hagiography sometime before the middle of the twelfth century, when this version was written. Apart from its curiosity as a tale of friendship, therefore, it is also an interesting example of the conflation of medieval literary genres.

There is no historical basis for either Amicus or Amelius. The story is set at the court of Charlemagne, king of the Franks and emperor. While the final scene in which Charlemagne battles with the Lombard king, Desiderius, draws heavily on two historical accounts of this war which occurred from 773 to 774, the presence of two soldiers with these names is not mentioned there nor is there any legend about their miraculous burial. It has been suggested that a legend sprang up around two tombs existing side-by-side in a church in Mortara, Italy, and became the basis for the story.

The earliest reference to the legend comes from about the year 1090. Ralph Tortarius, a monk at the monastery of Fleury in central France, wrote a letter to a friend that included the summary of a story about friendship he had heard and which he said was well known "among the Gauls and Saxons." That story was more or less that of Amicus and Amelius, although Ralph placed them at the court of a king of Aquitaine named Gaiferus, who may be the same individual as the duke of the Aquitaine who rebelled against Charlemagne at the beginning of his reign. Ralph does not appear to have considered the men to have been saints: in his version, for example, Amicus is cured by the command of doctors, not of an angel. And Ralph either did not know or omitted the final episodes in which Amicus and Amelius are killed in battle and find burial together.

The Latin hagiographical version translated here was written sometime in the half-century following Ralph's mention of the legend, but by the end of the twelfth century another version of the tale was written, also anonymously. That version was written in a Norman dialect of Old French as an epic poem of the genre called *chansons de geste*. Again, there is no talk of these men being saints. They are adventurers, even if they are ones with a strong faith in

God. There are other distinct differences: the role of the women in the story is expanded, and the two men remain with their wives after the miraculous cure. Again, the final battle and burial scenes do not appear, although the two men die at the same town of Mortara on the return from a pilgrimage to Jerusalem. Even the men's names have changed to Ami and Amile.

The names of the men further remind us that these are not historical persons. *Amicus* means "friend" in Latin, as does *ami* in French. Amelius is not a Latin word, but it is close to *melius*, "better," and as it happens, Amelius turns out to be the better friend. Other names have a symbolic meaning. The name of Amicus's eventual bride, Belixenda, called Belissant in French, is derived from the word for "beautiful," and in Middle English, Mirabele, which recalls both "beautiful" and "wondrous." Ardericus, the villain of the tale, is the Latinized form of a Germanic name, Hardrich, which means "cruel ruler." Ralph had called him Hardradus, or "cruel counsel."

From beginning to end, friendship is what this story is all about. The friendship between Amicus and Amelius's fathers is repeated and intensified in their sons, whose physical resemblance to each other merely reflects how they "mirror" each other through their intimacy. Throughout the story, their true and lasting friendship is contrasted with its opposites: the evil desire for intimacy experienced in lust for a woman, the wicked deceit in the false friendship offered by the traitor, the faithless desertion by military retainers and servants. The depths of the friends' devotion to each other is also surely the point of what Amelius must do to cure Amicus of his leprosy. Even the men's marriages do not fulfill their need for mutuality and intimacy in the same way, and so ultimately they abandon their wives and end their lives together.

It is curious that the later, poetic version of the legend leaves off this ending, and has the two men part company to rejoin their families. French society by the end of the twelfth century was much different than it had been at the beginning of the century. Ecclesiastical authorities, in particular, had exerted much pressure to enforce the indissoluble bonds of marriage. It seems also that political authorities, especially the kings of twelfth-century France and England, were becoming more and more uncomfortable with the bonds of loyalty between men and attempting to undermine this loyalty in favor of greater ties of obedience to themselves. It is possible, therefore, that the legend was amended to reflect changing social realities.

Is this story really hagiography, however, or merely a variant of a *chanson de geste*? After all, the men presented here are hardly typical saints. One seduces an unmarried woman, the other deceives his sovereign in impersonating his friend and commits bigamy in marrying when already married, both men abandon their wives, and both die not in martyrdom but in battle against a king who, despite being depicted as a dishonorable individual, was a Christian. Still, as in most hagiographies, there are immediate consequences to immoral actions: Amicus's affliction with leprosy is but one example. In the end, it is perhaps Amelius's recollection of the lesson of Abraham that provides the best clue to interpreting this tale. In his Letter to the Galatians, Paul offers the opinion that Abraham's faith "was reckoned to him as righteousness" [Gal 3:6, quoting Gen 15:6] and that "those who are men of faith are blessed with Abraham who had faith" [Gal 3:9]. The mention of Abraham reminds the reader of his near sacrifice of his son, Isaac [Gen 22], a sacrifice that Amelius was required to complete. Even then, the blood sacrifice serves as a reminder of the baptism that first joined Amicus and Amelius, and a portent of their deaths together.

The legend proved extremely popular in the Middle Ages, and versions of it survive from regions as distant as Wales and Hungary, Scandinavia and Italy. It even became the basis for a fifteenth-century miracle play. The poetic legend was translated into Middle English by the early fourteenth century; in that version, the two men were known as Amys and Amylion. What follows is the first translation into English of the hagiographical version of the story.

SOURCES AND FURTHER READING

The best Latin edition of the *Vita Amici et Amelii carissimorum* (*Bibliotheca hagiographica latina*, no. 386) is found in Eugen Kölbing, *Amis and Amiloun*, Altenglische Bibliothek 2 (Heilbronn, 1884), although there are some errors which are emended in this translation. Kölbing also provides editions of the legend in various vernacular languages; of these, the Old French version has been edited several times since then, and translated into English by Samuel Danon and Samuel Rosenberg as *Ami et Amile* (York, SC, 1981). The Middle English version, with notes, has also been edited by Françoise Le Saux as *Amys and Amylion*, Exeter Medieval English Texts and Studies (Exeter, 1993).

A good background to the legend, in both its versions, can be found in the introduction to MacEdward Leach's *Amis and Amiloun*, Early English Text Society 203 (London, 1937), also an older edition of the Middle English text. There is a collection of articles on the legend, mostly dealing specifically with the Old French version, in *Ami et Amile (Une chanson de geste de l'amitié)*, ed. Jean Dufournet (Paris, 1987). An article in this collection by Geneviève Madika entitled "La religion dans *Ami et Amile*" discusses the numerous biblical parallels generally in the legend. See also Ralph Hexter's *Equivocal Oaths and Ordeals in Medieval Literature* (Cambridge, MA, 1975), who uses the legend as an example of his subject. There are only a few articles that compare the hagiographical legend with its variations, see Kathryn Hume, "Structure and Perspective: Romance and Hagiographic Features in the Amicus and Amelius Story," *Journal for English and Germanic Philology* 69 (1970): 89–107; Ojar Kratins, "The Middle English Amis and Amiloun: Chivalric Romance or Secular Hagiography?" *Proceedings of the Modern Language Association* 81 (1966): 347–54; and Alexander Haggerty Krappe, "The Legend of Amicus and Amelius," *The Modern Language Review* 18 (1929): 152–61.

Life of the Dear Friends Amicus and Amelius

During the time of Pepin, the king of the Franks,[1] a boy was born in the castle at Bourges[2] from a German father, a man of distinguished nobility and great holiness. Since he was an only son, his parents had made a vow to God and to the blessed apostles Peter and Paul, that he should be brought to Rome to be held over the baptismal font, if God in His grace granted him life.

At the very same time, a vision appeared to the count of Auvergne[3] in his sleep, as his wife was pregnant: he seemed to see the Roman pontiff baptizing and confirming with holy chrism many boys of Auvergne in his palace. The count awakened, wondering and turning over in his mind what the vision foretold. He revealed what he had seen to the wise among his retainers and implored them to interpret it. One venerable old man, given the idea through divine assistance, said: "Rejoice, count, rejoice, my Lord, because your son is about to be born with great goodness and holiness, and it is him whom you should take, as directed by divine providence, to the Porch of the Apostles and to be lifted over the font of rebirth in the hands of the supreme pontiff." The count approved of the advice of the old man and rejoiced.

So the boy was born and brought up with the utmost care. Then, a little more than two years later, his father was filled with a longing to do what he had intended and brought him to Rome. They reached the town of Lucca,[4] where according to God's disposition they met a nobleman, a German by birth but with lands among the French.[5] He was making his way likewise with his young son to the Porch of the Apostles and also hoped for him to be washed in the font of holy baptism. When the two men had saluted each other and agreed to talk with each other, they each asked in turn from where they were and who they were, and first one then the other replied, and they assured each other of mutual friendliness. They went on their way after that, continuing together to the city of Rome. What an ineffable companionship was seen between the young boys, and what a oneness of will between both of them! Neither wanted to have a meal if not practically in the same amount as the other, and neither enjoyed the rest of sleep if not in the same bed as the other.

In this way their parents brought them before the presence of the Roman pontiff, whose name was Deusdedit,[6] and said: "Most holy Lord and father, whom we know and believe to act in place of St. Peter, the first of the apostles, the count of Auvergne and the distinguished knight of the castle of Bourges entreat the clemency of Your Holiness, that you should deign to wash our sons in the water of holy baptism and also that you should receive from our hands some sort of gifts, brought from the most profound affection of the heart." At these words, the holy man responded: "Your gifts to me are certainly welcome, but not at all necessary: spend them instead on the poor, for whom you must acknowledge they are more useful! Satisfying your first request, however, I will give the sacrament of baptism to your little ones, although I am a sinner, and may the Father and the Son in his mercy preserve them and may the spirit of both inflame them to love of the entire Holy Trinity!"

After the little boys were christened, he gave them the washing of baptism, as was done at that time in the basilica of the Holy Redeemer.[7] The son of the count was given the name Amelius and the son of the knight, Amicus. A large group of Roman knights received them from the font with great joy and with cheerfulness of spirit, as God intended. After the complete office of holy rebirth, the Roman pontiff—a man of venerable holiness—ordered to be brought two wooden drinking vessels, encrusted with gold and jewels, alike in bulk and size and artfully made, and gave them to them, saying: "Receive this gift, and may it be an eternal reminder to you, because I have baptized you in the basilica of the Holy Redeemer." They received them freely and gave thanks in many ways, and then they returned to their homes, praising and exulting.

As an adult, God decorated the boy of Bourges with such wisdom, that you would think him to have been sort of another Solomon. His father, already an old man and seized with a languorous fever, forewarned him with this admonition when he was thirty years of age, saying: "Listen, dearest son, listen, sweetest son! Already the time draws near, when I must suffer the law common to human nature and leave you to your own authority. Remember, son, especially to keep God's commands, to fight in the army of Christ, to keep the Lord's faith! Yield to the help of friends and associates, defend widows and orphans, the wretched and the distressed, support those suffering from want, and always have your last day in mind! Furthermore, never allow the companionship and friendship of the son of the count of Auvergne to be lost. For the Roman pontiff baptized you on the same day, and he honored you both with the same gift. You are both of the same appearance, both of equal height, and, if you were placed alongside the count's own relatives, you would appear to be brothers." With such last words, and after the reception of the eucharist, the old man passed over to the Lord. As was befitting, his son honored his father's corpse with the required rites and handed it to the tomb.

As it happened, the evil and wicked young men of Bourges, inspired by the bitterness of sin, soon began to attribute many evils to him, to deceive him, and to prepare plots secretly against him. But he loved everyone and bore these injuries patiently. What more can I say? The wickedness of the impious was increased against him, so that he—for shame!—was expelled with all of his family from the castle that was his inheritance from his beloved father. Then, remembering the commands of his father, he said to the ten servants who went with him: "The vileness of the impious is directed against us, my companions, and the homeland of our ancestors has been removed from us and ours. But I hope that God in His mercy will make us prosper. Let us make our way to the court of the Count Amelius, who is joined to me by companionship and friendship. Perhaps he will enrich us with possessions and his goods. If not, let us go to Hildegard the queen and wife of Charles, king of the Franks,[8] who is known always to have a regard for the exiled." All of them answered, saying: "We are ready to follow you and obey you in all things!"

Taking to the road after this, they arrived at the court of the count. The count of Auvergne had marched out, however, to visit his companion Amicus, whose father he had heard was deceased. When he had not found him, he sadly departed. He decided then that he would not return to his homeland and his own inheritance, if he did not first find Amicus, the wise and glorious knight. He sought him in places throughout Gaul and France, he sought him also in the land of Germany, where he had heard were his relatives, but he was not able to hear anything certain about him.

Amicus also did not cease to seek the count with his men, until such time as they found hospitality with a certain nobleman. When he had heard a series of declarations about Amicus's misfortunes, the nobleman spoke in this way: "Stay with me, dearest knights, let me hand over my daughter to your lord, about whose prudence and wisdom I have heard, and I will enrich you with possessions, with gold and silver!" This speech was pleasing to them and they celebrated the wedding with the utmost joy. After spending a year and a half there, Amicus the glorious knight said to his ten servants: "Let us do now what we should have done: let us set out to seek Count Amelius!" And leaving there two of his servants, with the drinking vessel that he had from his baptism, he made his way to Paris.[9]

The count had searched for Amicus incessantly for two years already. When he neared Paris, he found a pilgrim whom he questioned, as he had done with so many, asking him if he had seen Amicus, the knight of Bourges, who was expelled from his homeland. And he said that he had never seen him. Then the count pulled off his tunic and gave it to him, saying: "Intercede for me with God and His saints, that He might show me His mercy to find the glorious Amicus and put an end to my labor which I have willingly suffered for two years!"

Thus the count came to the court of Charles the king, but he did not meet Amicus there. The pilgrim, in fact, making his way, found Amicus at about the time of Vespers,[10] and, when the two had greeted each other, Amicus said: "Pilgrim, servant of God, I wish to learn from you, if you have heard of Amelius, the son of the count of Auvergne, and where on earth he is." The pilgrim replied immediately, bewildered: "Who are you, knight, who are making fun of me, a pilgrim? Because you appear to be Amelius, the son of the count of Auvergne, as you have said, who asked me today if I had seen Amicus, a knight of Bourges. I don't know why you have changed clothes, companions, horses, and arms, but let me assert that you were sound of mind today when at the third hour you gave me this shirt." Amicus said to him: "Don't be upset, dearest brother, for I am not, as you believe, the son of the count of Auvergne, but Amicus, a knight of Bourges, who does not stop from looking for him! Accept with peacefulness the charity of this money and intercede to God with your prayers, that He might find me worthy to grant to me that Amelius find me!" Having accepted the mercy, the pilgrim then answered, saying: "Make haste, knight, to Paris, where I hope you will find him you seek so longingly!"

And making haste, Amicus went after him. But the next day Amelius had already departed from Paris and was feasting with his knights in a meadow very much in bloom alongside the Seine River. When they saw the armed men of Bourges approaching, they rose up quickly and ran out toward them with their weapons drawn. The knight of Bourges had already observed them, however, and called out to them in such a manner: "My companions, see the Parisian knights who are strong and unbeatable! Raise up your spirits, fight strongly, and manfully defend your lives! If we are able to escape this danger, indeed, we will go to Paris with great joy and we will be received magnificently at the royal court." And they rode out with slack reins on both sides, lances raised, swords hacking to and fro, so much so that you would not believe that any one of these men assaulting each other could escape the danger of death. But almighty God, who changes all things to work for His will and to put an end to the labors of the just, made both parties to resist the first advance.

Then the knight of Bourges said: "Where do you come from, knights so very strong, who want to kill the exile Amicus and his companions?" At this voice, Amelius was astounded, grew pale, and recognized Amicus, the glorious knight. The count said: "Dearest Amicus and rest to my labors, I am he your companion, whose name is Amelius, the son of the count of Auvergne, who has not ceased searching for you in exile already for two years!" Dismounting, they soon drew each other together with embraces, exchanged kisses, rejoiced with joy, and from such newfound happiness gave thanks to God. They then both pledged their faith to each other over the sword of Amelius where there were relics of the saints. They made their way together to the court of Charles the king, where he perceived them to be modest, wise, and very handsome young men, peers alike in their education as in their appearance, loved by all and honored by all. What more could I add? Amicus was made the king's treasurer and Amelius his cup bearer.

When already three years had passed, Amicus said to Amelius: "My comrade, solace of my life, I wish to see my wife, whom I have left already fully two years ago, and to whom I will soon be able to return. You must remain at court, but guard yourself against the daughter of the king and especially from the false friendship of the most wicked count Ardericus!" Count Amelius answered him: "I will guard myself according to your suggestion: but I entreat you to make hasty your return!" And thus the glorious knight departed. As it happened, Count Amelius cast his eyes on the king's daughter and she was quickly able to subdue him. Alas! Where were the warnings of the most faithful Amicus, warnings that ought to have remained in the depths of his heart and restrained his ignorant will? This lapse is not an unfamiliar one, though, since the same thing conquered both the holier David and the wiser Solomon.[11]

Meanwhile, Ardericus the traitor, who rejoiced in iniquity and envied all honesty, spoke to Amelius in these words: "You don't know, count, you don't know, dearest friend, that Amicus has plundered the king's treasury and for this reason has accepted flight? Now, make an alliance of friendship with me and accept my faith and indivisible companionship over the relics of the saints!" Once they had both sworn their vows, Count Amelius did not hesitate to disclose his secrets to the wicked Ardericus.

Then one day Amelius was standing before the king, so that he might offer him water for his hands, and the impious Ardericus spoke thus to the king: "My king, you do not want to accept water from the hand of a sinful man, who is more worthy of death than honor, since he has taken the flower of virginity from the princess your daughter!" At this, Count Amelius fell down, trembling and stupified, and said nothing in response. Then the king kindly raised him up and said to him: "Rise, Amelius! Don't be afraid, and defend yourself manfully against this accusation of evildoing!" Then, rising, Amelius said: "Most just king, do not believe in the lying words of the traitor Ardericus, you who hold the reins of justice and do not divert from the path of right either out of love or out of hatred! I ask that you might grant to me the opportunity for support,[12] so that I might fight a duel in your sight with the traitor Ardericus over this accusation of evildoing, and that with the court standing all around I might prove that it is an utter lie!" Then the king said: "Let both of you seek support and may you return to the court quickly this afternoon!"

At the predetermined time, both of them stood in the presence of the king. While Ardericus had count Heribertus with him, Count Amelius was abandoned by all, and, sighing at the absence of the most wise Amicus, he suffered with exceeding grief. Then the pious queen Hildegard undertook the cause of Count Amelius's defense. She thus procured for Count Amelius the opportunity of support, binding herself in such a manner that had he not returned to the court at the predetermined time, she would not have dared to return to the king's conjugal bed any more.[13]

Amelius then hurried off to seek support. He found Amicus returning to the king's court, and prostrating himself at his feet, said: "Solitary hope of my salvation, woe is me, I have badly served the faith placed in me, because I have stumbled into sin with the king's daughter, and also arranged a duel in his presence with the false Ardericus." With a sigh, Amicus said: "Let us leave my companions here and go into the shelter of this grove of trees!" He upbraided him roughly, then gave him this advice, offered from the depth of a wise heart: "Let us change our clothes and horses. You set out for my house without delay, and let me make war with the treacherous count on your behalf with God's help." Count Amelius answered him: "How shall I set out for your house, my comrade, I who do not know your wife and household and have not seen their faces?" Amicus answered: "Hasten with confidence to my house, and ask prudently who my family is and who my wife is. But be careful, and in no way touch my wife!"

They then separated, both weeping. Amicus went to the king's court in the guise of Amelius, and Amelius to the house of his companion in the guise of Amicus. And when Amicus's wife saw Count Amelius, believing him to be her husband, she stretched out her arms in her usual manner, wanting to offer him kisses. But he responded: "Get away from me, because a time for weeping is approaching, not a time for rejoicing. Since I departed from you, in fact, I have suffered many awful things, and many more remain yet to be endured!" That night, when the two of them got into bed, he placed his sword between himself and her. "See," he said, "do not approach me in any way, because you will die instantly by this sword!" And in this way they passed each night until the night Amicus returned unexpectedly, wanting to test if Amelius had served well the faith placed in him concerning Amicus's wife committed to his care.

Already the outcome of the situation was nearing. Amelius, who had not returned, worried that the queen might be trembling fearfully, because the traitor Ardericus, whom everyone served after the king, was saying to everyone openly that the queen should not dare to approach the king's conjugal bed, and that she had permitted Count Amelius to violate the king's daughter. Meanwhile, Amicus, dressed in the clothing of his companion, returned at about the sixth hour[14] and entering before the presence of the king, spoke to him with these words: "Most gentle king, you who raise up the fallen and defend the innocent, I am ready to make war with the false Ardericus and to defend the pious queen and her daughter, and also myself from the accusation of evildoing which he lays against us!" The king, answering kindly, said to him: "Do not fear, my count, because if you are the victor I will give you this same daughter of mine, whose name is Belixenda, to be your wife!"

In the morning, when the first hour of day was completed,[15] Ardericus and Amicus went out armed into the countryside, with the king and the whole people of Paris standing around. And the very pious queen, with virgins and widows and a multitude of other such women, kept the holy churches filled, where they poured out many tears in prayer, honoring the altars with gifts and lighting candles. Then Amicus began to think to himself, saying: "Woe is me, I who desire the death of this count so fraudulently! I know, indeed, that if I do slay him, I shall be accused of that crime before the Supreme Judge, if He in fact hears the case of my life. He will be told about [this crime committed by] me forever with eternal hatred." After this, then, he spoke thus to Ardericus: "Count," he said, "I have too readily accepted bad advice, so that you so ardently desire my death and commit your life so imprudently to the danger of death. But if you want to swear that the crime that you accuse me of is false, and cancel completely this duel which can only bring death, you can have my friendship and service always!" Furious, Ardericus replied: "I do not want your friendship or your service, but the truth of the matter, just as it appears, and I will swear it in front of everyone, because I want to carry away your head!" Ardericus swore that the man had wronged the king's daughter, and Amicus swore that Ardericus was lying.

After this oath, they ran together. They battled from the third hour of the day, however, until the fifth,[16] when Ardericus was overcome—that most impious traitor!—and Amicus cut off his head. The king, grieving because he had lost Ardericus, but rejoicing for his only daughter whom Amicus had liberated from the accusation of evildoing with God's help. It pleased him to hand her over to Amicus, the glorious and very wise knight, as his wife, with the rest of her household and a large quantity of gold and silver. And he gave to them a city along the coast, recommending to them that they should live there.

Amicus received her happily and then hurried home, as quickly as he could, where Count Amelius was. When Amelius saw him coming with an army, he took to flight, thinking that Amicus had been defeated. Amicus, sending after him, said: "Do not flee, count, but make haste to return to me! I have freed you from Ardericus, that traitor, and have married the king's daughter for you." When Amelius returned, he accepted her and lived thereafter in the aforementioned city with his wife.

Amicus remained with his own wife, but God smote him with the disease of leprosy, so much so that he could not rise out of bed. This was in accordance with that which is written: "Every son, whom God rescues, he rebukes, he scourges, he chastises" [Prov 3:12]. Amicus's wife, whose name was Obiae, so detested him that many times she wanted to suffocate him.[17] Amicus called his servants[18] Azo and Horatus to himself and said to them: "Take me away quickly from the most vile hands of my wife, bring the drinking vessel I have hidden, and carry me to the castle of Bourges!"

When they had approached the castle, however, a band met them and questioned them, saying: "Who is this invalid, who is it you are carrying here?" They said: "He is Amicus, your lord, struck with leprosy, who comes to you asking that you have mercy on him [and give him hospitality]." Immediately these impious ones fell upon the servants and threw Amicus from the cart in which he was being carried, saying: "Abandon him quickly, and do not let that name be heard here anymore, if you do not want give up your lives!" Then Amicus, bursting into tears, said: "God, most pious Father, whose way for all is mercy and truth, grant either death to me or deem me, wretch that I am, worthy to obtain the counsel and assistance of Your mercy!" He then said to his servants: "Wretch that I am, lead me to the Porch of the Apostles. Perhaps God will look after me, wretch that I am, in His mercy!"

When they had arrived at Rome, the Roman pontiff, Constantius,[19] a man of great piety and holiness, ran up to them with many Roman soldiers, the same men who had received Amicus from the baptismal font, and with great humanity they supplied him and his men with what they needed. After three years, a famine arose in the city, so severe that a father might even banish his son from him because of it. Then Azo and Horatus said to Amicus: "Lord, we have served you faithfully from the day of your father's death and have not held back from your commands in any way. But we no longer have the strength to be with you in this land or to take care of you, if we do not want to risk death when the famine grows worse. For this reason we ask that you give us the freedom by which we might be able to escape this death-bearing plague!" Amicus, immediately erupting into tears, said: "My sons, not my servants, my solitary help, I beg you by God that you do not abandon me here, but lead me to the house of Count Amelius, my friend and companion!" And they answered him, saying: "We have always obeyed your commands and, insofar as we are able, we will be obedient to you."

They quickly led him to the town where Count Amelius lived, and as they approached his court, they hit sticks together [to warn others of their presence] as is usual with persons of that disease. When Count Amelius heard them, he said to one of his servants: "Take bread and meat and fill my Roman drinking vessel with the best wine and bring it to that invalid!" The servant obeyed the command and replied: "By the faith, lord, that I have sworn to you, if it were not your drinking vessel that I hold, I certainly would believe it to be the same one that the sick man has, since the two vessels appear to be of the same beauty and magnificence." And the count said: "Hurry and bring him to me!"

As he was brought before the count, the count demanded to know who he was, and how he had acquired such a drinking vessel. He said that he had been born at the castle of Bourges and that he had received the drinking vessel and baptism at Rome from the high pontiff Deusdedit where he had received his name. When he heard these words, the count suddenly knew that it was his companion, who had dragged him back from death and handed to him the daughter of the king of the Franks as his wife. Accordingly, he threw himself on him, making loud exclamations and often exploding into tears, kissing and embracing him. When the count's wife heard about it, she ran to him with her hair all loose, and dissolved into many tears over him, reminding him how he had bravely battled the traitor Ardericus. After much lamentation, they brought him into their home and even settled him in their own precious conjugal bed, saying: "Stay with us, lord, until your spirit passes from this prison of the flesh. All things that are ours will be yours and whatever you want will be done with only a nod from you!" So he remained in their home with his two servants.

One night, Amicus was lying in the same bedchamber as the count, his wife being absent. Suddenly, the angel Raphael[20] appeared, sent by God. He called to Amicus and said to him: "Amicus, are you asleep?" Thinking that it was Amelius who had called him, he answered: "I am not at all asleep, dearest companion!" And the angel said to him: "You have answered well, because you have been made a companion to the citizens of heaven, and an imitator of the patience of Job and Tobias. I am Raphael, the angel of the Lord, who has come, sent to you, that I might announce to you the medicine for your health, because your prayers have been granted. Hear, therefore, the command of the Lord: 'Say to Count Amelius that he should kill his two sons and wash you in their blood, and in this way you will receive your health!'" Amicus said to him: "Let it not be, my Lord, that on account of my health the count should murder his own sons!" But the angel said: "Thus it must be, since the Lord has so ordained."

When he had said these things, he left. Amelius, half asleep, heard it and was terrified, and questioned Amicus, saying: "Who was speaking with you just now?" Amicus answered him: "No one, lord, I have just been pouring out my prayers to the Lord in the usual manner for my sins!" But the count said: "That is not it, because someone was speaking with you." Then, rising up, he hastened to his guest's bedchamber and found it shut and said: "Tell me, brother, who spoke these words to you tonight?" Then Amicus began to weep most bitterly and said: "Since you compel me, my lord, let it be unwillingly and with great trembling that I tell you what is commanded. The angel of the Lord, Raphael, came to me and said: 'Amicus, the Lord says this: "Let Count Amelius kill his two sons and let him wash you in their blood, and thus you will be cured from leprosy!"'"

When the count heard this, he was distressed, and said: "Amicus, I have received you in my home, I have made both male and female servants and all my things available to you. For what reason do you so deceitfully demand this and contrive that an angel told you that I should kill my sons?" Amicus, immediately bursting into tears, said: "It is only that I am compelled to say these burdensome things to you. I beg of you not to expel me from your home!" The count answered: "What I have promised you, I will do gladly until the day of your death. But I beg you by your faith and our companionship and the baptism that we received on the same day at Rome, to tell me if an angel said these words, or just a man!" Amicus answered: "It is just as I said. An angel spoke to me tonight, and said that God would thus free me from this leprosy!"

Amelius began then in secret to weep and think to himself: "If he was ready to die for me before the king, should I not kill my sons for him? If he kept faith with me until death, how should it be that I will not do the same? Abraham was saved by faith, the saints conquered kingdoms by faith,[21] and the truth of the gospel says: 'And as you wish that men would do to you, do so to them'" [Lk 6:31].

He hurried, therefore, to the bedchamber of his wife and asked her to [go to church and] hear the sacred mysteries.[22] Without delay, the countess hurried to the church in her usual way. The count, with his sword drawn, went to the bed where the boys were resting, and found them sleeping. He leant over them and wept most bitterly, saying: "Whoever heard of a father having willingly killed his sons? Woe is me, my sons, from this moment I will not be a father to you, but a bloodstained attacker!" And because his tears were dropping onto them, they were awakened. The boys, who were already three years of age, gazed at their father's face and began to smile. He said: "Your laughter—alas!—will be changed into mourning, because in this hour your innocent blood will be shed by an impious father!"

When he had said these things, he cut off their heads. He replaced their heads on their corpses in their bed, and covered them as if they were alive. The blood which he collected from them he sprinkled over his companion, saying: "Lord Jesus Christ, You who has enjoined that all humanity have faith and You who has cured leprosy mercifully according to Your word, deem this my companion worthy of cure, for whose love I did not fear to shed the blood of my own sons!"

And suddenly Amicus was cured of leprosy. Exulting with great joy, they gave thanks to God, saying: "Blessed be God the Father of our Lord Jesus

Christ, who saves those who believe in him!" Afterward, the count clothed Amicus in his best clothes. They then ran to the holy church, and when they arrived, they gave thanks to God. The church bells immediately began to sound by themselves, according to God's will, and when the people of the city heard it, they ran to them from all sides, amazed.

The count's wife also began to wonder, when she saw the two of them approaching side by side, which of them was her husband. "I recognize the clothing of both of them," she said, "but which of them is the count, I absolutely do not know." To her the count said: "I am Amelius and he is my companion Amicus, who has been made healthy." And the countess, amazed, said: "I see that he is completely cured, but how this was done, I wish to know." The count answered her: "Let us give thanks to Almighty God, who wished to cure him because of his piety, and since He has done it, let us not try to investigate it!"

Already the third hour of the day had passed, but neither the father nor the mother had gone in to see their sons. Notwithstanding, the count sighed repeatedly, and thought about the death of his sons. Then the countess demanded that the boys be brought to her, so that she could wish them joy. But the count said: "Let the boys rest in peaceful sleep!" He then entered the bedchamber alone, so that he might weep over his sons, but he found them playing in their bed, with scars around their necks, scars in the shape of a red line that remained there until their deaths.

And taking them up in his arms, the count carried them to the bosom of his wife and said: "Oh wife, rejoice, because your sons live, who were killed by the command of an angel, and with whose blood Amicus was cured!" When she heard this, his wife said: "Count, why did you not reveal to me that you had taken a vessel for collecting my sons' blood and that you had sprinkled Amicus, your companion and my lord, with it?" Then the count said to her: "Cease these words! Let us pursue hereafter the faithful service of God, because today in our home God has seen fit to work great miracles!" And up to the end of their lives, they served God through chastity.

For ten days there was great joy in that city. And on that same day, the wicked wife of Amicus was seized by a demon, fell off a cliff, and died. After the period of celebration, Amicus moved against the rebels of Bourges and besieged them for a long time, until at last he was restored, having conquered them. He received his men kindly, and acquitted them of all guilt of their offense. He lived peacefully with them, keeping the firstborn son of Amelius with him, and he served God further in fear [of the Lord].

After a few years, it happened that Hadrian, the pope of the city of Rome,[23] sent his legates to Charles, the king of the Franks, pleading for the defense of the Church of Rome, since he was being vehemently afflicted by the king of the Lombards, Desiderius.[24] Seeing that Charles was then in the place called Thionville,[25] Hadrian, the apostolic lord, sent his legate, whose name was Peter, and asked him with the prayers of the pope that Charles might hasten to the defense of the Church himself and might liberate the Roman people from the hands of that arrogant king. Charles, the most Christian and most gentle king of the Franks, immediately sent his agents to Desiderius, pleading that he peacefully restore the towns and the rest of the things he had taken away from St. Peter, and that he do full justice to the territory of the Romans, promising in addition that Desiderius would be given a sum of fourteen thousand solidi in gold and silver.[26] But Charles was not able either with pleadings or with gifts to soften Desiderius's most fierce heart.

Then the great king Charles brought together himself from all over his kingdom a host of bishops, abbots, dukes, princes, marquesses, and very powerful knights, with whom he occupied the lands adjoining Chiusa di San Michelo [where Desiderius was encamped].[27] From there, he sent some men from his army, among whom was the venerable Albinus, bishop of the city of Angers, whose life and merit was already apparent in his own day.[28] The king himself, with many of his Frankish fighters, approached that same Chiusa by Mont Cenis Pass, and he instructed his uncle Bernard with other loyal followers to enter Italy by Great Saint Bernard Pass.[29]

Desiderius and all of his host made their stand in that same Chiusa, where they hoped to resist strongly, since its buildings and all its other materials might serve to defend them. In the very same hour as he had indicated beforehand, the most Christian king approached Chiusa, and immediately sent his officials to the aforementioned Desiderius, pleading again that he peacefully restore the towns which he had violently taken away from St. Peter.[30] But Desiderius utterly refused to acquiesce to his prayers. While the violent king Desiderius persisted in such hardness, Charles, the most Christian king of the Franks, who so desired to restore peacefully the rights of St. Peter, sent agents to the king of the Lombards. He offered to hand over three hostages [that Charles had with him], sons of judges of the Lombards,[31] but only in exchange for the return of the towns [that Desiderius had occupied]. Directly and without further enmity or battles, Charles would return with his Frankish armies to his own lands. But Charles did not thereby succeed in deflecting Desiderius's evil mind.

Almighty God himself observed the wicked faithlessness and the intolerable boldness of the evil Desiderius, even while the Franks wanted only to return some day to their own lands. So He sent a terror and a strong fear into Desiderius's heart and into the hearts of all the Lombards, so that in that same night, Desiderius abandoned his own tents as well as all his belongings, and all of the Lombards took flight together, no one pursuing them. When Charles realized what had happened, he pursued them with his army, an army so large that they seemed to flow as waves of the sea, and in that army you would have seen the peoples of the French, English, Germans, and other peoples entering Italy.[32]

Count Amelius and Amicus, his companion, accompanied this army, acting in their prior offices in the king's court. They also nonetheless applied themselves daily to the works of Christ, fasting, praying, paying alms, aiding widows and orphans, frequently mitigating the king's wrath, enduring the wicked, and advising the governments of the Romans.[33] It happened, then, that a great army had gathered together in Lombardy from everywhere, but King Desiderius with his small army of those who had returned to him nonetheless held out in Campania.[34] Where, for instance, King Desiderius had a priest, Charles had a bishop, if the one had a monk, the other had an abbot, if the one had a knight, the other had a prince, if the one had a foot soldier, the other had a duke or a count. What more can I say? Where Desiderius had one knight, Charles was able to send thirty into war.

And with banners raised and battlelines arrayed, a huge shout was made on both sides and rocks and spears began flying here and there,[35] knights rushing in from all sides. The Lombards fought so fiercely for three days that they yielded for no other reason except because of the innumerable host of various peoples against them. But Charles, having been inflamed by a divine fire, called together the leaders and strongmen of his army after the third day, saying: "Either perish in battle or win victory for yourselves!" So it happened that King Desiderius fled with the army of the Lombards to the place which is now called Mortara, which was then named Beautiful Woods, because it was so charming.[36] He paused there, saying to his men: "Most fierce knights, eat bread with me, drink water, arrange relief for the horses!" In the morning, when the day was begun, Charles the king closed in with his army and found the armed Lombards. Both armies fought manfully there, and there died in that place not a small multitude of both armies. You may be sure that it is on account of that slaughter of the armies of Charles and of Desiderius that the place is called to this day Mortara.

There was also killed the son-in-law of Charles the king, namely Amelius, with Amicus his companion. Those whom God had joined in the concord of one spirit and in love in life, so in death He did not want them to be separated. With them were butchered many bodies of the bravest knights. Desiderius, indeed, altogether fled on that account at full speed with his judges and with a multitude of the Lombard people back to Pavia.[37] Charles pursued him with his armies, and formed a wall [with his men] around the town of Pavia, surrounding it on all sides. He also directed forthwith to France, and had his most excellent wife, Hildegard the queen, with his sons, brought to him.

Then blessed Albinus, bishop of the town of Angers, with other bishops and abbots, gave the following advice to the king and to the queen: they proposed that the bodies of the slain be buried and that a church be built there. That advice pleased the king and queen. Two churches were built, one by the order of Charles and dedicated in honor of St. Eusebius of Vercelli,[38] the other by order of the queen and consecrated in honor of St. Peter. Because the king greatly loved his son-in-law and Amicus, his companion, he sent to Milan and ordered two stone arches to be brought, one to decorate the tomb of Amelius in the church of Saint Peter, the other to decorate the tomb of Amicus in the church of Saint Eusebius. The remains of their bodies were buried, the one here, the other there. In the morning, however, and done according to divine disposition, the body of Amelius was found with his tomb next to the tomb of Amicus in the king's church.

What an admirable companionship between these two friends, what ineffable devotion between both, which not even in death deserves separation! For their love, almighty God wanted to make of them a venerable and memorial sign, He who gave this virtue to his disciples, that with love of this kind they might move mountains [see Mt 17:20–1]. The king and the queen rejoiced on account of this miracle, and remained there for thirty days, performing the offices of the dead, and bestowing the greatest number of gifts on the basilica dedicated in honor of St. Peter.

The army of Charles, meanwhile, labored at the siege of the town [of Pavia]. The wrath of God pressed and labored against all of the Lombards, who were in that town, and already many of them had deserted because of the illnesses and the disaster of the numbers dead. With the compliance of God, the most excellent king of the Franks captured the town he had besieged for ten months, together with King Desiderius and all who were with him, and subjugated their kingdom to his power. Desiderius and his wife with him, he led into France. So blessed Albinus, who had already raised the dead and given sight to many of the blind, ordained priests, deacons, and other clerics for the aforementioned church of Saint Eusebius, warning them that they should take care of the bodies of the two companions.

These soldiers of Christ, Amicus and Amelius, suffered death under Desiderius, the king of the Lombards, on the twelfth of October, our Lord Jesus Christ reigning, who lives and reigns with the Father and the Holy Spirit forever and ever. Amen.

NOTES

1. Pepin, called the Short, was king of the Franks from 754 until 768, and father of Charlemagne.

2. Bourges is in central France, and there was a fortified castle there from at least the end of the tenth century.

3. The Auvergne is a region in south-central France.

4. Lucca is near Pisa in north-central Italy on the medieval road to Rome.

5. This odd statement would have made little sense in the time of Pepin, but is one of the many historical inaccuracies that indicate this legend is later than the era of Charlemagne.

6. There was never a pope named Deusdedit, which means "God has given" in Latin. Popes Stephen II and Paul I held office during the reign of Pepin.

7. Probably the church which was at the site of the modern church of Santa Maria della Pietà della natione Tedesca, which had the name of Holy Redeemer in the Middle Ages, and which is located close to the southeast corner of the basilica of Saint Peter.

8. This Charles is Charlemagne, king of the Franks from 768 until 814, later also King of the Lombards from 774, and emperor from 800. Hildegard was his second wife; she died in 783.

9. Paris seems to be identified here as Charlemagne's capital, but his capital was at Aachen in modern Germany.

10. Vespers was the hour of the monastic liturgy that preceded the evening meal.

11. The reference here is to David's lust for Bathsheba [2 Sam 11] and Solomon's marriage to hundreds of women [1 Kings 11].

12. What the men are asking for is to get another person to act as "second" in the duel. The Latin term is *consilium*, which means advice, the person who gives it, and the means by which it is given.

13. Either the pledge that Hildegard gives is such that if broken, she would not be permitted to join the king in their bed, or simply that she would fear his displeasure too much to want to join him.

14. The sixth hour was about midday.

15. The first hour was that which followed sunrise.

16. The third hour to the fifth hour spans most of the morning.

17. In the French and English versions of the legend, Amicus's wife, whose name there is Lubias, is said to be the niece of Ardericus, and both are said to be related to Ganelon, the villain of *The Song of Roland*, another popular *chanson de geste*.

18. What kind of servants these men are is unclear. They are probably serfs, only semi-free and legally bound to Amicus, since they demand their freedom later, and since they also do not attempt to defend him with weapons in the episode that follows. The French and English versions of the legend have Amicus assisted not by servants but by his nephew, Amourant, a name that means "loving" in Old French.

19. There was never a pope named Constantius. There was an antipope named Constantine, who attempted to hold the office in 767, but the pope who held office during the early reign of Charlemagne was Stephen III.

20. Raphael was the name of the angel who appeared to Tobias in the biblical book of Tobit, a book included in the Septuagint, and thus in the medieval and modern Catholic bible but excluded from the canonical books of Protestant denominations.

21. This reference is unclear.

22. There is a discrepancy in the text. Amelius's wife was earlier said to have been absent from their home, but here she is in the next bed.

23. Pope Hadrian I served from 772 until 795.

24. King Desiderius of the Lombards ruled from 756 until 774.

25. Thionville is in northeastern France near the modern border with Luxembourg. It was the site of a royal residence during the era of Charlemagne.

26. The solidus was the basic unit of currency in the era of Charlemagne. The territory of the Romans refers to the lands around Rome and not to any political unit, although these lands were held by the pope.

27. Chiusa di San Michelo is in northern Italy between Turin and Milan, and very close to Mortara, mentioned below.

28. The presence of St. Albinus of Angers in the company of Charlemagne is a curious detail, because this abbot and bishop died in 550, more than two hundred years before Charlemagne became king.

29. Both Mont Cenis Pass and Great Saint Bernard Pass led through the western Alps into northern Italy.

30. The lands held by the pope were considered to belong to St. Peter, whose representative the pope was held to be.

31. The "judges" (*iudici*) of the Lombards were officials of the kingdom who were also men of high social status.

32. The English were certainly not involved in any of Charlemagne's military campaigns, since they were not part of his empire.

33. The governments of the Romans seem to be those nobles holding lands from the pope in the area around Rome.

34. Campania is the region south of Rome. Here the geography is confused, since the battle immediately following takes place in northern Italy.

35. The rocks were presumably thrown by catapults, a practice typical of medieval siege warfare.

36. There is no other evidence to assign an earlier name to the place called Mortara, but it serves to emphasize the hagiographer's point, as does the later reference to its name being derived from the many casualties in war, since *mortalis* means "deadly" in Latin.

37. Pavia is in northern Italy, and was the capital of the kingdom of the Lombards.

38. St. Eusebius of Vercelli was a fourth-century bishop. Mention of his name here is not too surprising, since Vercelli is not far from Mortara.

CHAPTER 22
THE BOOK OF ELY
Translated by Jennifer Paxton

INTRODUCTION

The *Book of Ely* (or *Liber Eliensis*), from which the following extracts are taken, is different from most of the other works contained in this anthology because it is not conventional hagiography, although it contains most of the material one might expect in a saint's *Life*. Rather, the *Book of Ely* is a history of the monastery of Ely, a Benedictine house in Cambridgeshire in eastern England, from its foundation in the seventh century by the virgin queen St. Æthelthryth (or Etheldreda) to the time of the text's composition, the mid to late twelfth century (sometime between 1133 and 1174). The *Book of Ely* is a highly polemical work that depicts the monastic community's past in ways designed to comment on the present political circumstances in which it found itself. Crucial to the text's purpose of casting the best possible light on the church of Ely is its depiction of the intervention of St. Æthelthryth and her saintly kinswomen in the history of the church. The patronage of St. Æthelthryth is the thread that ties the narrative of Ely's past together.

Such a thread is badly needed in the *Book of Ely* because of the peculiar genre to which it belongs. Instead of being a conventional chronicle or history, it incorporates within its narrative transcriptions of many legal and administrative documents from the monastery's past, as well as long extracts from other literary works relevant to Ely. Because of this mixture of narrative and documents, historians call this kind of text a "charter-chronicle." Several other important charter-chronicles stem from the same region of England at around the same time. Much hagiographic material is embedded within this history, and to a certain extent, the whole work, even its most prosaic sections, is concerned with the story of St. Æthelthryth's guardianship of the church. Still, the long transcriptions of legal documents make the text somewhat indigestible to the modern reader, and this has led scholars to neglect its very interesting literary qualities, including the rhetorical purposes served by the inclusion of the saint's miraculous interventions in Ely's history.

Rather than reflecting the views of a single author, the *Book of Ely* claims to represent the perspective of the brothers as a group. In fact, the question of the authorship of the *Book of Ely* has never been conclusively settled, largely because it was not so much written as compiled or designed. Many of the individual chapters were written for other purposes at other times, although

459

some were clearly commissioned for inclusion in the *Book of Ely*. Hence, we must separate the activity of the compiler from that of the authors of individual sections. The different origin of the various pieces that make up the *Book of Ely* makes it more difficult than usual, but certainly not impossible, to determine the plan behind the compilation of the text.

There are indications that the compiler may have been Richard, the subprior and later prior, who represented the convent in a crucial legal dispute over property at the papal court in Rome. The editor of the text, E.O. Blake, has suggested that the compilation of the *Book of Ely* may have grown out of Richard's legal activities (see *Liber Eliensis*, p. xlvii). In any case, the composite nature of the *Book of Ely* means that each chapter must be examined separately to determine authorship, where possible, and then the design of the whole text must be analyzed to appreciate the purposes for which it was created. The different origin of the various miracles also accounts for their diversity of style.

The creation of a complicated text like the *Book of Ely*, a monumental undertaking in an age before computers or even useful filing systems, can often be traced to a specific political context that prompted one or more members of a monastic community to attempt a thoroughgoing presentation of the community's history. A series of developments at Ely, beginning with the Norman Conquest but accelerating in the early twelfth century, combined to place the monks on the defensive, in need of the self-justification that a well-tailored history of their house could provide. The most important event in the recent history of Ely was the creation there of a new bishopric in 1109. Before that time, Ely had been a wealthy Benedictine abbey ruled by an abbot, under the diocesan authority of the bishop of Lincoln. As was not uncommon, conflicts arose between the bishops of Lincoln and the fiercely independent monastery about the right of the bishops to intervene in monastic affairs. As a means of gaining independence from episcopal control, Abbot Richard of Ely (1100–1107) proposed that a new diocese be carved out of the overly large diocese of Lincoln, with its see at Ely. Several other prominent English bishoprics were also centered at monastic churches, so there was nothing unusual about this suggestion. The proposal was not carried out, however, until after Richard's death. At that time, King Henry I (1100–1135) sent Bishop Hervey the Breton, who had previously been expelled from his diocese of Bangor by the rebellious Welsh, to Ely to be maintained there at the expense of the monks. The scheme of creating a new bishopric was revived, and Hervey became the first bishop of Ely.

The monks had at first believed that it would be to their advantage to have their own bishop rather than be subject to the bishop of Lincoln, but they soon changed their minds. Hervey's reign was marked by a prolonged dispute between the bishop and the monks over the division of the church's estates, a matter that caused tension at many English churches at the same time. Beginning around the time of the Norman Conquest, most monastic communities, whether or not they were connected with bishoprics, began to separate the estates from which the monastery derived its income into two portions, one designed to supply the needs of the monks, and the other to support the bishop or abbot. This division accomplished several goals, one of which became urgent after 1066, when William the Conqueror reorganized all landholding in England along feudal lines. From then on, every piece of land in England was held either directly of the king or indirectly through one of the king's vassals. Abbots and bishops by and large held their offices directly from the king, and when they died, their fief was considered to be vacant. The king thus took custody of the church's estates until a new bishop or abbot was chosen, appointing a guardian to run the estates who was responsible for looking after the needs of the monks. Since the monks had no control over this guardian, and since the delay before a new leader was chosen could be quite lengthy, it was advantageous for the monks to separate the portion of the estates directly used to support their needs from the abbot's, so that those estates at least would not pass into the king's hands.

The desire to protect the church's estates during a vacancy was by no means the only purpose of dividing them, or even the most important. The simple desire for autonomy on the part of both monks and bishops also played a large role. As the *Book of Ely* amply attests, the interference of the bishop or abbot in the affairs (and finances) of the monks could often be just as disruptive and necessarily more prolonged than that of royal officials. At Ely the division dragged on as the monks contested the bishop's allotment of estates to each portion, and unresolved matters persisted into the reign of Hervey's successor, Nigel. The *Book of Ely* reflects the monks' persistent resentment at what they claimed was an unjust distribution of resources.

If Bishop Hervey was not unambiguously loved by the monks, then his successor, Nigel of Salisbury, was positively despised. He can justly be described as the villain of the *Book of Ely*. Nigel was a courtier-bishop, whose primary activity was centered not in his diocese but at court, where he served first King Henry I and then King Stephen (1135–54). He was the nephew of Roger of Salisbury, Henry I's powerful treasurer, head of an important family of "new men" who had risen in royal service. The whole Salisbury clan, including Nigel's cousin Alexander, bishop of Lincoln (whom we will meet below), was thrown out of power in 1139 by King Stephen, precipitating a civil war that had been brewing ever since Stephen had managed to succeed his uncle Henry I in the place of Henry's daughter, Stephen's cousin Matilda. Nigel switched sides several times during the civil war (often referred to as the "Anarchy"), and his political activities impinged directly on the affairs of the monks at Ely. They had two main grievances against him, both stemming from his involvement in the wider affairs of England.

One of the prime consequences of Nigel's political commitments was his perpetual need for money. His repeated efforts to raise funds from the church of Ely for his own purposes continually aggravated the Ely monks. First, he needed money to try to stay in the good graces of King Stephen despite his wavering loyalty. Later, he required substantial funds to buy the office of treasurer for his son, Richard FitzNigel, who went on to a glorious career (the famous *Dialogue of the Exchequer*, which explains the workings of the English treasury in the late twelfth century, is attributed to him). It is important to keep the division of the church's estates in mind, since it explains why Nigel had to bargain with his monks, albeit from a position of strength, in order to obtain their financial support for his external activities. He was not in fact entitled to the proceeds from their estates and was ultimately sanctioned by the pope for diminishing the church's holdings. Hence, he often resorted to a method of fund-raising that particularly irritated the monks: the pawning or sale of church ornaments that were made of precious metals and thus represented a substantial asset to be liquidated.

Quite apart from Nigel's raiding of the church's resources, the monks of Ely deeply disliked the household of political and military advisers that Nigel gathered around him. Although many were clerics, they were certainly not monks, and thus these men did not fit in well with the ordered monastic life of the church; the brothers greatly resented their presence and their influence over the bishop. These advisers plainly owed their loyalty to Bishop Nigel personally, and not to the church that he was supposed to serve. If Nigel is the chief villain of the *Book of Ely*, then his followers certainly play a large supporting role.

The structure of the *Book of Ely* is designed to emphasize Ely's past glories and to express disapproval of the current regime of the bishops. It is divided into three books, each of which covers a distinct phase in the history of the church. The first deals with the foundation of Ely as a double monastery by St. Æthelthryth and runs until the devastation of the church by the Vikings in 870 and the subsequent abandonment of religious life there. The second book carries the story from the refoundation of the church by St. Æthelwold in 970 as a monastery for men through the Norman Conquest of England in 1066 until the reign of the last abbot of Ely. Finally, the third book treats the time of the bishops. The portions of the text translated here have been taken from this last book. For reasons of space, I have translated only the most important miracles from the reign of Bishop Nigel; these miracles also provide a particularly strong example of how the compiler of the Book of Ely deployed his hagiographic material in order to comment upon the reign of the bishop.

The miracles translated here do not occur together in one place in the text but are instead scattered throughout the account of Bishop Nigel's reign (I have provided summaries in square brackets of the material omitted). The pattern is neither random nor strictly chronological. The story of Nigel's rule is presented as a series of conflicts, usually between the bishop himself and the monks of Ely. First, the compiler gives his own version of the particular case at issue. Next, he transcribes any supporting documents that pertain to the conflict, including charters and papal letters. Finally, after the conflict has been resolved in one fashion or another, whether favorably for the monks or not, the compiler then includes a group of miracle stories. Their function in the text is clearly to reinforce the spiritual authority of the house of Ely at a crucial point in its history, after the resolution of a dispute. Usually the miracles do not deal directly with the substance of the conflict just presented, but they often allow comparisons to be drawn that make the compiler's larger points about ecclesiastical authority and its proper exercise.

Furthermore, each group of miracles, which can be either quite short or very lengthy, tends to contain a good assortment of different miraculous manifestations, as if to prove the diversity of St. Æthelthryth's talents. Usually there is a blend of healing miracles and chastisement miracles, with the occasional miraculous rescue thrown in for good measure. The cures are largely straightforward, but the chastisements require some comment.

At first it may seem surprising that saints would behave in what seems like vengeful ways, but in fact, to a monastery of the twelfth century, the protection offered by a saint against the Church's enemies was often one of the most potent weapons they possessed in difficult times. The chastisement miracles in the *Book of Ely* are especially striking. They highlight the matters that worried the monks and made them feel vulnerable. Among these were attacks on the monks' estates and disrespect paid to the monastery's patron saint and the other saints venerated there. Both the material and spiritual possessions of the church were important to the continued success of the community.

Obviously, the monks' lands provided the income and goods in kind from which they derived their livelihood. Less immediately apparent is the material importance of the saints. Their cults also provided revenue to the church in the form of donations. There was stiff competition among the churches in a given geographical area for the lucrative pilgrim trade. The protagonists of miracle stories in the *Book of Ely* are often enjoined to go to the church itself for a cure, sometimes from quite far away. Donations and the prestige that went with them were more likely to flow to the church if they were solicited at the source. On the other hand, St. Æthelthryth is also shown healing at a distance, to demonstrate the breadth of her authority. The wider the area in which the saint's power could be felt, the more successful the church would be in attracting patrons and prestige.

Whether the audience for the *Book of Ely* extended beyond the walls of the monastery itself is not certain, since all the surviving manuscripts come from Ely. It is clear that the text was meant for the monks themselves, as a vehicle for teaching the history of the church and fostering pride in belonging to a community with a proud tradition. However, it may also have been used for a kind of community outreach, either directly, by dissemination of the text, orally or in writing, or indirectly, by serving as a primer for monks who would then spread material gleaned from the text in their interchanges with the inhabitants of Ely and its surrounding area. The miracles recorded in the *Book of Ely* contain a varied cast of characters ranging from individual monks to prominent local laypeople to obscure residents of the Ely estates, perhaps lending these stories a broad appeal. While the cures may have been meant to attract pilgrims and donations, the chastisements may well have been noised abroad as a warning to Ely's enemies.

Several of the miracles translated here may not look much like miracles at all. The reason for this is that they were actually derived from charters concerning specific legal transactions and were later dressed up as miracles in an attempt to show the intervention of the saint in the monastery's affairs. These odd miracles, that read more like dry legal documents with a few supernatural flourishes thrown in, usually at the end, offer an important window onto twelfth-century views of sanctity and the role of saints in the life of a church. It was just as important to the monks that their patron saint protect them in legal disputes over property as that she demonstrate her power to cure disease. Because the *Book of Ely* contains so many legal documents, it is especially noteworthy when a charter has been converted into a miracle; this indicates that the compiler is making an important point about the saint's ability to protect the house in all its undertakings.

Since the miracles presuppose some familiarity with the *Life* of St. Æthelthryth, a brief summary here will be useful. She was born in the early seventh century to King Anna of the East Angles. She was married twice, first to Tonbert of the Gyrwi and then to King Ecgfrith of Northumbria, but in each of her marriages she managed to preserve her virginity. When her second husband tired of her piety, she fled his court and took refuge in the Isle of Ely, a very remote spot at the time, in the marshy fenlands of eastern England, where the best way to travel even very far inland was often by boat. There she founded a monastery for both men and women and ruled over it as abbess until her death, when she was succeeded by her sister Sexburga, who had her body translated (moved) from her original tomb into the church. At the time her tomb was opened, it was found that the body was uncorrupted, a very important criterion of sanctity. Sexburga herself was succeeded by her daughter Eormenilda and granddaughter Werburga, all of whom were venerated at Ely in addition to St. Æthelthryth, along with another of Æthelthryth's sisters, Withburga, who had been a recluse at Dereham in Norfolk. Several of these relatives of the founder recur in the miracles, often as messengers for St. Æthelthryth.

Above all, however, it is St. Æthelthryth to whom the monks of Ely turn for help, especially when more worldly forms of protection, such as wealth and legal privilege, fail to safeguard their material and spiritual interests. Although the *Book of Ely* records all the sources of the community's power—its property and its treasures as well as its saintly patronage—it was ultimately in the power of the saint to confer healing, ensure prosperity, and punish enemies (even if these included the bishop himself) that the monks of Ely placed their faith.

SOURCES AND FURTHER READINGS

This translation was made from the edition of the *Liber Eliensis* by E.O. Blake, Camden third series 92 (London, 1962). References to the text in the notes are to Blake's edition. All the texts here translated are whole chapters from Book 3. The intervening material between the selections has been summarized by the translator in brackets. The text has not previously been translated. Blake discusses the value of the *Book of Ely* as a historical source in "The *Historia Eliensis* as a source for twelfth-century history," *Bulletin of the John Rylands Library* 41 (1959): 304–27. For the best study of the cults of St. Æthelthryth and her royal kinswomen, see Susan Ridyard, *The Royal Saints of Anglo-Saxon England: A Study of West Saxon and East Anglian Cults*, Cambridge Studies in Medieval Life and Thought, fourth series 9 (Cambridge, 1988), pp. 50–61, 176–210. For the history of Ely's landed endowment, see Edward Miller, *The Abbey and Bishopric of Ely: The Social History of an Ecclesiastical Estate from the Tenth Century to the Early Fourteenth Century*, Cambridge Studies in Medieval Life and Thought, new series 1 (Cambridge, 1951; reprinted, 1969). For a study of the relationship between bishops and their chapters in England after the Norman Conquest, see Everett Crosby, *Bishop and Chapter in Twelfth-Century England: A Study of the Mensa Episcopalis*, Cambridge Studies in Medieval Life and Thought, fourth series 23 (Cambridge, 1994); Ely is discussed at pp. 151–74. A useful orientation to the events and problems of Stephen's reign can be obtained by reading both R.H.C. Davis, *King Stephen*, third edition (London, 1990) and Marjorie Chibnall, *The Empress Matilda: Queen Consort, Queen Mother and Lady of the English* (Oxford, 1991). Finally, for an overview of the latest scholarship on the Anarchy, see the volume of papers edited by Edmund King, *The Anarchy of King Stephens's Reign* (Oxford, 1994).

The Book of Ely

[**Translator's note:** Nigel of Salisbury has been received as bishop by the monks at Ely. An account follows of the misdeeds of Nigel's servant Ranulf, to whom he had entrusted the day-to-day affairs of the church of Ely. St. Æthelthryth causes his perfidy to be revealed, and he is forced to flee. Bishop Nigel, terrified by his servant's fate, is frightened into restoring some of the church's possessions that he had appropriated and issues a charter confirming the monks in possession of certain properties. From the group of five miracles that follows, only one is translated here.]

(60.) On a girl, blinded in the right eye, whose sight was restored before the body of blessed Æthelthryth.

In the second year after the consecration of our lord and father Nigel,[1] the venerable bishop of the holy church of Ely, at dusk on the octave of the ides of June [June 6], a most celebrated miracle occurred at the tomb of the blessed virgin Æthelthryth. For a beautiful virgin, of noble descent, distinguished character, and praiseworthy reputation, as those who knew her maintain, who could only see with her left eye, since her right eye had been completely destroyed, was deemed worthy of having her sight restored at the tomb of the sacred virgin and of drinking in beauty with both her eyes. This notice will give a true account of how this happened as the result of a sacred revelation. The girl was born of an illustrious family in the province of the Mercians, in the ancient city called Cirencester.[2] When she lost her father while still a child, she and her mother moved to the region of the East Saxons.[3] There her mother remarried, to a prominent man in the celebrated city of Wallingford named Ranulf, called *grossus* because he was rather corpulent, who was highly esteemed due to his many good deeds for men of faith.[4] As befitted his worldly position, he determined that the girl should enjoy a sparkling reputation for purity, just as if she were his own daughter, and that she should aspire both to beauty and to wealth of moral character. One night, while she was lying in bed, she was taken gravely ill after being terrified by an apparition. For there appeared to her a splendid, heroic woman of high color and piercing glance whose indomitable resolve was unmistakable.[5] She stood by the bed and struck the half-awake girl sharply in the face, so that a great rush of blood poured out from her nostrils in a flood and stained the bedclothes, and after striking a great blow on her right side, she solemnly withdrew, greatly agitated and with wildly inflamed eyes, without addressing her at all. And when the girl awoke, she was at once seized by a very grave illness, and the whole household was worried about the adverse state of her health. When they approached nearer they realized from the sight of the blood that the vision she had related was true. And since Solomon says, "The rod and reproof give wisdom, but a child left to himself will bring shame to his mother" [see Prov 29:15], perhaps God saw fit to instruct her by means of an affliction of this kind, so that after this she might not be subject to any threat to her virginity. Thus the infliction of bodily disfigurements serves in this way as a safeguard for a girl's humility. The next day was Friday, the day on which Christ fought for the world with Zabulus.[6] Evidence of the seriousness of her infirmity mounted, so that if she had had anything worth distributing, she should have speedily made a will. The girl was sick for a whole week until the day that the pagans designate by the name of Jove.[7] Since she almost completely lacked the breath of life, she asked earnestly for ministers of the church, and having made a confession and faithfully received the sacraments of the Lord, she immediately fell silent. When the night which precedes the day on which man was created came again, a noble personage appeared, clad in white garments, a woman of imposing authority indeed.[8] "Hey, Reinburgis," she said, "are you asleep or awake?" And when she made no response at all, but lay absolutely speechless, turned toward the wall as if resolved on death, the saint again addressed her, calling her by name a second time. "Reinburgis," she said, "why do you make no reply? In all the world there is no prince's or emperor's daughter who does not readily heed my voice and take care to answer my questions." The girl heard all these things, but she was unable to respond. Then the woman said a third time, "Awake, Reinburgis, awake. I see you are truly overcome by a wondrous insensibility." After a while the illustrious saint said to herself, "I am waiting too long; I am wasting too much time in talking." And producing a flower from her bosom, she quickly put it in the girl's mouth. The power of speech was forthwith restored to her; nevertheless, she was not roused from sleep. And the woman said, "Do you not recognize, Reinburgis, the face of the one who is speaking to you? Do you not know who I am, whence and why I have come? Or are you well enough to hear that I will restore to health this sick flesh that you bear?" The young girl replied, "I hear you, lady, I hear you, and with your intervention I will recover by the grace of God." Then the noble and praiseworthy saint said: "Your body has borne a heavy blow from my right hand, but you will duly receive healing from me. Your cheeks are pale and thin from my blows, and your black and blue side quakes in suffering. Therefore my lady, the virgin and remarkable Queen Æthelthryth, who could no longer bear the tears of your mother, sent me with a remedy that she designed for you. This cure has come down to you from her through me from the highest heaven. She orders you to appear before her, so that you might hereafter be saved from dangerous misfortunes." From the first day of the illness, her mother had continually battered at the door of clemency of the most holy virgin Æthelthryth and had directed her prayers and tears of great devotion to her alone, in preference to all the rest of the saints. "Thank you," the younger one replied, "for there is no sign of any suffering remaining in my body." The sickness departed, her strength returned, and the illness which had seized her body receded. "You have hitherto borne the burden of a grave illness, but you will not recover completely in the way that you suppose," she said. "But be a daughter for a little while and bear up and you will be completely cured of this disease." And applying her hand gently to her side and piercing it without pain, she inserted her arm up to the elbow and lightly stroked her heart with the tips of her fingers. Then the young girl said: "There is no danger, lady. Behold, I am strong and healthy, and everything harmful to my health has now been completely removed." "The grave illness," she responded, "has been taken from you and yet perfect health has not yet been restored." The woman drew back her right hand and again inserted it, so as to soothe her. And she performed the same action as before for a second time. "Now, lady," said Reinburgis, "I am healed. I am entirely restored to health." And she replied: "This cure has nearly been accomplished; it will be completed by the third application of the remedy." Therefore, by doing what she had done twice before she completed it in the name of the Holy Trinity, and removed her hand from her heart and her arm from her insides. And she smeared the side that she had pierced with ointment and thereby restored the part that she had anointed to its original healthy state. She again admonished her vehemently to go to the tomb of the blessed virgin and not to become mired in delays while preparing for the journey. The girl promised the woman that she would adhere to whatever she ordered. "I am ready," she said, "to perform what you command and to be brought to the sacred church of the blessed virgin." "Go," said the figure a third time, "do not delay, lest you fail to fulfill what has been enjoined upon you. Remember the great perfection of the queen whose goodness will restore you to health, and when you come to her, you will be completely cured." The girl very quickly added that she would by no means be willingly thwarted in what she had promised, if only a companion were at hand who could offer her help. "What kind of protection, girl," she said, "do you seek?" She replied: "I am a powerless girl, deprived of a father's aid, subject to the rule of my mother, and I cannot be placed under anyone else's counsel without her consent." The girl's brother, who was at her bedside, taking pity on his sister's misfortunes, silently and attentively took in the words of the one who was responding,[9] but he could neither see nor hear the person addressing her. His mind thus did not by any means conjure up in error this truth, that the execution of a celestial command compels the performance of virtuous deeds without delay. The woman, however, showing her full stature and exhibiting a more severe expression than usual, addressed the girl with authority in these words: "I am here to convey orders and set out rewards and punishments," she said, "and I am offering you what you need to be saved. The queen has commanded; let her commands be fulfilled. Let the order of Æthelthryth the most holy virgin—she is my lady—be obeyed for her sake, although it is proclaimed by the voice of another. Now, since you are holding out an excuse and showing uncertainty and are not speedily taking up your journey toward her, whose copious grace goes before you, through this mark you will recognize a sign for you of the greatness of her power and her dignity. And you will not soon forget this decree, the truth of which you will experience." She rebuked her with bitter words; she reproved her with a menacing expression; and since she demonstrated that the matter was not at all difficult for her, by the wrath she displayed she rendered her more wary. Having seized her right eyelid, she pulled it over the pupil, and threatened her in these words: "Since you are ignoring sound advice, and since you are avoiding the gift of useful medicines, your right eye will be disordered because your faith is disordered, so that you will be unable to see human things, and you will not recover the sight you previously enjoyed until you appear before the holy virgin of God, Æthelthryth." After she said this, the woman disappeared. When the girl awoke, she placed faith in the truth of the vision and wept shamefaced tears, nor could pain torment her more than shame. However, we should preach the compassion of grace rather than the die of fortune: Although for the praise and glory of God she took away the girl's sight, she preserved the complete freedom of her mind. Although she rages in the sea of misfortune, in the land of the wise man she makes use of tools. Reason tempered her blindness, discretion added trust to her good faith, so that she might not fall away from virtue and be tormented by despair. The girl concealed the heavy misfortune of her sore eye as best she could for a whole week. Thursday was over, and the light of Friday was beginning to break forth. Her companions had lain down to rest, and she was also settled in her bedroom to sleep, when behold, the woman who had come before came again a third time and addressed the girl by name: "Reinburgis," she said, "I have appeared again, indeed, I have come to you again because I am worried about you." At these words she invited the noble lady to sit against the adjoining area wall. Suddenly, a woman of middle height appeared,[10] dressed in female attire, who with a fierce expression uttered a stern proclamation, full of bitterness and threats: "What," she said, "Oh abominable youth, have you dared to do such a wicked deed? Have you failed to perform the order of my lady that has been proclaimed so often? Why were you, with your impudent brow, not ashamed to put off what such a great queen commanded you to do? How have you fallen into such great folly and confusion that you are violating the precept especially enjoined upon you? Why have you delayed in completing, out of the idleness of a perverse mind, what the blessed virgin Æthelthryth ordered you to do? Since due to extraordinary fickleness and inconstancy you have refused to be swayed by the dictates of reason, you will suffer the consequences of your lack of judgment. Therefore, I will carry out a suitable punishment at my lady's command. So that she may respond as you so richly deserve to the injury you have done, you will meet your downfall." Then the woman who had come first said: "O servant and message-bearer of such a great virgin, put compassion before justice and stay the scourge of such a heavy penalty. Take the rod [see, for example, Ex 7:9], so that she might perceive your unaltered purpose." "I cannot delay, as you implore," she said, "nor do I dare concede what you ask of me. The incorruptible virgin ordered me to punish the fault of her heedlessness so that hereafter you might give heed to the severity of the verdict and its cause." Hearing this, the noble lady lamented and interceded for the girl a second and third time, and when her petition was totally in vain and the smaller woman could not be brought to forgiveness even by many prayers, the avenger of sin pulled her up by the hair, and taking a very long iron key, which she had previously concealed about her person, she stuck it into her head cruelly, into her eye and her brain, penetrating her with unbearable pain. "I have carried out the order enjoined upon me," she said, "obedient to the will of the one who commands me." After she said this, she disappeared. Then the worthy lady quickly poured a drop of healing liquor onto the iron key, which sprang out of her neck, and all the pain in her head was relieved. And Reinburgis was once again rescued from destruction, saved by celestial medicine. This event, which shines forth with all the splendor of miracles, is entrusted to divine witness. The woman had summoned her in the guise of a guardian, soothing her moreover with soft words, but now, speaking as a person of command, she exclaimed to the girl with the greatest authority: "I am the harbinger of a remarkable deed. Since you have now struggled much concerning your success and health, you ought to have discharged gladly what must instead be exacted from you with torments, and to worship willingly instead of being afraid. It is ordered by blessed Æthelthryth that you delay no longer, but go to her as quickly as you can, and you will not enjoy this cure, unless you help by providing a good inner disposition. Visit the place which we favor and adorn with the presence of our bodies alongside our lady. When you have come there, between the reliquary and the tomb of the glorious virgin and queen, which is fittingly located in the northern part, while lying there with a lit candle you will fall gently into a sweet sleep, and when you awake, you will receive the sight that you have lacked for many days. I forbid you to drink any cider until you appear at the place I have named. Due to the great worry about you that had arisen in me, I caused your cup of water to be emptied out yesterday at the entrance to your bedroom as a safeguard against death. If you had swallowed that drink, and if your throat had not vomited up what it had drunk, the disease that lay hidden in the vessel of death would have exposed you to eternal ruin. I fight you and have struck you between the shoulders and have freed you from this kind of death. Therefore, do the best and healthiest thing for you, which is to proceed swiftly to the virgin, whose command you have heard so many times. Let your recollection of this vision remain firmly fixed, so that it may not easily fade from your memory. On the day of the expedition thither, do not by any means tarry in this region until evening, if you wish to obtain the recovery that has been promised. If indeed you remain, and do not leave the town, and the flame of your devotion does not increase, then the passion of her who gave the order will grow cool in this matter, since a lesser love was stronger in you. You will neither recover through her nor attain the health you desire. Instead—indeed and it is very important that you hear this—sudden death will seize you to himself with his nimble arms and drive you from your body." Once she had said this, the image vanished, and when the girl awoke, she arose and imparted what had been revealed to her to her mother and urgently begged that she might hasten on the journey. All that she had seen was quickly told, and her stepfather and mother did what was asked. The girl's brother even appeared unexpectedly, having been released from his duties, after having been absent from the region a long time. He prepared provisions for the journey and hastened to set out on the appointed day, and they quickly reached the Isle of Ely. And what the girl said happened to her on the same day on which she took the way to St. Æthelthryth for her betterment should be solemnly noted. As her faith burned in her breast, her body was soon completely cured, except that she could not open her right eye. However, never did sleep creep over her on that journey; instead, her troubled eyes were wearied by continual sleeplessness. At last, when she arrived at the tomb of the most holy virgin at around the time of Vespers, she kept a pious vigil there, and when the virgin lay down in the northern aisle with her lamp lit, just as she had been ordered, she gently fell asleep on the pavement. Shortly before, she had fearfully revealed to the senior religious of the church what had happened to her and the blindness that plagued her. And the severe punishment inflicted by the celestial hand made her ashamed, despite the fact that her unworthy blood would not stain her lineage and the distress of her private affair would not blacken the noble name of her own people. When the wellborn maiden had thus lain her head to rest for a little while before the tomb of the most holy virgin and remarkable Queen Æthelthryth, blood suddenly poured from her right nostril, which quickly roused her from sleep. She used the sleeve of the garment she was wearing to stem the flow of blood, lest the outpouring stain the floor. And with the greatest devotion she nobly exclaimed, "I thank you, brightly shining virgin, venerable and glorious queen, that I can now see the worldly things that had been hitherto closed to my eye." And placing the candle that she was holding in her hand on the wall, she closed her left eye with her left hand and with her right hand made a sign with her right eye to indicate that she had most definitely experienced the effects of a sacred revelation. The faithful who were present, who about an hour before had seen her eye disordered and swollen, were astonished when they saw that it was now bright and quite free from all deformity. The joyful cry of the saints reached up to the stars, and the voice of the people rang out joyfully with unbounded celebration. The news did not fail to go out to the congregation, who had gathered from different parts of the kingdom out of love for the queen and virgin for the praise and glory of God. The radiant and beautiful girl was led before the sacred table of Christ, with her happy expression and her beautiful face now subtly changed. She described the divine favor that had been conferred on her to all who wished to know, laying it out very clearly just as I have told it. Therefore, good Jesus, in these and in the rest of your miraculous works we praise you, God, and profess that you are the Lord of heaven and earth, who thus glorifies the miracles of your blessed spouse and most intact virgin Æthelthryth far and wide, so that they may appear full of grace to all who may hear and judge them. The precentor of the church, moreover, solemnly began the hymn that I mentioned [the *Te Deum laudamus*], and the whole congregation joyfully honored God's great works with tears of spiritual joy.[11] It is fitting that all the faithful should know that just as those three revelations were made to her on the evening which takes its name from that of Jove,[12] she also deservedly attained the improvement of her health on the same day, at the hour of evening worship. She remained praying at the tomb of the consecrated virgin, pouring forth abundant tears, and having received her release, she returned home, where her family and friends were filled with joy that her health had been restored to her by heaven. From that maiden who had been deprived of sight there emerged one who found in herself the grace of such a great cure. Perhaps the sacred virgin of Christ and famous queen Æthelthryth has in fact shown us other things in our time secretly, but in modern times no miracle as joyous as this one has appeared so clearly.

[**Translator's note:** There follows an account of the difficulties Ely and Bishop Nigel suffered during the Anarchy [ca. 1139–44]. Several times Nigel changes his allegiance from King Stephen to the Empress Matilda and back again, and he must ultimately buy back the king's favor for three hundred marks, a considerable sum.[13] He strikes a bargain with the monks that he will pawn certain church treasures to raise the necessary funds, pledging to turn over his estate at Hadstock if he cannot redeem them, with the members of his household acting as the guarantors of the agreement. In the end, he fails to raise the money and is forced to concede the estate to the monks, but the loss of their precious treasures galls them, as the first miracle in the next group shows. It is really an inventory that has been converted into a miracle to demonstrate the vengeance of the saint for the loss of her church's possessions. Many of the items listed here can also be found in another inventory ordered by Nigel at the beginning of his reign (see Book 3, Chapter 50).]

(92.) The bishop's guarantors for the money taken from the church and the misery that befell them.

And now indeed, while I have pen in hand, I will write down what should be remembered about the men mentioned above,[14] lest sloth hamper this work from the very outset. Indeed, these guarantors of the church's monies hung on the lord bishop, always advising him, while they were engaged in ruining the church's property, to seize its riches and its most valuable possessions for himself and to reduce and finally eliminate the allotment for the monks' needs, so that they could thus in the end compel the monks to leave the church and their possessions to them, which they knew would please their lord.[15] For he did not call to mind the grants or the charity that they had formerly dispensed to their father [Bishop Nigel] from their allotment, out of pity for him. Indeed, none of these things forestalled his raging, and he still reached out his rapacious hand to seize control of all the profits of the church. Since it had been completely stripped of sacred vessels, he now chose it as a dwelling place for his own advisers rather than for divine worship; he was perpetually cruel and hostile toward the monks, so that it was impossible to tell if he was waging war more on men or on God. Thus he took the remaining ornaments of the Lord's temple,[16] which had formerly been adorned but was now indeed powerless and miserably overthrown, and pawned them to the bishop of Lincoln,[17] namely the cape and girdle of King Edgar of blessed memory,[18] and the alb with the fringe of Thurstan the monk, provost of the same church, and his *stola,* which would all certainly have been lost if the monks had not swiftly come to his aid with the thirty-nine marks that he had requested. They handed it over to him via the prior,[19] who then was, although they had obtained it with difficulty by deducting it from their allowance for food and clothing, but when he received it he spent it on his own concerns; and so on the final day appointed for the monks, when they would either have to redeem these objects or lose them forever, William the sacrist made another payment of sixty-seven marks of silver on the church's behalf.[20] Likewise, the church then redeemed for seven marks and six shillings and eight pence the pledges which the bishop had previously put out to Nicholas the clerk at London, namely a large chalice and silver tower-shaped pyx,[21] from which the enclosed relics had been stolen. Also, for a small golden book and for a silver handle it paid five marks to a man of Thetford,[22] and besides that in one year [Bishop Nigel] carried off from the sacristy twenty-four marks and six shillings.[23] Before this he had indeed likewise pawned to the Jews at Cambridge the aforementioned cross and book,[24] which the glorious, oft-cited Edgar had given to the church as a token of his generosity and munificence, and in order not be done out of such an important and famous possession, the monks gave two hundred marks via Prior William. Moreover, [Bishop Nigel] spent on hawking and hunting all the dues and offerings that had come in at the altar of St. Æthelthryth for three years. But he would neither read about nor listen to these matters; he considered that we had said a great deal about nothing much rather than just a few small things about very important matters, namely that he should at last take pity on the shattered and wounded church and stop injuring and harassing those who ministered there to the Lord. For the Lord will also take vengeance on his enemies and will make expiation at last for the land of his people [see Deut 32:43]. I will set out in order, albeit unwillingly, the account I promised of what he in fact did to lands and villages, dues and possessions, and the outcry of the people accuses him, and his excessive insolence is evident from afar. The doers of such deeds, to be sure, were also the said criminous clerks, namely Gocelin,[25] supreme in [the bishop's] counsel, crafty by nature, first in trickery, second to none in shameful deeds. He worked on Bishop Hervey shrewdly at the beginning of his reign and got him to promise to remove from his ministry the very lord who had cultivated him, Thurstan, provost and monk of the church [of Ely], by accusing him before King Henry, and he had no doubt that he would thus succeed to this ministry by deceit.[26] And although he ought to have used everything he had to repay the church fittingly, on the contrary he requited good with evil and caused the loss of the golden chalice of Wulfwine the monk, worth four and one-half marks. Moreover, he took on a colleague for himself, his equal in every sort of cunning, called Osbert of Wattisham, and both of them proved hostile to God and St. Æthelthryth, as if one were a Diocletian and the other a Maximian;[27] they unceasingly stole, wasted and alienated her property; and made a point of inflicting inestimable damage as they did their many cruel deeds. And indeed Gocelin, the war leader, boldly presumed to break into the tomb of the virgin Æthelthryth at night, and just as one reads that all violent plundering is effected with a tumult [see Is 9:5], he, too, totally transported by mad rage, boldly entered and was the first to lay hands on it and remove gold, silver, precious stones, and all the ornaments with axes and hatchets, and he ordered those chosen for the crime to carry out the orders of the lord bishop without delay, not knowing, miserable man, how swiftly he would pay the heaviest divine penalties as vengeance for the sacred virgin Æthelthryth. For he was seized by a sudden grave sickness of the feet, which the doctors call in Greek *podagra*,[28] and was rendered completely unable to walk, and although he wasted away for a long time due to this great misfortune and bore the reproof from heaven impatiently, he still did not want to understand that he should do good. Nor did he desist from his sinful, depraved ways, for he had spent his time as a priest living luxuriously and had squandered all the property of his provostship in pride and misuse. Therefore, he ended his life in poverty and tribulation, and neither he nor anyone associated with his offense felt any remorse at all; thus, the very memory of them has now perished [see Ps 9:6], as I will describe fully in the proper places.[29] Another member of the wicked league, the previously mentioned William of Shelford,[30] who took part in everything, advanced rashly with mattocks, hammers, and craftsmen's tools, prepared for the evil deed, and was himself the second to lay hands on the bier. He removed the money,[31] but he was soon most bitterly sorry for the deed. Although he was truly very rich and needed for nothing, he fell due to a mischance into such great poverty, that he did not even have the necessities of life, and when all his property was consumed, he did not know what to do or where to turn. At last, after asking for a very long time, with difficulty he obtained from the brothers reception into monk's estate in Ely, where he engaged in persistent tears and lamentation, vigils and prayers, and he spent the rest of his life in repentance, bemoaning his guilt. Then Prior Thembert and Sacrist Ralph,[32] devoid of good will and human kindness, who ought to build themselves up as a wall for the house of Israel [see Ezek 13:5], took part in the vile league and complied with the bishop in his heart's desires, although God should be obeyed more than men, and those who please men were put to shame, for God has rejected them [see Ps 53:6], just as a miraculous occurrence revealed. Suddenly the just felt the protection of God the judge while the guilty suffered and were plagued by sorrow and tribulation, that is to say they fell ill, and there was no one who would help [see Sir 51:10]. The former of these two was struck by an incurable paralytic illness and was deprived of almost all motion in his limbs and of the power of speech. The other one received a deadly injury to his face, and it began to swell due to the extreme pain, turning his whole jaw into gore, while the unwholesomeness of the disease spread throughout the wound. Thus, continually groaning in their suffering, both men were rendered powerless by their illness. Since no doctor's efforts could profit them, they died lamenting, after being horribly tormented for a long time due to the vengeance of God and St. Æthelthryth, because they rewarded her evil for good and hatred for love [see Ps 109:5]. Although she had reared them and brought them up, they however have scornfully rebelled against her [see Is 1:2].

(93.) How a pleasing vision of blessed Æthelthryth was revealed.

There are many things that belong in this history which even the greatest of poets would handle with extreme difficulty, while an unskilled one with an ignorant tongue might scarcely be able to understand them, but trusting in the Lord God, who makes the tongues of babes speak clearly and opened the mouth of the dumb beast [see Wis 10:21], I believe I will share in the resurrection with my most beneficent mistress Æthelthryth. I declare that after God and his most pious mother, she who brought me up and led me to this day of light and had mercy on me will always be a refuge for me and a remedy for sorrow, sighing heavily over my sins and crimes, for which I deserved her anger and the darkness of exile. For her glory I have put together this little book, a sort of new testament, as it were, as an account of and monument to her miracles, which I have uncovered by diligent searching, and I have gathered the scattered things written about her in one place,[33] not by my own efforts but with the help and inspiration of God's glory. I don't say these things to magnify my own voice or because I consider myself to be worth anything. My strength has failed me, and the light of my eyes—it also has gone from me [see Ps 38:10], and all day my words pursue me, so that every day it is said to me: "Where is your God? Where is your hope [see Tob 2:16, Vulgate], or your Æthelthryth, whom you have continually asked to bring you aid? In what ways has she helped you before or does she help you now? You praise her and cherish her, love her and venerate her, you attempt to commemorate her with your heart and with your mouth as well as with written memorials. Make sweet melody, sing many songs, that she may be remembered [see Is 23:16], but we do not acknowledge your writings or sayings, we despise them, we cast them off." But while I recount these things, I shrink back, weakened, from the purpose of my journey. Now I ask the grace of the reader, that his pious eye heed what I have added. For when the people of England, who were bitterly divided into two factions, were savagely harrying, burning, and slaughtering everywhere, nobles were expelled from their manors, and the local inhabitants, afflicted by many misfortunes, fled through town and countryside but were driven together to be killed, while a few barely saved themselves by hiding in churches.[34] Among these, along with innumerable others, was a teacher named Julian, who, since he had not found rest for his foot [see Deut 28:65], landed in Ely while lord Nigel was bishop. He was a man of admirable learning, second to none in grammar, more skilled in fact than some of the Latins, most adept at laying bare and expressing an argument, very prominent in every field of knowledge. His wisdom was swiftly recognized, and he was received with great reverence. He had first taught grammar and the arts which are called liberal overseas, as well as philosophy and rhetoric in his own city, London, the capital of England, and in the course of time he taught theology to some of the more industrious monks. In intimate conversations he was famous for his clever humor, and he uttered words and phrases adorned with rhetorical figures, always soberly, and of these he committed many most fittingly to writing. Indeed, he (may God have mercy upon him) urged the younger monks to study. He set especially earnestly and diligently about the task of educating two of them before all the rest, encouraged them to pursue what was honorable, and admonished them to shun what was improper and avoid the defilements of the world, earnestly instructed them from the depths of his knowledge, brought them up like sons as long as the job remained to be done, and endeavored by his encouragement to lead their souls to the Lord. I won't mention their names, because everyone living who knew the Ely community could serve as my witnesses. These had both been professed during childhood and received into the monastery. The younger one was the first to take up the monastic life, but he was arrogant, proud and vain, and neither the severity of the rule nor the rigor of discipline could at all tame him, and as he grew older in years, he increased correspondingly in vice. Having despised the fear of God and reverence for the holy habit, he was completely brought low; although he was in the house, nay in the citadel of forgiveness, he did not understand; he was compared to foolish cattle, and was made like them [see Ps 48:13, Vulgate]. He always delighted in rods,[35] and was hateful, turbulent, angry, and insolent in speech; he sought out discord and planted disputes among the brothers, disturbing the whole congregation so much that hardly anyone could tolerate him. And when he had led a life of every misdeed, so that he was considered infamous for his shameful acts, he was impelled to repentance at last by the mercy of God. He tried to wash away the filth of his prior crimes with fountains of tears, and he did not lift his eyes to Heaven or invoke the name of the Lord, but persisted solely in moaning, as if buried alive, and producing groans and heartfelt sighs. Thus through the grace of God he now trusted in the hope of salvation, which he had earlier given up on, and although he had wasted his time in heedlessness, he nevertheless loved the virgin of God, Æthelthryth, with all his mind, and moved to devotion by his ardent love for her, he produced by his own labors a little book of her life and virtues. The other monk, who was older in age but younger in profession,[36] had likewise been professed in the monastery. He was humble of mind, gentle of expression, most well versed in sacred Scripture, and due to grace, divinely conferred on him, he was very learned about many things, which the other monk did not know, and used to instruct him. He was indeed youthful in age but mature in character, governing himself strictly in the rule of holy conduct and leading a life given over to simplicity and prayer. He followed in all respects the life that he had learned that the venerable Æthelthryth had led. And when he had grown in fear of the Lord, so that he was praised even by those outside the monastery for the extraordinary austerity of his life, he was chosen there for the office of the priesthood. After his ordination, it was revealed to him in a vision that his death lay not far off. And he did in fact meet his end, overcome by a fever. However, not long after his burial, he appeared to the aforementioned heedless companion in a certain place in the monastery, in the porch of the blessed Paul. The latter, thinking he was in the midst of a vision, was struck dumb for a long time at the sight of him. When he asked whether he had died, he responded joyfully, with a peaceful expression, just like that of the man of extreme simplicity and innocence that he had been: "Do not be afraid of me because you think I am dead! I am alive and very happy." The brother considered this, and understanding that what he had seen was in no way a specter, and not at all afraid of the dead man, he took him by the hand and had him sit down alongside him. What I have to report is wondrous, and exceedingly pleasing to men in their present infirmity, and divine mercy does not wish to conceal from us what was done secretly. He added the following to what he had already said; indeed, he said: "I was in heaven before the divine majesty, where I also beheld the most holy virgin Æthelthryth, kneeling humbly before the supreme God and holding in her hand a book bearing the name of the man who produced that same book as a testament and a perpetual memorial to her glory. Moreover, she was recounting her works of mercy to the aforementioned brother." After saying these things, the apparition vanished. Indeed, the brother who had seen this here is faithful, and we trust his words; he set it down in writing, which I took not long after and hastened to set down on this page, so that all might reflect upon and understand our venerable advocate Æthelthryth and the great charity and sweetness with which she embraces and fosters those who love her and devotedly assist in her ministry. Blessed be God, who chose himself such a servant, that we might rejoice and be glad for her, and be satisfied with her consoling breasts [see Is 66:10–11]. Amen.

(94.) On St. Æilgetus, the steward of St. Æthelthryth.

I will not keep silent what many witnesses remember. A certain man was living in the village of Gretton,[37] and although he did not have many possessions, he was nevertheless considered in that neighborhood to be of outstanding faith and virtue. Indeed, he acquired the daily bread for his small household by the labor of his hands, going out in the morning to his work, and remaining thus at his labor until the evening. In the sweat of his face he ate his bread [see Gen 3:19], and since his body was weakened by hunger, his mind did not lust after pleasure and was accordingly quicker to meditate upon celestial matters. One day, when he was resting in his bed, while neither completely asleep nor completely awake, he saw a man appear to him in a dream, dressed in shining clothes, who roused him by striking him lightly with his hand, and exhorted him to keep watch, saying: "Arise, swift one, and in the morning hasten as quickly as you can without delay to St. Edmunds.[38] Diligently seek out the lord Ording, the abbot of that place.[39] When he has been summoned, you will make known the following commands. Saluting him in the name of the Lord, you will say that he should come prepared hither to the church of this town, and in the place in its cemetery that has been revealed and designated, he will find hidden under the ground the most blessed man Æilgetus, who was hitherto unknown to men. He was formerly the steward of the venerable queen Æthelthryth, who is mentioned above, namely in the first book about the virtues of the same virgin.[40] He should bring him forth from the earth and place him where he might be held in reverence." When the man awoke from the dream, he pondered the vision that he had seen. He arose and hastened to St. Edmunds. There he was led before the abbot, and he recounted the command he had received while he was asleep, just as he had received it. When the abbot heard it, he glorified the Lord, because He wished to reveal His saint through him in his lifetime, and he would have completed the mission divinely entrusted to him without delay, but he wished to put it off awhile due to some pressing misfortunes, wherefore, hindered by great worry, he could not afterward complete the task at all.

[**Translator's note**: There follows a long account of the monks' attempt to recover the estate of Stetchworth from a certain clerk named Henry, to whom (they claimed) the estate had been improperly alienated. During the dispute, Subprior (later Prior) Richard, who may have been one of the compilers of the *Book of Ely*, is sent to Rome to plead Ely's case before the pope. The monks are ultimately successful. It is no accident that the first miracle in the group that immediately follows is an account of the evil that befalls someone who has attempted to cheat the monks out of their rightful revenues.]

(115.) How a man who owed a debt to the monks of Ely committed the crime of perjury.[41]

In the year 1154, it happened that Stephen de Scalers, who by succession to his father's rights held of the monks of Ely in the village of Shelford two and a half hides and nine acres with one church for an annual rent of seven skeps, was withholding two years' rent from the monks.[42] And since indeed a mother should not fail to help her children when necessity presses in, Lord Nigel, who at that time held the bishopric of the church of Ely, after hearing the complaint of his monks and learning of the injury done to them, decreed that the aforesaid man should be bound by the chains of anathema if he had not paid the monks by the next Palm Sunday. Indeed, on the said day Stephen came before the bishop at Ely and swore vehemently that he had sunk into such great poverty that he was wholly unable to pay the said rent as he had in the past. The rent which he was able to pay was valued at forty marks in those days. The monks would even have taken their land back into their own hands at that time, if they themselves or any of their other adherents could have made out where it lay. But since time consumes the world itself, and those things that are of the world, the said land was completely unrecognizable even to the monks, on account of the passage of so much time, because certain boundary stones were broken and certain boundary lines completely erased. Wishing therefore to plan for their future and that of their church, the brothers took counsel with the bishop and agreed to forgive Stephen the whole two-years' debt, on the condition that he undertake under oath to make clear to them where their land lay and to pay the rent annually. Stephen agreed, promised, and swore. He swore indeed with his right hand placed on the altar of the holy cross, with the [consecrated host] and relics of many saints placed upon it, that he and his men would establish the limits of the land that he held from the monks in Shelford, namely two and one half hides and a church with nine acres, for those same monks as certainly as it could be shown, and he agreed on the annual payment of the rent for that same land under oath. If any of the said land be left over, that neither he nor his men knew about, he should pledge it out of his military fief, which he held in Shelford from the bishop,[43] and the bishop indeed agreed to this. At this Robert de Conington and Theobald de Scalers and William son of Roger, knights who have often been mentioned, promised on their faith with Stephen that they would not advise their lord to withdraw from the agreement and, if it were necessary, that they along with the monks would prove this against Stephen. These are the witnesses of this matter: Bishop Nigel, Archdeacon William de Lavington, David archdeacon of Buckingham, Richard of Saint Paul's, Roger the chaplain, Ingeram the chaplain, Ærnald de Lavington, John of Saint Albans, Richard of Stuntney, Master Roger, Grælangus de Tenet, Gilbert his brother, Ralph the steward, Alexander the butler, and Alexander the clerk, with the people of the town of Ely in attendance.[44] When the solemnity of Easter was over, Prior Alexander and Archdeacon William came to the church of All Saints in Shelford.[45] Stephen was also there with his men who dwelled in that town. Therefore, at Stephen's order, the priest, Richard, and all the inhabitants of Stephen's village swore that they would by no means conceal any facts about the land in question that they had learned from anything said by their predecessors or by any other means. These were the witnesses to the oath: Archdeacon William, Nicholas the chaplain of Cambridge, Robert Trencehart, Richard of Stuntney, Roger the prior's clerk, Peter and Osbert, clerks of Shelford, Robert de Conington, Theobald de Scalers, William the monk, Nicholas his son, Brand, and Gilbert of Shelford, Hervey son of Vitalis of Cambridge, Roger de Fossa of Melbourn, William, kinsman of the prior, Serlo of Hauxton and the inhabitants of the villages of Newton and Hauxton, Alfred the sacristan's man, Adam the son-in-law of Serlo. With these men present, neither Stephen nor his oath-helpers revealed the full extent of the fief, as they had promised, but instead committed perjury. Therefore the monks still have a grievance against him. Without delay, divine vengeance followed the perjury that the same Stephen had knowingly entered into to contribute to his damnation. For he came down with a serious and unbearable malady of the feet, and none of the doctors could cure him thereafter, and thus, suffering from the same disease, he grew old unhappily and died.

(116.) How mercifully God acted toward a sick man who was cured by St. Æthelthryth's merits at her spring.

It is known that all the miracles and the miraculous favors that have been performed in Ely by the grace of the Lord Jesus Christ, with the help of the powers of the virgin saints who dwell there, have taken place for the consolation of the simple, so that, seeing their good works, they might glorify the Father who is in the heavens. Much about these miracles has been laid out in the great book, mingled with the charters,[46] so that the saving cures people have experienced may not be hidden from another generation, but instead, the children who will yet be born and arise may not forget the works of the Lord and keep his commands [see Ps 78:6–7]. Therefore, our discourse begins there, and let no faithful one refuse to believe, wherefore let the hand of the writer not turn away from the path of truth. I intend to describe this one thing out of the many that Queen Æthelthryth in her many mercies, in accordance with the clemency of God, used to perform in the generation of those seeking her and seeking the face of the God of Jacob. In the province of Northampton lived a very poor man who was nevertheless renowned for his goodness;[47] hampered by infirmity, he mourned and languished for a long time [see Is 33:9]. For a poison, coursing through him to all his limbs, had caused a swelling in the shape of a wineskin, which weighed him down so much that he could neither walk nor stand, lie nor sit. But this infirmity, as the outcome demonstrated, was not mortal, but was rather meant to test his patience, so that the glory of God and the merit of the dear virgin might be made manifest in him. He was thus tormented incessantly, and his illness persisted and indeed grew worse. And when he had gone to bed one night after heaving many sighs, he fell asleep slowly and with difficulty, as is often the case for those who weep and suffer affliction. He now wholly despaired of his deliverance, indeed he had given up on anything that was not full of sorrow and invoked Christ alone with his perpetual weeping. But God, who hears all things, visits the sick, and comforts the troubled, did not scorn or despise the prayer of the poor man [see Ps 21:25, Vulgate], but consoled him in his tribulation, and saw fit to reveal to him in a vision through the person of a certain venerable lady that he would be able to receive healing from his illness. She offered him the means of a cure thus, saying: "O man, believe me, relief from your wretched infirmity and the restoration of your health lie in Ely. Hasten there and you will quickly rejoice in the health you desire." After hearing this, and turning over in his mind the vision he had seen, the man immediately arose to see if what he had perceived while asleep was true. The saint added these words of comfort to what she had already said: "There the glorious spouse of God, Æthelthryth, blooms wholly undefiled in body, continually resplendent with miraculous signs and wonders; she restores to health the people who flock there suffering from any kind of illness." Gladdened by these words, he believed these things had been shown him by God to give him greater hope; comforted, he began to rejoice, and he confidently undertook the journey that had been enjoined upon him, although it was burdensome and difficult for his feeble limbs. It happened, however, that he arrived at the courtyard of the said church at the hour when the brothers are summoned to take their daily food and bodily refreshment, when it is customary for all entrances and exits to be barred and particularly well guarded. Nevertheless, at that moment he found one of the guards hastily closing the door, in the very process of fastening the bars. The man cried out to him, producing more of a sob than actual words, and asked to be allowed to go inside a little ways. He refused and called the wretched man uncouth and lazy, and moreover, stirred to fury, he gave him a slap and ordered him to be gone. He stood there beseeching him and praying and earnestly admonishing him that for the love of God and of His lady St. Æthelthryth, he might at last be allowed to go up to the spring of the dear virgin. The harsh and cruel servant, roused by the poor man's misery to anger rather than pity, nevertheless feared that if it reached his masters' ears that he had offended a pilgrim, then he could scarcely endure the punishment that would result, so he said: "Behold, the door lies open, but there is no ewer at the well, and you do not have anything with which you could draw water, and the well is deep." He persevered in his prayer, however, that he might at least be able to go in to pray and go up to the well. When he was finally permitted to enter, although unwillingly, he looked all around, and although he had never been in that place to pray before, he miraculously reached the spring without any directions, as if he had known just where it was. He was looking around, since he had no bucket, when a branch of the spring suddenly burst forth and presented its services to the servant of God at the mouth of the well, and, as I speak truly, offered itself for drinking and flooded the surface of the courtyard all around with its waters, producing a large area suitable for healing. Taking the water up in his hand he poured it over his whole body, frequently invoking the name and aid of St. Æthelthryth. When he had tasted it, it splashed over all his limbs, and he immediately felt relief and began to recover, for the swelling deflated completely. He gave thanks to God and His dear virgin Æthelthryth. But the cruel and good-for-nothing servant awaited the pilgrim's return thus: He banged on the door, urged him to leave at the top of his lungs, and asked whether he was sufficiently full from drinking up the whole spring. But when he heard what had happened, he refused to believe it. At last, when the poor man had brought him a cup of water, he understood and believed, and so that he might be more sure of it, he rushed to the spring, which he found had overflown all around, so he himself became a witness to the event. Thus, as we have shown, the man drank from this water and washed and then came and happily and eagerly related to the aforesaid servant of the church what had happened, and how, when he came to the fountain, he found no ewer or any other vessel. Therefore, he went out and preached everywhere the grace of God miraculously performed in him through His ever-pious savior Æthelthryth. Indeed, those who came thither in hope often experienced the healing of their afflictions. The dropsical drank there and were cured. The blind washed and could see, as is contained in the following chapter for the praise of the most sacred virgin Æthelthryth.

(117.) Another miracle about the spring of St. Æthelthryth.

This water is truly a living spring, and the flowing stream perpetually gladdens the city of God that had been made sacred by the divine resting place of the mortal remains of the dear virgin Æthelthryth.[48] For she had originally been interred not there, but where she had died, in a wooden coffin buried in the cemetery deep in the bosom of the earth, where the choir stall of the bishop has now been built, in the midst of her people according to their rank.[49] There, with blessed Wilfrid and the doctor Kenfrid in attendance and an assembly of brothers and sisters gathered around, both her body and her vestments were observed to be completely uncorrupted by the working of miraculous powers, just as Bede tells us in the *History of the English*.[50] From there she was translated with great rejoicing by her sister Sexburga into the church of the ever blessed Virgin Mary, which she herself had founded, and placed by the altar, where she lay with reverence for a long time, namely for 435 years, until the nineteenth year of the pacific king of the English Henry,[51] when Abbot Richard again translated her into the new monastery as lady and abbess, located more prominently in a place of rest that had been prepared behind the high altar.[52] However, the monks turned the remaining hole in the ground where, as we have said, the virgin had rested for a long time, into a cistern, where the living waters by her miraculous powers constantly worked cures and continually cured the sick in her name. A girl who had been blind for a long time was brought to these same living waters by her neighbors and friends. On account of the mercy of the holy virgin that had been shown to innumerable people, they admonished her to fear nothing, have steadfast hope, and pray to her with mouth and heart. She placed her faith in what her family had said, prayed intently, and immediately her prayer was heard. Thus she came led by another, reached the spring crying out and invoking the support of the most pious Æthelthryth, immediately moistened her face with tears, and then likewise washed her face and eyes with water from the spring. She could then see clearly and rejoiced greatly. Therefore, she rendered thanks to her patroness Æthelthryth and to God for all His good works. She who had arrived blind, in mourning and sorrow, returned home without a guide.

(118.) Another miracle concerning the same spring.

Recently in summertime, while the brothers were performing the Divine Office in the choir at the first hour of the day, an event occurred that I will recount, of which I was myself a witness. A young girl came to the spring to drink the water, along with a crowd of hurrying people. But they turned her aside everywhere and roughly elbowed her out of the way, forcing her to go back. Nevertheless, when they had gathered in the middle in a rush, she plunged in, although she had to push to do so. While she was trying to outstrip the rest and retreat quickly after drawing her water, the vessel she was holding accidentally fell from her hand, and she fell in after it. When the people who were standing around quarreling with each other over the ewer realized this, they abandoned their dispute and ran away, calling out: "St. Æthelthryth, help." They saw her head pointing down toward the depths of the spring within, while her feet stuck out on top. She was immersed for a rather long time, for three or four hours. No one came by in the meantime who could save her, though Stephen and Richard, two clerks sitting nearby at their books, ran up. Fearing that she had been killed in the water, and both lamenting, alas, alas, they pulled her out by her feet. Not only had she not suffered any harm from being in the cistern for such a long time, by the virtue of St. Æthelthryth she in fact seemed to be unhurt. And thus the Lord preserved her uninjured in the depth of the whirlpool, just like Daniel of old in the lions' den [see Dan 14:34–42], lest the waters, consecrated by Christ to the glory of his beloved spouse, from which so many good works customarily arose, should be stained by a record of dishonor due to the shedding of blood. The place [Ely] should be venerated because of the help of our mediator Æthelthryth, who drives out various diseases from the sick, and heals the ills of the body with either a taste or a sprinkling from her abundant spring. Magnify it with me greatly, we who shall be satisfied with the goodness of thy house [see Ps. 64:5]. The temple of God is wondrous in equity [see Ps 64:6, Septuagint]. Let us cry out to God from the bottom of our hearts and say to the savior: "You, Lord of all things, in whom nothing is lacking, preserve this house intact forever, Lord. Amen."

(119.) How God severely avenged injuries to his beloved virgin Æthelthryth.[53]

Although the barbarians came to England from Denmark for a long time and ravaged it everywhere with fire and sword, at last, by the provident mercy of God, their strength failed, and in the end they were forced to return to their native soil and relinquish the land they had occupied, especially in the days of the venerable King Edgar, so much so that if one of them was found left behind, he would either be killed or subjected to torture.[54] By his order and authority the holy Bishop Æthelwold restored the monastery to the old rule and reformed the place and enriched it with estates, both by purchase and by acquisition.[55] He also bought the village of Downham, which is a very fertile village close to the monastery.[56] First he agreed to pay fifteen pounds for two hides to Leofsige and his wife Siflæd at Cambridge, and he fulfilled his bargain via Leofwine, a monk and provost of the church, in the presence of many faithful men. Meanwhile King Edgar died. When he was dead, the said Leofsige, an enemy of God and deceiver of men, and his wife, voided the entire agreement made with the bishop. At one point they offered Abbot Brihtnoth part of the money that they had received from him, and at another point they utterly denied that they owed him anything.[57] They believed that they would thereby recover by fraud the land that they had sold, but the church's witnesses always refuted them in everything. Thus, when the king had died, as I said, they disturbed and harassed us for a long time, so that for a long time no one either plowed or sowed the land or cultivated it in any way, and thus all the work of cultivation that had been done on it went to ruin. Therefore, when God saw that that deceiver was afflicting His servants with many great injuries and tribulations, He had mercy on their labors, and by His mercy the holy church of Ely recovered what it had unjustly lost. For, just as it is written in the Psalm, the righteous cried out for help and God heard them and delivered them out of all their troubles [see Ps 34:17]. While these things were going on and that miserable man was confident that he would freely and securely retain both what he had received from the holy church and St. Æthelthryth's property, and had not stopped troubling the servants of God, he died shamefully and miserably due to the raging of divine vengeance, in revenge for the virgin of Christ, and it was fulfilled in him, what is read in Solomon: "the righteous shall rejoice, but the wicked are overthrown by calamity" [see Prov 24:16]. I have taken this from the book of lands that they call the book of St. Æthelwold, so that those who read or hear these things may be afraid to seize or diminish the properties and goods of the holy virgin Æthelthryth; for judgment fell on whoever did such things [see Rom 2:2].

(120.) How God again wreaked vengeance on the enemies of blessed Æthelthryth.[58]

Another miracle follows and, although it is similar in kind, nevertheless it turns out to have entailed a different degree of risk. The brothers, however, were present and were thoroughly acquainted with the matter, and they set it down in English in what is now called the book of St. Æthelwold, but now we wish to bring it to the notice of all, translated into Latin, and we believe that if it has been listened to attentively, it will have been set forth as a warning for many. At a time when the troublemakers of England had assembled in London, a man named Wihtgar, who was not meanly endowed with property and possessions, offered to sell Bishop Æthelwold five hides at Brandon and Livermere.[59] When the bishop and the abbot heard this, they gave him twenty pounds for the land. They paid fifteen at that time with many venerable men as witnesses and sent one hundred shillings to him afterward via the aforementioned Leofwine, provost of the church, and Wine of Witchford, a most excellent man, who gave him the money at Brandon with the whole hundred in which that land lies as witnesses.[60] However, when King Edgar departed this life, a certain Ingulf unjustly and forcibly took Brandon away from God and St. Æthelthryth. "O miserable and unfortunate man, you will not be able to retain what you seize for as long as you think. You will very swiftly pay a grave penalty for this." Indeed, it is written: *No wisdom, no understanding, no counsel, can avail against the Lord* [Prov 21:30]. For so that the miraculous power of God and the merit of the blessed virgin could be revealed, from the day on which he invaded the properties of the church, he tasted nothing to eat or drink, for his heart was immediately ruptured. And thus it happened, that he who unjustly seized what is God's when he was alive could not retain it when he died, but lost himself and it along with his life. Once he was dead, his wife and his sons usurped that land in the same way, but since they did not give honor to God or to blessed Æthelthryth, neither did they preserve their lives. Divine vengeance thus blazed up over them, and within a year they had all died miserably. Then Siward, Ingulf's brother, greatly lamenting their deaths and seeking to protect himself, began to fear the judgment of the Lord, and against the will of many, especially Egelwine the Ealdorman,[61] he offered the land to St. Æthelthryth and freely relinquished it, so that with regard to this matter it would well be fulfilled what is read in Wisdom: "The house of the wicked will be destroyed, but the tent of the upright will indeed flourish" [see Prov 14:11]. However, the Lord destroyed the house of this impious man so that his posterity should not remain always in his sight [see Ps 60:8, Vulgate], because he had hated the holy church and the most blessed Æthelthryth without cause [see, for example, Ps 35:19; 69:4]. But God, who sees and judges all people, who pronounces their rewards and punishments, demonstrates that the wicked suffer reverses precisely when they believe that things seem easy for them, as it was shown in this man. However, as I will truly relate, and as it is very clear to all, not just he but all those in the realm of England, whether prince or potentate, who threatened or diminished the dignity or property of the place from which the virgin Æthelthryth was taken up from the prison of the flesh, suffered horrible bodily torments and always died miserably. These things should cause great fear and wonderment, for no one should doubt or ridicule what we relate, as if he might aim to perpetrate the like. Instead, chastened by the afflictions of others he should learn not to offend the virgin of God with injustice, but rather to please her with obedience.

(121.) The priest who refused to celebrate the feasts of our saints.

Just as we are taught in the Old Testament that the salvation of the righteous is from the Lord [Ps. 37:39], salvation is on the other hand correspondingly far from sinners, of whose number and assembly was one by the name of Gervase, who by much flattery obtained from Ralph the steward, an innocent and simple man, the office of the priesthood of Saint Cross, namely a parish of the town of Ely, but not in order to care for the souls of those entrusted to him, but rather so that he could exact a worldly profit and unrighteous mammon [see Lk 16:9]. For his sin swelled out with fatness, his heart overflowed with follies, he scoffed and spoke with malice; loftily he threatened oppression, and set his mouth against the heavens, and his tongue strutted through the earth [see Ps 73:7–9]. Besides this God gave him a worthless disposition, so that he would not do what was called for, as the result of his deeds confirmed, when he undertook to invalidate and destroy the solemnities and glories of our saints, namely of blessed Withburga, Sexburga and Eormenilda, so that their memory should not be perpetual and their name not persist from generation to generation. For he had pledged to master Ranulf the ex-monk that he would inflict damage on the servants of God and St. Æthelthryth, provoke them with insults, and oppress them with injuries.[62] For it happened once in the month of July that the priest had no desire to announce the feasts of the blessed Withburga and Sexburga before the people on the preceding Sunday, but wished to make no mention of them, since they fall in the same week.[63] Indeed, many who were there wondered aloud to each other why he did not mention their feasts, indicating to him in a whisper that he had not announced to the people the solemnities of their ladies. However, he refused, and exasperated by the matter, he pretended not to hear and proceeded hastily with the rest of the mass. But God, in whose sight all things are laid bare and open [see Heb 4:13], and who is glorified in the assembly of the saints, strengthened his hands and raised the right one to wreak vengeance [see Ps 89:7, 89:13] on behalf of those saints on their impious enemy, so that those to come might learn to observe the glorious solemnities and cherish the deeds of the virgins resting at Ely. Not long after this, namely within the week, by his hard and impenitent heart he stored up wrath for himself on the day of wrath [see Rom 2:5], since he went to a gathering to which he had been invited, and ate a great deal and drank with much enjoyment. After he had passed a whole night in lewdness and drunkenness, and had thus spent a whole week dedicated to gluttony and illicit pleasures, on the day in question he belched up still-undigested food at a mere touch. He made everyone laugh because he was unable to keep to the right path; nevertheless, he ascended undaunted to the altar. He did not fear the judgment of the Lord, nor did he feel in his heart that he should not presume to receive the life-giving mystery of the body of Christ unworthily. He arrived, put on the sacred vestments, and finished the rest uncertainly, as if distracted. He stood ready in all his priestly apparel until the Introit of the Mass, when, as a punishment from the Lord in revenge for his saints, in full view of all the people he fittingly met with bewilderment and disgrace, as he deserved. Because of his nausea, he vomited copiously from his upper orifice, and then with a rather loud noise he expelled the products of digestion through the lower one; thereupon, he collapsed on the ground. The people who were there, feeling for him in his misery, carried him to a more removed spot and took off his sacred vestments, which were thereafter no longer fit for the service of the altar. He led a miserable life for a short time, until he at last unwillingly acknowledged his offense, and he revealed that not only had he refused up to that point to publish the solemnities of the saints, but he had even forbidden that it be done. Therefore let God be praised in his saints, who are to judge the nations of the peoples.

(122.) On the altar cloth of St. Æthelthryth that was miraculously restored to the church of Ely.

When the most pious king of the English, Stephen, had held the kingdom for almost nineteen years, but very laboriously and with great difficulty, he grew sick with dysentery, from which he then died.[64] He was succeeded in the kingdom by his kinsman Henry, whom he had chosen as his heir after him, born of Lady Matilda, formerly empress, daughter of the old king Henry, begotten by a venerable father, Geoffrey, count of Anjou.[65] After he was received as king and consecrated by Theobald, archbishop of Canterbury,[66] he prohibited unjust laws, restored the peace that had been long absent, brought down punishment on transgressors, demolished adulterine castles,[67] and expelled factious men from the kingdom. No one was able to prevail against him; a hostile part of Wales alone held out in opposition.[68] He collected a great treasure, a large amount of gold and silver to pay for the expenses of knights to attack the city of Toulouse, a city in Aquitaine that he wished to bring under his sway.[69] Thereupon Bishop Nigel, realizing that the lord king needed money for such a great undertaking, made an agreement with him and bought for four hundred pounds an office at court, namely the treasury, for his son Richard,[70] who had been brought up at the monastery in Ely, a youth of great cunning and intelligence, who caused that house great misfortunes. And since [Bishop Nigel] did not have the means to pay, he appropriated the vestments and vessels and anything else of value from the house of St. Æthelthryth, saying that what was left was always sufficient. Moreover, he took an altar cloth, exquisitely worked with gold and gems, that Queen Emma had presented as a covering for the sepulcher of the holy virgin, and against the monks' wishes, he pawned it to the bishop of Lincoln, just as he did on another occasion, as it is written above, when he pawned it along with other goods of the church, but the monks redeemed it from there out of their own meager resources, lest they be deprived of such a great ornament.[71] For the bishop of Lincoln happened to go to Rome on his church's business, when lord Eugenius was pope,[72] and he wished to offer the altar cloth to the pope in order to acquire his favor. But when the apostolic lord saw the vestment, he was astonished at its great value, and upon looking at it more carefully in bright light, he realized that it came from some famous and ancient church. He asked where such an ornament might come from, and when he discovered that it was from Ely, he ordered under apostolic sanction that [Bishop Alexander] should return the ornament thither, with no excuses. Therefore, when all the business that had compelled the bishop to come to Rome was completed, he returned to England, bearing with him the altar cloth that he had brought. He wished to remove the gold from it, however, so he found goldsmiths and workers in gold fringe to carry out his plan. But although they used their hands, applied tongs, and set about cutting the precious gold fringe, it held up as firm as stone or brass against the sharpest implements. They tried again and again, but their effort was in vain. We tell this truthfully and believe that it must have been done at the will of the holy virgin, for the monks there were lamenting in sorrow that the altar cloth of their mother had been taken away, and when they had paid a price, they got back what they had unjustly lost, giving thanks to her for all her favors.

[**Translator's note**: There follows an account of how Bishop Nigel was suspended by the pope for allowing the alienation of some of Ely's estates. He was ultimately reinstated after promising to do all in his power to recover them for the church. After three miracles not translated here, there is a report of the efforts Bishop Nigel made to keep his promise to the pope of restoring the alienated estates. The two final translated texts represent two slightly different accounts, derived from a common original, of the deaths of Bishop Nigel and his servants; the translation attempts to reproduce the verbal parallels between the two versions, of which the second is clearly much more negative in tone.]

(137.) How Bishop Nigel fell ill and about his death.

In these days the paterfamilias of Ely, Bishop Nigel, fell ill, and his sickness was so severe that the breath of life scarcely remained in him. But I am talking about the first misfortune of his dread illness, and I will reveal how unhappily things turned out for us thereafter. A certain very poor woman dwelled at Ely, sustained by alms from the brothers and living a religious life.[73] She overcame her bodily desires with vigils and strict abstinence. On a certain night, while she slept, it seemed to her that she stood in the church at the door, looked at the altar of blessed Æthelthryth and entered to supplicate God and the saints who rest there. There she saw a nun descend toward the [tombs of the] saints from above the altar and then advance down the steps toward her. She looked into her upraised eyes and said to her: "Do you not see, good woman, how everything here is going to ruin, and there is no one who is taking any thought about it?" She was carrying under her shroud a staff, which she raised high before her and said: "With this staff I have destroyed the enemies who disperse the goods of this place, and by the command of God I will likewise use it further to destroy those who remain, as vengeance for the dear virgin queen Æthelthryth." To this the woman replied: "My lady, tell me your name and who you are, so that I may in truth know from whom I have learned these things." She replied: "I am Withburga,[74] the virgin whom God the heavenly bridegroom deigned to unite with, sister of the most sacred Æthelthryth. Relate faithfully what you have in truth heard and seen, and when morning comes you will meet the monk Augustine praying. To him you will reveal my greatest secrets." The woman, greatly terrified by these things, awoke, and just as it had been shown to her, she then found the said monk coming in, to whom she recounted the contents of her vision. When he heard it he was greatly astonished and said: "I put faith in these things without doubt, nor will I be amazed, if evil befalls us, because we always expect losses in this house." And not long after, when the Easter feast had arrived, the bishop, while sitting in the church, was seized with a grave illness and could scarcely be relieved by doctors' potions. And thus for three whole years he had to be carried in a chair by his followers because he was almost totally paralyzed. He persevered in confession and in beseeching God continually until the end of his life, but he was not thus transformed so as to do good to Jacob and the house of Judah [see Zech 8:15]. He died in the year of the Lord's Incarnation 1169, the thirty-sixth of his episcopate, on the third of the Kalends of June [May 30], on Friday at the ninth hour, and on the Sunday after he was buried by the venerable monk William, bishop of Norwich,[75] and honorably placed in the church of blessed Æthelthryth near the altar of the holy cross, in the seventeenth year of the younger Henry, king of the English.[77] The monks there indeed bewailed their orphaned state, mourning the death of their father and sorrowing greatly, beseeching God all together with prayers and tears that He not leave them orphans, but that He send them the Holy Spirit as a counselor and champion [see Is 19:20], and that He provide a worthy bishop and a suitable prior for their house.

(138.) How God severely avenged the injuries of his virgin Æthelthryth, and how Robert the Chamberlain gave Denney to St. Æthelthryth.[77]

Since the Lord had thus struck down the strong and powerful, proud and arrogant man, at the same time he consigned all the adversaries of his beloved virgin Æthelthryth to amazement and error, to hissing and blasphemy against all these round about [see Jer 25:9; 19:8, and elsewhere], as was described in the preceding chapter,[78] that is to say those who devised iniquity and gave the worst counsel against her [see Ezek 11:2], whom I have put off citing by name, wherefore I am considered by many to be guilty of untruth. And I went in too much bitterness in the heat of my spirit [see Ezek 3:14] to bring forth my recollections of the continued miseries of these men, which they had incurred as the result of their sins, since they moved me rather to lamentation than to scorn. Nevertheless, lest I be judged, both by monks within and by laymen without, to have accepted the grace of God unworthily, let me name those who acquiesced in the worst counsel, as the virgin of God had shown through a dream.[79] Indeed, just as the blessed virgin had predicted, the previous prior, Thembert, and the previous sacrist, Ralph, whom the Lord had made watchmen for the house of Israel [see Ezek 33:7], died, followed by the constable Adam, about whom horrible things were seen and revealed after his death.[80] The ruin of Alexander the butler followed theirs, for he was struck by an acute illness at the time of his betrothal, so that for a long time, until his death, he was deprived both of his wits and of the power of speech. No one doubted that he had been struck by the saint. Then William of Shelford, whom we have mentioned above, and Henry Peregrinus were struck down and lived in great pain for three years.[81] Next, indeed, Ralph Fitz Olaf, who deprived this house of our best altar cloth valued at forty pounds, and who had always been especially active in planning and carrying out the dispersal and theft of many of the church's valuable possessions, was now indeed, by the judgment of God, overcome by a sudden sickness.[82] There arose under his breast a bladder like tumor which the physicians call a carbuncle; after it was cut out, he could not be cured. Then Richard of Saint Paul's fell ill and so miserably declined, that his relatives and associates abandoned him completely.[83] One day when William, archdeacon in the same church of St. Æthelthryth, was pleading against his own lord, he was himself suddenly struck both deaf and dumb in front of everybody.[84] What else is there to say? He was carried by the monks to the infirmary, and after being plagued for a week by many different ailments, he expired nine days later without having stirred. Thus we call to mind the many malefactors of this house; we omit those of whom the people remind us incessantly, lest we make unreasonable demands on the reader. In the end, when the bishop was likewise sitting in the church conversing with those to whom he had undeservedly dispersed the possessions of the saint, he became seriously ill. With the breath of life scarcely remaining in him, he was carried outside lifeless, so that he who hears ought not to doubt that the Lord truly exacts vengeance against the enemies of His dear virgin Æthelthryth. But many had gathered to visit him, and concerning his reproof they zealously offered to God in his saints the fitting prayers of devotion. At last, when he had been rescued from the workhouse of the flesh, the monks most nobly, and with the greatest mourning and wailing, handed over the body of their father for burial in a fitting place in the church itself. When he had been buried, his son the above-mentioned Richard,[85] always an adversary of the church of Ely, feared that evil would be in store for him if the man whom the church would send to the king got there before him, so he went speedily to the king across the sea, to whom he accused [the monks] of many things, relating many sinister and dishonest things about them. He stirred up

The Book of Ely

the lord king so much that he sent an order to England via a certain clerk of his, Wimer the ex-priest, that the prior of Ely should be deposed from his ministry and the monks be proscribed in all their goods.[86] It was done.

[**Translator's note**: After Nigel's death, the *Book of Ely* gives an account of the acquisition of an estate at Denney, and then a brief history of the martyrdom of Thomas Becket. The text ends rather abruptly.]

Notes

1. That is, in 1135.
2. Cirencester is located in Gloucestershire, in the West Midlands.
3. The "region of the East Saxons," or the former kingdom of Essex, is located in southern and eastern England.
4. Wallingford is located in Berkshire, in southern England.
5. The "heroic woman" in question is probably St. Sexburga, the sister of St. Æthelthryth, who succeeded her as abbess of Ely.
6. Zabulus is another name for the devil.
7. That is, Thursday.
8. This is again a Thursday.
9. That is, the girl.
10. This woman is probably St. Withburga (d. ca. 743), the sister of St. Æthelthryth. She lived for many years as a recluse at Holkham and Dereham, and was buried at the latter location, but in 974 Abbot Brihtnoth had her translated to Ely, much against the will of the inhabitants of Dereham.
11. The precentor is the monastic official in charge of conducting religious services.
12. This is, once again, a Thursday.
13. A mark is a unit of money equivalent to two-thirds of a pound, or thirteen shillings and four pence.
14. The guarantors of Bishop Nigel's agreement with the monks, which is described in Book 3, Chapter 89.
15. There is no independent evidence for an attempt to convert Ely into a secular cathedral.
16. That is, the church of Ely.
17. Bishop Nigel's cousin was Bishop Alexander of Lincoln (1123–48).
18. King Edgar the Peaceable reigned from 959 until 975.
19. The prior in question is presumably Prior Thembert, who ruled for some part of the period between 1135 and 1151, when his predecessor and successor are attested.
20. The sacrist was the monastic official in charge of the furnishings of the church, including its treasures.
21. The pyx is a sacred vessel for preserving Eucharistic wafers.
22. Thetford is in Norfolk, in East Anglia.
23. This suggests that Bishop Nigel was using the income set aside for the sacristy, a serious infringement of the monks' independence.
24. There were several prominent Jews in Cambridge engaged in money lending. The book in question was mentioned in Book 3, Chapter 50.
25. Blamed in Book 2, Chapter 65 and Book 3, Chapter 50 for the loss of two chalices. A member of Bishop Nigel's household, he was one of the sureties for the money Bishop Nigel took from the monks in Book 3, Chapter 89, and is depicted here as the chief despoiler of the church's treasures.
26. Bishop Hervey served from 1109 until 1131. It is not exactly clear in which office Gocelin replaced Thurstan. King Henry I reigned from 1100 until 1135.
27. The Roman emperor Diocletian, who ruled from 284 until 305, appointed Maximian as his colleague in 285 to rule the western half of the empire while Diocletian took up residence in the east. Due to the Diocletian persecution of Christians begun in 303, neither man would be beloved of medieval Christian writers.

28. *Podagra* is gout in the feet.

29. See below Book 3, Chapter 138.

30. See Book 3, Chapter 78. A royal goldsmith who had helped Bishop Nigel raise money to buy King Stephen's favor. The tools he used to strip the shrine were probably goldsmith's tools. For his career, see Elisabeth Van Houts, "Nuns and Goldsmiths: The Foundation and Early Benefactors of St. Radegund's Priory at Cambridge," in *Church and City 1000–1500: Essays in Honour of Christopher Brooke*, eds. David Abulafia, Michael Franklin and Miri Rubin (Cambridge, 1992), pp. 59–79, at pp. 66–68, 72–73.

31. That is, the offerings of the faithful that had been deposited at the shrine.

32. The sacrist was an ally of Prior Thembert in despoiling the church's treasures.

33. This miracle is taken from a lost life of St. Æthelthryth; this passage looks like the preface to the lost work.

34. This passage refers to the so-called Anarchy, the effects of which were particularly severe in eastern England.

35. Which he used for meting out punishment.

36. See Gregory the Great, *Dialogues*, trans. Odo John Zimmermann (New York, 1959), bk 3, chap. 18, p. 148.

37. Gretton is in Northamptonshire, in the East Midlands.

38. The abbey of Bury Saint Edmunds in Suffolk, in East Anglia.

39. Abbot Ording of Bury (1146–56).

40. Refers to Book 1, Chapter 23.

41. This miracle is derived from a document dated 1154 that details the transaction between Stephen de Scalers and the monks of Ely. It has been converted into a miracle story.

42. For more on the career of Stephen de Scalers, see Van Houts, "Nuns and Goldsmiths," pages. 70–73, (see note 30 above). Shelford is located in Cambridgeshire. A "hide" was an Anglo-Saxon unit of land equivalent to about one hundred and twenty acres in this part of England. A "skep" was a dry measure usually used for grain. Note that the rent was paid in kind rather than in money.

43. Stephen de Scalers held land both of the bishop and of the monks. He is pledging here to count any excess land toward the land he holds of the bishop.

44. William de Lavington was Archdeacon of Cambridgeshire from 1150/1152 until at least 1159. He had been involved in a dispute with the monks of Ely over the exercise of the archdeacon's rights. David, archdeacon of Buckingham, was the brother of Bishop Alexander of Lincoln (see note 16 above).

45. Alexander served as prior from 1144/1151 until approximately 1163. He went to Rome on the priory's business (see Book 3, Chapter 64) and is the author of the letter to Pope Eugenius III about the Stetchworth case in Book 3, Chapter 103.

46. That is in the *Book of Ely* itself. This is an interesting statement of the purpose of compiling a charter-chronicle.

47. Northamptonshire lies in the East Midlands.

48. The "city of God" is a reference to the church of Ely.

49. The choir stall is the part of the church where the monks stand during services.

50. The Venerable Bede tells the story of St. Æthelthryth in his *History of the English Church and People*, trans. Leo Sherley-Price (New York, 1955), bk. 4, chap. 19, pp. 238–41.

51. This is an error. The translation of St. Æthelthryth and her sisters took place in 1106; King Henry I ruled 1100 to 1135.

52. That is, when Abbot Richard (1100–07) moved the relics of the saint into a new monastic church which had been built.

53. This miracle is derived from the *Libellus Æthelwoldi,* or *Book of St. Æthelwold*, an account of the acquisition of Ely's estates written in English shortly after the refoundation of the monastery in the late tenth century and translated into Latin at the order of Bishop Hervey. The same miracle also appears earlier in the *Book of Ely* at its chronologically appropriate point in the narrative (Book 2, Chapter 11). The rhetoric has been heightened to emphasize the chastisement. See Blake's introduction, pages xii-xiii.

54. The Danes who began invading and settling in England in the 860s. They were progressively driven out in the tenth century by the kings of Wessex (in the southwest),

The Book of Ely 493

who consolidated the various English kingdoms in their own hands, creating the first unified English monarchy. On King Edgar, see note 17 above.

55. Bishop Æthelwold of Winchester (963–84) was the refounder of Ely, which had been destroyed during the Danish invasions in 870.

56. Downham is located in Cambridgeshire.

57. Abbot Brihtnoth of Ely (970–81?). For his career, see especially Book 2, chaps. 6–56.

58. This story is also derived from the *Book of St. Æthelwold* and used earlier in the *Book of Ely* (Book 2, Chapter 35).

59. Both Brandon and Livermere are located in Suffolk, in East Anglia.

60. One hundred shillings is the equivalent of five pounds. A "hundred" is an Anglo-Saxon political and territorial unit, notionally equivalent to one hundred hides of land. Here the reference is to the assembled inhabitants of that territory.

61. Egelwine was Ealdorman of East Anglia, that is the official in charge of Cambridgeshire and Northamptonshire, from ca. 962 until 992. A major patron of nearby Ramsey Abbey, but not remembered as a benefactor at Ely. For his activities regarding Ely, see Book 2, Chapters 7, 11, and 24.

62 For Ranulf's activities, see Book 3, Chapter 47, where he is portrayed as a second Catiline in language borrowed from Sallust's *The Conspiracy of Catiline*, translated, together with his *The Jugurthine War*, by S. A. Handford (Baltimore, 1963).

63. St. Sexburga's feast falls on July 6, and the feast of St. Withburga's translation (when she was solemnly transferred into a new tomb) falls on July 8.

64. King Stephen reigned from 1135 until 1154. Grandson of William the Conqueror, he succeeded his uncle, Henry I.

65. King Stephen was succeeded in 1154 by King Henry II, who ruled until 1189. Henry was the son of the empress Matilda (who lived ca. 1102–1167), daughter of King Henry I of England (who reigned from 1100 until 1135) and widow of the German emperor Henry V, she later married Count Geoffrey of Anjou (who lived 1112–1151).

66. Archbishop Theobald of Canterbury served from 1139 until 1161.

67. That is, castles erected without a royal license.

68. King Henry II led a partially successful expedition into north Wales in 1157.

69. King Henry II besieged Toulouse, located in southwestern France, in 1159.

70. Richard FitzNigel, later also bishop of London (1189–98), was probably the author of the *Dialogue of the Exchequer*, which describes the inner workings of the English treasury.

71. Queen Emma (d. 1052) was married from 1002 to 1016 to King Æthelred II (978–1016) and from 1017 to 1035 to King Cnut (1016–35). She was the mother of both King Harthacnut (1040–42) and King Edward the Confessor (1042–66). Bishop Nigel thus pawned the same altar cloth to Bishop Alexander twice; the miracle here refers to the first occasion when Nigel pawned church treasures to Alexander, described in Book 3, Chapter 89, though the altar cloth itself is not mentioned there. Also see note 18 above.

72. Pope Eugenius III served from 1145 until 1153.

73. That is, living a monastic life in the manner of a nun.

74. On St. Withburga, see note 10 above.

75. Bishop William Turbe of Norwich served from 1146 until 1174.

76. This is an error. Since Bishop Nigel died in 1169, the regnal year for Henry II (1154–89) must have been incorrectly calculated.

77. Denney is located in Cambridgeshire.

78. See above Book 3, Chapter 137.

79. This account of the punishment inflicted on members of Bishop Nigel's household, as well as on Prior Thembert and Ralph the sacrist, continues the story begun in Book 3, Chapters 78, 89 and 92. See Blake's introduction, page xxxix.

80. On Thembert, see above note 19. On Ralph, see note 32 above.

81. William of Shelford was a member of Bishop Nigel's household, accused in Book 3, Chapter 78, of prompting Bishop Nigel to harass the monks.

82. Ralph Fitz Olaf was a member of Bishop Nigel's household. See Book 3, Chapter 52. He served as a guarantor for the money Bishop Nigel took from the church.

83. Richard of Saint Paul's was a member of Bishop Nigel's household.
84. William de Lavington (see note 44 above) was pleading in the bishop's court.
85. On Richard FitzNigel, see note 70 above.
86. During a vacancy in the bishopric, the king could take custody of the church and its possessions.

Chapter 23
The Tract on the Conversion of Pons of Léras and the True Account of the Beginning of the Monastery at Silvanès

Translated by Beverly Mayne Kienzle

Introduction

Pons of Léras was a saint without supernatural powers, an imitable holy man and a lifelike, practical example for men of his time who could be moved to join the Cistercian lay brotherhood. His actions demonstrate step-by-step how an unlearned knight, even a notorious sinner, could become a Cistercian lay brother and a model of service, hard work, and dedication to the community. Formerly a brigand, Pons repented, placed his wife and children in monasteries, sold his immovable possessions, and restored whatever he owed or had robbed from anyone. After doing public penance during Holy Week and undertaking pilgrimages with a group of followers, he and his companions in 1132 constructed a monastery at Silvanès, located in southern France (in the modern *département* of Midi-Pyrénées), and affiliated with the Cistercian order in 1136. Pons remained a lay brother until his death on the first of August sometime after 1146. The only miracle in the account of Pons's life—a miraculous multiplication of grain—occurs during his absence, after his departure to seek help for a starving crowd that encircled the monastery during a famine. In contrast to the prominent role hagiographers often accord to miracles at the place of a saint's burial, Hugh Francigena, author of the *Tract*, reports nothing about Pons's relics or his final resting place; instead he relates that the conversions of knights inspired by Pons's example brought peace to the area.

The Cistercian order was founded in 1098, when a group of monks, led by their abbot Robert, left the Benedictine monastery of Molesme and founded what they called the "New Monastery" at Cîteaux, a site located southeast of Molesme and approximately halfway between the towns of Dijon and Beaune in the Burgundian region of France. Their intent was one of reform: critical of past departures from the purity of the *Rule* of St. Benedict of Nursia, particularly in monasteries affiliated with the powerful abbey of Cluny, they advocated returning to a more austere lifestyle governed by a pure interpretation of the *Rule*. Rejecting the wealth and worldly involvement of

Molesme and other monasteries, they espoused ideals of poverty and isolation: a return to the early monastic ideal of inhabiting the wilderness, but still retaining the core of community life. Despite these ideals of poverty, simplicity, and austerity, the Cistercian order rose to the heights of power and influence. Under the leadership of Bernard, chosen abbot of Clairvaux in 1115, the order expanded rapidly, governing over three hundred and fifty abbeys across Europe by the middle of the twelfth century. Bernard himself intervened in numerous affairs of ecclesiastical politics, advising bishops and popes, including Eugene III, a monk of Clairvaux elected pope in 1145, who persuaded Bernard to preach the Second Crusade.

At the time Silvanès was incorporated into the Cistercian order, the Cistercians were expanding the number and influence of their monasteries in southern France. The *Tract* recounts both the founding of the abbey in 1132 and the decision to affiliate with the Cistercian order in 1136. The story of the abbey's growth and expansion goes hand in hand with praise for the simplicity of the early Cistercians, their austere way of life and their care for the poor in the region. At a time when heterodox movements were gaining adherents, Pons of Léras and his followers offered praiseworthy examples of orthodox piety.

Pons represented the model lay brother *(conversus)*, whose work was essential for maintaining the order's expanding properties. Lay brothers, who worked the land, tended the animals, and prepared and took the products to market, were recruited primarily from tenants of land that came into Cistercian ownership. According to Constance Berman's extensive study of Cistercian agriculture, a peasant could acquire protection from crop failures or physical disability if he relinquished to the monastery his rights to his land and thereby became a lay brother. Evidence exists that some husbands separated from their families and relinquished their cultivation rights in order to enter the monastery. At the time the *Tract* was written, a lay brother's status was not very different from a monk's, according to Berman, so that even knights like Pons of Léras became *conversi*. The portrait of the lay brothers in the *Tract* belongs to the period before they began to be treated as lesser members of the community and before the discontent and violence that became more and more frequent during the thirteenth century, as James Donnelly has illustrated.

The manuscript rubrics of the *Tract on the Conversion of Pons of Léras and the True Account of the Beginning of the Monastery at Silvanès* identify its author as Hugh Francigena, but little beyond that is known about him. The cartulary of the same monastery mentions a monk called Master *(magister)* Hugh, probably indicating someone who would have sufficient education to be the author of the *Tract*, but the designation "Francigena" does not accompany the name there. Two letters addressed from Hugh Francigena to bishop Gaucelin of Lodève (1161–87) are bound with the manuscript of the *Tract* (Dijon, Bibliothèque municipale, MS 611), but neither of those contains any biographical information about Hugh; nor does a third letter—the bishop's reply to Hugh's first correspondence. Furthermore, no other known extant works are ascribed to Hugh Francigena. In the *Tract* he relates that he was writing out of obedience to his abbot, Pons, and he describes himself formulaically as the lowliest of all monks and a man "for the most part" of "no learning." Certainly this is an exaggeration; the Latin of the *Tract* has a rustic character, but that of the letters is more elevated and conforms to the norms for epistolary composition.

The mention of Abbot Pons together with other information contained in the *Tract* and in the monastery cartulary allow for dating the *Tract*'s composition between 1161 and 1171, the years of Pons I's abbacy, when Silvanès was competing for endowment with neighboring abbeys and for parish tithes with the military orders. A reference in the *Tract* to monastery buildings being renovated and rebuilt and an 1164 cartulary entry mentioning construction at the monastery ground supports the supposition that the *Tract* was written around 1164, in the early years of the abbacy of Pons I. Its goal was perhaps to attract benefactors to fund the construction. Praise and prayers are accorded to donors named in the text, and in some cases, the amount of money given is specified and its purpose identified. Arnaud du Pont, for example, offers the hermits the land for the first monastery, provides grain during a famine, and eventually joins the monastery, presumably after his wife's death. Gifts from du Pont and his family are also confirmed in the monastery cartulary.

SOURCES AND FURTHER READING

The Latin text of the *Tractatus* has been edited recently by Beverly Mayne Kienzle in "The Works of Hugo Francigena: 'Tractatus de conversione Pontii de Laracio et exordii Salvaniensis monasterii vera narratio; epistolae' (Dijon, Bibliothèque municipale MS 611)," *Sacris erudiri* 34 (1993): 273–311. Kienzle discusses the text at greater length there and in "The Tract on the Conversion of Pons of Léras and the True Account of the Beginning of the Monastery at Silvanès," *Cistercian Studies Quarterly* 30 (1995): 219–43, and "Pons of Léras: A Twelfth-Century Cistercian," *Cîteaux: commentarii cistercienses* 40 (1989): 215–26. Derek Baker brings to light the background of popular and dissident religious movements in "Popular Piety in the Lodèvois in the Early Twelfth Century: The Case of Pons de Léras," in *Religious Motivation: Biographical and Sociological Problems for the Church Historian*, ed. Derek Baker (Oxford, 1978), pp. 39–47; and Beverly Kienzle and Susan Shroff focus on questions of Cathar and orthodox doctrine debated during the mid-twelfth century in "Cistercians and Heresy: Doctrinal Consultation in Some Twelfth-Century Correspondence from Southern France," *Cîteaux: commentarii cistercienses* 41 (1990): 159–66. Constance Berman provides an excellent overview of the Cistercians' expanding presence in southern France during this period in *Medieval Agriculture, the Southern French Countryside and the Early Cistercians. A Study of Forty-three Monasteries*, Transactions of the American Philosophical Society 76.5 (Philadelphia, 1986). The cartulary of

Silvanès Cartulary has appeared as *Cartulaire de l'abbaye de Silvanès*, ed. P.A. Verlaguet, Archives historiques du Rouergue 1 (Rodez, 1910). Important work is underway on the Cistercian lay brotherhood but until its publication, the standard reference remains: James Donnelly, *The Decline of the Medieval Cistercian Laybrotherhood* (New York, 1949). A recent study of the Cistercian order during its first century is undertaken in Martha Newman, *The Boundaries of Charity. Cistercian Culture and Ecclesiastical Reform, 1098–1180* (Stanford, 1996). One final note on the translation itself. Although all translations of Scripture are mine, I have tried to stay as close as possible to the RSV.

The Tract on the Conversion of Pons of Léras and the True Account of the Beginning of the Monastery at Silvanès

Here Begins the Tract on the Conversion of Pons of Léras, and the True Account of the Beginning of the Monastery at Silvanès.

In the name of the holy and undivided Trinity, of the one true, highest, eternal and ineffable deity, of the Father, Son, and Holy Spirit. I, brother Hugo, of all monks the most lowly, have taken care to recount for our monastery, that is, the monastery at Silvanès, its early beginnings, the first cradle of its childhood or infancy, as it were. [I have done so] according to the capacity of my intelligence, the measure of my natural talent, and with whatever style possible. I have attempted to record with written records how, as if under the solicitude and diligence of a good nurse, it grew into manly strength under the care of heavenly grace, and how with God's protection it reached the state we now perceive it to occupy. [I have undertaken this task] for the honor, glory, and praise of the one who customarily made great things out of small, who with five loaves of bread fed five thousand people to satisfaction [see Mk 6:38–44; Mt 14:17–21; Jn 6:10–13]; indeed the one who at the beginning of the world created all things out of nothing [see Gen 1:1–2]. [I recall these things] also for the memory of future [monks] so that all who follow in our path may know how many and how great were the fathers who gave the religious life of our house its beginning. Once this generous root of [our] good tree is known, [our future brothers] may endeavor to bring forth fruit according to the species of its kind, and they may never shrink from the witness, praise and glory of this very beautiful tree, namely our mother church at Silvanès. From the beginning, the hand of the heavenly farmer has always cultivated [it] like a humble thicket. Still he continues to cultivate [it], bestowing growth and increase upon it, watering it with numerous benefits as if with heavenly rain. With diligent care, he has elevated [it] to such heights among the other trees of the forest that its shadow may cover the mountains. [In our mother church] spiritual souls painted with colors of diverse virtues nourish [their] brood of good practices just as heavenly birds building nests, while the brood continually sing out praises of the Creator with [their] voices. In our mother church's shadow, the simple and gentle, like the good animals of God, continually take rest from the heat of carnal vices, just as the Psalmist says: Your animals shall dwell in it [see Ps 67:11, Vulgate].

If anyone should reproach me—a man of little natural talent, encumbered eloquence, and for the most part, no learning—because I have presumed to put a hand to a matter so great as this, let him know that it was not bold presumption that led me nor the wind of vain glory that moved me. I began this [work] under the bond of salutary obedience. My lord abbot Pons instructed me about this [work] and suggested specific things that he either saw himself at the beginning [of our monastery], or heard from those who saw and were present, even from those who were the first establishers and founders of this site. Some of our brothers also gave information for this work; they learned all [they know] only by hearing. Our account rests more on the witness of Hugh the Presbyter and Raymond Alzarrani, who have known everything since the beginning and who shared in the toil and long-suffering of the first [founders]. No one is allowed to doubt the truth of their testimony. Now these things should suffice for a preface.

Here ends the preface.

Here begins the tract [on the conversion of Pons of Léras and the account of the beginning of the monastery at Silvanès].

Louis, son of Philip, was reigning,[1] lord Peter was presiding as bishop of Lodève,[2] our Lord Jesus Christ was ruling over the heavens, the earth and the sea, when there lived a man in the region of Lodève, who had the standing of a knight [and] who went by the name of Pons of Larazio, which was his impregnable castle. According to the world's [standards for] worthiness, this man was of an outstanding sort, wealthy with property, fortunate in his possessions, keen in natural talent, mighty in strength, agile with arms, powerful in town. He stood out above others in all worldly glory. Indeed at an early age he followed worldly desires, and he was troublesome to many of his neighbors. In fact he overcame some with astute speech [while] others he disturbed with the violence of arms. Day and night he robbed as many as he could of their possessions and pressed upon them the actions of his greediness. Although he was notorious for that vice, he was considered no less reprehensible for others. But his heart was pierced with the spear of the gracious Lord who desires not the death of a sinner, but [his] repentance [see Ezek 18:23 and 33:11], who *has mercy on whomever he wishes,* and *strengthens whomever he wants* [Rom 9:18]. Fear of the Lord transformed him completely from his earlier actions. For when he recovered his senses, he began to consider the evil things he had done, [and] to think about the judgment that threatened such actions. Inwardly moved by his heart's pain, he turned wholly to repentance. In order to wash away the disgrace of his crimes, day and night he poured out rivers of tears. Alone and in silence he continuously pondered how, that is, with what sort of reparation he might appease the anger of the eternal judge, or with what sort of actions he might obtain mercy. Suddenly he resolved to leave behind everything of this world and henceforth to spend the remainder of his life doing acts of penance. However, he had a wife without whose agreement he would not be able to do this. He confided to her the secret of his intention, and implored her with insistent entreaties to do as he intended. As she was of a noble family and more noble in mind, she willingly annulled the sacred vows of her husband. Nonetheless, moved with inner devotion and wholly drenched in tears, she prevailed upon the father for the sake of her children. For she had a son and a daughter, [and] her heart beat with a mother's love for them. But the father was provident, and while he strove to care for himself, he also provided well for his children. For he dutifully placed the mother and daughter with a large portion of his fortune in the monastery of nuns called respectfully *Brinonia*.[3] He introduced his son into the company of monks at the monastery called Holy Savior in Lodève. This was his first offering, by which he offered three pleasing things to the Three.

His neighbors and all his friends too marveled, wondering one by one what he wanted to do or what he would arrange. Pondering all this in their hearts, some said one thing and others something else. Then a group of friends spoke intimately with him. All of them wanted to know what he had in mind or what action he was pondering. He opened the secret of his heart to them, and recounted the design of his plan in an orderly fashion. He took this occasion [to speak to them] since, even though [he was] a lay person, he was well spoken and eloquent. He delivered a brilliant sermon on contempt for the world, fear of divine judgment, the fruit of penance, the punishment of evil, and the joy of the blessed. By his eloquence some were kindled and goaded to reject all pride of the world, and they were converted on the spot to repentance. Desiring to stay near him thereafter, they promised him their inseparable company and vowed to remain readily with him in life and in death. The first of these was Raymond of Pireto, a man remembered well who later distinguished himself in the monastic life; the second Guiraud, a priest; the third Peter Alzarran, a knight; the fourth, William of Roca; the fifth, Hugh Magnus; the sixth, William of Esparron; the seventh was Pons himself who converted them with his word and example. Their very number conveyed the understanding that they were enlightened with sevenfold grace [see Is 11:2–3].[4] They would bring to perfection the religious life and calling, because they began with the perfect number.

Freed from the bonds of carnal love and strengthened with the companions prepared for him by God, [Pons] undertook the Gospel teaching where the Lord says: *If you want to be perfect, go, sell all that you have and give it to the poor and you will have treasure in heaven; and come, follow me* [Mt 19:21]. A proclamation was made and he laid open all his possessions to purchasers. Then many men, knights and peasants, wealthy and ordinary, clerical and lay, having brought their purses, came together from all parts, desiring to purchase for themselves what pleased them. When their money ran out, many things had been bought, but many still remained to be purchased. He then gave advice to the buyers about the price, saying that he would accept as payment animals of every type including beasts of burden and all the fruits of the earth which sustain the life of mortals. He wanted to do this for a certain reason, as it will appear from what follows. For he knew what he was going to do.

It happened that with the sale of all the immovable goods, he would have a more substantial group of movable things, namely horses and mares, mules and she-mules, oxen and cattle, sheep and goats and many others that it takes too long to enumerate. Following the Lord's commandment, he wanted to distribute all [his] things to the needy: churches and monasteries, hospices and hostels for strangers, the poor and pilgrims, widows and orphans. But he believed that this would perhaps be less acceptable to God if he did not first return those things which he had once taken by force. Therefore he sent messengers throughout the area and all around through cities and castles and villages, wherever people came together in public for trade or markets. [He also sent messengers] throughout the churches so that they might proclaim publicly that all to whom Pons of Léras either owed something or from whom he had taken something by force, should come to him at the village called Pégairolles on Monday, Tuesday, or Wednesday after the solemnity of Palms, to receive one by one their goods. For it was near Easter, the feast day of Christians.

The Lord's day called Palm Sunday arrived. In Lodève, after the procession [and] when the Gospel had been read, the bishop [was] standing with his clerics on the step which was made for speaking in the square, [and] the people were standing around. Pons of Léras, undressed and barefoot, came with very great concern about his salvation, [and] with [him were] his companions named above. Someone led him just like a criminal, and his neck was bound in a wooden collar, popularly called a *redorta*. The one who led him whipped him continually with sticks, for he himself had ordered that done. Coming to the bishop like a runaway serf who had left a good master, he delivered himself to God through the hand of the bishop [and] on his knees he begged forgiveness. He gave the bishop a letter that he brought in hand; in it he had described all his sins. He implored [the bishop] repeatedly that it be read for the hearing of the whole people. The bishop, [wanting to] spare him that shame, at first prohibited that this be done. But Pons persevered most insistently in his petition and secured [the bishop's agreement] that this be done. Thus with the bishop's consent the letter was read. The beating and driving with sticks continued and he pleaded even more intensely that he ought to be driven more harshly. He said in a loud voice that he was answerable for very great crimes. He flooded the ground with tears and moved all the people to weeping and tears. All who were present marveled and revered him with great affection. They acclaimed his repentance and affirmed that the Lord had truly looked upon him. They also prayed for him, that the one who had given him the grace of repentance would also give him perseverance in the good. This confession was useful and necessary not only for the one who confessed, but also for the many others who, timid from embarrassment at their shame, had hidden their sins for a long time. Now moved by his example, they saw him confessing this way [and] rushed to the bath of penance and confession. After these things were done and the rite for the solemnity of Palms was duly completed, he went to the church. Then on the second day, that is the second day in Holy Week, and also on the third and fourth day, many claimants came to the place we mentioned above, coming together from various parts, each and everyone seeking the things they had once lost. Coming together then before him as before a judge, they cried out to him just as [they would] to a judge; with him as the accused, by his own witness they pressed testimony against him [see Lk 22:71]. He in fact was his own accuser and judge, defendant and witness; he took upon himself all the roles of a trial while he desired to satisfy all. He accused himself; he brought witness against himself; he judged himself like a judge; like the defendant, he accepted the punishment. Then, prostrate at the feet of each and every one, he first begged forgiveness and then, according to the amount of items lost from their possessions, he restored to each and every one the things mentioned before. Since, as we said above, he also possessed a multitude of diverse animals and all the money necessary for a man's use, each one received things comparable to those he had lost. Thus they believed they had not so much received other people's things as found their own. Turning old maledictions into benedictions, bidding him farewell and blessing him, they were joyously returned to their own [possessions].

Then seeing a certain local man and neighbor of his standing nearby, he said: "Ho there, what are you waiting for? Why don't you state the reason for your claim?" He said, "I, my lord, have no reason to make a claim against you, but I praise you greatly and bless you because you helped me in many matters and defended me in several cases against my adversaries. You have never harmed me at all, nor injured me in any way." Pons said to him, "But I did harm you. I did do evil. I did inflict loss on you, but perhaps you do not know. Did you lose your flock from your fold at such and such a time, on such and such a night?" He said, "I did lose [my flock], my lord, I did in fact lose but I did not know who inflicted that loss on me. I did not realize that you were aware of my loss." "I," said Pons, "did that; I arranged it all through my partners and accomplices. For that reason I beg you to forgive me and then I will return what I took from you." "May the Lord in heaven pardon you," he said, "for I willingly forgive you for this." "Accept," he said, "these remaining animals and let them take the place of the ones that were once lost to you." Then the man accepted the money and believed it had fallen from heaven, and proclaimed with joy that he who had once inflicted a loss on him was not an evildoer but a bestower of a great gift. In truth, Pons distributed to the needy all of his remaining possessions, just as it was written: *He distributed, he gave to the poor, his justice remains forever* [2 Cor 9:9; Ps 111:9, Vulgate].

Now on the fifth day, which is also called [the day of] the Lord's Supper, he chose thirteen poor people, [and] lavishly fed them with foods appropriate for the season, washed their feet, *rinsed them with* [his] *tears, wiped them with* [his] *hair* [Lk 7:44; also see Lk 7:38 and Jn 13:5], and faithfully completed all things in accordance with the Lord's mandate. Now when evening fell, [and] the sun had set, keeping in mind the Lord's passion, he did not wish to give his eyes sleep nor his eyelids dozing. Just as that same night our Lord Jesus Christ of his own will hastened to bring his passion to completion for the sake of sinners, so he too of his free will went out to bring works of penance to completion. He wanted to be made a participant in the passion of Christ so that he might deserve to become a sharer in his resurrection and glory. Therefore, in the silence of the dead of night he and his associates with him went out from their land and their kindred and from the house of their father[s]. Each wore nothing except a simple garment, ordinary and appropriate to the religious life, and [bore nothing but] a staff and a bag. They eagerly undertook a journey of pilgrimage which led to Saint-Guilhem[-le-Désert].5 Now they were going barefoot, to which they were hardly accustomed, and so they bore this with more difficulty. Now the road they walked along was very difficult, not only for those walking barefoot, but also for those going with shoes and traveling on horseback and even during the day. For the road is rough with stones and utterly horrible; it winds and bends, rises over hills, and drops in valleys. While they walked along there, they talked and encouraged each other to bring to completion works of penance. I don't know by what divine judgment something sad and terrible befell them. But I believe that the will of God was [such] that they be tempted, so that once tempted they would be tested and once frightened they would be purged [see Job 41:1–6]. Now suddenly a powerful wind rushed in from the desert region, shattered the heavens and disturbed the air. Then the moon which was shining earlier suddenly concealed itself and the spheres of the stars, too, all fled [from sight]. But also a thick cloud hid the mountains and darkness set in. Then thunderbolts began to crash, lightning to flash, and hailstones to tumble down. Fright and fear about the severity of the storm rushed over them. Finally, amidst the repeated lightning bolts, they carefully looked for and sought out some place of habitation which would [offer] safety and shelter from the storm and the rain. Nonetheless, before they came to that place, they endured so many things that it can rightly be said about them that they were stoned, injured, and tempted [see Heb 11:37].

When morning broke, they set out rejoicing in the sight of the Lord because they were considered worthy to suffer hardship for the sake of his love. Arriving finally at Saint-Guilhem[-le-Désert] they found there a crowd of knights and other men who had come together as they had customarily done on that day every year for the purpose of venerating the cross. With these people, they also devoutly venerated the life-giving wood, on which [our] Author made the sacrifice which expiated our actions. All marveled at their humility and devotion, and when they found out that they were from Lodève, they revered them all the more. Present among them was a certain rich and powerful man, namely Raymond Peter of Ganges who assembled them all and with his repeated entreaties persuaded them to spend the day of the Lord's Resurrection with him at Ganges in order to give honor to such a great solemn feast.6 They agreed and left with him. They were there on the next day afterward which was the day before the Sabbath, and also on the day of the Lord's Resurrection. There they heard holy Masses and received a parting meal of the Lord's body and blood.

On the next day, that is the second day of Easter Week, they bade farewell to their host and began a journey to Saint James.7 They wholly desired to find Him in foreign guise and they sought Him, just as it is read that on that same day [following the Resurrection] He appeared to two disciples traveling to Emmaus in pilgrim dress [see Lk 24:13–28]. Only He who witnessed and rewarded their hardships knows how many troubles and crosses they endured on that journey—*distress and tribulation, vigils, fasts, hunger, thirst, cold, and nakedness* [2 Cor 11:27]. But God gave them grace in the sight of all who saw them, so that all would easily recognize from the very sight of their faces that they were truly religious and men of virtue. Wherever they needed provisions, many willingly ministered to them. If at any time the wealthy offered them many things, they accepted only as much as would suffice for one day's provisions; they returned the rest. In fact, when they were compelled to accept many provisions, they distributed them on the spot to the poor. Lest they seem to place hope in money when they had placed it wholly in God, they kept nothing for the future, believing Him who said: Do not think about tomorrow [see Mt 6:34]; and also that [teaching]: *Seek first the kingdom of God and his justice and all these things will increase for you* [Mt 6:33]. For that reason they spent many days without the sustenance of food, but they gave no less thanks to God. At every point on this journey they took the greatest care to visit notable sites of the saints and everywhere to seek out religious men. They requested the approbation of [their] prayers and they also sought to learn more about the way of life in which they could thereafter and at all times serve the Lord blamelessly. Among all who gave them advice there was one opinion—the same intent, the same word, the same advice—for all were of course instructed by the one spirit. They all praised them and said that they [ought to] cultivate a place in the wilderness, obtain their provisions with the labor of their hands, construct a monastery for themselves in which they might serve God in purity and simplicity of life, and leave after them heirs to their religious life. The archbishop of [Santiago de Compostela] greatly confirmed and urged on them that advice. Indeed at first he wanted to keep them in his diocese and assign them an appropriate place. Later he thought to himself that if they were to remain among people [who spoke] another language, they could be of little benefit. Since they would not be understood when speaking, they would be considered foreigners by those [who were] foreigners [to them]. Finally he took care to send them back to the lands they knew. He admonished them to persevere in their holy plan, and trusting in the goodness of God, he promised them great things from God.

Confirmed by his words, strengthened by his blessing, they returned along another road to their homeland. They went to the memorial of Michael the Archangel, which is located on the Mount-in peril-of-the-sea; they visited the church of blessed Martin of Tours; they went to Limoges because of [the church dedicated to] St. Martial; [and] they entered the basilica of blessed Leonard [of Noblat].[8] They entered the last city, Rodez, [and] when they prayed at the church of blessed Mary, Virgin and Mother of God, they were announced to the bishop and summoned by him. He was Lord Ademar, bishop of Rodez,[9] a man of esteemed memory and great authority. When he learned that they were known [to be] men of Lodève, and also neighboring and generous noblemen, he received them quickly and with great reverence. Knowing their wish, he promised that he would be useful to them in every way and offer them counsel and assistance if they wished to stay in his diocese. When the Count of Rodez heard that Pons of Léras was in the diocese, he wanted to see him, as much as [he was] a knight known and familiar to him and once [was] his friend. When [the Count] knew his wish he promised him that he would be his assistant and defender in all matters. The count as well as the bishop offered them certain locations for constructing a monastery, namely villages and deserted churches. They however [wished to] flee from throngs of people [and] preferred the secret hidden places of forests and woods.

With the favor of the count and the blessing of the bishop, they departed and came to the region which is called Camarès. That land is woodsy, covered with forests, steep with mountains, sloping with hills, watered by fountains, streams and rivers. A certain great and powerful noblemen ruled over the land; he was named Arnaud du Pont. Now they had known him for a long time, knowing that he was a benevolent and cheerful man, ready for every virtuous deed. When he saw them coming toward him, before he recognized them he said to them: "My lords, why are they coming to me? What do they want? Know that I am ready for whatever you want." Now after he recognized them, he received them with great honor and devotion and diligently inquired about their reason for coming. In response they told him that they wanted a location appropriate for the religious life, hidden and removed from people, where they might stay and serve God. "Who," he said, "can satisfy these wishes of yours as I can, and what land could be found more suitable for such a plan? Behold the land is before you: settle wherever it pleases you, build, sow, plant, set out new vines, and pray for me."

They chose for themselves a certain location which formerly was called Silvanès. They or their followers called it Salvanès, changing the *i* to *a*, so that what before was called Silvanès for the forests, would thereafter be called Salvanès for salvation. They remained there building huts with their own hands, [and] living in company with the animals. Insistent in daily labor, they rendered an uninhabitable place inhabitable, cutting back thickets with sickles [and] plowing the earth with hoes.

The fame of their religious life then spread everywhere [and] reached the ears of the neighboring bishops, namely [those] of Rodez, Lodève, and Béziers. From there [it reached the ears] of all the people. Then many people began to visit them, bringing gifts, [and] assisting them in all things. In what follows we will more fully show that people of Lodève are known to have done so much.

At that time an incomparable famine took place in that region. For the earth denied fruit to its cultivators and all who cultivated it mourned. Because they had been frustrated in their hope and mocked, they went to the oak trees with faith in Ceres.[10] In that year, in accordance with Isaiah's prophecy, *thirty measures of seed* are said to have made scarcely *three measures* and *ten acres of vines* could fill scarcely *one small bottle* [Is 5:10]. Then a crowd of poor people gathered at Salvanès. The enormous multitude surrounded the house just like an army, placing all hope for their life on its food stuff. Now from the beginning this custom was established for the house and the brothers: it was considered like a law that they would receive everyone in the hospice, feed the hungry, refresh the poor, clothe the naked, bury the dead and fulfill other deeds of piety and mercy. With God's protection, that practice is observed to continue up to the present day in as far as possible. Now when the brothers saw such a great throng of troubled and shaken poor people, they said to one another: "Either we must flee from this place or we must die with them. See what we must do. Who will be able to sustain them even for a few days? If this place with its houses and inhabitants were made of bread, it would be devoured in a short time by such a huge crowd."

Then Pons of Léras curbed their grumbling [and] said:

If we want to flee, we will not escape, for a road to escape is not open out of the east, nor out of the west, nor out of the desert mountains, because God is [our] judge. Then those who hasten to flee show that they have been conquered. Disgrace awaits the conquered, but glory the conquerors. Now we have come not for flight but to fight. It is therefore fitting for us to stand, not to escape, and to contend bravely because no one will be crowned *unless he has legitimately done battle* [2 Tim 2:5]. You remember the early days of your conversion, when you endured a great struggle of hardship and suffering, and how the Lord freed you from all anxieties and difficulties. Now too believe that he will assist you in the same way. Remember that once for forty years God fed the people of Israel in the desert without earthly bread [but] with heavenly manna [see Ex 16:1–36]. In the days of Elijah in Sarepta of Sidon, for many days he fed the widow and her family at her home along with the prophet from a jar of meal and a flask of oil, because the jar did not run out of meal and the flask did not run out of oil [see 1 Kings 17:9–16]. But also in the time of Elisha when Samaria was besieged, and the besieged were put to the test by worry of hunger, God in one day provided them with such a great abundance of food that *one measure of fine wheat flour* sold *for one shekel and two measures of barley for one shekel at the gate of Samaria* [2 Kings 7:1]. In the Gospel, too, you heard that the Lord fed five thousand men with five loaves of bread [and that] after their meal the apostles took away twelve baskets of scraps from the five loaves that were left by those who ate [see Mk 6:38–44; Mt 14:13–21; Jn 6:10–13]. *Has the hand of the Lord been made weak* [Num 11:23] so that now He cannot do such things? It is as great now as it was then. It can not be lesser, nor can it be greater. Let us believe in Him, brothers, because *all things* are *possible to a believer* [Mk 9:22]. Let us place all our hope in Him because He frees *all who hope in him* [Ps 17:31]. Let us fear Him knowing that He *will do the will of those fearing him* [Ps 144:19, Vulgate]. Let us love Him because *He takes care of all who love Him* [Ps 144:20, Vulgate]. But now the moment demands that you, brothers, do again what you remember once doing. Sell what you own and give alms. Once it was your own [that you sold]; now it is the community's [that you sell]. Behold you have oxen and sheep, mares and cattle. Let nothing remain from a piece of thread to a shoelace that is not sold and given to our needy brothers. For they too are our brothers. With us they have the same father, God, [see Jn 8:41] to whom all of us say: *Our Father* [Mt 6:9; also see Lk 11:2]. They were redeemed by the same price as we [were], that is, by the blood of Jesus Christ. If after all these events it should happen that we die, *let us all die in our innocence* [1 Mac 2:37], knowing that just as Christ laid down His life for us [see Jn 10:17], so too we ought to lay down our lives for our brothers. Meanwhile I shall go to the rulers of the people who are in the world and I shall become a beggar for the beggars.

Having said these things he mounted a little ass, and carrying a whip in his hand he set off.

The brothers truly made ready to sell all the things they possessed just as he had ordered. Upon hearing that, Lord Arnaud du Pont prohibited that this be done in any way, fearing lest the place again become a wilderness. Opening his storehouses, he gave them some provisions to sustain the poor for a short time. Then seeing their faith, the Lord gave his blessing on that house for that day and henceforth. For when a few grains were ground by the milling machine, the jars were filled by the flour collected, and when the dough was made, the kneading troughs overflowed with the yeast of divine blessing. Although the oven took the loaves in small form, it returned them in large form. When the same loaves were broken, from a few [loaves] large baskets were filled; they were scarcely emptied by those to whom they were given. The bread was multiplied even more at its distribution and in the mouths of the eaters the bread grew under their teeth. Thus the grace of divine blessing overflowed, [and] the people in this wilderness were fed as if by heavenly manna all that time until the season of new crops.

Pons of Léras came back after a few days. Bringing back no small amount of divine consolation, he gladdened the house and all its inhabitants. Hearing what marvelous things God had done, he rejoiced *with truly great gladness* [Mt 2:10]. All along with him likewise blessed the Lord in hymns and praises, saying that *the merciful and compassionate Lord established the memory of His wonders* [and] *gave food to those fearing Him* [Ps 110:4–5, Vulgate]. When the time until the birthday of St. John the Baptist had passed, on that same day [Pons] made a meal for all the people, and when all were fully fed, he bade them farewell and ordered all of them to go to their own places in the name of the Lord. Then going forth they proclaimed everywhere that *God is truly in* that *place* [Gen 28:16] and there *it is nothing other than the house of the Lord* [Gen 28:17].

Finally after a short time, the place rose in authority and grew so much, not only in things but also in religious persons and possessions, that it was said to be suitable for having an order and constructing an abbey. A disagreement then arose among them [over] which order seemed to be better. Some praised the Cistercian order, others the Carthusian order, and some even said [that it would be] fitting to construct a monastery for nuns. Then they resolved to put their case before the Carthusians. For that purpose Pons of Léras traveled to Chartreuse [and] explained the case to the prior and other brothers.[11] Observing the rule of truth, they praised the Cistercian order above all other orders and ordered Pons to seek after it instead. To that advice they added this: that [their] order be derived from the abbey of the order which seemed nearer to that location, so that they not endure excessive hardship in going [there] or returning.

Then Pons of Léras bade them farewell. Arriving at Mazan, he entered the chapter house. By the hand of Lord Peter, the abbot who was then present at that place, he gave the house of Salvanès over to the Cistercian order and placed the care of said house with that abbot. Then Dom Peter, first abbot of Mazan, a holy man of esteemed memory and worthy of God, sent some selected men to that place to get workshops ready and prepare the place for the order. He instructed the Salvanian brothers to come to him, and when they had been tested and instructed according to the Rule of blessed Benedict for one year, he clothed them in the monastic habit, blessed them, and sent them away. He placed one man over the others-a wise and good man, learned in letters, namely Dom Ademar—and established him as abbot; he handed over and released the care of the house to him.

Then the church of Salvanès first became an abbey, specifically in the year 1136 since the incarnation of our Lord. Then the religious life began to flourish in [the abbey], the order to increase, and charity to burn fervently. Then famous men and faithful people began to give it many things from their belongings and possessions, and [these were] not only neighbors but even people from distant places and from abroad. For the religious life of the house was not unknown to princes of the world, who sent offerings there for the salvation and redemption of their souls. The emperor of Constantinople did this; also the king of Sicily, Duke Roger; also the marvelous man, Count Thibaut, [of Champagne] known by the whole world for his holiness and devotion; also many others who have been inscribed on the register of eternal blessedness [and] have received rewards for their devotion from the Lord.[12] Among them should be especially counted and commended to eternal remembrance a certain noble and wealthy man by the name of William, who sent two hundred marks of silver from abroad for building the Salvanès church. His memory is celebrated and cherished among our special friends and acquaintances with a blessing not only on his anniversary but even as a daily practice. But also a certain noble and very wealthy man, a citizen of Lodève by the name of Peter Aibrand, had the dormitory [built]; he offered one hundred marks of silver for doing that work. His son, Aibrand, had the refectory [built].

Later, after some time had passed [and] because of the insolence of people of the world and many other bothersome matters, Dom Abbot Guirald and all the brothers, decided that they ought to move the monastery to another place which seemed better and more suitable for the religious life and which seemed to abound in many other advantages. That place was not far from the monastery, only as far as a ballista's bow can send [an object]. It was, however, not in the possession of the monastery and could not be had except for a great price. Hearing that, the above-mentioned William, who had sent two hundred marks of silver for building the church, desired and instructed that from the same money a place be purchased on which a church might be founded. That was done. The place, with all belonging to it, was bought at the price of one thousand solidii—a beautiful and delightful farm very appropriate for the religious life. They then began to build the new monastery on it. On that place Peter Aibrand venerable sacristan of the church of Lodève [and] son of the aforementioned Peter Aibrand, had [built] a dormitory of greater size and more excellent beauty than was the first. Richard of Clarius, venerable cleric of the aforementioned church, had the refectory [built]. These are the builders or founders of the Salvanès monastery who for the merit of their devotion, have deserved to be first among our friends and acquaintances; their memory will never be forsaken, because as long as the Cistercian order will be able to last, not a day will pass on which they are not commemorated, and a solemn prayer not made for them.

Truly those who by their labors first began the place remained there in holiness of life, in humility and obedience until their earthly bodies rendered their souls to heaven. Now brother Pons of Léras, who always strove to choose a rather humble position, remained a lay brother wearing the lay-brother's habit so that he might provide for the entire house more freely and always be a servant of the servants of God. This too he did until he rested in God at his blessed end. This [man] was

> pious, humble, modest,
> sober, chaste and calm;
> while present in life he quickened
> the strength of his body.[13]

In the month of August, on the first day of the month, entering the way of all flesh, he did not pass away but he went away to his fathers, from death to life, from toil to rest, from exile to his homeland.

Those living in the flesh established this church by their labor; now they are crowned and they receive the palms of their labors. We are all indebted to their souls as are all who will be in this place until its end, because they toiled and we entered into their labors [see Jn 4:38], they sowed and we reaped. Although we may stand in need of their prayers more than they of ours, by their merits and intercessions God always guides and protects this place.

By their example many men of the military order in this place have converted to the Lord. One of them was Lord Arnaud du Pont, whom we mentioned above; it was he who gave the very place where he later rested in peace.[14] Many others too put aside material arms there and took up spiritual arms to do battle against spiritual wickedness; they cast *their swords into plowshares and their lances into sickles*. They will no more raise *their sword against the people, and no longer will they exercise themselves in battle* [Is 2:4]. For in them that [saying] was fulfilled: *The wolf shall dwell with the lamb and the leopard shall lie down with the kid* [Is 11:6]. *The wolf and the sheep shall feed together, the lion and the ox shall eat straw* [Is 65:25].

Meanwhile, the brothers were occupied with divine praises and persisted in daily labors; they sowed fields and planted vines and made new fruit. God blessed them and they multiplied greatly. Their desire was useful to them; they were not deceived by their desire. God gave them houses of people and they took possession of the labors of people so that they might guard His justifications and look after His law.

I have omitted writing about the site of the place because we see it daily. Let it suffice to say only this for the absent: the mountains are all around it and the Lord is around His people [see Ps 124:2, Vulgate]. I have determined it superfluous to discuss the materials and buildings, since they are being renovated every day. The old are being destroyed and new ones built, and with God's grace, they are continuously being altered for the better.[15]

Concerning spiritual matters it ought to be known that this house was founded on firm rock [see Mt 7:25 and Lk 6:48], that is [on our] Lord Jesus Christ. The house erected with seven columns [see Prov 9:1] goes through the clouds with its height.[16] It transcends the heavenly bodies and reaches the throne of the Eternal judge, where the King of kings and Lord of things holds the scepter and regulates the reins of the world and steadfastly guides the flying chariot. In the house large stones, *living stones* [1 Pet 2:5], precious stones are cut, shaped and polished; from them the heavenly Jerusalem is built *as the city whose participation is of itself* [Ps 121:3, Vulgate] and for itself.

The first abbot of this place was Dom Ademar who lived in it for six months. Second was Desiderius who ruled it for eight years.

The third was Guirald who by the law of the rule tightly governed the monastery for seventeen years, increased it with many possessions and accomplished many good things in it. Among those things he also founded the house at Nonenque and with it added the religious life of nuns. He died in the year of grace 1161, in the month of September, the fifteenth calends of October [September 17]. In that same year in the month of October, Dom Pons, my abbot, succeeded him with the approval of the entire community and rose from prior to abbot; he was fourth in the order of abbots. It is he who instructed us to write this and who gave written testimony to things we said that he either saw or heard. *We know that his testimony is true* [see Jn 21:24].

Rejoice then, church at Salvanès, kind mother, render thanks and give shouts of joy, *enlarge the place of your tents and extend the curtains of your tabernacles; lengthen your cords, for you will enter on the right and on the left and your descendants will inherit* [Is 54:2–3] the mountains. Rejoice and exult in the Lord your God. While the wild boar will love the tops of the mountains [and] the fish the rivers, while the bees will feed on thyme,[17] [and] the cicadas on dew drops, your honor, your name and praises will always remain, with the aid of our Lord Jesus Christ who lives and reigns God forever and ever. Amen.

Here ends the Tract on the Conversion of Pons of Léras, and the True Account of the Beginning of the Monastery at Silvanès.

NOTES

1. King Louis VI, who ruled France from 1108 until 1137, was the son of King Philip I, who ruled from 1060 until 1108.

2. Bishop Peter I of Lodève (ca.1106–42).

3. *Brinonia* is possibly to be identified as Celle-Sainte-Perpétue. The difficulties of identifying this monastery are discussed by Vincent Ferras, *Pons de Léras: Un cistercien occitan au XIIième siècle*, second edition (Toulouse, 1979), p. 51, note 3. The abandonment of wealth constituted an important conversion motif in medieval hagiography. Pons's renunciation of marriage, along with the relinquishment of the property that would have been inherited, ran counter to cultural expectations for knights. The wife's entreaties persuaded Pons to reserve a large portion of his wealth to endow her and her daughter as they entered the above monastery. A wife normally received a dower (share of the husband's wealth) upon the husband's death. Since Pons's wife was from a noble family, part of his wealth may have derived from her dowry. For further information on medieval marriage customs, see Frances and Joseph Gies, *Marriage and Family in the Middle Ages* (New York, 1987), pp. 121–41.

4. Hugh here refers to the seven gifts of the Holy Spirit.

5. The monastery of Saint-Guilhem, later called Saint-Guilhem-le-Désert was founded in 804 by William (Guilhem in Old French or Guillaume in modern French) of Orange, friend of Charlemagne, who distinguished himself for his military exploits, celebrated in an epic poem named for him: *La Chanson de Guillaume*. At the time the monastery was founded, Charlemagne awarded it a relic of the true cross. William died there in 812, and the monastery became an important pilgrimage site, where visitors flocked to venerate the relic and William's tomb. It was also a recommended stop on the pilgrimage route to Santiago de Compostela (see note 7 below). See also P.-A. Verlaguet's introduction to his edition of the *Cartulaire de l'abbaye de Silvanès*, Archives historiques du Rouergue 1 (Rodez, 1910), p. xv.

6. Ganges was incorrectly identified as Aniane in Beverly Mayne Kienzle, "Pons of Léras: A Twelfth-Century Cistercian," *Cîteaux: commentarii cistercienses* 40 (1989): 215–26.

7. Santiago (or Saint James) de Compostela, located in Galicia, a province in the northwestern corner of Spain, was one of the major pilgrimage sites of the Middle Ages. In 830 what were presumed to be the remains of the apostle James were located under a field of stars *(compostela* in Latin*)*, and the site attracted many pilgrims, becoming the most frequented pilgrimage site in the West after Rome. There were four principal routes leading through France to Compostela and converging to cross the Pyrenees at two points. A guide to the pilgrimage, the *Liber Sancti Jacobi (Book of St. James)*, was written in the twelfth century. Recent publications on the route to Compostela include: Mary Jane Dunn and Linda Kay Davidson, *The Pilgrimage to Compostela in the Middle Ages. A Book of Essays* (New York, 1996), and by the same authors, *Pilgrimage to Compostela. A Comprehensive Annotated Bibliography* (New York, 1994).

8. The first site named is the spectacular Mont-Saint-Michel, located on an island off the French coast, between Normandy and Brittany, and completely surrounded by water at certain times of the year. The abbey there, founded in 966, was and still is a popular pilgrimage site. The other sites listed were stops on the pilgrimage routes to Santiago de Compostela. The church of Saint-Martin in Tours was located on the so-called Via Turonense, originating in Tours. The abbey of Saint-Martial in Limoges and the abbey of Saint-Léonard of Noblat were both located on the so-called Via Lemovicense, which was named for Limoges. (For more guidance on the routes to Compostela, see note 7 above). Hence Pons and his followers first headed southwest to Spain, then north to Mont-Saint-Michel, and finally southward again to reach home.

9. Bishop Ademar of Rodez (1099–1144).

10. Here the Latin reads *quoniam spe sua frustrati fuerant et illusi Cereris fide quernas ibant ad arbores*. Ceres may mean grain by metonymy, with the resultant translation: "Disappointed in regard to grain, they went to the oak trees." I prefer, however, the notion that the peasants were going to the oak trees to appeal to Ceres, the grain goddess, since representations of Ceres and Terra Mater (Earth Mother) were still visible in twelfth-century works. On Ceres, see Pamela Berger, *The Goddess Obscured: Transformation of the Grain Protectress from Goddess to Saint* (Boston, 1985), pp. 44–45.

11. The prior of La Grande-Chartreuse in question was Guigo I (1110–37).

12. Emperor John II Comnenus, who ruled the eastern Roman (or Byzantine) Empire from 1118 until 1143, or Emperor Manuel I Comnenus who ruled from 1143 until 1180; King Roger II, the Norman who ruled Sicily from 1101 until 1154; Count Theobald IV (Thibaut le Grand) of Champagne, who served from 1125 until 1152.

13. This is a stanza from a pre-1970 hymn for the Vespers of a Confessor Pontiff found both in the Roman and the Cistercian breviaries.

14. Arnaud du Pont retired to Silvanès in 1153 and died a few years later (*Cartulaire de l'abbaye de Silvanès*, ed. P.-A. Verlaguet [Rodez, 1910], p. xlvii).

15. Note this important reference to monastery buildings under construction.

16. The "seven columns" is another reference to the seven founders.

17. On *mel thymosum* (thyme-flavored honey) see C. Plinius Secundus, *Naturalis Historia*, 11.15.15 (Pliny, *Natural History*, ed. and trans. H. Rackham, Loeb Classical Library [Cambridge, MA, 1940], 3:456). On *mel thyminum* (honey made from thyme) see L. Iunius Moderatus Columella, *De Re rustica*, 6.33.2 (Columella, *On Agriculture*, ed. and trans. E.S. Forster and Edward H. Heffner, Loeb Classical Library, [Cambridge, MA, 1954], 2:211).

Chapter 24

Thomas of Monmouth, *Life and Passion of St. William of Norwich*

*Originally translated by Augustus Jessopp
and Montague Rhodes James and
edited by John M. McCulloh*

Introduction

On the Saturday before Easter in 1144, the mutilated body of William, a twelve-year-old skinner's apprentice, was discovered in a wood outside Norwich, England. Within a few weeks, the child's uncle, Godwin Sturt, a priest, appeared before a meeting of the clergy of the diocese of Norwich, charging the Jews with the murder of his nephew. From this incident developed the first recorded example of the accusation that Jews practice the ritual murder of Christian children. Despite a complete lack of any reliable evidence that Jews ever performed such rites and in the face of specific denials of the charge by Christian authorities, including several popes, variations of the ritual murder libel have surfaced on hundreds of occasions from the twelfth century to the twentieth.

The beginnings of the ritual murder myth fit into a larger pattern of change in medieval European society. The high Middle Ages was a period of growing religious intolerance. On the frontiers of Christendom, Europe was expanding at the expense of non-Christian peoples, notably against the Muslims in Spain and the Mediterranean. In 1095, Pope Urban II launched the First Crusade, a military expedition that recaptured the Holy Land from the Muslim Turks. In 1096, forces assembling for the crusade in northern France and Germany carried out the first widespread, large-scale violent attacks upon Jews in Latin Europe. The twelfth century also saw the rise of both popular and official applications of violence for the suppression of heretics, religious dissenters from within the Christian community.

Although the Norwich case is the earliest known example of a ritual murder charge, we are unusually well informed about it as a result of the work of Thomas of Monmouth. On the other hand, the only information available about Thomas personally is what he chose to record in his account of the life, passion, and miracles of St. William. At Norwich the cathedral chapter, the group of clergy responsible for maintaining the liturgical life of the bishop's church, was a house of Benedictine monks, and Thomas apparently entered the chapter in the later 1140s. He gives no indication that he witnessed any of the events surrounding the murder in 1144. However, by Lent of 1150 he had been in the monastery long enough to have absorbed some of its history and traditions. At that time he claimed to have experienced a series of visions in which he was visited by Herbert Losinga, the first bishop of Norwich. Bishop Herbert directed Thomas to have the boy's body translated from the monks' cemetery to a more honorable tomb in the chapter house where the monks held their daily meetings. After much hesitation, Thomas conveyed the message to his superiors, participated in the subsequent translation, and recorded not only the story of William's life and death but also the numerous miracles attributed to the child saint.

The series of locations in which William's body rested during the decade following his death provides an index of gradual progress toward official recognition of his sanctity. William's corpse was discovered on Saturday, March 25, 1144, but it lay exposed in the wood until the following Monday, when it was temporarily interred on the spot. A month later, after Godwin's accusation of the Jews, the monks of the cathedral chapter exhumed the body and reburied it in a prominent tomb in their cemetery beside the church. A few miraculous events occurred during and after this translation, but then enthusiasm for William apparently waned until 1149 and early 1150, when certain members of the chapter began to encourage a renewal of interest. One of these was Thomas of Monmouth, whose visions during Lent of 1150 led to the translation of William's body from the cemetery into the chapter house. William remained in the new location for only a little over a year. In July 1151 he was moved again and buried under the floor of the cathedral near the main altar. Finally, in April 1154, he was translated within the church to a special chapel dedicated to the holy martyrs. Each of these moves reflects a desire to increase the honor shown to the young saint by placing him in ever more prestigious locations.

The various burial sites also show the need to balance the demands of accessibility and security. The monks wanted the tomb in a place where pilgrims could approach it in order to seek favors and cures from the saint and to leave offerings in expression of their gratitude. At the same time, the sepulchre had to be in a location where the traffic would not disrupt the daily affairs of monastic life. The body also needed protection from potential thieves, for the relics of saints were a valuable commodity in medieval Europe. The tomb in the cemetery was accessible, but it offered little honor or security. The chapter house was more prestigious and safe, but the crowds of visitors interfered with monastic routine. The tomb in front of the altar of the church provided both honor and protection, but the chapel offered both of those advantages and moved the activity out of the center of the cathedral as well. William's body apparently remained in that location until the fifteenth century. Interestingly, however, as the official recognition of William's cult increased, the level of popular enthusiasm apparently declined. The highest concentration of recorded miracles—which presumably had some relationship to the number of visitors to the tomb—occurred during the year that William lay buried in the chapter house.

Thomas of Monmouth most likely composed his *Life and Passion of St. William of Norwich* with the goal of obtaining papal canonization for the boy whom Thomas considered a martyr. There is, however, no evidence that the process proceeded any further, and William's cult never received papal confirmation. The selections included here represent most of Book 1, in which Thomas tells the story of William's life from a prenatal prophecy of his future holiness to his burial in the monk's cemetery. Many of the features of the *Life* are hagiographical commonplaces. Nevertheless, as a saint William was unconventional in so many respects—his youth, his lay status, and his social class, as well as the striking tale of ritual murder—that Thomas took pains to stress the conventional features of his *Life*.

Thomas's second book is directed specifically at allaying doubts about William's sanctity, and it is unusually argumentative for a hagiographical work. In the first half of the book he describes, as proof of William's holiness, five miracles that occurred between 1144 and 1149/50. These include accounts of two visionaries who claimed to have seen William in Heaven in the presence of God himself. In the second half of Book 2, Thomas presents evidence for the guilt of the Jews, most of which is entirely circumstantial. He does state, however, that human sacrifice was part of a Passover ritual performed each year in one Jewish community chosen by lot from all those in Europe, and he claims as his source the testimony of a former Jew of Cambridge who had converted to Christianity when he heard of William's miracles. Similar stories in later ritual murder accusations elsewhere suggest widespread Christian belief in an international Jewish conspiracy.

The third through the sixth books of Thomas's work are for the most part quite conventional. They present a chronologically ordered account of William's three translations in the years between 1150 and 1154 and the numerous miracles that occurred in the same period. The seventh and last book begins with a series of miracles that date from the mid-1150s. They are followed by a few more stories, much more widely spaced in time, suggesting that in later years Thomas occasionally appended an additional anecdote to his essentially finished composition. Conveniently he notes that the last miracle he records took place in 1172.

Thomas's *Life* was unknown until the 1890s, and most of the scholarly investigations of it over the past century have sought to explain young William's death. Despite these attempts at armchair detective work, the crime remains unsolved. During the last decade researchers have emphasized the more significant issue of the place of William's murder and Thomas's book in the history of medieval relations between Christians and Jews. Here the fundamental point at issue is whether Thomas of Monmouth personally created the fiction of ritual murder, or whether he simply reported a story of the killing that was widely accepted in the Norwich community and possibly based on an existing, but otherwise undocumented, popular belief that Jews sacrificed Christian children.

SOURCES AND FURTHER READINGS

For over a century the only edition and the most detailed discussion of Thomas of Monmouth's work (*Bibliotheca hagiographica latina*, no. 8926) have been those in *The Life and Miracles of St William of Norwich by Thomas of Monmouth, Now First Edited from the Unique Manuscript*, ed. and trans. Augustus Jessopp and Montague Rhodes James (Cambridge, 1896). The text printed here is a modernized and occasionally corrected version of Jessopp and James's translation. A new text is now forthcoming from Oxford Medieval Texts: *Thomas of Monmouth: The Life and Miracles of St William of Norwich*, ed. and trans. Willis Johnson. Two recent studies of the significance of Thomas's work are Gavin I. Langmuir, "Thomas of Monmouth: Detector of Ritual Murder," *Speculum* 59 (1984): 820–46, who sees Thomas as the inventor of the ritual murder libel, and John M. McCulloh, "Jewish Ritual Murder: William of Norwich, Thomas of Monmouth, and the Early Dissemination of the Myth," *Speculum* 72 (1997): 698–740, who argues that Thomas is a reporter rather than the creator of the charge. Kenneth Stow, *Alienated Minority: The Jews of Medieval Latin Europe* (Cambridge, MA, 1992), provides a recent history of the Jews and their relations with Christians in the Middle Ages, while R.I. Moore, *The Formation of a Persecuting Society: Power and Deviance in Western Europe, 950–1250* (Oxford, 1987), offers a broad interpretation of the growth of persecution. Hagiographical studies of Thomas's work have emphasized his descriptions of William's miracles: Ronald Finucane, *Miracles and Pilgrims: Popular Beliefs in Medieval England* (Totowa, NJ, 1977) and Benedicta Ward, *Miracles and the Medieval Mind: Theory, Record and Event, 1000–1215* (Philadelphia, 1982), especially pp. 68–76. M.D. Anderson, *A Saint at Stake: The Strange Death of William of Norwich, 1144* (London, 1964) is a readable popular account of the events surrounding William's murder and the efforts to promote his cult as a saint.

Thomas of Monmouth, Life and Passion of St. William of Norwich

(1.) Concerning the forewarning in his mother's dream.

The mercy of divine goodness, wishing to display itself to the see of Norwich, or rather to the whole of England, and to give it in these new times a new patron, granted that a boy should be conceived in his mother's womb without her knowing that he was to be numbered among the illustrious martyrs and worthy to be honored among all the army of the saints. Moreover divine mercy brought it about that he should grow up little by little as a fragrant rose from the thorns.

His father was a certain Wenstan by name. His mother was called Elviva, and they passed their lives as honest people in the country, being very well supplied with the necessities of life. It should not seem absurd to anyone that a boy of such sanctity and destined for such honor should by God's will be born from lowly parents, when it is certain that He Himself was pleased to be born from among the poor. Accordingly his mother, although ignorant of the fact, had by divine goodness conceived, and, while still unaware, was with child. But it happened that she was chosen to receive a marvelous forewarning by a vision worthy of our honor, which revealed to her how great should be the sanctity and dignity of the child whom she bore in her womb. As she slept it seemed to her that she was standing in a road with her father Wulward, a priest, a very famous man in his time.[1] And there as she looked down, at her feet, she saw a fish known as a luce. The fish had twelve fins on each side, and they were red as if they were dabbled with blood. And she said to her father, "Father, I see a fish, but I wonder very much how it should have come here or how it can live in so dry a spot." Her father answered, "Pick it up, my daughter. Pick it up and put it in your bosom." When she did so, the fish seemed to move in her bosom and by degrees to grow so large that she could no longer hold it. So it glided out, and escaping by her sleeve and suddenly acquiring wings, it flew away, and passing through the clouds, it entered into heaven, which opened to receive it.

The woman awoke after her vision, and in the morning she told her father what she had seen in her dream. Her father having much experience in explaining visions, wondering what was presaged and what it portended, first thought it over privately and, considering all the facts, after a while he responded to his daughter. "Know for certain, my dearest daughter, that you are with child, and rejoice with joy because you shall surely bring forth a son who shall attain to highest honor on earth, and after being raised above the clouds shall be exalted exceedingly in heaven. Know, too, that when your son shall have reached the age of twelve, then he shall be raised to this pinnacle of glory." Now we can hardly believe that the father would have spoken these words to his daughter with so much certainty on the basis of his own knowledge, but rather on behalf of the Holy Spirit, to whom alone all things are present, even those things which are to come.

In accordance with her father's words, the daughter did bring forth a son, who also at twelve years of age arrived at the height of honor that had been foretold.

(2.) Concerning his birth and infancy.

After some time had passed and the day had arrived for his delivery, a son was born to the woman, and he was called William. But he was born on the day of the Purification of the Blessed Virgin Mary, that is on Candlemas.[2] Perhaps this also indicated how great the purity and sanctity of the child would be, and that he would greatly love candles and their brightness. But I have judged that I should not omit one event, which I later learned of from his mother and his brothers and the priest who had baptized him, so I have inserted it here. On the day of his weaning, when his father Wenstan was entertaining his relatives who had been invited to the feast, a man who was undergoing penance, with iron bands upon his arms, presented himself to the guests as if begging for alms. After dinner the man cheerfully held up the child in his hands, and the baby, wondering at the iron fetters in the innocence of childhood, touched them with his little hands. Suddenly the bonds broke and fell to pieces. The guests, amazed at the sight, were greatly astonished, and attributed what had occurred to the merits of the child. The penitent, set free by divine favor, went his way giving thanks. The priest, who was among the guests, collected the broken rings and placed them in a conspicuous place in his church at Haveringland, not only for keeping up the memory of those who were living but also as a record for those who should come after; and he carefully preserved them for a long time.

The mother, loving her child exceedingly, reared him with very great care, and by carefully educating him she brought him up from his infancy to the age of reason. When he was only seven years old, as I learned from the mother's narrative, he became so devoted to abstinence that, although his elder brothers did not fast, he himself fasted on three days of the week—namely Mondays, Wednesdays, and Fridays. He also celebrated with devout fasting the vigils of the apostles and of other saints that were announced to the people.[3] And his zeal gradually increasing, he used to pass many days content with nothing but bread and water. With his heart overflowing with piety, whatever he could save from his own portion of food or extort from his mother by his pleas, he used to distribute to the poor, sometimes openly and sometimes secretly. But while doing these things he conducted himself so dutifully, kindly, and prudently, that as far as possible he at the same time benefited the poor and did not cause his parents any annoyance. He attended church joyfully, learned his letters and the Psalms and prayers, and treated all the things of God with the greatest reverence. With divine grace anticipating him in all things, he strove with earnest effort by kindness to all, to be loved by all and to be burdensome to none. Divine providence worked in the child (who was knowingly ignorant and wisely untaught) the mighty works of grace and pointed out by sure signs even then how great his merits were going to be later on.

(3.) How he was accustomed to associate with the Jews and, rebuked by his own people for doing so, how he withdrew himself from them.

When therefore he was flourishing in this blessed boyhood of his and had attained his eighth year, he was entrusted to the skinners to be taught their craft. Gifted with a teachable nature and eagerly applying hard work, in a short time he far surpassed lads of his own age in the craft, and he equaled some who had been his teachers. So attracted by a divine command, he left the country and moved to the city and lived for some time with a very famous master of that craft. He was seldom in the country, but was occupied in the city and diligently gave himself to the practice of his craft, and thus he reached his twelfth year.

Now, while he was staying in Norwich, the Jews who were settled there and needed to have their cloaks or their robes or other garments (whether held as security for loans or their own property) repaired, preferred him over all other skinners. For they thought him to be especially suited for their work, either because they had learned that he was honest and skillful, or because attracted to him by their avarice, they thought they could bargain with him for a lower price, or as I believe instead, because by the ordering of divine providence he had been predestined to martyrdom from the beginning of time, and gradually step by step was drawn on toward that fate. And the Jews, thinking him to be somewhat naive and thus more suited to their purpose, had chosen him to be mocked and sacrificed in scorn of the Lord's passion. For we have learned from certain Jews, who were afterward converted to the Christian faith, that at that time they had planned to do this very thing with some Christian. And in order to carry out their evil purpose, at the beginning of Lent they had chosen the boy William, who was twelve years old and unusually innocent. When therefore the holy boy, ignorant of their treacherous plan, had frequent dealings with the Jews, he was taken to task by Godwin the priest, whose wife was the boy's aunt, and by a certain Wulward with whom he was staying, and he was prohibited from associating with them any more. But the Jews, annoyed that their plans were thwarted, tried with all their might to salvage their wicked scheme. They were especially eager because the day for carrying out the crime they had decided upon was approaching, and the victim whom they had thought they had already secured had slipped out of their wicked hands. Accordingly, collecting all the cunning of their crafty plots, they found a man—I am not sure whether he was a Christian or a Jew—who was a most treacherous fellow and just the fitting person for carrying out their detestable crime. With great haste—for their Passover was only three days off—they sent him to find and bring back with him the victim who, as I said before, had slipped out of their hands.

(4.) How he was deceived by the Jews' messenger.

At the dawn of day, on the Monday after Palm Sunday, that detestable messenger of the Jews set out to execute the business that was committed to him, and after searching with very great care, he at last found the boy William. When the child was found, the man deluded him with cunning wordy tricks and deceived him with lying promises. For he pretended that he was the cook of William, archdeacon of Norwich, and that he wished to have him as a helper in the kitchen, where if he should continue steadily with him he would get many advantages in his situation. The simple boy was deceived and trusted himself to the man. However, wishing to have his mother's approval—for his father had died by this time—he started with the fellow to find her. When they had come to where she was, the boy told her the reason for his visit, and the traitor, repeating his previous offer, cast the net of his treachery. So with many promises that son of perdition easily prevailed upon the boy's mind with his tempting offers. Yet at first he could not at all gain the mother's consent. But when the scoundrel persisted, the innocent boy agreed though his mother resisted, moved by forebodings and in her motherly affection feeling some fear for her son. On one side was the traitor, on the other the mother. He begs; she refuses. He begs, but only that he may make away with the boy. She refuses, afraid lest she should lose him. He asserts that he is the archdeacon's cook, but she does not believe him at all. So between her and him you might have seen a struggle as between a sheep and a wolf (who seemed at first sight far the strongest) in defense of a third. The lamb was between them. Here stood the sheep and there the wolf. The wolf persists so that he may rend and devour; the sheep holds her ground that she may rescue and save. But because the boy, being led astray, favored the one and kept on incessantly begging the consent of the other, the mother, partly overcome by her son's prayers and partly seduced by the man's rosy promises, at last was compelled against her will to give way. She begged, however, for delay till after Easter; but the traitor swore he would not wait three days, not for thirty pieces of silver. The mother refused to let him go, and vowed she would not release him before Easter. So the traitor took three shillings from his purse with intent to weaken the mother's devotion and to bend the capricious stubbornness of a fickle woman, seduced by the glitter of money to the lust of gain. Thus the money was offered as the price of the innocent's service, or rather in truth as the price of his blood. But not even yet was the mother's devotion shaken, nor the intuition of a coming evil easily removed. The wrangling still went on: on one side with prayers, and on the other with the pieces of silver, so that, if he could not wear down her stubbornness by his continual offers, the brightness of the coins that smiled at her might arouse her avarice. So the mother's mind was cruelly disturbed by these, even though her motherly affection only slowly gave way under the temptation and, persuaded at last by the shining pieces of silver, she was the victim of her greed, and once overcome, willingly or not, she came to accept that which she still opposed. Briefly told, the mother being won over, the lamb was handed over to the wolf, and the boy William was given up to the betrayer.

(5.) How on going to the Jews he was taken, mocked and slain.

In the morning accordingly that traitor, an imitator in almost everything of the traitor Judas, returns to Norwich with the boy, and as he was passing by the house of the boy's aunt he went in with him and said that the mother had entrusted the boy to him, and then he went out again hastily. But the boy's aunt said quickly to her daughter, "Follow them at once, and take care you find out where that man is leading the boy off to." Thus the girl ran out to explore the way they were going, and she followed them at a distance as they turned about through some private alleys. At last she saw them entering cautiously into the house of a certain Jew, and she observed that the door closed right after them. When she saw this, she went back to her mother and told her what she had seen.

Then the boy, like an innocent lamb led to the slaughter, was treated kindly by the Jews. Ignorant of what was being prepared for him, he was kept until the following morning. But on the next day, which in that year was their Passover, after the singing of the hymns for the day in the synagogue, the leaders of the Jews assembled in the house of the Jew mentioned earlier. Suddenly they seized hold of the boy William as he was having his dinner and in no fear of any treachery, and they ill treated him in various horrible ways. For while some of them held him from behind, others opened his mouth and gagged him with a wooden rod, fixing it by thongs through both jaws to the back of his neck, they fastened it with a knot as tightly as they could. After that, taking a short piece of rope about the thickness of one's little finger and tying three knots in it at certain distances marked out, they bound it around that innocent head from the forehead to the back, forcing the middle knot into his forehead and the two others into his temples. The two ends of the rope were stretched most tightly at the back of his head and fastened in a very tight knot. The ends of the rope were then passed around his neck and carried around his throat under his chin, and there they finished off this dreadful engine of torture in a fifth knot.

But not even yet could the cruelty of the torturers be satisfied without adding still more severe pains. Having shaved his head, they stabbed it with countless thorn-points, and made the blood come horribly from the wounds they made. And they were so cruel and so eager to inflict pain that it was difficult to say whether they were more cruel or more eager in their tortures. Indeed, their skill in torturing gave strength to their cruelty and provided it with implements. Thus, while these enemies of the Christian name were reveling in the spirit of malice around the boy, some of those present decided that he should be fixed to a cross in mockery of the Lord's passion. And they did it as if to say, "Just as we condemned the Christ to a shameful death, so let us also condemn the Christian, so that, uniting the Lord and his servant in a like punishment, we may turn back upon them the pain of His reproach that they attribute to us."

Conspiring, therefore, to accomplish the crime of this great and detestable malice, they next laid their bloodstained hands upon the innocent victim, and having lifted him from the ground and fastened him upon the cross, they vied with one another in their efforts to make an end of him. And we, after inquiring into the matter very diligently, both found the house and discovered in it some most certain and clear marks of what had been done there. For people say that there was there instead of a cross a post set up between two other posts, and a beam stretched across the middle post and attached to the others on either side. And as we afterward discovered, from the marks of the wounds and of the bonds, the right hand and foot had been tightly bound and fastened with cords, but the left hand and foot were pierced with two nails. Thus, the deed was planned so that, in case at any time he should be found and the fastenings of the nails discovered, it might not be detected that he had been killed by Jews rather than by Christians. But while in doing these things they were adding pain to pain and wound to wound, still they were not able to satisfy their senseless cruelty and their inborn hatred of Christians. Indeed, after all these many and great tortures, they inflicted a frightful wound in his left side, reaching all the way to the center of his heart, and as though to make an end of the matter they extinguished his mortal life so far as it was in their power. And since many streams of blood were running down from all parts of his body, they poured boiling water over him to stop the blood and to wash and close the wounds.

Thus the glorious boy and martyr of Christ, William, dying the death of time in mockery of the Lord's death, but crowned with the blood of a glorious martyrdom, entered into the kingdom of glory on high to live forever, in the year of our Lord's Incarnation, 1144, on Wednesday, the 22nd day of March.[4] His soul rejoices blissfully in Heaven among the shining hosts of the saints, and his body works miracles upon earth by the omnipotence of divine mercy.

(6.) How they conferred about hiding him.

Thus, their wicked purpose having been accomplished, the Jews consulted with one another about what else was to be done. They took down the lifeless body from the post and began to plot what they should do with it . . . [They discussed their problem on Wednesday without reaching agreement. Meeting again on Thursday, they concluded that they should dispose of the body well away from their neighborhood in order to divert suspicion from themselves. Nevertheless, because the Thursday before Easter was Absolution Day, when penitents from throughout the diocese gathered at the cathedral to receive absolution of their sins, the Jews decided that it would be safer to wait until Friday to dispose of the corpse.]

(7.) How he was carried out and hidden in the wood.

The next day dawned, when everywhere the Christian religion specially celebrates the adoration of the venerable Cross.[5] On that day it is the custom among all Christians not only to fast but also to abstain from all amusements and pleasures, and while going around to the churches of the saints to be diligently engaged in devout attendance at prayers. At daylight, therefore, on this day the Jews who had been chosen the day before namely, Eleazar[6] and another, tied up the body of the blessed martyr William in a sack and carried it out. And when they had got out of the city with the body and were just entering Thorpe Wood, it happened that a certain citizen of Norwich—indeed,, one of the most eminent and richest of the citizens—met them. His Christian name was Elward and his surname was Ded. After visiting all the churches in the city during the previous night, he was returning from the church of Saint Mary Magdalen, which is the church at the hospital near the wood, and was making his way with a single servant along the edge of the wood to Saint Leonard's church. Divine grace arranged for this to happen so that there might be a lawful witness,[7] and when the body was afterward discovered, the matter might not be concealed from the Christians. So Elward, coming upon the Jews as they were going along, recognized them, but he could not tell what it was that one of them was carrying in front of him on his horse's neck. However, being suspicious and considering what sort of business the passers-by were conducting and what it could possibly be that they were carrying with them, and why they should have gone so far from home on a day when Jews did not normally leave their houses,[8] he halted for a moment and asked them where they were going. Then, going nearer and reaching out his hands, he touched what they were carrying with his right hand, and he found it was a human body. But they, frightened at having been discovered and in their terror having nothing to say, gave their horses free rein and rushed into the thick of the wood. Whereupon a suspicion of some mischief suggested itself to the mind of Elward; yet he turned his thoughts once again to the road he had been traveling with the pious enthusiasm of devotion.

Meanwhile the Jews, picking their way through the tangled thickets of the wood, hung the body by a thin flaxen cord to a tree and left it there, and then returned home by another path. And because they were extremely terrified and conceived new fears at every meeting with anyone that they saw, I conjecture that the same thing happened to them that usually occurs to very timid people who are feeling guilty. For in such a case they look with suspicion at everyone they encounter, and they see pitfalls everywhere, and they suppose that tree trunks and stones seen at a distance are men. At any rate when they got back, the Jews told the others the mishap that had occurred to them on the road.

(8.) How by giving a hundred marks to the sheriff they were rid of their fear.

The enemies of the Christians, being very much alarmed, were quite at a loss to know what to do. And in despair, while one was suggesting this and another that measure for their common safety, they decided at last to hasten to John the sheriff, who in the past had been their refuge and their one and only protector.[9] So by common consent it was arranged that certain of them who were their chief men in influence and power should go to him and deal with him so that, supported by his authority, they should have nothing more to fear. So they went and passing within the castle walls, were admitted to the presence of the sheriff. They said that they had a great secret to divulge and wished to communicate secretly with him alone. Without delay, when all who were present had withdrawn, John bade them immediately to declare what they wanted, and they replied, "Listen, we are placed in a position of great anxiety, and if you can help us out of it, we promise you a hundred marks." He, delighted at the number of marks, promised that he would keep their secret and that, according to his power, he would not fail to give them his support on any occasion.

Accordingly, when the great secret had been revealed, Elward was hastily summoned. When he arrived, he was immediately ordered, or rather compelled, by the sheriff, whether he wished to or not, to take an oath that he would reveal no information against the Jews nor divulge what he had seen during his lifetime, or at any rate until he himself was at the point of death. But the ordering of the divine goodness by no means wished that event to be hidden forever, which He determined should be revealed in many ways to the praise of His illustrious martyr and to keeping alive the memory of His own passion in the future.

Accordingly, when five years had gone by, this Elward, overtaken by infirmity, was brought to the end of his life. But as his last hour was drawing near, he was admonished in a vision by the holy boy, William himself (who was already now becoming very famous throughout the whole province by his frequent miracles), not to neglect to reveal the things he had seen to whomever he pleased. So, he invited to his bedside certain persons whom he thought worthy to receive the revelation of such a great secret, namely Wicheman, a monk to whom the bishop had committed the responsibility for receiving the confessions of penitents and . . . , priest of Saint Nicholas.[10] At last on his deathbed, and almost with his last words, in obedience to the martyr's command, he set forth in order what he had first seen and afterward had come to know was certainly true.

All of this I, Thomas, a monk of Norwich, after hearing it from their lips and knowing it to be certainly true, have been careful to hand down in writing, because I did not think that the story of so important a truth ought to be lost or concealed by silence.

(9.) How a light from heaven gleamed over his body like a ladder of fire.

While these things were going on in the city, on the very same day, that is the Friday before the sacred feast of the resurrection of the Lord, the divine grace, which is never absent from His servants, condescended to exhibit around about the body of the glorious martyr, which was lying in the wood, certain glorious testimonies of his piety. For toward evening of that same day a fiery light suddenly flashed down from heaven, which, extending by degrees as far as the place where the body was, blazed in the eyes of many people who were in different places. Particularly Henry de Sprowston, formerly the keeper of the stable to Bishop Eborard,[11] saw it as he was standing at the door of his house with all his family. The lady Legarda, formerly wife of William of Apulia, with her attendants saw it too. She, for the love of God, lives near the hospital of Saint Mary Magdalen, looking after the sick, and engaged in such services, she lives as a beggar for the salvation of her soul. But in the same night, when the sick people of the hospital were getting up for the midnight office in the silence of the night, they saw the brightness of that same light when Legarda showed it to them. Indeed some of them say that even on the morning of Holy Saturday the brightness was apparent to them as they gazed until sunrise. Moreover, that light divided into two rays and seemed to take the shape of a very long ladder, extending from below into the sky to the eastward. And, as they who first found the body lying in the open air in the wood testified, one of these rays stretched as far as his head and the other to his feet. What else did the divine grace wish to signify to His faithful ones with this sign except that it was His pleasure to declare, by a clear indication to all, how great was the merit of him whom He was so glorifying by signs from heaven? For the form of the ladder typifies his ascent to glory, and the brightness of the light declares his deserving of the martyr's crown.

(10.) How he was discovered and by whom.

[On Saturday morning, the nun Legarda and some of the residents of the hospital went out before sunrise to find the spot where the light had appeared. When they got there, they found the boy's body at the base of an oak tree, where two crows were trying to feed on the corpse. Nevertheless, their efforts were in vain because "divine providence, having foreseen to preserve him . . . , wished him to remain undefiled by birds and wild beasts."]

(11.) How he was found a second time.

On that same Saturday, after sunrise, Henry de Sprowston, the forester whom I mentioned before, mounting his horse, went into the wood to see if he could find anyone who might be doing mischief by cutting down anything in the wood without permission. As he was going along, either chance or, as I rather believe, the divine will inclined his mind toward the place where he had seen the beams of the bright light gleaming on the day before. While he was passing back and forth in that part of the wood, suddenly he observed a man cutting wood who said that he had discovered there close by a boy who had been slain. Then, led by the peasant, Henry found the boy, but who he was or how he had got there he could not understand. But when he had looked at him very carefully to find out if by any chance he knew him, he perceived that he had been wounded, and he noticed the wooden torture in his mouth. Becoming aware that the boy had been treated with unusual cruelty, he now began to suspect, from the manner of his treatment, that it was no Christian but in fact a Jew who had presumed to slaughter an innocent child of this kind with such horrible barbarity. So, observing the place very carefully and taking note of the quarter of the heavens, he became certain that this was the same place where on the day before he had seen the rays of light gleaming and flashing upward. Accordingly, when he had considered these things with much astonishment, Henry went back and told his wife and all his household all he had seen. Then summoning a priest he announced to him that the body of a little innocent who had been treated in the most cruel manner had been discovered exposed in the wood, and that he very much wished to take it away from there and, if the priest approved, to bury it in the churchyard of Sprowston. After very earnestly deliberating about carrying out this intention, they came to the conclusion that, because the festival of Easter was coming the next day, they should defer their arrangement until the third day[12] and so carry out their devout intention more fittingly.

(12.) How he was buried in the wood.

So the business of burying him was put off. But in the meantime by one man after another telling others their versions of the story the rumor got spread in all directions, and when it reached the city, it struck the hearts of all who heard it with great amazement. The city was stirred with a strange excitement, the streets were crowded with agitated people, and already many of them asserted that only the Jews would have done such a deed, especially at that time. And so some were standing about as if amazed by the new and extraordinary affair. Many were running here and there, especially the boys and the young men. Drawn by a divine impulse, they rushed in crowds to the wood to see the sight. What they sought they found, and on detecting the marks of the torture in the body and carefully looking into the method of the act, some suspected that the Jews were not guiltless of the deed; but some, led on by what was truly a premonition, asserted that it was so. When these returned, they who had stayed at home got together in groups, and when they heard how the case stood, they too hurried to see for themselves, and when they returned, they described the same evidence to others. And thus all through the Saturday and all through Easter day all the city everywhere was occupied in going and returning time after time, and everybody was excited and astonished at the extraordinary event.

And so the earnestness of their devout fervor was urging all of them to destroy the Jews, and they would there and then have laid hands upon them except that restrained by fear of Sheriff John they kept quiet for awhile.

While things were going on in this way for two days in the city, Henry de Sprowston, with his wife and family, on the Monday after Easter Sunday got ready to carry out his intention, and about the first hour of the day, he hastened to where the blessed martyr's glorious body was still lying in the open air. But when he got to the place with his party, forewarned I think by a divine impulse, he decided that he must change his plans because he was afraid to carry out his intention without the bishop's permission. Accordingly with all reverence he adopted another plan and buried the body in the place where it had been found.

But this fact I think ought to be mentioned, that while the body was being carried by the hands of those who were going to bury it, suddenly a fragrant perfume filled the nostrils of the bystanders as if there had been growing there a great mass of sweet-smelling herbs and flowers. And I think it was divinely determined that the burial happened to take place there, so that afterward the body might be transferred for greater veneration, and although he was translated, yet in this place, too, divine grace wished to make him illustrious with many miracles.

(13.) How the priest Godwin took pains to learn whether it was he.

When the illustrious martyr's body was buried, the word spread through some of his former companions that this body was the body of William who had formerly had dealings with the Jews, and at last the news came to the ears of Godwin the priest, whose surname was Sturt, and who was married to the martyr's aunt.

And when he learned from the boy's companions that it really was so, he took care the next day to visit the place with his son Alexander, then a deacon, and with Robert, the martyr's brother. He did so first in order to make sure whether it was William himself, and also so that, if the boy were recognized, Godwin might perform the burial service right away. But because he could not be recognized until the earth that was laid upon him had been removed, they determined to dig him up. However, while they were digging and throwing out the earth, when they got near the body, suddenly the earth before their very eyes seemed by some strong force to be lifted up from below and thrown out. When the diggers saw this, immediately a great horror and amazement penetrated their hearts, and falling back they left off what they had started. But when the priest called them back, they took courage and resumed their interrupted task. But when the same thing happened again the same way as before, it seemed to them certain that here was one who was not yet dead but alive. At that the priest crying out ordered them to hurry, for he believed that they would find him still alive. They were hastening eagerly, when they actually touched the body with their hands. When the soil was removed, the face was exposed, and they plainly distinguished whose it was. Brother recognized brother and friends their friend. Brother wept for his dead brother and friends bewailed their murdered friend. The more they had loved him living, the more they grieved for him slain. And when they came closer they were greatly astonished because, although so many days had passed since the time when they suspected he had been put to death, yet absolutely no bad smell was perceptible. But what seemed more deserving of their wonder was—that though there was never a flower there nor any sweet-smelling herb growing thereabout—yet there the perfume of spring flowers and fragrant herbs was wafted to the nostrils of all present. At last having celebrated the burial rites they replaced the earth that had been dug up and disturbed, and commending the soul and body to God they went their way.

(14.) Concerning the warning to his aunt in a vision.

When the priest Godwin got home he related to his wife Liviva, who was the boy's aunt, exactly what had happened. Immediately clapping her hands and breaking out into loud cries, she said, "It is true, and my dream was only too true. It came to me on the Saturday before Palm Sunday, when the Lord was pleased to reveal to me plainly—in spite of my ignorance—the most certain truth of this business. I saw in a vision of the night, in which I was standing in the middle of the street of the marketplace when suddenly the Jews came upon me running up from all sides, and they surrounded me as I fled and they seized me. And as they held me they broke my right leg with a club and they tore it away from the rest of my body, and running off rapidly, they seemed to carry it away with them. O, how true was the forewarning of my vision! O, how happy I would be if I had not dreamed a true dream! I remember what you, my lord, said to me when I related this dream to you: that soon I would lose one of my dear ones through the Jews, and one whom I certainly loved more than all others. Behold, I am now suffering what you predicted. See, I'm sad to say it has happened just as you predicted." She had scarcely finished speaking when a chill pierced her to the marrow, her face grew very pale, she lost consciousness, and as though dead she slipped from the hands of the bystanders and fell to the earth.

Recovering consciousness after a while, the woman rose, and immediately bursting into tears, she bewailed the nephew whom she had so greatly loved. For a long while afterward she could scarcely be restrained from her lamentations, and she kept on lamenting him whom she had so dearly and tenderly loved.

(15.) Concerning the mother's lamentations.

Just at this time as the report was spreading, the story of her son's murder came to the ears of his mother who, naturally overwhelmed by the sad news, immediately fainted away as if she were dead. After a while, however, recovering herself, she hastened to Norwich without delay to inquire into the truth of the matter. But when she learned by the report of many people that her son was dead and was buried in the wood—immediately tearing her hair and clapping her hands, she ran weeping and wailing through the streets like a mad woman. At last going to the house of her sister, whom I mentioned before and inquiring of both the priest Godwin and her sister, she could learn nothing about the circumstances and the truth except that he had been slain in an extraordinary way. Nevertheless, from many probable indications and conclusions she was convinced that they were not Christians but Jews who had dared to do this sort of deed. With a woman's readiness of belief she easily gave credence to these conjectures. Whereupon she at once burst forth into denouncing the Jews publicly with insults and indignation. Sometimes she behaved like a mother moved by a mother's love; sometimes she bore herself like a woman with a woman's passionate rashness. And so, assuming as certain what she only suspected, asserting what she imagined as though it had actually been seen—she went through the streets and open places. And carried along by her motherly distress, she kept calling upon everybody with dreadful screams, protesting that the Jews had seduced and stolen her son away from her and killed him. This conduct worked very greatly upon the minds of the populace to accept the truth, and so everybody began to cry out with one voice that all the Jews ought to be utterly destroyed as eternal enemies of Christians and the Christian religion.

(16.) How the priest Godwin accused the Jews at a synod and offered to prove by ordeal that they were guilty of the death of the boy William.

When some days had passed, the day for holding the synod drew near, and according to custom Bishop Eborard presided. The sermon having been preached, the aforesaid Godwin, the priest, arose, saying that he was about to bring to the ears of the bishop and his brother priests a distressing complaint and one which had not been heard of in the present time. Wherefore, after everyone had been ordered to be silent, he began in the following manner:

"Very reverend Lord, Father, and Bishop, may your goodness, which has been so well known in the past and will continue to be for all time, deign to incline your ears graciously to the words of our complaint. May also the reverend assembly of my brethren and fellow priests, whom I see attending the present synod, condescend to listen patiently to my sad complaint and receive it without indifference. Truly I have come forward to plead not so much a private or domestic case as to make known to you an outrage that has recently been done to the whole Christian community. Indeed I think it is not unknown to you, Father and very reverend Prelate, nor do I think it is a secret to most of you, my dear brethren, that a certain boy—a very little boy and a harmless innocent, too—was treated in the most horrible manner in Passion Week, was found in a wood, and up to this time has been buried there without a Christian funeral. He was indeed a cousin of my own children, and because of the tie of kinship which united us he was very dear to me. Therefore, when I lay my complaint before you all concerning his death, I can hardly keep the tears from my eyes. To begin with, I excuse all Christians as innocent in this detestable act of murder. But, in the second place, I accuse the Jews, the enemies of the Christian name, as the doers of this deed and as the shedders of innocent blood. Third, I am ready to prove the truth of my statements at such time and place and by such proof as is allowed me by Christian law. You should not consider me hasty or unwise in the present business. If I were not certain of the truth of the charge I have laid before you, I certainly would not have come forward so confidently to establish the proof I have promised. And that the facts are so you can judge for yourselves, not only from the practices that the Jews are bound to carry out on the days specified, but also from the manner of the punishment inflicted and the character of the wounds as well as from the many circumstances that fit together. To these and many other most evident proofs must also be added Leviva, the boy's aunt, with her very remarkable warning vision. There is also the weeping mother who laments that she was circumvented and seduced by the crafty tricks of a very cunning messenger of the Jews, and so her son was taken away. Thus, since these things are so certain and I too am concerned when my neighbor's house is in flames, therefore I come before you as my one and only protection, and I present my complaint to you with greater confidence because I firmly believe that you will by no means deviate from the laws of right and equity."

With this conclusion he brought his speech to an end and was silent. With attentive ears, eyes fixed on the ground, and an anxious heart, he waited for the bishop's answer. Accordingly, while all were disturbed and stunned at what had occurred, they say that the prelate, very much moved by the atrocity of the deed and motivated by his zeal for justice, replied as follows:

"What you affirm to be certain is so far clearly uncertain to us; however, we shall take care to arrive at reliable knowledge of this business. And if indeed it turns out to be as you say, you may be sure that the rigor of our justice shall not be found wanting in any respect. But since it is not proper that a just judge should pronounce upon those who are absent and unheard, let the Jews be summoned and have a hearing tomorrow. Then, if they are convicted, let them receive the punishment they deserve."

The handling of this business being thus put off until the next day, and the business of the synod having been dealt with in part, all dispersed intending to return the next morning. But on the same day, by order of the bishop, the dean[13] of Norwich summoned the Jews to appear and ordered them to present themselves before the bishop in the morning to answer before the synod regarding such an important matter.

The Jews were greatly disturbed and ran to Sheriff John as their only refuge, seeking help and counsel in so difficult a cause because by trusting to his patronage they had often escaped many dangers. So John, having taken counsel and being one who was not ignorant of the truth, did not allow the Jews to come to the synod on the following day. Indeed he sent word through his servants that the bishop had nothing to do with the Jews, and that in the absence of the king the Jews should make no answer to such nonsense on the part of the Christians. But the bishop having received this message (and the priest wishing to repeat his complaint of the previous day in full synod), inquired of Dom Aimar, prior of Saint Pancras,[14] and other very learned and prudent men who happened then to be present at the synod, what answer they thought ought to be given. They declared unanimously that a clear outrage was being done to God and Christian law, and they advised that it should be quickly restrained with rigorous ecclesiastical justice. In the meantime, however, the bishop, not wishing to appear hasty, and yet not shrinking from doing what was right, decided that the aforesaid enemies of Christ should be summoned a second and a third time, lest too much hurrying of the sentence should either go beyond moderation or exceed the ordinary limits of custom. The dean did not delay in executing what the bishop had decreed. But the Jews refused to appear. When the synod had come to an end, the bishop again consulted with the wisest men as to what was to be done under the circumstances. Accordingly it was determined by common consent that notice should be given to John that he should not protect the Jews against God, and to the Jews that peremptory sentence would be passed upon them, and that unless they at once came to clear themselves of the charge they must understand that without doubt they would be exterminated.

Of course John moved by these words came with the Jews without delay, intending to hear what might be said against them, and presented himself, grumbling, before the bishop.

Thereupon the aforesaid priest rose and explained his previous complaint, and what he asserted in word he promised that he would prove without delay by the judgment of God.

The Jews on the advice of the sheriff denied the charge brought against them, but as to the proposed ordeal, they asked for a short delay to deliberate.

But when the priest refused this and protested against any kind of delay, with the assent of the bishop they proceed to take counsel intending to confer secretly about it. The sheriff was consulted as to what remained for them to do in such a critical situation, since they perceived that on the one hand any delay was denied them, and on the other they were dreadfully afraid of the trial by ordeal. After seeking some way of compromise, with a great deal of discussion, and after dealing with each alternative on its merits, they found no safe escape from such a great difficulty except by obtaining some truce and delay. If they could obtain that, they hoped they could easily extort from the king with money the favor of getting a chance to argue the case, and so utterly put an end to the rumor of the crime of which they stood accused.

When the greatest part of the day had been spent in this kind of discussion, at last they sent to the bishop asking that they be allowed some sort of delay. When this was denied them, the sheriff departed with the Jews, without making the customary request for permission to leave. But because it was not safe for them to remain outside, the sheriff protected them within the defenses of the castle until, their security having been guaranteed by a royal edict, they might be safe for the future and out of harm's way. When it was told to the bishop and his supporters that they had gone away, the bishop said nothing at the time because he feared openly to oppose the king and his officers. Instead he reserved the speech which had been thus interrupted, intending to repeat it when a future occasion should arise.

(17.) How Aimar, the prior of Saint Pancras, asked leave to take away with him the body of the holy martyr.

But Aimar, the prior of Saint Pancras, having seen and heard and pondered all that had taken place and moved by inward devotion of heart, drew aside a certain priest from whom he took pains to inform himself very fully and carefully about the facts of the case as far as the priest knew them. But when he learned the manner of the boy's death, both the kind of torture and the marks and number of the blows, what else could he infer with all of this evidence except that the most holy boy had truly been killed by the Jews as an insult to Christ?

So, moved by a certain inward warmth of devotion, he went straight to the bishop and earnestly begged with many prayers that he might be allowed to take away with him the body of the holy boy. But when he could not succeed in obtaining his request, it is said that he answered that if he had been so fortunate as to get him to Saint Pancras, no amount of silver or gold would have induced him to allow the boy to be taken away. Instead, he would have kept him very diligently like a most precious treasure, and the boy would have been properly glorified according to his merits and become famous by frequent veneration and worship. These words of the prior so affected the mind of Bishop Eborard that they became an incentive to his veneration and served to increase his devotion toward the holy boy. Urged by this and affected by the advice of very many, he determined that the body of the blessed boy should be brought into the cathedral church and be buried in the monks' cemetery.

(18.) How after being laid out and washed he was found to be uncorrupted.

Then the bishop chose certain of the monks along with some of the clergy to bring the boy in, and he directed them to carry out his orders on April 24. While they were carrying out their instructions and were just returning, so large a crowd of the common people met them that you would have thought very few had stayed behind in the city. Thus that precious and desirable treasure was carried with immense delight of clergy and people and brought by the venerable convent of the monks in procession and carried into the cathedral church and placed with its bier before the altar of the Holy Cross. Moreover the bier was covered with a festive drapery, and candlesticks were placed upon it on both sides at all four corners, and they gleamed with burning tapers. The mass of requiem was solemnly sung by the monks, and the whole church was filled from end to end with crowds of citizens.

And when the Mass had been celebrated, the body was laid up between the pulpit and the monks' choir lest the crowds of people that were pressing in desiring to kiss the bier, and if possible to rush forward to see the body, should hinder rather than help the brethren who were performing the proper ministry of washing the corpse. For it was a joy to be present at so great a spectacle and good fortune to be standing nearby. So some of the brethren were chosen to wash the body and, when it was washed, to wrap it in an alb[15] and linen that had been blessed and, when it was wrapped, to place it again upon the bier. And they whose business it was took off the martyr's coat and the shoes from his feet and prepared to wash him as is the custom with the dead. But while they were washing him, behold, this wonder, this more astonishing than all wonders, happened. For although thirty-two days had passed since his death, he was found to be unchanged and without corruption in any part.[16] For, while he was in the hands of those who carried him, his fingers, arms, and other limbs seemed so pliant that you would have believed him to be sleeping rather than dead. But what was even more wonderful, while they were washing his face, fresh blood suddenly issued from his nostrils, so that the company of those present were amazed. As the blood kept flowing drop by drop, those who were helping at the service caught it in linen cloths, and when it ceased they again washed his face. But they who were present at the wondrous sight afterward assured us that, both while they were washing him and especially while the blood was flowing, so strange a fragrance of exceeding sweetness greeted their nostrils, that the perfume itself made clear to them that the giver of all sweetness had truly come to honor the holy body. For what else could the sweetness of the divine presence have intended to signify to us except that in this way He was openly declaring how great were the martyr's merits in the sight of Heaven? We also learned from the report of these same men that they discovered sure and obvious indications of martyrdom in him. First when his head was washed and their hands carefully passed over it, among the numerous punctures of thorns they came upon pieces of the actual thorns. They extracted these and took care to preserve them with utmost reverence. Next, while they examined one by one all the portions of the sacred body, they found evident signs of martyrdom in his hands and feet and side. Moreover there were plain indications that he had been doused with boiling water. At last after washing the body they clothed him in an alb, wrapped him in linen, and put him back upon the bier.

While these things were being done, a search was made through the whole city for a sarcophagus in which the martyr's sacred body might be laid, but none could be found. So a grave was dug in the cemetery at the foot of the wall of the chapter house, where the body might be entombed in a wooden coffin. But while they were digging, strange to tell, a sarcophagus was actually found there resting upon another. Both were clean and pure inside because no corpse had ever been placed in them. Indeed this discovery was immediately accepted as a miracle, since among the great men of the church and its first founders not one was found who remembered these sarcophagi, or who had brought them, or when they had been hidden there. Consequently we conjecture that divine providence had preserved these intact and unused for such a long time for St. William.

(19.) Of his entombment in the monks' cemetery.

When these things had been accomplished as we have related and his soul had been commended to God as is customary with the dead, the glorious martyr was taken into the inner cemetery to be buried with the whole convent of the brethren going before in procession with Psalms and praises. The cemetery was filled with thousands of people who entered by the gate on the other side, and the area was hardly large enough for those who kept coming in. On the one side were the clergy and the monks who were celebrating the funeral service with songs of praise; on the other were the laity who were standing by with the greatest of joy. But although they who were present differed in grade and in sex, they were all of one mind in wishing to see the sight. At last, after the service had been properly celebrated and the sepulchre had been decently prepared at the entrance of the cemetery on the side next to the cloister, the body of the most blessed martyr was taken from the bier and laid within it. And as it lay in the sepulchre it was exposed to view for a period of several hours to those who were permitted to look upon it, wrapped in an alb. But to those who happened to be standing near, as I was informed afterward by some of them, it was granted to sense there the sweet-smelling fragrance that I mentioned before. Lastly, instead of a slab, because no slab was to be had, the concave half of the other sarcophagus was placed over him and stone was fixed to stone with cement. When all was finished, leaving the Lord to watch over him, the convent of monks returned to the church chanting, but the rest returned to their homes glorifying the wonderful works of the Lord.

NOTES

1. Celibacy for priests had been an ideal in the Western Church since Antiquity, but in the Early Middle Ages clerical marriage was common. Since the mid-eleventh century, papal reformers had legislated against the practice, but a century later it was still common in England. The priest Godwin Sturt, an important figure in the events following William's

death, was married to the boy's aunt, and Bishop Eborard of Norwich also had a wife and children.

2. This feast commemorates the ritual purification of Mary on February 2, forty days after Jesus' birth. The day was called Candlemas in English because its celebration included a candlelight procession.

3. A vigil was the day before a major festival, of which the best known example would be Christmas Eve. William's fasting on vigils demonstrates that he was unusually pious.

4. In the manuscript, the entire expression of the date ("in the year—March") is written in the margin in the hand of the scribe who copied the text.

5. Good Friday, the Friday before Easter, was celebrated as the day of Christ's death. The rituals of the day included the adoration or veneration of the cross as the instrument and symbol of Christ's passion.

6. Thomas here refers to the Jew as *Deus-adiuvet* (May-God-aid), a Latin translation of the Hebrew name Eleazar.

7. Neither of the other witnesses was legally competent. William's young cousin who supposedly saw him enter the Jew's house (see Chapter 5 above) was too young. Similarly a Christian maid in the house (mentioned only in Book 2), who claimed to have caught a glimpse of William during his torture, was disqualified because she was employed by a Jew.

8. Jews, being generally regarded as the killers of Christ, were expected to remain indoors on Good Friday, when the Christians commemorated Jesus' death on the Cross. At the Fourth Lateran Council of 1215, Jews were prohibited from showing themselves in public during the three days before Easter.

9. The Jews of England were directly subject to the king, and the sheriff was the king's representative.

10. There is a blank in the manuscript where the priest's name should appear.

11. Eborard (or Everard) of Calne was bishop of Norwich from 1121 until 1145.

12. This discussion took place on Holy Saturday, so the third day—by Latin reckoning—was Easter Monday.

13. The dean of a cathedral was the bishop's assistant.

14. Aimar was prior of the Cluniac monastery of Lewes in Sussex. St. Pancras (Pancratius in Latin), to whom Aimar's house was dedicated, was martyred at Rome in the early fourth century, reportedly at the age of fourteen.

15. An alb is a white garment made of linen, worn by priests at Mass and by monks for important festivals. Its whiteness symbolizes purity.

16. Thomas states that William died on March 22 and that his body was translated from the wood to the cemetery on April 24, but those dates are more than thirty-two days apart. In fact, following the Latin convention of counting the days at both ends of a specified period, thirty-two days before April 24 was March 24, which in 1144 was Good Friday.

Chapter 25

The Jewish Martyrs of Blois
Edited and translated by Susan Einbinder

Introduction

From the time of Charlemagne, official Christian policy toward its northern European Jewish minority had been one of uneasy tolerance. The First Crusade (1096) brought an abrupt end to this period, with crusader attacks on local Jewish communities.

Both Christian and Jewish sources describe the crusader armies that passed through the Rhineland en route to the Holy Land. "Behold we journey a distant path," one Jewish chronicler quotes them as saying, "to seek the idolatrous shrine and to take vengeance upon the Muslims. But here we behold the Jews who dwell among us, whose ancestors killed him [Jesus] and crucified him without cause. Let us take vengeance first among them . . ." In prose and poetry, Jewish authors left vivid descriptions of desperate communities that sought through prayer, diplomacy, and bribery to placate mobs of crusaders and local Christians. Finally, in anguished acceptance, entire communities of Jews submitted to "the will of Heaven." Some Jews were slaughtered by their attackers; others, anticipating the ultimatum of conversion or death, voluntarily slaughtered their families and friends and then themselves. Whether active or passive, both sorts of victims earned the title of martyrs—in Hebrew, *qedoshim*, or sainted ones, those who have died *beqiddush haShem*, in sanctification of God's Name. The literature which served to memorialize these martyrs and their deeds constitutes the beginnings of medieval Hebrew martyrology.

Over the next two centuries, under conditions of intensified persecution and expulsion, the Jewish literature of martyrdom flourished and evolved. In the twelfth century, along with the Second and Third Crusades, and the expulsion from French royal lands in 1182, new accusations arose that Jews compulsively murdered Christians (especially male Christian children). These accusations, known as libels, were elaborated over time to include accusations of ritual murder, cannibalism, crucifixion, and ultimately desecration of the eucharistic host, as in the case of the alleged martyrdom of the Christian youth Thomas of Monmouth described in the previous chapter. Of course, such charges were entirely without foundation, but they proved useful to both secular and religious authorities who sought to pressure Jewish communities (many of which subsisted on moneylending) into large ransoms or fines.

Pressed to the limit, Jews were offered the option of conversion or death; stories of the many who chose death found a home in the martyrological literature as well.

One of the most interesting questions modern scholars have had to ask about the literature of Jewish martyrdom is where it came from. Prior to the Middle Ages, Jewish tradition did not overly venerate martyrdom; the stories of martyrdom preserved from earlier eras were few. These consisted mainly of the tales of martyr-zealots in the books of Maccabees, the martyrs of Masada in Josephus, and the legend of the Ten Martyrs of the Hadrianic persecutions, in the second century, preserved in rabbinic sources. While the first two sources were known only indirectly to medieval Jews, the stories of the Ten Martyrs were a part of the annual liturgy for the Day of Atonement.

Many scholars now believe that medieval Jewish martyrological traditions originated in southern Italy and passed from there to the Rhineland region known as Ashkenaz. Significantly, the Jews in Muslim Spain, the other major center of continental Jewish settlement, did not produce a martyrological literature. Under Islamic rule, the situation of the Jews was not one of persecution, but of a high degree of cultural achievement (at least among the Jewish elite) which history has called a "golden age." Even under Christian rule, when they did experience persecution, Spanish Jews produced relatively little martyrological literature; its presence may be a rare example of Ashkenazi influence on Sephardic literature and thought.

The attempt to root Jewish martyrological traditions in an earlier set of traditions was important to medieval Jews. Like modern scholars, they were aware of the novelty of martyrdom as an ideal in literature and in life. And like most medieval thinkers, they were not comfortable with originality, but preferred anchoring themselves to ancient precedents and authorities. The Jewish authors of martyrological compositions were deeply immersed in Jewish law and learning, who often held positions of authority in their communities. They needed to represent martyrdom as an ideal ratified and even recommended by Jewish tradition; in word and deed, the martyr-heroes of their stories taught shaken communities how they should interpret and respond to their terrible losses. The stories argued strenuously that God had not abandoned His Jews to their oppressors, that His anger would subside and turn to love once more.

As will be obvious from other readings in this anthology, Jewish martyrology owes something to the motifs and conventions of its Christian counterpart, particularly to the stories of Christian martyrdom composed during the period of our concern. In a general sense, the type of the ideal martyr reflects the shifts in the hagiographical ideals found in northern European literature. The *qedoshim* of the First Crusade chronicles were men, women, and children, young and old, rich and poor, elite and common folk. By the middle of the twelfth century, a different, less pluralistic, ideal has emerged; almost always a male, the *qadosh* is also ideally a scholar and community leader, a righteous and blameless man whose death will atone for communal sins.

However, the forms and themes of martyrological writing in Hebrew also testify to a literary heritage of their own, drawing on biblical and rabbinic sources. These traditional resources anchor what is new in a secure harbor of Jewish belief.

Hebrew martyrology was written in verse and prose. Prose was a new medium for Hebrew, whose emergence may be linked to the general efflorescence of vernacular prose writing in the twelfth century. Because it was new, Hebrew prose authors were less confined by preexisting models and conventions of representation than they were when writing verse. Nonetheless, the surviving number of prose narratives is small, beginning with three prose chronicles of the First Crusade, by Solomon bar Samson (a relative of the northern French exegete Solomon bar Isaac, or "Rashi" of Troyes), Eleazar bar Nath an (the "Raban," himself a scholar in Mainz) and an anonymous author. The Raban's nephew, Ephraim of Bonn, wrote the *Sefer Zekhirah*, a two-part chronicle of persecutions covering the period from 1146 to 1196, and Eleazer bar Judah of Worms (the "Rokeah") has left us a prose description of the Third Crusade attack on his household that cost him his wife and daughters. A few letters and scattered references in legal and exegetical prose complete the list.

Although the medieval authors of Hebrew prose depended upon their readers' ability to decode its allusions, quotations, and textual references, this was not a difficult task for a literate Jewish male of the time. With modest aids, the mechanics of reading these texts is not overly complex for the modern reader either, especially because narrative prose is a familiar medium. This is not the case with medieval verse, a much larger corpus which has yet to be properly studied.

Hebrew verse martyrology is a subset of a vast corpus of liturgical verse called *piyyut* (plural: *piyyutim*). The origins of the *piyyut* are shrouded in mystery, but the practice is well formed and documented by the fifth and sixth centuries in Palestine and then Babylonia (modern Iraq). At this time there was no fixed liturgy for Jewish prayer, but a generally agreed upon sequence of benedictions which were included in the daily service, with alterations for Sabbaths and holy days. Local cantors, who led the congregations in prayer, could and did compose their own poetic prayers, often linked in theme to the weekly or holiday scriptural portions. The benedictions, which concluded each composition, acted as guideposts for the congregation.

By the ninth century, however, this liturgical freedom began to disappear, as a fixed liturgy replaced the ever-changing poetic texts. The language of the liturgy was canonized by Rabbi Saadia Gaon (882–942), the head of the Jewish academy in Babylonia; however, the effort to eliminate variation in the liturgical service was not totally successful. A liturgical compromise emerged, in which it became the custom to adorn the fixed liturgical stations (still marked by the same benedictions) with poetic inserts on Sabbaths and special occasions. These poetic inserts were composed in cycles of poems, of preordained types, and with little room for innovation.

The first known Hebrew poetry written in Europe comes from ninth-century Italy, whose Jewish community inherited an intriguing combination of Palestinian and Babylonian styles and traditions. Most of their sacred poetry was either occasional or for those liturgical sites that the classical poets, or *paytanim*, had left relatively unadorned. The *selikhah*, a petitionary poem inserted into the liturgy during the ten days between Rosh haShanah and Yom Kippur, or on the ninth of Ab and other fast days, was a genre they particularly developed. The *qinah*, or lament, typically recited on the ninth of Ab, in commemoration of the destruction of the Temple and Jerusalem, or on fast days, was another. Formally, these were simple poems, unburdened with the heavy ornamentation of other types of *piyyut*. Most were written in stanzas, often without rhyme. Although the practice of ending each stanza (most often a quatrain) with a biblical quotation was already common, the *selikhah* did not prominently feature this device.

Like the Jews themselves, Jewish sacred poetry traveled from Italian soil to the region known as Ashkenaz some time during the tenth century. For a while, the chief influence on the liturgical practices and poetic composition of northern European Jews was from Byzantine Italy. By the eleventh century, there are signs that the Jewish poets of the Rhineland and France were aware of the poetic and prosodic revolution that had taken place in Hebrew writing in Spain, and had their own interests as well.

The Jewish poets of the Rhineland and northern France further developed the *selikhah* and *qinah* forms. To them we owe the form of *selikhah* known as an ʿ*akkedah* (plural: ʿ*akkedot*), a poetic meditation on the near sacrifice of Isaac by his father Abraham, as described in Gen 22. This genre flourished especially, because the Jewish survivors of the Crusade massacres, as well as those who voluntarily slaughtered their children to prevent their abduction and conversion or death in Christian hands, interpreted their experience as a new kind of ʿ*akkedah*. In their eyes, the medieval Jewish communities outstripped the virtue of their father Abraham, who was saved from the awful command they fulfilled.

The French and Rhenish Jewish poets also developed a new type of *selikhah* called *gezerot*, to commemorate the ravages of the Crusades and subsequent persecutions. The introduction of historical subject matter and realistic detail seems to be an original contribution of the twelfth-century writers. There are hints of this tendency in earlier Italian Jewish composition, but not nearly on the order exhibited in Rhenish and French *piyyutim*. The medieval *selikhot* and *qinot* also became more diversified formally. Although some still retain the preference for simple monorhymed quatrains, many others experiment with a variety of strophic forms, rhyme, and stress patterns. Most of the language is biblical, with some rabbinic expressions or phrases; the last verse of a quatrain is generally a direct biblical quotation.

Thus the martyrological poems that follow fall into a known genre of composition and one developed nearly exclusively by the medieval Jews of this period and region. The poems would have been chanted in a synagogue

The Jewish Martyrs of Blois

setting, probably as part of a service of mourning such as typifies the liturgy of the ninth of Ab or other commemorative fast days. Indeed, a letter written by the Jewish community in Orléans, the closest to Blois, indicates that a special fast day was to be instituted for the martyrs of Blois.

The chronicle entry and poems that are included in this selection refer to an incident that took place in Blois in the late spring of 1171. Blois was an important county whose rulers had often been at odds with the king; in 1171, the count of Blois was Thibaut (or Theobald) V, one of whose brothers, Henry, was the count of Champagne, and another, William, the archbishop of Sens and bishop of Chartres. They were closely allied to King Louis VII of France. Henry and Thibaut were married to Louis's daughters by his first wife, Eleanor of Aquitaine; their sister, Adèle, became Louis's third wife. Henry's wife Marie earned fame, about this time, for her patronage of Chrétien de Troyes, the author of the first Arthurian romances. Alix, the younger daughter, was married to Thibaut. The complexity of these marital alliances and political appointments indicates how important it was for Louis to bring this family into the fold and to guarantee their loyalty. While, in the long run, royal policy succeeded, in the short run, as the Blois incident illustrates, it was shaky in times of stress.

According to the Jewish sources, a Christian servant watering his master's horse by the Loire at dusk encountered a Jew named Isaac about the same task. Isaac, however, was carrying a roll of untanned skins under his cloak and dropped one, which fell into the water. The servant concluded that he had seen Isaac throw a "child, murdered by the Jews" into the river. He confided this story to his lord, who saw in it a way to avenge himself on a local Jewish enemy, whose political power had hitherto restrained him from causing her harm. This was the woman Pucellina, who had also earned the enmity of Countess Alix and her governess. The letter written by the Jewish community of Orléans and sent to inform other Jewish communities of what had happened indicates strongly that Pucellina was a moneylender who had treated her clients harshly while enjoying the protection of Count Thibaut. However, the count's affection for his protégée (or his willingness to protect her in the face of mutinous vassals) faded, for upon hearing the libelous report he arrested nearly the entire adult Jewish community of Blois.

The mass arrest of Jews, called a *captio*, was becoming a popular way for powerful lords and even kings to frighten wealthy communities into making large cash payments in exchange for their release, and this is apparently what Thibaut had in mind. However, the ransom negotiations broke down early, when the Jews made an absurdly low offer, and an Augustinian canon in Blois suggested the alternative route of validating the servant's testimony through the ordeal by water. When the servant "passed" this test, the Jews were sentenced to be burned. Offered the choice of conversion, the majority refused, and on May 26, 1171, thirty-two Jewish men and women were burned. Three of the martyrs receive particular attention in the laments that follow, because they were not burned with their fellows but tied separately to a stake. When the ropes binding their hands burned loose, the men leapt from the flames and insisted their innocence had been proven. But the Christian mob beat and slew them and returned them to the pyre. According to the letters sent after the execution, the Jews sang a beautiful tune while they were burning, identified as the prayer ʿ*aleinu leshabeakh la'adon hakol* ("we must praise the Lord of all"). Furthermore, their bodies remained unburnt in the flames. Jewish delegations to the French king, Louis VII, and to Henry of Champagne and William of Sens, achieved assurances of protection for their Jews and the ransom of forced converts, children and sacred books from Blois.

The Blois incident made a profound impression on the surrounding Jewish communities of France and the Rhine valley, because it was the first time a secular ruler had collaborated in the prosecution of his Jews on such a charge. The outpouring of literary compositions to commemorate the event testifies to the shock it inspired. In addition to four letters written shortly after the burning, and two lists of martyrs' names, we know of seven martyrological poems for the Blois martyrs, who also feature in Ephraim of Bonn's late twelfth-century chronicle, the *Sefer Zekhirah*.

The following prose selection is from the *Sefer Zekhirah*, a prose work describing persecutions from the Second Crusade through the end of the twelfth century. The Blois story is included as the first incident in the second part of the chronicle, a sequel detailing specific incidents of persecution from 1171 to 1196. Ephraim carefully shaped the more documentary accounts of the letters which were his sources to idealize the behavior of the Jews and villify the Christians; in addition, his portrait of Pucellina, in particular, has been constructed to suggest a medieval kind of Esther, and indeed implies strongly that Pucellina's attachment to Thibaut was a romantic one. While this is not impossible, it is hardly likely to have in itself been the cause of such hatred for her among the Blois aristocracy, and the Orléans letter describes her activities in very different ways.

The poetic laments vary greatly in style, and this in itself testifies to the wide development of the lament genre in Hebrew over this period. One reason I have chosen the poems of Ephraim (the same Ephraim who wrote the chronicle version) and his brother, Hillel, is that their versions are unusual for their narrative coherence, normally not a striking feature of martyrological poetry in Hebrew. It is significant that Ephraim, a prose writer, and his brother should have tried to import some of the new narrative techniques into their verse. Because we have several prose documents that permit us to fill in the narrative background to the poems, documents also known to Ephraim and Hillel, the poems provide a rare opportunity to see how the authors wove and arranged their poetic texts out of the sources at their disposal.

Despite its narrative style, Hillel's poem is written in monorhymed quatrains, an extremely traditional form in which the final line of each stanza is a direct biblical quotation. Ephraim's lament is extremely unusual in form, beginning with five stanzas of ten lines apiece in which the last line may have served as a refrain. The sixth stanza, however, mimetically portraying the author's loss of restraint, floods into a long burst of outrage and grief that continues for sixty more lines. Again, the startling structure of this poem indicates to what extent Ephraim was willing to experiment with new literary forms.

Yom Tov Joigny, a well-known scholar of the Tosafist school, used yet a different poetic format, one that evokes the strophic forms of Sephardic poetry and also of local northern French poets. Yom Tov's lament is composed of four strophes and a rhyme pattern that indicates the use of a refrain and a coda. This is a common song or balladlike form, found in Arabic and Hebrew poetry from Spain (where it is called a *zajal*) and also in the vernacular lyric of northern France. Similarly, Yom Tov has employed a syllabic meter, uneven but creating approximately twelve-syllable lines divided by a caesura, evoking Spanish Hebrew sacred poetry on the one hand, as well as the alexandrine line of Old French as well.

In both the prose and poetry, the shift away from the pluralistic depiction of martyr types found in the First Crusade narratives and verse is evident. The Blois selections pay close attention to select "heroes" who fit their authors' ideals of a noble and scholarly martyr-type. Only the prose mentions Pucellina, and according to romanticized conventions. All the Blois texts minimize the overwhelming percentage of women among the martyrs, and single out, instead, the scholar-martyrs Yehiel, Yekutiel and Yehudah. Because these men are described as part of the same scholarly network that includes the authors, the poets may have known them personally. However, by emphasizing these figures, the authors also stress the highly ideological nature of this literature, which seeks to preserve the institutions of medieval Jewish authority even as it consoles the bereaved.

SOURCES AND FURTHER READING

The prose account of Ephraim of Bonn appears in his chronicle, the *Sefer Zekhirah* [The book of remembrance], ed. Abraham Habermann (Jerusalem, 1970), pp. 30–34. The *Sefer Zekhirah* is also included in the two classic anthologies of persecution literature: *Sefer Gezerot Ashkenaz veTsarefat* [The book of persecutions in Ashkenaz and France], ed. Abraham Habermann (Jerusalem, 1945), pp. 142–46 and *Hebräische Berichte uber die Judenverfolgungen während der Kreuzzage*, eds. A. Neubauer and M. Stern (Berlin, 1892), pp. 31–35. The poems by Ephraim and by Hillel of Bonn are both easily accessible in Habermann's *Sefer Gezerot* (see above), respectively on pp. 133–36 and 137–41. Ephraim's poem is also included in the selection of verses appended to Habermann's edition of the *Sefer Zekhirah* (see above), pp. 91–95, as well as in his edition of the entire corpus of Ephraim's liturgical verse, *Piyutei Rabbi Ephraim berabbi Ya'aqov meBonn*, ed. Abraham Habermann (Jerusalem, 1968), pp. 54–58. Yom Tov Joigny's poem was published in Hayim [Jefim] Schirmann, "Qinot ʿal Hagezerot be-Eretz Ysrael, Afriqa, Seferad, Ashkenaz veTsarefat" [Laments concerning the persecutions in the land of Israel, Africa, Spain, Ashkenaz, and France], in *Qobetz ʿal yad*, new series 3 (1939): 36–37. None of these poems has previously appeared in English translation.

For a general overview of Jewish history and intellectual life in this period, the major works are in Hebrew, such as Abraham Grossman, *Hochmei-Tsarefat haRishonim* [The early sages of France] (Jerusalem, 1995) and Ephraim Urbach, *Baʿalei-haTosafot* [The Tosafists] (Jerusalem, 1955). The standard introduction to medieval Hebrew liturgical poetry is also in Hebrew, Ezra Fleischer's *Shirat Haqodesh Haʿivrit Bimei-habeinaiyim* [Hebrew liturgical verse in the Middle Ages] (Jerusalem, 1975), but also see the selected translations in T. Carmi, *The Penguin Anthology of Hebrew Verse* (Harmondsworth, 1981). Some of the most useful general studies of the history of Jewish-Christian history relations in the High Middle Ages include: Robert Chazan, *European Jewry and the First Crusade* (Berkeley, 1987) and *Medieval Jewry in Northern France* (Baltimore, 1973); William C. Jordan, *The French Monarchy and the Jews: From Philip Augustus to the Last Capetians* (Philadelphia, 1989). Specifically on the First Crusade literature, see also Ivan Marcus, "From Politics to Martyrdom: Shifting Paradigms in the Hebrew Narratives of the 1096 Crusade Riots," in *Prooftexts* 2 (1982): 40–52, and Alan Mintz, *Hurban: Responses to Catastrophe in Hebrew Literature* (New York, 1984), specifically the chapter entitled "Medieval Consumations," pp. 84–108. Also on the literature and phenomenon of medieval Jewish martyrdom, see Ivan Marcus, "Mothers, Martyrs and Moneylenders: Some Jewish Women in Medieval Europe," *Conservative Judaism* 38 (1986): 34–45; Shalom Spiegel, *The Last Trial: On the Legends and Lore of the Commandment to Abraham to Offer Isaac as a Sacrifice: The Akkedah* (New York, 1979); Israel Yuval, "Haneqem vehaqelalah, hadam vehaʿalilah: Meʿalilot qedoshim leʿalilot-dam" [Vengeance and curse, blood and libel: from the deeds of saints to the blood libel], *Sion* 58 (1993): 33–90 (as well as the special issue of *Sion* 59 [1994] devoted to responses to Yuval's article). Specifically on the martyrs of Blois, see Robert Chazan, "The Blois Incident of 1171: A Study in Jewish Intercommunal Organization," *Proceedings of the American Academy of Jewish Research* 36 (1968): 13–31; Susan Einbinder, "Pucellina of Blois: Romantic Myths and Narrative Conventions," *Jewish History* 12 (1998): 29–46; Shalom Spiegel, "In Monte Dominus Videbitur: The Martyrs of Blois and the Early Accusations of Ritual Murder," *Mordecai Kaplan Jubilee Volume* [Hebrew section] (New York, 1953), pp. 267–87.

The Jewish Martyrs of Blois

1. EPHRAIM OF BONN, FROM THE *SEFER ZEKHIRAH*, ENTRY FOR 1171

What shall we say to God, how to speak and justify ourselves, the Lord found out our sins in 1171, too. For evil looms in France,[1] and great destruction in the city of Blois. There were about forty Jews who lived in the city, and on that evil Thursday toward evening,[2] the calamity occurred: a certain Jew rode to water his horse and beheld a servant there—may his name be blotted out of the Book of Life!—watering his lord's horse. The Jew was carrying some untanned skins in his arms,[3] and one of the rolls of leather slipped so that it was visible under his cloak. The servant's horse saw the whiteness of the leather in the darkness and was frightened. He jumped backward, so the servant could not bring him to the water. Then the Christian servant panicked and returned to his lord, saying: "Listen, my lord, to what so-and-so the Jew did. I rode after him to the river to water your horse, and beheld him throwing into the river a Christian boy killed by the Jews. When I saw this, I panicked and hastened to return lest he kill me as well. And even the horse underneath me was frightened by the stirring of the waters when he threw the boy into them, and it did not want to drink." Now he knew of his lord that he would rejoice in disaster,[4] because he hated a certain haughty Jewish woman in town, and that is why he spoke this way.[5] Then he [the lord] answered, "Now I shall take my revenge on Madame so-and-so, Madame Pucellina." The next morning, he rode to the count of the city, that is Thibaut the Evil the son of Thibaut—who is worthy of cursing!- evil curses and bitterness on his head!–the ruler who hearkens to lies!—all of his servants are liars![6] When [Thibaut] heard [this], he grew angry and took all the Jews in Blois and put them in prison. Then Madame Pucellina encouraged them all, for she trusted in the count's love, since he had loved her greatly until now.[7] But Jezebel his wife, the enemy, incited him, because she, too, hated Madame Pucellina.[8] Now all of them were in chains except for her. But the count's servants who were guarding her would not let her speak to the count at all, lest she change his mind. Meanwhile, he, for his own reasons, was considering ruses to enact as a pretext to attack and seize them.[9] But he didn't know how to do this, for there was no evidence against them. This was until a certain priest came—may his memory be lost and uprooted from the land of the living!—and said to the count: "Come, I will counsel you how to execute judgments against them. Command the servant to be brought who saw the Jew throw the boy into the river, and let him be tried by water ordeal to see if the truth is with him." So he commanded that they bring him and strip off his clothing and put him into the pool full of polluted waters to see: if he floated to the top, his words were true, and if he sank to the bottom, he had not spoken truly.[10] For these are the judgments of the Christians, how they try matters according to their faith—laws which are no good and judgments it is impossible to live by [compare Ezek 20:25]! So they did as they wished and swam the servant and raised him up: and they acquitted the wicked and condemned the innocent.[11]

Now, before the arrival of the priest, whom I've mentioned, who incited him not to take a ransom for the boy's life, the count had begun negotiating a ransom for financial settlement.[12] He sent a Jew to the Jews to ask them what they would offer him. They consulted with their Christian friends and, also, with the Jews [imprisoned] in the tower, who suggested only one hundred pounds, in addition to one hundred eighty pounds owed them from outstanding debts.[13] In the meantime, the priest arrived. From the time of his arrival, the count didn't turn to them again or listen to what they had to say. He just wanted to please the priest—so wealth did not help on the day of wrath [see Prov 11:4].[14] Then the count, the foe, commanded that they bring them and put them in a wooden building, and to surround the building with brush and bundles of kindling. When they brought them outside, they said to them: "Save your souls by leaving your God [literally, the One you worship] and turning to us!" Then they afflicted them and beat them and tortured them [to see if perhaps] they would exchange their Glory, but to no avail [Jer 2:11]. They refused [to convert], and each man helped his fellow by saying: "take strength in fear of the Almighty [*Shaddai*]."[15] Then the foe commanded [his men] to take two priests of righteousness, the pious Rabbi Yehiel bar David the Kohen [Priest] and the righteous Rabbi Yequtiel bar Judah the Kohen [Priest],[16] and they tied them to a single stake in the burning building, because both were men of valor, [who were] students of Rabbenu Samuel and Rabbenu Jacob.[17] They also tied the hands of Rabbi Judah be-rabbi Aaron. Then they ignited the kindling and the fire caught and severed the bonds about their hands. The three of them came out and said to the foe's vassals: "Behold the fire has no power over us—why can't we go free?" Then they said to them: "Not on your lives will you get out of this." But they struggled to get out. Then they returned them again to the fire. But they kept getting out, and they caught hold of a Christian to bring with them into the fire. When they drew near the fire, the uncircumcised ones gained strength and took the Christian from them.[18] Then they slew them there with swords and cast them into the fire. But they were not burned, not them and not the others,[19] thirty-two souls; just their souls were burnt but the body endured.[20] The uncircumcised ones saw and said to each other in wonder: "Surely these are saints!" There was a Jew there, Rabbi Baruch bar David haKohen, who saw these things with his own eyes, for he also dwelled in the land ruled by the count the foe [that is, Thibaut], and had gone in order to seek a compromise on behalf of the Jews in Blois. Because of our sins, it was to no avail, but for the sake of the remainder of those [Jews] who dwelled [under] the accursed count, he [the count] was appeased with one thousand pounds. In addition, he [Baruch] saved the Torah scrolls and the rest of their books. This was in the year 1171 on Wednesday the twentieth of Sivan, and it is fitting to make it a fast day like the Fast of Gedaliah.

All these matters were written about in Orléans, the nearest city to the Sacred One's slain ones, and Rabbenu Jacob was informed. Furthermore, it was written that when the flames rose, they lifted up their voices in song together. At first the song was soft, but at the end it was [in] a great voice. They [the Christians] came and said to us: "what is this song of yours? for we have never heard a song like this." Then we all knew that it was ᶜaleinu leshabeakh.[21] O Daughters of Israel, weep for the thirty-two souls burned in sanctification of God's Name.[22] And may your brothers, all the House of Israel, weep for the burning! Because of [our] sins, they were not permitted burial except in the place where they were burned beneath the mountain. Afterwards, Jews came and buried their bones. About thirty-two holy souls sacrificed themselves as an offering to their Creator, and God smelled the savory offering—whom He shall choose will make an offering to Him [see Gen 8:21; Num 16:5].[23]

Wednesday, the twentieth [day] of Sivan, 1171, was adopted by all the communities of France and England and the Rhine as a day of mourning and fasting, of their own free will and at the commandment of the Gaon Rabbenu Jacob ben harav Meir who wrote them letters to inform them that it was fitting to mark it as a fast day for all our people, a fast day that would be even greater than the Fast of Gedaliah ben Ahiqam, "for it is a day of atonement." That is the language of Rabbenu's writing,[24] and so it was established and adopted by the Jews. And the poem "We have sinned, O our Rock" was based on this, as the whole evil incident was written in it, and it is referred to in the penitential poems for the Blois persecutions [I have appended] above.[25] May the righteousness of all those who gave themselves for the unification of the name endure for Israel, Selah.[26]

2. HILLEL OF BONN / BLOIS, *EMUNEI-SHELUMEI YSRAEL* [THE FAITHFUL, PEACEABLE ONES OF ISRAEL]

The faithful, peaceable ones of Israel, whose form is like onyx—
Like a vanquished warrior, You cast them off and abandoned them
When You gave [them] over into the hand of filthy Thibaut.[27]
*The princes of the people have been extinguished, the people of the
   God of Abraham* [Ps 47:10].   4

On the 20th of Sivan,[28] when the fruits ripen and bloom,
In 1171, they were handed over to him to compel [them].
Declaring God's Unity, they were accepted as savory offerings,[29]
Sweet-smelling as date clusters grown fragrant [Song 7:14].[30]   8

He decided to end their lives without ransom.
On the advice of the degenerate priest [who said] to end their
   imprisonment and burn them,
He [Thibaut] put them in a tower to cut them off from the Awesome One.
Surely He turns His hand against me all the day [Lam 3:3].[31]   12

When they heard this, they unanimously reconciled themselves
To saying as one, "We will obey and hearken," as at Sinai.
They are all one man's children, a perfect family. They would not deny [God].
"Hear O Israel, the Lord Your God is One" [Deut 6:4]. 16

We will give our burden to Him
And not put our hopes in gods of gold.
He commanded [us] to arrange the altar, to make holy sacrifices.[32]
And when the blaze rose . . . [Judg 13:20]. 20

They were ordered to bring them out to the pyre;
The martyrs all rejoiced as if they were bringing a bride to the wedding canopy.
"We are obligated to praise," they praised with yearning spirit.
"How beautiful you are, my beloved, how beautiful! [Song 1:15; 4:1]!"[33] 24

The flowers of the biblical priesthood were tied in a pair
Yehiel and Yequtiel, in priesthood and service.
For their love, they were stretched on the stake to be tied
They who were pleasing in their lives and in their death were not separated [2 Sam 1:23].[34] 28

Young men and old sealed their love with a sacred seal
There were thirty-one of them.[35]
Judah and Isaac, Moses, pious and valiant men—
And Judah still goes with God and with the saints [Hos 12:1]. 32

Made of the same stamp, four without flaw:
Baruch and Samuel his brother died together;
Menahem and Judah were brothers in dread and fear.
How good and pleasing it is for brothers to dwell together [Ps 133:1]. 36

Together the women go to the fire.[36]
Each woman rushes her companion to hurry and go.
Seventeen of them were counted, working women.[37]
With joy and happiness they are led along [Ps 45:16]. 40

When the flames reached the bonds of the Jewish priests' hands,
The ties were severed from the children [of Israel]'s hands.
They cried out: "The fire has tested us and we have emerged innocent!"
The kings and princes of the earth are stationed [Ps 2:2]![38] 44

The tormentor's rage against them did not diminish.
He commanded his servants to return them to the fire,

The Jewish Martyrs of Blois

Beaten and wounded. They were struck with clubs and with their
    staves—
Requite them, O Lord, according to their deeds [Lam 3:64]!   48

Angels on High will weep for my anguish,
For my pains have multiplied and my sorrows grown great.
The three warriors who fell before me
Were laid out before the Lord [Josh 7:23].   52

Awesome and Mighty One who observes the insult to those who
    worship Him!
To select for his offerings from his beautiful singers of praise,
From among these pious ones called "those who will be called,"
The Lord prepared an offering and consecrated His guests [Zeph 1:7].[39]   56

As a support and a strength, a great sign and wonder:
The soul was burned but the body was not destroyed.
Eyes saw and ears heard and wondered,
A banner to wave for Truth's sake, Selah [Ps 60:6].   60

They stood the test and accepted judgment gaily.
No heart retreated or eyes flinched.
It's fitting that we establish mighty prayers for them
And that we fast and entreat concerning this [Ezra 8:23].[40]   64

Redemption and atonement shall be legislated for Yeshurun.
This day will be a Day of Atonement for atoning.
May their worthiness merit their people collectively, to annul wrath—
Let the community atone for the priests and for the people [Lev 16:33].   68

Let the righteous man cry out: "Gather up the pious sacrifice!
Hananiah and his companions submitted themselves to slaughter,
Rabbi Akiba and his companions, the epitome of those slaughtered,[41]
Those who made a covenant with me with offerings" [Ps 50:5].   72

O Holy One, remember this Binding [*Akkedah*]
That it be connected with the Binding [*Akkedah*] of Isaac.[42]
Acceptable and performed according to law and testimony:
This is the law of the burnt offering [Lev 6:1, Heb = Lev 6:9, RSV].   76

Look at the affliction of God's righteous ones,[43]
And be zealous for your great Name and for the desolation of Ariel,[44]
For the spilled blood of Your pious ones and servants, may it please
    You to
Avenge the children of Israel [Num 31:2].   80

Acknowledge the shedding of the pious ones' blood before our eyes.
How long will You be like a warrior who cannot save?
Contend with my enemies and spill their blood—
The Lord is a God of vengeance: O God of vengeance, appear [Ps 94:1]!   84

May my prayer come before you in the highest heights.
[May] the prisoner's sigh and the blood of Your pious ones be received.
When You bring total destruction upon the enemy,
My lips will express praise [Ps 119:171].   88

The voice is the voice of Jacob, crying out and groaning,
[Seeking] revenge for the blood spilled by Esau,
The burning of the Temple and Your exalted Torah:
"*The Law [Torah] of the Lord is perfect*" [Ps 19:8].   92

The slaughtered of Blois will rejoice in their lot,
They will not be content to say, "Is there a God in our midst?"[45]
[But] they will draw courage in their fortress like the lion and great cat
Endowing those who love the One who Is [Prov 8:21].   96

For the sake of His Name, He will always contend for them.
Let His sweet salvation be known among the nations before our eyes.[46]
May He swiftly take vengeance against those enemies who first committed wrongs against Israel.[47]
Praise His people, O nations [Deut 32:43]!   100

They brought them down to the valley with no graves to be judged.
Look and see, O Lord of Judgment.
Fulfill the vision and judgment against my enemies
that I may bring them down to the valley of Jehoshafat [Joel 4:2, Heb = Joel 3:2, RSV].[48]   104

Give heed to my moaning, my God, my praise and hope.[49]
Put the tears of my cheeks into Your bottle before You,[50]
Fulfill quickly the vision of my prophecy:
"*I will avenge their blood and I will not clear the guilty*" [Joel 4:21, Heb = Joel 3:21, RSV].   108

Because they have transgressed the law and violated testimony
They have plowed under my sanctuary and Zion to put up their emptiness
Take vengeance together for the blood and violence,
The violence done to the children of Judah [Joel 4:19, Heb = Joel 3;19, RSV].   112

Receive my outpouring of prayer, O God on high.[51]
Hasten [to provide] shelter, and save Your wretched people.
Resettle Your city and dwelling as it looked of old
And the Lord will dwell in Zion [Joel 4:21, Heb = Joel 3:21, RSV].   116

Be strong and of courage, may it be so and be confirmed in faith.[52]
He will hasten and hurry to fulfill His good word,
filling the city with a multitude and founding it a palace,
And the Lord's redeemed ones will return and enter Zion in joy
   [Is.35:10; 51:11].   120

3. Ephraim of Bonn, *Le mi oy le-mi avoy* [Who has woe?]

Who has woe? Who has sorrow and strife?
Who has grievances? Who has wounds and disgrace?
Who has eyes reddened from weeping and grief [see Prov 23:29]?
Those who tarry in captivity, who come looking for ransoms,[53]
Who hope for peace and healing, but misery behold.
Those who are stoned and burned and sentenced by various judgments,
Who go through fire and water and by them are judged.
Who offer up their families, fathers and children,
by stretching forth [their necks] for slashing, [or as] whole offerings to
   blaze up in flames:
This is the law of the burnt offering, the offering on the hearth [Lev 6:1,
   Heb = Lev 6.9, RSV].   10

Woe to us, for we have sinned!
We have not even fulfilled our obligations to our Father[54]
Because of our sins, the Sanctuary was trampled and the Tabernacle seized,
Nebuchadnezzer swallowed us up, devoured us and confounded us,
Titus and Vespasian and Hadrian and Trajan uprooted us.
You chose us to be special—but behold us for a curse.
Surely we are dead and destroyed, all destroyed!
In 1096 You gave us over to destruction and in 1147 to be injured,[55]
In 1171 slaughter and burning were planned in Blois:
This is the law of the burnt offering, the offering on the hearth.   20

Woe to us, for we have been plundered, and the tender beauty,
The lovely community of Blois, known abundantly for both Torah
And law went up in fire.[56]
How did you merit conflagration and devouring?
Princes made libels and spoke deviously:
"You killed a Christian and drowned him in the river!"
And they brought them into prison and chained them to afflict them

They tortured them and beat them to make them exchange their religion
 and their faith.
But they stood the trial and test, in the flames and in the blaze:
This is the law of the burnt offering, the offering on the hearth.   30

Woe and evil to the wicked one, may his memory be wiped out![57]
He counseled evil, and conspired with wicked men,
To swim a man in the water [in order] to clarify the matter.[58]
And they acquitted the wicked and condemned the righteous to uproot
 him.
Then the ruler listened to his lies,[59]
Thibaut, may his name be cursed!
He refused to negotiate a ransom and spoke without mentioning it;
Riches did not profit to avert the day of wrath.[60]
Then he commanded that my children be brought, the children of the
 Bound One, to a Binding:[61]
This is the law of the burnt offering, the offering on the hearth.   40

Woe to me for my hurt, my wound is grievous [see Jer 10:19]![62]
When the wicked one opened his mouth—may his name be blotted out
 from the earth!—[and said]
To burn the pious ones of the One on High, who were so full of wisdom,
They brought them into the building to burn them there.[63]
They said: "*Exchange your glory for what cannot help you one bit*"
 [Jer 2:11].[64]
The righteous ones uttered, putting dust in their mouths,[65]
"To be burned and cooked is not a jot[66]
Against the teaching of God's Unity [and] pure devotion."
Then they sang, "We must praise [the Lord of All]," to mark the unity
 of the One God.[67]
This is the law of the burnt offering, the offering on the hearth.   50

Woe is me, my mother! For you have given birth to me for sorrow!
They gathered like the people of Sodom to surround the house[68]
Fiery snakes [and] bundles of kindling to increase [the fire]
And thirty-two offerings were burned as a sacrifice.[69]
The women ran and hurried their companions to be burned,
And they offered up their children as a voluntary offering—
Plump lambs as a whole burnt offering, freely offered.
On Wednesday the twentieth of Sivan by the calendar—
Great was the humiliation of that day![70]
Let it be a fast day forever and one of distress for a wretched nation.
Remember me, my Lord, for good,
For [only] death will come between us—
This is the law of the burnt offering, the offering on the hearth.   63

The Jewish Martyrs of Blois

Woe is me, my soul is weary from the pain caused by killing
Woe is me, for God has added sorrow to my pain [see Jer 45:3]
Woe is me, for I have been silenced, and my heart aches.
Oh woe is me, I have lived so long among my enemies![71]
Woe, who can live when the Lord sets men to raking my flesh?[72]
Woe is me, the traitors have acted contemptuously to cause me grief!
Woe to the father who has exiled his sons—so my father laments— 70
Woe is me for I have sworn an oath and there is no one to undo it
Woe is me for I have destroyed my household and exiled the one who loves me
Ah lord and his majesty! Let them mourn my fortress [compare Jer 22:18]!
Woe to the sons who have been banished from your table, my patron,
Or to the ship that has lost its pilot at sea[73]
Woe, for the disgrace and shame with which my accusers have shamed me
Woe, for within and without they surround me!
Woe is me, that my willfulness has perverted my path,
Woe is me, that my Creator has held me guilty.[74]
Woe is me, if I speak or meditate on the One who fashioned me,[75] 80
Woe is me, if I speak to distract myself from worry,
Woe is me, for my good days have passed,[76]
For my kin and consoler has gone far away.
To whom shall you compare me—whom am I like in my misery?
For what nation among all those surrounding me
Has sinned and been chastised as I have?[77]
All Your wrath has swept over me to cause me misery:
I am stoned, I am caught in disgrace,
I am burned, I am beheaded in humiliation,
I am slain, I am cut down by my debt,[78] 90
I am strangled, I am choked by my foes,
I am beaten, I am lashed on my back,
I am put to death, I am killed by the lion,
I am crushed in the olive press to make my blood flow
I am hanged, I am belittled and exiled to cause me pain,
I am trampled, I am destroyed to cause me misery,
My blood is shed, my beautiful skin reversed,[79]
I am pursued and repulsed by my foe,
I am forced, I am fined by my enemy,
I am hidden, I am made a captive. 100
All the nations, my destroyers, have grown strong
And I, how long shall I wait to be restored
By David's descendent and Elijah the Prophet?
Ah, may evil befall all my evil neighbors
Woe to their lives, for they have earned evil for destroying me
Surely Your hand is not too short to benefit me.

May Your word be fulfilled, that we may honor You in the city of my abode.
I will offer bulls on Your altar as an eternal offering
And the eternal [offering] will perpetually endure:
This is the law of the burnt offering, the offering on the hearth. 110

4. Yom Tov Joigny, *Yah Tishpokh* . . .

Lord, pour out Your wrath on the / [foe] who has stripped away the bark [of the fig trees][80]
And let it be known that You are God— / look down from above.[81]
There is no Redeemer but You / to whom my eye sheds tears.
Beat down the polluted [foe] / and the blaze that gathered [them] up.[82]
Your children are like young calves / split on the altar.[83]
Before I ask, / answer a weary soul
And let all Israel / weep for the burning. 7
Woe, days of mourning have drawn near! / and [we] have been gathered to eulogize them
Thirty-three souls, weakened from pain, / who were destroyed.
Refusing a worthless faith, / they mocked at death.[84]
They set them ablaze like the foundations of the earth / and evil surrounded them.
Their children were shackled / and their skin destroyed.[85]
. . . / bitterness . . . for the flock[86]
Hasten to crush them / and loft [Your sword] over them. 14

When they behaved courageously, / refusing to exchange You [for another god]
They spurned other gods / and were given over to thorns and briers.[87]
They were covered with incense and cloud / like a flaming torch among the sheaves [Zech 12:6].
They melted their flesh and organs / to declare the glory of Your Name.
They died violently / so that the voice of song turned bitter.[88]
My enemies afflicted [them] / with hearts of stone.[89]
Among Your pious ones, remember Yehiel / who fought with brandished arm.[90] 21

Why do You look on, O God, / [while] they put incense before You?
The wicked ones burned them / to make an offering of flesh and skin[91]
And men of strife roasted them in fire / like spring barley parched [in fire].
They surrounded my priests / with wood and thorns and kindling.
Destroy them as I wish! / Like Zeboim and Gomorrah![92]
Avenge my priests / who were burned unjustly.
As for the blood of Your priest Yekutiel/ his soul yearned for Your Name.[93] 27

Before I ask / answer a weary soul:
And let all the house of Israel / weep for the burning. 29

NOTES

1. Compare Jer 6:1, "For evil looms out of the north and great destruction" and Radaq (Rabbi David Qimhi) who comments on the first half of that biblical verse: "the language is hyperbolic, because they have no place to flee."

2. This may be a reference to the Christian feast of Holy Thursday.

3. The phrase Ephraim uses here, ʿora vair(e), combines the Hebrew for "skin" with the Old French for "fur." Its translation as "untanned skins" is conjectural. The phrase I have rendered as "in his arms" literally means "in his chest."

4. Compare Prov 17:5, where the conclusion of the verse may be intended to echo also: "he who rejoices in disaster will not go unpunished." Notice the servant has also reversed the order of events as Ephraim portrayed them: the servant claims he arrived after the Jew, while the text says the opposite. Ephraim thus emphasizes the untrustworthiness of the servant's report.

5. "Haughty" might also be rendered as "high-ranking."

6. Thibaut (or Theobald) V, count of Blois (1152–91), brother to Henry of Champagne and brother-in-law to King Louis VII of France.

7. The documentary letter from Orléans, the earliest written report of what had transpired at Blois, does not use the word "love" as suggestively as Ephraim does. Even in Ephraim's case, where he may be alluding to a romantic liaison between Pucellina and Thibaud, the word still denotes loyalty and devotion—in the feudal sense—more than it does romantic love. There was some relationship between the count and Pucellina that was expressed in his favoritism, and the ebbing of that favoritism is partly behind the downfall of the Jews of Blois. See my analysis of this relationship in Susan Einbinder, "Pucellina of Blois: Romantic Myths and Narrative Conventions," *Jewish History* 12 (1998): 29–46, where I suggest as an alternative reading that Pucellina was a moneylender.

8. "Jezebel" is Countess Alix of Blois, the second daughter of Eleanor of Aquitaine by Louis VII, conceived during their trip to the Holy Land on the Second Crusade. If I am correct, she hated her because she owed her money. The Hebrew word used here for "enemy" is *tsorreret*, evoking the rivalry between Peninah and Hannah in 1 Sam 1.

9. Compare Gen 43:18. I am following the Jewish Publication Society translation rather than the RSV, which is awkward ("so he may seek occasion against us and fall upon us").

10. The phrase "polluted [or impure] waters" is Ephraim's derogatory way of saying the waters were blessed by the priest. Baptismal waters were also described as "polluted" or "impure" by medieval Hebrew writers. Scholars have generally missed the fact that Ephraim has this backward. Actually, the person who underwent a water ordeal was vindicated if he (or she) sank. It is only in the fire ordeal that the "unnatural" result (imperviousness to flame) indicates innocence. In Ephraim's narrative, his misunderstanding lends extra pathos to what is to come, for it seems to him that even though the ordeal indicates the servant lied, the count perverts the judgment and condemns the Jews anyway.

11. This passage reverses the language of Deut 25:1: "acquitting the innocent and condemning the guilty."

12. Ephraim's use of "ransom"—or, more simply a bribe—indicates that this was not a financial payment to settle the case of the "murdered boy." Curiously, no corpse was ever produced in this case, so that Gavin Langmuir does not consider it a true case of a blood (or murder) libel.

13. This sentence requires considerable commentary. The word Ephraim uses for "their Christian friends" is *'ohavim*, but here it is clearly not "lovers," rather patrons or supporters. The fact that Ephraim includes this detail illustrates that the relations among Jews and Christians in Blois was not one of unrelieved hostility, but something far more complex and fascinating. Since we know there were only "about forty [adult] Jews" in Blois, and that either thirty-two or thirty-three were burned, it is not clear if the negotiations were only with the remnant of the Jewish community in Blois, although this is what Ephraim is implying. The negotiator, we know from a letter he sent which still survives,

was Nathan be-rabbi Meshullam from Paris. The "outstanding debts" of the community resulted from their moneylending activity.

14. In the phrase "to please the priest," I am emending *limtzot* (from the editon by Habermann) to *lirtzot*, as the former makes no sense.

15. Remember that, according to the list of the names of the deceased, seventeen or eighteen of the martyrs were women. The Hebrew generic *'ish* is masculine. *Shaddai* is a name for God, rendered here as "the Almighty."

16. A Jewish *kohen* (plural: *kohanim*) was a descendant of the biblical priesthood. The word used for the Christian priest, who is a canon of the Augustinian order, is *komer*. From the time of the destruction of the Second Temple in C. E. 70, the Jewish priests had very little ritual function but retained social status within their communities. Their ritual privileges included the right to utter the priestly benediction (Num 6:23–27) and to be seated or called to read from the Torah before other Jewish males.

17. That is, these men were students of the Rashbam [Rabbenu Samuel] and Rabbenu Tam [Rabbenu Jacob], the foremost Tosafist scholars of the day. The former was in Caen, while the latter was in Troyes.

18. The phrase "uncircumcised ones" is a derogatory one meaning "Christians."

19. This phrase literally means "both them and all of them."

20. The expression "the souls were burnt but the body endured" is rabbinic, and used in midrashic discussions of the death of Nadab and Abihu (see Num 3:1–5). Ephraim uses it here in a positive sense, indicating that the bodies of the martyrs were incorruptible and undamaged by the flames.

21. *ʿAleinu leshabeakh*: the liturgical composition beginning "we must praise" and often referred to now as the "Adoration." The prayer also includes an affirmation of God's unity. Interestingly, until the incident at Blois, it was only recited on the Day of Atonement (Yom Kippur). Its insertion in the daily liturgy began after the Blois martyrdom.

22. The phrase *beq'dushat haShem* ("in sanctification of God's name") is the standard expression for martyrdom.

23. Ephraim cleverly re-reads the verse from Num 16:5, which says "him who He will choose He will cause to come near to Him." But the Hebrew *yaqriv* not only means "to draw close" but "to sacrifice" or "make an offering." Ephraim changes the antecedent of the verb to refer to the martyrs and not God.

24. That is, Rabbenu Tam in Troyes.

25. The phrase "I have appended" is not in the Hebrew but is implied by the word "above." As Habermann notes in his edition, "apparently the author attached his *Sefer Zekhira* to his commentary to the penitential poems, and this is what is intended by his words." As for the poem Ephraim explicitly mentions, *hatanu tsurenu* ("We have sinned, O our Rock"), it is not among the surviving poems commemorating the Blois martyrdom. There are several liturgical verse compositions beginning with this phrase, and Ephraim may be "interpreting" one of them to predict or refer to the massacre at Blois.

26. The phrase "unification of the name" was a technical term, used to describe the act of martyrdom.

27. Thibaut is Count Thibaut V of Blois (see note 6 above).

28. The thirty-two (or, according to Rabbi Hillel, thirty-one) Jews were executed on May 24, 1171. Here the mention of the date also introduces a May theme to the poem, anticipating, however, a very different kind of love story.

29. It is a commonplace for the Jewish martyr to die reciting Deut 6:4, affirming God's unity. According to rabbinic tradition, the second-century martyr, Rabbi Akiba, died reciting this verse.

30. The use of this verse appears to be exegetical, as Rashi (a twelfth-century biblical commentator from Troyes) interprets it within the already-familiar allegorical tradition. Here it implies that the Jews (that is, the date clusters) had matured in faith to yearn truly for their God (that is, the dates give off fragrance).

31. The prose texts explain that the Jews tried to enter into ransom negotiations with the count, but that the amount they offered was so low it was rejected out of hand. Why they offered such a low sum has been the subject of some, inconclusive, conjecture.

32. The phrase can be read in two ways, as was intended: to make holy offerings, as in the literal meaning of cultic sacrifice, but also, to offer up the holy ones, that is the martyrs or saints.

33. The Song of Songs is a scriptural book routinely cited in martyrological texts, affirming the mystical union of martyr and God in terms of love and marriage.

34. The phrase "were not separated" is supplied by the biblical verse but is not in the poem itself. It would have been filled in automatically by the medieval listener.

35. There were thirty-two martyrs, but one seems to get lost in the original count, perhaps dying later than the others. The prose accounts mention the confusion.

36. The exact meaning of this line is unclear.

37. The phrase I have translated as "working women" literally means "spindle-users," and was attested early as referring to craftswomen. Here, perhaps, it might even mean moneylenders.

38. The verses of this stanza rely on the language of the ordeal by fire. There has already been an ordeal by water in this story, to validate the testimony of the servant with the libel accusation. The prose leaves open the possibility that the Jews who leaped from the flames were playing upon the Christian belief in such "miracles" in the hope of saving themselves. However, as we can see, the prose and poetic texts also allude to the failure of the martyrs' bodies to burn, testifying to a belief in the incorruptibility of the martyrs in fire as well; see lines 57–60 below. The audience of the poem would automatically have completed the biblical phrase quoted in line 44 (*The kings and princes of the earth are stationed*) with the remainder of the verse *against God and His anointed* [Ps 2:2].

39. The verses of this stanza confirm the notion that God selected the pure and righteous to die for the sins of the community.

40. Apparently, although it was authorized by Rabbenu Tam, the plan to institute a fast day for the Blois martyrs never materialized; see David Wachtel, "The Ritual and Liturgical Commemoration of Two Medieval Persecutions," M.A. thesis, Columbia University, 1995. However, much later, after the Chmielnitzki massacre (1648), the Blois laments enter the fast-day commemorative liturgies.

41. Hananiah, Misael, Azariah were the three young companions of Daniel who survived the fiery ovens of the king; see Dan 1:6–7, 3:13 ff. Rabbi Akiba was perhaps the most famed of the Jewish martyrs of the Hadrianic period. A great rabbi and scholar, known also for developing a hermeneutical method for interpreting biblical and rabbinic texts, he was killed by the Romans in the wake of the failed Bar Kokhba revolt.

42. The term *Akkedah* (binding) refers in Hebrew exclusively to the "binding of Isaac." It was adopted by the Jews of medieval Ashkenaz to refer to the suicide martyrdoms of the First Crusade and later pogroms, especially those in which parents killed their children lest they fall into Christian hands. A special form of liturgical poem, called an Akkedah, was devoted to elaborated descriptions of Gen 22 and its later reverberations.

43. *Yishrei-el* meaning "the righteous of God" is a pun also evoking *yisra-el*, that is Israel.

44. Ariel is a tag name for Jerusalem, and by extension, Israel. Desolation is used in the sense of destruction.

45. "Is there a God in our midst [or not]?" is from Ex 17:7, where, ironically, it is the rebellious Israelites who pose this question of Moses.

46. This line continues the verse allusion of line 79 above, taken from Ps 79:10. Approximately halfway between them, in line 85, the poet alludes to Ps 79:11, so this is a Psalm he wants his readers to hear in the background to his text. Indeed, the Psalm refers initially to the desecration of God's Temple by the nations, and the slaughtering of God's servants, who are left unburied in disgrace. We know, in fact, from the letters written following the Blois incident, that negotiations with Bsihop William of Sens for permission to bury the martyrs' bodies, were unsuccessful.

47. "Those who first committed wrongs against Israel." The phrase, concluding Deut 32:42, is now translated as "from the long-haired heads of the enemy" in the RSV. However, in the poet's time, it was not understood in this way. Rashi interprets the expression *rosh para^cot oyev* as meaning that God will avenge Israel by going back to the first (*rosh*)

of those who attacked her. Rabbi Abraham ibn Ezra, a twelfth-century exegete from Spain, reads the expression as "split heads." I have instead followed Rashi's reading, as it was more likely to have been followed by Hillel also.

48. King Jehoshafat of Judah was buried in Jerusalem (1 Kings 22:50), and tradition puts the valley in this general area, possibly in Kidron Valley (as it is called in the RSV). The context of the prophetic passage is that God will bring the nations to judgment in this valley because they have scattered Israel and mistreated her. The pun is on the name "Jehoshafat," which means "God shall judge."

49. Compare Ps 5:2 and Rashi, who comments there, "listen to my prayer when my heart is stopped with sorrow."

50. Compare Ps 56:9. The addition of "before You" may come from the commentary of Rashi, who explains the verse as "put my tears in Your bottle and keep it before You."

51. Compare Is 26:16. The word *tsaqun* was understood as both whispered prayer and as an outpouring of prayer.

52. Alternatively, "may it be affirmed and confirmed in affirmation" (*amen ye'amen ba'emunah*).

53. At this point the poet diverges from the biblical text [Prov 23:30] which reads "those who tarry in the taverns . . ." It was customary for the Jewish community to try and negotiate a payment toward the freeing of Jewish prisoners. The Christian government's ability to exploit the eagerness of the Jews to do this led at least one famous prisoner of the thirteenth century, Meir of Rothenberg, to refuse to be redeemed. The famous scholar and poet insisted that the exorbitant price of his release was a dangerous precedent, and he acceded merely to an improvement in the conditions of misimprisonment, which lasted another eight years until his death.

54. The word *ketormos* suggests that "we haven't even done as much as a *tormos*," which is the small plant known in English as the lupine. See the use in the Babylonian Talmud, Beitzah, no. 25b.

55. The pun in this line is untranslatable. The years in Hebrew are written in letters, which thus potentially have semantic meaning also. The abbreviation for 1096 (TTN"U) can mean "you will be given" (or "you will give"), and is echoed in the following *netananu* ("we were given"). Similarly, 1147 (TTZ"Q), is echoed in *huzaqnu* ("we were injured").

56. I have rearranged the lines slightly to make the English translation less awkward.

57. "The wicked one" is either Count Thibaud V or the Augustinian canon who served as his advisor.

58. The ordeal by water of the servant is mentioned in the prose texts. In Ephraim's prose account, it is not clear whether he understands the process of the ordeal (and he had no reason to, as Jews were exempt from ordeals). The servant is indeed vindicated, as he sinks, but Ephraim seems to think that this verified the falsity of his testimony, a "true" outcome that is nonetheless overruled by the evil canon.

59. The phrase "listened to his lies" refers either to the servant, who claimed he had seen one of the Blois Jews throw a murdered child into the Loire, or to the Augustinian canon who was advising Thibaud. Compare the account in Ephraim's prose version above.

60. Compare Prov 11:4. Literally, Ephraim's line reads "riches did not profit to make the day of wrath pass over." Compare his use of the same expression in the prose account above.

61. The "Bound One" is Isaac, who was "bound" by his father, Abraham, as an offering. The term *Akkedah*, or binding, refers to this story exclusively, until the medieval Rhenish Jews revive it to draw an analogy to their own sacrifices. As Ephraim points out in another lament, the medieval Jews exceeded Abraham in faith, because he was ultimately spared from sacrificing his son while they slaughtered theirs.

62. The medieval exegete, Radaq (David Qimhi) connects the pain of Israel to persecutions they suffer.

63. As the prose account describes, the prisoners were brought into a wooden building, which was surrounded by kindling and set on fire.

64. In other words, to exchange your glory (your God and faith) for Christianity, which can do you no good (because it is false).

65. The precise meaning of this line is unclear.

66. "Not a jot" is literally, not worth a mishnah, that is, the smallest unit of the legal literature known collectively as Mishnah, compiled ca. 215.

67. "We praise [the Lord of All] . . ." is the beginning of a liturgical passage associated with the Day of Atonement (Yom Kippur). It is the Blois incident that marks its use in the daily liturgy.

68. This line literally reads: "They were like the people of Sodom as they surrounded the house to surround it." Actually, the syntax is even more complex, but I have translated to the obvious sense.

69. As in the refrain, Ephraim is referring to the martyrs in the language of biblical sacrifices. Here the point is that of the two types of biblical offerings, those mandated and those considered voluntary, the martyrs fall into the latter category.

70. The meaning of the line is not at all clear. Literally it means "Surely, there was greatness that day to humiliate?"

71. Or, perhaps, "I have lived in chains [compare Job 38:31] among my enemies." The dominant use of *meshek* in the rabbinic literature and by Rashi seems to be in the sense of continuity or duration.

72. This phrase literally means "to raking my back," alluding to the death of the second-century martyr Rabbi Akiba, whose back was torn by the executioner with an iron rake.

73. Ephraim here quotes from the Babylonian Talmud, Baba Batra, 91a, writing on the death of Abraham. Literally, the phrase reads, "woe to the ship that has lost its pilot while coming and going."

74. Lines 78–79 revolve around a pun on *yitsri* (my will, or wilfulness) and *yotsri* (my Creator). Thus, literally, "My *yetser* (will) led me astray, and my *Yotser* (Creator) held me to account."

75. The phrase "fashioned me" may be more literally rendered as "hewed me."

76. The phrase "for my good day has passed" has been translated literally, but the colloquial use in English has so trivialized the expression that I have used the plural.

77. The phrase "and been chastised" may be literally rendered as "and been broken out against," that is, had God lash out against them in punishment for their sins.

78. In the phrase "cut down by my debt," Ephraim uses *nidrag* in a very unusual way here. The word generally refers to being graded, or in steps. However, Talmudic usage also includes reference to tree stumps, which are cut in graded heights, and I am guessing that Ephraim drew on these passages.

79. The probable meaning of "reversed" is "flayed."

80. The poet here fuses Jer 10:25 and Joel 1:7. The fig trees in question are Israel.

81. Compare 1 Kings 18:36, where a very similar phrasing is used by Elijah as he awaits God's ignition of his offering on the (watersoaked) altar. Rashi and Radaq both comment that Elijah means to say that when God sends down fire to ignite the offering, people will know that he was acting at God's command and not on his own initiative, especially since such offerings (on private altars) were forbidden. The poet may be implying that here, too, the audience is to understand the martyrs as human offerings are desired by God, despite the Jewish prohibitions on voluntary death. For the second half of the verse, see Deut 26:15.

82. For the second half of the verse, I have followed Schirmann's suggested reading in his edition.

83. The poet here fuses Ezek 43:15 and Joel 1:7 (which he also used above in line 1). Rashi explains *qetsafah* as "dismay," and Ibn Ezra connects it etymologically to *qetsef*, "like foam on the waters which has no substance."

84. "Refusing . . . god" because they refused to convert (exchange their God for a "worthless" or "nothing" one). "Mocked at death" renders a phrase which literally means "belittled their lives to death," following the JPS translation; see Judg 5:18.

85. See Schirmann's note in his edition and Ps 105:18, as well as Job 19:26.

86. The gaps in the text marked by the ellipses are due to the mark of a censor.

87. The poet draws on Is 10:17 and Rashi's exegesis of that line.

88. Literally, "their lives and spirits were done violence."

89. Compare Zech 12:6.

90. Compare Is 30:32, RSV.

91. These two lines in essence mean: "Why do You (God) look on and do nothing while your Jews are martyred?" The incense is associated with sacrificial offerings.

92. Zeboim is a city punished by God with destruction (see Deut 29:22–23).

93. Yehiel and Yekutiel are the martyrs singled out in Ephraim and Hillel's poems, as well.

Chapter 26

Liturgical Offices for the Cult of St. Thomas Becket

Edited and translated by Sherry Reames

Introduction

Thomas Becket, also known as St. Thomas of Canterbury, was such a prominent saint in the late Middle Ages that the date of his martyrdom—December 29, 1170—was annually commemorated all over Europe with special prayers and lessons, and often with special music as well. On July 7, 1220, almost fifty years after Thomas's death, his body was solemnly translated from its original resting place, the crypt of Canterbury Cathedral, to the famous shrine in the cathedral proper; and the anniversary of the translation became a second annual feast day in his honor, observed with special prayers and lessons of its own almost everywhere in England and in some continental churches as well. Most of these liturgical texts about Thomas and other saints were incorporated into the daily office, which was celebrated by members of the clergy and monastic orders, rather than into the Mass, which was intended for Christians at large; so they are found in breviaries and antiphonals rather than missals and books of hours. But their influence inevitably extended well beyond the clergy, since they helped to determine which ideas about a given saint would be incorporated into sermons, vernacular literature, and works of visual art.

The standard office for Thomas's December feast day was evidently written soon after the canonization in 1173 by Benedict of Peterborough, a monk who belonged to the community of Christ Church, Canterbury, until 1177 and served as the first recorder of miracles at the saint's tomb. Benedict derived the lessons in the office largely from the accounts of Thomas's life and martyrdom by John of Salisbury and others; but both the texts and music of the chants were his own, and they represent a notable artistic achievement. For one thing, the form is much more challenging than necessary. To create chant texts, many medieval offices simply chose brief excerpts from the accompanying lessons or the Bible. But Benedict's chant texts are newly written poems in demanding kinds of accentual verse, using very regular meters and difficult rhyme schemes. Generally they comment in some way on the lessons that precede or follow them, singling out particular phrases, images, or motifs for further development. But they are full of surprises as well—paradoxes, wordplay, unexpectedly rich combinations of images and allusions.

Their musical settings are also unusually effective, according to Andrew Hughes. So the exceptional popularity of this office, which was imitated in many later saints' offices, may be due as much to the high quality of Benedict's work as to the fame of Thomas himself.

Although the original version of Benedict's office was evidently monastic, using twelve lessons, twelve responsories, and thirteen antiphons at Matins, the version given here is the somewhat briefer one in the Sarum liturgy, which was adopted by the majority of English churches.

The principal architect behind the great translation ceremony of 1220 was Stephen Langton, archbishop of Canterbury, and a later tradition at Canterbury credits Stephen with having composed or at least approved the set of special lessons used to commemorate this event. If so, the original lessons for the feast of the translation must have been composed between 1220 and 1228, the year of Langton's death. As with the feast-day office, the original version was probably monastic. But the closest approximations that have come down to us are those found in a few manuscripts of the Sarum Breviary, which preserve a good deal of material that has been omitted both from other secular breviaries and from the few surviving monastic ones.

Special chant texts for the feast of Thomas's translation may never have been widely adopted, even in southern England, since they are found in less than half of the earliest Sarum manuscripts. But the rhyming office found in two of these manuscripts, London, British Library, MSS Stowe 12 and Additional 28598, dovetails so nicely with the longest Sarum version of the lessons that it was obviously designed to be used at the same time. The lessons provide the necessary context for understanding the sometimes cryptic allusions in the rhyming office, and the rhyming office enhances the meaning and effect of the lessons by providing poetic commentaries on them. Both the lessons and the chant texts show the influence of Stephen Langton, drawing key themes and images from his *Tractatus on the Translation* and also paying tribute to his efforts as diplomat, peacemaker, and sponsor of the translation and shrine. The translation office also pays tribute to Benedict's rhyming office for Thomas's feast day, borrowing most of its metrical forms and music, and echoing its wording at key points.

Although the present edition includes only the texts of the chants, it will be helpful to have some general information about how they were sung. In all cases the basic kind of music was plainsong, or Gregorian chant; but the various parts of the service were performed in different ways. Antiphons, which were sung to introduce and follow prescribed psalms and canticles in each service, were fairly brief and straightforward pieces of music, generally using just one or two notes per syllable of text. Such simple music would preserve the most striking feature of the antiphon texts in these two rhyming offices for Thomas: their regular, strongly marked meter, which typically takes the form of a goliardic stanza (four lines, alternating seven and six syllables, and rhyming *abcb*). Responsories, most of which were sung after lessons, tended to have much more flowing and elaborate musical settings, with extended melismas on individual syllables. More complex poetic and musical effects were also possible in the responsories because they were sung dialogically, with the response itself (sung by the choir) followed by the verse (sung by the cantor) and then the *repetenda* (the last part of the response, repeated by the choir). The third, sixth, and ninth responsories ended with the *Gloria Patri*, followed by an extra repeat of the *repetenda*. The Sarum office for Thomas's feast day also has a *prosa*, an even more elaborate composition in which every line ends with the vowel *a*. The lines of the *prosa* were ordinarily sung by two soloists, alternating with each other and with the choir, which echoed the melody of each line in a long melisma on the final *a*.

SOURCES AND FURTHER READING

The Sarum office for Thomas's December feast day has been published in full only once since the sixteenth century: in the first volume of Francis Procter and Christopher Wordsworth's edition of the Sarum Breviary, *Breviarium ad usum insignis ecclesie Sarum* (Cambridge, 1882), which essentially reprints the 1531 folio edition. The version given below is based on Procter and Wordsworth. I know of no previous English translations of the office as a whole, though some of the sources behind the lessons have appeared in translation (including John of Salisbury's initial account of the martyrdom, translated in *The Letters of John of Salisbury*, ed. W.J. Millor and C.N.L. Brooke, vol. 2 [Oxford, 1979]), and some of the chant texts have been translated in studies of the music by Andrew Hughes and others. A good recent account of Thomas's life and the early development of his cult, with bibliographical suggestions preceding the notes to each chapter, is Frank Barlow's *Thomas Becket* (London, 1986). The liturgical lessons have been generally neglected by scholars, but Andrew Hughes has written a very informative article on the chant texts and music in the monastic version of this office ("Chants in the Rhymed Office of St Thomas of Canterbury," *Early Music* 16 [1988]: 185–201).

The Sarum lessons for Thomas's Translation have yet to be published in their entirety; the version in the 1531 folio edition, reprinted by Procter and Wordsworth, omits a good deal of material, both in the middle and at the end, which I have supplied from the fullest surviving medieval manuscript, London, British Library, MS Cotton Appendix 23. The set of chant texts given below for Thomas's Translation is based primarily on British Library, MS Stowe 12, with some emendations from British Library, MS Additional 28598. The only previous edition is a transcription by Andrew Hughes, issued on disk as text TH28 in *Late Medieval Liturgical Offices: Resources for Electronic Research: Texts* (Toronto, Pontifical Institute, 1994). Neither the lessons nor the chants have previously been available in English. Three useful historical studies of Thomas's translation are Raymonde Foreville, *Le Jubilé de saint Thomas Becket du XIIIe au XVe siècle (1220–1470)* (Paris, 1958), esp. pp. 1–11 and 89–95; Anne Duggan, "The Cult of St Thomas Becket in the Thirteenth Century," in *St Thomas Cantilupe, Bishop of Hereford: Essays in His Honour*, ed. Meryl Jancey (Hereford, 1982), pp. 21–44; and Richard

Eales, "The Political Setting of the Becket Translation of 1220," in *Martyrs and Martyrologies*, ed. Diana Wood, Studies in Church History 30 (Oxford, 1993), pp. 127–39. Both Foreville and Duggan include some discussion of the printed Sarum lessons for the Translation.

I give the Latin texts of the chants in both offices, followed by literal translations, in order to convey as much as possible of their poetic quality. Even readers who don't know Latin should be able to appreciate the strongly marked rhythms in these brief poems, their varying uses of wordplay and rhyme, and the effects the translation office creates by echoing key words and images from the corresponding parts of the feast-day office (most obviously, in the first responsory at Matins and the first antiphon at Lauds).

Liturgical Offices for the Cult of St. Thomas Becket

1. RHYMING OFFICE AND LESSONS FOR THE FEAST DAY OF THOMAS BECKET (DECEMBER 29)

First Vespers.
Procession (where there is an altar of St. Thomas)
Responsory
Jacet granum
oppressum palea,
justus caesus
pravorum framea,
[The seed lies dead, smothered by the chaff; the just man falls, cut down by the sword of the wicked,]
Repetenda
Caelum domo
commutans lutea.
[Trading a house of clay for heaven.]
Verse
Cadit custos
vitis in vinea,
dux in castris,
cultor in area.
[The keeper of the vines falls in the vineyard, the commander in the camp, the laborer in the field.]

Prosa.
Clangat pastor in tuba cornea
ut libera sit Christi vinea,
quam assumptae sub carnis trabea,
liberavit cruce purpurea.
Adversatrix ovis Erronea
fit pastoris caede sanguinea
pavimenta Christi marmorea;
sacro madent cruore rubea.
Martir vitae donatus laurea
velut granum purgatum palea
in divina transfertur horrea,
Caelum domo commutans lutea.
[Let the shepherd blow on the trumpet of horn so that Christ's vineyard may be free, which He claimed when He donned His royal robe of flesh, and redeemed with His beautiful cross.[1] Wrongdoing, the adversary of the sheep, bloodies the marble floors of Christ with the shepherd's slaughter;[2] the floors are drenched with the sacred blood. The martyr, endowed with

the crown of life, like the wheat cleansed from chaff is gathered into God's storehouse [see Mt 3:12, 13:30], Trading a house of clay for heaven.] [3]

Magnificat Antiphon (where there is no procession)
Pastor caesus
in gregis medio
pacem emit
cruoris precio.
O laetus dolor
in tristi gaudio:
grex respirat
pastore mortuo;
plangens plaudit
mater in filio,
quia vivit
victor sub gladio.
[The shepherd cut down in the midst of his flock has purchased peace at the cost of his blood. O joyful sorrow in sorrowful joy: the flock is revived by the shepherd's death; the grieving mother[4] applauds her son, who lives and triumphs beneath the sword.]

Matins: First Nocturn.
Invitatory
Assunt Thomae
martyris solennia;
virgo mater
jubilet Ecclesia.
[The feast of Thomas the martyr is at hand; let the virgin mother Church rejoice.]

Matins Antiphon 1
Summo sacerdotio
Thomas sublimatus
est in virum alium
subito mutatus.
[When raised to the highest priestly office, Thomas was suddenly transformed into another man.]

Matins Antiphon 2
Monachus sub clerico,
clam ciliciatus,
carnis carne fortior,
edomat conatus.
[A monk under priestly robes, secretly clad in haircloth—stronger than the flesh, he subdues fleshly impulses.]

Matins Antiphon 3
Cultor agri Domini
tribulos avellit
et vulpes a vineis
arcet et expellit.
[Planter of the Lord's field, he rips out the thorns, holds off the foxes, and drives them from the vineyard (see Song 2:15).]

(*Lectio* 1) When we celebrate the birthday of the glorious martyr Thomas,[5] dearest brothers, we cannot do justice to all the distinguishing marks of his life and behavior; so let our brief discourse focus on the manner and cause of his passion. Just as blessed Thomas had shown himself to be peerlessly vigorous in fulfilling the duties of his offices as chancellor and archdeacon, so after receiving the pastor's office he became faithful to God beyond human appreciation. Indeed, once he had been consecrated he was suddenly transformed into another man. He secretly put on a hairshirt and also breeches of haircloth, down to his knees, and he concealed a monastic habit beneath the outward dignity of his clerical garments. Thus he compelled his flesh wholly to serve the spirit, striving to please God with the uninterrupted practice of every virtue. And recognizing himself as the laborer sent into God's field, the keeper of the vineyard, the shepherd in the sheepfold, he zealously fulfilled the ministry entrusted to him. He labored to recover and fully restore the rights and prerogatives of the Church, which the power of the state had appropriated for itself.

When a serious disagreement arose between him and the king of England, over the law of the Church and the customs of the realm, the assembled council proposed a set of customary rules which the king stubbornly insisted should be confirmed in writing by both the archbishop and his suffragans.[6] But the archbishop steadfastly refused, declaring that these rules would clearly destroy the liberty of the Church. As a result he was punished with great insults, worn down with more serious injuries, and provoked with countless injustices. Finally he was threatened with death, and since the Church's case had not yet become clearly known and the persecution seemed to be personal, he decided the best course was to remove himself from such wickedness. Thus he was driven into exile, but Pope Alexander honorably received him at Sens[7] and warmly committed him to the protection of the monastery at Pontigny.[8]

Matins Responsory 1
Studens livor
Thomae supplicio,
Thomae genus
damnat exilio.
[Envy, eager to punish Thomas, condemns Thomas's family to exile.]

Repetenda
Tota simul
exit cognatio.
[His whole kindred departs together.]
Verse
Ordo, sexus,
aetas, conditio,
Nullo gaudet
hic privilegio.
[State of life, sex, age, rank—these here enjoy no privilege at all.]

(*Lectio* 2) Meanwhile his enemies confiscated everything in England which belonged to the archbishop, ravaged his estates, pillaged his possessions, and devised a new kind of punishment by outlawing his entire family at once. All those who were his friends or members of his household, or who were alleged to belong to him in any way, were banished, regardless of their own rank or fortune, merit or state of life, age or sex. Even elderly and decrepit men, infants crying in their cradles, and women ready to collapse in childbirth were sent into exile. And all those who had reached the age of discretion were forced to swear on sacred objects that they would present themselves to the archbishop of Canterbury as soon as they had crossed the Channel, so that he would be pierced to the heart with compassion for their sufferings and would bend the inward sternness of his spirit to the king's will. But the man of God, committing himself to acts of courage, for the sake of Christ's name endured exile, losses, insults and reproaches, and the outlawing of his relatives and friends, not in the least broken or changed by any injustice. So great was the steadfastness of Christ's confessor that he seemed to be teaching all his fellow exiles that the whole earth is the homeland of the courageous.

Matins Responsory 2
Thomas manum
mittit ad fortia,
spernit damna,
spernit opprobria.
[Thomas commits himself to courageous deeds, scorns losses, scorns reproaches.]
Repetenda
Nulla Thomam
frangit injuria.
[No outrage breaks Thomas.]
Verse
Clamat cunctis
Thomae constantia:
omne solum
est forti patria.

[Thomas's steadfastness cries out to all: to the courageous man, the whole earth is his homeland.]

(**Lectio** 3) When the king heard about his unshakable steadfastness, he sent threatening letters through certain abbots to the general council of the Cistercian Order,[9] in order to drive him away from Pontigny. And in fact blessed Thomas left there voluntarily, to prevent holy men from suffering loss on his account. But before he departed, God comforted him with a vision: he was shown by heavenly revelation that he would be gloriously restored to his own church and would go to God thereafter with the palm of martyrdom.

After he was driven out of Pontigny, he was received with great honor by Louis, the most Christian king of France, who treated him with the highest courtesy until peace could be restored.[10] Nevertheless, frequent attempts were made, though in vain, to persuade Louis not to extend even the least human kindness to the betrayer of the king of England. Indeed, the savage rage of Thomas's enemies went so far that its cruelty is shocking to pious ears. For, although the Catholic Church prays for heretics and schismatics and perfidious Jews, everyone was forbidden to help him with the support of their prayers.

Thus for six successive years he lived in exile, afflicted with diverse and countless injustices. Like a *living stone* [1 Pet 2:4–5] that is shaped for building the heavenly palace by many kinds of carving and compression [see Is 28:16], so the greater the pressure on him to fall, the more firmly and immovably he was proved to stand. Nor indeed with such effort could assayed gold be burned up [see Wis 3:5–6; Zech 13:9] or *a house built on solid rock* be destroyed [Mt 7:25].[11]

Matins Responsory 3
Jacet granum (as at Vespers, above, but with no *prosa*)

Second Nocturn.
Matins Antiphon 4
Nec in agnos sustinet
lupos desaevire:
nec in hortum olerum
vineam transire.
[He does not allow wolves to rage among his lambs, nor his vineyard to be reduced to a vegetable patch.[12]]

Matins Antiphon 5
Exulat vir optimus
sacer et insignis:
Ne cedat Ecclesiae
dignitas indignis.
[The great man lives in exile, holy and distinguished, lest the worth of the Church submit to the unworthy.]

Matins Antiphon 6
Exulantis praedia
praeda sunt malignis:
sed in igne positum
non exurit ignis.
[The exile's estates are plunder for the wicked; but though he is tested by fire, the fire does not consume him.]

(*Lectio* 4) Eventually, by the efforts of the pope as well as the king of France, many days were set aside for peace negotiations. But since the servant of God was not willing to accept any terms that did not preserve both the honor of God and the integrity of the Church, his opponents withdrew one by one. At last the pope took pity on the desolation of the English Church, and managed with difficulty to thwart the plans of Thomas's adversaries, so that peace would be restored to the Church. The kingdoms rejoiced because the king had received the archbishop into his favor, although some people believed that the truce was genuine and some guessed otherwise.

Thus in the seventh year of his exile the noble shepherd returned to England, so that he might either free the flock of Christ from the jaws of the wolves or sacrifice himself for the flock entrusted to him. He was received with inexpressible joy by both the clergy and the people, with everyone weeping and saying, *"Blessed is he who comes in the name of the Lord"* [Ps 118:26; Mt 21:9]. But after a few days he was again beset with injuries and injustices beyond measure and number, and forbidden by a royal edict to go beyond the walls of his church. Anyone who dared to show a friendly countenance to him or any member of his household was considered an enemy of the state. During all these afflictions his spirit was not broken, but his effort continued to be focused on freeing the Church. He sighed for that goal, persisted for its sake in vigils and fasts and prayers, fervently desired to spend himself to obtain it.

Matins Responsory 4
Ex summa
rerum laeticia
summus fit
planctus in Ecclesia
de tanti
patroni absentia.
[After the pinnacle of joy comes the bitterest lamentation in the Church, mourning the absence of so great a champion.]
Repetenda
Sed cum redeunt miracula
redit populo laeticia.
[But when miracles return, joy returns to the people.]

Verse
Concurrit
turba languidorum,
et consequitur
gratiam beneficiorum.
[Crowds of needy people gather in haste and give thanks for blessings.]

(*Lectio* 5) On the fifth day of Christ's nativity,[13] four courtiers came to Canterbury—men of illustrious birth, but notorious for their evil deeds. As soon as they arrived, they attacked the bishop with abusive words, provoked him with violent insults, and made serious threats against him. The man of God answered with restraint, saying what reason required on each point, and adding that many injustices had been inflicted on him and on God's Church since the restoration of peace. In saying this he was not setting himself up as the corrector of faults, but he was neither able nor willing to dissemble instead of fulfilling his duty of pastoral care. The foolish-hearted men, disturbed by his words, shouted inexcusable things and rushed out.

Once they had left, the bishop went on into the church for the Vespers service of praise to Christ. The accomplices of Satan followed along behind, now wearing mail coats and with their swords drawn, with a great force of armed men. The monks blocked the entrance to the church, but the priest of God, soon to be sacrificed for Christ, hurried to unbolt the door for his enemies, saying, "The church is not to be barricaded like a fortress."

When his enemies burst in, some of them furiously shouted, "Where is the traitor?" others; "Where is the archbishop?"

The fearless confessor of Christ advanced toward them, and said to those threatening him with death, "I myself freely accept death for the Church of God, but I warn you in God's name not to harm any of my followers." Thus he imitated Christ, who said at the time of His passion, *"If you seek me, let these men go"* [Jn 18:8].

Then they rushed forward—greedy wolves upon the faithful shepherd, degenerate sons upon their own father, terrible executioners upon Christ's sacrificial victim. They cut off the consecrated crown of his head with their deadly swords and, hurling the Lord's anointed one to the ground, most cruelly (as is horrible even to tell) splattered his brain and blood across the paved floor. And so, as the grain of wheat is crushed by the chaff, and as the keeper of the vines is struck down in the vineyard, the commander in the fortified camp, the shepherd in the sheepfold, the laborer in the field—so the just man, slain by the unjust ones, exchanged his house of clay for a heavenly palace.

Matins Responsory 5
Mundi florem
a mundo conteri,
Rachel plorans,

jam cessa conqueri,
Thomas caesus
dum datur funeri;
[While Rachel laments that the flower of the world is trampled by the world,[14] already giving way to bitter grief,
Thomas, cut down, is taken to burial;]
Repetenda
Novus Abel
succedit veteri.
[The new Abel succeeds the old.[15]]
Verse
Vox cruoris,
vox sparsi cerebri
caelum replet
clamore celebri.
[The voice of blood, the voice of splattered brain, fills heaven with the resounding cry.]

(*Lectio* 6) According to those standing very close to him, the martyr's final words, which could scarcely be heard above the noise of shouting, were these: "To God and the blessed Mary and St. Denis[16] and the patron saints of this church I commend myself and the Church's cause." In all the torments endured by the invincible athlete of God, he neither cried out nor groaned nor raised his arm or robe to defend himself against his attackers. Rather, he exposed his head to the blows, bending it and remaining immobile until the deed was completed and he slept in the Lord, lying prostrate as if in prayer.

Then the wicked men returned to the holy bishop's palace and, to conform the passion of the servant more completely to the Passion of the Lord, *they divided his garments among them* [Ps 22:18; Mt 27:35], along with the silver and gold, the precious vessels, the best horses, and whatever they could find that was valuable, deciding who should carry off what. And the soldiers carried out these instructions.

As for the rest, who can recall it without weeping? So strong was everyone's grief, so bitter the weeping of each person, that you would have thought the prophecy had been fulfilled again: *"A voice was heard in Rama, a great weeping and lamentation"* [Jer 31:15, Mt 2:18]. However, the divine mercy soon provided comfort along with tribulation, and through certain visions—as if foreshadowing by present signs that the martyr would return in order to be glorified by future miracles—signaled that sorrow would be followed by joy, and the turmoil of the needy by thankfulness for blessings.

Matins Responsory 6
Christe Jesu
per Thomae vulnera,
quae nos ligant

relaxa scelera,
[Christ Jesus, through the wounds of Thomas, pardon the evil deeds that bind us,]

Repetenda
Ne captivos
ferant ad infera
hostis, mundus
vel carnis opera.
[lest we be carried as captives to the depths by the devil, the world, or the deeds of the flesh.]

Verse
Per te Thoma
post [leve] munera,
amplexetur
nos Dei dextera.
[Through you, Thomas, after deeds of ill omen,[17] may the right hand of God welcome us.]

Third Nocturn.
Matins Antiphon 7
Sathanae satellites
irrumpentes templum:
inauditum perpetrant
sceleris exemplum.
[The accomplices of Satan, bursting into the temple, commit an unheard-of example of crime.]

Matins Antiphon 8
Strictis Thomas ensibus
obviam procedit;
non minis, non gladiis,
sed nec morti cedit.
[Thomas goes on toward the drawn swords; he yields neither to threats nor swords nor even death.]

Matins Antiphon 9
Felix locus,
felix ecclesia,
in qua Thomae
viget memoria:
felix terra
quae dedit praesulem:
felix illa
quae fovit exulem:
felix pater,

succurre miseris,
ut felices
jungamur superis.
[Blessed is the place, blessed the church in which the memory of Thomas flourishes; blessed the land which gave him as protector, and blessed the land that welcomed him as exile. Blessed father, help the wretched ones so that we—also blessed—may be united with those above.]

(*Lectio* 7) The Gospel according to John: At that time Jesus said to his disciples, "*I am the good shepherd. The good shepherd lays down his life for his sheep,*" etc. [Jn 10:11].[18]

A homily by the blessed Pope Gregory: In the Gospel reading, dearest brothers, hear the lesson for you and the danger for us. Note well that He who says, "*I am the good shepherd,*" is good not just by an extrinsic gift but by His very essence. And He specifies the nature of the goodness we are to imitate, saying, "*The good shepherd lays down his life for his sheep.*" He Himself did what He taught, showed what He was ordering. The Good Shepherd laid down His life for His sheep in order to transform His body and blood into our Eucharist, feeding the sheep He had redeemed with the nourishment of His own flesh.[19]

Matins Responsory 7
Thomae cedunt
et parent omnia:
pestis, morbi,
mors et daemonia;
[All things yield to Thomas and obey him—plague, illnesses, death, and demons;]
Repetenda
Ignis, aer,
tellus, et maria.
[Fire, air, earth, and seas.]
Verse
Thomas mundum
replevit gloria,
Thomae mundus
praestat obsequia.
[Thomas filled the world with glory; to Thomas the world gives homage.]

(*Lectio* 8) In truth blessed Thomas, precious athlete of God, deserved to be glorified. By virtue of the cause for which he died, since it is the cause that makes a martyr, which of the saints has ever manifested the title "martyr" in a more glorious way? He died fighting for the Church and even in the church, in a sacred place, in the season of the Lord's nativity, among fellow priests of God and in the arms of monks. Thus all the details of the bishop's ordeal came together in such a way that they will forever enhance the glory of the man who suffered and expose the ungodliness of his persecutors, staining their names with eternal disgrace.

Indeed, divine vengeance fell on the martyr's persecutors with such fury that in a short time they were cut off and ceased to exist. Some of them were snatched away suddenly, without confession and the last sacrament. Some died tearing apart their own fingers or tongues with their teeth; some with their whole body wasted away, streaming with diseased blood, and tortured before death with unheard-of afflictions; some undone by paralysis; some rendered senseless; some perishing in a frenzy—all leaving clear proofs that they were paying the price for their unjust persecution and deliberate treachery.

Therefore let Mother Church rejoice that a new martyr has obtained victory over her enemies. Let her rejoice that a new Zechariah has been sacrificed in the temple for her freedom, and that the blood of a new Abel cries out to God for her against the murderers [Mt 23:34–35].[20] Truly, the voice of the blood shed, the voice of the brain splattered by the swords of the deadly accomplices, made earth and heaven together resound with the famous cry.

Matins Responsory 8
Novis fulget
Thomas miraculis:
membris donat
castratos masculis,
[Thomas shines with extraordinary miracles: he gives genitalia to castrated men,]
Repetenda
Ornat visu
privatos oculis.
[He provides sight to those deprived of eyes.]
Verse
Mundat leprae
conspersos maculis,
solvit mortis
ligatos vinculis.
[He cleanses those covered with marks of leprosy, releases those bound by the chains of death.]

(*Lectio* 9) Indeed the earth was shaken by the cry of this blood. It trembled, and even the heavenly powers were moved, so that as if in retribution for the innocent blood nation rose against nation and kingdom against kingdom, or rather the kingdom was divided against itself, and omens and great signs came from heaven. Yet the martyr in the first days after his passion began to shine with extraordinary miracles, restoring sight to the blind, mobility to the lame, hearing to the deaf, speech to the mute, and thereafter cleansing lepers, strengthening the paralyzed, curing dropsy and all kinds of incurable maladies, and resurrecting the dead [see Is 35:5–6; Mt 11:5]. Miraculously commanding demons and all the elements, his power extended even to remarkable and unheard-of miracles, for men who had lost eyes and genitals were found worthy by his merits to receive new ones. And certain individuals who had dared to scoff at the miracles of this saint were suddenly stricken and compelled to praise them willingly. At last the martyr prevailed so far against all his foes that within a few days you could see what was written about the Only-Begotten Son repeated in the servant: *"Those who despised you will come to you and bow down at your feet"* [Is 60:14].

Thomas, the distinguished athlete of God, suffered in the year of the Lord's Incarnation 1171 (according to the reckoning of Dionysius),[21] on the fourth Kalends of January, a Tuesday, at about the eleventh hour,[22] so that the time of the Lord's birth into toil became the time of his birth into eternal rest. May the same God, our Lord Jesus Christ, deign to bring us there as well—He who lives and reigns with the Father and the Holy Spirit, one God, now and forever. Amen.

Matins Responsory 9
Jesu bone,
per Thomae merita,
nostra nobis
dimitte debita,
domum portam,
sepulchrum visita;
[O kind Jesus, through Thomas's merits, release us from our debts; watch over our home, city gate, and tomb;]

Repetenda
Et a trina
nos morte suscita.
[And arouse us from threefold death.[23]]

Verse
Actu mente
vel usu perdita,
pietate
restaura solita.
[Restore, by your wonted mercy, what we have lost by act, thought, or habit.]

Lauds.

Lauds Antiphon 1
Granum cadit, copiam
germinat frumenti,
alabastrum frangitur,
fragrat vis unguenti.

[The seed falls and puts forth an abundance of grain (Jn 12:24–25); the alabaster jar is broken, and the fragrance is released (see Mk 14:3)].

Lauds Antiphon 2
Totus orbis martyris
certat in amorem:
cujus signa singulos
agunt in stuporem.
[The whole world competes in love of the martyr, whose miracles stir everyone to astonishment.]

Lauds Antiphon 3
Aqua Thomae quinquies
varians colorem,
in lac semel transiit,
quater in cruorem.
[The water of Thomas,[24] changing color five times, was transformed once into milk and four times into blood.]

Lauds Antiphon 4
Ad Thomae memoriam
quater lux descendit:
et in Sancti gloriam
cereos accendit.
[In memory of Thomas a light descended four times and lit candles to the saint's glory.]

Lauds Antiphon 5
Tu per Thomae sanguinem
quem pro te impendit:
fac nos, Christe, scandere
quo Thomas ascendit.
[Through Thomas's blood, O Christ, which he shed for thee, make us too to rise where he ascended.]

Benedictus Antiphon
Opem nobis,
O Thoma, porrige,
rege stantes,
jacentes erige,
mores, actus,
et vitam corrige:
et in pacis
nos viam dirige.

[Extend your help to us, O Thomas; guide those who stand; lift up the fallen; correct our habits, deeds, and life; and lead us into the way of peace.]

Second Vespers.
Magnificat Antiphon
Salve, Thoma, virga justiciae,
mundi jubar, robur Ecclesiae,
plebis amor, cleri deliciae,
salve, gregis tutor egregie,
salve tuae gaudentes gloriae.

[Hail, Thomas, rod of justice, light of the world, strength of the Church, love of the faithful, delight of the clergy, hail, distinguished protector of the flock, greet those who rejoice in your glory.]

2. RECONSTRUCTED OFFICE FOR THE TRANSLATION OF THOMAS BECKET (JULY 7)

First Vespers.
Antiphon 1
Adest Thome martiris
optata translacio,
que divini muneris
fulget beneficio.
Gaudeamus et psallamus
ad honorem presulis,
ut virtutem et salutem
suis prestet famulis.

[The longed-for translation of Thomas the martyr approaches, which shines with the blessing of God's generosity. Let us rejoice and sing Psalms in honor of our protector, that he may grant his servants strength and salvation.]

Magnificat Antiphon
Thomam armat
in ma[rt]em nacio
hinc, principum
adversa sessio,
exilium,
et Dei visio,
hinc regressus,
hinc sancta passio
ut vincatur
mors, septenario
die Martis
fit, et translacio.

[On this day a race arms Thomas for war[25]; on this day a hostile meeting of princes; on this day exile and vision of God; on this day he returns; on this day his sacred passion so that death is defeated; and his translation makes a seventh Tuesday.]

Matins.
First Nocturn.
Invitatory
Ubi Thomas
victor est in gloria,
nos translati
transferat memoria.
[Where Thomas is victorious in glory, may we be transported by remembering the one who was translated.]

Matins Antiphon 1
Motus humor redolet
quod intus habetur;
sic fulget miraculis
Thomas dum movetur.
[As a fluid when stirred emits the odor held inside, so Thomas shines with miracles when he is besought.]

Matins Antiphon 2
Testis Christi martiris
dum martyr transfertur,
mari puer veniens
mersus aquis fertur.
[In witness to Christ's martyr,[26] when the martyr is translated a boy nearly drowned en route is borne aloft by the waves.[27]]

Matins Antiphon 3
De Divisis veniens
dum vir invocavit
Thomam, mersus quinquies
mortem non gustavit.
[When a man coming from Devizes called upon Thomas, although he sank five times he did not taste death.]

(*Lectio* 1) As we remember the translation of the glorious martyr Thomas and offer due praises to God, dearest brothers, let us reverently consider what things came together in this translation, as if by blessed foreknowledge. Although his translation was earlier aimed at by several pontiffs of the holy Roman church and commended by the guardians of the holy church of Canterbury at the time, nevertheless what was sought could not be achieved before the times noted below. Indeed, the timing should be ascribed to God's dispensation, not man's. Our Lord and Redeemer, arranging all things with wisdom, preordained this too, so that Thomas's translation, like his passion, would be a benefit to the holy Church.

Therefore, lest those who come after us should be uncertain about what happened in the blessed martyr's translation, let us consider how many years from his passion, on what day, in whose times, and how the precious body of the glorious martyr Thomas, which had been buried in a humble place, was translated to a glorious one—touching briefly on one point at a time, so that we may be permitted to remain longer in contemplation of today's celebration in honor of this martyr.

Matins Responsory 1
Absorbetur
pleno iam gaudio,
livor tristi
precedens odio:
[Rancor, worse than bitter hatred, is already swallowed up by abundant joy]
Repetenda
Dum agitur
Thome translacio.
[When the translation of Thomas is carried out.]
Verse
Omnis gaudet
confinis regio,
etas, ordo,
sexus, condicio.
[Every adjoining land rejoices, every age, rank, sex, and way of life.]

(*Lectio* 2) In the fiftieth year after his passion, the translation of the most blessed martyr Thomas was carried out. Dearest brothers, let us consider the mystery of the fiftieth year. The fiftieth year is the jubilee year, and the jubilee year means the year of forgiveness or the forgiving year.[28] Just as in the Law during the jubilee year, burdens of debt and states of bondage used to be remitted, so in the jubilee year of this martyr's translation, the burdens of penitents are lifted.[29]

For this reason the holy father Pope Honorius III, as a mark of the jubilee year, granted to those coming to celebrate the blessed martyr Thomas's translation during this year such a remission from penances previously imposed as nowhere in past times do we remember Roman pontiffs to have granted to anyone.[30] Hence not unfittingly the blessed martyr says what our Redeemer said: *"Come to me, all you who labor and are heavy laden, and I will give you rest"* [Mt 11:28]. And as in the Law ancient possessions would also return to their former possessors, so the aforementioned pope determined that English churches transferred to Romans or foreigners should, after their deaths, return to their true patrons.[31] Therefore let us say with the prophet, "The sun has risen, and the moon has stood firm in its order" [Hab 3:11].[32]

Matins Responsory 2
Linguis preit
ut resureccio
agnus legem
quinquagenario:
[As the Resurrection shows the way for Pentecost, so the Lamb outstrips the Law in the number fifty]
Repetenda
Jubilei
sacro misterio.
[By the sacred mystery of the Jubilee.[33]]
Verse
Thomam transfert
acto martirio,
quinquagena
sit revolucio.
[Let it be the fiftieth anniversary of the completed martyrdom that translates Thomas.]

(*Lectio* 3) Let us also recall that the translation of the blessed martyr Thomas was first celebrated on a Tuesday. I do not know by what foreknowledge of events, if indeed it should be called foreknowledge rather than destiny, things pertaining to the blessed martyr tended to happen especially on Tuesdays.[34] Let us call some, if not all, of these to mind. Thus the blessed Thomas issued from his mother's womb, as if into the light for war, on a Tuesday.[35] On a Tuesday the princes first assembled and spoke against him.[36] He went into exile on a Tuesday.[37] On a Tuesday the Lord appeared to him near Pontigny and said, "Thomas, Thomas, my Church will be glorified in your blood." On a Tuesday he returned from exile.[38] On a Tuesday he attained the palm of martyrdom. On a Tuesday he was gloriously translated. These seven Tuesdays I have named, dearest brothers, did not happen without foreknowledge, so that he who had experienced battle and conflict on Tuesdays also won the glorious victory, completely defeating his enemies, on a Tuesday. Regarding these seven Tuesdays, one can understand what God says through the prophet: "On one stone there are seven eyes" [Zech 3:9].

Matins Responsory 3
Dante papa
nobis Honorio

que penarum
fit relaxacio:
[Since Pope Honorius is granting us a suspension of punishments,]
Repetenda
Jubilei
ne cesset racio.
[Let the reckoning of the Jubilee go on.]
Verse
Basilice
cuius colleccio
fit, Romanis
redit possessio.
[Property returns from Romans to the church to which it belongs.]

Second Nocturn.
Matins Antiphon 4
Elevate pauperem
manus cor absentes,
corpus movent martiris
magnates presentes.
[Upraised hands far away move the martyr's heart with respect to a poor man, as the great men present move his body.]

Matins Antiphon 5
Elevatis manibus,
mortuum levavit
miles Northamtunie
quem prestrangulavit.
[With upraised hands a knight of Northampton held up the body of the boy whom he had choked.]

Matins Antiphon 6
Plus quam turbe fimbria
Christum movit tacta,
Thomam plus absencium
manus quam ab acta.
[Touching the hem of his robe affected Christ more than crowds did; so Thomas is moved more by the hands of absent ones than by a public act.]

(*Lectio* 4) The blessed martyr is *the very stone that the builders rejected, which has become the chief cornerstone* [Ps 118:22, Mt 21:42]. Just as the cornerstone joins together two walls that come together from different directions, so the glorious martyr through his passion creates unity between the kingdom and the priesthood, which come as it were from opposing sides. As for the seven eyes, this seven appears in the seven Tuesdays, by the provision of the Holy Spirit. About these Tuesdays one can also understand what is said in the Apocalypse: that *John saw a lamb that seemed to have been slain, which had seven horns and seven eyes* [Rev 5:6].[39]

Let us notice as well that the glorious martyr was translated from his grave with the joy and praise of everyone, into a place adorned with gold and precious gems, on the same month and day when the late renowned King Henry of England, in whose time he had suffered, was committed to burial with the sorrow and lamentation of his household.[40] From such evidence let us conclude that such things happened on Tuesday in order to show that on the day of Mars, in the manner of combatants, one conquers and the other is conquered.

Matins Responsory 4
Die Thomas
quam cum tristicia
sepelivit
regem familia,
[Thomas, on the day when the king was sorrowfully buried by his family,]
Repetenda
Ingemmata
transfertur atria.
[Was translated to a bejeweled burial place.]
Verse
Ut lucescat
auri memoria
tanti martis
felix victoria.
[So that the blessed victory of such a warrior would shine with a monument of gold.]

(*Lectio 5*) The translation was most gloriously carried out in the fifth year of the pontificate of the holy father Honorius III, when Henry III, the illustrious king of England, was in the thirteenth year of his life[41] and the most holy father Stephen was archbishop of Canterbury. And deservedly in the times of such men, since he had lived so innocently that it was fitting and honorable that he be translated by innocent men and in the times of innocent men— whereas to some extent those before this had been unworthy to honor such a martyr as he deserved. What if the holy martyr's translation had been celebrated before the ordained time? If it had occurred while seven monks of the Canterbury church were in exile or, after their return, while more than civil wars were raging among the English, then wouldn't his coffin have been incomparably adorned with gold and gems while his body itself was unprotected from the arrogance of madmen, who cared nothing for saints or the Church?[42] Therefore, the most blessed martyr, as if he had foreknowledge of future events by divine revelation, wished to wait for days of peace in the time of rulers who desired peace, since *in peace was made his seat and his dwelling in Zion* [Ps 76:2].

Matins Responsory 5
Innocentum
qui vixit moribus,
passus martyr
cum Innocentibus:
[He who lived with the habits of the innocent, having died a martyr with the Innocents,[43]]
Repetenda
Non transferri
vult sub predonibus.
[Does not wish to be translated under the rule of robbers.]
Verse
Pape regis
piis temporibus
transfert hunc
presul manibus.
[In devout times the bishop translates him by the hands[44] of the pope and king.]

(*Lectio* 6) Let us hear how the most blessed martyr's translation was carried out. At dusk on a certain night,[45] when everything needed for such a ceremony had been carefully prepared, the venerable fathers Stephen, archbishop of Canterbury, and Richard, bishop of Salisbury,[46] together with prior Walter and the whole monastery,[47] came to the tomb of this martyr with due reverence. There they remained devoutly in prayer for a time, as long as the brevity of the night allowed, as if they were asking and saying in the manner of the holy women at Christ's tomb, *"Who will roll away the stone for us from the mouth of the tomb?"* [Mk 16:3] When the stones had all been expertly rolled back without any damage, they arose from their prayers. Gazing into the tomb, they found that instrument of the Holy Spirit, wrapped as was proper in episcopal vestments. Then, while everyone else lay prostrate again, with devout prayers and tears of great joy, certain men—chosen from those present for their life and holiness—lifted that precious treasure from the tomb and laid it honorably in a wooden casket covered very securely with iron. When they had carefully closed this with iron nails, since day was already at hand they carried it to an honorable and secret place, until everything was solemnly prepared for the day of the translation.

Matins Responsory 6
Monumenti
nox tollit hostium;
nox extollit

in locum alium:
[Night takes away the door of the tomb; night lifts up into another place]
Repetenda
Deitatis
testem eximium.
[The distinguished witness of God.]
Verse
Tenebrarum
nox pellit tedium,
sed lux transfert
in lumen omnium.
[Night overcomes the loathsomeness of darkness, but daylight transforms it into the light of all people.]

Third Nocturn.
Matins Antiphon 7
Quem matrone nobilis
fides invocavit,
alienam filiam
martyr suscitavit.
[Invoked by the faith of a noble woman, the martyr resurrected the daughter of another.]

Matins Antiphon 8
Dum ingrata gratias
mater non peregit,
redivivam virginem
item mors subegit.
[When the ungrateful mother did not complete her thanks, death again overcame the revived girl.]

Matins Antiphon 9
Mater castigacior
orat mente pura;
surgit virgo tercia
morte moritura.
[The mother, sorely chastised, prays with her whole heart; the girl arises, someday to die a third death.]

(*Lectio* 7) Such a multitude of bishops, abbots and priors, courtiers and noblemen, rich and poor, gathered in Canterbury for the translation that the city and the neighboring towns could scarcely hold them. When the day appointed for the translation arrived, the aforementioned coffin was carried on the shoulders of the venerable fathers Pandulf, legate of the Apostolic See,[48] the archbishops of Canterbury and Reims, bishops and abbots, the noble man Hubert de Burgh, then Justiciar,[49] and several courtiers and noblemen, in the presence of the illustrious Henry III, king of England, who did not join them in carrying it because of the weakness of his young age and the tumult of the crowd. They carried it on their shoulders in the sight of the people, with tears of joy and hymns of jubilation, to the altar of the Holy Trinity, where they placed it very reverently and safely within another wooden casket or reliquary, this one incomparably adorned with gold and precious stones. Thus every devotion or honor that could be bestowed on such a martyr, not only the great but also the small very piously contributed, spending what remained of the day in praises of the martyr and joy of heart.

Therefore the most blessed martyr, as if repaying his faithful ones in turn, did not withhold the consolations of his grace. Indeed, he adorned the whole celebration of his translation, both at that time and later, with the most glorious signs and miracles: the blind restored to sight, the lame to mobility, the mute to speech, the dead to life. Therefore let everyone rejoice together who has been found worthy to take part in such a translation. Let all the English people exult in the Lord, since the heavenly King particularly distinguished this people above others when He forechose from it a man without spot, in order to make one of the English, set among the angels,[50] an intercessor for the people's salvation. Let the spirit of the most holy father Stephen, Archbishop of Canterbury, also magnify the Lord and rejoice in his beneficent God—Stephen, who took charge of such a ceremony of translation and brought it to glorious effect. Dearest brothers, *this is the day which the Lord has made; let us rejoice and be glad in it* [Ps 118:24]. Let us honor the celebration of such a day with worthy praises to God, resolved that whatever prayer or honor we bestow on such a martyr belongs to the glory of God, in whose name he was translated.

Thus the most holy translation of the precious body of Thomas in the church of Canterbury was completed in the year of grace 1220, the Nones of July, at about the third hour,[51] in the fiftieth year from that same martyr's passion. Glory to almighty God, who exalted such a saint. Glory to the only-begotten Son, who redeemed him. Glory to the Holy Spirit, who enlightened him with His grace. Praise and thanksgiving to the one, sole, living and true God, forever and ever. Amen.[52]

Matins Responsory 7
Cuius erat dulci misterio
sub Henrico
secundo passio,
[By a sweet mystery, he who suffered under Henry II]
Repetenda
Sub Henrico
transfertur tercio.
[Is translated under Henry III;]

Verse
Ut lucescat
ipso ternario
Trinitati
grata translacio.
[So that his dear translation in this threefold time may begin to shine for the Trinity.[53]]

(*Lectio* 8) Shortly before the translation of the blessed martyr Thomas, a certain woman from Kemble had a little daughter, the only one surviving of four whom her husband had given her.[54] When the little girl became severely ill and died in her mother's arms, the mother's tears and groans seemed to exceed all bounds. Moved by her loud weeping, a certain noble widow, who was the lady of that town, hastened to her. When she learned the girl was dead, the lady took her body to invoke divine assistance and measured her,[55] calling on the help of the blessed martyr Thomas; and the girl arose.

Later, however, when her mother had made the candle and thought about sending it to St. Thomas, the little girl again became sick and, as her mother testified, again died. Then the mother realized that she had been insufficiently grateful and loyal to the martyr. She vowed to take the girl to St. Thomas herself, if he would recall her from death a second time. Therefore the glorious martyr, tempering strict justice with the kindness of his grace, again restored the dead girl to her mother, alive.

A certain knight of the countess of Eu,[56] a man named Robert, was traveling toward Canterbury with his twelve-year-old son, little Robert, in order to pray at the tomb of St. Thomas the martyr. Embarking on the sea at Wissant,[57] he sailed without incident to the middle of the Channel. There, however, his son walked half-asleep to the outer edge of the ship, either to urinate or for some other reason, took a careless step, and fell overboard.

When his father saw this, he cried out, "St. Thomas, have mercy on me, and save my son for me!"

The boy himself, barely immersed in the sea and then quickly tossed back to the surface, said, "St. Thomas, you can save me if you want to."

Meanwhile, the wind drove the ship away from the place where the boy had fallen, as far as the distance a bow can shoot two or three arrows. Finally the sailors, responding to the knight's cries, turned the sail and managed to turn the ship around to look for the boy. By now an hour had passed or, as the knight himself testified, as much time as it takes a horse going at medium speed to cover two leagues or three *gallicas*.[58]

When they reached the boy, they found him sitting on the water completely unhurt, except that in his fall he had swallowed a little sea water. When the boy had seen the ship leaving him, he had despaired of his life with great sorrow and hopelessness. Hoping to shorten the time of his suffering by hastening his own death, in fact, he had submerged his head in the sea. When the boy was pulled into the ship, he reported these things to his inquiring father. But he added that, although he himself wanted to sink, a certain bishop had held him up so that he could not drown.

Matins Responsory 8
Sunt presules
auctores operis,
archipresul
cum multis ceteris;
[Bishops are the authors of this deed—the archbishop with many more.]
Repetenda
Aliorum
transfertur humeris.
[He is carried on the shoulders of others,]
Verse
Perplaudentium
turbis innumeris,
regis parvi
membris pro teneris.
[Because of the enormous crowds of cheering people, on behalf of the delicate limbs of the small king.]

(*Lectio* 9) A certain man from Devizes,[59] wishing to pray at the tomb of St. Thomas, was traveling with many others toward Canterbury for the translation. When he was crossing the bridge at Brantford, near London, the wagon turned over near the middle of the bridge, and he was thrown into the water. Keeping his head, he repeatedly called on St. Thomas, begging him not to allow his pilgrim to perish. Five times he sank to the bottom of the river, but was always returned to the surface and was finally thrown out onto dry ground. He testified with great wonder that he did not feel any discomfort from the water, either in his mouth or nose or ears. Another man, accompanying this same pilgrim, lost a cloak in the same place where the former fell into the water, and no one has yet been able to find the garment, which sank into the rapidly flowing water.

A certain knight from Northamptonshire married a widow who had a three-year-old son by her first husband. One day, while the boy was standing at the table next to the knight, he took in his mouth a small piece of meat from the knight's hand. When he attempted to gulp down the bite of meat, the child choked and died.

The boy's mother was suspicious of the knight's role in her son's death and, crying and weeping with repeated lamentation, called him a murderer. Although the knight's conscience was clear, nevertheless as the boy's stepfather he was profoundly disturbed. Rising up, he bent a silver coin over the boy,[60] vowing to take him to St. Thomas himself if the saint would restore him to life.

A little while after this vow, while everyone was waiting to see what God would do, the piece of meat that had shut off the boy's breath suddenly sprang back from his throat into his mouth. And indeed the boy, reviving within a little while, was completely restored to life and to his friends through the merits of the blessed martyr.

Matins Responsory 9
Cecis visus,
mutis locucio,
claudis datur
recta progressio:
[Sight is given to the blind, speech to the mute, mobility to the lame;]
Repetenda
Sic ornatur
Thome translacio.
[Thus Thomas's translation is adorned.]
Verse
Ut res fixo
stet testimonio,
mortuorum fit
resureccio.
[So that the truth may endure with unshakable proof, the dead are resurrected.]

Lauds.
Lauds Antiphon 1
Granum quod in tempore
moritur brumali,
frumentum multiplicat
surgens estivali.
[The seed which died in the depths of winter springs up in the summer, multiplying the grain.]

Lauds Antiphon 2
Thomam brume frigore
genusque mactatum,
transfert estas temporis
et etas magnatum.
[Thomas and his offspring, slain in the cold of winter, are translated by a season of summer and an age of great men.]

Lauds Antiphon 3
Aurum fulvum martire
clauso deauratur,
et gemmarum numerus

per hunc geminatur.
[Tawny gold is made rich by the martyr it encloses, and the worth of gems is doubled by this.]

Lauds Antiphon 4
Auro congaudentibus
in translacionis,
Christe, da topazion
benediccionis.
[To those rejoicing together in the gold of the translation, O Christ, give the topaz[61] of your blessing.]

Lauds Antiphon 5
Martyr aurum proximis
splendet et remotis;
hic est lapis efficax
in cunctis devotis.
[The martyr shines with gold to those near and far; this is the stone with healing power for all the faithful.]

Benedictus Antiphon
Thoma, celis
quem iunxit passio,
tua nobis
assit compassio,
et nos celi
iunge palacio.
Recensita
prestet translacio.
[Thomas, whose passion united you to the heavens, let your compassion be present to us, and join us to the heavenly court. Let your translation be powerful when it is recounted.]

Second Vespers.
Magnificat Antiphon
Salus datur
lesis demonio;
liberantur
mersi naufragio;
defunctorum
fit resureccio.
Sic gemescit
Thome translacio,
sit obrisum
nostra devocio.

[Health is given to those wounded by the devil; those drowned in shipwrecks are set free; the dead are resurrected. As Thomas's translation becomes a gem, so may our devotion be fine gold.]

NOTES

1. The Latin adjective *purpurea* ("purple") can mean either "regal" or "bloodstained"—an ambiguity that made it a favorite poetic term for suggesting the paradoxical nature of the Cross.

2. This office is pervaded by allusions to the central metaphor in the Gospel lesson appointed for Thomas's feast day, Jn 10:11–18: the good shepherd who lays down his life to save his sheep.

3. Notice that the last line of the *prosa* repeats the *repetenda* of the preceding responsory.

4. This is the Church (see the Invitatory, just below), which will be visualized later in the office as the biblical figure of Rachel (see Matins Responsory 5 and *Lectio* 6).

5. That is, the date of the saint's martyrdom, when he was born to eternal life.

6. This is presumably a reference to the Constitutions of Clarendon, though historians give a much more complicated account of Thomas's position on them. The king, of course, was Henry II, who ruled both England and extensive domains in France from 1154 until 1189.

7. Pope Alexander III (1159–81) was himself in exile in France during most of his papacy because of a schism.

8. Pontigny, a Cistercian monastery in eastern France, was outside Henry's jurisdiction and not far from the papal court at Sens.

9. Henry's message to the council, in September 1166, threatened to expel all the Cistercians from his domains if they continued to shelter Thomas at Pontigny.

10. King Louis VII, who ruled France from 1137 until 1180, opposed Henry on a number of territorial and political issues.

11. The responsory *Lapis iste* in the longer, monastic version of the office clarifies the point behind these biblical allusions: "This stone is hammered for six years; thus it is polished, thus made square, Yielding less the more it is beaten. Verse: The furnace tests gold, and it is not consumed; the solid house is not shaken by winds."

12. This is probably an allusion to the story of Naboth, who was killed for refusing to hand over his ancestors' vineyard to King Ahab, who wanted the land for his own vegetable garden (1 Kings 21).

13. That is, December 29; as in the familiar carol, the first day of Christmas is December 25 itself.

14. An allusion to the grieving Church; see *Lectio* 6, below.

15. On the "new Abel," see *Lectio* 8.

16. St. Denis, an early bishop of Paris and a martyr, was the patron saint of France.

17. The Latin text plays on the opposition between *leva*, which literally means "left hand," and *dextera*, "right hand."

18. The prescribed Gospel for the day went on to verse 16, but medieval breviaries saved space by giving just the beginning.

19. The source is Gregory the Great's *Homiliae in Evangelia*, homily 14 (*Patrologia latina*, ed. Jean-Paul Migne, 221 vols. [Paris, 1844–64], 76:1127).

20. For the actual stories of Zechariah and Abel, see 2 Chron 24:17–22 and Gen 4:1–16, respectively.

21. Dionysius Exiguus (or Denis the Short), a Roman monk and scholar who died around 545, originated the system of reckoning dates from the year of Christ's birth.

22. That is, about an hour before dark.

23. Either sinful acts, thoughts, and habits (as at the end of the verse) or the effects of the world, the flesh, and the devil.

24. Water which supposedly contained a drop of the martyr's blood.

25. Literally, "for Mars." The subject of this puzzlelike antiphon is the series of memorable Tuesdays ("days of Mars") in Thomas's life. See *Lectio* 3 of this office for the historical details.

26. This is probably wordplay on the original meaning of *martyr*, which was "witness"; so this line would read, "in witness to the witness of Christ."

27. All the specific miracle stories mentioned in these Matins antiphons are retold below in *Lectiones* 8 and 9.

28. This sentence and part of the next one are omitted from Procter and Wordsworth's edition of the Sarum Breviary, but British Library, MS Cotton Appendix 23 and many other manuscripts have them.

29. For the Old Testament teaching on the jubilee year, see especially Lev 25:8–55.

30. Honorius—who held the papacy from July 18, 1216, to March 18, 1227—did indeed grant unusually generous indulgences, by the standards of the time, to pilgrims who came to Canterbury Cathedral around the time of the translation. But there are conflicting reports as to both the exact size of the indulgences and the exact period during which the visit had to occur. Raymonde Foreville discusses the evidence in *Le Jubilé de saint Thomas Becket du XIIIe au XVe siècle (1220–1470)* (Paris, 1958), pp. 37–45.

31. This concession amounted in effect to a temporary suspension of the pope's practice of appointing his own candidates to vacant church livings in England; for further information, see Jane E. Sayers, *Papal Government and England during the Pontificate of Honorius III, 1216–1227* (Cambridge, 1984), pp. 189–90.

32. The quotation is based on the Septuagint (the Greek version of the Hebrew Scriptures) instead of the Hebrew version that underlies most English translations of the Bible. Additions in British Library, MS Cotton Appendix 23 explain the references: "the sun (that is, the blessed martyr); . . . the moon (that is, the church)."

33. The idea seems to be that Easter comes fifty days before Pentecost in the liturgical year, and mercy exceeds justice in the fiftieth year.

34. The list of memorable Tuesdays in Thomas's life was a favorite motif in his legend. The first such list, with five Tuesdays, is found in the Old French *Life* of Thomas by Guernes de Pont-Sainte-Maxence, written in the 1170s.

35. Raymond Foreville, who attempted to work out the exact dates of the famous Tuesdays in "Tradition et comput dans la chronologie de Thomas Becket," *Bulletin philologique et historique, Années 1955–56* [1957]: 7–20, concluded that he was probably born on December 21, 1118.

36. Presumably a reference to the Council of Northampton, in October 1164, which accused Thomas of financial wrongdoing in his earlier post as chancellor.

37. If his exile in fact began on a Tuesday, the date would have been November 3, 1164. But some of his biographers say he landed in France on All Souls Day, November 2.

38. That is on December 1, 1170, according to Foreville.

39. After this point the text in the printed Sarum Breviary adds a transitional sentence and then skips to the account of the public translation (beginning of *Lectio* 7 below).

40. Henry was buried on July 7 or 8, 1189.

41. King Henry III (1207–1272) succeeded his father, John, in October 1216, when he had just turned nine.

42. The most obvious "madman" being alluded to here is King John, who reacted to the election of Stephen Langton rather than his own candidate as archbishop of Canterbury in 1206 by forcing both the Canterbury monks and Langton himself into exile until 1212 or 1213. When Pope Innocent III declared an interdict over John's whole kingdom, John's response was to seize ecclesiastical property and drive out most of the bishops. John was also a chief protagonist in the civil wars of 1215–17, refusing to compromise with his rebellious barons even after he had signed Magna Carta.

43. Thomas was martyred on the day after the feast of the Holy Innocents (December 28), commemorating the male infants of Bethlehem who were slain by King Herod when he heard about the birth of Jesus [see Mt 2:16].

44. That is, by their followers.

45. Raymond Foreville concluded that this was probably July 4, the Saturday preceding the public translation (see *Le Jubilé*, page 8 and note 3).

46. Richard Poore, who held the see of Salisbury from 1217 to 1228, made important contributions to the Sarum liturgy and began the construction of Salisbury Cathedral.

47. That is, the cathedral priory of Christ Church.

48. One of Pandulf's responsibilities in England was to help protect the monarchy of the young king, whose father had finally staved off a crusade against him by ceding England to the pope. Pandulf was especially powerful in the period from the death of the regent, William Marshall, in 1219, to young Henry's fourteenth birthday in 1221.

49. The chief justiciar was ordinarily the second most powerful position in England, since he acted as the king's chief deputy and as regent when the king was absent. Hubert de Burgh, Earl of Kent, held this office from 1215 to 1232.

50. This kind of wordplay on *Anglici* and *angeli* is a favorite pun in legends of English saints.

51. That is, about a quarter of the way through the period between sunrise and sunset on a long midsummer day.

52. The last lesson in the printed editions ends here.

53. Part of the point is that Thomas's new golden shrine was located in the cathedral's Trinity Chapel.

54. Kemble is a town in Gloucestershire.

55. The idea was to make a vow to the saint, promising a thank offering of a candle as long as the thread required to measure the body or part of a body for which healing was sought.

56. Eu is a town on the French coast, northeast of Rouen. The first Count of Eu was Geoffrey, illegitimate son of Richard I, Duke of Normandy; but by the early thirteenth century the county was held by the Lusignan family.

57. Wissant is a port between Calais and Boulogne sur Mer; its original name may have been English, "Whitesand."

58. If an English league was about three miles, this French unit of distance must have been about two miles long.

59. Devizes is a town west of London and Reading.

60. The gesture indicates the intention of using the coin as a shrine offering.

61. A precious stone described in some medieval sources as more valuable than gold and brighter than any other gemstone.

CHAPTER 27
SAGA OF BISHOP JÓN OF HÓLAR
Translated by Margaret Cormack

INTRODUCTION

At the instigation of the Norwegian king, Óláfr Tryggvason, Iceland adopted the Christian faith in the year 999 or 1000. It acquired its own bishop, Ísleifr Gizurarson, in 1056. His son, Gizurr, succeeded him as bishop in 1082 and donated the estate Skálholt to be the episcopal see. In 1106 the populous Northern Quarter was designated a distinct see with Jón Ögmundarson, the subject of this saga, as its first bishop. His see was established at Hólar.

Jón's cult does not date from his own liftime. Its development reflects the ecclesiastical concerns of the end of the twelfth century, that is of the third generation after Jón's death in 1121. The intervening period had seen the establishment in 1152/53 of Trondheim as the archdiocese for Norway and the Norse Atlantic settlements, the promotion of St. Óláfr as perpetual king of Norway a decade or two later, and the increasing interest of Norwegian religious and secular authorities in Icelandic affairs. These events must have made the Icelanders feel the lack of a saint of their own. An attempt in the early 1190s to promote Óláfr Tryggvason in this role was a failure, but the translation of Bishop Þorlákr Þórhallsson of Skálholt five years after his death in 1193 was a spectacular success. The translation established him as the country's first native saint, and his cult spread rapidly throughout Iceland.

The promotion of Þorlákr's cult appears to have begun in the diocese of Hólar, whose clergy immediately tried to repeat their success with one of their own bishops. The translation of St. Þorlákr's relics had taken place on July 20, 1198; in December of the same year the remains of two bishops of Hólar were disinterred, washed, and placed under a wooden vault in the churchyard. Those chosen for this honor were Jón Ögmundarson, the first bishop to hold the see, and the most recent bishop, Björn Gilsson (d. 1162). Jón eventually obliged by performing miracles, and his feast was declared a holy day in 1200.

Of those responsible for Jón's sanctification, only Bishop Brandr Sæmundarson of Hólar and a future bishop, Guðmundr Arason (1161–1237), are known by name. The latter is mentioned as a purveyor of relics and as the recipient of accounts of miracles and visions. He was sufficiently important that the formal translation of Jón's relics was postponed until his arrival, and he succeeded Brandr as bishop of Hólar in 1203.

After the translation of his relics, Jón was venerated primarily in his former diocese, where his miracles were recorded, and where most of them occurred. Although his primary relic, his body, remained in the cathedral, by the mid-fourteenth century the church at his birthplace, Breiðabólstaður in Fljótshlíð, had acquired one of his arms. The anniversary of his death on April 23 was celebrated as an established feast day throughout Iceland, and the anniversary of his translation on March 3 was observed as a feast day in the diocese of Hólar by order of Bishop Auðunn of Hólar (1314–20) in an attempt to encourage Jón's cult. In spite of Auðunn's efforts, Jón never attained the popularity of St. Þorlákr or of Guðmundr himself, whose cult Bishop Auðunn also promoted, with greater success.

Guðmundr Arason was responsible for the composition of a Latin *Life* of Jón by the monk Gunnlaugr Leifsson (d. 1218/19) of Þingeyrar (the monastery whose foundation is described in Chapter 17); he had earlier sent him some visions of St. Þorlákr to write up. In addition to Jón's *vita*, Gunnlaugr is known to have composed a rhymed office of St. Ambrose, a Latin *Life* of Óláfr Tryggvason, and a poetic translation of Geoffrey of Monmouth's *Prophecies of Merlin*.

None of Gunnlaugr's Latin works has survived; they are known only through Icelandic translations that have been subject to an unknown amount of revision. Like other Icelandic prose narratives, whether translated or composed in the vernacular, these translations are referred to as "sagas." The original contents of Gunnlaugr's Latin *Lives* and their relationship to extant sagas have been the subject of much scholarly discussion, necessarily of a highly speculative nature. As regards the *Saga of Bishop Jón of Hólar* (hereafter *Jóns saga*), there are three versions, of which A, the shortest and oldest, has been chosen for translation. It is generally assumed to have been composed in conjunction with, or on the basis of, Gunnlaugr's Latin *Life*.

The saga, which was probably written in the years immediately following the translation of Jón's relics, is our only source of information about Jón's life and episcopate. The century that had passed since Jón's lifetime gave the author a certain amount of leeway for the exercise of his imagination; there can have been few still living who had firsthand knowledge of Jón's life and career. Major events such as the foundation of the first Icelandic monastery at Þingeyrar, the rebuilding of the church at Hólar, and the establishment of a cathedral school, were presumably common knowledge at the institutions concerned, although the saga's descriptions of life at the cathedral and school have undoubtedly acquired a golden glow with the passage of time. The school, indeed, was known primarily through its famous graduates; in Gunnlaugr's time, only ruins were visible (see below Chapter 11).

The historicity of the remainder of the saga is far less certain. The descriptions of the visits of Jón's parents and grandparents to royal courts are examples of a hagiographic commonplace in which prominent individuals comment on the future saint. Jón's own voyages abroad are paralleled in the careers of the heroes of secular sagas, for whom a period of travel during which they made names for themselves at the courts of kings was de rigueur.

Definitions of Icelandic terms and institutions will be found in the notes. However, mention of a few points here may prevent confusion. First, the medieval Icelandic economy was primarily pastoral, and the population depended for its survival on the growth of enough grass to feed the livestock through the winter. Given the island's location just south of the Arctic Circle, even a slight change in temperature, or an excess or absence of rain, could prove disastrous. The weather miracles which occur at key points in the saga meant the difference between survival and starvation. Secondly, Iceland was administratively divided into four quarters. Local assemblies met within each quarter. Thirdly, Iceland did not become subject to the king of Norway until several decades after *Jóns saga* was composed (1262–64). Before that time, the nearest thing Iceland had to a government was the General Assembly (*alþingi*), a legislative and judicial body which met annually at þingvöllr in southwestern Iceland from the Thursday that fell between the eighteenth and twenty-fourth of June to the Wednesday between the second and the eighth of July. Only laws approved at this assembly were valid; this applied to ecclesiastical as well as secular matters.

The resemblances and differences between the Icelandic Church and hagiography and those of the rest of Europe will be apparent from the text. One feature that will probably strike most readers is the ubiquity of married priests. Clerical celibacy did not become an issue in Iceland until the second half of the thirteenth century; it was first imposed in the Christian Law of Bishop Árni Þorláksson of 1275. Priests' wives are mentioned in the sagas and miracle collections of the Icelandic saints with no suggestion that they were unusual or undesirable. Bishops, however, were another matter; it was apparently understood that they should separate from their wives after being consecrated, and authors are careful to refer to such women as "former" wives. This did not, however, mean that all contact between the couple was at an end; when *Jóns saga* was being written, Herdís, the "former" wife of Páll Jónsson, bishop of Skálholt, functioned as housekeeper of the cathedral estate in the same way as Jón's anonymous wife had done a century earlier at Hólar.

Sources and Further Reading

The following translation is based on the edition by Guðbrandur Vigfússon of "Jóns saga helga hin elzta" in *Biskupa Sögur*, 2 vols. (Copenhagen, 1858) 1:149–202, which also appears in *Byskupa Sögur*, ed. Guðni Jónsson, 3 vols. (Reykjavík, 1948) 2:79–156. The 1948 edition titles the saga "Jóns saga helga eftir Gunnlaug munk (yngri gerð)." The only previous translation is to be found in *Origines Islandicae: A Collection of the More Important Sagas and Other Native Writings Relating to the Settlement and Early History of Iceland*, ed. and trans. Gudbrand Vigfússon and F. York Powell (Oxford, 1905; reprint Millwood, 1976) 1:534–67. This translation is confined to the "biographical" portion of the saga and omits the miracles. Expanded versions of some episodes are found in a younger version of the saga and have been translated by Jacqueline Simpson in *The Northmen Talk: A Choice of Tales from Iceland* (London and Madison, Wisconsin, 1965), pp. 65–76 (see note 13 below).

The best survey of medieval Icelandic history is Jón Jóhannesson, *A History of the Old Icelandic Commonwealth. Íslendinga saga,* trans. Haraldur Bessason, University of Manitoba Icelandic Studies 2 (Winnipeg, 1974). Icelandic society in the thirteenth century can be approached through William Ian Miller, *Bloodtaking and Peacemaking: Feud, Law and Society in Saga Iceland* (Chicago, 1990). Early Icelandic ecclesiastical history can best be introduced through reading the primary sources, notably Ari Thorgilsson, *The Book of the Icelanders (Íslendingabók)*, ed. and trans. with an introductory essay and notes by Halldór Hermannsson, Islandica 20 (Ithaca, NY, 1930) and the "Christian Laws Section" of the law code, translated by Andrew Dennis, Peter Foote, and Richard Perkins as *Laws of Early Iceland: Grágás I, The Codex Regius of Grágás with Material from Other Manuscripts,* University of Manitoba Icelandic Studies 3 (Winnipeg, 1980), pp. 23–51. The Church's attitude toward women has been examined by Jenny Jochens, "The Church and Sexuality in Medieval Iceland," *Journal of Medieval History* 6 (1980): 377–92. For the cult of Jón and other saints venerated in Iceland, and the historical sources that provide information about these cults, see Margaret Cormack, *The Saints in Iceland: Their Veneration from the Conversion to 1400,* Subsidia Hagiographica 78 (Brussels, 1994). An excellent introduction to the miracles in the Icelandic saints' lives is that of Diana Whaley, "Miracles in the Sagas of Bishops: Icelandic Variations on an International Theme," *Collegium Medievale* 7 (1994): 155–84. The same volume contains a study of some of the visions found in this corpus by Margaret Cormack, "Visions, Demons and Gender in the Sagas of Icelandic Saints" on pp. 185–209. *Medieval Scandinavia: An Encyclopedia,* eds. Phillip Pulsiano, Kirsten Wolf, Paul Acker, and Donald K. Fry (New York, 1993) is an invaluable English-language reference work which contains articles on "Jóns saga ens helga," "Biskupa sögur," and other related topics.

The proper names in the text are transcribed from the Icelandic and thus contain two letters unfamiliar to some readers which are pronounced as follows:

ð "th" as in "the"
þ "th" as in "thorn"

In Icelandic, accent marks over vowels indicate length, not stress. Stress is always on the first syllable of a word.

Although composed in Icelandic, the saga contains a number of words and phrases in Latin, notably dates; familiar prayers such as the Our Father (Pater noster), Hail Mary (Ave Maria), or Creed (Credo in Deum); and brief liturgical quotations, which may or may not be accompanied by a vernacular translation. I have left the Latin as it is found in the text, providing a translation in brackets if one is not provided by the saga's author.

My translation follows *Jóns saga* through the translation of St. Jón's relics. There are an additional twenty nine miracles, whose total length is about half that of the translated text. Due to considerations of space, I have included only a miracle experienced by the anchoress Hildr, referred to earlier in Chapter 14, and the final chapter of the saga.

The chapter numbers in the translation are those of *Biskupa Sögur* (see above). I have occasionally modified the paragraphing found in that edition. One or two obvious omissions in the main manuscript have been silently filled in from a closely related version of the saga. The main difference between my translation and the language of the saga is that the latter is strikingly oral. Sentences frequently consist of long chains of clauses connected by "and" or "then." In the interest of readability, such chains have been shortened to produce sentences of a more manageable length. I have also omitted numerous adverbs of time such as "then" and "next" which are redundant in written English.

I am happy to acknowledge the assistance of the many institutions and individuals who made this translation possible. A research grant from the College of Charleston for the summer of 1996 enabled me to travel to Iceland and make use of the facilities of the Stofnun Árna Magnússonar in Reykjavík, whose staff were more than generous in putting their time and collection at my disposal. Of the many individuals who provided aid and advice in the course of the project, special thanks are due to Peter Foote and Hermann Pálsson, who carefully read and commented on the whole translation; Ólafur Halldórsson and Russell Poole, for thoughtful discussion of difficult passages; and Nona Flores, who read the resultant draft and pointed out numerous deviations from acceptable English usage. These and many others have saved me from errors and infelicities of expression; for those that remain, I am solely responsible.

Saga of Bishop Jón of Hólar

(1.) We begin our story or narrative about the holy bishop Jón at the time when Haraldr Sigurðarson ruled Norway and twenty-two winters had passed from the fall of King Óláfr the Saint.[1] The holy bishop Jón was born on the farm on Fljótshlíð called Breiðabólstaðr. His father was named Ögmundr, and his mother Þorgerðr. The father of Ögmundr was named Þorkell and was the son of Ásgeirr *kneif*. The mother of Bishop Jón was named Þorgerðr; she was the daughter of Egill, son of Hallr of Síða, to whom it was granted to be first of all the chieftains in the East-fjord Quarter to accept baptism and the true faith. Þorgerðr's mother was named Þorlaugr, daughter of Þorvaldr from Áss.

The holy bishop Jón grew up at home with his father at Breiðabólstaðr until he was four winters old. At that time there came to pass great events which were a cause of great joy to all the people of the country; Ísleifr,[2] the son of Gizurr the White and son of the daughter of Þóroddr *goði*,[3] was consecrated bishop at the request of all the people. He was consecrated bishop by Archbishop Adalbert in Bremen in Saxony, in the days of Pope Leo the ninth.[4] Ísleifr was educated in Saxony, in the town called Herford.[5] He was first of the bishops who have held the see here to be consecrated to this country. Many bishops had come to this country previously, who were not consecrated to it; some were here for very many winters, some for only a short time. Ísleifr was in Norway the winter after he was consecrated bishop. He then traveled to Iceland and arrived the summer after the Famine Winter, and had his see and home on his own patrimony, Skálholt.

It was soon prophesied by wise people what sort of person the holy bishop Jón would be, because wherever he went, people who considered his appearance were very impressed by him. A man named Guðini was called "Guðini the Good," and people think that he was good. He saw St. Jón when he was a child, and spoke these words of him: "This boy is handsome, and has a great appearance of holiness about him." This reflects what is said, that "the words of the wise amount to prophecy."

(2.) When Jón was a child, his father and mother made a change in their way of life and went abroad. They came to Denmark and went to King Sveinn,[6] who received them honorably. Þorgerðr was appointed to sit next to Queen Ástríðr herself, the mother of King Sveinn. Þorgerðr had her son, St. Jón, with her at the table; and when all sorts of delightful delicacies, with good drink, were set on the king's table, it happened that the boy Jón stretched his hands toward the things he desired, as children always do. His mother wanted to forbid this, and slapped his hands. When Queen Ástríðr saw that, she said to Þorgerðr, "No, no, my dear Þorgerðr, don't strike those hands, because they are bishop's hands." Now from such events one may observe that which we mentioned above, how greatly wise people were impressed by Jón. They also foresaw certain things concerning the holy bishop Jón which later came to pass, in accordance with divine providence.

It is also proper to mention what the holy King Óláfr said about Þorgerðr, the mother of the holy bishop Jón.[7] She was eight years old when she went to Norway with her father and mother. Egill went to the court of the holy King Óláfr and was honored there, like all other distinguished men who came from Iceland. But as Christmas approached Egill became melancholy. The king noticed it and asked the cause. Egill said it was nothing. But when the king insisted, Egill told him that if he had to suggest a cause, he thought it was mostly because his wife Þorlaug would not be as honorably placed as he at the glorious feast which was approaching. The king said he would have the matter taken care of, and invited her, along with her daughter, to stay with him at Christmas. On Christmas evening, when mother and daughter were walking through the royal hall with Queen Ástríðr,[8] having been appointed seats close to her, the king recognized the girl. He later said to her father, Egill, "This daughter of yours seems to me a lovely girl with a favorable appearance, and I can tell you that she will have great good fortune, and the line that descends from her will be the noblest in Iceland." Now that which this holy man said has beautifully come to pass, as was to be expected, and is revealed in this holy man, her son Bishop Jón; for he is truly noble, having been adorned with many virtues and honored with episcopal rank while he lived in this world, and now he shines with beautiful miracles, and is of great help to all those who seek his intercession with Almighty God.

(3.) When Jón's father and mother had been abroad for as long as they thought advisable, they returned to Iceland and settled down on their farm at Breiðabólstaðr. When St. Jón had passed through his early childhood, his father entrusted him to Bishop Ísleifr for his education;[9] he grew up under his supervision, and quickly flourished in holy learning and good habits because he had an excellent opportunity to learn both from Bishop Ísleifr. Many chieftains and other distinguished men handed over their sons to Bishop Ísleifr for fostering and teaching, and had them ordained priests; many of these later became important clerics, and two of them were bishops: St. Jón, bishop of the Northern Quarter, of whom we are now speaking, and also Kollr, bishop of the people of Vík.[10] Bishop Ísleifr had three sons, and all of them became great chieftains: Bishop Gizurr and Teitr and Þorvaldr. Gizurr was educated in Herford in Saxony. Hallr in Haukadalr fostered Teitr. Teitr, son of Bishop Ísleifr, fostered and taught many clerics, and two of his pupils became bishops: Bishop Þorlákr the first and Bishop Björn.

Bishop Ísleifr soon saw how well his foster son Jón made use of what he learned, and of the other good things which he taught him by his own excellent example and good habits. Then he began to love him very much and honor him greatly in many ways, and others immediately followed his example. St. Jón was a man of tall stature, very handsome and manly, with very fine eyes, flaxen hair, great strength, and most pleasant in his entire appearance. And as pleasing as he was to everyone on account of his appearance, it was no less important how gentle and easygoing he was in speaking to the common people. By his discreet demeanor he succeeded in becoming dear to both God and good people.

Now one must also say something about how the holy bishop Jón esteemed Bishop Ísleifr, his foster father, because thoughtful and learned people say that whenever Bishop Jón was present and people were discussing among themselves those considered most accomplished, Jón always said: "My foster father, Bishop Ísleifr, was the most handsome, most eloquent, and best of men." Then those who had been talking together answered the bishop, "Lord, who said anything about Bishop Ísleifr?" And the holy bishop Jón would answer: "I will always mention him, whenever I hear a good man mentioned." Now that was a fair testimony to Bishop Ísleifr, that a saint should speak of him in that way, and a great honor to Bishop Jón, that such a man should have fostered him. It is also said that there was one quality in particular in which St. Jón surpassed others: that his voice was uniquely excellent, and some examples of this will be told later in the narrative, showing that wise people thought so.

St. Jón wanted to go abroad again. At that time he was a deacon, and correspondingly mature. He wanted to see the customs of good men and add to his learning, for his own benefit and that of many others, as it later turned out. So he went first to Norway and then to Denmark, and did not break his journey until he had reached Rome and visited the holy apostle Peter. Then he returned and arrived in Denmark on the feast *in passione domini* [Palm Sunday]. King Sveinn was still alive, and Jón went to seek him out; and when he came to the place where the king was, it so happened that the king was at Mass. The priest who was to sing Mass began to read the account of Christ's passion just as St. Jón came into the church. He read slowly and with difficulty, and people who stood there thought it tedious and boring to listen. And when St. Jón perceived that the priest had virtually become a laughingstock, then St. Jón put a stole over his shoulders and went to the priest and humbly took the book from his hand and read the account of the passion with such spirit and understanding that all those who were present marveled. And when Mass was finished, the king sent for him and invited him to come and stay with him for a long time, and honored him so much that he seated Jón next to himself. It was a matter of some importance to him that Jón should stay as long as possible; Jón stayed there for a while.

(4.) On this occasion, while St. Jón was with King Sveinn, he was honored by God with remarkable visions. The day afterward, when he came to the royal table, he himself told the king what had appeared to him. "Last night it seemed to me that I was in the choir of an exceptionally splendid cathedral, and I saw Our Lord Jesus Christ as if he were sitting in the bishop's seat, and I saw holy King David sitting on the footstool at his feet, playing his harp with outstanding skill and beautiful sound. And it seems likely to me, lord! that some of the beautiful music that he played may have remained in my memory. Now, lord, have a harp brought, and in your presence I will see if I am able to remember anything of what he played." The king ordered that a harp be brought to Jón; and he took the harp and tuned it, and played with such great skill that the king himself and all those who were present commented on how well he played. Everyone who was told of this event thought it most noteworthy, and everyone praised Almighty God, who sees fit to reveal the glory of His saints.

It is only proper to mention how much assistance Icelanders received from the holy bishop Jón, both at home and abroad. We count as the first example the fact that he induced Sæmundr Sigfússon to return to Iceland with him, a man who has also been of the greatest service to God's Church in this country. He had been abroad for a long time, and there had been no news of him. But St. Jón was able to find out where he was and bring him from the south, and they traveled north together, across the sea to their kindred and fatherland.

(5.) When St. Jón was abroad on this occasion, King Magnús son of Óláfr, son of Haraldr, son of Sigurðr, ruled Norway.[11] When St. Jón came north to Trondheim, the king was there.[12] At that time there were many Icelanders in Norway; Teitr, son of Bishop Gizurr, was there. It happened that an Icelander called Gísl committed a killing, and the victim was a retainer of King Magnús. Gísl was driven to this abrupt action by the obligation to avenge his father. The man he slew was called Gjafvaldr, and had taken part in the killing of Gísl's father, Illugi. Immediately after the slaying Gísl was seized and put in irons by the king's men. As soon as the Icelanders learned of this they all went to the place where Gísl was imprisoned. Teitr led the group, and he struck the fetters off him and led him away. After these events the king had an assembly called, and was extremely angry; disaster appeared to be imminent. At this assembly all the Icelanders except St. Jón were forbidden to speak. The king permitted Jón to speak, and he made a long and exceptionally eloquent speech about the case, to such good effect that the king's anger was softened, and those who had virtually been condemned to death obtained peace and reconciliation.[13]

After that Jón and Sæmundr returned to Iceland and settled down on their farms, each on his patrimony, Jón at Breiðabólstaðr and Sæmundr at Oddi, and farmed there for a long time. Between them there was always brotherly love and holy concord, for they were very similar with regard to many good things. They were also nearly of an age, according to our estimate, and Jón was two years older. They both greatly adorned in many ways the holy churches which were in their care, and served them humbly in their priesthood and greatly increased their ability to support resident clerics whose duty it was to serve each church, so that there were more [clerics] than before. They might truly be called pillars of the Church, because they supported her beautifully in their holy teachings and many other blessings which they dispensed to all the people in the vicinity, or anyone who would accept or comply with their wholesome advice. St. Jón married, and had two wives, the first of whom lived only a short time; he did not have children who survived childhood with either of them, as far as we know.

(6.) When Bishop Ísleifr had held the see at Skálholt twenty-four winters, he took ill at the General Assembly, and died at home at Skálholt on Sunday, the third *nonas iulii* [July 5], eighty winters after the fall of Óláfr Tryggvason. One thousand and eighty years had passed since the birth of Christ.[14] After that Gizurr, the son of Bishop Ísleifr, was consecrated bishop at the supplication of all the people of the country; he was forty years old. That was in the days of Pope Gregory the seventh,[15] and in the days of King Óláfr Haraldsson,[16] two years after the death of Bishop Ísleifr. Gizurr went south to Rome and there asked for consecration, because Archbishop Liemar was not reconciled with the pope and was forbidden to perform consecrations.[17] Pope Gregory sent Gizurr to the archbishop named Hartwig in Magdeburg in Saxony; he consecrated Gizurr bishop at the command of the pope.[18] Of the two winters between the death of Bishop Ísleifr and the return of Bishop Gizurr, Gizurr spent one here in this country and the other, the winter after he was consecrated, partly in Denmark and partly in Gautland; he came out to this country that summer. At that time Markús Skeggjason was lawspeaker. According to what the priest Ari Þorgilsson said, Bishop Gizurr was the greatest chieftain and noblest man in all Iceland in the estimation of the populace.[19] It was due to his popularity and the persuasion of the priest Sæmundr,[20] and also in consultation with the lawspeaker Markús, that it was made law that everyone in Iceland should count up all his property and swear an oath to the total, whether in land or movable goods, and pay tithe on it, in the manner that has been observed since.[21] Bishop Gizurr had it made law that the see of the bishop of Iceland should be at Skálholt; formerly it had been nowhere. He donated the land of Skálholt to the see, as well as many other valuables in land and movable goods.

(7.) When Almighty God wished to raise up his servant St. Jón to a higher grade of ecclesiastical rank than he had been before, the Northerners asked Bishop Gizurr to establish a bishopric in the Northern Quarter, because they thought they were distant [from Skálholt], and that their Quarter was the most populous and the largest, and therefore had greatest need of episcopal visitation, but hitherto there had very rarely been opportunity for it. Bishop Gizurr presented the matter to the wisest men, and it seemed to all of them that it would be advisable to accede to this request, primarily because it appeared that it would greatly exhalt God's Church; furthermore it seemed likely that the country would be without a bishop for shorter periods if there were two bishops. The solution adopted was that Bishop Gizurr gave more than a quarter of his bishopric to establish a see in the Northern Quarter, as its inhabitants had requested. And for this responsibility and honor, to be bishop of the Northern Quarter and its inhabitants, Bishop Gizurr chose the priest Jón Ögmundarson, with the consent of all the clergy and laity of the Northern Quarter. Although at first St. Jón was very reluctant to undertake this responsibility on account of humility, he finally acceded to the prayer of Bishop Gizurr and agreed to travel abroad and receive episcopal consecration, "if God wants this to come about." Afterward many meetings were held about the matter, and it was decided that the see of the bishop of the Northerners would be established up north in Hjaltadalr, on the estate called Hólar.

A distinguished priest called Illugi lived there; of the noble men of the Northern Quarter only he was prepared to depart from his patrimony for the sake of God and needs of Holy Church. Previously there had been long arguments among the chieftains as to who should depart from his patrimony and residence, and no one was prepared to do so, except Illugi alone. It may be clearly seen by everyone that he did it for God's sake and in expectation of that which must now have come to pass, that God would give him a fair dwelling in the eternal bliss which may truly be called the patrimony of the good.

(8.) That same summer the bishop-elect went to his ship with the companions and the funds that had been allotted to him, and took with him the letters and seal of Bishop Gizurr, which bore witness to his business. When they were ready they put out to sea, and nothing is told of their journey before they arrived in Denmark after a good voyage. St. Jón the bishop-elect at once went to Archbishop Özurr,[22] arriving rather late in the day at the place where he was. The archbishop was in church at Vespers; when St. Jón the bishop-elect came into the church, Vespers were nearly finished. He stopped outside the choir and began to sing Vespers with his clerics. The archbishop had prohibited his clergy, young and old, from looking out of the choir when the Divine Office was being sung, and imposed a punishment if his order was disobeyed. But as soon as the archbishop heard the singing of St. Jón, he looked out into the nave, and wanted to know who it was who had such a voice. When Vespers were finished, the archbishop's clerics accosted him to his face: "What's this, Lord Bishop? Haven't you yourself just broken the rules you established?" The archbishop answered: "I admit that what you say is true, but it was not without cause, because a voice reached my ears the like of which I have never heard before; it was more like the voices of angels than of men." This shows what we mentioned earlier in the narrative, namely how much St. Jón's voice surpassed most others in the opinion of wise men.

When Jón had concluded Vespers, he went to the archbishop who received him honorably and invited him and all his companions to stay with him. When St. Jón had been with the archbishop a short time, he explained his business to the archbishop, and showed him the letters and seal of Bishop Gizurr. After discussing the matter for a few days with other members of the clergy to whom the archbishop wanted to present the case, and considering it carefully, the archbishop said to the bishop-elect: "I recognize, most dear brother! that you possess virtually all the qualities that make you suitable to be a bishop, and I believe that the people would be blessed who might have such a bishop over them. But because of one thing that you have told me—that you have had two wives—I dare not consecrate you without the permission and cognizance of the pope himself. Therefore we advise you to go to the pope as quickly as you can, and we will send with you a letter with our seal, explaining your case to the pope. And if it turns out as we would like to hope, that he permits you to receive consecration, and us to perform it, come back to me as soon as possible and I will joyfully conclude your business."

(9.) After that St. Jón the bishop-elect went to Rome, and when he arrived, his case was favorably heard by the pope. When St. Jón came south to Rome the pope was St. Paschal the second.[23] St. Jón presented all his business to the pope, and showed him the archbishop's letters and seal which explained all the details of his case. When the pope had seen the letter, he graciously granted that which had been humbly asked of him, and directed St. Jón the bishop-elect to Archbishop Özurr, to whom he wrote under his seal giving him permission to consecrate St. Jón as bishop. When Jón had received the pope's blessing, he departed, and he and his companions returned to Archbishop Özurr. When the archbishop learned from the pope's letters, which St. Jón brought from his audience with the pope, that he had been given full permission to consecrate him, he rejoiced exceedingly, and thanked Almighty God that it should be granted to him to conclude St. Jón's business in accordance with people's wishes. Now Jón stayed with the archbishop himself, waiting until the time that the latter would find suitable to consecrate him. Then the archbishop called together the clergy who needed to be present at the ceremony, and when everything had been prepared, he consecrated St. Jón as bishop on Sunday, two nights before the feast of the two apostles, Philip and James, which is the third *kalendas Maii* [April 29]. After St. Jón was consecrated he stayed with the archbishop and received much salutary advice from him, to the great benefit of himself and of the people over whom he was placed. St. Jón was consecrated bishop, as has just been told, when he was fifty-four winters old. That was in the days of Pope Paschal and of Eysteinn and Sigurðr, kings of Norway.[24] At that time Bishop Gizurr had ruled God's Church in Iceland as long as his father, Bishop Ísleifr, and that was twenty-four winters.

(10.) Bishop Jón came out to Iceland the summer after he had been consecrated, and had a good passage. Soon after he had landed the news of his arrival spread; all good people rejoiced, and came flocking to meet him. He heard everyone's business with equal mildness, and showed in every way that he had not forgotten the holy humility he had before he was consecrated as bishop; on the contrary, he had it even more copiously, along with all other virtues, as was even more necessary for him now that he had been raised by Almighty God to a position of great honor. When St. Jón had disembarked, he went to his see at Hólar, and at once began to rule the Church of Almighty God, over which he was set, well and beautifully. He spent that winter at his see. When summer came he rode to the General Assembly, and there he and Bishop Gizurr met with great rejoicing, and Bishop Gizurr made known to the people the great benefit for which they were indebted to God: that joyous event, which had then come to pass, that there were two bishops in the country, because that had never happened since Christianity had come to Iceland. The bishops discussed many profitable things with each other, and, in consultation with other clergy, decided what rules they should lay down for those under them.

(11.) That summer Bishop Jón began his visitation of his diocese, and began to rule God's Church very strictly; he chastised wicked people with the power that was given him from God, and strengthened good and virtuous people in many ways. St. Jón had been bishop at Hólar only a short time before he had the church there pulled down. That church had been built after the one that Oxi Hjaltason had built. People consider that the church that Oxi built was the largest wood-roofed church in all Iceland, and he had donated much property to the church and had it decorated with great care inside and had the roof entirely covered with lead. But that church with all its ornaments burned up completely according to the secret judgment of God. The holy bishop Jón had a large and noble church built at Hólar which stands there to this day, although it has been reroofed and received many other repairs since that time. In building this church the holy bishop Jón spared nothing that would increase God's glory and make the building and its decoration as beautiful as possible. He chose a man called Þóroddr, who was considered one of the most skilled craftsmen at that time, to build the church. St. Jón was not sparing in paying him large and handsome wages, and Þóroddr performed his task well and conscientiously. It is said of this man that he was so quick to learn that when he was at work and overheard the priestlings[25] being taught the art called *grammatica*[26] it stuck so well in his ears because of his great quickness and attentiveness that he became highly accomplished in this kind of learning.

When Jón had been bishop a short time, he founded a school on the cathedral estate, west of the church doors, and had it constructed well and carefully; the traces of the buildings can still be seen. To direct the school and teach the people who attended it he chose an outstanding and extremely eloquent cleric from Gautland, called Gísli, son of Finni. He paid him a large salary both to teach priestlings and to provide, with the bishop himself, such support for holy Church as he could, by his teachings and sermons. Whenever he preached to the people he had a book in front of him, and took from it everything he said to them. He did this through prudence and humility, so that it would seem more valuable to those who listened if they saw that he took his teachings from sacred books and not solely from his own understanding, since he was rather young. Such grace accompanied his preaching that those who listened were much affected and undertook great changes for the better in their way of life. And that which he taught with words, he illustrated in deeds. All good people found his teachings light and easy to bear, and wise people considered them appropriate and pleasing; but to evil people they caused great fear and true chastisement. On all major feast days there was a great crowd there, because many people made it their business to come, first to listen to the Divine Office, which was so beautifully performed there, and also to the commandments of the bishop and the wonderful preaching which it was possible to hear there, whether delivered by the bishop himself or by the man [Gísli] who has just been described.

(12.) St. Jón had been bishop only a short time before he began to change people's habits and way of life to something very different from what they had been before. He became strict with people of bad morals, but was pleasant and gentle toward all good people. He himself illustrated his teachings, in that everything he taught in words he also performed in deeds. It seemed to those wise people who best knew his way of life that he was seldom forgetful of that which the Lord himself said to his disciples: *Luceat lux vestra coram hominibus, ut videant opera vestra bona et glorificent patrem vestrum, qui in celis est* [Mt 5:16]. These words mean: *Let your light shine before men, so that they may see your good deeds and glorify your Father, who is in heaven.* The holy bishop Jón was strict about something that has been observed ever since: that people should attend the Divine Office on holy days or at other obligatory times,[27] and he commanded priests to repeat frequently the things people needed to know. He commanded people to have daily customs suitable to Christians, namely to visit daily, late and early, a cross or church, and there to recite their prayers attentively. He commanded people to have the sign of the Holy Cross in their room as protection for themselves, and that as soon they awoke, they should cross themselves and sing first Credo in Deum, and thus recite their faith to Almighty God, and thereafter go for the rest of the day armed with the sign of the Holy Cross, with which they had signed themselves when they woke, and never take food or sleep or drink without crossing themselves first. He ordered everyone to know the Pater noster and Credo in Deum, and to remember the canonical hours seven times a day, and to sing every evening without fail, before going to sleep, the Credo in Deum and Pater noster. And to conclude this matter in a few words, with God's aid he was able to improve the customs of those under him in such a short time that Holy Church had never flourished so in the Northern Quarter, either before or after, as when the people were so blessed as to have such a bishop's rule over them. He also prohibited entirely all evil customs and paganism and sacrifice, spells and sorcery, and opposed them with all his strength; they had not been entirely wiped out while the faith was young. He also prohibited all superstitions which men of old had derived from the moon's phases or special days, or the dedication of days to heathen men or gods, as is done when one calls a day Óðinn's day or Þórr's day, and everything else that he thought grew from evil roots.[28]

(13.) An unseemly pastime was popular in which people recited back and forth, a man to a woman, and a woman to a man, verses which were disgraceful and shameful and disgusting. He abolished it and prohibited it unequivocally. He would not listen to erotic poems or verses, or permit them to be recited, but he was unable to abolish them entirely. It is told that he became aware that Klængr Þorsteinsson,[29] who later became bishop of Skálholt but was at that time a young priestling, was reading a book called *Ovidius epistolarum*.[30] In that book there is much erotic poetry, and he forbade him to read such books, saying that it was difficult enough for someone to preserve himself from bodily lust and evil passion without kindling his mind to it by [bad] habits or poetry of this sort.

He was also diligent in pruning ugly vices away from people, and went about it so adroitly that hardly anyone came to him whom he was unable in some way to guide and correct through divine love and the pains he took to help each individual. If he imposed heavy penances on people on account of their great crimes, and they submitted to them well and humbly, there was but a short time to wait before his most holy breast, which the Holy Spirit had chosen as a dwelling place, began to commiserate with their sufferings so that he lightened the penance somewhat, and those same people whom he had previously chastised through divine love and zeal he healed mercifully when they had separated from their sins. He who loved all those under him like brothers or sons did not profit from anyone's faults or misconduct, but rejoiced in things that went well for others, and lamented everything that turned out otherwise. He was so good-hearted that he could hardly bear to see or know of anything that harmed people, and so generous and charitable to the poor that his equal could hardly have been found. He was a true father to all poor people; he comforted widows and orphans, and no one who came to him was so grief-stricken that he did not receive some comfort through Jón's spiritual advice. He was so beloved of all the people that hardly anyone would do anything to oppose him, and that was due more to the godly love which everyone bore him than to bodily fear. And because he crushed his own desires in many ways, and did God's will if he found that the two were not identical on account of carnal nature, God repaid him at once in that He subjected all his people to him in holy obedience.

(14.) St. Jón lived his life according to divine commandments and the example of good men. He prayed night and day, held frequent vigils and long fasts, and mortified himself in many ways so that he might render to God a greater return than before from all those things which had been entrusted to him. In order that he might be freer than before to perform the Divine Office or to preach, or to accomplish other things which would most exhalt God's Church, he chose people to supervise the cathedral estate with him, to look after its possessions, in company with the noble housewife to whom he had previously been married. One of these people was a distinguished priest called Hámundr, son of Björn; he was the grandfather of the nun and anchoress Hildr, who will be mentioned again later in this work [see Chapter 40]. Next in authority after Hámundr was a priest called Hjalti, a kinsman of the bishop. A man of noble family called Örn, son of Þorkell of Víðimýri, had more say in the administration than other laymen. These people took care of nearly everything that pertained to the estate, and appointed people to their tasks: some to bring necessary things to the estate, some to work, others to serve poor people—and the bishop was very particular that this be done mercifully. Some were responsible for receiving guests, because on every feast day people came to the bishop, a hundred or sometimes two hundred, or even more, because the holy bishop Jón made it known in his sermons that he would be satisfied only if everyone in the district who had the means came to visit the cathedral at Hólar at least once at year. Because of this it was so crowded on Holy Thursday or Easter that there were no less than four hundred people in total, men and women. Although many of these people brought provisions with them, there were even more who stayed at the bishop's expense, and were filled by him with both spiritual and bodily nourishment, so that, strengthened with the episcopal blessing, they returned to their homes rejoicing. Many virtuous people moved to the estate and donated money for their keep, some supplying their own provisions, in order to listen to the bishop's teachings and [the Divine] Office. They built dwellings for themselves around the churchyard.

The holy bishop Jón took many people as students, and provided good masters to teach them: Gísli son of Finni, whom we mentioned before, to teach grammar, and the priest Rikinni, Jón's chaplain and close friend, to teach chanting or versification, because he was also extremely learned. There was hardly a building in which some useful work was not done. It was the custom of the older men to teach the younger ones, and in between lessons the young men wrote. They were all in accord with each other and did not quarrel, and no one envied anyone else. And when the bell was rung for the Divine Office, they all came and performed their hours with great attentiveness; nothing was to be heard in the choir except beautiful singing and holy prayer. The older men knew well how to conduct themselves, and the small boys were disciplined so strictly by their masters that they dared not misbehave. The following clerics were brought up under the supervision of Bishop Jón: Klængr, whom we mentioned before, who later became bishop in Skálholt and adorned that place with his bookmaking; he was at Hólar in the days of Bishop Ketill and of Bishop Björn,[31] and was popular with all good people; Vilmundr, first abbot of Þingeyrar, was also taught there, as was Abbot Hreinn. Bishop Björn, the third bishop of Hólar, was also taught there. Many other eminent clerics were brought up and educated there, even though we do not name them.

(15.) Many things took place during the episcopate of the holy bishop Jón that were very noteworthy and amounted to great miracles, although people didn't have the confidence to call them miracles while the holy bishop Jón was alive, because Holy Writ commands: *ne laudaveris hominem in vita sua*, which means: you shall not praise a man during his lifetime.[32] This is commanded because it can happen that a man inclines his ears excessively to human praise, and this decreases his merit somewhat in the sight of God. In the present instance it came about otherwise, as the same writing says: *lauda post mortem praedica securum*, [that is] "praise him after death, and preach him secure." Now it is permitted to preach his glory and rejoice in his secure merits before Almighty God.

The following event is told concerning the holy bishop Jón. A man came to him and requested him out of great love to give him a relic of the bone of the holy bishop Martin.[33] Jón did not like to deny his request, and fetched the bone and held it in his hands. He was upset by the thought of cutting the bone of such a holy man. Then he vested himself for Mass, and when he came to the canon, he took the holy bone and laid it on the altar under the corporal, by the chalice, and then sang Mass until it was finished. After Mass, before he removed his vestments, he reached for the bone, which had broken into two pieces. When the holy bishop Jón saw that, he rejoiced exceedingly and gave thanks to God and the holy bishop Martin. Then he presented the smaller part to the one who had requested it, and preserved the larger part honorably at Hólar.[34]

Many people who had various afflictions or diseases came to the holy bishop Jón, and received rapid cures of their ailments after he prayed over and blessed them. A man named Þórir was a servant of the holy bishop Jón and looked after the sheep on the cathedral estate. He was a young man, active and rather heedless, who did not guard his words and rarely attended the Divine Office, even when he was at home on the cathedral estate. The holy bishop Jón admonished him to do better, because he was deeply concerned about all his servants, that they should have good habits and attend the Divine Office whenever they were at home, as long as essential tasks were not neglected; however, the bishop had no effect on this man. On the evening of a feast day, when the holy bishop Jón was at Vespers, and all virtuous people had gone to listen to the office, this man Þórir remained inside, according to his bad habit, and began to play and wrestle with the young people. He was told that the office was going on outside, but paid no attention. He soon received punishment on his own person for breaking the commandment of the bishop; he fell during the game, and the same tongue that he would never curb was caught between his teeth and he was terribly hurt. His tongue swelled up and was extremely painful, and became so stiff and swollen that he was unable to speak. Then it occurred to him how he had behaved, ignoring the bishop's commands, and he repented sincerely. He immediately went to the bishop and asked for healing by means of gestures. And the holy bishop Jón, that man of God, immediately commiserated with his injury and misery, and took his tongue with his hand, and stroked it, and with his prayers cured him in a few days, as if he had never received this injury.

(16.) There was a man called Sveinn, son of Þorsteinn, who was so horribly bewitched by the devil that he nearly cast off his faith and forgot all the conduct that Christians should observe. It came about in this way, that he went mad for a certain monster, which appeared to him to be an exceedingly beautiful woman. She succeeded in maddening him so that he would have nothing to do with other people, and went around as if lost in thought, and paid no attention to any of his needs.[35] But by the mercy of Almighty God, who does not desire the destruction of any of his people, but rather desires to help them all, this man was seized and brought to the holy bishop Jón; that was shortly after he came to the see. The blessed Bishop Jón received him warmly and cheerfully, led him into the church, and fastened the doors. He began to ask him closely about everything that had happened, and then incited him urgently to repent. And with his holy admonitions, this young man began to feel great contrition, and eventually he told the holy bishop Jón truthfully about everything, about all the deceits and ambushes of the devil in which he had been entangled. And when the holy bishop Jón saw true repentance in him, he was so happy that he should be able, like a good shepherd, to bring this sheep back to the flock of the Lord, that he wept. After that he began to impose penance on Sveinn with holy prayers and admonitions, and commanded him first of all that, to the detriment and disgrace of the devil, he should be zealous to tell what had happened to everyone who would listen. Sveinn did so, and stipulated in exchange from every priest to whom he told the story that when the priest heard of his death he would sing a requiem Mass for his soul. When they went out of the church, such a great change had taken place in Sveinn's condition that he who up to then had lived a life hateful both to himself and others was from then on cheerful and pleasant to everyone, and took good care of himself; as long as he lived he thanked God and the holy bishop Jón for his health.

(17.) When St. Jón had been at the see a short time, people found themselves in desperate straits. Severe famine and cold weather oppressed the land so that the ground had produced no growth by the time of the spring assembly.[36] The holy bishop Jón went to the spring assembly at Þingeyrar; when he arrived there he made a vow for a fruitful season, with the agreement of everyone at the assembly. They vowed that a church and farm should be built there, and that everyone should contribute until the estate should be completed. After the vow the holy bishop Jón took off his cloak and himself marked out the foundation for the church, and the situation improved so quickly that in that same week all the ice, which to a great extent had caused the famine, disappeared and was nowhere to be seen. The earth produced growth so quickly that in that same week there was nearly enough grass for the sheep.

There was a spell on the estate at Hólar: there was one stall in the byre in which it was pointless to tether an animal, because every animal tethered there in the evening lay dead the next morning. One autumn the holy bishop Jón went with the steward to decide which of the cattle should be kept on the episcopal estate through the winter, but when they had decided, the cowherd informed them that there were not enough places for the cattle, because one of the stalls was useless. The bishop said that it should be as he had determined and intended, and said that that stall should be used along with the others, and so it was done. The next morning, when people came to the byre, the cow in that stall lay dead. The bishop was told, and he ordered that another beast be put there, and then a third; and they died. Then the cowherd said to the bishop, "How long shall we go on in this way?" The bishop answered: "As long as there are any cattle left, if God wishes that the estate be laid waste on account of this." After that it stopped; Bishop Jón had overcome that oppression through his faith and steadfastness.

Yet another year spring came so late that the ground had little growth at the moving days.[37] The holy bishop Jón rode to the General Assembly and made a vow for the improvement of the weather on the feast of John the Baptist [June 24]. When he had specified the vow and it was confirmed, he spoke these words: "I wish that God would give us rain immediately!" thus showing that he was a very impatient man. The summer had been dry until then, so that there had been no trace of moisture, and as a result there was hardly any grass. And when the holy bishop Jón made the vow, the weather was so clear and transparent that not a cloud could be seen in the sky. But when he began the *Gloria in excelsis* that day at Mass, so much rain came from the sky that people thought it hard to stay outside on account of the wet weather. From then on for the rest of the summer there was drizzle at night and sunshine during the day, and it went on like that for a while. The grass that summer was about average.

This holy bishop Jón was graced by God with many noteworthy visions and beautiful revelations. It was not really strange that many things were shown to him in sleep, since he had no more sleep than the bare minimum, and his mind was always, before he fell asleep and as soon as he woke up, on God's service and holy prayers.

(18.) Jón had a vision on the very night that his foster brother, the priest Þorkell, known as Þorkell *trandill*, a most excellent priest, died south in Skálholt. It was after Compline, when the holy bishop Jón was in bed. As soon as he reclined against the pillow he fell into a doze, and it seemed to him as if a man he did not know came in and stopped in the middle of the room. It seemed to him that the man was asked by those who were present if he had any news to tell, and he said, "Þorkell holy." He said nothing more. The bishop awoke and jumped up at once and called Rikinni his archpriest, and said to him: "Get up, brother, and let us go to church and praise Almighty God, because our brother, the priest Þorkell, has departed from this life, and let us now commend his soul to Almighty God." They had heard that he was sick. They went to church and recited an office of the dead, and then he told the priest Rikinni the vision that had appeared to him.

(19.) In the twelfth year of the episcopate of the holy bishop Jón many great events took place. Bishop Gizurr died in Skálholt, thirty nights after Þorlákr Runólfsson received consecration as bishop; that was Tuesday the fifth *kalenda Junii* [May 28]. Þorlákr had been elected bishop at the request of Bishop Gizurr the summer before Bishop Gizurr died. Gizurr was bishop thirty-six winters. At that time one thousand one hundred and eighteeen years had passed since the birth of Christ. In that same year died Pope Paschal, King Baldwin of Jerusalem, the patriarch Arnald of Jerusalem, King Kirjalax of the Greeks, and King Philip of the Swedes. One hundred and eighteen winters had passed since the fall of Óláfr Tryggvason.[38]

Once when St. Jón had lain down to sleep at night, a vision appeared to him. He thought that he was praying before a large crucifix, and then it seemed to him that the image on the cross bent down and spoke a few words in his ear, but we do not know what they were. He told this vision to the priest Rikinni, but there was no one who could interpret it. However, on the following day people who had just arrived from overseas came to the holy bishop Jón, and brought him a book. In that book was written an occurrence which was then completely unknown in this country; it told how some Jews tortured an image of our Lord Jesus Christ in the same way as they had formerly tortured our Lord Jesus Christ; they beat the image with whips and spat on it and struck it on the neck; after that they crucified it, and then went before the cross and mocked the image, after the example of the Jews of old. After that they took a spear and thrust it viciously into the side of the image. Then a wondrous and unheard of event took place; water and blood gushed from the side of the image, and from that blood and water many sick people received their health. And when the Jews saw all these things they repented with all their hearts and turned to God. When the holy bishop Jón and the priest Rikinni had read this account, the priest, smiling, said to the bishop, "See here, father, the dream which the Lord showed you last night." Then they both praised the Lord Jesus Christ.[39]

(20.) Now we have recounted some of the miracles which we have heard told or seen written concerning the life of the holy bishop Jón, even though people took care not to call them manifest miracles during his lifetime. Nonetheless all those who could see most clearly were very much impressed by such things and by many others which Almighty God performed for his dear friend. But it was considered no less noteworthy how gloriously he maintained the estate and the clergy who were there with him, and how even-tempered he was in all good things. His humility was constant, as was his love for the people and first and foremost for Almighty God. His compassion was constant, so that he could never bear to see anything miserable. He fasted frequently, stayed awake praying virtually night and day, and was always doing something useful. And whatever he did, his lips were never silent from the praise of God Almighty.

(21.) When the time had come that Almighty God wanted to reward eternally the holy bishop Jón for the toil and trouble and many hardships that he had borne for His sake, the holy bishop Jón fell ill, and in that same illness departed from this life. The illness was not violent, and he was therefore able to consider and arrange everything as he wished. When he was in bed with this sickness, but had not yet received the last rites, one of his pupils came to him, a good scribe and a popular man in priestly orders named Þorvarðr *knappi* from Knappadalr. He had with him a book which he had copied and made for a priest who lived far away and who had entreated him to make the book. They had agreed between them that the bishop should set a price on the book for which the priest would purchase it. The bishop was pleased to see the priest [Þorvarðr *knappi*] and spoke joyously to him: "Come to me, my son, and give your father the kiss of peace before I die, like your other brothers." The priest went to him and kissed him. Then he showed him the book, and told him what they had agreed on concerning the price, and asked him to set a price on the book. The bishop examined the book and praised it highly and then said: "This is a good book and well copied, but he is not destined to enjoy it; someone else will have the benefit of it." The priest replied: "Why, father? Put a price on it, and he will be happy to purchase it for that price, because he entreated me to make such a book for him." The bishop answered: "I can do that, and set a price on the book, if you want me to, but there is no need, because the priest for whom you have intended the book is now dead." Some time passed between this and the news of the death of this same priest, and he had been dead when the bishop told of his death. Everyone was very impressed that the holy bishop Jón was able to know such things when he was far away.

(22.) Now the sickness of the holy bishop Jón began to worsen; but even though his strength waned, he nonetheless continued his accustomed prayers. He received the last rites, and all the clerics at the cathedral were present, along with others who were dear to him. He had already arranged things as he thought most propitious. After that he received the *corpus domini* [the Eucharist] and when he had tasted it, he sang first the following *communio*:[40] *Refecti domini pane celesti ad vitam quesumus nutriamur eternam.* ["We beseech Thee that we, refreshed by the heavenly bread of Our Lord, may be nourished unto eternal life"]. After that he began the following psalm: *Benedicam dominum in omni tempore, semper laus ejus in ore meo* [Ps 33:2; Vulgate 34:2].[41] These words are translated as follows: "I will praise the Lord at all times, and may His praise be always in my mouth." And while he had this Psalm on his lips, and his tongue was still moving with these holy words, his holy soul departed from his body, and was carried by God's angels to those joys which were prepared for it by Almighty God, where he will praise Almighty God eternally in the company of other saints, just as he promised in the Psalm which he sang last. The holy bishop Jón departed from this world to eternal joys on Saturday, the ninth *kalendas Maii* [April 23]; one thousand one hundred and twenty one winters had passed since the birth of Christ. He was consecrated bishop when he was fifty-four years old, and he spent fifteen winters in his see. When he had lived a total of sixty-nine years in this world he died in a good old age. That was in the days of Pope Calixtus the second. It was also in the days of the kings of Norway Eysteinn and Sigurðr, but their brother, King Óláfr, had died.[42] Þorlákr Runólfsson was bishop at Skálholt.[43]

The clerics who were present prepared the corpse of the holy bishop Jón well and carefully, and when they had reached the stage where the corpse was vested and prepared for the grave and the funeral office sung, up to the point when the corpse should be carried out, those of the priests whose duty it was to carry it approached, and took hold of the bier and tried to lift it. Then something happened which greatly impressed everyone who was present: the corpse became so heavy that those who were appointed to carry it out were completely unable to move it. This caused great concern to everyone, and they discussed among themselves what could be the cause. Then one of the clerics began to speak well and wisely, and said: "This occurrence must be due to our negligence, and we must have done something disrespectful in our service to our bishop. Now search carefully to see whether he has all the items in his vestments which are appropriate and pertain to his rank." They investigated, and it turned out that they had not put his ring on the hand of the holy bishop Jón.[44] They took the ring and put it on his hand, and after that the same men as before approached, and easily took up the corpse and carried it to the grave. The corpse of the holy bishop Jón was buried outside the church, south of the choir, and a vault was made over it. His bones lay there for slightly less than eighty winters until God revealed his glory with beautiful miracles, and his relics were taken from the ground. The venerable lord Bishop Brandr had the relics taken up and brought into the church and arrayed honorably with great magnificence, to the praise of our Lord Jesus Christ.[45] May He see fit to deliver us from troubles and dangers, and when we depart from this world, may He unite our souls with His chosen ones, through the merits and prayers of this his holy and dear friend.

(23.) When seventy-seven winters had passed since the death of the holy bishop Jón, the venerable chieftain Bishop Brandr, fourth bishop of Hólar, had the bones of the holy bishop Jón washed and a new coffin made, and deposited them in it with great care. He had the skull of the holy bishop Jón washed separately in pure water, and had that water carefully preserved. At the same time he also had the bones of Bishop Björn washed and a new coffin made for them.[46] Then he had both coffins put under a vault, but without earth over it. The bones of the holy bishop Jón were taken from the earth on this occasion on the nineteenth *kalendas Januarii* [December 14, 1198].

At that time there was a young girl called Hjálmgerðr. She was ill for a long time, and she began to have severe pains in her eyes as well from frequent insomnia. Then at the advice of Bishop Brandr the water that the skull bones of the holy bishop Jón had been washed in was taken and dripped on the girl's eyes the next three evenings and three nights; then she slept sweetly, and within a short time was completely cured of this ailment.

(24.) The next year, at the beginning of winter, a girl called Arnríðr got a dangerous ailment. It was of this nature, that she felt bad pains and great discomfort in her chest and through to one side. The ailment caused her such pain that everyone thought she was near death. Along with this she exuded such a stench that people could hardly bear to sit by her. She was unable to sleep or eat. Her father was in great distress on account of her ill health. When he thought she was near death, he took her up gently in his arms and tried to see if he could feel with his hands the nature of the ailment, because he was a good healer. As he ran his hands over her, he felt a large and horrible abscess above the navel, by the ribs on one side. Then he said, "If one of my livestock had such a sickness I would cut it open, but now I dare not do so before God." After that he made a vow to the holy bishop Jón for intercession with Almighty God, to have a candle made that was as tall as the girl, and another that would reach about her. The candles would be lit in the church at Hólar on the anniversary of Bishop Jón. He and his wife also vowed prayers, to sing the Pater noster fifty times, and the Ave Maria along with it. As soon as the vow was confirmed the girl fell asleep and slept until morning. Then those who sat up with her dripped into milk some of the water in which the bones of the holy bishop Jón had been washed, and had the girl drink the mixture. And as soon as she had tasted it she vomited up a huge amount of foul-smelling vomit. After that she lay quiet until evening. Then her father picked her up and ran his hands over her again, and he felt that the abscess had burst and the swelling separated into three lumps. And when three nights had passed after the vow was made, the girl was as completely cured as if she had never been sick. Everyone present praised God and the holy bishop Jón. This event took place shortly before Advent.

(25.) The following event took place there at the cathedral that same winter, the day before the feast of the apostle Andrew [November 30]. A man called Einarr, a deacon, had the duty of serving in church. When he was supposed to be adorning the church for the feast day he got such a bad headache that he was unable to perform his task because of it. He took some medicine of the relics of Bishop Jón and laid it against his head, and afterward he went out. When he headed for the living quarters intending to lie down, he received such a rapid cure that he felt no ailment in any part of him, and turned back again to the church and gave thanks to God and the blessed Bishop Jón, and faithfully completed his service.

On the sixth day of Christmas [December 30] it happened that a man called Grímr was hurt in a game with others of his own age. His leg was dislocated at the knee joint, and blood immediately flowed between the leg bone and the kneecap; for that reason his leg could not be completely reset. A great swelling developed in his leg and made it as stiff as a board, and he was unable to walk. When the thirteenth day of Christmas [January 6] came, and everyone had gone to Nones, he was alone, and became melancholy on account of his injury, and called with all his heart on Almighty God and on the holy bishop Jón for intercession. He also vowed to chant to the glory of God and the holy bishop Jón all the Psalms he knew from the Psalter every day as long as he lived. He knew the [psalms for] Vespers, and at once began to chant them. When he had finished chanting, he soon perceived what the merits of the holy bishop Jón could accomplish with God, and got on his feet and went out to the church without a stick; he met those he lived with and told them what had happened. He immediately left the homestead and went to find the priest Guðmundr,[47] a virtuous cleric, and told him everything that had happened. He [Guðmundr] rejoiced in this and thanked God.

(26.) A women named Rannveig was married to a priest called Jón. She came down with a serious ailment the Sunday before Christmas; a great swelling and very painful infection developed in her face, and she felt the inflammation elsewhere, as well as other discomforts. The priest Jón, her husband, made a vow for her to the holy bishop Þorlákr, but there was no change. After that the holy bishop Þorlákr appeared to a certain girl and said to her: "Don't be surprised if I don't respond to everyone's vows, because there are others who also have great merits, and some things are reserved for others in the way of miracles." After that he vanished from the girl's sight, and she told people about the vision. Now Christmas passed, and the woman's discomfort only increased. The Sunday before Epiphany her sickness increased so much that she was completely unable to speak or sleep. When night fell, she began with great misery to invoke the intercession of the holy bishop Jón, that she might be cured by means of it. She made a vow to sing five Pater nosters every week to the glory of the holy bishop Jón, and the verse of Queen Mary [the Ave Maria] as well, on the day of the week on which his feast day had fallen the previous year. Through the intercession of holy bishop Jón, Almighty God at once heard her prayer, because as soon as she confirmed the vow she fell asleep, and did not wake before the morning, when the priest woke her. All the swelling was gone from her face, and she was completely cured within a few days.

It happened further that on the Tuesday before Candlemas [February 2] a priest named Jón went to see his mother. As he returned home and was riding hard, it happened that his horse fell; his leg landed under the horse and was badly hurt. After that he mounted the horse and rode home. A bad pain developed in his leg, and it swelled up, and became as stiff as wood. On the feast day of the virgin Brigid [February 1] he called with all his heart on the holy bishop Jón for a cure, and that things might not turn out so badly that he would be unable to celebrate Mass on the feast day that was approaching. He vowed to sing the Pater noster ninety times and the Ave Maria as well, and completed the prayers at once on the feast of Brigid. On Candlemas day itself he awoke when it was time for him to go to the Divine Office, and all the swelling was gone from his leg, and he rose up completely cured and performed his office rejoicing.

(27.) There was a man named Sveinn; he went to Mass on the feast of St. Brigid [February1]. It happened that he had a bad fall, striking his head, which split open; it was a very bad wound and bled terribly. Nonetheless he managed to complete his journey and reached the priest who was serving at the church he had intended to go to, and was responsible for celebrating Mass there. Sveinn showed him the wound and asked him to stop the bleeding; he did so. When Mass was over, Sveinn went home. When he reached the farm where he lived, the wound began to bleed again, even worse than before, but this time there was no one there who was able to staunch it. He sought divine aid, since there was no possibility of human assistance, and called with all his heart on the holy bishop Jón for intercession, and vowed to pray every day of his life for Ögmundr, Jón's father, and Þorgerðr, his mother, and to visit the cathedral at Hólar once every twelve months if he was resident in the Northern Quarter. And as soon as he had formally announced the vow, the bleeding ceased, and in a few days the wound was healed. He rejoiced greatly at this event and all those who were present thanked God and the holy bishop Jón.

Now word of Jón's sanctity began to spread, and many people received great relief from their ailments, and beautiful miracles, on account of his intercession with Almighty God. These joyful tidings were told by one to another and were soon known far and wide. It also happened at this time that a girl called Svanhildr was very ill, so that she never left her bed. Her back and hips were knotted, and her legs crippled. Her mother made a vow for her to the holy bishop Jón, to sing fifty Pater nosters every Saturday until his anniversary, and then to go herself to Hólar and present two candles there. The woman also vowed that the girl herself should sing every day for a week a number of Pater nosters equal to her age; she was seven years old at the time. Then they confirmed the vow. The next Sunday after they made the vow, the girl was able to walk alone across the living room, and she improved day by day until Easter. By that time she was as completely cured as if she had never had such an ailment. Everyone thought this extremely noteworthy, most of all those who had seen the girl previously and knew most about her ailment, and now saw her completely cured. They praised God and the holy bishop Jón.

(28.) A man was called Áslákr. He had an ailment that made his skin break out in a rash and scabs with great itching and burning, so that he was utterly unable to keep still. A man called Þorfinnr asked him why he was so scabby, and he said he would show him what caused it, and asked him to come away from other people. When the two of them were alone in a building, Áslákr showed himself to Þorfinnr and took his clothes off. His body, from neck to heels, was covered with blisters, accompanied by a pain like burning. Þorfinnr then took the water of the holy bishop Þorlákr, and applied it all over his body; and when people went to bed in the evening, Áslákr lay awake in great discomfort all night. The next morning Þorfinnr came to speak to Áslákr, and asked how he was. "Not well," he said, "and I think I have received a great increase in my complaint; now all my skin is like a single scab, and there is such searing pain and burning that I don't know what to do on account of this horrible itching." Then he burst into a flood of tears from misery and wretchedness. In addition to everything else a great swelling had come into his face, so that one could hardly see the eyes in his head. It then occurred to him how much was said concerning the sanctity of Bishop Jón, and how many miracles God had performed on account of his intercession. He called on him with all his heart, that he alleviate his ailment somehow. He vowed to sing the Pater noster five times for seven consecutive days to the glory of God and the holy bishop Jón. After that he prayed and at once fell asleep, and when he awoke the next morning his entire body was smooth and whole and free of the burning pain. His face was still a bit swollen, but for the rest he was completely cured. Then Þorfinnr took the water of the holy bishop Þorlákr and applied it to his face and at once all the swelling vanished. Áslákr rejoiced greatly at recovering his health, and thanked God and his saints with all his heart.

(29.) A man was called Þorbjörn. He became dangerously ill, and it happened so suddenly that one evening he lay down healthy and cheerful and fell asleep, and awoke with such a bad stitch in his side that he could hardly draw breath for the pain that accompanied it. The pain was mostly in his side and chest; he wanted to see a priest, but there was no one who could go for one. Then he called on the one from whom relief is most assured, Almighty God, through the intercession of the holy bishop Jón, and vowed to chant seven Pater nosters for a total of seven days in honor of the holy bishop Jón. He began to chant at once; his chanting went haltingly on account of the illness. When he had reached the seventh and had barely finished it, he dozed off, and as he was dozing a man in a black cope appeared to him, tall and very clerical looking. It seemed to Þorbjörn that he was afraid of the man and dared not speak to him. Then it seemed to him that the man who had come took his right hand from under his cope. The hand was so bright and radiant that he could not look directly at it. The man put his hand on his breast and pushed so hard that he thought he could hardly bear it. After that the man raised his hand and blessed him and then vanished. Þorbjörn wished he had asked him who he was, but there was no time to do so. After that he woke up, cured, so that he felt neither sickness nor ailment anywhere. He was deeply impressed by that event, and thanked God and the holy bishop Jón.

At that time it happened that a man called Auðunn had a foot ailment that had affected him for eighteen months. It was of such a sort that on one toe there was a sore which was always open. He had shown healers his foot, and they said that the foot would never be healed unless it were both cut and cauterized; but he thought that horrible and therefore sought a more skillful healer. He called on the holy bishop Jón for intercession and mercy, and vowed to give a mark of wax to the cathedral at Hólar, and chant five Pater nosters every Saturday until Easter. It was then the feast of St. Gregory [March 12]. Then he bandaged his foot as usual, and did not take off the bandage until seven days had passed. The foot was so whole that there was no sign of a sore on it. He himself told this event to many people, and they all praised God and the holy bishop Jón, and were deeply impressed by how frequently miracles now occurred.

It also happened that a woman called Guðrún got such a severe headache during the night that she did not think she would be able to bear it. She called on the holy bishop Jón with all her heart, praying that, if he had such merits with God as she heard told, he would now help her. She also vowed to have a candle made that would go around her head. Then she confirmed the vow and soon afterward fell asleep, and awoke completely cured, and got up at once and dressed and thanked God and the holy bishop Jón.

(30.) In the same year that most of these miracles which have just been told, and many others, occurred, the following events took place at the estate of Hólar during Lent. There was a poor and weak woman there, truthful and harmless and firm in faith. At this time people were oppressed by bad storms and cold weather, and the outlook was for the worst sort of famine and distress. It was like this all over Iceland. The woman whom I mentioned before lay awake in her bed one night, praying; and when her prayer was finished, she leaned back on the pillow and fell asleep. Then it appeared to her that a man approached her, tall in stature and of noble appearance; she thought she was afraid of him and did not dare to greet him. He then greeted her with these words: "Don't you people find this weather hard to bear, and aren't you afraid of the terrible blizzards which are raging?" The woman answered: "People are certainly very much afraid, and can't see clearly when there will be an end to this terror. There are many who have already become poor and destitute and are in great affliction, even though those who live on this holy place are fortunate." Then the man who appeared to her said "And aren't people seeking a solution, considering that they are in such danger?" The woman answered: "They aren't so sure what is best to do about such things." He then offered the following advice: "Let them take from the earth the coffin of the holy bishop Jón, and venerate [him] as best they can, and see what happens then." When he had said that he vanished from sight, and she woke up and told people of the apparition, and everyone thought it highly significant.

(31.) At the same time Bishop Brandr was very ill, so that he could not even get to church with assistance, and he had the Divine Office and Mass read in his room. That was the first week of Lent, and this was done both on the Wednesday and on the Thursday. People urged Bishop Brandr to send people to open the vault over the grave of Bishop Jón, and bring the bishop some of the relics. When they opened the grave, they found herbs of a kind that was completely unknown, green as in summer. The greenness of the herbs at that time of year seemed wonderful to them, and they picked some and put them in the bishop's drink. As soon as he had tasted it he felt a bit better. He then announced publicly that he would have the relics translated, and immediately that same day he ordered the place in the church prepared where he intended that the relics should be. When everything was ready they waited the rest of the day because they were unwilling to translate the relics before the arrival of the distinguished cleric, Guðmundr Arason,[48] who later was bishop after Bishop Brandr, because they had sent for him. He arrived in the evening, and on the next day, Friday, they translated the relics. At that time the weather was cold and dark, steady snowfall alternating with flurries. At midday all the clerics had come to church vested in surplices and copes with crosses and candles and censers and relics, and formed a *processio* [procession] inside the church. The bishop sat in his chair in a cope, and when everything was completely prepared, all the bells were rung. Then the clerics went out of the church. As for Bishop Brandr himself, who earlier had barely been able to get to church with the aid of two men, his strength increased so rapidly by the grace of God that he now sprang up from his chair and went out in the *processio* guided by one man as usual. They all went together to the grave with fair songs of praise and took up the relics and bore them into the cathedral with great glory and rejoicing, and deposited them in the place which had previously been prepared. Then they all solemnly sang Mass to the glory of God and the holy bishop Jón.

(32.) The relics of Bishop Jón were taken out of the ground in the way just told in the third year after Bishop Brandr had had the bones washed. This translation was performed *quinto nonas Marcii* [March 3], and so that it would be shown by clear tokens that this translation was performed in accordance with God's will, the weather changed so quickly on the very day when the relics were translated that it turned so mild that in a few days all the snow was gone, not only in that district but throughout Iceland; in fact in the very hour when the relics were translated the weather changed in the sky. Everyone, wherever he was, was deeply impressed that the weather changed so suddenly, and when the tidings were heard as well, that the relics had been taken from the earth at that time, everyone thanked God and the holy bishop Jón . . .

[**Translator's note**: The following story was referred to above, see Chapter 14.]

(40.) It is now especially necessary to mention an event which took place after the death of holy bishop Jón, during the interval between his death and his translation. He had consecrated as a nun a woman called Hildr, who became an anchoress before the holy bishop Jón died. He consecrated a cell for her south of the church, and it so happened that he was buried opposite the cell. And after his death something happened that was a great trial to her. There was such an infestation of mice in her cell that she could hardly stand it. Everything that people could think of was tried to destroy those noxious creatures, but nothing worked. They tried to wainscot the cell and panel it carefully, but that did not improve things either. No one could think of a solution to the problem. And when Hildr saw that people were going to give up on the matter, she said to herself while she was alone one night, "If my lord, the holy bishop Jón, could know what a torment these creatures are to me, and if he would be as concerned with my bodily welfare now as he formerly was with my spiritual welfare, when he lived here in the world with us, things wouldn't go on like this any longer." And when she had said this she saw a man come into the cell, priestly and noble, and thought she recognized the holy bishop Jón. He had an aspergillum in his hand, and sprinkled holy water throughout the building, and thus drove away all the mice, so that from that time on they were never observed again in her cell . . .

(45.) Now we have recounted something of the life and miracles of the holy bishop Jón, according to what we have found written in discerning books, and some of it we have received from discerning and truthful people. And now it is our request to all those who have this narrative in their hands that they by no means despise our narrative, when they make another more noteworthy one, and permit us to justify ourselves before they judge it inaccurate. Also and in particular we request everyone who has heard the narrative—and for me it is a matter of the greatest importance, and my duty, to do this—to appeal one and all to this sublime saint of God, the holy bishop Jón, for his intercession, and call on him in our need. Let us consider it as so much the more our duty to revere him as we hear more glorious things told of him, both of his life and the performance of miracles, through which Almighty God, to His own honor, makes [Jón's] glory known to men. Then let us wholeheartedly pray with great devotion to this good friend of God, that through his intercession he may obtain for us from the Lord all those things which are most needful for us while we live in this world, and that God may call us from the world only when we have received all the preparation for our death which may give us most hope of salvation. And when this life is over may He grant us a dwelling place in paradise until the day of judgment, and after the day of judgment an eternal dwelling in heaven with Himself and all His saints *in secula seculorum. Amen.*

NOTES

1. King Haraldr *harðráði* of Norway reigned from 1046 until 1066; King St. Óláfr Haraldsson of Norway reigned from 1016 until 1029, and died in 1030.

2. Bishop Ísleifr Gizurarson of Iceland served from 1056 until 1080.

3. A *goði* is one of thirty-nine chieftains who participated in judicial and legislative proceedings at the General Assembly.

4. Archbishop Adalbert of Hamburg-Bremen served from 1043 until 1072. Iceland and the rest of Scandinavia were part of the archdiocese of Hamburg-Bremen until a Scandinavian archdiocese was established at Lund in 1103 or 1104. Pope Leo IX served from 1049 until 1054. If the date of Gizurr's consecration (1056) is correct, Leo cannot have performed it.

5. Ísleifr, the first bishop of Iceland (1056–80), had been educated in Herford, Germany, and must have been the only Icelander of his time with a thorough ecclesiastical training.

6. King Sveinn (Svend, Svein, Sweyn) Estridsson (Estridsen, Úlfsson) of Denmark, who reigned from 1047 until 1074.

7. On St. Óláfr, see note 1 above.

8. St. Óláfr's wife Ástríðr is not the same woman as King Sveinn's mother.

9. It was common in Iceland for a child of good family to be brought up by someone other than its parents (see William Ian Miller, *Bloodtaking and Peacemaking: Feud, Law and Society in Saga Iceland* [Chicago, 1990], pp. 122–24). Although there had been other bishops in Iceland before Ísleifr and during his episcopate, they were foreigners whose knowledge of Icelandic was probably quite limited. Ísleifr's episcopate appears to have seen the growth of the Church as an institution rather than the adoption of Christian ethics. While *The Book of the Icelanders* informs us that many chieftains sent their sons to Ísleifr to receive an ecclesiastical education and be ordained, a source contemporary with *Jóns saga* notes that most of Ísleifr's contemporaries paid little attention to his teachings on Christian morality. The main issue seems to have been sexual morality, specifically concubinage on the part of Icelandic chieftains, which had been the subject of a letter from the Archbishop of Trondheim in 1180.

10. That is, Oslo Fjord and the surrounding territory.

11. King Magnús bareleg, who reigned from 1093 until 1103.

12. Trondheim, also known as Nidaros, was the Norwegian town with which Iceland had the closest ties in the eleventh and twelfth centuries. Kings often held court there, and its cathedral contained the relics of St. Óláfr. In 1152 or 1153, Trondheim was raised to the status of an archdiocese comprising Norway and the Scandinavian settlements in the Atlantic (Iceland, Greenland, the Faroes, Orkneys, Hebrides, and the Isle of Man).

13. It should be emphasized that in taking vengeance for his slain father, Gísl is doing no more than his duty, as required by the Icelandic code of honor. A younger version of *Jóns saga* contains more elaborate—and more miraculous—accounts of how Jón saved Gísl, who had actually been hanged, and Sæmundr, who had lost his sense of identity while studying in Europe. The younger version of the Gísl story adapts a miracle well known from the hagiography of St. James and the Virgin Mary, in which a hanged man is saved from death; the Sæmundr episode contains the earliest recorded account of Sæmundr's knowledge of the black arts, for which he became famous in later Icelandic folklore. These extracts from the younger version of the saga have been translated by Jacqueline Simpson in *The Northmen Talk* (London, 1965), pp. 65–76.

14. Coordinating internal chronology with that of Europe was the accomplishment of the priest Ari Þorgilsson (1068–1148), who used the succession of lawspeakers as a basis of his calculation of the *Anno Domini* dates of key events in Icelandic history. The results

of his calculations are preserved in *The Book of the Icelanders*. When *Jóns saga* was being composed, an alternative chronology was fashionable, one which assumed the birth of Christ took place seven years before the traditional date. Oddly enough chapter six of *Jóns saga*, which is based largely on *The Book of the Icelanders*, uses this alternative dating system. To avoid confusion, I have silently corrected all dates.

15. Pope Gregory VII served from 1073 until 1085.

16. King Óláfr Haraldsson of Norway reigned from 1067 until 1093.

17. Archbishop Liemar of Hamburg-Bremen served from 1072 until 1101, but was removed from office and excommunicated during the period between 1075 and 1076/7.

18. Archbishop Hartwig of Magdeburg served from 1079 until 1102.

19. On Ari Þorgilsson, see note 14 above.

20. Sæmundr Sigfússon is discussed above in Chapters 4 and 5 and note 13.

21. The tithe was a 10 percent income tax levied by the Church. In Iceland, however, it was treated as a property tax, 1 percent of the total value of property. Since interest and rental rates on land and livestock were 10 percent, the 1 percent property tax was the equivalent of a 10 percent income tax. When this practice was challenged in the second half of the thirteenth century (1281), the Icelanders claimed to have received papal permission from Pope Innocent to calculate it in this fashion; see *Árna saga biskups,* ed. Þorleifur Hauksson, (Reykjavík, 1972), p. 81.

22. Arcbhisop Özurr (Asser) of Lund served from 1102/3 until 1137. Iceland was part of the archdiocese of Lund from its creation as the Archdiocese for all of Scandinavia in 1102/3 until the establishment of the Archdiocese of Trondheim in 1153/4.

23. Pope Paschal II served from 1099 until 1118.

24. Eysteinn, Sigurðr, and Óláfr, sons of Magnús Bareleg, ruled Norway from 1103; Óláfr died in 1116.

25. In the term "priestlings," I have anglicized the term used for boys studying for the priesthood.

26. Grammar, the most basic of the seven liberal arts, consisted of instruction in Latin.

27. A list of established feast days, with rules for the preceding fasts, is included in the Christian Laws Section of *Grágás*, composed between 1122 and 1133; see *Laws of Early Iceland: Grágás,* trans. Andrew Dennis, Peter Foote, Richard Perkins, (Winnipeg: 1980), 1:39–51, especially 45–46. The Christian Laws Section also contains the requirement that everyone know the Pater noster and Creed, as does a lenten sermon included in the Icelandic homily-book, a manuscript from ca. 1200. The Icelandic homily-book also mentions other points in Jón's program: regular church-attendance, singing the Creed upon awakening and before going to sleep, and observing the hours of the Divine Office by reciting an appropriate number of Pater nosters, with the Creed at Prime and Matins. In spite of its appearance in vows in *Jóns saga,* the Ave Maria was not part of required Christian learning until 1275.

28. The Christian Laws Section of *Grágás* (see previous note) contains provisions prohibiting magic and various kinds of supersititions; see *Laws of Early Iceland, Grágás,* 1: 38–39.

29. Bishop Klængr Þorsteinsson of Skálholt served from 1152 until 1176.

30. This book is possibly the *Heroides Epistolae* [Letters of Heroines], a copy of which was owned by Hólar cathedral in 1525. Another version of the saga gives the work as *De Arte*, that is Ovid's *Ars Amatoria* [The Art of Love]. Both works are typical of the literature of courtly love popular in Europe.

31. Bishop Ketill Þorsteinsson of Hólar served from 1122 until 1145. Bishop Björn Gilsson of Hólar served from 1147 until 1162.

32. This is perhaps a reference to Sir 11:30 in the Vulgate: *ante mortem ne laudes hominem quemquem* ("praise no man before his death").

33. That is, St. Martin of Tours (ca. 316–397).

34. On the evidence of this passage relics of St. Martin are presumed to have existed at Hólar and at Grenjaðarstaðir, the church served by the priest according to another version of the saga. The church at Grenjaðarstaðir was dedicated to St. Martin.

35. In Scandinavian folklore, wandering around distracted is a sign of seduction by a supernatural being (a reference for which I thank a personal communication from John Lindow).

36. The spring assembly lasted from four nights to a week between May 7 and 27.

37. Days on which people changed their legal residence: the Thursday that fell between May 21 and 27 through the following Sunday.

38. In 1118, Pope Paschal II died on January 1, King Baldwin of Jerusalem on April 2, Patriarch Arnulf on April 14, Emperor Alexios Komnenos on August 8. The date of the death of King Philip of Sweden is unknown. This passage is based on Ari Þorgilsson's *Book of the Icelanders,* which refers to the Greek emperor as "Alexios" rather than "Kirjalax." The latter form of the name is generally used in the sagas.

39. This is the earliest reference to the *Flagellatio Crucis* (the legend of the flagellation of the Cross) in Iceland. The earliest extant Icelandic manuscripts of this text date from the fourteenth century.

40. A *communio* is a prayer that accompanies the giving of the Eucharist. The passage quoted is actually a postcommunion prayer.

41. In the translation of the RSV, "I will bless the Lord at all times; his praise shall continually be in my mouth."

42. See note 24 above.

43. Bishop Þorlákr Runólfsson of Skálholt served from 1118 until 1133. On the kings of Norway, see note 24 above.

44. A ring was part of episcopal insignia.

45. Bishop Brandr Sæmundarson of Hólar served from 1163 until 1201.

46. On Bishop Björn Gilsson of Hólar, see note 31 above.

47. Identified as Guðmundr Arason (d. 1237) in a closely related version of the saga.

48. See previous note.

Chapter 28

GAUTIER DE COINCY, *MIRACLES OF THE VIRGIN MARY*

Translated by Renate Blumenfeld-Kosinski

Introduction

Gautier de Coincy was born around 1177/78 near Soissons in northern France. He came from an important family that had connections to the abbey of Saint-Médard, where Gautier became a monk in 1193. At the abbey school Gautier probably studied some of the classics, but he believed that a true Christian should be more interested in Christ and the Virgin Mary than in Virgil. He finished his theological education most likely in Paris and became prior at Vic-sur-Aisne in 1214 and later at Saint-Médard in Soissons. About four years later Gautier began compiling and translating his vast collection of miracles of the Virgin Mary as well as composing a series of songs in her honor.

In the thirteenth century the cult of the Virgin reached an unprecedented intensity. In the Gospels Mary's role had been relatively small, although she was mentioned as Christ's mother and shown to be present at the Crucifixion. In the early centuries of Christianity she became more and more important, and she gained new attributes commemorated in feast days. For example, the Council of Ephesus (431) proclaimed her *Theotokos* or Mother of God, and in the seventh century the feast day of her assumption into heaven was instituted (August 15). Throughout the Middle Ages theologians debated the question of Mary's immaculate conception (that is, was she conceived without the stain of original sin?), but this concept did not become a dogma until 1854. In the twelfth century the cult of the Virgin grew dramatically, and in addition to theologians poets began to celebrate her in French and Provençal. For some of the troubadours of this period Mary equaled or replaced the beloved lady in their love songs.

Gautier de Coincy, as one of the most ardent supporters of Mary's cult, certainly saw himself as a lover and champion of his venerated lady. His devotion to her, expressed in songs in her honor, once angered a demon who appeared to him and threatened him. The demon predicted that a great misfortune would befall the abbey, and only a few days later the precious bones of the patron, St. Léocade, were stolen. Shortly afterward they were found in the river where the thieves had thrown them and Gautier was profoundly grateful for this miracle. He tells this story in miracle number 44 in the first volume of his collection.

But most of the over fifty miracles in his collection are translations and adaptations of Latin stories that had circulated for many generations. Unlike the miracles of various saints which were essential for a holy person's canonization, the miracles of the Virgin did not serve the purpose of underscoring her holiness; that was taken for granted. Rather, her miracles are offered as a consolation to suffering humanity, a sign of hope in a hostile and dangerous world.

From a core of seventeen miracles, known as the Hildefonsus—Murieldis Group (the two saints whose miracles were told in these stories), the collection of Marian miracles grew to a group of forty-three that formed the foundation for all Western legend collections, as Wilson has shown in her introduction to John of Garland's thirteenth-century collection of Marian miracles, the *Stella maris*. Gautier certainly used such a collection as his source, but he also made the miracles very much his own. He often interrupts the telling of the miracle story with asides, criticizing various groups of society: lawyers, physicians, the rich, women, and many others. Further, he adds so-called *queues* or "tails" to a number of his stories. These are usually passionate diatribes against those people who do not venerate the Virgin Mary as ardently as he does or who are guilty of assorted other vices. There is also virulent anti-Semitism in these passages as well as in the miracle of the converted Jewish boy you will find below. In the stories assembled here the Virgin Mary comes to the aid of a variety of sinners and people in trouble: from an abbess who gets impregnated by her steward to a nun about to sin, from a worldly clerk who falls grievously ill to an abbot whose party at sea is in danger of drowning, we find people who in the moment of greatest need turn to the Virgin. That the Virgin is the ultimate intercessor becomes clear in a number of passages where Gautier insists that all other saints derive their power only from her. Our writer establishes a clear hierarchy where Mary is the one with the most direct access to God and Jesus Christ.

For whom did Gautier write? Although at one point he claims to write his stories for "those men and women who are illiterate," it is more likely that he had an aristocratic audience in mind. In number 33 of the second volume he sends his book on the way with the words: "Greet all the kings and queens, dukes, duchesses, counts, countesses, bishops, abbots, and abbesses," suggesting that the lowest segments of the society were not his target audience.

Nearly eighty manuscripts of Gautier's collection survive to this day, a testament to the text's lasting popularity and influence. Gautier's poetry became a model for the pious literature in the vernacular that began to flourish in the thirteenth century. Even after the completion of his vast collection of miracles and songs, Gautier vowed to compose a song in honor of the Virgin Mary every year, and he did so until his death in 1236.

SOURCES AND FURTHER READING

The standard edition of the miracles is V. Frederic Koenig, *Gautier de Coinci, Les Miracles de Nostre Dame*, 4 vols. (Geneva, 1955–70). In Old French the miracles are written in verse, in lines of eight syllables with rhyming couplets. I will translate them in prose. The miracles were chosen to reflect some of the major types of Marian miracles: healing miracles; stories of conversion, rescue from seemingly hopeless predicaments, and punishment of unbelievers. The best study of the genre of the miracle story in French literature is Uda Ebel, *Das altromanische Mirakel: Ursprung und Geschichte einer literarischen Gattung* (Heidelberg, 1965). An insightful study on the theme of human weakness in Gautier's miracles is Brigitte Cazelles's *La Faiblesse chez Gautier de Coincy* (Saratoga, CA, 1978). H.P.J.M. Ahsmann explores the influence of the cult of the Virgin on vernacular literature in *Le Culte de la sainte vierge et la littérature profane du moyen âge* (Utrecht, 1930). The complex tradition of the different collections of Marian miracles is traced in the introduction to *The "Stella Maris" of John of Garland. Edited Together With a Study of Certain Collections of Mary Legends Made in Northern France in the Twelfth and Thirteenth Centuries*, ed. Evelyn Faye Wilson (Cambridge, MA, 1946). On the cult of the Virgin (with many passages on Marian miracles) see Marina Warner, *Alone of All Her Sex: The Myth and the Cult of the Virgin Mary* (New York, 1976) and Jaroslav Pelikan, *Mary Through the Centuries: Her Place in the History of Culture* (New Haven, 1996).

Gautier de Coincy, Miracles of the Virgin Mary

(1.) About an abbess whom Our Lady delivered from great anguish.[1]

There once was an abbess who very much loved the lady from paradise (Mary). She put her entire heart and good sense into serving her and tried very hard to keep the rules of her order and to manage the convent, so much so that her nuns spoke ill of her and viciously complained about her. They were very jealous of her, for they found nothing in her life with which they could reproach her: they found nothing they could latch on to. For a long time things went on like this and they saw her do nothing of which they could accuse her. But the enemy [the devil] who knows how to fool people, was often furious and very distraught because she had lived for such a long time in such a saintly manner. The devil who knows how to play tricks busied himself so much around her that he inflamed her heart so much that she fell in love with her steward. The devil made her break the seal of virginity which she had vowed and promised to the king of truth.

After a very short time the lady felt in her flanks a seed that germinated and grew so much that she saw the truth and knew that she was pregnant with a child. Soon her face which had been so fresh and well colored grew pale and spotty, and her nuns right away noticed this and were overjoyed. Some of them said: "By rights she should be burned, the traitor and hypocrite! She only brings shame upon us." "No," another one said, "we couldn't do that, but we can make her pay. We couldn't even blow our noses without her wanting to punish us. But, thank God, she has done something that will bring her great sadness and shame. God, who can do anything, may give her plenty!"

They secretly sent word of this matter in briefs and letters to the bishop. He promised them that he would bring shame upon her if he could prove the matter and at the end of the letter he told them that he would be at their chapter house the next day.

The abbess rose in the morning without knowing anything about this. In her chapel, the good lady had a solemn Mass said for Our Lady. After Mass she remained alone and sighed and cried, all heartbroken. She felt clearly that she was close to giving birth. If it pleased God she would have liked to give birth secretly so that she would not be exposed shamefully. The unhappy woman did not know what to do and became desperate. She did not know what to do or say, for there was no one to whom she could reveal her situation. She began softly to invoke the sweet mother of Christ: "My Lady," she said, "you whom the king of heaven chose to be his sweet mother, have pity on my misery. Ah, sweet, glorious lady, you are so sweet and merciful that your pity and sweetness overflow in the whole world. Ah, mother of God, whatever I have done I implore your forgiveness for my crime. Noble lady, noble queen, through your kindness have pity on this unhappy orphan. My heart is all stained and blackened because I angered you so much. With clasped hands and tearstained face I implore you to listen to me. Whatever I have done, I have never renounced you but have served and invoked you, and I will serve you, my sweet lady, as long as my poor soul will reside in my poor body which is so vile. My lady, please condescend to asking your son, who is so devout, to give me counsel for I am lacking in all human counsel. In the world I find so much harshness that I don't dare to speak of my purity nor to confess to man or woman. Ah, sweet merciful lady, I entrust my heart entirely to you. Sweet Lady, Holy Mary, I commend my affairs to you. I know well that you are so good, so full of sweetness and friendship, that you will have pity on me. The woman who commends herself to you is no longer lost. I therefore give over my body to you: you shall henceforth be its guardian."

The lady, kneeling and praying, fell asleep in front of the altar. My lady, the holy Mary, came to her with two angels. She was so beautiful that twenty writers like me could not describe her and the two angels were brighter than the summer sun. For a long time the abbess was frightened by all this brightness. "Be not afraid, dear friend," said Our Lady. "I am God's mother, Mary, who prays ceaselessly, night and day, to her sweet son for all the sinners. I have seen your hot tears and heard your prayers. For all the service you have given me the king of heaven forgives you all your misdeeds for the sake of my prayer and sends you his grace." Then the sweet lady told the two angels to approach and to deliver the lady of her child and to take it to her friend, the saintly hermit, who lived seven miles away. He should keep it with him to the age of seven and guard it like the apple of his eye. After having received these orders, the angels approached the abbess and took the child from her stomach and took it to the hermit, a man of great merit.

"Dear friend," said Our Lady, "I delivered you honorably from the great shame and infamy about which you cried so much. I delivered you of a beautiful son. I advise you that from now on you should beware of further dangers: you would anger me too much and would alienate your noble husband, your noble spouse, whom you married a long time ago.[2] The woman who marries my sweet son is not badly married. But the woman who cheats such a husband should have a sad heart. And you, because you cheated on him, must drink this morning a very bitter soup: the bishop will scold and insult you violently, but nonetheless you will come out of all this lightly, for I cannot in any way permit that those who serve me with a sincere heart should have to bear any trouble or shame." With these words Our Lady, the holy Mary, left her.

The abbess awoke and was greatly surprised that she felt so light. She was so filled with joy that she did not know what to say. She slipped her hands under her habit and felt nothing. Since she did not feel her big stomach anymore, she was overcome by such joy and astonishment that she did not know whether she was asleep or awake. She was flabbergasted with joy. "Sweet Lady, Holy Mary," the poor woman said, crying, "I have found help in you. Sacred, glorious Virgin, how tender and merciful are you! How sweet and indulgent are you! Noble, saintly and worthy Lady, is there a man or a woman who could describe your sweetness and goodness? No, my Lady, no one could. No one could ever praise you enough."

While she was intent on praying and weeping softly with the joy she had received, the bishop, who had been informed of her condition by the nuns, arrived at the abbey, all fired up with doing her harm. The nuns had a great council and gossip was all over the convent. They all agreed that they would put the abbess to shame and would say the worst about her. They went looking for her around the abbey. One of them said, "I can find nothing." Another one said that she was probably hiding. "Perhaps she gave birth somewhere," said another one. "Let's go look for her quickly. She must be found and we will apprehend her and expose her." There was not a room nor a closet nor a cottage that was not searched immediately. They looked for her for such a long time that they finally found her in her chapel, on her knees and in tears, in front of the statue of the Virgin who is always willing and ready to help and comfort her followers. The abbess refused to be distressed when she heard that her bishop had sent for her and waited for her in the chapter house. She crossed herself and commended herself to the Savior's mother. She did not desire any other lawyer or jurist.

In the chapter house she sat down by the bishop's side as usual, but the bishop, who was boiling with rage and ill will, began to insult her. He made her get up shamefully and her angry nuns threw her out of the chapter house. She could not make herself heard. The saintly lady suffered but endured in the name of penitence the great blame and infamy. She took great comfort in the protection of Our Lady, Holy Mary. To make sure of the facts, the bishop sent two mature clerks after the abbess. "Go," he said, "and see in secret whether she is pregnant or not. She had a very good reputation: I do not want to do her an injustice before I know her condition." The two clerks went to the lady. She was very troubled and ashamed when she had to undress. She remembered Our Lady and invoked her softly. The two clerks prodded her here and there for a long time—but all for nothing. For they could find nothing to reproach her with. They returned to the bishop to tell him. "It was crazy to search her," they said. "She is slimmer and smoother than a girl ten years old. Women are such slanderers and want you to believe such tall stories that no honest man should believe them."

The bishop was not pleased when he heard his two clerks speak in this manner, for he believed that they had been bribed and had pocketed a large sum. "Dear sirs," he said, "I believe your eyes, but I believe my own eyes by half more. I want to see her myself. My eyes will tell me the truth." The bishop came to the abbess who did not stop to pray to God for advice. He insulted and attacked her very much and swore that right away she should be undressed once more. While the lady was undressing, her heart's fountain moistened and dampened her face. She was so ashamed she did not know what to do. When she had taken off all her clothes and the bishop saw her sides and her stomach all slim and smooth, he was overcome by great pity for her and fell down by her feet, crying. "My lady," the bishop said, "I have been badly tricked and deceived. In the name of the noble Lord who does not lie, I beg you to have mercy on me. My heart was all sullied and blackened when on bad advice I defamed you whom I loved so much." Crying, he asked for her mercy. The abbess humbled herself before the bishop and quickly kneeled down. Sighing, she said to him: "Get up, dear sir, I forgive you everything and may God do so as well by His sweetness and mercy." They kissed each other.

The bishop was determined to make trouble for and punish those who had put forward and maintained this matter. He could feel no joy until he had cleared up this affair. He returned to the chapter house. To shame them, he wanted to throw out of the abbey all the women who had done this. But the abbess quickly drew the bishop aside, fell to his feet, and in tears told him how Our Lady had delivered and protected her. It was much better to tell him the entire story than to see her nuns unhappy or wandering as poor beggars from abbey to abbey. In praise of Our Lady the saintly woman told him everything. While listening to this miracle the bishop often crossed himself and marveled. He cried and sighed so tenderly that he could hardly utter a word. With clasped hands he thanked God and my lady, Holy Mary.

He took the two clerks to the side and sent them quickly to the saintly hermit at the hermitage. Both of them saw the child that Our Lady had sent there. The saintly hermit was very happy that God had revealed the story. He told them openly that Our Lady protected the child. She who is the guardian of all good told him to keep him until the age of seven. He was so beautiful that no one could get tired of looking at him. When the bishop heard these news he found them most pleasant and good.

When the child was seven years old he had him fetched and had him educated in letters. He was very solicitous of the child for he was so gracious, so amiable, and so friendly that everyone loved him. In a very short time he learned so much that he became very learned and much valued. When the noble man felt his end approaching, he remembered the child and succeeded in having him elected bishop. During his lifetime he was a most saintly man and did a lot of good for his bishopric. From deep in his heart and soul he honored Our Lady and served and exalted her. And when God decreed that he should leave this life he died a saintly and glorious death.

Our Lady is truly marvelous: God help me, she thought up such a sweet miracle that no one could have invented it. Who would have dared to think that a woman could have a child without it leaving a visible trace? Or who would have dared to think that one could deliver a woman without tearing or hurting her flesh? God's mother handled this matter skillfully. The sweet lady did not want to begin something without finishing it. She reconciled the abbess who had sinned with her sweet Son. God's mother arranged a good outcome for many a misdeed. May God grant us, whatever we may have done, that we never sin against her. May His sweet mother make us so good that we can see His face in paradise.

(2.) Of a Jewish child who converted to the Christian faith.[3]

Now listen to the marvelous story about an evil Jewish glazier in Bourges that I found in my book. You have not heard a story like this for a long time.

Gautier de Coincy, *Miracles of the Virgin Mary*

A Jew had a little boy, more intelligent and more beautiful than all the other little Jews. Because he was so pleasant and pretty, he was the favorite of all the students in the city who held him very dear. He often went to their school. But his father often beat his soft and tender flesh because he enjoyed himself with them. He spent so much time with them that, as it please God, when one Easter a group of them went to receive Communion in a church, he did likewise. There was a statue above the altar, very beautifully made, which had a veil on its head and in front of it held a baby. The little Jew approached and looked at it intently for he found it most beautiful. His heart clearly told him that never before had he seen anything as beautiful. In his heart it seemed to him that the statue came forward instead of the priest. She took the host that had been consecrated by the priest from the altar and gave him Communion with such sweetness that his heart was all filled with it. He went back home, his face shining with joy.

When his father saw him so beautiful he ran toward him and embraced him. He kissed him on the mouth, his forehead, and his face. "Where does this beauty come from?" he asked him. "Dear father," said the little Jew (for he was a child who could not lie), " I come from Communion with the students from the school." But before he could finish his sentence his father threw him to the ground and almost killed him. Full of ill will and fury, he began to speak to the little Jew: "You fell into an evil trap! In order to spite the Christians and to dishonor their religion, I will do something extraordinary to you." In his fury he grabbed the child by the hair and though he struggled he dragged him to the furnace where he made his glass. Then he threw him into the furnace which was full of live coals. And so that the child would be engulfed more quickly, this dog ran to get dry wood and filled his furnace with it. The mother came running, crying and screaming, and threw her headdress on the ground. Clapping her hands and tearing at her hair she ran into the street. "Help, help!" she cried. "Come quickly to this monster!" In a very short time there was a crowd, more than ten thousand people; the whole city was assembled. They created a great uproar and made a lot of noise. They rushed to the huge brazier and extinguished the fire in the furnace. They found the child on the live coals stretched out as happily as if he were lying in a beautiful bed. His hair and clothes showed no sign of burning. All those who saw the child gave thanks to Jesus Christ with loud voices and great cries. They quickly grabbed the furious dog and after beating him threw him into the furnace. The fire revived immediately.

After the father had been grilled and burned completely, the crowd gathered around the child. They asked him sweetly how it was possible that he was not completely burned and consumed in this great fire. Everyone, whether wise or stupid, was astonished. "By my faith," he said, "the beautiful statue who smiled at me this morning when I was taking Communion accompanied me into the furnace. Right away I fell asleep and was all at ease. And it seems to me that she covered me with the veil that she wears on the altar.

Then I felt neither the fire nor the smoke but slept on the live coals so well that I still feel all refreshed." Everyone cried with pity and was thankful and prayed with joined hands to the beautiful lady who through her sweetness had saved him from the live coals and the flames.

They gave the child to a priest who baptized him with great joy. His mother had herself baptized after him in the name of the Holy Trinity. Many Jews in the city converted to our faith after having seen this miracle. All their life they served God and Our Lady, Holy Mary who deigned to perform this miracle in order to bring them to the true faith. She showed them well that all the Jews were blind who did not believe that she was the flowering virgin of whom God spoke through Isaiah.[4] The young lady showed them well that she was the virgin in whom Jesus Christ assumed flesh and blood. But until the coming of the Antichrist they will not believe the prophecy, no matter what one tells them: they have persisted for too long in their error! They are so hardened that they are harder than hard stone. Certainly, those highly placed people who tolerate them will not last much longer. May Our Lady not tolerate those who accept them, nor may her sweet Son tolerate them. To tolerate them is too hard! I am so hard toward them that, if I were king, I would make it a rule not to tolerate that a single one of them endured.[5]

(3.) Of a child who put a ring on the finger of a statue.[6]

Be quiet, good people! I want to tell you a beautiful miracle to exhort the sinners to fulfill their promises to God. Those who make promises to God and His sweet mother and do not keep them are evil debtors who seek their death and go crazy.

My book where I find my subject matter says that some people put a statue in front of a church they were renovating. Passersby put their offerings at the foot of the statue. The young people often gathered on this square in order to play ball and chase each other around. One day there was a big crowd of students playing ball in front of the portals of the church where the statue was standing. One of the students, who was very good-looking, had on his finger a ring that his girlfriend had given him. He was crazy with love and he absolutely did not want the ring that belonged to his girlfriend be lost or broken. He walked toward the church to put his ring in a safe place until he was done with his game. With that in mind, he looked around and saw the statue, all fresh and new. When he saw how beautiful it was he knelt down in front of it. With tears in his eyes he bowed down and greeted it. In a short span of time he changed heart completely. "My lady," he said, "from now on and my entire life I will serve you, for I have never seen, my lady, a young girl or woman who was as pleasing and beautiful to me. You are a hundred thousand times more beautiful and pleasing than the girl who gave me this ring. I had given my heart entirely to her, but for love of you I will leave her and her heart and jewels. I want to give you this beautiful ring out of pure love[7] as a promise that I will never have another girlfriend or wife than you, sweet beautiful lady."

Right away he pushed the ring onto the statue's finger which was completely straight. Immediately the statue bent its finger so strongly that no one could have removed the ring without cutting it. The young man was very much afraid and cried out in fear. All the people in the square, great and small, came running and he told them what the statue had said and done. And everyone crossed himself and marveled. Everyone commended him and advised him that he should not wait a single day before leaving the world and entering into religion in order all his life to serve God and Our Lady, Holy Mary who had shown him through her finger that he must love her and never have another girlfriend.

But he did not have enough good sense to keep his promise but put it out of his mind so that he remembered very little about it. The days passed and the student grew up and changed. His girlfriend's love blindfolded him so much that he could see nothing else. He completely forgot the mother of God. He was so fickle that he broke his promise and did not stop loving the girl to whom the ring had belonged. His heart was so set on his girlfriend that for her he abandoned Our Lady and married the girl and made her his wife. The wedding was a splendid affair for he was from the upper classes and came from an important family and lineage. At night, the bed was beautifully prepared in a handsome bedchamber. The clerk who loved the noble woman, who was very dainty and beautiful, with great intensity desired very much to lie with her in order to assuage his great desire. But as soon as he got to bed he forgot all about his pleasure and went to sleep without doing anything. The sweet and noble lady, who was sweeter than flowing honey, suddenly appeared to him. It seemed to the clerk that Our Lady was lying between him and his wife. She showed him the finger with the ring which suited her to perfection for her finger was smooth and straight. "You have not acted in the right way," she said. "You were unfaithful to me. You treated me very badly. Here is your girlfriend's ring which you gave me out of pure love, saying that I was a hundred thousand times more beautiful and pleasing to you than any girl you could think of. You would have had a loyal friend in me had you not left me. You leave the rose for the nettle, and the brier for the elder tree.[8] Miserable man, you are so deceived that you leave the fruit for the leaf, the eel for the lamprey. For poison and gall you abandon the sweet flow of honey."

The clerk, amazed by this vision, woke up. He was completely stupefied. He thought the statue was lying beside him. He touched the bed around him but he found nothing. Then he felt he had been fooled because he had not lain with his wife. But again he did not succeed and fell asleep. The mother of God quickly appeared to him again; she was furious. She appeared very proud to him, frightening, fierce, and disdainful. It seemed to the clerk that she did not deign to turn her face in his direction; rather it seemed that she hated him, she insulted and threatened him and told him all sorts of shameful and insulting things. Several times she called him false perjurer, faithless, and a traitor. "The demons possessed and blinded you," said Our Lady, "when for your miserable wife you renounced and repudiated me. If you fill yourself with the stinking stink of this stinking woman you will find yourself stinking at the bottom of Hell."[9] The clerk got up, completely flabbergasted. He knew very well that he was dead and lost because he had angered Our Lady. He knew that if he touched his wife just a little bit he would perish and die. "Counsel me, Holy Spirit," said the clerk in tears, "for if I go on I will instantly be lost." He jumped from the bed without waiting any longer. Inspired by the holy lady, he woke up no one and fled to a hermitage where he took a monk's habit. All his life he served God and my lady Holy Mary. He did not want to remain in the world any longer and went to live with his girl friend, the one on whose finger he had slipped the ring out of love, as a pure lover. He left the world in order to marry Mary. The monks and clerks who marry my lady Holy Mary are very nobly married, but those who marry Marion are very badly married.[10] Through the Marions they married are their souls badly married. For God's sake let us not marry badly! Let us leave the Marottes and Marions in order to marry Mary who marries her husband in heaven.

(4.) Of a nun who wanted to sin but Our Lady saved her.[11]

My book tells me a beautiful and pious miracle, delightful to listen to, of a beautiful nun. I found in this book that there once was an abbey where a noble group of ladies lived and among them were many saintly women. One of them was a girl of very good family who was extremely religious. She served the sweet glorious lady with great devotion. The devil was extremely angry at her religious feelings. He lay in wait for her, until one day she went to visit some friends to entertain herself. A nobleman from the region began to love her ardently because of her beauty and was so crazily in love that he almost lost his mind. The devil who encourages such sentiments made him give such presents and made him beg her so much that eventually her reticent heart began to yield. He begged her through his messengers and besieged her with such handsome presents that the only thing missing was opportunity. Things got to such a point that they agreed on and named a day when he would secretly come and get her to take her to his lands and marry her and make her his beloved and his lady.

The nobleman did not forget the day that his beloved had named and she did not forget it either. Around midnight, when the painful and bitter hour was approaching, when she would abandon God and father and mother for vanity and sensuality, she happened to fall asleep. Right away it seemed to her that two demons, blacker than blackberries, took her away at great speed and left her all alone at a great pit which had such a hideous, horrible, dark, gloomy, deep, huge, and perilous opening that it seemed—and I am not lying—that it meant to swallow up the whole world. This pit, this hole, this abyss stank a thousand times more than sulfur. Such stink came from it that all the air was polluted and so much smoke issued from it that daylight lost its brightness. She was very frightened and distressed, fearing that she was going to fall into the pit and disappear. The pit stank so much and troubled her so much that her heart was about to break. She heard the toads croak which were fat and swollen like pigs. There was a lot of vermin inside: serpents with sharp teeth, huge lizards, and large vipers. Those who had committed stinking crimes were thrown into this pit where they were stung, bitten, and gnawed by this vermin. There was a lot of gnashing of teeth and wringing of hands. From time to time she heard a scream, a great lamentation, and a howl so horrible and atrocious that she almost went crazy. Then she saw devils and demons, extremely horrible and ugly, come running from all sides. They were dragging and hauling souls in great affliction and hurling them without delay into this pit and abyss. Suddenly she thought that all the devils were running in her direction. They wanted to drag her into this pit but she began to scream and cry for help: "Help! Help! Sweet Lady, Holy Mary!"

While she was screaming in this manner she noticed in the distance a lady who resembled Our Lady, but she looked so proud, it seemed to her, that she would not condescend to look in her direction, and she seemed so far away to her and made such slow progress that she did not appear to want to help her. Nonetheless she screamed as loudly as she could: "Noble Virgin, help, help!" When she had pleaded long enough Our Lady came closer to the pit which contained such a disgusting bath and said to her: "Who are you that you call me so loudly?" "Oh, mother of the noble king who never lies," she answered in tears, "I am your nun and your virgin who has served you so many times. Sweet Lady, Holy Mary, I am the unhappy and suffering one who was never slow in serving you. Sweet and noble queen, without the help of your great sweetness this huge pit will swallow me up, if you do not have pity on me. All these devils here will drag me into the pit and will let me fall into it. Noble lady, noble Virgin, help your poor servant who belongs to you in body and soul." "Leave me alone," said Our Lady. "You are neither my servant nor my friend. Why don't you ask for help from the man for whom you have abandoned me? I don't have to defend you, he does! For you are no longer mine but his. Let him come to you and help you. May he, for whom you have left me and my son, come and get you out of this danger!"

When the nun heard this, it seemed to her that the devils all together dragged her into this horrible pit, but Our Lady right away blocked the opening of the pit and said to her: "I cannot allow you to perish in this pit for you have served me so much." She stretched out her hand toward her without delay and pulled her away from the abyss. All the devils fled at the sight of the mother of God. "Dear friend," said Our Lady, "if you want to have mercy on your soul, stay away from vanity and lewdness. Those people make their bed in hellfire who give in to their desires and delight in their foul flesh. Keep the man away from you who wanted to estrange you from God. You wanted to make your bed in the fires of hell when you wanted to cheat on my son to whom you were consecrated. Out of love for Him you have to remain pure and chaste. I showed you well what happens to people who indulge in lewdness. Dear daughter," said Our Lady, "sensuality takes over body and soul: it debases the body and kills the soul. But chastity makes body and soul purer than fine gold. Chastity is of such a nature that it cleans the body and purifies the soul; it honors the body and exalts the soul and lifts it up so much that it sends it straight to paradise. Chastity is the straight path, the straight way, the right address that sends the chaste to heaven."

At this moment that lady woke up, marveling at the miracle she had seen. Without delay the messengers arrived whom her friend had sent to her secretly. "Go away! Go away! Enemies of God!" she cried. "I do not want to have any other friend or husband than the King of Kings who is called God. He is my beloved and my husband; I do not ever wish to have another husband. My heart relies on Him. Go away from here! Go away! Go away! You are the devil's messengers who wanted to take me away from my beloved by guile." She made them so ashamed and refused so adamantly that they returned to their lord. He was furious, his heart bitter and confused.

The nun arranged to return to her cloister. From then on she never wavered. She realized that she could not frequently leave her abbey and amuse herself with her friends without the devil trying to trip her up. The devil knows so many tricks that he quickly would have caused her to have a falling-out with the one who put the ring on her finger. Oh, God! how careful must a woman be who has such a noble Lord. She should not abandon herself to any baron or prince of this world, however many gifts he may give her. I am saying this because the wives and servants of the noble Lord, of the noble spouse who knows all their thoughts without taking their pulse, are not always acting as they should. Certainly, if they reflect well on all this, they must devote all their heart and thoughts to this spouse, for He sees all their thoughts before their hearts have even thought them. The woman who thinks of such a spouse can not lose.

(5.) Of two women whom Our Lady converted.[12]

Since you would like to listen, in order to entertain you I will tell a miracle and a marvel which makes my heart cross itself and be astonished. I found in my book that there were two ladies who violently hated one another. The one felt toward the other such hostility that she would gladly have strangled her, for the second one had robbed the first one of her husband. It is therefore not surprising that she was full of resentment, for a woman feels great sadness when someone takes her husband away from her. But she would rather have torn out one of her teeth than to say or do anything, for her lord was so cruel, so depraved and evil that he would instantly have killed her. With his glance he had subdued her so cruelly that she was not bold enough to do anything against his mistress. She was so ashamed and angered that she did not dare do anything.

On her naked knees she often prayed to Our Lady, Holy Mary that she should send shame and dishonor to the woman who had estranged her husband from her and who had taken him so completely from her that she could not get any pleasure from him. Thus the unhappy woman implored Our Lady many times. She was overwhelmed by anger and prayed so long that one day Our Lady appeared to her. "Tell me," she said, "are you crazy to ask me all day long for vengeance against the unhappy woman who has placed all her hopes in me? She serves me so dutifully that I could do her no harm. She pronounces her sweet greetings to me with such a sincere heart that I could under no circumstances permit that she should be dishonored." When Our Lady thus failed her she did not know what should become of her. Her heart was so full of burning fury that she did not know what to do or say.

One day, while she was in this state of fury, she met the woman she hated so deeply. In her anger and craziness she addressed her most cruelly: "Tell me! Tell me! Tell me, you tramp, how do you dare meet me? How do you dare be in the same place as I am? If it were not for God, I would strangle and kill you with my two hands. My heart is so hurt and wounded, it is so afire with burning fury that there is no one who could tell how ardently I hate you, for you make the man who used to love and cherish me beat and strike me. Certainly, the old disloyal man used to be sweet and faithful toward me, but you have so enchanted him and made him so angry at me that he no longer loves or esteems me. Rather, he beats me up and breaks me when I dare to say a single word. I'm not lying when I say that I am sadder than any other unhappy woman. I had hoped that Our Lady, to whom I appealed as sweetly as I could, would take vengeance on you. But I have no more hope, for she told me recently that however you may manage your affairs, she will not let anything bad happen to you because you so often salute her sweetly and diligently. This makes me so furious that I'm just about ready to renounce God." "So help me God! What am I hearing?" said her beautiful friend. Throwing herself at her feet, she implored her sweetly, with hot tears running down her face, to tell her truly whether what she had said was true. The wife swore on the Holy Spirit and on everything she could think of to assure her that everything was true and she should not doubt her. She cried and sighed so tenderly that she could hardly pronounce a single word. Right away and with her face moist and tearful she swore to her that she would with the help of God and Our Lady never again steal hers or any other woman's husband, but would live so chastely that she would keep company with no man as long as she lived. Straight away, she vowed chastity to Our Lady and she kept her vow and extinguished the fire of vanity and lewdness in herself so well that she no longer had any desire for these vices. The other lady likewise devoutly served the Creator's mother. Having asked forgiveness from each other, they kissed and embraced and made peace. As long as they lived they loved one another and led a good life.

Thus the lady who always brings peace and harmony imposed her peace on them. The devil ties his ropes around those men and women who do not honor or serve Our Lady who day and night leads so many sinners back on the straight path. Whoever does not honor her has a crazed soul! There is no woman, however crazy she may be, whom Our Lady, if she serves her well, will not bring back from her folly. There is no man, however sinful, evil, and lecherous he may be, that she will not force to do good things, if he turns to her service. There is no one, however crazy, who will not turn into an honorable person before he dies, if he serves her well. God's mother has the power to save whoever serves her well. Let us hurry to serve her: as long as we live—and we do not know how long that will be—let us greet her devoutly and from all our hearts. Let us kneel before her statue. There is no one so stupid and so silly that he would not be led to the haven of salvation if he moistens his lips with her savory salutation. He who does not greet her often holds his tongue too dear, for the sweet greeting pleases her very much. May God save all those who salute her. I advise everyone to make a habit of this greeting!

(6.) About a clerk who was gravely ill and whom Our Lady healed.[13]

In order to warm your hearts and so that you will love Our Lady even more, I want to tell you a miracle about a wealthy clerk who had many friends and possessions; he wanted to possess everything he could. He abandoned all restraint and gave himself over to the world. All he cared about were worldly things and he became exceedingly worldly. He could not care less about his soul but nonetheless in his heart he loved Our Lady so much that he never passed before her statue without saluting her on his knees, his head bent: neither laziness nor tiredness, nor being busy or in a rush kept him from this. After saying the twelve greetings[14] which have been so useful to so many people, he joined his hands together and knelt on the ground with great devotion and said humbly to himself: "Blessed be the holy womb that carried You, King Jesus Christ, blessed be the breasts that gave you milk. You are our Lord and Savior and the Redeemer of the whole world."

He kept up this habit for a long time until he fell so ill so that he was confined to his bed for so long that he lost his memory and his mind. Then he fell into madness, a grievous disease. He bit people like a crazy person and he would have hurt a number of them very badly had he not been taken in and bound.[15] His severe illness made him so crazy and made him rage so much that he tore his tongue with his teeth. He chewed up his lips with his teeth inside and out and he would have torn the fingers of his hands if one would have let him. His face swelled up so horribly that no one could recognize him anymore; you could no longer see his nose or his mouth. Thus he was lying in bed like a tree trunk. He was horrible to look at. He was so stinking and filled with foul matter that no one dared come and see him, for whoever falls into a disabling illness—be he ever so rich and good-looking—quickly finds that his acquaintances disappear.

The clerk was getting so much worse that he could find no relief, neither from a doctor nor from any medicine. But the lady who heals everything and has a medicine for any illness sweetly cured him. He was lying ill for so long a time that it seemed to him that an angel came near the bed where he was lying and said, crying, in a low voice and with great compassion: "My Lady, you who are the stream, fountain, and duct of all pity, how can your great sweetness permit that your clerk endures such illness? My Lady, in the olden days you were not so hard, clever, proud, and disdainful. Oh, sweet glorious Lady, what can this be that I see? Oh, mother of God! Help! Help! Please do no longer tolerate that this man, who has loved you for such a long time and prayed to you and implored you, languish like this and perish so shamefully.

Sweet Lady, Holy Mary, if your sweetness does not help him of what use was it to him that he said so many Hail Marys? Where are his beautiful lips and his tongue which always blessed your breasts, your holy sides and your holy flanks? My Lady, from whom all sweetness comes, why are you waiting for such a long time to help him? If *you* do not help your own people, my Lady, who would then help his own people? If you do not help, who will help? If you can not do it, who will? Are you not the lady of the archangels? Are you not seated above the angels to the right of Jesus Christ, the heavenly king? Are you, my Lady, not the virgin who gave milk through your breast to the king of heaven as your son? Does He not want whatever you want? Oh, sweet mother of the Savior, what are sinners going to do if their hope in you is disappointed? Do you not represent all their faith? Highest lady, highest queen, are you not the physician and medicine who heals and cures all illnesses? How can you take care of anyone else if you do not have pity on this one? If you do not show friendship toward him who so many times knelt before your statue with a devoted heart, what will you show toward others? Oh, mother of God, it never happened that the sweetness that suffuses you does not flow out toward the sinners. There is no sinner who, if he loves you sincerely, does not receive help if he begs for it. You look at him with sweetness. I am his guardian angel: if it is possible, I do not want him to end his life in this way." When the angel had said this the Virgin descended on his bed and she was so comely and so beautiful that no one could describe her. And she was so generous that she said very sweetly: "Dear sweet friend, I am bringing you what you have waited for such a long time. You honored my holy womb so many times and blessed it so often that it is only right—if any friendship resides within me—that I should have pity on you." Very sweetly and with great delight she pulled out her breast which is so sweet, mild, and beautiful. She put it into his mouth, and she touched him everywhere and moistened him with her milk. Then she left, leaving him asleep.

Right away he woke up and was very much astonished when he saw that everything was over. He found himself more sprightly than he had been before. It would take me an entire day to recount the great joy and the giving of grace and praise celebrated by his friends and by strangers. The clerk turned away from the world and changed his way of life. Now the only prowess that interested him was to do good works. From then on he led a very saintly life. He loved Our Lady Holy Mary with such a loving heart that for her love he abandoned everything else. To be closer to her, he gladly left his former acquaintances. Whoever has her acquaintance should stick to her and abandon all bad acquaintances. Never will he who is acquainted with her not be close to God. No other acquaintance is so beautiful.

(7.) Of an abbot who was on a sea voyage.[16]

Listen well, all clerks and lay people! I want to tell you without delay a miracle that she whom we should love so much performed in the sea. There were some people—I do not know where they were going—who were passing on the sea before Brittany. At that moment, it was around midnight, a storm began that troubled and frightened them so much that they were sure they'd perish instantly. They were neither calm nor composed when they saw death before their eyes, but they all screamed, one more than the next, and implored their saints when they saw how the sea was battering them. Some screamed: "What shall we do? May St. Nicholas help us!" The others wailed loudly and clearly to implore St. Clarus. Others called to St. Andrew that he may come and help them in their predicament. Everyone implored and called to the saint whom he trusted most and loved best.[17] They made vows and promised pilgrimages should they be delivered from this great peril.

In this ship there was an abbot, a valorous and wise man. He screamed at them with tears in his eyes: "Woe! Woe! Dear people, what do I see? You are doing the right thing, but believe me, you would do better by half if you loudly called on My Lady, Holy Mary and commended your troubles to her. For no saint can bring you such great or quick help. No storm or wind or tempest can rage for any length of time in a place where she is named. Therefore you should name her first, and then the other saints. You should implore her on the sea for she is the star of the sea."[18]

Instantly no man or woman failed to implore the sweet lady. Loudly everyone exclaimed: "Highest Lady, Holy Mary, have pity on us in our misery! Our Lady, you who are the sweet mother of Him who governs everything, by your sweetness, generosity, pity, and power please help these wretched people who are perishing and being tormented right away." While they were thus crying and lamenting, the abbot who was so frightened and tormented by all the suffering that in two entire days he had eaten nothing but an apple, got back his courage and began to chant loudly together with his companions the *Felix namque*, the sweet response that we chant in memory of the glorious sweet lady.[19] As soon as they had pronounced the verses everyone saw with his own eyes how a big candle appeared and descended from paradise. Beautifully and gently it came to rest on the ship's mast. It illuminated the entire ship and instantly their suffering ceased. The sea, which had been so churned up, so stormy and swelling that it seemed that every wave was going to drown the entire world, became quiet so quickly that it seemed that it dared not even to produce a wave.

This is the lady you should love and pray to. She is the lady of the air and of the sea. She is the lady here, and she is the lady there. You should know the truth that no one who calls on her from his heart will fail to be delivered from adversity. The people from the ship felt great joy over the miracle Our Lady had performed for them. There was no man or woman on the ship who did not give thanks to her, with joined hands and wet faces. Whoever is helped by her is truly helped. Whoever asks for her help from a good heart will never lack for her help. The mother of God helped them sail so far that they joyfully arrived in their port. The good abbot did not forget Our Lady, Holy Mary but served her his entire life with a good heart and good sense, and he had this miracle written down which you have just heard me tell.

Oh, mother of the King who created everything, no heart ever prayed to you that you would turn a deaf ear to. My Lady, you perform so many marvels that you amaze the entire world. Your great sweetness exhorts us to serve you, pure virgin. You are the star who governs and guides the world day and night. Sweet Lady, Holy Mary, it is so sweet to call to you! Those who were drowning in the sea called to St. Andrew and St. Nicholas until they were exhausted. They screamed for St. Clarus, but I am not sure he hears very well, for this time he certainly did not hear anything. Powerful virgin, there is no doubt that you can help people more than they could even wish for. My Lady, St. Clarus and St. Thomas,[20] St. Andrew, and St. Nicholas should not be ashamed if your power surpasses theirs. Their power comes from yours. They would not even dare to look at paradise if you were not there and unlocked and opened the door for them. Eve had closed it so firmly that all of them together would not have succeeded in entering it. If your miracles surpass theirs and if you hear more clearly than they do, this means no shame or reproach for them, for you are the lady of all of them. All your miracles must be quicker, more elevated, and better than theirs, for all their miracles derive from yours: for this they give grace to you. There is no saint, however great his reputation may be, who does anything but through you.

You are so great that you can do all alone what they could and cannot do, all those who existed and exist today. But you are so filled with grace, goodness, and pity that you help them to achieve what they cannot do by themselves. Through you they perform all their exploits. You are more daring than St. Christopher, who was tall, bold and courageous,[21] for many times you ask from God what all of them together do not dare ask. They often take a rest when you do all their work. You are the one who takes care of everything, who thinks about everything, you are the one who through your sweetness cleans away from the world all offenses and misdeeds. You are milder and sweeter than anyone else. My Lady, one should rather call on you than on any saintly man or woman and more than anyone else it is right that you should be loved.

Most supreme virgin, he who calls on the saints and honors and names them does very well. But by rights, sweet lady, one should name you first and serve and implore you, for from your hands comes all the good that comes to us from them. Highest, purest virgin, the sweetness that flows from you submerges us through them. Sweetest Lady, there is no doubt that we should serve them sweetly in order to deserve their help. We must honor them on this earth, and pray to them and implore them that they should come to our aid and they should sweetly pray to you for us that in this bitter sea which is the world—which is so huge and deep and where there are so many storms—you do not let us perish, for our ship is so shaky that many people fall out of it. Sweet Lady, Holy Mary, our ship is so threadbare that it is about to break and sink. The sea of this world has such strong waves which attack us that they constantly burst into our ship. Lady, you who are the star of the sea, put your wind into our sails, that it may guide and carry us to the great shore and haven of paradise where all those are enjoying themselves who honor you. Nobody honors you that you do not carry him to the King whom you carried in your womb. There is much pleasure in serving you, for you are heaven's window and door. The one who was carried there to enjoy himself was very lucky!

(8.) Of a woman who was healed in Arras.[22]

My book tells us that in the rich city of Arras[23] there once lived a very sweet and simple girl. As it pleased God, one day she went into her father's garden all alone, without company. Our Lady Holy Mary, the sweet mother of Jesus Christ, wished to appear to the girl and she was so glorious and so beautiful that I do not know how to tell about it. The little girl was very much afraid and was so astonished that she did not know whether she was asleep or awake. The lily, the fresh rose who contains all courtesy, who truly loves true simplicity, spoke to the simple girl: "Dear friend, dear little girl, do you know who I am and what my name is?" She answered, trembling: "No, I don't know you, my sweet Lady." Thereupon the clear jewel said to her: "Dear little girl, dear friend, I am the mother of God, Mary." When the other heard this pleasing name, she sighed and stretched out her hands toward her and bowed down before her. When she was a little more reassured she spoke to her very simply: "Ah, beautiful mother of God, how is it possible that you condescend to appear to such an ordinary girl?" "Dear girl," said Our Lady, "it is because I wish to benefit your soul, this is why I appeared to you. I have come because I want you to be one of my virgins and one of my servants. If you want to follow my commandment I admonish and command you to be pure as a rose and to preserve above all other things your virginity. Avoid false love and vanity and flee this world. If you want to be truly clean and pure and serve me purely, keep your body so clean that you will never agree to having a husband or touching a man. Thus you will be one of my servants, one of my virgins." Our Lady, Holy Mary then left her and the girl for her part left as well, filled with joy, and returned to the house.

In her heart and mind she hid this event so well that she never revealed it to anyone. From then on she lived such a simple life that everyone was astonished. But when she reached marriageable age, a handsome and noble young man asked her friends and family for her hand. Her friends, who thought this marriage a very good thing, quickly consented to it. The girl did not want to consent, for as long as she lived she did not want to touch or know a man. But her father and mother thought her refusal crazy and cowardly. Her father beat her cruelly and her mother mistreated her badly. The girl who was very much afraid finally told them about the vision she had had. But the father did not believe her and ridiculed her vision. He deprived and tormented her so much that she was forced against her will to marry the young man.

As the marriage approached she began to feel pain and she lamented in her heart: "Oh, mother of God, pure virgin," said the unhappy woman, "help your servant. If no help issues from you I will find the whole world deaf toward me. I cannot find anyone to give me advice. Everyone beats me, everyone assaults me, everyone brutalizes me and makes me feel like a stupid girl. Sweet Lady, Holy Mary, I am in such pain and feel so lost that I do not know what to say or do. High and noble queen, pitiful lady, pious virgin, if I do not get your help my chastity will be violated and my soul dead and lost." In this way the suffering woman complained and lamented bitterly. If Our Lady does not remember her she sees well that she will be forced to break her holy commandment.

Here we have to speak a little too openly, but I can not do otherwise if I want to tell you the miracle as my book shows it to me. If chaste ears are too astonished at the marvels they are going to hear, I pray to reason that she will defend me for I have to tell things in such a way that people will understand me. The text indicates, it seems to me, that the first night they were alone together in a beautiful bed the husband wanted to enjoy her as one enjoys a wife. But Our Lady, to whom she called from her sweet heart, protected her so that he could not vanquish her by any means. Whatever her husband tried to do to her chastity was not tainted, for her heart did not consent and so her body was not sullied. And finally, when the poor woman was lying there in a faint, he could still not fulfill his desire. He felt so ashamed and so thwarted that he was going almost crazy with rage. He found the passage so narrow that he could not breach it despite all his fighting. This struggle lasted a good half year. Every evening at nightfall he came back to the struggle with renewed force, but the door was so tightly closed and locked that there was no way for him to enter.

One night he felt his desire so hotly that, spurred on by the devil, the scoundrel, the murderer, took a knife and in order to cool his great ardor he stuck the knife into nature's door so violently that she almost lost her entrails through the door of her jewel. Blood flowed from her everywhere. He wounded her so mortally that as long as he lives he will never be able to sleep with her. Soon the bed was as bloody as if an oxen had been killed there. The poor woman screamed and cried. She complained to Our Lady Holy Mary, she was filled with pain and lamented pitifully. Her wound was so painful that she did not know what to do or say. She could never find a physician—however, skillful he may be—that could help her. Her pain, anxiety, and rage were such that she could not leave her bed but remained there by necessity. She bitterly complained to Our Lady; she begged her to think of her soul, for her poor body was gone.

At the time there lived a bishop in Arras who had a great reputation; his name was Aloysius. The poor woman succeeded in having herself carried to him. Like a half-dead woman she confessed to him and told him about the vision she had had in her childhood, and then she told him everything that she had done and that had happened to her. When the bishop saw that her intentions were so pure and reasonable his heart almost began to bleed. He had such great compassion for the terrible tribulations he saw the poor woman endure that right away he wanted to punish her husband severely and immediately divorce them. But he reflected that the man who kept her as his wife would be able to take care of her better than a stranger, by reason and by law. The bishop took great care to comfort her as best he could. He exhorted the husband to learn to be her brother for the love of the heavenly King, for he could no longer be her husband. And if she lacked something that she could not provide for herself, he, the bishop, would make sure she would get it, every single day of her life. Thus the bishop comforted her. She was carried back to her house but the woman was in excruciating pain and her wound got worse day and night. She lived for such a long time in this misery that it would be tedious to tell about it.

While the poor woman languished and could not leave her bed it pleased the highest Judge—who always judges wisely and sometimes mysteriously—that in the whole region of the Artois the fire from hell[24] erupted and it spread so violently to so many men and women that I do not know how to tell you about the suffering, the screaming, and crying in the entire region. If the merciful Father of Glory had not sent at the time a saintly woman as physician to heal His Christian people in the rich city of Arras truly everyone would have been burned, clerks and lay people all together. The text indicates that at that point the sweet King and Father gave such power to His sweet and mild mother that in everyone who came to see her in her beautiful church in Arras the painful burning was immediately extinguished on the condition that they showed contrition and repentance for their sins.

This hellish fire gripped the breast of the poor woman of whom I have been telling you so cruelly that she had herself quickly carried to the church of Our Lady. The longer she stayed there the worse her pain became. Hell's fire so attacked her that soon her entire breast would be burned. The disease hit her so badly that the burning fire burned nine big holes into her, so hideous that no one dared look at her for she looked so horrible and hideous. Thus the poor woman languished for a long time in the church of the glorious lady. Her chest was falling to pieces and the fire attacked her sides. Between her teeth she prayed to the mother of God to liberate her from this life, for her life was so hard and she suffered so much from the burning that she thought that life was worse than death. But when the lady in whom all comfort resides saw that her illness was so severe that no one even dared to think that she could survive, she decided that she wanted to cure her. When she saw the pure and clean virgin whom everyone—her husband, her father, and mother—abhorred, the clear star who illuminates the world and so cures and purifies it that everyone is amazed began to act. She who does marvels amazing all of us, she who knows so well when it is necessary to watch over her friends, saw the woman's situation at a point when everyone wished for her death, and decided to help her. She took things into her hands and showed without delay her great sweetness and power.

The text tells us that one night there were so many sick people suffering from the burning disease in the church that it was tightly packed. At that point the poor woman cried out to Our Lady, Holy Mary; she lamented for a long time: "Oh, Mother of God, Holy Virgin," said the poor, miserable woman, "do not let me live any longer in such pain and martyrdom. Sweet Lady, I can say truly that there never was a creature born who was more beaten down and despised than I am. It weighs on me and makes me unhappy that my life lasts so long. Oh, sweet lady, your heart is harder than iron when you let hell's fire burn my chest and stomach. Oh, Mother of God, I am still the one you held so dear in my childhood when you appeared to me. Then you said, pure virgin, that in your sweetness you had elected me to be your servant. Did you deceive me, my Lady? And your most holy vision, was it an illusion, a lie and a phantom?" Thus the poor and suffering woman complained to Our Lady, Holy Mary and finally she lamented, screamed, and cried so much that she began to annoy all people around her, whether healthy or sick. But around midnight she was forced to be quiet for she could no longer move her tongue. She was so weak and so afflicted that nothing remained in her save her spirit. The poor woman closed her eyes and commended her body and soul to divine mercy.

Our text tells us that once the poor woman was asleep she saw the church so illuminated that she thought a thousand stars and a thousand candles and torches were burning in it. When her heart was all filled with the great shining light she saw a great lady and queen come down from heaven. She was so light, pure, fine, and so pleasantly beautiful that it seemed that her clear face illuminated the whole church better than any lamp or the sun, even at its zenith, could have done. This Lady went straight to the spot where the poor woman was lying and said to her very sweetly: "Dear friend, if you want to be cured quickly of your illness get up immediately and without delay go and stretch out before my holy altar. There you will be cured right away, provided you have faith." "Oh, mother of God," she answered, "I cannot take a single step even if one offered me all the riches of this world." The Mother of God by her sweetness and mercy quickly took her by the hand and led her up to the altar. She was so exhausted and in such pain when she arrived there that she felt she had to go sleep immediately. She fell asleep sweetly before the altar, but before long Our Lady reappeared. "You should know, dear woman," she said, "that you will be healed completely and so that your heart may believe truly and firmly that you actually spoke to me, all the people suffering from the burning disease that you will kiss tomorrow when you wake up will be cured from hell's fire."

The good woman slept soundly in front of the altar till late morning. When she woke up the entire church of Our Lady was filled with people and the poor woman felt great joy. Everyone was very astonished when they saw this woman asleep so close to the altar of Our Lady. Someone who did not know her quickly ran toward her and kicked her viciously with his foot. "Get up! Get up!" he cried, "hurry and get out of here. It was not a good idea to fall asleep here." The woman, who no longer felt any pain, jumped quickly to her feet, as lightly as if she had never felt any pain. When she felt that she was cured and that she was more lively and healthy than a fish swimming in the

Seine, she cried as loudly as she could: "Sweet Lady, Holy Mary, help! Help! Help! Help!" Everyone in the church ran toward the good woman. The poor woman embraced the altar and cried till her face was wet; she embraced and kissed the altar more than a hundred times. She was so joyful and felt so good that she did not know what to do. All the people wept with joy and right away everyone, clerks and lay people, thanked Our Lady. The woman did not forget what the glorious one had told her: she quickly went and kissed all those who suffered from the burning disease; a mass of people crowded around her. The mother of the King of truth then let flow in great waves the fountain of her pity. Here everyone can see with his own eyes the great virtue and power of the sweet mother of God. A miracle like this should not be considered child's play. The sweet mother of Jesus Christ, by her sweetness and grace, then gave such efficacy to the poor woman's kiss that in whomever she kissed—be he ever so invaded by the hell's fire, ever so burning or tortured or oppressed—the fire was immediately extinguished.

The Mother of God was working well here: the woman herself recovered her health so completely that, unless my source is lying, the burned breast was whiter and more beautiful than the other. And the nine holes which the bishop and all the people of the city knew so well, which had been so horrible that the bones could be seen through them, were healed and so closed up that no one who examined her could perceive them. The wound in her body which had been filled with worms and rot until she could no longer live was now so perfectly healed that she was healthier than ever before. A week would not be enough to tell about the great joy displayed by everyone. I don't have to dwell on how much joy and cheering there was among so many cured people. Throughout Arras the bells were rung loudly. Very sweetly and with clasped hands the bishop Aloysius thanked the queen from above. The good bishop, the good lord, had this great miracle written down and made sure it enjoyed great authority in the great city of Arras.

May the nonbelievers, those who are false and without faith, come forward if they have anything to say against this miracle, those who contradict and beat down so many miracles. They are such felons, they are such scoundrels that they stink more than mud. Their life is stinking and bitter: they stink before God and His mother and before all saints. They think the great miracles we are telling them are fables and fictions. They should be ashamed! They will be ashamed, do not doubt it, for they have as little faith as dogs. By St. Giles, they rather listen to tales or funny stories they are told (such as the one where Tardius, the little creep, read and sung three lessons above the bier of lady Coupee whose back Renart the Fox had broken),[25] than to a good sermon from the Scriptures. They ridicule and contradict those men and women who tell them good things. They think that the *Lives* of the saints are fables and fictions. May their tongues burn up! Sometimes they even contradict the miracles of Our Lady. Truly, I hate them so much that I can't even express my thoughts. Always they find something to contradict and bicker about [. . .] Sometimes some of them say that there are various miracles written down that are neither true nor authentic. What an outrage, oh God, oh God! Whoever loves such criminals, such minstrels, I have a mortal hatred for. And so do God, His sweet mother, and all her saints. Holy Mary! May God help me! There are some goliards[26] and tricksters who vilely perform every day with reliquaries and little bells and do false miracles, and because of them those who lack in faith and whom no one should believe say that the miracles of Our Lady are also false and invented. Oh! Oh! Oh! Oh! Proven criminals! Criminals! Criminals! Criminal murderers! You are worse than someone who just committed a murder! You can't conceal anything. No one is so stupid and so silly that he does not know without a doubt that the mother of God can ask the King of Kings, who is seated above, whatever she pleases, whatever suits her. The sweetest God, the sweetest Father, performs great miracles for His mother, far and wide, and I can tell you no one could number them or write all about them. Everyone knows that the great miracles, the great deeds that Our Lady, Holy Mary performs day and night all over the world are not trumped up miracles that tricksters perform in churches, at the crossroads, and at fountains. So true and certain, so clear and light, so great and full of authority are the deeds of the pure virgin through whom God has saved the world that neither clerk nor layman should doubt them [. . .] Those people who do not love the miracles they are shown and who do not want to tell about the great miracles and deeds Our Lady is performing are of an evil nature. Everything encourages and incites us to get good people to love her and do her sweet service and to love her courtesy. Whoever is not inflamed by love for the sweet lady cares not a fig about his body or soul. The Holy Spirit loves the person who learns how to serve her, but the devil makes the person freeze who feels cold toward serving and loving her. And whoever does not serve or love her and implore her day and night can truly call himself miserable, for him heaven is cold and frozen and he is on the way to the devil. Whoever does not serve her, may God help me, cannot be on the right path. Whoever does not serve her wholeheartedly has lost the way to heaven. He believes poorly and has poor feelings if he does not agree to love her: all those who consent will go on the straight path to God. He who does not agree with this has no memory or good sense. Whoever wants to find the way to God should consent to well loving His mother.

(9.) About a monk in whose mouth were found five new roses.[27]

I wish to tell you a pretty and brief miracle about a simple monk. He was simple and simply and devoutly served God. He was not as learned as St. Anselm.[28] He said the litany and the seven Psalms[29] he had learned in childhood with good faith according to his simple understanding. He served the mother of God with great devotion and loved her dearly. On his naked knees he often implored her, all the while crying. But he was very distraught and disturbed by the fact that he could not remember the proper prayer for the glorious lady. He thought about it deeply and finally made one up according to his abilities: he took the five Psalms and put them together to form the five letters of MARIA. He was clever enough to put a Psalm to go with each letter; he did not need any other philosophy. In the name of the Virgin Mary, whom he loved very much and held very dear, he often said this prayer. Here are the names of the five Psalms: *Magnificat, Ad Dominum, Retribue servo tuo;* the fourth is *Inconvertendo, Ad te levavi* is the fifth. In honor of the sweet and holy name he said these holy Psalms as long as he lived and when it pleased God that his life should come to an end, a beautiful miracle happened: one found in his mouth five fresh roses, with bright red petals, as if they had just been cut.

This miracle clearly shows us how loving and good the mother of the glorious King is. Those who remember her every day cannot be harmed, everyone must believe this. This miracle should teach us that we should strive to serve her, for she rewards us greatly. I exhort all learned people to say the five Psalms I mentioned, which are signified by the five roses, at least one a day, on their knees and with clasped hands before the statue of the Virgin who gave milk from her breast and thus nourished her Father and her Son. He who serves His Mother well serves God. No one can earn her love except by serving her. Those who serve her well earn rich rewards. They deserve joy eternal, those who serve her. May God grant that we all may serve her so that we deserve her sweet love.

Notes

1. Source: V. Frederic Koenig, *Gautier de Coinci, Les Miracles de Nostre Dame*, 4 vols. (Geneva, 1955–70), 2:181–96.

2. Marriage here means her marriage to Christ, that is, becoming a nun.

3. Source: Koenig, *Gautier de Coinci*, 2:95–100. For a study of the history of this miracle see Gilbert Dahan, "Les juifs dans les Miracles de Gautier de Coincy," *Archives Juives*, 16 (1980): 41–49, 59–63.

4. This is probably a reference to Is 7:14: "Therefore the Lord himself will give you a sign. Behold, a young woman shall conceive and bear a son and shall call his name Immanuel."

5. Gautier uses one of his preferred techniques here: a wordplay on one term. Here he uses French *dur* (hard) and *endurer* (to tolerate or endure). For French policy regarding the Jews at this time see William Chester Jordan, *The French Monarchy and the Jews: From Philip Augustus to the Last Capetians* (Philadelphia, 1989).

6. Source: Koenig, *Gautier de Coinci*, 2:197–204. The story of the ring on the statue originated in Roman times when the statue was that of the goddess of love, Venus. William of Malmesbury in the twelfth century was the first to substitute the Virgin Mary for Venus. See Ebel, *Das altromanische Mirakel*, pp. 40–46.

7. Gautier uses the term *fine amor* here (line 55), expressing the concept of courtly love.

8. This is the tree Judas hanged himself from.

9. This is a rather nonladylike word game on French *puer* (to stink), *puante* (stinking) and so forth. Variations of the word are mentioned nine times.

10. Old French "Marion" is a generic name for a simple girl. "Marotte" is the diminutive of Marion.

11. Source: Koenig, *Gautier de Coinci*, 2:246–54.

12. Source: Koenig, *Gautier de Coinci*, 3:35–41.

13. Source: Koenig, *Gautier de Coinci*, 2:122–29.

14. The twelve greetings correspond to the greetings the angel Gabriel and Elizabeth addressed to the Virgin Mary (see Lk 1: 26–45). They were later transformed into the prayer "Hail Mary."

15. On the symptoms and treatment of madness in the Middle Ages, see Muriel Laharie, *La Folie au moyen âge, XIe-XIIIe siècles* (Paris, 1991).

16. Source: Koenig, *Gautier de Coinci*, 3:51–59.

17. St. Nicholas was one of the most popular saints of the Middle Ages. His cult began in the sixth century, and in the eleventh century he began to be venerated in Normandy, near where this miracle story takes place. One of his specialties was to help people in storms at sea. St. Clarus was bishop of Nantes in Brittany in the fourth century. St. Andrew was one of Christ's apostles. His cross (in the shape of an X) was believed to protect against lightning.

18. The Latin term *Stella maris* (star of the sea) was frequently used to designate the Virgin Mary. John of Garland's text listed in the bibliography has this term as its title. On the significance of this designation see Marina Warner, *Alone of All Her Sex: The Myth and the Cult of the Virgin Mary* (New York, 1976), pp. 262–64.

19. *Felix namque* (for happy is he who) was a response (in Latin, *responsorium*), one part of a chant where chorus and solo voice alternated.

20. St. Thomas was one of Christ's apostles.

21. St. Christopher transported the child Jesus safely across dangerous waters. He was often depicted as a giant.

22. Source: Koenig, *Gautier de Coinci*, 4:295–320. On this miracle see Renate Blumenfeld-Kosinski, "Sexual and Textual Violence in the 'Femme d'Arras' Miracle by Gautier de Coincy" (in *Translatio Studii: Essays in Honor of Karl D. Uitti*, eds. Renate Blumenfeld-Kosinski, Kevin Brownlee, Mary Speer, and Lori Walters [Amsterdam, 1998, pp. 51–64]).

23. Arras, in northwestern France, was a rich city famous for its commerce. It was best known for its textile industry.

24. "Hell's fire," also known as "St. Anthony's fire," is the disease of ergotism, caused by the ingestion of fungus-infected rye. See Mary Kilbourne Matossian, *Poisons of the Past: Molds, Epidemics, and History* (New Haven, 1989), especially pp. 55–58.

25. This is a reference to a minstrel performing the *Roman de Renart* (Renart the Fox), a thirteenth-century satirical romance. The line here is directly borrowed from the romance. (*Le Roman de Renart*, ed. Hermann Breuer [Halle, 1929], branch M, vol. 6, p. 318).

26. The goliards were wandering poets, minstrels, and scholars, a group of whom Gautier did not approve.

27. Source: Koenig, *Gautier de Coinci*, 2:224–26.

28. St. Anselm of Canterbury (1033/34–1109) was elected prior (1063) and then abbot (1078) at Bec in Normandy. Later (1093–1109) he served as archbishop of Canterbury. He was one of the great teachers of his time, favoring a rational approach to theology.

29. The French term for "litany" is *miserle*. (It can also mean "complaint.") A litany is a form of prayer, often of a penitential character. The seven Psalms are the seven penitential Psalms. They are Psalms 6, 32, 38, 51, 102, 130, and 143. For a history of the assemblage and the meaning of these Psalms see the introduction to *Les sept psaumes allégorisés of Christine de Pisan, a Critical Edition from the Brussels and Paris Manuscripts,* ed. Ruth Ringland Rains (Washington, 1965), pp. 24–50.

30. *Magnificat* refers to Psalms 96 and 98 which were believed to announce the "new song" mentioned in Luke 1: 46–55. *Ad Dominum* comes from Psalm 120 (119):1: "I called to the Lord in my distress and he answered me." *Retribue servo tuo* is the first line of Psalm 119 (118):17: "Deal bountifully with thy servant, that I may live and observe thy word." *In convertendo* (written as one word in the Old French text) is from Psalm 126 (125):1: "When the Lord restored the fortunes of Zion, we were like those who dream." *Ad te levavi* comes from Psalm 123 (122):1: "To thee I lift up my eyes, O thou who art enthroned in the heavens."

CHAPTER 29
THE CULT OF MARY MAGDALEN IN LATE MEDIEVAL FRANCE
Edited and translated by Raymond Clemens

INTRODUCTION

From the time of Gregory the Great (590–604) until the publication of Jacques Lefèvre d'Etaples's *De Marie Magdalena* (*Concerning Mary Magdalen*) in 1519, the figure known as Mary Magdalen was actually a composite of three biblical women: the unnamed sinner in Luke 7 who washed Christ's feet with her tears and dried them with her hair, Mary of Bethany (the sister of Martha and Lazarus), and Mary Magdalen, the woman to whom Christ appeared first after His resurrection. In later medieval legends, Mary Magdalen traveled to Marseille, where she preached to the inhabitants, converting the pagans in southern France to Christianity. In separate legends, Mary retreated to a nearby cave and remained in penitent seclusion for thirty years, fasting and being raised daily to sing with the angels. When she died, her body was interred by Maximinus, one of her traveling companions, in his basilica where it remained until the eighth or ninth century, when it was stolen and brought to Vézelay.

The legends concerning the Magdalen's voyage to Marseille were most likely the creation of the monks of Vézelay, an important and prosperous abbey in Burgundy. They hoped to convince doubters that, although Mary was reputed to have died in Palestine, they nonetheless possessed her relics. The monks at Vézelay were successful in their endeavor; most if not all of western Europe believed that the abbey possessed the saint's relics from the eleventh until the late thirteenth century, when a rival claim to possess the relics of the saint arose in the rural town of Saint-Maximin, twenty miles northeast of Marseille, in Provence, in a shrine entrusted to the Dominican order. Both assertions rested on a common history of the saint, formulated in the mid-eleventh century to substantiate the claims of the monks at Vézelay. In an ironic twist, the legends written by the monks at Vézelay were subtly altered and used against them by the promoters of the cult at Saint-Maximin.

Before composing more substantial accounts, the earliest claim to the Magdalen's relics composed by the monks at Vézelay stated simply that "all things are possible with God" and that it was divinely intended that the body of Mary Magdalen rest at Vézelay. This enigmatic explanation, translated below (Text 1), was followed by a vision in which the saint appeared to the anonymous hagiographer above her reliquary confirming her presence at Vézelay.

This explanation was quickly abandoned in favor of more convincing stories. According to one account, written in the mid-eleventh century and called the *Sermo de sancta Maria Magdalenae* (Text 2), following the stoning of the protomartyr Stephen, Mary traveled to Marseille where she and her siblings Lazarus and Martha converted the region to Christianity. When Mary died, she was buried at Arles. Many years later, a knight named Adelelmus was sent by the abbot of Vézelay to Provence, where he found Mary's body and brought it to Vézelay under the saint's protection, thereby authenticating her relics by demonstrating that the saint herself wished to be translated.

The *Sermo* was then abandoned in favor of yet another account of Mary's life and translation called the *Vita apostolica* and the *Translatio posterior* (available in translations published elsewhere, see below). According to this account, Mary traveled to Marseille with Maximinus, one of the seventy disciples of Christ, and together they converted the region to Christianity through their preaching. When Mary died, she was buried in Maximinus's church in Aix in an alabaster sepulchre with the history of her life depicted in sculpted images on its surface. In 745 (or 749, according to some accounts), Count Gerart of Burgundy, wishing to build a monastery in honor of Mary Magdalen at Vézelay, sent a monk named Badilo to Provence to obtain some part of her body. Although Aix had been devastated by the Saracen invasions, Badilo was able to locate and identify her tomb by its unusual material and the sculpted history on its exterior. One night, determined to succeed in his mission, he broke off a piece of the tomb and peered at the body inside, which he found to be remarkably preserved. Although the flesh was desiccated, the body was still covered with skin. He and his party fled with the relics, stopping at Nîmes to dismember the body so that it would take up less space and the theft would be less likely to be discovered. By the time Badilo's party arrived at Badilon-sur-Vézelay, a small town outside Vézelay, the body had become too heavy to move and could only be lifted when the abbot and monks received it in solemn procession. (It was a common topos in medieval hagiography that a saint's body become too heavy to move until it was received with appropriate dignity: this was one way the body of the saint continued to express his or her will [either to be or not] after death.) The *Vita apostolica* and the *Translatio posterior* were made popular through their inclusion in numerous abbreviated legendaries including those of John of Mailly and Jacopo da Voragine, which effectively gathered the many conflicting versions of her life into a single coherent narrative.

By the mid-thirteenth century, pilgrims to Vézelay had begun to doubt the presence of Mary's body at the abbey because so few of her relics were shown to the public. Their doubts were serious enough to prompt Pope Clement IV (1265–68) to send his legate Simon de Brion, the future Pope Martin IV (1281–85), to Vézelay to investigate charges of temporal and spiritual decadence. Realizing their predicament, the monks staged a revelation of the relics before the legate's arrival in the presence of two local authorities, Guy of Mello, bishop of Auxerre (1247–70), and Peter, bishop of Césarée-de-Philippe. On the night of October 4, 1265, in the presence of the bishops and the monks of the community, a bronze coffer was opened revealing the bones of the saint wrapped in silk along with a great quantity of hair and an undated charter issued by King Charles the Bald (840–77) authenticating the relics. After the ceremony, the monks returned the silk-covered bones to the bronze coffer, sealed it, and restored it to its original place. In the morning, the bishops drew up an account of the authentication, which the monks preserved.

Two years later, on April 24, 1267, the relics were translated from the bronze coffer into a silver reliquary before the papal legate Simon de Brion and a crowd of dignitaries, including Louis IX (1226–70). As they were being transferred, some of the relics were given to the king and some to Simon de Brion. In July of the same year, Louis returned one of the saint's arms in an arm-with-hand-shaped reliquary and an upper jaw/cheekbone (*gena*) with three teeth in a gilded vessel held by a silver angel. In addition, he presented the monks with several relics of the passion of Christ, which he encased in the hand of the arm reliquary that had been brought to him by crusaders in 1204 from the imperial treasury at Constantinople. After he became pope, Simon de Brion gave one of these Magdalen relics to the bishop and the community at Sens.

The relics' authentication in 1265, and their ostentation, translation, and distribution in 1267, were clearly intended to revive pilgrimage to the Magdalen's shrine at Vézelay, which, according to the translation account, had declined. On one level, the monks were successful in their claim to possess the Magdalen. Moreover, in 1267, they gained an important royal ally in Louis IX, who not only revealed a personal devotion to Mary Magdalen but also provided fitting jeweled reliquaries for the saint and even added to Vézelay's store of relics. However, on another level, it is clear that the cult at Vézelay was in decline. The 1265 authentication of the relics did not report that the monks had found the body (*corpus*) of the saint wrapped in silk but, rather, only certain holy relics (*quasdam venerandas reliquias*). If pilgrims had doubts about the quantity of the relics before 1265, how much greater must that doubt have been after 1267, when several of the remaining relics were distributed to those in attendance at the revelation and translation?

The decline of the cult of Mary Magdalen at Vézelay provided fertile soil for the birth of the cult at Saint-Maximin. The promoters of the relics at Saint-Maximin appropriated most of the legendary material concerning the life of Mary Magdalen in Provence and her death and burial by Maximinus in his church in Aix. They even appropriated the legend of Badilo's theft of the relics from the sarcophagus of Mary Magdalen. They added, however, one element to the story which altered the course of Magdalen devotion in western Europe: they contended that in the confusion of the Saracen invasions, a mythical king named Odoyno had taken the precaution of hiding Mary's body in an adjoining marble sarcophagus. Thus, Badilo could not have taken her body, they argued, because it had already been removed from its original sarcophagus. In this way, the proponents of the cult at Saint-Maximin were able to preserve most of the Vézelay tradition but claim the body of Mary Magdalen—and thus the power of her relics—for themselves.

The remainder of the documents translated in this chapter reflect the various means employed by the Dominicans at Saint-Maximin to support their claim to the Magdalen's body. The first document (Text 3) is the earliest *inventio* (that is, discovery) account of the relics; it describes the discovery by Charles II of Salerno of the saint's body and the charters authenticating it in the crypt of the church of Saint-Maximin in Provence on December 9, 1279.

The second account (Text 4) is taken from the Dominican inquisitor Bernard Gui's chronicle of the lives of the popes. An ardent supporter of the Provençal cult, Bernard Gui (d. 1331), wrote his *Flores chronicorum* between 1311 and 1316, and dedicated it to Pope John XXII (1316–34). Although Bernard was not the first chronicler to record the discovery of the relics at Saint-Maximin (that distinction belongs to a Franciscan, Salimbene de Adam (1221–1287)), his account greatly influenced the histories of later chroniclers.

The next document (Text 5) comprises four miracles (Chapters 5, 10, 41, 84) taken from the *Book of Miracles of Blessed Mary Magdalen*, compiled by the third prior of the convent, Jean Gobi the Elder (1304–28). Organized in its present form between 1304 and 1314, this book contains eighty-six miracles grouped according to the affliction remedied or danger averted. The miracles authenticate the body in several ways and establish Saint-Maximin as the center of the saint's sacral power on earth. The "Raymond miracle" (miracle number 4) was the earliest recorded at the shrine at Saint-Maximin. According to this miracle, Raymond of Uzès was preserved from execution by the Magdalen after he killed another man for disparaging the relics at Saint-Maximin (calling them "the bones of an ass or other animal"). The miracle demonstrates the authenticity of the relics by revealing the lengths to which the devoted would go to defend them and the rewards offered to those who defend the Magdalen. It exists in substantially different versions in Salimbene de Adam's chronicle, the *Book of Miracles of Blessed Mary Magdalen* (translated here), and the *Libellus hystorialis* of Philippe Cabassole (ca. 1355).

The Dominicans not only needed to prove that the relics at Saint-Maximin were those of Mary Magdalen, but they also needed to demonstrate the tremendous power that was localized in those relics and in Saint-Maximin where they were kept. Miracle number 10 tells an unusual story about a man who, although devoted to the Magdalen, could not help sinning. After touching his ring to the saint's reliquary, he found himself unable to perform the sexual act while wearing the ring until he repented and confessed his sins. This miracle functioned as a moral story to persuade sinners to mend their ways. Miracle number 41 illustrates the concentric circles of miraculous power that emanated from the relics and the resulting inward gravitation of pilgrims to the shrine.

In addition to promoting their own relics, it was essential that they cast doubt on the authenticity of their competitors' relics housed at Vézelay. Miracle number 84 serves to prove that the relics at Vézelay were not those of Mary Magdalen by using the authority of a supernatural power (a demon in this case) who testifies to their identity.

The final document translated here is the *Dominican Legend of Mary Magdalen*, written in the second half of the fifteenth century (Text 6). This account ascribes motives to Charles II that cannot be found in any earlier source. Although many of the events it chronicles are anachronistic (for example, it refers to Charles as king of Sicily in 1279, a title he did not have until his father died in 1285; it confuses Charles's confessor, Peter of Alamon, with the first prior of the convent, William of Tornay; and it places Charles in a Barcelona prison in 1279, although he was not imprisoned until 1284), it demonstrates the growth of the legend and the progressive need for greater and more detailed explanations of how Mary's body was discovered at Saint-Maximin.

Sources and Further Reading

The most popular *Life* of Mary Magdalen in the late Middle Ages is that included in Jacopo da Voragine's *Golden Legend*. Jacopo's work includes the *Translatio posterior* and several Vézelay miracles. A translation may be found in *Jacobus de Voragine, The Golden Legend: Readings on the Saints*, trans. William Granger Ryan (Princeton, 1993), 1: 374–83. The most influential early accounts of the saint's biblical life were the sermons of Gregory the Great, which can be found in *Forty Gospel Homilies*, trans. David Hurst, Cistercian Studies Series 123 (Kalamazoo, 1990). Another influential *Life* is that of Pseudo-Rabanus Maurus found in *The Life of Saint Mary Magdalen and of Her Sister Saint Martha: A Medieval Biography*, trans. David Mycoff, Cistercian Studies Series 108 (Kalamazoo, 1989). Some of the materials composed to authenticate the Vézelay relics in 1265–67 are found appended to a translation of Hugh of Poitier's chronicle: *The Vézelay Chronicle and Other Documents from MS. Auxerre 227 and Elsewhere*, trans. John Scott and John Ward (Binghamton, 1992), pp. 334–41. Aside from this chapter, the only material available in English on the Saint-Maximin cult is Salimbene de Adam's account of the discovery of the relics in 1279, which can be found in *The Chronicle of Salimbene de Adam*, trans. Joseph Baird, Giuseppe Baglivi, and John Robert Kane (Binghamton, 1986), pp. 530–32.

The most influential work on the cult of Mary Magdalen at Vézelay remains Victor Saxer's *Le Culte de Marie Magdeleine en Occident des origines à la fin du moyen âge* (Paris and Auxerre, 1959). Few modern studies on the Magdalen's relics are widely available in English, although several works are either in preparation or in press. Patrick Geary, *Furta Sacra: Thefts of Relics in the Central Middle Ages*, revised edition (Princeton, 1990) discusses accounts of the theft of the saint's relics from Provence in several places (especially pp. 108–28). Katherine Jansen, *Mary Magdalen in the Middle Ages* (Princeton, forthcoming) examines the image of Mary Magdalen disseminated by the mendicant orders in the later Middle Ages. Helen Meredith Garth, *Saint Mary Magdalene in Mediaeval Literature* (Baltimore, 1950) provides a survey of the literary sources that mention Mary Magdalen. On images of Mary Magdalen in art, see Martha Mel Edmunds, "La Sainte-Baume and the Iconography of Mary Magdalene," *Gazette des Beaux-Arts* 114 (1989): 11–28; Susan Haskins, *Mary Magdalen: Myth and Metaphor* (New York, 1993); Marjorie Malvern, *Venus in Sackcloth: The Magdalen's Origins and Metamorphoses* (Carbondale and Edwardsville, 1975).

The Cult of Mary Magdalen in Late Medieval France

1. FROM THE *VÉZELAY MIRACLES* [*BIBLIOTHECA HAGIOGRAPHICA LATINA*, NOS. 5471–72][1]

Many have wondered how it was possible that the body of St. Mary Magdalen, who was born in Judea, was brought to Gaul from such a distant region. But they can be answered in a few words: because all things are possible for God, and He did what He wished. It is not difficult for Him to do whatever He pleases for the salvation of men. This ought also to be asserted—that Mary Magdalen does not fail to punish most of those who doubt or contradict this. Those who have approached her and confessed their unbelief have received salvation through the intercession of Christ's companion. Indeed, she makes herself known, often appearing to those she leads to visit this place, as she appeared to us when we ventured to write this account.

On Saturday, as I placed the cover over the relics after Matins, as is the custom, an image appeared to me of a virtuous woman standing before the small door of the shrine in which the bones of Christ's companion are preserved. As I watched her, these words seemed to come from her mouth: "I am she who is thought by many to be here." It also must be noted that no place except Vézelay (as might be expected) is said to have her body and what is believed to be there is proven plainly by the power of the miracles [that occur there].

2. THE *SERMO DE SANCTA MARIA MAGDALENAE* [*BIBLIOTHECA HAGIOGRAPHICA LATINA*, NO. 5488][2]

The mercy of the almighty God, seeing mankind, whom He had formed in His image and likeness, entangled in diabolical snares, [and] desiring to give it the aid of his protection, decided to send His only begotten son into the world through the incarnation of the divine mystery, with whom and through whom He created all things, [so that] by making Him a saved man, He might lead mankind to a recognition of the truth. All these things, as they happened, were like a thundering evangelic and apostolic trumpet to all the faithful throughout the world. Therefore, among the twelve [Christ] chose, He enticed many of both sexes to an understanding of the faith so that the sound of their preaching reached into every land and their words progressed to the ends of the earth. From this famous progression [came] our protectress, St. Mary, three and four times blessed, who is called Mary of Magdalen from the castle Magdalo, as we know from the Gospel story. In this sinner, he instilled such grace that she deserved to hear from him: *your many sins have been forgiven, because you have loved much* [Lk 7:47], and *Mary has chosen the better part, which shall not be taken from her* [Lk 10:42].

What she did in life, whom we know to have been more glorious among all women, after the death of the Lord, beyond what the evangelic history tells, is considered uncertain to some, where or with whom she stayed, except what one reads in the book of the Acts of the Apostles: *The apostles remained together in prayer, with the women* [Acts 1:14], and so on. Certainly a truthful history of many things has her depart with St. Lazarus, her brother and St. Martha, her sister, during the persecution of the people by the Jews, just as the rest of the apostles [did].

Truly she was also the apostle of the apostles to those who remained [i.e., the gentiles] as the apostle says: *Because you have rejected the word of God and judged us unworthy, behold we turn to the Gentiles* [Acts 13:46]. After she left the seaport, she came to the outskirts of the city of Marseille, where she was strengthened in the company of the remaining saints, with those who were welcome company, as it is recorded by the inhabitants of that place in the writings of those ancients and confirmed up to the present by the narration of the entire community. She came to Marseille to spread the grace of the word of God to the people. But knowing that it was prohibited for a woman to be heard in public and that she should not initiate divine discourse, she gave that work to her brother Lazarus to complete, so that, just as he had merited resurrection in spirit and body from Christ the Lord, he should resurrect people to the spiritual life. Afterward, they withdrew to the place they had chosen earlier, and persisting in the divine work for a long time, they came to the end of this present life with glorious virtues. And having been brought to the joys of eternal life, they contemplate the face of Him whom they loved so ardently.

The church of the confessor St. Maximinus, in the bishopric of the abovementioned city in which the bodies of the saints are known to be buried, is still pointed out [to pilgrims]. The walls of the church, which were built to a wonderful size and adorned by their many virtues, still stand decorously, although because of the violence of the Saracens, the territory they conquered remains very much deserted.

How the relics of blessed Mary Magdalen and those of the most holy bishop Maximinus came to the French town of Vézelay ought to be commented on briefly. In the time of the king of the Franks, Carloman,[3] not by chance, but, I imagine, by divine providence, it happened that one day Adalgaire,[4] bishop of the holy church of Autun came to the monastery in Vézelay. Among his liegemen, he brought with him the famous knight Adelelmus.[5] Adelelmus was the brother of Odo, the devout abbot of Vézelay.[6] Then the bishop, in conversation with the monks, mentioned with what great love Mary Magdalen had followed Christ. Waiting until it was appropriate, the knight Adelelmus, drawing out his words with pious sighs, said, "From the time I was a child I have seen and known the burial place of Mary, whom you venerate with pious words." When the abbot Odo heard this, inspired by God, he fell on his knees to kiss the hands of the bishop and his brother Adelelmus and excitedly asked for the relics.

What followed? The necessary funds were raised and the monks were chosen along with the soldiers who, with Adelelmus, were strong enough to complete this work. But when they arrived in the city of Arles, they learned that the entire region had been utterly ravaged and deserted, so that no men could be found except the Saracens who had brought this destruction. After hearing this, they were greatly disturbed, [but] at length they recalled the thoughts of Pope Gregory, saying: "Let us always will to do good works, for they will be brought to completion through divine intervention."[7] Strengthened by his prophecies, [and] also relying on the prayers of both the bishop and the abbot, they continued their journey and came to the place in which was hidden the most precious treasure of the bodies of the saints. But as they quickly gathered the bodies of the most glorious Mary Magdalen and blessed Maximinus, confessor of Christ, a great number of Saracens came upon them. Suddenly they were overcome with terror and called on the protection of the saints whose precious relics they carried in their hands. Because of the helping mercy of God, a great cloud appeared among them, lasting until they withdrew to [their] native lands and arrived at a welcome place of defense. Our protectress Mary, whose sins had been washed away at the pious font, obtained this for us. After these signs of her powers were revealed, the monks of Vézelay came successfully to the place, where afterward the saint was made known by her many signs, because she was the one who wiped away her guilt with [her] hair.

By your intervention, O Lady, who merited to be called the beloved of the Lord, wash away the various crimes of our sins. Let it be pleasing to our Lord, your beloved, that He restore us to God His father, with whom He lives in the unity of the Holy Spirit, forever, Amen.

3. The Saint-Maximin Invention and Translation Account[8]

In the year of the Lord 1279, on the ninth day of December, the Lord Charles, firstborn son of the king of Sicily and Jerusalem,[9] found a document in a marble sepulcher that had been opened by him at Saint-Maximin, in the diocese of Aix, which states:

> During the reign of Odoyno, most pious king of the Franks, in the year of the Lord 700, on the sixteenth day of the month of December, this body of the precious and venerable blessed Mary Magdalen was moved secretly at night from her alabaster sepulchre into this marble [sepulcher] (once the body of Sidonius[10] was moved) so that it might be better hidden during the invasions of that treacherous people, the Saracens.

He found another document on the fifth of May in the year 1280 in the presence of the archbishops of Narbonne, Aix, and Arles, and many other bishops, abbots, and monks in the same sepulcher, which states: "Here lies the body of blessed Mary Magdalen." And her revelation is celebrated on the same day.

4. From Bernard Gui, *Flores chronicorum* [*Bibliotheca hagiographica latina*, no. 5506][11]

On the ninth of December in the year of the grace of Jesus Christ 1279, in that town—which by papal designation is now called Saint-Maximin—Prince Charles, son of King Charles of Sicily, count of Provence, and later king of Sicily, searched with great care and devotion for the body of St. Mary Magdalen in the holy oratory in which St. Maximinus (one of the seventy-two disciples of the Lord Jesus Christ and first bishop of Aix) once entrusted her burial, which is related widely in ancient and authentic histories. Once he had opened all the tombs that lay on both sides of the crypt in the oratory, the gouged-out earth remaining in the middle, with a strong fragrance, as if a storehouse of sweet spices had been opened, [and] with subsequent signs and many glorious miracles, the holy body of the most sacred Magdalen was discovered. It was not in the alabaster tomb in which she had first been buried and which is still there, identified by the written descriptions of it and by the sculpted images [on the surface of the sarcophagus], but in another tomb in that same place, made of marble from the region, placed to the right of those entering the crypt. Clearly seen with their own eyes by all who were present admiring [her] was a root with a small branch of fennel, stuck in her throat, which emerged from her most sacred tongue (still in her head), and extended from the body at some length. And I who write this have often heard from the faithful and devout report of others that a divided root with a small branch is currently used in various places for the preservation of certain relics.

In testimony of the evident truth, in the same tomb next to the sacred body there was also found a very ancient charter, enclosed in wood to protect it from putrefaction, containing this writing:

> During the reign of Odoyno, most pious king of the Franks, in the year of the Lord 700, on the sixteenth day of the month of December, this body of the precious and venerable blessed Mary Magdalen was moved secretly at night from her alabaster sepulcher into this marble [sepulcher] (once the body of Sidonius was moved) so that it might be better hidden during the invasions of that treacherous people, the Saracens.

I who write this read this most ancient charter and saw it there, preserved in the sacristy, in testimony of the truth.

Having most diligently examined all the things discovered [in the crypt], the prince and count Charles (later king of Sicily) called together the archbishops of Narbonne, Arles, and Aix, and many other bishops, abbots, and monks, and his nobles with the clergy and the assembled people. On the appointed day (i.e., May 5, 1280), he raised the sacred body of blessed Mary Magdalen from [the crypt] and placed it, with fitting honor, in a sumptuous reliquary, which he prepared, made of gold, silver, and precious stones. Her head was afterward enclosed in a most precious case of pure gold and very precious stones, constructed with wonderful and fitting craftsmanship. The place where the head and body are preserved is venerated and revealed by manifest miracles. The same Charles with the prelates then found in the tomb another very ancient script on a charter, whose exterior was entirely covered in wax and whose antiquity made it difficult to read. It said: "Here lies the body of blessed Mary Magdalen."

It is evident from the aforementioned, without dispute, hostility, or jealousy of the one judging, where on earth the body of St. Mary Magdalen truly lies, whose blessed spirit enjoys the eternal vision of God in heaven with all the saints. Moreover, although it is said in many places and written in chronicles that the sacred body of blessed Mary Magdalen was translated by Gerart, count of Burgundy, from her sepulchre of alabaster to the monastery at Vézelay, which he had built, in the time of Constantine V[12] (son of the emperor Leo III)[13] and Pope Zachary[14] in the year 745, it appears more clearly from the writing placed above, which was found next to the body of St. Mary Magdalen, if fitting faith ought to be applied to it, that twenty-five[15] years earlier that body had been moved from her sepulchre of alabaster and transported into another sepulchre of marble after the body of Sidonius had been removed from it. The recent deeds of Prince Charles (as just mentioned) and truth, uncovered and revealed by such evident signs, clearly indicate and faithfully manifest that the translation of the body of the Magdalen to Vézelay, commonly broadcast and written, is not able to be truly accepted because her body was not then in the sepulchre of alabaster where it was first placed, but [it was a translation] of some other body or perhaps some part of her body.

The revelation, discovery, and translation of the sacrosanct body of blessed Mary Magdalen was celebrated in the town of Saint-Maximin in the diocese of Aix, on May 5, 1280, in the third and last year of the pontificate of Nicholas III,[16] and therefore it was established that it should be celebrated in that same place by future generations on that same day.

In that place, in the years following, Charles, now king of Sicily, endeavored to construct and establish a convent of preaching brothers.[17] After removing the monks of Saint-Victor of Marseille from there, by the order of Pope Boniface VIII[18] in 1295, [he established] a church in honor of St. Mary Magdalen and the many other saints whose remains lay in the oratory—that is, Sts. Maximinus, Sidonius (the man born blind and healed by Christ in the Gospel), and Marcella, handmaid of St. Martha, who said to the Lord Christ, *Blessed be the womb that carried you, and the breasts that sustained you* [Lk 11:27]. The same king ordered a great and beautiful [church] to be built with royal funds, and he gave the place as much in books as in jewels and precious ornaments to celebrate the worship of God, according to princely magnanimity.

5. SELECTIONS FROM THE *BOOK OF MIRACLES OF BLESSED MARY MAGDALEN* [*BIBLIOTHECA HAGIOGRAPHICA LATINA*, NO. 5510][19]

(5.) Another miracle concerning prisoners.

A man named Raymond from the city of Uzès reported (and he maintained this under oath) that [after] he visited the relics of blessed Mary Magdalen in Saint-Maximin, he passed through Marseille where he happened to meet a man named Stephen. When he heard that Raymond had visited the relics of the above-mentioned saint in Saint-Maximin and that he had kissed her arm there, Stephen erupted irreverently with invective against the saint, asserting and affirming that the Magdalen did not lie in Saint-Maximin and that what he had kissed there was not the arm of the Magdalen but the bones of an ass or some other animal. The pilgrim rebuked the detractor, saying to him "if the inquisitors knew this, they would punish you when they had heard what you said, which seems to sound sacrilegious." That blasphemer not only repeated what he had said but also belched forth more words of abuse. No longer able to patiently endure those insults against the saint for whom he had a singular devotion nor the detraction of that place in which the body of the saint (he believed) certainly lay, Raymond attacked the blasphemer with his sword. By inflicting several wounds on his body, he deprived Stephen of his life, of which he was not worthy because of the blasphemy he had unfairly hurled at the saint. He fled quickly to Saint-Gilles, supposing that he was safe there from the court of Marseille, but was captured some days later. During the time he was held prisoner in Saint-Gilles, he turned with great faith to Mary Magdalen for her intercession. Mindful of his vow, she consoled him in prison by appearing to him with a great company of diverse persons and with greatest clarity. At length he was led from that prison and taken to Marseille, where he was sentenced to death by hanging. And although, as is the custom in such things, his eyes were veiled, he was able to see everything as if he had no blindfold or impediment over his eyes. And when he ascended the scaffold, a voice from heaven said to him repeatedly: "Do not be afraid! Do not be afraid!" With great devotion, Raymond commended his spirit and soul to Mary Magdalen.

He was hanged, and although he had no bodily support while hanging in the gallows, he suffered no injury. And when the messengers of the court, who were separate from all the others present at the scaffold, withdrew, the stone pillars of the scaffold totally collapsed. And although the wood that transversed the scaffold was solid and appeared new, it had been split through the middle. The hanged man walked away alive and healthy, having no injury; divine virtue had protected him and kept him safe through the merits of the Magdalen. Those who had left, seeing and considering the miracle, returned immediately, gave thanks to God and the Magdalen, released Raymond and permitted him to go free out of reverence for the saint.

That man went immediately to Saint-Maximin and gave thanks to his liberator. He narrated to all the miracle, which had been worked in him through divine power by her merits, and presented himself as a servant of the Magdalen at her shrine . . .

(10.) Concerning the touch of the relics against impurity.

There was a man who, although lewd and unclean in body, was nonetheless moved by devotion to come to Saint-Maximin to visit the relics of blessed Mary Magdalen. At the time, he wore a ring which (out of devotion) he touched to the arm bone of the Magdalen commonly shown to those coming [to Saint-Maximin] so that they might kiss it. And because a habit (whether of virtue or vice,) leads one to an act that is similar to it, the habit of vice, in which that man had long labored and which strengthened in his mind, led him (after he completed his pilgrimage) as it had before to an act similar to his habit.

When the man attempted to consummate the act of vice as he was accustomed, he found himself totally immobile and powerless. The woman was amazed, and the man was stupefied because such an obstacle had never prevented him from committing his wickedness. Asked by the woman whether he was wearing anything that prevented him from completing his wickedness, the man responded that he did not, except per chance the ring with which he had touched the relics of the Magdalen. Quickly setting aside the ring on the woman's advice, he consummated his nefarious act immediately just as [he had] at other times. After perpetrating his wicked deed, taking back his ring and wishing to replace it on his finger, as it was before, he [found] he was unable to do it, although he tried repeatedly.

Returning to his senses, ashamed about this thing that had happened to him and grieving and penitent over the sin he committed, he returned to Saint-Maximin that same hour, sought the lector of the brothers, and asked forgiveness for his sins from the Lord in confession with appropriate contrition and many tears. After he had confessed and been absolved of his crimes, commending himself devotedly and humbly in prayer to the Magdalen, he attempted to place the ring on his finger. And because, through appropriate confession and contrition, the original slimness was restored to the finger which had become inflated from carnal knowledge, he was able to place the ring (the material of which was consecrated through contact with the relics of the Magdalen) on his finger easily and without any difficulty just as before.

And because he knew, according to the testimony of angels in Tobit, that *it is honorable to reveal and confess the works of God* [Tob 12:7], wishing that these divine works should no longer remain hidden, he gave permission to his confessor (the lector) to reveal to everyone all things pertaining to this matter, which had been made manifest to him. [Therefore] he made this miracle known to the brothers and many others for the glory of God and the exaltation of his lover, the Magdalen, and in order to increase as much as possible the devotion of those coming to that place . . .

(41.) Here begin [the miracles] concerning physical infirmity:

At the time when the most serene Prince Charles II . . . wished to gather together a great multitude of prelates and nobles and others in Saint-Maximin to reveal the relics and body of the blessed and glorious Mary Magdalen, there was a man from Corsica in Marseille, who for two years had been so afflicted by paralysis that he was unable to use any limb of his body. Hearing that the revelation was to take place . . . he vowed he would attend if he were able.

And because he was unable to travel there through his own efforts, his wife and son procured a cart mounted on four wheels. After placing the man on it, they brought him to Saint-Maximin by dragging the cart. When the moment of the revelation arrived, all those present celebrated with devotion and reverence, [and] the infirm man directed his continual prayers to God and blessed Mary Magdalen. But because of his many sins, or perhaps because he did not have as steadfast a faith and as complete a hope as he ought, he did not obtain from her the complete healing he asked for but, instead, gained only the ability to move his hands and feet. In the rest of his body he remained as powerless as before.

After returning to Marseille in the cart, he remained infirm for five years. Because he was troubled in his soul by the torments and afflictions he endured continually, he came to understand and believe that the wonders that he had heard concerning the Magdalen were true and that he ought to return to her more devotedly and confidently than he had the first time. With greater confidence and firmer faith, he began to implore the aid of the Magdalen repeatedly with his whole heart, promising her and God to return to Saint-Maximin to visit her relics.

Wonderful thing! Marvelous and stupendous to all! Immediately after he uttered his vow, that man, who for almost seven years had been so oppressed by illness that he was unable to move, began to rise of his own power, and supported by two crutches he began to walk, nor did he allow himself any delay but began his journey to Saint-Maximin with the aid of the crutches. The closer he came to the place where the body of the Magdalen is, so much the greater did he perceive the power of God and the Magdalen aiding him, so that as soon as his feet touched the territory of Saint-Maximin, his limbs received the power of God and the help of the Magdalen to such an extent that he put aside one of his crutches [and] was able to walk with the aid of only one [of them].

When next he confidently entered the church in Saint-Maximin, in which the body of the saint lies, and gave himself completely in prayer with many tears and great devotion, the divine power strengthened all that man's limbs, so that each was restored to its original function. That man, fully and perfectly cured by God through the merits of the Magdalen, gave praise to God and the Magdalen, as he ought, and he left the cart (in which he was first brought) and the crutches (with which he came the second time) in the same place in the church as testimony to the miracle.

(84.) Concerning diverse things that happened, were revealed, or said, or done to the honor, praise, and glory of blessed Mary Magdalen.

A brother who lectured on theology to the canons in Lyon and who was the lector of the Dominicans in Lausanne narrated this miracle to Jean Gobi, then the prior of Saint-Maximin, to Brother Raymond Bartholomei, prior of the Dominicans in Marseille, and to Brother Rostan of Saparono, also a Dominican, while they were traveling to Metz to the general chapter meeting.[20] This brother was present when these things happened that are narrated below, and he both saw and heard them.

There was a time when those who rule and watch over the church in Vézelay gave some relics—so they claimed—to the Preaching Brothers in Lausanne, stating that they were from the body of the Magdalen, which—they claimed—they had in their church.[21] Perhaps they were moved by this intention because many doubted whether they had the body of the saint in Vézelay. The brothers, who preach the words of God in diverse parts of the world, might believe better, and in their preaching they might induce others to the belief that the body of the Magdalen was truly in Vézelay.

The brothers gratefully received the gift with both joy and devotion, believing firmly that it was thus; and the relics were accepted with such great devotion that not only those brothers, but also through all that country and roundabout they believed for certain that they were from the body of the Magdalen because those from Vézelay firmly asserted it. And all who had fevers or other infirmities, or were bothered by whatever sort of troubles, came to the church of the brothers with devotion and faith hoping that, in their needs, blessed Mary Magdalen would not deny her aid. The relics were promoted to such an extent through that region in the church of the brothers, by reason of those relics, devotion grew in those brothers so that they were no longer known by the name Preaching Brothers but, rather, were commonly called Magdalen Brothers by all. Among those who sought the blessed saint's help, there was a person brought [to the shrine] by parents and friends, who was gravely vexed by the presence of a demon. Once in the church of the Dominicans, friends asked that the relics of the Magdalen, which the brothers had, be presented to the demoniac, hoping that the demon who inhabited the body of that person would not be able to resist the power of the saint, nor endure the presence of her relics.

Therefore, at the urging of the demoniac's friends, the brother who was the sacristan carried the relics, presented them to the demoniac, and began to adjure the demon by the power of the Magdalen, whose relics were there. When the demon heard this, he responded to the brother with these words: "Brother, what are you saying? What are you saying? Brother, consider what you are saying!" The brother then said to him more strongly: "I adjure you through blessed Mary Magdalen, the relics of whose body we have here, that you leave this body and do not vex it any more!" Then in the presence of that brother who narrated this to the brothers mentioned above, and of all those standing there, with a certain indignation, and as if with anger, the demon responded within the hearing of all: "Certainly, brother, you do not know what you say or even what you are talking about, indeed I say even more to you—you truly speak falsely because there is nothing there of the body or relics of the Magdalen, and that is why I will not leave this person!"

Hearing these words with great amazement and wonder, all those who were there were forced to believe that the body in Vézelay from which the brothers had received the relics was not the Magdalen's.

6. The Dominican Legend of St. Mary Magdalen at Saint-Maximin [*Bibliotheca hagiographica latina*, no. 5512][22]

Wonderful and glorious in his saints [Ps 67:36], God is most glorious in his apostle and representative, the exemplar of penitence, blessed Mary Magdalen whose *many sins were forgiven because she loved much* [Lk 7:47]. The Lord who *gives generously to all and does not reproach* [Jas 1:5] bestowed the gifts of grace in the life and death of the notorious sinner he made a penitent. For who has sought the aid and patronage of the holy penitent-sinner and great lover of our Lord Jesus Christ and devotedly run to her for help who was not listened to and freed from whatever difficulties held him? And certainly I will plainly recount for the glory of the almighty God and the praise and singular devotion of St. Mary Magdalen a matter new and worthy of commendation, and I will reveal a great miracle.

For in the year 1279, when Charles II, famous king of Jerusalem and Sicily and count of Provence, was captured by the king of Aragon in a naval battle and cruelly bound and held in an iron cell, his freedom and absolution from such harsh chains was not hoped for by prayer, price, or any human support.[23] When the vigil of glorious Mary Magdalen came, he was persuaded by his confessor, Master William of Tornay, professor of sacred theology—who was inspired by divine grace—[to observe] the vigil with great desire, devotion, and purity of heart. Having made sacramental and beneficial confession, the king fasted, and after he heard a long collation and sermon from the above-mentioned spiritual father, he recalled the most sacred body in Villa Lata, now called Saint-Maximin, and the place of the saint's penance, called Balma, which was in his province, and [he recalled] the translation of the body of this most holy saint to the duchy of Burgundy. He was completely confident of her merits, which were so great because she undertook her penitence in the region of Provence and renounced the life of preaching the gospel. He devoted himself totally to her from the bottom of his heart and with a clean conscience, he begged her for aid and support.

Then in a dream in the middle of the night, *when all things held their silence* [Wis 18:14], the most pious St. Magdalen, consoling her devotee with her most sweet presence, roused him from his dream with a sonorous delightful voice and said to him, "O my devotee, what do you seek from me, or what do you want me to do?" He said to her, "O most merciful and sweet lady, because I am destitute of all human hope and under the most cruel detention in this prison, you are my only confidence. O sweet patron, free me. For all things are possible for you with God." The most blessed Mary Magdalen answered, "Your prayer has been heard. Rise quickly and follow me." The famous king said to her, "O venerable lady, pray for the company established under captivity." The Magdalen responded, "Your prayers have been heard." And taking his hand, she liberated him from the prison with his servants and set them free.

A little while later, the glorious Magdalen asked the king where he was. And when he supposed he was still in the palace of Barcelona, the saint said, "You are about three miles from Narbonne, where the body of blessed Paul Sergius, disciple of the apostle Paul, lies." From whence the king, delighted by his liberation and restoration and desiring to be more certain of whom to give fitting thanks, asked the woman whether she was blessed Mary Magdalen.

She responded, "Indeed I am, and I obtained your liberation from God." The king thanked her and spoke to her with these sweet words: "O most sweet representative and apostle of Jesus Christ, who merited to see Christ first among mortals after His resurrection from the dead! O exemplar of penitence, who washed His feet with frequent tears and dried [them] with the hair of your head! O most sweet lady! O my sole hope! O most holy patron, what praise shall I offer you? What can I do for your glory? Because of the innumerable gifts I have received from you, I know without doubt that I am unable to offer fitting acts of thanks. Nonetheless I devote myself totally to you."

Then St. Magdalen said, "I assign this to you, and I demand it of you because you believe. You must demonstrate to the pope and the Christian people that my body is in Villa Lata (which is now called Saint-Maximin), and not in Burgundy. You will find my body in the church of Saint-Maximin, beside the great altar, to the right of the altar, in the tomb, next to which lie, in the same church, the bodies of Sts. Maximinus, Blasius, Sifredus, and Sts. Marcella and Susanna. Believing that the body of blessed Sidonius, blind from birth, which lay in my tomb, was mine, Addonus,[24] king of the Franks translated it from Provence to the region of Burgundy after the expulsion of the infidels. And so that you will be more certain, you will find the bark of a tree which will never decompose above my tomb, and in the bark you will discover the writing of blessed Maximinus that says, 'Here lies the body of blessed Mary Magdalen.' You will also find my bones, destitute of flesh, except on the part of my head where our Lord Jesus Christ touched me saying, 'Do not touch me,' after his glorious resurrection. Also, beside my left jaw, you will find a small crystal jar, in which is the earth soaked with the blood of Christ, which I gathered during his passion and carried with me in perpetual remembrance. You will also find the hairs of my head transformed into ashes, except for those which touched the feet of our most holy Lord Jesus Christ when, by crying with tears and drying with the hairs of my head, I obtained remission of my sins. You will also discover the palm branch with green leaves, proceeding from my mouth. God wishes that all these things be shown to the Christian people to increase faithful devotion in the place of Saint-Maximin where my body lies. And because the church is poor, and the divine cult is celebrated there with little propriety, you will order to be built in reverence for me a convent and a church of brothers of the Order of Preachers (since I was an apostle), and you will endow and magnify [them] with the cave of Balma, in which I completed my penitence. God arranged and ordained that these monasteries are to be ruled and governed by the Dominicans (after removing the monks), and you will cause those monasteries to be united by the pope and gathered together for the Order of Preachers. You will cause the feast of my translation to be celebrated and solemnized, and you will order that my office be arranged to be spoken by those same friars." (The king himself composed that office, which begins: "Your servants, sons, [and] preachers, proclaim you with unceasing voice: Holy, Holy Holy." And ends:

"Therefore, come to the aid of your sons, those whom you have chosen as your servants.") After these things were assigned to the famous king by the glorious saint, she disappeared, leaving him much consoled.

With dawn breaking, the king with his company saw the most noble city of Narbonne about two miles distant. There he made himself a vow to erect a cross on that road (to which blessed Mary Magdalen had led the king and his company), and it was done and today is called the cross of Leuca.[25] And when his arrival came to the attention of the archbishop of Narbonne, his clergy, and the illustrious viscount of Narbonne, and the whole city, they rushed to meet the king in procession and received him into the city and palace with honor. He told them his solemn story and grand miracle, and he built a chapel in honor of St. Mary Magdalen in the palace.

At last he took with him the most reverend archbishops of Narbonne, Arles, and Aix, the bishops of Avignon, Marseille, and Sisteron, many other prelates, and his confessor [William of Tornay], and he set himself to the advancement of the veneration of glorious Mary Magdalen. He arrived at the place of Saint-Maximin, and after fasting and offering up prayers, the pious king and his prelates dug in the place revealed to the king and at length found, with the greatest fragrance, the most sacred body of St. Mary Magdalen with the foretold signs. In that place, the Lord displayed and demonstrated many signs and great miracles for the praise and glory of his apostle and beloved confidant, as is demonstrated more clearly and in greater detail in the bulls of her revelation, which the seals of the most reverend prelates prove.

After the most sacred body was revealed and the monks were expelled from Saint-Maximin and Sainte-Baume by the promise and will of the pope, the king, following the divine will revealed to him by blessed Mary Magdalen, placed the preaching brothers (dedicated to preaching the Gospel and following the apostolic life) in the said places and united them under the Order of Preachers, and for these places, which were small and poor at that time, the most merciful king gave appropriate compensation to the monks of Saint-Victor and the nuns of Saint-Zacharie.

He began [to build] and completed the greater part of a church with a convent in Saint-Maximin, wonderfully sumptuous in its structure and royal work. He offered gold and silver vessels and other ornaments to the prior and brothers of the convent and gave a most generous sum from the proceeds from the *gabelle*[26] of Nice for the sustenance of the Dominicans, the completion of that church and convent, and the enlargement of several others in the region of Provence. He instituted and ordained the number of Dominican brothers living there under the prior at one hundred. By the holy and religious authority of the highest pontiff, he made his confessor the first prior, who was divinely chosen and preordained. That holy king commanded (by his order and the approval of the highest pontiff) that the office of St. Mary Magdalen be said devotedly and piously, as much in the dormitory as in the choir, night and day, by the prior and the present and future brothers for the praise and glory of Our Lord Jesus Christ and the honor of St. Mary Magdalen, by whose merits and prayers we will be able to arrive in the heavenly kingdom. Amen.

NOTES

1. Paris, Bibliothèque nationale, MS latin 5296B, p. 142.
2. Baoudouin de Gaiffier, "Hagiographie Bourguignonne: A propos de la thèse de doctorat de M. René Louis sur Girart, comte de Vienne," *Analecta Bollandiana* 69 (1951): 145–47.
3. Carloman II reigned from 879 until 884.
4. Bishop Adalgaire of Autun served from 875 until 893.
5. No biographical information is available on Adelelmus.
6. Abbot Odo of Vézelay (827–911).
7. This slightly altered fragment is taken from Gregory the Great's Easter sermon on Mary Magdalen. See *Forty Gospel Homilies*, trans. David Hurst, Cistercian Studies Series 123 (Kalamazoo, 1990), p. 157.
8. Paris, Bibliothèque nationale, MS nouvelle acquisition latine 2672, fo. 3r.
9. Charles II was count of Provence and king of Sicily from 1285 until 1309. In addition to discovering the Magdalen's relics in 1279, he was Saint-Maximin's primary benefactor, gaining papal approbation for the relics in 1295 and providing money for the foundation of a Dominican convent.
10. According to Jacopo da Voragine's *Golden Legend* (itself based on earlier texts), Sidonius was the man born blind and given sight by Jesus who later traveled to Marseille with Mary Magdalen and Maximinus.
11. Paris, Bibliothèque nationale, MS nouvelle acquisition latine 1171, fols. 99r-100r.
12. Emperor Constantine V reigned from 741 until 775.
13. Leo III was emperor from 717 to 741; from 720 to 741 he ruled with his son, Constantine V (see previous note).
14. Pope Zachary served from 741 until 752.
15. Bernard corrected his mistake in later editions of the *Flores* to forty-five years.
16. Pope Nicholas III served from 1277 until 1280. Nicholas never confirmed or denied the presence of the Magdalen's relics at Saint-Maximin; they were authenticated by Pope Boniface VIII in 1295.
17. The Dominican order (*Ordo Fratrum Praedicatorum*), was founded by St. Dominic (ca. 1170–1221) and approved by Pope Honorius III (who served from 1227 until 1241) in 1216. Founded to help stem the threat of Catharism, the order's primary mission was preaching; the members were commonly known as "preaching brothers" (*fratrum praedicatorum*)
18. Pope Boniface VIII served from 1294 until 1303.
19. Jacqueline Sclafer, "Iohannes Gobi senior OP, Liber miraculorum b. Mariae Magdalenae," *Archivum Fratrum Praedicatorum* 63 (1993): 143–45, 149–50, 171–72, and 201–3.
20. The Dominican general chapter meeting was held in Metz during Pentecost, 1313.
21. The Dominican house at Lausanne was founded in 1234 under the name of St. Mary Magdalen.
22. Bernard Montagnes, *Marie Madeleine et l'ordre des prêcheurs* (Marseille, 1984), pp. 28–34.
23. On Charles II, see note 9 above. Charles was at war with King Peter of Aragon (1276–85) because Peter had accepted the crown offered by the Sicilians in 1283 after the uprising in Sicily known as the Sicilian Vespers (March 30, 1282). Peter was excommunicated by Pope Martin IV (the former Simon de Brion) who was elected with the strong support of the Angevin Charles I (who reigned from 1246 until 1285), Charles II's father, who became king of Sicily in 1266. Charles II was captured by Peter in a battle at sea on June 5, 1284; a battle he had been warned to avoid by his father. Charles I died shortly thereafter, on January 7, 1285, and his son became count of Provence and king of Sicily while still in prison. On October 4, 1288, a treaty negotiated by Edward I of England (under pressure from Pope Nicholas IV) with Alphonse III of Aragon (who reigned from 1285 until 1291) freed Charles but required him to mortgage three of his sons (one of whom was the future

St. Louis of Toulouse) as ransom for his own release; Charles's children were not freed until 1295.

24. There was no King Addonus; perhaps the author of this legend has confused King Odoyno, who was reputed to have translated the Magdalen's relics from her alabaster tomb to Sidonius's marble one in the early eighth century, with Count Girart, who founded the monastery of Vézelay and ordered the relics translated from Provence to Vézelay. In Paris, Bibliothèque nationale, MS nouvelle acquisition latine 2672, a later scribe has rubbed out "Addonus, king of the Franks," and written "Girart, Count of Burgundy."

25. The cross was located on the road from Narbonne to Béziers (Montagnes, *Marie Madeleine*, p. 33, note 17 [see note 22 above]).

26. This was a form of salt tax.

Chapter 30

Three Thirteenth-Century *Lives* of St. Margaret of Antioch

Edited and translated by Wendy R. Larson

Introduction

St. Margaret, or Marina, as she is known in the Eastern Orthodox tradition, was a victim of the Roman persecution of Christians under Emperor Diocletian in the early fourth century. After it was introduced to the Latin West in the twelfth century, Margaret's cult developed into one of the most popular in the Middle Ages. Margaret was, for example, one of the voices that Joan of Arc (1412–31) claimed to have heard. Margaret's first known appearances in both Greek and Latin martyrologies, or lists of saints, were in the ninth century. In his *Martyrology*, the Carolingian scholar Rabanus Maurus (d. 856), listed separate entries for Margaret on July 13 and for Marina on June 18, although the lives he provided were identical. Eventually, Margaret's feast day settled on July 20 in the West and July 17 in the East. Iconographically, Marina is typically portrayed with a raised hammer in one hand and the other around the throat or head of a demon; Margaret is usually shown either emerging from a dragon, or standing on top of one, and piercing it with a spear.

Aspects of Margaret's legend have been controversial from the beginning of the textual tradition. The tenth-century Greek hagiographer Metaphrastes called the saint's dramatic encounters with demonic foes "malicious interpolations." The Rebdorf manuscript claims to have "corrected" the story, and presents curtailed accounts of the dragon and demon scenes, and leaves out the saint's final intercessory prayer. Finally, in 1969, the Holy See suppressed Margaret's cult because of doubts about her historicity.

One reason for the ambiguous response by Christian ecclesiastical institutions to Margaret is her encounter with a dragon. The dragon itself is not controversial—it is part of a long biblical tradition as a symbol of evil from Job to the Book of Revelation—but rather the circumstances of its destruction. Other saints' *Lives* include dragons with no damage to their reputations. Like Margaret, for example, the fifth-century Byzantine St. Elisabeth the Wonderworker defeats a dragon using the sign of the cross (see below). Elisabeth, however, simply confronts the dragon in its lair and destroys it with the sign of the cross. Margaret, instead, makes the sign of the cross while inside a dragon which has swallowed her; it bursts open, and she escapes unharmed. Two of the lives of Margaret included in this chapter contain clerical objections to this dragon scene. In the *Golden Legend*, Jacopo da Voragine proposes a scenario much like Elisabeth's as an alternative, suggesting that ingestion of the saint by the dragon is what specifically troubles the author, while the author of the *South English Legendary* offers another difficulty posed by Margaret's feat—the impossibility of actually killing a devil.

Although the dragon scene in Margaret's life met with ecclesiastical disapproval, it could not be easily removed from the legend. The dragon is featured in Margaret's iconography, and the saint's safe emergence from the dragon's split womb also became associated with her role as patroness of women in childbirth.

In addition to objections about the fantastic elements in Margaret's life, her role as an intercessor—established by her lengthy prayer before her execution, in which she promises forgiveness of sins in return for veneration—raised theological difficulties. This was further compounded by the strong correspondence between Margaret's life and Christ's established through many quotations and echoes of Scripture. Church authorities were concerned about inappropriate attributions of power to saints, as well as what Nicholas of Cusa, a fifteenth-century reformer, called "superstitions," or the belief in the magical effects of acts of devotion to saints (see also Sherry Reames, *Legenda Aurea: A Reexamination of Its Paradoxical History* [Madison, WI, 1985], p. 50).

Margaret's final prayer also lists the means by which supplicants might invoke her intercessions, and includes dedicating churches or a votive lamp, owning a copy of her life or asking to have it read, in addition to the veneration of her relics. This element in her life provides an unusually concrete sense of the wide array of cultic practices associated with Margaret.

Margaret's cult cut through the spectrum of medieval society, as the list of devotional acts, ranging from building a church to asking for a reading of her life, suggests. Mothers of every economic position relied on her during pregnancy and childbirth, and both male and female monastics turned to Margaret as role model and guardian in their struggles with the temptations of the flesh, represented by the dragon and demon. Parishes both large and small were dedicated to Margaret; in England, she ranks third behind the Virgin Mary and St. Catherine of Alexandria in the number of churches dedicated to women.

This chapter provides translations of three *Lives* of St. Margaret written in the thirteenth century and read in England: the *Golden Legend*, the *South English Legendary*, and *Seinte Margarete* from the so-called Katherine Group. Although the Katherine Group text was composed earliest, it is presented last in this chapter because of its complexity. The *Golden Legend* will be presented first, as it offers the most succinct account of Margaret's life and provides the best basis for comparison with the other two versions. As these three versions of the same story will illustrate, competing interests and different audiences shaped the presentation of the saint's life, and reflect the wide range of concerns within the cult of St. Margaret. They highlight the need for caution regarding overly simple constructions of the "meaning" or significance of an individual saint.

The Golden Legend was a collection of one hundred and eighty-two saints' lives compiled by the Italian Dominican Jacopo da Voragine around 1260. Drawing from over one hundred and thirty different sources, Jacopo sought to bring consistency and rationality to the hagiographic material available to him, in the form of a source book for Dominican preachers. The *Golden Legend* was eventually translated from the original Latin into every known western European language, and was, after the Bible, the most popular book in the late medieval West (in the early days of printing, it was *the* most popular book).

Usually beginning with an etymological discussion of the saint's name and its spiritual significance—in this case the convenient fact that *margarita* means pearl—Jacopo goes on to recount the life, clarifying any contradictions in his sources, and providing a clear commentary on the lessons which may be drawn from the saint's experiences. In the *Life of St. Margaret*, Jacopo faces the challenge of simultaneously acknowledging and critiquing the dragon scene.

Jacopo knew and used both known major versions, or recensions, of Margaret's life, which are known, after the names of their later scholarly editors, as the Mombritius (from Bonino Mombritzio, d. ca. 1482) and the Rebdorf (from an anonymous monk of that abbey) recensions. Jacopo clearly favors the latter. The figure of Theotimus, for example, is only briefly mentioned by Jacopo as the original author of Margaret's *Life*, but is an important aspect of the Mombritius recension, which introduces Theotimus as witness and chronicler, and offers an unskeptical description of the dragon and demon scenes. In contrast, Jacopo firmly declares "apocryphal" the story of the saint's ingestion by and escape from the dragon. Following the Rebdorf recension, Jacopo is notably spare in details about the appearance of either the dragon or demon, a creative opportunity which other authors favoring the Mombritius recension use to great effect.

In his succinct account, Jacopo includes many of the other themes which the following two versions in this chapter will develop further, including Margaret as patroness of women giving birth and her endurance in the face of physical pain. The quotation Jacopo cites to conclude the Margaret legend strikes the important note of Margaret as a young girl who substitutes the earthly father who rejected her with a loving heavenly one. Joined to the etymological analysis with which she was introduced, Margaret's value as a model of exemplary chastity and perseverance makes clear her appeal to the compiler even if he is not entirely comfortable with all the aspects of her legend.

Dated between 1260 and 1288, the second text, the *South English Legendary*, is an anonymous verse collection of saints' *Lives* in Middle English. Its close proximity to the date of the *Golden Legend* has caused some scholars to view the *Legendary* as a translation of the *Legend*, but such a direct relationship is unlikely. The authorship and audience have not been definitively determined, although monastic authorship for a lay audience, perhaps to be read aloud on the saint's feast day, seems most likely.

The *Legendary* text makes a point of placing Margaret into a historical context, dating the events to 289, and noting that her martyrdom occurred during the reign of Emperors Diocletian and Maximian. It also stresses the influence on young Margaret of the stories of earlier martyrs such as St. Stephen and St. Lawrence. In turn, she will become a role model for the readers of her life.

In the original Middle English, the text is written in rhymed couplets which this translation does not attempt to reproduce. The account conveys a great deal of emotional tension as Justice Olibrius and the crowd encourage Margaret to renounce her faith. They use arguments based on perverse reversals of Christian ideals, such as calling Margaret a "whore" for preserving her virginity. The lavish quality of the descriptions of her tortures also heightens the intensity of the text's play between crude sexual images and the display of the wounded, yet pure, martyr's body. Of particular interest is the handling of the dragon scene, in which an uneasy compromise is reached between sources which question the veracity of the dragon's destruction from within, and the seeming ubiquity of the dragon in Margaret's legend. The scene is framed in disclaimers, setting out the case both for and against belief in this aspect of the saint's tradition. The text ends with a reassertion of Margaret's efficacy in intercessions for birthing mothers, as well as further insight into popular cultic practices.

The collection of texts known as the Katherine Group include the *Lives* of three female saints: Margaret, Catherine of Alexandria, and Juliana; as well as other devotional materials in Middle English for a female audience, specifically a group of anchoresses. They were probably composed between 1200 and 1230, in the West Midlands of England.

The intended female audience is explicitly addressed at the beginning of *Seinte Margarete*: "Listen, all who have ears and hearing: widows with the wedded, and maidens especially." In another Katherine Group text, *Ancrene Wisse*—a handbook for anchoresses—reference is made to "your English book of St. Margaret," and the saint's victory over the demon Rufus, as part of a discussion on handling temptation. The particular emphasis on sexual temptation, emphasized in the demon's account of his activities, would be appropriate for a monastic audience (of either gender), for whom sexual continence would be a priority. An audience of people who had dedicated themselves as *sponsae Christi*, or spouses of Christ, by taking monastic vows, would have especially appreciated the prevalence of affective language, as Margaret addresses Christ as not only Lord, but also as lover, and anticipates union with her bridegroom at the end of her sufferings. This reflects a popular kind of piety which encouraged the believer to form an emotional connection with Christ which was described in physical, often sexual, terms.

Repetition is a key ingredient in the rhetorical style of *Seinte Margarete*, which cannot be fully conveyed in a translation. The author delights in the alliterative repetition of sound as well as of concepts, often stating the same idea twice or more, in thesaurus-straining bursts of artistry which illustrate Margaret's spiritual power through her verbal control in the midst of her physical trials. The idea that this text may have been composed for public presentation is appealing, although the complexity of the text, and our knowledge that it was part of the meditative practices of at least one anchoress, also points to private readings.

SOURCES AND FURTHER READING

The Latin edition of *The Golden Legend* from which this translation was made is *Legenda Aurea*, ed. Theodor Graesse (Leipzig, 1850) pp. 400–403. A complete English translation of the text may be found in *Jacobus de Voragine, The Golden Legend: Readings on the Saints*, trans. William Granger Ryan (Princeton, 1993). See also Sherry Reames, *Legenda Aurea: A Reexamination of Its Paradoxical History* (Madison, WI, 1985) for more on Jacopo da Voragine's technique and audience. An English translation of the story of St. Elisabeth the Wonderworker may be found in *Holy Women of Byzantium*, ed. Alice-Mary Talbot (Washington, DC, 1996) pp. 117–35.

This translation from the *South English Legendary* is based on the Middle English text found in the Cambridge, Corpus Christi College MS 145, printed in *The South English Legendary*, eds. Charlotte D'Evelyn and Anna J. Mill, 3 vols., Early English Text Society, old series 235–36 and 244 (London, 1956–59), pp. 291–302. For the relationship between the *Golden Legend* and the *Legendary*, see Klaus P. Jankofsky, "*Legenda Aurea* Materials in the *South English Legendary*: Translation, Transformation, Acculturation," in *Actes du colloque international sur la Legenda Aurea: texte latin et branches vernaculaires*, ed. Brenda Dunn-Lardeau (Montreal, 1986) pp. 317–29. Annie Samson provides a useful discussion of the authorship and audience for the *Legendary* in "The *South English Legendary*: Constructing a Context," in *Thirteenth Century England*, eds. P.R. Cross and S.D. Lloyd (Cambridge, 1986), 1:185–95.

The Middle English source for the translation of the Katherine Group *Seinte Margarete* is printed in *Seinte Marherete*, ed. Frances M. Mack, Early English Text Society, old series 193 (London, reprint edition, 1958). This edition is based primarily on London, British Library MS Bodley 34, with reference to London, British Library MS Royal 17A, xxvii. A modern English translation of all the Katherine Group texts, including *Ancrene Wisse*, along with a helpful introduction, may be found in *Anchoritic Spirituality: Ancrene Wisse and Associated Texts,* ed. and trans. Anne Savage and Nicholas Watson (New York, 1991). An excellent discussion of the handling of the dragon and demon scenes is provided by Jocelyn Price, "The Virgin and The Dragon: The Demonology of *Seinte Margarete*," in *Sources and Relations: Studies in Hon-*

our of J.E. Cross, eds. Marie Collins, Jocelyn Price, and Andrew Hamer, Leeds Studies in English 16 (1985), pp. 337–57. For a literary study of the Katherine Group texts, see Elizabeth Robertson, *Early English Devotional Prose and the Female Audience* (Knoxville, TN, 1990), especially Chapter 6. Karen Winstead offers a useful overview of the Margaret legend's development in late medieval England, including reference to the three texts translated here, in *Virgin Martyrs: Legends of Sainthood in Late Medieval England* (Ithaca, NY, 1992).

Three Thirteenth-Century *Lives* of St. Margaret of Antioch

1. Jacopo da Voragine, The Life of St. Margaret of Antioch *from* The Golden Legend

The name Margaret is also that of a precious gem which is called *margarita*, or pearl. This gem is dazzling white, small, and powerful. Thus the blessed Margaret was dazzling white through her virginity, small through humility, and powerful through her miraculous works. The power of this gem is said to work against the effusion of blood, against the passions of the heart, and for the strengthening of the spirit. Thus blessed Margaret possessed power against the effusion of her blood through constancy, since in her martyrdom she remained most constant; against the passion of the heart, that is, the temptations of the demon, through her victory because she overcame the devil; and she strengthened the spirit through doctrine, for through her doctrine many souls were strengthened and converted to the faith of Christ. Her legend was written by the learned man Theotimus.[1]

Margaret of Antioch[2] was the daughter of Theodosius, a patriarch of the pagans. She was given to a nurse and when she came to the age of discretion, she was baptized, and for this her father hated her. One day, when she had arrived at the age of fifteen, she was watching her nurse's sheep with the other young girls. The prefect Olibrius[3] was passing by, and when he saw such a beautiful girl, he was inflamed with passion and sent his men hurrying after her saying, "Go and seize her. If she is freeborn, I will take her for my wife; if she is a slave woman, I will have her as my concubine."

Thus she was presented for his inspection, and he questioned her about her lineage, and her name, and her religion. She responded that she was of noble lineage, that her name was Margaret, and her religion was Christian.

The prefect said, "The first two fit you properly, for you possess nobility and are as beautiful as a pearl; but the third—that such a beautiful and noble girl should have a crucified God—is not at all fitting."

She asked, "How do you know that Christ was crucified?"

And he replied, "From the books of Christians."

Margaret said, "Since you have read of both Christ's suffering and glory in them, you should be ashamed to believe one and deny the other." Then she went on to claim that He had willingly been crucified for our redemption, but now He lived in eternity. The angry prefect ordered her put into prison.

The next day he ordered her brought to him and said, "Proud girl, pity your beauty and adore our gods, and all will be well for you."

She said, "I adore Him for whom the earth trembles, the sea rages, and all creatures are afraid."

The prefect said, "Unless you give in to me, I will have your body butchered."

Margaret responded, "Christ gave himself to death for me, and so I wish to die for Christ."

Now, by the prefect's order, she was suspended on a rack and cruelly beaten with rods, then scratched with iron rakes and torn so that her bones were laid bare, and the blood poured from her body as if from a pure fountain. The people who were standing by wept, and said, "Oh Margaret, we truly grieve for you, because we see how cruelly your body is torn. Oh what beauty you have lost through your lack of belief: in order to live, at least believe now."

She replied to them, "Oh bad counselors, go away and leave me alone. This torment of the flesh is the salvation of the soul." And she said to the prefect, "Impudent dog and insatiable lion, you may have power over the body, but the soul is held by Christ." [see Lk 12:4] Then the prefect covered his face with his cape, so that he would not see so much blood.

Then she was taken down and returned to the prison, where a wonderful light shone. When she was there, she prayed to the Lord, that He make visible her enemy who was fighting against her, and an enormous dragon appeared there, but when he came to devour her, she made the sign of the cross and he disappeared. Or, as one may read elsewhere, it opened its jaw over her head, and stretched out its tongue under her heels, and swallowed her up; but as it was trying to digest her, she defended herself with the sign of the cross and by the power of the cross the dragon broke open and the virgin came out from there. What is said, however, about the dragon devouring her and then breaking open, is considered apocryphal and frivolous.

Again, the demon, still trying to deceive her, changed into the form of a man. When she saw him she fell to prayer, and when she arose, the devil came to her, took her hand, and said, "Let all that you've done be sufficient for you, and let me be!" [see Lk 8:28] But then she seized him by the head, pushed him to the ground and set her right foot on his neck and said, "Lie there, proud demon, under the feet of a woman!" [see Ps 110:1, Acts 2:35]

Then the demon cried out, "Oh blessed Margaret, I am overcome! If I had been defeated by a young man I would not care, but I am overcome by a tender girl. I feel even more sorry because your father and mother were my friends."

Then she forced him to truly say why he had come. He said it was to urge her to obey the prefect's orders. She also forced him to say why he tempted Christians in so many ways. He responded that it was his nature to have hatred toward virtuous people. Although he was often repulsed by them, nevertheless, he was infected with the desire to seduce them, because he envied humans the happiness which he had lost and could not retrieve for himself, and so he strove to steal it from others. He added that Solomon[4] had enclosed an infinite number of demons in a vase, and after his death the demons sent out fire from the vase, and caused men to suppose that it contained a great treasure. They broke the vase and the demons escaped and filled the air. When this was said, the virgin lifted her foot and said, "Be gone, miserable thing," and the demon immediately vanished. As a result, Margaret was confident: because she had defeated the leader, she would surely overcome his assistant.

The following day, before a gathering of people, she was presented to the judge. Disdaining to sacrifice, her body was stripped and burned with flaming torches, so that all wondered how such a tender girl could stand the torment. Then she was tied up and put into a tub filled with water, so that by varying the punishment, the intensity of the pain might increase; but the earth shook and all saw the virgin emerge from there [see Mt 27:51].

Then five thousand men believed and for the name of Christ received death sentences. But the prefect was afraid; so that no others would be converted, he ordered that the blessed Margaret be beheaded. However, she requested that she have time to pray, and prayed devoutly for herself, for her persecutors, and for all who would honor her memory and invoke her. She added that any woman in perilous childbirth who invoked her would give birth to a healthy child. A voice from heaven said that her petitions had been heard. She rose from her prayer and said to the swordsman, "Brother, take your sword and strike me!" He struck her head off with one blow, and thus she received the crown of martyrdom. She suffered on the twentieth of July, as we find in her story, or, as we may read elsewhere, on the twelfth of July.

A certain saint says this about the holy virgin, "Blessed Margaret was filled with the fear of God, endowed with righteousness, covered with religion, infused with compunction, praiseworthy for her virtue, singularly patient, and nothing could be found in her contrary to the Christian religion. She was hated by her father and loved by our Lord Jesus Christ."

2. *The Life of St. Margaret from the* South English Legendary

St. Margaret was a holy maiden and good,
She was born in Antioch[5] and came of noble blood.
Her father was named Theodosius, a high-ranking man then,
He was a very high patriarch and master of the law.
He did not believe in Jesus Christ because he was a heathen.　　　　5
He was not pleased with his young daughter Margaret
Because in her heart she wished to be a Christian;
The false gods she saw every day she believed to be devils.

She heard tell of St. Stephen[6] and of St. Lawrence[7] also:
How in painful martyrdom they were put to death,　　　　10
And also of other martyrs who suffered pains here.
She fervently wished to be their companion.
This maiden was very young when her mother died,
Her father soon learned that she was drawn to Christianity.

He made great trouble about her; he sent her from home,　　　　15
To a nurse to guard her well, to turn her heart.
Fifteen miles from Antioch, this pure and gentle maiden
Was sent into the land of Asia, far away.
This pure maiden was very young when she went from home;

She was scarcely fifteen years old when her father sent her away.   20
It was also two hundred years and four score and nine[8]
After God was born to bring us out of torment.

Evil was the emperor, Diocletian.[9]
Evil also was his deputy who was called Maximian.[10]
They destroyed all Christian men and sought them far and wide,   25
And when they might find any, they put them to a painful death.

They appointed many justices who went across the land
In every direction to seek Christian men and kill them.
One who was named Olibrius[11] went into Asia;
The emperor had sent him there to seek out Christian men.   30

This young maiden who was there at the end of Asia,
Privately night and day did cry to our Lord:
To send her a steadfast heart, in the name of Our Lady Mary,
So that she might endure the torments of death without cowardice.
Her nurse that had care of her loved her dearly,   35
But she was not fully aware of what Margaret's heart was drawn to.
This pure maiden who was so young, of scarcely fifteen years,
Always wished to be put to death for Our Lord's love.
Her nurse sent her every day with her sheep into the field,
To watch the sheep with other maidens her age.   40
One day as this maiden was with her sheep in the field,
Justice Olibrius came passing by.

He beheld this pure maiden and he thought her very fair,
He was immediately drawn to her with lecherous love.
He longed greatly for her; he sent his men forth,   45
And commanded them that they hastily inquire about her.
If she were of noble blood she should be his wife
And lead a life of great nobility, and if she were not a free woman,
He would buy her at great price to possess her for lust
Without marriage, as his lover, in the sin of lechery.   50

When she saw this she began to cry loudly:
"Lord," she said, "I pray you, who were born of Mary
And died on the tree, in order to bring us out of misery:
Preserve my body in purity so that it will not be defiled;
Body and soul I commit to you because I foresee death.   55
I am beset by evil men so that I may flee nowhere.
Lord, give me a steadfast heart to suffer death,
So that I shall not flinch from it because of powerful torments."

St. Margaret was brought forth before the evil justice
Who intended to fully have his lecherous way with her. 60
Intently he beheld this maiden: "Damsel," he said,
"Tell me from whom you come and of what kin.
Tell me also what your name is and what life you lead."
This maiden answered him without any fear:

"My kindred," she said, "is so well-known it may not be hidden. 65
My father is a great man, well-known among you here;
Theodosius is the highest master of our temple.
You ask also what my name is: Margaret I am called.
That is and was my original name, but I have taken a higher name:
I shall be called a Christian woman for my Christian faith, 70
For that is my highest name and therefore I must confess,
That I believe in Jesus Christ and I will never forsake Him."

When Olibrius heard this he was completely at a loss
As if he were in another world. "Noble maiden," he said,
"The two things fair and sweet which you said first become you: 75
That you come from noble blood and you are named Margaret,
These become you very well, such a noble and free maiden.
But the third is not at all becoming to you, as you may see.
That you should honor that false god whom Jews slew on the tree,
Such a noble maiden as you are, God grant that it should not be. 80
It is more fitting for such a gracious body as yours to be in the bedroom,
Lying embraced in my arms, than to honor a false god."

The maiden gave him a quick answer with a most gracious speech:
"Sir," she said, "The evil Jews that slew God on the Cross,
Were brought into the pains of hell for their evil deed, 85
And yet they did us good though they loved us not,
For we were brought out of torment through His death,
Even though they who brought Him to it had not intended that."

Then for wrath Olibrius began to shout and cry very loudly.
He ordered the holy maiden to be taken and led into a secure prison 90
That was so deep and dark that men might be terrified
And turn to their false gods to do sacrifice.
The next morning he called knights of the law, great and wise,
And sat himself amidst them all as a high justice,
And had this holy maid fetched in order to receive their judgment. 95
Before these tyrants, mildly, this holy maiden came,
And made the sign of the cross and gave all her anger to Our Lord,
And was completely ready to receive martyrdom for His love.

Olibrius spoke very courteously and said, "Margaret,
Think about your nobility, how gentle and sweet you are, 100
And have mercy on your fair body so that you not injure it.
For tonight I think you had best consider:
Choose whether you wish to be brought to a painful death with shame,
Or honor our high gods who have made all things."

"Sir," said this holy maiden, "Our Lord himself accepted 105
A painful death and forsook worldly joys to bring us out of torment.
For him I will accept death, I have no doubt,
Rather than bow down my head to venerate your false gods."

Then the justice turned as if he were insane with wrath.
He called the torturers so fiercely, it would frighten men. 110
"Take this whore now," he said, "and hang her on a tree,
And tear her skin and flesh so that I can see her guts.
Bind her tight, completely naked, so that she can never flee,
So that our gods may be avenged for her evil, sinful deeds."

The tormentors were very ready, for their hearts were drawn to evil. 115
They quickly stripped the maiden naked and bound her very tightly.
High off the ground they hung her up and beat her all over.
They gave her many wounds with scourges and sharp pricks.
They tore her tender flesh completely apart, so that it is a pity to tell,
In streams her blood flowed down as water does from a well. 120
Because her limbs were tender, and the scourges sharp and keen,
In pieces the flesh fell down, the bones could be seen.
Alas, her sweet tender body was so villainously torn apart!
Alas, for pity's sake, how might any man do such a deed!

With awls they ripped open her abdomen; the guts were visible. 125
Alas, for such a sinful deed: they tore apart her dear limbs.
And for shame the justice would not look,
But held himself back and hid his eyes and many others also.
The men who stood in that place and saw all that suffering
Sorrowed and grieved greatly and wept with their eyes. 130
"Maiden," they said, "Margaret, who are so noble and lovely,
Have pity for your fair body so that this torment may stop,
For you will still be very worthy if you will change your mind."
The maiden cast up her eyes and answered at last.

And said, "You wicked counselors, go from me immediately. 135
I have taken another counsel; I forsake all of you."
Olibrius sat and beheld how her limbs were dripping blood;
He could not look at it for grief nor could many who stood there.

Because of pity and grief he hid both his eyes with his mantle,
So too did many others, that they might not see the suffering. 140
"Maiden," said Olibrius, "change your mind, I advise you,
And you shall lead the best life among all women that I know."

"Be quiet," said this holy maiden, "keep your evil hand still.
You have power over my body, therefore do your will [see Lk 12:4];
But my Lord knows my soul well, you cannot kill her. 145
You, with all your might, may not injure her at all."

When the evil man saw that he might not succeed,
He could not for grief see her terrible bleeding.
He made the men leave off their torturing and lead her to prison
While he decided what he would do with her. 150
This maiden lay in a strong prison by herself, all alone;
She did not know to whom to complain of her wounds.

But angels came down to her and comforted her [see Mt 4:11]
She was deep in prayers by day and also by night.
She asked Our Lord by His grace that He send her some vision 155
Of the devil that worried her and reveal his power.

I am told that the devil came silently to this maiden
In the form of a dragon, but I know not whether they lie.
He yawned and put his upper jaw over her head,
And his lower jaw and his tongue underneath at her heel. 160
He gaped open very wide and swallowed up the maiden.
She went into that accursed stomach, but she would stay there only
    a little while.
Because she made the sign of the cross, the devil immediately burst,
And this maiden whole and sound came out of the worm.

But I cannot say if this is true for it is not written as truth; 165
But whether it is true or not, no man knows.
But it would be against nature if the devil were made to die,
For he may not suffer death; I cannot believe it.
Yet I also cannot not believe that his power was so strong
To take such a holy creature into his womb. 170
But truly it is written that in a man's likeness
The devil came to this maiden to try to deceive her.
Suddenly he came to this maiden in order to test her.
This maiden arose very boldly and gripped him by the hand
"You have done enough," she said, "you shall do no more; 175
You shall bow down at once for your false teaching."

She seized him by his evil head, and cast him forcefully to the ground,
And promptly set her right foot firmly on the back of his neck [see
   Ps 110:1; Acts 2:35].
"You devil," she said, "are so strong, full of pride and envy.
It would be better if you had remained at home than to come test me.   180
Bow down; you are overcome! I shall stand upon you [see Lk 10:19];
You may report back home that you were under a maiden's hand."
Firmly she bound this foul creature [see Mt 12:29] and scourged him
   most severely.
Terribly he yelled and often said, "Noble maiden, mercy!"

"Alas that I came here; my might is taken from me!   185
Alas that a tender maiden should thus overcome me!
If it were a man of some strength, I would think nothing of it,
But I am ashamed that a young girl has brought me to the ground.
Maiden, by your graciousness, have mercy on me.
Let me go this one time; I will never harm you again.   190
I ask you for love of your kin who are—every one of them—my friends,
And serve me well, as you know, all but you alone."

"Oh thief," spoke this holy maiden, "you will stay longer.
You, who fly around so widely, will tell me about your trickery.
Why do you bother Christian men most above all others?"   195
"Certainly, maiden," said the devil, "because they love us least,
And of all men shame us the most and are our greatest foes.
They have great strength from their God to go among us.
If by natural right each one may try to destroy his foe,
Then we ought not to be blamed for acting in our way.   200
Among men of the Old Law we behaved so for a time,
They served well their high God, which made us envious.

"Then came King Solomon,[12] who was wise regarding the law;
Who served Almighty God well, and was drawn into His service.
Therefore we became envious and tested him most severely.   205
But his Lord gave him such power that he overcame us at last,
And put us in a strong vessel, and cast us in a pit,
And sealed it well all around, and shut us up tight in there.
While he was alive, we had no power
To go among men, we were so tightly locked in.   210
Nor after his death either, if men had wished it.
But instead, men brought us out of there because of greed for gold.
For when we were shut in we did blow and blast
And cast fire glowing bright red out of the earth.
Therefore men came there often and saw fire there   215
And said that there had to be great treasure near:

'Look how red the vapor comes out! As we can see,
If we dig quickly we will be rich men soon.'
They dug and found the vessel in which we were put.
'Aye,' they said, 'we have found the treasure shut up here.' 220

"This vessel they broke immediately and expected truly to take it.
But they found a poor treasure at first opening;
Not much at all for their benefit or for other men either.
But we were very glad when we were let out of prison,
And went and filled all the air above and thus in every direction, 225
We wander and harm men throughout the land.
Now I have told you, Margaret, of all our deeds.
Have pity on me, I beg you, and bring me out of this wretchedness,
And be like a maiden should: full of mildness and grace.
I promise that I will never trouble you any more." 230

At last this holy maiden let the foul thing go;
The demon was very glad that he was out of bonds.
On another day, the justice was seated on his throne
And had the holy maiden Margaret fetched before him.
He asked whether she were willing yet to change her mind. 235
"Truly, sir," said the maiden, "you speak about nothing."

Then the justice in great wrath ordered a fire made immediately
And had the maiden stripped naked and cast into the fire.
But the fire was quenched instantly and she was not burned at all;
She was whole and sound and again brought before the justice. 240
There was great wrath and sorrow; they bound her feet and hands,
And cast her in a deep well of water, head down.
But Our Lord's might was much greater; her bonds immediately burst,
And, all unharmed, she came out of the water easily.

The justice was nearly out of his wits when he heard this tiding. 245
"Surely," he said, "in some way we can put her to death."
He ordered hot water all seething, and when it boiled,
He ordered the holy maiden seized and cast into the water.
When she was put in there, simultaneously the earth quaked [see
    Mt 27:51]
So terribly that all of the people were afraid. 250
The maiden came out of the boiling water,
And none were injured among all that crowd.
Lord, great is your might as one may always see,
That anything in such torment might be alive.
Five thousand men in the place when they saw this, 255
Converted instantly to Christianity and praised Our Lord most high.

When the justice saw that, he began to cry out and groan.
He took the men who converted and cut off each of their heads,
And also ordered the holy maiden seized and her head cut off too,
So that she would be put out of life and out of woe. 260
Thus an executioner was commanded; Maltus was his name.[13]
He pondered how he might treat this maiden with the most shame:
He led her outside the town where, at the break of dawn,
Thieves and other men were judged by the law.

When Margaret was brought to the vile place, 265
She asked the executioner first to give her time to say her prayers.
Maltus gave her that and told her to be quick.
The holy maiden sat kneeling and cast her eyes to heaven.
"Lord," she said, "Jesus Christ, who redeemed me on the Cross,
And the source of all goodness, I thank you with my heart and mouth, 270
If your will is to bring me out of this world's wretchedness,
To be led to the joy of heaven, without stain on my body.
Grant me, I pray you, for your five wounds,
Lord, that if any man has a good remembrance of my life,
And of the suffering which I have endured, for your grace, 275
Or my life is written with good intent and read in any place,
If they pray with good intent, grant them mercy and grace.
If they are in any distress, bring them out of pain.
If any one in honor of me builds a chapel,
Or any altar in a church, or provides for any lamp there, 280
At his cost, in honor of me; Lord, I ask you,
If they pray for a thing that is proper to pray for, grant it to them for
    love of me.

And if any woman calls to me in the labor of childbirth,
Or better, reads my life, Lord be merciful to her.
Nor let her die, but bring forth that child to view 285
All safely from his mother's womb with all his limbs in place.
Save both mother and child, Lord, for love of me.
Lord, for your mother's love, may this prayer be granted."

Instantly, when the maiden had said this prayer,
There came a very strong thunderclap and great lightning, 290
So that the people that stood about fell down for dread
And lay there, as if they were stunned, they seemed dead so long [see
    Mt 28:4].

A dove whiter than any snow came down from heaven
To the maiden in the thunder after her prayer.
"Maiden," it said, "Margaret, you are blessed and noble; 295

Our Lord grants you your prayer until the world's end.
Come now to rest after your death, Our Lord sends for you;
You shall go after your great suffering, to the joy of heaven."

The dove flew back to heaven from which he came.
The maiden arose very meekly to receive her martyrdom. 300
"Maltus," she said, "come forth now and do your lord's bidding,
For in my Lord's name I am now ready."

"O, Margaret, mercy," this executioner said immediately,
"For all the world, I dare not do so foul a deed:
I see so much light from heaven around you on every side. 305
Instead, I wish I might die with you and go with you thither."

"Maltus," said the holy maiden, "unless you do this deed,
You will have no part henceforth with me, therefore do what I advise you."
Maltus drew his sword: "Sweet Lord!" he said,
"Forgive me this dreadful deed, for I do it with great fear." 310
He cut off the holy head and immediately when he had done so,
He fell down by her right side and died with her.

Just as this maiden died, all the people saw
A white dove fly out of her into heaven on high.
In this manner the holy maiden brought her life to an end. 315
Her life was very virtuous, who ever thinks about it:
When women bear a child, in the company of other women,
It is good that they read her life, for certainly it is the truth.
Now St. Margaret, the holy maiden, we ask at the last
That you pray for us so that we may go to the joy of heaven. 320

3. *The Katherine Group* Seinte Margarete

In the name of the Father and of the Son and of the Holy Spirit, here begins the life and the passion of St. Margaret.

After our Lord's pain and His Passion and His death on the Cross and His rising from death, and after His Ascension when he rose up to heaven, there were many martyrs, both men and women, put to various deaths for the name of the Lord; and as renowned champions they overcame and cast down their three kinds of foes—the fiend, and this weak world, and their bodies' lusts—and went from these woes to joy and to eternal pleasure, crowned by Christ.

There were many more misbelieving men then than now, who praised and glorified heathen idols, wretched things made of stones and sticks. But I, one of God's servants named Teochimus,[14] learned in God's law, read and searched through many and various pages; and never in any place did I learn of any who was worthy to be revered as is fitting to a lord, except the high Savior who is in heaven. He lived, while he wished to, among worldly men;

and cured the dumb and deaf; and raised up the dead to light and to life [see Mt 11:5]; and crowned his chosen ones who suffer death or any other hardship; and has granted all Christian men—so that they profit by that name—that life which lasts eternally. I, baptized at the font in the Almighty Father's name, and of the wise Son, and of the Holy Spirit, was living in the land at the time when that blessed maiden, Margaret, by name, fought with the fiend and with his earthly limbs, and overcame and cast them down. Then I obtained what was written by the scribes, all about her passion and her painful death which she suffered for the Lord.

Listen, all who have ears and hearing: widows with the wedded, and maidens especially, listen very eagerly to how they should love the living Lord and live in maidenhood,[15] which is the power dearest to Him; so that they may, through that blessed maiden whom we remember today with the honor of maidenhood, sing the blessed maidens' song, with this maiden and with the heavenly throng in heaven.

This maiden whom we remember was named Margaret; and her fleshly father was called Theodosius, patriarch and prince of that heathen people. But she, as the dear Lord ordained it, was brought into a village to be fed and fostered, fifteen miles from the great city Antioch. When she was fifteen years of age, and her mother had gone the way which all earthly men must go, she was more dear to the one [her foster mother] who had guarded and weaned her. All loved her who looked on her, as one whom God loved. The heavenly Lord gave her the grace of the Holy Spirit, so that she chose Him as beloved and as her lover, and committed into His hand the honor of her maidenhood, her will and her work, and all that she would ever own in the world, with her whole self, to guard and to rule. Thus, the meekest of the mild, she tended and guarded her foster mother's livestock with other maidens in the field. She heard everywhere how Christ's chosen ones were put to death for true belief; and yearned and desired eagerly, if it were God's will, that she might be one of the many mother's children who suffered so much for the Lord.

It happened after a time that there came out of Asia to Antioch the fiend's own fosterchild, to honor his heathen gods in the great city. He was named Olibrius,[16] sheriff of the land, who destroyed and condemned all who believed in the living God. As he went his way, he saw this blessed maiden Margaret. As she tended and guarded her foster-mother's sheep out in the field, she shimmered and shone all over her face and body. Fiercely, he ordered his troops: "Seize her quickly. If she is a free woman, I will have her and take her as my wife; and if she is a slave, I will choose her for a concubine, and will free her with treasure and with gold, and because of her lovely face, all I have will be for her benefit."

As the knights were about to lay hands on her, she began to cry out and call to Christ: "Lord, have compassion and mercy on your woman; nor let my soul perish with the lost, nor my life with the wicked [see Ps 35:9, Vulgate], who are completely bloodied with sin. Jesus Christ, God's Son, be my joy and my gladness forever; I will greatly praise and exult you. High Lord, hold my heart, I beseech you, in true belief, and protect my body, which is absolutely committed to you, from fleshly filth, so that my soul may never be soiled in sin, through the body's lust, which pleases only for a little while. Lord, listen to me. I have a dear gemstone, and I have given it to you—my maidenhood I mean—the brightest blossom in the body that bears and guards it well. Never let the evil one cast it in the mire, for it is dear to you, and to him it is the most loathsome thing, and he continually wars against it and makes attacks on it with all kinds of tricks. Lord, guard me, and always protect my maidenhood for yourself; never allow the evil one to attack my mind or to lessen my wisdom. And send me your messenger from heaven, Savior, who will instruct me and tell how I should answer this devil's sheriff. For I see myself, Lord, beset and surrounded like a lamb by mad wolves, and like the bird caught in the fowler's trap, like a fish hung on a hook, like a roe deer taken in a net. High Savior, help me, never leave me in the hands of evil men."

Because she spoke like this, the knights all returned and said to their lord: "You cannot share power with this maiden, for she worships none of our heathen gods, but believes in the Lord whom the Jews condemned and put to death, and whom the heathen hung high on the cross." When Olibrius the evil one heard this, his expression changed, and he ordered her immediately brought before him. As soon as she had come, he spoke to her. "Tell me," he said, "whether you are the child of a free man, or a slave woman."

The blessed maiden Margaret quickly answered him and softly said: "I am a free woman, and God's slave."

"Yes," he said, "but what god do you exult and honor?"

"I exult," she said, "the high Father, the Savior in heaven, and His dear Son, named Jesus Christ; and to Him, I, a maiden, have given my maidenhood, and love Him as lover and believe in Him as Lord."

"How now!" he said, "Do you believe in and love the one who pitifully died miserably on the Cross?"

"No," she said, "those who intended to kill Him—your forefathers—have died miserably and are wretchedly lost; and He lives, a royal child, crowned in His kingdom, king of kings, eternally in heaven."

At these words the villain became exceedingly angry and ordered her cast into prison and into the torture chamber, until he had a better idea of the way he would mar her maidenhood; and then he went into Antioch, and worshipped his heathen gods, as was proper and fitting to his evil faith. The next day he ordered her brought before him. She was quickly brought out, and he began to say: "Maiden, have mercy and compassion on yourself: think of your youth, and of your seemly shape, and of your shining face. Follow my will and worship my idols, and you shall be above the highest in my household, with all that I own and possess in the world."

Margaret, mildest and meekest of maidens, answered: "Now know this, if you will—for He knows it full well, who has sealed me and my maidenhood for Himself—that you may not in any way, with wealth or with pleasure, with woe or with tribulation, or with any worldly thing, turn or pull me from the path which I have begun to follow. And you know that your words to me are unworthy; for I love and believe Him alone, who rules and guides with His mind the winds and weather, and all that is circled by the sea and sun. Both above and beneath, all bow to Him and obey [see Phil 2:10]. And besides this, because He is so mighty and so powerful, He is the most lovely living thing to look at and sweetest to smell; nor can His sweet scent, nor His almighty power, nor His matchless loveliness, decrease or end; for He will never end, but lives eternally in honor, and His great might will last forever."

"Stop!" said Olibrius, "These words are worth nothing. But know one thing: unless you stop them, my sword shall destroy and swallow up your flesh, and afterwards your bones shall be consumed by burning coals [see Ps 102:3]. But if you will believe me, you shall be my beloved and my wedded wife, and rule as lady all that I own and am lord over."

"I believe your promise," she said, "but keep it and your love, for I have a lover whom I will not lose or leave for anything. You are trying too hard and I am afraid you are wasting your time, for your flattery and anger are all one to me. I will commit my body to every bitterness that you can think of, no matter how sorely it hurts, that I might have the reward of maidens in heaven. God died for us, the dear Lord, and I am not afraid to suffer death for Him. He has His mark on me, sealed with His seal [see 2 Cor 1:22]; nor may either life or death divide us in two[see Rom 8:39]."

"Is that so?" he said. "Take her now," he said to his executioners, "strip her stark naked and hang her up high, and beat her bare body with wounding rods." The accursed scoundrels beat so wickedly on her lovely body, that it broke open all over and lathered with blood. The blessed maiden lifted her heart up high toward heaven and cried to Christ: "Lord, in you is all my hope! [see Ps 25:2] Hold my mind and my will to you so firmly that they will not stray, despite the woe or any pleasure my enemies do to me. Never allow my enemies, the fiends I mean, to possess or mock me, as they would if they were able to cast me down; but they never will, me or others who rightly love you. Heavenly Lord, blessed be your name. Lord, look to me and have mercy on me. Soften my pain, and salve my wounds, so that the fact I suffer affliction will appear nowhere on my face."

The executioners beat so wickedly on her body that the blood burst out and flowed down from her body as a stream does from a well.

While men scourged her so grievously, Olibrius, that evil sheriff without pity, said, "Stop now and cease your unwise words, and listen, maiden, to my advice, and it will be well for you." All those who were there, men and women, cried out with pity and lamented this maiden, and some of them said, "Margaret, Margaret, maiden so worthy if you wished it, woe is us that we see your soft lovely body torn apart so horribly! Alas! Woman, what beauty you let go and lose because of your lack of belief. The sheriff is pitilessly angry and will surely kill you—but love and believe him now, woman, and you will have the greatest happiness and wealth."

"O," she said, "wretches, fools without wit, alas, what do you think? If my body is torn apart, my soul shall rest with the righteous: suffering and the body's pain are the soul's healers. But I advise you, believe in the living God, mighty and powerful and full of every good, who hears those who cry to Him and opens the heaven-gates. For I will not listen to you, nor praise any of your gods, which are dumb and deaf, and blind and without might, made with human hands.

"But you," she said then to the evil Olibrius, "do your father's work, the fiend of hell [see Jn 8:44]. But the high Savior is my help, you heathen hound. If He has given you my body to tear apart, hateful sheriff, He will deliver my soul out of your hands and raise her into heaven, though you hang me here. And you, horrible devil, you evil lion hateful to God, your power will diminish and melt to nothing, and you will forever suffer in pain and sorrow when I rejoice with God and am glad forever."

He was nearly out of his mind with wrath, and ordered her most cruelly hung and hauled up higher than she was before, and her beautiful flesh was torn and rent with sharp swords and awls of iron. But she looked up on high and began to say:

"Lord, hellhounds have surrounded me, and the tormenting crowd has beset me; but you, high Savior, are all around to help me. Merciful God, deliver my soul from the sword's edge and from the hound's hand, for I have her alone. Save me, Lord, out of the lion's mouth, and my meek mildness from the horns of unicorns. [Ps 22:16, 20–1] Gladden me, God, with your joy and give me the hope of salvation, that my prayer will pierce through to heaven. Send me your messenger in the shape of a dove to come help me, so that I may preserve my maidenhood for you unstained. Further, if it is your will, Lord, let me see the accursed being who makes war against me; and make known your power in me, Almighty God, that I may overcome him, so that through me all maidens forever will trust more in you. Blessed be your name, brightest face of all, world of all worlds forever into eternity."

While she spoke like this, she was so torn that neither the wicked sheriff nor anyone else who was there could look toward her for horror because of the strong flow of the bloody stream; but the hardest-hearted hid their heads under their mantles because of the painful wounds they saw on her.

Then the wicked Olibrius spoke again: "What does it mean, maiden, that you will neither submit to me, nor have pity or mercy on yourself? Yes, don't you feel your flesh all ripped and torn because I have ordered it? But submit now and obey me before you suffer and die a cruel death. For if you do not, you will suffer by the sword with all your limbs sundered, and when you are completely torn apart in the sight of all who now sit and watch you, I will count all your sinews." [see Ps 21:18; Ps 22:14, 17, Vulgate]

"But, hateful hound," she said then, "though you do all that, you will not shame me. When my soul is before God's sight in heaven, what you do with my body on earth does not matter. But you should be ashamed, you shameless devil—if you knew how to be ashamed—you argue with such a young maiden, and waste all your time and achieve nothing. For if I followed the will of the flesh, for you to do as you wish with it, my soul would sink, as you will, to suffering in hell. Therefore, I am most willing for my flesh to perish here, so that gentle Jesus will crown my soul in the joys of heaven, and after Doomsday join them both together, in everlasting joy and eternal happiness."

He became so angry that he nearly went mad. He ordered her cast into the prison house, on pain of death, and men quickly obeyed. It was about the seventh hour of the day that men dragged her thus into the darkest dwelling, the worst one to enter. And she lifted up her hand and blessed all her body with the sign of the holy cross. As she was drawn inside, she began to pray this prayer to Our Lord: "Dear Lord, though your judgments are secret, they are all beneficial. All things both heavenly and earthly submit to you and obey. You are hope and help to all who praise you. You are fosterer and father to helpless children. You are the treasure of the wedded, and the protector of widows, and the maiden's reward. You are the joy of the world, Jesus Christ, kingly Son: God born from God as light is from light.[17] Look to me, Lord—my life, my love, my lover—and pity me, your maiden. My own fleshly father did drive me away, his only daughter, and my friends are, for your love, Lord, my enemies and foes; but I hold you, Savior, as both father and friend; do not let me go, living Lord. Look on me and help me, and allow me to set my eyes on the wicked one who wars against me, and let me judge him, Lord of judgment [see 1 Cor 6:3]. He afflicts and hates me, although I never knew that I had harmed him. But such is his kind, and his envious heart is so full of poison that he hates everything good, every holy and sanctifying thing. Lord, you are the judge of the quick and dead.[18] My joy, judge between us two, do not be angry because of the words which I say. I always beseech you for one thing above all others: that you preserve my maidenhood unharmed for yourself, my soul from sin, my wit and my wisdom from the thoughtless one. My Savior, all that I wish for is in you. May you be blessed forever, beginning and end, without end and beginning, forever in eternity."

Her foster mother was one who tended her, and came to the prison house and brought her bread for food and drink from the spring, so that she lived. Then she and many more watched her through an eyehole as she prayed her prayers. Suddenly out of a corner a demon of hell came toward her in a dragon's likeness, so horrible that they were terrified by that sight. The evil creature glistened as if he were covered with gold. His locks and long beard shone like gold, and his horrible teeth seemed to be of black iron. In his horned head on either side of his high hooked nose, his two eyes shone brighter than the stars or gemstones, broad as basins. Fire sparked out from his disgusting mouth, and from his nostrils issued smothering smoke, most hateful to smell. He let out his tongue, so long that he swung it around his neck, and it seemed as though a sharp sword shot out of his mouth, which glistened as a flame and lit everything in fire. All that place was full of strong and powerful stench, and because of this demon all the shadows shimmered and shone. He stretched himself and steered toward the meek maiden, and with his jaw gaping at her threateningly, he began to crane his neck and draw back as if he would swallow her completely. If she was terrified by that horrible demon, it was not much wonder! Her face began to grow pale, because of the horror that gripped her, and because of fearful terror she forgot her prayer that she might see the invisible demon, nor did she think that her prayer was granted, but she promptly fell to the earth on her knees and lifted her hands up high toward heaven and spoke this prayer to Christ:

"Invisible God, full of every good thing, whose wrath is so fierce that the inhabitants of hell and heaven and all living things quake before it; help me Lord, against this terrible creature, so that it not harm me. You created and rule all earthly things. Those who praise and honor you in heaven, and all the things that dwell on earth—the fish who float in the waters with fins, the flying birds who fly in the air, and all that is created—perform your will and keep your commands, except for man alone. The sun runs her course without any rest; the moon and stars who move through the air neither stay nor stop, but move forever more, and they never turn from the way that you wrought for them. You steer the sea-stream so that it may not flood farther than you mark. The winds, the storms, the woods, and the waters, submit to you and obey. Fiends and angels have fear of your anger. The serpents and wild beasts who dwell in the wood live after the law that you ordained, beloved Lord. Look to me and help me, your handiwork, for all my hope is in you. You harrowed hell, and as a champion overcame the accursed spirit who tries to destroy me. But hear me now and help me, for in my affliction I have no other kin but you alone. Protect me against this evil creature, because I trust entirely in you alone, and revere your will, dear Lord; through your strength I may stand against him, and cast down his great arrogance. Look, he hurries to swallow me entirely, and intends to bear me into his baleful hole where he dwells. But by your blissful name I bless myself now."

And then she drew on herself from top to bottom and then across, the beloved sign of the dear cross that Christ rested on. At that moment the dragon rushed to her and set his horrible, greedy and huge mouth over the top of her head, and reached out his tongue to the soles of her feet, and swallowing, swung her into his wide belly—but for his evil fate, and to the glory of Christ. For the sign of the cross with which she was armed quickly delivered her and was instantly his slayer; his body burst open in the middle, and that blessed maiden came out of his belly all unharmed, without any stain at all, praising on high her Savior in heaven.

Then looking to her right, she saw where an invisible demon sat, much blacker than any black man, so grisly, so loathsome, that no man might briefly describe it, and his two hands were bound fast to his gnarled knees [see Mt 12:29]. When she saw this she began to thank and praise her Savior:

"Brightest face of all who were ever born, blossom bloomed and born from a maiden's bosom; Jesus, God and God's Son, may you be blessed. I am joyful and glad for your goodness, king of kings, immortal Lord. You preserve and lift up true belief. You are the well of wisdom, and each joy grows and awakens from you. You are the angels' joy, who rules and guards them without ceasing. I am utterly joyful and glad with spiritual mirth: but is that any wonder, mighty and matchless God? Yes, Lord, I see my faith blooming. I have seen how the fiend who meant to defeat me fell exactly in two, and felt how his foul stench flowed and floated away. I have seen the devil of hell cast down here, and the man-slayer slain, the strong demon destroyed. I have seen his arrogance and his foolish pride suddenly fallen [see Is 13:11]. I have seen how the Cross, which delivered me so quickly from his cruel jaws, made that baleful worm and bitter beast burst. I have seen holy and blessed oil as it descended to me, and I myself smelled you, sweet Jesus, always sweeter than anything on earth. I have seen bliss and because of it I rejoice. In blessing and joy I live now, nor was I ever so sad as I am happy now. I thank you for it long-suffering Lord. I have dashed down the dragon, and cast over his fierceness; and he died who intended to swallow me. I am champion and he is vanquished and overcome. But I thank you for it, who are crowned king of kings eternally; refuge of the sorrowful and suffering and sinful; guide of the wandering, and wretches, and the hopeless; castle of strength against the strong demon; maidens' mirth and martyrs' crown; softest banquet-seat and golden scepter; purest gold and most glistening gemstone; the dearest and sweetest of all visible and invisible things; the shaper of all created things; threefold Trinity and yet One, threefold in three persons and One in high dignity. High holy God, full of every good, be forever and ever glorified and praised without end."

When she had praised Our Lord this long, the grisly thing came creeping toward her and held her by the feet and like the sorriest thing sadly said:

"Margaret, maiden, you have injured me enough: do not pain me anymore [see Lk 8:28] with your blessed prayers that you pray so often; for it painfully binds me up completely and makes me so weak, I can feel no strength in myself. You have brought my brother down horribly and slain the slyest devil of hell, whom I sent in a dragon's likeness to swallow you, and harm the might of your maidenhood with his great power, and make it so that you were never more remembered among mankind on earth. You destroyed and killed him with the holy Cross, and you are making me die with the strength of the prayers which are in your mind. But leave me and let me go, lady, I ask you."

That mild maiden Margaret grasped that grisly thing which did not frighten her at all, firmly took him by the hideous hair of his head and lifted him up and dashed him right down to earth, and set her right foot on his rough neck and went on to speak:

"Stop now, wretched pestilence, at least be quiet, deceitful black devil, so that you afflict me no more. My maidenhood will not help you at all, for I have my Savior in heaven to help, and the world's ruler is my protector everywhere. Though you were strong when you attacked me, He who had me in protection was much stronger."

With this, then she pressed hard on the demon with her foot at each of these words:

"Stop making me more angry now, evil spirit. Stop now, old man-slayer, from now on you will not destroy Christ's crowned ones. Disgusting thing, now stop suffocating me with the stench rising from your mouth. I am my Lord's lamb, and He is my shepherd [Ps 23:1: Jn 10:14]. I am God's servant and His slave to do all that is His dear will. Blessed is He forever who has made me glad in endless bliss."

While she spoke to that horrible thing, a shining light from heaven came into the prison house and it seemed as though she saw in the glistening beam the beloved Cross reaching to heaven. A dove sat on it and said to her:

"You are a blessed maiden, Margaret, for the gates of paradise are now open to you."

And she bowed low to her dear Lord, and thanked him eagerly with a fervent heart. The light faded little by little, and then she turned around and said to the demon, "Tell me," she said, "quickly, most hateful of all things, what your nature is."

"Lady," he said, "most blessed maiden, if you lift your foot from my neck and at least loosen me so that I can breathe, I must obey. Nevertheless, doing your will is against my will."

The mild maiden did so; she loosened and raised her heel a little and he began to break into disgusting speech:

"Do you want to know, lovely lady, what my name is? [see Lk 8:29–30] But whatever my name is, I have been the greatest curse of man after Beelzebub, and swallowed their labor, and made the rewards that they had prepared themselves for many years vanish. Thus, with some of my wiles I wrenched them down when they least expected, and never yet has anyone overcome me until you now. You hold me in bonds, and have blinded me here, and are the curse of my brother Rufus, the boldest and wisest in counsel of all those in hell.[19] Christ dwells in you, therefore you can do with us whatever you wish. Woman, you are not like other women. It seems to me that you shine brighter than the sun, but especially your body, which shines with light [see Rev 12:1]. I cannot look at that light which seems to me so shiny and bright; those fingers especially seem so beautiful to me, so wondrously fair and so brightly shining, with which you blessed and made the mark of the mighty Cross, which bereaved me of my brother, and which bind me bitterly with cruel bonds."

"You flatter, foul thing," she said, "but tell me what I asked."

"Woe is me! Lady," he said then, "woe for my life, for I am he who always wars against the righteous. It seems to me that I am always confident concerning foolish sinners. But I am continuously busy with the good, and I most diligently follow those who try to be pure about sex, and flee the filths of the flesh, to see if in any way I can make them fall and foul themselves. I have cast down many who certainly expected to escape my wiles in the following way. Sometimes I let a pure man remain near a pure woman; I do not attack them at all or fight them, but leave them completely alone. I let them talk about God, and debate about goodness, and truly love each other without evil wishes or any evil desires, so that each will truly trust both his own and the other's will and feel more safe to sit by themselves and play together. Then because of this security, I first attack them, and quickly shoot secretly, and wound their unwary hearts with a swift, venomous drug before they know it. All lightly at first, with loving looks, with passionate gazing each at the other, and with playful speech, I incite them to more, so long that they tease and tussle together. Then I force into them loving thoughts, at first against their wills. Therefore, because they allow it, as that affliction grows, it seems good to them. And thus, when they have permitted me and do not prevent me at all, nor bestir themselves, nor stand strongly against me, I lead them into the bog and the loathsome lake of that foul sin. If they want to withstand my evil wiles and my deceitful tricks, they must wrestle and struggle with themselves; they cannot cast me off before they have overcome themselves.

"It is hateful to me, but nonetheless I will do it: I will tell you how they may best overcome me. Meanwhile, loose me, lady, and undo me.

"These are the weapons that worst wound me and preserve them spotless, and strengthen them most strongly against me and against their weak lusts. They are: eating simply and drinking more temperately; keeping the flesh in some need; never being idle; and holy men's prayers for them, along with their own prayerful thoughts, which they should think while they are praying against the evil thoughts which I put into them. They should remember that through me their lust leads them to act shamefully; and consider that if they obey me, they obey a bitter beast, and remember whose love they lose. What a lovely thing they have lost: that is their maidenhood, the maiden's honor, and the love of the lovely Lord of heaven and of the lovely queen, lady of the angels. And they make themselves vile before all that heavenly host, and dishonor themselves among worldly men, and lose the love not only of the high in heaven, but of low ones on earth, making the angels mourn and us to laugh so loud with great mirth, who see them fall so low from so high, from the highest in heaven to the lowest in hell. This they must often remember in themselves: to think about what a dark and sooty thing sin is, to think about hell-woe and of heavenly joy; and to frequently remember their own death and the Lord's, and the terror and horror that will be at the judgment; to think that the pleasure of fleshly lust perishes so very soon, and the pain of it lasts forever more. And as soon as they have any guilt, not to delay, but to go straightaway to reveal it in confession, even if it is a little or light sin. For that is the thing I hate most under the sun, that one should run to confess their sins often. For I can make that little sin to grow immeasurably if one hides and conceals it, but as soon as it is shown with repentance in confession, then it shames me, and I flee from them, shuddering as if I were put to shame.

"However, they may be steeped so far in foolish love that while they are together they cannot stir their hearts, nor stop, nor withstand the strength of my tricks, in any way. Then there is no remedy but fleeing, so that they are never alone with the other, or see them, or meet, or sit together, without a witness who can see what they do and hear what they say. If they do not prevent me, but permit me and tolerate me, and yet expect to escape, I lead them with false love little by little into such deep dung that they drown in it. And I ignite in them sparks of lusts so evil that they burn up within and are blinded by that fire, so that they do not have the sight with which to see themselves. The strength of their heart melts in the heat and enfeebles their wit, and attacks their wisdom, so that they do not want to know what they ought to know well. Now look at a wonder: they are so completely overcome, and I have so blinded them, that they blindly go ahead and disregard God and forget themselves. Therefore, fatally, when they least expect it, they suddenly fall foully and filthily into fleshly defilements; and for one lust that fades in a moment, they lose both the love of God and the world's praise.

"But those who are stalwart and strong, because they vigilantly defend against me, they seem so evil to me that I am utterly unhappy until they have been injured somehow by me. I am very busy about them in their beds so that they will soil themselves somehow while sleeping. But the mark of the cross injures me most and the worst was made by you now."

And with this he began to cry out and yell: "Margaret, maiden, what will become of me? Woe is me, my weapons are all overthrown. Even if this happened through a man—but it is through a maiden. This seems to me the worst yet, that the whole race you come from are all in our bonds, and you have escaped from them. It is the greatest of all wonders, that you alone have overcome your father and mother, kinsmen and kinswomen both, and all the region that you and they dwelled in, and have chosen Christ alone as lover and Lord. You beat us and bind us and put us to death. Alas! We are weak now and not worth anything at all, when a maiden brings down our great pride."

"Sorry thing," she said, "stop and tell me where you usually live, what kin you come from, and through whose command you afflict and harm holy men and attack their works."

"But tell me," he said, "blessed maiden, by whom you were granted your lovely limbs so sturdy and strong; from what nature comes your love and belief, which lay me so low? Woman, tell me now, and explain to me why the world's ruler lives in you, and how He came into you, and I will make you aware of all my wiles."

"Be still," she said, "and stop your asking. Accursed thing, you are not worthy enough to hear my voice, and especially to understand such hidden and difficult things as God's mysteries. But whatever I am and wherever I am from, it is through God's grace: an undeserved, voluntary gift which He has given me, for me to give to Him in return. But quickly speak and tell me what I am asking."

"Yes," he said, "I must do it. Satan the wicked, who because of his pride fell so low from paradise, is emperor and king, crowned by us all. But why must I tell you tales, lovely lady, of our kin and our kind, when you can see it yourself written in the books of Jannes and Mambres?[20] Because in visions I see Christ come to you, I feel such fear that I dare not speak, but quake and tremble, as the most downcast of all things. However, since you want to know, we live in the air for the most part, blessed maiden, and our paths are above, with the winds [see Eph 2:2]. We are always ready to do all that we can against mankind, and especially righteous men and maidens such as you. For Jesus Christ, God's child, was born of a maiden, and through the might of maidenhood mankind was reborn, and we were bereaved, and all that we owned was taken away. Lady, now you know what you wanted: where we usually live and why we afflict and hate maidens most. Yet, if you wish to know why we war most against righteous people, I answer you: because of envy which always and forever eats our hearts. We know they are made to rise to that place from which we fell, which seems a mockery and very unreasonable to us, so that injury inflames us and we become mad through the anger that ever enrages us against the good. That is our nature, which I must make known to you. To be sorrowful and sorry for each man's happiness; to rejoice when he sins, and never be glad except for evil alone: this is our nature, matchless maiden.

"But, dear Lord's lamb, loosen me a little and lift your foot, lady, which presses so hard on me. I ask you in God's name, the high heavenly Father, and in Jesus' name, His wondrous Son, that man nor woman may never more cast me away. Bright lady, bind me on earth and do not cast me down into hell. For Solomon the wise,[21] when he lived here, enclosed us in a barrel, and the men of Babylon came and thought they found a gold hoard and broke open that vessel, and we came forth and filled the wide world."

"Be quiet forever," she said, "most miserable of all things. Old devil, you will not dispute more with me, but fly from my eyesight, sorrowful fiend, and descend to where you can injure man no more." With that, the earth split in two and swallowed him, and he fell roaring backward into hell.

In the morning the evil Olibrius sent his men to bring her before him. She crossed herself and came out boldly. Men made their way from every street to see the pain that would be inflicted on her lovely body if she would not bow and obey the sheriff's command.

"Maiden, " he said, "Margaret, I still bid and command that if you do my will and worship my idols, and the day and time that you were born will be blessed." "No," she said, "I do not care to be blessed so. But it would be both for your gain and your good, that you who are unblessed seek after blessing and worship God almighty, the high heavenly Father, and His wondrous Son, Jesus Christ, who is true man and yet God. But you create witless things, worthy of you, bloodless and boneless, both dumb and deaf, and yet you do worse, for unseen demons live within them, and you love and worship them as your lords."

He began to grow angry, and cried out in rage: "Strip her stark naked and haul her up high so that she hangs in reward for her mockeries, and burn her body with lit tapers." The worthless menials did so quickly, so that her snow-white skin blackened as it became scorched, and burst into blisters as the flames rose up all around, and her lovely body crackled from them, and all who saw that rueful effect on her soft sides cried out. And she began to pray David's prayer: "High Savior, God, with the hallowing fire of the Holy Spirit, the comfort of mankind, inflame my heart and let the flame of your love blaze in my loins. [see Ps 25:2, Vulgate]"

But Olibrius, the most evil sheriff, said: "Take my advice maiden: do what I want before you lose your life dishonorably."

"I would live dishonorably," she said, "if I believed you, but if I die like this, my death is honorable and will continue into eternal life. You strain yourself and do not succeed with what you do to me –lone maiden that I am— but only weary yourself. My Lord has specially sealed my limbs, and in return for my gemstone which I gave Him, has prepared and given me a champion's crown. [see 2 Tim 4:7–8]"

Then he become absolutely mad and in wrath ordered a vat full of water brought out, and had her bound, both the feet and hands, and thrown to the bottom, so that she would suffer death and drown in there. It was done as he ordered, and she looked up and cried to heaven: "King of all kings, break my bonds so that I and all who see it will praise and worship you. May this water be pleasant and harmless for me, and grant that it will be a bath of bliss and baptism at the font for me, the blessing and light of eternal salvation. Let the Holy Spirit come in the likeness of a dove who may bless these waters in your blissful name [see Mt 3:16–17; Mk 1:10–11; Lk 3:21–22; Jn 1:32]. Bind my soul to yourself with baptism, and with these same waters wash me within, and cast away from me every sin, and bring me to your bright bedchamber, bridegroom of joy. I undergo baptism here in the dear Lord's name and in His dear Son's, and in the Holy Spirit's: One God enveloped in goodness and undivided."

She had only just spoken when all the earth began to quake and to quiver, and a dove came, burning as bright as if it were on fire, and it brought a golden crown and set it on that blessed maiden's head. With that, her bonds broke and burst, and as bright as the shining sun, she came up out of the water singing a praise-song which David the prophet[22] wrote long before to honor Christ. "My lovely Lord," she said, "makes known like a king that He rules rightly. Beauty and strength are His garments, and He has girded them on so that they may appear comely and fit well. [see Ps 92:1, Vulgate]"

"Come," said the dove with a resounding voice, "and rise up to the joy and the wealth of heaven. You were blessed maiden, when you chose maidenhood, which is queen of all powers; therefore you shall enjoy the brightest of crowns forever in bliss without end."

At the same time five thousand men, not counting children and women, turned to Our Lord, and all were immediately beheaded, as the sheriff ordered, for Christ's kingly name, in a town in Armenia named Caplimet,[23] all praising God with uplifted voices, and all rising up as martyrs with joy to heaven.

The sheriff was so enraged, he reddened all over in anger, and was so wroth and so maddened, that in a fit he condemned her to death. With a hot heart he ordered that her head be severed from her body with a shimmering sharp sword, with a blazing and biting blade. Those who were ordered laid hands on her and bound her so that the blood burst out at the nails and led her outside the town to be beheaded.

"Maiden," said Malchus,[24] "stretch out your neck to receive the sharp sword, for I must be your death, and that is a sorrow for me—if I can do it—for I see God Himself with his blessed angels surrounding you."

"Then wait for me, brother," she said, "while I pray and commit to Him both my spirit and body to repose and rest."

"Pray boldly then," he said, "as long as you like."

And she began to kneel and blissfully lift her hands up to heaven with this prayer:

"Lord, God of the people, all your judgments are right, although they are mysterious and difficult. I am now condemned to death here and granted life with you; I thank you for your gentle mercy. Father of all the people of creation, you shaped all that is made. Wisest Creator of all, you marked and measured out the heavens with your outstretched hand, and the earth with your fist. Steersman of the sea-stream; guardian and ruler of all created things, seen and unseen; bend your ears, Savior God, incline to my prayers. I beg and beseech you who are my wealth and joy, that whoever writes a book of my life, or obtains the text, or owns it and has it often in hand; and whoever reads it, or eagerly asks a reader for it; may all their sins be immediately forgiven, ruler of heaven. Whoever in my name builds a chapel or church, or endows one with a light or lamp, give them and grant them the light of heaven, Lord. In the house where a woman is pained by childbirth, as soon as she remembers your name and my suffering, Lord, quickly help her and her child. Lord, do not let any child be born in that house misshapen, or lame, or humpbacked, or dumb, or deaf, or injured by devils. And whoever remembers my name with their mouth, lovely Lord, deliver them from death at the last judgment."

With this, it seemed as though it thundered, and a dove came from heaven, so bright as though it was burning, with a cross blazing with flame and light, and the maiden fell headlong to the ground, and the dove came and touched her and raised her up with the cross, and said to her sweetly with the softest of voices:

"Maiden, you are blessed among all women [see Lk 1:28, 42], who have sought after holy oil and healing, and remembered all sinful men in your blessed prayers. I swear by myself and by my heavenly host, that your prayers will be truly granted for all those who hear what you have asked. And much more is granted to those who recall your name, and many things given to them which you have not mentioned now. Wherever your body or any of your bones are, or an account of your suffering, if a sinful man comes and lays his mouth on them, I will heal his sins. Nor may any demon dwell in a house in which your martyrdom is written, and the whole house will rejoice in God's peace and in spiritual love. And I am prepared to give to all who pray to you remedy for their transgressions. You are blessed, and blessed is the place where you stand, and blessed are all those who through you shall turn to me. Come now, bride, to your bridegroom, for I await you. Come, beloved, to your life, for I wait longingly for your coming; the brightest bedchamber waits for you. Beloved, hurry to me [see Song 8:14]. Come now to my kingdom. Leave these lowly people and you will rule with me all that I own."

The voice stopped, and she stood up, the happiest of women, and began to beg those who were around her, weeping for her death, that they should endure it [see Lk 23:28] "Now let be," she said, "your loathsome noise and all rejoice with me who wish me well, for you have heard—if you listened rightly—what the high Savior has promised me. And as you love yourself, I counsel you lovingly, that you have my name often in mind, because I will gladly pray for you in heaven, who often remembers my name and invokes it on earth. With a blissful heart join me in praising the high king who has chosen me, the world's Creator, and ruler of all created things. Heavenly Savior, I thank you for it; I praise and worship you. For your dear name I have undergone hardship, and now suffer death. Take me to you, God, beginning and end of all that is good. May you always be blessed, and your blissful Son—Jesus Christ by name—with the Holy Spirit,[25] who proceeds from them both: yes, three and yet One, divided in persons, in high dignity undivided, tied together and enclosed in one divine image. Worship and honor be to you alone from world into world forever into eternity."

After this prayer, she bowed her neck and said to the executioner, "Now brother, do quickly what you have been ordered." [see Jn 13:27]

"No," he said, "I will not, because I have heard how the dear Lord's mouth has spoken with you."

"You must do it," said the maiden, "against your will, for if you do not, you will have no part with me in the heavenly kingdom."

And with that he lifted up the cruelest of weapons, and smote swiftly down so that the stroke sank in and the body bent, and that sharp sword sheared across the shoulders, and the body bowed to earth, and the spirit rose up to the starry chamber, blissfully to heaven. At that same time, he who gave the stroke cried out: "Lord, be merciful to me and grant forgiveness for this deed; Lord, heal me of this sin." And he fell down in fear by her right side.

Then came down angels of light [see Jn 1:51], and settled gently on her body, and sang, and blessed it. The fiends, who were fatally afflicted, began to cry: "Margaret, maiden, at least now loosen and undo our bonds: we well know that there is no Lord but God in whom you believe."

Then through this, very many turned to Christ; and the dumb and deaf came to her body as it lay and all were healed. The angels, as they bore her soul in their arms, rose toward heaven and sang as they rose up with the sweetest voices: "*Sanctus, Sanctus, Sanctus, Dominus deus sabaot*, and so on. Holy is, holy is the Lord of the heavenly hosts: heaven and earth are full of his glorious riches. Ruler of all creatures, save us on high. Blessed is that child's coming who comes in the name of the Lord; salvation on high!"[26] With that, the spirits of hell began to howl and yell then, and the infirm all went to her body and were healed.

I, Theochimus, came, and took her lovely body, and carried it and brought it again into Antioch with immeasurable joy, and placed it in a sepulchre at the house of her grandmother who was named Clete. I know this well, for in the suffering of the prison where she was put, I found her sustenance and fed her food, and I saw where she fought with the fearful fiend, and the prayers that she prayed, and wrote them on vellum, and set down her whole life on these pages and sent it truthfully written throughout the wide world.

Thus the blessed maiden, Margaret by name, died by torment, in the month that our language—which is Old English—calls *Efterlithe*, and *Julius* in Latin,[27] on the twentieth day, and went from these miseries to life that lasts forever, to bliss without death, to joy without any woe.

All those who have heard this in their hearts, gladly remember this maiden in your prayers, so that in the bliss of heaven she may still pray for you the prayers she prayed on earth. There she shines sevenfold more brightly than the sun, in victory and in joy, more than any mouth could tell it; and sings forever unsullied, in that host of angels—which no man or woman may do whose flesh is soiled—and through her intercession, we may yet see her among the angels and hear her sing.

May God the Father be magnified, and His Son be blessed, and the Holy Spirit be praised, these three in One, served by angels and by those on earth without end. Amen.

Notes

1. Theotimus's name derives from the Greek for "God" and "honor." Apparently fictional, Theotimus is part of the Mombritius recension of the Margaret legend. A figure such as Theotimus, who acts as eyewitness to a saint's passion, and records his or her life, is common in early saints' *Lives* as a means of authorizing a text. Mentioned briefly at the beginning of the *Golden Legend*, Theotimus's narrative frames the *Seinte Margarete* account.

2. Antioch is a Syrian city now in west central Turkey, twenty miles upriver from the Mediterranean Sea; it was the seat of one of the patriarchs of the early Christian church.

3. Although Olybrius does not appear in the historical record, Olybrius's position—described as "prefect," "justice," and "sheriff" respectively, in the three Margaret legends—suggests that he was a local Roman official.

4. Solomon was the son and successor of David, king of Israel. He built the first temple. Early tradition attributed three books of the Hebrew Bible to him: Proverbs, Ecclesiastes, and Song of Songs. *The Testament of Solomon* records Jewish tradition concerning Solomon's power over demons and is the basis for the story which the demon in the Margaret legends recounts. An English translation of the *Testament* is in D. C. Durling and J. Charlesworth, *The Old Testament Pseudepigrapha* (Garden City, NY, 1983), 1:935–97.

5. On Antioch, an important city in Syria, see note 2 above.

6. St. Stephen (d. 35), a deacon, and the first Christian martyr (thus often known as "the protomartyr"), was stoned to death for blasphemy. His story is recounted in Acts 6, 7. In iconography he is often shown with stones protruding from his head. His feast is December 26.

7. St. Lawrence (d. 258), a deacon, was martyred in Rome under Emperor Valerian. He is typically shown with a gridiron, on which tradition says he was roasted to death. His feast is August 10. St. Stephen and St. Lawrence are often paired because they were both deacons.

8. That is, 289.

9. Emperor Diocletian reigned from 284 until 305.

10. In 286 Diocletian made Maximian co-emperor. In 293, the Tetrarchy was formed, with Galerius serving as Caesar under Diocletian in the eastern Roman Empire, and Constantine serving as Caesar under Maximian in the western empire. Diocletian's systematic persecution of Christians began in 303. Diocletian and Maximian abdicated in 305 and were succeeded by Galerius and Constantine. Maximian was villainized by later writers, but the persecutions under him in the western empire were less severe than those under Diocletian.

11. Olibrius is the same character met under the name Olybrius in *The Golden Legend*; see note 3 above.

12. Solomon was the son and successor of David, king of Israel; see note 4 above.

13. Margaret's executioner is named Maltus (in the *Legendary*) and Malchus (in the Katherine Group *Margarete*). In the account of Jesus' arrest found in Jn 18:10, Malchus is the slave of the high priest whose ear is cut off by Peter with a sword. In the Margaret story, Malchus is the one wielding a sword, rather than the victim of one.

14. Teochimus is the character known as Theotimus in *The Golden Legend*; see note 1 above.

15. Maiden / maidenhood. In modern English "maiden" designates a young girl, but in Middle English, the word can mean both a young girl and a virgin of either gender. Thus, the word "maidenhood" describes the state of virginity, and may be applied to males or females of any age. In Geoffrey Chaucer's *Canterbury Tales*, the Wife of Bath refers to St. Paul as a "maid."

16. Olibrius is the character known as Olybrius in *The Golden Legend*; see note 3 above.

17. "God born from God, light from light" is a phrase from the Nicene Creed, which would be recited as part of the Mass.

18. "Judge of the quick and dead" is also a phrase from the Nicene Creed.

19. Rufus, from the Latin for "red," is a common name for a devil (note that the demon has named his "brother" and another demon, Beelzebub, but not himself). The author of another Katherine Group text, *Ancrene Wisse*, refers to this scene when discussing the power of prayer to defeat temptation by physically binding demonic tempters: "Have you not heard of Ruffin the devil, Belial's brother, in your English book of St. Margaret?" The advice offered in this section (4) of *Ancrene Wisse* is very similar to the demon's upcoming discourse on the power of thought in overcoming sexual temptation in particular. See *Anchoritic Spirituality*, trans. and ed. Anne Savage and Nicholas Watson (New York, 1991), p. 137.

20. Jannes and Mambres were the names of two Egyptian magicians, mentioned in 2 Tim 3:8, who opposed Moses before Pharaoh [Ex 7:11]. Their names occur often in writings of both Jewish and classical antiquity. The demon is referring to a lost work bearing their names, which must have existed at least as early as the third century C. E., because the patristic writer Origen cites it in his *Commentary on Matthew*. See *Seinte Marherete*, ed. Frances M. Mack, Early English Text Society, old series 193 (London, reprint edition, 1958), p. xxix.

21. Solomon was the son and successor of David, king of Israel; see note 4 above

22. David, king of Israel and the father of Solomon, was credited with writing the book of Psalms. He is here called a prophet because the Psalms were interpreted by Christians as referring to Christ, who lived one thousand years after David.

23. Caplimet is a town not mentioned in the Greek sources, and its name varies greatly in the Latin. It has been suggested that this is referring to the ancient *Limnai*, a region of double lakes southwest of Antioch, where a town may have once existed. See William Mitchell Ramsay, *The Historical Geography of Asia Minor*, Royal Geography Society, Supplementary papers 4 (London, 1890; reprint, Amsterdam, 1962), p. 414.

24. Malchus was encountered earlier as Maltus in the *South English Legendary*; see note 13 above.

25. "With the Holy Spirit who proceeds from them both" is a phrase from the Nicene Creed; see notes 17 and 18 above.

26. This liturgical text (presented here partly in Latin and partly in Middle English translation) is the central part of the Mass known as the Sanctus. This prayer marks the beginning of the Canon of the Mass and the approach of the blessing of the eucharistic elements.

27. This is the only recorded appearance of the word *Efterlithe* in Middle English, and is also the first known use of the term "Old English." Margaret's feast is on July 20.

Chapter 31

The Middle-English Version of Jacques de Vitry's *Life of St. Marie d'Oignies*

Translated by Sarah McNamer

Introduction

The *Life of St. Marie d'Oignies* is one of the most important documents for the study of beguine spirituality and women's piety in the later Middle Ages. Its subject was born in 1177 near Liège in what is now Belgium. As her *Life* relates, she married young, but persuaded her husband to live chastely with her; together with other beguines, she served lepers in a small hospital from 1191 to 1207, when, seeking to escape her fame, she retired to the priory of Saint-Nicholas at Oignies-sur-Sambre, not far from Namur. She died in 1213.

Jacques de Vitry first encountered Marie in 1208. Born to a wealthy family near Reims around 1170, Jacques studied in Paris before hearing of the charismatic Marie, traveling to Oignies to meet her, and becoming one of her most ardent disciples. Although he served as Marie's confessor, he spoke of himself as her follower and instrument, calling her his *mater spiritualis* or "spiritual mother" and crediting her as the chief inspiration behind his preaching. Even after her death, Marie continued to exert a strong influence on Jacques; according to his contemporary and friend Thomas de Cantimpré, Marie often appeared to Jacques in visions, advising him on spiritual matters. Indeed his attachment to her was so great that for many years he wore a relic of her finger in a silver reliquary around his neck; it was this, he says in a letter to a friend, that twice saved him from drowning.

During the years immediately following Marie's death, Jacques traveled throughout Europe, preaching against the Albigensian heresy and observing the ideals and practices of other holy women such as the Poor Clares and Umiliati of northern Italy. In 1216 he became bishop of Acre in the Holy Land, and served in that post until 1228. He returned to Italy in 1229, when he was appointed cardinal of Tusculum. Throughout his life, however, the diocese of Liège remained his spiritual home; he visited Oignies frequently, and it is there that he was buried after his death in 1240.

In part, Jacques's purpose in writing this *Life* was to promote Marie's candidacy for sainthood and to gain ecclesiastical sanction for the beguines. Marie was never made a saint, attaining only the title *beata* (blessed). But

Jacques did obtain the approval of Pope Honorius III in 1216 for the women's religious movement that had been flourishing in the Low Countries since the late twelfth century. Known by the simple Latin appellation *mulieres sanctae* (holy women), as well as by the vernacular *beguines* (a term of uncertain origin, probably derogatory), this group of women had no founder or official hierarchy and took no formal vows. Though they often lived together in clusters of buildings known as *beguinages*, the cloistered life was not, at first, their ideal; whether wives, widows, or virgins, they sought merely to dedicate their lives to good works and prayer in loose affiliation with each other. Many came from aristocratic families, but in seeking to fulfill the ideal of the Gospels (the *vita apostolica*) they rejected their wealth, supporting themselves and those they served through manual labor, usually clothmaking. In their devotion to the humanity of Christ, service to the poor, intense eucharistic piety, and often extreme asceticism, they shared much in common with other religious women of the late twelfth and thirteenth centuries, no matter what their institutional affiliation. Some men, too, sought to join this movement; relatively few in number, they were known as the *beghards*.

Much of what we know about the beguines in the early thirteenth century comes from Jacques's prologue to the *Life of St. Marie*. He writes of observing "crowds of them in different places and how they scorned carnal enticements for Christ, despised the riches of this world for the love of the heavenly kingdom, clung to their heavenly bridegroom in poverty and humility and earned a sparse meal with their hands." Their intense desire for intimate union with Christ interested Jacques deeply. He writes of "women wasting away with such an intimate and wondrous state of love in God that they were faint with desire and . . . could only rarely rise from their beds." He admired, too, their longing for the eucharist: "Some of them ran with such desire after . . . such a great sacrament that in no way could they be deprived of it, and unless their souls were frequently invigorated by the delights of this meal, they obtained no consolation or rest but utterly wasted away in languor." All of these qualities, he writes, were fully exemplified by Marie. "She shone wondrously among the others like a jewel among other stones, like the sun among the stars." Although Marie never had an official leadership role among the beguines, she clearly inspired many women to imitate her, not only while she was alive but after her death through the vehicle of Jacques's *Life*. Indeed, during the half-century after her death the beguine movement reached its peak; thousands of women joined the movement, not only in Liège but in Cologne and various urban centers in the Low Countries. For reasons that remain unclear, the beginning of the fourteenth century witnessed a decline in the number of beguines and a movement toward enclosure and stricter regulation. By the fifteenth century, the beguine movement had virtually died out.

The Middle English version of the *Life of St. Marie d'Oignies* follows the Latin original very closely, with a few important exceptions: the anonymous translator calls Marie "St. Mary," even though she was never canonized, and he omits Jacques's lengthy prologue on the beguine movement. The Middle

English *Life* survives in a single fifteenth-century manuscript which also contains the *Lives* of two other continental holy women, Christina Mirabilis and Elizabeth of Spalbek. These texts witness to a larger wave of interest in continental women's *Lives* and visionary literature in late-medieval England. Such writings include works by or about Bridget of Sweden, Catherine of Siena, Mechthild of Hackeborn, Marguerite Porete, and Elizabeth of Hungary. The type of piety exemplified by these women is often very different from the native English tradition, which generally prized a more sober form of prayer over the enthusiastic, mystical strain we see in Marie's *Life*.

In providing alternative models of sanctity for English readers, texts such as the *Life of St. Marie d'Oignies* helped to foster the kind of religious sensibility exemplified by one of the most interesting figures of the late-medieval period, Margery Kempe. There are several close correspondences between the *Book of Margery Kempe* and the *Life of St. Marie d'Oignies*. Whether or not Margery herself knew the *Life*, her scribe certainly did. In Chapter 62 of the *Book*, Margery's scribe describes his doubts about the authenticity of her "holy tears," doubts that nearly caused him to abandon his role in the composition of her *Book*. At this crucial juncture, reading about Marie d'Oignies reconfirmed his belief in Margery's holiness: "he loved her more, and trusted more in her weeping and her crying than he ever did before":

> For . . . he read of a woman called Mary of Oignies, and of her manner of life, of the wonderful sweetness that she had in hearing the word of God, of the wonderful compassion that she had in thinking of His Passion, of the abundant tears that she wept, which made her so weak and feeble that she could not endure to look upon the Cross, nor hear our Lord's Passion repeated, without dissolving into tears of pity and compassion.

Thus, the *Life of St. Marie d'Oignies* served to convince Margery's scribe that copious weeping and intense devotion to Christ's Passion were legitimate signs of holiness. We may assume that the *Life* served this function for other English readers as well.

SOURCES AND FURTHER READING

This translation was made from the edition by Carl Horstmann, "Prosalegenden: Die Legenden des MS Douce 114," *Anglia* 8 (1885): 102–96. Horstmann's edition is a transcription from the single surviving manuscript of the Middle English text, Oxford, Bodleian Library, MS Douce 114. Like many medieval manuscript copies, this one contains several errors, which Horstmann did not emend; I have altered it when necessary for the text to make sense, placing my emendations in square brackets. Since the Middle English version refers to Marie as "Mary" and to Jacques as "James," I have retained the anglicized names in the text. My translation includes only Book 1 of the *Life*. Book 2, which repeats some of what is in Book 1, is organized according to the ways in which Marie exemplified the seven gifts of the Holy Spirit.

No other translations from the Middle English *Life* exist, but a translation from the Latin text (*Bibliotheca hagiographica latina,* no. 5516) has been completed by Margot H. King: *The Life of Marie d'Oignies by Cardinal Jacques de Vitry,* second revised edition (Toronto, 1989). King's translation includes Book 2; it also includes Jacques's original prologue (quoted above in the introduction). Thomas de Cantimpré's supplement to the *Life of Marie d'Oignies* (*Bibliotheca hagiographica latina,* no. 5517) provides further insight into the relationship between Marie and Jacques; see the translation by Hugh Feiss, *The Supplement to Jacques de Vitry's Life of Marie d'Oignies, by Thomas de Cantimpré* (Saskatoon, 1987).

The most thorough study of the beguines is that by Ernest W. McDonnell, *The Beguines and Beghards in Medieval Culture* (New Brunswick, NJ, 1954). Herbert Grundmann situates the women's religious movements of the twelfth and thirteenth centuries in the context of related cultural currents in *Religious Movements in the Middle Ages,* trans. Steven Rowan (German original, 1935; Notre Dame, IN, 1995), especially Chapters 4, 5, and 6. For a more concise overview of women's piety during the early thirteenth century, see Brenda M. Bolton, "*Mulieres Sanctae,*" in *Women in Medieval Society,* ed. Susan Mosher Stuard (Philadelphia, 1976), pp. 141–58 and "Vitae Matrum: A Further Aspect of the Frauenfrage," in *Medieval Women,* ed. Derek Baker, Studies in Church History, Subsidia 1 (Oxford, 1978), pp. 253–73. The most perceptive analysis to date of the asceticism, devotion to the humanity of Christ, and eucharistic piety practiced by women such as Marie d'Oignies is Caroline Walker Bynum's *Holy Feast and Holy Fast: The Religious Significance of Food to Medieval Women* (Berkeley, 1987). The influence of the *Lives* of continental women saints on medieval English culture is explored in a collection of essays edited by Rosalynn Voaden, *Prophets Abroad: The Reception of Continental Holy Women in Late-Medieval England* (Cambridge, 1996). For the original Middle English *Book of Margery Kempe,* see the edition by Sanford Brown Meech and Hope Emily Allen, Early English Text Society 212 (London, 1940; reprint 1993); for the Penguin modernization (quoted above in the introduction), see *The Book of Margery Kempe,* trans. B.A. Windeatt (Harmondsworth, 1985).

The Middle-English Version of Jacques de Vitry's Life of Marie d'Oignies

A little prologue by the English translator

The honorable James, bishop of Acre, wrote a long prologue to the following *Life* addressed to the bishop of Toulouse.[1] In this prologue he describes at great length the marvelous and commendable deeds of the devout and holy women in the diocese of Liège and the surrounding area. His writing style includes figurative language and learned allusions that are well suited to those trained in theology and rhetoric. But these cannot easily be translated into the English language without lengthy explanation; moreover, if one extracted only some of the prologue, the meaning would not be clear. Therefore I omit the entire prologue, except for this short introduction: Here begin the chapters of the first book of the *Life of St. Mary of Oignies*, which Master James, Mary's confessor and friend and subsequently bishop of Acre and cardinal of the Court of Rome, wrote in Latin in the year of grace 1215.

Here begins the *Life of St. Mary of Oignies*

(1.) Of her childhood.

In a town called Nivelles in the diocese of Liège, there was a young maiden named Mary who was as illustrious in name as in life.[2] She was born to [noble] parents,[3] and though they enjoyed an abundance of riches she was never enticed by worldly goods, even when she was a child, so that almost from her mother's womb she was cast up to Our Lord [see 1 Pet 5:7]. Never, or very seldom, did she play as others do, nor did she mix with vain girls who indulged in frivolous pastimes. Instead, keeping her soul from all covetousness and vanity, in God's providence she revealed in childhood what she would be like when she was older. In her youth she often knelt beside her bed and offered to Our Lord prayers that she had learned as the first fruits of her life.

Indeed, such mercy and pity grew within her from the time she was a little child, and so much did she with a natural inclination love religion, that one day when she caught sight of some brothers of the Cistercian order walking by her father's house she secretly followed them, marveling at their habits. And when she had gone as far as she could, she showed her desire to imitate those lay brothers or monks by setting her own feet in their footprints.

And when her father and mother wished to dress her in delicate and pretty garments, as is the manner of worldly people, she was saddened and rejected them, as if St. Peter's words about women were naturally imprinted in her mind: *Let not yours be the outward adorning with braiding of hair, decoration of gold, and wearing of robes . . .* [1 Pet 3:3], and as St. Paul says, *not with braided hair or gold or pearls or costly attire . . .* [1 Tim 2:9]. At this her father and mother, laughing and mocking the maiden, said, "What kind of woman will our daughter be?"

(2.) Of her marriage.

Disdaining her virtuous deeds, her parents married her off to a young man when she was fourteen years old. Removed from her father and mother, she was kindled into such spiritual fervor and chastised and subdued her body with such determination that often when she had worked with her hands much of the night, she remained for a long time in prayer. During the rest of the night, she slept but little, upon a few wooden planks which she had hidden at the foot of her bed. And because she did not have power over her body in public, she secretly wore under her dress a rough belt which girded her very tightly. I do not say this to praise the excess, but to point out her fervor. In this and many other things that she did through the privilege of grace, let the discreet reader take heed: the privilege of a few makes not a common law. Let us follow her virtues; the special form of her virtues, let us not imitate without special privilege. For though the body exists to serve the spirit, and though we ought to bear in our body the wounds of Our Lord Jesus Christ [see Gal 6:17], nevertheless we know that the worship of the King requires law and justice, and sacrifice from the robbery of the poor [see Is 61:8] does not please Our Lord. Necessities are not to be denied to the poor flesh, but vices are to be rejected. Therefore, when we read about what some saints have done because of the intimate counsel of the Holy Spirit, we should admire rather than attempt to imitate them.

(3.) Of the conversion of her spouse, and how they rejected the world and lived chastely.

When she had lived for a time in matrimony with John, her spouse, Our Lord beheld the humility of His maiden and graciously heard her prayers; for John was inspired to commend Mary, whom he had lived with first as his wife, to a life of chastity. The Lord made the chaste man tutor of His maiden, so that she should have solace from her guardian, and left her a faithful provider, so that she might more freely serve Our Lord. Out of natural goodness John did not oppose the holy intentions of his wife, as is the custom among other men, but patiently supported her in her good works and had compassion on her. He was inspired by Our Lord not only to promise to live an angelic life of continence and chastity, but to give all that he had to poor men for the love of Christ and to follow his companion in her holy purpose and religious life. Indeed, the further he was separated from her by carnal affection, the closer he was bound to her by the love of spiritual wedlock. Because of this, Our Lord later appeared in a vision to His maiden and promised that He would reward her in heaven for undertaking this form of matrimony with her spouse, who for the love of chastity had abstained from indulging in fleshly lusts on earth.

Therefore wretched lechers who foul yourselves out of wedlock with illicit unions, may you be ashamed and afraid, seeing these blessed young people abstaining from lawful embraces for God's love and overcoming the fierce heat of burning youth through the fervor of religion. They deserve crowns as their reward.[4] It is fitting for the Lord to give them a place in His house and a position in heaven higher than that which He gives to ordinary sons and daughters, since they, in a kind of blessed martyrdom, burning not where there was fire, slaying their lust where lust abounded, thirsting not where fluids were near, and hungering not where meat was plenty, pierced their flesh with the nails of the fear of God. Indeed, utterly degrading themselves for Our Lord's love, they served lepers for a time at a place near Nivelles called Willambrouk.

(4.) Of her rejection and persecution by her relatives.

Devils saw and envied them; their relatives and other worldly people, who had respected them when they were rich, gnashed their teeth and scorned them once they had become poor for Christ's love. They were made vile and abject for God; they endured many reproaches for Our Lord's sake.

Fear not, Christ's maiden, to approach the humiliations of the Cross with your Christ, and to set aside the joy and esteem which this world offers. It is better for you to be abject and lowly in the house of Our Lord than to dwell in the halls and chambers of sinners [see Ps 84:10]. You have lost the good graces of your relatives, but you have found Christ's grace. Indeed, have you lost the love of your relatives? No, for they never loved you, but your riches—just as flies follow honey, wolves seek carrion, and thieves pursue their prey rather than the man.

(5.) Of her compunction and tears.

Lord, you are very good to those who trust in you [see Lam 3:25]; you are true to those who abide in you. Your maiden rejected the kingdom of the world and all worldly honors for your love: and indeed, you have given her back one hundredfold in this world and everlasting life in the world that is to come. Let us then consider how you bedecked and adorned your very dear friend with great jewels of virtues, just as a heavy vase of gold is adorned with every precious stone; let us consider with what great miracles you honored her who was scorned and cast out by worldly people.

The beginning of her conversion to you, the first fruits of her love, was your Cross and your Passion. Hearing you, she listened and was filled with awe; beholding your works, she was afraid. One day when, inspired by you, she considered the benefices that you had mercifully shown in the flesh to mankind, she received such grace of compunction and such an abundance of tears at the memory of your Cross and Passion that her tears ran down copiously on the church floor, leaving a path where she walked. For a long time after this visitation, she was unable to behold an image of the Cross or to speak or hear other people speaking of the Passion, without falling into a swoon from the overflowing desire of her heart. And so, to temper her sorrow and restrain such an abundance of tears, she sometimes left the memory of Christ's manhood behind and lifted her mind up to the divinity and majesty of God, that she might find comfort in the part of His nature that transcended all suffering. But the more she tried to restrain her weeping, the more her tears marvelously increased. For when she considered how great He was who suffered so much humiliation for us, her sorrow was always renewed, and her soul was refreshed with new tears through a sweet compunction.

One day before Good Friday, when she had offered herself to Our Lord with abundant tears, sobs, and sighs, a priest from the church who seemed to enjoy rebuking her exhorted her to pray softly and stop weeping. She did her best to obey, being always humble and as simple as a dove in all things. But knowing her weakness, she slipped out of the church and hid herself in a secret place far from all people, tearfully asking Our Lord to teach that priest that it is not in man's power to restrain a flood of tears when a great blast blows and the water flows [see Ps 147:18]. Thus, while the priest was saying Mass that same day, he was so overcome by tears that he nearly suffocated; the more that he tried to restrain his tears, the more not only he but also the book and the altar cloths became soaked with the water of weeping. And so it was that this unwise man who had rebuked Christ's maiden learned through shameful experience what he had refused to learn through humility and compassion. For after many sobs and stammerings, he barely escaped death. (This was related to us by one who witnessed it himself, and we know that his testimony is true). A long time after the Mass had ended, Christ's maiden returned and, berating the priest, miraculously described what had happened to him just as if she had been present. "Now," she said, "you have learned by experience that it is not possible to withstand the fierceness of the gale when the south wind blows."

Day and night, water fell continuously from her eyes. In order to keep these tears from running down her cheeks and onto the floor, she caught them with the veils that covered her head. She used many of these linen cloths, changing them often so that when one was wet another could dry. When compassionate men asked her if she felt any of the usual soreness, aching, or lightheadedness after her long fasts, frequent vigils, and copious weeping, she replied, "These tears are my refreshment; these are my sustenance night and day; they do not afflict the head, but feed the mind; they do not cause pain, but refresh the soul with enlightenment; they do not empty the brain, but fill the soul and soften it with a gentle anointing when they are not wrenched out through effort and violence but given graciously by Our Lord."

(6.) Of her confession.

Now, after her compunction, let us briefly consider her confession. I take God as my witness: never in all her actions or conversation did I perceive one deadly sin. And if it happened to seem to her that she had committed any little venial sin, she confessed to a priest with such sorrow of heart, such shame, and such contrition that sometimes she was compelled to cry out loudly in the manner of a woman in labor, so great was the anguish in her heart. Indeed, she was so vigilant about avoiding small and venial sins that she could sometimes go for fifteen days without even having a sinful thought in her heart. And since good minds often experience guilt where there is no cause, she often knelt at the feet of priests and, chastising herself, tearfully confessed something of which we were barely able to suppress laughter, such as some childish words she remembered she had spoken in vain in her youth. But truly, once she had grown past childhood, she strove to guard her soul with great fear, her wits with great diligence, and her heart with great purity, having always in mind Solomon's words, *He who sets no store by small things falls little by little* [Eccles 19:1]. Never or seldom were we able to discern idle words in her, or immoderate looks, or pretentious mannerisms, or excessive laughter, or unseemly comportment. Sometimes, however, when she could not contain her abundant joy, she was compelled to show the rejoicing of her heart through enthusiastic bodily gestures and gladness of expression, either through the purity of her heart bursting out into joyful laughter, or through her goodness greeting her friends with a small and modest embrace, or out of heartfelt devotion kissing some priest's hands or feet. And when she came to herself again in the evening as if after a kind of mental inebriation, she took stock of all her deeds. If she perceived that she had gone even a little bit too far, she repented with a wondrous contrition of heart and punished herself, often fearing when there was no true cause to fear. And in this alone we sometimes reprimanded her, seeking solace for our own sloth; for she confessed such small sins more often than we desired.

(7.) Of her penance and satisfaction.

Now, after her confession, let us consider how much and how marvelously she punished her body, with what great love and delight in embracing Christ's Cross she pained her flesh. Let us see that first school lesson of Our Lord Jesus Christ, that first instruction of the Gospels: *If any man would come after me, let him deny himself and take up his cross daily and follow me* [Lk 9:23]. She reflected on this often in her heart and strove to follow Christ in these three steps. For she not only refused to accept other men's goods, but rejected even her own, coveting nothing; she not only punished her body, but her very self, completely relinquishing her own will. She renounced her own self, submitting herself to another man's will through obedience; she took up the Cross, chastising her body by abstinence; and she followed Christ, regarding herself as nothing through humility.

Since she had tasted of the spirit, all fleshly delight was distasteful to her. Once, after a great sickness, it was necessary for her to regain her strength by eating food and drinking wine. Afterward, the memory of this delectation was so abominable to her that she had no rest in spirit until she had punished herself and made satisfaction. She tormented her flesh exceedingly for the delights she had experienced before, such as they were! For with fervor of spirit, loathing her flesh, she cut away great pieces of her flesh and hid them in the earth for shame; and because she was enflamed with the great heat of love, she saw one of the seraphim (a burning angel) standing by her in this state of ecstasy. When her body was washed after she was dead, women found the places of the wounds, and marveled greatly; but those who had heard her confession knew what this was about. Those who marvel at how the worms welled out of St. Simeon's wounds, and at how St. Anthony's fire burned his feet: why are they not amazed at such great strength in the body of a frail woman, who, wounded by charity and quickened by Christ's wounds, set no store by the wounds of her own body?[5]

(8.) Of fasting.

Christ's maiden excelled so greatly in the grace of fasting that on those days when it was necessary to refresh the body she approached meat as if it were medicine. She ate only a little, once a day: in summer, at evening, and in winter at the first hour of night. She drank no wine, she ate no meat, and she never ate fish, except for small fishes occasionally. She was sustained by greens, soup, and the fruits of trees. For a long time she ate bread that was so black and hard that even dogs would not eat it; indeed, it was so dry and rough that it tore the inside of her mouth and blood came out of the wounds. But thinking of Christ's blood made this sweet to her, and with the wounds of Christ her wounds were healed, and the sharpness of the hard bread was sweetened with the softness of heavenly bread.

One day while she was eating she saw the ancient enemy looking tormented with envy. When there was nothing more he could do, he taunted her, saying "Hey, you glutton, you're filling yourself up too much." Indeed, she often had trouble eating, due to so much lengthy fasting; moreover, her stomach ached and churned and became bloated and cold, as if it loathed food. But she knew the tricks and wiles of the enemy, who, knowing her to be God-fearing, would be glad if she weakened herself through too much abstinence. Therefore, the more that that venomous spirit became tormented when she ate, the more she forced herself to eat in defiance of him. For whether she ate or fasted, she did all for the worship of God.

For three years she fasted on bread and water from the feast of the Holy Cross until Easter;[6] yet she suffered no harm to her body nor to the work of her hands. She would refresh her body with a little bread and water in her cell in church at evening or during the night; and from the grace before meals until the prayer of thanksgiving, holy angels appeared before her at her frugal supper, moving up and down as if through a bright window. From their presence she took such comfort and such joy of spirit that a spiritual sweetness surpassed all sweetness of taste.

St. John the Evangelist, whom she loved with a special affection, sometimes came to her table while she ate; and in his presence her physical appetite was so diminished by devout desire that she could hardly eat any food. And truly, Our Lord rewarded her soul for the physical delights she had forsaken for the love of Christ, for it is written, *Man shall not live by bread alone* [Mt 4:4; Lk 4:4]. Sometimes this heavenly bread gave her such comfort that she neither ate nor drank for eight days, and sometimes eleven, that is from the Ascension of Our Lord until Pentecost; and amazingly, her head never ached, nor did she rest from manual labor, since she was as strong the last day as she was the first. Even if she had wished to eat during those days, she was unable to do so, for her senses were entirely overcome by her spirit. As long as the soul was so completely satisfied with spiritual nourishment, it would not allow her to receive any refreshment from ordinary food.

Sometimes she would rest peacefully with Our Lord for thirty-five days in a sweet and blessed silence, eating no food and uttering no words but these alone: "I desire the body of Our Lord Jesus Christ." And when she received the sacrament, she would dwell with Our Lord for the whole day in silence. Indeed, during those days she felt as if her spirit had departed from the body, the body being like an earthen vessel hiding the soul or a garment of clay wrapping and covering it. She was thus abstracted from material things and swept away in ecstasy. Returning to herself after five weeks, she opened her mouth and spoke and received bodily food, and those who stood nearby were amazed.

A long time after this, it happened that she could in no way tolerate the smells of meat or of any fried food or wine, except when she took wine in the rinsing after the sacrament [of the Eucharist]; then she was able to endure the smell without any trouble. And when she went through various towns on her way to receive the sacrament of Confirmation from the bishop, the smells that she was unable to tolerate before did not bother her a bit.

(9.) Of her prayer.

The more that she made her body lean with fasting, the freer was her spirit and more replete with prayers; the body was weakened through abstinence, and the soul was strengthened in Our Lord. She received from Our Lord such great and special grace for praying that by night and day never or seldom was her spirit released from prayer. She prayed without ceasing, either crying to God with a still heart, or else verbally expressing her heart's desire. While she worked with her hands or spun, she had a Psalter set before her and sweetly said Psalms to Our Lord. In this way she fastened her heart to God as if with nails, lest it wander in vain. When she prayed specially for anybody, Our Lord revealed himself to her spirit and answered her; for she was able to know either by the uplifting or depression of her spirit whether she was heard or not.

One time when she prayed for a dead man's soul, she received the answer, "Do not pray for him, for he has been condemned by God." And indeed, this man received a mortal wound and was wretchedly killed in a tournament and was damned forever.

One day when she was in her cell beside the church of Oignies, she saw a multitude of hands before her as if praying. Astonished, and wondering what they were, she took fright and sought refuge in the church. She saw the same hands again another day while she was in her cell, and was afraid; and when she wished to flee to the church, she was held back and detained by the hands. Then she went to the church and prayed to Our Lord to tell her what those hands signified. And God answered that the souls who suffered in Purgatory asked the help of her prayers or the prayers of others; through them their pains were soothed as if by a precious ointment.

Sometimes she substituted the sweetness of contemplation for ordinary prayers; and sometimes she was unable to open her mouth or to think of any other thing except God.

For pilgrimage and prayer, she often used to visit the church of Saint Mary near Oignies, where she received great comfort from Our Lady. This church was a little over two miles distant from her. During one particularly harsh winter, she walked barefoot to that church over snow and ice without any harm or injury to herself. And once when she had only one maiden with her and did not know the way because the path was wild and overgrown, a light went before her, showing her the way so that she did not get lost. On the same day she had eaten nothing and kept vigil in the church all night long; yet when she set forth for home in the morning and would have nothing to eat until evening, she was able to make the journey without any difficulty, since holy angels escorted her on both sides.

Sometimes on the same path when a great downpour seemed to be gathering in the clouds and she had no garments to protect her from the rain, she looked up and saw obedient stars holding back the rain. Thus, even when it was raining she came home again untouched.

Sometimes when her soul was more replete and pure than usual she was unable to cease from prayer. She honored Our Lady both night and day by genuflecting one thousand one hundred times, continuing this extraordinary and unprecedented salutation for forty days in a row. First, with intensity of spirit, she would genuflect six hundred times without stopping; second, she would read the whole Psalter while standing, kneeling after each psalm to say the Hail Mary; third, she would strike herself with a sharp stick each time she genuflected, thus offering herself to God in a kind of martyrdom. Indeed, in order to make this sacrifice more sweet she made her body bleed with the last three strokes; then she ended the service by genuflecting fifty times. She did this not with physical strength, but with the help of angels, who sustained and comforted her.

The virtue of her prayer not only gave strength to men, but tormented fiends. She had such power over the latter that it was as if she bound them with ropes. They were compelled to come to her through the fire of her prayers, sometimes gnashing their teeth against her, sometimes quarreling and complaining to her, and sometimes as if humbly beseeching her.

When any of her friends were troubled by temptation, she was moved by the spirit of compassion and did not cease praying until the enemy was overcome and her friend delivered. Once one of her special friends was tempted very subtly and therefore more dangerously by the devil who walks in darkness. That sly enemy, transforming himself into an angel of light, appeared to this man in a pitying and friendly guise while he was sleeping. He reprimanded him for some vices, and cunningly advised him to do certain good deeds; thus he first gave him treacle, so that he would be able to impart venom more surreptitiously afterward. Then when he was accepted as though he were trustworthy, in the manner of a sophist that traitor mingled lies with truth, deceptively concealing wickedness by mixing it with goodness. At last his trickery reached this point: this brother would have been totally confounded if Christ's maiden had not perceived the simulation and subtlety of that sly sophist through a revelation of the Holy Spirit. But when she told her friend that his revelation was not from God but was the deception of a wicked spirit, he objected, saying, "Since that spirit has done many good things for me and has predicted things that came true, he will in no way deceive me." At this she gave herself over to prayer and weeping and did not rest until that spirit stood before her one night in her cell while she prayed. Beholding his false radiance, she said, "What are you, or what is your name?" He scowled at her in his arrogance. "I am he," he said, "whom you, cursed woman, have stolen from my friend and compelled to come to you through your prayers. Sleep is my name, for I appear in sleep as Lucifer to many, especially to religious, and they obey me and fall into pride through my seductions, imagining themselves worthy to be visited by God and angels." In the end, it became clear that that man had been deceived by the fiend.

There was a young virgin in a Cistercian abbey serving Our Lord under the habit of religion among nuns. Seeing her take up the vocation of the ascetic life despite the fragility of her sex and her tender age, the old serpent became exceedingly envious. Since he knew that this virgin was God-fearing and virtuous, he assailed her with blasphemous and unclean thoughts in order to cast her down into despair through fear and excessive dread. Because she was afraid and not used to such thoughts, the first time such a thought entered her mind she believed that she had lost faith; she thus struggled in anguish for a long time. Refusing to open up to anyone the wound of her heart, she finally fell into despair. So greatly had the enemy depressed her mind that she was neither able to say the Our Father nor the Creed, nor would she confess her sins. And if she was sometimes coerced with entreaties or threats to confess some things, she could in no way be brought to ask forgiveness. She would not partake of the sacraments of Holy Church; she would not receive the sacrament of the altar; in her distress she often tried to kill herself; she despised God's word and preaching for her salvation; she hated all goodness; and the devil spoke many words of blasphemy and scorn through her mouth. And when her devout sisters had prayed much for her to our merciful Lord, they were unable to free His dove from the devil's jaws, nor could this kind of demon be cast out through fasting and prayer –not because the merciful spouse despised the prayers of so many holy virgins, but because He wanted to allow that particularly cruel kind of demon possession to be overcome by His maiden Mary, who had the ability to pierce through the cheeks of the fiend with the efficacy of her prayers and mightily draw the prey from his mouth.

Therefore, when that young virgin was brought to Christ's maiden, she received her benignly, with liberal and generous hospitality, not only in her cell but also in her heart through the spirit of charity, since she was full of compassion and spiritual sweetness. And when she had prayed much for her to Our Lord, he who wanted to hold her fast still would not let her go. Then Mary sacrificed herself more to Our Lord and fasted forty days with weeping and prayers, eating only two or three times a week. At the end of this fast, that most hideous spirit left the virgin and was constrained to come to Christ's maiden in pain and sorrow and shame, tightly bound and tormented by

Christ's angel, so that it seemed as though he had cast out all his bowels and wretchedly bore on his neck all that was within him—for what Our Lord works invisibly in the spirit, sometimes He reveals visibly through outward signs. Wailing and beseeching her to have mercy on him, he begged Christ's friend to give him penance; for, he said, he was under her power and must do whatever she enjoined him to do. Since she never presumed of herself nor would do anything without counsel, she called on a close friend and teacher in whom she trusted. He advised her to send him out to a deserted place, where he would be able to annoy no man until the Day of Doom. Just then another man came along who was very familiar to them both, and when he heard this advice, being more fervent on account of the fierceness of his passionate spirit, said, "By no means shall that traitor escape so easily! Bid him to go down at once into the depths of hell." So she commanded that evil spirit to do so. He wailed as he fell, and in her spirit she heard a great cry from the fiends when they saw so great and mighty a prince come to them. At this Christ's maiden marveled greatly and thanked God for his abundant grace and goodness. And the young virgin was delivered the very same hour, and confessed and received the Sacrament, and, thanking God, went home again safe and sound.

Another time, while she rested in her bed after many vigils, the fiend appeared to her in various disguises, gnashing his teeth against her and cursing. "By your rest," he said, "you disturb our rest in hell. I am no less tormented by your rest than I am by your labor and your prayers." And smiling, she blessed herself and ordered this hideous ghost to go his way.

(10.) Of her vigils and sleep.

This strong, wise woman thought that wasting time was reprehensible and intolerable, for days pass and do not come again; and unlike other material things, lost time may not be recovered, nor lost days be restored. Therefore she kept as busy as she could, so that no hour of the day or night should pass in which she was unoccupied or idle. She seldom slept at night, knowing that sleep was mercifully given to us by Our Lord simply as refreshment for mankind's frail weakness, rather than as something meritorious in itself. And indeed it is just that we earn no reward by sleeping, since we have no use of our free will or judgment in that state. Therefore she abstained from sleep as much as she could, serving Our Lord through vigils, and she was so devout in these vigils that no noise or hustling or bustling could distract her. The virtue of abstinence made her body hard and lean, and the fire of God's love burning within, easily prevented her from becoming drowsy. The sweet songs of the angels, who often kept her company in her vigils, kept sleep from her eyes without causing her any bodily harm. Thus, removed from the company of men at night, she enjoyed the fellowship of hosts of blessed spirits, whose wondrous sounds delighted her ears as much as a harmonious and merry melody sung by a chorus of people. This music shook away sloth, refreshed her mind, and comforted her spirit with a wondrous sweetness; it stirred devotion, inflamed desire, and incited her to praise and thank the Lord, singing *sanctus, sanctus, sanctus Dominus*; that is, holy, holy, holy Lord.

Let wretched and foolish women take heed and repent of their sins; with their wanton and lascivious songs they kindle the fire of lust and make coals burn with the breath of their mouths. Alienated from the song of angels, they shall perish in their vanity and pride; their laughter shall be turned to weeping, joy into sorrow, and song into a mournful wailing. The Lord shall substitute a rope for their bright belts, stench for their sweet fragrances, and a bald head for their crimped and colored hair. Indeed, our Mary, spurning worldly songs and all the devil's vanities for the love of Christ, deserved to dwell most happily and sweetly among the merry melodies of holy angels.

Many precious relics of saints adorned the church of Oignies where she kept her vigils; and because she kept watch over them, they gladdened her spirit with a marvelous joy, as if to show that they appreciated her guardianship. Later, in her final illness, they had compassion on her and comforted her, promising her their help before God for her labor and vigilance.

In her cell she had a bed with a little straw, but she seldom rested there; for very often she remained in church and, leaning her head against the wall, was refreshed with a little sleep before returning once again to the sweet labor of vigils. Even then, she did not spend the time of her sleep without fruit; for while she slept, her heart remained awake [see Song 5:2]. She who clung to Christ while awake held Him in her heart [while she slept], dreaming of nothing but her Christ. For just as a hungry man dreams of food, so in her dreams she had Him whom she desired always before her eyes; for where love is, there is the eye; and truly, where her treasure was, there was her heart [see Mt 6:21]. As Christ says of Himself, *where I am, there shall my servant be* [Jn 12:26].

Often Our Lord showed her many things while she slept and visited his maiden with many revelations, lest sleep should pass in idleness. As Joseph and other saints were warned in their sleep, and as God promised through the prophet Joel: *your old men shall dream dreams, and your young men shall see visions* [Joel 2:28].

Sometimes she was able to rest in her cell; but sometimes, most often during solemn feast days, she could find no rest except in the church in the presence of Christ. At such times she had to remain in the church night and day. For above all things it was necessary for her to obey her familiar angel, who was her guardian, just as she would obey an abbot. When she was afflicted with too much fasting, this angel advised her to rest; and when she had rested a little, he would wake her and lead her back to the church. Once, through this angel's influence and the power of virtue and strength, she clung to the floor of the church from the feast of St. Martin until Lent.[7] Wherever she sat or lay, she would not permit even a little straw to be between her and the bare earth. And while she slept, she used the bare earth or the plank which stretched across the pedestal of the altar instead of a pillow. Indeed, I remember that there was such bitter cold and frost that winter that the wine suddenly froze into ice in the holy chalice while the priest chanted. Nevertheless she felt no cold, nor did her head ache, since the holy angel mercifully supported her with his hand.

Woe to you who are luxury lovers, sleeping in soft sheets and ivory beds and used to soft and silken things: you are both dead and buried in the lusts and desires of your flesh. You who lead your days in this world's wealth, you will fall down in a flash to the depths of hell, where vermin shall be strewn under you and your covering shall be worms. Behold, the earth served Christ's maiden, lest she be hurt by her hard practices, for she devoutly served Our Lord; the winter spared her, lest she be destroyed by the cold; holy angels ministered to her, lest she suffer in any way. Against you, vain fools, the world shall fight for God; for that which He made shall be armed to avenge Him on His enemies, and the creature who serves the Maker shall show great anger toward you.

(11.) Of her clothes.

She who was clad in the holy Lamb's fleece, she who was inwardly adorned with the bridal garment, she who had clothed herself with Christ, cared nothing for outward array. Her clothes were ordinary, for neither filth nor fastidious cleanness pleased her. Indeed, she eschewed both fair and foul attire alike; for one signified delight and vanity, and the other hypocrisy and [the desire to gain] praise from people. Nevertheless she knew that St. John the Baptist was praised by Our Lord for the harshness of his clothing, and that Christ himself said, *those who wear soft raiment are in a king's house* [Mt 11:8]; therefore she did not wear a linen smock next to her skin, but a coarse undergarment called *estamin* in the vernacular. She also had a white woolen tunic, and a cloak of the same color without any ornament or fur, knowing that Our Lord covered the nakedness of our first father and mother after their fall not with luxurious or ornately colored clothes, but with leather garments. She who burned within was satisfied with the simplicity of these clothes and feared no cold, nor did she need any material fire to chase away the chill in winter; but in a wondrous manner, when the winter was bitter and the frost severe, she was as warm in body as she was fervent in spirit when she prayed, so much so that her clothing sometimes smelled of her sweet, fragrant sweat. Sometimes the aroma of her clothing was like that of incense, for she offered her prayers to Our Lord with the censer of a pure heart.

What do you say to this, you superficial women, full of pomp and pride, who burden your carcasses with layers of clothes and dress up like unnatural beasts with long tails, disgracing yourselves with horns and hooves and adorned like a temple? Your clothes are gnawed with moths and stink. But the clothes of this holy woman are kept as relics and smell very sweet. They are precious garments, impervious to the cold no matter how thin, and therefore sanctified because of the cold; and indeed, because they are sanctified they are carefully guarded and honored with pious affection by devout people after her death.

(12.) Of her manual labor.

This wise woman knew well that Our Lord had meted out penance to the first father and mother after they had sinned, and through them to their children, namely, *In the sweat of your face you shall eat bread* [Gen 3:19]. And so for as long as she could she labored with her own hands in order to mortify her flesh with penance, to provide necessities for the poor, and to obtain food and clothing for herself, since she had forsaken all things for Christ's sake. Indeed, Our Lord had given her such abundant grace and skill in working that she far surpassed her companions, so much so that she was able to make a living both for herself and for one companion through her diligence, bearing in mind what the apostle says: *If anyone will not work, let him not eat* [2 Thess 3:10]. Indeed, she considered each act of labor sweet when she recalled that the only-begotten Son of Heaven, who opens his hands and fills every creature with his blessing [see Ps 145:16], was nourished by the manual labor of Joseph and the work of a poor little virgin. Therefore in calm and silence, as the apostle says, she obtained her bread by the work of her hands, for her strength was *in quietness and trust* [Is 30:15]. Indeed, so much did she flee the noise and company of men and love stillness and calm that one time from the feast of the Holy Cross until Easter she kept silence, barely speaking a word.[8] And Our Lord was so pleased to accept this offering of silence that the Holy Spirit revealed to her that God would allow her to pass straight to Paradise without suffering the pains of Purgatory. This reveals how serious the vice of loquaciousness and idle talk is, since silence and stillness are so pleasing to Our Lord.

Multiplying every day the talents given to her [see Mt 25:14–30], she climbed up the ladder of Jacob from virtue to virtue until at last she reached the highest level and pinnacle, leaving all material things behind. In this state her physical being was so absorbed by spirit that she was unable to concern herself with anything but the bread that does not perish, as the Gospel says [see Jn 6:27], for she was completely fulfilled and preoccupied with Christ. Thus, freed from all manual labor at such times, she rested like a hermit with Our Lord, who had endowed His handmaiden with this special liberty.

(13.) Of her bearing and appearance.

The inner disposition of her mind was reflected in her physical bearing and appearance, and the pleasantness of her aspect would not let the joy of her heart be hidden. Often, however, she tempered the heaviness of her heart with gladness of expression, or hid the mirth of her mind with the simplicity of a serene face. And since the apostle says that women shall pray with their heads veiled [see 1 Cor 11:5–10], the white veil that covered her head hung before her eyes. She moved modestly, with a slow and easy gait, bending her head and looking at the ground. Indeed, so much did the grace of her soul shine in her face through the fullness of her heart that many who looked upon her were spiritually refreshed and moved to devotion and pious weeping; reading in her face the unction of the Holy Spirit as if in a book, they knew that virtue resided in her.

It happened one day that a virtuous man named Guy, formerly a cantor of the church at La Cambre, went out of his way to visit her, for he was a friend to religious people. One of his companions, who until then did not know by experience how much good it may do to humble minds to visit virtuous people, scorned the pious labor of this devout man and asked, "For God's love, sir cantor, what do you seek? Why are you going out of your way? Why do you want to chase after flies and butterflies like a child?" But since this man was humble, patient, and forbearing, he did not waver from his proposed journey on account of these words but devoutly went to Christ's maiden, from whose presence he had taken not a little comfort once before. While he spoke with her, his companion, who put little store by his words in the manner of worldly people, was occupied in idle conversation. Then when he was bored and tired of waiting, he came to the cantor to tell him to hurry up. And when he happened to look directly at the face of Christ's maiden, suddenly and astonishingly he dissolved into tears and was unable to tear himself away from that place and her presence for a long time. Then the cantor, though he wanted to restrain himself out of modesty, recognized what had happened and rejoiced. Mocking his companion, he said, "Let us go hence, what are we waiting for? Perhaps you want to chase after butterflies." And after many sighs and tears his companion was finally able to draw himself away from the place, saying, "Forgive me, Father, for I did not know what I was saying before; now, truly, I have perceived God's virtue in this woman through experience."

Another time, when her body was no longer able to bear the fervor of her spirit, she fell into a serious illness. So much, indeed, did the gracious Father discipline His daughter whom He loved that the limbs and members of her body became strangely twisted; for sometimes the pain caused her arms to form into a circle, and she was compelled to beat her breast with her hands. And when the power of the sickness abated somewhat, she thanked Our Lord (who chastises like children those whom He loves) with so much joy that the apostle's word was plainly fulfilled in her: *for when I am weak, then I am strong* [2 Cor 12:10]. After Our Lord had tested His chosen child with this infirmity like gold in a furnace, purifying and polishing her completely [see 1 Pet 1:7], she obtained such great strength from God for vigils, fasting, and other deeds that strong men could scarcely endure a third of her labor.

Nevertheless, when any of her friends were afflicted with disease or cast down with any temptation, she was sick with the sick and burned with the sorrow of those who had been led astray; sometimes she even felt their afflictions in her own limbs. Then at once she would call a priest, who would make the sign of the cross with his finger on the place that ached; and in a miraculous manner the pain fled to another place, as if dreading the power of the Holy Cross. Again and again he made the sign of the cross, until this migratory evil dared no longer abide the power of the Cross but finally went away completely from the body of Christ's maiden, thus revealing the power of the crucifix in an astonishing and unprecedented manner. Truly she who had gazed with the eye of faith at the brazen serpent and had been delivered from the bite of the evil adder thanked God and the Holy Cross many times.

Many men obtained the grace of devotion not only by beholding her face, but also through conversation with her; she gave plenteous sweetness to some, not only spiritually in the heart, but literally in the mouth, for they could taste the sweetness of honey. Men who are slow to believe may hear this and mutter; but those who have experienced such consolations themselves will believe easily when they hear this: Spouse of Christ, your lips are a honeycomb distilling nectar, and milk is under your tongue (see Song 4:11). One day when an eminent but humble man from a distant country came to visit her out of piety and great charity, he received such comfort from the sight of her and such sweetness from her words that for the rest of the day the taste of real food was unable to displace from his mouth the honey-sweet savor he had received. I deliberately omit this holy man's name here, since he is very distressed when he is praised; indeed he is tested in the mouths of those who praise him just as gold is tried in a furnace. [But suffice it to say that] he was an exiled bishop.[9]

Now let us put an end to this first book, in which we have spoken of those things that pertain to the exterior person, that is to say the body, and things that are manifest to the senses; and since half our day's journey is done, let us rest a little before going on to more inward and subtle things.

NOTES

1. Jacques dedicated his *Life of St. Marie d'Oignies* to Bishop Fulk of Toulouse, who visited Marie in 1212.

2. The diocese of Liège was the center of beguine life in the early thirteenth century. It is in modern Belgium.

3. The Middle English translator has written here that Marie's parents were "common," but the context makes it clear that this is an error; they were *not* common, that is, they were of noble lineage.

4. Jacques refers to the crowns which martyrs were believed to receive in heaven.

5. St. Simeon Stylites (390–459), born in what is now Syria, came to be revered in both Eastern and Western Churches for practicing extreme forms of bodily mortification. These not only included self-inflicted wounds and severe fasting, but the curious habit of living on tall pillars for years at a time. His feast is celebrated on September 1 in the East and on January 5 in the West. St. Anthony of Egypt (251–356) lived for many years in complete solitude in the desert, where he suffered many temptations and afflictions including a form of ergotism which came to be known as "St. Anthony's fire." He was an extremely popular saint in the later Middle Ages. His feast is celebrated on January 17.

6. The feast of the Holy Cross is celebrated on September 14.

7. This is almost certainly a reference to the feast of St. Martin of Tours, which occurs on November 11.

8. Since the feast of the Holy Cross is on September 14, the time period referred to here is six or seven months.

9. Jacques is probably referring to Bishop Fulk of Toulouse. Fulk left Toulouse in 1211 to protest the support given to Albigensian heretics by the people of the city.

Chapter 32

PETER OF THE MORRONE (POPE CELESTINE V), *AUTOBIOGRAPHY*

Translated by George Ferzoco

Introduction

Peter of the Morrone was born in late 1209 or early 1210 in the region of Molise, south-central Italy; the precise place is likely Sant' Angelo Limosano, a small agricultural town. After an introduction to monastic life, Peter became a hermit in the early 1230s, living in the Apennines of Abruzzo (the region just north of Molise), notably on Mount Maiella and Mount Morrone. Just as his fame as a thaumaturge attracted constant visitors, his holiness attracted many followers, obliging him to obtain ecclesiastical approbation for the group; this was granted by Pope Urban IV in 1263, who incorporated Peter's men into Benedictine monasteries. To ensure the stability of the new congregation, Peter went to Lyon and obtained a privilege from Pope Gregory X in 1275. In 1293 Peter established the seat of his congregation at the new Abbey of the Holy Spirit of the Morrone, near Sulmona; Peter himself lived in a hermitage on the mountainside overlooking the monastery.

This move occurred during the interregnum following the death of Pope Nicholas IV (April 4, 1292). The cardinals, divided between the Orsini and Colonna factions, could not agree on a new pope. But pressure exerted by Charles II of Anjou and others helped break the impasse, and on July 5, 1294 in Perugia the octogenarian Peter was unexpectedly and unanimously elected pope. Although Peter was known to some important clerics and secular leaders, he was likely selected not for his leadership potential but for his usefulness as a compromise candidate, whose reign would not be long. Peter was crowned Pope Celestine V in L'Aquila on August 29, 1294; he established an unusual indulgence which granted complete absolution to those who visited, under certain conditions, the church where he was crowned. Celestine appointed twelve new cardinals, accommodated the Franciscan Spirituals in the specially created congregation named "The Poor Hermits of Lord Celestine" (*Pauperes Eremite Domini Celestini*), and granted many favors to his monastic congregation, but it soon was apparent that he had little talent or inclination for his new tasks. When the curia moved to Naples in November of 1294, Celestine considered renouncing the papacy and returning to his eremitical life; and he did so — the only time a pope has ever voluntarily resigned his office — on December 13, 1294, after consultations with cardinal Benedetto Caetani. This same prelate was elected Pope Boniface VIII eleven days later, and fearing that Peter might change his mind regarding his abdication, the new pope sent emissaries to bring his predecessor to him. Peter was arrested trying to flee across the Adriatic and was brought to Fumone, where he was confined until he died on May 19, 1296. Under pressure from French king Philippe le Bel, Pope Clement V canonized Peter on May 5, 1313 in Avignon.

This canonization was the fruit of lengthy investigations of Peter's sanctity, which may well have been doubted by many contemporaries. Opinions concerning several aspects of Peter's life were often intransigent and conflicting, particularly regarding his renunciation of the papacy: indeed, the legitimacy of this act was the subject of scholastic debates, and its rationality was (tacitly, at least) questioned in vernacular literary works, such that many people hold that Dante was referring to Celestine when mentioning the sight of someone in hell as "he who through cowardice made the great refusal" (*Inferno* 3:59–60).

And although little seems to have been made of it in canonization documents, the so-called *Autobiography* may also have raised the eyebrows of readers, given its unusual style and content. The work's beginning and ending assure us that the work was written by Peter's own hand and left behind in his cell, presumably when he left to accept the papal tiara. But it seems that the work — in the form we know it, at least — could not have been actually written by Peter. Its inconsistent grammar and meandering narrative are incompatible with the possibility of one person (whether it be Peter or not) having been its sole author; for example, the evolution of the narrative's content clearly illustrates the progressive loss of an authentic autobiographical tone. This loss is paralleled by a similar diminution of precise elements of popular culture while monastic hagiographical features become more pronounced. Nonetheless, it does seem likely that the work primarily comprises a series of reminiscences told by Peter to his monks, later recorded by a hagiographer. Taken together, these "oral relics" form the story of Peter's youth and early monastic experiences.

The work, divided into four parts, is preceded by a prologue which is biblical in content and monastic in tone. Each of the prologue's six sentences is a biblical citation or is directly inspired by a scriptural verse. One of the verses, "Lord, open my lips, and my mouth will send forth your praise" [Ps 50:17; 51:17 in Vulgate], is the very one used in the great monastic legislative guide, the *Rule* of St. Benedict, in regard to readings which accompany meals in the refectory. The fact that this work emerged from a monastic milieu further underlines the strong probability that its many edifying episodes would have been a part of the *lectio divina*.

The first part of the narrative proceeds with accounts of the young Peter and his mother; the second with the beginning of his eremitical life; the third with his solitary life on Mount Morrone, which was to be his home for many years and was to give him the name by which he became widely known; and the fourth narrates his life in the company of several followers on Mount Maiella. Each part of Peter's life begins with a miraculous event which marks a break with what has gone before. As one might expect, Peter's birth is a cause for wonder, as he came out of the mother's womb "dressed as if in a religious habit," wearing the amniotic sac; this clearly echoes folkloric beliefs that such a birth marks the baby for a fortunate, and in some cases spiritually gifted, life. The second part begins with a divine test of Peter's new eremitical vocation in the form of a violent storm in a strange new place. A particularly significant episode marks the beginning of the third part. Peter had just become a priest at the insistence of the people who frequented the region where his hermitage stood, but after his ordination, Peter left the area and moved to Mount Morrone where he underwent a spiritual crisis. He felt compelled to request that he be relieved of the sacerdotal duties he had just accepted, because it interfered with his ascetic vocation. But after long winter weeks of doubt, a vision convinced him to continue on the path he had undertaken. So, here we have an emotionally charged episode: because of public demand, Peter is ordained; he moves to Mount Morrone; he then desires to abandon the priesthood in favor of his previous lifestyle. It is striking that this is a precise mirror image of the events of Peter's papacy. On the demand of the princes of the Church, Peter is made pope; he moves with the curia to Naples; he then desires to abandon the papacy in order to return to his eremitical ways. The parallel is so precise that it must either reflect a constant indecisiveness on the part of Peter, or that the hagiographer hoped to deflect possible criticism of Peter's abdication by showing that his act had some precedent and was not inherently a negative decision.

This part of Peter's life as narrated in the *Autobiography* is followed by a final section, in which a devastating fire and initial disagreements between Peter and his followers are overcome successfully and are followed by a series of miraculous events; indeed, Peter's move to Mount Maiella may have been influenced by its traditional status as the holy mountain of central Italy. But this work, even though it ends abruptly and prematurely, finds a continuation beyond even this fourth and final section, for the *Autobiography* is not found in any extant manuscript to be unaccompanied by a Latin prose *vita* which continues the narrative of Peter's life from the point at which the autobiography ends. It clearly served as an integral element of Peter's hagiographical dossier, and moreover serves today's readers as a fascinating record of not only the hagiographical world of Peter and his followers, but also more generally of the popular and religious culture of thirteenth-century central Italy. Its hagiographical commonplaces combine with many idiosyncratic details of visions, miracles, asceticism, and social life to create a short yet fascinating work.

SOURCES AND FURTHER READING

The Latin text on which this translation is based (*Bibliotheca hagiographica latina*, no. 6733) is to be found in Arsenio Frugoni, *Celestiniana*, Istituto storico italiano per il Medio Evo, Studi storici 6–7 (Rome, 1954), pp. 56–67. There is no scholarly biography of Peter/Celestine in English, but the most accessible in another language would be Paolo Golinelli, *Il papa contadino. Celestino V e il suo tempo* (Florence, 1996). For a study of the documents comprising Peter's canonization dossier (and for bibliography), see George Ferzoco, "Church and Sanctity: The Hagiographical Dossier of Peter of Morrone," in *Normes et pouvoir à la fin du moyen âge. Actes du colloque "La recherche en études médiévales au Québec et en Ontario" 16 – 17 mai 1989 — Montréal*, ed. Marie-Claude Déprez-Masson, Inedita & Rara 7 (Montréal, 1990), pp. 53–69.

Peter of the Morrone (Pope Celestine V), Autobiography

> Here begins the life of the most holy father, brother Peter of the Morrone or Pope Celestine the Fifth; to begin, this is the treatise of his life which he wrote with his own hand and left behind in his cell.
>
> Come, and listen to me, and I will tell you, all of you who fear God, how much He did for my soul [see Ps 65:16; 66:16 in Vulgate]. God, create in me a pure heart and put a righteous spirit in my innards [Ps. 50:12; 51:12 in Vulgate]. Lord, open my lips, and my mouth will send forth your praise [Ps 50:17; 51:17 in Vulgate]. Let whatever we say be in praise of God and for the edification of our neighbour [see 2 Cor 12:19]; for the Scriptures say: "Mercy and truth will not desert you: gird your mouth with it and inscribe it on the tablets of your heart" [Prov 3:3]. And elsewhere: "The mouth which lies kills the soul" [Wis 1:11]. Thus in everything I say I shall say the truth in Christ, and will not in any way lie.
>
> Thus, first I shall say something about my parents, whose names are these: Angelerius and Mary. Both of them were just before God, so I believe, and were greatly praised before men. They were simple and upright and God-fearing; humble and peace loving, they were not ones who would exchange evil for evil, but they freely gave alms and hospitality to the poor. Just like the patriarch Jacob, they brought forth twelve children, always praying the Lord that one of them might become a true servant of God. Because of this motive they dedicated their second son to the study of letters. This son, becoming a good and most beautiful man according to the pomp of this world, was not as careful of the service of the Lord as his parents had desired. However, the father having died at a ripe old age, the widowed wife was left with seven children (because the others were dead). The good woman, seeing that her son the cleric was not as spiritual as she had hoped, shook with all her heart and said, "Oh my, poor soul that I am! How many children did I bear and nourish, yet I see none of them a servant of God." However, the eleventh son was then five or six years old, in whom God miraculously extended His grace, because he perceived all good things that were said, hid them all in his heart, and told them to his mother. And he often told his mother: "I want to be a good servant of God" [see Ps 85:2]. Truly the mother, considering this, said to herself: "I shall give this son of mine to the study of letters, and maybe the Lord will give him better grace than he gave to the other son; and if he should die, at least this son will remain with me." That which she thought did indeed happen, because he became a monk and after a short while died, and that boy survived, although knowing little of letters.
>
> But the devil, who is always opposed to every good thing, struggled, through himself and through his own forces. First, he tempted the boy not to want to study, and did not allow the boy's brothers to study. Thus, whenever they could they opposed their mother, saying "One son who does not work is enough for us," because in that town the clerics did no work. The devil also tempted a certain rich man of that land, who praised the boy saying, "I want

to make you my heir." There was also (as I truly believe) a certain demon, because he seemed to be one to me who was a boy, who said he was a seer and said to the mother: "What did you do? Remove him from study and teach the other smaller son, because he will not be a servant of God, as you believe, but will soon die this kind of death"; concerning which my mother was very sad, but notwithstanding this she did not cease to do the best she could.

She remembered something that occurred at the birth of the boy: that, as she said, when the boy came out of the womb of the mother, he was dressed as if in a religious habit. And she recalled something else that took place when the boy began to read: that night her man appeared to a certain godmother, saying "My wife has directed our son to the study of letters. Oh, there is such joy for me, for her, and for many others! So tell him on my behalf that if he loves me, he will exert himself in this as much as he is able, and he will finish what he began." Whence the mother, against her sons' will, took the valuables which belonged to her and gave them to a teacher so that he would instruct the boy, to whom God sent such grace that in a short time he could read the Psalter.

He, when he was still a boy and unlearned insofar as he could not recognize the Blessed Virgin and St. John who are depicted on the Cross, saw them however descend from the Cross; and taking the book in which the boy was reading, and in it both of them, namely the Virgin Mary and John, chanted in the sweetest fashion.[1] This the boy told to his mother with great joy. Concerning which the mother said: "See, son, that you tell no one."

Also, when the boy went to play with the other boys, he was tempted by the devil so that he would say words which were not allowed, and which the boy did not know. But with the coming of the night, he saw in a dream that he was in church, where he read during the day, and was before the altar: and here angels descended from the heights, and being on all sides of the boy, threatening and saying: "Why did you say such things? Beware that you do not say other such things," and one said to the other, "Hit him; why did you say those things?" However, he did not strike.

He saw these and many other good things continually in visions which he would relate to his mother. She forbade him to tell them to anybody else, and he did not tell them to anybody.

The mother also saw in a dream that this child was the shepherd of many sheep which were as white as snow. This dream made the mother very sad, and even when she arose she remained sad. But being the next day with her son, who was already twelve years old, she said, "Son, I saw a particular dream regarding a certain cleric." To which the son immediately responded: "He will be the guardian of good souls" [see Prov 16:17]. And she, hearing this, happy and joyful she said to her son: "Son, it is you. Take comfort in the Lord" [see Eph 6:10].[2]

God did many wondrous things for the mother of this boy, which he saw with his own eyes. First of all, being infirm for a period of thirty or more years on account of a serious illness such that she had lost the use of the right side of her body, she thus one day thought in her heart to go to a certain holy place. This she did and she was cured in one night.

Also, this very son of hers, when he was a child of three years, wounded his eye with a pointed stick. The eye became blind in such a way that doctors and all who saw it said that the eye was lost. She however, trusting in the Blessed Virgin, brought him to a certain church dedicated to the Blessed Virgin and remained there with her son for the entire night. And so, in this way, the morning found the eye healthy and without any marks.[3]

Likewise, another son who was married, while gathering the harvest, had a grain of cereal enter his eye, and in such a way that no one was capable of finding it. And thus for many days he wandered here and there seeking help and not finding it. And he cried out night and day on account of the very great pain. His mother, sad and mourning, turned to the Blessed Virgin that one night and said to her: "My Lord, return sight to this son of mine as you recently did to my other son." And when dawn broke this cleric son of hers looked into the eye of his brother and said that the grain was in the middle of his eye and was protruding outward. And he took it with his own fingers and pulled it out of his eye.

Similarly, a period of famine deprived the mother of bread, and she was unable to find any assistance. And so one night she turned to God, asking the Lord that he might mercifully provide for her sons so that they would not die of starvation. And arising in the morning she said to her son, "Son, take your scythe and go to the field and look in the field. Perhaps God will show us mercy and we will not die of hunger." And it was near harvest time, and her son did not want to go, saying "Why should I go? The grain is still green and won't be good for anything." Eventually he consented and went to the field and found in the middle of it much grain which was yellow and dry, as much as they needed. He gathered and threshed the grain then brought it to the mill and gave thanks to God.

Also this mother greatly honored the saints and venerated their feast days. So on the feast of the beheading of St. John,[4] because the next day she had to make bread, on the eve of that night she wanted to make the dough. Thus she began to put, with fear, water in the flour. And then suddenly all the flour seemed to be transformed into worms. And then shaking all over she fell to the ground, praying to God and saying, "Have pity on me"; and soon the flour returned to its normal state.

The youth desired ever more to serve God and especially to serve him in the hermitage. He did not know that a hermit could live with a companion, and indeed he thought that a hermit had to remain always alone, and he had a great fear of the night on account of phantasms. And being thus in doubt he did not know what to do; indeed there was in his hometown not one servant of God with whom he could discuss things.

Thus he went from year to year until he was twenty years old, and even older. This youth had a friend who was older than him in age to whom he began to say, "What shall we do? Let us leave our land and go far away in the service of God. But first let us go to Rome so that we might do what we want to do with the advice of the Church." He the friend agreed and they began to undertake their trip. And after a day's journey the older friend reconsidered and said, "Let's go back, let's not abandon our homeland and our relatives." Peter, inspired by God said to him, "I trust in God that if you abandon me, God will not abandon me. I will certainly not go back." And he remained alone.

And walking a day's journey he arrived at the ninth hour at a place named Castel di Sangro.[5] And as soon as this youth entered that town the air became turbulent and there was a great tempest of wind and rain, and this although before he arrived at that town the weather was wonderful. But he wanted to walk farther. Thus he arrived at the bridge over the river which was outside the town, and when he was on the middle of the bridge, then the wind came down upon him and gave him a great fright such that, deeply shaken, he turned back. And there was at the end of the bridge the church of Saint Nicholas, in which he entered and prayed to the Lord and to St. Nicholas that they give him help.[6] Comforted by God, he stayed there many days and while he was there he came to know from certain people that there was a hermit on the mountain near that town. Happy and joyful he went to him; but before he arrived to meet him, the Spirit of the Lord forbade him to reveal his secrets to the hermit.

So he went to the hermit and before he entered his cell, God showed him the dishonest life of this hermit. Accordingly he told him nothing except of his plan to travel to Rome, because the hermit had told him that he himself wanted to go to Rome. Thus the hermit fixed the day the youth would come back to him, so that they could begin the journey. But the Lord did not permit that he should return on that day; for if this would have happened, it would have been a bad thing for him, as was indeed clear.

Another day, he bought two loaves of bread and two fish and went up the mountain. And when he was already near the place there appeared before him two very beautiful women who fiercely struggled with him, taking him by the hands and telling him, "Do not go, because there is no hermit in that place; come with us." He was barely able to free himself from their hands. And arriving at the place he found the cell open and a burning fire and water. And bringing the two loaves and fish, he found no one there. This happened in the month of January and there was a great snowfall; indeed, it was snowing even then. And immediately the Spirit of God was with him and he began to reflect, saying, "Stay and try, and you will see what God will do for you." And so he remained in great fear and doubt. But after a long vigil, exhausted with fatigue he fell to the ground and slept. And a great crowd of angels and saints was around him, so clear and visible that he thought himself to be awake. And in the mouths of each one of them there were red roses, and with these roses they blossomed with very great joy, such that when he was awakened from his sleep he heard that song for the space of time which it takes to say the Our Father.[7] Thus made more happy than one could say, and by now reassured, he remained there alone for ten days with those two loaves, sated with joy and delight.

And after this the Lord showed him a place on another mountain where he found a large rock, and under this rock he dug a bit such that he could barely in this excavated space arise or stretch out. And he stayed there for a period of three years, in which place the Lord showed him many good things.

First, every night, and at the proper hour, he heard the sound of a great bell. Then there arrived a certain person from a good hermit saying, "Why does that brother have a rooster who sings at night? Why don't you have it?" And then a certain matron who was present there said to him immediately, "I have a very beautiful rooster; if you want I shall bring it to you." And this man, like a simple person responded, "I want." And this was done. But the rooster never sang, and the sound of that bell disappeared. And he understood that which he had done wrong. He returned the rooster but he never rediscovered the grace of the sound of the bell which he had lost.

Also, often while he prayed at night he often saw here and there near him two very beautiful men dressed as bishops who sang the Mass. It seemed to him they were saying the Psalms with him.

Indeed, at the beginning of his conversion he had to withstand many temptations, both while awake and while sleeping. In fact two demons took the form of certain women he had seen earlier in the world, who were very beautiful. And often the eyes of his heart presented both of them to him. And while he slept one of them, naked, was on one side of him and the other was on the other side. And thus they struggled with him. And he upon awakening folded his tunic under his feet and these devils took away these clothes from under his feet and put them back on his body. But with God's help they did not prevail.[8]

Also in that place there were reptiles: snakes, scorpions, lizards, and the like. Sometimes when he slept those animals known locally as toads went on his chest and attached themselves to his flesh because he did not have any other clothing except his tunic with a cowl, with which he covered his head. They would attach themselves to his flesh while he slept. And even when he would get up he would not notice them and say the entire Matins, genuflecting many times. And when he did notice, he would loosen his belt and thus they would fall to his feet. And a marvelous thing happened: he would not notice these animals before, but when they fell to his feet he would kick them and water would spurt from their mouths, and he then would see what they signified. Many were the good and bad things that befell to him in that place, which would take long to recount; thus I shall turn to other matters.

After spending three years in that place, all the people persuaded him to take the sacerdotal order, on which occasion he went to Rome and there he was made a priest. Then he came to Mount Morrone, and there he found a certain cave which was very pleasing to him. But immediately when he entered he sat down and behold, a large snake came out before him and it left that place in which God brought many good things to him over the space of five years.[9] And since he always desired solitude and poverty, therefore he knew at once to give up the office of Mass, and to seek the counsel of the pope. But this was in the winter; seeing there was a lot of snow on the mountain, therefore he was unable to descend. Therefore he was there for many days in this temptation, and when the day was near on which he was supposed to take the road to Rome, behold, in the night, he was thinking in a vision that he was going to Rome, and while he was going he kept getting lost on the way. And then there was before him, behold, two brothers coming whom he asked about the way. To him they said nothing; but rather they laughed among themselves about him, whence he was seated in sorrow and sadness. And behold a certain matron came, who having been asked about the way responded in this manner: "You ought to have petitioned God when you were in the crypt," and she said nothing else. He understood that he had not prayed concerning this. He petitioned God and behold in the night a certain abbot who had died (and this abbot had first given him the religious habit) came to him in a vision in such a manner. It seemed to Peter that he was before an altar and behold, he appeared before this man dressed in an exceedingly white vestment saying to him, "O son, pray for me and remain with God." And Peter wanted to walk away, but this man apprehended him by the collar and would not dismiss him, although he said humbly, "Give up, O son, give up, O son," to whom he replied, "I swear to you by the living God and the Holy Trinity and through the other saints," he said to swear, "so that you say to me what I should do concerning such a deed." But he responded saying, "Say Mass, O son, say it." And he, "John the Baptist and Blessed Benedict and many other saints did not wish to touch so great a ministry. How can I, who am such a great sinner, I who am not worthy to carry out such a task?" To whom he said, "O son! Worthy? And who is worthy? Say Mass, O son, say it with fear and trembling." And immediately he disappeared. Moreover on the same day a certain holy monk came to him, to whom he was accustomed to confess, who said similar things to him just as the abbot in the vision had said to him.

Also, at another time a great temptation befell him. He was greatly disturbed, wanting to know what he should do when he had a nocturnal emission, namely, to know whether that day he should or should not celebrate Mass. Asking advice of many religious, one would say one thing, another would say another thing. And thus he was in great doubt, not knowing what to do. He asked God's counsel so that He might help him in this matter. And so one certain night while sleeping he seemed to mount toward a certain castle placed on high. And mounting he saw a large cloister and in the middle of it the door of this castle, and all around this cloister several cells, in which there were brothers wearing white habits. He wanted to enter the palace, and brought with him a certain small donkey which he was unable to leave behind. Thus he began to mount the steps of the palace's staircase, on which the donkey moved with ease. And thus going up three or four steps, that bad little donkey began indecently to eject excrement from its body, as if it had been eating unripened grasses. And he, watching this and seeing the steps sad and mourning did not dare to go up. And he saw at the top of this staircase, at the entrance to this palace, three similar persons and equal to the point that they seemed one person. And all looked at him, of which one, who looked like Christ, said to him, "Come up, come up. Why don't you come up? Perhaps because the little donkey has acted in accordance with his habits, what does this matter to you? Come up, come up." And he awakened from his sleep filled with every joy and delight, praising and blessing God. Many and unrelatable good things befell him at that place over the space of five years.[10]

But since this man always sought solitude, and because all the woods around this place had been destroyed and cultivated by men, he went away from this place and went to Mount Maiella. And there he found a large cave which he liked very much. But the two companions he had did not like this cave, and neither did any of his friends; in fact, all of them were opposed except one of them and thus he remained alone in this place. Yet after a few days his friends also followed him because they loved him greatly. Thus they made bunches from branches of trees and tied them together. Thus did they close the crypt and they lived in it. And since this was a very hot period of summer (that is, in the month of June) the trees were very dry, thus one night the tempter appeared to him, and looking, it seemed to Peter that the entire cell was on fire. And he called the brothers saying "Get up quickly and throw everything outside." And others getting up saw the cell burning. In great haste, they took everything they could and went out and began to grumble about him who had come to this place. And they believed that the fire had come down the mountain from above. But he, comforted by God, said in his heart, "Even if my whole body should burn, I will not abandon this place." And when he said these words, the entire fire disappeared as if it were a dream. Many of his devotees went to him and reproached him, saying, "Everyone murmurs against you and are in disagreement about this, and if they didn't fear you out of devotion they would protest against you. And you know very well they love you very much. But we are so tired that we can barely come here because of the length and difficulty of the road which we must take. And even those of the nearby town don't want to come here any more." And he, with a peaceful heart humbly responded: "My dear ones, go with God's blessing. And return here when you have a greater desire to do so." A few days later, one of them went to him and begged to be received as a brother, and this was done. And many, from that moment on, began to abandon the world and went to him. As often as possible, he refused to see them on account of his simplicity and his constant desire to live in solitude. But finally, conquered by charity, he sometimes agreed to receive them. Many great signs appeared there, which demonstrated that God had chosen this place to be consecrated to the Holy Spirit.

From the first days, a dove appeared there and lived with them. It ate at the spot where the altar was later built. And it walked among the brothers as if it were domesticated by them. And once the oratory was built, the dove was often there, even when office was said. One day visitors were there for the Mass, and the dove was among them, and one of them crouched down in order to capture it but was unable to do so. And thus the dove, for a period of two or three years, appeared there.

After this a beautiful oratory was built in honor of the Holy Spirit. Many pilgrims visited, even from faraway towns. One day they came even from his hometown, and the brother sitting with them spoke of the word of life. And there came four men from another town, and as soon as they arrived a spirit of love and great ardor so overcame this brother that he could barely restrain himself. Then he sent away those from his hometown and remained with the others and with his brothers. It was the ninth hour, and he said to them "Let us first say Lauds, and then we will have the joy of consolation." And they entered the oratory and began to say the office. And these people began to hear the sound of many large bells. But this place was so removed from all human habitation that no sound of bells could ever be heard there. And, stupefied, they were greatly surprised to hear these things. And so two of them left the oratory lifting their eyes and ears to heaven and everyone cried. And the brothers, upon going out of the office, went to Peter full of tears saying: "Where is the place where the bells are ringing?" And the brother, hearing the words, understood the cause. He said "It is not very far from here." And he began to change the subject. And they stayed seated, speaking of many good subjects until Vespers. And when it was time they went to the office and immediately they began to hear the sound of large bells until the end of the office. And thus it was at each hour, night and day, until the third day, when they left. And afterward every time they were in the houses of lay people they heard those sounds. And from this they could prove that the sound came from God.

One of them suffered a grave illness, which was this: while he slept he would suddenly get up and scream and run outside from place to place and hide in any hiding place he was able to find and nobody was able to restrain him. But from that day on, he felt nothing of the sort. Another, on the other hand, suffered from a spiritual weakness, such that each night he would have at least two nocturnal emissions. And from that day he was so freed from that vice that he never felt anything again. Every night devils would assault him but they never conquered. All four of these were converted; they took the religious habit and gave all their goods to the poor. Two of them, who were young, conducted such lives that God showed them many things in life and in death. The other two, who were already old, led a good life for many years and died in peace.

After these four, many people heard the sound of these bells. And when they heard them there, they heard them from everywhere except in cities and towns. From one city there were twenty people who heard that sound, and many others from other parts. And these were lay people and seculars, and no clerics and no religious, giving cause to great wonderment. But all the brothers of that place did hear them, and on major feast days they heard the sound of even more bells. And all the brothers heard them, but not all in the same way; some would hear them more clearly and would hear different bells; and a certain brother heard one bell which gave a sweeter sound than all the others, and this bell sounded when the Body of Christ arrived. This bell was always heard at the same spot on the mountain; in another spot another two bells were heard; and a bit farther yet another two. And it seemed that many doves were in the air above that place. And the more one paid attention to hear the bells, the less one heard them, and vice versa. And that sound so filled the ear that it was barely tolerable.[11]

Often one heard a loud singing of the office, sometimes in the oratory, sometimes in the cell of this brother. And they understood what was said in this office in these places. A certain brother, while celebrating the office, often heard other very sweet voices mixed with the voices of the brothers in such a way that when the voices of the brothers were silent the other voices could be better heard. On the feast of St. Stephen, in the evening, this brother Peter said to his fellow brothers, "Let us do a good office in honor of St. John and tomorrow I shall give you a good meal."[12] It was a Friday, and they arose very hurriedly to the Vigils, and after the Vigils the brothers returned to their cells. And this brother, returning to his cell, prayed as much as he desired. And then he laid down on the table, and immediately taken by sleep, he began to hear the office in the oratory. And soon awakening, listening, he heard very clearly the voices. And the cell was ten steps away from the oratory. And there were many at the office, among them children; and one of them, who seemed to be superior to all the others, emitted a voice like a trumpet. The office being said, they left the choir and made a procession before the Cross and there began to say many good things, particularly with regard to this place. And afterward, the superior among them turned to the brother's cell and said aloud, "Peter, make abstinence." And immediately they vanished.

Also, one day after Matins this brother was lying on his table sleeping. And suddenly he seemed to be in the oratory, and it seemed they were to say the Mass but he did not know who was to celebrate it. At that time he saw a few men in the oratory; and suddenly the oratory was filled with men dressed in white. And then there appeared someone at the right side of the altar who said the Mass. And he seemed to be the abbot of this brother, but he did not recognize him. And after he awakened, it seemed to him that it was the Holy Spirit, whom everyone held with great reverence. And the brother of whom we are speaking was to the right of that abbot. And when the body of Christ was raised, a certain bell was sounded, the power of its sound drew everyone to the altar after having thrown them to the ground. And then this brother, having awakened, found his head where his feet had been, and heard this glorious sound even after he awakened.

And another time at the break of day he was sitting in his cell. He had a book before him, and read it. The window was already open. And suddenly outside the cell near the window many glorious-looking personages appeared who said among themselves, "Let us build this cell." And they began to say the office of the dedication, circling around the cell. And this brother said the office with them. And this brother marveled at this, saying to himself: "What's happening? I'm not sleeping!" And he looked at the book, and put his hands on the letters of the page which were true, because it was already daytime. And the office being finished, he clearly felt freed and stripped of a vestment which I did not feel having been on me before. And immediately these people vanished.

One Sunday, one of the brothers had a vision of a shining man who said: "See that this oratory is dedicated to God. And I give you this sign. This morning, when you enter the oratory, the lamp which is before the altar will move back and forth." And this happened in the sight of all the brothers; and this was a marvel because the lamp, even though it was full of oil, did not let any oil escape, even though the lamp was seen to move greatly from here to there.

Also, certain brothers saw a great crowd of devils in the woods around the place who rutted and bleated like sheep and wanted to enter this place. And in another higher place there was another crowd of good spirits who battled against them and did not permit them to enter.

Also, a certain Lent the brothers dedicated themselves to a great abstinence, prayer, and silence and other good works to the utmost of their capabilities. But the devil tempted them interiorly, in their hearts, and they could do nothing about it. Consequently, he openly confronted them on the Sunday of the Passion at night, before the brothers arose for Vigil. And while they were in their cells, he struck four of the brothers with great fear in such a way that arising for Vigil they all began to scream and say, "Help us, help!" One of them had lost both his hands, such that the fingers of each hand were useless. And all the brothers who were in the choir saw very ugly devils in the air and all over the place, such that everyone abandoned the office. But the brother who was in the cell, when he heard this, went to tell them that those who could, should never abandon their office. And at daybreak all these phantasms disappeared.

And everything which has been related here occurred repeatedly for a period of three years, that is, as long as the small oratory existed. Afterward, such things occurred rarely and to few people.

Here ends the life of the most holy father of ours, St. Peter the Confessor of the Morrone, which he wrote with his own hand and left behind in his cell.

NOTES

1. This commonplace of a work of sacred art coming to life is also found, for example, in accounts of the conversion of Francis of Assisi.

2. That this should occur when Peter is twelve years old is an indication to the reader that he has reached an age of intellectual maturity, such as seen in the episode of Jesus at the same age, teaching the rabbis.

3. Both here and in the previous paragraph, we see examples of the practice known as incubation, in which people spent the entire night in a church or holy place in prayer, in the

hope of a miraculous cure or assistance. This practice is still in evidence in parts of central Italy known to Peter.

4. That is, August 29. This feast was of great significance to Peter, as he chose it to be the date of his papal coronation as Celestine V.

5. Castel di Sangro is a town in Abruzzo; the ninth hour is equivalent to approximately three o'clock in the afternoon.

6. St. Nicholas was renowned as a protector of travelers; churches dedicated to him were not uncommonly found along roads and near significant spots for pilgrims.

7. In central Italy the recitation of the Our Father (or Pater noster) is used as a unit for measuring time, especially crucial episodes; for example, it might be said that an earthquake lasted "three Our Fathers" (that is, the length of time needed to recite this prayer three times).

8. It should be noted that throughout his eremitical life, Peter was widely known for his refusal to be in the presence of women.

9. One region close to Mount Morrone, the Marsica, enjoyed a reputation since the classical period of producing spiritually gifted men who were also snake charmers.

10. A contemporary literary description of the beatific vision is found in the final canto of Dante's *Paradiso*; however, the pilgrim of the *Commedia* who reached this point had not encountered anything quite like that described by Peter in this account. With regard to nocturnal emissions: medieval canonists (including the most renowned of all, Gratian) in fact considered the question as to whether priests could celebrate mass after such occurrences; so for Peter to take this matter so seriously would indicate that he was not trained in canon law, nor did he have at hand a suitable book he or one of his followers could consult.

11. Although likely a coincidence, it may be worthwhile to note at this point that Peter's native region has had a particularly long tradition in the manufacture of church bells.

12. The feast of St. Stephen is December 26, the day before that of St. John the Evangelist.

CHAPTER 33

THE *LIFE OF ST. DAVID* SET DOWN BY AN ANCHORITE AT LLANDDEWIBREFI

Translated by Elissa R. Henken

INTRODUCTION

St. David (Dewi Sant), a sixth-century monk and missionary, patron saint of Wales and the only Celtic saint canonized by Rome (by Pope Calixtus II, in the early twelfth century), belongs to the Age of Saints, the period in the fourth to eighth centuries when Wales became Christianized and helped to Christianize its neighbors in the British Isles and on the Continent. Christianity had been introduced not only in the Roman-held areas of Britain but also, through the western sea routes, to the north and west. In the Romanized areas, Christianity was organized with bishops and dioceses, although in the west, where there were no towns, this meant that bishops became associated with particular tribes. The sea routes brought Christianity to Wales from both Gaul and the eastern Mediterranean, with its concepts of monasticism and eremetic desert life. The blend of influences created the peculiarly Celtic Christianity characteristic of David's time and which was already in full flower when the Anglo-Saxon invaders pushed Christianity out of what is now England. The Welsh clerics, monks, and anchorites, who came to be known as *seint* (singular, *sant*; derived from the Latin *sanctus, sancti*, "saint, saints") traveled out from the centers of learning, preaching and establishing churches, and generally at some point living as hermits. Most of the Welsh saints were associated with a particular area, though some, and most especially David, developed influence over much broader territories.

We have no contemporary reports of David's life. The earliest references are in Irish texts—the *Catalogue of the Saints of Ireland* (ca. 730), *The Martyrology of Tallaght* (ca.750), and the *Martyrology of Oengus the Culdee* (ca. 800)—which among other references give David's death date as 589 and his feast day as March 1; the *Life of St. Paul of Léon*, compiled ca. 884 in Britanny by Wrmonoc, which names David as fellow student of Sts. Paul, Samson, and Gildas; and Asser's *Life of King Alfred the Great* (ca. 983), which mentions him as a powerful saint. The first strong Welsh statement about David appears in the vaticinatory poem *Armes Prydein* (ca. 930), which calls on David to help free the Welsh of foreign oppression.

Although saints' *Lives* had become popular in Brittany and Ireland by the seventh century and in England by the eighth, they were not significant in Wales until the end of the eleventh century when changing religious and political circumstances necessitated them. During the centuries of conflict with the Anglo-Saxons, the Welsh Church had remained essentially undisturbed, but the Normans threatened great upheaval. The old system of the *clas* or monastic community and the traditional centers of learning, such as St. David's and Llanbadarn, were to be replaced by newly created dioceses and Latin monastic orders, and the whole brought under England's and Rome's hierarchies. All along their route, the Normans replaced local saints with ones better known in the Roman Church. In the twelfth and thirteenth centuries, some saints' *Lives* were composed by Welsh clerics defending the honor and rights of their own saints and supporting claims of the Welsh Church against the imposition of Canterbury's authority, and some were composed by Anglo-Norman clerics interested in the traditions of their newly acquired territories and eager to assert their ecclesiastical rights. Churches established their rights through the rights of their patron saints, showing that their particular saint had been granted land and privileges by kings and were superior to other saints. Through manipulation of the traditions, the clerics vied with the supporters of other saints for recognition by secular authorities and by the pope of their supremacy over other churches in Wales.

The first known, extant *Life* composed in Wales is Rhigyfarch's *Life of St. David*, written in Latin at the end of the eleventh century. Rhigyfarch's father Sulien (1011–1091) was twice bishop of the see of St. David's in Dyfed (the southwest corner of Wales), and re-established as a center of learning the *clas* at Llanbadarn, in Ceredigion (west-central Wales), where his four sons, continuing the family tradition of clerical service and learning, labored. Rhigyfarch (1056?-1099), the oldest and most noted of the four, has left his writing preserved in only a few examples—the *Ricemarch Psalter* (Trinity College, Dublin, Trinity College MS 50 [A 4.20]), which includes a martyrology of Jerome, a translation of the Hebrew Psalter, and Rhigyfarch's own verses in Latin; "Lamentation," a poem composed ca.1093 about the wretchedness of Ceredigion under subjugation by the Normans; and the *Life of St. David*, which seemingly provided the model for subsequent *Lives* of Welsh saints. According to Rhigyfarch himself, he gleaned his information about David's life from old manuscripts at St. David's. He probably also drew on the prayers, lections, and sermons used on David's feast day and on oral traditions heard in and around St. David's. Rhigyfarch's *Life of St. David* apparently served several political functions in addition to its religious one. It may have been written, as Nora Chadwick suggests, in 1081, during Sulien's second episcopacy, to support Sulien's policy in encouraging a pact between the Welsh princes Gruffudd ap Cynan and Rhys ap Tewdwr, as well as to show to William the Conqueror at the time of his pilgrimage to St. David's. The *Life of St. David*, with its documentation of St. David's as a place of power and influence, may have been used to urge William to protect the Welsh Church from encroachment by Canterbury. Alternatively, as suggested by A.W. Wade-Evans, J.W. James, and other scholars, the *Life of St. David* may have been composed a few years later, around 1093 or 1095, as a protest against an already encroaching Canterbury. Its composition may also have been a response to a first, now lost, text of Lifris's *Life* of St. Cadog, who was David's main rival in south Wales. Whenever its composition, it became an effective part of the struggle both for an independent Welsh Church and for the primacy of St. David's, rebutting claims being made by other churches such as the new, Norman-created diocese of Llandaff which, assuming the rights and authority of Sts. Dyfrig and Teilo, tried to establish its own supremacy (documented in *Liber Landavensis* or *Book of Llandaff*, ca. 1130). In addition to recounting David's wondrous deeds, his demonstrations of piety and learning, the *Life of St. David* establishes David as chief saint in the island, twice makes him archbishop, and carefully places in a subordinate position each of his rivals (except for Cadog, whom it neglects even to mention). For example, when David, Teilo, and Padarn (of Rhigyfarch's own Llanbadarn) go on pilgrimage to Jerusalem, David alone is given the gift of tongues so that they will not need an interpreter en route, and while the patriarch of Jerusalem consecrates all three as bishops, he raises David alone to the archiepiscopacy. At the Synod of Brefi, where David is selected as chief saint in the island and again made archbishop, it is Sts. Dyfrig and Deiniol (representative of the foremost northern house, Bangor) who are sent to fetch him. David is also given precedence over St. Patrick, who is forced to make way for David thirty years before the latter is even born.

Rhigyfarch's *Life* went through a number of recensions and continued to play a role in St. David's fight for an independent Welsh Church, which in turn was part of the fight for an independent Wales. For example, at the end of the twelfth century, Gerald of Wales, pleading the case for archiepiscopal status for St. David's, wrote his own *Life* of the saint and made three trips to Rome, on the third of which he carried letters of support from Llywelyn Fawr and some of the other Welsh princes who were striving to forge the separate principalities of Wales into one political entity.

Latin *Lives* of the Welsh saints were composed in both strongly Welsh houses and in more Normanized ones, but *Lives* were compiled in Welsh for only two of the saints—David from St. David's and Beuno from Clynnog Fawr, Gwynedd (northwest Wales)—both of which texts were recorded in a manuscript dated 1346 by an anchorite at Llanddewibrefi. The text included in this volume is of this Welsh *Life*—entitled *Buchedd Dewi* or *Life of David*—which has survived in fourteen manuscripts. The demand for Welsh texts suggests something of fourteenth-century concerns. These Welsh texts were written at a time of deep despair and suffering for the Welsh, after the fall of Llywelyn II (the last English-recognized prince of Wales) and the loss of independence. These Welsh *Lives* were just as much a political protest against English exploitation in the fourteenth century as Rhigyfarch's Latin text was against Norman subjugation in the eleventh century.

The Welsh version departs in numerous ways, both large and small, from its Latin source, such as leaving out the pilgrimage to Jerusalem (David is instead consecrated archbishop on a journey to Rome, the seat of real rather than merely symbolic power), paying less attention to David's Irish disciples and connections, omitting many of his miracles as well as a lengthy description of the daily routine at St. David's, putting less stress on David's extreme asceticism, and removing discussion of the Pelagian heresy from the Synod of Brefi. As D. Simon Evans points out, the Welsh *Life* tends to create a more intimate and familiar atmosphere with its emphasis on David's essential integrity, simple goodness, piety, humility, and devotion.

David's *Life*, whether in Welsh or Latin and like the other *Lives* of Welsh saints, which draw on local oral traditions, follows a basic biographical pattern, one which parallels the lives of secular heroes. The male saints, whose sanctity is declared before their births, are generally born of royal blood and have unusual conceptions and births. David's birth was prophesied thirty years in advance; he was conceived in rape (one way to keep the mother symbolically pure); Sts. Patrick and Gildas gave way before the unborn child; from the time of conception he (and his mother) ate only bread and water, perhaps contributing to his epithet *Dyfrwr* or *Aquaticus* (Waterman); and his birth was marked by special storms and the leaping of stones. Just as secular heroes show precocity in strength and growth, saintly heroes display precocity in learning and religion. At his baptism David raised a fountain and healed a blind faceless man. After a demonstration of his power (David healed his teacher's blindness), the saint goes out into the world. Secular heroes have adventures, gather companions, and supernatural aids; saints go on pilgrimage, missionary travels, or into the wilderness, gather disciples and objects such as the crosier and bell, through which they often work their supernatural powers. On his journey, David founded churches, depoisons and warms the waters at Bath, healed a blind king (healing blindness seems to be David's leitmotif), and acquired disciples. Next, through combat with a secular power, a struggle in which no amount of physical force can stand up against the saint's spiritual force, the saint gains land and the privileges of rule, such as sanctuary and freedom from taxation. David's conflict with secular power was with the Irishman Boia. Since marriage (except, occasionally, for the avoidance of it) is not part of the saint's biographical pattern, the only remaining stage is death. The Welsh saints tend not to be martyrs; their deaths are natural not violent, and are usually foretold and then accompanied by angelic visitations and heavenly visions, as was David's.

David's biographical pattern may be the same as other saints', but he gained a status and an identification with Wales far beyond that of any of the others. By the fourteenth century, his cult was more widespread than the cults of any other Welsh saints—fifty three churches dedicated to him and thirty two wells (though none in the north). In the medieval mathematics of pilgrimages, two journeys to St. David's equaled one to Rome, and three journeys equaled one to Jerusalem. David's identification with Wales is reflected in the weekly celebration in his churches, where he is termed "champion of the Britons, the leader and teacher of the Welsh," and in poetry, where Wales is referred to simply as *tir Dewi* (David's land). By the end of the Middle Ages, David's feast day on March 1 was celebrated with both religious and secular-nationalist customs (church sermons and wearing of the leek). With the Protestant Reformation, Welsh reformers did not discard David and the other saints but rather decided that the pre-Anglo-Norman British Church, the original Celtic Christianity of the Age of Saints, had been in essence a Protestant church free of the corruptions of Rome. The nineteenth-century nationalists were, therefore, free to call on David as a nationalist symbol, and his feast day, both in Wales and among expatriates, has become a day of national consciousness, a reaffirmation of the cultural and historical ties which bind the people in one nation, and a nation quite distinct from neighboring England. The fourteenth-century Welsh *Life of St. David* is a religious tract but it is also one of the tools in a centuries' long fight for Welsh independence.

SOURCES AND FURTHER READING

The most recent edition of the Welsh *Life*, and the one used here, is D. Simon Evans, *The Welsh Life of St. David* (Cardiff, 1988), which provides the text from Oxford, Jesus College, MS 119, fols. 93a-103b and gives the notes and introduction in English. Previously, Evans published a Welsh-language edition of *Buched Dewi* (Caerdydd, 1965), based on Aberystwyth, National Library of Wales, MS Llanstephan 27. A diplomatic edition of the text in Jesus College, MS 119 was published by J. Morris Jones in *The Life of Saint David and Other Tracts in Medieval Welsh from the Book of the Anchorite of Llanddewivrevi A.D. 1346* (Oxford, 1912). The earlier Latin *Life* (*Bibliotheca hagiographica latina*, no. 2107) has twice been published by A.W. Wade-Evans, first in an English translation as *Life of St. David* (London, 1923) and then a Latin edition in *Vitae sanctorum Britanniae et genealogiae* (Cardiff, 1944); both cases follow London, British Library, MS Cotton Vespasian A.xiv. J.W. James published the Latin text from London, British Library, MS Cotton Nero E.i, with an English translation, in *Rhigyfarch's Life of St. David* (Cardiff, 1967). For additional information see E.G. Bowen, *The Settlements of the Celtic Saints in Wales* (Cardiff, 1956) and *Dewi Sant / Saint David* (Cardiff, 1983); Glanmor Williams, *Religion, Language and Nationality in Wales* (Cardiff, 1979); Elissa R. Henken, *Traditions of the Welsh Saints* (Cambridge, 1987).

The Life of St. David *set down by an Anchorite at Llanddewibrefi*

Here is related David's genealogy and something of his life.

David son of Sant, son of Ceredig, son of Cunedda,[1] son of Edern, son of Padarn Peisrudd [Padarn of the Red Cloak], son of Deil, son of Gorddeil, son of Dwfyn, son of Gorddwfyn, son of Amguoel, son of Amwerydd, son of Onud, son of Perim, son of Dubim, son of Ongen, son of Afallach, son of Eugen, son of Eudoleu, son of the sister of the Virgin Mary, mother of Jesus Christ.[2]

King Ceredig ruled many years and from his name, Ceredigion got its name. He had a son, and the name of the son was Sant. An angel appeared to that one in his sleep and said to him, "Tomorrow," he said, "you will go to hunt and you will obtain three finds by the river Teifi, namely, a stag, and a salmon, and a swarm of bees in a tree above the river, in the place which is now called Henllan.[3] Give the right of the land to be kept for a boy who is not yet born; he will own the two places until judgment day, those which were mentioned above, Llin Henllan and Liton Maucan."[4]

Then Patrick[5] came to Glyn Rhosyn[6] and intended to spend his life there. An angel came to Patrick and said to him, "Leave this place," he said, "for a boy who is not yet born." Patrick became angry and said, "Why did the Lord despise His servant who since a boy has been serving Him in fear and love, and why has He chosen at this time a boy who is not born and who will not be born for thirty years?" And Patrick prepared to depart and to leave that place to the Lord Christ. The Lord, however, loved Patrick greatly, and sent an angel to him to placate him. And the angel said to him, "Patrick, be joyful. The Lord has sent me to you to show you the island of Ireland from the hill which is in Glyn Rhosyn (and which is now called Patrick's Seat). You will be an apostle in the island which you see, and you will suffer much there for the love of God; and God will be with you whatever you do." Then Patrick's mind was quieted and Patrick left that place to David. He prepared himself a ship in the harbor, and raised from death a man who had been buried there in the sea-marsh for fifteen years; Kruchier was his name. Patrick went to Ireland and that man with him; and that one, after that, was a bishop.

And thirty years after that, as the king who was called Sant was walking by himself, lo, a nun met him. He seized her and raped her. The nun conceived (the nun's name was Non[7]), and a son was born to her and he was named David. And she did not have a man either before or after; chaste was she in thought and deed.

The first miracle which David did: from the time she conceived, she did not desire in her lifetime any food except bread and water. And David consumed no food except bread and water.

The second miracle which David did: when his mother went to church to hear a sermon by St. Gildas,[8] Gildas began to preach and could not do it. And then Gildas said, "All of you go out of the church," he said. A second time, he tried to preach and could not do it. And then Gildas asked was there anyone in the church except himself. "I am here," said the nun, "between the door and the wall." "Go," said the saint, "out of the church and ask the congregation to come in." And each one came to his place to sit as he had been. And then the saint preached clearly and loudly. Then the congregation asked him, "Why could you not preach to us a while ago, and we gladly wishing to hear you?" The saint said, "Call in the nun whom I sent from the church earlier." Non said, "Here I am." Then Gildas said, "The boy who is in the womb of this nun is greater in his power and his grace and his dignity than I, since to him only did God give the privilege and chieftainship of all the saints of Wales eternally, before judgment day and after. And because of that," he said, "there is no way for me to dwell here longer because of the son of yonder nun, to whom God gave chieftainship over everyone in this island. I must," he said, "go to another island and leave this island to this boy."

Another miracle David did: in the hour of his birth, thunder and lightning came. A stone which was opposite Non's head split until it was in two halves, and one half leapt over the nun's head to beneath her feet when she was giving birth.

Another miracle David did: when he was baptized, a spring appeared from the earth where a spring had never been. And a blind man who was holding David for baptism gained his sight then. And then the blind man knew that the boy he was holding for baptism was full of grace. And he took the baptismal water and washed his face with the water. From the hour of his birth he had been a blind flat-face. And then he gained his sight and all that belonged to it.[9] Then everybody praised God as they should.

David was taught in a place called Vetus Rubus; in Welsh it is Henllwyn.[10] There he was taught psalms for the whole year and its lessons and the masses. There his fellow pupils saw a dove with a golden beak teaching David and playing around him.

From there David went to a teacher called Paulinus,[11] who was disciple to a holy bishop in Rome. And that one taught David until he was a teacher. And then it befell that David's teacher lost his sight, from exceeding pain in his eyes. The teacher called all the disciples to him one after the other, and sought their help regarding his eyes, and not one was able to help. And last of all, he called David. "David," said the teacher, "look at my eyes; they're causing me pain." "Lord teacher," said David, "do not ask me to look at your eyes. In the ten years since I came to you to study, I have not yet looked at your face." The teacher then thought and marveled at the boy's modesty and said, "Since it is thus," he said to the boy, "put your hand on my face and bless my eyes, and I will be completely well." And when David put his hand on his eyes, they were completely well. And then Paulinus blessed David with every blessing found written in the Old Testament and the New. Then an angel came to Paulinus and said to him thus: "It is time," he said, "for St. David to go from here, to do the things which are ordained by God for him to do."

Then David came to Glastonbury, and there he built a church. David came to the place where the water was full of poison, and he blessed it and made that water warm until judgment day. And that is called the Warm Bath [i.e., Bath].[12] Then David came to Croyland and to Repton. Then he came to Colva and Glasgwm. Then he built Leominster on the banks of the Severn. Then he gave relief to Peibiaw, king of Erging, who was blind.[13] Then he built a church in Gwent, the place called Rhaglan. Then he built a church in the place called Llangyfelach in Gower.[14] Two saints were in Cydweli, who were called Boducat and Nailtrum, who gave themselves as disciples to him.[15]

Then David returned to the place called Vetus Rubus. And there was a bishop called Goeslan, who was brother in faith[16] to David. And David said to him, "An angel of the Lord told me that scarcely one in a hundred in this place will go to the kingdom of heaven. And he showed me another place, and from that place no one will go to hell of those who have good faith and belief. And also of those buried in the cemetery in that place, no one will go to hell."

And one day, David and his disciples, namely, Aeddan and Eliudd and Ismael,[17] came, and many together with them, to the place God had indicated to them, that is, to Glyn Rhosyn; that place is called Hoddnant.[18] That was the first place in which they kindled a fire under the sky. And when they lit a fire there early in the morning, the smoke rose and that smoke encircled the whole island and much of Ireland, and that from early morning until the evening.[19]

And then a prince called Boia (who was an Irishman)[20] saw the smoke. And in anger, he sat on a high rock from morning until evening, without food and without drink. And his wife came upon him there and asked him why he did not wish either food or drink. "Indeed," said he, "I am sad and angry. I saw smoke today," he said, "rising from Hoddnant and encompassing many cities. The man," he said, "who lit that fire, his authority will travel the way the smoke traveled." His wife said, "You're crazy. Get up," she said, "and take your servants with you, and kill the one who lit that fire on your land without your permission."

And then Boia came, and his servants with him, intending to kill David and his disciples. And when they came to where David was, they fell into a fever so they could not do any kind of harm to David or his disciples, except mock them and say insulting words to them, and returned home. And while they were thus, lo, Boia's wife met them and said, "Our shepherds told me our whole stock has died, that is, our cattle, our oxen, our stud horses, our sheep, and they are all dead and their eyes open."

And then Boia and his wife and his household lamented and wailed and moaned, and said, "The saint," they said, "whom we were mocking did this." This is what they decided: to beseech the saint and seek his favor and that of his household. And then Boia gave Hoddnant in perpetuity to David, and Boia returned home and his household with him. And when they came home, they found their animals alive and healthy.

And then Boia's wife said to her handmaidens, "Go," she said, "to the river near the saint, and take off your clothes, and naked say to them rude, shameful words."[21] It was hard for all of David's disciples to suffer that shame, and they said to David, "Let us flee from here," they said, "we cannot suffer this, nor look upon the wicked women." And then the saint said, "Isn't it better for us to cause them to leave this place to us?" And then David and his disciples fasted that night until the next day.

The next day, Boia's wife said to her stepdaughter, "Come, girl," she said, "rise and let us two go to Glyn Alun to seek nuts." The maiden said to her stepmother, "I am ready," she said, "to go." And they walked to the bottom of the valley. And when they came there, the stepmother sat and said to the stepdaughter, "Put your head in my lap and I will examine it." Thus did the good, chaste, gentle, accomplished maiden put her head in her stepmother's lap. Thus did the stepmother, drew a knife and cut off the head of the saintly maiden. And in the direction the blood fell to the ground, a spring appeared. And many people obtained health and deliverance there. And till today that spring is called Dunawd's Well, since Dunawd was the maiden's name.[22] Then the wicked stepmother fled, and nobody in the world knew what death took her. And Boia began lamenting, and David and his disciples rejoiced.

Then Boia planned to kill David and his disciples. However, it happened the next morning that his enemy came to the tower in which Boia was sleeping, after finding the gates open, and cut off Boia's head in his bed. And straightaway a fire from heaven came and burnt all the buildings to the ground.[23] Let everyone know that the Lord God killed Boia and Satrapa his wife[24] for the sake of David.

Then David built in Glyn Hoddnant. And there was not any water there, except a little running water. And then David prayed to the Lord, and immediately a clear spring arose. And in David's lifetime that fountain was full of wine, so that he never lacked good wine in his lifetime.[25] That is a worthy gift from God to a man such as that.

After that, Bishop Goeslan, brother in faith to David, and a disciple of David who was called Eliudd, both fasted to entreat God for springs of fresh water,[26] since there was no water in the city and because the weather was so dry. And then they obtained from God two springs, which are still called today Goeslan's Well and Eliudd's Well. And the crippled, the blind, and the sick may get relief in those two wells.

And in the meantime, St. Aeddan was in his own church in the city of Ferns, praying, namely, the night before Easter, when, lo, an angel of the Lord came to him and said to him, "You, good blessed man, don't you know," he said, "what is being prepared for St. David, your teacher, in Glyn Rhosyn?" "I don't know, indeed," said Aeddan. The angel said, "Three of his monastery household have plotted his betrayal, that is, have put poison in bread, and that bread will be given to him tomorrow to eat. Therefore, send a messenger to your teacher, and tell him to avoid the bread with the poison in it." Thus the saint became sad and wept. "Lord," he said, "how will I send a messenger there? The time is so short and there's no ship ready to be had." "Send," said the angel, "your fellow disciple, namely, Sguthyn, to the beach and I will get him across." Sguthyn gladly did what was asked of him, and came to the beach, and walked ahead into the water until the water came to his knees. And immediately, here is a monster from the sea taking him on his back, and bearing him across until he was on the other coast. And by midday Easter day, he was with his teacher.

And as David was coming to the church after Mass, and after preaching to all his brothers, lo, he could see the messenger meeting him in the place called Bedd Ysgolan. David then welcomed and embraced him, and asked after St. Aeddan, his disciple; greatly did David love his disciple. And after the messenger described completely the condition of his disciple Aeddan, Sguthyn called David aside and revealed to him his message, and how and in what manner the angel had told St. Aeddan. David then was silent and thought and said great thanks to God, and came ahead to the monastery.

And after everybody sat in the appropriate prescribed manner, after finishing the grace, the deacon who served David rose to serve him with the poisoned bread. Thus did Sguthyn rise up and say, "You," he said, "will not serve today. I myself," said Sguthyn, "will be server today." Thus the former went to sit and wondered greatly; he knew the sin which was in his mind. And then David took the poisoned bread and divided it into three parts, and gave one to a bitch who was standing outside the door. The hour the bitch devoured the bread, she was stone-dead, and all her hair fell out in the blink of an eye, and her skin cracked, and all her entrails fell to the ground. All the brothers, when they saw this wondered greatly. And then David sent the second part of the bread to a crow that was lying in her nest in an ash tree which was between the refectory and the river to the south. The hour she took the bread in her beak, she fell from the tree to the ground, dead. The third piece of bread, David took and blessed it and ate it. All the brothers watched him and wondered greatly, and feared exceedingly for David. And then David declared the incident to all the brothers, that the deceivers had tried to poison him. And then all the brothers cursed those men, and together with that gave prayer to the Father of heaven that they should not ever receive a portion of the kingdom of heaven.

And after strengthening faith and belief in this island, all the laborers of this island came together before the Synod of Brefi.[27] And the bishops, and the clerics, and the priests, and the kings, and the princes, and the earls, and the barons, and the noblemen, and the squires, and the entire clergy, and everybody, innumerable, assembled for the Synod of Brefi. And an agreement was made in that assembly: whoever of the Synod of the saints would preach so that the multitude in general could hear, they would grant that one of them to be chief of the saints of the island of Britain. And then the saints began to preach in turn. And then on behalf of the assembly in general, one said, "Only one man in a hundred of this assembly hears anything of the sermon; you labor completely in vain." Then all the saints said to each other, "There isn't one of us who can preach to this crowd, and we tried each in turn; and we see there is not grace for any of us to preach to this crowd. Look and think whether you know whether there is anyone so deserving that he can preach to this crowd."

Then St. Paulinus, who was an old bishop, answered, "I," he said, "know a young man—fair, gentle, with an angel always as a companion to him. And I know," he said, "that he is wise and chaste, and loves God greatly, and I know that God loves him, and that he partakes of all good virtues. I," he said, "know that the man in this island most having the grace of God is that one and he is called St. David. First he learned letters which were appropriate for him to learn at the beginning. And after that, he learned with me the Holy Scriptures, and was a cleric, and in Rome was ordained an archbishop. And I," he said, "saw an angel come to him, and call to him, and command him to go to his land to inhabit the place which God had reserved for him in the kingdom of Dyfed, that is, Mynyw[28] in the south. Go and call that one, he who loves God greatly and preaches of Christ, and I know that he is the one to whom God has given the grace."

And then the saints sent messengers to Dinas Rubi,[29] where St. David was, a servant of God, praying and teaching. And when he heard the messengers' errand, here is the answer he gave, namely, "I will not go there," he said, "I prefer to pray to God here. Go," he said, "in the peace of God and His love." And a second time the saints invited St. David, and he gave the same answer he had given earlier. A third time, by agreement of all the saints, there were sent to David the two chief saints who were present, namely, Deiniol and Dyfrig.[30] And that night before the messengers came to David, David said to his disciples, "My sons, know you that messengers will come here tomorrow. Go fish in the sea and bring here," he said, "fresh water from the well."

And the messengers came the day David told them, and he prepared for them their dinner. David's disciples put on the table before the saints an abundance of fish and water from the spring, and the water became wine straightaway. And David said to them, "Eat joyfully, brothers." And then the two saints said to him, "We will not take either food or drink," they said, "unless you promise to come with us to the great, wonderful Synod, where an innumerable host awaits you. Therefore," they said, "come with us for God's sake, and for the blessing of those saints, if you do not wish to incur their curse." Then David said, "I will go," he said, "for the love of God, to those companions. However," he said, "this which you ask of me, I cannot do. I," he said, "will travel with you to the Synod, and you, pray to the highest Father that He will give aid to us wretches, and I will pray with you, brothers, so that you will take food and drink from the alms and the charity which were given to us from heaven."

And after that, David arose with the messengers for the Synod of Brefi. And before they came to that assembly, lo, they saw coming toward them a widowed woman whose only son had died, and the woman crying and screaming. And when David saw the woman in such lamentation, he stopped and let the messengers go ahead. Thus did the wretched woman who had heard David's renown: she fell to her knees and told him that her only son was dead. David took pity on her and turned aside with her to where her son was dead by a river called Teifi, and came to the house where was her son's corpse.

The *Live of St. David* set down by an Anchorite at Llanddewibrefi

And David fell on the body, and put his mouth to the mouth of the boy, and prayed to the Lord and said, "My Lord God, you who did descend from the lap of the Father of heaven to this world because of us sinners, to redeem us from the jaws of the ancient enemy, have mercy, Lord, on this widowed woman here, and give to her only son his life again, so that your name may be glorified over the whole earth." And when David finished his prayer, the boy rose completely well, as if he were rising from sleep, and David raised him by his right hand and gave him in complete health to his mother. Thus the boy, from the place where he was raised from the dead, followed David in thought and deed. And he was together with David through many years serving God. And everybody who saw that praised God.

Then David traveled with the saints' messengers to the Synod where he was awaited. And when David came there, all the saints rose to welcome him as they saw him coming. And they greeted him and fell on their knees and, raising him to the top of a high mound where there had been a sermon earlier, beseeched him to preach. And he excused himself for a short while from them and said that he dared not and could not do what they were asking of him. However, he took the blessing of the assembly in general and obeyed them. He refused to ascend to the top of the mound, and said he did not wish any place to stand except on level ground. And David began to preach from there of the law of Christ and the Gospel, and that was like the cry of a clarion horn, and clear to every man, as clear to the furthest as to the nearest, and as universal as would be the sun for everyone at midday. And that was a marvel for everyone.

And when David was on the flat ground, which was mentioned above, preaching, that ground rose like a high mountain beneath his feet, and everyone of that assembly looking at that, which is still a high hill manifest to everyone, with level ground on every side of it. And God did that miracle and wonder for David in Llanddewibrefi.[31]

And then, agreed among themselves, they praised St. David and, united, acknowledged that he was leader of the saints of the island of Britain, saying thus, "As God placed a ruler over every kind of fish in the sea, and as God placed a ruler over the birds on the earth, thus God placed David as ruler over the men in this world. And in the same way that God placed Matthew in Judea, and Luke in Alexandria, and Christ in Jerusalem, and Peter in Rome, and Martin in France, and Samson in Brittany,[32] he placed St. David to be in the island of Britain. And with that David was made leader and ruler over the saints of the island of Britain, because he preached in that great synod to all the people, at which none but him was able to preach. And that day, all the saints of this island and all the kings went down on their knees to adore David, and they placed him as chief over the saints of the island of Britain. And he deserved it.

And that day David was given his refuges and defense for every kind of man of those who might do wrong and flee to David's sanctuary land. This is the sanctuary of David for everyone who may be in Dinas Rubi, in David's refuge and under his protection: if it is necessary, [his protection] may run from the river Tywi as far as the river Teifi,[33] and if it is necessary for it to run farther, then it has priority over every saint and king and man in this island. David's sanctuary is wherever there may be land consecrated to St. David, and no king nor prince nor bishop nor saint may dare give sanctuary to him before David, since he had right to sanctuary before everyone and none got it before him, since it is he whom God and men set as chief of the whole island. And then these saints by agreement of the kings excommunicated whomsoever might break St. David's sanctuary.

And then as David on the last Tuesday of February was listening to the clerics serving God, lo, he could hear an angel conversing with him, and saying to him thus: "David," said the angel, "that which you long sought from your Lord God is ready for you when you desire it." He then raised his face up and rejoiced and spoke thus: "This hour, Lord, take your servant into your peace." The clerics who were listening to these two speeches were greatly amazed and fell like dead men.

And close on that, lo, they heard a pleasant voice and smelled the fairest aromas filling the city. Thus David a second time spoke aloud, "Lord Jesus Christ," he said, "take my soul and do not let me remain longer in these tribulations." And after that they heard a second time the angel saying to David, "St. David, prepare yourself; the first day of March, your Lord, Jesus Christ, will come and nine orders of heaven with him, and a tenth of the earth, to receive you and will call together with you those whom you wish of clerics and laymen, innocent and sinner, young and old, youth and maiden, man and woman, lewd buffoon and harlot, Jew and Saracen, and those will come together with you."

And the brethren, every one, when they heard that, through weeping and wailing, and howling and sighing, raised their cry and said, "Lord St. David, help our sorrow." And then David said to them, comforting them and cheering them, "My brothers, be constant and of one mind, and whatever you have seen and heard from me, keep it and perfect it." From that day until the eighth day, David did not leave the church on account of preaching to everyone and praying.

The news, however, in the space of a day went throughout this whole island and Ireland with the angel. Thus was the angel saying, "Know you that it is in the next week which is coming that St. David, your lord, will go from this world to the Lord." Then was seen a gathering together of the saints of this island and the saints of Ireland, from every part coming to visit St. David. Oh! who then could suffer the wailing of the saints, or the sighs of the anchorites, or the clergy and the disciples saying, "Who will teach us?"; lament of the parsons saying, "Who will succor us?"; despair of the kings saying, "Who will ordain us, who will be a father as merciful as David, who will pray for us to our Lord?"; lamentation of the poor, and the sick moaning. The monks and the virgins, and the married ones and the penitents, the youths and the maidens, the boys and the girls, and the newly born at their [mothers'] breasts dropping tears. What will I recount but one lament by everyone: the kings lamenting their brother,[34] the old lamenting their son, the youths lamenting their father.

On Sunday David sang Mass and preached to the people. And its like had not been heard before, and will never be heard after him. Eye never saw so many people in one place. And after finishing the sermon and the Mass, David gave his blessing in common to everyone who was there. And after he had given his blessing to everyone, he said this speech: "Lords, brothers and sisters, be joyful and keep your faith and your belief, and do the little things which you have seen and heard from me. And I myself will journey the way along which our fathers went, and farewell," said David. "And may you be strong on earth, and never again shall we see each other [in this world]."

Then a general cry was heard rising with lamenting and wailing and tears, and saying, "Woe, that the earth does not swallow us! Woe that fire does not come to burn us! Woe, that the sea does not come across the land! Woe, that the mountains not fall upon us!" And almost everyone there was as if going to his own death. From Sunday until Tuesday, after David's death, they did not consume either food nor drink, did nothing but pray in sorrow.

And Tuesday eve, at cock crow [i.e., Tuesday morning], lo, a host of angels filled the city, and every form of songs and delights everywhere in the whole city. And in the small hours, lo, the Lord Jesus Christ came, and with Him nine orders of heaven, as He had left them in their majesty, and the sun clearly shining for all the hosts. And that Tuesday, the first day of March, Jesus Christ took St. David's soul with great triumph and joy and honor. After his hunger and his thirst, and his suffering cold, and his labor, and his abstinence, and his charity, and his weariness, and his tribulation, and his trials, and his concern for the world, the angels took his soul, and bore him to where there is light without end, and rest without labor, and joy without sorrow, and abundance of every kind of good, and triumph, and brightness, and beauty, where there is praise of Christ's champions, where the evil rich are despised, where there is health without disease, and youth without old age, and peace without discord, and glory without vanity, and songs without weariness, and rewards without end, where Abel is together with the martyrs, where Enoc is with the living, where Noah is with the sailors, where Abraham is with the patriarchs, where Melichisedech is with the priests, where Job is with the long-suffering, where Moses is with the princes, where Aaron is with the bishops, where David is with the kings, where Isaiah is with the prophets, where Mary is with the virgins, where Peter is with the apostles, where Paul is with the men of Greece, where Thomas is with the men of India, where John is with the men of Asia, where Matthew is with the men of Judea, where Luke is with the men of Achaea, where Mark is with the men of Alexandria, where Andrew is with the men of Scythia, where are the angels and archangels, and cherubim and seraphim, and the King of kings in the age of ages. Amen.

And as we have commemorated David in his own life, and his deeds on this earth, thus may he be a helper, and may his interceding for us avail before the true Creator that we may receive mercy in time to come.

Notes

1. Cunedda, a fifth-century chieftain of the northern British Manaw Gododdin (present-day eastern lowland Scotland), resettled in Gwynedd (in north Wales), driving out the Irish. According to tradition, his eight sons, including Ceredig, became the eponymous ancestors of Welsh kingdoms. Cunedda became a valued and frequently claimed ancestor in the genealogies.

2. Welsh saints commonly establish their privileged position through showing descent from both royalty and Jesus' family.

3. This motif of animals from three realms (land, water, air) at a tree, with its suggestion of representing all nature, appears several times in Welsh saints' *Lives*, marking land assigned to the saint. Henllan is on the banks of the Teifi, near its estuary in Cardigan. The angel's comment on the current name of the place may originally have been a gloss.

4. "Two places" (*deu le*) may have been a scribal error for "right" (*dylyet*). "He will own the right until judgment day" would have made more sense since no two places are previously mentioned. Liton Maucan has not been identified, though several places with possibly related names along the Teifi and in north Pembrokeshire have been suggested.

5. Patrick, a fifth-century saint, probably from western Britain, helped convert Ireland to Christianity and became its patron saint.

6. Glyn Rhosyn (Vallis Rosina), popularly understood as "Valley of Roses," although the root word is a diminutive of *rhos*, "moor" or "swamp." This location, which became the site of St. David's, was ideal, especially in David's time. St. David's is tucked into a river valley deeply incised into the plateau, so that the settlement is invisible from the sea but, at the same time, the monks had direct access to the seaways, the main travel routes for medieval Wales. The sea traffic made Saint David's an important place for the meeting of people and exchange of information.

7. Non a fifth-century saint; traces of her cult are found in Wales, Cornwall, Devon, and Brittany.

8. Gildas (ca. 495-ca.570), British cleric and saint, thought to have been born in the northern British kingdom of Strathclyde, trained in the Church in south Wales, and eventually settled in Rhuys in Brittany. He wrote *De Excidio et Conquestu Britanniae* (Of the ruin and conquest of Britain), a diatribe against the excesses of secular and ecclesiastical society.

9. "Flat-faced" (*wynepclawr*) means without eyes or nose, a deformity possibly caused by leprosy. In restoring not only the man's sight but also "all that belonged to it," that is his facial features, David is the only Welsh saint to heal a *wynepclawr*, although several Irish saints are recorded as having done so.

10. Vetus Rubus, or Henllwyn, may be either Henfynyw in Cardiganshire or an unspecified place near St. David's.

11. Paulinus (ca. 470?), a Carmarthenshire saint who may have resettled in Brittany where he was known as St. Paul Aurelian and later became patron saint of the town and see of Saint-Pol-de-Léon. His *Life* was written ca. 884 by Wrmonoc.

12. Although the Welsh *Lives* leave it as understood that the water is depoisoned, the Latin *Lives* and fifteenth-century Welsh poetry explicitly state that by blessing the water David caused it to become health-giving as well as warm.

13. Peibio king of Erging (Archenfield) in southeast Wales; traditionally the grandfather of St. Dyfrig, with whose church at Llandaff, St. David's was competing for authority.

14. This list of places reflects both actual missionary movements out of St. David's (one of the characteristic activities of the Celtic "saints" was to travel through the countryside, establishing churches) and the author's declaration of how widespread was David's authority and his cult. Glastonbury, Somerset, by the eighth century claimed David as a patron; Bath, Somerset; Croyland, Lincolnshire, founded by St. Guthlac; Repton, Derbyshire; Colva, Radnorshire, had a chapel dedicated to St. David; Glasgwm, Radnorshire, had a church dedicated to St. David; Leominster, Herefordshire, actually on the banks of

the Lugg; Erging an early lordship and later *cantref* (administrative unit), now in southeast Hereford; Rhaglan, Gwent; Llangyfelach, Glamorgan; Gower, Glamorgan.

15. Cydweli, Carmarthenshire, lies between the rivers Loughor and Tywi. Nothing is known of Boducat or Nailtrum.

16. Goeslan, Gwestlan, Guistilianus. *Brawd ffydd*, "brother in faith" appears to have been a mistranslation of *fratruelis*, "father's brother's son," which probably can also mean "father's brother" or "uncle," the relationship reported by Gerald of Wales.

17. Aeddan, identified by name and narrative with Aedán or Maedóc (ca. 560–626), bishop of Ferns, County Wexford, although some scholars suggest that this is a conflation of traditions for two individuals. Eliudd, the baptismal name for Teilo (ca. 500), a saint with churches mainly in southwest Wales and variously named as disciple and companion of David. His *Life* in the twelfth-century *Liber Landavensis* promoted the claims of Llandaff against St. David's. Ismael or Ysfael (d. ca. 540), a saint to whom churches are dedicated in southwest Wales.

18. Hoddnant (pleasant valley).

19. According to both Welsh and Irish laws, lighting a fire was one step required in laying claim to land.

20. David's conflict with an Irishman reflects actual conditions; Irish settlers invaded southwest Wales in the fifth and sixth centuries. Since the family of David's great-grandfather Cunedda was instrumental in driving the Irish out of northern Wales, David may be seen as continuing the effort in the southwest.

21. The tactic of sending naked or bare-breasted women is a recurring motif in Celtic tradition. In this usage, David is being treated like a great warrior who cannot be overcome simply by force.

22. The motif of luring someone to death through an offer of delousing is an internationally recurring motif. Severed heads and springs are commonly associated in Celtic tradition and several Welsh saints' *Lives* in particular report a well springing from the blood of an innocent who has been beheaded. This particular well has not been located.

23. The motif of a fire from heaven occurs several times in Irish saints' *Lives* and in Welsh tradition, most famously in the case of King Vortigern, who betrayed his people to the Saxons. Boia's fortress has been identified as an Iron Age hill fort on a rocky hill about a mile from St. David's.

24. The author appears to have misunderstood the Latin *satrapa* (chieftain) to be the name of Boia's wife.

25. The *Lives* of Welsh saints record many incidents of saints raising springs or causing them to run with wine or milk or in other special ways. Since David drank only water, this wine was presumably for the Eucharist and for guests (as seen later in the text when he serves wine to Dyfrig and Deiniol).

26. Fasting is recognized as a powerful means of compulsion in Celtic law and tradition. Later in the text, Sts. Dyfrig and Deiniol use the same technique in forcing David to attend the Synod of Brefi.

27. The Synod was held at Brefi, located on the banks of the river Brefi, a small tributary to the Teifi, and near the Roman fort Llanio, placing it in a spot with the rare quality of being accessible to all of Wales. Although David's Latin *Life* suggest that the Synod was called to fight Pelagianism, scholars debate whether that would have been a pertinent issue in David's time. In both the Latin and Welsh *Lives*, the Synod has the more immediate significance of showing that saints representing all of Wales recognized David as the primary saint and (anachronistically) his monastery as the Metropolis. St. Cadog's *Life* denies David's supremacy by claiming that Cadog was in Jerusalem at the time.

28. Mynyw, an old name for St. David's, which in the *Lives* is more commonly called Glyn Rhosyn or Vallis Rosina.

29. Dinas Rubi, another name for Saint David's.

30. Deiniol (d. 584?), patron saint of Bangor, with his cult centered mainly in north Wales. Dyfrig or Dubricius (ca. 465?), a saint associated mainly with southeast Wales; traditionally named as an early leader and teacher of Welsh saints.

31. Llanddewibrefi, with a church standing on a hill of this description, is located near Lampeter.

32. St. Martin of Tours (ca. 316–397). Samson of Dol in Brittany (b. 486?), a Welsh saint who settled in Brittany.

33. Tywi (emended from Tyfi), Teifi. The area mapped out by these two rivers covers a major portion of southwest Wales.

34. *Brawd* can mean either "brother" or "judgment." I have translated it as "brother" because it seems to fit—while the young and the old see him as a father or son, the kings see him as a brother. However, "judgment" may be the more authentic translation in the light of the term used in the London, British Library, MS Cotton Vespasian A.xiv text, the Latin *arbitrum* "arbitrator, judge," which the Welsh translator has taken to be "judgment."

Chapter 34

THE OLD CZECH
LIFE OF ST. CATHERINE OF ALEXANDRIA
Translated by Alfred Thomas

INTRODUCTION

Catherine of Alexandria was one of the most popular saints of the Middle Ages, beloved in the Western and Eastern Churches alike. According to legend, she was martyred in the year 307 and in the eighth century her body was discovered by Egyptian Christians and translated by them to a monastery on Mount Sinai. This monastery was founded by St. Helen (ca. 250–330), the mother of the emperor Constantine and was embellished by the emperor Justinian I and renamed in Catherine's honor in 527. Here her bones were said to exude the heavenly oil with which her wounds were miraculously healed by Christ when He visited her in her cell after torture. The first versions of the legend were written in Greek, but from the eleventh century we find Latin adaptations of the Greek sources. All of these stories deal exclusively with the martyrdom and the debate with the pagan scholars whom Catherine converts to the true faith. At a later point, two other episodes (Catherine's conversion through the agency of a hermit and her mystical marriage to Christ) were added to the basic story of the debate and the martyrdom.

The cult of St. Catherine was one of the most popular in medieval Europe. Numerous images and literary representations of her life and martyrdom survive, most of them based on the immensely popular *Golden Legend* by Jacopo da Voragine. The presence of her relics at the abbey of Sainte-Trinité-du-Mont in Rouen during the first half of the eleventh century probably inspired several of the Latin versions of her *Life*. In fact it was Rouen that was largely responsible for disseminating the saint's cult in northern Europe. Her renown as a teacher and protectress increased, the former no doubt aided by the spread of the universities, such as the Sorbonne at Paris, of which she became the official patron. Her cult was also important in England where her legend was one of the most frequently represented subjects in late medieval churches. Several versions of her *Life* are extant in English, ranging from a twelfth-century prose version written for anchoresses to a fifteenth-century verse adaptation by the Augustinian canon Osbern Bokenham.

St. Catherine owed much of her popularity in fourteenth-century Bohemia and Moravia (corresponding to the present-day Czech Republic) to the Holy

Roman Emperor Charles IV (1346–78). She had become his personal protectress after the Battle of San Felice, fought on Catherine's feast day, November 25, 1332, when the sixteen-year-old Charles and his army had successfully relieved the fortress besieged by the armies of the Italian League. A passionate collector of holy relics, Charles built a church in Catherine's honor in the New Town of Prague (1356) and dedicated his private oratory to her in his castle of Karlstein near Prague (after 1347). This chapel provided an architectonic mirror-image of the monastery of Saint Catherine on Mount Sinai, where her relics were said to be preserved. Encrusted with semiprecious stones, the chapel at Karlstein also forms an intriguing parallel to the description of the jeweled hall, the setting of Catherine's second vision in the medieval Czech version of her *Life*.

The Old Czech *Life of St. Catherine of Alexandria* was composed sometime between 1360 and 1375 by an anonymous author, most probably a clerical member of Emperor Charles's court. Although highly original in parts, it was based on Latin sources. There are seventeen extant Latin manuscripts of the Catherine legend in Prague. These can be divided into three groups: those which relate the conversion and passion (five); those which confine themselves to the conversion (four), and those which deal with the passion alone (eight). The Czech author of our legend seems to have used two sources, one belonging to the first category and known by its opening words as *Tradunt annales historiae* ("The annals of history relate") which tells the whole story but concentrates on Catherine's dispute with the scholars, the other belonging to the second category (the conversion) and known by its opening words as *Fuit in insula Cypri rex quidam, nomine Costus* ("There once lived on the island of Cyprus a king named Costus"), which tells only of Catherine's conversion and her mystical marriage to Christ. The Czech author includes all the episodes found in the two Latin sources (the conversion, the mystical marriage, the debate and the passion) but reduces the debate with the pagan scholars while amplifying the descriptions of the mystical marriage and the scourging scene.

At 3,519 lines long, the verse legend was written in the standard trochaic meter and octosyllabic line of medieval Czech poetry. Although the poem can be dated to the second half of the fourteenth century (largely on the basis of morphology and rhymes), it survives in a unique manuscript dating from the beginning of the fifteenth century (Brno, Moravian Provincial Library, MS III F 6). The same codex contains four other works in Czech, all of which are of a devotional nature but which do not compare in quality with our legend and therefore are probably not written by the same author.

The legend begins with the banishment to Alexandria of Catherine's father, Costus, king of Cyprus, by Emperor Maxentius because of a slander leveled against him by his enemies at court. This episode is expanded in the Czech version and probably reveals something about the author's personal preoccupation with the hazards of court intrigue. One interpolated passage, which is absent from the Latin sources, complains of the invidious influence of treacherous rivals, the wording of which corresponds closely to a similar complaint against disruptive social inferiors in the prose *Life of St. Procopius*, a Bohemian saint popular in the second half of the fourteenth century. This work has been attributed to a Dominican in the entourage of Emperor Charles and has been linked with Jan (John) Moravec, his personal confessor and a professor of theology at the University of Prague (founded by the emperor in 1348). Although it is impossible to prove that Jan Moravec was the author of our legend, his erudition as a theologian and his prestigious status as a courtier and confidant of the emperor certainly correspond to the profile of the anonymous author of the verse *Life of St. Catherine*.

The most probable audience for our legend was an aristocratic, courtly public. Although the Czech literary language had been the principal medium of the provincial gentry and peasantry up to the middle of the fourteenth century, by the reign of Charles IV it was becoming one of the languages favored at the court at Prague. Descended on his mother's side from a long, illustrious line of Slavic rulers of Bohemia (the native dynasty had died out in 1306), Charles IV spoke Czech fluently and identified with it as well as with Old Church Slavonic, originally the literary language of the Bohemian Church until it was abolished in 1097 when Latin became the official language of the liturgy. Even though the Bohemian Church had remained Roman Catholic ever since then, Charles decided to revive the Old Church Slavonic liturgy and gained a papal dispensation to found a *Monasterium Slavorum* in Prague. Known as the Emmaus Monastery, this new foundation was populated with Benedictine monks whom the emperor invited specially from Croatia.

Just as the emperor endeavored to promote Czech as a courtly and even diplomatic language and rekindle Old Church Slavonic as its liturgical counterpart, so did he promote the lives of local and eastern saints. Among the local saints who found his personal favor were Ludmilla, a princess of the Bohemian ducal house and the first martyr in the region, her grandson Wenceslas who became the official patron saint of Bohemia (907–929 or 935), Procopius, the founder of the Sázava Monastery where the Old Church Slavonic liturgy was first celebrated on Bohemian soil, and Adalbert, bishop of Prague (956–77), who was martyred during an evangelizing mission to pagan Prussia. The emperor himself wrote a Latin *Life* of St. Wenceslas, which presents him as a courtly knight in the latest fashion. (One might compare this chivalric representation with the lovely polychrome statue of the saint by the court sculptor Henry Parler, now in the Saint Wenceslas chapel of the Cathedral of Saint Vitus in Prague). In addition, two Czech *Lives* of St. Procopius survive from this period, one in verse, the other in prose, the latter part of a large vernacular collection of saints' *Lives* known as the *Passional* and based on the popular *Golden Legend*. In addition to these Bohemian saints, Charles also promoted the cult of Catherine of Alexandria, whose mythic origins, as we have seen, were in the East. The cultivation of these local and eastern saints was all part of the emperor's dynastic and political ambition to make his kingdom of Bohemia the de facto center of a Holy Roman Empire which would reunite the schismatic Eastern and Western Churches.

An important aspect of the originality of the Old Czech *Life of St. Catherine* is its courtly treatment of the relationship between the virgin saint and Christ. In the second celestial vision Christ is represented as a handsome lover with long golden hair who sings an epithalamium to His new bride. Even the grisly description of Catherine's flagellation at the hands of the emperor Maxentius's henchmen (for refusing to apostatize) provides the author with the pretext for a courtly meditation on the symbolic significance of colors as the maiden's skin constantly changes hue under the relentless lashes of the whip. At the end of the torture scene, the author compares Christ and Catherine with the Celtic lovers Tristan and Isolde and their mystical union with the love potion made famous by the poet Gottfried von Strassburg in his courtly romance *Tristan*. These features clearly indicate that the audience for whom the legend was intended was aristocratic and familiar with the refined vocabulary of the courtly love lyric and the romance. Moreover, the emphasis on Catherine's literal *imitatio Christi*—her flagellation and subsequent martyrdom—suggests that she was intended as an exemplar of female piety, since in the later Middle Ages women were encouraged to identify with Christ's human suffering.

Catherine's eloquence as a teacher and theologian in converting the fifty pagan scholars to the Christian faith reminds us that the legend was not simply intended as harmless entertainment for a court audience of initiates but served an important ideological purpose. The frequent references to "error" (*blud*) in Catherine's discourse on the Christian faith suggests that the author and his orthodox contemporaries were concerned to warn the faithful against the dangers of heretical sentiments emanating from the pulpits of Prague. In the 1370s, the Austrian Conrad Waldhauser and the Moravian Jan Militsch of Kremsier, were advocating the radical reform of the Church to the German- and Czech-speaking populations of the Bohemian capital. Jan Militsch is known to have preached his passionate sermons in the church of Saint Giles in the Old Town, close to where the famous religious reformer Jan Hus later preached in Czech at the Bethlehem Chapel. The church of Saint Giles was linked with the Dominican Order of Preachers, and Militsch's wayward teachings must have caused alarm in their orthodox circles. The Old Czech *Life of St. Catherine* can be seen as an eloquent riposte to this vociferous clamor for religious reform. St. Catherine herself was traditionally equated with orthodoxy; and her success in converting the fifty pagan philosophers to Christianity was deemed a token of her powerful ability to witness to the true faith in the face of theological error and doctrinal deviance. The author's vision of the world, and of the deity who made it, is similarly orthodox and comports with what we know of Charles IV's personal and public piety. His immediate entourage consisted principally of clerics (hence his appellation *rex clericorum*), among whom the Dominicans were especially prominent, no doubt due to their time-honored role as royal confessors and teachers. As previously suggested, one of these Dominicans—Jan Moravec—may well provide the name behind this anonymous text. Certainly his university training, theological learning and courtly artistry are all consistent with what we can glean about the sophisticated author's view of the world from the internal evidence afforded by the extant text. It is a vision of a static, immutable Godhead whose mysterious power and essence must remain forever inaccessible to the human mind. True to this orthodox spirit Catherine addresses the pagan scholars—and through her, the author his contemporaries—in some of the most moving and rhetorically original language in the entire poem (lines 1,838–53):

> The almighty Godhead of my Savior and Healer of my soul encompasses such expanse and multitude of qualities free of all distress that no reason can grasp His power and His strength, the beginning and ending of His everlasting Being, its foundation and its dome, its length and its width, its solidity and its transparence, its farness and its nearness, its angularity and its circularity, its smallness and its immensity.

SOURCES AND FURTHER READING

The edition from which this translation was made is *Dvě legendy z doby Karlovy* (Two legends from the time of Charles IV), ed. Josef Hrabák (Prague, 1959), pp. 119–219. The Old Czech verse has been rendered into English prose. Due to considerations of length, certain sections have been summarized in brackets. For a detailed study of the Old Czech *Life of St. Catherine* in its European context, see Alfred Thomas, *Anne's Bohemia: Czech Literature and Society, 1310–1420*, Medieval Cultures at Minnesota 13 (Minneapolis, 1998), Chapter 6.

A particularly useful comparison with this late medieval Czech version of the saint's *Life* is provided by the late-twelfth-century Anglo-Norman rhymed version composed by the English nun Clemence of Barking. This version is based on the so-called Vulgate Latin source, which focuses on Catherine's dispute with the fifty pagan philosophers and her martyrdom. For an English translation of Clemence's work, see *Virgin Lives and Holy Deaths: Two Exemplary Biographies for Anglo-Norman Women*, trans. Jocelyn Wogan-Browne and Glyn S. Burgess (London, 1996). Several other comparative texts are available in English translation. A translation of the early Middle English *Seinte Katherine* is contained in *Anchoritic Spirituality: Ancrene Wisse and Associated Texts,* ed. and trans. Anne Savage and Nicholas Watson (New York, 1991); a late-Middle-English version of the *Life* of Catherine is contained in *A Legend of Holy Women: A Translation of Osbern Bokenham's Legend of Holy Women*, ed. and trans. Sheila Delany (Notre Dame, IN, 1992); a thirteenth-century Old French version is contained in *The Lady as Saint: A Collection of French Hagiographic Romances of the Thirteenth Century*, ed. and trans. Brigitte Cazelles (Philadelphia, 1991). All three collections include many other *Lives* of female martyrs and other texts relevant to late medieval female spirituality.

For a classic study of virginity in late-Antique Christianity, see Peter Brown, *The Body and Society: Men, Women and Sexual Renunciation in Early Christianity* (New York, 1988). For the female body in late-medieval religious culture, see Caroline Walker Bynum, *Holy Feast and Holy Fast. The Religious Significance of Food to Medieval Women* (Berkeley, 1987).

The Old Czech Life of St. Catherine of Alexandria [1]

Once upon a time, long ago, in Greece, a pagan emperor ruled over the earth and all the kings of pagandom, both near and far. Maxentius[2] was the name of that evil man, as the sources tell us. His angry, cruel character was so well-known that everyone had to cart his name about in grief like a pile of rocks. The pagans feared him and trembled at the sight of him like a hen faced with a buzzard. He replaced God for them; they bowed to his idols and whatever he commanded, whether great or small, was carried out immediately. Under the rule of this emperor, a rich, respected, and well-renowned king reigned on the island of Cyprus. His name was Costus; he was named thus because there was a town in Cyprus where the sea surrounds it, called Nicosia, as it is still named.[3] Costus was given power over all the kings of pagandom. He ruled in benevolent glory with honor, splendor, and worldly goods, and lived with his flawless queen, as with a rose, in kindness, justice, freedom, and nobility. He was wise, generous, helpful, true to all and sundry, and brave in conflicts with his enemies. His glory was renowned throughout all the world and in all lands, so that the emperor had none more reliable than he at his court; nor was anyone more diligent, whatever he ordered him to do, night or day. Until the day treacherous rivals appeared, who just like today cause harm to others, whisper slanderous gossip in people's ears, hate their lords and envy those good people in service, heap everything onto their own plate, invent lies and repeat them, and impede the faithful in their service. Such were these rivals who envied the king's office. They changed their minds and wished to denounce him, saying: "Know this, emperor, true as we stand living before you now, Costus recently plotted with your enemies and is their sworn conspirator. Believe us, we are not boasting: he is set on your destruction, so beware of him."

The emperor thanked them, said nothing about it, and ordered Costus to leave his land and his home. King Costus had no children apart from a daughter, whom he gave the name Catherine. They took ship for Alexandria, where they began to reside in the castle. Although the emperor was angry, he consulted with his wise men and banished Costus from the land. Nevertheless, Costus was allowed to keep his kingdom, land, and castles since the emperor did not believe all the slanders against him. So the only harm Costus suffered was his banishment from the court. In the town of Alexandria Costus and his queen lived in honor with their desirable daughter. He loved her with all his might, as was appropriate, for she was his only daughter. He was often elated by her until he sent her to be educated at the highest level. She was instructed in much wondrous learning, familiar only to the most erudite scholars: wisdom, the meaning of literal and allegorical texts, about the essence of everything, as best it can be reached by all kinds of philosophical inquiry. All that the maiden mastered in just a few years, surpassing in learning all the learned students in the world.

A short time later Costus died; his kingdom, and all the powers attached to it, were inherited by her. This dear, desirable maiden, as I have heard from my elders, was eighteen years of age and of such extraordinary beauty that she had no equal on the entire earth. Her widowed mother took great pains to protect her and brought her up to lead a pure life, a hundred times more than was known to her mother. "Many a powerful king, therefore, would be blessed if she became his wife and would have much joy," she said. But Catherine's desire was not what others thought it was. Powerful kings wooed her. But she paid no attention for she knew in her mind that it is wicked to lead a life of slavery and therefore she did not wish to marry. Because of her noble morals she promised to maintain her virginal purity according to wisdom and learning to the end of her days.

At that time the news came out that Maxentius's son, being his only son, had been elected emperor of those lands. Because he loved his son so much, Maxentius tried his utmost to have him married at an early age. So he sent upright messengers to all the pagan regions and lands to find out whether an emperor or king had a beautiful daughter who would be worthy and able to marry his son. Ignorant of such a king, the envoys enquired diligently wherever they went. Among those enquiring envoys, some stopped in Alexandria and spoke to the townspeople, asking them who was their ruler. The townspeople replied: "If you travel through the whole world, over mountains, water, and seas, you will never see a maiden of such a translucent complexion and such exquisite beauty as the modest Catherine, our noble queen. In learning, wisdom, loveliness, and nobility no one has ever seen her equal." The envoys' joy and consolation increased when they heard this. Missing nothing, the guests enquired further of the townspeople who showed them to the castle. Thither they went to woo the maiden on the emperor's behalf alone. When they came to the queen's court, they met her mother walking with her desirable daughter, who blossomed in precious beauty. All this seemed a miracle of miracles to those envoys. They said to each other: "No one alive will believe what we tell them about such beauty; our description will not do it justice." They secretly told her mother to give them her word and not marry Catherine to anyone else and they wished to betroth her to the emperor's family. This the queen promised them.[4] They bade her farewell and set off to the emperor to tell him the news.

The emperor immediately summoned his wisest counselors and most learned men and sent them to Alexandria. These obeyed the emperor's command without delay and set off with great pomp and pride. When they arrived at Alexandria, they went straight to the castle where they once more rendered praise to the queen. Her daughter stood next to her. It seemed to them all that there was nothing more lovely in the world that shone or blossomed than this maiden. She stood there enchantingly attired in garments whose value no one could estimate. At that moment the visitors delayed no further. One senior counselor stepped aside with the queen and quickly agreed on a time when they should return and take the maiden home—with great honor and splendor as is appropriate when conducting the daughter of a powerful king to be the bride of an emperor. The queen did not reprimand them for this but was extremely happy and joyful. At that time the maiden knew nothing about the plans. The queen began to make the wedding arrangements, wishing to give away her dear daughter with pomp, lavish entertainment, and display, which was quite within her means.

The most desirable Catherine was taken aback by all this and even took offence at so much wealth, saying: "What does my mother want? What does she intend by embellishing her halls? What is all this extravagance for?" She asked one of her ladies who said: "O princess, you must start to feel differently about the emperor's son, so get ready for the festivities." Catherine went into her chamber and locked herself in. The news grieved her. Sitting down, she said to herself: "All the wisdom acquired by the most learned masters is known to me; everybody who desires considers me a great beauty and would not want anyone else among the female sex. Moreover, I am very high born and my wealth is immeasurable. Furthermore, I am wise and learned. Why then should I live in slavery if I can avoid it? I don't wish my mother to expend any more effort on all this shameless work. I will not be the empress! I would be mad to take a husband whom I have never set eyes on and whom I do not know, whether he is hunchbacked or handsome, whether he has castles or run-down houses, whether he is blind or can see, hideous or lovely, generous or stingy, beautiful or ugly, foolish or wise, false or true, sickly or healthy, or what his manners are like. I would rather preserve my chastity forever until I die, since no one alive is equal to my wisdom and my beauty."

She stopped talking to herself and, with a firm resolve, got up, closed the door behind her, went to her mother, sat down lightly beside her, and said: "Dear mother, listen to me for a while. I see that you earnestly and sincerely desire me to marry and that you are working hard to bring it to a speedy conclusion. Nevertheless, I do not want to marry the emperor's son, be sure of that. So don't give him false hopes and strive to no avail. I assure you that I will not change my mind." Alarmed by these words, the queen said: "My dear daughter, why are you being so unreasonable? I advise you to be silent. Where on earth could you find a better husband? All kings serve him; he has great treasures, villages, even towns, castles, and many lands large and wide. It would be a terrible blow for me if it all came to nothing. Dear daughter, we have had to bear our lot for many years and always desired to change it. Finally your time has come. I advise you, do not let it go, but pursue it gladly. The honor has now come about for which your father yearned; for many years he served the father of your fiance. Daughter, do bear this in mind." The maiden answered boldly: "Mother, your words to me and your anger with me are in vain. I shall persuade you once and for all: I shall not marry any man before judging him and finding that he excels in beauty, honor, riches, birth, and wisdom. And if it is not so, then know, mother, that I shall never marry him. Neither should you strive for it nor let anyone else meddle in the matter." From that point on the queen began to grieve.

And when Catherine's friends tried to persuade her to change her mind and marry the emperor, she answered: "You say that you are not aware of a man as beautiful, as brilliant, as bright with wisdom, and as shining with learning as I am. So why don't you leave me in peace? If you don't want me to offend you and do your will, according to all sorts of advice, then look for a husband who is equal to me alone in learning, beauty and wisdom. Such a man I shall certainly marry, above all to please you." Her friends answered: "Perhaps we ought to know a wiser, nobler, and richer man than you; but we should admit that we do not know one wiser, more beautiful, more famous in learning than you are. Maybe there isn't one in the whole world. You only imagine it wrongly." The maiden said: "If you yourselves say that no one is my equal in all the world, then know that I am delighted by that and swear to you today that I will never wed." From that time on her resolution burned even more ardently in her heart.

In the meantime the queen recalled a hermit who was a learned and noble teacher and who was born in the same city. The journey from Alexandria to him was very long for he lived in deserted and thick forests, in a cave among the mountains, praising the Lord Jesus Christ and his blessed mother. He was a man full of grace, noble, honorable, steadfast, wise, worthy, and helpful. He dwelt there in true purity, leading a God-pleasing life, without blemish, and of an upright mind. The queen gladly went to him for advice for she often derived great comfort from the elegance of his speech and the beauty and wisdom of his words. While preoccupied with her troubled thoughts, she suddenly remembered him and persuaded the young maiden to go and see him with her and to take from him some advice about her predicament.

[**Translator's note**: In lines 426–471 Catherine and her mother visit the hermit at his cave in the wilderness. When the hermit hears of her refusal to marry the emperor's son, he tells her about the ideal bridegroom, that is Jesus Christ.]

The Hermit Describes Christ to Catherine

"The kind of husband you desire I do not know anywhere. But I will tell you something if you are graceful enough to keep a secret: I know a famous king of enormous wealth, learned and just, wiser than all wisdom; more beautiful than all radiance. This king is his mother's only son. And his dear mother is the purest maiden, brighter than the morning star, and blossoms above all women; his distinguished father is the lord of all lands, he never had a knowledge of a woman's body, and is the king of kings. His kingdom is so wide and long that it cannot be measured and is so conceived that no one who enters it will ever die but will live forever joyfully, without enemies, free of sorrow and without longing. This king has innumerable devoted servants and pages each of whom has more wealth and wisdom than your father, Costus, king of Cyprus. And I tell you, furthermore, that even his youngest child surpasses you infinitely in wisdom, learning, and beauty. His life will never end, his wealth will never decay, his love will not perish, his beauty is admired by the stars; his wisdom is so dazzling that no one can fathom it by guessing or by reason, how it increases and how it is dispensed. All the shining angels serve him joyfully and obediently; they do not grieve, are not sad in his mansions but always rejoice; his mighty rule has no end and does not diminish, will not perish, will not change, perpetually renewing itself."

[**Translator's note**: In lines 527–638 Catherine enthusiastically expresses the desire to learn more of the ideal bridegroom described by the hermit.]

The First Celestial Vision

Seeing that the princess was so keen, the hermit joyfully removed a picture from a crack in the rock of his cave. On it were painted two beautiful images: a faithful image of the Virgin Mary, holding her son, the meek Jesus Christ. Taking hold of this picture, he wiped it surreptitiously with his sleeve and concealed it within a fold of the princess's gown, saying: "See this with joy! This is a painting of the young Lord, whom I told you about, with His mother. Take the picture and go home with your mother. When you are in your room, lock yourself in and kneel humbly before this picture, raise your eyes to heaven, and earnestly request this dear, lovely, most radiant, and gracious virgin to reveal her son to you. It is my firm hope that your prayer will always be heard." Catherine took her leave of him, slid the picture under her arm, and set off home with her mother and with those maidens who were her servants. She was overcome with the immense desire to behold the face of that young lord very soon.

When dinner was over at court, everybody had fallen asleep, and the lights had been put out, it occurred to Catherine to enter her chamber and put on the light. She took out the beautiful painting and placed it before her. Not sparing both her hands, she struck her breast with them, wept bitter tears and eagerly implored the Virgin not to delay but kindly to reveal to her her beloved son. Thus she tormented herself, saying: "Let Him take me, poor little thing, not as His bride but as His servant!" Tears poured down her lovely white cheeks and, such was the extremity of her desire, that her eyes became murky and bloodshot. When she had wept a great deal in this fashion, she collapsed onto the floor and fell asleep from sheer exertion. At that moment she had a wondrous, lovely, and vivid vision. She dreamt that she was sleeping in a long and wide, perfect and pleasurable meadow. It gleamed with fresh summer grass and was in full, gorgeous bloom. She had never in her life seen more beautiful or wondrously delightful clearings and meadows. Among those precious sights was enthroned Mary, that blossoming maiden, whose mother is St. Anne,[5] holding her precious one, Christ, Her dear little son, and loving him most fervently. Above His dear little shoulders His white neck shone as a white lily gleams from the most radiant love. And His desirable hair shone immaculately as pure, precious gold glints more preciously than any other gold. In His hair, falling over His shoulders, curls curved like gold rings wrought beyond belief.

[**Translator's note:** In 740–945 Following the first vision, Catherine returns alone to the hermit's cave and tells him of her experience. Realizing that she has been chosen by Christ as his potential bride, he instructs her carefully in the tenets of the Christian faith and baptizes her. She returns to the palace and has a second vision. This time, as a baptized Christian, she is privileged to see her bridegroom's face and is wedded to Him.]

The Second Celestial Vision

When the time came that everyone had dispersed and was fast asleep in bed, Catherine quickly entered her chamber, took out the painting once more, and knelt before it, weeping and imploring, with many a prayer, that Mary, God's Mother, ask her child to reveal Himself and take her as His servant and bride of eternal ornament. Praying made her faint and a dream appeared to her in which she entered a delightful, strange, and beautiful vision. That maiden, faultless and of great renown, truly found herself in a hall more beautiful than anyone living had ever seen. It contained wondrous wonders fashioned from the richest material: the floor was made of beryls, the walls from diamonds set in gold, many windows were fashioned from emeralds and sapphires and, instead of glass, were glazed with precious stones: hyacinths, rubies, turquoises, carnelians, spinels set in ivory; there were jaspers, chalcedons, topazes, garnets, olivines, amethysts, and pearls, all most beautifully cast and assembled.[6] On the ceiling of the hall a sun, moon, and stars, depicted with their orbits, shone just as they move in heaven day and night through God's power, measuring every moment of time. She saw more beautiful wonders rejoicing in their beauty and beheld two thrones, placed side by side, next to the rising sun. On one sat God Almighty on His radiant throne; on the other, wearing a precious crown, sat Mary, His mother by the power of the Word, the Empress of the Archangels. Both held scepters in their hands. All this brilliance and joy consoled Catherine so much that the sadness she had recently felt vanished from her heart. And she thought to herself: "God willing, my wish will be granted because my bridegroom let me behold Him with His mother. I will no longer want when I look upon His face."

At that moment Mary the protectress summoned Catherine with a gesture of the hand; she approached, shy and humble, bowed and knelt before them. Seeing this, Mary said: "My beloved son, welcome your bride! For you know that she has carried out all that you commanded her." Christ said: "I have already decided that I want to take the radiant, lovely Catherine as my bride. She will reign with me in my kingdom forever." Kneeling devoutly, Catherine said: "My dearest king, today I pledge my purity to your mercy, and as best I am able, with a faithful, ardent heart, shall serve you until my death." At that moment, Christ made himself so beautiful to behold by so many pleasing features that His radiant splendor filled her heart in her body with wondrous melodies. Without a doubt she felt within her heart a joy of which she had neither read nor heard from her youth. What she had so deeply sighed for she now saw with her own eyes. He who was sitting in the hall with His dear mother, surrounded by a radiance with which the walls gleamed, stood up, approached the maiden, and stopped in the middle of the hall, clad in the most precious garments. Immediately Mary raised Catherine by the arm and said: "No longer fear reproach, grief, or harm, for my son has taken you as His bride and His handmaiden. Be comforted, full of joy, and free from all sadness." At these words, the Son of God began quietly to sing in an appealing, sweet, precious voice, which filled Catherine's heart with vigor. He went up to her and sang these words to her: "Welcome, my most precious one! Welcome, my lovely bride! Come here to me, little face that I have chosen, my dear little dove! I have prepared an eternal abode and have kept a spotless crown for you in my kingdom." When He had finished singing most sweetly to this girl, He took a ring from His right hand and put it on her palm; Catherine devotedly closed it softly in her hand and began to sing a new song in a sweet voice: "Now I am the bride of the spouse who has maintained my purity and betrothed me with His ring for which I was faint. Now I need no other mirror, for my husband is more precious than all the world and the most beautiful. My eyes will forever see my spouse, my heart will forever belong to Him, defying all evil." Having finished her song of praise, Catherine woke, stood up and beheld, in fact and not in illusion, on her lovely white hand a ring of heavenly gold.

[**Translator's note**: In lines 1098–2234, following Catherine's mystical marriage to Christ, she continues to resist the blandishments of Emperor Maxentius. In an attempt to return her to apostasy, he orders fifty pagan philosophers to dispute with the brilliant young woman. But not only is she victorious in the debate; she also succeeds in converting them to Christianity. The furious emperor orders the philosophers to be executed and is determined to exact revenge on Catherine for humiliating him.]

The Emperor Orders Catherine to Be Tortured

When all that was completed, Emperor Maxentius roared with rage and, looking at the maiden, became angry at witnessing the strength of Catherine's faith and was unable to prevail against her. He ordered his servants to seize and torture her without mercy. Without hesitation, the servants tied up the desirable girl, immediately stripped her of her garments, and began to beat her with whips. These whips had been made exactly as the emperor had ordered for that maiden's punishment, for he wished her to believe in their pagan gods. Each whip had three tails threaded from coarse horsehair; to the end of each tail was fastened a little knot, half of which was cunningly coated with lead in which had been inserted strong hooks. When the servants obediently struck the body with the whips, even if the tail spared the skin, the knots pierced the precious, innocent skin. The hooks got lodged in the wounds and tore the flesh from the body, painfully ripping it into shreds. Oh Jesus Christ, what a piteous sight of the maiden who promised herself to you, the maiden who in her youth at the court of her father, Costus, the powerful king, excelled in honor and glory, worthily brought up in her mother's household, where neither pain nor wounds ever hurt her, where she was never insulted, but enjoyed plentiful wealth, lands, castles, and towns, as befits a daughter who is the only child of her father and mother. Oh Jesus, how your bride stood pitifully naked for the greater glory of your name, as she promised herself to you, not desiring any spouse apart from you. Therefore she gladly and humbly suffered dire torture, for the executioners did not take pity on the softness of her body and ripped her desirable skin with their whips with all their strength, so that one could see great harm and injury caused by the tails on her purest body.

She bore on her body ribbons of six colors, signs of true love for her beloved as a lady should for her beloved. The first color quickly appeared in her cheeks, which used to blossom white and red, but these two were changed by her suffering. Her cheeks did not lose their blood but lost their beauty and became green with shame as she stood naked in front of these insensitive pagans. Full of ardent love, she clasped her hands together, closed both her eyes and silently lowered her head. The pagans were lashing her fiercely and their strokes made her eyes glisten in hot droplets that the pain caused to trickle across her lovely little cheeks. A second color she wore was of the purest white, the color of hope. Indeed, whenever had there been a spouse more loved than this precious one, whose pure white body shone before the pagans, on which blossomed the red color from her holy blood with which the accursed henchmen sprinkled such gleaming whiteness? Many a flowering rose appeared among the skin and flesh, which the hooks had ripped from the bones. These wounds congealed and turned painfully black. A fifth color she next bore from fidelity to her beloved husband like a steadfast, faithful handmaiden. Many bruises made by the tails, sore and swollen with blood under the skin, were turning dark blue and contracted among the wounds wherever the tormentor had aimed with his scourge. I would not believe that a lady nowadays would be so devoted to her husband, and so faithful in her love, that she would withstand for him even a single blow endured by St. Catherine, her mother's delightful daughter. Now her body assumed a sixth color, that of her desirable hair which had also to suffer and which shone more preciously than all the gold in the world. In this grievous torture her hair shook over her shoulders, and wherever the whips struck her, the locks got entangled up with them and were torn from the scalp; and when the whips lashed back, the hair got matted in the flesh, where it glistened through the blood. Thus these colors shone, one next to the other, here in the skin, here in the bruise: white, black, green, blue, gold, and red, each in its own substance. O, how this love had pitched so richly all its tents that this maiden beloved of God is able to suffer such torture! The precious drink of Isolde had previously been given to her when, in her dreams, she was betrothed to Tristan, who is the lord of all things, above whom none is more powerful.[7] The fire of the Holy Ghost burned in her heart. Thus even when the tears bitterly trickled from her shining eyes, her little heart at that time was not at all frightened by that torture and anguish but simply sighed to God.

The Old Czech *Life of St. Catherine of Alexandria*

[**Translator's note:** In lines 2342–3293 Catherine is returned to her dark cell where she is visited by an angel who comforts her. Then several of Christ's angels arrive to anoint her wounds with celestial oil, which is later exuded by her miraculous relics. Completely cured, Catherine is visited by the empress and Porphirius, the emperor's captain of the guards, both of whom embrace the Christian faith. The increasingly demented Maxentius orders both his wife and Porphirius to be executed in a grisly fashion. The emperor now devises an instrument of torture consisting of two rotating wheels with spikes attached to them which are intended to slice up Catherine's lovely body. But just as the maiden is about to be strapped to the instrument, an avenging angel descends and smashes it into a thousand pieces which kill several thousand pagan onlookers. By now the emperor is in despair and orders Catherine to be decapitated with a sword, thereby providing her with a martyr's death. Before her execution Catherine offers a prayer to her beloved Christ on behalf of all those true Christians who in the future will invoke her name and honor her memory.]

Catherine's Final Prayer and Christ's Response

"I now see the meek Jesus Christ, who is the joy of my heart, whose power conquers all, who calls me lovingly to Him. From Him I derive my strength, for His love I die; He is my king and powerful emperor, He is my soul's helper, He is my glorious, radiant spouse and my precious, beautiful bridegroom; all my mind is taken by Him. He is the complete reward and powerful compensation of the holy and those whose faith takes them from the world."

After saying these words the holy maiden politely asked the executioner to delay a while so that she could pray to God and request Him as best she could what she had in her heart. To this the executioner agreed, not in any hurry to spill innocent blood. Putting aside his sword, he said: "Do what you please, and be at peace, beautiful maiden." Then that honorable and brave warrior of Christ sighed once more from the depths of her heart, stepped back, sank to her knees, clasped her beautiful hands, raised her bright eyes to heaven, and said: "Jesus Christ! From you derives the source of all joy, you are the glory of all holy maidens. Whoever is with you at any time, partakes of your great work. My charming spouse, my beloved, strong and victorious God, I praise and thank you that you deigned to make me a bride of your virginal kingdom, hearing my longing and making yourself well known to me. O kind one, look down upon me and pity my torment today, and grant with your sweet deeds what my heart thirsts after. I beg you, oh Lord, to grant me this wish: if men and ladies living in the Christian faith and not recognizing error, but permanently serving your name in honor and glory, appeal to me in need and request your help, remembering my dire torture; those whom befalls some evil occurrence on dry land or on water, in court or in prison; those who in their suffering, in humiliation and in poverty, in deceit and in illness, call out for my protection, deign to hear them, oh Lord, and please grant them everything they desire. Fulfill me this wish: those who have my sufferings painted on the walls of their house, illuminated in a book, or faithfully write about my life, please grant them what they deserve: do not let their houses be visited by sudden death or lightning, or any other danger; but let good fortune prevail there, no ill-hap befall them; let no deformed children be born there but rather healthy and well-formed ones. And whoever dies and must go to the other world and asks my help, being of true faith as is proper, let not his soul, oh God, be surrendered to the devil but kept with you! Lord, having made my request and having completed my battle, my eyes dark with tears, I kneel, awaiting death for you from a sharp sword, which the executioner can barely handle from shame, which will fall on my neck today, for I am to die from it. Dear God, deign to receive my little soul kindly and lead it joyfully to that place and peace where there is the consolation of all holy maidens and eternal gladness through the hands of your angels and your holy archangels."

And as she completed this ardent prayer, immediately a voice descended over her from heaven, which most delightfully filled her ears and comforted her, saying: "You have waited a long time, my renowned beloved! Come here into this bliss, beautiful in honor, my dear desirable bride! My prepared mansions await you, the gates of paradise are open. A dwelling in eternal and blessed peace is ready for you, my dear, precious bride! Come to it quickly, achieve heavenly joy, free of care, beloved! Everything you have requested, my lovely one, you have received; to all those who give you praise and remember your torture I readily promise that I will help them in their need."

[**Translator's note**: In lines 3485–3519 Having heard her beloved spouse, Catherine is beheaded. She dies at the sixth hour like Christ on the Cross. Milk, instead of blood, pours from her neck, a miraculous token of her virginity. Her body is translated by angels to Mount Sinai, where her holy relics remain to this day.]

NOTES

1. I would like to thank Dr. Karel Brušák for his helpful and detailed comments on this translation.

2. Emperor Marcus Aurelius Valerius Maxentius (306–12). He was defeated by Constantine I (the Great) at Saxa Rubra on October 27, 312, and drowned in the Tiber while in flight.

3. The author is claiming that the name Costus derives from the place-name of Nicosia (Ni-cos-ia) in Cyprus. This assertion is unlikely, but it illustrates the medieval love of trying to find the etymological origin of place-names in proper names and vice versa. For example, the place-name Britain was thought to be derived from the proper name Brutus, the famous Roman general who was allegedly the mythical founder of the British Isles.

4. The original Czech speaks of both Catherine and her mother as queen. To avoid confusion, I refer to Catherine as "princess" and her mother as "queen" even though Catherine technically became the queen regnant upon the death of her father. It is for this reason that she is often represented wearing a crown in medieval book illuminations, paintings and statues. Her other attributes are a sword, a book, and a spiked wheel.

5. The Virgin Mary's mother, St. Anne, is not mentioned in the Latin source of our text. She became very popular in the later Middle Ages, largely through her inclusion in *The Golden Legend* by Jacopo da Voragine. The patron saint of midwives, she was especially venerated by pregnant women. She is frequently represented in paintings and sculpture teaching her daughter, Mary, how to read. One of the most famous examples of her

representation in art is Leonardo da Vinci's painting of the Virgin and Child with St. Anne (in the Louvre, Paris), the cartoon of which is now in the National Gallery, London.

6. Precious gems were extremely popular in the Middle Ages. Accounts of them are found in books called lapidaries, which often attributed to them magical and religious powers. The probable models for the description of the jeweled hall in the second vision, which is absent from the Latin source, was the description of the heavenly Jerusalem in Rev 21:18–21 and the Ezek 28:13 which refers to the virginal bodies in paradise being clothed in jewels. In the description of Jerusalem in the Book of Revelation the city and the jewels which adorn it are closely identified with the virginal bride of Christ. Thus the gems which encrust the hall in the second vision symbolize Catherine's chastity and purity as the *sponsa Christi*.

7. The reference to the Celtic lovers Tristan and Isolde in connection with Catherine's betrothal to Christ probably originates in the German courtly romance *Tristan* by Gottfried von Strassburg (ca. 1210). This work tells how Tristan, the nephew of King Mark, and Isolde, Mark's intended wife, accidentally drink a love potion during their voyage from Ireland to Cornwall which makes them fall passionately in love with each other. In the prologue to his poem, Gottfried draws a parallel between his initiated courtly audience of "noble hearts" and the Christian community which eats the body of Christ in the form of the sacramental bread of Holy Communion. This leads Gottfried to link the tragic power of the love potion to change the lives of his protagonists with the mystical transformation of the eucharistic bread and wine into the body and blood of Christ. If Gottfried audaciously maps a religious conceit onto his secular material, our Czech poet does the opposite by associating the mystical marriage of Christ and Catherine with the passionate union of Tristan and Isolde. In this manner he reveals his thoroughly orthodox approach (as a clerical writer) to his religious subject-matter as well as his concern (as a courtly writer) to dramatize his hagiographic material in terms of the kind of secular romance which would have been familiar to, and popular with, his noble audience.

Chapter 35

THE CANONIZATION PROCESS FOR ST. VINCENT FERRER

Translated by Laura A. Smoller

INTRODUCTION

What follows are depositions taken from witnesses at an inquest held in Brittany in 1453–54 as part of the process of canonizing St. Vincent Ferrer. Vincent Ferrer was born in Valencia, in the kingdom of Aragon, in the year 1350, and died in Vannes, in Brittany, in 1419. His adult life coincided with the years of the Great Schism (1378–1414), when western Christendom divided its allegiance between a pope housed in Avignon and another in Rome. A serious and pious child, Vincent joined the Dominican order at the age of twenty-two, became a doctor of theology, and began to preach and lecture in theology in Valencia. A gifted speaker who clearly knew how to move a crowd, Vincent presided over the "spontaneous" conversion of twenty-five thousand Jews, according to Pietro Ranzano's *Life* of the saint. He attracted the attention of the Aragonese cardinal Pedro de Luna, accompanying him to Avignon as confessor, when, in 1394, Pedro became Pope Benedict XIII in the Avignon line. In 1399, Vincent had a vision of Christ standing between Sts. Dominic and Francis, who bid him to go forth and preach repentance and the impending day of judgment. Thus began a twenty-year mission that would take Vincent through most of Europe, from as far south as Sicily to as far north as Normandy. Daily he would celebrate Mass and preach in the open air. Throngs of people came to hear Vincent's sermons, and the sick and infirm would crowd around the master afterward to beg for his healing prayers and touch. Enthusiastic auditors would follow Vincent for days, months, or as long as they could, and a small group of flagellants attached themselves to his entourage. Vincent was most famous for preaching the imminence of the apocalypse, and he wrote a letter to Pope Benedict XIII in 1412 informing the pontiff that the Antichrist had already been born and was at that point nine years old.

In February 1418, Vincent came to Brittany at the invitation of the Breton Duke John V. He toured the duchy for fourteen months, adhering to his usual grueling schedule of open-air Masses and sermons, despite the fact that at sixty-eight he was not as agile as he once had been. In May he headed into Normandy, then in English hands, and preached in Caen before the English king Henry V. By June he was back in Brittany, where he toured in the southwest and the interior of the duchy. In the spring of 1419, dangerously ill, Vincent returned to Vannes, where on April 5, 1419, he died. His body was buried in the Vannes cathedral, to the dismay of both the Dominican and the Franciscan orders, both of whom wished to house what would doubtless be a profitable pilgrimage site. Only thirty-four years later the papal curia opened the local inquest in Brittany that was a first step in any canonization, taking testimony largely in and around Vannes in 1453–54. Other inquests were held in Avignon (now lost), Toulouse, and Naples.

In the later Middle Ages, a canonization inquest such as that generated on behalf of Vincent Ferrer took place when the pope looked favorably upon the petition of important lay and religious postulators on the putative saint's behalf. For the local inquest the pope would appoint a panel whose duty it was to take sworn and accurate testimony into the life, merits, and miracles of the proposed saint at the site of popular devotion (usually the tomb). Particularly by the fourteenth century, such canonization inquests were often highly scripted. Before the papal commissioners ever went out into the field to gather their testimony, interested procurers would line up witnesses for the inquest and, in most cases, prepare a set of questions to ask the witnesses. These questions were frequently based on a biography of the proposed saint crafted by the parties promoting his or her canonization. No such articles survive for the Brittany inquest into Vincent Ferrer's sanctity, and we know that the first *Life* of Vincent was in fact that composed by the Dominican Pietro Ranzano, after Vincent's canonization and based upon the information elicited in the canonization inquest. The testimony of the Brittany witnesses is relatively free-form and has few interruptions; they seem to have responded not to a specific set of questions, but rather to prompts about larger categories such as Vincent's preaching, chastity, eating habits, and an open-ended query about miracles.

The testimony from Brittany, thus, is less scripted than many late medieval canonization inquests. Through the testimony there emerges a picture of an eloquent preacher and thaumaturge. Bretons remembered Vincent as a holy man and treated him, since he was buried there, as a local saint. He was strongly identified both with the dukes of Brittany and with the cathedral in Vannes in which his body lay. Hence the insistence of most witnesses that they did not testify out of favor for the cathedral of Vannes or the duchy of Brittany. Bretons turned to him for assistance in all sorts of problems, such as sickness, paralysis, death, missing items, shipwrecks, deafness, and blindness. Their testimony is set against a backdrop of plague, which ravaged the duchy in the years 1452 and 1453, and there are many reports of miracles in which Vincent's intercession was said to have cured plague victims, protected the healthy from plague, or caused plague to abate in a particular village. Among some, it was rumored that plague would not leave the duchy until Vincent Ferrer was canonized. While the Brittany inquest affords us a glimpse of the holy preacher at work, it also gives us a window into the lives of people from all walks of life in the mid-fifteenth century: their troubles, their hopes, their fears, their beliefs, and their relations with the holy.

SOURCES AND FURTHER READING

The canonization inquest into the sanctity of Vincent Ferrer is *Bibliotheca hagiographica latina*, no. 8656b. The selections below are translated from the sole fifteenth-century manuscript copy of the testimony gathered at the Brittany inquest: Vannes, Archives Départementales du Morbihan, MS 87J11 (which is an unfoliated manuscript). That text has been edited and slightly abridged in Henri Fages, *Procès de la canonisation de Saint Vincent Ferrier pour faire suite à l'histoire du même saint* (Paris and Louvain, 1904), which was also published separately as Volume 3 of Fages's *Histoire de Saint Vincent Ferrier* (Paris and Louvain, 1901–04). The standard accounts of Vincent's life and career are found in *Acta Sanctorum quotquot toto orbe coluntur*, eds. Jean Bolland, et al., first edition (Antwerp and Brussels, 1643–1971), April I, pp. 476–527; Fages, *Histoire de Saint Vincent Ferrier*; Matthieu Maxime Gorce, *Saint Vincent Ferrier (1350–1419)* (Paris, no date [ca. 1924]); and P. Sigismund Brettle, *San Vicente Ferrer und sein literarischer Nachlass*, Vorreformationsgeschichtliche Forschungen 10 (Münster, 1924). The most recent treatment of Vincent's mission in Brittany is found in Hervé Martin, *Les ordres mendiants en Bretagne, vers 1230-vers 1530. Pauvreté volontaire et predication à la fin du Moyen-Age* (Paris, 1975), pp. 317–23; a good English-language survey of the duchy's history is found in Patrick Galliou and Michael Jones, *The Bretons*, The Peoples of Europe Series (Oxford, 1991). For the late medieval process of canonization, see André Vauchez, *Sainthood in the Later Middle Ages*, trans. by Jean Birrell (Cambridge, 1997) and Aviad M. Kleinberg, "Proving Sanctity: Selection and Authentication of Saints in the Later Middle Ages," *Viator* 20 (1989): 183–205. Recent works on miracles in English include Ronald C. Finucane, *The Rescue of the Innocents: Endangered Children in Medieval Miracles* (New York, 1997) and *Miracles and Pilgrims: Popular Beliefs in Medieval England* (London, 1977; reprint, New York, 1995); Michael Goodich, *Violence and Miracle in the Fourteenth Century: Private Grief and Public Salvation* (Chicago, 1995). See also Laura Smoller, "Defining the Boundaries of the Natural in the Fifteenth Century: The Inquest into the Miracles of St. Vincent Ferrer (d. 1419)," *Viator* 28 (1997): 333–59; and "Miracle, Memory, and Meaning in the Canonization of Vincent Ferrer, 1453–54," *Speculum* 73 (1998): 429–54.

In the following translation, the names of the witnesses have been rendered exactly as they occur in the Latin text of the *processus*. Thus Latin forms are mixed with forms from the local vernacular languages, both Breton and French.

The Canonization Process for St. Vincent Ferrer

(Witness 8.) Petrus Floc'h, a citizen of Vannes, aged around fifty-five, as he says and as his appearance confirms. The witness, having been given notice, summoned, brought forth, received, put under oath to testify the pure truth, diligently examined and questioned concerning the life, manners, and miracles of said Master Vincent Ferrer, and the circumstances under which they occurred, testified under oath that, around the time of Carnival[1] about thirty-four years ago, the witness had his first knowledge of said Master Vincent Ferrer, who then appeared to be in his seventies. This was in the city of Vannes. Master Vincent was received in procession by the former bishop Amauricus, ecclesiastics, nobles, and a great multitude of citizens of Vannes united for that purpose.[2] The procession went from the suburbs of Vannes toward the chapel of Saint Lawrence to meet Master Vincent, who was riding on a poor ass, and thusly entered the city. And [the witness] does not know if [Vincent] went then to the cathedral or not, but he well knows that he then was a guest in the home of Robin Le Scarb, which was between the Franciscan convent and the castle "Lermine" [L'Hermine].[3] And he wore the habit of a Dominican, and he was commonly said to be a member of that order and to be a native of Aragon. [The witness] doesn't know any more about his origins. And he says that from the time that he entered the city, he celebrated Mass and preached every day, because the witness, who then was a youth, was urged by his parents to be at his Masses and sermons every day. And he remembers that the theme of his first sermon was "*Gather up the fragments left over*, etc." [Jn 6:12]

Asked how [Vincent] carried himself during his Masses and sermons, [the witness] responded that before [Vincent] mounted the pulpit, he appeared to be very weak and was often supported by others, and he carried a cane to hold himself up. But when he was preaching, he had a clear, very strong voice, as it seemed, to the point that men marveled at this. And [the witness] added that when [Vincent] came down from the pulpit, it seemed that he was not the same person who had preached.

[The witness] did not know how [Vincent] lived in his lodgings, but he heard that he fasted daily and abstained from meat up until the illness from which he died, during which—as he heard—Master Vincent ate broth made from meat on the persuasion and command of the aforesaid lord Amauricus, then bishop of Vannes. And he moderately partook of good wine.

Next, asked, he testified that [Vincent] was very humble, because [the witness] often associated with him on the roads coming and going from his sermons, and he freely greeted men and bowed to them, and when he spoke he would often say "in the name of Jesus." And he was very devout in his attitude both toward his Masses and his sermons.

And [the witness] heard many good things said about [Vincent] and nothing bad. And he is considered by all to be a saintly man and of saintly life, so that the lord duke and duchess and others—great and humble—hold him in reverence. And also commonly it was said that he did not lie down in a bed until his last illness, and that he appeared to be simple, chaste, sober, calm, peaceful, and very modest. And that his sermons were very sweet and gracious to people, and the witness speaking never was bored during his sermons and when he followed Vincent's entourage. And that Bretons who spoke Breton, although they could not understand French, nonetheless understood his sermons—as it is told.[4] And the same witness saw many who did not know the French tongue who in effect recited many of his sermons. And also those far away heard as perfectly as did those who were close, because the same witness was sometimes near and sometimes far, and heard perfectly. And he has also heard many others saying that similarly they understood [Vincent].

Next, he said that [Vincent's] sermons were very fruitful in these parts because the faith was greatly exalted and better understood through them, blasphemies ceased, and the great and small were taught to invoke and honor the name of Jesus, to say the Lord's Prayer and the Apostles' Creed, to hear Masses, to make the sign of the cross, and many other things concerning the faith and divine duties which he cannot describe in any more particulars. But he knows very well that men in these parts lived and still live in a holier, better, and more devout manner afterward than they did before his advent.

Next, asked about the death of Master Vincent, he answered that he saw him in bed on the day he died in what was then the home of a certain Dreulin, now that of Johannes Le Fauchour, in the city [of Vannes]. And at that point he was near death and had lost his powers of speech, and lady the duchess and Lady de Malestricto were attending to him, along with many other ladies, many from his [Dominican] order, many of his disciples, and other priests, who continually were urging him to think of God and His passion. And when one of the priests, whose name the witness does not know, asked Master Vincent if he understood what had been said to him, he lifted his hand, as a sign that he understood. At last he died on that day, and as the witness believes, it was a Wednesday in the week following *Vindicate me* [Ps 43], and around the third hour after noon.[5] He does not remember which month. And after [Vincent] died, at once the house was closed up because it was said that the Franciscans and also the Dominicans desired to have his body. And on that day, around sunset, those from the cathedral in Vannes with a great multitude of people took the body to the cathedral in Vannes, and it was placed in the choir of the cathedral. And [Vincent] was wearing the habit of a Dominican in his open coffin, and the body was watched over with great diligence. And everyone, without distinction, touched his body or his habit with great reverence and devotion. In what manner the body was watched over thereafter in the cathedral before it was buried, the witness does not know, but he heard it said that it had been kept in the sacristy of the cathedral.

Asked why it was guarded thusly and not quickly buried, he answered that he heard it said that members of the Dominican order were petitioning the duke that they might have Master Vincent's body and that he would not be buried in the Vannes cathedral. But upon receiving permission from the duke, the aforementioned lord Amauricus [the bishop], with a great multitude of clergy and the people, at once buried him in the choir of the cathedral, in front of the episcopal seat at the base of the choir toward the great altar. And, as he remembers, iron bars and great stones were placed there. And he testified that Guillermus Roberti, a stonecutter, made his tomb.

Next, asked if Master Vincent chose his burial [place], he answered that he heard that in his illness Master Vincent had said that if there had been a Dominican convent in the aforesaid city or nearby, the prior of that convent could have made the arrangements for his burial as it pleased him. But because there was not, he left the arrangements up to the lord bishop of Vannes. And on account of that, the former lord bishop had him buried as related above.

Asked if there had been any Dominican convent, [witness] said that there was not one, nor is there a convent belonging to that order in the diocese of Vannes, except for the convent of Quimperlé, which is fifteen leagues from Vannes.[6] Nor is there another convent of that order outside the diocese for ten leagues.

Next, he testified concerning the miracles of Master Vincent that it is commonly said that God worked many miracles by the prayers of the said Master Vincent during his lifetime, and many ran to him to recover their health, and when he had made the sign of the cross over them with his hand, they recovered their health. [The witness] nonetheless would not know how to describe them, except that he once saw that a certain Alanus Hervei, then a citizen of Vannes, lead one of his serving maids, then pregnant, whose name the witness does not know, to Master Vincent at the maid's great urging. Master Vincent laid his hands on the serving maid, making the sign of the cross and touching her belly, and said to her that she should go home in Jesus's name and that she would give birth to a son at once. She left and, immediately after her entrance into the house, gave birth to a son. The witness said that he was not present at the birth, but he saw and heard Alanus, who was the witness's neighbor, and others living with him saying, reciting, and telling about this miracle. And there was common parlance, *fama*,[7] and reputation about these matters in the area.

Asked what is *fama*, he answered, "That which is commonly said by people in a region."

Next, he testified that after Master Vincent's death, he saw a certain Perrinus Hervei, also known as Grasset, the previous witness, then in the parish of Blessed Mary of Le Mené in the suburbs of Vannes, lying on a mattress near the fire in his home, tied down with cords and linens and invoking a demon and blaspheming God and the saints. [Perrinus] was carried to the church of the Blessed Mary of Bondon near Vannes, and there cried out horribly and more horribly, and became much worse when holy water was sprinkled on him. And he spat on the image of the Blessed Mary. Nor could he hear anything said about God. Seeing this, a certain Brother Thomas (as he best recalls the name), a friar of the Carmelite order in the said church of Bondon, commanded Perrinus to be taken to the tomb of Master Vincent. And then, there, he saw Perrinus taken down and his hands and arms shackled with iron chains. Whether his legs were tied up or not, he doesn't recall. He knows nonetheless that it was necessary to carry him; he could not have gone in any other way. Perrinus was set down on the base under the altar at the tomb and there slept a while, about the space of an hour, as it seemed to him. And at last, waking up, Perrinus asked why he was tied up so and who had brought him there. The response to him was that he had been brought there because he was demented or possessed by a demon. And then Perrinus said that he had been cured by the merits of Master Vincent, whom—as he asserted—he had seen there talking to him. And he asked the bystanders in these words, "Didn't you just see Master Vincent talking with me?" And he was released from his chains and went away from there cured and thereafter did not have that infirmity, because this witness has seen him from then up to now, and he is still alive.

Asked who was there, [the witness replied]: Symon Maydo, Johannes Gibon, and innumerably many others. And then a great crowd rushed there, and the bells were rung. And this was considered by all to be a miracle.

Next, he testified that in the year in which Master Vincent died, and thereafter for five or six years, God worked miracles through Master Vincent's merits that were so many and so great that he does not know how to describe them. And there was a great convergence of people at his tomb up to the above time. But after five or six years from the time of his death, there were not so many miracles worked, although there were always some. For the last two or three years again the confluence of people and the multitude of miracles has grown and continues greatly to grow. And the witness saw many people coming there, carrying sudaries and crosses and saying that they had been resuscitated from the dead by the intercession of said Master Vincent.[8] [And he saw] others [carrying] crutches by which paralyzed persons and others with weakened limbs were sustained, asserting that they were liberated by the intercession of said Master Vincent. There were so many that [the witness] could not specify or recall their names; nor did he know how many people [he saw there].

He said also that the people of Brittany and especially those in the city of Vannes have a great devotion toward said Master Vincent and that when someone is sick or loses anything, at once they emit a vow to Master Vincent, and many are healed and many things found by the merits of Master Vincent, as the witness also believes most firmly. And his tomb in the said cathedral of Vannes is held in great veneration; and he says that there is an almost infinite number of wax images, wooden crutches, crosses, coffins, and iron shackles there in sign of the miracles of the said Master Vincent. And he added that at another time there were four times more images there than there are today.

Next, he testified that Master Vincent is held and commonly considered to be a saint by all in Vannes, and [it is held] that God operates many miracles through his intercession. And he asserts that citizens of Vannes commonly visit his tomb once a day.

Next, he testified that concerning the above and in this region there is public discussion and *fama*. And that he spoke for the sake of truth, and not on entreaty, promise of reward, or favor for the said cathedral of Vannes or Brittany, and not under any sort of compulsion or force.

(Witness 41.) Johannes Le Vesque, a married cleric and resident of Josselin, in the diocese of Vannes, age around thirty-five, as he says and as his appearance confirms. The witness, having been given notice, summoned, brought forth, received, put under oath, questioned, and diligently examined concerning the miracles of said Master Vincent Ferrer, testified under oath that on the vigil of the last feast of the blessed Apostles Peter and Paul [June 29], a little after noon, the witness, who was then on a river bank called "Augusta," saw that Alanus Bouic, age about twenty, who knew how to swim, had brought the son of Thomas Gueho, named Johannes (as he believes), age about fifteen, who did not know at all how to swim, to the riverbank to bathe and teach the said Gueho to swim. And at length he led him to a place along said riverbank beneath a mill there, where the water was the depth of two lance lengths or more. And there they both went under. And Bouic, seeing that he and Gueho were in such danger, escaped by swimming. And he left said Gueho there, who twice went under the water. And when he went under for the third time, a *domicella* named Margareta Boudard, aged forty or so, who never was married and is of the highest reputation and life, concluding—as did the witness and all the others who were there—that the boy was dead and drowned, devoutly commended [*vovit*] him to Master Vincent, praying that he might miraculously restore Gueho to life and free him from this danger, since the parents of Gueho were then at the "pardon" at the cathedral at Vannes where the body of Master Vincent was buried.[9] At once after the vow was uttered, Gueho appeared on the surface of the water, [still] dead as the witness firmly believes. And all alone, without moving his body any more than a log would move, he floated near the shore, for a distance of three lance lengths across the water. A certain son of Tournemote (he does not know any more) caught him up in his arms. And at once following this, although Gueho's throat and head appeared almost as if they had been disconnected from his body, and he was the color of a dead person and had his eyes closed, he began to cry out, "Jesus."[10] And since the witness and the others present thought that he would be full of water, they put him on a grassy spot with his head lowered so water would come out. Nonetheless Gueho emitted no water. And after he remained there a while wrapped in a tunic by the *domicella*, he was completely recovered.

Asked how long he remained in the water, he said for half of a quarter of an hour.

Asked if he believes that [Gueho] was dead, he said that he firmly believes this because of the above reasons and because said Gueho appeared dead when he was taken up [from the riverbank].

Asked who was there, he said the aforementioned *domicella*, Johannes Barbe, Petrus Cadier, and more than forty others. And the witness and all those present held and believe most firmly that Gueho was resuscitated and freed miraculously through the intercession of the said Master Vincent. And he said that he testified for love of truth, without any favor for the cathedral of Vannes or the duchy of Brittany and without fear or any other sort of corruption.

(Witness 48.) Katherina, wife of Johannes Guernezve, a citizen of Vannes, aged fifty-five years or so. The witness, having been given notice, summoned, brought forth, received, put under oath, questioned, and diligently examined concerning the life, manners, and miracles worked by Master Vincent Ferrer and the circumstances [under which they were worked], testified under oath that she saw said Master Vincent in the city of Vannes celebrating Mass and preaching, and so acting and having such a reputation as Guillermus Connannou, the previous witness, testified.

She testified further, when questioned concerning miracles, that five or so years ago, around the feast of the blessed Lawrence [August 10], a certain person called Johannes Guerre, from the diocese of Tréguier, as she believed, an archer of the illustrious prince lord duke of Brittany, as the witness had commonly heard both from him and from other archers of the said lord duke and many others, went to Johannes de Veneto [or Johannes of Vannes], then chief of the archers of Brittany, to request and recover money from him, by way of stipend, so that with this [money] Guerre might better satisfy his creditors, of which he had many at the time. And, indignant, said de Veneto wounded the same Guerre in his head, arm, leg, and kidneys, by beating him as well as by pushing him down the stairs in the home of said de Veneto. And thus wounded, he went to the home of the witness and there was cared for by her servant and a certain Yvone Gourhaut, an acquaintance of hers, for eight days or thereabouts. And the witness then visited Guerre and, being berated by her neighbors that she might leave Guerre to die without confession and seeing the signs of death coming over him, sent for Lord Oliverius Bourric, priest and rector of the parish church of Montcon, and chorister in Vannes, who was asked to lead said Guerre in confession. But because Guerre was not conscious, nor could he speak, she believed that the priest, giving up on Guerre, left. But this she does not know well.[11] But Guerre afterward became cold and rigid such that he neither talked nor exhaled any breath from his body, and such that, in the judgment of this witness, he was completely dead. And all those present judged him dead, for one woman from the parts of Lanval by the name of Johanna made the sign of the cross over his brow with a candle, as is the custom with dead people in those parts. And Richarda, the wife of Master Johannes Anglici, held feathers to the mouth and nostrils of said Guerre so that she might perceive if he had any breath. And the witness, sorrowing greatly that he had thus died without confession, urged those present that they should kneel and invoke Master Vincent so that he might restore the soul to his body. And she, with the others, in one voice commended him to the said Master Vincent. When that vow had been uttered, [Guerre], sighing, began again to speak, saying that he had seen Master Vincent in white robes and that many species of demons had been vexing him [Guerre], and that he had been freed and resuscitated by the said Master Vincent. And that after the arrival of Master Vincent those demons had ceased their torments; nor did he see them afterward. And immediately afterward and again in the morning and several other times and days in succession, he confessed to said Lord Oliverius [the priest]. And at length, within five weeks, when he was totally healed, he, the witness, and many neighbors and other diverse associates—barefoot and dressed in linens—went to the tomb of the said Master Vincent and there had a Mass celebrated and left a wax offering. And this resuscitation was held and considered by all those present to be an evident miracle.

Asked further if she believed that he had been dead, she said that she believed this because all the signs of death were apparent in him.

Asked for how long he remained dead, she said that it was longer than a half hour.

Asked who was present, she replied: the daughter of the witness, Bodeac, the wife of Master Johannes Anglici, said Johanna from Lanval, and many others.

And asked about this, she said that she most firmly believed that he had been resuscitated at the intercession of said Master Vincent. And further she said that she often had heard said Guerre saying that he believed the same.

She testified also that there is a great confluence of people at the tomb of said Master Vincent; and that Almighty God daily operates an infinite number of miracles at his intercession, about which she was not able to testify specifically on account of their number; and that there is great popular devotion at the tomb of said Master Vincent and toward him, both in his life and after his death up to the present. The said Master Vincent was commonly held and considered in those parts by all to be a saintly man and [she said] that at his intercession there had been and were miracles worked daily. And about these there is the common public reputation in these parts and parlance and *fama*.

Asked about this, she said that *fama* is common and public talking about a certain thing among the people of one place. And through her oath she affirmed that she testified the above for love of truth alone, and not by compulsion out of fear, favor for the cathedral of Vannes, or any other corruption.

(Witness 52.) Oliverius Bourric, priest, rector of the parish church of Montcon in the diocese of Vannes, chorister in the cathedral of Vannes, aged thirty-six, as he says and as his appearance confirms. The witness, having been given notice, summoned, brought forth, received, put under oath, questioned, and diligently examined concerning the same and other miracles of the aforesaid Master Vincent Ferrer, testified under oath that now some four or five years ago, in which time the same witness was called to hear the confession of Johannes Guerre, who then was wounded by Johannes of Vannes, as commonly was said, he went to see Guerre at the home of Johannes Guernezve in which he was lying in bed. And when the witness arrived there, said Guerre lost his ability to speak, nor could he confess to him. But at once, in the witness's judgment, he gave up the ghost and was dead.

Asked how he knew this, he said because he touched and palpated him in the mouth, nose, ears, throat, chest, and many other parts of his body, and in all parts he was cold, hard, and rigid, just as the dead are, of which the witness has seen many. Nor did said Guerre emit any breath; nor did the nerves and veins continue in his throat or other parts of his body;[12] and he was colored like the dead. And the witness and the other bystanders all firmly judged him to be dead. Discerning this and sorrowful that he had died without confession, said witness, along with the others present, remembering that God works many miracles at the intercession of Master Vincent, exhorted them that they should kneel and say an Our Father. And, directing *his* prayer to Master Vincent, he asked that Master Vincent might deign to restore [Guerre's] life so that at least he might confess his sins. Upon this, at once said Guerre sighed and said he had seen Master Vincent in white robes and had been freed by him. And afterward, the witness heard his confession and within fifteen days or so afterward, he had totally recovered, although he still had a large wound in his head, and he went to the tomb of said Master Vincent barefoot and in white clothing. And there he had a Mass said by the witness and gave a wax offering.

Asked how long Guerre was dead, he said about an hour or so.

Next, asked, he said that he and the others present believed and the witness still believes most firmly that he was resuscitated through the intercession of Master Vincent, and that this was undoubtedly a miracle. And the witness had this [miracle] made public on the Sunday following in the cathedral of Vannes by a certain Master Peter Heremite, then a canon in Vannes. And this was well known in said city of Vannes and considered to be a miracle.—Asked who was present, he said Master Johannes Anglici, Bodeac Gourhaut, the wife of the said Master Johannes Anglici, the wife of the said Guernezve, and several others.

Next, he testified that he had heard recited in the said cathedral an infinite number of miracles of Master Vincent: resuscitations from the dead; liberations from demons, the plague, fevers, pains in the head, and many other bodily infirmities; restorations of lost sight, hearing, and speech. And as to the pilgrims in white robes, the convergence of people at the tomb, their devotion, and the wax images left at the tomb, he testified in conformity with the preceding witness. And further the witness, who has resided in the cathedral of Vannes for twelve or more years and still resides there, has seen many miracles and things listed above which are so numerous that he doesn't know how to tell them all, but he knows well that in the cathedral, city and surroundings, Master Vincent is esteemed to be a saint, and that God works miracles through him. And about the above, there is in the region of Vannes public parlance and *fama*. And he testified under oath that he had spoken truthfully, not motivated by reward or favor for the cathedral at Vannes or Brittany or compelled by fear of anyone.

He added also that two months later he heard it commonly said that a son of Oliverius Rouxel had been dead for an entire day and afterward resuscitated at the intercession of Master Vincent.

He heard also about the son of Johannes de Vannes junior, that said son was sick with plague now four months ago and at last remarkably swollen and so colored with signs of death [*pinatus*] from the said infirmity that one despaired for his life.[13] His mother devoutly commended him to Master Vincent, by means of which vow the same son recovered his health. And it is said that he was thus cured miraculously. Which also he testifies out of truth and in no way under compulsion to do so.

(Witness 56.) Katherina, wife of Oliverius Rouxel, a citizen of Vannes, aged thirty-nine, as she says and her appearance confirms. The witness, having been given notice, summoned, brought forth, received, put under oath, questioned, and diligently examined concerning the miracles of the aforesaid Master Vincent Ferrer, testified under oath that around five years ago Guillermus, her son, then around age four, had been very sick—with what illness, she did not know. He did not lie in his bed but walked around, even though he was very weak. At length one day, she is not sure which, but she thinks a Wednesday, the said son in the morning, around the hour of Prime,[14] lost consciousness,[15] and his body became cold and stiff, and he did not emit any breath, although the witness often held a burning candle to his mouth and nostrils so that she might ascertain if he was breathing, and she held some warm tiles to his feet, and by various other ways wished to warm up his body. Nonetheless, no breath of life was apparent in him, and he remained this way until the morning around the hour of Prime again. And on that second day, a little before Prime, the witness asked her husband if he had been to the tomb of said Master Vincent on behalf of his son. He responded that he had not, but on the persuasion of the witness speaking, he did then go to the tomb of said Master Vincent, and there he prayed for the son and left a burning candle and brought another to the witness. The witness, because she was not able then to go to the tomb, went to the Franciscan church which was much nearer to her home and there had a Mass celebrated before the image of the Blessed Mary, commending the son to God, Blessed Mary, and Master Vincent. And because she was not able to hear the Mass, she went out of the church as quickly as possible so that she might arrange for the coffin and burial of her son. And, on the way home again she commended her son to Master Vincent, promising two pennies each year for him. When she got home, she told her husband about this, who was happy with both the vow and the promise of the pennies. As she came into the house, a certain daughter of the witness named Anthonia stopped her, saying that the son was still lying there as if dead just as before. And while the witness was standing there in the entrance to the house, greatly sorrowing, the son turned his head toward the witness and asked for an apple which he saw in the house, saying that he was cured and was hungry. And then the witness gave her son this apple and, seeing that he ate the apple, with great joy went to her husband, who was then in another room of the house, telling him that their son was talking and had eaten an apple. And that day, the son got up and was well, and this son is now nine years old and still alive.

Asked if she believes that the son was dead, she said yes, both because of the above reasons and also because all the signs of death were apparent in him, and everyone who saw him thought he was dead and upbraided her for not burying him, asserting him to be dead. And she believes most firmly that her son was resuscitated miraculously at the intercession of said Master Vincent, swearing that she testified truthfully, and not in any way under compulsion.

(Witness 73.) Noble woman Oliva de Coatsal, the widow of the former Silvester Loiveloux, a squire, from the parish of Ploescob, now living in the parish of Ploeneret, age around fifty, as she says and as her appearance confirms. The witness, having been given notice, summoned, brought forth, received, put under oath, questioned, and diligently examined concerning the life, manners, and miracles of the aforesaid Master Vincent, testified that she often saw him celebrating Mass and preaching the word of God to the people, and she saw and heard him commonly considered to be a good and holy man.

She testified further that, now thirty-three or so years ago, around the feast of the Nativity of St. John the Baptist [June 24], a certain infant of hers named Guillermus, then aged one year or so, was gravely ill for around seven days. At length, in a manor house of her former husband called Kaerlovenan, two leagues or so from the city of Vannes, one day he died from the said illness, around noon (she does not recall anything more specific [about the time]), for he was cold, stiff, and the color of a dead person. Nor did he breathe, because the witness checked this in several ways in his mouth, nostrils, and ears. And then, remembering the life, sermons, and saintliness of said Master Vincent, whom she often had seen alive during the time he was in Brittany, and toward whom she had great devotion, and [recalling] that commonly it is said that he is a saint and that God works miracles for him, she took up the said infant and put him in a shroud. The former Father Alanou from the said parish of Ploescob (who is now dead), had him carried on a horse, wrapped in the shroud, to the tomb of said Master Vincent, and she came with him. And she said that along the way [the infant] always looked dead, and in the church she picked him up, thus dead, and carried him to the tomb and put him on it and then prayed that, if Master Vincent were a saint and could accomplish things with God, as this witness believed and as commonly was said about him, he would restore her infant to life. When her prayer was over, at once the said infant moved, looked well, and ate some cherries that aforesaid Alanou had brought with him, and from then on he was totally cured and never had that illness thereafter. And he lives to this moment. And the witness said he was [present] in the house in which she was testifying.

Asked who was present in the said manor at the aforesaid events, she replied: the aforesaid Alanou and certain others who are now dead. She said that in the cathedral at this miracle there was a great crowding of people on account of this, with the bells ringing. But she does not recall any particulars about them.

And she believes that this was the second miracle made public in the cathedral of Vannes after the death of said Master Vincent. And she believes most firmly that said infant was really dead and miraculously resurrected by the merits of said Master Vincent, because all the signs of death were apparent in him. And she and all those present esteemed him dead and resuscitated and healed at the tomb, just as she described. And she and the others present considered this to be an evident miracle. And thereafter she made said Guillermus visit the tomb yearly, and she herself similarly visits it and there leaves twelve pennies yearly.

She added that immediately after the resuscitation of said infant, [there arrived] the parents (as they said) of another infant who appeared to be a year and a half or so old and who (as they said) had been cut into two parts through his head by the mother. And a sign of this division was apparent in the infant's head. The infant's father said the reason was that the mother was pregnant and desired to eat some meat, which they did not have [and apparently planned to eat the child]. And they brought the infant to the tomb of said Master Vincent, asserting and certifying that he had been divided in two parts as said above, and had died, and after a vow made by the parents to Master Vincent, he had been resuscitated and totally cured by [Vincent's] intercession.

Asked if she knew said parents, she said no, nor did she know where they were from except that they spoke French and not Breton.

Asked if she knew for how long said infant remained divided and dead and how long thereafter he was brought to the said tomb, she said that she did not know that or anything else about the said infant beyond what she had testified.[16]

And she attests that she had testified the above truthfully, not motivated by entreaties, gift, fear, affection, or favor for the cathedral of Vannes or Brittany, or under compulsion by any human graces.

Then the said witness immediately preceding brought to us Oliverius, her firstborn; Peter; and the said Guillermus, her sons, who similarly were summoned, brought forth, received, and put under oath. And we questioned and diligently examined them under oath concerning the aforesaid miracle worked on the person of the aforesaid Guillermus. They said to us and testified that they had heard about that miracle and its circumstances in all [details], just as their mother testified, both from her and from Guillermus Le Vigoroux and his wife and children, who are now dead. And they knew nothing further except that the said Guillermus told us that on account of this miracle he was and is a pilgrim to the aforesaid Master Vincent once each year, and in his memory he comes to the cathedral at Vannes and visits Master Vincent's tomb yearly. And they asserted that they testified the above truthfully and without corruption of any sort and without compulsion.

(Witness 74.) Johannes Guezou, a fisherman from Calmont, of the parish of Saint Patern in Vannes, aged around fifty-five, as he asserts and as his appearance confirms. The witness, having been given notice, summoned, brought forth, received, put under oath, questioned, and diligently examined concerning the life, manners, and miracles of the aforementioned Master Vincent Ferrer, and their circumstances, testified under oath that he saw the same Master Vincent celebrating Mass and preaching the word of God to the people in the city of Vannes in the place designated above. And he says that he preached very well in his estimation, and is commonly considered to be a saintly man and of a good and holy life, and is also said to be humble, peaceful, and full of all virtues because it was thus apparent from his deeds, manners, and habits, which the same witness often saw in the city of Vannes, as well as from his exterior actions. And he has commonly heard an infinite number of good things said about him and never a bad word.

Next, he testified that last Wednesday, which was the twenty-eighth day of the month of November of the present year, around midnight, the witness, Johannes Rochelart, Perotus Kaeranroux, and Natalis Guezou (the witness's son) were fishing in a certain boat in the sea near an island named An Maluec, near the island De Haut, at a distance of eight leagues over the water from the city of Vannes. They were planning to raise their nets that they had set out in the sea there to catch fish the previous March. An enormous tempest came over them, such that the sea was more terrible than the witness had ever seen it, and he had been accustomed to go to sea frequently from his youth to fish. On account of this storm, the witness with the others mentioned above, fearing for their lives, untied the ropes and the anchors, hoping to allow the boat to drift to shore wherever it might, as it pleased God. But the tempest was so strong that the boat was unable to leave that place. And after it had remained there for three hours or so, having no further hope for their life or liberation, the aforementioned Rochelart said first to Natalis (the witness's son and the most innocent), then to the witness and the others, that they should get down on their knees and commend themselves to Master Vincent, promising that as soon as they were freed from this danger they would devoutly visit his tomb. And they all, on bent knees, weeping and sighing, devoutly did so. When the vow was made, at once the tempest ceased, and the sea appeared most clear and peaceful. And they recovered their anchors, ropes, and nets, which they had thought were broken and lost. And he believes and all [the others], according to this witness, believe most firmly that the above happened miraculously through the intercession of the said Master Vincent, because this witness is very skilled in the art of navigating, and he saw no sign that the tempest would cease. And at once after the utterance of the vow, the tempest stopped. And in the witness's judgment, this could not have happened so rapidly and suddenly except miraculously. Also because immediately after the vow the sea appeared so calm, as if no tempest had been there. Nor would the witness have believed that they would not all have died there. And at once after they made land, they all at once visited said tomb, rendering thanks to God and to Master Vincent, who, as he says, in these parts is commonly and publicly considered to be a saint. And he affirms that he testified this under no sort of compulsion.

(Witness 101.) Oliverius Herbelt, a barber-surgeon, a native of Nouzay in the diocese of Nantes, now living for more than thirty years in the city of Vannes, age fifty-five years or so, as his appearance confirms. The witness, having been given notice, summoned, brought forth, received, put under oath, questioned, and diligently examined concerning the miracles of the aforesaid Master Vincent Ferrer, testified under oath that on a Wednesday, three weeks ago, the witness had a sudden infirmity by which his mouth twisted around toward his right side, beyond the center of his face, although he did not feel any pain, except that he could not speak. Nonetheless, his tongue and face were noticeably swollen, and his right eye had turned a little bit toward the right side, and he felt that his right arm was weak and as if it were asleep, although he could use it a little. And since the witness did not recognize the state that he was in, he went upstairs in his house, and when he wished to draw near the fire, he commended himself devoutly to said Master Vincent. And when the vow was made, at once his mouth went back to its place and the swelling ceased, and he began to talk. And seeing this, the witness sent his offering to the tomb of Master Vincent, and each year he will visit the tomb, as he says, as long as he shall live.

Asked who was present at the above events, he says that Mariona, the wife of Bernard Kaerscab (who told the witness about the state he was in before he went upstairs), the witness's wife, and many others saw him thusly. But he believes that when he made the vow, no one was present. Nonetheless, he told his neighbors afterward both about the vow and about the miracle. And afterward, he devoutly personally visited the tomb. And he would have visited it immediately [on his cure], except that he did not leave his house for a few days on medical advice. And he believes that he was cured totally at the intercession of said Master Vincent, because he had no other medicine.

Next, he testified about the crowds, devotion of the people, and common reputation and *fama*, as the preceding witnesses. And he believes firmly that Master Vincent is a saint and that God daily operates miracles for him. And he swears that he testified the above for love of truth and that he did not testify other than the truth.

(Witness 113.) Petrus Le Chanteur, a farmer, from the parish of Lizmerzel in the diocese of Vannes, age thirty-five years or so, as he says and as his appearance confirms. The witness, having been given notice, summoned, brought forth, received, put under oath, questioned, and diligently examined concerning the miracles of the aforesaid Master Vincent Ferrer, testified under oath that, when the witness was seven or eight years old, a certain infirmity came over him with such force that his face turned around backward toward the left side so that he saw his backside and indeed could not see in front of him. And he remained like this for seven months or so. His parents brought him to many physicians and sought many remedies for him, from which no remedy followed. And at last the witness was in the town of Questelbertz with a certain physician named Alanou Tricherie, who daily tried to cure him from the said infirmity and, after he knew the nature of the infirmity and for some time had applied various medicines to him, said that he was incurable. Then the witness's father, who was in the parish of Lizmerzel, one league distant from the said place of Questelbertz, despairing otherwise for the witness's health, commended him to the aforementioned Master Vincent, as he afterward told the witness. And after the vow had been uttered, he returned to the said place of Questelbertz and asked said physician if the witness was getting better, and he responded no. And totally despairing for his health, the father said to the physician that it was necessary for him to take the witness with him and that it was not possible to find another better physician unless he could be cured through the merits of said Master Vincent, to whom he said he had commended him. And thence he came to the chamber where the witness was lying in bed, and then at once, feeling himself cured, he got up, healthy and joyful, and showed himself to his father with his face entirely turned around to its right place. And at once the rejoicing father led him to the tomb of said Master Vincent in the cathedral of Vannes.

Asked about the time, he says that it was in the month of August. And he believes that this was twenty-four or twenty-five years ago, at which time the witness, confirming the vow, promised to visit the tomb yearly. And at some point afterward he was impeded by other business and did not visit the tomb at that time [for his annual visit]. And however often he omitted his personal yearly visits to the tomb (even though he would nonetheless send his oblation with another), the infirmity would come back over him with this lapse, and his face would turn backward as before. And as soon as he would promise to go personally to the tomb, the infirmity would cease and his face would return to its place and normal position.

Asked how often he thus neglected to visit the tomb and the infirmity returned as described above, he says that it was six or seven times. And he says that the last time was in the month of August, two years ago, from which time he has not omitted [his pilgrimage], nor has the infirmity returned.

Asked about those present, he says that he does not know who was present at his father's vow. In Questelbertz there was present the said physician, who afterward died, and no one else. But he says that many neighbors of the witness saw him with that infirmity and afterward cured, among others Michael Savine, Alanus Savine, Johannes Lechesne, and Yvo Lechesne. And the witness swears that he testified the above not due to entreaty, the promise of a gift, fear, or favor for the cathedral in Vannes or in any other way under compulsion, but solely for the truth.

(Witness 124.) Johanna du Clerigo, the wife of Yvo Locquemeren, a *domicella*, of the parish of Lentive in the diocese of Vannes, aged sixty or so, as she says and as confirmed by the appearance of her body. The witness, having been given notice, summoned, brought forth, received, put under oath, questioned, and diligently examined concerning the miracles of the aforesaid Master Vincent Ferrer, testified under oath that Ludovica, her daughter, age twenty or so, was sick with plague around the last feast of the blessed Mary Magdalen [July 22]. And on the fourth day of the illness, the witness, trusting in the merits of

Master Vincent, devoutly commended [the daughter] to him, promising that if her daughter—whose death everyone who saw her expected to occur right away, and who already had received extreme unction and the other sacraments to prepare her to die—should be able to recover her health, she would visit the tomb barefoot and in white garments, and from the portal of the cathedral up to the tomb, she would go on her knees, and offer there a wax offering. And when the vow had been uttered, she says that her daughter at once felt better and over the course of time, although not all at once, she recovered and escaped the plague. And she believes firmly that [this was done] miraculously through the merits of Master Vincent because the infirmity had come to the point of death, and she gave her [daughter] no medicine, but rather, when she made the vow, promised that she would give her no medicine.

Asked about those present, she says that no one was present at the vow, but many saw the daughter when she was so sick, and then afterward cured. And this witness visited the said tomb and fulfilled what she had promised.

Next, she testified that Petronilla, the wife of Johannes de Alrayo, a farmer, from the same parish, had an infirmity in her right arm such that the arm was greatly swollen entirely up to her shoulder and right breast. Whence she and everyone who saw her concluded that she would lose that arm or would die. She asked a neighbor of hers who said that he knew some medicine for similar infirmities, and [the neighbor] visited her and having seen her said to her that he would not lay a hand on her unless she commended herself devoutly to Master Vincent beforehand and asked for his assistance. [Petronilla], hearing this, humbly commended herself to Master Vincent, devoutly asking that he might deign to pray the Almighty for her and her health. And she put an offering at the tomb. When this was done, the pain in her arm, which had been very great, stopped for the most part, not entirely, however. But afterward the said "physician" placed an unguent between the woman's body and arm, and at length she was cured. And the witness believes [that this was a miracle]—considering the infirmity, from which two or three neighbors living in the same village as the witness and the woman recently died. And the witness was present when the woman commended herself as described above, and also urged her to commend herself. And before the vow, she believed that [Petronilla] would doubtless die very shortly, within two hours.

Next, she testified that Johanneta, the daughter of Corffman, was gravely ill with plague, because she saw her thus sick. And she heard from her mother that she had commended her to Master Vincent. And that after the vow, she recovered her health. But she was not present at the vow, nor at the recovery of health, although afterward she saw [the daughter] totally cured.

About the crowds of people, the devotion, the common reputation, and *fama*, she testified as did the preceding witnesses. She asserts that she testified truthfully, not out of fear or favor of anyone, and not forced in any way.

(Witness 213.) Yvo an Daguat, of the parish of Noyal Muzuillac, age forty-five, as he says and as his appearance confirms. The witness, having been given notice, summoned, brought forth, received, put under oath, questioned, and diligently examined concerning the miracles of the aforesaid Master Vincent Ferrer, testified under oath that last August, Pcrrina, his daughter, then aged nine, had two buboes, namely one in each side of her groin, and she was so sick from these that the girl went for five days without talking, seeing, eating, and drinking. And then there appeared in her the deadly black signs,[17] and everyone who saw her judged that she would soon die from that illness. And on account of this there were made for her a cross and a wooden coffin, and a lighted wax candle was put in her hands. And then the witness, seeing his daughter in such a state, around the hour of Vespers,[18] commended his daughter to Master Vincent, promising to offer Master Vincent ten pennies in local money and to bring the coffin to Master Vincent's tomb for the daughter if she should escape death. And after the vow was made, around midnight the daughter began to cry, and the next day, around the hour of Vespers, she began to speak and to get better. And the buboes began to suppurate, and afterward, when they perforated, they emitted putrid humors. And finally she recovered her health entirely. And the witness fulfilled his vow. And he believes that his daughter thus got better miraculously through the merits of Master Vincent and was not forced [to testify] in any way.

(Witness 222.) Perrotus Mauret, of the parish Saint Patern in Vannes, aged around thirty-five years, as he says and as his appearance confirms. The witness, having been given notice, summoned, brought forth, received, put under oath, questioned, and diligently examined concerning the miracles of the aforesaid Master Vincent Ferrer, testified under oath that around the last feast of St. Michael [September 29], a certain daughter of the present witness, named Perrina, then one year old, was so ill that she departed from this world and was dead for two parts of an hour. And then, greatly grieving for his daughter thus dead, the witness humbly and devoutly commended her to Master Vincent, promising that if she were resuscitated he would bring her to the tomb in her cradle and there offer a candle of the length of his daughter. When the vow was made, thence the said daughter began to open her eyes and her mouth and then to cry, and a little after nursed from her mother. The next day the same witness took the daughter to the tomb and there left the aforementioned candle. And within two days thereafter she totally recovered her health.

Asked how he knew that she was dead, he replied that he knew this because he saw her have all the signs that appear in dying men: she closed her mouth, turned her eyes up, and emitted sputum from her mouth, and was cold and stiff and emitted no breath.

Next, asked how he knew that the signs he specified above are the signs of death, he responded that he knew this because he had been present at the deaths of many dying men and women who, after they gave up the ghost, had those signs. And as soon as the said signs of death appeared in them, they were considered dead.

Next, asked how he knew that these signs were in his daughter, he responded that he saw, touched, and palpated her, and found her thus, and therefore assumed her to be dead. And she was judged [to be dead] by her mother and by all those who saw her. And he believes most firmly that she was thus healed and resuscitated miraculously by the merits of Master Vincent.

And asked, he says that he testified to these things for the love of truth and not because of a promise of reward, fear, favor for the cathedral of Vannes or duchy of Brittany, or in any other way corrupted by forceful persuasion.

(Witness 247.) Guillermus de Liquillic, a licentiate in laws from the parish of Lehonio, near Dinan, in the diocese of Saint Malo, age forty-five years or thereabouts, as he asserts and as his appearance confirms. The witness, having been given notice, summoned, brought forth, received, put under oath, questioned, and diligently examined concerning the life, manners, and miracles worked by Master Vincent Ferrer and the circumstances [under which they were worked], testified under oath that, in the year of Our Lord 1418, he saw the aforesaid Master Vincent celebrating Mass and preaching several times in a certain public space called, in the vernacular, the field of Dinan, and on this matter he testified as did the preceding witness. And further he testified that he had heard from Johannes de Liquillic, his father—who had been named "Misor" or administrator of the city of Dinan by the body of the burghers and inhabitants and thus was in charge of getting foodstuffs necessary to nourish Master Vincent during the time in which he was preaching in Dinan—that the same Master Vincent every day ate fish and no meat, and ate only once a day.

Asked about miracles, he testified that he had also heard from his father that during the time in which the aforementioned Master Vincent was in Dinan—just as was said before—when the same Johannes, the witness's father, had provided two candles that it had been the custom to burn in front of the same Master Vincent when he celebrated Mass, after Master Vincent had left the said city, [the father] brought said candles or the residual wax left from them to his house in that town, and Johannes's wife, the mother of the present witness, put them in a certain chest next to their bed. And afterward one time, a little before the feast of the Purification of the Blessed Virgin Mary [February 2],[19] while Master Vincent was still alive, said wife with all diligence sought for those candles in that chest to convert them into blessed wax candles for the aforesaid feast of the Purification [of the Blessed Virgin], as is the custom, and was not able to find them. At length, after the passage of time, the same Johannes one night, waking from sleep, saw two lit candles on the said chest, and, having seen these, the same Johannes woke up his aforementioned wife, who also saw those candles after she was awakened, just as Johannes did. And afterward, said Johannes heard it commonly said that the aforesaid Master Vincent had gone the way of all flesh on the day and hour—or thereabout—in which the said Johannes had seen the candles; and from this, the same Johannes, recalling all the above, believed that the aforesaid candles had been lit miraculously in honor of the aforesaid Master Vincent, and otherwise he might know nothing.

Further, he testified that when the aforesaid Master Vincent was in the above mentioned town, and a certain Guillermus de Liquillic, the brother of the witness, then aged ten, suffered from a certain pain or infirmity in one side, the aforementioned father of the said Guillermus presented Guillermus to Master Vincent, who was then at the Dominican convent in Dinan, and showed him Guillermus's infirmity. Having heard [about the pain] and on the father's supplication, Master Vincent touched said Guillermus and signed him with the sign of the holy cross. And then said Guillermus began to convalesce and never felt any pain from this infirmity any more.

Asked how he knew this, he testified that he saw the previously related incidents and heard and believed that Guillermus had recovered his health miraculously through the merits of said Master Vincent. And he said that he testified truthfully, not compelled out of fear, the promise of a gift, or favor or honor for Vannes, or at the instigation of others.

Notes

1. Carnival refers to the period of time before Lent (the forty days prior to Easter). Carnival (from the root *carnes*, meat) was a time of feasting prior to the deprivations of the Lenten season.

2. Vincent entered the city of Vannes on March 5, 1418.

3. L'Hermine was a ducal castle in Vannes.

4. The eastern half of the duchy was French speaking, and the western half spoke Breton.

5. "Vindicate me, O God," Psalm 43 (42 in the Vulgate), was recited at the Introit of Mass on the First Sunday of the Passion, that is, the Sunday before Palm Sunday. Vincent died April 5, 1419.

6. A league was about 1.4 miles.

7. *Fama* literally means the talk of the multitude, what everybody is saying. *Fama sanctitatis*, or a public reputation for sanctity, was one of the requirements for canonization, and the panel in Brittany apparently was careful to elicit testimony about Vincent's *fama*.

8. A sudary was a piece of cloth wrapped around a dead person's head.

9. This sentence includes several confusing terms. The term *domicella* can refer to a young noble woman or maid of honor; I take it in this testimony to refer to a woman of minor nobility, the female equivalent of *domicellus* (in the sense of a nobleman who is not a knight; a squire). The verb *vovit* literally means "s/he vows." Most witnesses refer to their invocations of the saint (which usually include a promise of a pilgrimage or counter-gift) as vows (*vota*). The "pardon" was literally a sale of indulgences. Pardons, or days of pilgrimage on which there is a remission of sins, are still common in Brittany.

10. Le Vesque may be thinking of the martyrdom of St. Paul, on the vigil of whose feast day the miracle occurred. Paul was martyred by beheading and, according to legend, his disembodied head began to intone the name "Jesus Christ" upon his beheading. See Smoller, "Miracle, Memory, and Meaning."

11. As the following deposition of Oliverius Bourric, the priest, makes clear, this was a point of contention. Katherina Guernezve and several other women contended that the priest had been absent at the moment of the vow to Vincent Ferrer, which they said Katherina initiated. The priest, backed up by another male witness, insisted that he alone had made the vow; see Smoller, "Miracle, Memory, and Meaning," pages 443–54.

12. Apparently the son had no pulse.

13. The witness refers to the visible effects of the plague having progressed to septicemia. Disseminated intravascular coagulation causing diffuse hemorrhage is a well-known complication of gram-negative septicemia.

14. That is, around daybreak.

15. The phrase *perdidit loquelam* literally means "he lost his powers of speech," but here it is used probably to indicate a loss of consciousness.

16. It is interesting to compare Oliva de Coatsal's version of this story with the testimony of a witness at the inquest held in Naples (a man identified only as a herald of arms from Valencia, witness number 18): ". . . this witness heard it said in the city of Vannes in which the body of the Blessed Vincent lies, that there was a certain man who had a demented wife who desired to undertake brutal deeds [reading *brutalia* for *butalia*]. He commanded his wife that at lunch time she should prepare him lunch for when he should return to the house. The woman, who had a fourteen-month-old son by her husband, took up a sword, demented, and killed her son, dividing him through the middle. And she took up a quarter part of the son's body (from the upper part) and put it in a pot. When the husband came in for lunch, she presented him with the said part of the son, boiled with broth and saffron, in which there appeared a hand and a certain part of the body of the boy. [The husband], on seeing this, was stupefied and said to his wife, with tears and great sorrow: 'What did you do?' She replied, 'This is the quarter part of your son and mine; eat.' [The husband], at once rising from the table with tears, wailing, and lamentation, took up the quarter part of his dead son and went to the cathedral in which is the body of Blessed Vincent, placing the parts—one cooked and the other cut-up parts—on top of the body of Blessed Vincent. And he stood there until nightfall, with weeping and lamentation. And given leave to go by those presiding in the cathedral, he went back to his house, and there he found his son playing under the bed in the manner of boys, still with that quarter part of his body tinted with saffron, just as it had been cooked. The father, seeing such a great miracle, at that instant offered his son to the aforementioned cathedral to assist in serving the said Blessed Vincent. And six days after said miracle, the witness himself saw said boy alive and well, still retaining said sign [i.e., the saffron color] and all the aforesaid. And [he said] that these matters were and are still widely publicly known in said city of Vannes and other places.—Asked about the time, he said that it was at the time of the Jubilee in Compostela." Valencia, Biblioteca Universitaria, MSS, "Proceso de la canonizacion de San Vicente Ferrer, 9 del junio 1590", fol. 256r-256v; see Fages, *Procès*, page 442.

17. That is, the marks witnesses call *pinae*, a sign that the plague had progressed to septicemia.

18. That is, at sundown.

19. This feast was also known as Candlemas. On Candlemas it was customary for every parishioner to join in procession, carrying a blessed candle which was then offered to the priest. The candles were often then burned before the image of the Virgin in the church.

CHAPTER 36
THE MISSION OF JOAN OF ARC
Edited and translated by Nadia Margolis

INTRODUCTION

Joan of Arc stands out in hagiography by doing more than experiencing visions and hearing voices: she made her visions a reality and thereby affected the course of her country's history, both before and after her martyrdom. Her persona spectacularly combines the attributes of Christian soldier, patriotic Amazon and virginal visionary. Few saints continue to spark political and personal passions as she has, whether in France or other countries, even to this day. Passages from her letters, trial testimony, and related documents have been selected, translated, and chronologically rearranged here to provide as complete a picture as possible of her life and deeds as a saint, within a chapter's length. Because her story was often so unbelievable even to her contemporaries, her judges returned repeatedly to certain problematical points throughout the duration of her trial, as is evident from the varied dating of the different passages grouped under similar topics.

She was born in 1412 in the pastoral village of Domremy, in the Lorraine-Champagne region, near the German border. Other than their names, not much else is known about Joan's family, although it is significant that Joan's father had once dreamed that his daughter would leave home to join soldiers. We surmise that her mother, Isabelle, was a woman of strong character, judging by her decades of effort to restore her daughter's name after Joan's death. Despite her father's name, Jacques d'Arc, Joan would call herself "*Jeanne la Pucelle*" (Joan the Maid)—never *Jeanne d'Arc*, a modern appellation. They were a pious family of reasonably well-off peasants.

Joan grew up learning from Isabelle how to sew, manage a household, and help tend cattle. We learn that her mother was also her primary spiritual teacher who gave her the usual rudimentary religious education to which women of her class were entitled. Joan therefore probably could neither read nor write, except to sign her name. She knew her Pater noster and other basic prayers by heart and went to Mass regularly. Local festivals of spring renewal and fall harvest, uniting both lord and peasant around special fountains, trees, and an oak forest—all vestiges of pre-Christian folklore—equally influenced her spiritual development.

Such well-entrenched, nonliterate religious practices helped preserve these people's simple faith from the top-level ravages of the Great Schism (1370–

1417) dividing the papacy between Avignon and Rome. Joan would have been five years of age when the Council of Constance returned the reintegrated papacy to Rome, under Pope Martin V. She would later suffer repercussions from this at her trial.

On the secular side, the people of Joan's province were fervently patriotic and loyal to the dauphin Charles, the future Charles VII. Closer to German domains than Paris geographically, they were all the more eager to maintain their French identity, while out of touch with Parisian political corruption and civil strife. Joan's compatriots were therefore more immune than other sections of France to efforts to dethrone the dauphin. Charles's claim as rightful heir to the throne was threatened after a series of developments comprising the Hundred Years' War (1337-1453): most immediately the miraculous (for Henry V) English defeat of the French at Agincourt in 1415 and the ensuing Treaty of Troyes in 1420, which named Henry king of France as well as England. Pro-English propagandists also sought to disinherit Charles on the grounds of his mother's marital infidelity. By the time Joan was formulating her mission in 1428, civil war had been raging for a decade, with marauding Burgundians even looting pro-Armagnac Domremy. Charles had retreated to Chinon, on the opposite side of the country from Joan.

Nevertheless, these events would manifest themselves in Joan's visions and mission as set down by her voices for the rest of her life. She also would gain popular acceptance thanks to various political prophecies circulating at this time, of which she became aware early in her mission but professed not to believe in her testimony.

The three saints whose voices guided her during her mission were among the most popular and frequently celebrated in fifteenth-century France. In 1425 she first heard, then saw, St. Michael the Archangel: protective warrior saint of France and especially of the Valois line, the French royal family. Michael was depicted either slaying dragons or carrying scales with which to appraise good and bad souls. Soon thereafter Joan experienced similar interaction with St. Margaret of Antioch and St. Catherine of Alexandria. If Michael acted as a patriotic saint for her, corresponding to Joan's youthful visions of vengeance against her country's enemies, the two women held even more profound significance by their militant virginity and associated attributes. Margaret, whose statue graced the village church at Domremy, fiercely guarded her purity and excelled at verbal combat with her suitor, who finally beheaded her. Catherine displayed similar skills on a larger scale as she defended her fellow Christians against Maxentius, the Roman emperor, and successfully debated fifty of his most skilled philosophers. For this she risked mutilating torture by a spiked wheel. When an angel came and destroyed the wheel, Catherine was decapitated, from which wound milk flowed instead of blood. Together with such primally female characteristics, both women saints possess certain "manly" dimensions aside from their debating skills, bravery, and steadfastness. Margaret, in some versions of her legend, engaged in what we now call "cross-dressing": she so guarded her virginity as part of her sacred union with God that to thwart marriage plans she cut off her hair and disguised herself as a monk. While Joan's wearing of men's clothing is one of her key features, it is less well known that she also broke an engagement arranged for her by her parents, for which she was sued. Yet the two women made an even greater impact through their deaths as Christian martyrs, an essential aspect of their saintliness not lost on the sixteen-year-old Joan as she set out on her mission.

Her fulfillment of this mission parallels biblical and heroic epics in its narration of signs requested, then given, then obeyed, disobeyed, or misread between mortals and God. These signs prove useful when dealing with unenlightened or evil rulers, as in any saint's life, who reject or torment the heroine along the way, and who often repent or are punished after her death.

In Joan's case, in 1428, when she first approached the local official, Captain Baudricourt, he rebuffed and insulted her. Eventually, however, especially when she gave a sign of her prophetic powers by predicting the dauphin's defeat at the Battle of Rouvroy, she gained Baudricourt's support. He even helped outfit her for war and provided an escort to Chinon, where she traveled to gain an audience with the dauphin. She impressed Charles straightaway by recognizing him even when he had disguised himself at their first meeting. She then persuaded him more by revealing what is known as "the secret" or "sign." What form it took has been strenuously debated: was it a prayer, mark, or pronouncement? More important was its message that he was the rightful king of France and that she had been sent by God to lift the siege at Orléans and have him crowned at Reims. Elated but circumspect, Charles then commanded his theologians, including Jean Gerson, chancellor of the University of Paris, to examine her at Poitiers. These learned men also asked for a sign—a biblical similarity evident to them, as the Poitiers record shows. Joan appears to have given one, since they approved her mission, citing such Old Testament heroines as Judith, Esther, and Deborah and classical Roman ones like Camilla.

Royal matrons also verified her virginity, an essential facet of her identity as Joan the Maid, *La Pucelle*. Joan's virginal presence would counteract English propaganda vilifying the circumstances of Charles's birth and repurify the French blood royal, whose purity also was symbolized by the white lilies (fleur-de-lys), as she states in her letters. Joan would therefore restore the French national identity weakened by division into the pro-English Burgundians and Charles's supporters, the Armagnacs. The Anglo-Burgundians would attempt to undercut *La Pucelle*'s symbolic effectiveness by labeling her "harlot of the Armagnacs."

Charles consequently allowed her to ride with his army, although she never held true rank. She nonetheless acquired her own banner, depicting her favorite symbols: the lilies of France, Christ, and the world supported by two angels, inscribed with the words *Jhesus Maria* ("Jesus Mary"); and her own special sword, mysteriously recovered from the abbey of Saint Catherine at Fierbois.

Another arm she wielded to great effect was the epistolary one, even though she was mostly illiterate. She dictated many letters to towns she and her men were about to enter, often beginning "Jesus Mary" and warning the townspeople to support the dauphin or suffer destruction. She even wrote, as have been translated here, rather unabashed letters directly to the English and the duke of Burgundy. One wonders how such powerful men must have reacted before the demands of an unknown peasant girl claiming to lead an army enabled by God to defeat them.

But the irrefutable sign or proof of Joan's authenticity was the French army's miraculous defeat, under her "command," of the English at Orléans on May 8, 1429, thus lifting the long, demoralizing siege. Having foretold her mission to last "one year, scarcely more," she went on to other victories, and managed to have the dauphin properly anointed at Reims on July 17, 1429.

She then seemed to extend her goals to expelling the English, and thus led more attacks throughout northern France and even Paris, though unsuccessfully. Despite additional victories, her fortunes definitely waned after the Reims coronation. She was finally captured at Compiègne in May 1430, a year after Orléans, by one of John of Luxemburg's men. The duke of Luxemburg sold her for a high price to the Anglo-Burgundians, who then delivered her to the Inquisition and the Church at Rouen after three months' exhausting journey from prison to prison. We note that she was too dangerous a figure, because of her visionary status, to be tried simply as a military prisoner.

Her prison itinerary and trial (January-May 1431) constituted a horrible ordeal for her, as befits a true martyr. The arduous treks to some fourteen prisons around northern France, from Compiègne to Rouen, bring to mind Christ's stations of the cross, while she, like Catherine, was threatened with a torture wheel to make her recant. Yet it is thanks to her testimony and the recollections of witnesses at both the condemnation trial and later rehabilitation (1450-56) that we have her story preserved. For in a sense both damage-control procedures—the first to erase her, the second to exonerate the institutions having allowed such injustice to happen—only heightened her glory and contributed to her eventual canonization. The judges at Rouen, the most potent legal, ecclesiastical, and political minds of her time, ended up cast as Maxentius and his philosophers for her to defeat in the long run.

The conduct of the condemnation trial, extolled by chief magistrate Pierre Cauchon as a *beau procès* ("fair process / trial") and which modern scholars now assess as a good trial conducted in bad faith, strikes us as questionable by today's standards. Joan had no defense counsel. Much of the testimony is related only via paraphrase and indirect speech. The six-month process was conducted in French, then, about four years after Joan's death, the pro-English court notaries translated these records into the more official language of Latin. These notaries, under orders from Cauchon, also tampered with the testimony to tarnish Joan's image. Five copies were made of this Latin record and sent to Pope Eugenius IV, King Henry VI of England, chief judge Cauchon, vice-inquisitor Lemaistre, and the notary Manchon who helped make the copies. The only surviving original record in French was the so-called trial "minute" or summary—now called the d'Urfé fragment. This was copied into a longer, somewhat later, French record, also incomplete, now called the Orléans manuscript. Thus, along with her letters, the Orléans manuscript affords us the closest semblance we have of the real trial proceedings and Joan's own words, though her personality shows through even in the official Latin version.

The Rouen judges repeatedly questioned her on those aspects that had perturbed the Poitiers examiners—the origin of her voices and her male clothing—but now more viciously. Her visions and voices obsessed her judges, all Church officials, because such direct contact with the divine undercut the authority of the Church Militant, meaning the Church on earth. Joan instead was bypassing these clerics and communing with the Church Triumphant—or Church in Heaven. This particularly irritated her judges, who were also affiliated with the University of Paris, because the Council of Constance, by removing the papacy from France and returning it to Rome, cost the Parisian clerics much prestige as supreme theologians. Moreover, Joan did not help matters by declaring her preference for the Roman pope, instead of the Avignon pope, during her trial. They therefore not only labeled her a witch and heretic, but also an "apostate" (one who has abandoned Christianity) and "schismatic"—rather ironic for these pro-Avignon-papacy clerics. To make these accusations stand they tried to entrap her into describing her visions of these saints, only to prove them false by sophisticated doctrinal argument.

Her clothing generated another theological problem for her judges. They branded her wearing of male attire "unnatural"; another form of her defiance of the Church's teachings. Joan countered by asserting that, aside from the practical benefits of such attire for military life and its desexualizing advantage in preserving her virtue, her masculine clothing denoted obedience: not to the clerics but to her voices and thus to God. Such mystically symbolic accessories as her banner, imprinted with *Jhesus Maria*, and sword of Catherine, engraved with five crosses, were viewed by these judges as her tools for blasphemy.

As for secular politics, although these judges and notaries were solidly French by birth, the Anglo-Burgundians controlled them. These pro-English judges thought that if they could prove Joan, savior of France and of Charles's claim to the throne, to have been guided by satanic voices instead of angelic ones, they could thereby discredit Charles's legitimacy as king by divine right. They thought they had scored a clear victory during her brief "abjuration"—the high point of the trial—when, on May 24, exhausted from months of harrowing interrogation, sick and frightened by threats of torture, advised to save herself by the more sympathetic priests, Joan appeared in a dress to sign a form stating that she disowned her voices. Yet she quickly recovered and negated that recantation by reaffirming her belief in her voices and resuming male attire. Although she was surrendering her life she was not renouncing her faith.

That Charles VII did nothing to help Joan has branded him one of history's ingrates. This image came to overshadow the achievements of his otherwise laudable reign (1422-61) in the popular memory. Encouraged by his ambitious courtiers, Charles's inaction on her behalf has been ascribed to insufficient funds to raise an army or ransom, his jealousy of Joan's popularity among his subjects, and his passive but calculating realization that her unorthodox presence and spiritual claims, after a certain point, had made her a political liability.

She was thus burned at the stake at Rouen on May 30, 1431. It was only after the English had been virtually expelled from France that Charles ordered, in conjunction with Pope Calixtus III, the revision of her condemnation (1450-56). Although it yielded some memorable testimony revealing her saintly allure, this so-called rehabilitation sought to whitewash Charles's regime rather than actually to clear Joan's name and resolve the religious issues surrounding her case.

Because of this underlying malaise, even though Joan had been a national saint in the popular mind since her death, efforts toward her canonization did not seriously begin until the mid-nineteenth century, during a wave of intense patriotic feeling continuing through World War I, in whose wake soldiers reported heartening visions of her in the trenches. Various miracles were reported, in addition to those she performed during her lifetime. She was finally canonized on May 16, 1920 by order of Pope Benedict XV. As Sackville-West declares in the last sentence of her biography, "The real miracle was the whole career, not a few isolated incidents."

Sources and Further Readings

Joan's trial testimony, the primary source of her biography, has been extracted, rearranged, and translated from the Latin and Middle-French original texts of Joan's trial as edited, annotated, and translated into modern French by Pierre Tisset and Yvonne Lanhers, *Procès de condamnation de Jeanne d'Arc*, 3 vols., Société de l'Histoire de France (Paris, 1960-71). Important additional information from witnesses comes from her posthumous "rehabilitation" trial of 1450-56, especially in Volumes 3 and 4 of Pierre Duparc, *Procès en nullité de la condamnation de Jeanne d'Arc*, 5 vols., Société de l'Histoire de France (Paris, 1977-89). Both Tisset-Lanhers and Duparc supersede two highly popular and influential earlier editions: Jules Quicherat, *Procès de condamnation et de réhabilitation de Jeanne d'Arc, dite La Pucelle*, 5 vols. (Paris, 1841-49) and Pierre Champion, *Procès de condamnation of Jeanne d'Arc*, 2 vols. (Paris, 1920-21). The latter is an informatively annotated update of Quicherat, of which Champion only completed parts concerning the condemnation trial. My translation of the Poitiers conclusions is based on Jules Quicherat's text of the Middle French original in his Volume 3, pages 391-92. Volumes 4 and 5 of Quicherat, containing literary and historical excerpts culled from almost all known fifteenth-century European sources, have yet to be replaced. This is part of an ongoing project at the Centre Jeanne d'Arc in Orléans. Tisset-Lanhers and Duparc also incorporated additional trial materials, notably what is called the Orléans manuscript—the most complete surviving fragment of the original French record—plus other documents unknown to or underestimated by Quicherat and Champion. Because the Orléans text is closer to the actual trial, whenever a disparity has arisen between it and the Latin text, I have always chosen the French text as the basis for this translation. In some striking instances, however, I have indicated modifications to the French record by the later Latin one, to enable the reader to see the differences possibly inspired by the pro-English sympathies of the notaries as they Latinized the legal record. Previous English translations have not done this.

English readers of Joan's condemnation trial should welcome the appearance, in the "Visionary Women" series, of *The Trial of Joan of Arc*, ed. Marina Warner (Evesham, 1997). This is basically a reprint of the Scott translation (see below) with an introduction by Marina Warner. Prior to Scott's work, and even since, the classic translation has been by W.P. Barrett, *The Trial of Jeanne d'Arc* (New York, 1932), based on Champion's text. For the Orléans manuscript, underestimated by Champion, see the translation and lucid analysis of the entire authenticity puzzle by W.S. Scott, *The Trial of Joan of Arc* (London, 1956). For a translation of extracts from the rehabilitation process, see Régine Pernoud, *The Retrial of Joan of Arc*, trans. J.M. Cohen (New York, 1955). To my knowledge, there exists no previous complete English version of the Poitiers conclusions.

Joan's letters—partially published in Quicherat's volumes and the Tisset-Lanhers update, with more by Doncoeur (1960) and others—were translated into English in part by Barrett in his translation of the trial, and in their entirety, with commentary, by Claire Quintal and Daniel Rankin (Pittsburgh, 1969). I have based my translation on the French texts of the letters provided in Régine Pernoud and Marie-Véronique Clin, *Jeanne d'Arc* (Paris, 1986), pp. 377-90. Records of deliberations concerning her beatification and canonization are contained in *Acta Apostolicae Sedis*, vol. 1 (Vatican City, 1909), especially pp. 167-69 (translated here) and pp. 390-94. For a revealing study of her canonization process, see H. Ansgar Kelly, "Joan of Arc's Last Trial," in *Fresh Verdicts on Joan of Arc*, eds. Bonnie Wheeler and Charles Wood (New York, 1996), pp. 205-36.

Astoundingly enough, it is safe to estimate that Joan, whose aura among authors is second perhaps only to that of Jesus, has inspired some fifteen thousand literary, historical, musical, graphic and cinematographic works by writers from around the world, a substantial sampling of which appears in Nadia Margolis, *Joan of Arc in History, Literature and Film: A Select, Annotated Bibliography* (New York, 1990). The most complete information center for these and other aspects of the heroine is housed at the Centre Jeanne d'Arc at Orléans. Collections at the Boston Public Library (Cardinal Wright Collection), Harvard University (Widener Library) and Columbia University (Acton Griscom Collection) are indispensable for research in areas beyond the Orléans center's holdings.

For Joan as autobiographer, Willard Trask's artful yet faithful reconstruction and translation is based on original materials: *Joan of Arc: A Self-Portrait* (New York, 1936). Among several good modern biographies of Joan in English, the most readable, informative and sensible remains that by Victoria Sackville-West, *Joan of Arc* (London, 1936; most recent reprint Norwalk, CT, 1990) though many histories continue to appear from divergent, often deeply passionate, points of view. Richly illustrated surveys of her changing cultural-historical image are those by Marina Warner, *Joan of Arc: The Image of Female Heroism* (New York, 1981), and Régine Pernoud and Marie-Véronique Clin, *Joan of Arc*, trans. Jeremy Adams (New York, 1996). New interpretations of various aspects of Joan can be found in: *Fresh Verdicts on Joan of Arc*, eds. Bonnie Wheeler and Charles Wood (New York, 1996); Susan Crane, "Clothing and Gender Definition: Joan of Arc," *Journal of Medieval and Early Modern Studies* 26 (1996): 297-320; and Charles Wood, *Joan of Arc and Richard III: Sex, Saints and Government in the Middle Ages* (Oxford, 1988), Chapter 7. The best web page, by the St. Joan of Arc Center in Albuquerque, New Mexico, linking with a growing variety of other Joan sources, is at: http://www.stjoan-center.com.

The Mission of Joan of Arc

JOAN'S ACCOUNT OF HER EARLY LIFE
[*From trial testimony of the first public session, Wednesday, February 21, 1431*]

On that very day, the said Joan was asked her name and surname. She responded that, in the place where she was born, they called her Jeannette, and in France, Joan; and of her surname she knew nothing.[1]

Asked her birthplace: she answered that she was born in the village of Domremy which is the same as the village of Greux, and that the principal church is in Greux.

Asked the name of her father and mother: she answered that her father was named Jacques d'Arc and her mother Isabelle.

Asked where she was baptized, she answered that she was baptized in the church of Domremy.

Asked who were her godfathers and godmothers, who baptized her . . .[2]

Asked how old she was, she answered that she thought she was nineteen or so. And she went on to say that her mother taught her the Pater noster [the Our Father], the Ave Maria [Hail Mary] and the Credo, and that no one but her said mother taught her the Creed . . .[3]

[*From trial testimony of Thursday, February 22*]

Asked at what age she left her father's house, she said she could not state her age officially.

Asked if she knew any trade or craft, she answered yes: that her mother had taught her to sew and that she believed that no woman in all Rouen had anything more to teach her about sewing.

She went on to say that she had left her father's house for fear of the Burgundians, and that she went to Neufchâteau, in Lorraine, to the house of a woman known as *La Rousse* [the Redhead], where she stayed for about two weeks. In that house she [Joan] did household tasks but did not go to the fields to tend lambs and other animals.[4]

Asked whether she went to confession every year, she said yes, to her own priest. And when he was too busy or unavailable, she confessed her sins to another priest, with the former's permission. She also said she went to confession two or three times before mendicant friars,[5] and that she received the Eucharist every year at Easter.

Asked if she received the Eucharist at feasts other than at Easter, she replied, "Next question."[6]

[*From trial testimony of Saturday, February 24*]

Interrogated concerning a tree in her neighborhood, she answered that quite close to Domremy there is a tree called the Ladies' Tree; and that others called it the Fairy Tree; and nearby there is a fountain; and she had heard that people sick with the fever went to drink from it as a cure, and that she had even seen them in search of this fountain. But she did not know whether or not they recovered.

She also said she had heard tell that sick people, when they could get up, went to the tree to stroll about; and she said it is a large tree, called a beech, from which comes the "may sprig" [*le beau mai*], and that it belonged to Lord Pierre de Bourlément.[7]

She said that she had gone walking there [by the tree] several times with other young girls in the summer and used to make wreaths for Our Lady of Domremy.

She said that she had heard old people, not of her family, say that fairies frequented the tree; and had heard her godmother, one Joan, wife of the mayor of Domremy, say she had seen them there. But she [Joan] did not know if this were true.

She said as far as she knew, she had never seen a fairy by the tree nor elsewhere. She also said that she had seen young girls place garlands on the tree's branches, and that sometimes she too had put them there . . .

She said that ever since she learned she had to come into France, she played very little, as seldom as she could. And she did not know whether, since reaching the age of reason, she had danced by the tree. But sometimes she may have danced around there with children; or rather that she had done more singing than dancing.

She said that indeed there was a forest there called the "Oak Forest" [*Bois Chesnu*], that one could see from her father's house; and that it was not farther than about three miles away; but that she did not know nor did she hear that fairies appeared there.

Joan's First Voices and Visions
[*From trial testimony of Saturday, February 24*]

She said that had heard tell from her brother that they were saying in our region that she had experienced her revelations at the Fairy Tree. But she had not done so, and told her brother to the contrary. And she went on to say, when she came before the king, several people inquired whether in her country there was a stretch of forest called the Oak Forest; for there were prophecies saying that from out of the forest should come a maiden who would work miracles; but that she did not put any faith in this.[8]

[*From trial testimony of Thursday, February 22*]

She then said that, since the age of thirteen, she had been having revelations from Our Lord through a voice that taught her how to behave. And that the first time she was very afraid. And she said that the said voice came at noon, in summertime, when she was in her father's garden during a fast day, and that the said voice came from the right, toward the church. And she said that the said voice is rarely without light, which always comes from the same direction as the said voice. [**Translator's note:** Latin record adds here: And when Joan herself came to France she heard that voice often. Asked how she could see the light of which she spoke, since it came from the side, she answered nothing to this, but went on to other things. She said that if she were in a forest, she could clearly hear voices coming to her. She said in fact that it seemed to her a worthy voice and she believed that this voice was sent from God].

She went on to say that after hearing the said voice three times, she knew it was the voice of an angel. She also said that this voice had always taken good care of her.

Asked what advice this voice had given her for the salvation of her soul, she answered that it taught her how to conduct herself and that she should go to church often. And then the voice told her it was necessary that she go into France . . . and told her two or three times a week that she must leave to go into France. And that her father knew nothing of her departure.

With this, it said to her that she must hasten to go and that she should lift the siege at Orléans; and that she should go to Robert de Baudricourt, captain of Vaucouleurs,[9] and that he would provide her with men to accompany her.[10]

To which she responded that she was nothing but a poor girl who knew neither how to ride a horse nor how to lead an army.

And after her words with this voice, she went off to the house of an uncle where she remained for a week. And that afterward her uncle led her to the said Robert de Baudricourt, whom she recognized even though she had never met him before. And this she knew because the voice had told her who he was.

She went on to say that the said Baudricourt refused her twice. Then on the third occasion, he welcomed her and gave her men to escort her into France, just as the voice had told her . . .

She then said that when she left Vaucouleurs, she assumed male clothing, and also a sword Baudricourt had given her, but no other armor or weapons. And she said she was accompanied by a knight and four other men; and that on that day they took lodging in the town of Saint-Urbain, where she slept in the abbey.[11]

She also said that on the way to Chinon, she passed through Auxerre where she heard Mass in the great church; and that she often had her voices with her . . .

She said she never asked anything of the voice except at the end, for the salvation of her soul.

[*From trial testimony of Saturday, February 24*]

Questioned as to when she last heard her voice,

She answered that she had heard it yesterday and today.

Asked at what time she had heard it,

She said that she had heard it three times: once in the morning, once at the hour of Vespers, and another at the hour of the Hail Mary;[12] and sometimes more often than this.

Asked what she was doing yesterday when she heard this voice,

She answered that she was sleeping and that the said voice woke her.

Asked whether the said voice woke her by its sound or by touching her on the arm or elsewhere,

She answered that the voice woke her without touching her.

Asked whether the voice were still in her room,

She responded that to her knowledge, no; but that it was in the castle ...

Asked what the voice told her, once awake,

She replied that it told her to seek advice from Our Lord.

Asked if it said any more to her than what she asked of it,

She answered ... "You say that you are my judge; take care what you do with me; for in truth I have been sent by God and you are putting yourself in grave danger" ...

Questioned as to whether the voice told her in her youth to hate the Burgundians, she responded that ever since she heard that the voices were for the king of France, she has not liked the Burgundians.

[*From trial testimony of Tuesday, February 27*]

Questioned as to whether she fasted every day of this Lenten season, she answered, "Does this pertain to your trial?"

To which Beaupère [the interrogator] said, "Yes, it really is relevant to the trial."

She responded, "Yes, truly, I have been fasting every day."

Asked if, since Saturday [February 24] she had heard her voice?

She replied, "Yes, in fact quite often."

Asked if she had heard it in this chamber since Saturday,

She replied, "This has nothing to do with your trial." And afterward said yes.

Questioned as to what the voice said to her on Saturday,

She said, "I could not hear it very well; and could not understand anything I could recall for you, until I returned to my room."

Asked what it said to her when she had returned to her room,

She responded, "May you answer boldly." And she said she asked it for advice on things asked of her ...

Questioned as to whether it was the voice of an angel that spoke to her, or of a male or female saint, or directly from God,

She answered, "The voice is from Sts. Catherine or Margaret. And their heads are crowned with beautiful crowns most lavishly and preciously. And I have Our Lord's permission to tell you that. If you doubt me, then send to Poitiers or other places where I was interrogated.[13]

Asked how she knew they were those two saints and if she could tell one from the other,

She answered that she certainly knew who they were and one from the other.

Asked how she knew one from the other,

She responded that she recognized them by the greeting they gave her. She said that it was seven years ago that they first taught her how to behave. She said she also knew them by the way in which they named themselves to her.

Asked if they were dressed in the same cloth,

She answered, "Now I shall tell you nothing else." And that she was not permitted to reveal more. "And if you do not believe me, go to Poitiers."

She said, "There are revelations that belong to the king of France and not to those interrogating me."

Asked if they were the same age,

She answered, "I am not allowed to tell you."

Asked if they spoke together or one after the other,

She answered, "I am not allowed to tell you; and in any case I am always receiving advice from both of them . . ."

Questioned as to which came first,

She answered that it was St. Michael.

Asked if it were long ago,

She answered, "I don't know that I identified St. Michael's voice in itself, but rather I could tell by the great comfort it brought me."

Asked who was the first voice coming to her when she was thirteen years old,

She responded that it was St. Michael whom she saw before her eyes; and that he was not alone, but with angels from heaven. And she added that she would not have come to France were it not under orders from God.

Asked whether she saw St. Michael and the others bodily and in real form,

She answered, "I see them with the eyes of my body, just as I see you." And when they left her, she wept and wanted them to carry her away with them.

Asked in what form St. Michael appeared,

"I have not yet answered such questions of you and do not yet have any permission to do so."

Questioned as to what St. Michael said to her that first time,

She answered, "You will have no other answer."[14]

[*From trial testimony of Thursday, March 1*]

Asked if he were naked,

"Do you think that Our Lord cannot afford to clothe his angels?"

Asked whether St. Michael was carrying his scales,

She said, "I don't know . . ."

[*From trial testimony of Saturday, March 3*]

Whereupon, by order of my lord the bishop of Beauvais, the said master Jean Beaupère interrogated the said Joan by reciting to her that she had said that St. Michael had wings, and with this, that she had not spoken at all about the bodies or members of Sts. Catherine or Margaret,

She answered, "I have told you before what I know of this, and will answer nothing further."

She said that she had seen them so well that she knew them certainly to be saints in Paradise.

Asked if she had seen anything but their faces,

She answered, "I have told you before what I know of this, and would rather you have my head cut off. . . ."

Asked whether St. Michael and St. Gabriel[15] have natural heads,

She answered, "Yes, as far as I could see. And I believe it was they just as firmly as God exists."

Asked whether she believed that God had made their heads in the way in which she saw them,

She answered, "I saw them with my own eyes. I shall tell you no more . . ."
[*From trial testimony of Thursday, March 15*]

Asked if she had anything against the orders or wishes of her voices,

She answered that whatever she was able and knew how to do, she accomplished under her own power. And as for leaping from the tower at Beaurevoir,[16] which she did against their orders, she could not keep herself from doing this; and when they saw her dire need of them, and that she could not survive on her own, her voices saved her life and kept her from killing herself.

And she went on to say whatever else she did, in her great undertakings her voices always came to her aid; and that is the sign they are good spirits.

Asked if she had other signs that these were good spirits,

She answered, "St. Michael assures me of it, even before my voices come."

Asked how she knew it was St. Michael,

She answered, by the speech and language of angels. And she believes firmly that they were angels.

Asked how she recognized it as the language of angels,

She answered that she knew it right away; and strongly wished to believe it. And she went on to say that St. Michael, when he came to her, said that Sts. Catherine and Margaret would come to her, and that she should do what they advised her to do, and that they were ordered to lead her and counsel her in whatever she had to do; and that she should believe what they would tell her, and that it was at Our Lord's command . . .

Asked what [St. Michael] taught her,

She answered, above all he told her that she should be a good child and that God would help her; and that, among other things, she must come to the aid of the king of France. And that the largest part of what the angel taught her was in this book [of the trial record]; and the angel recounted to her the pitiful state of the kingdom . . .

JOAN'S WEARING OF MEN'S CLOTHING
[*From trial testimony of Thursday, February 22*]

Questioned as to who advised her to wear men's clothing, to this question I have found in one book that her voices had commanded her to assume male attire, and in another, I found that, no matter how many times she was interrogated on this, she never gave a reply other than "I charge no one." And I found in this book that several times she gave different answers to this question.[17]

[*From trial testimony of Saturday, February 24*]

Questioned as to whether she would like some women's clothes, she answered. "If you would give me leave to do so, provide me with a dress, and I'll take it and go away. But otherwise no. I am content with the clothes I have on, since it pleases God that I wear them."

[*From trial testimony of Saturday, March 3*]

... She answered that they [Poitiers examiners] asked her where she first assumed male attire; and that she told them it was at Vaucouleurs ...

She said that a young lady from Luxemburg and a lady from Beaurevoir offered her a woman's dress or cloth with which to make it, and asked her to wear it; and she answered she did not have permission from Our Lord and that it was not yet time to do so ...

Asked if she believed she would have been delinquent or sinned mortally by taking women's clothes,

[She replied that it was better to obey God than people, even noblewomen.

Asked whether, when God revealed to her that she must change her clothing, it was through the voice of St. Michael, St. Catherine, or St. Margaret.

She answered, "You will have no more on this."

Joan Meets with the Dauphin
[From trial testimony of Thursday, February 22]

She said she found her king at Chinon where she arrived at around noon; and stayed in an inn. After dinner she went before the king who was in the castle.

She said she went right into the room where the king was, and that she recognized him from the others because of the voice's guidance.

She said she told the king that she wanted to make war against the English.

Asked whether, when the voice pointed out the king, there was a ray of light over him, she answered, "Next question."

Asked whether she saw an angel over the king, she answered, "Spare me, next question."

She said that, before the king put her to work, she had had several apparitions and beautiful revelations.

Asked which revelations, she answered, "I cannot tell you yet, but go to the king and he'll tell you about them."

She said that the voice promised her that, soon after her arrival, the king would welcome her.

She said that those of her entourage knew well that the voice was from God, and that they saw and knew the voice, and that she knew it well.

She said the king and several others of his council heard and saw the voices coming to her, and among them was Charles, duke of Bourbon.

[From trial testimony of Thursday, March 1]

Asked what sign she gave her king to show him that she had been sent by God,

She answered, "I have always answered you that you will never pull it out of me. Go ask the king."

... Asked to whom she had promised [not to reveal the secret between her and the king],

She replied that it was either to St. Catherine or St. Margaret; and this was demonstrated to the king ...

JOAN IS ALLOWED TO EMBARK UPON HER MISSION
[*Summary of Conclusions of the Examination at Poitiers (March-April 1429)*]

This is the opinion of the doctors summoned by the king in the matter of the Maiden sent by God.

The king, given his needs and those of his realm, and in consideration of the continuous prayers by his poor people to God and all others who cherish peace and justice, must neither rebuff nor reject the Maiden, who claims herself sent by God to help him, even though these promises be only human efforts. Nor must he believe her too readily and without reflection. But in following the Holy Scriptures, we might test her in two ways: by human prudence, in inquiring about her life, her habits and intentions–as St. Paul the apostle has said, *Probate spiritus si ex Deo sint* (Test the spirits to see if they are of God) [1 Jn 4:1]; and by devout prayer, requesting a sign of some divine work or expectation, by which we might judge whether she has truly come via God's will. God also commanded Ahaz[18] to ask him for a sign, when God promised him victory by saying to him: *Pete signum a Domino* (Ask a sign of the Lord) [Is 7:10]; likewise did Gideon,[19] who asked for a sign [see Judg 6:17], and several others, etc.

The king, since the arrival of the aforementioned Maiden, has observed the two conditions cited above: that is, by examination using human prudence and also by prayer, requesting a sign from God. Concerning the first, by human prudence, he has probed details of her life, her habits and intentions, and has had her stay with him for a period of six weeks, in order to demonstrate her worth to all—be they clerks, men of the Church, devout practitioners, men at arms, women, widows and others. She has conversed with all manner of people, both publicly and secretly. In her they have found no evil; only goodness, humility, virginity, devotion, honesty, simplicity. Of her birth and life many marvels have been spoken of as true.

As for the second means of examining her, the king asked her for a sign, to which she responded that she would demonstrate it at the city of Orléans and nowhere else, for that is what God commanded of her.

The king—given the examination performed on the said Maiden, inasmuch as it was possible for him, having found no evil in her, considering her response promising to give a divine sign at Orléans, in light of her consistent and unwavering words, and her insistence on going to Orléans in order to give the sign of divine aid—should in no way prevent her from going to Orléans with her men at arms, but rather should have her escorted there honestly and hoping in God. For to doubt or abandon her without any evidence of evil would be to reject the Holy Spirit, and to abase God's help, as Gamaliel said during a council of Jews regarding the Apostles [see Acts 5:39].[20]

[*From Jean Gerson's treatises on Joan (ca. March-May 1429):* **Concerning a Certain Young Girl**[21]]

It is in harmony with the Holy Scriptures that God made use of the weak sex and of the age of innocence to offer people and kingdoms the joy of salvation.

Such a proposition is evident because, according to the Apostle's account, God chose what was weak in the world to confound all that which was strong. From there, proceeding with examples, one can read about Deborah, Esther, and Judith,[22] how they obtained salvation for God's people ... For it is thus through a humble Virgin that redemption of all mankind was born ...

[Jean Gerson's treatises on Joan (ca. March-May 1429): **On a Marvelous Victory**[23]]

The people are thrilled with delight, a pious and deep persuasion has filled them; they are transported in the praise of God to the enemies' confusion ... The Maid and her men at arms are not neglecting the limits of human prudence: they are acting according to their feelings. We cannot see that they are tempting God more than is reasonable. It is evident that the Maid is not obstinate in her own sentiments and that she is not exceeding the orders and inspirations she believes she received from God ... Similar deeds could be recalled [as precedents]: those of Deborah, of St. Catherine converting the philosophers no less miraculously ... Included in all these cases is the constant aspect of natural order[24] ... many other reasons could still be added, borrowing from sacred and secular history, recalling Camilla[25] and the Amazons.

Joan's Military Campaign: The Road to Reims and After

[From Joan's letter to the English (dictated ca. March 22, 1429, and sent from Blois in late April, 1429)][26]

Jesus Mary,[27]

King of England and you, duke of Bedford,[28] who call yourself regent of the kingdom of France; you, William Pole, earl of Suffolk; John, Lord Talbot; and you, Thomas, lord of Scales[29] –who call yourselves lieutenants of the said duke of Bedford: set things aright with the king of Heaven and render unto the Maid,[30] who has been sent here by God, the king of Heaven, the keys to all the good cities that you have pillaged and ravaged in France. The Maid [*La Pucelle*] has come on behalf of God to reclaim the blood royal. She is ready to make peace, if you are willing to settle with her by evacuating France and making restitution for whatever you have stolen. And all of you—archers, companions in arms, gentlemen. and others who are before the city of Orléans—go away, return to your country, by order of God. And if you do not do this, await news of the Maid, who will shortly pay you a visit, much to your disfavor, to inflict great damage upon you. King of England, if you do not do this, I am chief of the army[31] and am waiting to confront your men wherever they are in France; and I will make them leave, whether they wish to or not. And should they not obey, I will have them all killed. For I have been sent here by God, king of Heaven, to chase you completely out of France, body for body,[32] if necessary. Should they wish to obey me, then I shall take mercy upon them. May you have no other thought than this, since you do not hold the kingdom of France by order of God, king of Heaven, son of Mary— but rather it is Charles who shall hold it as true heir. For God, king of Heaven, so wishes it, as revealed by the Maid unto Charles, who shall soon enter Paris in good company. If you do not believe this news sent on behalf of God via the Maid, then we shall strike you down, with such fury as has never been seen in France for a thousand years, wherever we might find you, if you do not comply with us. You may be sure that the king of Heaven will send more might to the Maid than you shall ever be able to muster against her and her good men, no matter how many times you attack; at the end of which we shall see on whose side God truly sits in Heaven. You, duke of Bedford, the Maid pleads and requests of you not to destroy yourself thus. If you comply with her, you may join her there where the French will achieve the greatest exploit ever for Christianity. Give us your answer whether you wish to make peace in the city of Orléans; and if you do not, much devastation will come to remind you.

[From Christine de Pizan, **The Tale of Joan of Arc** (July 31, 1429)][33]

Stanza XXVIII
I have learned of Esther, Judith, and Deborah,[34]
Who were women of great worth,
Through whom God saved his people,
Who had been sorely oppressed,
And of other gallant women,
All Worthies, every one,[35]
Through whom God performed many miracles,
But through none more than this Maid.

Stanza XXXI
For Merlin, the Sibyl, and Bede,[36]
Foresaw her coming five hundred years ago,
Committed her to their writings,
As the remedy to France's troubles,
And made their prophecies foretell,
That she would carry a banner,
In the French wars, and they also told
All she would accomplish and how she did so.

Stanza XXXIV
Oh! What an honor for the feminine sex!
It is obvious that God loves it
That all those vile people,
Who had laid the whole kingdom to waste—
By a woman this realm is now made safe and sound,
Something more than five thousand men could not have done—
And those traitors purged forever!
Scarcely anyone would have believed it before this.

[*From Joan's Letter to the Count of Armagnac (August 22, 1429, from Compiègne)*][37]

Jesus Mary,

Count of Armagnac, my good and dear friend, Joan the Maid informs you that your message has come before me, that which you say you have sent me to find out from me which of the three popes mentioned in your message you should believe in. Of this I cannot rightly tell you at present, but later when I am in Paris or elsewhere at a more peaceful moment; for I am now too involved in making war. But when you hear that I will be in Paris, send me a message and I will let you know everything you should believe in, and that I will have had the advice of my rightful and sovereign lord, the king of all the world, as to what you should do, as well as I can. I commend you to God; may God protect you.

[*From Joan's letter to the Clergy, Burghers, and Common Folk of the City of Riom (November 9, 1429, from Moulins)*][38]

Dear and Good Friends,

You know well how the town of Saint-Pierre-le-Moûtier[39] has been taken by force, and with God's help I intend to empty the other places of those contrary to the king. But for this attack on the aforementioned town we have expended much powder, weapons, and other munitions for war, so much so that we find supplies wanting for the siege before La Charité, to which we are now marching.[40] I beg of you, for the love of your king's honor and worth, and also for that of all others on our side, please to send any powder, niter, sulphur,[41] arrows, crossbows, and other weapons at once to aid this siege. In so doing, please do not make us do without these said powders and other equipment for long, and may we not have to call you negligent or unwilling to meet our request. Dear and good friends, may Our Lord protect you. Written at Moulins the ninth day of November.

Jehanne[42] (Joan)

[*From trial testimony of Thursday, February 22*]

She said she had led a great attack on Paris. Asked whether she had led the said attack on a feast day, she answered, after being questioned several times, that she had indeed believed it was a feast day.

Asked if she thought it a good thing to launch an attack on a feast day, she answered, "Move on to the next question."[43]

Condemnation Trial (January 3–May 30, 1431)

Key figures for the prosecution: Judges: Pierre Cauchon, bishop of Beauvais (chief judge); Jean Lemaistre (vice-inquisitor, adjunct judge); Counsel: Jean de La Fontaine (Cauchon's delegate); Promotor of the Case: Jean d'Estivet (chief prosecutor);

Notaries: Guillaume Manchon, Boisguillaume, Nicolas Taquel; Prison Escort: Jean Massieu, dean of Rouen Cathedral.[44]

[*From trial testimony of Wednesday, February 21. Jean Massieu petitions for Joan to be allowed to hear Mass before the trial. The request is denied by the promotor in his own petition*]:

Having read these letters [Massieu's request], Jean d'Estivet, promotor appointed to this case by the aforesaid bishop [Pierre Cauchon], ordered and requested that the said maiden be brought in and interrogated according to law as he was empowered to do by the said bishop. And concerning the said Joan's plea to be permitted to hear Mass, the said bishop said that he had consulted several wise and distinguished personages, from which he found that, given the crimes of which she stood accused, and also because she had worn men's clothing, the aforesaid request ought to be denied and so he declared it . . .

[*First exhortation to Joan*]: [Wherefore, desiring to fulfill the function of our office to preserve and exalt the Catholic Faith,] we did first [with the kind help of Jesus Christ (whose cause this is)] charitably admonish [and require the often-mentioned Joan, then seated before us] her that to accelerate the present trial and unburden her own conscience, she should swear on the Holy Gospels to speak the whole truth to anything she should be asked [the questions put to her in matters of the faith] and not seek to use subterfuge or cunning which would divert her from truthful confession . . . [45]

[*The oath is administered to her*]: Will you swear to tell the truth about all that will be asked of you concerning the Catholic Faith and all else of which you have knowledge?

To which the said Joan answered that about her father and mother and all things she had done since she had taken the road to France,[46] she would willingly swear. But concerning the revelations God made to her, that she would never reveal nor tell them to anyone except for Charles, whom she calls her king; and that even if they were about to cut off her head, she would not reveal them; for she knew through her visions that she was to keep them secret; but that in a week she would know whether she could reveal them.

After these words, the said bishop admonished her and asked that she swear to tell the truth in matters concerning the Faith. The said Joan knelt down, put both hands on the book—namely, a missal—and swore that she would tell the truth about everything asked her, including matters of the Faith, but that, concerning the aforesaid revelations, she would tell of those to no one.[47]

On that same day, after several questions were asked of the said Joan, such as the name of her father and mother and her birthplace, and her age, the said Joan, having complained about the irons binding her legs, was told by the said bishop that because she had tried to escape from prison several times, it was ordered that she be put in irons to hold her more securely. To which the said Joan answered that she had in fact tried to escape from prison but that it was lawful for every prisoner to do so. She said furthermore that, if ever she were to escape, she could not be recaptured unless she were to falsify or break with her faith before someone; and that she had never relinquished it in the presence of anyone . . . [48]

The Mission of Joan of Arc

Asked to recite the Our Father and Hail Mary, she answered she would say them willingly, provided that Monsignor the Bishop of Beauvais, then present, would hear her confession. And no matter how often we asked her to recite the Our Father and Hail Mary, she responded that she would not say them at all if the said bishop would not hear her confession.

And then the said bishop proclaimed, "I will summon one or two notable people from this group to whom you will say your Our Father and Hail Mary." To which she replied, "I will not say them at all if those men will not hear my confession."

[*From trial testimony of Thursday, February 22. Questioned by Jean Beaupère, Lemaistre's vicar, in the latter's absence*]

He first asked her if she would tell the truth. She replied, "You may well ask me some things which I will answer truthfully, others not." She then added, "If you knew anything about me you would like me off your hands. I have done nothing except by revelation . . ."[49]

[*From trial testimony of Saturday, March 17*]

Asked to give a description of the form and type, size and clothing of St. Michael when he came to her,

She answered: "He was in the form of a truly gallant knight"; and of his uniform and other things, she will say no more.

As for angels, she has seen them with her own eyes, and she has no more to say about it.

She said she believes firmly in the sayings and deeds of St. Michael who appeared to her, just as she believes Our Lord Jesus Christ suffered death and the Passion on the Cross for us. An that what moved her to believe this was the good advice, comfort, and good teaching that St. Michael gave her.

Asked whether she would submit all his sayings and deeds, whether good or bad, to the judgment of our mother, holy Church,

She answered that, as for the Church, she loves it and would like to sustain it with all her might for our Christian Faith; and that it is not she [Joan] who should be harassed or prevented from going to church and hearing Mass. As for the good works she has accomplished since her coming, she must refer to the king of Heaven, Who sent her to Charles, son of Charles, king of France, who will be king of France.[50] "And you will see that the French will soon win a great boon that God would send them, so much so that it will shake up the entire kingdom of France." And she said she was saying this so that, when this shall all have happened, she will be remembered for what she said . . .

Asked to say whether she would submit to the Church's judgment,

She answered, "I refer to the Lord Who has sent me, to Our Lady and to all the blessed saints, male and female, in Paradise." And it is her opinion that the Lord and the Church are one, and that one should not create difficulties over this, and asked why they try to argue that they are not all one. [**Translator's note**: The judges then explain the different Church hierarchies to her, between the Church Triumphant (in Heaven) and the Church Militant (on earth), site of their jurisdiction . . .]

And for all that, questioned as to whether she would refer to the Church Militant, in light of the said explanation,

She answered that she was sent to the king of France by God, the Virgin Mary and all the saints in Paradise of the triumphant Church on high, and at their command; and it is to that Church that she submits all her good deeds and all that she has done and will do. And to answer whether she would submit to the Church Militant, she said she would have no further reply . . .

[*From trial testimony of Wednesday, May 2*]

Asked whether she would submit in the church of Poitiers, where she was examined,

She answered, "Do you think you can trap me that way and thus draw me toward you?"

In conclusion she was abundantly and once again admonished in general to submit to the Church [Militant] upon penalty of being abandoned by the Church; and that if the Church abandoned her, she would be in great danger for both body and soul and could very well endanger herself by the fires of eternal damnation, for her soul, and of worldly fires for her body, by the sentence of other judges.

She answered, "You will never do what you say against me, not without evil overtaking you, body and soul."

Abjuration (May 24, 1431)

Here follows the tenor of the schedule that the bishop of Beauvais and the other judges said was made by the said Joan and signed by her hand, which I do not believe, and it is not believable that she intended that which is here shown.[51]

I Joan, commonly called *La Pucelle*, miserable sinner, after I recognized the snare of error in which I had been held, and now that I have, by the grace of God, returned to our mother, holy Church, so that it may be clearly apparent that I have returned with good heart and good will, I confess that I have gravely sinned by pretending dishonestly to have had revelations and apparitions from God and His angels St. Catherine and St. Margaret, by deceiving others, by believing foolishly and making superstitious divinations, by blaspheming God and His saints, by trespassing against divine law, Holy Scripture, and canon law; by wearing clothing that is dissolute, deformed and an indecent affront to nature, and closely cropped hair like a man, against all modesty of the female sex; by bearing arms most presumptuously, by cruelly desiring to spill human blood [. . .] and all my words and deeds that are contrary to the Church, I do revoke; and wish to live in union with our mother, holy Church and in obedience with our Holy Father, the pope in Rome. And this I say, affirm and swear to by Almighty God and by the Holy Gospels. In witness thereof my manual sign.

[Signed]: Joan+[52]

The Mission of Joan of Arc

Sentence (May 24, 1431)

We have condemned you, and now condemn you by this definitive sentence to life imprisonment, with the bread of sorrow and the water of affliction, that you may weep for your sins, and nevermore commit them . . . [**Translator's note**: She then willingly accepted a woman's dress, and that her hair be shorn completely]

Relapse (May 28, 1431)

[**Translator's note**: They find her in her cell, now dressed again as a man and citing her voices who had chastised her for damning her soul by renouncing them and urged her instead to behave boldly toward her judges.] She said further that she had taken on men's clothing again because they had not kept their promise that she be allowed to hear Mass; that she should receive the Body of the Lord, and that she be relieved of her leg irons. And that she would rather die than be kept in irons . . . She said also that everything she had said and revoked, she had done only through fear of the fire.

Asked if she believes the voices to be those of St. Catherine and St. Margaret,

She answered yes; and that they come from God . . .

Final Sentence (May 30, 1431)

[**Translator's note**: Pierre Cauchon, after a final attempt to make Joan recant again—even allowing her to receive Communion, reads a proclamation before her at Rouen turning her over to the secular authorities to be burned.] Wherefore we declare you excommunicated as properly befits a heretic and, since your errors have been condemned in a public sermon, we judge that, like a limb of Satan cut off from the Church, infected with heretical leprosy, so that you may not infect the other members of Christ, we must abandon you and hand you over to secular justice, praying the same powers to humanely temper its penalty of death and mutilation of your body. And if true signs of repentance appear in you, may they administer the sacrament of penance.[53]

Execution (May 30, 1431) and Aftermath

[*From the deposition of Jean Massieu given during the rehabilitation inquest, 1456*]

Brother Martin Ladvenu administered the Eucharist to Joan in the presence of this witness.[54] After that was done, she was led in woman's clothing and taken to the place where she was burned. On the way, Joan made such pious laments that the witness and Brother Martin could not restrain their tears. She in fact commended her soul to God with such devotion that she moved all who heard her to tears. She was taken to the Old Marketplace where Nicholas Midi stood ready to preach a sermon. After this was done, Midi declared to Joan, "Joan, go in peace! The Church can no longer defend you and places you in secular hands." At these words Joan, kneeling, said most pious prayers to God and asked this witness for a cross. Whereupon an Englishman present made a little cross out of sticks, which she kissed and placed upon her breast most devoutly.

However, she also wished to have a church crucifix. This she obtained, and kissed it while squeezing it in her arms and weeping while commending herself to God, to St. Michael, St. Catherine, and to all the saints. She embraced the cross one final time while bidding farewell to those present. Then she descended the platform and went to the scaffold, where she died most piously.

Also at that time [Massieu] heard Jean Fleury, clerk and bailiff, say that, according to the executioner, after her body had been burned and reduced to ashes, her heart remained intact and full of blood. They thus ordered the executioner to gather all her remains and throw them into the Seine, which he did.

[*From the deposition of Brother Ysambart de la Pierre given during the rehabilitation inquest, 1456*]

... the bishop of Beauvais, one of the judges, wept during the occasion [Joan's burning]. Then an English soldier, who hated her tremendously and had sworn to place a log onto the fire with his own hands, after having done this and having heard Joan invoke the name of Jesus during her last moments, he was struck dumb and stupefied, as though in a moment of ecstasy... Later he confessed to having gravely sinned, and repented of all he had done to Joan, whom he judged a good woman. For it seemed this Englishman had seen, during Joan's last breath, a white dove take flight from out of the flames... the executioner also... said he feared damnation because he had burned a saint.

Beatification and Canonization

[*From the decree by Cardinal Cretoni, December, 1908*]
Whether and concerning agreement on what miracles there is a case with which we are dealing.[55]

The name of the Maid of Orléans, given to immortality, soon to be inscribed in the list of the blessed in Heaven, just as she attests the divine power, which *chose the weak in the world to shame the strong* [1 Cor 1:27], likewise also condemns the laziness of those who, feigning love of their country or patriotism, care for nothing but their own business amid the ruins of their country and religion. Let these people remember that *to do and suffer great things is the task of Christians*;[56] and not only male Christians. For more than once has a woman been summoned by God *to free her people and gain a name for herself in eternity* [see 1 Mac 6:44].[57] God has renewed miracles of this kind of armed sainthood, in another, *Why should you look upon the Shulammite, as upon a dance before two armies?* [Song 6:13].[58] They, *empty men who have no knowledge of God* [see Wis 13:1], are astonished at this, while others who have knowledge cry out, *Come and see what God has done* [Ps 66:5].—*The bows of the mighty are broken, but the feeble gird on strength* [1 Sam 2:4].

The siege of Orléans had now been dragging on toward precipitous destruction, both for the city itself and for the fortunes of Charles VII, king of France. In those final agonies, in the town of Domremy, which was distant from that seat of tumult, about three hundred miles, by an unknown maiden, devoted to grazing her flock and on the offices of religion and piety, was heard the voice of Michael, prince of the Heavenly Host, as once it sounded to Judas Maccabeus: *take this holy sword, a gift from God, with which you will strike down the adversaries of Israel, my people* [2 Mac 15:16]. At first Joan resisted, and only after the voices were repeated did she at last reveal the matter to her parents. But although she could not convince anyone else nor indeed herself that she could be summoned to take up arms and lead the king to be consecrated in Reims, *He gives power to the faint, and to him who has no might he increases strength* [Is 40:29]. God gave the untutored maiden such wisdom, learning, skill in military matters, and arcane knowledge, that no longer could anyone doubt that the salvation of her people had been divinely entrusted to her. So, inspired by some secret spirit, linking mortal arms with the shield of faith, dressed in the clothing of a military leader, with drawn sword, she mounts a horse, routs the enemy, flies to victory, leads King Charles to the city of Reims for royal consecration. When this had been completed, she attained the laurel worthy of heaven, given over to be burnt by the fire by men intensely hostile to the Apostolic See, greatly angry that they had been vanquished by a girl.

Although the life of the Venerable Joan appeared to be one constant miracle, and her reputation for sanctity and achievement had become so well known that the praise given to Judith was fitting for her: *Among every people that shall hear your name the God of Israel shall be glorified within you* [Jud 13:31]. Nonetheless, it was pleasing to divine providence to confirm the judgment of the Church about the supreme virtues of the same venerable maiden with new miracles. Concerning three of these a careful investigation was conducted and the judicial records were reviewed and approved by the Congregation of Sacred Rites.

In the order in which they were reported, the first miracle occurred in the house of the Sisters of the Order of St. Benedict, in the year 1900. Sr. Theresa of St. Augustine had been tormented for three years by a stomach ulcer: her illness grew worse day by day and all hope of cure had been abandoned; she was about to receive last rites of the dying. But lo, on the final day of the novena, in the morning she rises from her bed to beseech the aid of the Venerable Joan, attends Mass, eats freely, returns to her former duties and is immediately and completely cured.

The second miracle occurred in the year 1893 in the town of Faverolles. Julia Gautier de Saint-Norbert, of the Congregation of Divine Providence at Evreux, was suffering for more than ten years from an incurable cancer in her left breast. Tormented with unspeakable pain for fifteen years, all hope of cure abandoned, with eight girls as attendants, she made the difficult journey to the church to beg the help of the Venerable Joan. There she prayed for help, and on that same day she felt herself to be immediately and completely cured, while the doctors and others present were astonished.

In the year 1891, in the town of Fruges, Sr. Jeanne-Marie Sagnier of the Congregation of the Holy Family, experienced the third miracle. For three months now she had been afflicted with the most excruciating pain in both legs, as each day new ulcers and abscesses appeared and grew. The doctors could achieve nothing but judge that they were dealing with a chronic case of tuberculosis of the bones. But Joan of Arc, when called upon, brought unexpected healing, from the fifth day after she had begun to pray, on which day the sick woman arose in the morning, unexpectedly and completely healed.

[The three miracles were approved on January 12, 1909.]

Notes

1. While one might simply ascribe this to the simplicity of peasant families, the blank Joan draws here also derives from her self-image as divinely chosen, devoid of mortal connections, especially carnality, hence her self-naming as *La Pucelle*.

2. She goes on to name six out of ten of them, several of whom were important citizens of Domremy.

3. A Credo, or Creed, is a capsule statement of essential tenets of Christian doctrine for recitation during important Christian religious events such as baptism. The most frequently invoked creeds in Western Christianity from the Middle Ages to the present have been the Creed of the Apostles, the Nicene, and the Athanasian Creeds. The Latin term *Credo* comes from their opening words: "I believe . . ."

4. The Latin record makes this look like a pointed denial that Joan was ever a shepherdess, a most engaging facet of her historical persona. This denial puzzled various scholars until discovery of the French original, which makes it clear that Joan did not tend sheep at La Rousse's house, but that she normally did. See W.S. Scott, who, in his notes to his translation of the French record, page 19, points to tampering by Courcelles, one of the notaries who altered the text while translating it into Latin in order to blacken Joan's image here and elsewhere. The Latin record's denial of her sheep-tending fueled other theories, especially the "Royal Bastardy" theory, which, together with her surprisingly rapid persuasion of the dauphin, and other details, postulates that she was of royal birth, though illegitimate.

5. The mendicant friars were so called because they were forbidden to own property, unlike monks in monasteries, and thus wandered about in unstable poverty. This lack of convent base also helped free them from Church jurisdiction and made them more mobile so that they became particularly effective preachers and confessors among townspeople. The most important mendicant orders are the Dominicans (Black Friars) and the Franciscans (Grey Friars).

6. This expression, translated from the original Middle-French *passez oultre*, became a trademark tactic by Joan to avoid answering any questions she did not wish to. She used it with remarkable success. It is often cited as an example of her truculent attitude, surprising to many accustomed to thinking of her as a simple, innocent country girl.

7. Pierre's family were lords of Domremy. They celebrated the May festival along with the peasants. The "may sprig" is a decoration made from a beech tree for that festival.

8. This is the so-called Merlin prophecy, fusing secular and religious concerns: *Ex nemore canuto puella eliminabitur ut medelae curam adhibeat* ("a maiden shall come from out of an oak forest to take care to heal all ills"), which we see the judges trying to use to discredit her by associating her with fairies and other apparitions. This prophecy would also be cited during her rehabilitation trial (1450-56) to defend her. See also note 36 below.

9. Vaucouleurs functioned as the county seat for Domremy.

10. That is, on the trip to Chinon to meet with the dauphin.

11. Here Joan reveals her awareness of decorum. She not only slept separately from the men, but also in the guest house of the abbey, the only place where women could stay.

12. Vespers, occurring just before dark, and "the hour of the Hail Mary," also called "the Angelus," at night, were among the seven canonical hours of the Divine Office dividing the Christian day.

13. This fateful refers to the (now lost) transcript of Joan's examination before the theologians held at Poitiers before Charles allowed her to ride with his army. Her judges at Rouen indeed did consult that record; but as a means to convict her, not to support her testimony. Since the practice of using testimony from another trial for devious purposes was not condoned even back then, this may explain the disappearance of the Poitiers records. See Charles Wood's essay in *Fresh Verdicts on Joan of Arc*, eds. Bonnie Wheeler and Charles Wood (New York, 1996), pp. 19-29.

14. At this point there is an unsignaled ten-page disparity between the original French record and the Latin record, indicating either an error in the French (Orléans) record or the addition of false extra pages to the Latin one. I am thus not including any part of those pages here, and have continued where the French record recommences (March 1).

15. Although the archangel Gabriel is not one of the three principal figures in her visions, Joan alludes to seeing him at several points in her testimony, usually with St. Michael, as depicted on her banner and in conventional iconography. In the Hebrew scriptures [see Dan 8:15 ff.], Gabriel helps Daniel understand his visions.

16. This refers to her famous attempt to escape imprisonment by leaping from the top of Beaurevoir tower (some sixty to seventy feet) and miraculously surviving, although she knocked herself unconscious, and thus was easily recaptured by her enemies.

17. The "I" here is probably the voice of d'Estivet or one of the other interrogators. "This book" or, as Joan refers to it at times, "your book," signifies the trial records.

18. Ahaz, son of Jotham, ruled Judah from 736 until 716 BCE. Contrary to God's advice, Ahaz refused to ask for a sign, and despite repeated warnings, his continued disobedience caused his kingdom great suffering, as is recorded in the Hebrew Scriptures: 2 Kings, 2 Chron, and mentioned by most of the prophets, especially Isaiah.

19. Gideon, son of Joash, a biblical hero [see Judg 6-8], was invoked more than once among the Poitiers theologians. The future liberator of Israel, judge, and reformer received a visit from an angel of the Lord appointing him leader of his people against the Midianites. When the angel first came to him, Gideon asked for a sign.

20. Gamaliel, grandson of Hillel and himself an important Jewish rabbi, balances Gideon here in that his story is told in the Christian Scriptures [see Acts]. He was also a pre-Christian teacher of the future St. Paul, yet unlike his illustrious pupil, Gamaliel was known for his tolerance of different religions, including the emerging Christians.

21. Jean Gerson (1363–1429), the chancellor of the Sorbonne at the University of Paris, was Joan's strongest and most prestigious supporter at the Poitiers examination. Although his treatise as a whole would strike us as very cautious, it may nonetheless be judged quite courageous, since Gerson, in favoring Joan, stood virtually alone among his pro-English colleagues at the university, protected only to a certain extent by his rank. For a complete translation in English of this Latin treatise, see H.G. Francq, "Jean Gerson's Theological Treatise and Other Memoirs in Defence of Joan of Arc," *Revue de l'Université d'Ottawa* 41 (1971): 58-80.

22. These are all heroic women from the Bible: Esther and Deborah in the Hebrew scriptures (Esther and Judg 5, respectively), and more on Esther and Judith are in the Apocrypha (Esther 10–11 and Jud, respectively). Each was chosen by God to liberate her people from tyranny. Gerson was not alone in citing these biblical precedents for Joan, though he may have been the first and most eloquent in so doing.

23. This treatise is no longer credited to Gerson but is rather an anonymous reworking composed after Orléans; see Francq, note 21 above.

24. That Joan is a "natural" creature and a real human is intended to answer a major question among her Poitiers judges: is she a real, natural human being or a Satanic creature disguised as a woman, that is, a witch? Anglo-Burgundian detractors of course sought to prove the contrary.

25. Camilla is the warrior heroine whose moving story dominates the second half of Book 11 of Virgil's *Aeneid*.

26. This is Joan's most important and best known letter since it so clearly states the main goals of her mission: the divinity of her inspiration; the affirmation of Charles's legitimacy as rightful king; and the expulsion of the English from France. The letter also shows her state of mind just two weeks before her triumph at Orléans. In his notes to his edition of the trial, Pierre Champion considers it the most significant of all documents in this respect, calling it a "cry from the heart" fused with the spirit of the Crusaders against the infidels, echoing Deut 20:10: "When you draw near to a town to fight against it, offer it terms of peace." (*Procès de condamnation de Jeanne d'Arc*, 2 vols. [Paris, 1920-21], 2:400).

27. Joan used this popular invocation on her standard and several of her letters. The words were also inscribed upon the ring she always wore, a gift from her mother. St. Catherine of Siena (ca. 1340-1387) began her letters with a similar phrase.

28. Since King Henry VI, who reigned from 1422 until 1471, was only nine months of age at the death of his father, King Henry V, Duke John of Bedford (1389-1435) became regent. By the Treaty of Troyes (1420), and because he was also the principal architect of the Anglo-Burgundian alliance, Bedford ruled France as well as England. Controlling northern France including Paris and Rouen, he was thus Joan's most powerful adversary, both on the battlefield and at the Rouen trial.

29. Earl William Pole of Suffolk (1396-1450), a career soldier from a very young age, served under and replaced Salisbury as head of the English forces in France after the latter's death at Orléans; he would then be taken prisoner by Joan's men at Jargeau (June 1429) from which he was later freed by ransom. A literate man, he composed verse as a diversion from army life and befriended the famous prince and poet Charles d'Orléans during the latter's captivity in England. His pro-French sympathies cost him his life.

John Talbot (1388?-1453) was considered the most daring of the English generals and a model of chivalry. Bedford made him governor of Anjou as a reward for his valor before Orléans, in which siege he also participated. Later, he would be taken prisoner by one of Joan's allies at Patay (June 1429). After regaining his freedom in 1433, he continued an illustrious career, becoming governor of Rouen and marshal of France, perishing at Castillon in the final stages of the French expulsion of the English. Thomas of Scales (ca. 1399-1460) devoted his entire career to the Hundred Years' War in France as Bedford's lieutenant, and the War of the Roses, supporting the Lancastrian cause. He served at Orléans, would again be defeated at Beaugency by Joan's army, then taken prisoner at Patay (June 1429) and ransomed.

30. In her testimony on February 22, Joan says that she had originally said "Render to the king" here. Pro-English notaries may have changed it to make her seem more vainglorious.

31. In her testimony on February 22, Joan affirms she never called herself "chief of the army" [*chef de guerre*]. This also would make her look more delusional.

32. In her testimony on February 22, Joan states that she had never said this originally. This may have been added by detractors to make her seem more bloodthirsty.

33. Christine de Pizan (1365-1430?) was France's first professional woman of letters. A prolific writer pioneering in many topics and styles of expression, she devoted much of her writing to defending women. Dated shortly after the Reims coronation and Joan's victory at Château-Thierry, Christine's poetic tribute to Joan was the first non-anonymous French work composed during the heroine's lifetime. For a complete English translation, with the French original and notes, see *"Ditié de Jehanne d'Arc," Christine de Pisan*, ed. and trans. Angus J. Kennedy and Kenneth Varty, Medium Aevum Monographs, new series 9 (Oxford, 1977).

34. For these biblical heroines, see note to Gerson's treatise (note 22) above. Christine was a friend of Gerson, from whom she probably culled material on the Poitiers examination deliberations.

35. The cult of the Nine Worthies, flourishing since the early 1300s in Europe, is a pantheon of valiant men from Old Testament, ancient Greek and Roman, and medieval Christian traditions. Shortly thereafter, female counterparts were devised, stemming pri-

marily from the Amazon tradition distilled from Greek and Roman literature. During the Hundred Years' War, the great warrior Du Guesclin was inscribed as the tenth Worthy, and Joan the tenth female Worthy.

36. These are the three great sources of various versions of the prophecy mentioned in note 8 above. "Merlin" is the magician and seer in Arthurian literature. His prophecy is cited by Geoffrey of Monmouth in the *Historia regum Britanniae*; "the Sibyl" refers to a tradition of (eventually) ten female seers from classical and late Antique Greek and Roman literature, the closest being the Tiburtine or Erythraean or Cumaean Sibyl, credited with predicting the Coming of Christ to the Roman emperor Tarquin via the so-called Sibylline Books; the Venerable Bede (ca. 673-735) was a respected source of historical information and legend, in Joan's time associated with a numerical puzzle (chronogram) predicting Joan's coming.

37. This letter attests belief in her divine wisdom among certain nobles, if outcasts, as well as the common folk. The three popes were Martin V (in Rome, approved by the Council of Constance), Clement VIII (at Peñiscola), and the secretly-elected Benedict XIV. The duke of Armagnac had refused to recognize Martin V and had thus been excommunicated prior to writing Joan. See Charles Wood, *Joan of Arc and Richard III: Sex, Saints and Government in the Middle Ages* (Oxford, 1988), pp. 127-29 for an analysis of this letter's significance.

38. This letter reflects Joan's practical military competence and her ability to raise support among the common people. That a girl of her age and background was able to master this has been cited as further proof of her divine inspiration, to defeat the argument that she was merely a lucky mascot for the French army. Jules Quicherat records having seen this letter's seal, containing a strand of black hair, thus a relic of Joan, back in the mid-nineteenth century. The "relic" is now missing.

39. Joan's army had just conquered the old abbey town of Saint-Pierre-le-Moûtier (Nevers).

40. Joan's campaign at La Charité-sur-Loire would be unsuccessful (November 29, 1429).

41. These were important components of early gunpowder.

42. This letter also bears the first known signature of Joan, who otherwise could not write.

43. To attack on a religious feast day was blasphemous, which Joan knew and also knew the judges' strategy in repeatedly framing this question. The failure of the attempt to take Paris is often blamed on this impious act.

44. Note that Joan has no defense counsel. Massieu is often portrayed as the closest approximation to a supporter-confessor, although even Jean de La Fontaine was accused of helping her with her testimony. Sackville-West nicely sketches the highly diverse personalities of the magistrates and notaries, all of whom were under control of the English, in *Saint Joan of Arc*, Chapters 15-17.

45. Bracketed insertions are from the official Latin record.

46. France was not yet a unified nation. Joan makes the distinction, as did her contemporaries, between her home province in the disputed eastern borders and "France," especially the part loyal to the dauphin.

47. Joan's obstinacy in these matters surfaced each time they administered the oath to her during the trial.

48. As is understandable from these passages intended to convey some of the atmosphere of her trial, the self-righteous attitude of the judges, together with the unnecessary physical and spiritual hardship imposed upon her during this process, has fostered repeated comparison with Christ's trial and Passion through the centuries.

49. In other words, "I have done nothing I was not ordered to do by my visions and voices, and you know how tricky that business can be!" This is probably one of her several moments of astounding awareness in regard to controversies over Church doctrine. She seems here to be alluding to the almost hopelessly vexed question of visions and other forms of revelation among theologians at the time. Even theologians who differed too strongly with the Church on these questions risked accusations of heresy. Ironically, it was the treatises of one of her Poitiers supporters, Jean Gerson, as in his *Discretio spirituum*

["On the distinction between good and evil spirits"], that unwittingly provided the manual for convicting Joan of heresy, although she did elude them on witchcraft.

50. We recall that the dauphin is Charles VII and that his father was Charles VI, who died in 1422, seven years before Joan's arrival on the scene.

51. This of course is the voice of the Latin notary, writing perhaps years after the fact, alluding to her upcoming retraction of this abjuration.

52. Joan's abjuration elicited much debate over the centuries, since her admirers did not wish to believe she would ever have done this. Along with the justification by physical duress and threat of torture, another theory rests on her use of a cross after her signature, a secret signal she had used among her men in the event her written orders were intercepted by the enemy. An X meant the order was not to be followed; an O meant that it should be obeyed.

53. The last two sentences of this passage are pure formality. In fact, Joan's scaffold was set higher than usual so that the flames would take longer to consume her, thereby prolonging her pain.

54. Jean Massieu and Martin Ladvenu were the clerics most sympathetic to Joan during her trial.

55. Joan's posthumous journey to sainthood involved a long, complex process of deliberations even after her case reached the Vatican. The three major steps were these: in 1894 Joan was declared Venerable by Pope Leo XIII; in 1909 she was beatified; in 1920 she was canonized. The above extract comes during an important middle phase, that of approving her miracles—occurring after her death—for beatification and canonization. The principal miracles effected by her in her lifetime were: (1) her prediction of the outcome of the Battle of Rouvroy before Captain Baudricourt or anyone else not at the battle could have known; (2) how she knew of the sword buried at the abbey of Saint Catherine at Fierbois, which became her own; (3) her prediction of her wound at the battle of Orléans two weeks beforehand; (4) the Orléans victory and lifting of the English siege, specifically the change of wind facilitating it; (5) resuscitating a dead infant at Lagny, long enough for it to receive last rites before expiring permanently.

56. The author gives no source for this phrase which is so generic as to be untraceable.

57. This passage, in its original context, speaks of a male hero in battle, Eleazar, not a woman.

58. The Song of Songs, the most erotic book of the Bible, uses these words in a very different context: to praise a young woman's comeliness.